P9-DTQ-295

THE OXFORD HISTORY
OF
THE AMERICAN PEOPLE

Other Books by Samuel Eliot Morison

The Life and Letters of Harrison Gray Otis, 2 vols., 1913

The Maritime History of Massachusetts, 1921, 1941

The Oxford History of the United States, 2 vols., 1927

Builders of the Bay Colony, 1930, 1964

The Tercentennial History of Harvard University, 4 vols., 1929–36

Three Centuries of Harvard, 1936, 1963

Portuguese Voyages to America, 1940

Admiral of the Ocean Sea: A Life of Christopher Columbus, 1942

History of U. S. Naval Operations in World War II, 15 vols., 1947–62

By Land and By Sea, 1953

The Intellectual Life of Colonial New England, 1956

Freedom in Contemporary Society, 1956

The Story of the "Old Colony" of New Plymouth, 1956

John Paul Jones: A Sailor's Biography, 1959

The Story of Mount Desert Island, 1960

One Boy's Boston, 1962

The Two-Ocean War, 1963

Vistas of History, 1964

Spring Tides, 1965

WITH HENRY STEELE COMMAGER

The Growth of the American Republic, 2 vols., 1930, 1962

WITH MAURICIO OBREGÓN

The Caribbean as Columbus Saw It, 1964

BENJAMIN FRANKLIN, by Houdon, 1780

THE OXFORD HISTORY
OF
THE AMERICAN PEOPLE

SAMUEL ELIOT MORISON

NEW YORK · OXFORD UNIVERSITY PRESS

1965

COPYRIGHT © 1965 BY SAMUEL ELIOT MORISON
Library of Congress Catalogue Card Number: 65-12468

PRINTED IN THE UNITED STATES OF AMERICA

TO MY BELOVED WIFE

PRISCILLA BARTON MORISON

WHO HAS HELPED ME TO UNDERSTAND

THE MOVING FORCES IN THE HISTORY

OF OUR NATION

I find the great thing in this world is not so much where we stand, as in what direction we are moving. . . . We must sail sometimes with the wind and sometimes against it, — but we must sail, and not drift, nor lie at anchor.

Oliver Wendell Holmes *The Autocrat of the Breakfast Table* (1858)

The role of government and its relationship to the individual has been changed so radically that today government is involved in almost every aspect of our lives.

Political, economic and racial forces have developed which we have not yet learned to understand or control. If we are ever to master these forces, make certain that government will belong to the people, not the people to the government, and provide for the future better than the past, we must somehow learn from the experiences of the past.

Bernard Baruch, presenting his papers to Princeton University, at the age of 93. *The New York Times*, 11 May 1964

Preface

THIS BOOK, in a sense, is a legacy to my countrymen after studying, teaching, and writing the history of the United States for over half a century.

Prospective readers may well ask wherein it may differ in form and content from other American histories of similar length. Politics are not lacking; but my main ambition is to re-create for my readers American ways of living in bygone eras. Here you will find a great deal on social and economic development; horses, ships, popular sports, and pastimes; eating, drinking, and smoking habits. Pugilists will be found cheek-by-jowl with Presidents; rough-necks with reformers, artists with ambassadors. More, proportionally, than in other histories, will be found on sea power, on the colonial period in which basic American principles were established, on the American Indians, and the Caribbean. I am offering fresh, new accounts of the Civil War and the War of Independence. A brief account of the parallel history of Canada, so near and dear to us, yet so unknown in her historical development to most citizens of the United States, has been attempted.

Having lived through several critical eras, dwelt or sojourned in every section of our country, taken part in both world wars, met and talked with almost every President of the United States in the twentieth century, as well as with thousands of men and women active in various pursuits, I have reached some fairly definite opinions about our history. At the same time, I have tried when writing about great controversial issues, such as war and peace and the progressive movement, to relate fairly what each side was trying to accomplish.

Since this is not a textbook, but a history written especially for my fellow citizens to read and enjoy, footnote references, bibliographies, and other "scholarly apparatus" have been suppressed. Readers may take a certain amount of erudition for granted! Of course nobody, much less myself, can possibly read every printed source and monograph on American history from the beginning through 1964. This is particularly true of social history, comprising ideally, though impossibly, all human activities. Consequently, I have depended for particular subjects on the information and advice of experts, some my colleagues or former pupils, many my friends, but others who were strangers; and it has been most gratifying to find people so generous with their special knowledge. Moreover, having learned from my naval experience the value of oral testimony by participants, I have sought out, talked with, and profited by conversations with many of the civilian and military leaders of the past fifty years. These, excepting a few who wish anonymity, are named in the following section on Acknowledgments.

For many years I have been interested in collecting the popular music of American history, from that of the Indians to the present. The Oxford University Press has given me the opportunity to use some appropriate tags and choruses of these at the ends of appropriate chapters, and more could have been added to the later chapters but for the reluctance of music publishers to part with copyrighted material.

The illustrations have been chosen as much for their artistic appeal as for illustration in the strict sense. The late Dr. Harold Bowditch helped me to make the point that the English Colonies were not originally democratic, by selecting and delineating coats of arms of colonial founders to which they were entitled, and which they used on bookplates, silver, and in other ways.

One thing has deeply impressed me as I swept through the history of North America — the continuity of American habits, ways, and institutions over a period of three centuries. The seeds or roots of almost everything we have today may be discerned in the English, French, and Spanish colonies as early as 1660. Nobody has better expressed this fundamental unity of American history than George E. Woodberry in his poem "My Country."

> She from old fountains doth new judgment draw,
> Till, word by word, the ancient order swerves
> To the true course more nigh; in every age
> A little she creates, but more preserves.

SAMUEL ELIOT MORISON

44 Brimmer Street
Boston
Christmastide 1964

Acknowledgments

M Y BELOVED WIFE Priscilla Barton Morison not only encouraged me to write this book but listened critically to the reading of draft chapters, and greatly contributed to my happiness and well being while the work was going on.

General acknowledgments are due to my secretaries during the period of writing, Diana G. Hadgis and Antha E. Card. Miss Card, especially, has helped me by repeatedly checking facts, and by research and suggestions, as well as making the Index.

To Dr. Sydney V. James, Jr., who for a year helped me by research on the Indians, the Jacksonian period, and other subjects.

To my daughters Emily M. Beck, editor of the latest edition of Bartlett's Familiar Quotations, for looking up and checking quotations, and to Catharine Morison Cooper for research on American music.

To the many naval and military officers and civilians who are mentioned in the prefaces of my earlier books, especially in the fifteen-volume *History of U. S. Naval Operations in World War II.*

To my colleagues at Harvard and other American universities, and at the Universities of Oxford, Paris, and Rome, from whom I have learned very, very much, through friendly conversation and correspondence.[1]

Special Subjects of Acknowledgment

AVIATION: Professors Secor D. Browne and Jerome C. Hunsaker of M.I.T., and Dr. J. Howard Means of Boston.

CANADA: Professor A. R. M. Lower of Queen's University, Professor John J. Conway, formerly of Harvard, and the Honorable William Phillips.

CATHOLIC CHURCH HISTORY: Professor Marshall Smelser of Notre Dame University and Monsignor George Casey of Lexington, Massachusetts.

COLONIAL PERIOD: Professors Edmund S. Morgan of Yale and Carl Bridenbaugh of Brown; both Professors Schlesinger and the late Perry Miller of Harvard, and the Rev. Arthur Pierce Middleton of Brookfield Center, Connecticut.

CONSERVATION: Mr. Ernest C. Oberholtzer of Ranier, Minnesota, Mr. Edmund Hayes of Portland, Oregon, Mrs. Marguerite Owen of Washington, D.C., and Professor Arthur A. Maass of Harvard.

1. My Balzan lecture at Rome on "The Experiences and Principles of an Historian" is printed in *Vistas of History* (Knopf, 1964).

ECONOMICS, especially the Great Depression: Professors Edward S. Mason of Harvard, Joseph Stancliffe Davis of Stanford, and Adolf A. Berle of Columbia Universities.

FEDERAL CONVENTION: Professor Henry S. Commager of Amherst College.

HORSES AND SPORTS: Mrs. Thomas E. P. Rice of Boston, Mr. Franklin Reynolds of Mount Sterling, Kentucky, Dr. George G. Simpson of the Harvard Museum of Comparative Zoology, and Mr. Colin J. Steuart Thomas of Baltimore.

ILLUSTRATIONS: Addison Gallery of American Art, Andover; American Museum of Natural History; Archives of Canada; Mrs. Bern Anderson of Newport; Atkins Museum of Fine Arts, Kansas City; Mr. David W. Barton; Boston Athenaeum; Boston Museum of Fine Arts; British Museum; Mrs. Richard E. Byrd; Corcoran Gallery, Washington; Mrs. John Duer; the H. F. DuPont Winterthur Museum; Mrs. Frederica F. Emert; the Franklin D. Roosevelt Library; Harvard University; Historical Society of Pennsylvania; Professor M. A. de Wolfe Howe of the Harvard Law School; Mrs. Mabel Ingalls; the John Carter Brown Library; Johns Hopkins University; Karsh of Ottawa; Mrs. Fred C. Kelly; The Mariners Museum, Newport News; Maryland Historical Society; the National Archives and National Gallery of Art, Washington; New-York Historical Society; Pach Brothers of New York; Peabody Museum of Cambridge; Peabody Museum of Salem; Pennsylvania Academy of Fine Arts; Princeton University; the Syracuse Savings Bank; Tennessee Valley Authority; Virginia Chamber of Commerce; United States Navy.

IMMIGRATION: Professor Oscar Handlin of Harvard.

INDIANS AND PRIMITIVE MAN IN AMERICA: Mr. Leonard Ware of the Bureau of Indian Affairs, Department of the Interior; Professor J. Otis Brew of Harvard University and the late Samuel K. Lothrop, curator of Andean Archaeology in the Peabody Museum, Cambridge.

LATIN AMERICA: Professor Roland T. Ely of Rutgers; Colonel Robert D. Heinl Jr. USMC (Ret.); the Honorable Mauricio Obregón of Colombia; the Honorable Aaron S. Brown, American Ambassador to Nicaragua.

MARITIME: Mr. Marion V. Brewington of Peabody Museum, Salem; Professor K. Jack Bauer of Marcus Harvey College, Charleston, West Virginia; Rear Admiral Ernest M. Eller, Mr. Jesse R. Thomas, and Mr. Donald R. Martin of the Navy Department; Mrs. John M. Bullard of New Bedford.

MEDICINE: Drs. Paul Dudley White, J. Howard Means, and Sidney Burwell of the Harvard Medical School; Dr. J. Whittington Gorham of New York.

MUSIC AND THE FINE ARTS: Mr. Erich Leinsdorf, conductor of the Boston Symphony Orchestra; Professor G. Wallace Woodworth of Harvard; Mr. George Biddle of New York; Mr. Joseph A. Coletti; the late Maxim Karolik; the several music publishers who have allowed me to quote snatches of their songs.

PSYCHOLOGY: Professor Erik H. Erikson of Harvard.

SUEZ AFFAIR: Marshal of the R.A.F. Sir John Slessor; the Honorable Winthrop Aldrich, former Ambassador to Great Britain.

TEXAS: the late Walter P. Webb and J. Frank Dobie of the University of Texas; Professor Allan Ashcroft of the Texas Agricultural and Mechanical University.

WITCHCRAFT: Miss Esther Forbes of Worcester.

Contents

List of Illustrations

xvii

List of Maps

MAPS BY VAUGHN GRAY

List of Songs

THE OXFORD HISTORY
OF
THE AMERICAN PEOPLE

America Under Her Native Sons

1. *The Origin of Man in America*

HISTORY IS THE STORY OF MANKIND; but when we try to tell the story of man in America from the beginning, the lack of data quickly brings us to a halt. There are plenty of surviving objects which antedate the coming of Europeans, but no written records; none, except the Maya calendar, that anyone as yet has been able to read. The historian trying to find out when and whence man first came to America, and how he lived during the hundreds of centuries before Europeans arrived, is like a child trying to solve a picture puzzle with only one per cent of the pieces. Under such circumstances no two people would make the same design. Archaeologists, anthropologists, plant geneticists, and others who have gone into the subject of man's arrival and spread in America, do not agree. New discoveries — new pieces to the puzzle — are made almost yearly, new methods of dating these finds are being devised, and new patterns are set up which confuse an historian who is used to working with dated documents, monuments, and books.

Thus, what we mean by the history of the American People is the history in America of immigrants from other continents. Mainly they came from Europe, and there were many unwilling ones from Africa, and not a few from Asia. But we cannot ignore the "Indians," as Christopher Columbus, making one of the worst guesses in history, called the natives whom he encountered on 12 October 1492. These natives first welcomed the Europeans, then fought them, and finally were subjugated by them. They gave the Europeans some of the world's most valued agricultural products — maize, tobacco, the potato, cassava, and chocolate. They taught their conquerors hundreds of skills and so frequently mated with them that millions of people in the United States, Canada, Mexico, Central and South America have Indian blood in their veins. The Indians have so influenced, indeed so transformed, the lives of white and black men in North America that we are eager to know where they came from and how their culture developed. But in this search we find little but silence, darkness, and mystery.

Nothing certain is known of the origin of man in the continent we call America. One guess is as good as another, and some speculations have been repeated so often as to acquire the force of fact. The existence of people here before the Indians has always been suspected, often asserted, but never proved. Our European ancestors entertained a low opinion of Indian culture.

3

Hence, when they came upon a remarkable monument like an inscribed rock or a serpentine mound, or the stone temples of Yucatán and Guatemala and the cyclopean walls of Peru, they were apt to ascribe them to Phoenicians, Egyptians, or anyone but the natives. Theories of the Lost Continent of Atlantis (a literary conceit of Plato), or of a land bridge between Africa and Brazil, have been brought up to prove that Europeans or Africans were in America thousands of years before Columbus.

There is no reason to deprive the American Indians of credit for developing their own civilization. There is no doubt that they themselves, without external aid or example, designed and built the marvelous pre-Columbian monuments and sculpture of Central America, and produced the beautiful examples of goldsmiths' work, pottery, and implements which are now treasured in museums. Similarities (such as the use of the bow and arrow, pottery making, and the Mexican game *patolli* resembling the Hindu game *parchesi*) have been pointed out as evidence of a continuing contact between Asia and America. This argument assumes that the Indians were incapable of inventing anything; an argument which, in view of the unchallenged fact that they developed corn and the potato from wild plants, and made boats from birch bark, is untenable. Reversing the argument, one may point out that, if the Indian had enjoyed even occasional contact with the Old World, he would certainly have imported things that even the Maya and the Inca lacked — steel implements, the wheel, and built-up wooden boats. The Indians had no iron, no wheel in any form, and their boats were either dug out from a log or stripped from the bark of a single tree, or were rafts of reeds and balsa. The Indians of Ecuador and Peru taught themselves to sail balsa rafts, and invented the centerboard to help them point up to the wind; but, unlike the Polynesians, who were among the world's boldest sailors, they stayed close to shore.

It is generally agreed that *homo sapiens* originated in Central Asia, whence he gradually spread into every region of the globe except Antarctica; and now he is there too. Physical characteristics of the American Indian are either definitely Mongoloid or a mixture of that with something else. They probably first began coming from Asia to America during the pleistocene, or Ice Age, which started in remotest antiquity and ended at some time between 8000 and 5000 B.C. During that era a large part of North America was covered by an ice cap which alternately advanced and retreated, each period taking thousands of years. This movement radically affected plant, animal, and human life. As the ice cap retreated, temperature rose and rain decreased until (around 8000 B.C. in the southwestern United States) the big mammals that fed on grass starved to death, and the men who hunted them died or moved on. After an arid period that lasted until about 2000 B.C., the temperature again declined, the rain returned, and the prophecy was fulfilled that "the desert shall rejoice and blossom as the rose." For about a millennium the American Southwest enjoyed more moisture than it does today. Then the climate gradually grew drier, and by the beginning of the Christian era had reached about the same degree of humidity that it still retains.

At Bering Strait, between America and Asia, only 23 miles of open water separate the northeastern cape of Siberia from Great Diomede Island. That island belongs to the U.S.S.R., but only three miles of water separate it from Little Diomede Island, which belongs to the U.S.A.; and from Little Diomede it is only another 22 miles to the Seward peninsula of Alaska. A primitive people, pressed by enemies from behind, could have crossed Bering Strait by raft. The first comers were not very advanced in culture. They brought little to mark them as humans except speech, fire, and the arts of making flint spear points and of scraping animal hides for clothing and shelter. Even that far back, they were accompanied by dogs, man's ever faithful companions.

Again assuming that the geologists are right, the last great ice cap that covered a large part of the United States began to melt about 40,000 years ago. Until then, living conditions in North America could hardly have been attractive even to Mongoloid aborigines. The ice first melted along the Northwest Coast. Studies of soil and rock formation prove that a fertile, relatively warm corridor first emerged from the ice along the Alaskan coast, and then up the Yukon, Mackenzie, and Fraser river valleys, and southeast of the Rocky Mountains. We may suppose that successive waves of immigrants from Siberia pushed down this corridor, thrusting the first comers further and further afield, into the buffalo country of the Great Plains, thence to New Mexico and Arizona. There the Cliff Dwellers maintained themselves against later invaders who, finding the cliffs too formidable, swept around them into Mexico and Central America. Some groups built dugout canoes by means of which they were able to settle the Caribbee islands. Others passed over the jungle-covered cordillera into South America, spread fanwise over that immense continent, and finally reached Patagonia, where Magellan in 1520 encountered the clumsy giants who worshipped the god Setebos and gave Shakespeare his character Caliban. These diverse branches of American Indians cannot have descended from a single group. There must have been innumerable crossings of the Strait, over thousands of years; a procession of refugees from Siberia. The Eskimo were the last to cross, and some of them stayed in Asia. We are challenged to find out what went on in this bottomless pit of American prehistory. We must assume that it took many, many thousands of years after the first coming for the continent to be peopled with tribes and nations differing as much in physique and language as do the nations of modern Europe. For the civilizations of Mexico, Peru, and Colombia to have developed from a crude hunting people can hardly have taken less time than it did for paleolithic man, the "cave man" of Europe, to develop the civilizations of Egypt and Greece.

Science has come to the aid of imagination in the shape of three methods of dating. One is known as dendrochronology. The rings on trees make a definite pattern, owing to the differing amounts of moisture and sunlight that they receive annually, and these rings persist even when the wood becomes charcoal. In a region such as that inhabited by the Pueblos of the Southwest, where wooden beams are found in varying levels under modern native buildings, the rings of a recently cut tree may be compared with those of a pueblo destroyed a century ago, and those with the rings of an earlier pueblo, and so on until we have a chain of overlapping tree-ring patterns extending over 2100 years. That does not get us very far back, as archaeology goes; but we can get much farther with the method known as Carbon 14.

Carbon 14, that is, carbon with an atomic weight of 14, exists in all organic matter, and disintegrates at a constant rate. Half the "life" of Carbon 14 is gone in about 5600 years, and another quarter goes in the next 5600 years; after 20,000 years it is all gone. This disintegration can be measured if a sample is placed in a small chamber surrounded by Geiger counters. Thus, if a sample, when measured for Carbon 14, is found to have been reduced by 75 per cent, it must be about 11,200 years old. While this method is not foolproof, it is the best that has yet been devised; and the findings based on it, in the past twenty-five years, have upset earlier calculations as to the antiquity of man in America. Very recently, Dr. John N. Rosholt has developed a third method of dating, by utilizing "daughter" products of uranium. This may prove to be more accurate.

Who the first paleo-Indians or proto-Indians were, is another matter. But archaeological finds, starting in 1926 with the one at Folsom, New Mexico, and dated by the Carbon 14 method, have taught us much about how they lived. At Folsom a party from the Denver Museum of Natural History, digging up the bones of a long-extinct type of bison, found some twenty two-inch points, laboriously chipped out of flint and beautifully fluted so as to fit on the head of a spear. These are unlike the arrowheads later made by American Indians, and also different from European Stone Age implements. Accompanying the spear points were flint rasps for scraping the hides that these people used for clothing and shelter. Since then, over twenty-five similar caches have been found, all the way from Canada down to Patagonia, and from California to Massachusetts; and the organic matter in some of them has been dated.

The Clovis finds of 1932 are some of the most important. In a region near the Texas-New Mexico border there have been excavated fluted spear points sticking into mammoths' bones, together with bone shafts for the spears. These have been carbon-dated at about 8000 B.C. The Fort Rock, Oregon, find of 1951 yielded several dozen spear points, scrapers, bone awls and drills, and a pair of sandals made of shredded sagebrush bark which, when given the Carbon 14 treatment, could be dated as having been made around 9053 B.C. The people who made these points knew the use of fire. They were hunters of big game; for, in a dozen different sites, weapons have been found sticking into or lying near the bones of Ice Age bison, hairy elephants and mammoths, jaguars, ground sloths, camels, and other big mammals that became extinct far beyond the memories of the Indians that Europeans first encountered.

Most surprising of all these finds is a pair of caves in Patagonia, excavated by Junius Bird in 1951, where human remains were found in conjunction with spear points, and bones of the primitive horse, and which the carbon test gave an average age of 8639 years. This means that somewhere around 6700 B.C., descendants of the hunter folk who had crossed Bering Strait had reached the southern tip of the American continent, traveling through forests, plains, and jungles, along rivers, valleys, arroyos, and mountain ranges, and possibly part of the way by dugout canoe. And as primitive man seldom moved unless forced by pressure of other men or savage beasts, or scarcity of food, this safari must have taken thousands of years.

It is anyone's guess when the first crossing from Asia took place; estimates run all the way from 12,000 to 25,000 B.C. The geologists put a ceiling — or bottom — on it at 38,000 B.C., at which time they believe the ice cap started to melt. But we must remember that the Bering Strait route is only one of numerous assumptions that have been made. Man may have reached America from Asia in big dugout canoes such as the Polynesians built, and such as those observed by Columbus in the Caribbean.

Somewhat more developed than the people who made the Folsom points were those of the so-called Cochise culture along the southern borders of Arizona and New Mexico. The Ventana Cave in the Castle Mountains, about 75 miles south of Phoenix, shows evidence of having been occupied continuously by Indians for thousands of years prior to A.D. 1800. Archaeologists have dug down through layer after layer of debris to one of about 2000 B.C. that contains stone mortars for grinding wild seeds. And at the other end of the continent, in Boston, a deep excavation for a skyscraper in the Back Bay uncovered an elaborately woven fish weir, which has been carbon-dated at about 2000 B.C. These two finds indicate that the primitive American was getting on, but very slowly. His great burst of material progress came not earlier than 500 B.C., even in Guatemala.

Very old human remains are rare in America because the primitive Indian (it is conjectured) exposed his dead on raised platforms, so that they disintegrated. The oldest hitherto found in America are those of the hunter folk who made the spear points, but not enough of these have as yet been discovered to establish a definite pattern. The subject is complicated by jokers who like to tease scientists by pretended finds of "cave men" in the bowels of the earth.[1]

Some of the ancient human remains that are generally accepted as genuine are: (1) The "Tepexpan man," a skeleton found in the Valley of Mexico in 1949 under an ancient lake bed and in a stratum with mammoth bones. Both

1. The "Calaveras skull" from California and the "Piltdown man" of England are noted examples of these fakes.

geological and carbon datings of a nearby peat sample yield dates between 9000 and 10,000 B.C. The man, about sixty years old, showed no markedly primitive features, so that some scientists think that he was just another Indian of the Aztec period who happened to be buried very deep. (2) The "Midland man," a female skull and fragments of human bones with numerous spear points, a hearth, and bones of extinct species of antelope, camel, bison, and mammoth, discovered in 1953–54 at the bottom of a sand blowout near Midland, Texas. The bones are those of a woman about thirty years old, and there is nothing about them to suggest that her race was different from that of the American Indian. By using the latest uranium isotope method of dating, it seems that this woman was buried at some time between 13,000 and 17,000 B.C. She is America's oldest inhabitant, so far. (3) The "Minnesota man," the remains of a fifteen-year-old girl who fell or was pushed into the glacial Lake Pelican, Minnesota, discovered in 1931. The teeth and jaws of this young lady were of such exceptional size as to encourage the belief that here, at last, was a pre-Indian; but a careful examination of the remains by her discoverer, Professor A. E. Jenks, proves that her buck teeth are definitely Mongoloid, similar to those of modern Eskimo girls. With Miss Minnesota were found an elk-antler dagger which was probably the instrument of her death, and a small conch shell from the Gulf of Mexico, evidently the poor girl's jewelry. No carbon dating was possible, but the geographical stratum in which she was found points to a maximum age of 11,000 years.

On the basis of these few finds — a fraction of one per cent of our picture puzzle of early man in America — one may make the following tentative conclusions:

(1) At an era prior to 10,000 B.C., people of a Mongoloid type began crossing the Bering Strait from Asia to America, and after many vicissitudes spread throughout the length and breadth of the continent, reaching Patagonia by 8000 B.C.

(2) These people were racially akin to the American Indians whom Europeans later encountered, but not necessarily their ancestors. Our Indians may have come later by the same or other routes, they may have exterminated the primitive folk or assimilated them, or driven them into undesirable corners.

(3) The first comers subsisted by hunting big game, which they killed by means of spears tipped with flaked-flint or other hard stone points. Pelts of bison and other now extinct animals were dressed with stone scrapers and used for clothing and shelter, although caves were the preferred homes. These people supplemented their diet with nuts and wild seeds and, presumably, with fish, but did not plant corn or other seeds or keep domestic animals other than the dog. Ignorant of the use of metal, they correspond, roughly, to early Stone Age man in Europe.

Thus, our knowledge of man in America, and the appearance and habits of these first Americans, is recent, fragmentary, and subject to controversy. We are just beginning to let a little dim light down that bottomless well.

2. The Indians' America

Coming from the study of these primitive Americans to the Indians whom the first Europeans met is like stepping out of darkness into a blaze of brilliant light. For the Indians are still with us, in North, Central, and South America; their society and folklore have been studied for over four hundred years, and the results have been incorporated in thousands of volumes.

Yet, even now we cannot write "The History of America before 1492," because history presupposes a more or less continuous and dated story. Even the most advanced Indians, those in Mexico and Peru, could not write, and recorded nothing of their past except remembered myths. In that respect they were like the earliest Greeks before Hellas burst into radiant life. They knew little and cared less whence or when they came. The most that the first Europeans who questioned them could ascertain was a few leading events of a century or two back.

It challenges our imagination to re-create this unrecorded gulf of American history between the passing of the primitive hunter folk and the rise of civilized empires in Mexico, Peru, and Colombia, and the high development of the Pueblos in the southwestern United States. Most archaeologists believe that the hunting culture of the Folsom points lasted from the first crossing to somewhere between 500 B.C. and A.D. 500. Within that millennium, "progress" hit the inhabitants of America. They learned agriculture, basketry, and pottery; in some regions they began to weave cotton and other fibers, to build with stone, and to smelt copper with gold. The entire race moved upward, but some groups moved much faster than others. Those that went furthest were the Maya of Central America, the Inca of Peru, the Chibcha of Colombia, and the Aztec of central Mexico.

Out of the silence of the centuries, archaeologists are attempting to reconstruct the complicated Maya Empire which was already falling apart when the first Spaniards reached these shores. But the glistening white pyramids that rise out of the tangled jungles of Yucatán, the ornate palaces of the kings, the great stone courts for a game of ball that was once played from the West Indies to Paraguay, the temples of fire and human sacrifice, the massive walls covered with reliefs of strange human figures, repulsive serpents, and the magnificently plumed Quetzal bird — these, although recovered physically by archaeology, still guard the secrets of that amazing people.

Over 800 sites of Mayan cities have been discovered, but no more than a dozen have been carefully excavated, and even in the four that have received the most attention — Piedras Negras, Uxmál, Copán, and Chichén Itzá — only some of the monuments have been cleared of jungle growth. Sequences of picture carvings, which conveyed something to the Maya as hieroglyphics did to the ancient Egyptians, have never been deciphered. But their carved calendar glyphs have been solved and these afford us a few dates to the pre-

Columbian history of Mexico. The starting date of their calendar, which was more accurate than the Julian calendar which English-speaking lands used until 1752, corresponded to 613 B.C. in our reckoning. The Maya empire began in Guatemala, whose stone-built cities were completely abandoned in favor of new homes in Yucatán. There Mayan civilization reached its height around A.D. 1100. About a century later a warrior tribe from the north called Toltec, traditionally led by a remarkable king named Quetzalcoatl, conquered most of the Maya and absorbed their culture, much as the Romans did that of the Greeks. The Toltec empire fell before the onslaught of a new warrior race from the north, the Aztec, who reached Mexico City about A.D. 1325 and founded an empire, whose last ruler, Montezuma II, was overthrown by Hernando Cortés. We can date the Maya temples from their stone calendars, but we know nothing of what happened in the Maya cities; not even the names of their prophets, priests, and kings.

In South America, other high and complex civilizations were attained by the Chibcha of the Colombian highlands, and the Inca of Peru. Yet the most striking achievements of the Indians, north and south, were in agriculture. Maize, which our European forebearers called "Indian corn," they probably developed from a wild grass of the Mexican highlands. Little pod-like ears of it have been found in caves in New Mexico with objects that are at least 2000 years old. The white potato is derived from a wild tuber that grew in Peru. The cacao bean was cultivated to make chocolate as a drink and a confection, and the Indians flavored it with vanilla. Tobacco, an aromatic wild herb, was planted by the Indians and esteemed for its narcotic effects; and tobacco spread throughout the world faster than any religion. Quinine they also discovered and used as a febrifuge. Many varieties of beans and tomatoes were cultivated, cordage was twisted from sisal and henequen fiber, the wild caoutchouc tree was tapped for latex from which the Indians made rubber balls for their games, and even waterproof shoes and clothing. Indian organic chemists learned how to leach poison out of cassava so that they could cover their arrowheads with the deadly *curare* and use the flour to bake bread.

Through tens of thousands of years, successive migrations and intertribal wars raged over the surface of the Americas; empires rose and fell, arts and skills were developed, with no discernible trace of outside influence. But the Indians were never united. As among Melanesians in the interior of New Guinea today, adjoining villages spoke different languages and frequently warred with one another. A few groups of the Indians — the Iroquois confederacy in northeastern United States and the empires of Mexico, Peru, and Colombia — evolved a political organization; but the rest did not grow beyond tribal units. There is evidence of trade passing from north to south or vice versa — the products of a good pipestone quarry might be carried over 1000 miles; but in general each tribe, occupying an area covering only a few hundred square miles at most, lived in a state of permanent or intermittent hostility with its neighbors. The Indians of the same region or language group did not even have a common name for themselves. Each tribe called itself something like "We, the People," and referred to its neighbors by a word that meant "the Barbarians," "Sons of She-Dog," or something equally insulting.

Thus Europeans could impinge here and there on the New World without arousing any general hostility. On the contrary, they were usually welcomed as allies against a nearby enemy. Firearms, little used by the first Europeans, were not responsible for their conquest of the Indians; the natives fell victims to their own disunity and primeval isolation. The principle of union, which in North America has created one of the strongest nations in modern history, was almost unknown to them. Hiawatha, a Mohawk chief who flourished around A.D. 1570 (not to be confused with Longfellow's hero), created the Iroquois League of the Five Nations; but he is an almost unique figure. Some of the most advanced tribes in North America at the period of European discovery were those of the Northwest Coast, extending from Alaska into Oregon. Their economy was based on salmon and other fish, which they learned to preserve by smoking, so that everyone had plenty to eat the year round and an abundance of leisure. The Northwest Coast Indians wove baskets so close that water and food could be boiled in them by using hot stones, built great dugout canoes, and ornamented their dwellings with carved genealogical trees, the totem poles, which told every passerby who you were and from whom descended. These Indians accumulated inherited property, and were such keen traders as to be more than a match for the first white men who came their way. Strangely enough, their culture did not extend into California, where numerous small tribes, contemptuously called "Diggers" by outsiders, lived until very recently on small game and acorn-meal bread.

In the area north of Mexico, only in New Mexico and Arizona can any long historical sequence be given to Indian life. Here a hunting nation which knew the rudiments of agriculture settled somewhere about the beginning of the Christian era. They built adobe-walled towns with apartment-house dwellings, community courts, and buildings where religious dances were held and other ceremonies practised. These pueblos (which is merely the Spanish word for "towns") were so defensible that succeeding waves of Indian conquerors passed them by, and they have been less molested by Spaniards and Americans than other North American Indians. Today the Pueblo Indians, as we call them, afford the best example in the United States of a well-rooted Indian culture. With a tree-ring method of dating, it has been possible to establish a sequence of basket weaving and pottery for them, in different styles, from the first centuries of the Christian era to the present. In the 1300 years that elapsed between A.D. 217 (year of the oldest Pueblo roofbeam that can be dated) and 1540, when the Spaniards burst into this region, there gradually grew up what archaeologists called the Anasazi culture — from a Navajo word meaning "the old people" — and this culture is divided into six consecutive periods. In the oldest, that of the Basket Makers, the people, who lived in caves or round adobe huts, wove baskets in which they stored wild seeds and little nubbin-like ears of corn which they cultivated with a digging stick. They kept dogs and possibly turkeys, hunted with flint-headed spears, smoked tobacco in a pipe shaped like a cigar-holder, and went naked except for sandals and furs. Owing to the dry climate, and a custom of burying their dead in dry caves, many human remains of these people have been found.

In their next or second stage, the Basket Makers learned to make pottery, as Mexican Indians had done earlier; and this art spread throughout America. The proof that it did not come from Asia is that American Indians never used the potter's wheel, which the Old World possessed thousands of years earlier. The second Basket Maker people wove crude fabrics from plant fibers, and the women adorned themselves with bracelets of shell, seed, and turquoise beads. The bow and arrow, another independent invention of the Indians which had earlier been adopted in the Old World, replaced the spear.

The third Pueblo period, from about A.D. 1050 to 1500, curiously corresponds to the "glorious thirteenth century" in Europe. It was the golden age of the Anasazi culture, that of the best cliff houses, great masonry-walled communal dwellings built in the open, with terraced setbacks like modernist skyscrapers, and big *kivas* like built-in drums, where the priests danced and produced awe-inspiring burps and booms. The close-woven basketry and decorated black-on-white pottery of this period are both remarkable. After 1300 the area occupied by the Pueblo civilization was seriously reduced by drought, arroyo erosion, and invasion; the people were forced into larger pueblos where there was a good supply of water, and their arts, ritual, and organization expanded. These were the ancestors of the Zuni, Hopi, Tewa, and Kere nations of today. Navajo and Apache of the Athabascan language stock moved in during the sixteenth century and absorbed the Anasazi culture, which the Navajo still maintain. These people have been very tenacious of their way of life so that nowadays at Acoma, Walpi, Orabi, Laguna, Taos, and other modern pueblos, one can observe Indians living very much as they did before the Europeans arrived.

Of the Indian history of North America east of the Rockies, even less is known because the Indians there did not stay put, like those of the pueblos. Whence came the "Mound Builders," as the older Indians of the Ohio and Upper Mississippi valleys are popularly called, we do not know. Certainly they did not arrive there until about the beginning of the Christian era. They traded with other Indians, replaced the pointed sticks with which the Anasazi tilled the earth by hoes of stone and shell; carved elaborate stone tobacco pipes into realistic pictures of birds and fish, and painted their bodies with red ochre, of which a plentiful supply is often found in their graves. They made elaborate ornaments out of shell, bone, and copper that they obtained from the Lake Superior deposits. Mound Builders were the best metal workers north of Central America before the European discovery, and even had a musical instrument — pan-pipes of bone and copper. These disappeared

when they disappeared, along with the tunes that a thousand years ago re-
sounded through the oak groves of our Middle West. Above all, these people
recorded themselves by gigantic earthen mounds, often built in shapes of serpents and birds. The Cahokia Mound at East St. Louis is a hundred feet high
and covers sixteen acres. Within these mounds the Indians buried their dead
almost as elaborately as the ancient Egyptians did, and the contents of their
tombs tell us how they lived.

At the time the first Europeans arrived, the Indians of the Great Plains
between the Rocky Mountains and the forested areas bordering on the Mississippi lived partly by corn culture but mostly by hunting the buffalo on foot
with bow and arrow. Although Europeans regarded all Indians as nomads (a
convenient excuse for denying them the land they occupied), only the Plains
Indians really were nomadic. Even they did not become so until about A.D.
1550, when they began to break wild mustangs, offspring of European horses
turned loose by the Spaniards. Use of the horse gave the men mobility in
pursuit of the buffalo herds, while women followed with children and baggage on *travois*, earth-trailing shafts attached to big dogs or old horses; or, in
winter, on toboggans, another Indian invention.

The Algonquian language group included the Abnaki of Maine and Nova
Scotia, all tribes of southern New England, the Delaware and Powhatan of
the Middle states and Virginia, the Sauk and Fox, Kickapoo, Pottawatomi,
and Blackfoot in the Middle West. This complex of tribes, semi-sedentary
and agricultural, we know fairly well from the observations of the English and
French with whom they made their first European contacts. They cultivated
beans, pumpkins, tobacco, and maize which, on many occasions, saved English colonists from starvation. The Algonquin, living sociably and filthily in
long bark-covered communal houses, was an excellent fisherman and hunter.
He invented a light and efficient small boat, the birch-bark canoe, and the
snowshoe, hunted deer and moose for their meat and skins, and trapped
beaver for their fur, of which the womenfolk made smart jackets. The men
went almost naked, even in winter, except for short trousers and moccasins of
deerskin. These tribes produced some great and noble characters: Powhatan,
Massasoit, King Philip, Tammany, Pontiac, Tecumseh, and Keokuk. The
Algonquin were susceptible to Christianity and assimilated European culture
better than most Indians, although some of the chiefs we have named tried
to unite their people against the English and perished in the attempt.

The Five Nations (Mohawk, Cayuga, Oneida, Onondaga, and Seneca) of
the Iroquois confederacy had the reputation of being the toughest fighters in
North America; and they had to be, to hold their own against the Algonquin.
In 1600, when first seen by Europeans, they occupied the territory from Lake
Champlain to the Genesee river, and from the Adirondack Mountains to
central Pennsylvania. Hard pressed when the Europeans arrived, the Iroquois
survived, and even extended their dominion, partly owing to Hiawatha's
league, which prevented war among themselves, and later through alliance

with the Dutch and English. Their folkways were similar to those of the Algonquin. Among their famous leaders were Hendrick, Cornplanter, Red Jacket, Brant, and Logan. The Tuscarora, who in 1720 moved north and became the Sixth Nation, and the southern Cherokee, were also of Iroquoian stock. The Cherokee produced one of the greatest of American Indians, Sequoya, who invented an alphabet for his people and vitally advanced their culture.

In southeastern United States the Muskhogean stock, which included the Apalachee, Chickasaw, Choctaw, Creek, Natchez, and Seminole nations, was regarded by Europeans of the colonial era as the elite of North American Indians. They had an elaborate system of castes, from the "Suns" down to the "Stinkards," who were not allowed to intermarry. All Muskhogean tribes were planters of maize, which they accented with the annual "busk," or green corn festival; and they were expert potters, weavers, and curers of deerskin for clothing. They quickly learned from Europeans to plant orchards and keep cattle. Like the Cherokee, they for the most part were forcibly removed to Oklahoma over a century ago.

We know nothing of the development of the many and complex Indian languages before the curious Europeans tried to transpose the sounds to their own languages and write them in their own letters. The language stocks with which Europeans first came in contact in North America were those of the Pueblos (basically akin to Aztec), the Algonquian, Iroquoian, and Muskhogean. Algonquian dialects, differing no more than French from Spanish, were spoken as far north as Hudson Bay, west to the Rockies, and south to the Carolinas; but there was no mutual knowledge or connection between the widely separated tribes who spoke them. Not one of these Indian tongues has any connection with a known European or Asiatic language.

Not all Indians lived in a continual state of intertribal war, but war was part of the social pattern. Bringing back scalps was equivalent to a high school certificate for the young braves; if you didn't do it you were a despised underdog. Any Indian group that tried to shift its dominant values from war to peace was doomed to extinction by another. That is probably what happened to the Mound Builders, whose burial objects display ornaments and gadgets rather than weapons; and it is known to have happened to the Hurons in Canada.

On the negative side it was the Indians' lack of union, and on the positive side it was European sea power, which enabled white men to overrun the New World. Once a European established a beachhead, he had a bridge of ships bringing supplies and reinforcements from the Old World. An isolated garrison like Columbus's at Navidad, or Raleigh's on Roanoke Island, might be wiped out; but this was no longer the eleventh century, when the Norsemen abandoned their colony because the natives were too much for them. The European invaders of the sixteenth and seventeenth centuries had the means and the determination to keep coming. The Indian was incapable of bringing up anything better than local defense forces to counterattack. Time and again he tried, but almost always he failed. Only in the remote fastnesses of the Andes and Amazonia, where Europeans have never penetrated, and in the Sierra Nevada de Santa Marta and the Isthmus of Panama, where the Cuna-Cuna managed to protect themselves, have the Indians succeeded in keeping their civilization intact. If the European discovery had been delayed for a century or two, it is possible that the Aztec in Mexico or the Iroquois in North America would have established strong native states capable of adopting European war tactics and maintaining their independence to this day, as Japan kept her independence from China.

The population of the Americas in 1500 is largely a matter of conjecture, aided by a few fragmentary estimates by early Europeans. The latest scholarly estimates of Indian population in the present area of Canada and the United States vary from 900,000 to 1,500,000; of Mexico, 3 to 4.5 million; of Central and South America and the West Indies, 4.5 to 10 million. The Indian population of the United States and Canada in 1960 — counting only those who are purebloods or consider themselves Indians — was not far short of the lowest estimate of 1500; a remarkable recovery, considering the stresses to which that race has been subjected.

There is no reason to regard the North American Indian as an inferior race. Backward in many respects he was, but he has proved to have every potentiality common to other human beings. Americans of European stock, from Bishop Las Casas to John La Farge, who have taken the trouble to live with the Indians and understand their ways, find them inferior to none, and superior to many in firmness and integrity of character. They were far more "rugged" than any of the Europeans who claimed to be individualists; and in contrast to the Negro, who adopted the culture of each European race that enslaved him, the Indian has firmly resisted four centuries of intense European pressure.

As children of nature who "take no thought for the morrow," and give their last bit of bread to an unknown guest, the Indians follow the New Testament better than many who profess and call themselves Christians. The names they gave to our lakes and rivers are still on the map, as are those of states like Utah, Arkansas, and Massachusetts, and cities like Keokuk and Chicago. They have mated successfully with people of European stock; it has become something of distinction in the United States to claim Indian ancestry. One President of the United States (Coolidge) and one Vice President (Curtis) had Indian blood and were proud of it.

In peace as in war the Indians have had a profound effect on later comers to America. Our culture has been enriched by their contribution. Our character is very different from what it would have been if this continent had been uninhabited when the Europeans arrived. It was a good thing for our forebears that they had to fight their way into the New World; it will be a sorry day for their descendants if they become too civilized to defend themselves. As the Algonquian warrior of old drank the blood of his fallen enemy in order to absorb his courage, so the people of America may thank the brave redskins who made their ancestors pay dear for the mastery of a continent.

ANCIENT NAVAJO WAR CHANT

The European Discovery of America

1. *The Heritage of Classical Antiquity*

WE NOW REACH THE FASCINATING SUBJECT of the European discovery of America. Who was the first "white man" to set foot on these shores? Where did he step off? How long did he stay? There is no reasonable doubt that Christopher Columbus made the *effective* discovery, from which all American history stems. But was Columbus really the first? And what advances, scientific or otherwise, made his voyage possible?

To answer the last question first, the 1492 discovery was the culmination of two or three centuries of maritime exploration, all based upon geographical knowledge and theory left by the ancients. A Greek named Pytheas made furthest north prior to the Christian era. In the fourth century B.C. he sailed to a point where the night lasted only two hours in the summer, and reported an island six days' sail north of Britain, where the sun shone at midnight, which he called Thule. We do not know what island he meant, but his narrative was so widely read that *Ultima Thule* became the designation for any far-off, never-never land. That is why the Danish explorer Knud Rasmussen in 1909 named his northernmost base in Greenland, Thule.

Homer and Herodotus regarded the world as a flat disc edged by the ocean, but the Pythagorean school of philosophers in the sixth century B.C. advanced a spherical theory. Aristotle took it up, and Claudius Ptolemy, a Greek geographer who lived at Alexandria in the second century of the Christian era proved it by pointing out that the shadow of the earth on the moon during an eclipse is always round, and that you can see the masts of ships at sea when their hulls are below the horizon, or the mountain tops of islands before you can see their bases. To these proofs the medieval theologians added the argument that since the sphere is the most perfect form, God must have made the world that way. The spherical globe was taught to every lad who attended a medieval university. Columbus never had to argue for it. No doubt the uneducated majority, and people who lived on flat plains far from the sea, continued to think of the earth as flat; but so do some people even today. There is still in existence a flat-earth fraternity, founded by the late Wilbur G. Voliver of Zion, Illinois.

Although a spherical world was assumed, nobody cared how big it was until Alexander the Great became master of a large part of the ancient world. Close figuring was required to march troops from Greece to India, or to send a fleet from Suez to Ceylon. Accurate maps and charts were necessary, roads had to be laid out, ocean trade routes established. So Alexander and his successors called on the scientists. A school of geography was set up at Alexandria; Hipparchas, who flourished there about 150 B.C., was the first to divide the globe into 360 degrees and to use the device of latitude and longitude in order to give co-ordinates of every place. Even earlier, Eratosthenes made a successful effort to measure the length of a degree, and so figure the size of the earth. His estimate of the circumference of the earth was nearly correct — 21,420 miles instead of 24,975. Ptolemy, however, made a new set of calculations which allowed a shorter degree and estimated the world to be only about five-sevenths its true size. That was a fortunate error, because it encouraged Columbus to sail. Ptolemy's work, with the maps that accompanied it, was the geographical bible of the Renaissance and remained the basis of all geography for a century after Columbus. Strabo, a Greek geographer, wrote about A.D. 50, "Those who have returned from an attempt to circumnavigate the earth do not say they have been prevented from continuing their voyage by any opposing continent, for the sea remained perfectly open, but through want of resolution and the scarcity of provision." They were obviously defeated by the lack of really seagoing sailing vessels. Sail, in the ancient world, was an auxiliary to oar-power, and the row galleys that made both short and long voyages had to land every few days to replenish food and water for their big crews. When the Egyptian Pharaoh Necho, around 600 B.C., sent Phoenician galleys to circumnavigate Africa, they had to stop over twice to sow and reap grain, and it took three years to complete the voyage.

By the second or third century A.D. the ancient world had lost its zest for discovery, and geographical knowledge made no advance for a thousand years.

2. *Irish and Norse Discoveries*

On any globe or map of the northern polar region you will note a series of island stepping-stones from Europe to America, parallel to those from East Asia to Alaska. These stepping-stones are the Shetland and Faroe Islands, Iceland, Greenland, and Baffin Land. The longest gap measures only 250 miles across; but, for small boats, these were formidable crossings over tempestuous northern waters, far more difficult than the short hops across the Bering Strait that the ancestors of the American Indians must have made. By this short route Norsemen discovered the New World about the year 1000, and an unknown Irishman probably did so even earlier.

It is an historical fact that Irishmen discovered and settled Iceland when it was empty of human life, and that Norsemen expelled them about A.D. 850. The same sagas which describe the Norse discoveries call certain lands west of Greenland, "White Man's Land," or "Ireland the Great," and add a few interesting details. An Icelander named Bjorn put to sea with a northeast wind one day in the tenth century, and never returned. Years later, Gudlief

Gudlangson, driven west by a gale, landed in a country where white people rushed down to the beach and would have killed him but for their leader, whom Gudlief recognized as Bjorn, who told him that these people were rough Irish and he had better get out, which he did. The saga of Eric the Red states that natives encountered on the continent told of white people living far off who "wore white garments and yelled loudly, and carried poles before them to which rags were attached." Just what an Irish religious procession would have looked like to Indians! But if Irishmen did reach America in the ninth or tenth century, they never returned, and left no trace. Probably there were too few to contend with the natives. Some day, perchance, authentic Irish relics will be found in northeastern Canada; but until that time comes we have only these elusive stories of an Irish colony glimpsed vaguely through northern mists.

The Norse discovery of America rests on a sound basis of documentary evidence, supported by ruins and remains on Greenland, although not as yet by anything indubitably Norse on the American continent. These Norsemen, bold adventurers, seafarers, and colonizers, left a permanent stamp on the institutions and the architecture of England, Normandy, and Sicily. For them, as later for the Portuguese and English, the one way to wealth and independence was to follow the sea. For raiding they used the Viking warships, but for trading, the stubby, one-masted vessel some 40 to 60 feet long, called *knörr*. In the knörr they made long voyages without knowledge of the compass.

Greenland was discovered and colonized from Iceland by Eric the Red about 985 A.D. He founded two settlements on the west coast; and as the climate was warmer then than of late, cattle could be raised and some food crops grown. These Norse settlements lasted for several centuries. Sixteen churches were built, and even a small stone cathedral for the bishop. Danish excavations have uncovered the ruins of this church, of hundreds of houses, and bodies of small undernourished Europeans buried deep and clothed in fashions of the thirteenth to fourteenth century. A letter of Pope Alexander VI at the time of Columbus states that the Vatican had received no word from Greenland for some eighty years. What had happened? It seems probable that around A.D. 1400 the climate became so severe that Norwegian and Icelandic traders found voyages thither no longer profitable, and that the Norsemen in Greenland died off or were killed by the Eskimo.

Now for Vinland. Two Icelandic sagas tell how Leif the Lucky, Eric's son, on a visit to Norway in the year 1000, was ordered by King Olaf to bring Christianity to Greenland; how he missed Greenland in a storm and made a land where wild grapes and self-sown wheat grew, which he named Vinland the Good. According to one saga, he sought out Vinland after it had been discovered by another Norseman, built huts and a large house, and spent a winter before sailing back to his father's settlement in Greenland. The Eric family seems to have brooded over Vinland without doing anything about it; but about twenty years later Thorfinn Karlsefni, a Greenland trader, attempted to establish a colony there. Sailing in his knörr with wife Freydis, about 150 people and a few cattle, he crossed Davis Strait to Labrador and coasted until he found an estuary suitable for settlement. The party landed there and passed two winters which were mild enough for cattle to live outdoors. The Norsemen were disappointed at finding no wild grapes, and their relations with the natives, whom they called *skrellings* (dwarfs), were unfriendly. In a surprise skrelling attack on the settlement, Freydis, showing more courage than her menfolk, routed the enemy with a sword; but Karlsefni decided that the country was too dangerous, embarked his people, and sailed back to Greenland.

We would all like to locate Leif's Vinland, and the site of Thorfinn's colony, but data in the sagas are contradictory and confusing. If Leif really did find wild grapes, his Vinland could have been no further south than Nova Scotia. The description of Thorfinn's site fits the topography of northern Newfoundland better than that of any other region; and in 1962 a Norwegian archaeologist excavated a site at L'Anse aux Meadows facing the Strait of Belle Isle, which by carbon dating he believes to have been constructed around the year 1000, and where he thinks he has found the ruins of Leif's house. Possibly authentic Norse remains will be found there; but the evidence so far produced indicates that the site was used for smelting iron by early French colonists. Thus, the sites of Leif's Vinland and Thorfinn's colony are still anyone's guess. All alleged relics hitherto "discovered" were either built centuries later, such as the stone tower at Newport, or are forgeries such as the "Kensington Rune Stone" and the "Beardmore Weapons," inscribed or planted by practical jokers.

If Europe had been ready for expansion in the eleventh century, and interested in finding new regions, the Norse discovery might have led to something; but Europe was not ready, and nothing that the Norsemen found suggested that Vinland was worth following up. Fish, fir trees, and wild grapes were not worth fighting natives to get. Nor did anyone suspect that Greenland and Vinland were keys to a New World. Greenland appears on several early maps both before and after 1500 as a promontory of Europe or Asia curving west over Iceland. Vinland is on no pre-Columbian map; nor does even the name appear in print until 1595. And nothing in the saga descriptions of Vinland could have attracted later European explorers, who were looking for gold, gems, and spices.

The Norse occupation of the American continent was ephemeral. It made no change in the balance of nature and left no trace on native folklore. Yet there is a fascination about it to this day. Across the centuries one can spare a thought for the Greenlanders, struggling against starvation in a frigid climate becoming colder, beset by bands of surly and belligerent Eskimo. During the short summer the Norsemen stare out to sea, hoping and praying for the ship that never comes. Then the winter closes in; and, knowing that no ship can get through until next spring, they do their best to survive. One by one they drop off, until none are left.

3. Genoese and Portuguese

We now shift our attention to the Mediterranean. Here was the cradle of the civilization which eventually spread into the New World; here were born and trained the seamen who brought Europe into Africa, America, and the Far East.

During the Dark Ages the Mediterranean nations were weak and poor, owing in great part to the depredations of Arab pirates on the ports of the decrepit Roman Empire. But in the eleventh century the Christian nations began pushing the "Moors," as they called the Arabs, out of Spain and Portugal, and conducting crusades to recover the Holy Land from the infidel. The crusaders' need of water transportation stimulated commerce and ship-building in Italian seaports and brought their people into contact with the Middle East. Genoa, the birthplace of Columbus, set up trading posts in the Aegean isle of Chios and on the shores of the Black Sea. The long overland journey of Marco Polo to Peking, and his stories told after his return, gave the late medieval world its first direct knowledge of the fabulously wealthy empire of China, and indirect knowledge of an even richer island that Marco called *Cipangu* — Japan. All this suggested that Europeans attempt to tap that wealth by sea, instead of by long and expensive camel caravans across Asia.

So far as we know, the first to make the attempt were the Vivaldi brothers of Genoa. In 1291 they led an expedition of two galleys along the West African coast; and their object, according to a contemporary chronicle, was "to reach India by an ocean route." But the Vivaldi never returned. Moslem merchants later reported that one of their ships was wrecked on the African coast and that the other landed, but its crew was enslaved.

The fourteenth century was a period of political degeneracy, civil strife, and dissension, leaving slight scope for maritime energy. But in the next century a distinct advance was made by the Portuguese. Portugal, the ancient Lusitania, was a small country but she had the right situation for dominating the Western Ocean, "Where endeth land and where beginneth sea," as Luis de Camoëns wrote. Portugal did more to enlarge the boundaries of the known world and to improve methods of navigation then all other nations of Europe combined. Today the mark of her navigators is written on the map of the world in places so remote as Cape Race, the Azores, Brazil, Angola, Mozambique, Timor, and Macao.

An able royal family, the house of Aviz, ruled Portugal in this era. A son of that house, Prince Henry the Navigator, invited Jewish, Moslem, and Christian mapmakers and astronomers to Cape St. Vincent, which he made a center for exploration "through all the watery roads." Between 1451 and 1470 his captains discovered all eight islands of the Azores, and colonized most of them. Corvo, remotest of the group, is only 1054 nautical miles from Cape Race, Newfoundland. Why, then, did it not become a stepping-stone to America? Largely because of the westerly winds, which prevented several Portuguese mariners, who set forth from the Azores in hope of finding more and bigger islands out in the ocean, from sailing far enough to discover anything. There was a persistent legend of an island called Antilia, where Portuguese Christians, thrown out by the Moors in the eighth century, had settled, much as the Irish expelled from Iceland were said to have gone to America. But Antilia was never found, though it has left its mark on the map of America in the name "The Antilles."

Portuguese explorations of Africa opened to commerce the entire west coast and a part of the east coast of that continent. For such voyages the design of seagoing sailing ships had to be improved so that they could beat back against prevailing northerly winds; and navigation by the sun and stars had to be invented so that a sailor could know where he was. The Portuguese invented the caravel, a sharp-built vessel rigged with lateen sails and so designed that she could sail almost as close to the wind as a modern racing yacht. These were the first European sailing vessels to make progress against the wind, necessary if you were to make long voyages over wide stretches of ocean, since you could not always count on fair winds. In addition, the Portuguese developed celestial navigation. They learned how to tell latitude by measuring the height of the sun, or of the North Star, above the horizon; a method of navigation not entirely superseded to this day. The early instruments, however, were so inaccurate on a rolling and pitching ship that the Portuguese took their sights ashore whenever possible; and that helped them to map the African coast.

By the time of Prince Henry's death in 1460, trade in gold, ivory, pepper, and Negro slaves had been opened up with the Gold Coast and Sierra Leone. African exploration was then carried forward by the prince's nephew Alfonso V, and so profitably that Portugal became the envy of Europe. The culmination came when Bartholomew Dias made one of the greatest voyages of all time. He had already been at sea six months in 1487, touching now and again on the West African coast, when he lost sight of land and was driven southeastward by a heavy gale, expecting at any moment to be cast ashore. When the wind moderated and shifted, Dias turned northward, and on 5 February 1488 his lookouts reported land on the *port* bow. Dias then knew that he had rounded the southern end of the African continent. He followed the east coast of Africa for a few days, when his seamen mutinied and he was forced to turn back, leaving the glory of actually reaching India to Vasco da Gama. On the homeward passage Da Gama sighted the promontory which his sovereign named the Cape of Good Hope.

4. Columbus's First Voyage

America was discovered accidentally by a great seaman who was looking for something else; when discovered it was not wanted; and most of the exploration for the next fifty years was done in the hope of getting through or around it. America was named after a man who discovered no part of the New World. History is like that, very chancy.

Toward the close of the fifteenth century the wings of discovery began to brush very close to the shores of America. Portuguese sailors looking for fabled Antilia may have come within a day's sail of Newfoundland. Doubtless the New World would eventually have been discovered as men became more venturesome; for instance, a Portuguese navigator named Cabral accidentally raised the coast of Brazil in 1500 when on a voyage to India. But that does not detract from the glory of Columbus, whose discovery really opened America to Europe. Most Europeans at that time were not looking for a New World, but a new way to get at the oldest part of the Old World — the Indies. By that word they meant all Asia east of Suez, together with Oriental islands such as Sumatra and Japan, of which Marco Polo had brought home tall tales. An ocean route was sought to countries of fabulous wealth in the hope of tapping them directly instead of paying tribute to a horde of caravan conductors, camel jockeys, junk sailors, Oriental brigands, and miscellaneous middlemen. But even the most practical promoters looked for something more; they hoped to convert the heathen to Christianity, whose area had been contracting since the rise of Islam. First the Arabs overran North Africa and most of Spain; now the Turks had conquered the Byzantine empire and were threatening Austria. If Europeans could only get in touch with "Prester John," as they called the Christian emperor of Ethiopia, supposed to live somewhere in the Indies, they might form a Holy League against the Turks and recover the Holy Land.

Bartholomew Dias, as we have seen, returned to Lisbon in 1488 after opening up a sea route to India around Africa. In the receiving line was a sailor destined to even greater fame. Cristoforo Colombo, as he was christened at Genoa in 1451, we know by the latinized form of his name, Christopher Columbus. A sailor since his early years, he had swum ashore on the Portuguese coast at the age of twenty-six, after his ship had been sunk in a naval battle, and cast his lot with Portugal. In partnership with a brother he conducted a chart-making business and made voyages under the Portuguese flag north to Jan Mayen Land, south to the Gold Coast, and out to the Madeiras and Azores.

For several years Columbus had been promoting a plan for a direct ocean route to the Indies. It was simple enough — to drop down to the Canary Islands and sail due west along lat. 28° N, which according to his best

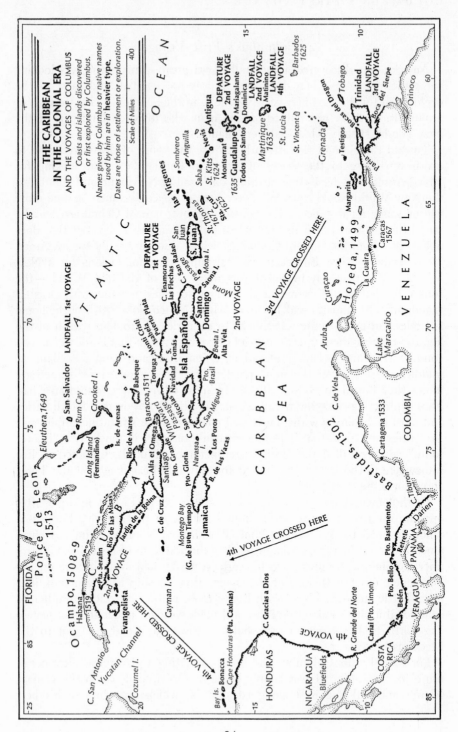

THE CARIBBEAN IN THE COLONIAL ERA

AND THE VOYAGES OF COLUMBUS

Coasts and islands discovered or first explored by Columbus.

Names given by Columbus or native names used by him are in **heavier type**.

Dates are those of settlement or exploration.

Scale of Miles

0   400

ATLANTIC OCEAN

CARIBBEAN SEA

24

information would hit Japan. Actually, that parallel does run between Japan proper and Okinawa. Since everyone agreed that the world was spherical, nobody doubted that this voyage was theoretically possible, just as nobody today doubts the possibility of landing a man on Mars. Distance was the obstacle, then as now. By air from the Canaries to Japan is about 10,600 miles; but Columbus figured out that it was less than one-fourth of that distance — 2400 miles. He not only made the smallest estimate of the size of the globe in modern history; he followed Strabo in declaring that the ocean was relatively narrow and the European-Asiatic continent about twice its actual length. Thus, he calculated that Japan would be about the same distance west of Spain as are Haiti and New York. His critics, and the experts who turned him down in Portugal and Spain, were really better geographers than he; and their attitude was natural enough. For nobody suspected the existence of an American continent to bar the sea route to the Indies; and a voyage of 10,000 miles over an empty ocean, with the same distance to sail back, was more than the seamen of those days could take. The logistics problem alone would have rendered it impracticable even if the wind were fair all the way out and home.

Columbus was not the kind of man to take no for an answer. He was sure he could do it, certain that God meant him to do it; his name meant "Christ Bearer," so he was destined to carry the good tidings to heathen lands. But he also insisted on a proper reward. As a poor boy and a self-made mariner he had been pushed around all his life, and he intended to take no more of that. So he demanded three ships, the hereditary title of Admiral of the Ocean Sea, control of all trade between Spain and whatever Oriental port or island he discovered, and a cut on all precious metals that he brought home. Preposterous!, said the princes to whom he applied. Columbus felt he could afford to wait. But he might have waited until death if the intuition of Queen Isabella had not flown out to meet his supreme self-confidence and irritating conceit.

Early in 1492 it was settled between him and the joint Spanish sovereigns, Ferdinand and Isabella. On 3 August Columbus set sail from Palos in southern Spain in the ship *Santa Maria*, accompanied by two caravels owned and captained by the Pinzón brothers of Palos. All three were manned by local men and boys. He had a letter of introduction from the sovereigns to the "Grand Khan," the supposed title of the Emperor of China, and blank letters in which Columbus could insert the name of any potentate at whose dominions he touched. He had a Latin passport stating, "By these presents we dispatch the noble man Christopher Columbus with three equipped caravels over the Ocean Sea toward the regions of India for certain reasons and purposes." He shipped a learned Jew who knew Arabic, which he hoped would enable him to converse with Orientals who knew no Latin. The more you look at it, the more naïve Columbus's enterprise seems. The only solid thing about it was his faith in God and his mission. And what he asked faithfully he obtained effectually.

Columbus was not so simple as to assume that one could land in Japan or China with ninety sailors and take over the country in the name of Spain. He proposed to set up a trading post colony, the only type of colony that Europe then knew, on some outlying island off the Asiatic coast. He had visited the chief trading post in West Africa, São Jorge da Mina, where nearby Negro kings welcomed the Portuguese; so why should not the Chinese or Japanese roll out a Persian carpet for an honorable admiral from Spain? Actually, that is what eventually happened in the Philippines. Manila became a Spanish trading post where products of East and West were exchanged.

The most important voyage of discovery in all history was also one of the easiest, outward-bound. Columbus sailed south to the Canary Islands, topped off with provisions, and made his departure thence on 6 September 1492. From earlier voyages he knew that down there his ships would be wafted along by the northeast tradewind, as they were.

After they had been out of sight of land for a full month and had logged over 2700 miles from the Canaries, the sailors threatened to force Columbus to turn back, fearing that they could never get home again. Columbus naturally was not going to be done out of his discovery after coming that far. He spoke cheering words, assured them there were plenty of provisions, appealed to their desire for gold and to their sense of honor; then set his jaw and remarked, "It is useless to complain. I made this voyage to go to the Indies, and shall continue until I find them, with God's help." Signs of land now became frequent. On 12 October 1492 at 2 a.m., a lookout in *Pinta* sighted in the moonlight a limestone cliff on what turned out to be an island in the Bahamas. Columbus named it *San Salvador*, and it is so called today. They drifted for the rest of the night, made sail at dawn, rounded the southern shore, and anchored under the lee of the land. There Columbus and his captains went ashore and in the presence of wondering natives took possession in the name of Ferdinand and Isabella.

San Salvador, the Admiral insisted, was an outpost of "the Indies," so he called the natives Indians. They were Arawaks, gentle and unwarlike, who wove cloth and made pottery; but, to Columbus's vast disappointment, possessed no gold except for a few nose plugs obtained by trade. So, picking up a few Indians as guides — they learned to speak Spanish surprisingly quickly — Columbus sailed through the Bahamas to Cuba, which his pilots, eager to please, led him to believe was the source of gold, and which he therefore assumed to be a part of China. No gold was to be found; but some of Columbus's shipmates, returning from a trip upcountry, discovered something that has created more well-being than gold. They met "many people with a firebrand in the hand, and herbs to drink the smoke thereof, as they are accustomed." These Cuban natives rolled their own cigars, which they called *tobacos*. A walking party, such as the Spaniards encountered, would carry one big cigar with a lighted firebrand; at every halt they "lit up" and everyone took a few puffs and felt refreshed. Cultivation and use of tobacco had already spread all over the Americas — Jacques Cartier at the site of Montreal in 1555 found Indians inhaling the smoke from pipes — and it was not long before Europeans carried Lady Nicotine to the Old World.

Columbus was disappointed at finding no spices of the Orient, such as cloves and cinnamon, but he noted maize and cassava, which have spread world-wide, native cotton, dugout canoes, and the hammock, which European natives soon adopted for their seamen. And at the great island which he named Hispaniola, he found the Indians wearing massive golden ornaments which they made from gold dust panned out of river beds. So, when flagship *Santa Maria* hit a reef on Christmas Eve and became a total loss, Columbus had no trouble getting volunteers to build and man a trading post colony; everyone wanted first whack at the gold. He named the place *Navidad* (Nativity), and on 16 January 1493 the Admiral in *Niña*, accompanied by *Pinta*, began the homeward passage. In an unusually rough winter, the caravels did well to weather two bad storms and to reach Palos on 15 March 1493.

The momentous discovery had been made; yet neither Columbus nor any member of his company realized it. The Bahamas, Cuba and Hispaniola, to them, were no new world such as we mean by that phrase, but island outposts to Asia. Japan and China were just around the corner.

5. *First Colonizing Attempts*

Back in Spain, Columbus reported to Ferdinand and Isabella, who confirmed his titles and privileges and promptly organized a second voyage under him, with some 1200 men to colonize Hispaniola. This fleet of seventeen vessels raised the island of Dominica on 3 November 1493 and coasted along the Lesser Antilles, discovering and naming, among others, Guadeloupe, Antigua, Nevis, St. Croix, the Virgin Islands, and Puerto Rico. Thence Columbus sailed along Hispaniola where he met his first setback — the discovery that his Navidad trading post had been wiped out. The Spanish garrison, roaming about Hispaniola in search of more gold and girls, ran afoul of a stout cacique named Caonabó, who killed them and destroyed Navidad.

Columbus abandoned that site and founded a new and more ambitious colony some 75 miles east of it at a place he named Isabela. But as soon as he stepped ashore and exchanged his sea command for that of governor, he got into trouble. Spaniards had signed on for one purpose only, to get gold; but there was none nearby and the Indians brought none in. Columbus intended everybody to live at Isabela and trade only at stated seasons, under license; but he could not prevent the men slipping off to the bush and trading with a gun. The soil was excellent and food crops could be grown in a few weeks; but, as one of the Admiral's friends wrote, nobody would work the land because, as soon as they found gold could not be picked up on the beach, they all "wanted home." The trouble about trading for gold was simply that the natives of Hispaniola had little of it and wanted less. Consumer demand for the cheap trading truck that the Spaniards brought — glass beads, tinkly hawk's bells, and strips of scarlet cloth — was soon satisfied. So, in order to keep his colony going, Columbus was forced to desperate expedients. First, he required a gold tribute from every native, a tribute too great for them to collect with the best will in the world. Next, he divided up the land — with the Indians who lived on it — among the Spanish colonists. In other words, he set up a system of forced labor for private profit. At the same time the smaller islands were raided for more laborers, and Indians who refused to work were either slaughtered or shipped home to be sold as slaves. Within fifty years the natives of Hispaniola, estimated by ethnologists to have numbered around 300,000 in 1492, and those of the Bahamas too, were extinct. Negro slaves were then imported from Africa to work sugar and cotton plantations and sift the earth for gold.

Columbus still insisted that Hispaniola was in "The Indies," and in the spring of 1494 he explored the south coast of Cuba, hoping to contact Chinese mandarins or Japanese shoguns; but he only met more Arawaks. He turned back before reaching the westerly cape of Cuba, satisfied that it was a promontory of China. Leaving his brother Bartholomew in charge of the colony at Isabela, he returned to Spain, and with difficulty convinced the sovereigns that his discoveries were valuable. They allowed him to fit out a relief expedition, recruited partly among peasants, draftees from the army, day laborers who were paid 14 cents a day, and girls who were paid nothing since they were expected to work their passage and then find husbands. Also, a free pardon was offered to criminals in jail who would spend a year in "The Indies," but not many takers were found. Ferdinand and Isabella gave Columbus three more vessels to make another voyage of discovery, in the hope of tapping the Indies further south. But before that voyage started, England had unveiled another corner of the New World.

6. First Northern Voyages

In the West Country of England the port of Bristol enjoyed a prosperous trade with Iceland and the Azores, and became the principal breeding place for English mariners who did business in great waters. To this thriving city there came to live around 1490 a countryman of Columbus named Giovanni Caboto, whom we call John Cabot. As the man who gave England her title to all North America east of the Rockies and north of Florida, Cabot and his voyages have been the object of intense research. Yet to this day we know very little about them.

King Henry VII of England, first of the House of Tudor, had been offered Columbus's enterprise but turned it down. After hearing the results of the first two voyages, in 1496, he granted authority to John Cabot and his three sons to sail "to all parts, contreys, and seas of the East, of the West, and of the North . . . upon their own proper costs and charges." They are to "seek out, discover and finde whatsoever isles, countreys regions or provinces of the heathen and infidels . . . unknowen to all Christians," raise the English "banners and ensignes," and in return may monopolize the trade. Obviously Cabot's main object, like that of Columbus, was to set up a trading-post colony adjacent to the Indies. According to one who interviewed Cabot, he had been to Mecca in Arabia, on the main caravan route for spices from the Far East to Europe. Since England, at the end of this line, paid the highest prices for spices, it occurred to Cabot to sail west along the high, short latitudes to tap the spiceries of the Indies and undercut the camel merchants.

His expedition was small but bold, braving the high seas and strong wester-lies of the North Atlantic in the little ship *Matthew*, with a crew of eighteen men. We have no details of the outward passage, only that it started from Bristol in May 1497, and that on Midsummer Day, 24 June, Cabot made landfall on some part of the North American coast. Exactly where, we cannot determine from the scanty sources that have survived; in my opinion it was on the northeast coast of Newfoundland. The Englishmen landed and raised the banner of St. George. They saw not one native, but picked up Indian fishnets as souvenirs and reported the vast store of codfish in those waters. The weather was so warm and pleasant that Cabot was sure he had discovered a northern promontory of Asia, and that on his next voyage he could reach Japan. It was a common delusion of explorers of North America for the next hundred years or more, arriving in the American summer, warmer than that of England or France, that they had found a semi-tropical country. As the wife of an early settler of Massachusetts wrote, after the disillusion of her first New England winter, "When I remember the high commendations some have given of the place, I have thought that they wrote surely in strawberry time." John Cabot reached our shores in strawberry time.

Matthew was back in Bristol on 6 August 1497, having made the ocean passage from "the new isle" (as it was called in the royal records) to Brittany in fifteen days. This indicates that Cabot had only three weeks for explora-tion, and that he must have taken his departure from southern Newfound-land to have made the 1860-mile crossing so rapidly. Henry VII gave him a pension of £20 per annum for adding "the new isle" to his dominions. But what lay behind the rockbound coasts of that northern land? Cabot tried to find out in 1498. We know nothing more of this voyage than that he started, but never returned; apparently the ships were lost with all hands. In 1501 an Azorean, a former *lavrador* (farmer) named João Fernandes, joined some other Portuguese and two Englishmen in making a northwesterly voyage from Bristol; and because João the farmer made the landfall, they named the country "Tierra del Lavrador." The Land of the Labrador it is to this day.

Except for a few entries in the English royal accounts of presents given to seamen who brought the king an eagle, a "popinjay" (woodpecker or blue-jay?) and "cat of the mountain" from the "New Founde Lande," this is all we know of English exploration in the first era of discovery. To the English of that day, it was a story of failure. No gold, no spices, no Japan; only trees, rocks, and codfish.

But the humble codfish brought northern America into fame. Catholic Europe (and all Europe then was Catholic) consumed enormous quantities of fish, and the best to cure and keep, in the absence of refrigeration, was the firm-flaked cod of northern waters. Portugal had found her passage to the Indies around the Cape of Good Hope, but she could use more fish; and by a treaty with Spain, King Manuel of Portugal claimed all newly discovered lands up to the meridian 1100 nautical miles west of the Cape Verde Islands. Assuming that the English discoveries were really within his bailiwick, he authorized Gaspar Corte Real, an Azorean, to make a voyage of discovery in 1500. That summer Corte Real rediscovered Newfoundland. On a second voyage next year he was lost, but his shipmates brought back Indians as slaves, and Venetian objects which Cabot must have left behind. Shortly after, Portuguese and French fishermen began plying their calling on the Grand Bank and curing their catches ashore. Some twenty place names on New-foundland today, from Cape Ray to Cape Race, are of Portuguese origin. Fagundes, a Portuguese, was the first to explore the Gulf of St. Lawrence, and the post of governor of Newfoundland remained hereditary in the Corte Real family until the last of that gallant line fell fighting the Moors in 1578.

Long before that, France had picked up the ball of northern dominion. For Portugal, by that time, had a great trading empire in the East to attend to. As a missionary once remarked, "God gave the Portuguese a small country to be born in, but a whole world to die in."

7. Searching for the Strait

Largely to forestall what they feared the Portuguese might do, Ferdinand and Isabella ordered Columbus in 1498 to take a more southerly route than on his two earlier voyages, in the hope of discovering the Asiatic continent. After a sultry but otherwise easy voyage, he made an island on the last day of July which he named Trinidad, and for the first time set foot on the Ameri-can continent in a harbor of what is now Venezuela, on 5 August 1498. Again he was disappointed in finding only naked Indians, not bejeweled gentlemen of Japan; but here he did find pearls. And from the vast volume of fresh water emptying into the Gulf of Paria he concluded that this was not the Indies which he had sought, but *un otro mundo*, an Other World. By this he meant that it was a land unknown to the ancients. His conception of the South America which he had discovered was that of a land mass tailing off from the Malay Peninsula, much as Indonesia actually does. And if that were so, there must be a strait through it; for Marco Polo had sailed all the way home from eastern China.

So Columbus's fourth and last voyage, in 1502–4, was largely a search for that strait. He sailed from the Canaries to Martinique, then coasted along the chain of islands to Cuba and crossed the Caribbean to what is now Honduras. He spent a very tempestuous winter exploring the coast of Central America to the Gulf of Darien, sailing into almost every navigable river or bay in the hope of finding a passage to India. But he had no luck. After a terrible bout of foul weather, he passed Christmas and New Year's, 1502–3, near the northern entrance to the present Panama Canal; but without any Indian to interpret, he never learned that he was on the narrowest part of the Isthmus. He tried to establish a trading post on the coast of Panama, but was driven off by the local Indians. Two worm-eaten and waterlogged caravels had to be abandoned, and with the other two he just managed to make Jamaica, where he was marooned for a year before being rescued.

Columbus then returned to Spain to die, despised and neglected. In the eyes of the royal court his West Indies had turned out to be useless. He alone of the early discoverers predicted their value for humanity, which is one reason why we honor him. Before he died he could declare, with no exaggeration, "By the Divine Will I have placed under the sovereignty of the King and Queen an Other World, whereby Spain, which was reckoned poor, is to become the richest of all countries."

By a strange comedy of errors, this Other or New World came to be named after a man who never commanded a voyage of discovery. Amerigo Vespucci, the most controversial character in our early history, was a Florentine who settled in Seville, where he ran a ship-chandlery business and helped to fit out Columbus's voyages. It is probable that in 1499 he joined a voyage commanded by Alonso de Hojeda, one of Columbus's captains, along the Pearl Coast to the Gulf of Maracaibo. Later he made three voyages, again as a passenger or junior officer, along the coast of Brazil. In 1504–5 there were printed in Florence what purported to be letters from him about these voyages; they were very chatty and amusing but, except for several spicy items on the manners and customs of the Indians, they might have been based on Columbus's and Hojeda's voyages. Whoever did write or compile these letters intimated that Vespucci was the captain of all four voyages and that the first, in which he (or his editor) claimed that he discovered the continent, took place in 1497, a year before Columbus. And in Vespucci's mouth is put the significant statement, "These regions we may rightly call *Mundus Novus*, a New World, because our ancestors had no knowledge of them. . . . I have found a continent more densely peopled and abounding in animals than our Europe or Asia or Africa."

It so happened that a young instructor named Waldseemüller at the College of St. Dié in eastern France was then bringing out a fresh edition of Ptolemy, with a new map of the world. Charmed with these printed letters, he wrote in his *Cosmographiae Introductio* (1507), "Since Americus Vespucius has discovered a fourth part of the world, it should be called after him . . . America, since Europe and Asia got their names from women." The idea spread, and by 1530 every European country except Spain and

Portugal was calling the New World, America. Yet it was a mistake even to credit Amerigo, or whoever wrote the letters on his alleged voyages, with a new geographical idea. His *Mundus Novus* was the same as Columbus's *otro mundo*, a continental appendage to eastern Asia. Waldseemüller, however, went a step further and joined Columbus's and Cabot's discoveries to those of the Portuguese in Brazil as one continuous continent, with Japan about 600 miles west of the Isthmus of Panama; and on his map the name AMERICA appears at about the site of Uruguay.

To give the Vespucci letters their due, they gave Europe for the first time some conception of the vast extent of South America. But nobody as yet had any knowledge of the Pacific; even Balboa who in 1513 gazed on it "with a wild surmise — silent, upon a peak in Darien," supposed that he was seeing the Indian Ocean. But Magellan took the measure of the vast Pacific.

Ferdinand Magellan, greatest seaman in the world's history, was a thirty-nine-year-old Portuguese who had already visited the source of spices, two little islands of Indonesia named Ternate and Tidore. The voyage there and back around the Cape of Good Hope was so long and tempestuous that he conceived the idea of finding a short way through America, and Spain financed him. He discovered the Strait that bears his name, and it took him 38 days to get through it. On 28 November 1520, says the narrative of the voyage, "We debouched from that Strait, engulfing ourselves in the Pacific Sea." By ill chance the great captain shaped a course that missed every island until he reached Guam, fourteen weeks later, with crews so hungry as to have eaten the leather chafing gear on the yards. They then crossed the Philippine Sea and sailed through Surigao Strait, scene of the great naval battle of 25 October 1944. Magellan landed on the island of Limasaua, where on 31 March 1521 there occurred an intensely dramatic encounter. The captain's Malay servant Henriquez, whom he had engaged on an earlier voyage to Indonesia, made himself understood by the Moslem natives. He was the first human being to encircle the globe. Magellan never did. He was killed at Mactan when attacking the enemies of his new ally, the rajah of Cebu. Of his fleet, originally five strong, *Vittoria*, under Captain Juan Sebastian del Cano, reached home in 1522, three years after the voyage began, with only eighteen survivors out of several hundred.

This voyage told Europe for the first time the width of the Pacific, and where the real Indies were situated with reference to the New World. But the search continued for another strait of easier access and navigation than Magellan's.

In the meantime Hispaniola was making good as a colony. It exported about a million dollars' worth of gold in 1512, the high point. Negro slaves were being imported to replace the wretched Indians; cattle raising and sugar planting had begun. Settlers who quarreled with the government moved on. Balboa was one of those, and Juan Ponce de Leon, granted Puerto Rico in 1501 if he could conquer it from the Indians, which he promptly did. Feeling debilitated at the age of fifty-three, Ponce embarked on a voyage in search of the fabled fountain of youth, in the course of which he discovered and named Florida at Eastertide 1513. But the fountain eluded him, and the natives were unfriendly. Spanish settlement of Jamaica began in 1510; of Cuba in 1512.

Such, in briefest outline, is the history of the earliest period of European discovery and colonization. After initial curiosity was satisfied, the New World aroused slight interest. Down to 1516, when Peter Martyr brought out the first attempt at an American history — *Decades of the New World* — there was not a single work that attained the dignity of a book; only a few pamphlets such as Columbus's *Letter* and Vespucci's *Mundus Novus*. For, from the European point of view, America was a disappointment. It blocked the western route to China, Japan and India; its precious metals appeared to be exhausted; the spices brought home by Columbus had turned out not to be spices, and the only valuable wood found so far in the New World was guiacum, an essence of which was supposed to cure the blight inflicted upon Europe by the West Indians — syphilis. The climate was unhealthy, the native food unwholesome, even some of the fish were poisonous. Spain would have been glad to write off the New World and withdraw, but for the teasing thought that some other country might move in and make something of it.

SALVE REGINA

III

The Spanish Century

1492-1580

1. *Spain Conquers Three Indian Empires*

WHAT NATION would put her stamp on the New World? That, we may say, was the greatest question in American history for two centuries after the discovery. We know the answer: Spain stamped America from Cape Horn up to the Rio Grande, and even beyond; but England, entering the contest late, placed the stamp of her language, law, and custom on the major part of North America, which became the United States and Canada; and France placed hers on Quebec. All three did it by colonization, a form of conquest in which a nation takes over a distant territory, thrusts in its own people, and controls or eliminates the native inhabitants. Conquest is as old as human history; but modern colonization, as we understand it, started when Europeans began that amazing expansion of trade and settlement which resulted in world dominion. This process produced lasting results in America, Australia, New Zealand, and South Africa; even in those countries of Asia and Africa which have won their independence since World War II.

We have now witnessed the fall of colonialism, affecting the world almost as deeply as did the fall of the Roman Empire. Even the words "colonial" and "colonialism" have become pejorative. But non-Indian Americans have no reason to join this hue and cry. For colonialism brought the New World into the orbit of Western civilization. Even the concepts of freedom and democracy, which almost every independent American nation, and many others too, have embraced, were imported from Europe. And the more viable of these new nations have set up governments based on the English parliamentary or the American republican system.

One may divide modern colonies into three kinds: the trading-post, the fringe colony (an enlarged beachhead on the edge of the sea), and the all-out settlement colony. The first was what Columbus tried to set up in Hispaniola. But a trading-post colony, works only when planted among a relatively advanced people who are used to commerce. The Portuguese had done that among the Negro kingdoms of West Africa and would do it in Africa and India — where the last Portuguese colony, Goa, was grabbed by Nehru in 1962. The Portuguese never emigrated in large numbers; they merely established garrisons and left the natives alone as long as they did not try to rush

34

the trading post and make off with the goods. But in Brazil, her portion of
the New World, Portugal found she had to establish a fringe colony, just as
Columbus did in Hispaniola. Both had to expand trading posts to fringes, and
eventually to all-out settlements, because the natives of Central and South
America were not traders; Europeans had to spread out and settle, in order to
produce anything. And it was not long before all Europeans in the New
World were importing Negro slaves to do the heavy work that Indians would
not or could not do, and that Europeans were too proud or lazy to do.

The transition of the Spanish empire in America from trading post and
fringe to settlement began with the conquest of Mexico in 1519–21. That
date is as important as 1492 in American history, since it signaled a complete
change of attitude by Europe toward the New World.

In 1519 the governor of Cuba, wishing to establish a trading post on the
Mexican coast, sent an expedition of eleven ships, carrying about five hundred
Spaniards under thirty-two-year-old Hernando Cortés, to set it up. His conquest of Mexico was one of the most amazing military and diplomatic feats in
the world's history. The march from Vera Cruz to the great interior plateau,
the audacious capture of Montezuma's lake-rimmed capital, and the defeat of
a vast army on the plains of Teotihuacan completed the ruin of Aztec power
and firmly established Spain as sovereign of Mexico.

The only other conquests to be mentioned in the same breath were those
of Peru and New Granada. Balboa, after crossing the Isthmus of Panama, got
word of the Inca empire which was said to surpass even that of the Aztec in
wealth and magnificence. Spain ordered Francisco Pizarro to conquer it. He
built a fleet at Panama, invaded Peru in 1531, treacherously seized and murdered Atahualpa, the Inca emperor who had welcomed him, founded Lima in
1535, and two years later frustrated the last efforts of the natives to surround
and cut him off.

Cartagena, a trading-post colony founded by Pedro de Heredia in 1533, was
the jumping-off place for an expedition under Gonzalo de Quesada which
pushed up the Magdalena river, crossed the mountains to the site of Bogotá,
and overthrew the Chibcha, third of the great native empires. Quesada then
established the government of New Granada, famous among other things as
the birthplace of Simon Bolívar, the future liberator.

The relative ease of these conquests is explained by complete surprise, and
the Spaniards' superior equipment and technique. It was as if a horde of
conquerors should descend on us from another planet with weapons that
would make our latest nuclear gimmicks of no more use than bows and
arrows. By any standards, the ruling classes of the Aztec, Inca, and Chibcha
empires were their conquerors' equals. As Cunninghame Graham wrote:

Their chieftains, treated as gods, borne on the shoulders of their subjects, refined,
intelligent, and far more reasonable in controversy than were their conquerors,
boldly met the onslaught of a race of men who fell upon them, as it were, from the
skies — a race of beings sheathed in steel, riding on animals that seemed a part of

them who breathed out fire, as the Indians thought, taking the harquebus as in some way connected with the horse. With their poor arms and quilted cotton doublets, their poisoned arrows and their fire-hardened spears, they faced those "children of the sun," dying in heaps, just as Leonidas and his three hundred Spartans died for their fatherland.

These conquests put a new face on Spanish America. Mexico, Peru, and New Granada were far more valuable than anything Columbus had found: rich, populous native empires with a small ruling class which the Spaniards had merely to supplant in order to exploit the masses and extract the wealth. Labor was there, already organized. It was as if Chinese invaders should move in on General Motors, kill all the top executives, and force the technicians and artisans to work for them.

Up to 1522 comparatively few Spaniards had settled in America, and most of those who did were sorry for themselves. Now that these mining empires were opened up, everyone wanted to go. Entire regions of Spain where living was hard, and the West Indies too, were depopulated in favor of Mexico, Peru, and New Granada. A census taken of the Greater Antilles in 1574 revealed that Hispaniola then contained only 1000 Spaniards — fewer than Columbus had brought over in 1493 — and 12,000 Negro slaves; Cuba and Jamaica each had only 250 Spaniards. The islands now became agricultural, raising cotton, sugar, and tobacco for Spanish consumption, and cattle and corn for export to the American mainland.

Thus, in South and Central America the Spanish colonial system was based on the exploitation of semi-servile Indian labor and wholly servile imported African labor. Tens of thousands of Spaniards came over; but they were the plantation owners, the overseers, and the skilled artisans. The mines of Mexico and Peru were to sixteenth- and seventeenth-century Spain what oil, steel, and minerals are to twentieth-century Europe and America — the basis of power, feeders of defense and conquest.

The settlement type of colony has almost always been characterized by exploitation. That is the main reason why colonialism is so unpopular today. Europeans went to new countries primarily to get rich, and many did; but in the course of time the people they exploited, whether natives or imported slaves, had their revenge. And of the greater colonizing powers, only England, profiting by her experience in the American Revolution, has had the wisdom to help her overseas subjects to make a peaceful transition from colony to nation.

2. The Adelantados in North America

The results of this conquest in terms of treasure were spectacular, but the prospect of more to come was infinite. It might be supposed that liquidation of three native empires would employ the energies of Spain for a century; but these conquests were only the beginning. The whole southern section of the

United States from South Carolina across to California was explored by Spanish conquistadors in search of more valuable treasure, of new empires that might challenge Mexico; and for the fabled Strait of Anian which was supposed to cross North America from east to west, and might be the long-sought passage to India. These conquistadors were called *adelantados*, advancers. They were given special exploration permits by the King of Spain or the Viceroy of Mexico.

Pánfilo de Narvaez, who had been badly treated by Cortés, chose Florida for his field of glory in 1527. Most unfortunate of all conquistadors, Pánfilo lost two ships in a hurricane, landed somewhere on the Gulf coast of Florida, fought his way up to the site of Tallahassee, and retreated to the coast. There he built a fleet of boats from native wood fastened with spikes fashioned from spurs and stirrups, rigged with cordage and sails made from the hair and hides of horses eaten by his men. In these crazy craft he sailed past the mouth of the Mississippi, only to be wrecked on the coast of Texas. The survivors — Cabeza de Vaca, two other Spaniards and a Negro — spent six years among the Indians, eventually reaching Mexico with tales of wild "hunchback cows" that covered the plains as far as the eye could see, and of cities with emerald-studded walls, of which they had heard. These "Seven Cities of Cibolá" were more readily believed in than the buffalo.

In 1539 the viceroy of Mexico sent Fray Marcos, accompanied by Esteban, the Negro companion of Cabeza de Vaca, up into the future New Mexico in search of the fabled Seven Cities. There they discovered the disappointing foundation of this myth, the Zuñi pueblos, and so reported. But the honest tale of Fray Marcos was so blown up by popular imagination that the viceroy now sent out the most splendid exploring expedition of all, that of Francisco Vásquez Coronado, while a co-operating fleet sailed up the Gulf of California. One of Coronado's lieutenants discovered the Grand Canyon in 1540; Coronado himself marched eastward across the panhandle of Texas into eastern Kansas, only to prick another rumor of wealthy cities and a strait. Disappointed, he returned to Mexico.

Hernando de Soto, who had served under Pizarro in Peru, obtained a grant of Florida from the king. Landing at Tampa Bay, he marched about the interior of the future Gulf states for many months, led on by tales of splendid cities. In 1541 he reached the Mississippi near Memphis, crossed to the west bank, spent the winter near the site of Fort Smith, Arkansas, returned to the Father of the Waters, and there died. His men built boats, descended the Mississippi, crossed the Gulf of Mexico, and reached Tampico in safety after an absence of over four years.

Owing to their failure to find treasure or a strait, these Spanish explorations of North America had no immediate result; the tide of conquest turned south. Only at the end of the sixteenth century, when the frontier of Mexico had been pushed so near to the Rio Grande that conquest of the Pueblo Indians seemed desirable, did Juan de Oñate formally take possession "of all the kingdoms and provinces of New Mexico." The Pueblos promptly submitted, colonization began, and the next governor founded Sante Fe in 1609. Thus New Mexico was settled at the same time as the first permanent English colony in Virginia.

Gifts of untold value that Oñate gave to the future United States were domesticated cattle and horses. Texas longhorns are descended from the cattle that he turned loose, and his mares and stallions are ancestors of the mustang or bronco. Those that Oñate turned out to graze were first killed by the Indians for food; but some converted Pueblo ranch hands who had learned to ride brought their mounts to the wild Indians beyond the Spanish pale. The latter found that horses were just what they needed to hunt the buffalo, and each other. By 1700 almost every tribe between New Mexico, the Mississippi, and Kansas had domesticated the horse, and enormous herds of wild mustangs roamed the Great Plains.

By 1600, Spain had conquered almost the whole of coastal South America except Brazil, and much of the interior as well, down to the River Plate. Thus, foundations had been laid for every one of the twenty republics of Central and South America, excepting the Argentine. No other conquest like this has there been in the annals of the human race. In one generation the Spaniards acquired more new territory than Rome conquered in five centuries. Genghis Khan swept over a greater area but left only destruction in his wake; the Spaniards organized and administered all that they conquered, brought in the arts and letters of Europe, and converted millions to their faith. Our forebears in Virginia and New England, the pathfinders of the Great West, and the French pioneers of Canada, were indeed stout fellows; but their exploits scarcely compare with those of brown-robed Spanish friars and armored conquistadors who hacked their way through solid jungle, across endless plains, and over snowy passes of the Andes, to fulfill dreams of glory and conversion; and for whom reality proved even greater than the dream.

On the institutional side, the Spanish empire more closely resembled the Roman than the British empire. All European institutions suffered a change before emerging in America, the Spanish not excepted. The English colonists of North America were able to select the more vigorous and valuable features of English political institutions, and consciously adapt them to New World needs, rejecting the useless residue of feudalism; but the Spanish colonists' institutions were selected for them at Madrid. The Spanish crown, having emerged triumphant from struggles with the nobility and the burghers, took good care that no rivals to royal authority developed in America. Proper machinery was devised to this end, in marked contrast to the lackadaisical English colonial policy. Laws for Spanish America were drafted in Spain by the Council of the Indies. The American trade, monopolized by the merchants of Seville, was regulated in minute detail by the Casa de la Contractation, the official board of trade. The New World was first divided into two great viceroyalties of Nueva España (Mexico) and Peru, to which La Plata

(Argentine and Chile) and Nueva Granada (Colombia and Venezuela) were later added. They in turn were divided into eleven *audiencias*, roughly corresponding to the national boundaries of today; and these were subdivided into minor administrative units. The officials, from viceroys to alcaldes, were responsible to the king and held their posts during his good pleasure. Thus, Spanish America grew up understanding no form of government but autocracy tempered by corruption; a pattern not wholly broken today.

There is another side to the picture: first, the conversion of Indians, whose religion required the killing of thousands of innocent people annually to appease angry gods, to Christianity. From the Spanish *hidalgo* the South Americans inherit the chivalrous courtesy that one finds among their poorest people today; the Puerto Rican immigrant to New York City cherishes his *dignidad*, he cannot be pushed around. And the fine arts of Europe followed close on the trail of conquest. Lima, the "City of Kings," and Mexico City became seats of urban civilization within fifteen years of the conquest; in each a university was founded in 1551. The first printing press in the New World was set up at Mexico City in 1539. To this day an air of superb magnificence rests on the churches and palaces built by the Spaniards and their native subjects in their provincial capitals.

Thus, the Spanish empire in America had more than a century's head start on the English and French; and the results of that conquest, materially as well as spiritually, were amazing, stupendous, and the envy of every European power. Spanish prestige reached its height in the year 1580 when Philip II succeeded to the throne of Portugal as well as that of Spain, uniting under his person two empires that now stretched their arms around the world: the left arm to the west coast of Mexico, the right arm to Manila. At that time, not another nation had placed a single permanent settler on the shores of the New World.

But the end of the Spanish monopoly was near. The autumn gales of 1580, blowing up the English Channel, brought into Plymouth Francis Drake's *Golden Hind*, returning from a three-year voyage around the world, laden with the spoil of a Peruvian treasure ship, and eager for more. Only eight years later, the Spanish Armada invading England was decisively defeated. Within a few more years, Virginia and New France were well seated, and Spain could do nothing about it.

But before we relate the small beginnings of the English colonies which in 1776 became the United States, we must tell about a colony that put a permanent stamp on the Province of Quebec.

3. The Beginnings of New France

These were modest indeed. There is no Leif the Lucky, Cabot or Columbus in the annals of French discovery. Humble fishermen and traders were the heralds of empire for that nation. For a century after the first Frenchman arrived in New World waters the story of New France is one of small things; petty expeditions ill-equipped by small merchants of the seaport towns, harassed by the fluctuating policy of successive kings, abandoned as soon as hope of finding gold or other quick assets was lost. Throughout her French period Canada was a trading-post and fringe colony in which the tasty codfish and luxurious peltry played the same role as the spices that brought wealth to Portugal, and the precious metals of Mexico and Peru.

French fishermen sailing in the wake of John Cabot and the Corte Real began to frequent the Grand Bank as early as 1504; but the first French voyage of discovery came twenty years later. Francis I, admirer of Italy and Spain, decided that he needed a Genoese navigator to do what Columbus and Cabot had failed to do — find a strait leading to the Indies. So he engaged Giovanni Verrazano and persuaded to finance him the silk merchants of Lyons, who wanted a short sea route to China.

Verrazano's first port of call after the West Indies, in April 1524, was the site of New York. He looked up the great river later named Hudson and decided that it was no strait. He then tried Narragansett Bay with the same result. Rounding Cape Cod, he ranged the coasts of Maine, Nova Scotia, and Newfoundland to the Strait of Belle Isle. The results of this voyage were negative, from the viewpoint of the French court; but Verrazano founded a new geographical delusion. The map of North America that his brother drafted has a narrow-waisted isthmus at the site of Virginia, with the legend "Indian Ocean" on the other side. This northern isthmus concept persisted into the eighteenth century, when Governor Spotswood of Virginia expected to play the role of Balboa on the crest of the Blue Ridge.

Jacques Cartier, mariner of Saint Malo in Brittany, was responsible for directing the attention of France to the Laurentian region. He made two voyages to America in 1533 and 1535, sailing up the river which he named the St. Lawrence, turning back a little above the site of Montreal, wintering under the Rock of Quebec. Friendly and humorous Hurons beguiled the Frenchmen through a long, cold winter with tall tales of a Kingdom of Saguenay inhabited by white men who had mines of gold, silver, and rubies, and even grew spices; Chief Donnaconna, elaborating, declared that among them were men who had only one leg, flew like bats, and never ate. Cartier not only "bought" the whole package but persuaded the Huron chief to accompany him to France and sell it to the king, which he did. Here, thought Francis I, was the opportunity to acquire a Mexico of his own and run the King of Spain out of business. So he sent Cartier on a third voyage in 1541, with ten ships and so many people and such rich equipment that the King of Spain seriously thought of sending a fleet to break it up. This expedition pushed up the St. Lawrence, but the wealthy kingdom was always beyond the next rapid. Cartier's partner Roberval explored in boats the river now called Saguenay but found only the walls of the northern wilderness closing in on him. They returned to France with a heap of iron pyrites which they believed to be gold, and quartz crystals that they hoped were diamonds. "Canadian diamonds" became a standard joke in France, and the only tangible result of this voyage.

French efforts to colonize Canada were now suspended, owing largely to civil wars at home. But two futile attempts were made to found French trading posts on the coast of Florida, where the Spaniards had neglected to take possession. The first, by Jean Ribault, set up a pillar at the mouth of the St. John river below Jacksonville in 1562, and established a trading post on the site of the present U.S. Marine Corps reservation at Parris Island, South Carolina. That did not last long. René de Laudonnière made a second attempt, with four shiploads of French Protestants, in 1563. They located Ribault's stone column, and Jacques Le Moyne, an artist in the party, made a charming watercolor sketch of Laudonnière and Outima, chief of the Timucua Indians, fraternizing. The leader decided to pitch his trading post there, named it Fort Caroline, then returned to France for reinforcements. In his absence some of the Frenchmen stole a ship anchored in the river and went a-pirating in the West Indies. This stirred up the Spaniards, and the French left in Fort Caroline reached the verge of famine because they were dependent on the Indians for food. In the summer of 1565 the Spaniards caught up with them. Fort Caroline was captured and the survivors who surrendered were slaughtered, every one. Spain founded St. Augustine the same year and studded the coast as far north as the Carolinas with forts and missions. For the treasure galleons returning to Spain passed that way, and it would not do to let foreigners locate at a spot whence small boats could put out and capture a becalmed ship.

The only permanent result of this short-lived French colony in Florida was the introduction of tobacco both to France and England. John Hawkins of Plymouth called at Fort Caroline and brought home a parcel of it, which he described as follows: "The Floridians have a kind of herb dried, who with a cane and an earthen cup on the end, with fire, — doe suck through the cane the smoke thereof, which smoke satisfieth their hunger."

Even though Cartier's last voyage shattered the Saguenay myth, French fishermen resorted every summer to the Grand Bank, and to cure their codfish some landed on the shores of Newfoundland and Cape Breton Island, so called by fishermen from Brittany. These landings led to trade with the Indians, who had valuable fur to barter for axes and other iron tools. Gentlemen of that era required fur for trimming coats and to make the felt of which wide-brimmed, high-crowned hats, fashionable for over two centuries, were made. So the fishermen learned to bring over a supply of cloth, axes, iron kettles, and other goods that the Indians wanted, and every fishing station became a trading post. This led to special fur-trading expeditions pushing into the Gulf of St. Lawrence, and to the establishment of a chain of trading posts — Port Royal, Quebec, Montreal, Trois Rivières — which eventually became towns or cities.

In 1590 Henry of Navarre — Henri IV whose gallant soul and bristly-bearded countenance live in the pages of Parkman — won the Battle of Ivry and brought an end to the Wars of Religion. It was time to make an effort to colonize Canada, ahead of the English. The chosen method was natural enough in a poor country lately torn by civil strife. A monopoly of Canadian fur trade was granted to individuals or small companies, on condition that they settle a certain number of colonists per year at their own expense. The government undertook to find colonists if the company could not, by rounding up vagabonds and relieving congestion in the jails.

The immediate results of this policy were not impressive. The companies seldom complied with the terms; and when they did, the former inmates of His Majesty's prisons either died or ran away. Other fur traders in the meantime brought pressure on the king to cancel the monopoly and give it to themselves; and the monopoly so frequently changed hands that it was no longer respected. Yet one of these short-lived companies was responsible for bringing to Canada Samuel de Champlain, rightly regarded as the father of New France.

That was in 1504. A company attempted to establish a colony on the river which now divides Maine from New Brunswick. The settlement was first pitched on Dochet Island (since renamed St. Croix), for protection against the Indians. After one cold and miserable winter it was transferred to Port Royal on the Annapolis Basin in the present Nova Scotia. Champlain in a small pinnace explored the coast of "Norumbega," which later became known as New England, as far as the south side of Cape Cod, looking for a better site. He found none, because the further south he sailed, the less fur the Indians had to sell. But Port Royal did very well. Under Poutrincourt and a Parisian lawyer named Lescarbot, a stout palisaded *habitation* was raised, a treaty concluded with the nearby Micmac sagamore, corn and other vegetables were planted, and a jolly winter was spent by great log fires, beguiled by songs and a pageant in which the Indians took part.

4. The Elizabethan Prelude

Henry VII, first monarch of the House of Tudor, took over a small, weak, and war-weary England in 1485. Elizabeth I, last of that royal line, left an empire to her successor James I.

Since Henry VII had been second only to Ferdinand and Isabella in New World discovery, it may seem strange that England was slow to follow up. But there were good reasons. Cabot found no passage to India and reported nothing of value in the land that he discovered. England was afraid of Spain, and the example of what happened to the French colony in Florida deterred her from attempts to settle near the Spaniards. The English kings were chronically broke, largely because of their dependence on Parliament for money. And England needed time to accumulate venture capital so that individuals could finance overseas enterprise.

English mariners reached America the hard way, the long way, and (as we shall see) the back way, instead of taking the short route traced by Cabot. The first big effort came in 1553 when the Muscovy Company was formed to find a northeast passage to the Indies. That was more than any ship could get through without an icebreaker, but the Muscovy Company did open a profitable trade with Russia, which at that time was hardly better known in England than the Iroquois Confederacy. The next target for English overseas enterprise was West Africa, for gold, ivory, and slaves. These led to the voyages to America by Sir John Hawkins.

Under Elizabeth I (1558–1603), England embarked on a course of expansion, spiritual and material, such as few nations have ever experienced. It was the age of Sir Philip Sidney and Shakespeare, of Sir Humfrey Gilbert and Sir Walter Raleigh, of highest skill in matters maritime, and supreme achievement in poetry, prose, and music. In England during that happy era, the scholar, the divine, and the man of action were often one and the same.

Yet every attempt at colonization in Elizabeth's reign failed. The efforts of Philip II of Spain (Elizabeth's brother-in-law) to rub her out as a heretic and a usurper led to a breach between the two countries, and a long war which was fought mostly on the ocean. Venture capital found it more profitable to finance privateering expeditions against Spanish treasure fleets than to search for a passage to India or set up a North American trading post. Yet, somehow, the preliminary work got done.

Sir Humfrey Gilbert was the Englishman who sparked it off. His first quest was for the nonexistent Strait of Anian. In 1566, when he was twenty-seven years old, he wrote "A Discourse To Prove a Passage by the Northwest to Cathaia"; i.e. China. Eleven years later, Francis Drake departed on a voyage with the hope of finding it.

Drake had commanded a ship in Hawkins's fleet, treacherously attacked by Spaniards at Vera Cruz. He had raided the Isthmus of Panama in 1572, sighted the Pacific, and "resolved to sail an England ship in these seas." And he wished to check another unfounded geographical theory that a great Terra Australis ran around the world just below the Strait of Magellan. Sailing through that strait in the *Golden Hind*, Drake ascertained that there was no Terra Australis, only barren Tierra del Fuego. He turned north, captured a rich treasure galleon off the coast of Peru, landed at or near the place now called Drake's Bay not far north of San Francisco, and took possession of that country for Queen Elizabeth I, naming it Nova Albion — New England. He had no doubt that the western opening of the northern strait lay nearby, and he probably sailed as far north as Vancouver Island in the search. Not finding it, he turned west, picked up a valuable cargo of cloves in the Spice Islands, and returned to England around the world. The profits of this voyage were almost $9 million in gold, and the Queen was so pleased with her share that she knighted Drake on the deck of the *Golden Hind*, which was as good as telling the King of Spain, "North America belongs to England — hands off!"

In the meantime Sir Humfrey Gilbert had obtained from the Queen a

charter to discover "remote heathen and barbarous lands not actually possessed by any Christian prince or people . . . and the same to have, hold,
occupy and enjoy," providing that all settlers who go out with him shall
"enjoy all the privileges of free denizens and persons native of England"; and
that any laws or ordinances that he may pass for his colony "be as neere as
conveniently may, agreeable to the forms of the laws & policy of England."
Although Sir Humfrey never made good on this grant, the last two principles,
new in the history of colonization, became basic in English colonial policy. A
freeborn Englishman lost no rights by moving overseas; and the lord proprietor of a colony, such as Gilbert intended to be (and Lord Baltimore and
William Penn later became), most not play dictator but must govern by
English law.

In June 1583 Gilbert sailed from Plymouth in command of four vessels.
His ultimate object was to find and secure the northwest passage, but he
first took possession of Newfoundland, which he thought blocked its eastern
entrance. Entering St. John's harbor in August, he set up a pillar with the
English arms and told the fishermen from over thirty vessels which he found
there at anchor that they must obey him and the Queen. He attempted to
explore the coast southward, sent one ship home, lost another on Cape
Breton; and then, as the sailors became mutinous, turned homeward. Gilbert
sailed in the tiny pinnace *Squirrel*, which the larger vessel tried to keep in
sight through raging gales and "outrageous seas." On a rough September day
she closed the *Squirrel* so near that Sir Humfrey with a book in hand was
heard to call out, "We are as neere to heaven by sea as by land!" Then the
sun set, and of a sudden the light on the pinnace went out, for she had been
"devoured and swallowed up of the Sea."

The book that Sir Humfrey was reading on the last day of his life was
undoubtedly Sir Thomas More's *Utopia*, in which is found the maxim, "The
way to heaven out of all places is of like length and distance." That book,
which has given its name to all other utopias, may be called the blueprint to
the American dream of a good life. More's imagination fused the ideal world
of Plato's *Republic* and the New World of America. He foretold that a model
republic might be founded somewhere in the new countries recently discovered; and that there mankind might find what they had always sought —
plenty, peace, liberty, and security, under a government of calm philosophers;
a six-hour day, leaving time "for the free liberty of the mind and garnishing of
the same."

Gilbert's charter was inherited by his thirty-one-year-old half-brother, Sir
Walter Raleigh, Elizabeth's favorite courtier. In 1584 Raleigh sent a reconnaissance fleet under Captains Amadas and Barlow to the future Croatan
Sound, North Carolina. They brought back a glowing account of the air, soil,
and Indians — "most gentle, loving and faithful, void of all guile and treason,
and such as live after the manner of the golden age." Raleigh now decided to
colonize in earnest. As encouragement, the Virgin Queen knighted him and

graciously permitted him to name the new land Virginia. This Virginia meant all North America that England could seize and hold, from sea to sea. Next year, Sir Walter sent out, under Ralph Lane, a colonizing expedition of a hundred men who settled on Roanoke Island, in what is now North Carolina. The colony included artist John White, surveyor Thomas Hariot, and a Bohemian Jew named Joachim Ganz to prospect for minerals. He found none; but Hariot's account of the expedition, illustrated by White's drawings, is the most careful description of North American natives from the pen of an Englishman in the first century of colonization. Sir Francis Drake, who had been raiding the West Indies, looked in at Roanoke Island on his way home. He found the colonists unhappy and hungry, and at their request took them back to England.

Sir Walter now obtained and organized "The Governor and Assistants of the City of Raleigh in Virginia." In 1587 he sent out a fresh colony consisting of 117 men, women, and children in three ships, with John White as governor. This colony might have been permanent if, like the later Jamestown, it had been supported from home. But it was a bad time and a poor place to leave a small colony to its own devices. The region around Pamlico Sound had a dense Indian population, and the local tribe did not appreciate the insatiable demands of Englishmen for food and labor. It was the wrong time, too, to look for help from home. A Spanish armada was being prepared to invade England, where nobody could spare the effort to succor a tiny outpost in Virginia.

The Armada was defeated in 1588, but two years passed before anything could be done about Virginia. Then Raleigh arranged for some privateers to carry supplies to his colony. They spent most of the summer roistering about the Caribbean and only reached Roanoke in mid-August. As their commander tells the story, "We let fall our grapnel neere the shore and sounded with a trumpet a Call, and afterwardes many familiar English tunes of Songs, and called to them friendly." But to these genial sounds there was no answer; and when the Englishmen landed, they found only rummaged and rifled chests, rotten maps, rusty armor, grass-grown palisades, and the word CROATOAN carved on a tree. That was the native name of the island on which Cape Hatteras is situated, about a hundred miles southwest of Roanoke. The sailors refused to linger at so depressing a place, and the relief expedition returned to England.

Nobody knows what became of the "Lost Colony." The best guess is that some starved to death, and others were killed by the Indians, who adopted the surviving children. To this day the Croatan (now called Lumbee) Indians of southeastern North Carolina believe that the blood of Raleigh's colonists runs in their veins.

Thus the sixteenth century closed like the fifteenth, without England's having planted a colony or even a trading post in the New World. It was largely the war with Spain, which lasted until 1604, which kept her back. But that war, waged mostly on the sea, was no loss to the future of English civilization. Through fighting Spaniards the English acquired confidence wealth, and strength. They improved the designs of ships and methods of navigation. They ceased to be insular; they acquired a world ambition.

England, too, felt that she was fighting for freedom against a despotism that covered half the world, but Elizabeth I resolutely refused to send armies into the European continent. How wise she was! How different, and worse, the world might have become if the energy that the English displayed between 1550 and 1650 had turned to the dominance of Europe; if no Virginia, no New England, had been founded overseas, and England had become a military nation. But sea power has never led to despotism. The nations that have enjoyed sea power even for a brief period — Athens, Scandinavia, the Netherlands, England, the United States — are those that have preserved freedom for themselves and have given it to others. Of the despotism to which unrestrained military power leads we have plenty of examples from Alexander to Mao. So let us not write off the forays and sea battles of the Elizabethans as failures. The efforts of blithe, lusty spirits like Drake, Gilbert, and Raleigh, under that great queen whom they called Gloriana, blazed the way for the United States of America and the British Commonwealth.

VIVE HENRI QUATRE!

Vive Hen - ri qua - tre, Vi - ve ce roi vail - lant!

Ce diable à qua - tre A le tri - ple ta -

lent De boire et se bat - tre, Et d'être un vert ga - lant!

Two Founding Decades

1607-1627

1. *The Setting*

O N 30 JULY 1607, owing to a royal annulment of his monopoly, Lescarbot with a heavy heart abandoned the French trading post so happily seated at Port Royal, Nova Scotia. Most of the colonists returned with him to France, but Poutrincourt, Champlain, and a handful of men remained. It must have seemed to them that all was over, that New France would now be victim of freebooters from all nations. Actually the history of Canada and the United States had just begun. Unknown to the French, a band of enthusiastic Englishmen a few months earlier had founded Jamestown, nucleus of the Old Dominion of Virginia. Champlain began in 1608, under the Rock of Quebec jutting into the St. Lawrence, the first French post in America destined to be a great city. There, more than 350 years later, the royal lilies of France are still displayed on the banners of the French-speaking Province of Quebec.

Another year passed, and the waters of the Hudson, unruffled (so far as the record goes) by any European ship since the brief visit of Verrazano in 1524, were cloven by a little Dutch vessel called the *Half Moon*, captained by Henry Hudson. He was the herald of a short-lived Dutch empire in North America, as Cabot and Cartier were of the more permanent English and French empires. And in 1620 a band of a hundred Pilgrims, as they called themselves, set up a trading post on the shores of Northern Virginia, which had just been renamed New England. Their Colony of New Plymouth became the second nucleus of the English American empire; and in 1625 a third was established on the island of St. Kitts in the Caribbean.

Port Royal was not dead. Madame de Guercheville, a pious lady-in-waiting to the Queen Mother of France, paid the bills for a joint fur-trading and missionary expedition to reoccupy the almost deserted post, and to establish others. Her men found Port Royal so depressed that in 1613 they set up a missionary station on the island of Mount Desert in the present State of Maine. This was wiped out the same year by Captain Samuel Argall in command of an armed ship from Virginia. He then inflicted the same punishment on Port Royal for venturing to exist on a continent claimed by England. In the valley of the St. Lawrence, French and Dutch had already taken sides in the bitter Indian rivalry of Iroquois and Huron; and the king of Spain almost decided to rub out Jamestown.

Such was the unhappy relation between the four European nations which claimed most of America north of Brazil. One could have been an optimist indeed in 1620 to predict that any good could come out of this. Nobody suspected that the seeds of democracy had already been sown at Jamestown and Plymouth, and those of the future Canadian nation at Quebec.

Fruitless as were the Roanoke colonies, the English learned from them that the seating of a colony was a highly expensive business, ruinous to any individual or small group who attempted it. Raleigh is said to have lost £40,000 in his efforts. The first twelve of the English continental colonies, and all English island colonies except Jamaica, were founded and settled by private enterprise, personal or corporate. The English crown, claiming the entire American continent north of Mexico, had neither the money nor the aptitude to found colonies. So it gave concessions to individuals and companies.

Most of the English colonies of the early seventeenth century, such as Jamestown (1607), Plymouth (1620), and Massachusetts Bay (1628), started as trading posts, owned by English merchants and settled by their employees. The first English colony to be agricultural from the beginning was Bermuda (1612), where there were no natives to trade with — only the wild hogs left by the Spaniards. In no one of these colonies was private ownership of land permitted until communal ownership proved to be a failure. Except for a few gentlemen adventurers, the original planters were hired men working under a boss called a governor, who was responsible to owners living in England. This was true of Virginia until 1616, of Plymouth until 1623, of Massachusetts Bay until 1630, and of Canada and New Netherlands until much later.

It was not, however, the English colonial intention to be satisfied with mere trading posts. In the literature of English colonization at least six main ideas are stressed: (1) England is overpopulated — "The land grows weary of its people." In the shires "the beggars are coming to town," as the old ballad states; in London the unemployed sleep in the streets. What better solution than to give the poor and unemployed a new lease on life overseas? (2) England wants markets for her woolens. What better one can be found than North America, with its cold climate? Not only settlers but Indians might be persuaded to swap furs and skins for coats and blankets. (3) England sorely needs precious metals. Surely there is as good a chance to find gold in Virginia as in Hispaniola — or Saguenay? (4) England has been paying good money to Mediterranean countries for olive oil, currants, and wine. If these could be produced in English colonies, she would be much better off. She is dependent on the Baltic countries for ship timber, tar, and cordage. Surely the Royal Navy would be better prepared if a source of supplies could be found in Virginia? (5) England needs a short route to the Indies. Maybe one can be found up one of the unexplored bays on the coast of Virginia. (6) England has the duty to propagate Protestant Christianity and prevent the Catholic Church from converting the entire native population of America.

And "a place of safetie" — a Protestant refuge — might there be found "if change of religion or civil warres should happen in this Realme."

These were the basic motives of English colonization for a century and a half. And from the first it was understood that any English settlement must have English law and English liberty. The first charter of the Virginia Company (1606) declared that the colonists and their descendants would enjoy "all liberties . . . to all intents and purposes as if they had been abiding and born within this our realm of England." These became fighting words in the 1770's.

2. Virginia

As soon as James I made peace with Spain in 1604, the energy and gallantry of the English nation that had been engaged in fighting the Spaniards concentrated on setting up Virginia; and for that purpose they chose an admirable vehicle for private enterprise, the joint stock company. This combined the venture of many small investors (in the case of the Virginia Company £12 10s or about $62 in gold per share) into one joint or common stock which was administered by a governor, treasurer, and assistants elected by the stockholders at quarterly "courts" or meetings in London. Public-spirited Englishmen of all classes, laymen and divines, nobles and knights, merchants and the trade guilds of London, launched a drive for stock subscriptions; the king gave the company a charter, and on 20 December 1606, 120 colonists embarked at London in three little ships, *Susan Constant, Godspeed,* and *Discovery.* Upon their departure they were cheered by this merry ballad by Michael Drayton:

> Britains, you stay too long,
> Quickly aboord bestow you,
> And with a merry gale,
> Swell your stretched sayle,
> With vows as strong
> As the winds that blow you.
>
> And cheerefully at sea,
> Successe you still intice,
> To get the pearle and gold,
> *And ours to hold,*
> VIRGINIA,
> Earth's only Paradise.

Captain Christopher Newport conducted this task force to Virginia, and the Company gave him "sole charge and command." They raised the Chesapeake Capes on 26 April 1607, after eighteen weeks at sea. Captain Newport and his council (which included Captain John Smith, George Percy, and Edward-Maria Wingfield) explored the lower reaches of Chesapeake Bay for a suitable home site, but made the usual mistake of firstcomers in America by settling on a low, swampy island. This they named Jamestown after the King, and there the people began going ashore on 14 May. They lost no time in building a fortified trading post, with wattle-and-daub thatched houses, a church, and storehouse of similar construction, which have been well reproduced in the modern National Park. They were just in time to repel an Indian attack on 26 May.

The early history of Jamestown was miserable indeed. After Captain Newport sailed for England in June, the population was 104 men and boys. Within six months 51 died of disease and starvation; and it was only Captain Smith's skill in making friends with Powhatan — via daughter Pocahontas — and the return of Captain Newport with a supply ship around New Year's day, that the rest were saved. That supply ship brought between 70 and 100 more settlers, including two women, and five Poles who had been recruited to begin the production of pitch, tar, and turpentine. Thus, from the start, England rejected the Spanish system of excluding foreigners from her colony; and there is no evidence that these or the forty-five other Poles who were sent to Virginia within a few years were under any civil disability.

The Virginia Company planned no mere trading post but a settlement colony. The leaders had courage and vision, but the general run of the early settlers were ill chosen; they seem to have been divided into those who could not and those who would not work. As Captain Smith wrote, "In Virginia, a plaine Souldier that can use a Pick-axe and spade, is better than five Knights." And although more men were procured, for several years Jamestown remained a fortified trading post where employees of the Company worked for their absentee stockholders. No private property was allowed, hence there was no incentive. The Company provided the colony with a poor sort of government — a council appointed in England, of which each member became president by turn; and under this council's direction the people wasted time looking for gold and failed to produce the necessary provisions to keep them alive. They sickened on the local food that they bought from friendly Indians, caught malaria from the hordes of mosquitoes, and died like flies in autumn.

Reports of those who returned to England were so discouraging that the Virginia Company reorganized with a new charter in 1609. This brought in new blood and new money, and a change of system. Lord de la Warr (from whom Delaware is named) was appointed governor of "London's Plantation in the Southern Part of Virginia," official name of the Jamestown settlement. As the governor was not ready to leave, Sir Thomas Gates took command of an expedition of nine ships, the largest fleet that England had yet sent to America. The flagship was wrecked on Bermuda, and a contemporary account of this event inspired Shakespeare's *Tempest*. The survivors built a boat out of Bermudian cedar and in her sailed up Chesapeake Bay in May 1610. When they reached Jamestown, they found the settlement reduced to the last stage of wretchedness. The colonists were discouraged, diseased, and starving; they

VIRGINIA 51

had eaten all the livestock that skulking Indians had not killed, and their houses were in ruins. Gates decided to embark the survivors in ships already in the harbor and return them to England. The entire company was on board, anchors aweigh, and sail made in June 1610, when up the river came a gig bearing Lord de la Warr, whose ships, with 300 men on board and ample supplies, were becalmed down the bay. De la Warr ordered Gates and his people ashore, vigorously took charge, and the Jamestown colony was saved from collapse or extinction.

Under De la Warr and his energetic successor, Sir Thomas Dale, strict military discipline was established and severe measures to punish laggards and delinquents were adopted. But the colony was still in a bad way. Governor Dale wrote home in 1611:

Every man allmost laments himself of being here, and murmurs at his present state. [The colonists were] sutch disordered persons, so prophane, so rioutous, so full of treasonable Intendments, besides of sutch diseased and crased bodies which render them so unable, fainte, and desperate of recoverie, as of three hundred not three score may be called forth or imploied upon any labor or service.

He begged the king,

If it will please his Majestie to banish hither all offenders condemned to die, it would be a readie way to furnish us with men, and not allwayes with the worst kinde of men either for birth, spiritts or Bodie.

Jamestown was still a semi-military trading post. The colonists owned no property; they were working for stockholders overseas. Twice a day the men were marched to the fields or woods by beat of drum, twice marched back and into church. They led an almost hopeless existence, for there seemed to be no future. The local Indians were no traders, had nothing but a little corn to offer; the only "cash crop" profitable in England was cedar board for wainscoting. No empire could have developed from a colony of this sort. The only thing that kept Virginia alive in these difficult years was the patriotism and deep religious faith of some of the leaders. This was well expressed by a poetical paraphrase of one of Governor Dale's reports, printed in England in 1610:

Be not dismayed at all
For scandall cannot doe us wrong,
God will not let us fall.
Let England knowe our willingnesse,
For that our work is good;
Wee hope to plant a nation
Where none before hath stood.

Virginia needed more than faith and a gallant spirit to be permanent. It needed a profitable product, a system of land-holding that would give colonists a stake in the country; discipline, to be sure, but also liberty. In about eight years, 1616–24, it obtained all these. During that time the colony was transformed from an almost desperately maintained trading post, ruled by iron discipline, into something like the Virginia of the Byrds and Lees.

The first factor in this transition was tobacco. Its value for export was discovered in 1613 when John Rolfe, who married the Indian "princess" Pocahontas, imported seed from the West Indies, crossed it with the local Indian-grown tobacco, and produced a smooth smoke which captured the English market. Virginia then went tobacco-mad; it was even grown in the streets of Jamestown. We hear of one man who by his own labor raised a crop of tobacco that brought £200, another with six hired men making £1000 in one year; and the last governor sent out by the Company, Samuel Argall, who came out "with nothing but his sword," took home £3000. As early as 1618 Virginia exported 50,000 pounds' weight of tobacco to England. This encouraged settlers, but made the colony more dependent on England for supplies. To keep Virginia supplied with food, a special organization called "The Magazine" was formed by the wealthier members of the Company. It sent out food supplies and in return received the monopoly of selling Virginia tobacco in England. A fair enough solution, but politically unwise because tobacco was of ill repute with King James. At his behest Parliament would have prohibited the import of tobacco into England in 1621, had the Virginia Company not persuaded the House that this would ruin the colony.

The institution of private property was the second factor that saved Virginia. When, after seven years, the terms of the Company's hired men expired, those who chose to stay became tenant farmers and later were given their land outright. This made a tremendous difference. As Captain John Smith put it, "When our people were fed out of the common store, and laboured jointly together, glad was he who could slip from his labour, or slumber over his taske, he cared not how; nay, the most honest among them would hardly take so much true paines in a week, as now for themselves they will doe in a day." By 1617 a majority of the hardy, acclimated survivors were tenants. Within ten years tenant plantations extended twenty miles along the James river, and the total European population of Virginia was about a thousand.

The third factor that ensured the success of Virginia was political, in the broadest sense. Again it was Captain John Smith who put the issue in one sentence: "No man wil go from hence to have lesse freedome there than here"; and in the English conception of freedom the first and most important was "a government of laws, not of men." The Company ordered Governor Sir George Yeardley to abolish arbitrary rule, introduce English common law and due process, encourage private property, and summon a representative assembly. This assembly would have power, with the appointed council, to pass local laws, subject to the Company's veto.

The fourth factor was sex. There had been a few women in the colony from the first, but they stood the hardships even less well than the men and boys, and few were alive in 1620. The Company then undertook to recruit "young and uncorrupt maids" and ship them to Jamestown, where a planter who wanted a wife paid the Company 150 pounds of best leaf tobacco. Every lass promptly found a husband, and every married couple had the right to build a house for themselves, whilst bachelors continued to bunk in barracks.

All these reforms except the last were passed by the general court of the Company in England in 1618, under Sir Thomas Smyth. Sir Thomas has had a bad break from most historians; his successor, Sir Edwin Sandys, has been given the credit. Smyth was an experienced business man, governor of the Muscovy Company and director of the East India Company; but he lacked the personality of Sandys, an Oxford graduate and parliamentary leader, tolerant in religion and liberal in politics, who appeared to later Americans as a primitive Thomas Jefferson. Sandys hoped to "plant a nation, where none before hath stood"; but the less voluble and expressive Smyth may have had the same vision even though he did not talk about it.

The year 1619 brought a political upset within the Company. The small stockholders, each of whom had contributed his £12 10s, hoped to receive a dividend before they died. They suspected that the Magazine was taking all the profits while stockholders were put off with promises. So the cry went up that the Smyth party had been too long in power; and the spring election of the Company in London in 1619 was won by Sandys. As Sir Edwin Sandys had no commitments elsewhere, he was able to concentrate all his efforts on serving the Company and Virginia, and implementing the reforms of 1618.

In consequence of the votes passed by the Virginia Company in London, Governor Yeardley summoned a legislative assembly, the very first in America, in 1619; and it seems to have been elected by manhood suffrage, including that of the foreigners. The next step, equally important for the future, was to abolish the military regulations of Dale and place Virginia under the rule of law — the common law of England. That law, and orderly process to change the law, have proved to be the surest safeguards of human rights known to modern man.

Despite the new tobacco prosperity, the rate of mortality continued to be appalling. Between Easter 1619 and Easter 1620, the population fell off from about 1000 to 866. During the next twelve months, ten different ships landed 1051 more people in Virginia. But by Easter, 1621, what with deaths and the departure of the discouraged, only 843 remained alive in the colony.

Sir Edwin Sandys worried over the exclusive attention paid by the colony to tobacco, partly because a one-crop system is unhealthy for the economy (as Cuba has learned to her cost), partly because King James I was down on smoking. Sandys therefore persuaded the stockholders' meeting in London to adopt a five-year plan for Virginia. These measures were directed toward making the colony self-sustaining in food, producer of many products that England then had to purchase abroad, and a market for English goods. Vines, vintners, and olive trees were imported from France, the Company spent £5000 to establish an iron industry at the falls of the James river, sawmill workers were imported from Hamburg, and expert lumbermen from the Baltic provinces. To implement these plans more settlers were needed, and as a result of intense publicity some 4000 English people emigrated to Virginia in four years. Yet a census in February 1624 showed that only 1277 of them were still alive. "What has become of the five thousand missing subjects of His Majesty?" was asked at an investigation by the Royal Council in 1624. Except for those who returned home, they had died or had been killed in the Indian massacre of 1622.

This event, which checked Virginia when on the brink of prosperity, was due primarily to the neglect of defense by the Virginia Company and its local government. They trusted that the marriage of Pocahontas to John Rolfe would keep the Indians friendly. That it did, for a time; but Powhatan was succeeded by his brother Opechancanough who, resenting the steady encroachment of the English on his cornfields, decided to clean up. He almost did, too; in a sudden, secret onslaught, 347 colonists, at least one-third of the white population, were killed.

That calamity knocked out the five-year plan of Sir Edwin Sandys. His ambitious schemes for iron works and a college were given up, outlying plantations were abandoned, and the Virginia Company came under political attack. The king directed his attorney general to enter suit against the Company, alleging that none of its professed objects had been carried out, and the crown won, in 1624. The charter under which the Virginia colony had been seated was annulled, and the Company whose liberal policy set the pattern for English colonization was dissolved.

Virginia now became a crown colony, with a governor and council appointed by the king; but the local people welcomed the change because the king continued their representative assembly, the house of burgesses, and respected the rule of law. And under Charles I, who succeeded his father James I in 1625, a really prosperous era began.

Among the inducements to settlers offered by the Virginia Company under Sandys was this: any Englishman who agreed to take out at least 250 people at his own expense was allowed to choose a tract of unallotted land anywhere in the colony, 1250 acres or more, with powers of local self-government. These tracts, known as Hundreds or "Particular Plantations," are the origin of names such as "Martin's Hundred," "Archer's Hope," and "Bennett's Welcome" on the map of Virginia today. And, by a curious set of circumstances, this was the origin of Plymouth Colony, the first permanent settlement in New England.

3. Plymouth Plantation

Since 1600 there had been a number of English and French voyages along the coast of the future New England. Officially the region was Northern Virginia, granted by James I in 1606 to a Northern Virginia Company similar to the one that founded Jamestown. This company, of which the leading lights were Chief Justice Sir John Popham and Sir Ferdinando Gorges, attempted in 1607 to establish a trading post on an island inside the mouth of the Kennebec river. Raleigh Gilbert, the twenty-four-year-old son of Sir Humfrey, was the governor. They built a small vessel and sent her home with a load of mast timber, but the winter set in "extreme unseasonable and frosty," the north wind howled down-river and congealed the settlers' blood, the Indians refused to trade; and when a relief ship showed up in the spring of 1608, everyone scrambled on board and went back to merry England.

The Northern Virginia Company then employed Captain John Smith to explore the coast. He wrote an enthusiastic *Description of New England*, which was published in 1616. He praised the soil, the climate, and especially the fishing. English and French fishermen frequented the coast for the next few years, but there was no attempt to settle until the Pilgrim Fathers practically stumbled in.

These were a group of Separatists — Puritans who had seceded from the Church of England, unhappy exiles in the Netherlands. The Dutch gave them good usage, but hard living, and they wanted a place of their own to live where they could worship as they chose and also prosper. Their leader William Brewster, through a connection with Sir Edwin Sandys, got them a patent to a "particular plantation" in Southern Virginia. They intended to locate near the mouth of the Hudson (then within the boundary of Virginia and unoccupied), there to set up a trading post and fishing settlement. Poor in worldly goods though indomitable in spirit, they could raise money only by agreeing to remain in virtual servitude for seven years to a group of loan sharks in London. Owing to various delays their ship, the *Mayflower*, did not clear England until the autumn of 1620. After a rough voyage of 64 days, she made Cape Cod on 9 November. The wind headed her, and the shoals were so terrifying that the Pilgrims turned about and made Cape Cod (now Provincetown) harbor. Since this place was outside Virginia, which made their patent useless, a few rugged individualists who had joined the Pilgrims in London announced that "when they came ashore they would use their own liberty, for none had power to command them." Brewster, Bradford, Winslow, Standish, and other leaders of the expedition then drew up the famous Mayflower Compact, which almost all the adult men signed. Therein they formed a "civil body politic," and promised "all due submission and obedience" to such "just and equal laws" as the government they set up might pass. This compact, like the Virginia assembly, is an almost startling revelation of the capacity of Englishmen in that era for self-government. Moreover, it was a second instance of Englishmen's determination to live in the colonies under a rule of law. We must never forget this; for in colonies of other European nations the will of the prince, or his representative, was supreme.

After prospecting Cape Cod and deciding that it was incapable of supporting human life, the Pilgrim Fathers decided to settle at the place which

Captain John Smith had already named Plymouth. On 16 December the *Mayflower* arrived there and began landing her passengers. The English had no sooner landed and built crude shelters than the "great sickness" bore in on them as it had on the Englishmen at Jamestown; and only 50 of the 102 immigrants survived. Hope returned with spring, when "the birds sang in the woods most pleasantly"; and when *Mayflower* set sail for England on 5 April 1621, not one of the stout-hearted survivors returned in her. With the help of a friendly Indian they learned how to plant and cultivate corn; Miles Standish taught them how to shoot game; fish, clams, and lobsters were plentiful. In October they invited friendly Wampanoag Indians to share their first Thanksgiving feast, and concluded a treaty with sachem Massasoit.

William Bradford, aged thirty-one, was elected governor after the first one died; and thereafter the Plymouth Colony had annual elections of governor and assistants. Several times the colony was at the point of starvation; it would have perished but for food bought from a Virginia shipmaster who was fishing off the coast. He also brought news of the Indian massacre of 1622 which almost finished off Virginia. This put the Pilgrims on their guard; they built a fort on the hill overlooking Plymouth harbor, and by firm diplomacy kept the hostile Indians of Massachusetts and Cape Cod at bay. In June 1625 Bradford wrote to a friend in England that the Pilgrims "never felt the sweetness of the country till this year." They managed to get along as a trading-post colony, growing corn which they traded with the Indians for beaver pelts; and by this fur trade they eventually managed to get out of debt to the loan sharks in London, to obtain a patent from the reorganized Northern Virginia Company (now the Council for New England) for their land, and even to set up branch trading posts on the Kennebec river and at the sites of the Cape Cod canal and Hartford, Connecticut.

4. New Netherland and New France

At these last two posts the Pilgrims encountered friendly rivals — Dutchmen from "the Manhatoes," the site of New York City, where the Pilgrims themselves originally intended to settle.

New Netherland, the Dutch colony which at one time comprised the entire Hudson Valley and the shores of Delaware Bay and Long Island, stems from the voyage of Henry Hudson, an Englishman in Dutch employ. In the yacht *Half Moon*, even smaller than *Mayflower*, he sailed in 1609 up the river named after him, hoping that it would prove to be a northwest passage to the Indies; and only gave up when he reached the rapids north of the site of Albany. But he had discovered the greatest fur-bearing region in North America south of the St. Lawrence, and made friends with the Mohawks by giving some of their chiefs their first taste of hard liquor. Adrien Block, Cornelis May, and other Dutch sea captains sailed thither to trade, but no real attempt to colonize was made until the Dutch West India Company was founded in

1621. This Company founded trading posts at Fort Orange (Albany) in 1624, and at New Amsterdam (New York City) in 1626. That was the year when the Company purchased Manhattan Island from the local Indians for sixty guilders' worth of trading truck — the "greatest real estate bargain in history," the sixty guilders being roughly equivalent to forty 1965 dollars.

The United Provinces of the Netherlands, having lately won their independence from Spain, were powerful and enterprising. During the seventeenth century the English regarded the Dutch as their greatest rivals and potential enemies. The two countries were very much alike in their Protestant religion, love of liberty, and other respects; but they drifted into war because of rivalry in foreign commerce. In matters maritime and many others it was difficult to "beat the Dutch." The Dutch West India Company might have planted a strong colony, a real challenge to New France and New England. But the Netherlands had no surplus population to emigrate, and the capitalists were mostly interested in wresting valuable possessions from the Portuguese in the Far East, such as the Spice Islands, Java, Malaya, and Ceylon.

The Dutch at first got along well with their English neighbors and even taught them the use of wampum, the Algonquian shell money, for trading with the natives. French Canada was a far more formidable rival to the English empire, although England did not yet know it.

Just as the founding of Jamestown in 1607 is a turning point in the history of Anglo-America, so the year 1608, when Champlain set up a trading post at Quebec, is a milestone in the history of New France. The French did not immediately abandon their posts on the Bay of Fundy, but these never wholly recovered from the effects of Samuel Argall's raid. Eventually, enough French peasants settled the Grand Pré of L'Acadie to present England with a problem, Longfellow with "Evangeline," and Louisiana with the "Cajans." But in the seventeenth century the French applied their main efforts along the St. Lawrence and in the West Indies. Champlain, by keeping a firm hand on Quebec and by founding Montreal, put his king in possession of the one great valley that led from the heart of North America to the east coast. The St. Lawrence drained the greatest source of beaver fur on the continent; but whether the French, the Dutch, or the English obtained the bulk of it depended on how their colonists handled the Indians.

Champlain quickly discovered that the St. Lawrence was a fulcrum of power politics between the Five Nations of the Iroquois, and the Huron, Montagnais and other tribes of the valley. He tried to secure for these neighboring Indians a firm mastery of the great river by helping them fight the Iroquois. Even before the Dutch occupied the site of Albany, Champlain had helped the Montagnais to win a fight with Mohawks on the lake named after him, had explored the Ottawa river by canoe, and reached Lake Huron where he wintered with the Huron nation and won their allegiance. This put the Huron in a fair way to become middlemen for the fur trade between the French at Montreal and the Indians who trapped in the basin of the Great

Lakes. The Iroquois, determined to prevent this, in 1624 ambushed a fleet of Huron canoes carrying fur down the Ottawa to Montreal. That showed the French what to expect, for the Iroquois were famous for long-distance forays and surprise attacks on Indian villages, followed by savage scalping and the torture of prisoners.

Quebec was still a trading post, controlled by Champlain under whatever brief monopoly had won the royal favor. He and the fur merchants welcomed the missionaries, but wanted no white settlers. When in 1617 Louis Hébert, a Paris apothecary who had made a voyage to New France and wished to settle there, proposed to bring out his family, he was discouraged. Champlain, not relishing the prospect of Indians hanging around a drugstore, allowed Hébert to stay only after he had promised not to serve the natives. For thirteen years his family comprised the only real settlers in Canada, all the rest being missionaries or employees of trading companies; not until 1628 did ploughing or planting begin.

Twenty-five years had then elapsed since Champlain's first voyage, but the French hold on Canada was still so feeble that in 1629, during a brief Anglo-French war, an English privateer captured Quebec easily; and a Scottish laird, Sir William Alexander (who is responsible for the name Nova Scotia) occupied the abandoned trading post at Port Royal. But Charles I returned both Quebec and L'Acadie to France in return for payment of overdue installments on the dowry of his Queen, amounting to $240,000. This was as good a bargain for France as the Louisiana Purchase later was to be for the United States. And by 1633 Champlain was again at Quebec as governor for a new and powerful company, the Hundred Associates of New France. But he was already sixty-six years old, and on Christmas Day 1635 he died.

Samuel de Champlain was the most versatile of colonial founders in North America: at once sailor and soldier, scholar and man of action, artist and explorer. Sailors admire him, not only for exploring the rugged coast of New England without serious mishap, but for his *Treatise on Seamanship* in which his description of "The Good Captain" well applies to himself: "An upright, God-fearing man, not dainty about his food or drink, robust and alert, with good sea-legs, and in a strong voice to give commands to all hands; pleasant and affable in conversation, but imperious in his commands, liberal and courteous to defeated enemies, knowing everything that concerns the handling of the ship," and of sailors. Champlain's accounts of his coastal cruises and explorations of the interior were embellished with drawings of flora, fauna, and Indians that are not lacking in artistic merit, and accompanied by maps which were not surpassed for accuracy in fifty years. Loyal to his king and his church, he endeavored with success to lead the New Testament life in an age of loose morals; many years after his last visit to the Huron nation they were marveling at his continence. The death of this great leader closes the first chapter in the history of New France.

5. Beginnings of the Non-Spanish West Indies

Within the space of fifteen years English, French, and Dutch made their first settlements in the Lesser Antilles, which Columbus had discovered but the Spaniards had bypassed in favor of the big islands and the continent. After several initial failures in that region by Sir Walter Raleigh and others, Thomas Warner organized a company, and in 1624 sailed with a group of choice cutthroats to colonize St. Christopher (St. Kitts). Taking no chances with the Caribs, Warner surprised them after a drinking bout, slaughtered a number, and drove off the rest to nearby islands. His men then settled down somewhat nervously to plant tobacco, knowing that nearby islands were full of Caribs.

That same year the French, who had sailed the Caribbean for a century as pirates and privateers, began their first West Indian colony, more or less by accident. A French privateer captain whose lieutenant was named Pierre Belain D'Esnambuc, following an unfortunate encounter with a Spanish galleon, anchored in the roadstead of St. Kitts. The English settlers welcomed his men with enthusiasm, fearing a dugout canoe counterattack from nearby Nevis. That is exactly what the Caribs did. The combined English and French defense force broke up this Carib amphibious landing; and then, marvelous to relate, instead of fighting each other, divided St. Kitts amicably. The island is only 23 miles long, but the English took the middle and the French the two ends, and both found tobacco planting there very profitable.

St. Kitts was not big enough for ambitious men such as Warner and D'Esnambuc. Both sailed home to obtain royal grants. Warner received from Charles I in 1625 a patent creating him governor of the Leeward Islands with the right to colonize St. Kitts, Nevis, Barbados, and Montserrat; Louis XIII gave D'Esnambuc a patent for the middle of St. Kitts, with the right to colonize Guadeloupe and Martinique at his own expense, if he cared to try.

Warner was a little fellow without much influence, and no sooner had he obtained his Leeward Islands patent than he had to reckon with a "big shot" at the Jacobean court. This was James Hay, a Scot who followed King James to London, obtaining all manner of favors and the earldom of Carlisle. Warner, knowing Hay's power at court, attempted to use him as window dressing, but the Scot was too smart to be content with being a mere front man. He allowed Warner and his friends to raise the money; but the charter created Lord Carlisle absolute proprietor of the English Caribbee Islands from St. Kitts to Barbados, inclusive. Warner and his friends were glad to settle for permission to keep the land that they had been cultivating in St. Kitts.

In his new Caribbee Islands proprietary, Carlisle found Barbados the most profitable, and it became the wealthiest and most successful English colony in the first half of the seventeenth century. Barbados is only 300 square miles in area, but all good soil. By the end of 1629, according to Captain John Smith, no fewer than 3000 English had settled in Lord Carlisle's Caribbee Islands, most of them in Barbados but some in St. Kitts, Nevis, and Antigua. The profits from cotton and tobacco were immense, and emigration went rapidly forward.

Thus, in the twenty years 1607–27, the English, Dutch, and French had firmly begun their New World empires. The French had a string of trading posts in Canada, a plantation on St. Kitts, and were about to take over Guadeloupe. The Dutch trading posts on the Hudson were about to spread into a fringe colony along its banks and onto Long Island. And three years later, the Dutch began founding colonies in the West Indies.[1] English Virginia was spreading along the shores of Chesapeake Bay, Plymouth Colony was still struggling along, and the Caribbee Islands proprietary was doing very well. England, moreover, had performed a service to the future unlike that of any other country in modern times. She had planted the seeds of the common law and of representative government.

1. See Chapter VII, below.

CONFESS JEHOVAH

V

New England Takes Shape

1628-1675

1. The Puritan Movement

PLYMOUTH COLONY was founded in 1620 by the *Mayflower* Pilgrims, who brought Puritanism in one of its purest forms to America. But New Plymouth would long have remained a poor and isolated colony, and New England a mere string of trading posts and fishing stations, but for the great Puritan migration of the 1630's.

Puritanism was essentially and primarily a religious movement; attempts to prove it to have been a mask for politics or money-making are false as well as unhistorical. In the broadest sense Puritanism was a passion for righteousness; the desire to know and do God's will. Similar movements have occurred in every branch of Christianity, as well as in Judaism.[1] Puritanism was responsible for the settlement of New England; and as the Congregational, Presbyterian, Methodist, Baptist, Unitarian, Quaker, and other Protestant sects of the United States are offshoots of seventeenth-century English and Scottish Puritanism, it is not surprising that Puritan ways of thinking and doing have had a vast effect on the American mind and character, precursors of what is commonly called the Protestant Ethic.

The English Puritans who founded New England were nearer in doctrine to the Catholic Church than to liberal Protestant sects of the nineteenth and twentieth centuries. They agreed that man existed for the glory of God, and that his first concern in life should be to do God's will and so receive future happiness. They insisted, however, that the Catholic Church had taken a wrong turn after the fifth century by adding forms, ceremonies, and dogmas unauthorized by the Bible. The Church of England, they felt, had made a good start by repudiating Rome, but had slowed up the Reformation by retaining bishops, vestments, and ritual. Puritans proposed to worship as they imagined the early Christians did; their learned men combed through the Epistles and Acts of the Apostles to discover exactly how the primitive churches were organized. The Congregational Church in New England happened to be organized on a democratic basis, not because Puritans were in

1. Jansenism in eighteenth-century France was a Puritan movement within the Catholic Church which still has a pervasive influence in Ireland. The French Huguenots, and Scots, German, Scandinavian, and Netherlands Calvinists were essentially Puritan in doctrine and attitude, differing only in detail from the English Puritans.

love with democracy but because leaders such as John Cotton and Thomas
Hooker insisted that the First Church in Boston and the First Church of
Hartford copy the exact organization of the First Church of Corinth and the
First Church of Philippi, about which they knew very little, since the apostles
and evangelists did not say much about them.

The English Puritans were radical, in that they proposed to get at the root
of everything, no matter who or what stood in their way; but in a larger sense
they were conservative, even reactionary, since their aim was to restore "the
church unspotted, pure" of the early Christians and so to reform society that
one could lead the New Testament life and at the same time earn a living.
They wished to sweep away the practices of the Renaissance, to get back to
apostolic times when the men who had seen Jesus plain were still alive. God,
they believed, had dictated the Bible as the complete guide to life; the Trinity
maintained a line of communication to each individual Christian through
conscience. They were deeply impressed by a story that their favorite church
father, St. Augustine, told in his *Confessions*. He heard a voice saying, *tolle et
lege*, "Pick up and read." Opening the Bible, his eyes lit on Romans xiii:
12–14: "The night is far spent, the day is at hand; let us put on the armour
of light. Let us walk honestly, as in the day; not in carousing and drunkenness, not in debauchery and lust, not in strife and jealousy. But put ye on the
Lord Jesus Christ, and make no provision for the flesh, to fulfil the lusts
thereof."

In response to the light of conscience and the written Word, the Puritan
yearned to know God and to approach Him directly without intermediary. If
the Puritan rejected the ancient pageantry of Catholic worship, it was not
because of any dislike for beauty. He loved beauty in women and children
and, as his works prove, achieved beauty in silverware, household furniture,
and architecture. He rejected ritual as a distorting screen erected by man
between him and his maker. Stained-glass windows, images of the saints,
organ music, and Gregorian chants, he thought, threw a jeweled, sensuous
curtain between the worshippers and the Almighty. As soon as the Puritan
acquired the means to beautify the exterior of his meetinghouse (as he called
his church building), he did so with classic columns, Palladian windows, and
spires; but the interior he preferred to leave cold and bare so as not to distract
the attention of the congregation.

Puritanism spread rapidly over northern Europe, especially in Switzerland,
the Netherlands, and the British Isles. People seemed to acquire a longing
for Bible study, extemporaneous prayer, and long, meaty sermons on duty and
doctrine. We hear of men and women running from town to town to hear sermons; of churches hiring an extra preacher to deliver a sermon when their
regular parson could not or would not. And Puritanism appealed to merchants
because it taught that a man could serve God as well in business or a profession
as by taking holy orders, and that all "callings" were equally honorable in His
sight. As George Chapman expressed it in his play *Eastward Ho:*

> Whate'er some vainer youth may term disgrace,
> The gain of honest pains is never base;
> From trades, from arts, from valour, honour springs;
> These three are founts of gentry; yea, of kings.

A series of dissatisfactions with the situation in England was the main reason for thousands of Puritans emigrating to the New World. Their main grievance was religious. Puritans looked to Elizabeth I and her successor to carry through the reform and reorganize the church on an apostolic basis. Queen Bess was much too clever to do that. A large segment of her subjects had become Puritan, but many were still Catholic at heart, and would be driven into open rebellion by abolishing ritual. And James I cordially disliked the Puritans; he boasted that he would make them conform, or harry them out of the land. The Pilgrim Fathers, anticipating a crackdown, took flight to Holland and then to New Plymouth. But the great mass of English Puritans, called nonconformists, remained, hoping to reform the church from within.

Charles I, who succeeded in 1625, gave his ear to Bishop William Laud, a saintly cleric who wished to order and discipline the Church of England on an Anglo-Catholic, high church pattern. He looked on Puritan practices as blasphemous; he aimed to restore candles and the cross to the altar, kneeling and chanting, and other forms of worship that had been brushed aside in earlier reigns. The government now purged the universities of Puritans and put pressure on the Puritan clergy to conform, or get out.

Not only religion but everything else was going wrong, from the Puritan point of view. In Europe, the Catholic counter-reformation, implemented by Spanish power and financed by American gold, seemed to be winning. France tried to suppress her Protestants, the Huguenots; Bohemia and the Rhineland were overrun by Spanish armies. The tide seemed as irresistible as Hitlerism did three centuries later, and the Puritans suspected that Charles's Catholic queen, Henrietta Maria, was nourishing a "fifth column" at home.

The internal situation, too, dismayed the Puritans. King James, coming to wealthy England from starved Scotland, became wildly extravagant, replacing the statesmen of Elizabeth's reign by glamor boys and flatterers; the revels of his court were scandalous. His example of heavy and luxurious spending went right down the social line. Business flourished, fortunes were made in foreign trade, speculation, and through monopolies that the king conferred on his favorites. The newly rich were buying up land, all prices were inflated, fixed incomes bought less and less, foreigners like the banker Pallavicini were throwing modest farms together to make great country estates; Sir Edward Coke, the great barrister and judge, acquired over sixty manors. It was becoming increasingly difficult for the simple country gentleman or business man to hang onto his land, much less keep up with the Johnny-come-latelys. A ballad of the day tells more of this tendency than any description:

> You talke of Newe England; I truly beleeve
> Oulde England's growne newe and doth us deceave.

I'le aske you a question or two, by your leave:
    And is not ould England growne new?

And what is become of your ould fashiond clothes,
Your longsided Dublett and your trunck hose?
They'r turn'd to new fashions — but what the Lord knowes!
    And is not ould England growne new?

Now your gallaint and his tayllor some half yeare together
To fitt a new sute to a new hatt and fether,
Of gould or of silver, silke, cloth stuff, or lether.
    And is not ould England growne new?

New trickings, new goeings, new measurs, new paces,
New hedds for your men, for women new faces;
And twenty new tricks to mend ther bad cases!
    And is not ould England growne new?

On the political side, King Charles's attempt to govern England and levy taxes without a parliament brought Puritanism and political liberalism into alliance. By March of 1629, when Charles dismissed the last parliament to meet for twelve years, it looked as if he had succeeded in suppressing the traditional liberties of Englishmen. It was time for the weak, the indifferent, and the faint-hearted to run to cover. But the Puritan, doubting nothing and fearing no man, undertook to set all crooked ways straight and create a new heaven and a new earth. If he were not permitted to do that in England, he would find some other place to establish his City of God.

2. The Founding of the Bay Colony

New England was the answer. Virginia was Anglican, the Dutch had seized the Hudson, but the Pilgrim Fathers had proved that human life could be supported on a "stern and rockbound coast," and the Council for New England, to which this region had been granted, was looking for business. The Council issued several land patents in the 1620's, one to a group of Puritans who in 1628 received the coast between the Charles and Merrimack rivers, with an indefinite extension inland. Under a stout soldier named John Endecott, this group settled Salem. Next, just as modern business men buy a small concern and build it up, other groups of Puritans got control of this organization and obtained a royal charter as the "Governor and Company of the Massachusetts Bay in New England."

These men had long been talking about emigrating to America in order to set up a colony after their own hearts. Among their leaders were Thomas Dudley, who had been captain of a foreign legion, his son-in-law Simon Bradstreet; Thomas Leverett, alderman of Boston in Lincolnshire, whose pastor, John Cotton, was one of the leading Puritan divines; Sir Richard Saltonstall and Theophilus Eaton, merchants of London; William Pynchon, Squire of

Springfield in Essex; and a lawyer just turned forty, named John Winthrop. These men met somewhere in Cambridge University, of which most of them were alumni, in August of 1629 and signed an agreement to emigrate to New England within seven months, provided they could carry over the government and charter of the Massachusetts Bay Company. The reason for this important proviso was to protect themselves from the king, who otherwise might confiscate their charter, as had happened to the Virginia Company only five years earlier. And it so happened, whether by chance or design, that the Massachusetts Bay Charter did not require the stockholders to meet in any particular place. The stockholders voted for the transfer and elected John Winthrop governor. Many families sold both land and goods, and during the first six months of 1630 some fifteen ships, carrying over 1000 men, women, and children, cleared from English ports for Massachusetts. The movement gathered force as Bishop Laud put the screws on the Puritans, until by 1634 some 10,000 of them had settled in New England.

These Puritans had a definite mission — to establish a community rather than a mere colony, where they could put their ideals into practice. New England, to them, was a New Canaan which the Almighty had set apart for an experiment in Christian living. They felt, as Winthrop remarked on the way over, that they were "a city upon a hill," "with the eyes of all people" upon them; an example to prove that it was possible to lead the New Testament life, yet make a living.[1] These immigrants, organized in neighborhood groups and led by their ejected pastors, made several settlements around Boston. For a generation the fur trade was important, especially on the Connecticut river, where William Pynchon established a new Springfield. The Reverend Hugh Peter, from a fishing center in Cornwall, organized fisheries at Marblehead and found a market for dried codfish, an industry which became so important that a wooden image — "the sacred cod" — was hung up as a symbol in the assembly chamber at Boston, and is still there. But for several years the main business of the Massachusetts Bay Colony was raising cattle, corn, and other foodstuffs to sell to newcomers who came supplied with money and goods. The Puritans' connections with London merchants, who extended credit to their friends overseas, were essential to sustain a colony that doubled its population every year.

This system ended in 1637 when the Puritan migration stopped, owing to the troubles that heralded the English Civil War. Puritans now hoped to prevail at home, as indeed they did. This occasioned the first major American depression — the "fall of cow," as a local poet described it — which forced the Puritans to look around for other means of livelihood. These were found through shipbuilding and the West Indies trade. In the Caribbee Islands, where it paid planters to concentrate on raising tobacco and sugar with slave

1. John Winthrop, A Modell of Christian Charity, p. 20; quoted by President-elect John F. Kennedy in his speech to the General Court of Massachusetts, 9 January 1961, at a time when Massachusetts had become a bad example of political corruption.

labor, there was a great demand for New England products — dried fish, salt beef and pork, ground vegetables, poultry, even horses — and for ships to transport them. By selling these in the West Indies, the New Englanders obtained a balance to buy goods in England. Around 1670 they began distilling West Indies molasses into rum, which replaced hard cider and home-brewed beer as the drink of the country. This West Indies trade was the main factor in New England prosperity until the American Revolution; without it the settlements on the northern coast would have remained stationary or declined.

The transfer of the Massachusetts Bay charter from London to Boston had an important influence on future American institutions. It made the colony virtually independent of England. There was no royal governor or judge, no English army garrison, no parliamentary agent; nothing to keep it in line with English colonial policy. And the form that this colonial government took, following the terms of the charter, became the standard American pattern. As a business charter, the corporation consisted of freemen (stockholders), meeting in an assembly called the general court where were annually elected, on a stated date, the governor, deputy governor, and assistants (councillors). But transfer overseas turned the company into a colonial government. The free-men were now the voters, the governor and deputy governor the two chief magistrates, and the assistants doubled as governor's council and supreme court. By 1644, owing to a typical small-town dispute over a stray sow, the general court separated into two houses, and Massachusetts Bay had something approaching a modern state government. The franchise was confined to church members in good standing; but this excluded very few adult men, and the annual election of all officials made the government responsible to the people. They exercised their power, too; on occasion electing another governor than staid and conscientious John Winthrop. One of Winthrop's friends wrote from England that people were wondering why the electorate "doe toss and tumble about" their leaders so disrespectfully.

This government was not a democracy, but an important step toward it. And a further check on autocracy was established by a body of laws and a bill of rights. Winthrop and his elected assistants, who also served as judges, liked to pass judgments based on their own intuition and the Bible. The people observed that this allowed too much discretion to the judges. Hence the Massachusetts "Body of Liberties" adopted in 1641, and the "General Fundamentals" of Plymouth Colony which may have been earlier, contained the classic safeguards of English liberty, such as jury trial, no taxation without representation, free elections, nobody to be deprived of life, liberty, or property save by due process of law, or compelled to incriminate himself. These are the same principles later incorporated in the Bill of Rights of the Federal Constitution. In certain aspects, the Body of Liberties was ahead of English practice. Torture and cruel and barbarous punishments were prohibited, feudal dues were abolished, foreigners were assured equal protection of the law (as they already had been in Virginia), and cruelty to animals was forbidden. Cruelty to wives, too; a husband was forbidden to beat his wife "unless it be in his own defense upon her assault!"

Winthrop   Dudley   Saltonstall

Higginson   Winslow   Ludlow

Mason   Clarke   Gorges

ARMS OF FOUNDERS OF NEW ENGLAND

3. A Clutch of New Colonies, 1630–1650

The Massachusetts Bay form of government was copied in three New England colonies that sprang from the Massachusetts trunk, as well as in the older Plymouth Colony. Connecticut Colony was established by the earliest western migration in North American history. The Reverend Thomas Hooker and the Reverend Samuel Stone, and John Haynes, a wealthy landowner who had been elected governor of Massachusetts Bay, felt cramped in Cambridge and declared that the "bent of their spirits" required a move. In 1636 they marched cross-country and settled three towns, Hartford, Windsor, and Wethersfield, on the Connecticut river, which became the nucleus of Connecticut. Two years later, a company of London Puritans led by Theophilus Eaton and the Reverend John Davenport, chose New Haven as a likely site for a trading city to rival New York and Boston. Their colony of that name spread along and even across Long Island Sound. Each group of emigrants in 1639 drew up a written constitution — the Fundamental Orders of Connecticut and of New Haven, providing representative governments which served them well until 1662, when Charles II combined them under a corporate charter as the Colony of Connecticut. That charter remained the fundamental law of colony and state until 1818. The social and political institutions of both these colonies were similar in all essentials to those of the Bay.

Very different was the Colony of Rhode Island and Providence Plantations, founded by left-wing Puritans who, finding the atmosphere of the other New England colonies stuffy, protested loudly against their system of church and state. Rhode Island's founders were the Reverend Roger Williams, who has a deserved fame as an early exponent of religious liberty, Samuel Gorton, and the first woman to play a leading role in American history, Anne Hutchinson. All three, banished from Massachusetts Bay or Plymouth as troublemakers, founded the four settlements on Narragansett Bay, which received a colonial patent from the Long Parliament in 1644, and, later, a charter from Charles II which protected them from being forcibly annexed by their orthodox Puritan neighbors. As hardly any two Rhode Islanders shared the same beliefs, and Williams floundered among a number of sects, the only possible basis for unity in that colony was religious liberty. This was accorded to all Christians. It not only worked, but slowly spread; in 1964 Cardinal Cushing, Archbishop of Boston, proposed that his Church adopt religious liberty as a principle.

Roger Williams was the most beloved of colonial founders prior to William Penn. The Indians, whose language he studied, lodging with them "in their filthy, smoky holes," adored Williams because he respected their individuality, protected them against land-hungry members of his race, and never tried to convert them unless they asked for it. Williams stoutly maintained what everyone else in his day considered a monstrous heresy: that, for aught anyone knew, the Indians' religion was equally acceptable to God with Christianity. It was typical of Williams that in the *Key to the Indian Language,* which he had printed in England, the vocabulary starts with "*Cowammaunsh* — I love you," and that his rules of grammar are interspersed with little rhymes such as:

> Sometimes God gives them fish or flesh,
> Yet they're content without.
> And what comes in, they part to friends
> And strangers round about.
>
> If nature's sons both wild and tame
> Humane and courteous be,
> How ill becomes it sons of God
> To want humanity!

In addition to the five Puritan colonies, two small proprietary colonies were set up in New England — New Hampshire and Maine. The future Granite State, which began as a personal estate of Captain John Mason, consisted of a few hundred people in Portsmouth, Exeter, and other settlements on tidewater. Mason eventually sold out to the crown. Maine to the Kennebec river belonged to Sir Ferdinando Gorges, who entertained grandiose schemes for a feudal domain which came to naught, and his heirs sold out to Massachusetts.

4. New England People and Institutions

Important for the development of New England, and of the Chesapeake and West Indies colonies too, were events in England itself. The troubles which led to the English Civil War, beginning in 1637, prevented Charles I from suppressing the Bay Colony as his friends and its enemies wished him to do. Civil war between "Cavaliers" (the king's party) and "Roundheads" (Parliament's party and the Puritans) broke out in 1641 and continued, except for a short truce, until January 1649, when Charles I was executed. Parliament then set up a republic, the Commonwealth of England, keeping sovereign power in its own hands. This worked so ill that in 1653 the Roundhead army created Colonel Oliver Cromwell Lord Protector of England. Oliver almost established a new dynasty; but after his death on 3 September 1658 his son and successor, Richard, proved a weakling and resigned. Charles II was restored to his father's throne in 1660 and resumed the Stuart policy of trying to govern without a parliament.

During these two decades 1640–60, England's American colonies were left very much to themselves. The New Englanders naturally sympathized with the Roundheads, but refused to go along with their fellow Puritans in England. Massachusetts even defended her neutrality in the Civil War by twice preventing a parliamentary privateer from capturing a royalist merchant ship in Boston harbor. On another occasion the Bay Colony assembly declared: "Our allegiance binds us not to the laws of England any longer than while we live in England, for the laws of the parliament of England reach no further, nor do the king's writs under the great seal go any further." The colony sent Edward Winslow to London with defiant instructions from Governor Winthrop, ending, "Our charter gives us an absolute power of government."

A striking proof of English capacity for self-government was the New England Confederation, formed in 1643. This was a loose federal union, precursor of the Confederation of 1781. The professed objects were to settle boundary and other disputes among the four member colonies of Massachusetts, Plymouth, Connecticut, and New Haven, and mutual protection against aggression by French, Dutch, or Indians. Each colony appointed two commissioners who met annually, handled Indian affairs, and had power to declare war by a vote of three to one. They managed to settle several intercolonial disputes, and in 1675–76 helped to concert military measures in King Philip's War.

The New England people, almost to a man, were English and Puritan. About the only non-Puritans to emigrate were some of the indentured servants; this class never became as important in New England as in Maryland or Virginia, though numerous enough to make trouble for the authorities.

After their time was up they often hired out for wages. The only joke in Governor Winthrop's journal (and he didn't think it a joke but a piece of insolence) is the retort of a servant. His master, having been forced to sell a yoke of oxen to pay the man's wages, said he could keep him no longer, since he knew not how to find any more money. The hired man replied that he would accept cattle for wages as long as his master had any: "You shall then serve me, and so you may have your cattle again!"

The great mass of emigrants to New England were middle-class farmers, tradesmen, and artisans who had enough property to make wills — to the subsequent delight of genealogists. As Puritanism put no stigma on manual labor, and as every man, no matter how poor, could vote if he joined the church (and in Rhode Island did not even have to do that), independent yeomen and workmen became the backbone of the community. In New England you could always find a blacksmith, wheelwright, carpenter, joiner, cordwainer, tanner, ironworker, spinner, weaver or whatnot, — to make things which the Southern colonies at that era had to import from England. New Englanders, however they differed in property and occupation, had a common belief in the Bible as the guide to life, and a uniform method of land division and settlement. When members of a village community felt crowded for space, they petitioned the colonial assembly for a new township, the ideal size being six miles square. A committee was appointed to satisfy Indian claimants, to settle on a village site and lay out lots. Home lots and the meeting-house, which served both as church and town hall, were laid out around a village green, with a surrounding belt of planting lots for growing crops. Salt meadows on the coast, or river meads in the interior, valuable for the wild grass which could be cut and stored for winter forage, were laid out in long strips and usually cultivated in common. The rest of the township for many years remained the property of the community, where anyone could cut firewood and timber, or pasture cattle. Houses of this period, with high-peaked gables and leaded glass casement windows, bore little resemblance to the white-painted New England village of later colonial days; but the village pattern remained constant until the eighteenth century when, owing to no further danger from Indians, and the increase of population, people began laying out farms far from the central village.

Although the Puritans objected to the prevailing religious and social customs of their mother country, they were none the less loyal Englishmen, determined to embrace and perpetuate both English liberties and English culture. They had the Englishman's love of field sports, especially hunting and fishing; they bred horses for their own use and for export to the West Indies, and raced them, too. Yankee settlers of Long Island, as early as 1670, held annual horse races on Hempstead Plains for the prize of a silver cup.

One trait in which New Englanders even excelled the old country was their emphasis on education. Free popular education has been the most lasting contribution of early New England to the United States, and possibly the most beneficial. As Gertrude Stein once put it when writing on education: "In New England they have done it they do do it they will do it and they do it in every way in which education can be thought about." Compact villages made it possible to have and do, as well as talk about education. It is no accident that almost every educational leader and reformer in American history, from Benjamin Franklin through Horace Mann and John Dewey to James B. Conant, has been a New Englander of the Puritan stock.

Elementary education — the "three R's"— became a parental responsibility by act of the Bay Colony in 1642; and five years later, settlements with fifty or more families were required to appoint a schoolmaster "to teach all such children as shall resort to him to write and read." The same act of 1647 (shortly copied by Connecticut and New Haven) required towns of 100 families or more to set up a grammar school on the English model. These grammar schools took in boys at six or eight years of age and kept them for six years, during which they studied Latin and Greek grammar and literature, and arithmetic. Four of these schools — Boston Latin, Cambridge Latin, Roxbury Latin, and Hopkins Grammar School of New Haven — are still flourishing as public high schools. Ezekiel Cheever, a graduate of Emmanuel College, Cambridge, taught successively at New Haven, Ipswich, Charlestown, and Boston, wrote Latin textbooks, and died in harness at the age of ninety-two, without ever missing a day of school. To the boys of all four towns he was a kind and beloved master, and in his rhymed advice to later pedagogues he says:

> The lads with Honour first and Reason rule;
> Blowes are but for the refractory fool.
> But, Oh! first teach them their great God to fear;
> That you, like me, with joy may meet them here.

This religious sentiment was basic. The dynamic motive in colonial education, and in American higher education generally, until the rise of the public high school and the state university, was religious as well as humane. Boys had to learn to read in order to read the Bible, to write and speak "pieces" in order to communicate; to "cipher" in order to do business. Knowledge of Latin and Greek opened to them the best world literature and prepared them for college. Some 130 alumni of the universities of Oxford, Cambridge, and Dublin emigrated to New England before 1646. These men wanted the same advantages for their children as they had enjoyed in the old country; and now that the English universities were closed to Puritans, the only way they could obtain a supply of learned ministers for their Congregational churches, and of educated men to carry on the work of civil government, was to set up a college of their own. Without waiting for a wealthy benefactor, they went ahead and founded one through a grant of £400 by the assembly of the Bay Colony in 1636. Two years later the college opened at the new Cambridge, in a small house in a cow-yard given by the town, and was named after its earliest benefactor, the Reverend John Harvard, who, dying at the age of thirty, left the college half his fortune and a library of 400 volumes. In 1650 Harvard College was given a charter by the Bay Colony, which declared its purpose to be "the advancement of all good literature, arts and sciences."

The first president, thirty-year-old Henry Dunster, set up such high standards in the liberal arts as to attract students from Bermuda, Virginia, and England as well as the New England colonies. Throughout the depression of the 1640's the college flourished, students paying term bills with farm produce, clothing, and cattle on the hoof. Scholarships were provided, at the request of the New England Confederation, by voluntary contributions of a shilling, a peck of wheat, or a string of wampum from each family. Having no rivals in the English colonies until William and Mary College was founded in 1691, and Yale in 1701, Harvard set both the pace and the pattern for higher education in North America. The traditional four-year liberal arts course was followed, mostly in Latin textbooks. Instruction was by lectures, recitations, and Latin disputations; dormitories were provided for the students, who dined in hall with their tutors. A great show was made of commencement. Catalogues were issued, in which graduates were grouped under the year of taking their bachelor's degree. Three years more was required to study theology and take an M.A. Somewhat more than half the Harvard graduates in the seventeenth century became ministers.

The first printing press in the English colonies, and the second in North America, was set up in 1639 in the Harvard College Yard, as the former village cow-yard is called to this day. Here were printed the *Bay Psalm Book* of 1640 (now the most valuable of early Americana), the *New England Primer*, and an annual almanac compiled by some college "philomath" who was allowed to fill vacant spaces with his own poems and essays. But the amazing achievement of this press was to print the entire Bible in the Algonquian language, for which the Reverend John Eliot of Roxbury devised the first equivalents in Roman letters. This was the first Bible to be printed in the New World, and the first translation of it into a barbarous and hitherto unwritten language since Bishop Ulfila turned the Old Testament into Visigothic in the fourth century of the Christian era.

New Englanders, popular illustrators to the contrary, did not dress in black with steeple-crowned hats; they liked bright colors for clothing, furniture, and hangings. They mostly made their own furniture and silverware, both for domestic use and for "The Lord's Supper," as they and their successors call Holy Communion. John Hull, first of the colonial silversmiths, was also a pillar of the church, merchant, shipowner, and farmer. He owned vessels and traded with the West Indies, England, and Spain, lent money at interest, served as treasurer of the colony, and made the dies from which were coined the pine-tree shillings and sixpences, oldest of English colonial coinage. He melted down Spanish dollars ("pieces of eight") obtained in the West Indies trade, and from the silver bullion fashioned cups, beakers, and other articles that compare well with the best contemporary work in England; and he taught an apprentice, Jeremiah Dummer, to continue the business after his death.

Besides the arts of the husbandman and the crafts of the household, organized industry began in New England. Fullers from Rowley in Yorkshire set up a fulling mill at Rowley in the Bay Colony, where home-woven cloth could be shrunk and sheared. John Winthrop Jr., later governor of Connecticut, in 1645 set up an ambitious and, for a time, successful ironworks at Saugus near Lynn. Here iron ore dug out of swamps and ponds, smelted with oak charcoal and flux from nearby rocks, was fashioned into pots and pans, anchors, chains, and other ironware for local needs. The men who ran it, mostly of a Welsh family named Leonard, later established other ironworks, and from these descended the iron and steel industry of the United States.

Another line of John Hull the mintmaster was horse-raising on Cape Cod and Point Judith, Rhode Island. Neat cattle, sheep, goats, and horses were brought to New England in the first wave of settlement, and the breeding of them became a leading industry. There was great demand for horses in other English colonies, especially in the West Indies, where the poorest jade could earn her keep by turning the rollers of a sugar mill. As early as 1668 the Massachusetts general court took measures to improve the breed by allowing only stallions "of comely proportions and fourteen hands in stature" to run free on the town commons; all others had to be stabled or gelded. Most of the stock imported into New England was nondescript, but there are records of sires being brought over from Leicestershire, traditional home of the English hunter, and draught mares from Flanders. Either the Galloway pony of Scotland, or the Irish hobby, a small hardy sorrel, was the ancestor of the once famous Narragansett pacer, so called because raised in Rhode Island as a saddlehorse with an easy gait. Every colonial lady expected to be provided with this comfortable means of transport, at a time when few roads fit for wheeled vehicles existed. And this breed remained famous for over a century. The great Edmund Burke in 1772 asked his friend James Delancey of New York to send him by sea "two good New England Pacers."

Puritanism, with its stress on faith and works, was an excellent implement for subduing the rugged wilderness that was New England. "An hour's idleness is as bad as an hour's drunkenness," a maxim announced by the Reverend Hugh Peter of Salem, kept people busy when the climate did not; and, "Never waste precious time" became a basic American doctrine. The congregational organization of the New England churches gave almost every man a say in religious affairs, as the town meeting did in local government. On occasions such as raising the frame of a meetinghouse, or of some individual's house or barn, the entire community participated. The legislature and magistracy, following the form of the Massachusetts Bay charter, gave the colonies a representative system and embodied the seeds of democracy.

And of nationalism, too. Other European colonists in America, whether in

Canada, Virginia, New Netherland, the Caribbean, or South America, regarded themselves as Frenchmen, Englishmen, Dutchmen, or Spaniards
living in America, and looked forward to returning "home." Not so the New
Englanders. The first person on record to use the word *American* for a European colonist rather than an Indian was Cotton Mather, in 1684. The "Yankees," as they were called in the next century, regarded America as their
home. They had convinced themselves that their work here for God and the
English nation was supremely important; and was it not so? Puritanism was a
cutting edge which hewed liberty, democracy, humanitarianism, and universal
education out of the black forest of feudal Europe and the American wilderness. Puritan doctrine taught each person to consider himself a significant if
sinful unit to whom God had given a particular place and duty, and that he
must help his fellow men. Puritanism, therefore, is an American heritage to
be grateful for and not to be sneered at because it required everyone to attend
divine worship and maintained a strict code of ethics.

The effects went deeper and further than anyone could have predicted. Nor
was Puritan influence confined to America. Albert Luthuli, a graduate of
Adams College near Durban, South Africa, founded by New England Congregationalists in 1838, received the Nobel peace prize for 1960. Or, turn
to Turkey. Little Ali, who attends a missionary school and goes on to Robert
College in Istanbul, got his chance for an education because little John and
Elihu in the colonial era attended Boston Latin or the Hopkins Grammar and
went on to Harvard or Yale. And Ali's right to vote and be elected to the
Turkish parliament owes much to the fact that Englishmen in New England
and Virginia managed to make representative government work.

OLD HUNDRED

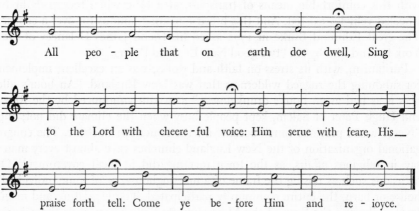

All   peo - ple   that   on   earth   doe   dwell,   Sing

to   the Lord with   cheere - ful   voice: Him   serue with   feare, His——

praise forth   tell: Come   ye   be - fore Him   and   re - ioyce.

From the Hudson to the James

1626-1675

1. New Netherland and New York

NEW NETHERLAND IN 1626 consisted of three trading posts — Fort Orange (Albany), New Amsterdam (New York), and Fort Nassau (Gloucester, New Jersey), under the Dutch West India Company. New Amsterdam by 1630 had neat gabled houses, a brick church, and about 300 inhabitants. The harbor was always full of ships and the town of sailors, since Long Island Sound and the East river was the best route between New England and Virginia. Beyond the wall at Wall Street, built by Governor Dongan to keep out Indians and wolves, stretched "bouweries," or farms. But the Company was not interested in settlement; it wanted only enough tillage to supply with food its employes, who alone had the right to engage in fur trade. Nevertheless several villages, such as Breukelen and Haarlem were founded, and a number of Netherlanders and Walloons — Belgian Protestants — came over.

Kiliaen Van Rensselaer, an Amsterdam jeweler and a stockholder of the Company, decided that fur trading alone would never make New Netherland a proper colony. In 1629 he persuaded the Company to issue a "Charter of Privileges to Patroons," in order to encourage farming and settlement. A patroon was a person who, in return for bringing out fifty people, received a feudal domain on the Hudson, with a fifteen-mile river front, exclusive fishing and hunting privileges, civil and criminal jurisdiction, and the right to share the fur trade with the Company, which promised "to supply the colonists with as many Blacks as they conveniently can." Van Rensselaer never came over himself, but his sons did; and he provided the settlers of Rensselaerswyck with materials to build their houses and barns, and tools to begin farming. In return, he received one-third of the tenant's crop as well as income from hunting licenses and a monopoly of grinding grain at his mills. These privileges came nearer to pure feudalism than any other land system in the future United States. They continued under English rule and even outlasted the Revolution, ending only with the Rent War of the 1840's. This explains why New York became the most aristocratic of English colonies, not excepting Virginia, and the leading Tory colony in the Revolution.

New patroonships along the Hudson were established by the Courtland,

Melyn, Philipse, Van der Donck, and other families. The ancestors of Martin Van Buren were tenants of Rensselaerswyck; other Dutch or Walloon families who became prominent under the Republic, such as the Van Wycks and Roosevelts, came first to "Breukelen" or New Amsterdam as farmers, clerks, or shopkeepers, and rose to merchant status in the next century. There were also settlers from outside Holland, such as Martinus Hoffman of Reval, son of an officer under Gustavus Adolphus, a founder of Esopus; and the Reverend Johannes Theodorus Polhemius of Flatbush, refugee from a Dutch colony in Brazil which the Portuguese had broken up in 1654. Englishmen from New England began to spill over into Long Island and Westchester County, where they obtained a concession of local self-government.

New Netherland, however, was a frustrated colony. The successive governors, whom Washington Irving depicted as figures of fun, were petty autocrats who ruled with a rod of iron, used torture to extract confession, and mishandled almost everything, including the Indians. The Dutch respected the powerful Iroquois Confederacy, with whom their relations were purely trading, but toward the Algonquian tribes that occupied the banks of the Hudson, Westchester County, and western Long Island they showed the same harsh unreasonableness that has made the Netherlands the most hated of all colonial powers in the present century. Governor Kieft, owing to an unprovoked massacre of the peaceful Wecquaesgeek tribe at Pavonia in 1643, sparked off a war that forced every white inhabitant to take refuge behind the wall at Wall Street. The Dutch only won by importing Captain John Underhill from New England to lead the local militia. The company now recalled Kieft and appointed Peter Stuyvesant, who had lost a leg while storming a French fort in the West Indies.

Peglegged Peter brought energy to the company's colony, but not much judgment. The stringent regulation of gin shops and the high customs duties that he imposed kept traders away and brought stagnation to New Amsterdam. His bad temper and autocratic methods offended even the patroons, and he drove out of the colony one of the two Protestant ministers already there. A prominent settler named Adriaen Van der Donck drew up a remonstrance to the Dutch government in 1649, begging it to take over the colony and establish schools, churches, and other apparatus of civilized life. And thirty English inhabitants of Flushing protested against Stuyvesant's decree that anyone who took in a Quaker for the night would be fined fifty florins. They were commanded by the Bible, they said, to do good to all men and they wished not to offend any of Christ's children. They would, therefore, continue to shelter Quakers "as God shall persuade our consciences."

Stuyvesant established a "co-existence" policy with the surviving Indians and with the New England Confederation, concluding a treaty at Hartford in 1650 that is the basis of the present New York-Connecticut boundary. But he annexed in 1655 the weak colony of New Sweden, which the Swedish West

India Company had established in 1638.[1] This Swedish colony, centering around Fort Cristina on the site of Wilmington, Delaware, had aroused Peter's ire by denying Delaware Bay to his traders. By 1660 New Netherland had only half the population of Connecticut. It was easy prey to an aggressor, who was not slow to appear.

Charles II, restored to the throne of England in 1660, had many friends and relations to take care of. And he hated the Dutch, who had refused to let him enter their country during his exile. So he decided to give New Netherland along with other territories to the Duke of York, and to declare war on Holland.

In March 1664, before that war even began, Charles II conferred on his brother the biggest territorial gift ever made by any English sovereign. The "Duke of York's Grant" included not only the present State of New York, but the entire region between the Connecticut and Delaware rivers. Thrown in for good measure were Long Island, Nantucket, Martha's Vineyard, and the present State of Maine east of the Kennebec. The Duke promptly appointed Richard Nicolls his deputy governor, and the king gave him four frigates to help him secure his prize. Nicolls sailed into the harbor of New Amsterdam on 18 August 1664 and called upon the governor to surrender. Peter Stuyvesant, after trying in vain to persuade his subjects to resist, decided to give up without firing a shot. By the end of October the English had taken over not only New Amsterdam, which they renamed New York, but Fort Orange, which they renamed Albany, and Fort Casimir on the Delaware, which they renamed Newcastle. The province, too, was renamed New York.

The Duke at the age of thirty was now owner and ruler of a section of America destined to be the wealthiest of its size in the world. What would he do with it? His charter made him sole proprietor of this vast domain, unhampered by any requirements to obtain popular consent to his laws and regulations. The government was his to arrange as he saw fit; the unoccupied lands were his to hold, sell, or lease as he chose.

One of the first things he chose to do was to slice off a large part of his gift, the Province of New Jersey, for two friends, Sir George Carteret and Lord John Berkeley, brother to the governor of Virginia. These fortunate gentlemen became "true and absolute lords proprietors of all the Province of New Caesaria or New Jersey." Philip Carteret, cousin to Sir George, was sent over to take possession in 1665. He found the grant inhabited by a few hundred Dutchmen and English Puritans, who had settled Woodbridge and Newark. Carteret and Berkeley then issued the "Concessions and Agreements of the Proprietors of New Jersey," the most liberal grant of political privileges made by any English colonial proprietor to the people. Freedom of conscience was

1. The Swedish colony, consisting of only 200 to 300 Swedes and Finns, brought log construction and the log cabin to America. This proved to be so well suited to pioneer housing that it spread all over the North American frontier in the eighteenth century.

guaranteed, generous land grants were promised, and a representative assembly, which first met, at Elizabethtown, in 1668.

In what was left of New York (and plenty there was), the Duke's rule was fairly enlightened. He ordered Nicolls to treat the conquered Dutch with "humanity and gentleness," and made no effort to impose the English language or his Catholic religion on them. But the Duke intended to get money out of his province, and to that end drew up his own schedule of customs duties and other taxes. These made trouble. Too much water had flowed under the English bridge since 1640 for anyone to impose taxes without representation.

The Province of New York was neither racially nor geographically homogeneous in 1664, and never became so. There were a few hundred Dutch, Swedish, and Finnish settlers in the Delaware river section, the former New Sweden. On the Hudson there were Dutch villages like Haarlem, Esopus, and Rensselaerswyck, and a frontier post at Schenectady, a few miles up the Mohawk. Westchester County and Manhattan Island were covered with thrifty Dutch farms, and at the tip of Manhattan the future City of New York had about 2000 inhabitants. On Long Island a few hundred farmers, mostly English, were trying to wrest a living from the sandy soil. To keep the English happy and to attract others, the governor made free land grants on Long Island and promulgated "The Duke's Laws," founded on those of the New England colonies. But the aristocratic element in New York profited most by the change in sovereignty. James confirmed all the Dutch patroonships, and both he and the English crown made enormous grants, under the name of manors, to the Livingston, Pell, Gardiner, Heathcote, and other English and Scottish families.

Many years elapsed before New York became a happy province. On Long Island the English settlers complained that they were "inslav'd under an Arbitrary power" because they had no hand in drafting the Duke's Laws or in levying taxes. The cost of administering a government that extended from the border of Canada to that of Maryland was so great that the Duke was still in the red when a new Anglo-Dutch war broke out in 1673. In the course of that conflict New York City was recaptured by the Dutch but restored to England at the peace next year. In order to get funds to keep the government going, the Duke then instructed his hearty Irish governor, Colonel Thomas Dongan, to summon an assembly. When that met, in 1683, it enacted "The Charter of Liberties and Privileges," declaring that the assembly had the supreme legislative authority and that no taxes were to be levied without its consent. By the time His Royal Highness got around to looking over this declaration of rights, he had become His Majesty King James II, and promptly disallowed it; and New York did not obtain another assembly until 1691. James might have kept New York as his private property when he became king, but it had cost him so much trouble and brought in so little money that he considered it a liability and unloaded it on the crown. Thus New York became a royal province like Virginia, but with no assembly.

In the meantime the history of New Jersey was becoming very complicated. There were two Jersies: East New Jersey with an assembly meeting at Elizabethtown, and West New Jersey with an assembly meeting at Salem or Burlington. By 1683 East New Jersey was in the possession of twenty-four proprietors and West New Jersey belonged to three or four other men. A bad confusion in land titles, which bedeviled the province for seventy-five years, resulted from these changes. In 1702 the proprietors were persuaded to surrender their governmental powers to the crown, and East and West were united as the Royal Province of New Jersey. But the two groups of proprietors retained their property rights, and are still doing a little land business today.

2. Lord Baltimore's Province of Maryland

The most lengthy local conflict in American history is the "oyster war" between Virginia and Maryland, in which fishermen were killed as recently as 1959. It started in 1632. Charles I, cutting a slice out of northern Virginia to oblige his friend Lord Baltimore, granted him as southern boundary "the further bank" of the Potomac river down to Chesapeake Bay. This unusual grant of an entire river, right up to highwater mark on the further shore, has always been resented and disregarded by Virginia crab and oyster fishermen, despite sundry attempts over a period of three centuries to placate them.

The proprietary form of colony, in which a large extent of land with all governing powers was given by a king to an individual, is the oldest form in the English and French colonies. It was tried, as we have seen, by Sir Walter Raleigh, the French, and many others, without accomplishing anything but temporary gain and eventual loss. But the Calvert family made a success of Maryland, and their province supported them in England in grand style down to the American Revolution.

Sir George Calvert, of an old Yorkshire family, has been well described as "the most respectable and honest" of the mediocre and greedy courtiers who came into power under the early Stuarts. He aspired to build up the family fortune by a proprietary colony of his own. First he tried it in Newfoundland on the Avalon Peninsula, including the site of the World War II naval base at Argentia. After five years of this (1622–27), Calvert had to write it off as a bad investment. In the meantime, he had been converted to the Roman Catholic faith and received the title of Baron Baltimore in the Irish peerage. His new religion forced him to resign his seat on the Privy Council when Charles I became king in 1625. But the new king, who liked him personally, compensated Lord Baltimore in 1632 with a rich slice of the Old Dominion. This was the section between the latitude of Philadelphia and the south bank of the Potomac, whose commerce and fisheries he intended his friend to monopolize. The province was named Maryland, ostensibly after Queen Henrietta Maria, but really in honor of the Virgin Mary.

ARMS OF FOUNDERS OF VIRGINIA AND MARYLAND

While the Maryland charter was being processed, George Calvert died, but the king confirmed the grant to his son and heir Cecilius, second Baron Baltimore. Cecilius never visited America, but proved to be a statesmanlike colonial founder and an excellent business man. The family fortunes he hoped to recoup in Maryland. And he also intended to make his colony a refuge for English and Irish Roman Catholics, as New England had become for Puritans. Although Catholics were much more severely discriminated against in Stuart England than the Puritans were, a far smaller proportion were willing to emigrate; never enough to make Maryland predominantly Catholic. Why more did not come is an unsolved mystery.

The second Lord Baltimore spent most of his property fitting out two ships, the *Ark* and the *Dove*, in the late fall of 1633, under the charge of his brother Leonard Calvert. The majority of the passengers were Protestants. Leonard picked up three Jesuit priests at the Isle of Wight, and after a long voyage reached the mouth of the Potomac in the spring of 1634. Profiting by the experience of Jamestown, Calvert selected a healthy town site, which he named St. Mary's, and there the two ships' companies disembarked. The colony prospered from the first; there was no "starving time," as food could be obtained from the Virginia settlements only a few hours' sail away. The neighboring Indians were weak and friendly, and the English treated them with firmness and justice.

This upper part of Chesapeake Bay which Lord Baltimore had secured for himself and his heirs is a very beautiful part of America. The land is low or gently rolling, the soil rich and fruitful; deep rivers and arms of the sea reach up into the land, both on the western and eastern shores; the waters teem with fish, crab and oysters. Even the birds seemed to welcome the English- men — the oriole which "by the English there is call'd the Baltimore-Bird," says an early description, "because the Colours of his Lordship's Coat of Arms are black and yellow"; the "Mock-Bird" which "imitates all other birds," and the red cardinal "which sings like the Nightingale, but much louder."

Lord Baltimore's plan for profits was based on the head-right system which had already proved a success in Virginia. To everyone who brought out serv- ants at his own expense, he offered free 100 acres for each able-bodied man and 50 acres for each woman or child; and to those who brought out a sufficient number to rate 2000 acres he granted a manor. His gains came not from selling land but from the quitrent on it of two shillings — raised to four shillings in 1669 — per 100 acres, to be paid annually forever. In practice, Lord Baltimore allowed quitrent to be commuted by a tax of two shillings on each hogshead of tobacco that the farm produced. This was collected and paid regularly (which never happened in Virginia) until the American Revo- lution.

The difference between a manor and an ordinary landed estate is that the lord of the manor has judicial powers. He can hold "court baron," or his steward can hold "court leet," to settle disputes between tenants and servants, and to punish them for minor offenses. Maryland lords of manors, like the seigneurs of Canada and the patroons of New Netherland, had this privilege; their Maryland grants were genuine manors, unlike the suburban estates and country restaurants which adopt the name nowadays. No fewer than sixty-two manors were granted to individuals, and about thirty more by the Lord Pro- prietor to himself, during the first fifty years of Maryland's existence. As exam- ples: "St. Elizabeth's Manor" and "Cornwalleys' Crosse," each 2000 acres in St. Mary's County, to Captain Thomas Cornwallis, a councillor appointed by Lord Baltimore who came out in the *Ark*; "De la Brooke" and "Brooke Place" manors, 4100 acres on opposite sides of the Patuxent river, granted to the Reverend Robert Brooke, an Anglican clergyman who came over in his own ship in 1650 with wife, two daughters, eight sons, seven maidservants, and twenty-one manservants. Brooke sent a son to Harvard College where, after establishing a high record for undergraduate spending, he proved the value of a college education by introducing the first pack of foxhounds into

Maryland. The Brooke manor house, built in 1652, and the slightly later one of "Cornwalleys' Crosse," are still standing.

The head-right system was an excellent device to keep the labor supply equal to the demand; a manor would have done its lord no good without labor to work it. Tobacco was the one great cash crop in seventeenth-century Maryland. In the old tidewater counties, rents and country doctors' bills were often paid in tobacco as late as the twentieth century.

Lord Baltimore kept an office in the City of London to deal with people who wished to emigrate, not only prospective lords of manors but servants. And for many years the majority of the white population consisted of the latter class. "Servant" in the colonial era meant about the same as employee in ours; and within the class there was as wide a variation as today between a migrant farm laborer in California and a master electrician. In the English and Dutch colonies, a servant was usually a person whose passage was paid, or assisted, in return for working for a certain number of years — usually four or five years for an adult, more for a minor. When released from this apprenticeship, the servant became a freeman like any other. An "indentured servant" meant one who had a specific contract with his employer called an indenture, because originally it was torn in two along an irregular edge. This system of exchanging the cost of passage and outfit for a few years' labor was the principal means of peopling the English colonies, and even for many years after they became independent.

Servants in Maryland — and the same is true of all English and Dutch colonies — might be of any class, from poor gentleman to convicted felon. The average servant was a respectable young person who wished to better himself in the New World but could not afford the cost of outfit and passage. During the four or five years he worked for his master, he became acclimated, learned how to grow tobacco and corn, and in many instances learned a trade. Some maidservants were employed in the manor house; others were dairy maids or worked hoeing tobacco alongside the young men. During the term of service the servant received only food and clothing; but at the end, each was entitled by Maryland law and custom — more generous than those of other colonies — to fifty acres of land, a complete suit of clothes, an axe, two hoes, and three barrels of corn. The former servant could then set up as a yeoman farmer, vote, and even be elected to the assembly.

Next below these respectable members of the servant class were ex-rebels, kidnapped persons, and convicts. James I began, and Oliver Cromwell and the later Stuart kings continued, the business of transporting to the colonies Scottish and Irish prisoners taken in the civil wars, and this practice continued until after the Rebellion of 1745. Most of these unfortunates were sent to the West Indies, where their descendants form a distinct class to this day; but some went to Virginia, Maryland, and New England. From the earliest times a class of London crooks specialized in "trapanning," kidnapping boys and girls. They were "spirited" on board a colony-bound ship, whose master sold their services on arrival to recoup himself for the cost of transport and the kidnapper's fee. In a popular ballad of the time, "The Trapann'd Maiden: or the Distressed Damsel," one of the victims is made to sing:

> Five years served I, under Master Guy,
>   In the land of Virginny, O,
> Which made me for to know sorrow, grief and woe,
>   When that I was weary, weary, weary, weary, O.

She tells how she has to do rough farm work from dawn to dark and sleep on straw, "instead of drinking Beer" to "drink the water clear," sing the children to sleep and do all that she is bid. It does not sound too bad; but this ballad was intended as an antidote to "The Maydens of London's Brave Adventures," which promises all "merry London Girls, that are disposed to travel," that they can get rich in the gold and silver mines of Virginia, or "have good ground enough, for Planting and for Tilling," and live on "fare most dainty."

Finally, there were the transported convicts. The English government under Charles II executed the worst convicts and shipped the rest to the colonies, where they had to labor for seven years to earn their freedom. Among them were juvenile delinquents, people imprisoned for nothing worse than stealing a loaf of bread, felons and habitual criminals, and highwaymen who saved themselves from hanging by "benefit of clergy" — proving that they could read. This curious exemption for the literate had come down from the middle ages, when anyone who could read was assumed to be a priest. Marylanders protested frequently against their fair land being made a dumping ground for "His Majesty's seven-year passengers," but were unable to do anything about it because the successive Lords Baltimore liked the system. And the convicts, on their part, were by no means eager for a free ride to America and subsequent hard work. These were the class of servants who gave most trouble from idleness and running away. The usual punishments for fugitives were whipping, adding months or years to their terms of service, or selling the delinquent's services to someone known to be a hard taskmaster.

There is some reason to believe that the first Negroes brought into Virginia and Maryland were regarded as slaves only for life, or until baptized; for it was church doctrine that only pagans could be enslaved. However that may be, the Maryland assembly passed a "black code" in 1664, which declared any Negro in the colony to be a slave for life by virtue of his color. And a law of 1671, following a similar Virginia enactment, declared that neither baptism nor conversion could affect a person's bondage or freedom. Until the end of the century, Negro slavery was no more important a factor in Maryland social life than in New York or Rhode Island; but after 1700 the importation of slaves increased, until at the time of the Revolution they numbered almost one-third of the population.

Lord Baltimore, shrewd as well as sincere, knew that as a Catholic proprietor in a Protestant empire he would have to watch his step very carefully. His instructions to his brother the governor were to "suffer no scandall or offence to be given to any of the Protestants, whereby any just complaint may hereafter be made." Catholic worship should be "done as privately as may be," Catholics should avoid arguments on religion and Protestants be treated "with as much mildness and favor as Justice will permitt." Leonard Calvert enforced these sentiments so well that at St. Mary's both Protestants and Catholics worshipped in the same building. But the proprietor had to crack down on three overzealous English Jesuits who came over in the first ships. They claimed the right to buy land from the Indians, as well as canon law privileges such as freedom from taxation, control of wills and marriages, and of being tried by an ecclesiastical court. Lord Baltimore sent over a Catholic layman to dissuade them from these pretensions, and when they refused to desist, appealed to Rome. The Vatican upheld the proprietor, and the Jesuits were sent home.

As the entire government of Maryland issued from the Lord Proprietor as fountain head, it is fortunate that Lord Baltimore, unlike the Duke of York, believed in representative government. He was, to be sure, required by his charter to obtain the "Advice, Assent, and Approbation of the Freemen of the same Province" to any laws he might enact; but how and when he should obtain this "triple-A" was left to his judgment. He appointed the governor, council, secretary, and all other officials, and the first assembly that he summoned, in 1649, consisted of twenty-one private gentlemen and four officials. As settlement spread, personal attendance at the assembly became irksome, and a representative system was worked out; after 1650 there were two houses, the council appointed by Lord Baltimore, and the elected house of burgesses. The proprietor and his governor retained the initiative in legislation; burgesses could not introduce bills. He was careful to keep all essential powers of government in family hands. Leonard Calvert's titles read like those of "Pooh-Bah" in *The Mikado:* he was governor, lord chancellor, chief magistrate, chief justice, and lieutenant general of the militia. After Leonard's death in 1647, Lord Baltimore, as a concession to the rising tide of Puritanism in England, appointed a Protestant governor, William Stone; but with the restoration of the monarchy in 1660 the chief office went back into the Calvert family. At all times in the seventeenth century, except for the decade of the 1650's, Catholics were the ruling class in Maryland, constituting a majority of the council and the permanent officials; and they governed well. Few lords proprietors ever visited Maryland, but the entire line derived a handsome revenue from the Province — some £13,000 a year around 1770.

Cecilius Calvert's astute statesmanship is again shown in the Toleration Act, which the assembly at his behest passed on 21 April 1649. This Act declared that no professed Christian should "be any ways troubled molested or discountenanced for . . . his or her religion, nor in the free exercise thereof . . . nor any way compelled to the belief or exercise of any other Religion against his or her consent." But anyone who denied the Trinity or the divinity of Christ should be hanged, and anyone who insulted the Blessed Virgin, the Apostles, or the Evangelists, should be fined or whipped. Lord Baltimore thus hoped to secure his fellow Catholics against persecution if the Protestants obtained control. Unfortunately, a community of Puritans ejected from Virginia and invited to settle near Annapolis made trouble. In alliance with William Claiborne, a Virginia trader who had been expelled from Kent Island, they rebelled, deposed Governor Stone in 1654, and attempted to repeal the Act of Toleration. The proprietor, however, handled his public relations in England with such skill that he kept his province, and after a period of turmoil the Act of Toleration was revived, only to be replaced in 1692 by the official establishment of the Church of England.

Nevertheless, the Roman Catholics had obtained a foothold in Maryland, including most of the real estate. As immigration increased, Maryland became overwhelmingly Protestant, but the Catholics have always been at the top of the social heap. Cecilius, who died in 1675, deserves high rank as a colonial founder; but good marks should also be accorded the English government which allowed and even encouraged Roman Catholics to live in Maryland without the disabilities under which they suffered at home. In no Catholic colonial empire — French, Spanish, or Portuguese — were Protestants allowed to exist, much less to acquire land and hold office. In Maryland, as earlier in Rhode Island and later in Pennsylvania, there grew up a system of legal religious toleration which became one of the cornerstones of the American republic. It was a gain for Protestants and Catholics to co-exist peaceably in the same community; this established a climate of toleration such as one does not find in countries like Spain, where a single Church has dominated the scene for centuries.

3. The Royal Province of Virginia

"Leah and Rachel, the two Fruitful Sisters," as an early chronicler called these colonies after Laban's fair daughters in Genesis, were peopled by the same sort of Englishmen who led the same sort of life; their differences were of degree rather than kind. Virginia, even after Maryland had been lopped off, remained a dominion of imperial extent, comprising at least seven later states of the Union. The younger sister's territory was always limited, and not until the census of 1960 did Rachel approach Leah in numbers — 3.1 million in Maryland and 4 million in Virginia.

We left Virginia in 1624, binding up the wounds of the great Indian massacre. She was now the king's province, to dispose of as he saw fit. Charles I appointed a royal governor and council but did not disturb the other institutions that the Company had set up: the house of burgesses, the rule of law, and the head-right system for granting land. Actually, the house of burgesses until about 1660 exercised more power under the crown than it had under the Company, and the new royal regime was more popular locally than that of the Company had been, because the Company regime interfered too much in the affairs of the people — Virginians never have liked economic planning. Charles I was much too busy to do any economic planning of his own; Cromwell accorded even more self-government than the king had, so the colony was left alone to develop in a natural way.

Under this "salutary neglect," as Edmund Burke described England's old colonial policy, Virginia prospered. The total population, a little over 1100 in 1624, had risen to about 15,000, together with 300 Negro slaves by 1648; and by 1671 to over 40,000 according to a report of Governor Berkeley. This meant that Virginia was easily first among England's continental colonies, and second only to Barbados among all English colonies.

Owing to the prevalence of tobacco culture and the head-right system, Virginia was settled in a dispersed, decentralized manner. Here is how the head-right system worked. Upon his arrival at Jamestown, the prospective planter obtained from the colonial secretary a warrant entitling him to 50 acres of wild, ungranted land for himself and for each person brought over at his own expense; and he received another 50 acres for every person he brought in later. He did not have to convert all head-rights into land at once; they could be saved for future use, inherited by his heirs, or even sold. But if he chose to start a plantation promptly, he had to find a site for it in un-granted land, lay it out with an official surveyor, record it at the county court, and then "seat" — that is, begin to build upon or cultivate the ground. After that he received a deed, and the land was his to have and to hold, subject to a quitrent to the crown of two shillings per 100 acres.

The quitrent was more often evaded than paid, because it was nobody's business to collect it; and the tax yielded only £800 around 1700, at a time when the Lords Baltimore were getting twice that out of little Maryland. Masters of ships collected head-rights for their sailors on every voyage. Seating was often perfunctory, as under the federal Homestead Act of 1862 — a few trees felled, a few furrows plowed, a shed clapped together. The indiscriminate location also had two disadvantages. It dispersed settlement, so that community life was next to impossible. Irregular or overlapping boundaries resulted from imperfect surveying, or using an "olde oake tree" as a mark. But it was a good method for equating land and labor supply; and as long as tobacco fetched a fair price in England it enabled a thrifty farmer to become a wealthy planter in a few years.

Take, for example, the case of Captain Adam Throughgood, who started life in Virginia as a boy servant. After his time was up he did so well that he returned to England and brought out wife, son, and 38 servants in 1628. Thereafter, by bringing out single men, maids, or couples, he accumulated in seven years 105 head-rights and an estate of 5350 acres. Robert Taliaferro by 1660 had acquired 6300 acres for the transport of 126 persons, 16 of them Negro slaves. John, the first Washington to settle in Virginia, arrived in 1657 as mate of a London ship and decided to stay. Within eleven years, in partnership with his brother-in-law Thomas Pope, he had obtained more than 5000 acres, including the estate where his famous descendant was born. One can trace the rise of John Washington not only by his increase of land-holdings but by his public offices: coroner, collector of the tobacco tax, justice of the court of Westmoreland County, vestryman, burgess, and officer in the militia.

Jamestown, where every arriving and departing ship had to call, had a goodly brick church (similar to St. Luke's, Smithfield, which has survived), and a brick State House where the assembly met, but not more than thirty other houses by mid-century. When the courts and assembly were not sitting, the town was almost deserted. A traveler of 1650, sailing up the James, the York, or another tidal tributary of Chesapeake Bay, found every few miles a clearing with a wharf, a modest mansion, a clutch of wooden cottages for servants, an orchard, kitchen garden and corn patch, and fields green with the tobacco plant. Beyond and between these plantations there was only the primeval forest in which cattle browsed and pigs rooted. Transport was largely by boat, along the natural waterways — "drowned river" estuaries up which the salt tides flowed to the line of falls. This gave every plantation a place on the tobacco pipeline to England. The Reverend John Clayton observed in a letter of 1688 that "this Conveniency" was an "impediment to the Advance of the country," because it forced ships to visit every plantation and spared the planters the necessity of sending their produce to a market town. "The Country is thinly inhabited; the Living solitary and unsociable; Trading confused and dispersed; besides other Inconveniences."

The method of trade is illustrated by the log of a small double-ended vessel, pink *Swan* of Poole in Devonshire. She sailed 18 November 1667, and after a rough crossing sighted the Capes of the Chesapeake 25 January 1668. The wind was blowing so strong out of the Bay that she was unable to enter for ten days. She then worked up and down the Patuxent river in Maryland and proceeded to Bush river, staying there until 16 April, peddling English goods and taking on tobacco. Still not fully laden, the *Swan* visited the Magothy and Severn rivers and again the Patuxent, loading three or four hogshead from each plantation. She checked out at Lord Baltimore's custom house at St. Mary's on 25 April, cleared the Capes 8 May in company with two other tobacco ships, and after an unusually prosperous passage reached her home port a month later.

Tobacco culture was so ruinous to fertility that every planter needed reserve land. Probably no more than 100 acres of a 1000-acre plantation were under cultivation at the same time. But tobacco was the life of the Old Dominion. All prices and salaries, even of the ministers, were expressed in pounds of tobacco; and when warehouses were built toward the close of the century, warehouse receipts passed like cheques drawn to bearer today. Even the wealthiest planters handled very little hard money; all transactions were made on credit, bills paid annually when the return of the crop was made from England. There, the tobacco grown in North America was processed into pipe tobacco and snuff — cigars were not used outside the Spanish empire, and the cigarette had not been invented. North American tobacco ran to two types, the sweet-scented, ancestor of the fragrant pipe tobacco of today; and Oronoko, a strong, heavy leaf preferred by European smokers, in which Maryland specialized. Down to the 1660's the English colonies could export their tobacco in English or foreign ships to any part of Europe, where there was an insatiable demand, and the Chesapeake colonies prospered accordingly. After 1665 the English government made it increasingly difficult to send tobacco anywhere except to England (not even to Scotland before 1707, or thereafter to Ireland) or in any ship not English or colonial.

The crown levied a duty of about four cents per pound on American tobacco imported into England. This became a hardship late in the century, when the wholesale price fell to a penny a pound or even less.[1] The planter selected a London or Bristol merchant and consigned to him his entire crop along with a list of his family's needs for the next year — clothing, guns and ammunition, farm implements, furniture, horses, and servants. The merchant sold the tobacco for what he could get, and made the desired purchases, charging the planter a commission each way; and almost inevitably got the planter into debt. It was a standard joke that a son inherited his father's debts to the merchant along with his land. Yet, despite this system of economic servitude — precursor of the later pioneer farmer's dependence on grain merchants and the railroads — and crop failures, and shipwrecks, Virginia prospered. Not only did the system enable thrifty, hard-working young gentlemen like John Washington to live comfortably and become wealthy; thousands of ex-servants and poor men, using only the labor of their own families, made a fair living and enjoyed plenty of sport too.

It so happened that on the first good road built in the English colonies, from Jamestown to Governor Berkeley's plantation of Greenspring, there was a quarter-mile straightaway. The Governor and his friends adopted the habit of racing their horses along this stretch on Sunday mornings after church; and from this informal contest there developed the "quarter horse." This American strain of racehorse, bred to run that short distance at terrific speed, lacked the thoroughbred's stamina to stay for a mile or more; he was the sprinter among horses. Until recently the quarter horse was the poor man's racehorse, as he could be raced anywhere; he is now bred for formal racing and rodeos, and for handling cattle.

Another poor man's sport that started early was running foxes at night with hounds, the original American form of the fox chase. It spread all over the English colonies, followed the frontier, and is practiced to this day. On a crisp autumn night, all over the land, you would find small groups of farmers

1. A part of the duty was repaid if the tobacco was re-exported to Europe; this was called the "drawback." London, for instance, imported 11.5 million pounds of American tobacco in 1678 and re-exported 5.5 million; Bristol re-exported half of what she received.

sitting around a fire in the open, passing around liquor in a jug, and talking in low voices while each man listened for the distinctive cry of his hound, running a fox in a nearby swamp or thicket.

We must now come to grips with the tradition that all white men in Virginia were "Cavaliers." That was nearly true, if we take cavalier in its then meaning of a royalist, an Englishman who, regardless of birth or rank, supported King Charles in the Civil War of 1641–49, as against the roundheads who supported Parliament and Oliver Cromwell. The humblest plowjogger who borrowed a horse and joined Prince Rupert's troop was as much a cavalier as the Duke of Norfolk. In this correct sense of the word, Virginia was nearly 100 per cent cavalier. The people sympathized with the royal cause, and were profoundly shocked by the execution of King Charles. The assembly promptly proclaimed his son in exile as Charles II, and let the world know it. Parliament's orders to discard the Book of Common Prayer were flouted; and although the assembly had to submit to a Cromwellian commission which deposed the popular governor, Sir William Berkeley, it elected him governor in 1660 when the joyful news arrived that the Cromwellian dynasty had come to an end with "Tumbledown Dick." Unfortunately for historical sanity, Virginians of the nineteenth century got the idea that cavalier meant a well-born gentleman or nobleman, a myth that in some measure contributed to secession and the American Civil War.

Who, then, were the Virginians of this half-century, 1624 to 1675? For the most part they were yeoman farmers with an upper crust of self-made men who accumulated a fortune in land. The first founders of Virginia, in the period 1607–24 were largely Oxford graduates, sons of knights or barons, men out of the top drawer of English society — like George Percy, son of the Earl of Northumberland, Lord de la Warr and his sons, and George Sandys. But few of these survived into the generation which we are now describing. They lost heart and returned to England, or died of the fever, or were killed in the massacre. The big men of 1625–45 were of middle-class origin who rose to wealth and power in Virginia itself — such as Samuel Matthews, who made his fortune by supplying tobacco ships with provisions. Most of these, too, passed from the scene, and around 1645 there arose other families of middle-class origin who became the First Families of Virginia. Such was John Carter, of unknown parentage, who arrived from England in 1645, made a fortune from tobacco, married in succession five wives who brought him more land, and left a son Robert, who became so wealthy as to be called "King" Carter. Such was the first William Byrd, son of a London goldsmith and a shipmaster's daughter, who reached Virginia in 1671 at the age of nineteen, inherited land from an uncle who preceded him, made a good marriage, got elected to the house of burgesses, purchased the plantation named Westover, built there a mansion, a shop, and a warehouse, and did very well with his tobacco crop. He imported, in his own ships, servants and all manner of goods. To the West Indies he sent provisions, grain, and barrel staves, and imported thence sugar, rum, and Negro slaves — in one shipment 506 slaves, most of whom he sold to his neighbors. He was also a successful Indian trader, sending goods by packhorse into North Carolina, there to obtain deerskins and furs. At the time of his death in 1704 he was rightly regarded as one of the first gentlemen of Virginia.

Among others of this class one may mention William Fitzhugh, Giles Bland, Daniel Parke, Lewis Burwell, Thomas Ludwell, and John Page. Their class, the rising generation of tobacco aristocrats, was strengthened by the arrival of refugee cavaliers, both during and after the English Civil War. Such were Henry Randolph of a distinguished English family, and Richard Lee. These men formed but a small minority of the 38,000 white inhabitants of Virginia around 1675. The dominant feature of the country at this period was the 100- to 300-acre farm, and the typical Virginian was an English yeoman, often an ex-servant, who worked himself, with his family and his few servants. They all had the vote and elected burgesses who went on record as being wholeheartedly cavalier, royalist, and Anglican.

Negro slavery did not become rooted in Virginia until after 1681, when according to the royal governor's estimate, there were 3000 "blacks" and 15,000 white servants, out of a total population between 70,000 and 80,000. Included with the blacks was a considerable number of free Negroes, some of whom had become wealthy. In Northampton County there was a community of free Negroes who acquired hundreds of acres by head-rights. They imported slaves from Africa and servants from England to such an extent that the assembly in 1670 declared it illegal for Negroes to own white servants. These Negroes had been emancipated by their masters, partly as a reward for faithful service, partly because of the feeling that it was wrong to hold any man a slave, once he had professed Christianity.

The early laws of Virginia forbade playing cards or throwing dice — doubtless for the good Puritan motive that they "wasted precious time." There was a fine of 50 pounds of tobacco, equivalent to a week's wages, for missing church on Sunday, when neither travel, business, nor loading of ships was allowed. Each Virginia parish was governed by a self-perpetuating vestry and two churchwardens who acted as moral policemen of the parish, like the constables of a New England town. The churchwardens presented to the county court all cases of bastardy, adultery, blasphemy, sabbath-breaking, slander, backbiting, and other "scandalous offences." County courts, composed of landowners appointed by the governor, punished by whipping, stocks, pillory, and ducking stools — rarely by imprisonment, as that was expensive and took labor out of production. The problem of five-month babies bothered Virginia like other rural societies; for where a man depended on the labor of his children, he could not take the chance of marrying a barren woman. Virginia couples caught that way had to confess premarital intercourse in open congregation while clad in the white sheet of penitence, as in New England or Old England. And there are even cases of

adulterers having to wear the scarlet letter A, and of women being punished
— but never executed — for witchcraft.

English men and women of that day, whether at home or in the colonies
and of whatever class, expressed anger or vexation in explosive, picturesque,
and bawdy language that shames the poor four-lettered profanity of today.
Against this practice church and state struggled in vain. In a crusade to clean
up Henrico County, 122 persons were indicted for uttering "wicked oaths,"
a woman was found guilty of swearing no fewer than 65 times, and John
Huddlesey was imprisoned for "oaths innumerable." And there were many
other indications that English tastes were the same in all latitudes. For a
homely example, we find that in Virginia, as in New England, cow-kind
were the favorite animals, adapting easily to the country and providing milk
and traction while they lived, beef and shoe leather when they were slaughtered. We find the same pet names for cows in Virginia as in Plymouth
Colony — Daisy, Bunny, Pretty, Whiteface; and for yokes of oxen, Buck
and Duke, Spark and Swad.

Although Virginians honored the king and preferred to worship according
to the Book of Common Prayer, their churches were conducted in a manner
that would have shocked Archbishop Laud, or even a bishop of today. Parts
of the liturgy were omitted, the surplice was seldom worn, holy communion
was administered to the congregation sitting around a table, Puritan fashion; and there was no altar with candles and cross, which Virginians of that
century regarded as faintly idolatrous.

The Anglican Church in Virginia suffered for want of ministers. Having
no college like Harvard where they could be educated, and few schools,
young Virginians found it too difficult to qualify for the ministry, and the
colony depended on obtaining a supply from England. Young English ordi-
nands naturally preferred a parish in Old England to roughing it in Virginia. But it is a mystery why cavalier clergy, ousted from their parishes by
the Long Parliament and Cromwell because they would not turn Presbyterian like the famous Vicar of Bray, did not flock to a colony where they were
desperately needed. By 1672 four out of five Virginia parishes were vacant,
and two out of three which were not vacant had lay readers instead of
ordained ministers. Virginia needed a bishop, as the Spanish and French
governments had given to their American colonies; and there was talk of
elevating the Reverend Alexander Murray, one of the most devoted and
intelligent ministers in the colonies, to the episcopate; but nothing came of
it.

Almost all Englishmen in the seventeenth century were interested in
religion, and everyone who read anything, read works on divinity. Invento-
ries of Virginian private libraries include a few Latin or English classics,
practical works on husbandry, and a surprising number of books of Puritan
theology, such as the works of the Reverend William ("Painful") Perkins,
which were favorite reading in New England. The Bible was as well known

and as thoroughly read in houses along Chesapeake Bay, as on the Merri-mack and the Connecticut. Yet, with all these resemblances, there was a fundamental difference between Puritanism in New England and in Vir-ginia. In the Northern colonies, it was a positive and pervasive way of life, difficult for anyone to escape. Puritanism in Virginia merely reflected the average Englishman's desire to support honesty and morality, in the absence of Anglican discipline and authority. Under conditions of dispersed settle-ment and immense parishes — some extending as much as 50 miles along a river — no minister could exercise much supervision. Most people in New England lived around a village green under the eye of the parson and the constable; if Elnathan Danforth was observed entering the house of Na-thaniel Cotton (who had recently married a young and pretty wife) when Nate was out mowing, the whole village watched developments with keen interest. But in Virginia the parson wore out his horse, his boatmen, and his legs, merely trying to get around, and much went on that he never could know about.

In their ideas on government, Englishmen in New England, Virginia, and Maryland saw eye to eye. All would have agreed with Governor Winthrop's famous "Little Speech on Liberty," that "Democracy is . . . accounted the meanest and worst of all forms of government," and that a "mixt" or balanced government, containing monarchical, aristocratic, and democratic elements, was the best. Virginia revolted against too much monarchy in 1675, New England in 1685; Maryland rebelled against a closed aristocracy, the lord proprietor's officials. Englishmen in the Southern colonies shared the Puritans' abhorrence of arbitrary power and dislike of undignified gov-ernment. As early as 1618 the Virginia Company, in order to "beget rever-ence" among the common people, ordered Governor Gates to hire a per-sonal guard, and the governors of Massachusetts Bay were always attended on public occasions by militiamen carryng halberds. This tradition of dignity in government lasted well into the early Republic but was largely lost under Jacksonian Democracy, which considered dignity incompatible with popular rule, and clowning more profitable than ceremony.

Governor Berkeley, in one of his many outbursts, thanked God that Vir-ginia had no printing press or free school. The former was true, and a pity, too; aspiring young writers had no chance to have their verse or prose published, short of London. But there were endowed free schools in Vir-ginia. The Syms School, established under a bequest of Benjamin Syms, was in operation by 1647; and the Eaton School twelve years later. Combined as the Syms-Eaton High School of Hampton, they are still in existence. And one finds in the records occasional mention of "old field schools," erected in some worn-out tobacco field, to teach children within riding or rowing dis-tance the three Rs. Wealthy planters depended on obtaining imported Irish or Scots schoolmasters to teach their children, and were not interested in public education.

Governor Berkeley tried to persuade Maryland and North Carolina to stop growing tobacco for a year in the hope of lessening the supply and raising the price, but Maryland refused to co-operate, and overproduction continued. "Forty thousand people are empoverished," Berkeley wrote in his *Discourse or View of Virginia*, "in order to enrich little more than forty merchants in England." In 1668 the price reached an all-time low — a farthing a pound at the wharf. This was due not only to overproduction but to the English prohibition of direct export to the continent of Europe. The English government, far from affording the colonial tobacco growers relief, such as lowering the customs duty of twopence a pound, scolded Virginia for her one-crop system and ordered the planters to pay more attention to cereals, timber, and the recalcitrant silkworm. Charles II received an annual revenue of £100,000 from the tobacco duty by 1675. But American farmers had to wait almost three centuries for price support.

Thus, during the first fifteen years of the reign of Charles II, Virginia, formerly a land of opportunity, had become a relatively poor and discontented community. Something was bound to happen; and, as we shall see in a later chapter, a minor Indian war and a young aristocrat named Nathaniel Bacon sparked off a serious rebellion.

V I I

Empires of the South and North

1625-1675

1. The Carolinas

CHARLES II, "THE MERRY MONARCH," most popular king that England ever had, was also the shiftiest. He had more brains than he cared to use, and the bright side of that defect, so far as the colonies were concerned, was an inclination to let them alone. No English subsidies bolstered the prices of colonial products, no royal bounty succored the settlers when they were starving, no royal troops helped defend them against Indians and pirates; on the contrary, this king disciplined but one colony, Massachusetts Bay, and that after repeated provocation. The colonies were allowed to grow any old way, which in the long run made them stronger than bounty-fed, regimented French Canada.

This king can hardly be said to have had a colonial policy. There was a drift toward closer control of colonial trade and government; but if a colonial assembly sent the right person to talk to the king, with a pocketful of money for important officials, it could get away with almost anything. For instance, Governor John Winthrop Jr. of Connecticut, who had access to the king through fellowship in the Royal Society, obtained for his colony the charter of 1662, which annexed New Haven and made Connecticut as independent as Massachusetts. Next year, Dr. John Clark of Rhode Island obtained a similar charter which recognized that colony's privilege of electing its own government, and protected it from partition by powerful neighbors.

Charles II was a good politician: he rewarded friends and punished enemies. His restoration set everyone who claimed a slice of the English empire to dusting off old charters, and brought in a new lot of office seekers. As there were not nearly enough plums on the government tree for all, an obvious way to reward deserving cavaliers was to create them colonial proprietors. We have already seen how this was done in the case of New York and New Jersey. A fortunate result of this policy was an expansion of that part of the English empire which became the United States. Six of the original Thirteen States were founded in the reign of Charles II, all as proprietary grants. In 1662 a group of eight promoters and politicians applied to the king for a grant of "Carolina," the region between Virginia and Spanish Florida, as a proprietary province. Their leading spirits were Anthony Ashley Cooper, later Lord Ashley and Earl of Shaftesbury, and Sir John Colleton, a wealthy Barbadian planter who sought new homes for the overcrowded white population of Barbados. Anthony, a poor cavalier, rewarded by the king with the chancellorship of the exchequer and created Lord Ashley, found that in the extravagant court he could not live on his salary. So he, Colleton, and Governor Berkeley of Virginia put their heads together and took in two important people as "front men." These were General George Monk, Duke of Albemarle, who had prepared the way for Charles's restoration, and the Earl of Clarendon, historian and statesman.

Their great talking point was the prospect of raising tropical commodities such as silk and wine, currants and olives, which had been hoped for but never realized in Virginia. And they obtained the Carolina Charter of 1663 which, with boundaries extended shortly after, gave them everything from sea to sea between the present southern boundary of Virginia and the latitude of Daytona Beach, Florida. The charter was in the form of a proprietary province, following that of Maryland, with the same limitation that all laws be consented to by the freemen and not be repugnant to those of England. In addition, it expressed the new policy of religious toleration, guaranteeing liberty of conscience to all settlers demeaning themselves quietly. The English government did not want its subjects to leave England for the colonies, and hoped to extend the empire by encouraging people to move from the older colonies to the newer, and to attract persecuted Protestants from continental Europe.

After two failures by the proprietors to establish settlements in northern Carolina, young and energetic Lord Ashley took hold and made himself the real founder. His first move, however, was oddly impractical. With the aid of his secretary, John Locke the philosopher, he drafted a curious document called, "The Fundamental Constitutions of Carolina." This was the longest, most fantastic and reactionary of all colonial frames of government. It created a Carolina nobility. Anyone who purchased 3000 acres could be a baron and lord of the manor; 12,000 acres gave the owner the title of cassique; and an owner of 20,000 acres could have the German title of landgrave. The common people could elect members of a house of commons, but no bill could become law unless consented to by a majority of the barons, the cassiques, the landgraves, and the proprietors! Naturally this constitution did not work in a pioneer society. Some forty great landowners, most of them absentees, did call themselves by the odd titles; but the house of commons (as the South Carolina assembly was called until the Revolution) ignored the requirement that every bill must pass through five winnowings, and prevented landgraves and cassiques from sitting on the governor's council by right.

The lords proprietors, having, as they fondly hoped, settled the form of government, made efforts to procure people to live under it. Three vessels were fitted out in England in the summer of 1669. Two were wrecked, but the third called at Barbados, picked up a couple of hundred emigrants and reached Carolina in the spring of 1670. Captain Joseph West, appointed first governor of the colony, turned down Port Royal as too near St. Augustine, "in the very chops of the Spaniards," and sailed along until he reached a big bay watered by two rivers that he named the Ashley and the Cooper, after his energetic proprietor. There he established Charles Town, not far from the site of modern Charleston. And here the settlement of South Carolina really began.

Lawndes   Huger   Butler

Leigh   Gordon   Bull

Oglethorpe   Wright   Houston

ARMS OF FOUNDERS OF THE CAROLINAS

For almost a quarter-century, Charleston was as unlike the romantic Charleston of the Jockey Club and St. Cecilia Assembly as Jamestown was unlike royal Williamsburg. The principal occupations were raising livestock, cutting timber or barrel staves for export to the West Indies, trading for fur and deerskins with the nearby Catawba and more distant Cherokee Indians, buying captives taken by these natives in their tribal wars and selling them as slaves in other colonies. Colleton was the only Proprietor ever to live in the province; most of the settlers were poor whites from Barbados whose names mean nothing to later history. So little was accomplished in the early years that we are tempted to carry this account beyond 1675.

In 1680 the lords proprietors persuaded a small group of Huguenots —

French Protestants — to settle near Charleston for the express purpose of cultivating the silkworm. And a band of rugged Scots was induced to start the settlement of Port Royal in 1683. They were attacked by the Spaniards three years later, since Spain claimed the whole of Carolina and had earlier established a mission at Port Royal. The few Scots who survived this fight took refuge on the Cooper river above Charleston.

This attack, proving that the Spanish empire was still alive and kicking, discouraged Englishmen from settling so near Florida. But Louis XIV of France inadvertently provided a high class of emigrants for South Carolina. In 1685 he repealed Henry IV's Edict of Nantes, which guaranteed toleration to French Protestants — and began to "harry them out of the land" more effectively than the Stuarts had done to the Puritans. Thousands emigrated to Prussia, England, and the English colonies, where they were welcomed. And as the Carolina proprietors were eager for Protestant settlers who knew how to cultivate olives and vines, they got the lion's share. Huguenot families such as Marion, Pingree, Petigru, Huger, and De Saussure gave a special character to South Carolina society. Liberty-loving people themselves, they were none the less responsible for fastening Negro slavery on the low coastland to cultivate rice. This proved to be the first step in the conquest of South Carolina by slave economy. Rice plantations were as much dispersed as the tobacco plantations of Virginia; but, owing to the social instincts of the French, as well as malarial fevers that prevailed in the rice country during the summer, leading planters built town houses in Charleston and developed an urban society.

Completely different in character were the first settlements in North Carolina, peopled largely by former indentured servants and other poor whites who had been squeezed out of Virginia by the low price of tobacco and the rise of Negro slavery. They hewed out small farms along the shore of Albemarle Sound, and exported tobacco, their only cash crop, in small vessels, through the shallow inlets, thus escaping export duties and other regulations imposed by Parliament. A head-right system more generous than that of Virginia was established by the lords proprietors to encourage a superior type of settler, and with success. Owing to the great distance of the Albemarle settlements from those on the Ashley and Cooper, they were given a separate governor and an assembly which was distinctly democratic in character, one of its early laws limiting individual land grants to 660 acres.

To anticipate later Carolina history, in 1710 the proprietors attracted the attention of Baron Graffenried of Bern to the possibilities of northern Carolina. He was made a landgrave and brought out over a thousand German and Swiss settlers, besides founding the town of New Bern. His colony tangled with the Tuscarora Indians, and was almost wiped out.

Although both Carolinas were successful colonies from the viewpoint of the settlers, they disappointed the proprietors, who had expected to grow rich from selling land. Like absentee landlords almost everywhere, they were robbed by their agents. The consequence was that in 1729 all but one proprietor (Lord Granville) sold out to the crown, and the two halves then became the royal provinces of North Carolina and South Carolina. The same thing happened to every other proprietary colony in the English and French overseas empires, excepting those of the canny Calverts and the popular Penns.

2. The Non-Spanish West Indies

During this half-century, the situation in the West Indies reached an uneasy balance between Spain, England, France, and the Netherlands. Spain retained Cuba, Puerto Rico, Trinidad, and the eastern part of Hispaniola, but lost Jamaica to England and Saint-Domingue (the future Haiti) to France. The French colonized Martinique, Guadeloupe, and half of St. Kitts and a few smaller islands. The English kept the other half of St. Kitts, together with Barbados, Antigua, Montserrat, and Nevis. In the Windward Islands of St. Vincent, St. Lucia, and Dominica the Carib Indians were still strong and hungry enough to keep Europeans out.

Admiral Piet Hein of the Dutch navy pulled off in 1628 the act that every French and English corsair had dreamed of for a century past, capturing an entire Spanish treasure fleet. Lying in wait off Matanzas in northern Cuba, he took nine great galleons laden with hides, ginger, cocoa, and cochineal, and eight treasure ships carrying 200,000 pounds' weight of silver. The lot netted the equivalent of $9.7 million to the Dutch West India Company which had financed him, not counting prize money to the sailors. Profits such as these go far to explain why the Company neglected New Netherland. No "pieces of eight" up the Hudson!

The king of Spain reacted to Piet Hein's exploit by sending, in 1629, a strong squadron of thirty-five sail to the West Indies under Captain Don Federigo de Toledo, to break up rival attempts to colonize the Leeward Islands. He devastated the English and French settlements on St. Kitts and Nevis, but most of the settlers made their escape in small boats, and some returned when the dons sailed away.

Pierre d'Esnambuc was the Champlain of the French Antilles. Expelled by Don Federigo from St. Kitts, he returned to France. Cardinal Richelieu, who had a keen sense of the value of colonies, was then in power. He reorganized and combined all the little companies that had begun settlement in Canada and the West Indies into two big ones, the Company of the Hundred Associates for Canada, and the Company of the Isles for the Caribbean. The latter company now encouraged D'Esnambuc to pick up more islands, and in 1635 one of his lieutenants planted the island of Guadeloupe, now France's oldest colony. Slaves were imported from Africa, a war of extermination was waged against the Caribs, and in a few years Guadeloupe became a prosperous sugar colony. Shortly after, Martinique was occupied, subdued, and settled.

Philippe de Poincy, appointed to command all French Antilles in 1638, governed in a style that completely outshone the English. At St. Kitts he built a stone château with formal gardens, orange groves, a model sugar plantation, and a sugar mill; he was served by a hundred French lackeys besides Negro slaves. An armed force of 8000 men was at his disposal. Almost the sole source of wealth in these tiny islands was sugar. It was in great demand in Europe, where the canes could not be grown; and its derivative, rum, helped Englishmen to endure the rigors of life from Hudson Bay to Albemarle Sound. Coffee, cocoa, indigo, and long-staple cotton were also cultivated in the West Indies; but sugar was king, like tobacco in Virginia, and it made these islands which Spain had neglected the richest and most heavily populated parts of the New World.

Refugees from Don Federigo's attack on St. Kitts, sailing down-wind to the island of Tortuga off Hispaniola, found it inhabited by beachcombers of all nations. These were called buccaneers because they lived largely on the meat of wild hogs and cattle, which they cured by smoking on a *boucan*, a framework of green wood. The refugees taught the buccaneers to use dugout canoes to capture Spanish ships becalmed in the Windward passage. The captured vessel would then become a pirate ship, and the buccaneers found pirating more profitable than hunting. Spain did not take this lying down: there were severe reprisals and counter-reprisals. Buccaneers who grew tired of constant fighting settled on the northwest shore of Hispaniola, which around 1665 was organized as the French colony of Saint-Domingue. This, by the end of the century, became the richest European colony in the West Indies, and eventually the Republic of Haiti.

Other and more reputable Frenchmen expelled the few Spaniards who inhabited the island of Santa Cruz and renamed it St. Croix, a name that it still bears as one of the Virgin Islands of the United States. The chartered company regime in the French Antilles was wound up by Louis XIV in 1674; Martinique, Guadeloupe, and Saint-Domingue became crown colonies.

About 1630 the Dutch West India Company decided to acquire a few islands before the French and English got them all. The first they took was St. Martin's, an island that one can drive across in half an hour. The big business there for the next three centuries was extraction of salt from sea water, to supply the Dutch fisheries. French refugees from St. Kitts were already present, and the two groups, after a few fights, concluded a treaty (1638) for dividing the tiny island, along a boundary that still exists. Two hundred Dutchmen settled in Tobago in 1632, but Spain decided to make an example of them. Landing next year, the Spaniards recruited Caribs who had retreated to the other side of the island, and massacred every last Dutchman. The West India Company, by no means discouraged, decided to extend its salt-making ventures and in 1634 sent out four ships which seized the islands of Curaçao, Aruba, and Bonaire off the coast of Venezuela, and established the salt business there. Eventually Curaçao became famous for a liqueur brandy and, in the present century, for processing fuel oil obtained from Venezuela.

After the death in 1638 of the Earl of Carlisle, proprietor of Barbados, Charles I made that island a royal province and granted the planters the right to elect an assembly. As early as 1650, the sugar crop in Barbados was worth £3 million, and the population had risen to 36,600 whites and 5680 Negro slaves. Ten years later, the white population had fallen to 23,000, but that of the Negroes had risen to 20,000. This little island, only 14 by 21 miles in area, contained more people than Virginia and had become the wealthiest English colony. Life here and in the other English Caribbean islands — Antigua, Nevis, Montserrat, and half St. Kitts — was rough and riotous. Sober merchants from England were shocked by the atmosphere of brutality and drunkenness. One of them in 1651 thus noted the invention of rum: "The chief fudling they make in the Island is Rumbullion, alias Kill-Devill, and this is made of sugar canes distilled, a hott, hellish and terrible liquor."

The planters of Barbados came from the same ambitious middle class as those who went to New England and Virginia, and their sentiments were as independent as the one and as cavalier as the other. The Barbados assembly proclaimed Charles II, and in 1657 protested against Parliament's trying to give them orders, declaring that to be under "a Parliament in which we have no representatives . . . would be a slavery far exceeding all that the English nation hath yet suffered." Parliament replied by sending a fleet to reduce Barbados to obedience. It blockaded the island, but the sailors were so weakened by scurvy and typhus that the commander granted easy terms of surrender. He agreed that no taxes be imposed in Barbados save by their assembly, and that free trade continue with the Dutch. It was this same fleet which sailed on to Virginia and deposed Governor Berkeley.

Unfortunately for Barbados, this was not its only visit from an English fleet during the interregnum. Oliver Cromwell adopted a vigorous policy of relieving Spain of her most valuable possessions. Late in 1654 he issued a ringing manifesto, written by John Milton, declaring that England was honor-bound to do something to redress the cruel wrongs and injuries inflicted on Englishmen in the Caribbean for the last thirty years. In revenge he proposed to capture the island of Hispaniola and make it an outpost of Puritanism. The expedition of 50 ships, commanded by Admiral William Penn (senior of that name), carried 2500 drafted soldiers under General Robert Venables. The fleet reached Barbados at the end of January 1655. Edward Winslow, a Pilgrim Father, accompanied the fleet as a sort of political commissar. It lay off Barbados for ten weeks, consuming all available food and recruiting 5000 servants and small landowners as auxiliary troops. Then, in attacking Hispaniola, Penn and Venables violated the first requisites of success in any amphibious operation. They lost surprise, landed troops too far from the objective, gave them no naval gunfire support, and made insufficient provision for their logistic supply. The result was a fiasco. The army was routed by one Spanish cavalry troop and was only saved from massacre by a disciplined English regiment of marines.

Wanting something to show for all this expense, Penn, Venables, and Winslow decided to attack another of the Greater Antilles. Jamaica was their choice because of its strategic position, "lying in the very belly of all commerce," an ideal base from which to raid Cuba or the Isthmus of Panama and engage in clandestine trade with the Spaniards. Conquest of Jamaica was easy because there were then only about 1500 Spaniards and Negro slaves in the entire island, and not 200 soldiers. The forts at the entrance of Port Royal Bay were surprised, the capital (later renamed Spanish Town) was taken, and the governor forced to surrender. Guerrilla warfare continued for several years, the guerrillas being supplied and supported from Cuba; and the Spaniards' slaves retired to the rugged interior above Montego Bay called the Cockpit Country. Their descendants, the "Maroons," with some justification claim to have been the first independent republic in America, as the English government finally had to negotiate a treaty with their "king."

Spain in 1670 recognized English possession of Jamaica, which became a highly valuable colony. Cromwell and his successors peopled the island largely with petty planters and ex-servants from the smaller islands, and with Negro slaves from Africa. The descendants of these slaves inherited no small measure of the Jamaica planters' pride, and after breaking up the British West Indian Federation by secession, have become the ruling class of an independent Jamaica in the British Commonwealth.

From Charleston it is a short sail to the Bahamas. Although Columbus here discovered the New World, Spain did nothing about the islands except to depopulate them; Englishmen filled the vacuum. The crown granted this group in 1670 to the Carolina proprietors, who sent in as governor Elias Hasket, a rough sea captain from Salem. He founded Nassau but had to make a deal with the settlers, predominantly pirates and buccaneers, in order to live; that displeased the proprietors, and Hasket was deposed. After sundry vicissitudes and the arrival of a group of respectable American loyalists, the Bahamas in 1787 became a crown colony.

Before English rule had been firmly established in Jamaica, England waged a short war with the Dutch, at that time allies of France and Spain. The buccaneers, more vicious than ever, were invited to settle at Port Royal by the governor of Jamaica, and given privateers' commissions. Their most famous exploits were on the Spanish Main, under that prince of ruffians Henry Morgan. In 1668 he raided Puerto Bello, slaughtered the garrison, looted the town and carried back to Jamaica a quarter of a million Spanish dollars. Next year he captured three Spanish treasure ships; and in 1670-71, with 37 ships and 2000 fighting men under his command, he took the Castle of San Lorenzo at the mouth of the Chagres river and marched across the Isthmus. Old Panama, then the richest city in the New World after Mexico and Lima, was sacked and destroyed by his men, who put prisoners "to the most exquisite tortures imaginable" to force them to reveal hidden treasure. Morgan's personal share required 175 pack animals to be carried across the Isthmus. And all this when England and Spain were supposed to be at peace! During the space of seven years, the buccaneers sacked eighteen cities, four towns, and numerous villages in Cuba, Hispaniola, and on the Spanish Main. The king knighted Morgan and appointed him lieutenant governor of Jamaica, and he died a rich and respectable planter.

3. New France

We left Quebec, the first permanent French settlement in Canda, mourning the death of Samuel de Champlain in 1635. Canada at that time was the property of a joint-stock company, the Hundred Associates. L'Acadie, the future Nova Scotia, was a chain of fishing and trading stations with about 250 settlers on the Bay of Fundy, disputed by two feudal lords. Nicolas Denys, given the entire island of Cape Breton as a feudal lordship in 1670, discovered coal deposits near the future Sydney but was unable to interest anyone in mining them.

The Hundred Associates' main object was fur trade in the valleys of the St. Lawrence and the Ottawa. They soon decided, as all colonial founders concluded sooner or later, that a trading-post empire could not exist without permanent settlement. The company then established a system of *seigneuries* or lordships, with manorial privileges, similar to the patroonships of New Netherland. A seigneur was granted anything from a few acres to 360 square miles, in return for procuring a certain number of *habitants* (settlers) who paid him a small annual rent, ground their corn at his mill, and worked for him free a certain number of days each year. This seignioral system, copied from the feudal regime in France, and meticulously planned by the crown after Canada became a crown colony in 1663, suited the habitants so well that it even survived the English conquest. But it never suited the fur traders.

Settlement in Canada advanced very slowly. In 1643, the year after a palisaded stronghold had been built at Montreal, there were not 300 Frenchmen in all New France, exclusive of L'Acadie. Seigneuries were laid out along the St. Lawrence and Richelieu rivers, where almost every habitant's farm had a frontage of from 190 to 250 yards on the water's edge and ran a mile or more inland. New France in the seventeenth century has been well described as a single village strung out along the rivers, broken only by the Rock of Quebec, center of government and of the church, by the tiny town of Trois Rivières, and the frontier trading post of Montreal.

Quebec in 1665 contained only 70 houses and 550 people. In contrast to towns in the continental colonies and the West Indies, one-quarter of this population consisted of religious — secular priests and Jesuits, Ursuline nuns and those of another order who ran the Hôtel-Dieu, the hospital. Both here and at Montreal, the church edifice was of a size and splendor that no English colonial capital could match for another century. At the head of the church in Canada was Bishop François de Laval-Montmorency, who reigned on the Rock for twenty-nine years from 1659, and remained a power in the colony until his death in 1708. Laval was an ecclesiastical statesman who defended church privileges against the state, and a stern disciplinarian who enforced a Puritanical code of manners and morals not unlike that of New England. Protestants, who had been fairly prominent in the early history of New France, were now excluded; one of them named Daniel Voil, who managed to get in, was condemned to death in 1661 for a bag of crimes including smuggling, witchcraft, and blasphemy, and was executed.

As Count Frontenac once remarked, there were but two kinds of business in New France — conversion of souls and conversion of beaver. Trading for beaver with *les sauvages*, as the French called the Indians, was the one great economic interest in Canada, corresponding to tobacco on the Chesapeake and sugar in the West Indies. All efforts of company or crown to persuade the habitants to grow a surplus of corn and cattle for export, or to build ships and set up home industries, failed for the same reason that English efforts to cultivate vineyards and silkworms in Virginia failed. Nothing paid like the big cash crop. The fur trade was conducted by young Frenchmen, called *coureurs de bois*, who penetrated deep into the wilderness by canoe, spent the winter hunting and trapping with the Indians, and collected quantities of furs. As soon as the ice melted they accompanied the Indian trappers down the St. Lawrence or the Ottawa to Montreal. One canoe could carry 600 beaver pelts, worth a gold dollar each in Montreal. As soon as the flotilla was signaled coming down river, there was a lively scrimmage among Montreal merchants for spots on the river front. Booths were set up with enticing merchandise such as muskets, blankets, kettles, and looking glasses; bars dispensed well-watered brandy, a quart of which bought a beaver pelt; and there were gaming tables where the Indian staked his pack on a few throws of the dice. The governor usually showed up to give a loyalty "talk" to the Indians, and several priests came to preach fair play and good morals; but after a day or two of trading the debauchery became such that the fathers departed. The coureurs de bois, who took a cut on this trade, grew rich if they did not squander their gains on drink and gambling, which they usually did. The business had a true "Western" appeal, and every young man of spirit in Canada got into it.

The French crown disapproved this fur-trading system; Louis XIV wanted New France to develop into a farming community like Normandy, where the people did what they were told by the seigneur, and were taught what to think by the parish priest. One reason why so many brisk young men became coureurs de bois was to get away from snoopy priests. The clergy in French Canada exercised the most effective system of thought control ever enforced in America north of Mexico. They saw to it that no printing press ever reached French Canada.

Beyond all praise, however, was the work of the Jesuit and other missionaries, devoted and courageous men, "pallid with the air of the cloister," who to save souls braved the terrors of the wilderness, lived amid the filth of Indian villages, and faced death in its most cruel and revolting forms. French Catholics were the most successful Christians of any European nation in dealing with American Indians. They appealed to their sense of dignity and most important, did not covet their lands. But all the missionaries' efforts broke down before the implacable hostility of the Iroquois. These Five Nations, whose fortified villages and extensive cornfields lay in central New York, were kept loyal to the English through the superior quality of English woolens and the high alcoholic content of West Indies rum. The Iroquois were largely middlemen, obtaining most of their furs from the southern watershed of the western Great Lakes, and rivals to the Huron, who acted as middlemen between the French and far western tribes. In 1648 the Iroquois conquered the Huron and tortured to death the missionaries living among them, Fathers Brébeuf and Lalemant. Father Isaac Jogues, who ventured into the heart of the Iroquois country, was also done to death. During the next few years the Iroquois almost choked New France by a blockade of the St. Lawrence and Ottawa rivers, capturing and killing every Indian they encountered bringing fur packs down by canoe. A young man named Adam Daulac led a forlorn hope of sixteen Frenchmen and five Indians against a war party of 700 Iroquois at the long Saut of the Ottawa. All were killed; but they gave the Iroquois such a tough fight that the planned assault on Montreal was abandoned.

It was largely because they were unable to cope with the Iroquois that the Hundred Associates threw in the sponge in 1663 and surrendered their charter. Louis XIV "Le Grand Monarque," then only twenty-five years old, and his energetic prime minister Colbert, took hold promptly. Canada, including L'Acadie, now became a crown colony like Virginia but with no representative institutions. "New France lived under a regime of complete absolutism," writes Gustave Lanctot, one of Canada's latest and best historians. "Her inhabitants possessed not one political right; they were even forbidden to hold any sort of public meeting without official permission, or to solicit signatures to a petition." And the severe laws made by the French crown for Canada were enforced by implacable justice; people were tortured (forbidden in all English colonies), and even punished by mutilation.

Canada's first military governor under the royal regime was the Marquis de Tracy, an elderly but energetic soldier who arrived at Quebec in 1665 with a fleet of ships. More important, he brought advance echelons of the

Carignan-Salières regiment, 1100 strong, who remained in the colony permanently and were given wives and land. No fewer than 961 girls were imported in ten years. Upon arrival they were sorted into three groups — *demoiselles* of good family, middle-class girls, and (most numerous) peasants' daughters. The plump little *paysannes* were snapped up first, as they worked hard and stood the severe winters well. Dowries were provided by a paternal king, and within two weeks of her arrival every girl found a husband. From these happy unions of soldiers and habitants with *les filles du Roi*, as the imported damsels were called, most of the millions of French Canadians of our day claim descent. But it is probable that the unconsecrated unions of coureurs de bois with young Indian girls have accounted for a goodly portion of this interesting and unique people.

Tracy lost no time in taking the first step to subdue the Iroquois. In 1666, 600 men of his regiment, an equal number of peasant volunteers, and 100 friendly Indians sailed up Lake Champlain and Lake George in 300 *batteaux* and canoes and, from the site of Fort William Henry, plunged into the wilderness that was then central New York. They accomplished little in the way of fighting, as the nimble Mohawks kept several jumps ahead of them. Food gave out and the French had to retire, but they gave the Iroquois Confederacy such a scare that it laid off attacking Canada for twenty years.

This campaign reopened the West to the French. Coureurs de bois and explorers now penetrated the country of the Potawottomi, the Sauk and Fox, and even the Sioux. Jean Talon, the intendant or civil governor, pushed this westward movement vigorously, enabled Père Marquette to set up a mission at Michilimackinac, sent the Canadian-born Louis Joliet to Green Bay, Lake Michigan, across country to the Wisconsin river, and down the Mississippi to the Arkansas. At Sault Sainte-Marie ("the Soo"), in 1671, Tracy's representative, Daumont de Saint-Lusson, in the presence of messengers from fourteen Indian tribes and with impressive ceremony, took possession of the entire west of North America in the name of Louis XIV.

English efforts to invalidate this vast claim form a large part of American history during the eighteenth century; and the feud, inherited by the United States and British Canada, continued well into the nineteenth. It was not really ended until the settlement of the Oregon Question in 1846.

The arrival at Quebec of a new governor, Count Frontenac, in 1672, marks the end of this period of transition. There were now about 500 French settlers in L'Acadie and 7000 along the St. Lawrence between the Gaspé Peninsula and Lake St. Louis. Frontenac established a new fort on Lake Ontario at the site of Kingston; but the expansionist policy which he inherited from Talon was opposed by Bishop Laval and the priests, on the ground that coureurs de bois corrupted the innocent Indians with brandy. The church had the ear of Louis XIV, and Frontenac in 1682 was recalled in disgrace.

Nevertheless, Canada had become a respectable colony with a military strength far greater than her numbers indicated. The time was fast approaching when she would have trouble with New England and New York. And when the clash came, fortunately for New France, Frontenac once more was governor.

England had already carved a slice out of France's potential western empire in the far north. The French sent overland expeditions to capture the Hudson's Bay Company's trading posts; but English tenacity and sea power triumphed; and the Company still exists.

Thus, in the fifty years between 1625 and 1675 the French and British, rivals of the next century, were firmly established in the New World. Starting in the north, trappers of the Hudson's Bay Company were exploiting the wilderness around the great inland sea where Henry Hudson had met his death in 1610. South of them, French Canada, with a settled strip along the lower St. Lawrence, was extending her tentacles into the far west; in L'Acadie there were a few hundred farmers on the Bay of Fundy and trading posts as far east as Canso. France was superb in discovery and exploration, more enterprising than the English or Dutch in staking out empire, and more skillful than either in handling Indians. France had at least twice the population of England in 1675, and many times her wealth; yet with all these advantages she proved incapable of peopling the continental empire that she claimed. New France, including the later acquisition of Louisiana, remained essentially a far-flung chain of trading posts while the English colonies were filling up with settlers and becoming commonwealths. The main reasons for this disparity were the preoccupation of the French kings with European wars which drained their country of men and money, and their insistence on their colonists' being 100 per cent French and Catholic.

The stage was set for one of the longest and bitterest struggles for power in American history.

VEXILLA REGIS

V I I I

Time of Troubles

1675-1691

1. King Philip's War

D ECENNIUM LUCTUOSUM, the Woeful Decade, was the title Cotton Mather used for the period 1685-95, when his beloved Bay Colony lost her charter and was placed under an arbitrary government. And we may add the next earlier decade, which began a time of troubles for New England, Virginia, and Canada.

Hitherto, New England had suffered but one Indian war, a short, sharp, and decisive conflict with the Pequots in 1637, which saved the land from savage warfare for nigh forty years. Why, then, should a war of extermination have broken out in 1675? Explanations by contemporaries are interesting, but hardly convincing. All agreed that it was a divine punishment on New England — but for what? Said the local clergy, retribution for sins of the younger generation who fidgeted under hour-long sermons, let their hair grow, wore fashionable clothes, and drank rum. Quakers believed that war came because Massachusetts Bay had been harsh to the Friends. Governor Berkeley of Virginia wrote home that the New England Puritans were being punished for their sympathy with the usurper Cromwell.

Although the Indians left no records in their defense, it is fairly certain that the underlying cause was the incompatibility of their way of life with that of the English. French Canadians could get along because their relations with the natives were mainly by way of trade, and their religion made few demands on converts. But English colonists wanted land, and it took about twenty times as much land to support an Indian as to feed an Englishman. The Algonquin tribes of New England wanted many things that the English offered, such as firearms and iron tools; but the Puritans wished to sell English civilization in one package, Congregational Church and all.

Up to a point they had an astonishing success. Missionaries such as John Eliot, John Cotton and Richard Bourne made great efforts to teach the Indians to read their own language, printed the Bible and other books for them, and trained native preachers. The colonial assemblies segregated converts in self-governing communities, and by 1675 there was a chain of these "Praying Indian Towns" between northeastern Connecticut and the Merrimack river, with some twenty more on and near Cape Cod. The converted

Indians hunted, fished, and raised their own food, and made a little cash selling game, canoes, and baskets to their white neighbors. Purchases of land from them, or from the "wild" Indians were illegal unless authorized by the colonial governments, and on several occasions overambitious realtors were heavily fined for breaking this law.

But the total number of converted Indians did not exceed 2500, out of about 10,000 in southern New England. By 1675 these "wild" Indians were beginning to feel badly crowded by the steady advance of the English frontier. They too sold land; but Indians never understood ownership of land in the English sense. Their idea of signing a deed to real estate, usually in return for a specified number of axes, kettles, and matchcoats or mackinaws, was to share it with the palefaces, not to move out; and they regarded the price as rent, to be repeated every so often. Their chiefs and medicine men resisted conversion because it undermined their authority.

The three unconverted tribes that made trouble were the Nipmuck of central Massachusetts; the Narragansett, who bordered on the bay of that name; and the Wampanoag, who inhabited eastern Rhode Island and western Plymouth Colony. The Nipmuck were being squeezed between the settlements of eastern Massachusetts and those along the Connecticut river, and dared not move west for fear of the Mohawk nation. The Narragansett, having threatened trouble in the past, had been roughly treated by the New England Confederation and were biding their time for revenge, under two able sachems named Pomham and Canonchet.

The Wampanoag, who started this war, were the original friends of the Pilgrim Fathers. Their territory had been greatly contracted by purchase, and Metacom (called King Philip by the English), chief sachem from 1662, had a taste for gay attire and ran up bills in Boston which he could only pay by selling more land. Plymouth seemed unable to prevent cattle from raiding his cornfields, or bootleggers from selling his people firewater. As he brooded over his wrongs, both real and assumed, Philip became surly and resentful. Plymouth heard from friendly Indians that he was planning a coalition against them; thrice he was haled into court and fined, which deeply offended his dignity.

War was brought on by the murder of Sassamon, a Harvard-educated Indian who had been Philip's secretary, and who tipped off Governor Winslow of Plymouth to the "king's" latest plot. The Indian murderers were arrested, tried, found guilty by a jury that included redskins, and hanged. That was too much for Philip. Indians thought it all right to kill in a fight, or to torture a prisoner to death; but to hang a man after trial violated their deepest feelings of morality. Two weeks after the hanging, on 24 June 1675, war broke out with an attack on Swansea, a frontier settlement near Philip's headquarters on Mount Hope, Narragansett Bay.

The Bay Colony came promptly to Plymouth's assistance, but their first joint operations were badly bungled. Philip, with his braves, women, and children, escaped to central Massachusetts, where they spurred into action the Nipmuck, and attacked the frontier settlements of Brookfield, Lancaster, Deerfield, and other places in quick succession. The New England Confederation declared war, bringing Connecticut Colony into the fight. By fall the westernmost settlements of Massachusetts Bay and Plymouth had been wiped out, and two striking forces sent to punish the Indians had been badly mauled. It looked as though Philip and his allies would soon drive the English into the sea.

New England presented a very grim aspect in 1675–76. The Indians, approaching stealthily through the surrounding forest, would burn and plunder every dwelling, barn, or mill, and kill or mutilate all livestock that they could not use, while the men in the designated garrison houses, where the villages gathered for defense, took potshots at them. The air was filled with terror-inspiring warwhoops, and the shrieks of tortured animals and people. This went on until the Indians retired, glutted with food and plunder, or the garrison was relieved by a troop of horse or company of infantry. The Indians, well supplied with muskets, bullets, and powder, were dead shots. They were waging total war, which the English could not do. Farmers had to plow, sow, reap, and feed stock; women had to cook, tend children, and milk cows; some soldiers had to guard each settlement so that normal activities could continue. As the Indians rubbed out one village after another, each community wanted to take the defensive and send no more striking forces into the woods where they were apt to be ambushed and slaughtered.

No outside help reached New England. Governor Andros of New York even took advantage of the situation by trying to annex a slice of Connecticut; Governor Berkeley of Virginia refused to allow a vessel sent from Boston to buy corn; King Charles II sent neither men nor money, although he could spare a fleet and 1000 soldiers to put down Nat Bacon in Virginia. Only in far-off Dublin a Protestant congregation passed the hat and sent a generous contribution to war victims in Boston.

Several factors saved New England. The Indians were not united. Pequot and Mohegan remained loyal to Connecticut; Wonalancet, the Penacook sachem in the north, remained neutral; and a large number of Praying Indians helped the English as scouts and fighters, teaching them proper tactics. This in spite of the fact that hundreds of the converted natives, unjustly suspected (like the Japanese-Americans on the West Coast in 1942) of being a "fifth column" were miserably interned on an island in Boston Harbor. And many others were killed by cowardly hoodlums. The Indians had no firm leadership — King Philip's role being largely that of an inciter to action — and no concerted plan; their warfare was all of the hit-and-run variety. The confederate New England colonies were under able governors — John Leverett, who had fought under Cromwell, John Winthrop, Jr., and Josiah Winslow. And the Confederation, taking a desperate step, decided in the fall of 1675 on a preventive war against the Narragansett, who were harboring Wampanoag refugees.

An army of over 1000 officers and men under Governor Winslow was transported by sea to a devastated settlement on Narragansett Bay. Winter closed in early that year; and on 19 November the army marched through snow, guided by a friendly Indian, to a "hideous swamp" in the present township of South Kingstown, Rhode Island. There some 3000 Narragan-setts were entrenched behind a triple palisade and blockhouses. In the early afternoon the van of the English army forced an entrance through a breach. Murderous gunfire flung back their first onslaught, killing five company commanders; but the rest pressed in, and all afternoon there was desperate fighting. No quarter was given on either side, the Indian wigwams were set afire, and about two-thirds of the enemy were killed or burned to death; the rest escaped. As light faded over this grim scene, and snow began to fall, Winslow gave orders to retire, and the weary survivors filed off through the woods, carrying their wounded comrades. They reached the Bay at two in the morning, having marched 36 miles and fought savagely for three hours within the space of a single day.

This was the toughest battle, not excepting Bunker Hill, ever fought on New England soil. The English losses were severe (eighty killed, including eight out of fourteen company commanders); and, owing to a breakdown in the service of supply, the survivors spent a Valley Forge winter at Wickford, Rhode Island. But it was worth the cost. The Great Swamp Fight broke the power of the Narragansett.

The war was not yet over. Canonchet escaped, and ambushed Captain Michael Pierce's company near Pawtucket; only one Englishman and nine friendly Indians survived to be put to torture. Canonchet then burned Rehoboth and Providence, telling Roger Williams, who parleyed, that he would never make peace until Plymouth Colony was wiped out. But his number was nearly up. Two weeks later, on 3 April 1676, Canonchet was ambushed and captured by a mixed company of English and friendly Indians. When told that he was to be put to death he said, "I like it well; I shall die before my heart is soft or I have said anything unworthy of myself." Pequot warriors shot him and sent his head to Hartford as a token of their fidelity to the English.

The war was still raging in central Massachusetts, but the English by now had learned to keep the enemy on the move so that he had no chance to strike back or even to obtain food. King Philip, too proud to give up, retired to his original home at Mount Hope, there to sell his life dear. His position, betrayed by an Indian whom he had offended, was surrounded by Captain Church's company, and when Philip tried to break loose (12 August 1676) he was killed on the run by a member of the Pocasset tribe who had joined his enemies.

Some Indians escaped to the northern wilderness, and a few even made their way to the Illinois country; but most of the enemy surrendered or were captured. The women and children were parceled out to white families as servants; warriors were sold as slaves in the West Indies and on the Barbary Coast of Africa. In Maine, where the Abnaki forced the evacuation of every English settlement, the war only ended in the spring of 1678, and by treaty, not unconditional surrender. These Indians retained their lands and their strength, and as allies of the French fought against the English in later colonial wars.

New England had won, at tremendous cost. Twenty years elapsed before all the destroyed villages were resettled, forty before the frontier advanced. In the meantime these colonies suffered other disasters, from the hands of kings and the powers of darkness.

2. Nat Bacon's Rebellion

What might have been an Indian war in Virginia similar to King Philip's, developed by chance into a rebellion led by a young Englishman. This strange turn was caused by a very different economic and political situation from that of New England. While the seaports from New York to New Hampshire were prospering through trade with the West Indies, the one-crop settlements on Chesapeake Bay were suffering from low prices for tobacco. In 1668 it reached the all-time low of a farthing (half a cent) a pound; and by 1675 had not recovered even to a penny. Taxes fell very heavily on poor people, while most of the ruling class, as members of the council, were tax-exempt. Northern colonial governments, annually elected, gave the New Englanders opportunity to ventilate grievances and correct abuses; but in Virginia there had been no election for fourteen years. In a wave of loyalty over the restoration of Charles II the colony had chosen a house of burgesses so pleasing to Governor Berkeley that he merely adjourned it from year to year. This "Long Assembly" even outlasted the Long Parliament of England. The Governor kept the burgesses loyal to himself by giving almost every member an office of profit or honor, often two or more. He appointed the councillors and county judges. The parish vestries, corresponding roughly to town meetings in New England, had become self-perpetuating, and for the most part were composed of the same men who made up the county courts. Thus, Sir William Berkeley, now nearly seventy years old, had the entire machinery of Virginia government in his hands.

The Indian situation, however, was similar to that of New England. Virginia as yet had made no attempt to convert the natives within her borders, but after Opechancanough's second rebellion in 1644 she had given reservations to a number of small tribes — the Pamunkey, Nottaway, Appomattox, and a dozen others. Owing to the growth of English population, these reservations had become enclaves surrounded by white people, who were constantly encroaching. By 1675 there were only 3000 or 4000 of these subject Indians, constantly dwindling. Berkeley treated them as king's subjects whom he was bound to protect; but the lower order of white people regarded them as vermin to be exterminated.

On the southwest border of Virginia, at the confluence of the Dan and Staunton rivers, lived the Occaneechee, a small tribe who acted as middlemen in the fur and deerskin trade between Virginia, the Carolinas, and the West. On the northern frontier were the Susquehannock. These, when dwelling on the river named after them, had been allies of Lord Baltimore against their ancient enemies the Seneca. But in 1674 Maryland let them down by making a separate peace with the Seneca, who then forced the Susquehannock to move south to the Potomac. Their presence there was a danger both to Maryland and Virginia.

In July or August 1675 three Virginia settlers were murdered by Indians. Both colonial governors called out the local militia; Virginia's contingent was commanded by Lieutenant Colonel John Washington, ancestor of the first President of the United States; and Maryland's by Major Thomas Truman, who was not an ancestor of the thirty-third President. On the north bank of the Potomac, near the site of Fort Washington and almost opposite Mount Vernon, Washington and Truman found the Susquehannock entrenched in a palisaded fort like that of the Narragansett in Rhode Island. The Indians sent out five chiefs to parley. An angry colloquy took place with the white officers, at the end of which the five chiefs were taken away and killed, by whose order is uncertain.

That unjust act, contrary to immemorial usage, sparked off an Indian war. The embittered Susquehannock broke into roving bands which attacked one plantation after another on the Virginia frontier, even more vulnerable than that of New England. Indian warfare was assuming the sadly familiar pattern that lasted for two centuries. If a white man could not find the right Indian to punish, he killed any Indian, feeling that the fewer there were the better; and the Indians similarly avenged themselves on any paleface they encountered.

Governor Berkeley, indignant at the outrage against the Susquehannock, and fearful of provoking a general war like King Philip's (of which he had heard the gory details), adopted the defensive strategy of building a chain of mutually supporting forts around the settled part of the colony. Frontier planters and Indian-haters were indignant; the word went around that Berkeley "doth not take a speedy course and destroy the Indians," owing to his "love to the Beaver" — he being an Indian trader. People who felt that way soon found a leader in Nathaniel Bacon.

This young man, variously estimated by later historians as a torchbearer for democracy and a desperate rabble-rouser, was cousin to the famous Lord Bacon. He had been withdrawn from the University of Cambridge for "extravagancies," and in 1673 packed off to Virginia, complete with bride and the generous sum of £1800 from a wealthy father. A cousin to Lady

Berkeley, young Bacon was warmly welcomed by the governor and appointed to the council at the age of twenty-eight. He bought two plantations on the James river above William Byrd's "Westover," and was by way of becoming a member of the ruling clique, when the overseer of his upper plantation was killed in a Susquehannock raid. Bacon's anger rose, and when he appeared before a muster of militia they cried with one voice, "A Bacon! a Bacon!" This went to the fellow's head. He was persuaded to assume command and lead the militia against the Indians. But, instead of going after the guilty Susquehannock, the militia, in typical frontier fashion, attacked the friendly, fur-trading Occaneechee, accusing them of harboring enemy fugitives, and killed their chief Persicles.

That exploit made Bacon a popular hero and began the rebellion. The lower order of white men, and a few great landowners like William Byrd who had plantations near the frontier, flocked to his standard. Governor Berkeley denounced him as "Oliver Bacon," but issued writs for a new assembly, the first since 1662. This body redressed several popular grievances such as plurality in offices and self-perpetuating parish vestries, and declared war on all neighboring Indians. Bacon appeared at Jamestown, made his submission to the governor, and was pardoned. He returned to his plantation; but, finding Indians still on the loose, cried "Treachery!" raised the country, marched on Jamestown, and forced the governor to flee to the Eastern Shore. Bacon now became a rebel indeed, summoning all true and loyal Englishmen to support him, setting up a *de facto* government, and denouncing the Berkeley clique as "sponges" who "have sucked up the Publik Treasure," "unworthy Favorites and juggling Parasites."

Back and forth rocked the fortunes of war. Bacon captured two ships on the James and organized them as a rebel navy. Berkeley called out the loyal militia of the Eastern Shore and begged King Charles to send him an army of regulars. Bacon planned to secure Virginia until a fair hearing of the people's grievances could be had in London; he hoped to capture Berkeley and send him home to be tried for failure to protect the colonial frontier. For a few months, "General" Bacon was master of all Virginia except the Eastern Shore. But he had no chance to win in the end. The Cromwellian usurpation was too recent for anyone to challenge the king's governor and get away with it; and Virginia's total population was less than 50,000. In vain Bacon exacted an oath of allegiance to himself and confiscated the property of loyalists. On sober second thought, many of the very men who had bawled, "A Bacon!" shrank from opposing their monarch's lawful representative, and deserted. And, marvelous to relate, the seventy-year-old governor managed to defeat the twenty-eight-year-old "general," with no assistance from home.

Bacon concentrated the remnant of his army, including servants and even Negro slaves, at Gloucester on the York river. Desperately he talked of beating the "Red Coates" who were on their way, and of creating out of

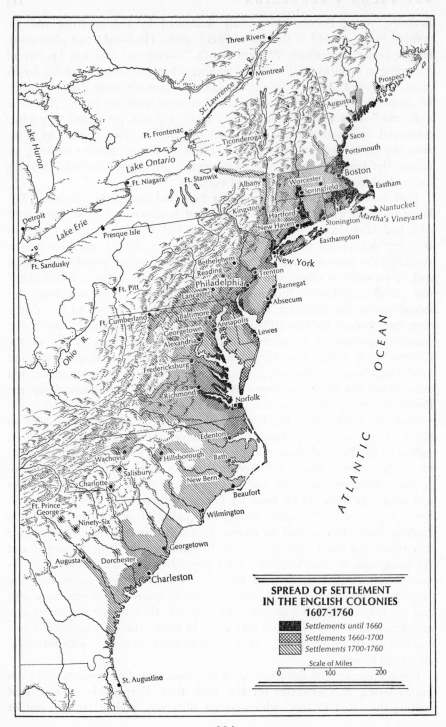

**SPREAD OF SETTLEMENT
IN THE ENGLISH COLONIES
1607-1760**

Settlements until 1660

Settlements 1660-1700

Settlements 1700-1760

Scale of Miles

0   100   200

Virginia, Maryland, and North Carolina a free state allied with the Dutch
or the French. In Maryland a rebellion had broken out which Bacon hoped
might spread and help his cause. But Charles, third Lord Baltimore, nipped
it in the bud and hanged the leaders before any liaison with Bacon could be
effected.

At his last stand, near Yorktown, Nat Bacon came down with a severe
attack of the "bloody flux" (dysentery) and there died miserably on 26
October 1676. His followers buried his body secretly so that it would not be
subjected to the indignities inflicted on the corpses of Canonchet and
Cromwell, and the rebellion flickered out.

Following the usual procedure against defeated rebels, the Governor court-
martialed and hanged all the gentlemen on Bacon's side whom he could lay
hands on — twenty-three in all. Most of this work had been accomplished
when a fleet arrived from England, bringing 1100 troops and a royal commission to find out what was wrong with Virginia. It also brought a general
pardon from Charles II to the rebels, and an order for Berkeley to come
home and give an account of himself. The governor returned to England in
June 1677 and died there, before having a chance to lay his case before the
king. Charles II, far from appreciating what his loyal servant had done,
remarked, "that old fool has hang'd more men in that naked Country, than
he had done for the Murther of his Father."

Although every effort was made by the new Virginia aristocracy to write
down Nat Bacon as a knave, the common people kept his memory warm in
folk tales and ballads until historians dared to do him justice.

> Nat Bacon's bones   The rich and proud
> They never found,   Deny his name,
> Nat Bacon's grave   The rich and proud
> Is wilderground: Defile his fame:
> Nat Bacon's tongue   The proud and free
> Doth sound! Doth sound!   Cry shame! Cry shame! 1

Bacon's rebellion accomplished some good. Most of the reform legislation
was re-enacted by the next assembly. No later royal governor dared rule
through such a close, tight oligarchy as did Berkeley; but the basic trouble,
the low price of tobacco, continued to harass the colony. And this brief civil
war contributed to building up an aristocracy of survivors. William Fitzhugh, one of them, wrote in 1687 that he missed "spiritual helps and comforts," that Virginia was no place to bring up a gentleman's son. "Good
education of children is almost impossible, and better be never born than ill-
bred," a sentiment in which Virginia gentlemen of every generation concur.
But transferring the capital to Williamsburg, where the College of William
and Mary was founded in 1692, marked the dawn of a better day in the Old
Dominion.

1. By Archibald MacLeish, reprinted with his permission.

3. The Dominion of New England

In 1677 the New England colonies had barely begun to recover from King Philip's War, and on the Maine frontier the war was not even finished. Some settlements had been abandoned altogether; in others the black ruins of houses and barns were being cleared away and new ones built. In the seaports, crowded with "displaced persons" who had no other place to go, ships laid up during the war were being repaired and merchants were begging their London correspondents for fresh credit.

At this juncture the Lords of Trade, a committee of the Privy Council appointed by Charles II to deal with the English colonies, informed the Massachusetts Bay authorities that they must accept royal officials to enforce obedience to the Acts of Trade. A reasonable enough request; but the Bay government stubbornly maintained its own theory of virtual independence. After trying to appease Charles II with a gift of "ten barrells of cranberries, two hogsheads of special good samp, and three thousand of cod fish," delicacies hardly suitable for the merry monarch's table, the general court replied in words that carry one back to the old Puritans, and forward to Samuel Adams and James Otis. "Wee humbly conceive," they said, "that the lawes of England are bounded within the four seas, and doe not reach America. The subjects of his majesty here being not represented in Parliament, so we have not looked at ourselves to be impeded in our trade by them."

The king chose to ignore this challenge. For several years he did nothing to curb this stubborn "Bay horse," except to send out a customs collector named Edward Randolph, who was thrown every time he tried to mount; illegal traders whom he arrested were always acquitted by the local courts. The English government finally concluded that in order to bring Massachusetts within the imperial system its charter must be revoked. And that obstacle was cleared by the High Court of Chancery in 1684.

Charles II died before making new arrangements about Massachusetts Bay. The next king, James II, gave Joseph Dudley, son of an old Puritan governor, a commission to rule Massachusetts, New Hampshire, and Maine, which now became the Dominion of New England. Sharing his authority were royal councillors, all of whom except Edward Randolph were New Englanders; but no assembly.

The practical effect of this change of government was to transfer political power from the Puritan oligarchy of the Bay Colony to an embryo Tory party. Joseph Dudley, the leader of this group, was a healthy young man who revolted against the grim atmosphere in which he had been brought up; and to his way of thinking were many merchants and Anglicans who wanted closer cultural and commercial ties with England. A minister who came over with Dudley celebrated the first Anglican service in Boston in 1686. Little by little, the customs of merry England, long proscribed in New England, began to creep in. When a maypole was set up in Charleston, the Reverend Increase Mather felt that the devil was indeed marching to victory in the Puritan citadel.

Dudley did not last long, as he refused to split with Randolph the proceeds of confiscating illegal imports. In December 1686, James II replaced him by the governor of New York, Sir Edmund Andros, and annexed Plymouth Colony, virtually independent for sixty-six years, to the Dominion. And James did not stop there. Like all Stuart kings an enemy to representative government, he decided to erect all colonies north of Maryland into a single viceroyalty. Rhode Island and Connecticut were annexed to the Dominion in 1687; New York and the Jersies next year; and the axe was about to fall on Pennsylvania when James II was deposed.

4. La Salle

In New France, successive governors refused to regard the Five Nations as an English satellite state, and sent one punitive expedition after another against them, usually with slight success. French explorers and traders then sought ways to get around them, into the West.

Greatest of these French explorers was Robert Cavalier de la Salle, who emigrated to Montreal at the age of twenty-three, obtained a seigneury on Lake St. Louis, and entered the fur trade. He learned the language of the Indians, became their friend, and decided to penetrate the great West. First, with an Indian guide, he followed portages across the future State of Ohio and descended the Ohio river to the site of Louisville. In 1679 he built a vessel on the Niagara river near Buffalo and sailed her to Green Bay, Lake Michigan; then paddled around that lake in a canoe; built a fort and left a garrison at the site of St. Joseph, Michigan; paddled up the St. Joseph river to its south bend near the present campus of Notre Dame University, carried over to the "Theakiki" (Kankakee) river, and paddled down the Illinois as far as Starved Rock. That hill he fortified, to defend friendly Indians against roving Iroquois. Then, back to Fort Frontenac (Kingston, Ontario) by canoe and carry, 1000 miles in 65 days. During the next winter season he retraced the greater part of this journey by canoe and on foot.

In the last month of 1681 his greatest adventure began. With 23 Frenchmen and 31 Indians, mostly refugees from King Philip's War, he struck out from St. Joseph fort for the Mississippi. As the rivers were frozen, the party made sledges on which they dragged their canoes across "the divine river, called by the Indians *Checagou*" and down the Illinois. On 6 February 1682 they joined the majestic stream of the Mississippi. Down they paddled, past the mouths of the Missouri and the Ohio, and the Chickasaw Bluffs. "More and more they entered the realm of spring. The hazy sunlight, the warm and drowsy air, the tender foliage, the opening flowers, betokened the reviving life of nature." [1] La Salle placated the fierce Quapaw, the cultured Taensa, the Natchez, and every other nation he encountered. On 6 April, after sailing past the site of New Orleans, he reached the point where the Mississippi separates into three channels. He and his men, divided into three parties, reached the Passes in three days, and met at a spot of dry ground on the Gulf of Mexico. There, with due religious ceremony, La Salle displayed the white banner of the Bourbons and took possession of "this country of Louisiana . . . in the name of the most high, mighty, invincible and victorious Louis the Great, by Grace of God King of France and of Navarre." Louisiana he defined as the valley of the Mississippi including all its tributaries. No claim so stupendous had been made by any European monarch since the voyages of Columbus.

Returning to Quebec, where he found the new governor unsympathetic, La Salle went on to France, where he gained the king's ear. Louis XIV, who at first regarded La Salle's descent of the Mississippi as "wholly useless," now decided to seize and hold Louisiana to annoy the king of Spain, his enemy for the time being. So he gave La Salle four ships, a company of soldiers, and both men and women emigrants, with orders to build a fort on the lower Mississippi "whence we may control the continent." This expedition, which started in 1684, was fraught with disaster. The fleet overshot the Passes by 400 miles — for La Salle had no means of finding the longitude of the spot where he had taken possession. He landed on the shores of Matagorda Bay, Texas, marched inland, and built a fort on a prairie bordering on the Garcitas river. The Frenchmen found plenty of buffalo for food, and friendly Indians of the Cenis tribe, but knew not where they were. So La Salle, with a few men, set forth overland to find the Mississippi. At a point near the site of Navasota, Texas, on 18 March 1687, he was murdered by mutineers, and the body of the man who had staked out an empire for France was stripped, dishonored, and left to the wolves and the vultures.

5. Revolutions and Rebellions of 1688–1691

These events were remote from New England and Virginia, but it was partly King James's knowledge of a French design to encircle the English colonies which persuaded him to combine all the northern ones, for purposes of defense, in one dominion. The dominion government was highly unpopular in New England. Sir Edmund Andros and his henchmen declared all land titles void unless validated for a price, and required everyone to pay the crown an annual quitrent. Taxes, instead of being voted by the people's representatives, were levied by executive fiat; selectmen and town clerks who protested were jailed; no money was provided to support schools.

1. This and other quotations about La Salle are from Francis Parkman's masterly biography of him.

Cape Codders, who had spliced out their slender gains from fishing and farming by trying out stranded whales, were deeply outraged by being ordered to hand over the oil to the royal governor, on the ground that whales were "royal fish." Boston merchants who had welcomed the change of government found themselves squeezed by Johnny-come-latelys on Andros's council and deprived of their accustomed lines of trade.

Andros proved to be an efficient military leader when bands of Indians led by French officers from Canada began to attack settlements on the New England frontier. But the people allowed him no credit for this. To the general run of New Englanders and New Yorkers, already accustomed to look for the cloven hoof in any action of Governor Andros, his military policy seemed evidence of a Catholic plot between James II and Louis XIV to hand over New York and New England to the French. England had recently been in a turmoil over a cooked-up "Popish Plot" in which Titus Oates played a role similar to that of Joseph McCarthy in the communist scare of the 1950's. Many colonists now imagined that there was a similar plot to turn all North America over to Rome. For, were not James II, Lord Baltimore, Governor Dongan of New York, and Governor Lord Howard of Virginia, Catholics? Two hundred families of French Protestant refugees who arrived at New York in 1687–88 spread stories of what Yorkers might expect if French dragoons were turned loose on them. If they could have read the instructions of King Louis XIV to Count Frontenac, when that stout governor returned to Canada in 1689, they would have been still more alarmed. Frontenac, with French regulars and Indian allies, was to proceed south by Lake Champlain and Lake George, capture Albany, bring the Iroquois to an alliance, and in boats descend the Hudson to its mouth, where a French fleet would be on hand to help him capture the city. He was instructed to ransom the merchants and gentlemen, exact forced labor of Protestant farmers and mechanics, and to send French Protestants home to be executed.

Fortunately for the English colonies, Frontenac's invasion stalled, the French fleet never arrived, and James II was so energetic in suppressing liberty at home that the English got rid of him. "Seven eminent persons," including a son of Sir Winston Churchill of Weymouth, sent an invitation to Prince William of Orange, who had married James's Protestant daughter Mary, to come over from Holland and save England. William landed in England with a small army on 5 November 1688. For several weeks the issue was in doubt; then James II, deserted by almost everyone, fled to France, and the "damned Dutchman" entered London. Parliament, meeting in January 1689, declared that James had abdicated, adopted a Declaration of Rights (one source of our federal Bill of Rights), and conferred the crown on William and Mary. This bloodless change of regime was ever after referred to as the "Glorious Revolution of 1688." It even made revolution respectable.

Months elapsed before this important news reached America. On 4 April

1689 a vessel arrived at Boston bearing an order of the new king and queen that "all magistrates who have been unjustly turned out" resume "their former employment." That touched off a parallel revolution in Boston. The machine-like precision with which it unrolled points to careful plans and leadership, which no one has yet unearthed. The townspeople rose, the countryside rose, Andros and some of his principal councillors were flung into jail; a meeting was held, presided over by the last governor under the Bay Colony charter. It issued a "Declaration of the Gentlemen, Merchants, and Inhabitants," drafted by the Reverend Cotton Mather, that the Dominion was dissolved and the old charter again in force. William III and Mary II were proclaimed amid such enthusiasm as the Puritan capital had never witnessed — a parade, lighted windows, barrels of wine broached in the street. A new election returned the old crowd to power, and as soon as news of these events reached Plymouth, Providence, and Hartford, they "trotted after the Bay horse" as usual, and restored their own pre-Andros governments.

In New York events took a very different course and reached a tragic end, partly because there was no charter government for a revolution to restore; partly because James II had many partisans among the Hudson river patroons.

Lieutenant Governor Nicholson, Andros's deputy for New York, was startled (to put it mildly) when news of the Boston uprising reached the city. He summoned three councillors of the Dominion, Nicholas Bayard, Stephen Van Courtlandt, and Frederick Philipse, together with the city fathers and leading officers of the local militia, to meet as an informal council. The mass of New Yorkers wanted this body to proclaim William and Mary; but the old councillors stood firm for James II. An incautious threat by Nicholson, when drunk, to burn New York City, sparked a popular uprising. Jacob Leisler, a German-born merchant and captain of the local militia, stepped forward and accepted responsibility for heading a provisional government. Delegates elected by six counties of New York and one of New Jersey met in convention at the fort near the present Battery, proclaimed William and Mary on 22 June 1689, and appointed Leisler military commander of the province and acting lieutenant governor until the new sovereigns' pleasure was known. But they reckoned without Albany and the grandees.

William and Mary for a long time could do nothing to help their loyal supporters in the colonies. Jacobite rebellions in Scotland and Ireland had to be put down first. England declared war on France. Not until 30 July 1689 did the English sovereigns come to any decision about America. In New England they accepted the situation as they found it. But they issued orders for New York that were liable to misconstruction. Lieutenant Governor Nicholson was to act as governor or, in his absence "such for the time being" in power "to take upon you the government of the said Province." Nicholson was then en route to London to try to get Leisler thrown out; so when this letter was delivered at New York in December, Leisler, who "for the time being" was in power, construed it as royal permission for his government to carry on. The Albany clique refused to go along, and the military situation was serious.

In October 1689 Count Frontenac, arriving at Quebec, learned of a raid on La Chine by the Iroquois, and that the French fort on Lake Ontario had been abandoned. These events forced him to give up the grand design for a military descent of the Hudson and subsequent purge of Protestants. He decided instead on the strategy of *la petite guerre*, a series of raids on the New York and New England frontiers. The first raid, comprising 200 French troops and friendly Indians, eluded the Mohawks and assaulted Schenectady on the night of 8 February 1690. They wiped out that frontier village, killed all but thirty of the inhabitants, and carried these captive to Montreal. Albany was in such a panic that it accepted a garrison under Leisler's son-in-law Milborne for protection.

Leisler now acted with energy and breadth of view. He called a meeting of delegates from all colonies north of Carolina to arrange a union for defense. The three New England colonies which responded agreed upon a joint military-naval expedition against Canada. Leisler was to direct a military expedition up the Hudson and Lake Champlain to Montreal; Massachusetts was to attack Quebec by sea. This left-and-right method of hitting Canada where it hurt was excellent strategy. It finally worked in 1759–60 after three tactical failures, of which that of 1690 was the first.

Leisler's expeditionary force, placed under Fitz-John Winthrop of Connecticut, where most of the troops were raised, suffered ill fortune. By the time it reached Lake Champlain smallpox had broken out among the troops and Winthrop retreated, to Leisler's rage and disgust.

In London, meanwhile, there were more delays. William and Mary commissioned an Irish army officer with the ominous name of Sloughter as governor of New York; but no ship could be found to take him out in proper style, as the royal navies of England and France were slugging it out in the English Channel and the West Indies. A small squadron of four or five sail finally left England for North America in November 1690 with Governor Sloughter on board, but the skipper of the flagship got lost, and one of the smaller vessels carrying a company of redcoats under Major Richard Ingoldsby reached New York first, in January 1691. Ingoldsby called on Leisler to hand over the government to him; Leisler refused, preferring to wait until the new governor arrived. With the backing of the Albany clique, Ingoldsby besieged Leisler in the old fort near the Battery. The garrison fired on the royal troops, they attacked, and after a brisk fight compelled Leisler to surrender on 17 March 1691.

Governor Sloughter, who arrived only two days later, had Leisler, Milborne, and three members of his provisional council tried for treason. The stacked court was mostly composed of the Albany councillors, with Joe Dudley, who was looking for a royal governorship, presiding. Leisler's services in keeping order and protecting the frontier availed him nothing. The fact that he had bought land with his own money to settle French Huguenot refugees at New

Rochelle, helped not one bit. He had put himself in the wrong by ordering his garrison to fire on the king's troops, and on that technical point he and his friends were found guilty of treason. His enemies were out for his blood, and got it. Leisler and Milborne were sentenced to a traitor's death. On 16 May 1691, on the site of City Hall Park, they were hanged by the neck, their bodies cut down while still alive, their bowels ripped out and burned before their faces, their heads cut off, and their bodies quartered. "The shrieks of the people," said a bystander, "were dreadful." The crowd carried off locks of Leisler's hair and bits of his garments as precious relics.

"These were the days of wrath and utter darkness," as a later petition of the New York assembly described this time of savage retaliation against a devoted servant of the people. After repeated efforts by the popular party, Parliament reversed the attainders of Leisler and Milborne. Their mutilated bodies were disinterred and given Christian burial, and in 1702 the assembly granted an indemnity to the heirs.

But that was not the end. New York politics for the next generation was divided between Leislerians and anti-Leislerians, and the last sparks of the feud had not died out when the American Revolution broke. Nicholas Roosevelt, first of that family to be in politics, was elected alderman because he had supported Leisler.

6. War and Witchcraft

The Glorious Revolution of 1688 in England saved both English and colonial liberties from a second Stuart despotism, but the English paid for their freedom by being dragged into war against France and Canada. In Europe it was called the War of the League of Augsburg; in America, King William's War.

Count Frontenac, who had a healthy respect for the Iroquois, left the New York frontier alone after the destruction of Schenectady; the New England frontier took the rap. For the past generation French missionaries and traders had been infiltrating the Maine wilderness to establish missions and trading posts among the Abnaki. In the summer of 1689 parties of Indians, led by French officers, began a series of raids on New England frontier settlements, and all forts and settlements on the coasts of Maine and New Hampshire were captured by the French and Indians before autumn. *La petite guerre*, as the French called it, looked pretty big to the frontiersmen.

These events aroused the feeling in New England tersely expressed by John Pynchon of Springfield: "We shall never be at rest till we have Cannida." Or, as Cotton Mather put it in classical style, *Canada delenda est*. To destroy Canada as a French colony became an objective of Massachusetts Bay, relentlessly pursued for seventy years. It is no wonder that the Canadians always referred to English colonists as "les Bastonnais," or that French kings planned the destruction of Boston.

The Boston authorities had the sound strategic sense to strike at the main centers of French power, Port Royal and Quebec, rather than to disperse their forces to defend a long frontier. Accordingly the Bay Colony, as the first offensive of King William's War, sent a small naval force in April 1690 to attack Port Royal, under the leadership of Sir William Phips.

This man was one of twenty-six children born to a poor fisherman's family on the Kennebec river in Maine. On a voyage to the West Indies, he became bitten by a bug that has made thousands of victims — hunting for sunken treasure. And, to this day, he has been the only person to make a real success of it. From a ship outfitted in England, he discovered the wreck of a Spanish treasure galleon north of Hispaniola and made the greatest haul ever retrieved from the ocean bottom — gold and silver bullion worth at least a million dollars. And, what was more, he got it safely to England despite his cutthroat crew, whose mutinous attempts he cowed with bare fists and a club. Each stockholder received a dividend of 8000 per cent; James II, delighted with his share, which was enough to build two capital ships for the Royal Navy, knighted Phips. Returning to Boston, Sir William led an expedition against French L'Acadie. He captured Port Royal with little trouble in May 1690, and brought the French governor to Boston as prisoner, together with plenty of loot. The colonial authorities, assuming that Quebec, too, would be easy meat, set up a second expeditionary force for Phips to command. It was too ambitious for one small colony, with no aid from England to undertake, and it started late through waiting for ammunition from England which never came. Phips's fleet of chartered merchant ships, carrying 2200 volunteers, mostly fishermen, reached Quebec on 7 October. Owing to the previous failure of Fitz-John Winthrop to reach Canada overland from New York, Count Frontenac was able to concentrate his slender defense forces on Quebec. They defeated the undisciplined Yankee landing force, and Phips decided to retreat.

Now all good effects of the Port Royal campaign were undone. The Abnaki and Penacook Indians went on the warpath, raided Haverhill, and destroyed Wells and York in Maine, and the French recovered Port Royal.

This Quebec fiasco, proving to the satisfaction of the English government that the Bay authorities were incompetent in military matters, ended all chance of the provisional government of Massachusetts being recognized as permanent. William and Mary in 1691 created the royal province of Massachusetts Bay with a governor appointed by the king, but with a charter which guaranteed an annually elected assembly. Sir William Phips, who happened to be in London trying to get support for a second attack on Quebec, was made the first royal governor of Massachusetts Bay, an office that his military incompetence had done much to create. His bailiwick included the old Bay and Plymouth colonies, together with Maine. Rhode Island and Connecticut, which had resumed government under their old charters, were not disturbed, and New Hampshire became a separate royal province.

The inauguration of Phips as governor (16 May 1692) occurred when the "Woeful Decade" of New England was at its nadir. King William's War was going full blast. The expense of the Quebec expedition of 1690, which the Massachusetts government had hoped to finance from loot, had forced that colony to issue paper money — a new device in the English-speaking world which undermined credit and increased poverty. The frontier was in grave danger and farmers were able to tend crops only at the risk of their lives. Worst of all, the new governor had to face the Salem witchcraft delusion.

Almost everybody in the Western world, including divines and men of science, then believed that a person could make a bargain with the devil, by virtue of which he could visit good or ill on friends or enemies. There had been 44 cases of witchcraft and three hangings in Massachusetts Bay before 1692; a few cases, too, but no executions, in Canada and Virginia.

To the already vast literature on witchcraft the Reverend Cotton Mather, boy wonder of the New England clergy, contributed a book on *Memorable Providences*, describing a case of alleged witchcraft in Boston for which a poor old woman was executed, and telling how he had handled the accusing children to prevent a witch-hunting epidemic. The second edition of this "how to do it" book, filled with data on how the "possessed" were expected to behave, got into the hands of a group of young girls in a poor settlement near Salem. More or less as a prank, they accused a half-Indian, half-Negro family slave of being a witch. She, flogged by her master into a false confession to save her skin, accused two respectable goodwives of being her confederates. The "afflicted children," finding themselves the objects of attention, and with the exhibitionism natural to young wenches, persisted in their charges for fear of being found out, and started a chain reaction. Governor Phips's appointment of a special court to try the witches only made matters worse, for the chief justice (William Stoughton) and his colleagues were not trained in the use of evidence and became panic-stricken themselves. Innocent people whom the girls accused implicated others to escape the gallows. They confessed broomstick rides, flying saucers, witches' sabbaths, sexual relations with the devil, and everything which, according to the book, witches were supposed to do. Honest folk who declared the whole thing nonsense were cried out upon for witches. It was a situation not unlike that which arose at the height of Joseph McCarthy's power. In 1952, if you criticized Joe, you were a communist sympathizer; in 1692, if you criticized the witch court or tried to help an accused kinsman, you were in league with the devil.

This vicious business continued through the summer of 1692 until fourteen women and five men had been hanged, and one man, Giles Corey, pressed to death for refusing to plead guilty or not guilty. At least four died in jail of the fever that swept through it; and one poor child, jailed with her mother who was hanged, went out of her mind. Some 55 others saved their skins by pleading guilty and accusing others. The frenzy was not halted until the witch-finders began to go after prominent people such as the Boston clergy, wealthy merchants, and Lady Phips. On the sound if tardy advice of Increase Mather and other clergymen, the assembly dissolved the special court on 12 October 1692 and released some 150 prisoners who were awaiting trial.

Although the Salem witchcraft scare was small compared with the contemporary ones in Europe, and the condemned witches were hanged, not burned to death as in Europe; and despite the fact that twenty years later the Massachusetts courts annulled the convictions and indemnified relatives of the victims, it was a stain on the community that time has never erased. The records reveal an appalling moral cowardice on the part of ministry and gentry, and of credulity and hatred among the common people. It was one of those times, unfortunately more rather than less numerous in the present century, when the safeguards of liberty, religion, and plain decency are ripped asunder by fear and passion, and the evil in human nature, whipped up by demagogues and tyrants, is given full sway. The one admirable thing that stands out is the integrity of those who preferred death with an easy conscience to saving their skins by implicating the innocent.

The dreary war dragged on. There were no more big expeditions, but frontier raids by French and Indians on Dover, Andover, Groton, and Kittery; the fort at Pemaquid, Maine, was captured and destroyed. In vain the Massachusetts assembly begged King William to help them in this "languishing and exhausting war," with ammunition, a naval force or, best of all, the capture of Quebec, "that unhappy fortress from which issue all our miseries." The king was too busy in Europe to heed. He ended his war in 1697 with the Treaty of Ryswick, but left his American subjects to end their war as best they could; and in New England it continued for two years more.

LILLEBURLERO

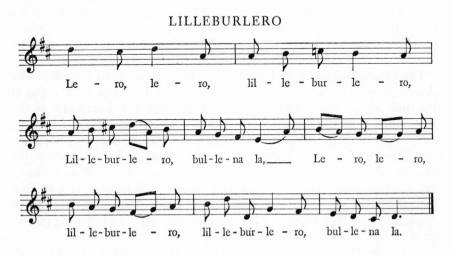

Pennsylvania and the West Indies

1688-1700

1. *Penn's Holy Experiment*

NO COLONY OR STATE of the Union so well fits Emerson's dictum, "An institution is the lengthened shadow of one man," as Pennsylvania. William Penn not only founded it but obtained settlers from Europe and firmly established the principle of religious liberty which is a cornerstone of the American political system. The Penn tradition still exerts a beneficent influence, even as his statue on top of City Hall dominates Philadelphia. Of our colonial founders he was one of the most able, and, with Roger Williams, the best loved.

William Penn, born in 1644, was the indulged son of a wealthy father, Admiral Sir William Penn, conqueror of Jamaica and friend both to Charles II and his brother the Duke of York. At an early age young William showed an interest in religion which puzzled his parents. Expelled from Christ Church, Oxford, for a prank which indicated his contempt for Anglicanism, he was first well thrashed by the Admiral, then sent on a grand tour of the European capitals. Upon returning to London he read law, then went to Ireland to look after the confiscated estates that Charles II had given to his father. On a visit to Cork, young William listened to a discourse by a Quaker preacher on the text from 1 John v. 4, "There is a faith that overcometh the world"; and the Friends' faith overcame him.

The Quakers, destined to have an influence on American life far greater than their numbers, were a left-wing Puritan sect founded by George Fox in England around 1650. The Puritans had substituted the authority of the Bible for that of the church; Fox, while he respected the Bible, found the direct word of God in the human soul. For him, no ministry was necessary. His followers, believing that all men were equal, called themselves the Friends. Hence their insistence on addressing everyone as "thee" and "thou," (at that time used only to children or inferiors), and refusing to take their hats off, which got them into trouble everywhere. They took literally the commandment "Thou shalt not kill," and so ran afoul of war-waging governments.

Some 3000 Quakers were imprisoned in England during the first two years of Charles II's reign; yet, like the early Christians, they gathered strength from persecution, and victory from defeat. They spread throughout the

British empire and into Holland, Germany, and even Russia. Severe laws were passed against Quakers in every colony except Rhode Island. Everywhere else they were whipped and imprisoned. In New York they were tortured; in Boston, hanged.

Finally by passive resistance the Friends won a grudging toleration in most of the English colonies. In England, by 1670, the sect had acquired a socially recognized position; and as Quakers had taken no part in the Civil War, they were regarded with more favor by Charles II than any other dissenting body. Thousands of converts were made among members of the middle class who had been repelled from Puritanism by the rule of Cromwell's major-generals.

ARMS OF FOUNDERS OF THE MIDDLE COLONIES

Tolerated though they were, many Quakers wished to emigrate for the same reason that Puritans had fifty years before — to get away from the corrupt society of England. Quaker communities were founded in Rhode Island, in the back part of Plymouth Colony, on the island of Nantucket, and in North Carolina. The political situation in England was not unlike that fifty years earlier, which impelled the great Puritan migration. Throughout society there was extravagance and corruption; and the body politic was shot through with plots and counterplots. Anything seemed likely to happen, from a Cromwellian comeback to Louis XIV conquering England and treating English

Protestants as he had the Huguenots. It was time for peaceably minded people to leave.

Admiral Sir William Penn, reconciled to his son, left him a small fortune at his death. In 1676, in company with George Fox, William traveled through northern Europe. There he ascertained that thousands of Quakers and other non-tolerated Protestant sects were eager to emigrate to America if they could have a colony of their very own where they could carry out their ideals of the good life. The old admiral had been a friend of the Duke of York and had even lent him large sums of money. A tactful reminder of this eased young Penn's application for a slice of the Duke's enormous grant, and in March 1681 he obtained the magnificent proprietary province that bears his name, together with a charter from Charles II guaranteeing his possession of it.

William Penn wasted no time; in 1682 he issued a tract called *Some Account of the Province of Pennsylvania*, which lacked the lyric enthusiasm of the booster pamphlets of early Virginia and New England and broke all canons of real estate promotion by modesty rather than overstatement. He told what sort of people he wanted, and gave instructions for the journey and outfit. He offered complete religious liberty and easy terms for land — 50-acre head-rights as in Virginia, 200-acre tenant farms at a penny an acre rent; and for £100 you could have a 5000-acre country estate with a city lot in Philadelphia thrown in. *Some Account*, translated into German, French, and Dutch, circulated widely on the European continent. Thus the population of Pennsylvania quickly became cosmopolitan, although the majority of earliest settlers were English and Welsh Quakers. Penn himself came over in 1682 and laid out Philadelphia in checkerboard fashion, a reflection of the tidy Quaker mind that has had a permanent influence on American city planning.

The neighborhood of Philadelphia was no wilderness. Several hundred Swedes and Finns, survivors of the short-lived colony of New Sweden, were already there; and, owing to the food that they produced, Pennsylvania passed through no pioneering hardships. In two years' time, Philadelphia contained 357 houses. The population of the province in 1685 was not far from 9000. Germans of the Mennonite sect, mostly linen weavers from Crefeld, settled Germantown in 1683 with Francis Daniel Pastorius, a learned minister whom Penn had met on his European tour. Welsh Quakers founded Radnor and Haverford. A corporation of English Quakers, called the Free Society of Traders, stocked a general store in Philadelphia, organized whale fishing in Delaware Bay, established brick kilns, tanneries, glass works, and trade with the West Indies. Almost the complete apparatus of English civilization was transplanted in a remarkably short time and extended to non-English peoples as well. William Penn could declare in 1684 without exaggeration: "I have led the greatest colony into America that ever any man did upon a private credit, and the most prosperous beginnings that were ever in it are to be found among us."

Although he was not averse to creating a valuable estate for his heirs, Penn looked upon his province mainly as a holy experiment. The founders of New England took the same view of their colonies; but there was a difference between their ideas and Penn's. Their object was to establish a particular sect and way of life; Penn's was to give liberty to any religion, and to many ways of life. The Puritans assumed that human nature was intrinsically evil, and framed laws to keep down sin and crime; Penn believed in the essential goodness of human nature and framed laws with that principle in mind. But, after experimenting, their respective law codes became very similar. In Pennsylvania, following a crime wave in 1698, the assembly passed and the proprietor accepted a new code so severe that the English Privy Council rejected most of it; whilst in New England the laws moved toward liberality and mercy. Both Puritans and Quakers regarded government as something more than a means to keep the peace and protect property; it was an agency in moral training. But the Puritans, like medieval churchmen, regarded government as the sword of St. Paul to uphold Christianity, whilst the Quakers, like Roger Williams, believed that a man's religion was nobody's business but his own.

Penn's charter was proprietary, like Lord Baltimore's, with a few essential differences. The crown reserved the right to hear appeals from colonial courts, to disallow acts of the assembly, and to appoint customs officials; the province was also required to obey the Acts of Trade and Navigation. This charge was more honored in the breach than the observance, since Quakers, like Puritans or Anglicans, held smuggling to be no sin. But William Penn was as free as any colonial proprietor to write his own frame of government. He wrote three in succession, modifying them to suit the people and his own tastes.

Everything went well in the local government when Penn was in Philadelphia as his own governor in 1682–84. He was a man of great charm and persuasiveness, still under forty, tall and athletic, able to impress Indians with his prowess at running and leaping. He entertained lavishly and well; he appreciated a fine horse, a well-built ship, and a handsome woman. But when the proprietor returned to England to mend his political fences, the colonial government almost blew up. The acting governor, Thomas Lloyd, quarreled with John Blackwell, an old soldier whom Penn sent over as governor. Blackwell, "driven by yells and jeers from the Council chamber at Philadelphia," consoled himself with a humorous description of Quakers as people who *prayed* for their neighbors on First Day (Sunday), and *preyed* on them the other six days of the week.

Penn made a worthy and successful effort to be just to the Indians of his province, although there never was a treaty "under the elm tree at Shackamaxon," the scene immortalized by a painting of Benjamin West. Of this treaty Voltaire wrote that it was the only one in history not ratified by an oath, yet never broken. One may say that had it been made, it was broken, since one of the slickest deals ever put over by Europeans on Indians was the famous "walking purchase."

In order to cash in on an alleged Indian sale to William Penn in 1686 of a tract of land "as far as a man can go in a day and a half," Thomas Penn, the second lord proprietor, had a good trail cleared, hired the three best runners in the Province, and started them off at dawn one September day accompanied by pacers on horseback and a few Indians to see fair play. The Indians, after vainly trying to persuade the runners to walk, gave up in disgust before noon; as one of them said, "No sit down to smoke, no shoot squirrel, just *lun, lun, lun* all day long." One runner quit, the second fell into a creek and was drowned; but the third, at noon of the second day, grasped a sapling which was then declared to mark the end of the one and one-half days' walking. This exploit gave the Penn family half a million acres of Indian cornfields and hunting grounds.

In 1699 William Penn returned to Philadelphia after an absence of fifteen years, and in 1701 issued his third frame of government, called the Charter of Privileges. Under it the proprietor appointed both governor and council, but the legislative power was lodged in an assembly consisting of four members from each county. This charter served as the constitution of Pennsylvania until 1776. The "Three Lower Counties," the future State of Delaware, had been purchased by Penn from the Duke of York, but were overlooked in the royal charter. The Charter of Privileges allowed these three counties to have their own assembly, but their governor was always the same as Pennsylvania's.

Penn now hastened back to England to forestall another attack on his propriety. In that he was successful, but his business affairs went from bad to worse. With Lord Baltimore he had a vexatious boundary controversy which was not settled until their respective heirs agreed on a line — latitude 39° 43' 26"—which surveyors Mason and Dixon began to run in 1764. Penn was cheated by most of his agents. None of the governors he appointed were any good. He ran deeply into debt and was even confined in debtors' prison for a few months. And for six years before his death in 1718 he was a hopeless invalid.

Although Pennsylvania was hospitable to all peoples and races and many, especially German sectarians, came over in the eighteenth century, the tone and temper of the province was set by English-speaking Friends. These were of the second generation of Quakers who had sloughed off the frenzy and fanaticism of Fox's early converts, yet retained the serenity, the high ideals, and the sturdy pacifism that are the finest flowers of their sect. Although their light-of-conscience faith tended to make them deficient in public spirit, the Quakers had the same ambition as the Virginians and New Englanders to transplant the finer things of English civilization. That they did remarkably quickly. By 1700 Philadelphia had outstripped New York as a cultural center, which was not difficult, and was pushing Boston for first place. It was the first English colonial town after Boston to have a printing press, and the third to set up a newspaper. Penn himself founded Penn Charter School in 1689, and Quaker compassion provided Philadelphia with the best hospitals and charitable institutions in the English colonies. James Logan, scientist and classical scholar who came over as Penn's secretary in 1699, accumulated the best collection of books in the English colonies after Cotton Mather's.

Pennsylvania was a portent of the America to be. Maryland had tried religious toleration but repealed her famous law in 1692; Rhode Island made religious liberty work on a small scale among English people only; but Pennsylvania was the first large community since the Roman Empire to allow different nations and religious sects to live under the same government on terms of equality. It is true that the Holy Experiment was not as successful as Penn had hoped. Quarrels among governor, council, and assembly distressed him. "For the love of God, me, and the poor country," he once wrote to Thomas Lloyd, leader of the opposition, "do not be so litigious and brutish!" Yet, for all that, English, Irish, and Welsh Quakers, Anglicans, Roman Catholics, Scots-Irish Presbyterians, and Germans of four or five different sects, managed to live in the same city and province, enjoying equality one with another; and, if not precisely in a state of brotherly love, at least not flying at one another's throats. Pennsylvania, as a successful experiment in the life of reason, deeply interested the liberals of eighteenth-century Europe. They held up the province as an illustration of their belief that man could lead the good life without monarchy, feudalism, or religious uniformity.

2. The Colonies in 1700

By the dawn of the eighteenth century most of the English colonies had acquired the character they long retained, even as states. At first glance the area of continuous settlement shown on our map is not impressive. Only a fringe of territory, nowhere more than fifty miles from the seacoast or a navigable river, had been brought under cultivation or settlement. It was fairly continuous from York, Maine, to Albemarle Sound, North Carolina. Thence to the settled fringe along the South Carolina coast there was a gap of 250 miles where the Indians were still undisturbed.

The best estimates of the population of the English colonies in 1700 are as follows:

New Hampshire	10,000		
Massachusetts Bay	80,000		
Rhode Island	10,000		
Connecticut	30,000	New England	130,000
New York	30,000		
New Jersey	15,000		
Pennsylvania and Delaware	20,000	Middle Colonies	65,000

Maryland	32,258		
Virginia	55,000	Chesapeake Colonies	87,258
North Carolina	5,000		
South Carolina	7,000	The Carolinas	12,000
Jamaica	50,000 [1]		
Barbados	71,000 [2]	West Indies	121,000

1. Of this number, only 5000 were white.
2. Probably 60,000 of these were slaves. There must have been some 2000 more English and 10,000 more slaves in the Leeward Islands, but no figures are available.

French Canada was still a string of farms, seldom more than one deep, along the St. Lawrence to Montreal, up the Richelieu river to Lake Champlain, and into the Minas Basin of L'Acadie. Its estimated population was 6200.

In the continental area, a scanty population had set the main patterns of government and society for the future United States. Every English colony had an elective assembly, and all except South Carolina had local self-government. Control from England would shortly be pressed, but it had not yet become oppressive. English culture had been transferred to America. The continental colonies now had two colleges: Harvard and William and Mary, with Yale about to be born; primary education was available for almost all white boys in the more closely settled regions north of Maryland. The printing presses of Boston had a greater output than any English city except London, and Philadelphia would soon be in the running. Religious exclusiveness, originating at opposite ends of the Protestant spectrum in Massachusetts Bay and Virginia, was breaking down. Religious liberty as practiced by Roger Williams and William Penn was becoming general. And the colonies were emerging with chins up from their troubled quarter-century, confident of the future, proud of their English liberties and heritage, and determined to protect them against all comers.

Racial homogeneity, too, had broken down. Negro slavery was established in every colony and strongly entrenched beyond likelihood of peaceful abolition in Virginia, South Carolina, and the West Indies. New York was still half Dutch. Scots, Irish, Germans, and French Protestants were pouring in.

The chief subject of anxiety among thoughtful North Americans in 1700 was war. England seemed poised on the edge of a struggle with France and Spain for control of both Europe and the Western Hemisphere. It would have been rash optimism indeed in 1700 to predict that England would win or that the United States, formed from the old thirteen English colonies, would aggressively push against Spanish America by war and diplomacy to the Pacific Ocean.

By 1700, England had placed her stamp on what proved to be the most valuable part of North America, as Spain had done in Central and South America; it was a powerful enough stamp to impress the immigrants from other countries. Above all, English concepts of liberty and self-government had been planted. This was the essential, outstanding fact which has made that section of North America which nobody wanted in 1600, the nucleus of the United States.

3. The Revolution Settlement

William and Mary became joint sovereigns of England and Scotland by virtue of a parliamentary bargain which the House of Commons never allowed them to forget. They were required to govern through and by Parliament, respect the traditional liberties of Englishmen, and support the Church of England. They did so well that, in accordance with the Act of Settlement of 1701, Mary's sister, Princess Anne, succeeded to the throne on the death of William III the following year. This, the first change of English rulers since 1625 to be unaccompanied by civil tumults, set a precedent for all later accessions. For Englishmen were heartily sick of tyrannical governments, five of which they had experienced in the preceding seventy years. As for rights, and liberties, Parliament had already passed the Habeas Corpus Act (27 May 1679) which prevents government prolonging indefinitely the detention of suspects in jail. Later it passed a law giving judges tenure during good behavior instead of at the king's pleasure. These two acts, with the Declaration of Rights of 1689, which confirmed Magna Carta and similar documents, gave England a modern bill of rights, except for free speech and a free press, which had to wait.

The English colonies shared almost all these benefits. They too were pleased to have no brawl over the succession; almost everyone from Maine to Barbadoes supported William and Mary. There were no Jacobite rebellions such as Scotland experienced in 1715 for "James III," and again in 1745 for "Bonnie Prince Charlie." Americans were pleased to be assured that there would be no more tampering with colonial charters, or attempts to abolish elected assemblies. But the colonies never became as completely self-governing as the realm of England; nor did they expect to be.

Almost everything that England did or did not do about her colonies until about the year 1774 can be referred to trading considerations. It was, essentially, a commercial empire. The general theory, common to all European nations but strictly enforced only by Spain and France, was that colonies existed for the exclusive benefit of the homeland. They should trade exclusively with her, produce such raw materials as she wanted, consume her wares, and not compete with her manufactures. She, in return, owed them protection. Although the first Navigation Act was passed in 1651, England did not get around to enforcing this "mercantile system" in the colonies until the reign of William and Mary. Except with respect to the Chesapeake Bay tobacco trade, Americans had hitherto traded pretty much where and how they pleased.

This mercantile system, which the colonies were expected to obey, and to which they successfully adjusted their economy, was expressed in a series of acts of Parliament known as the Acts of Trade and Navigation. The basic principles of these Acts were as follows:

1. Exclusive Navigation: All commerce between England and her colonies had to be conducted in vessels built, manned, and owned in England or the colonies. This principle greatly encouraged colonial shipbuilding; by the time of the American Revolution, some 25 per cent of the British merchant marine was colony-built. Most nations, including the United States, apply the same principle today; a French ship or airliner can take freight from New York to France, but not from New York to San Francisco.

2. The Entrepôt Principle: This meant that colonial trade with foreign countries should normally be conducted through the home country. England was much more liberal in this respect than other nations. On the outgo side, the laws "enumerated" certain products such as tobacco, sugar, and cotton, and, later, timber and furs, which could be exported from the colonies only to England or to another English colony. The purpose was to give English merchants the monopoly of processing and distributing colonial products to other countries. On the incoming side, colonies could import foreign merchandise only by way of England; it must be handled in an English port before going to America. Exceptions were made to accommodate certain colonial interests. The salt fish of New England could be taken anywhere, and the rice of South Carolina could be exported directly to southern Europe. In return, the colonies were allowed to import fruit, salt, and wine directly from the Mediterranean or the Azores and Madeira. And, although Scotland to 1707 and Ireland even later were "foreign countries" so far as these laws were concerned, the colonies were allowed to import "servants, horses and provisions" from them directly. This entrepôt principle created no hardship for the colonies, once they were adjusted to it, because the enumerated products enjoyed a monopoly in the English market, and the English government paid bounties to certain producers. And, since customs duties on foreign goods imported into England were in part repaid when re-exported to the colonies, Americans sometimes obtained such goods more cheaply than did the English.

The enforcement of the Acts of Trade and Navigation, as well as of all other acts relating to the colonies, was entrusted to political means. All proprietary colonies except the two belonging to the Penns and the Calverts became royal provinces; and of the corporate colonies only Hudson's Bay, Rhode Island, and Connecticut retained their charters. All royal governors, appointed by the king, were expected to enforce acts of Parliament both by executive means, and by vetoes over acts of colonial assemblies that conflicted with them. And the judges of colonial superior courts did not hold office during good behavior, as in England, but at the king's pleasure. Cases could be appealed from the highest court in a colony to the Privy Council in London, but this was expensive and seldom exercised. And a law of 1696 required all cases under the Acts of Trade and Navigation to be tried by royally appointed admiralty judges, without a jury. This prevented colonial juries from acquitting their friends engaged in smuggling.

The most effective means of control was royal disallowance. Acts of colonial assemblies, although duly passed and signed by the governor, could be disallowed by the Privy Council after a hearing. About 5.5 per cent of all colonial acts were thus revoked. The right was exercised judiciously, many of the disallowed laws being attempts to discriminate against religious sects, or against other colonies; but it caused great irritation.

The British government (as it should be called after the Act of Union with Scotland in 1707) included neither a colonial secretary nor a colonial office until 1768, when Lord Hillsborough was appointed the first secretary for the colonies. All colonial business went through a committee of crown appointees, called the Board of Trade and Plantations. This in general handled colonial business justly and intelligently, although it had no power of decision. The colonies were not represented on this board or in the House of Commons, but almost every colony kept a salaried agent in London to defend its interests and protest against unfavorable legislation.

Britain undertook to defend her colonies in time of war with fleets and armies, and Parliament usually repaid a good part of the colonies' war expenditures.[1] But it did not attempt to tax them directly until 1765, when the Stamp Act started the trouble that led to the American Revolution.

This system was neither unjust nor oppressive; rather, it was inadequate and ineffective to secure its professed object, welding the empire into an economic and political unit. For the most part, the colonies took it for granted, and under it colonial commerce increased and the people prospered. From the English point of view, however, the system was very unsatisfactory. There were several big cracks in it, one of them being Rhode Island, where no admiralty judge was ever able to hold court, and where, according to a governor of Massachusetts Bay, the government was one of "licentiousness and confusion," and "the administration of justice goes upon crutches." Another was Pennsylvania, where in William Penn's absence his governor winked at a surreptitious trade with the Dutch; and a third was South Carolina, where the assembly had the nerve to pass a law subjecting the admiralty judge to suits and penalties for his decisions! The Board of Trade in 1701 reported to the House of Commons that the entire colonial system should be overhauled, the power of assemblies curtailed, and that of the crown increased. But before

1. For instance, in Queen Anne's War, 1702–13, Massachusetts Bay spent £87,434 and got back £34,689; New York spent £84,098 and got back £56,150.

Parliament got around to doing anything about it, William III died, Anne succeeded to the throne, and a war began that involved all Europe and the colonies.

4. Queen Anne and Her War

Queen Anne, thirty-seven years old at her accession, though not of the caliber of the two Queens Elizabeth, was no cipher in government. A plump and amiable woman, she was deeply religious, but a glutton; at her first communion the Archbishop of Canterbury felt obliged to remark, "Your Highness must not drink it *all!*" She married Prince George of Denmark, an amiable nincompoop of whom her uncle Charles II once remarked, "I have tried Prince George drunk and I have tried him sober, and there is nothing in him." They never managed to produce a healthy child, and left no descendant to inherit the throne. But by a curious turn of fate this average, kindly woman, so middle class in her tastes that she insisted on friends calling her "Mrs. Morley," enjoyed one of the most glorious reigns in English history. Hers was the "Augustan age" of English literature — Addison, Steele, Defoe, and Swift; the *Tatler* and *Spectator*, and Alexander Pope, who saluted her thus:

> Here thou, great Anna! whom three realms obey,
> Dost sometimes counsel take, and sometimes tea.

Two months after her accession Europe was plunged into the War of the Spanish Succession. An imbecile king of Spain died without issue. Rival heirs were a grandson of Louis XIV, who backed him up, and a Bavarian prince, who was supported by England, Austria, and other powers. In this war General Churchill distinguished himself in the battles of Ramillies, Oudenard, Malplaquet, and Blenheim, and was rewarded with the dukedom of Marlborough; England captured Gibraltar and rounded out her American empire with Nova Scotia and Newfoundland. A war futile in its immediate objects, since the Bavarian prince died in the course of it and the grandson of Louis XIV got the throne after all; but the Treaty of Utrecht that ended this war in 1713 inaugurated thirty years of peace and became a landmark in modern history.

In America this conflict was called Queen Anne's War. And since Spain was an ally of France, there was conflict on the southern frontier, where a curious chain reaction had taken place. La Salle's accidental incursion into Texas when he was looking for the Mississippi stimulated Spain to establish her first mission in Texas, near the Neches river, in 1690: a few years later, she placed a garrison at Pensacola on the Gulf coast of Florida. Her purpose was to pinch out Louisiana, but Louisiana refused to be pinched. Louis XIV countered by sending Le Moyne d'Iberville and a group of pioneers to found Biloxi, in the present state of Mississippi, in 1699. And within a year the

French had founded three trading posts — Kaskaskia, Cahokia, and Vincennes — in the Illinois country. Also, to secure the water route linking the St. Lawrence, the Great Lakes, and the Gulf, the post at Michilimackinac was strengthened, and its former commandant, Cadillac, was allowed to found Detroit, key to the three upper Lakes, in 1701.

Le Moyne d'Iberville hoped to make Louisiana a southern Canada, but he could get no support from home. French peasants, who might have found Louisiana's climate more congenial than that of Canada, were forbidden to emigrate. French Protestants would have gone over if guaranteed toleration, but Louis XIV refused; his cardinal policy *Un roi, une loi, une foi,* applied to the French colonies too. So, instead of using the willing Protestants, who consequently went to swell the strength of Anglo-America, Louis XIV allowed himself to be persuaded by some half-witted courtier to colonize Louisiana with Canadian coureurs de bois, as a means of persuading these knights of the canoe and the snowshoe to become farmers. Iberville had to put them on the garrison payroll to keep them there.

The greatest threat to Spanish dominion of the Gulf was not this feeble attempt at French colonization, but the vigorous young colony that centered on Charleston. South Carolina, expanding and aggressive, occupied a position in respect to the Gulf colonies of France and Spain similar to that of Canada toward New York and New England. There being no Appalachian barrier here, the Carolinians quickly penetrated the Gulf region and applied the French fur-trading technique; except that on this frontier the desired Indian product was deerskin, not beaver. The Yamassee, nearest tribe to South Carolina, became her faithful ally and protected her from overland attack, just as the Iroquois protected New York.

France, threatened both by thrusting Carolinians and Spanish Pensacola, shifted her garrison from Biloxi to Mobile in 1702, concluded an alliance with the Choctaw, and egged on the Creek nation to attack the Yamassee. When Queen Anne's War broke out, Le Moyne d'Iberville begged his king to send ships and soldiers to throw the English out of Carolina. All that Louis XIV did, for the moment, was to send out a shipload of *filles du Roi* (who in this case were also *filles de joie*) to keep the Mobile garrison happy. Iberville returned to France in search of help, and obtained command of a squadron of warships and a regiment of soldiers, with orders to mop up all English colonies from south to north. First, the British West Indies; then "chase our adversaries from Carolina . . . insult New York, attack Virginia, carry help to L'Acadie and Newfoundland." This grand design fizzled because it was routed via Cuba. Iberville caught yellow fever at Havana and died, as did hundreds of his sailors and soldiers; the survivors returned to France.

England was equally backward in supporting Carolinian pleas for men and ships to mop up Pensacola and Mobile. In 1707 the Charlestonians themselves, with Chickasaw allies, burned Pensacola town but failed to capture the presidio, predecessor of the fort that held out for the Union right through the

Civil War. But without ships the English in South Carolina could not accomplish much except to rescue their sister colony, North Carolina, from a severe attack in 1711 by the Tuscarora. This Tuscarora war dragged on for several years, ending in the removal of that tribe to western Pennsylvania and New York, where they became the sixth nation of the Iroquois Confederacy. Their descendants still have a small reservation near Niagara Falls, of part of which they have been robbed to make a reservoir, after an unsuccessful appeal to the Supreme Court of the United States (1960).

The Treaty of Utrecht, which ended Queen Anne's War in 1713, left the vague frontier between Carolina and Florida exactly where it had been in 1700. The founding of Georgia in 1733 was the first sign of interest by the English government in its southern American frontier.

There were only twenty-seven French families in all Louisiana in 1717. Next year Le Moyne de Bienville, Iberville's brother, founded New Orleans at a strategic position to control the river traffic.

New York remained neutral during the first half of Queen Anne's War, mainly because the Albany fur traders wished to continue their contraband traffic with Canada. So the New England frontier took the rap, suffering a series of raids by Abnaki Indians led by French officers. This *petite guerre* was big enough to wipe out the Maine coastal settlements for the third time, to destroy Deerfield and carry its inhabitants into captivity, and to render northern New England insecure for settlement.

Joseph Dudley had now reached the goal of his ambition, the royal governorship of Massashusetts Bay. Acting on a tactical suggestion of the Reverend Solomon Stoddard of Northampton, he set up a system of frontier patrols. Select companies of the militia were equipped with snowshoes and moccasins for winter service, and bounties were given to farmers to raise hounds "to discourage and keep off the Indians in ranging and scouring the woods." But Dudley did not limit his strategy to defense. He had the right idea, that the only way to render life secure in northern New England was to destroy the bases of French power in North America.

Massachusetts first struck at Port Royal in L'Acadie, base for the French privateers which were preying on New England fishermen and traders. An attack in 1707 failed, but another, in 1710, was successful. Dudley now cooked up with General Francis Nicholson a sales campaign in fancy dress. Four sachems of the Iroquois Confederacy were sent to London, to plead with Queen Anne for men, money, and ships to throw the French out of Canada. Under the chaperonage of Major Peter Schuyler of Albany, the sachems, wearing matchcoats, feather headdresses, and full war paint, were presented to Queen Anne and made their plea through an interpreter. They saw the sights of London, heard a sermon by the Bishop, dined with William Penn, attended a cockfight, and stopped the show when they entered a theater to see *Macbeth*. And they managed to return safely to New York.

This really worked. The English government prepared a big operation against Quebec for the summer of 1711. Unfortunately, before it could be organized, Queen Anne had dismissed her Whig ministry and installed a Tory one, with her crony Mrs. Masham as the power behind the throne. The new favorite's incompetent brother was now promoted brigadier and made joint leader of an expedition against Canada with Admiral Sir Hovenden Walker, who sailed his fleet up from the West Indies for that purpose. This expedition was even more of a disgrace than Sir William Phips's of 1690. On 16 September, when 100 miles short of Quebec, the Admiral and General decided that winter was coming on, and they had better retreat. Several of the ships were wrecked, with great loss of life. This disaster prevented General Nicholson, who was leading an overland expedition against Montreal, from getting further than Lake George.

There was also plenty of fighting in the West Indies. By this time the buccaneers were dead, or had turned respectable; battles were between naval fleets, regular soldiers, and island militia. In August 1702 Du Casse of the French navy defeated a British fleet under Admiral Benbow off Santa Marta, a battle which lasted intermittently for six days. Benbow lost it because two of his captains flinched and he himself was mortally wounded. It was typical of the gentlemanly warfare of this century that, before he died, Benbow received this message from Du Casse: "Yesterday I had no better hope than to be taking supper in your cabin, as your prisoner. As for those cowardly captains of yours, *hang them up*, for, by God, they deserve it!" And hanged they were, when they returned to England. But this was the one blue-water victory for France. The British navy captured Gibraltar, Minorca, and Argentia in Newfoundland. The French navy, which Louis XIV had neglected, engaged largely in commerce destroying, *la guerre de course*, a strategy which eventually lost France her American empire.

In this war the value of navies was first clearly recognized — "the noiseless, steady, exhausting pressure with which sea power acts, cutting off the resources of the enemy while maintaining its own." And a governor of Barbados wrote, "All turns upon the mastery of the sea. If we have it, our islands are safe, however thinly peopled; if the French have it, we cannot hold one of them." British mastery of the sea forced Louis XIV in the Treaty of Utrecht to cede Newfoundland, Nova Scotia, Gibraltar, and Minorca to England, together with the right to participate in the *asiento*, the slave trade with Spanish America. Before Queen Anne's reign, England was *a* sea power; after 1713 she was *the* sea power, and long so remained.

"Never since the heroic days of Greece has the world had such a sweet, just, boyish master," wrote Santayana two centuries later, when British sea power was beginning to totter. "It will be a black day for the human race when scientific blackguards, conspirators, churls and fanatics manage to supplant him!"

Growth and Development

1713-1750

1. Expansion and Business

THE TREATY OF UTRECHT inaugurated an era of peace and expansion for England's continental colonies. Their population had grown from about
85,000 in 1670, to 360,000 in 1713. By 1754 it had quadrupled again to about
1,500,000. This increase owed much to heavy migration of non-English people — Irish and Scots, Germans and French — favored by a liberal naturalization act of the British Parliament in 1740. Only two new continental colonies,
Nova Scotia and Georgia, were founded between 1713 and 1754, but the area
of settlement almost tripled. In the North it spread into the hilly interior of
New England, the region west of the lower Hudson, and central Pennsylvania. In the Southern colonies it spread into the piedmont, the area between
the fall line of the rivers and the Blue Ridge and Smoky Mountains. And the
manner of settlement, as we shall see, created new tensions.

High prices prevailed in Europe for colonial products, especially tobacco,
rice, and sugar. The last-named primarily helped the West Indies, but the
continental colonies, which provided the islands with lumber, livestock, and
provisions, indirectly profited.

Before 1713 there had not been a real town on the continent between
Philadelphia and Charleston. Norfolk now grew up as an outlet for the lumber and naval stores of North Carolina. Baltimore, founded in 1730, soon
became a principal point of export for the wheat of Maryland and Pennsylvania. Philadelphia countered in 1733 by building the "Great Road" to the
mouth of the Conestoga river, Lancaster County. For wagon traffic over this
road in farm products, draft horses were bred from the Dutch and Flemish
stock brought over by early settlers; and the Conestoga wagon, which eventually
became the covered wagon of the Oregon trail, was developed.

Prosperity and a new influx of population greatly enlarged the ranks of the
colonial gentry. Both they and the middle class benefited by enlarged educational facilities. By 1713 there were only three colleges in the continental
colonies. The College of New Jersey (Princeton) was founded in 1746,
mainly to serve Middle-colony Presbyterians. Anglican King's College
(Columbia) was founded at New York in 1754; Philadelphia College (University of Pennsylvania) at Philadelphia in 1749; Codrington College at Bar-

bados in 1745. The publication of newspapers, little four-page weeklies though they were, increased the diffusion of knowledge, as did printing and publishing. But no colony south of Maryland had a printing press before 1730.[1]

The settled frontier expanded fast. In New England the old system of laying out new townships to groups of actual settlers broke down in favor of wide belts of speculative townships. In the Middle and Southern colonies, land began to be sold outright by assemblies, proprietors or speculators, instead of being granted by the head-right system.

In the province of New York, the population grew relatively slowly, partly because of the Six Nations, partly because the patroons and their successors engrossed so much land along the Hudson that settlers could come in only as tenants, which immigrants did not like. Lords of the manor paid no quitrents and dodged most of their other taxes by influence with the assembly. Ulster County in the lower Mohawk valley was settled largely by Scots-Irish; but there was not much room for expansion while the Iroquois Confederacy had to be respected, and among the thirteen colonies New York had to yield sixth place in population to North Carolina in 1760. Virginia was then first in population, Massachusetts Bay second, and Pennsylvania third.

Owing to the connections that William Penn had made in Germany, Philadelphia became the principal port of entry for foreigners. Mostly indentured servants, but including a number of people of substance and learning, they took up land in York and Lancaster counties, creating the prosperous farms and built the great barns that are still a feature of the landscape. The German immigrants belonged mainly to sects which were discriminated against at home: Mennonites, Moravians, Dunkards (German Quakers), Pietists (Puritanic Lutherans), and others. On their heels came Scots-Irish from Ulster who were under pressure by Catholics and by restrictive legislation of the British Parliament. These hardy people fanned out into the frontiers of all colonies from Maine to Georgia.

Crossing the Atlantic in a sailing ship could seldom be a pleasure before the clipper-ship era, but it was never tougher than in the eighteenth century. Gottlieb Mittelberger, who came to Philadelphia in 1750, described the misery during his voyage: — bad drinking water and putrid salt meat, excessive heat and crowding, lice so thick that they could be scraped off the body, sea so rough that hatches were battened down and everyone vomited in the foul

1. The first colonial town outside New England to have a printing press was Philadelphia in 1685; the second, New York in 1693. Next in order were Newcastle, Delaware (1724); Annapolis, Maryland (1726), Williamsburg, Virginia (1730), Charleston, South Carolina (1732), Newbern, North Carolina (1751), Hackensack, New Jersey (1755), Savannah, Georgia (1762). The earliest newspapers were the *Boston News-Letter* (1704), *Boston Gazette* (1719), Philadelphia *American Weekly Mercury* (1719), *New York Gazette* (1725), Annapolis *Maryland Gazette* (1727), Boston *New-England Weekly Journal* (1727), Newport *Rhode Island Gazette* (1732), and Charleston *South-Carolina Gazette* (1732).

air; passengers succumbing to dysentery, scurvy, typhus, canker, and mouth-rot. Children under seven, he said, rarely survived the voyage, and in his ship no fewer than thirty-two died. One vessel carrying 400 Palatinate Germans from Rotterdam in August 1738 lost her master and three-quarters of the passengers before stranding on Block Island after a four-month voyage.

Many foreigners who landed at Philadelphia, as well as indentured servants whose terms were up, migrated into the upper country of Maryland, Virginia, and North Carolina. This settlement of the southern piedmont began in 1716, at the instance of Governor Spotswood of Virginia, who led a gay cavalcade of gentlemen, whom he dubbed "Knights of the Golden Horseshoe," to explore the Shenandoah valley. That part of the valley between the Blue Ridge and the Alleghenies belonged to the Northern Neck grant of six million acres which Charles II had given to Lord Culpeper, whose heir the Earl of Fairfax, gave George Washington his first job as a surveyor. Fairfax sold land at rates that attracted immigrants from Pennsylvania, or let it on 99-year leases at £1 per 100 acres, while the Penn family was charging £15 10s and the Calverts £5, for the same amount of land. Migration from Pennsylvania and down the Shenandoah spilled over into the piedmont of Virginia and the Carolinas, peopling that region with Presbyterians and German Moravians who worked without slaves and resented control of the assemblies by slave-holding Anglican planters and merchants of the lowlands.

In North Carolina, where the piedmont was opened up by the Tuscarora removal to New York, land could be had at bargain prices. The royal governors were instructed to grant 50 acres free to each settler, and Lord Granville, who held the counties bordering on Virginia, charged only three shillings for 640 acres. It was he with whom Bishop Zinzendorf of the Moravian (United Brethren) sect contracted for the purchase of 100,000 acres for £916, a sale which resulted in the settlement of the Wachovia tract, centering on Salem. The popularity of North Carolina among yeomen, who wanted a farm where they would not be overawed by great slave-operated plantations, accounts for the phenomenal 1600 per cent increase in the population of that province between 1713 and 1763.

This up-country region of Virginia and the Carolinas, sometimes called the "Old West," lay so far from markets as to be almost self-sufficient. The people imported little but iron, gunpowder, and salt, and exported mostly peltry and cattle. Huge droves of cattle were rounded up annually in cowpens (one of which gave its name to a famous battle) to be driven to Baltimore, Petersburg, or Charleston for export. At the same time, the older English stock of the Southern colonies was expanding westward from the coast. Richmond was founded at the falls of the James in 1729; Petersburg at the falls of the Rapidan a few years later.

All English colonial exports were products of farms, forests and fisheries. The expansion of foreign and West Indies trade was enormous, even though canalized to some extent by the Acts of Trade and Navigation. Owing to

French protection of brandy against the competition of cheap rum, the French sugar colonies had a surplus of molasses which they were glad to sell to Anglo-American ships for distillation into rum at every seaport. West Indian planters, both English and French, consumed quantities of pickled beef and pork from New England, New York, and Carolina; onions and potatoes from the Connecticut valley; wheat and flour from Baltimore, and fed their slaves on New England codfish and Pennsylvania corn. They buil their houses from Northern pine lumber and exported their sugar and molasses in boxes and barrels put together out of pine shooks and oak staves axe-hewn in Northern forests. They rode to town on Narragansett pacers raised in Rhode Island, and ran their sugar mills with horsepower provided by superfluous "plugs" raised on New England farms. Many West Indies products were carried to England and exchanged for consumer goods for colonial consumption. Northern traders came to depend more and more on trade with the West Indies; their prosperity was conditioned by it, and any attempt to interfere with it was certain to be evaded or resisted.

Several American industries, besides distilleries, date from this period. Governor Spotswood, in addition to promoting western settlement, created an iron industry. Through his friend Baron Graffenried he obtained German iron workers, erected a settlement for them (named Germanna) at the junction of the Rapidan and the Rappahannock in 1715, and set up an iron furnace at Massaponax about five miles below Fredericksburg. At least three other furnaces had been set up in Virginia by 1732, one owned by Augustine Washington (the General's father) on the Potomac; and by 1750 the ironworks in the Chesapeake colonies were exporting over 2000 tons annually to England. In 1750 British iron interests induced Parliament to forbid colonials to establish mills for slitting bar iron into nail rods, or to set up plating forges using a triphammer, or steel tool furnaces. But this law had little effect. The prohibition was so flagrantly disregarded that Pennsylvania, New Jersey, and Massachusetts even granted bounties for new plants after the Iron Act was on the statute books. In 1775 there were actually more furnaces for producing pig iron, and forges for resmelting the pigs into bar or wrought iron, in the thirteen colonies than in England and Wales. So, even though the acts restraining manufactures were restrictive in motive, they were hardly so in practice; and before indulging in virtuous indignation over them we should remember that, before the Philippines became independent, Congress set quotas on Philippine products such as sugar, which competed with those of the United States, and that the President now has power to set quotas on a variety of foreign imports.

2. Currency Controversies

Far more serious handicaps to colonial trade than the Acts of Parliament were English restrictions on colonial use of money, and the attempts of colonial assemblies to get around them. No precious metals were produced in the colonies, and the balance of trade with the mother country was against them; so their want of metallic currency was constant. Yet Parliament refused to allow the export of English coin to English colonies, or to allow them to mint coinage of their own from foreign bullion that they obtained through trade with the West Indies. Colonial assemblies endeavored to meet this situation in a variety of ways. Each colony or group of colonies established a currency of account, "lawful money" as it was called, in pounds, shillings, and pence that were worth less than sterling in England. The standard for this lawful money was the Spanish milled dollar or "piece of eight," the commonest foreign coin that came into the continent from the Caribbean, and which eventually was chosen as standard for the United States silver dollar. This dollar was worth 4s 6d in terms of English sterling; but in South Carolina and Georgia it was valued at 4s 8d; in New England and Virginia at 6s; in New York at 8s, and in the other colonies at 7s 6d. This meant that a New York pound of account was worth only half an English pound sterling, and a "York shilling" only 6d sterling, or 12½ cents; in New England and Virginia a shilling meant 16⅔ cents.[1] The colonial assemblies fondly imagined that by this overvaluation of foreign coins in terms of £ s d, these coins would stay in the colonies and not be re-exported; but the only result was a corresponding markup of prices on English goods, and consignments of foreign bullion to England in order to pay for goods ordered there.

Since overvaluing the Spanish dollar and undervaluing sterling did not help the colonists, they resorted to paper money. Personal promissory notes, tobacco-warehouse receipts, and bills of exchange had long been used as currency in the colonies, even for very small sums. From this it was a short step for the colonial assemblies to issue official promissory notes to pay for unusual expenses in anticipation of tax collections. These "bills of credit" (whence we derive our phrase a dollar "bill") relieved the currency shortage in time of war. Consequently the demand grew up for issuing them in time of peace. The American farmer believed then (as in the main he still believes) that currency inflation, raising prices of farm produce, would ease his burden of debt. Massachusetts and South Carolina, which had borne a disproportionate share of the Queen Anne's War burden, continued issuing bills of credit after the Treaty of Utrecht. In some colonies, notably in Pennsylvania, where Benjamin Franklin urged the legitimate value of paper currency in a growing and expanding economy, issues of bills of credit were promptly redeemed, and depreciated very little. They were, in effect, a lien on future

1. Other foreign coins common in the English colonies were the half real (6¼ cents), called "fippenny" in New England and Virginia because it was worth 5d in their money of account; the English guinea, worth 21s sterling or $5; the Spanish gold pistole, worth $4; and the Spanish doubloon and Portuguese johannes, each worth $16. The "two shillings" of New York naturally became the "two bits" of the Far West, and reckoning in shillings died hard; the writer remembers Christmas wreaths being priced at "a shilling each, six for a dollar" in Boston.

growth and prosperity, like our terrific national debt of today. But in Rhode Island, a small colony whose possibilities of future expansion were limited, one issue of bills of credit succeeded another, until prices in terms of paper money rose about thirtyfold.

South Carolina thought up another scheme that the planters liked immensely — the so-called Land Bank. Under this system the colony created a paper "bank" or heap of bills and lent them to planters on the security of their land. It was a wonderful game, practically a gift; for if the planter was unable to redeem his paper debt, he and his fellows could generally induce the assembly to stay collection or let him discharge it in produce at inflated value. Massachusetts was almost torn apart by a land bank controversy in 1741. The merchants persuaded Parliament to declare a law of 1720, aimed at the South Sea Bubble and other wildcat English schemes of that speculative era, to have outlawed the Massachusetts land bank. This act, which ruined, among others, the father of Samuel Adams, was in part responsible for a clause in the Federal Constitution against *ex post facto* laws.

North Carolina, whose population increased so rapidly at this period, became the principal colonial source of naval stores — ship timber, pitch, tar, and turpentine — which the yellow pine of the uplands yielded in large quantities. South Carolina, too, produced them; but her most valuable export was rice — 42,000 barrels in 1731, tripled by 1765. Rice culture, like tobacco, required a great deal of labor before it was ready for market, and that had to be Negro labor; thus South Carolina became the greatest slave-importing colony. Indigo, the other staple of this colony, introduced from the West Indies about 1740, was encouraged by a British bounty, since it was wanted in England for dyeing woolens.

3. Colonial Society

Colonial prosperity brought about a change in the appearance of the older towns and villages. Merchants built themselves dwellings of a style and stature before unknown, and set the fashion for a change of architecture in farmhouses as well. Prior to this era one had only the Dutch colonial and the New England colonial styles in the North. The Dutch was generally a low, brick or stone, one-and-one-half-story house with hip roof; the New England dwelling, a two-story house with roof sloping almost to the ground in the rear, massive beams, overhanging upper story, a massive central chimney with fireplaces as long as fourteen feet, and casement windows with diamond-shaped leaded panes.

About 1720 there came a marked change. Houses were painted inside and out; the roomy gambrel roof was introduced, and sash windows with small square panes. Fireplaces grew smaller as wood became less abundant, and Ben Franklin in 1740 invented and presented to the public his "Pennsylvania Fireplace," better known as the Franklin stove, which saved at least 50 per cent on fuel. Wealthy merchants built pretentious three-story mansions, usually of brick in New England and of stone in Pennsylvania. One or more chimneys were built at each end of the house, down the middle of which was a broad central hall, and in the rear a second door or Palladian window framing a formal garden. At each side of the hall were two square parlors or reception rooms, paneled and painted white. In proportion and beauty of detail, these dwellings of the colonial grandees are among the finest types of domestic architecture ever produced in America; many are still lived in after more than two centuries.

Colonial society was not what the next century would have called healthy. The hottest colonial intellectual controversy between witchcraft and White-field took place over inoculation for smallpox. An epidemic hit Boston upon the arrival of an infected crew from the West Indies in 1721. The Reverend Cotton Mather, who had read in the Royal Society's *Philosophical Transactions* about protecting healthy people from smallpox by inoculating them with pus from those already down with the disease, persuaded Dr. Zabdiel Boylston to try this new method. He did so, inoculating some 250 persons of whom all but six recovered, whilst nearly half the uninoculated Bostonians who caught it "in the common way" died. In spite of this obvious success, a terrific hue and cry, led by the newspaper published by Benjamin Franklin's brother, was raised against Mather and Boylston. Stones and threatening messages were hurled through their windows; they were insulted in the street and threatened with death. Dr. Boylston persisted and in the next epidemic again demonstrated the success of inoculation, which was not replaced by vaccination until about 1790.

A chatty and observant traveler through the Northern colonies in 1744 was Dr. Alexander Hamilton of Annapolis, the thriving capital of Maryland. The Doctor took a dim view of society in New York City: "To talk bawdy and to have a knack at punning passes among some there for good sterling wit." Boston was more to his liking:

There is more hospitality and frankness showed here to strangers than either at New York or at Philadelphia. And in the place there is abundance of men of learning and parts; so that one is at no loss for agreeable conversation nor for any set of company he pleases. Assemblies of the gayer sort are frequent here; the gentlemen and ladies meeting almost every week at concerts of music and balls. I was present at two or three such and saw as fine a ring of ladies, as good dancing, and heard music as elegant as I had been witness to anywhere. I must take notice that this place abounds with pretty women who appear rather more abroad than they do at York and dress elegantly. They are, for the most part, free and affable as well as pretty. I saw not one prude while I was there.

Boston ladies had evidently learned to imitate the manners of the Court of St. James's. This bit of conversation was reported to Hamilton by his companion Samuel Hughes, who was strolling along King Street with a lady when Dr. Hamilton passed in the other direction: "Lord!" said she, "what strange mortal is that?" " 'Tis the flower of the Maryland beaux," said Hughes. "Good God!" cried the belle, "does that figure come from Maryland?" "Madam," said Hughes, "he is a Maryland physician." "O Jesus! a physician! deuce take such odd-looking physicians!"

The Doctor's observations of declining Puritanism are supported from many sources. One of Benjamin Franklin's first excursions into print was to attack the frivolity and luxury of Harvard students, of whom a committee headed by Judge Sewall reported in 1723, "There has been a practice of general immoralities particularly stealing, lying, swearing, idleness, picking of locks, and too frequent use of strong drink." Best sellers at a Boston book auction in 1744 were Richardson's *Pamela*, the satire on it called *Antipamela*, Ovid's *Art of Love*, and Edward Fisher's *Marrow of Modern Divinity*. Note the *modern*.

Colonial Americans were far more concerned with social status than is the present generation. The very word "colonial," to the average Englishman, meant inferiority; so everyone with social ambition had to prove that he was somebody, the best proof of which was to be appointed to the council of his colony. That, and ownership of several hundred acres of land, gave one a status that nothing could shake. Gentlemen unable to trace a pedigree had one made up in England, and adopted a coat of arms. The wealthiest men, who monopolized the higher colonial offices, got their sons elected to the house of burgesses and frequently visited "home," as they called England, to freshen contacts with English society.

Virginia society now became stabilized as the traditional Virginia of brave gallants and fair women, horse-races and fox hunting, six-horse coaches and ten-gallon punch bowls. The native aristocracy, which we earlier saw in process of formation, was now in its second or third generation. The planters were now building three-story brick dwellings with a porch or veranda for protection from summer heat, and detached kitchen and servants' quarters. The typical Southern mansion of this period, like Washington's Mount Vernon, had a main building with a tall colonnaded porch and two wings connected by a covered "breezeway."

To run a plantation successfully — and one man might have as many as eight or ten different ones scattered through tidewater and piedmont — called forth managerial ability. The great estates were closer together than in the earlier century, connected by good carriage roads as well as by water, and Negro servants were well trained, so there was constant visiting between families, and rounds of dances, fox-hunts, and card-playing. At the top of the social order was the governor, who kept court at Williamsburg. Everybody who was anybody had to be there when the assembly was sitting. This well-built little town attracted cabinet makers and other artisans, strolling companies of actors, and a dancing school and assembly. It held two annual fairs at which cattle and all sorts of merchandise were sold; and, "for the Entertainment and Diversion of all Gentlemen and others, that shall resort thereto," prizes were offered for running and leaping races, horse-racing, catching the greased pig, and marksmanship.

William Byrd the second may be taken as a good example of the Virginia gentleman of this era. Born in 1674, he was sent to England to be educated. On returning to Virginia at the age of nineteen with pleasant manners and plenty of money, he was elected a burgess. Next year he fell heir to his father's property, married into another first family, pulled down the old house and store at Westover, and built the brick mansion which is still one of the show places on the James. By this time trading was considered ungentlemanly both in England and Virginia, so William Byrd sold his father's rum, slave, and drygoods business, and with the proceeds accumulated a library and more land. Byrd was a man of breadth, culture, and public spirit. His scientific tastes led to his election to the Royal Society of London and his appointment as surveyor-general to run the boundary line between Virginia and North Carolina. His account of this mission, *The History of the Dividing Line*, is one of the most delightful works in our colonial literature. He speculated successfully in land (always a socially reputable way to make money), but left to his son an estate not quite so valuable as the one inherited from his self-made father. His shorthand diaries, recently deciphered and published, are the records of day by day life of a Virginia gentleman at the turn of the century. They also show that he was a good scholar, reading a little Greek or Hebrew before breakfast, and doing daily calisthenics to keep himself fit.

Byrd died in 1744. The career of his son, who succeeded him in the council, damped the fame of the Byrds of Westover for over a century. William Byrd III squandered his father's property and, in order to escape the consequences, committed suicide. Westover and his father's library were sold, his sons emigrated to the upper Shenandoah valley, and the Byrd family was heard of no more until the twentieth century, when it emerged in the persons of the famous brothers Tom, Dick, and Harry: Tom, who established the apple industry in the Shenandoah; Rear Admiral Dick, the polar explorer; and Senator Harry, the gentlemanly boss of the Democratic party in Virginia.

Horse-racing, which had been practiced on short stretches for a century, the horses becoming smaller for want of new blood, received a stimulus after 1750 through the importation of colts of three famous Oriental stallions, the Godolphin Barb, the Darley Arabian, and the Byerly Turk, which had revolutionized horse breeding in England. These thoroughbreds had greater staying power than the popular quarter horses of the previous century. Selima, daughter of the Godolphin, beat all comers in the Maryland *vs.* Virginia four-mile races of 1751–52, and reigned queen of the colonial turf for years. Janus, the Godolphin's grandson, arrived in 1756 and remained at stud down to the Revolution. Fearnought, grandson both of Godolphin and the Darley Arabian, after winning six King's Plates at Newmarket, was imported in 1764 and covered mares at £10 a time —" £8 if the money comes with the mare." From these, and from Kitty Fisher, granddaughter of the Godolphin, almost every famous horse of the American turf is descended. Colonial Americans everywhere loved horse-racing, but the most intense interest was found in the Chesapeake colonies and in New York. George Washington, whose diary reveals frequent losses and few gains from betting on races, acted as steward of those at Alexandria in 1761.

White indentured servants continued to be imported, especially Germans, much sought after for their skill and industry. English seven-year convicts were not wanted but had to be accepted. Many of the servant class had as good blood as their masters. William Byrd complained, when on a journey, of having to take his daily dose of quinine in water, "by reason a light finger'd Damsel had ransacked my Baggage, and drunk up my Brandy. This unhappy Girl, it seems, is a Baronet's Daughter; but her Complexion, being red hair'd inclin'd her so much to Lewdness that her Father sent her . . . to seek her fortune on this side of the Globe."

In every colony south of Maryland, Negro slaves outnumbered white servants by 1720, and the proportion continued to increase. In 1715, for instance, there were 23,000 Negroes in Virginia out of a total population of 95,000; in 1756, 120,156 Negroes out of a total of 293,474; and in the tidewater counties they outnumbered the whites at least two to one. North Carolina had only 19,000 slaves out of a total population of 98,000 in 1756; but in South Carolina, where the bounty-fed production of indigo opened a new area to profitable slave labor, the disproportion was so great that the assembly required each planter to keep one white servant for every twenty-five Negroes, and laid a sliding scale of duties on slave importations. South Carolina suffered the severest slave insurrections of the century — the Cato conspiracy of 1739, in which some seventy-five of both races were killed, and one the following year for which 50 Negroes were hanged. Of Northern colonies, New York had the largest proportion of Negroes — 19,883 out of a total population of 207,890 in 1771. The slaves here gave even more trouble than they did in the South. New York City became victim of a panic in 1741 which, for cruelty and sheer terror, surpassed the Salem witch-hunt. After several fires broke out, a rumor, supported by forced confessions, created the belief that slaves were conspiring with poor whites to burn the city. After a series of hysterical trials, 101 Negroes and 4 whites were convicted of criminal arson, 13 Negroes were burned alive, and 18 Negroes and 4 white people were hanged.

Every New England colony contained Negroes; Massachusetts the most (5235 out of a total population of 224,185 in 1746), but Rhode Island had the largest proportion (3077 out of 31,516 in 1749). Newport was a center of the African slave trade. Although it is part of the Southern historical myth that most of the Negroes sold in the Southern colonies were brought in by "damyankees," New England ships actually held a small share of this infamous traffic.[1] The Royal African Company of London handled most of it,

1. The tables in Elizabeth Donnan, *Documents Illustrative of the History of the Slave Trade*, IV, 175–81, leave no doubt of this. For instance, of 146 ships bringing slaves into

but every English colonial port including New York, Philadelphia, Annapolis, Charleston, Baltimore, Barbados, and Kingston, Jamaica, participated to some extent. The principal articles to exchange for slaves in Africa were rum, salt codfish, and Spanish dollars; and there is on record the instruction of a Captain Simeon Potter of Rhode Island to one of his masters, "Worter your Rum as much as possible and sell as much by the short mesuer as you can."

4. *The Great Awakening in Religion*

During this era there were three parallel but rival movements in religion: aggressive missionary work by the Church of England, a quiet but pervasive growth of liberal Christianity, and the Great Awakening, an emotional revival of orthodox Calvinism.

The first may be said to have begun at Yale Commencement in 1722. The Rector, the Reverend Timothy Cutler, concluded the exercises with what would seem to us an innocent enough exhortation: — "Let all the people say, Amen!" But it sent a shudder through the audience, for this was recognized as a rubric of the Book of Common Prayer, and a rumor of the Rector's having become an Anglican convert was already circulating. Next day the board of trustees held a grim meeting. Rector Cutler, tutor Daniel Brown, and the Reverend Samuel Johnson, recently a tutor, confessed that they had been convinced by reading Anglican books (given by a Harvard man!) in the Yale Library, that Congregational ordination was invalid. This created as great a sensation in the colonies as if, today, a college president should endorse communism. The trustees gave the errant brethren a month to recant; they refused, and were dismissed. Cutler and Johnson promptly went to England, where they received Oxford degrees, obtained Anglican ordination, and were sent back to be ministers, respectively, of Christ Church, Boston, and Christ Church, Stratford, Connecticut. Backed by two well-endowed Anglican organizations, the Society for the Propagation of the Gospel and the Society for the Propagation of Christian Knowledge, they began a militant crusade for religious liberty for Anglicans in New England, for the growth of their faith, and for the appointment of one or more bishops in the English colonies. The founding of King's College (now Columbia University) in New York City in 1754 was partly a result of this drive.

In New England, the once raging fires of Puritanism were banked. People in general attended "meeting," listened to sermons or slept during them, kept holy (outwardly, at least) the Sabbath, and attempted to observe the other commandments; but they were falling away from the antique faith. Some

Virginia between 1710 and 1718, 65 belonged to England, Scotland, and Ireland, 39 to Maryland or Virginia, 20 to the British West Indies, 4 to Philadelphia, 4 to New York, 1 to South Carolina, and 13 to New England; and all cargoes of 100 or more slaves were in English vessels.

were simply going through the recognized motions of piety. Others were becoming what was vaguely called Arminian, believing that only good works and a free catholic spirit were necessary for salvation. This movement went quietly on, culminating in the Unitarianism of the nineteenth century.

To combat so "soft" an attitude there began in 1734 among New England Congregationalists and Middle-colony and Southern Presbyterians, a revival known as the Great Awakening. This was the first important religious revival in the English colonies; no later one spread so wide or went so deep. At a time when people generally, and in the Old West in particular, were falling away from the established churches, the Awakening descended like a whirlwind to sweep up lost souls. It stimulated a fresh interest in religion, caused hundreds of new churches to be founded, strengthened the movement for religious liberty, gave the common man a new sense of his significance, and thus indirectly contributed to the American Revolution. Most important, the Great Awakening brought it about that Christianity expanded with the frontier, and that the new independent American, like the old dependent colonist, inherited a strong Christian tradition.

The seeds of the Awakening were sown in 1734 when Jonathan Edwards began to preach revivalist sermons at Northampton, Massachusetts. This man, pure and simple in his life, was an original thinker in the realms of theology and philosophy. In another environment he might have acquired the fame of George Berkeley, whose idealistic philosophy he anticipated at the age of fifteen; or of John Locke, whose *Essay on Human Understanding* he read in his sophomore year at Yale, with far higher pleasure, he said, "than the most greedy miser finds when gathering up handfuls of silver and gold from some newly discovered treasure." Equally remarkable are his boyhood notes on the habits of the flying spider, praised for their accuracy by leading entomologists of today; and his account of his conversion at the age of seventeen, one of the most beautiful records of that Christian phenomenon since St. Augustine's. Edwards might have been a naturalist or a great literary figure, but he chose theology because he believed that an exploration of the relation between man and God was infinitely more important. He would have considered our modern efforts to explore outer space as of minor importance, since their objects are merely to extend human knowledge. He looked beyond all stellar systems and galaxies, to save men's souls for eternal life.

Edwards rocked the Connecticut valley with a series of sermons that set people reading, discussing, and meditating the fundamental truths of Christianity. He recorded this revival in a pamphlet called *A Faithful Narrative of the Surprising Work of God in the Conversion of Many Hundred Souls in Northampton* (1736), which made an immense stir in the Protestant world. Edition followed edition at Boston, London, and Edinburgh. Within a year a German translation had been printed, within two years a Dutch one, and it became the classic of revivalism. The Reverend George Whitefield in far-off Savannah, Georgia, read the *Faithful Narrative* and began his amazing career as a revivalist. John Wesley read it on foot, walking from London to Oxford. "Surely, this is the Lord's doing," he wrote in his journal, "and marvelous in our eyes." Presently Wesley began to obtain the same effects with his preaching, and in a little while the Methodist Church was born. Edward's preaching at Northampton was the womb of all modern revivalism in the Protestant churches of the English-speaking world.

Whitefield preached a revival at Philadelphia (which made even skeptical Ben Franklin empty his pockets into the plate) and then made a New England crusade of 75 days, during which he rode 800 miles and preached 175 sermons. He was the first great preacher to travel widely in the colonies. His voice, unaided by amplifying devices, could carry in the open air to 20,000 people. He made violent gestures, danced about the pulpit, roared and ranted, to the huge delight of the yokels who were tired of gentlemanly, highbrow ministers from Harvard and Yale. He introduced the second stage of revivalism, in which congregations, mad with religious ecstasy, shrieked, rolled on the floor, ran amok. College exercises at Yale had to be suspended while the students held prayer meetings and compared the state of their souls. Freshmen even tried to convert their landladies!

Throughout New England and in the Middle colonies there was turmoil. Many ministers of the established churches embraced the Awakening and preached revival sermons. The majority, however, repudiated it as a vulgar travesty on religion. If they did, their congregations were apt to secede and set up "New Light" churches, many of which eventually became Baptist or Methodist. The revival probably improved people's morals and reduced the crime rate, at least temporarily. It checked the decline of Puritanism into that vague liberalism into which many sons of the Puritans have descended. It gave the common man a new interest in religion; it gave birth to three new colleges — Dartmouth, Princeton, and Brown. On the other hand, the excesses of the Great Awakening were similar to a protracted alcoholic jag. They gave the addict a thirst for more. Periodic outbursts rather than continuity, enthusiasm rather than serenity came to distinguish popular religion in Protestant America.

This Awakening was of absorbing interest to English dissenters, who kindled a backfire against the Church of England missionaries' request for a bishop. Nobody else, not even the Anglican laymen, wanted an American bishop; they feared danger to religious liberty and to lay control of the churches. Virulent pamphlets set up the Anglican bishop, in lawn sleeves, cope, and mitre, as the colonial bogyman of the 1740's, just as George III became in 1776. England decided to let that particular sleeping dog lie, which was well for imperial unity.

The backwash of reaction from the Great Awakening swept Jonathan Edwards from the pleasant village of his ministry. He had offended influential citizens by denouncing the "frolics" of their young people — which amounted to nothing worse than sleigh rides to a neighboring town to indulge in country square dances and rum-and-water. With his wife and eight children Edwards removed to the frontier settlement of Stockbridge in the Berkshire Hills, to be missionary to a small Indian reservation. There he found leisure to write *The Nature of True Virtue*, *Original Sin*, and *Freedom of the Will* which, together with his earlier treatise *The Religious Affections*, gave Calvinism a new lease on life. For they proved, at least to the satisfaction of people with a Puritan background, that man with no will of his own was yet perfectly free to choose a fate predetermined before he was born.

In 1757 the College of New Jersey, which had moved from Newark to Princeton and (as a result of the Awakening and a successful drive for funds) erected Nassau Hall, called Jonathan Edwards to be president. Immediately after he had been inducted into office, a smallpox epidemic broke out in the village; and within a few days New England's saint breathed his last.

Edwards's brand of revived Calvinist theology, carried forward by disciples such as the Reverend Stephen Hopkins, ran its course. The Andover Theological Seminary, formed to perpetuate it, closed its doors early in this century, and only the Evangelicals keep some measure of it alive today. But the works of Jonathan Edwards, after long neglect, are now reprinted; and today, whatever one's belief, one owes a respectful glance to that faith which made God everything and man nothing, which plunged some men into despair but to many gave fortitude to face life bravely; and, to a chosen few, the supreme joy that comes from union with the Eternal Spirit, and the supreme beauty that is the beauty of holiness.

AM I A SOLDIER OF THE CROSS?

Thy saints in all this glo - rious war, Shall con - quer, though they die; They view the tri - umph from a - far, And seize it with their eye.

Wars on the Spaniards and the French

1733-1763

1. Georgia and War in the South

THE FOUNDATION OF GEORGIA in 1733 led to a war between England and Spain. This merged into a war with France of vital concern to the Northern colonies, and that in turn led to the foundation of the fourteenth English continental colony, Nova Scotia.

By 1730, when Louisiana had become well established, the British government, realizing its mistake in not supporting South Carolina in Queen Anne's War, promoted a new colony on the border between Carolina and Florida. Imperial ambitions were implemented by philanthropy, and the person who combined them was General James Charles Oglethorpe. A gentleman of rank and fortune who had fought the Turks in the previous war, he had since, as a member of Parliament, interested himself in the lot of the poor and unfortunate. In particular he wished to help poor debtors, who under the harsh laws of that period were confined indefinitely in jail, and to give them a fresh start in the New World. In association with other English philanthropists, and members of Parliament interested in expansion, he obtained in 1730 a charter for the Trustees of Georgia. They were made proprietors of all the land between the Savannah and Altamaha rivers, and from sea to sea.

The Trustees of Georgia, prominent in politics and business, financed the biggest publicity campaign from which any English colony ever benefited. Flattering write-ups of the healthy climate and fertile soil were paid for in London newspapers; money was raised by popular subscription, and grants were voted by Parliament. In 1733 Oglethorpe himself, as governor, founded Savannah. He brought out in ship *Ann* the first load of 114 settlers, twenty-nine of whom died within a year. A group of Germans from Salzburg were settled up the Savannah river at a place to which they gave the biblical name Ebenezer, and members of several Scots Highland clans founded Frederica on the Altamaha.[1] Oglethorpe himself determined the sites of settlements, with a view to defense against Indians and Spaniards.

1. Down to the end of September 1741, the Trustees sent over 1810 charity colonists, of whom 45 per cent were foreign Protestants (Germans, Swiss, Scots, and 2 Italians), and the rest English. The number of those rescued from jail is not known, but the prevalence of crime in the colony suggests that it was large. More than a hundred different occupa-

Georgia did not prosper under the benevolent despotism of Oglethorpe and the Trustees, owing largely to their prohibition of Negro slavery and of hard liquor. They granted 50 acres of land free to each charity settler, which he was forbidden to sell; but this was not enough for a subsistence farm, and the climate was such that Englishmen insisted they could accomplish nothing without rum and slaves. The example of fortunes made in South Carolina by raising rice and indigo with slave labor caused many of the more energetic Georgians to move thither, even at the cost of their land being confiscated. Although the Trustees repealed the antislavery law in 1750, allowed prohibition to lapse, and granted Georgia a legislative assembly, the settlement made slow progress. In 1752, when Georgia had only 1735 white and 349 Negro inhabitants, the Trustees were glad to turn it over to the crown as a royal province, like the Carolinas.

Already "the extirpation of the English from the new colony of Georgia which they have usurped" had become a Spanish objective. But the Indian nations of the Gulf region, as well as the Cherokee of the uplands, had become alienated from Spain and were successfully wooed by Governor Oglethorpe. In 1738–39 they ceded to Georgia most of their coastal lands and offered to join her in a campaign to wipe out the Spanish posts in Florida.

At this point England declared war on Spain for other reasons. The English South Sea Company, a slave-trading organization recognized by Spain in 1713, had abused its treaty privilege of sending one slave ship annually to Porto Bello. It sent a whole fleet, whose cargoes were so eagerly purchased by the Creoles that Spanish trade suffered. Retaliation followed by Spanish revenue cutters, one of whose skippers cropped the ears of an English smuggler named Edward Jenkins. At a favorable moment, when English traders were urging a renewal of aggressive war against Spain, earless Jenkins was exhibited in the House of Commons; and the war, popularly called "The War of Jenkins' Ear," was declared in October 1739.

Spain began hostilities by forcibly occupying a fort which Oglethorpe had built on Amelia Island at the mouth of the St. Mary river. The General retaliated promptly. With 200 men from his own Highland regiment, 125 South Carolinians, several hundred Indian allies, and a small supporting fleet, he captured two Spanish forts at the mouth of the St. John river and boldly advanced on St. Augustine. That ancient presidio, with a population of several thousand and a strong garrison under the command of Don Manuel de Montiano, was so well defended that Oglethorpe retired in June 1740, after a siege of 38 days and one small battle. He blamed the South Carolinians, and they blamed him.

In the meantime, England had sent a fleet under Vice Admiral Edward Vernon to capture and sack Porto Bello, which was done with ease (Novem-

tions were represented, indicating that the Trustees planned a semi-industrial society. In the same period, 1021 persons came to Georgia at their own expense; and of these, 92 were Jews.

ber 1739), and another fleet around Cape Horn under Commodore George Anson to put a pincer on the Isthmus of Panama from the Pacific side. Anson's fleet, scattered by storms and decimated by scurvy, failed to make the rendezvous and returned home around the world, after capturing the Manila treasure galleon and taking temporary possession of Tinian in the Spanish Marianas. Without Anson's support, Admiral Vernon was unable to hold Porto Bello and returned to England. There he was greeted as a hero and given command of a more formidable expedition to overwhelm Cuba and the Spanish Main.

In this enterprise the English colonies from South Carolina to New Hampshire joined with enthusiasm, furnishing about 3000 volunteers under their own officers, in addition to a force of regulars provided by England. All that took time, and the expedition did not leave Jamaica until January 1741. Vernon decided to make his first objective Cartagena, on the coast of New Granada, now the Republic of Colombia. The Spaniards had made Cartagena the strongest place in South America. Vernon managed to break into the great harbor, but his assault on the castle was thrown for a loss by the Spaniards. While the warships and transports, anchored in the bay, awaited another chance to attack, yellow fever gripped the fleet, and of the 3000 colonial troops barely 1300 returned home.

Three curiously unrelated things came out of this fiasco. Among the Virginian officers who survived was George Washington's half-brother, Captain Lawrence Washington, who named his new estate on the Potomac "Mount Vernon" after the popular English admiral. Vernon's nickname "Old Grog," was applied to the mixture of rum and water which he ordered to be issued instead of the former ration of raw rum which was rapidly knocking the sailors out. And in the course of this expedition the colonial troops for the first time were called "Americans" instead of "provincials" by the English, and referred to themselves as such.

Disaster before Cartagena prevented Oglethorpe from making another attempt on Florida and gave Spain an opportunity to retaliate. A formidable expedition of 30 ships carrying 1300 soldiers sailed from Havana in May 1742 and, after picking up more men at St. Augustine, landed on St. Simon's Island and captured the fort. General Oglethorpe, having deployed his regiment and obtained several hundred Creek warriors, fell back on Frederica, ambushed an advancing column of Spaniards at the Bloody Marsh (7 July), and threw them back in disorder. That was the nearest the Spaniards came to "laying waste South Carolina and her dependencies," as Philip V of Spain had ordered them to do. Oglethorpe now returned to England but continued his interest in Georgia, which rightly regards him as a colonial founder in a class with Calvert, Winthrop, Penn, and Shaftesbury.

This war ended in 1748 without any settlement of the disputed southern boundary. But it was no longer possible for the English colonies to squeeze out Louisiana. That French colony was there to stay, a southern anchor to the chain that the French government would endeavor to stretch from Cape Breton up the St. Lawrence to the Great Lakes, and down the Mississippi to the Gulf of Mexico.

2. Canada and War in the North

It is not surprising that the French attempted an encirclement, or that the British endeavored to check it. The strategic position of France in North America had been greatly weakened by the Treaty of Utrecht, and loss of Newfoundland, Nova Scotia, and Hudson Bay. Her strength relative to the English colonies dwindled yearly. The population of Canada, 18,119 in 1713, did indeed double by 1734, but by that time the population of the English colonies north of the Carolinas had passed the half-million mark. And, starting with the Spotswood transmontane expedition of 1718, English America was expanding westward and threatening French communications between Canada and Louisiana.

Canada, weakened and impoverished by Queen Anne's War, needed manpower above all things, to hold firm against the English. But, at a time when the English colonies were attracting thousands of sturdy Germans, French Protestants, Scots and Irish farmers and artisans, the government of Louis XV allowed a mere trickle of emigrants to go to Canada, and not of the best sort at that — young libertines of whom their families wished to be rid, smugglers, poachers, and other petty criminals. The government authorized the introduction of Negro slaves, but few Canadians could afford to buy them. Even the fur trade, the one profitable business in New France, was partly strangled by the king's granting a twenty-five-year monopoly in 1717 to a private company. The export of forest products to France was fairly success-ful, but efforts to establish a profitable trade with the West Indies were defeated by the superior know-how of New Englanders. Poverty was the lot of most seigneurs, and the superior attraction of becoming coureur de bois continued to drain off their habitants. The bishops and the Jesuits contin-ued their secular feud with the governors and other officials. In one matter, however, Canada was definitely superior to the English colonies. She had a well-trained militia, partly paid by the crown.

French Canadian strategy during the thirty years after 1713 was defensive from their point of view, provocative from the English, and ultimately disas-trous. France spent about $6 million in gold building the "impregnable" fortress of Louisbourg on Cape Breton Island, which menaced the New Eng-land fisheries but proved useless in wartime because the relatively weak French navy could not maintain communications with it, or with Canada. On the eastern flank a series of clerical and lay emissaries kept the Acadians of Nova Scotia, and the Micmac Indians, loyal to France and expecting recon-quest, a policy which ended in deportation. In Maine, Canada incited the Abnaki to resist New Englanders who were resettling land whence they had been expelled during the last war, a policy which resulted in their missionary leader, Father Sebastian Rasle, being killed, gun in hand, and his fortified Indian town of Norridgewock, on the site of Madison, Maine, being destroyed.

In the west the French were enterprising and successful. They built a fort at Crown Point on Lake Champlain, Fort Niagara near the falls, and two forts on the Wabash. And they almost exterminated the Fox or Outagamie tribe of Wisconsin, which had threatened Detroit. Pierre de la Vérendrye, in a series of Western explorations between 1731 and 1744, built forts on the Lake of the Woods and on the site of Winnipeg, and marched into the Dakotas, Montana, and Saskatchewan.

But the fate of France in North America would not be settled there. Canada's roots were in the Atlantic, the St. Lawrence was her trunk, the Great Lakes her branches, and the Western forts mere twigs. Britain well knew that if the roots were grappled by her navy, and the trunk severed at Quebec or Montreal, French Canada could not survive.

In 1744 the War of Jenkins' Ear with Spain merged into the War of the Austrian Succession (called King George's War in America), in which England and Austria were allies against France and Prussia. Governor William Shirley and Massachusetts Bay now became aggressors on the northern frontier, as Governor Oglethorpe and South Carolina had been on the southern. Shirley, a local lawyer, had been appointed governor of Massachusetts Bay in the hope that he could settle the long-standing quarrel between the king's representative and the assembly. This he did so adroitly as to calm every faction, to receive an annual salary of £1000, and to be allowed by the assembly to run a war without their interference.

Shirley conceived and carried out the siege and capture of Louisbourg by New England militia led by William Pepperell, a merchant of Kittery, Maine, and the Royal Navy supported him with a blockading squadron under Admiral Sir Peter Warren. Pepperell's army on 30 April 1745 made a successful amphibious landing a few miles from Louisbourg, established a beachhead out of reach of the 150-gunned French fortress, and conducted the campaign in a spirit of rustic frolic, defying both military discipline and principles of strategy. The troops captured an outlying battery from the rear, dragged artillery through supposedly impassable swamps, chased French cannonballs to shoot them back from their own guns, and went fishing when they felt like it. But Pepperell knew how to handle Yankee country folk, and the net effect of their pluck and enterprise was so to discourage and confuse the French commander of Louisbourg that on 16 June he surrendered both town and fortress.

The French and their Indian allies now launched retaliatory attacks on New England frontier villages and Saratoga, New York, and the Iroquois raided Canada. In 1746 France sent a fleet of almost 100 ships under the Duc d'Anville, to reconquer Louisbourg and burn Boston. It eluded the British fleet sent to intercept, but was so battered by storms and decimated by scurvy during the three months' ocean passage that it returned to France minus 3000 soldiers and sailors, including the Admiral, and without firing a shot. The "Bastonnais" regarded this a direct answer to prayer.

Diplomacy, however, lost what valor and good luck had won. In the swapping of conquests that took place at the Treaty of Aix-la-Chapelle (1748), which concluded this war with France and Spain, England returned Louisbourg to France.

Although the mainland of Nova Scotia had been under British sovereignty since 1713, the only white inhabitants were several thousand French Acadians, mostly living on the Bay of Fundy. Toward them the British acted with exemplary liberalism. No attempt was made to interfere with their language, religion, or local self-government; but they firmly declined to admit British sovereignty, and during King George's War were actively hostile or sullenly neutral. This situation could not continue after the peace, when the British government began to people the hitherto unsettled shores of Nova Scotia. In the spring of 1749 some 1400 colonists from England, mostly objects of charity like those of Georgia, were sent out under an energetic governor, Edward Cornwallis. He founded Halifax, but the hostile attitude of the French Acadians and Micmac Indians long prevented any English settlement outside Halifax and Annapolis Royal. Before the next war broke out, the British authorities, supported by Governor Shirley, decided to deport all French who lived near strategic centers. They could not suffer this hostile minority to remain on an exposed flank.

The rights and wrongs of this policy have remained a subject of bitter controversy between French Canadian and English historians to this day. The real culprit was the French government, which sent secret agents to encourage the Acadians in the belief that France would return in might to reconquer L'Acadie. It was a situation similar to Hitler's fomenting rebellion among the Sudeten Germans in Czechoslovakia in 1938, and had equally tragic results — a wholesale deportation and a refugee problem. The Acadian deportation was carried out with unnecessary hardship. Families and neighbors were separated, as Longfellow described in *Evangeline*, which is based on a real episode that he heard from descendants of refugees. Many were quartered on towns and villages in the English colonies, where they were regarded as a potential fifth column; a few went back to France; many, after the end of the war, returned to Nova Scotia but not to their own farms, which had been confiscated and given to English settlers. The happiest were those who, like Evangeline, were sent to French Louisiana, where their descendants retained their language and to this day are known as "Cajuns."

Between 6000 and 7250 Acadians were deported, and many more escaped through the woods or by sea to Canada. It is not a pretty story; but to assert, as most French Canadian historians do, that it was completely inexcusable and the first wholesale deportation in history, is to ignore the provocation, the Old Testament, and the expulsion of some 400,000 Protestants from France after the revocation of the Edict of Nantes. Recent events in Algeria, Cyprus, Palestine, and other parts of the world indicate that it is almost impossible for two utterly different racial, religious, and language groups to live peaceably in the same region, if one or the other is encouraged and stimulated by an outside power.

3. Cold War Maneuvering, 1747–1755

It may now be said, with the privilege of hindsight, that the vital stake in all wars and diplomatic maneuverings since 1700 was the American West. Who was to rule the West — England, France, or Spain? Or, as nobody could then foresee, an American republic? Yet, until well after mid-century, the West was the last thing that politicians, whether English, French, or American, thought about. From the European point of view the principal objectives were the sugar islands in the Caribbean; that is why the major naval efforts of England and France were applied in that region. New England and New York were chiefly interested in the destruction of French power on their northern and eastern boundaries. For South Carolina and Georgia, the Spaniard in Florida and his Indian allies were the greater menace. But it was in the West that a new war began, even before the previous war ended.

In 1747 Thomas Lee, president of the Virginia Council, organized the Ohio Company, with the object of acquiring half a million acres on each side of the Ohio river. Other prominent Virginians, such as Thomas Jefferson's father, organized additional land companies and employed veteran Indian traders to push trade with the Indians in the Ohio country and to extinguish their prior claims to the land. This was a threat to French communications between Montreal and New Orleans that could not be ignored. In 1749 the governor of Canada sent a fleet of batteaux and canoes, commanded by Celeron de Bienville, to take possession of the Ohio valley.

A cold war for winning the West was on, and gradually it warmed up. In 1753 Governor Duquesne built a chain of log-walled forts on the Allegheny and the upper Ohio to defend French claims. Virginia could not ignore this challenge. The French pretention to reserve the entire West north of the Ohio ran counter to her charter boundaries, and to the claims of the new land companies. Governor Robert Dinwiddie sent young George Washington to the forks of the Ohio to protest. Protest being unavailing, Dinwiddie commissioned George (aged twenty-two) lieutenant colonal of Virginia militia and in 1754 sent him with 150 men to forestall the French. But the Canadians got there first, built Fort Duquesne on the site of Pittsburgh, and at Great Meadows in western Pennsylvania confronted the Virginia militia. Washington fired first, but lost the fight and had to surrender. This being nominally a time of peace, the prisoners were released and a somewhat crestfallen George was allowed to go home.

That shot in the Western wilderness sparked off a series of world-shaking events which reached their culmination thirty years later. In 1783 Major General George Washington, Commander in Chief of the United States Army, resigned his commission after winning independence for a republic not even dreamed of in 1753.

Virginia and New England were ready for hot war in 1754, but England and France were not. The Duke of Newcastle, the prime minister, fancied that he could maintain England's western claims by a local war. In the fall of 1754 he sent General Braddock to America with parts of two regiments to do the job.

In the meantime eight of the thirteen colonies had made an attempt to agree on a plan of union for common defense. The Board of Trade instructed the royal governors to meet representatives of the Six Nations at Albany and take measures "to secure their wavering friendship"; the Iroquois, impressed by the Great Meadows affair, were wondering which side to take. Leading Americans, however, wished the congress to undertake a more ambitious task. Before it met, Governor Shirley thus addressed the assembly of Massachusetts: "For forming this general union, gentlemen, there is no time to be lost: the French seem to have advanced further toward making themselves masters of this Continent within the past five or six years than they have done ever since the first beginning of that settlement."

The Albany Congress, meeting in June 1754, spent most of its time debating that question. The Plan of Union that it adopted was the work of Benjamin Franklin and Thomas Hutchinson. There was to be a president general appointed by the crown, and a "grand council" appointed by the colonial assemblies, in proportion to their contributions to the common war chest — a typical bit of Ben Franklin foxiness, to ensure that taxes would really be paid. The president, with the advice of the grand council, would have sole power to negotiate treaties, declare war, and make peace with the Indians; to regulate the Indian trade, to have sole jurisdiction over land purchases outside particular colonies, and to make grants of land to settlers and govern the Western territory until the crown formed it into new colonial governments. The Union would have power to build forts, raise armies and equip fleets, and levy taxes for the same, to be paid into a general treasury with branches in each colony.

This plan showed far-sighted statesmanship, but looked too far ahead, recommending a closer federal union than the thirteen colonies were willing to conclude during the War of Independence. Whether the British government would have consented is doubtful; but they never had a chance to express their views. Not one colonial assembly ratified the Plan. Every one refused to give up any part of its exclusive taxing power, even to a representative body. So the war which then began was carried through under the old system. No British commander had authority to raise troops or money from a colony without the consent of its assembly. The assemblies of provinces that were not directly menaced, and some of those that were, like Pennsylvania, refused to make any substantial contribution to the common cause. Even Virginia would not allow draftees to serve outside her borders until 1758.

English and Americans always seem to begin a war that they eventually win, with a bad thrashing. This time it was Braddock's defeat on the Monongahela, a bloody battle in that part of the Western wilderness which is now a suburb of Pittsburgh. The English ministry's strategic plan was sound: to capture four forts which the French had built on debatable territory and secure them before the hot war started. These forts, from east to west, were Beauséjour at the head of the Bay of Fundy, Crown Point on Lake Champlain, Fort Niagara at the falls, and Fort Duquesne. This last, the key to the West, was the objective of Major General Edward Braddock, forty-five of whose sixty years had been spent in the British army in Europe. He was given two of the worst regiments in that army, at half strength, which he was expected to fill with American recruits to a total of 700 officers and men each. The colonies were expected to provide additional troops, food, wagons, and Indian auxiliaries for a march from Alexandria, Virginia, across the Blue Ridge and the Alleghenies, and through a yet unbroken wilderness, to take Fort Duquesne.

Governors Dinwiddie of Virginia, Sharpe of Maryland, and Shirley of Massachusetts, enthusiasts for expelling the French from North America, met Braddock at Alexandria to make plans. Young George Washington became one of the General's aides-de-camp. So many things in this campaign went wrong that it is impossible to pin the blame on any one person; but Braddock made the most mistakes. Although a brave and energetic soldier, he knew nothing of wilderness marches or battles, and refused to learn from the Virginians. Instead of depending on pack animals for supply, he insisted on a great wagon train; and the only colony which provided its quota of wagons was Pennsylvania. Ben Franklin's diplomacy was responsible. He dropped the hint that if the farmers did not hire out their teams voluntarily, British "hussars" would come and take them; hussars were the storm troopers of that era. He procured some 150 Conestoga wagons, which Braddock said was "almost the only instance of ability and honesty" that he had "known in these provinces."

It took Braddock's army 32 days to cover the 110 miles from Fort Cumberland to Fort Duquesne through a trackless hardwood forest. A pioneer battalion of 300 axemen had to cut a crude road. By 7 July the van was only 10 or 12 miles from its destination. Braddock formed a "flying column" of his best troops, including both regulars and provincials, and pressed on ahead. To avoid a narrow defile, he twice forded the Monongahela river. George Washington, late in life, said that it was the most beautiful spectacle he had ever seen. Scarlet-coated regulars and blue-coated Virginians in columns of four, mounted officers and light cavalry, horse-drawn artillery and wagons, and dozens of packhorses, splashed through the rippling shallows under a brilliant summer sun into the green-clothed forest. Spirits were high and victory seemed certain; if the French did not attack at the fords, they surely never would. Rush the fort, and hurrah for old England!

But hark! What is that firing ahead, just as the last of the rear guard crosses the river?

It was a sortie from Fort Duquesne in head-on collision with Braddock's van, an engagement that neither side planned or wanted. The small French garrison at the fort had been strengthened by almost 1000 Indian warriors, who had flocked in from every part of the Old West. With the choosiness common to Indians they had refused to move the day before to ambush Braddock at the ford; but now, when the British column was safely across, they consented to go. No fewer than 637 braves, with about 150 French Canadian militia, led by 72 French officers and regulars, sortied in the early afternoon of 9 July.

Braddock had flankers out; he was not ambushed, only surprised. The head of his column saw a young French officer stop, turn, and wave his hat; immediately the English heard the Indians' war whoop, as the redskins deployed to right and left, took cover in the ravines that paralleled the road, and poured hot lead into the close ranks of scarlet and blue coats — the best targets they had ever encountered. The British troops could not see their deadly foes, but they could hear them plenty; and, never having fought Indians, were unnerved by the horrible war whoops. General Braddock, losing one horse after another, rushed about trying to rally his men; it was no use. His senior colonel and many other officers were killed, and he himself was shot in the lungs. Toward sundown, after the largely unseen Indians had mowed down scores of the huddled and almost leaderless redcoats, panic set in. The soldiers "broke and ran as sheep pursued by dogs" (so Washington recorded), abandoning wagons, artillery, and even muskets. Fortunately, the Indians were too busy scalping, looting, and torturing prisoners to pursue, or the entire flying column would have been massacred; as it was, of the 1459 officers and men engaged, 977 were killed or wounded.

Braddock died of his wounds after turning over the command to Colonel Dunbar, who made bad matters worse by abandoning Fort Cumberland and going into winter quarters at Philadelphia when the summer was but half over, leaving the Pennsylvania-Maryland-Virginia frontier completely defenseless.

4. The Seven Years' War, 1755–1763

Braddock's defeat was the Pearl Harbor of the Seven Years' War. It brought over all Indians of the Northwest to the French side, caused the Six Nations to waver in their allegiance, threw back the effective English frontier hundreds of miles, and exposed new settlements to a series of devastating Indian attacks. Thousands of men, women, and children who had settled the Shenandoah valley in the last forty years lost all they had, and were lucky to escape with their lives.

British operations of 1755 were inept though not disastrous. Governor Shirley failed to take Fort Niagara. General William Johnson "of the Mohawks," an able Irishman who acted as liaison between the English and the Iroquois, defeated the French at Lake George on 8 September and was made a baronet; but he was unable to capture Crown Point on Lake Champlain, and the French built Fort Ticonderoga south of it. Fort Beauséjour at the head of the Bay of Fundy surrendered to Colonel John Winslow of Massachusetts after two shells from the escorting British fleet had blown up an ammunition dump, and this secured the eastern flank.

In 1756 this "Old French and Indian War," as the Americans called it, merged into the Seven Years' War in Europe, where it was France, Austria, Sweden, and a few small German states against Britain and Prussia. England supported Prussia with money and engaged in naval warfare against France (and later Spain) in the Atlantic, the Mediterranean, the Caribbean, and the Indian Ocean. There was warfare on the continent of India between French under Dupleix and English under Clive and their respective native allies; hostilities even reached the Philippines, where an English fleet captured Manila. This should really have been called the First World War; hostilities were waged over as large a portion of the globe as in 1914–18.

The next two years were disastrous for England. The Earl of Loudoun, who succeeded Shirley as British commander in chief in America, was well described by his predecessor as "a pen and ink man whose greatest energies were put forth in getting ready to begin." Virginian militia under Colonel Washington with great difficulty held the Shenandoah valley against the Indians. Canada, reinforced by 3000 French regulars, took the offensive and the Marquis de Montcalm captured Fort Oswego on Lake Ontario and Fort William Henry on Lake George. In India, Clive lost Calcutta. On the continent of Europe, England's ally Frederick the Great was defeated by the French and Austrians; and the British commander in chief, the Duke of Cumberland, surrendered an army to the French.

How things looked to a colonial philospher, the Reverend Jonathan Edwards, may be seen in a letter that he wrote in the fall of 1756 to a friend who was chaplain to a Massachusetts regiment on Lake George:

God indeed is remarkably frowning upon us every where; our enemies get up above us very high, and we are brought down very low: They are the Head, and we are the Tail. God is making us, with all our superiority in numbers, to become the Object of our Enemies almost continual Triumphs and Insults. . . . And in Europe things don't go much better, . . . Minorca was surrendered to the French on the 29 Day of last June; principally through the wretched Cowardice or Treachery of Admiral Byng.[1] This with the taking of Oswego . . . will tend mightily to animate and encourage the French Nation . . . and weaken and dishearten the English, and make 'em contemptible in the Eyes of the Nations of Europe. . . . What will become of us God only knows.

1. Byng was court-martialed and shot for this, giving rise to Voltaire's quip that the British "kill an admiral from time to time to encourage the others."

Yet the entire aspect of the war changed in 1758 after William Pitt became secretary of state and prime minister. This Winston Churchill of the eighteenth century had a flair for grand strategy and a genius for choosing able men. While most Englishmen regarded the American war as secondary, Pitt saw that the principal object for England should be the conquest of Canada and the American West, thus carving out a new field for Anglo-American expansion. His strategy was simple and direct. He would send no more English troops to the continent of Europe, but subsidized Frederick to fight the French there. To the British navy he gave a triple task: to contain the French fleet in its home bases, escort convoys over the transatlantic route, and cooperate with the army in amphibious operations. And he concentrated the military might of Britain and her colonies in the American theater, under young and energetic commanders. The naval part was crucial. Canada, with a population under 60,000, could not hold out against the English colonies with a population of one million, unless the French could get reinforcements across the Atlantic.

At the Battle of Dettingen, 1743, four young English officers — Jeffrey Amherst, George Townshend, Robert Moncton, and James Wolfe had received their baptism of fire. Now the eldest was only forty-one years old and the youngest, Wolfe, was thirty-one. He was a lanky, narrow-shouldered young man with vivid red hair, the most earnest student of the art of war in the British army. In ambition, genius, and audacity, and in his fierce concentration on making himself master of his profession, Wolfe was the most Napoleonic soldier in English history. "An offensive, daring kind of war," he wrote, "will awe the Indians and ruin the French. Block-houses and a trembling defensive encourage the meanest scoundrels to attack us."

Such was his advice to Jeffrey Amherst, whom Pitt selected as commander in chief in America. Stolid and unemotional, Amherst had the right character to neutralize the impetuosity of Wolfe, his No. 1 brigadier general. These two, making a perfect team with Admiral Boscawen, in July 1758 recaptured Louisbourg, far better fortified than in 1745 and more skillfully defended. The same year, Colonel John Bradstreet, with a force of New Englanders, captured Fort Frontenac, where the St. Lawrence flows out of Lake Ontario; and Brigadier John Forbes, with George Washington on his staff, marched across Pennsylvania and captured Fort Duquesne, renaming it Pittsburgh after the great war minister.

Then came 1759, England's "wonderful year," so charged with British glory that it was said the very bells of London were worn thin pealing for victories, and British throats went hoarse bawling out "Heart of Oak." Guadeloupe in the West Indies fell to a well-conducted amphibious operation. The French power in India was destroyed, and the French fleet intended to reinforce Canada was smashed by Hawke at Quiberon Bay. Sir William Johnson and his Iroquois braves helped the British to capture Fort Niagara, key to the Great Lakes. And the campaign of Quebec surpassed all.

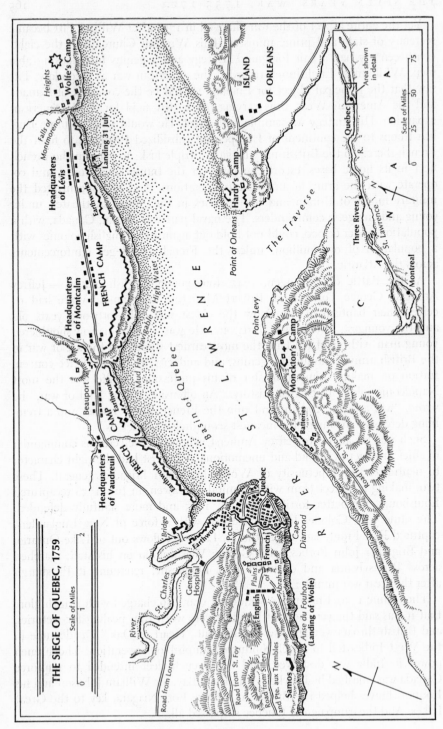

THE SIEGE OF QUEBEC, 1759

Scale of Miles
0   1   2

N

River St. Charles

Road from Lorette

Road from St. Foy

Road from Sillery
and Pte. aux Trembles

Samos

Anse du Foulon
(Landing of Wolfe)

English

Plains of Abraham

General Hospital

Bridge

Earthworks

St. Roch

French

Quebec

Cape Diamond

Boom

Earthworks

FRENCH CAMP

Headquarters of Vaudreuil

Beauport

Earthworks

Headquarters of Montcalm

FRENCH CAMP

Headquarters of Lévis

Earthworks

Landing 31 July

Falls of Montmorency

Heights

Wolfe's Camp

Mud Flats Navigable at High Water

Basin of Quebec

ST. LAWRENCE RIVER

Point Levy

Batteries

Monckton's Camp

Road from St. Nicolas

Point of Orleans

Hardy's Camp

The Traverse

ISLAND OF ORLEANS

Area shown in detail

Quebec

Three Rivers

St. Lawrence R.

Montreal

C A N A D A

N

Scale of Miles
0   25   50   75

166

The British army under Wolfe was transported by a fleet of over 200 sail, commanded by Vice Admiral Charles Saunders. Entering the St. Lawrence on 6 June, Saunders appointed Captain James Cook (of later Pacific fame) to sail ahead, take soundings, and buoy a channel through the Travers, the narrow, tortuous channel between Île d'Orléans and the south shore; and then performed the amazing feat of sailing his entire fleet up to Quebec in three weeks, without a single grounding or other casualty.

General Amherst, marching overland from New York, was supposed to co-operate. He recaptured Crown Point and Ticonderoga but was too slow and methodical to get within striking distance of Quebec. Thrice in previous wars this failure in co-ordination had saved Quebec for France, and in 1775-76 and 1812-13 similar American failures kept it British. But Wolfe was not discouraged. His total force, exclusive of sailors and marines, amounted to only 4000 officers and men, but included some of the crack units of the British army. Owing to Amherst's delay, the Marquis de Montcalm was able to concentrate some 14,000 French troops and militia in and around Quebec. His position appeared to be impregnable. The guns of the citadel commanded the river, and the land approach from the east was barred by two smaller rivers.

Admiral Saunders first landed a force on 27 June on the Île d'Orléans, four miles below Quebec. Montcalm's army was deployed along the north shore of the river, between the St. Charles and the Montmorency, with a detachment under Bougainville west of the city; but he neglected to secure the south bank. Wolfe's first bold stroke was to take advantage of this weakness and seize Point Levi, 1000 yards across the river from Quebec, whence his guns were able to bombard the lower town. At the same time he landed the better part of two brigades on the north shore, just below the Montmorency falls, to fox Montcalm (9 July). Ten days later, one of the frigates and several smaller vessels, slipping past the guns of Quebec under cover of a heavy bombardment from Point Levi, sailed over twenty miles upstream to confuse Montcalm and provide Wolfe with alternate points of attack. The British, owing to their command of the river, were now able to select time and place for their assault.

Wolfe first probed the Montmorency front but failed to make any impression there. He then quietly reinforced the up-river part of his force with men and ships, sailing them upstream and downstream with the wind and tide, forcing Bougainville's soldiers to march and countermarch to the point of exhaustion. His scouts spied out a narrow defile that led up the cliffs on the river's north bank to the Plains of Abraham. Montcalm, thinking this route to be inaccessible, had here posted only a small picket guard.

At sunset 12 September, Saunders put on a simulated landing at the Montmorency front, which pulled a large part of Montcalm's force off base. Late that evening, 1700 English embarked in boats from the transports up-river, and at 2:00 a.m. on the 13th, with a fresh breeze astern and an ebb tide under their keels, they began floating downstream, unobserved by Bougainville.

Wolfe, in one of the foremost boats, recited Gray's "Elegy in a Country Churchyard" to a young midshipman, solemnly pronouncing the famous line that his own fate would presently illustrate: "The paths of glory lead but to the grave."

The French were expecting a convoy of provision boats to slip down-river that night, and the British landing craft were mistaken for them. Only one French sentry on the shore challenged, "Qui vive?" A French-speaking Scot replied, "France." "De quel régiment?" "De la Reine," replied the Scot. The sentry was satisfied.

The boats reached the bottom of the defile. Twenty-four rugged volunteers climbed up the cliff, put the French picket guard to the sword, gave the prearranged signal, and the troops jumped ashore and swarmed up the steep path, muskets slung on their backs. As fast as the boats emptied they returned to the ships or to the south shore for reinforcements. Thus, by break of day, 13 September 1759, some 4500 British were deployed on the Plains of Abraham, a grassy field forming part of the Quebec plateau, close to the walls of the citadel.

Wolfe's object was to challenge Montcalm to an open-field battle, the only kind he knew how to fight; and the French accepted. Presently white-uniformed veterans of famous regiments — La Sarre, Guyenne, Languedoc, Royal-Roussillon, Béarn — were coming on the double from the Montmorency front, rushing through the narrow streets of Quebec and deploying on the other side to face the English. At 10:00 a.m. some 4000 of them, who had formed outside the walls, advanced to the attack, flying regimental colors and cheering "Vive le Roi!" For fifteen or twenty minutes they marched, and not a shot rang out; Wolfe had learned the value of precise, accurate, and concentrated fire power. Three-quarters of his 4500 troops were deployed in one line, which waited silently until the enemy was only 40 yards away. Then the command "Fire!" rang out and the muskets crashed in a rolling roar. A second volley followed and no more were needed; the ground was already covered with French dead and wounded. Then the English soldiers charged the dazed survivors with fixed bayonets, and kilted Highlanders, shouting wildly, attacked with claymores and broadswords, completing the rout of the French. Wolfe, personally leading a picked force of grenadiers, was shot down, and only had time to order the enemy's retreat to be cut off before dying on the field of glory. Montcalm, mortally wounded in the retreat, died next day. Each side suffered about equal losses, 640 killed and wounded. Quebec promptly surrendered to the British. Never did so short and sharp a fight have so important a result.

Soon Canada was sealed off from Europe by ice, but in the spring of 1760 a reorganized French and Canadian army under the Chevalier de Lévis moved against Quebec. Brigadier Murray, commanding a small, half-starved British garrison in the city, managed to hold them off. On 9 May a warship appeared down river, unannounced. Anxious eyes on both sides sought to make out her flag. Lévis, knowing nothing of the destruction of the French fleet at Quiberon Bay the previous November, was confident that he saw the white ensign of royal France, heralding a relief expedition. And when his aide made out a red cross of St. George on the ensign — for this ship was the van of a British fleet — the Chevalier's heart was broken. He abandoned the siege and fell back on Montreal. On 8 September 1760 after Generals Amherst, Haviland, and Murray had invested Montreal, Governor the Marquis de Vaudreuil, deserted by many French regulars and the Canadian militia, surrendered the whole of Canada to Great Britain.

In North America the war was over, except for the Pontiac conspiracy, a last flare-up by the Indians of the Ohio country who refused to accept the consequences of French defeat. In Europe, the Caribbean, and the Far East, the war lasted two years longer. A British fleet mopped up Martinique and all the French West Indies except Saint-Domingue. Spain's tardy alliance with France in 1761 gave a British naval squadron the opportunity to double Cape Horn and capture Manila. A British amphibious operation with colonial volunteers took Havana in 1762.

In that year George III, who had succeeded his grandfather George II in 1760, dismissed William Pitt, whose notions of conquest and glory had become immoderate. The king opened peace negotiations and obtained treaties with France and Spain by returning several British conquests in order to retain the most important. That was eighteenth-century war at its best. You beat your enemy, but did not try to annihilate him. Even so, the victory was too complete for the results to be permanent.

This Peace of Paris in 1763 marked the end of France as a North American power. Of the great empire won by Champlain, La Salle, and hundreds of explorers, warriors, traders, and priests, France retained only the two little islands of St. Pierre and Miquelon off Newfoundland. In the West Indies, besides a few smaller islands, she kept Saint-Domingue, Martinique, and Guadeloupe. Spain ceded to Great Britain East and West Florida, which became the sixteenth and seventeenth English continental colonies. France, in order to compensate Spain for the loss of the Floridas and Minorca, ceded to her the vast province of Louisiana, including all French claims to territory west of the Mississippi. Thus the Mississippi became a boundary between the English and Spanish empires.

Britain was now supreme on the seas, in the subcontinent of India, and in North America. English, Scots, Irish, and Americans boiled over with patriotism. "We doubt not," resolved Massachusetts Bay, "but as we are delivered from foreign Wars, we shall be equally free from intestine Divisions."

But that was too much to expect. A war may settle some things but creates new problems and tensions that beget another war.

Although Canada passed under British sovereignty, the year 1763 marks the beginning of French Canada as a self-conscious people, ill-rewarding the tolerance and justice of their English conquerors by indifference and disloyalty.

Their writers created a myth to the effect that they were sold or betrayed by the feeble Bourbon who reigned over France. There is no truth in this. France made strenuous efforts to defend her overseas empire, but these were not enough to counteract British energy and sea power, and the superior man-power of the English colonies. Two centuries after the fall of Montreal, the Province of Quebec, with 83 per cent of its five million inhabitants Catholic and French-speaking, was nourishing ancient grievances and a party aiming at complete independence.

HEART OF OAK

Triumph and Tribulation

1763-1766

1. The Thirteen Colonies in 1763

A GREAT ENTERPRISE had been concluded in the grand manner. For a moment the British Empire was not only a political and economic unit but a moral one. English, Scots, Irish, and Americans alike bellowed patriotic sentiments and slopped over with expressions of loyalty. George III, the attractive young man of twenty-two who succeeded his grandfather in 1760, and William Pitt the Great Commoner, were as popular in America as in England. But in the long run the Seven Years' War proved to be more of a solvent than a cement. What went wrong?

The victory had been too complete. The balance of power had been upset, and the French made it their business to tip the scales the other way. One obvious way was to envenom any future dispute between England and her colonies to the point of independence. For, even though the colonists had gained in loyalty, they had also grown in confidence and strength. From their point of view, they had won the war, with a little aid from the British army and navy. Causes of dissension inherent in the English colonial system had been sharpened. The royal and proprietary governors still carried instructions to maintain the prerogative against popularly elected assemblies. The royal disallowance of colonial laws was still in effect, and on the first important exercise of it after the war — the Two-Penny Act in Virginia — the voice of Patrick Henry was heard: "Caesar had his Brutus, Charles I his Cromwell, and George III [cries of 'Treason! Treason!'] may profit from their example." Imperial sentiments proved to be temporary; colonial attitudes permanent. Americans considered their own interests first, whilst the British governing class still thought of the colonies as their property, "to be regarded in no other light but as subservient to the commerce of their mother country," as an English publicist wrote. And the conquest of Canada, the Floridas, and of numerous nations of "wild" Indians, created new administrative problems that England was ill equipped to face, and which she could not solve within the existing framework of law and custom.

One principle upon which all Englishmen then agreed was the rule of law. When in the late eighteenth century, they spoke of the "liberties of free-born Englishmen," the rule of law was in the back of their minds: resistance to

Charles I in the name of law, vindication of law against James II. Colonial leaders were familiar with the works of Algernon Sidney, Harington, and Locke, who urged every Englishman to resist every grasp for power; to stand firm on ancient principles of liberty, whether embalmed in acts of Parliament or adumbrated in the "Law of Nature." Thus, in order to resist the government of George III, Americans had to prove to their own satisfaction that it was he who had broken the law. The maladroit persistence of George III and his ministers in trying to solve their administrative problems outside existing law served to smash all floating atoms of contention and produce a nuclear explosion in the political sphere.

British subjects in America, excepting of course the Negroes, were then the freest people in the world, and in many respects more free than anyone today. They argued and then fought, not to *obtain* freedom but to *confirm* the freedom they already had or claimed. They were even more advanced in the practice of self-government than the mother country. There was slight pressure from ancient custom, and few relics of feudalism. Land tenure was fee simple in New England, and subject elsewhere only to a light quitrent which was generally evaded. There were no tithes to support an established church. Maximum wages were not fixed, as in most European countries, nor were the rural laborers at the mercy of tyrannical justices of the peace, as in England and Ireland. Americans were exempt from naval press-gangs. Some form of military training was obligatory, but actual service in time of war was voluntary. Since the Zenger libel case in New York in 1735, almost complete freedom of speech, press, and assembly was enjoyed.[1] Trades and professions were open to the talented — there were no guilds or corporations or exclusive professional associations; indeed, very few professional men of any sort, other than lawyers, physicians, and divines. The hand of government rested lightly on Americans. Connecticut, for three years running, levied no taxes except local rates for roads and schools. In the absence of banks, merchants lent money privately, and the frontier offered an easy escape from debt. Victory had removed the French menace to security, and would have ended the Indian menace too, had Americans been content to live east of the Appalachians. Social classes existed, but, to British visitors like Janet Schaw, a "most disgusting equality" prevailed.

It did, near the wilderness. The frontier of settlement in 1763 left the coast near the Penobscot river in Maine, cut irregularly across New Hampshire and the disputed lands which later became Vermont, pushed up the Hudson to Lake George, and up the Mohawk about 100 miles from Albany. Thence it

1. John Peter Zenger, publisher of a newspaper that represented the opposition to the New York colonial government, was prosecuted for seditious libel. His friends obtained the services of Andrew Hamilton, a Philadelphia lawyer, who secured acquittal on the then revolutionary ground that truth was no libel. Although this Zenger decision was not always followed by colonial courts, it did establish the principle of a free press, which was of inestimable value to the radical party in 1764–76.

slashed across the southeast corners of New York and Pennsylvania and hugged the Appalachians until reaching North Carolina, where again it dropped down to the sea. Scattered settlements had already been made throughout the interior of the Carolinas and eastern Georgia.

This settled area of 1763, which two centuries later had a population approaching 100 million, then included about a million and a half people, almost one-third of them Negro slaves. By 1775 it had increased by another million. The bulk of the population was engaged in agriculture, but visiting Europeans regarded the country as a wilderness because over 90 per cent of it was still forested. Only near the Atlantic, in sections cultivated for over a century, could one have found anything resembling the farming areas of Iowa, Illinois, or Nebraska today. Elsewhere, and especially in the South, farms and plantations lay miles apart, separated by forest.

Let us now briefly survey the British continental colonies, starting at the southern end. West Florida, defined in 1763 as old Spanish Florida west of the Apalachicola, together with that part of French Louisiana including Mobile, Biloxi, and Natchez, had very few European inhabitants. Pensacola was still a stockaded fort; Mobile had only 112 Frenchmen. Governor George Johnstone, an energetic Scots naval officer, set up civil government at Pensacola, summoned an elective assembly in 1766, and advertised for English settlers, with good results; within ten years the population had risen to 3700 Europeans and 1200 Negro slaves, most of them at the Mississippi end. Johnstone cemented friendly relations with the Creek and Choctaw, who ceded their lands up to a line 35 miles from the sea.

In East Florida, when the British took possession, the only settlements Spain had to show for over two centuries of rule were St. Augustine and St. Mark. In contrast to Canada, where the French habitants loved their land more than their king and preferred English allegiance to exile, the people of St. Augustine, although granted toleration, chose to leave when England took over. No Spaniard could imagine living under alien heretics. The Spanish authorities provided transportation to Havana for all white inhabitants and several hundred fugitive slaves from Georgia and South Carolina who had settled near the garrison town. South of St. Augustine, where now the palm-bordered shores are broken by eruptions of resort hotels, there were only Indians living in 1763. These were mostly the Seminole branch of the Creek nation; no white man had yet penetrated the Everglades.

Colonel James Grant, who had made two successful campaigns against the Cherokee in the last war, became the first British governor of East Florida. He had to obtain both officials and settlers from Charleston. The Spaniards, before their departure, had cashed in on land claims earlier purchased from the Indians, by selling most of them to a shady pair of land speculators, a Gordon of Charleston and a Fish of New York, who claimed 10 million acres but sold out to the crown for £15,000. Other speculators obtained land grants on condition of settling a certain number of white Protestants. Little came of these efforts, because hardly anybody then wished to live in Florida. One Robert Turnbull recruited 1500 settlers from Minorca, Greece, and Italy, and established them at New Smyrna to grow indigo; their decendants there are still called Minorcans. In addition to these, the census of 1771 showed only 288 whites and 900 Negroes in all East Florida.

To travel in the 1760's from St. Augustine to Savannah or Charleston, one had to go by sea or Indian trail. Georgia had passed her heroic period; no longer did General Oglethorpe drill kilted Highlanders to raid the dons; no more evangelists like Whitefield and Wesley promoted the Kingdom of God on the Altamaha. A population of about 10,000, including a good proportion of Negro slaves, was engaged in planting indigo and rice.

South Carolina had passed the 100,000 mark and become very prosperous. The powerful Cherokee nation under their leader Attakullakulla or Little Carpenter, went on the warpath in 1759 but were badly beaten and forced to cede land which opened the back country to settlement. Charleston had become a gay little city with a goodly number of merchants and professional men, and a permanent theater. The wealthier Charlestonians sent their sons to England to be educated; but when it came to a showdown in 1775, your South Carolinian fresh from Christ Church or the Inns of Court became as flaming a patriot as any alumnus of Princeton, Yale, or William and Mary.

Josiah Quincy of Boston, who traveled through the Carolinas in 1773, wrote of the contrast between them: "The number of Negroes and slaves is much less in North than in South Carolina. Husbandmen and agriculture increase in number and improvement. Industry is up in the woods, at tar, pitch, and turpentine; in the fields, ploughing, planting, clearing, or fencing the land. Herds and flocks become numerous. Healthful countenances and numerous families become more common as you advance north." Many migrants from New England and the Middle colonies moved in during the expansion since 1740 and prospered at the expense of the poor "tar-heels." The back country in both Carolinas was seething with discontent, which broke out into rebellion in 1769.

In Virginia, in general, there was no middle class. If a white, you were either a First Family (F.F.V.) or a rough frontiersman. The gentry were openhanded, liberal, and hospitable; proud of their English blood. Andrew Burnaby, a clergyman who traveled through the province in 1759, observed:

They are haughty and jealous of their liberties, impatient of restraint, and can scarcely bear the thought of being controuled by any superior power. The women are, generally speaking, handsome, though not to be compared with our fair countrywomen in England. They have but few advantages, and consequently are seldom accomplished; this makes them reserved, and unequal to any interesting or refined conversation. They are immoderately fond of dancing, and indeed it is almost the only amusement they partake of.

An important accomplishment that Burnaby missed was the sound education in the ancient classics and political theory that young men obtained at the College of William and Mary. Running a plantation, serving on the council or in the house of burgesses, and reading Cicero, Polybius, and Locke gave Virginians excellent training in statesmanship.

Although progressive Virginia planters like Washington were substituting wheat for tobacco, prosperity in the Old Dominion was still largely based on tobacco. Owing to new lands being brought under cultivation in the piedmont, which could not be reached by ship, there grew up a new profession of tobacco "factors" or brokers. These, for some unexplained reason, were usually Scots connected with tobacco-processing firms in Glasgow. In 1774, for instance, William Cunningham & Co. operated six ships on the Glasgow-Chesapeake route, and maintained twenty-one agencies or stores in Maryland and Virginia, where they sold consumer goods, purchased tobacco direct from the grower, and arranged to have it carted to tidewater — sometimes by attaching a pair of shafts to a hogshead and rolling it down by horsepower. These canny Caledonians, through hard work and efficient marketing, replaced the English merchants who had handled the American tobacco crop for a century past; and, like them, were accused of depressing the price of tobacco and marking up imports. In view of the native Virginian's contempt for trade, his lack of currency and his credit requirements, he needed the brokers more than they needed him; but the antagonism that this system engendered made almost every Scot in the tobacco colonies a loyalist in the Revolution.

The Church of England was established in every Southern colony, but in none did it enjoy great influence. A clerical career did not appeal to the local gentry, and the church afforded a poor living in comparison with planting. The Two-Penny Act, which first called forth Patrick Henry's eloquence, was an attempt of the assembly to commute ministers' salaries, which had been set at 17,000 pounds of tobacco annually, at twopence a pound, at a time when it was worth sixpence.

The economic situation in Maryland was similar to that of Virginia, except that it depended less on tobacco and more on wheat, and had a growing seaport, Baltimore. That city owed its early prosperity to having waterpower close to Chesapeake Bay, making it a natural point for the grinding of grain from Maryland and Pennsylvania into flour for export. Annapolis, the capital, with tasteful brick houses and churches, was one of the liveliest little towns in North America; George Washington used to go there for enjoyment.

As travelers journeyed north from Baltimore along a tolerable road for wheeled vehicles, they found the aspect of the country changing. In Delaware, fifteen or twenty miles from Philadelphia, farms became smaller, more frequent, and better cultivated, with flower gardens and fruit trees. An Englishman crossing the Schuylkill and entering Philadelphia felt at home; the capital of Pennsylvania, remarked Lord Adam Gordon with evident astonishment, was "a great and noble city," like a large town in England, with an added Quaker primness and regularity. Some of the neatly laid out streets were paved, lined with sidewalks, lighted by whale-oil lamps, and policed at night. Philadelphia, with 18,766 people according to the census of 1760, was the largest and most prosperous town in English America. In another ten years it increased by another 10,000 and acquired some fine public buildings, including Carpenters' Hall and the State House, which would be the scene of great events in 1774–81. Philadelphia already had three semi-public libraries, a college, three newspapers (one in German), the only hospital in North America, and Benjamin Franklin. It was the only place in the English colonies outside Maryland which had a Catholic church. But the "brotherly love" principle of her founder had not worked too well. There were tensions between the English Quakers, who had the highest social standing, the German farmers, whom they regarded as uneducated boors, and the tough Scots-Irish, who had settled the frontier and back country. The province was run by an oligarchy of Philadelphia lawyers and merchants, many of them Quakers who were kept in power by a weighted system of apportionment and a property qualification for voting which excluded most of the artisans.

Proceeding north, our traveler of 1763 would cross the Delaware by ferry to Trenton and drive across New Jersey, probably spending a night at the pretty village of Princeton, where he could admire Nassau Hall, largest building in the English colonies. He crossed the Hudson by ferry from Perth Amboy to New York City. There he would find a compactly built little town, third in population in the English colonies, still bearing marks of its Dutch origin. The little city was cosmopolitan, as always, and exhibited vast differences in wealth. Not far from the stately merchants' mansions facing Bowling Green or the river were evil slums where day laborers, dockhands, and free Negroes lived. There were already enough Irish in New York to celebrate St. Patrick's Day, enough Jews to maintain a synagogue, enough Scots to support a Presbyterian church, and enough Germans to maintain four churches with services in their language. Trinity and St. Paul's, the two Anglican churches, worshipped according to the Book of Common Prayer, praying daily for "George, our most gracious King and Governour."

In this royal province the franchise was so restricted by a high property qualification that not half the white men could vote, and the landed gentry controlled elections. Up-river the Livingston and Van Rensselaer manors comprised almost a million acres; the Philipse family had two manors which amounted to little less; six manors covered over half of Westchester County; 200 square miles on Long Island belonged to four families; hundreds of acres on Manhattan were owned by the Stuyvesants, Bayards, De Lanceys, and De Peysters. Instead of political parties there were rival factions whose origins can be traced to Leisler's Rebellion: the Livingston or Presbyterian, and the De Lancey or Anglican. The former, more adaptable to rising tides, produced several leaders of the pre-Revolutionary period such as John Morin Scott and William Livingston the "signer." Later, under the leadership of Aaron Burr, it merged with the Jeffersonian party.

New England was racially homogeneous, with few Negroes, Irish, Scots, or Germans; and some 90 per cent belonged to Congregational churches. New England was also relatively democratic; almost every adult male had the vote, and inequalities of wealth were evident only in the seaports. Boston, with 17,000 inhabitants, was the largest town but no metropolis. There were a dozen prosperous coastal towns, each with some maritime specialty, and off-shore Nantucket had already embarked in deep-sea whaling. Portland (then called Falmouth) exported lumber; Portsmouth built ships and exported white pine masts and spars to Britain; Gloucestermen fished on the Grand Bank and carried dried fish to Surinam; Salem and Marblehead ships traded with the West Indies and the Mediterranean; Newport, New London, and New Haven were deeply involved in the West Indies trade. Few rivers in New England were navigable, and the roads were few and bad. Hence the principal land transportation took place during the winter when snow lay on the ground. Farmers would then load their butter, salt provisions, wooden ware, and maple sugar on a "pung," an ox-drawn sledge, and drive it to the nearest seaport, where they exchanged these products for rum and groceries.

Social life in the country revolved around each Congregational church, and town government gave everyone a chance to participate. Serving as selectman, or a representative in the assembly, afforded a political training which en-abled the Yankees to concert resistance against the new imperial policy; and, more important, to govern themselves during an upheaval.

Every seaport contained comfortable brick and wooden houses built in the Georgian style, with excellent interior decoration and well-kept gardens. The ship-owning merchants who owned most of them shared top status with the clergy and with a few lawyers and physicians. New England as yet had no landed aristocracy, no leisurely country life, no shooting and hunting in the English sense; but plenty of fishing for sport in the rivers and for profit in the sea. The wealthiest man in New England before the Revolution was Thomas Boylston, a Boston merchant whose property in land, houses, and ships was estimated at £80,000. But every seaport had a rough working class of sailors, fishermen, and shipbuilders, such as the caulkers who invented the political caucus. These were easily welded by agitators into mobs, as many crown officials and wealthy gentlemen were to learn unpleasantly, and were always ready to "run in" a cargo without paying duty.

Smuggling is a delicate subject. British writers on the American Revolution like to argue that it occurred because government tried to stop smuggling. It is true that the Yankees smuggled, Yorkers and Jerseymen smuggled, Phila-delphians smuggled, and Southerners smuggled; but so did the English smuggle, and in a big way, respectably organized. The latest English historian of smuggling, Neville Williams, calls the period 1713–76, "The Heyday of Illicit Trade," when smuggled tea became his nation's favorite beverage.

Apart from smuggling, however, the New England people were law-abiding, even on the frontier. A large part of the interior of New England was still wilderness; and much of the rest, settled in the last twenty years, was still in the log-cabin stage of development. But in parts that had been settled for forty years or more, one found the village green, the spired meetinghouse, and the white-painted dwelling built around huge brick chimneys, that still impart charm to rural New England. The necessities of life were plentiful and families were large, but Puritanism had preserved a certain simplicity and economy in social intercourse.

Although Benjamin Franklin was easily the first man of science in the colonies — his electrical experiments printed in 1751 were hailed by the intelligentsia of Europe — the New England colleges were centers of scientific activity. Professor John Winthrop not only taught physics, chemistry, and astronomy at Harvard, but led an expedition to observe a transit of Venus at Newfoundland in 1761. The Reverend Thomas Clap, President of Yale College, invented a new plow, maintained temperature charts, experimented with raising silk in Connecticut, promoted a spa at Stafford Springs, and observed sun spots, eclipses, and transits of Mercury with the college telescope. Throughout the country hundreds of men, many of them clergymen, were investigating natural phenomena and trying to relate them to the fundamental truths of Christianity; for science had not become so intricate as to discourage those who wished to know a little of everything.

2. The Imperial System in 1763

The loose-jointed system by which England endeavored to administer her colonies had not changed in 1763, owing to the failure of the Albany Plan of Union. Although no general opposition to this easy-going imperialism had yet been voiced by the colonies, there were several things about it that made them restless. They objected to the governor's instructions from the crown being considered mandatory. If the governor was energetic and conscientious, these instructions involved him in a row with the assembly, which naturally did not think it compatible with the liberty of British subjects that they should inflexibly obey directions from England. Nor did they like the admiralty courts, which gave verdicts without a local jury. But they particularly disliked the tenure of judges.

Tenure during good behavior (which we have for all federal judges today) had been secured in England by the Glorious Revolution of 1688; but in the colonies tenure "during the king's pleasure" prevailed. Easy-going royal governors had fallen into the practice of making judicial appointments during good behavior, to please the assemblies. The Board of Trade issued stringent instructions to stop this, and the death in 1760 of George II, voiding all royal commissions, brought on a crisis. The judges in New York and New Jersey refused to accept new commissions from George III except for tenure during good behavior. Lieutenant Governor Colden vetoed a bill of the New York assembly granting salaries to judges only on the condition of their holding office with this tenure. The Board of Trade then played a joke on New York. It obtained a royal warrant ordering the governor to appoint Benjamin Prat of Boston chief justice of the province during the king's pleasure. Colden complied; the assembly countered by voting no salary to the new chief justice. The board then ordered the governor to pay his salary out of permanent revenues. In the meantime, the other New York judges, outraged by the appointment of an imported Yankee, refused to receive new commissions from George III for king's pleasure tenure. The upshot was that poor Prat, performing the entire business of the supreme court without salary, overburdened with work and anxiety, died. The governor then found other men willing to accept judicial commissions during the king's pleasure, and the assembly gave in and paid their salaries.

In one colony after another, except North Carolina, which preferred to go without courts for several years rather than submit, the crown won this controversy, and in so doing caused a resentment which is expressed in the Declaration of Independence.[1] Americans could not understand why independent tenure of judges, a concession long since won by Englishmen, should not be extended to them. They could not grasp the English point of view that judges needed protection from the caprice and parsimony of colonial assemblies. The framers of the Federal Constitution saw both points, and provided against them.[2]

Thomas Secker, Archbishop of Canterbury, stirred up a new hornet's nest in 1763 by issuing a statement in favor of appointing colonial bishops. Presbyterian and Congregational ministers replied with hot pamphlets and passionate sermons; Anglican ministers gave as good as they got. Radical political leaders, especially Samuel Adams, made the most of the Archbishop's proposal as another instance of intended tyranny and the issue helped him to align most of the colonial clergy with the Whigs. The Reverend Jonathan Boucher, rector of St. Anne's, Annapolis, who returned to England in 1775 rather than submit to the Sons of Liberty, wrote that this controversy was the real background of the American Revolution, keeping "the public mind in a state of ferment and effervescence," and habituating the people to opposition. It certainly helped to create that "revolution in the hearts of the people" which John Adams declared to have been the real American revolution.

Although Americans found the imperial system occasionally irritating, they were not ready to do anything about it in 1763. They simply had the normal state of dissatisfaction that every free man of spirit should have with government, whatever its form. During the next twelve years of controversy, before the war started, American patriot leaders constantly referred to the situation

1. "He has made judges dependent on his will alone, for the tenure of their offices, and the amount and payment of their salaries."
2. Article III, Section I: "The Judges, both of the Supreme and inferior courts, shall hold their offices during good behaviour, and shall, at stated times, receive for their services, a compensation which shall not be diminished during their continuance in office."

before 1763 as the ultimate goal of their desires. John Adams even declared that at any time during the war he would have given everything he possessed to restore the old colonial system. That, however, was but a nostalgic dream. Long wars always change conditions so fundamentally that neither victor nor vanquished can ever re-create "the good old days." Never, never will they return, any more than an old man's lost youth.

In modern times we are used to war heroes and statesmen continuing in power during many subsequent years of peace. The Civil War generation governed the United States until 1901; The World War II generation governed Britain, France, the United States, and Canada for sixteen years or more. But immediately after the Peace of Paris, a new set of leaders, mostly in their twenties or early thirties, emerged in the Thirteen Colonies. Usually it was a local issue involving a constitutional question that brought them forward. Here are a few examples: — Christopher Gadsden successfully resisted an attempt of the royal governor of South Carolina in 1762 to void elections to the assembly of people he disliked. Patrick Henry and Thomas Jefferson came to the front on the Two-Penny Act and circular letter issues; Thomas McKean became embroiled with the governor of Pennsylvania; John Morin Scott led opposition to the Quartering Act; James Otis and the Adamses came forward on the Writs of Assistance and Revenue Act in Massachusetts. When old Governor Shirley, retired in England, was asked about the young troublemakers in Massachusetts, he burst out: "Mr. Cushing I knew, and Mr. Hancock I knew; but where the devil this brace of Adamses came from, I know not."

The world would soon know.

There was no American nationalism or separatist feeling in the colonies prior to 1775. Americans did not start off in 1763 like Ireland in 1798 or 1916, or Indonesia, India, and Pakistan in 1945, or the African colonies even more recently, with the conviction that they were entitled to be a separate and independent nation. They never felt, like Poland in her long, unhappy years, or Moslem dependencies in the 1950's, that they were so downtrodden by tyrannical masters as to make independence the only solution. On the contrary, Americans were not only content but proud to be part of the British imperium. But they did feel very strongly that they were entitled to all constitutional rights that Englishmen possessed in England. It took the radical leaders ten years after the Stamp Act to reach the position that Parliament had no rightful jurisdiction over the colonies, and even in the Declaration of Independence there was no complaint against the Acts of Trade and Navigation.

Thus there was nothing foreordained about the American Revolution; and historians who argue that the Revolution was inevitable can only make out a case by insisting that the Thirteen Colonies were becoming too big and self-conscious to continue as colonies. Yet Canada, which in 1960 had sevenfold the population of the Thirteen Colonies in 1776, and Australia, with four times their population, have managed to stay within the British Commonwealth; the "inevitable" argument would have made them independent long ago.[1] Nevertheless, one reason that they have remained loyal to the crown is that England, learning her lesson in time, relaxed imperial control; the American Revolution came about because she tried to tighten it.

Many interventions of the English government in colonial administration had been to protect minority groups against majorities, or small colonies against big ones; for instance, Quakers and Anglicans in New England against the dominant Puritans; Delaware against Maryland, New Hampshire and Rhode Island against Massachusetts Bay, which wanted to gobble them up; humble Georgia against proud South Carolina. The British government in the eighteenth century had a good record for religious and racial toleration. At a time when France, the German states, and even Switzerland were persecuting various Protestant sects, England welcomed foreign refugees and assisted their emigration to Pennsylvania and other colonies. Once in America they could be naturalized and enjoy all rights and privileges of British subjects, yet retain their own language, religion, and folkways, as many Pennsylvania Germans do to this day. No independence program would have got very far in the colonies before 1770, because these minority groups looked to the English government for protection. The frontiersmen in Pennsylvania and Virginia owed their safe deliverance from massacre in Pontiac's Rebellion to the British army under Colonel Bouquet, not to the militia of those colonies. American merchants and shipowners looked to the Royal Navy for protection from pirates and enemies on the high seas.

Outside the political sphere, Americans had many reasons to be grateful to Britain for contributions to their schools and churches. When Eleazar Wheelock wished to found a college in New Hampshire to educate Indians and New Hampshire frontiersmen, he knew that it would be no use to start an endowment drive in the American seaports. Instead, he dressed up a converted Indian as a parson and sent him to England to plead from the pulpit for money — and did it roll in!

When we boil down our colonial history, it is evident that by 1763 there had been worked out a compromise between imperial control and colonial self-government; between the principle of authority and the principle of liberty. King and Parliament had undisputed control of foreign affairs, war and peace, and overseas trade. Parliament canalized colonial trade into channels that it deemed profitable to all. In almost every other respect, Americans had acquired home rule. Their assemblies had secured the exclusive right to tax their constituents, to appoint officials such as colonial treasurers and fix their salaries; to commission military officers and raise troops or not as they chose; to control their own schools, churches, and land systems. They had acquired far more autonomy than Ireland then enjoyed, and infinitely more than the colonies of France, Spain, or any other country ever had before the

1. Thirteen Colonies in 1776, 2.5 million; Australia in 1960, 10.2 million; Canada in 1960, 17.6 million.

next century. And they confidently expected to acquire more control over their destinies as they increased in population and wealth.

So, apart from minor discontents over judges and currency, Americans were satisfied with this compromise in 1763. But the government of George III was not. It had devised no method of exacting a uniform contribution from the colonies for defense. In the last war, flank colonies like New England and South Carolina, directly menaced by the French and Spaniards, had made even more effort than England expected, but the Middle colonies did far less, and Pennsylvania the least, owing to Quaker pacifism. Moreover, England had piled up a war debt, which for the eighteenth century seemed tremendous, and which had been partly incurred in conquering French Canada and Spanish Florida. It seemed reasonable that Americans who benefited from these conquests should take part of the debt off the British taxpayer's back. Hence the Revenue Act of 1764 and the Stamp Act of 1765. There were still leaks in the enforcement of the Acts of Trade and Navigation, owing largely to the fact that royal customs officials in the colonies were so few in number, and so underpaid, that they could only make both ends meet by accepting presents from smugglers.

Thus the situation between England and her American colonies, while it had points of friction, was far from explosive. "The Abilities of a Child might have governed this Country," wrote Oliver Wolcott of Connecticut in 1776, "So strong had been their Attachment to Britain." But the Americans were a high-spirited people who claimed all the rights for which Englishmen had fought since Magna Carta, and would settle for nothing less. They were not security-minded but liberty-minded. That is why they met the attempts of the government of George III to impair these liberties, first with loyal expostulation, next with indignant agitation, finally with armed resistance.

Make no mistake; the American Revolution was not fought to *obtain* freedom, but to *preserve* the liberties that Americans already had as colonials. Independence was no conscious goal, secretly nurtured in cellar or jungle by bearded conspirators, but a reluctant last resort, to preserve "life, liberty and the pursuit of happiness."

3. Reform and Resistance

Successive ministries of George III tried to meet three problems at the same time: to settle what we may call the Western question (Indians, fur traders and land speculators); to plug holes in the Acts of Trade and Navigation; and to raise money from America for defense.

The British government approached these problems piecemeal, and usually too late. Governor Bernard of Massachusetts, in a series of letters addressed to leading English politicians, pointed out that to reform the Empire, England should reform colonial governments first, strengthen her royal governors and judges by paying their salaries, confer titles of nobility on leading Americans, and admit colonial representatives to the House of Commons. The Roman Empire was held together by such methods. All were citizens of "no mean city," as St. Paul remarked on a famous occasion; Gauls, Spaniards, Jews, Greeks, and Africans became senators; Emperors Trajan and Hadrian were sons of Spaniards. But the classically educated English politicians failed to profit by this example. Baronetcies for Pepperell and Johnson were the highest honors conferred on any American, and no colonial was ever given even a minor post in the British government. English-speaking politicians always prefer piecemeal reforms to comprehensive plans. Usually that works out all right, but sometimes events catch up with and overwhelm the politicians.

The law enforcement problem was the first to be tackled, William Pitt in 1760 ordered the Sugar Act of 1733 to be strictly enforced. That law put a prohibitive duty on molasses entering English colonies from the foreign West Indies. Since the Americans depended upon molasses from French and Spanish islands to feed their rum distilleries, the Sugar Act had been consistently evaded, usually by purchasing in Jamaica a false declaration that the molasses had been produced there. In order to enforce this unpopular law, the royal customs collectors at Boston applied to the superior court of the colony for writs of assistance. These were general warrants allowing an officer to enter any premises at any time in search of smuggled goods. As such, they were contrary to the traditional rights of Englishmen. A Boston lawyer named James Otis threw up his job as king's advocate general to argue against the issue of the writs in 1761. To young John Adams in the audience, "Otis was a flame of fire . . . the seeds of patriots and heroes were then and there sown." Otis made the significant argument, "An act against the Constitution is void; an act against natural equity is void." This invoking of a fundamental, "natural" law, "the unchangeable, unwritten code of Heaven" (as Sophocles puts it in *Antigone*), became more frequent during the next forty years. As expressed in our bills of rights, it has become basic doctrine in American law. And five years later, the British attorney general upheld Otis on the local issue.

The next problem to puzzle the ministers of George III was that of the West. Pontiac's Rebellion proved that it was not sufficient to conquer territory; something must be done to placate the Indians and defend the white frontier. Consequently, in October 1763, the king issued an important proclamation. Until further notice no colonial government could grant, and no white man take, land beyond the sources of rivers that flow into the Atlantic. This proclamation was probably intended to be temporary; but certain ministers regarded it as the cornerstone of a new policy, to discourage westward migration but encourage the peopling of Canada, Nova Scotia, and the Floridas. For in these flank colonies, as a cabinet minister declared, pioneers "would be useful to their Mother Country instead of planting themselves in the Heart of America, out of reach of Government, where from the great difficulty of procuring European commodities they would be compelled to commerce and manufacture, to the infinite prejudice of Britain." Lord Shelburne, the most intelligent of the ministers of George III in dealing with American affairs, was of another opinion; he wanted westward expansion as a safety valve; but the contrary idea became official policy.

In 1762 the ministers made another important decision, to leave a permanent garrison of 10,000 men in the continental colonies. It has often been asserted, but never proved, that this was done to create jobs for British army officers who otherwise would have been retired on half pay. General Amherst, the commander in chief in America, asked for only 6625 troops to keep the French and Indians in check; and he should have known what was necessary. When the troops arrived, most of them were garrisoned at places like Halifax and New York rather than at Pittsburgh, Detroit, and the Carolina frontier, which gave color to the charge, although the real reason was the increased expense of supplying a garrison beyond reach of water transport.

Another frontier blow-up showed that seaport garrisons were necessary to preserve order. A band of frontier hoodlums from around Paxton, Pennsylvania, furious over lack of protection during Pontiac's Rebellion by the Quaker-dominated assembly, took cowardly revenge by massacring peaceful survivors of the Conestoga tribe in Lancaster County. The "Paxton Boys" then made such dire threats against another remnant, the so-called Moravian Indians near Bethlehem, that these fled to Philadelphia. There the government quartered them in barracks and protected them by British regulars. The "Boys," 1500 strong, heavily armed and uttering "hideous outcries in imitation of the war whoop," marched on the capital in February 1764, bent on killing every redskin refugee. Philadelphia was in a panic, and it took Ben Franklin to talk the ruffians into going home, by promising more frontier protection and legislative bounties for Indians' scalps.

The first attempt of the government of George III to raise money toward defense and stop leaks in the Acts of Trade and Navigation was the Revenue Act of 1764. Its preamble stated frankly the purpose: "That a revenue be raised in Your Majesty's dominions in America for defraying the expenses of defending, protecting and securing the same." The law lowered the duty on foreign molasses from the uncollectable 6d per gallon, but levied additional duties on foreign sugar and on English or European luxuries such as wine, silk, and linen, when imported into the American colonies. It "enumerated" more colonial products such as hides and skins, which could be exported only to England, and withdrew some earlier exemptions that the colonies had enjoyed, such as free importation of Madeira wine. That favorite beverage of well-to-do Americans now became subject to a customs duty of £7 per double hogshead, as against 10s on port wine imported through England — an obvious attempt to change the drinking habits of the colonial aristocrats to profit the British exchequer.

Colonial leaders promptly seized on the declared revenue-raising purpose of this act as a constitutional point. As the New York assembly observed in a respectful petition to Parliament on 18 October, "Exemption from burthen of ungranted, involuntary taxes, must be the grand principle of every free state," without which "there can be no liberty, no happiness, no security." If Parliament got away with taxing their trade, it might proceed to tax their lands, or everything else. This seemed prophetic when Parliament on 22 March 1765 passed the famous Stamp Act.

In the meantime, a movement had begun to boycott the products taxed by the Revenue Act. This seems to have started at New Haven, as the New York *Gazette* smugly announced on 22 November 1764: "The young Gentlemen of Yale College have unanimously agreed not to make use of any foreign spirituous Liquors. . . . The Gentlemen of the College cannot be too much commended for setting so laudable an Example. This will not only greatly diminish the Expences of Education, but prove, as may be presumed, very favourable to the Health and Improvement of the Students. At the same Time all Gentlemen of Taste, who visit the College, will think themselves better entertained with a good Glass of Beer or Cider, offered them upon such Principles, than they could be, with the best Punch or Madeira." New England rum, however, did not come under the boycott.

Parliament's Stamp Act of 1765 was the first direct, internal tax ever to be laid on the colonies by Parliament; indeed, the first tax of any sort other than customs duties. It was a heavy tax, bearing on all classes and sections in America, the more so because the specified sums had to be paid in sterling. This meant that, in terms of colonial currencies, the tax was increased between 33 and 100 per cent. Almost every kind of legal paper, plea, demurrer, etc. would have to pay 3s, and an appeal or writ of error, 10s; every school or college degree diploma or donation to a school or college, £2; liquor licenses, £1 to £4 on top of the local licensing fee; a lawyer's license to practice, £10; land warrant or deed, from 6d to 5s; an appointment to office, £4. Every copy (not merely every issue) of a newspaper must pay 1s a sheet, and each advertisement in the same, 2s for each issue; and every copy of an almanac, 4d. Playing cards were charged a shilling a pack, and dice 10s a pair. All legal documents written in any other language than English must pay double duty, except in Quebec and Granada. All offenses against the Stamp Act were to be tried in an admiralty court, where the defendant would have no benefit of trial by jury. The Act also had a high nuisance value; every sheet or document subject to the duty had to be engrossed or printed on specially stamped paper sold by the official distributors, or brought to a stamp office to be embossed with the stamp, and the duty paid. One can imagine the inconvenience and trouble this would have given the publishers of newspapers and almanacs.

That age, as Horace Walpole remarked, was one of revolt. Ireland had her "Whiteboy" riots against forced labor and absentee landlords. In London, in May 1765, there took place the Bloomsbury riots against the unpopular Duke of Bedford. While the Duke was at dinner, a mob hurled stones through his windows and would have pulled down the house and roughed him up, had they not been driven off by the Horse Guards. Jack Wilkes, arrested on a general warrant for alleged indecency, became the hero of the London mob and of the Sons of Liberty in the colonies, where towns and counties were named after him. In Corsica, Pasquale Paoli unsuccessfully led a rebellion against the French and got his name, too, on the map of Pennsylvania. In Madrid there broke out *el motín de Esquilache*, a riot against the king's Neapolitan minister. Said Horace Walpole, "When the Spanish diadem totters, what royal head must not ache?"

The English colonies, chief contributors to the royal British headache, found the Stamp Act an easy mark, administered as it was by crown-appointed distributors of embossed paper which could be destroyed. Despite the few means of communication between the different colonies, their action against the Stamp Act was remarkably uniform from Halifax to Jamaica. In every continental seaport there was formed a group of middle-class citizens who called themselves "Sons of Liberty," a phrase first applied to the Americans by Isaac Barré in a speech against the Act in the House of Commons. These liberty boys, often disguising themselves as workmen or sailors, coerced distributors into resigning, burned the stamped paper, and incited people to attack unpopular local characters. On the very day (1 November 1765) that the Stamp Act came into operation, a howling New York mob led by a shipmaster, Isaac Sears, forced Lieutenant Governor Colden to take refuge on board a British warship. It then attacked the fort at the Battery, broke into the governor's coach house, destroyed his carriages, and forced the officer in charge of the stamped paper to burn it. The rabble then marched up Broadway to a country estate on the Hudson (between the present Chambers and Warren streets), then occupied by an officer of the garrison, who had threatened "to cram the Stamp Act down the people's throats." They gutted his house, destroyed furniture, books and china, drank up the liquor, uprooted the garden, and departed carrying the regimental colors as a trophy.

In Charleston Henry Laurens, wrongly suspected by the local mob of hiding stamped paper in his house, was pulled out of bed at midnight while the house was searched by his friends, whom he recognized under blackface and sailor disguise. In Boston the stamp distributor was hanged in effigy and his shop pulled down, after which the mob turned its attention to the royal customs collectors and Chief Justice Hutchinson. It gutted their houses, burned their furniture, and tossed their books and papers into the street. The voters, in town meeting next day, expressed their "utter detestation" of this "horrid scene," but nobody compensated the victims.

Newport, Rhode Island, provided a touch of humor. There the Sons of Liberty hired an unemployed sailor named John Weber to organize a mob and terrify the local customs officials and stamp distributors. When the liberty boys tried to pay Weber off, he decided that he liked the work too much to quit, and threatened to pull down the houses of the very "patriots" who had employed him. They were rescued from this fate by the attorney general, who had Weber cast into jail and whisked out of the colony.

Except for this instance, the Sons of Liberty kept the mobs well in hand, and no blood was shed anywhere. But the Stamp Act was completely nullified. After a couple of months the courts reopened, vessels cleared and entered, and business resumed without the use of stamps. It was an amazing exhibition of what a closely knit revolutionary organization could do, anticipating the Jacobins of the French Revolution and the Bolsheviks of the Russian.

An assumption that the law was unconstitutional and void justified this violence to respectable colonists. On 30 May 1765 Patrick Henry made his famous "Caesar had his Brutus, Charles I his Cromwell" speech, after which the Virginia assembly passed a set of resolves declaring that it had "the only and sole exclusive right and power to lay taxes . . . upon the inhabitants of this Colony," who were "not bound to yield obedience to any law" of Parliament attempting to tax them. These Virginia Resolves were "an alarum bell to the disaffected" everywhere, as Governor Bernard wrote. Massachusetts summoned her sister colonies to send delegates to a congress in New York City. Nine colonies responded. This Stamp Act Congress was the first spontaneous movement toward colonial union that came from Americans themselves; and it brought together for the first time men from widely distant colonies, such as James Otis of Massachusetts, Philip Livingston of New York, John Dickinson of Philadelphia, Daniel Dulany of Maryland, and Christopher Gadsden of South Carolina. They discovered that they saw eye to eye on the need for concerted resistance against encroachments on colonial rights. And, in October 1765, they passed a set of resolutions less violent in tone than Patrick Henry's, asking Parliament to repeal the act forthwith.

Hitherto there had been loose talk on the American side of having colonial representatives in the House of Commons. The Stamp Act Congress rejected the idea as impractical because of the distance; and also, no doubt, because it realized that a handful of colonial members could not check a British majority. The idea was now shelved in favor of asserting the colonial assemblies' exclusive right to tax themselves; and the wisdom of this shift was later proved by the sad experience of Ireland under the 1800 Act of Union.

In August 1765, the Grenville ministry fell, largely because George III grew weary of hearing lectures on duty from his conscientious prime minister. An Old Whig ministry led by the thirty-five-year-old Marquess of Rockingham now came into power. Parliament, at Rockingham's instance, after a hot debate but with the king's support, repealed the Stamp Act in March 1766. It did so because the Commons were convinced that the Act could not be enforced, even by military force, against such firm and united opposition as the colonies had shown. At the same time, Parliament reaffirmed its right to tax America in the Declaratory Act, declaring that as the sovereign legislature of the British Empire it could "bind the colonies . . . in all cases whatsoever." This was an almost word-for-word copy of the Irish Declaratory Act of 1719 which held Ireland in bondage.

News of the repeal, which began to trickle into the colonies in May 1766, aroused an ecstasy of loyalty; the more so because William Pitt had moved it. In New York City repeal and the king's birthday were celebrated simultaneously; every window was illuminated, oxen were barbecued, and free beer and grog were provided for a happy crowd. The assembly voted an equestrian statue of George III and a statue of William Pitt to be erected at the Battery. Tablets or busts of "the Great Commoner" were set up at Williamsburg, even in country villages like Dedham, Massachusetts. In Boston, after the news arrived, "The Morning was ushered in with the ringing of Bells, and the Discharge of Cannon, Liberty-Tree was decorated with Flags & Streamers, and all round the Town, on the Tops of Houses, were displayed Colours and Pendants."

The Americans had won a political victory. United opposition (and not for fifty years would they be so united again) had forced the repeal. Their fundamental loyalty is proved by their neither taking notice of the Declaratory Act, nor demanding repeal of the Revenue Act of 1764. In reality the British government had taken three steps forward — Proclamation of 1763, Revenue Act, Declaratory Act — but only one back.

X I I I

Crisis, Calm, and Again Crisis

1766-1774

1. *The Townshend Acts*

D URING THE GENERAL JUBILATION that followed the repeal of the Stamp
Act, no serious effort was made by the British government to find out
what, if anything, could be done to raise defense funds through colonial assemblies. No royal commission was sent to America to study and report;
agents of the several colonies in London were not even consulted. Instead,
Parliament made a fresh attempt to tax the colonies, and placed in effect a
plan of imperial reorganization without consulting them.

English politics at this period are difficult to grasp, because the Whig party,
dominant through the greater part of the century, had splintered into factions
— as later happened to the Jeffersonian Republicans in America after the
War of 1812. The faction that cared most about American affairs was known
as the "Old Whigs," not from their age but because they claimed to inherit
the genuine Whig principles of the Glorious Revolution of 1688. The Marquess of Rockingham, the Earl of Dartmouth, the Duke of Richmond, General Conway, Edmund Burke, and Lord Camden the chief justice, were
Old Whigs; their names, adopted by American towns and counties, testify
American gratitude for their efforts. But no government in England was
overthrown on an American question before 1781. Ministries rose and fell
largely on personal or trivial questions. One or more leaders, disgruntled because too few of their friends were given jobs, voted against the administration, the ministry had to resign, and the king asked another leader to construct a new ministry that could command a majority in the House of Commons. That happened in August 1766. The Rockingham ministry resigned,
and George III called upon William Pitt, whom he had created Earl of
Chatham, to construct a new one. Americans hoped for great things from a
ministry headed by Pitt and including other prominent friends of America
such as Isaac Barré and Lord Shelburne. Unfortunately Chatham fell ill
shortly after he became prime minister, and was succeeded by the thirty-one-
year-old Duke of Grafton, an amiable peer who had no sense of leadership
and allowed any member of his team to initiate bills.

To quote Edmund Burke, "While the western horizon was still in a blaze
with Pitt's descending glory, on the opposite quarter of the heavens arose

189

another luminary, and for his hour became lord of the ascendant." This was Charles Townshend, chancellor of the exchequer (corresponding to our secretary of the treasury) — "a statesman who has left nothing but errors to account for his fame." Under the influence of a bumper of champagne, Townshend delivered in the House of Commons on 8 May 1767 a speech which a spectator described as "extravagantly fine. It lasted an hour, with torrents of wit, ridicule, vanity, lies and beautiful language." He taunted the former premier, still angry over the repeal of his Stamp Act. Grenville retorted, "You are cowards, you are afraid of the Americans, you dare not tax America!" Townshend replied, "Fear! Cowards! Dare not tax America! *I* dare tax America!" Grenville retorted, "Dare you tax America? I wish to God I could see it!" Townshend declared, "I will, I will!" And he did.

The Townshend Act for taxing America, passed in June 1767, was based on an unfortunate distinction made by certain colonial pamphleteers, that external taxes (customs duties), which had always been laid on goods entering the colonies, were constitutional, whilst internal taxes like the Stamp Act were not. Taking these men at their word, Parliament levied duties on certain English manufactures entering America, such as paper, glass, and paint, and on the East India Company's tea. As a concession, British duties on colonial grain and whale oil entering England were removed, which led to the first substantial export of wheat and flour from the colonies to England. And bounties were voted on colonial hemp, flax, and timber.

Although the Townshend duties afforded colonial leaders their principal talking point, far more important in the long run was the administrative reorganization that Parliament adopted at Townshend's suggestion. A big loophole in the imperial trade system was the lax collection of customs duties in the colonies. Many customs officials remained in England and appointed deputies, for a part of their salaries, to do their work. These deputies were accustomed to eke out their scanty pay by accepting gifts from importers, for turning their backs while dutiable goods were run ashore. That system now came to an end. Absentee collectors lost their jobs, mostly to conscientious, hard-working Scots, and the service was reorganized. An American Board of Commissioners of Customs was set up, with headquarters at Boston, charged with the power to issue regulations, control the collection of duties on all continental colonies, and to use the hated writs of assistance. Admiralty courts were freshly empowered to try cases under the Acts of Trade and Navigation, without a jury. The double purpose of these regulations was to raise money from America not only for defense but to create a fund from which the salaries of royal governors and judges could be paid, to render them independent of the assemblies for their salaries.

These regulations were beneficial to the royal treasury. Even though the Townshend duties on English manufactures were repealed in 1770, and despite boycotts, non-importation agreements, and the Boston Tea Party, the Commissioners of Customs collected £257,000 in ten years. Of this sum

£92,000 were absorbed by administrative costs, £32,000 spent on a colonial civil list, and £83,000 remitted to England. Charles Townshend did not live to see this unexpected success of his measures. He died suddenly in September 1767 and was succeeded as chancellor of the exchequer by Lord North, of the Whig faction known as the "King's Friends."

The Townshend Acts took Americans by surprise. Their trade was in the usual depression that is apt to set in four or five years after the end of a great war. It was hard for them to find the sterling money to pay these new taxes, and the regulations of the Commissioners of the Customs required so many bonds and documents that for a time it was difficult to do business at all. But colonial leaders were hard put to find a legal argument against the Townshend duties. They wished to deny Parliament's power to tax them, yet to acknowledge Parliament's power to regulate their commerce. They were not prepared to break loose from the protective system of the Acts of Trade and Navigation, nor could they deny that many of the new regulations were designed to stop lawbreaking. The colonial leader who came closest to resolving this dilemma was John Dickinson of Pennsylvania, who styled himself "The Pennsylvania Farmer." He was a conservative Philadelphia lawyer, born in Maryland and educated in England, neither an agitator nor a politician, but a public-spirited citizen who abhorred violence and hoped to settle all pending disputes with England by persuasion.

The twelve "Farmer's Letters" which began coming out in colonial newspapers at the end of 1767 were exactly what Americans wanted, and the loyal, respectful tone of them appealed to the Old Whigs in England. Here are some of the key passages:

The Parliament unquestionably possesses a legal authority to regulate the trade of Great Britain and all her colonies. . . . We are but parts of a whole; and therefore there must exist a power somewhere to preside, and preserve the connexion in due order. This power is lodged in the Parliament; and we are as much dependent on Great Britain as a perfectly free people can be on another. . . .

The cause of Liberty is a cause of too much dignity to be sullied by turbulence and tumult. . . .

Let us behave like dutiful children, who have received unmerited blows from a beloved parent. Let us complain to our parent; but let our complaints speak at the same time the language of affliction and veneration.

The first quotation shows that Dickinson was moving, somewhat fumblingly, toward the principle of federalism which became implicit in the American Revolution and explicit in the Constitution of 1787. "We are as much dependent on Great Britain as a perfectly free people can be on another." In other words, Parliament as the supreme legislature of the Empire has certain distinct powers over the colonies; but they retain the residue, corresponding to state rights. Unfortunately no responsible Englishman of that day seemed able to grasp this federal principle. William Knox, an Irishman who had lived several years in Georgia as a crown officer, had fun with

Dickinson in his reply: "It is this *new invention* of *collecting taxes* that makes them burdensome to the Colonies, and an infringement of their rights and privileges."

Samuel Adams of Boston, master of the town meeting and member of the assembly, had already reached the point in his thinking that Parliament had no right to legislate for the colonies on any subject. But he was too good a politician to admit it. A middle-class Bostonian, austere and implacable, Adams alone among leaders of the American Revolution was a genuine revolutionary, resembling in several respects the communist agitators of our time. He was certainly the Western world's first orchestra-leader of revolution. He knew that voters are moved by emotion rather than logic. A master of propaganda, he realized that the general run of people prefer drama and ritual to a well-argued exposition. New England people lacked ritual in religion and drama on a stage; but Adams provided them with both in highly agreeable forms. There was dancing around the Liberty Tree (a big elm near Boston Common), the hanging of unpopular characters in effigy from its branches, serenading those whom the radicals wished to become popular, and damning the British ministers over bowls of rum punch. Adams employed classic symbols of liberty such as the Phrygian liberty cap, a liberty song with new words by John Dickinson set to the rousing tune "Heart of Oak," which everyone knew, and on every possible occasion organized a protest meeting. These devices were copied by Sons of Liberty throughout the continent; even at Charleston, where Christopher Gadsden selected a live oak as liberty tree. John Adams, after a Sons of Liberty dinner of 350 covers, attended by delegates from Philadelphia, observed that these things "tinge the minds of the people; they impregnate them with the sentiments of liberty; they render the people fond of their leaders in the cause, and averse and bitter against all opponents."

Samuel Adams, well educated in the ancient classics, thought in terms of Roman virtue, and his favorite motto, chosen from the unlikely source of Ovid's *Remedia Amoris*, was *principiis obsta*, "Take a stand at the start," lest by one concession after another you end in complete subjection. He was no orator — he had a quavering voice and a shaky hand; so he let other Sons of Liberty like Joseph Warren and the firebrand Otis make the speeches, while he wrote provocative articles for the newspapers and pulled political strings.

In February 1768, after the full impact of the Townshend Acts, began to be appreciated, Adams and Otis drafted and the Massachusetts assembly adopted a circular letter to the assemblies of all other continental colonies, to call their attention to the Acts. The assembly, stated this letter, has "preferred a humble, dutiful and loyal petition to our most gracious sovereign . . . to obtain redress." The new taxes are obviously unconstitutional, but they hope that "united and dutiful supplications" of "distressed American subjects" to George III "will meet with his royal and favorable acceptance."

Although the language of this circular letter was moderate and loyal, the

Grafton ministry decided to make it the occasion for a showdown. Lord Hillsborough, the new secretary for the colonies, ordered the Massachusetts assembly to rescind the letter, and Governor Bernard to dismiss them if they refused. The assembly did refuse, by a vote of 92 to 17. Samuel Adams and Sons of Liberty everywhere seized on this incident as a golden opportunity for propaganda, making the most of the patriotic ninety-two who refused to rescind. Jack Wilkes in England was still fighting to retain the seat in the House of Commons to which he had been duly elected, and his slogan was "45," the number of his scurrilous newspaper which the government had suppressed. The Boston Sons of Liberty sent him two turtles, one weighing 45 pounds, the other 47 pounds, "making in the whole 92 pounds which is the Massachusetts patriotic number." Paul Revere, silversmith, made a silver punch bowl dedicated to the "Immortal 92" and engraved all over with "Wilkes and Liberty," "No. 45," "No General Warrants," and other slogans and symbols. The South Carolina assembly voted £1500 to pay Wilkes's debts.

In Boston the chief contributor to the Sons of Liberty war chest for printing, banners, and free rum at liberty tree rallies, was a thirty-one-year-old merchant named John Hancock. The new Commissioners of the Customs therefore determined to put him out of business. He was "framed" by a prosecution of his sloop *Liberty*, falsely charged with smuggling Madeira wine. The Boston mob rescued him and his vessel, and gave the royal customs officials a very rough time, in consequence of which they retired to the castle in Boston harbor, and Governor Bernard asked for and got protection. Two regiments of the Halifax garrison were sent to Boston. Halifax inhabitants, annoyed by the loss of the soldiers' payroll, began to think that they should do a little rioting too!

The Boston radicals now overplayed their hand. When the troops arrived from Halifax and Governor Bernard refused to recall the dismissed assembly, Boston town meeting invited the province to elect delegates to a convention. This was a revolutionary act, recalling what had taken place in 1688–89. Sam Adams even buttonholed Bostonians in the street, urging them in his quavering voice to take up arms "and be free and seize the king's officers." But such towns as did send delegates to the convention warned them to do nothing rash, nor did they; and the delegates, seeing the folly of trying to resist British troops, passed some mild resolutions and dissolved the convention.

Although the Grafton ministry failed to intimidate Boston, it dealt successfully with New York, where two regiments of the British army arrived in 1766. The Quartering or Mutiny Act of Parliament required local authorities to provide quarters or barracks for the king's troops and furnish them free with certain supplies, including beer or rum. The New York assembly boggled at paying for these beverages, but voted all other supplies for 1100 men. Lord Hillsborough announced that this was not enough, and ordered the assembly to be suspended like that of Massachusetts. In the next election, in the fall of

1769, New York voters surprisingly returned a majority of the conservative De Lancey faction, and the new assembly voted everything that the British troops required. Sons of Liberty, led by Isaac Sears and Alexander McDougall, denounced this as a "contemptible betrayal," and Governor Colden threw McDougall into prison for sedition. Even after he was released, in January 1770, New York became the scene of a serious riot. British troops cut down a liberty pole put up by the radicals and piled up the pieces in front of Sons of Liberty headquarters. A fight followed on Gordon Hill, the mob using clubs and staves against the soldiers' cutlasses and bayonets, and one citizen was killed. This affair is New York's claim for having shed the "first blood of the Revolution"; but that lonely "martyr" was soon eclipsed by those of the "Boston Massacre."

2. *The Western Problem*

Although a school of American historians, working back from a time when the West was radical and the East conservative, have tried to prove that the American Revolution, too, was a Western movement, the facts are completely contrary. The American Revolution was brought about by radical groups in the seaport towns, usually in alliance with local merchants, and with planters of the Southern tidewater. The Sons of Liberty were no effete Easterners forced into rebellion by angry frontiersmen dressed in buckskin shirts and coonskin caps; they were well-educated, middle-class people who used mobs to terrify their opponents and nullify British attempts to tax and reorganize the colonies. This Revolution was made in seaports from Portsmouth, New Hampshire, to Savannah, Georgia. Here were enough people to give orators an audience, to stimulate grievances, and to organize committees; and in some there was a British garrison to cause trouble and create bitterness. The New England countryside, suspicious of seaport agitators, came slowly into the movement. "Boston folks are full of notions," was their favorite saying. Up-river New York; frontier Pennsylvania, which hated the Quaker oligarchy; the "Old West" or "back country" from the valley of Virginia into the piedmont of the Carolinas, were slow to catch fire — and many of these people never did.

Parts of the back country were full of turmoil. Their grievances, however, were not against England but against the clique that ran things in the colonial capitals. The frontier had expanded so fast since 1730 that, with the best will in the world, the colonial assemblies could not keep up with it in matters of representation and setting up courts of justice. From New Hampshire to South Carolina there were complaints that the back country was underrepresented or not represented at all; that settlers had to travel hundreds of miles to attend court, that the fees required for legal business were intolerable. The assemblies and councils did not want their state houses swamped by crude frontiersmen, judges did not care to ride circuit into the backwoods, and court officers "had to live." The fee table was a survival of the middle ages when the English kings were too poor to pay salaries to sheriffs and minor officials, who supported themselves by taking fees from anyone who required their labors. Today, although the system persists in American county government, fees are relatively moderate; but the litigant in 1765 had to pay anywhere from 5 s to £5 "every time he turned round," which meant that a poor man forced to go to law to defend his rights was apt to lose his shirt.[1]

Back-country discontent in the 1760's was most pronounced in the Carolinas. There, owing to thousands of pioneers from Pennsylvania pouring from the great valley into the piedmont, there had grown up a society differing in origin, religion, even race, from the people of the seaboard, and separated from them physically by a belt of pine barrens. Almost half the total population of South Carolina, and four-fifths of the white population, lived in the back country of that province in 1776. Yet the provincial government was completely centralized at Charleston, with neither counties nor courts in the back country, much less schools or police; a man had to own 500 acres and 20 slaves to qualify for membership in the assembly. Back-country settlers were at the mercy of border ruffians, horse thieves, and Indian raiders; a band of Creeks murdered fourteen people in the frontier settlement at Long Canes on Christmas Eve 1763, and were only driven off because Patrick Calhoun, father of John C., took command of the survivors. The people wanted government, pure and simple, and formed associations known as "Regulators" to refuse payment of taxes until they got it. They were furious to hear that the Charleston Sons of Liberty had persuaded the South Carolina assembly to lavish thousads of pounds on a statue to William Pitt, a gift to Jack Wilkes, and Christopher Gadsden's expense account attending the Stamp Act Congress, while denying schools, churches, roads, bridges, or protection to their region. In 1769 the assembly did set up six new circuit courts, and revised the fee table. But most of the Westerners' grievances in this province were still unredressed when the War of Independence broke.

In North Carolina the separation between coastal region and back country was even sharper. Here the Western grievances were not lack of government, but bad government — unequal taxation, extortion by centrally appointed judges and corrupt sheriffs, greedy lawyers, uncertainty of land titles, scarcity of hard money to pay taxes, refusal of the assembly to provide paper money or to allow taxes to be paid in produce, consequent tax levies "by distress," and government taking over poor men's farms. These grievances are strikingly similar to those of the Shays rebels of 1786 in Massachusetts; and Herman

1. The fee system is one of our less recognized abuses today. Alfred E. Smith in his *Story* admits that he raked in $103,000 in fees in two years, as a minor official in New York. A study by the Associated Press in 1951 brought out the fact that the treasurer of one Indiana county collected up to $40,000 in fees; that probate judges were making more than salaried justices of state supreme courts, and that many J.P.'s were collecting thousands annually in fees for simply witnessing legal papers. And the notoriously unfair apportionment of representatives in many states led to an important Supreme Court decision in 1964.

Husband, leader of the North Carolina Regulators, turns up twenty-five years later as a Whisky rebel in Pennsylvania. The five Western counties were well represented in the North Carolina assembly of 1769, but Governor Tryon dissolved that body before it could do anything about local grievances. In the meantime, the superior court at Hillsboro had been broken up by Regulators and some of the unpopular lawyers, such as Edmund Fanning, were beaten up and their houses wrecked.

Grievances accumulated for two more years, until some 2000 Regulators confronted half their number of loyal militia, on the banks of the Alamance river. There followed, on 16 May 1771, the so-called Battle of the Alamance. Only nine men were killed on each side, since most of the unarmed Regulators ran away after the first volley. But fifteen prisoners were tried for treason, and six were hanged. Governor Tryon and the army then made a triumphal progress through Regulator country and exacted an oath of allegiance from every male inhabitant.

That was the end of the War of the Regulation, the most serious internal rebellion in the English colonies since Nat Bacon's. It was put down largely by Whigs who later became Patriots. The next assembly passed some remedial legislation such as fixing maximum fees and establishing tobacco warehouses whose receipts could be tendered for taxes. But the North Carolina back country was still so discontented in 1776 that many former rebels emigrated to Tennessee to avoid taking part in the war, and others became Tories.

Back-country brawls from New Hampshire to South Carolina seem never to have interested the British government, which thereby missed a golden opportunity to win support from tough frontiersmen against the silk-stockinged Sons of Liberty and their wharf-rat mobsters. But the British government was deeply concerned with another Western problem. How far were land speculators to be allowed to encroach on the Indians' country? Would George III countenance Western expansion, or turn the Royal Proclamation of 1763 into a permanent policy?

In 1768 the two Indian superintendents who had recently been appointed made three important treaties: the Treaty of Fort Stanwix with the Iroquois, the Treaty of Hard Labour (a frontier post in South Carolina) with the Cherokee, and the Treaty of Pensacola with the Creek nation. These treaties set up a new frontier line somewhat west of the Royal Proclamation Line of 1763, not superseded until after the Federal Constitution went into effect. This new line failed to satisfy the land speculators. In 1768 George Washington and Captain William Crawford, who had accompanied him on the expedition against Fort Duquesne ten years earlier, set about obtaining deeds from Pennsylvania to a large tract in the western part of that province. Although this lay west of the Proclamation Line of 1763, Washington wrote to Crawford, "I can never never look on that proclamation in any other light (but this I say between ourselves) than as a temporary expedient to quiet the minds of the Indians and must fall of course in a few years. . . . Any person therefore who neglects the present opportunity of hunting out good lands and in some measure marking . . . them for their own (in order to keep others from settling them) will never regain it." "The scheme," he added, must be "snugly carried on by you under the pretence of hunting other game."

That sort of thing was going on all along the frontier: — bands of "hunters" roaming the hardwood forests, blazing trees and noting landmarks, then lobbying for a grant. Washington and Crawford were small operators in comparison with the big companies then being formed. The largest and most important was the Walpole or Vandalia Company promoted by Benjamin Franklin, George Croghan, and Thomas Wharton of Philadelphia, fur-trading merchants who believed that the peltry business was about played out. The Vandalia was organized on the basis of seventy-two shares, some of which were issued free to important English politicians like the Walpoles, Lord Camden, and George Grenville. Their original modest object of acquiring one and a quarter million acres in the Ohio valley, on Franklin's advice was swollen to ten million acres, for which they proposed to pay the crown £10,000. They had plenty of influence in London and even succeeded in getting rid of Lord Hillsborough the colonial secretary, who opposed the scheme because he was afraid it would depopulate Ireland, where he owned great estates. Some of the other schemes then pressing for crown grants were "Charlotiana," embracing most of Illinois and Wisconsin, promoted by Franklin and Sir William Johnson; General Phineas Lyman's "Military Adventurers," who asked for Kentucky and half Tennessee; and Major Thomas Mant's scheme for settling veterans on a tract covering somewhat more than the present state of Michigan. The Board of Trade and Plantations wrecked these big schemes, on the ground that "the proposition of forming inland colonies in America" was new and contrary to British interests. Let the restless Americans fill up Nova Scotia and the Floridas, where they will consume British manufactures, rather than settle on the Western waters, where the natural outlet for their products will be the Mississippi and New Orleans. This policy became official in a Royal Proclamation of 1774. It doubtless contributed toward making the big land speculators favor an independent America, which might look more kindly on their schemes.

3. The Non-Importation Movement

The New York assembly's cave-in and the Boston convention's collapse in 1768 convinced radical leaders that the only way they could make headway against the Townshend Acts was by co-operating with merchants to enforce a boycott of the taxed British goods. The new duties and regulations, burdensome to merchants and shipowners, gave them a common interest with the agitators. A result of this alliance was the non-importation movement of 1768–1770. Voluntary agreements were entered into by merchants, to boycott specific British or West India goods; not only those taxed but many untaxed luxuries, in order to put pressure on the British. Non-importation associations were formed in every colony and in almost every seaport. The leading merchants and, in the South, leading planters, agreed to import no British goods, or taxed tea, and to promote home industry. There began a vogue for spinning bees, wearing clothes of home-woven cloth, and brewing raspberry-leaf or Labrador tea. A freshman in the College of New Jersey who later became the fourth President of the United States, wrote to his father that every one of the 115 Princeton students was wearing homespun. The Harvard Corporation voted to let commencers wear homespun gray or brown instead of imported black broadcloth; commencement programs were printed on locally manufactured paper. Following the earlier example of Yale students in renouncing imported wines, Harvard students made the incommensurate sacrifice of giving up tea.

Non-importation agreements were difficult to enforce, as colonial sentiment was not nearly so united against the Townshend duties as it had been against the Stamp Act. Rioting alarmed many men of property, and the strong-arm methods by which the Sons of Liberty enforced "voluntary" agreements convinced them that British taxation was preferable to mob rule. Philadelphia took almost a year to come into the movement, and in Virginia and Maryland most of the merchants were Scots who had no sympathy with colonial liberties. Loyalist newspapers published statistics proving that supposedly patriotic merchants were smuggling British goods on the side; and this weakened the resolution of merchants elsewhere. Newport backed out in October 1769, on the ground that the Bostonians were not keeping faith. And non-importation was enforced very unequally. Imports decreased 45 to 50 per cent in Boston, Pennsylvania, and New Jersey, and as much as 83 per cent in New York; but imports into Virginia, Maryland, and the Carolinas actually increased. The effect on British industry and commerce was annoying but not disastrous, as new markets for English goods were opened elsewhere.

The Duke of Grafton resigned in January 1770, and the king turned to his friend Lord North to form a new ministry. He and the king, whom Americans later regarded as monsters, were responsible for the next concession.

George III, with ten years' experience as king, would have been called a "good guy" had he lived in the twentieth century. He was more popular in Britain and America than any English monarch since Charles II. Sincerely religious, temperate in food and drink, he had an impeccable private life; he never indulged in the clumsy frolics to which male members of the royal house of Hanover have been prone. He loved manly sports and country life, rode boldly to hounds and ran his own farm. George was very methodical and conscientious in his conduct of public business. But of the quality of statesmanship with which kings were supposed to be born, he had none.

His object was to substitute national leadership for party government; to rescue the crown from the clutches of leading Whig families, and to be his own prime minister. By 1770 George had got the hang of English politics and had become a manipulator second to none in the kingdom. He spent so much money sustaining Lord North's ministry and supporting "friendly" members of the House of Commons that the palace servants complained of not having enough to eat. In the general election of 1780 George spent the enormous sum of £104,000 to have the "right" people elected, and succeeded. It is not correct to say that George III introduced a new system of government, or that he aimed at absolutism. He simply put himself at the head of the old Whig system and used it for what, rightly or wrongly, he believed to be the national interest. After several attempts to find a prime minister who would be responsible to him rather than to the House of Commons, he got what he wanted in Lord North — and lost an empire.

The other Whig factions did not catch on to what was going on for two or three years. By that time they had persuaded themselves that the king was trying to subvert the British constitution through corruption, and set up a royal absolutism. This explains why Burke, Pitt, Richmond, and many other leading Englishmen backed the colonists against their own government, and encouraged Americans to feel that they were fighting for liberty in England as well as in America.

George III felt no prejudice against Americans. If he had had the sense to pay them a visit, and had chased foxes in Virginia, shot quail in Carolina, and gone fishing with the Yankees, he might have won their hearts and possibly learned something about colonial quirks. He had supported the repeal of the Stamp Act, and his first gesture toward the colonies in 1770 was conciliatory. With the king's support, Lord North brought in a bill to repeal the Townshend duties except the one on tea. George insisted that, in view of the Americans' boycott of British goods, and their infractions of law and order, the tea duty must be maintained "as a mark of the supremacy of Parliament." But all Townshend duties on British goods were wiped out.

The colonial radicals wished to continue non-importation until Parliament was forced to repeal the tea duty. But they found it impossible to keep merchants in line. They had sold out their old stocks and could not continue in business without fresh goods from England. So, after news of the repeal arrived, the merchants' associations in one colony after another lifted the boycott.

On 5 March 1770, the very day that Parliament repealed the Townshend duties, a bad brawl took place in Boston. The two British regiments quartered there were having a very unpleasant time. The local radicals got out a weekly scandal sheet, *The Journal of Public Occurrences*, which they circulated throughout the colonies, describing imaginary scenes of drunkenness and outrage. The British redcoats wished to be friendly with the populace but were taunted as "lobster-backs," ambushed, and beaten up by waterside toughs. If a solid citizen of Boston, whose daughters wished more exciting company than shopkeepers and Harvard students, invited a British officer to dine, word was passed around the town, unseemly cries were heard outside the house, the guest was apt to step into something nasty when he went down the front steps, and his host was likely to find a suggestive sample of tar and feathers on his front door.

The showdown came in early March 1770 after a few soldiers, to eke out their meager pay, had taken part-time jobs in a ropewalk where the regular workmen had gone on strike. That led to a riot in which a civilian was killed. On the evening of the 5th, a group which John Adams described as "Negroes and mulattoes, Irish teagues and outlandish jack-tars" began pelting with snowballs a redcoat who was standing sentry-go at the customs house on King (now State) Street. The main guard of about twenty men was called out and, with fixed bayonets, confronted a yelling mob of several hundred boys and men. After they had been taunted and stoned for half an hour, one soldier, who had been hit by a club, lost patience and fired without orders. Others followed suit; and when the smoke cleared, three men (one a sailor, another a Negro who was the most aggressive member of the mob) lay dead, and two more were mortally wounded.

Then what an uproar by the radicals! They named this affair the "Boston Massacre" and described it as a wanton killing of peaceable citizens by a brutal and licentious soldiery. The continent rang with outraged screams. But news of the repeal of the Townshend duties quenched the uproar, the non-importation agreements collapsed, and a wave of prosperity set in.

From the English side came strong hints that the colonial radicals had better pipe down. The Marquess of Rockingham said that the Americans seemed determined to leave their English friends with no shadow of an excuse to defend them. William Pitt, Lord Chatham, having recovered from his illness, took his seat in the House of Lords, saying:

I love the Americans because they love liberty, and I love them for the noble efforts they made in the last war. . . . I think the idea of drawing money from them by taxes was ill-judged. Trade is your object with them, and they should be encouraged; those millions who keep you, who are the industrious hive employed, should be encouraged. But (I wish every sensible American, both here in that country, heard what I say) if they carry their notions of liberty too far, as I fear they do, — if they will not be subject to the laws of this country, — especially if they would disengage themselves from the laws of trade and navigation, of which I see too many symptoms, as much of an American as I am, they have not a more determined opposer than they will find in me. They must be subordinate. In all laws relating to trade and navigation especially, this is the mother country, they are the children; they must obey, and we prescribe.

4. Calm and Crisis

This advice had no effect on Samuel Adams. He squeezed every ounce of propaganda out of the "Boston Massacre." The soldiers, defended by John

Adams and given a fair trial, were acquitted of murder, but Sam had the "martyr" version printed in a series of articles. On each successive Fifth of March — until the Fourth of July replaced it — the Sons of Liberty staged a procession to keep up resentment against the British. One would deliver a hot oration, and relics of the "massacre" would be displayed in the window of Paul Revere, who engraved a picture of "The Bloody Massacre" which shows the soldiers in line of battle firing a pointblank volley at twenty respectable citizens.

It proved difficult to whip up resentment against Britain when the colonies were enjoying the greatest prosperity within memory. Imports into New England alone jumped from £330,000 to £1,200,000, although the Acts of Trade and Navigation were being enforced by the efficient Commissioners of the Customs. Short harvests in Europe created a demand for American corn and wheat; and to pay for it, English specie was sent to America for the first time in history. In Boston, £8,921 in customs duties, almost twice as much as in New York, was collected in 1771; and during three years prior to the famous tea party, Boston imported almost half a million pounds of tea. The annoying regulations of the customs commissioners had been relaxed so that there was an immense traffic of sloops and schooners between colonial harbors — almost a thousand entries at Boston in 1773.

John Hancock told the royal governor that he was through with agitation. John Adams confided to his diary, "I shall certainly become more retired and cautious; I shall certainly mind my own farm and my own business." Ben Franklin, still in England, begged his countrymen to keep quiet; he pointed out that the North ministry had made a great concession and that America could well afford to bear the slight tax burden still placed upon her. New York, too, quieted down after 1770. Soldiers of the garrison could now promenade their wenches on the Battery without danger of insult or attack. Philadelphia was calm as usual. Virginia, wrote Thomas Jefferson "seemed to fall into a state of insensibility to our situation," that Parliament still claimed power to bind the colonies "in all cases whatsoever." "Still quiet at the Southward," wrote John Adams in 1772, "and at New York they laugh at us."

Samuel Adams felt this to be a very dangerous state of affairs. "It is to be feared that the people will be so accustomed to bondage as to forget they were ever free." "Every day strengthens our opponents and weakens us," are typical statements in his letters of this period.

To the Loyalists of the Revolution, and to many conservative Americans who have since studied that era, Adams's acts and words ring false, like those of an irresponsible rabble-rouser, greedy for power. That impression is incorrect. Adams had a perfectly coherent and reasonable policy. The British government, he believed, was clinching control over colonial liberties by means of the customs duties, which enabled it gradually to put crown appointees on the royal payroll. But this issue was rather arid; rural taxpayers were apt to say it was all right with them if the king paid the governor! Adams needed a spectacular, emotional issue.

In the meantime the Boston radicals picked on their new royal governor, Thomas Hutchinson, a native-born, scholarly, middle-aged New Englander. His appointment was received with general joy as a return to the happy days of Governor Shirley. Hutchinson was a man of integrity, devoted to Whig principles within limits, always an opponent to severe British measures; but he had an unhappy faculty for rubbing people the wrong way, and of making wrong decisions. One of these was to adjourn the Massachusetts assembly to Cambridge, ostensibly to free it from pressure by the Boston mob. This succeeded in annoying the members and inconveniencing Harvard College, whose lecture rooms were commandeered; but it delighted the students, who flocked to hear the oratory of Otis and Joseph Warren, and were indoctrinated into becoming radicals themselves. When the assembly voted Governor Hutchinson a salary, he replied haughtily that the king had already taken care of that. Shortly after, news arrived that the judges of the superior court of Massachusetts were also on the royal payroll. That started Samuel Adams off on another tack. Boston town meeting, instigated by him, inquired of the governor whether the rumor were true? He replied, in effect, that it was none of their business. The town meeting then adopted a scheme of Adams's, the appointment of a committee of correspondence to concert measures in defense of colonial liberty with similar committees in other towns and colonies. Thus began what a prominent Loyalist called "the foulest, subtlest and most venomous serpent ever issued from the eggs of sedition." It created an extra-legal organization, like the soviets in revolutionary Russia, that could be called into action when the radical leaders gave the word.

Hutchinson also indulged in a newspaper debate with Samuel Adams and his friends on constitutional principles. Both drew freely on ancient history and Latin and Greek literature. This was most imprudent on the governor's part, because not only did Adams put it over him on classical learning; he drove him into a corner, where he had to admit that Americans had no rights other than those that king and Parliament chose to recognize.

Pretty soon the radicals had a more explosive issue than judges' salaries — the *Gaspee* affair. This was a little revenue cutter commanded by a lieutenant of the Royal Navy, employed by the Commissioners of the Customs to enforce the laws in Narragansett Bay, particularly favored by smugglers. Owing to the vigilance of her commander, *Gaspee* became very unpopular with the Rhode Islanders. When chasing a smuggler, she ran aground on a sandpit below Providence; and that night (9–10 June 1772) a party of local patriots boarded her, captured the officers and crew, beat them up, and burned the cutter to the water's edge. An attack on a naval vessel has always been a very serious offense, and it is not surprising that the British government made strong efforts to arrest the culprits and send them to England for trial. The *Gaspee* affair became the signal for "agit-prop" articles in the news-papers about rights to jury trial, "worse than Egyptian tyrants," "court of inquisition," etc. The government was unable to find anyone who had taken part in burning the cutter, but the threat to bring accused traitors to trial in England became a noose around every radical's neck. And no principle of English liberty was more sacred than a man's right to trial by a jury of his own community. Hence the attempt to apprehend the *Gaspee* mob had wide repercussions. It persuaded the Virginia house of burgesses to appoint a com-mittee of correspondence, with Patrick Henry, Thomas Jefferson, and Rich-ard Henry Lee among the members. This was a wonderful boost for Samuel Adams's revolutionary machine; and by the early part of the year 1774 the assemblies of twelve colonies had appointed similar committees of corre-spondence. The machine might yet have broken down for lack of fuel, had not the North ministry come to its rescue with a tankful of explosives.

The Townshend duty of 3*d* the pound on tea entering the colonies had not been repealed, like the other duties, in 1770; and in the five years 1768–72 the thirteen colonies alone had imported and paid duty on 1,866,615 pounds of tea. At the same time, a very large amount had been smuggled in, mostly from Dutch sources. Parliament in May 1773 legalized a new arrangement designed to relieve the British East India Company from the results of its own inefficiency. It removed the duty on tea entering England and allowed the Company to be its own exporter to the Colonies, doing away with mid-dlemen. This added no new duty, but took one off; and, if enforced, would have enabled the East India Company to undersell the smugglers and give the colonial consumer cheaper tea.

It was difficult to find a constitutional issue in this device to undercut the tea-runners; but the radicals were equal to it. They had all summer to think it over, to write articles against the "illegal monopoly" given the great chartered company, and to write poems about the "pestilential herb," and "the cup infused with bane by North's insidious hand." The East India Company made matters worse by consigning their teas to "safe" merchants such as the sons of Governor Hutchinson in Boston, who were untainted by association with Sons of Liberty.

So, when the tea ships began to arrive in four continental ports in Decem-ber 1773, the Sons of Liberty were ready. In Charleston the tea was unloaded, but kept under bond in a damp warehouse; at Philadelphia and New York the masters of the tea ships were "persuaded" to turn back without entering harbor. The Boston Sons of Liberty, nettled by a criticism that Josiah Quincy had heard in the South, that "Bostonians were better at resolving what to do than doing what they resolved," determined to put on a better show. They let the two tea ships sail into the harbor. Samuel Adams summoned a convention of committees of correspondence to meet at Old South Meeting House and back up what he had planned to do. The convention sent a message to Governor Hutchinson demanding that he order the ships to take the tea back to England. This was unlawful, since the ships had already entered the customs limits. When the governor's refusal reached the mass meeting, Adams arose and said, "This meeting can do nothing further to save the country." Instantly a mob disguised as Mohawk Indians and Negroes rushed down to the waterfront and emptied 342 big chests of precious tea into the harbor.

This Boston Tea Party had the calculated effect of irritating the British government into unwise acts of reprisal. Destruction of property — and tea at that — seemed to arouse John Bull far more than having a revenue cutter burned or soldiers beaten up. At a cabinet meeting on 4 February 1774, the attorney general was asked to consider whether the "late proceedings" at Boston amounted to high treason. Easy-going Lord North, bored rather than irritated, wished to avoid trouble; but the king was furious. So was English public opinion, and the North administration could not stand unless it did something. It looked as if appeasement had twice failed and that it was time for Mother England to crack down on her naughty brat. Parliament was like-minded; in spite of warnings from Burke, Barré, and even General Burgoyne, Parliament in May and June passed the so-called Coercive or Intolerable Acts. "The dye is now cast," wrote the king to Lord North. "The Colonies must either submit or triumph."

That is why this comic stage-Indian business of the Boston Tea Party was important. It goaded John Bull into a showdown, which was exactly what Sam Adams and the other radical leaders wanted.

X I V

Coercion to Independence

1774-1776

1. The Coercive Acts

THE BOSTON TEA PARTY needled Parliament into passing, and George III into signing, a series of laws that Americans referred to as the Coercive, or Intolerable, Acts. These were, in order, the Boston Port Act which virtually blockaded Boston until it chose to pay for the tumbled tea; the Massachusetts Government and Administration of Justice Acts, chastising the government of that naughty province; and the Quartering Act, which empowered royal governors to commandeer private houses in any colonial town for quartering soldiers. Associated with these laws in the popular mind, but really directed to an entirely different problem, was the Quebec Act.

Although passed neither in heat nor in anger — the dates of enactment extended from March to June 1774 and all were debated — these Coercive Acts were a pretty bald assertion of power. Edmund Burke, writing to the New York assembly's correspondence committee, said that the real intent of the Boston Port Act was the necessity for "*some Act* of Power." He was right. As Lenin once said, "The basic question of every revolution is the question of power in the state." From the day that unhappy law was passed, the question between England and the Thirteen Colonies was one of power; who would rule, or have the final say? All other questions of taxation, customs duties, and the like faded into the background. Through all stages of remonstrance, resistance, and outright war, the dominant issue was one of power — should Britain or America dictate the terms of their mutual association, or separation?

Could these opposing claims of authority and freedom ever be reconciled? We who know the outcome can little appreciate the strain of those two years from June of 1774 to 4 July 1776, on men of good will, both sides of the Atlantic. Loyalty, tradition, pride of membership in a great empire, urged the colonials to submit; but cherished principles of English liberty impelled them to take a firm stand. In England the wrench was almost as severe. Many Old Whigs and prominent merchants opposed every step in Parliament's punitive program, and braved the charge of treason in applauding America's final decision to act on James Otis's motto, *Ubi libertas ibi patria* — "Where liberty is, there is my country."

The Quartering Act was intended to ease the military occupation for red-coats, who had been forced to sleep on Boston Common. The Government and Administration of Justice Acts altered the government of Massachusetts Bay by making the council (hitherto elected by the whole assembly) appointive by the governor, to hold office during the king's pleasure. The same principle was extended to all judges, marshals, sheriffs, and justices of the peace; and the towns were forbidden their favorite indoor sport of debating colonial rights and appointing committees of correspondence. These two laws, if enforced, would have sewed up Massachusetts Bay for the king; and they aroused apprehension that similar or worse alterations would be made in the governments of other troublesome colonies.

The Boston Port Act, first to be passed, created the most widespread indignation, and more definitely showed the hand of tyranny. All customs officials were removed to Salem, and the guilty port sealed up; even boat landings were illegal. It was to remain in force until "satisfaction" were made both for the tea and for losses sustained by royal officials in the Boston riots; and also until the king decided "that peace and obedience to the laws" were restored. Again to quote Burke, "The rendering the Means of Subsistence of a Whole City dependent upon the Kings private pleasure, even after the payment of a fine and satisfaction made, was without Precedent, and of a most dangerous Example." And this law was enforced by a squadron of the Royal Navy and by two regiments (soon increased to five) under General Thomas Gage, who at the same time was appointed governor and captain-general of Massachusetts Bay. The immediate effect was to start a bloodless insurrection in Massachusetts which confined the royal governor's authority to Boston and its environs. Committees of correspondence organized resistance so effectively that by the fall of 1774 the province was virtually independent, governed by an illegally elected convention.

Continent-wide, the effect was even more important. To the surprise even of the Bostonians, other colonies vied in sending food and money for the relief of the blockaded town. From South Carolina, for instance, came provisions to the value of £2700; Virginia sent 8600 bushels of corn and wheat and several hundred barrels of flour. The Old Dominion started rolling a ball which led to independence, with an assembly resolve of 24 May 1774. This resolve, drafted by Henry, Lee, Mason, and Jefferson, denounced the military occupation as a "hostile invasion," and designated 1 June, when the Port Act would go into effect, as a "day of fasting, humiliation and prayer." Governor Dunmore promptly dissolved the Virginia assembly, but before dispersing to their homes the burgesses met at the Raleigh tavern in Williamsburg and resolved that "an attack made on one of our sister Colonies, to compel submission to arbitrary taxes, is an attack made on all British America." They instructed their committee of correspondence to exchange views with similar committees in other colonies on the propriety of summoning a Continental congress. All the committees were in favor, and the First Continental Congress met at Philadelphia on 5 September 1774.

The fifty-five members of this Congress, which evolved into a federal government of a nation at war, were chosen by revolutionary conventions or committees in twelve continental colonies, from New Hampshire through South Carolina. Efforts of the extreme conservatives, whom we may now call Tories, to prevent these illegal elections were fruitless; the Continent seemed of one mind that concerted action must be taken. Congress included, besides the well-known radical leaders, a number of conservative Whigs such as the Rutledges of South Carolina, Joseph Galloway of Pennsylvania, and John Jay of New York. Peyton Randolph of Virginia was elected president of the Congress.

The Philadelphians outdid themselves in hospitality. John Adams, in addition to "generous, noble Sentiments and manly Eloquence" in Congress, enjoyed at Dr. Rush's "the very best of Claret, Madeira and Burgundy. Melons, fine beyond description"; and at Chief Justice Chew's four o'clock dinner, "Turtle and every other thing — Flummery, jellies, sweetmeats of 20 sorts, Trifles, whip'd syllabubbs, floating islands, fools, &c. I drank Madeira at a great Rate and found no inconvenience in it." These he shared with "all the Gentlemen from Virginia" and "Mr. Carrell of Anapolis a very sensible gentlemen, a Roman catholic, and of the first Fortune in America." But Samuel Adams, when he did dine out, called for bread and milk as appropriate to Roman virtue, and a balm for his stomach ulcer.

Congress faced a delicate task. America as a whole did not want independence; every path to conciliation must be kept open. But Congress had to do something about the Coercive Acts, and also to suggest a permanent solution of the struggle between *libertas* and *imperium*. It tackled that big subject first. Galloway brought forward a plan of union which proposed to settle the power problem by establishing an American parliament parallel to the British, each to have a veto over acts of the other relating to America. While this was being debated, word reached Philadelphia, via Paul Revere's saddlebags, of the sensational Suffolk resolves of 9 September, drafted by Joseph Warren and passed by a convention of the towns around Boston. These declared the Coercive Acts to be unconstitutional and void, urged Massachusetts to form a free state until and unless they were repealed, advised the people to arm themselves, and recommended economic sanctions against Britain. This news brought Congress up short, and made debating the Galloway plan seem like discussing insurance while one's house burned. Congress encouraged the Massachusetts patriots by endorsing their Suffolk resolves, which Galloway (who eventually became a Tory), called "a declaration of war against Great Britain." His plan was then rejected.

Constructive efforts were made to solve the power problem. John Adams, James Wilson and Thomas Jefferson wrote pamphlets advocating what amounted to dominion status — a reorganization of the British empire similar to that of the British Commonwealth prior to World War II. A colony's only connection with Great Britain would be the king, who, through his privy council, would conduct foreign relations and determine matters of war and peace, and even regulate imperial trade; but Parliament must keep hands off the colonies. This proposition went even further than the Continental Congress's resolves; so far, indeed, that it is doubtful whether even Chatham or Burke would have accepted it. But it was neither visionary nor impractical, as proved by the fact that in 1778 Lord North's government proposed to end the war and restore imperial unity on just such terms. Thus, the American Revolution was no irrepressible conflict. Everything the colonies wanted, the Old Whigs in England were ready to grant in 1775; but they were then out of office. And those in office, the coalition led by Lord North, were always too late with concessions.

The Continental Congress issued a Declaration of Rights stating that Americans were entitled to all English liberties, and citing a number of acts of Parliament of the past ten years which violated that principle. Congress then adopted a non-importation, non-exportation, and non-consumption agreement, virtually cutting off imports from Britain after 1 December 1774, and exports to Britain after 10 September 1775, if by that time the Coercive Acts had not been repealed. This agreement was called The Association. The American Revolution (as people now began to call the movement) showed a Puritan streak common to most revolutions, in a vote of Congress to encourage frugality and to "discourage every species of extravagance and dissipation, especially all horse-racing, and all kinds of gaming, cock-fighting, exhibitions of shews, plays, and other expensive diversions and entertainments," including elaborate funerals. Congress also voted to give up drinking imported tea, madeira, and port wine. But the local product, rum, was still permissible. The Congress rose on 22 October 1774, after resolving to meet again the following 10 May if by that time colonial grievances had not been redressed.

The weeks or even months then required for mail to cross the Atlantic allowed time for hotheads on both sides to cool off. But the time lag also meant that the situation got out of hand by the time England tried to do something about it. Franklin supported a common sense suggestion to send a royal commission to find out and report what the colonists really wanted. That eventually became the normal British way to deal with imperial problems, but George III would have none of it; he told Lord North that sending over a commission would look as if he were more afraid of Congress than they of him. The next sensible suggestion came from the Earl of Chatham. On 20 January 1775 he moved in the House of Lords to withdraw the British troops from Boston. Looking "like an old Roman Senator, rising with the dignity of age, yet speaking with the fire of youth" (as one present reported), he made what is now recognized as one of the greatest parliamentary orations of all time, declaring principles that apply to the nationalist revolutions of our day as well as to those of the 1770's. The Americans, he said, will never be reconciled until the troops are withdrawn. "What is our right to persist in such cruel and vindictive measures against that loyal and respectable people?" Americans have been abused, misrepresented, and traduced in Parliament in the most atrocious manner. And how have they behaved under this provocation? "With unexampled patience, with unparalleled wisdom." The Continental Congress for sagacity, moderation, manly spirit, and honor "shines unrivalled." All attempts to establish despotism over such a mighty continental nation must be vain, must be fatal. But "there is no time to be lost. . . . Nay, while I am now speaking the decisive blow may be struck, and millions are involved in the consequence. . . . Years, perhaps ages, will not heal the wounds." And the Duke of Richmond, in the same debate, warned the Lords, "You may spread fire, sword and desolation, but that will not be government. . . . No people can ever be made to submit to a form of government they say they will not receive."

The Lords' debate was followed on 23 January 1775 by one in the House of Commons on a petition signed by hundreds of English merchants to repeal the Coercive Acts. Edmund Burke then delivered the first of his famous speeches on reconciliation with America, but the motion to repeal was lost, 82 to 197. Next, Chatham managed to have introduced in the lower house on 1 February 1775 a bill "for settling the troubles in America." The principle was to preserve parlimentary control of trade and navigation, but to recognize the Continental Congress as a legal body, competent to grant money for imperial defense, The Coercive Acts, the Quebec Act, and the tea duty would be repealed, Boston set free, colonial judges would be appointed during good behavior, and the sanctity of colonial charters guaranteed. Although this bill was no clean-cut dominion solution of the imperial problem, it conceded every practical point for which Congress had contended. If it had been passed, there would have been no war and no Declaration of Independence. But the bill was roundly defeated. The only concession Lord North's majority would make was a resolve that if any colony promised to raise what His Majesty's government considered a proper quota for imperial defense, and assume the cost of its civil list, Parliament would exempt that colony from the revenue acts. North's "conciliatory resolve" naturally failed to conciliate because, as Benjamin Franklin wrote, it left ultimate power over colonial taxation to Parliament, and did nothing about the Coercive Acts.

Time was running out. Chatham warned Parliament on 1 February, "Great Britain and America were already in martial array, waiting for the signal to engage in a contest in which . . . ruin and destruction must be the inevitable consequence to both." Joseph Warren on the 20th wrote from Boston to a friend, in London, "It is not yet too late to accommodate the dispute amicably. But . . . if once General Gage should lead his troops into the country, with design to enforce the late Acts of Parliament, Great Britain may take her leave . . . of all America." That is exactly what Gage was planning to do.

As a sign that the North ministry wanted a way out, it attempted a secret negotiation in London with Benjamin Franklin. Lord North and his friends had abused the philosopher and ousted him from his job as deputy post-master general in America, but they looked on him as a "fixer." Three inter-mediaries, one a sister of Admiral Lord Howe, hinted in the course of chess games and social conversation that if Franklin would act as mediator he "might exact any reward in the power of government to bestow." They even offered him £1800 as down payment. Franklin replied that unless the Coer-cive Acts were repealed and the army withdrawn from Boston, even God Almighty could not bring about a reconciliation. The ministry's assumption that money and influence could settle everything so disgusted Franklin, hith-erto a moderate Whig working for peace, that he became an out-and-out radical for American independence.

Lord North now introduced another coercive bill, on the fatuous assump-tion that it would isolate New England and make it an example. This New England Restraining Act, signed 30 March 1775, forbade the four colonies of that region to trade with any part of the world except Great Britain and Ireland, and denied their fishermen access to the fishing banks off Newfound-land and Nova Scotia. To deprive the Yankees of their fisheries was like ordering Virginians not to grow tobacco. There might have been a revolution in the name of the "sacred codfish," had General Gage not made an excur-sion to Concord before news of the New England Restraining Act arrived.

2. Western and Canadian Interlude

The Boston Tea Party, among other things, spoiled the game of the Van-dalia and other land-speculating companies at a time when they had nearly won over the Board of Trade. But the pioneers were pushing west just the same, and Kentucky was the next scene of conflict. This "dark and bloody ground" over which many Indian tribes had hunted but where none dared dwell, was visited immediately after the French and Indian War by Daniel Boone and other "long hunters." They brought back tales of great hardwood forests, blue grass prairies, fertile meadows, and vast herds of buffalo and deer. These and other small-time speculators obtained the ear of the governor of Virginia, the Earl of Dunmore. He began granting crown lands beyond the Treaty of Fort Stanwix line to holders of land warrants issued to war veterans. This practice ran so counter to the Britsh Western policy already laid down, that the North ministry in February 1774 ordered governors to make no land grants except in areas already ceded by the In-dians, and such ceded land was to be advertised and sold by auction. This statesmanlike plan, which Congress imitated in 1785, was bitterly resented by the speculators and alluded to as a grievance in the Declaration of Independence.

By the time these royal instructions reached America, Virginia was engaged in a war with the Shawnee nation, which had never ceded its rights over Kentucky and was rendered desperate by the long hunters killing off the game. Governor Dunmore dispatched two armed parties of volunteers to take possession of the illegally granted lands. After one party had been ambushed by Shawnee braves on the Kentucky river in July, Dunmore ordered out some 1500 militia of western Virginia, and these under Colonel Andrew Lewis, on 6 October, defeated Chief Cornstalk of the Shawnee at Point Pleasant, where the Great Kanawha river joins the Ohio. Owing to Sir William Johnson's diplomacy, the Six Nations and the Western tribes left the Shawnee to their fate, and in the subsequent peace negotiations the latter ceded all their Kentucky claims to Virginia. So ended "Governor Dunmore's War."

The Continental Congress protested vigorously against the Quebec Act of 22 June 1774. This infuriated the Americans, partly because it picked up the southern boundary of Quebec and carried it to the Ohio river, as Louis XV and the Marquis Duquesne had claimed, thus depriving the four colonies which claimed lands north of the Ohio of the territory of four future states. There were good administrative reasons for this extension. The English government at Quebec had adopted a sound Indian administrative service, Scots immigrants were sending coureurs de bois to buy furs in the Ohio country, and the advantage of having these traders controlled from Quebec, and of keeping out hunters like Daniel Boone, were obvious.

The other and more important part of the Quebec Act is generally considered a landmark of toleration. It guaranteed to the French their seignorial system and civil law, and confirmed to the Roman Catholic church in Canada the right to "hold, receive and enjoy" its "accustomed dues and rights," which included control of education. The British government should have been commended for realizing that it could never make English Protestants out of French Canadians; but the Continental Congress denounced it for "establishing the Roman Catholic religion . . . abolishing the equitable system of English laws, and erecting a tyranny there, to the great danger . . . of the neighboring British colonies." Samuel Adams for years had been conducting a whispering (or, rather, shouting) campaign that George III, like James II, tended toward "popery." So here it was — the thin end of the wedge. As a Canadian historian quipped, "To the disordered imaginations of the American patriots, the northern province loomed up suddenly like a spectre from some barbaric and vanished past." Naturally, the French of Quebec declined pressing invitations to be represented at Philadelphia and to make common cause with the American Revolution.

Nova Scotia stayed quiet through all the pre-revolutionary agitation, although her Protestant inhabitants (mostly immigrants from New England) disliked the Quebec Act. Neutrality was an old Acadian tradition, now strengthened by a religious revival started by Henry Alline, which swept through the province and aroused far more interest than the war. The Floridas were too recently acquired and thinly populated to do anything. Georgia very nearly stayed out, a southern counterpart to Nova Scotia. She was not represented in the First Continental Congress; but the energetic efforts of a small group of settlers from New England, led by Lyman Hall, brought her into the Second. The West Indian colonies were too closely tied to England by trade and consanguinity even to contemplate supporting Massachusetts.

Fear of slave insurrection also tended to keep the West Indies loyal; the population of Jamaica in 1778 was 18,420 whites and 205,261 Negroes, mostly slaves. In Bermuda there was much sympathy with Congress, but the islanders, like the Nova Scotians, decided to stick to England and trade with both sides.

3. Fighting Begins

The Province of Massachusetts Bay became virtually independent in October 1774, when the assembly, dissolved by Governor Gage, met at Concord as a provincial congress under the presidency of John Hancock. This congress took over the government, ignoring both Gage and his newly appointed council. It appointed a new treasurer to collect taxes, and a committee of safety as a standing executive board. Boston was full of redcoats, and the harbor bristled with masts of naval vessels sent to enforce the Boston Port Act; but the governor could exert no authority outside the town. All winter long the committee of safety collected arms and munitions, organized and drilled selected militia (the minute men) for instant action, set up a system of intelligence to anticipate any British move, and prepared to resist any attempt of the royal government to take over the interior.

What made the farmers fight in 1775? Judge Mellen Chamberlain in 1842, when he was twenty-one, interviewed Captain Preston, a ninety-one-year-old veteran of the Concord fight: "Did you take up arms against intolerable oppressions?" he asked.

"Oppressions?" replied the old man. "I didn't feel them."

"What, were you not oppressed by the Stamp Act?"

"I never saw one of those stamps. I certainly never paid a penny for one of them."

"Well, what then about the tea tax?"

"I never drank a drop of the stuff; the boys threw it all overboard."

"Then I suppose you had been reading Harington or Sidney and Locke about the eternal principles of liberty?"

"Never heard of 'em. We read only the Bible, the Catechism, Watts' Psalms and Hymns, and the Almanac."

"Well, then, what was the matter? And what did you mean in going to the fight?"

"Young man, what we meant in going for those redcoats was this: *we always had governed ourselves, and we always meant to. They didn't mean we should.*"

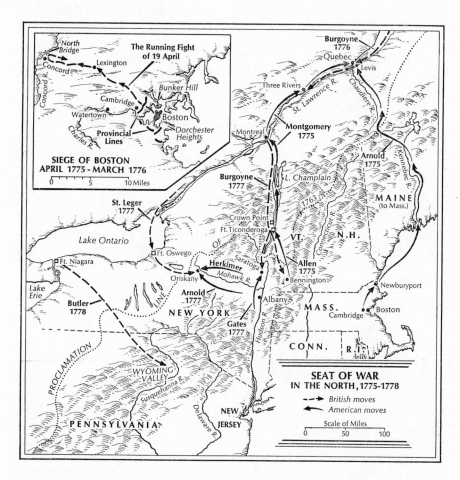

Old men's recollections so long after the event are not regarded by historians as good sources of history, but this gaffer's estimate of the situation is supported by a contemporary report by John Howe, whom Governor Gage sent out from Boston in early April 1775 to spy out the state of the countryside. On his way back Howe called at a small house beside the road, inhabited by an old man and his wife. The man was cleaning a gun. "I asked him," wrote Howe, "what he was going to kill, as he was so old, I should not think he could take sight at any game; he said there was a flock of redcoats at

Boston, which he expected would be here soon; he meant to try and hit some of them, as he expected they would be very good marks. I asked the old man how he expected to fight; he said, 'Open field fighting, or any other way to kill them redcoats!' I asked him how old he was; he said, 'Seventy-seven, and never was killed yet.' I asked the old man if there were any tories nigh there; he said there was one tory house in sight, and he wished it was in flames. The old man says, 'Old woman put in the bullet pouch a handful of buckshot, as I understand the English like an assortment of plums!"

Gage did not heed the warning. To destroy patriot munitions at Concord, he dispatched a strong detail under Major John Pitcairn on the night of 18–19 April 1775. Paul Revere and other riders aroused the countryside along their route; and minute men were on the march by break of day as far away as New Hampshire and Connecticut. When Major Pitcairn, after marching his red-coats all night, reached Lexington, he found a grim band of minute men lined up on the village common parallel to his line of advance. The British halted. The Major cried, "Disperse, ye rebels, disperse!" Someone, to this day nobody knows who, fired a shot from behind a stone wall. Firing then became general, and by the time the minute men dispersed they had left eight dead on the green. Sam Adams and Hancock, when the British approached, scuttled across lots, Adams exclaiming, according to tradition, "This is a glorious day for America!" It was what he had been working toward for years — a bloody clash that would bring on independence.

The British continued their march to Concord where, as in Emerson's poem,

> . . . the embattled farmers stood,
> And fired the shot heard round the world.

And do not imagine that it failed to go round the world. The local version of an unprovoked massacre of peaceful farmers reached England eleven days before Gage's official report and raised a furor against the North government. Sent south from New England by swift expresses (Philadelphia, 24 April, Richmond on the 30th, New Bern, 7 May), the story strengthenened the Patriot cause everywhere, and in Virginia and North Carolina civil war broke out. The Paris press gave full details; here were troubled waters in which France might fish with profit. In Venice the leading news sheet published an account of *la grande scaramucia a Concordia*. And, after a poet had woven the story into "The Midnight Ride of Paul Revere," it traveled the rest of the way around the world. In his opening speech at the Bandung Conference of 18 April 1955, Dr. Sukarno reminded the Asian and African members that it was the anniversary of "the first successful anti-colonial war in history," of the

> . . . cry of defiance and not of fear,
> A voice in the darkness, a knock at the door,
> And a word that shall echo forevermore!

And this first president of the Indonesian Republic concluded, "Yes, it *shall* echo for evermore!"

4. Second Congress and Olive Branch

On 10 May 1775, when all America was buzzing with the news of Lexington and Concord, the Second Continental Congress met at Philadelphia. No more distinguished group of men ever assembled in this country. The "brace of Adamses" and John Hancock came from the seat of war; Silas Deane and Roger Sherman from Connecticut; John Jay, Philip Schuyler, and a trio of Livingstons from New York and New Jersey; Caesar Rodney, Thomas McKean, and Thomas Read, from Delaware; Samuel Chase and Thomas Johnson Jr. from Maryland; Henry, Jefferson, Washington, Lee, and Wythe from Virginia. Gadsden, Middleton, and a pair of Rutledges represented South Carolina; Joseph Hewes and William Hooper came from North Carolina; Lyman Hall and Archibald Bullock from Georgia. Pennsylvania, the key colony, had a delegation that included "farmer" Dickinson, Galloway, Robert Morris, James Wilson, and venerable Franklin. After the death of Peyton Randolph, John Hancock, a New England gentleman of fortune possessing gracious manners and an impressive signature, was chosen president.

Within a few days Congress received another startling bit of news, together with a stand of British colors to decorate Independence Hall. Ethan Allen and 83 Green Mountain Boys had crossed Lake Champlain from the Vermont side and wrested Forts Ticonderoga and Crown Point from their British garrisons; the invasion route to Canada was open. But there was no question of independence as yet, or for almost a year to come.

Besides creating a provincial army and navy and sending diplomatic agents to Europe, Congress assumed sovereign power over Indian relations — an unconscious tribute to the imperial system. It created three departments of Indian affairs, and commissioners to handle them. In September 1775 Lewis Morris and James Wilson held a council with Blue Jacket, White Eyes, Cornstalk, and other chiefs of the Shawnee, the Delaware, and the Seneca, at Fort Pitt. Strings of wampum were exchanged for the usual trading-truck gifts, and the commissioners returned to Philadelphia believing their mission had been accomplished. The Delaware, then living in southern Ohio and Indiana, honored their long friendship with Pennsylvania, and Congress in 1778 concluded its first Indian treaty with this nation — a treaty containing the interesting suggestion (never acted upon) that an Indian fourteenth colony be created in the Northwest, with representatives in Congress. But the Iroquois Confederacy remained loyal to the Great White Father in London.

Congress represented a Whig, or Patriot, bloc, whose only common ground was resistance to unconstitutional acts of Parliament. Only a few members — namely, the Lees, the Adamses, Franklin, and Gadsden — believed independence to be the only solution, and they hardly dared breathe the word; loyalty to the king and to England was still so strong. Congress took a line which left the way open to conciliation. It approved the hot war that had broken out in Massachusetts, adopted the militia besieging the redcoats in Boston as the "Army of the United Colonies," appointed Colonel George Washington commander in chief, sent Benedict Arnold across the Maine wilderness in the expectation of bringing in Canada as the fourteenth colony, and authorized other warlike acts. All in the king's name!

In order to explain this inconsistent policy, Congress issued a Declaration on the Causes of Taking Up Arms, the joint work of Dickinson and Jefferson. It assured fellow subjects in other parts of the empire, "We mean not to dissolve that union which has so long and so happily subsisted between us. . . . We have not raised armies with ambitious designs of separation from Great Britain, and establishing independent States. We fight not for glory or for conquest." But "we are reduced to the alternative of choosing an unconditional submission to the tyranny of irritated ministers, or resistance by force. The latter is our choice." The army they were fighting was not the king's army but the "ministerial army"; George III was misled by bad counselors. The majority in Congress sincerely hoped that firmness and fighting spirit on the American side would cause the House of Commons to vote down Lord North's shabby group, and that the king would call to power someone like Lord Chatham who, when he heard the news of Lexington and Concord, exclaimed, "I rejoice that America has resisted!" Almost fourteen months elapsed between the opening of the war and the Declaration of Independence.

The war extended in a mild way to other colonies, usually taking the shape of militia forcing the royal governor to take refuge on a British warship. But the provincial congresses of four Middle colonies — New York, New Jersey, Pennsylvania, and Maryland — between November 1775 and January 1776 instructed their delegates in Congress to hold out against independence.

Our generation, sadly accustomed to blitzkriegs, Pearl Harbors, and the necessity for instant decisions, finds it hard to understand why the Americans of 1775–76 took so long to make up their minds. But they were going through an emotional travail comparable only to that of the first four months of 1861. Loyalties were being torn apart. Americans were members of the greatest empire since Rome. Although the word *revolution* aroused no terrors, owing to the bloodless affair of 1688, the word *republic* did. In the past, republics had been turbulent and of short duration; they required Roman virtue to maintain, and did we have it? John Adams feared not. There was "so much Venality and Corruption, so much Avarice and Ambition, such a Rage for Profit and Commerce among all Ranks and Degrees of Men even in America," he wrote early in 1776, that he doubted whether we had "public Virtue enough to Support a Republic." No European colony had ever thrown off dependence on a mother country, or even wished to. Would we not fight among ourselves and perhaps drift into becoming a satellite of France or Spain?

Independence meant sailing forth on an uncharted sea. America was not like Ireland, Poland, or other states which cherished romantic traditions of an independent past. All the mystic chords of memory which (as Abraham Lincoln said) make a people one, responded to English names and events — Magna Carta, Queen Elizabeth, the Glorious Revolution, the Bill of Rights, Drake, Marlborough, Wolfe. Dared one break with all English memories and glories?

It was a hard choice for a man who read and thought; easy only for the savage or the illiterate. If one looked into the Bible for guidance, there was St. Peter in his First Epistle urging his flock, "Submit yourselves to every ordinance of man for the Lord's sake." As freemen, said he, you are not to use "your liberty for a cloke of maliciousness; but as the servants of God. Honour all men: Love the brotherhood: Fear God: Honour the king." What could be more explicit? Were not some of the Sons of Liberty using "liberty for a cloke of maliciousness" ? There is even a touch of nostalgia in Jefferson's draft of the Declaration of Independence; "We might have been a free and a great people together."

General Washington started north from Philadelphia on 23 June 1775 to take command of the Continental army (as the Army of the United Colonies was generally referred to, even to 1783). He was met en route by the stirring news of the Battle of Bunker Hill. In May, General Gage received reinforcements which brought the British force in Boston up to 10,000, not including the sailors and marines in Admiral Graves's fleet. On 12 June Gage issued a proclamation (written by Burgoyne) to the "infatuated multitudes" who "with a preposterous parade . . . affect to hold the army besieged," promising pardon to all who would lay down their arms, except to John Hancock and Samuel Adams. Actually, the Continental army of homespun militia, which included a few good engineers, had the British hemmed in on every land side except Charlestown; and their fortifying of Breed's (not Bunker's) Hill on the night of 16–17 June 1775 brought on the battle. This was the first real standup fight between raw New England troops and British regulars; and although the redcoats won the hill, they lost 1054 killed and wounded out of 2200 engaged, against American losses of 441 out of an estimated 3200 engaged. "A dear bought victory," wrote General Clinton — "another such would have ruined us." And General Gage wrote home ruefully, "Those people shew a spirit and conduct against us, they never shewed against the French." Thus, although Bunker Hill was a tactical victory for the British, it was a strategic and moral one for the Americans. It aroused a spirit of exultation and confidence throughout the continent. Washington assumed command at Cambridge on 2 July, and began a remarkably successful job of whipping some 15,000 undisciplined militia into an army.

The Continental Congress now made a final attempt at conciliation: the Olive Branch Petition, drafted by John Dickinson and adopted by Congress 8 July 1775, largely out of respect for the author. According to John Adams, Dickinson was in a terrible quandary. "His mother said to him, 'Johnny you will be hanged, your estate will be forfeited and confiscated, you will leave your excellent wife a widow, and your charming children orphans, beggars and infamous.' From my Soul I pitied Mr. Dickinson. . . . I was very happy that *my* Mother and *my* Wife . . . and all her near relations, as well as mine, had been uniformly of *my* Mind, so that *I* always enjoyed perfect Peace at home."

The key paragraph of the Olive Branch Petition is this:

Attached to your Majesty's person, family and government with all the devotion that principle and affection can inspire, connected with Great Britain by the strongest ties that can unite societies, and deploring every event that tends in any degree to weaken them, we solemnly assure your Majesty, that we not only most ardently desire the former harmony between her and these colonies may be restored, but that a concord may be established between them upon so firm a basis, as to perpetuate its blessings uninterrupted by any future dissentions to succeeding generations in both countries.

Congress therefore begs the king to interpose his authority to stop the war, repeal the Coercive Acts, and bring about "a happy and permanent reconciliation."

The petition, signed by John Hancock and almost every subsequent signer of the Declaration of Independence, was sent over in duplicate to two colonial agents, who tried without success to persuade Lord Dartmouth to present it to the king. They were informed that His Majesty would receive no petition from a rebel body. That is not surprising, since the British government had already heard of Congress's launching the Arnold expedition against Quebec, which looked like a wanton aggression against a loyal and peaceful colony. On 23 August 1775, George III proclaimed that a general rebellion existed, and that "utmost endeavours" should be made "to suppress such rebellion, and to bring the traitors to justice."

On 16 November 1775, Edmund Burke submitted a proposal for reconciliation to the House of Commons, which rejected it by a vote of two to one; and on 22 December Parliament passed an act prohibiting "all manner of trade and commerce" with the Thirteen Colonies, declaring all colonial vessels lawful prize, and their crews subject to impressment into the Royal Navy. These were logical and conventional methods for repressing a rebellion; but as one English publicist remarked, "The fate of nations is not to be tried by forms." Samuel Tucker the Dean of Gloucester, Adam Smith the economist, even Lord Barrington the secretary at war, urged that all British troops be withdrawn from America and the colonists allowed to be independent if they chose, or to state their terms for staying in the empire. It is possible that if this policy had been followed, and the worst cause of friction removed, Congress would have concluded something similar to the Statute of Westminster of the Irish Free State treaty, leaving the home government more power over America than it now has over the British Commonwealth. It is highly unlikely that there would have been any revolt in America against such a treaty, for the people did not want war, and they were not yet conscious of separate nationality. But there was not sufficient imagination in English political circles to adopt such a policy. The obstinacy of George III did not matter; he was one with his people, a good John Bull to whom it was as unthinkable to yield to this American rebellion as it had been to yield to the Scots rebellions of 1715 and 1745.

American feelings of the time were well represented by the official American flag, which was first raised by Lieutenant John Paul Jones in Commodore Hopkins's flagship *Alfred* on 3 December 1775, and by General Washington on a hill near Boston on New Year's day. It carried thirteen stripes to mark the union of the colonies, but still displayed the Union Jack in the canton as a symbol of union with Great Britain. This flag was not replaced by the Stars and Stripes until June 1777.

5. The Declaration of Independence

News of the Act of 22 December 1775, prohibiting all trade and intercourse with the Thirteen Colonies, arrived in America shortly after the appearance of a remarkable pamphlet by a middle-class English Quaker, Thomas Paine, who had been in the colonies but a short time. Paine's *Common Sense* brought the discussion to a crisis by convincing doubters and strengthening those already convinced.

His arguments against continuing the war on a loyalty basis, and in favor of declaring independence, were logical and compelling. The Association boycott on trade with Great Britain had failed, hurting America more than it did England, and hampering the conduct of the war. To obtain the wherewithal to buy munitions, trade must be resumed with the British West Indies and other parts of the world. To be successful, a war must be waged for some great object. Reconciliation on any acceptable basis was no longer possible; and if it were, there was no guarantee against a renewal by Parliament of the attack on colonial liberties. Complete independence was the only real guarantee for American liberty. Only thus could foreign aid be obtained. An independent America can trade with the whole world, manufacture what she likes, and isolate herself from Old World brawls. "A thirst for absolute power is the natural disease of monarchy," and George III, as a brutal tyrant, had violated the "compact" between him and the people to protect their rights, and so forfeited his right to their loyalty and obedience.

These arguments won over General Washington, who had been toasting the king nightly at his officers' mess in Cambridge. On 31 January 1776 he wrote to Joseph Reed of Pennsylvania, "A few more of such flaming arguments, as were exhibited at Falmouth and Norfolk, added to the sound doctrine and unanswerable reasoning contained in the pamphlet *Common Sense*, will not leave numbers at a loss to decide upon the propriety of a separation."

The "flaming argument" of Falmouth was this: The minute men of Falmouth (Portland), Maine, roughed up Captain Henry Mowatt RN and attacked his ship at anchor, after which he took revenge by bombarding the town with red-hot cannon balls which destroyed it. The burning of Norfolk, Virginia, in December 1775, was done by Patriot forces on their retreat; but they succeeded in transferring the blame to Governor Lord Dunmore and the Tories. And there were other flaming arguments.

The royal governor of North Carolina managed to enlist a Loyalist force of 1600 Scots Highlanders, many of whom had been active in the Regulation of 1774. These were completely routed by Patriot militia at Moore's Creek Bridge near Wilmington on 27 February 1776. The result might have been different if a British expeditionary force mounted in Ireland and commanded by Lord Cornwallis had co-operated with the Loyalists, as the governor requested. Instead, Cornwallis chose to take a crack at Charleston, South Carolina. Before he arrived, the local Patriots had built Fort Moultrie, whose guns drove off the British fleet on 28 June when it tried to enter. These events removed all obstacles to the Carolinas' going for independence.

A fleet of the Continental navy of seven small ships converted from merchant vessels, under command of Commodore Esek Hopkins, sailed down to the Bahamas and captured undefended Nassau in March 1776, together with an enormous quantity of munitions. These were picked up by Washington's army when it was moving from Boston to New York.

The Canada expedition got off to a good start, but crashed against the Rock of Quebec. General Richard Montgomery led a force of about 1,000 New Englanders up the Hudson and Lake Champlain route and captured Montreal on 12 November 1775. Benedict Arnold's right punch to this left hook was a force of 600 Yankees who marched through the Maine wilderness to the St. Lawrence opposite Quebec, where they rendezvoused with Montgomery. On New Year's Eve 1775 the combined United Colonies force assaulted the citadel of Quebec, was bloodily repulsed, and Montgomery fell dead. General Washington, still besieging the British in Boston, received this depressing news on 17 January 1776. It meant that the British could now use Canada as a base, invade the Thirteen Colonies by the Champlain-Hudson route next summer, and isolate New England.

But the General was not discouraged. He occupied Dorchester Heights and forced General William Howe (who had relieved General Gage) to evacuate Boston on 17 March 1776. The American army then marched in.

The movement for independence received an important boost from a Virginia convention composed of the old house of burgesses sitting by itself after getting rid of Governor Dunmore and the council. Meeting at Williamsburg in early May, the members were outraged by the news that the king was sending 12,000 German mercenaries to put down the rebellion. On 15 May the convention instructed its delegates in the Continental Congress "to declare the United Colonies free and independent states." It then appointed a committee, presided over by George Mason, to report a declaration of rights and a plan of government for an independent state. Mason at the age of fifty-seven was regarded as the Nestor of Virginian statesmen. He hated politics and despised politicians, especially Patrick Henry; but when called upon, he always served. On this occasion he proposed, and the convention adopted on 12 June 1776, the Virginia Bill of Rights, parent of all American bills of rights. And on 29 June the convention adopted a constitution for an independent Commonwealth of Virginia.

In Congress, John Adams wrote, "By every Post and every day, Independence rolls in on us like a torrent." The Georgia delegates appeared, with full powers to vote for independence. South Carolina expelled her royal governor and voted for independence. North Carolina delegates had full powers. The Virginia resolves were read in Congress, and on 7 June Richard Henry Lee moved the Independence resolve:

That these United Colonies are, and of right ought to be, Independent States, that they are absolved from all allegiance to the British Crown, and that all political connection between them and the State of Great Britain is, and ought to be, totally dissolved.

That it is expedient forthwith to take the most effectual measures for forming foreign alliances.

That a plan of confederation be prepared and transmitted to the respective Colonies for consideration and approbation.

Consideration was postponed by vote of seven colonies to five, because the delegates of New York, Pennsylvania, Delaware, and South Carolina, uninstructed by their provincial congresses, were not prepared to vote; but on 11 June, Congress appointed a committee of five to prepare a Declaration of Independence: Thomas Jefferson, John Adams, Benjamin Franklin, Roger Sherman, and Robert R. Livingston. The committee delegated to Jefferson the task of making the first draft.

Between the day when he completed his rough draft and 28 June, when the report of the committee of five was presented to Congress, many alterations were made by Adams, Franklin, and Jefferson himself. Some interesting changes were also made in the course of a debate by the whole congress. Jefferson's draft included a bitter attack on the king for disallowing acts of the Virginia assembly directed against the African slave trade. The South Carolina and Rhode Island delegates objected, and it was deleted. The clause referring to the use of Hessians to put down the rebellion originally

read, "Scotch and foreign mercenaries," since a kilted Highland regiment
had already been sent to Boston. At that, the Reverend John Witherspoon
of Princeton, the only clergyman in the Congress, sprang to his feet and said
that he would not have the Scottish nation insulted. So the "Scotch and" was
deleted.

"I turned to neither book nor pamphlet while writing the Declaration,"
said Jefferson; but the principles and language of John Locke's *Second Treatise of Government* (1690) were so much a part of his mind that unconsciously he thought and wrote like Locke. The basic theory of the Declaration
was that of the social compact, precedent and justification for government.
But there are certain rights of which no government can deprive mankind;
and if a prince disregards these rights and establishes a tyranny, he dissolves
the compact and his subjects may throw off their allegiance. This doctrine was
a godsend to tender souls among the Patriots who could not get over their
duty to honor the king. It explains why the indictment of the Declaration is
directed primarily against George III.

Jefferson improved on Locke, who emphasized that man entered political
society to protect his property, by the statement:

> We hold these truths to be self-evident, that all men are created equal, that
> they are endowed by their Creator with certain unalienable Rights, that among
> these are Life, Liberty, and the Pursuit of Happiness.

Did Jefferson think of Negroes when he wrote, "All men are created
equal"? His subsequent career indicates that he did not; that in his view
Negroes were not "men." However that may be, the crisp challenge of the concluding paragraph allowed no exceptions:

> We, therefore, the Representatives of the United States of America [the first
> official use of that title] solemnly publish and declare . . . that as Free and
> Independent States, they have full Power to levy War, conclude Peace, contract
> Alliances, establish Commerce, and to do all other acts and things which inde-
> pendent States may of right do. And for the support of this Declaration, with a
> firm reliance on the protection of Divine Providence, we mutually pledge to each
> other our Lives, our Fortunes and our sacred Honor.

"Sacred Honor" to Jefferson and his colleagues was no empty phrase, no
echo of dying feudalism, but the proud declaration of free men that, once
their word was given, it would never be broken; and none who signed that instrument ever contemplated anything else.

The committee of five reported to Congress 2 June, and its report was held
over while Lee's independence resolution was debated. The first and essential
clause was barely passed on 2 July, because Dickinson and Robert Morris were
persuaded to stay away so that Franklin, Wilson, and John Morton could cast
Pennsylvania's vote for independence. Caesar Rodney turned up to break a
deadlock in the Delaware delegation; and the South Carolina members were
persuaded to go along. Only the New York delegation sullenly abstained. But

the principle of independence was adopted on 2 July, and the Declaration itself, after a few verbal changes had been made in committee of the whole, was adopted on the evening of 4 July 1776. Printed copies were sent next day to the former colonies, now states; and to the army. The Declaration was read from the balcony of Independence Hall on 8 July, and on the 19th, Congress voted to have the instrument signed.

If the American Revolution had produced nothing but the Declaration of Independence, it would have been worth while. The bill of wrongs against George III and Parliament, naturally, is exaggerated. Facts will not sustain many of the alleged "injuries and usurpations." But the beauty and cogency of the preamble, reaching back to remotest antiquity and forward to an indefinite future, have lifted the hearts of millions of men and will continue to do so:

We hold these truths to be self-evident, that all men are created equal, that they are endowed by their Creator with certain unalienable Rights, that among these are Life, Liberty, and the Pursuit of Happiness.

These words are more revolutionary than anything written by Robespierre, Marx, or Lenin, more explosive than the atom, a continual challenge to ourselves, as well as an inspiration to the oppressed of all the world.

CHESTER

Let Ty - rants shake their I - ron rod,

And slav - 'ry clank———— her gall - ing chains,

We fear them not, we—— trust———— in God,

New - Eng-land's God———— for - e - ver reigns.

Military and Naval Generalities

1775-1781

1. Condition and Organization

THE WAR OF INDEPENDENCE was not popular in America — few wars have been except the brief Spanish-American affair of 1898. Yet, even when people dislike a war, they may support it, as happened in World War II and the Korean War. In this instance a good part of the American people supported the war for independence as the only alternative to submission ("slavery" they called it); but by no standard, of that time or ours, was their support adequate. After Congress had declared independence, most of Washington's army expected to be discharged; George III should have quit when he read the ringing words of Thomas Jefferson! But the war went on. France joined as an ally in 1778, and again most American soldiers expected to go home and let the French finish the fighting; but the war went on. Many Americans were indifferent, and the Loyalist minority was actively hostile. John Adams was not heeded when he wrote in April 1776, "We shall have a long, obstinate and bloody war to go through." Most Patriots expected the war to be over in a year, and the British government had even more sanguine hopes. Had Americans been able to anticipate the length and difficulty of the war, they would probably have forced the Continental Congress to end it by compromise in 1776; even so there were sarcastic remarks about Congress risking *our* lives and fortunes to save *their* sacred honor. Conversely the British government, had it appreciated the tenacity of Washington, or foreseen the entry of France, Spain, and Holland into the war, might have conceded everything that Congress demanded.

General Washington, who had served with British regulars in the last war and respected them as a fighting force, attempted to form the Continental army on their model. The British army, with a stiff discipline enforced by flogging, was a hard and brutal service. It was recruited largely from the very young and adventurous or from ne'er-do-wells and drunkards. It may have been a mistake to try to create an American army on the British model, as the human elements to furnish that kind of army were not plentiful. But we cannot criticize Congress for not anticipating the French *levée en masse* of 1793, which created the first really national and democratic army in history. Congress made one concession to democratic social conditions by narrowing the difference in pay and privileges between officers and enlisted men. The result was to render officer procurement difficult. Almost every colony had a militia, in which all able-bodied white men were enrolled; but the militia officers were apt to be the bully boys of a neighborhood, good enough to drill yokels on a training field, but poor leaders in battle.

The best officers in the Continental army were either veterans of the previous war or young men commissioned from the ranks. Surprisingly few planters' sons in the South, or college graduates and professional men in the North, came forward to take commissions; in Maryland and Delaware, by exception, the majority of officers were local gentlemen, and the regiments of those states, by and large, were the best in the army. For naval officers the country had to depend largely on merchant mariners, and was lucky to get them away from privateering; a leading New Hampshire Patriot wrote in 1777 that if the pay and privileges of naval officers were not improved, the navy would be "officered by Tinkers, Shoemakers and Horse Jockeys." Nevertheless, in addition to Washington, America produced some field commanders in this war of whom any army could be proud — Anthony Wayne, Nathanael Greene, Henry Knox, John Eager Howard, Daniel Morgan, and Benedict Arnold; and a few naval captains who would have been an honor to any navy — Nicholas Biddle, John Barry, and John Paul Jones.

The other concession made by Congress to democracy was a short-term enlistment. This catered to the inherited English prejudice against "standing armies," and fear of the "man on horseback." Short-term enlistment is the most wasteful way to fill an army, because as soon as you get a lad trained, he is through; but America is still doing it. When a state committee in October 1776 called at Washington's headquarters to ask if one-year enlistments wouldn't do, he started from his chair and said: "Good God, gentlemen! Our cause is ruined if you engage men only for a year. You must not think of it. If we ever hope for success, we must have men enlisted for the whole term of the war." George Partridge of the Continental Congress, who told this anecdote, said that this was the only time he ever saw the General lose his self-control.

As a result of Washington's pleas, Congress before the end of 1776 authorized enlistments for three years, or for the duration. They offered liberal bounties to recruits, but found comparatively few takers, and one year continued to be the normal term under the colors. The average American hated to sign up for a longer period. Married men could not afford to, because nothing was done for dependents; and the young men's favorite contribution to the war was to turn out for a short campaign with the militia, then go home to plant the corn, get in the hay, or harvest the wheat, according to the season. Even in the first flush of enthusiasm, 1775–76, Washington was hampered by the original Yankee contingent of six-month volunteers; they felt that plenty more men were available, and should take their turn.

It must be remembered that Congress was composed of representative

Americans who knew their people, and knew that Americans could be led, not driven. Their dilemma was much the same as that of Lincoln at the beginning of the Civil War. They dared not call on their people at once to make the sacrifices necessary to win a quick victory; knowing that a certain way of life, the right to choose whether or not to fight, was more precious to the people than victory, and that they had to be shown that independence could not be won by talk. Thus, we have the paradox that the same spirit of liberty which made the colonists resist George III and choose independence, was an almost fatal handicap in the fight for independence. And it would have been fatal but for George Washington and French assistance.

The Continental army consisted mainly of infantry regiments, in theory composed of 500 officers and men each, recruited in and named after one state — hence terms such as "The Massachusetts Line," "The New Jersey Line." These were called line regiments because of the battle tactics of that day — soldiers firing almost shoulder to shoulder from a line three deep. In addition, there were special corps of cavalry, artillery, engineers, and light infantry. Congress set the quotas that each state was supposed to fill, but it had no authority to draft men to fill these quotas, and no means to enforce the requisitions. This was the same system that the British Empire had used in the French and Indian wars; and, as the colonies did then, so the states now, obeyed requisitions or not as they saw fit. In general, each state passed the buck by apportioning a number of men to each county or town, and these bid against each other by offering bounties to recruits to fill their quotas.

There had been no color line drawn in the last colonial war, and the Continental army and navy followed suit. There were Negroes in every line regiment and in John Paul Jones's ships. Virginian slaves who served in the armed forces were liberated at the end of the war. Rhode Island had the nerve to buy slaves to fill her quota, and send the bill to Congress. Even the South Carolina assembly authorized the recruiting of 1000 Negro slaves in 1780 as "pioneers, fatiguemen, oarsmen, or mariners."

In 1779, when uniforms began arriving from France, Congress passed the first uniform regulations for enlisted men. Blue coats were prescribed for all, with different-colored facings: buff for all officers and for the New York and New Jersey Line; red for the Virginia and Maryland Line, white for the New England regiments. Even after that, few enlisted men could get uniforms, for lack of supply. The general aspect of the average soldier was an eighteenth-century counterpart to Bill Mauldin's World War II cartoons, minus the helmet. He wore anything he could get, and at times that meant almost nothing. A German officer who surrendered with Burgoyne in 1777 reported that the Americans who beat him were upstanding men, slender and sinewy and of fine military bearing; but most of the officers from colonel down, and all enlisted men, wore ordinary clothes, not uniforms. A French observer commented on their "miserable, motley appearance!" Army morale undoubtedly suffered from the lack of uniforms, awards, and decorations. Not until 1782 did General Washington create the Purple Heart, to honor distinguished military service, and only three or four Purple Hearts were conferred before the end of the war.

The system of appointing and promoting officers in the Continental army was complicated. After the Battle of Trenton, Congress granted Washington power to make all promotions up to and including colonel, while Congress itself appointed the generals; but Washington usually had to consult state officials for promotions above the rank of captain. In general, troops from one state would not fight under regimental officers appointed from another. Officers' squabbles gave Washington more trouble than the discipline of enlisted men.

He had plenty of trouble, too, with the enlisted men. Leaders of the different states and sections mingled in the Continental Congress and came to appreciate each other's qualities; but it was not so with common soldiers. Provincials almost always detest people from other sections. We find the term "damn'd Yankees," later so popular in the South, used for the first time by "Yorkers" in General Schuyler's Northern army. The Yankees called the Virginians "buckskins," because Morgan's Rifles wore the frontiersman's fringed hunting shirt. In most of the line regiments from the Middle states and the South, the old-world distinctions between officers, presumed to be gentlemen, and enlisted men, were kept up. To them the fraternization between rank and file, common in the New England line regiments and in frontier units, was disgusting. When a Massachusetts colonel detailed one of his sons, a private soldier, as his batman, and allowed another son to set up a cobbler's bench to repair the men's shoes, Anthony Wayne's Pennsylvania regiment was so incensed as to attack the colonel's headquarters, destroy the bench, and drive his men from the tents with gunfire. A near-mutiny by the Connecticut Line in 1780 at Washington's Morristown headquarters was suppressed by the Pennsylvania Line, which itself mutinied the next year, killed several officers, and occupied Princeton. A mutiny in the New Jersey Line was forcibly put down by 600 troops from other states who marched down from West Point. These mutinies were not caused by treasonable intent — the Pennsylvanians even executed two British spies sent to seduce them to the king's service — but to logistic deficiencies, the lack of food, clothing, and shoes, as well as pay.

The colonial militia, which the independent states took over, included in theory every able-bodied man between the ages of sixteen and sixty. Militia turned out in great numbers whenever the British army marched inland and if properly stiffened by regulars, gave a good account of themselves. The first action of the war, at Concord, was a militia victory, pure and simple, and so was Bunker Hill. The surrender of Burgoyne would not have taken place but for the Green Mountain Boys and other militia who swarmed in to help Gates's regulars. Typical of the attitude of the average American is the story of Reuben Stebbins of Williamstown, Massachusetts. He had not seen fittin' to turn out until he actually heard the firing at Bennington. He then saddled his horse, called for his musket, and remarked as he rode off, "We'll see who's goin't' own this farm!"

The turning-out of an entire countryside to fight was new to the British. European armies marched safely through enemy country until they encountered a hostile army. Peasants and townspeople kept quiet or took to the forests and mountains, fighting was for professionals only. This phenomenon of a countryside in arms, both around Boston and in the Saratoga campaign, made British generals very loath to march far from the seacoast, where they were at the end of a logistics line maintained by the Royal Navy. After Burgoyne's surrender, and until Cornwallis cut loose in the Carolinas, no British army spent much time beyond gunfire range of the British fleet.

In 1776 the Thirteen Colonies, with a population of 2,500,000, could, within the framework of their social-economic system, have provided a regular army of 100,000. But they could never have fed and clothed so many, and 35,000 should have been enough, with militia support, to defeat the British, who never numbered more than that at any one time. The Continental army reached a top figure of 18,000 just before the Battle of Long Island, but by the end of 1776 had shrunk to 5000; by early 1778 it had recovered a strength of almost 20,000, and then declined again.

On the other hand, the war was even less popular in England than in America. Englishmen would not enlist in any appreciable numbers to fight overseas against their kith and kin; and the supply of German mercenaries was limited both by the rapacity of German princelings and the resources of the British treasury.

2. Logistics, Finance, and Foreign Volunteers

The principal reason why Washington's army, at Valley Forge and later, went hungry, unpaid, unclothed, and unshod, was no lack of supplies in the country, but the reluctance of farmers and merchants to exchange food and clothing for a Continental chit. One of the uncommemorated heroes of the war was Christopher Ludwig, a German baker of Philadelphia, who, when Congress proposed that he furnish 100 pounds of bread for 135 pounds of flour, offered to furnish as many pounds of hard bread as he was given flour, and did so. On the other hand, the merchants of Philadelphia, in 1781, refused to furnish General Greene with 5000 suits of clothes for the Southern army, although they had the cloth and the general offered them bills of exchange on France. Europe was used to armies helping themselves in wartime, and collecting from the government later, if one could; but in free colonial America the people had never experienced this, and Washington had to be pretty desperate, at Valley Forge, to "forage the country naked." The sufferings of the Continental army have not been exaggerated, but they were due to selfishness, mismanagement, and difficulties in transportation rather than to poverty or necessity.

An improvement took place after Washington persuaded General Nathanael Greene to accept the post of quartermaster general, which he did with reluctance since (as he truly remarked), "nobody ever heard of a quartermaster in history." By the spring of 1778 the army was sufficiently well fed to pursue Howe across New Jersey, but it was never properly clad until 1782. A Rhode Island colonel, writing to the governor of his state begging for more clothing, said that the condition of his men was so scandalous that they were called "the naked regiment." The Battle of Eutaw Springs was largely fought by barefooted soldiers in breech-clouts. Most American families in 1776 made their own clothing at home, and could not greatly increase the output; the well-to-do imported their clothing from England, and that supply was cut off. Wagon transportation was slow, costly, and subject to accident and depredation; the British controlled the usual sea routes from colony to colony. Supplies came from France and from prize cargoes; but clothing wears out fast in any army, and faster than usual in Washington's, where there was a shortage of tents and blankets. Procurement of blankets was a special problem since Americans, by and large, slept under quilts which were of no use to soldiers in the field. From Valley Forge General Washington wrote, "There are now in this Army . . . 4000 men wanting blankets, near 2000 of which have never had one, altho' some of them have been 12 months in service."

The medical situation in the army was so shockingly bad, even for that era of untrained "sawbones," that medical officers who survived the war got together to found American medical schools. Altogether, the private soldier of the War of Independence was so badly fed, clothed, and cared for, and often so badly led, too, that one is surprised and grateful that any continued to fight. Lafayette, De Kalb, and Von Steuben all expressed the opinion that no European army would have endured the hardships that the Americans suffered.

During most of the war, a principal source of food for Washington's army was Connecticut, where Governor Jonathan Trumbull, a business man, not only procured quantities of flour and beef but set up a cannon foundry, a shoe shop, and a plant for salvaging damaged muskets.[1] Yet the Connecticut Line was badly neglected in such items as clothing. Virginia throughout the war seemed paralyzed, so far as supplying her own line was concerned; her regiments at times were pinned down, not by the enemy but because the soldiers had neither shoes nor clothes. Although the revolted colonies showed considerable enterprise in producing arms and munitions, these supplies were never sufficient. Military cargoes from France, which slipped through the British blockade, in large measure armed and clothed the American army that

1. Governor Trumbull also backed the building of our first submarine, "Bushnell's Turtle," by David Bushnell of Saybrook. It was a hand-propelled, one-man job, supposed to screw a delayed-action torpedo into the side of an enemy ship; but it never succeeded in closing.

forced Burgoyne to surrender. But it was no easy matter to get supplies through that blockade. A large quantity of clothing and muskets that Lafayette persuaded the French to make for us in 1780, never reached America because Franklin could not find the merchant ships to load them or the warships to escort them.

France was also looked to for financial support. About a million dollars were advanced by the treasury of Louis XVI while France was still neutral, and about $1.6 million after she entered the war in 1778, together with about $6.4 million in loans. These, however, were but a small part of the war finance. The major financial operations were (1) bills of credit, the famous Continental currency, of which $241.5 million in face value was issued before 1781, together with state bills to the face value of $210 million; (2) domestic loans, both interest-bearing bonds known as loan office certificates in denominations of $300 up, and certificates of indebtedness for goods received or seized, amounting to about $20 million; (3) requisitions in money or in kind which were apportioned among the states on the basis of their estimated population. These yielded $5 million in paper money and $4 million worth of goods.

The loans, both domestic and foreign, as well as the states' debts, were repaid at par in the Washington administration, under Hamilton's funding scheme. But the Continental and state currency depreciated to a point where it cost more to print than it would buy. Robert Morris, appointed by Congress superintendent of finance in February 1781, at about the darkest moment of the war, succeeded in preventing a complete financial collapse. A loan of $200,000 in gold, brought over by the French navy, enabled him to found the note-issuing Bank of North America in November of that year, and to perform a financial miracle — putting the country on a hard-money basis before the war ended. Morris in finance accomplished as much for independence as Washington and Franklin did in their respective fields.

The officer problem was complicated by foreign volunteers. Twelve years of peace in Europe meant that many unemployed professional soldiers were eager to serve in the Continental army. They pestered Silas Deane and Benjamin Franklin, the American agents in France, for letters of recommendation. To get rid of these importunate volunteers, Franklin would give them passage money and a letter of introduction to Congress, whose president complained that French officers beset his door like bailiffs stalking a debtor. Congress appointed these soldiers of fortune to ranks as high as major general, and then left it to Washington to find something for them to do. And since Americans disliked serving under foreigners, there was nothing for most of them to do except to serve on Washington's staff, and tell him in French, German, or Polish as the case might be, that his army was lousy.

There were several exceptions. The Marquis de Lafayette was in a class by himself. A young and wealthy idealist, enthusiastic for liberty and avid of glory, he came out in 1777 in a ship equipped at his own expense; and Congress commissioned him major general in the Continental army one month before his twentieth birthday. Modest, handsome, and charming, La-fayette captivated every American with whom he came in contact, including Washington, who, before the end of the year, gave him a small independent command. The Marquis proved a brave and capable officer whom the Americans were as ready to follow as a native-born; perhaps more so, since he bought them clothing and comforts with his own money. But Lafayette's greatest service was political. The French court was flattered by the attention that the young nobleman received, and he, on a mission home in 1779, persuaded the king to send out the expeditionary force under Rochambeau which helped Washington to win the decisive Battle of Yorktown.

The Chevalier Duportail, a French engineer officer, thirty-four years old, came out in 1777 with three or four junior French engineers. Commissioned lieutenant colonel, he rose to major general and was extremely useful on Washington's staff as a designer of forts and other defensive works. Thaddeus Kosciuszko, a twenty-year-old officer of the Polish army, came to America in the summer of 1776. Pennsylvania employed him to construct forts for the defense of the Delaware river, which earned him a commission in the Continental Corps of Engineers. He designed the first fortifications at West Point. After peace was concluded he returned home and became a national hero of Poland, in one of her many wars of liberation. Casimir Pulaski, a Polish cavalry officer, was still under thirty when Franklin advanced him the funds to sail to America. He was given the top cavalry command under General Lincoln in the Southern campaign, and fell mortally wounded when charging the British lines before Savannah at the head of his troopers.

The self-styled Baron de Kalb, a middle-aged German soldier of fortune who had fought the last two wars in the French army, was also appointed major general by Congress. He proved to be a tough and able commander. Leading his troops in the Battle of Camden, he received a mortal wound.

One of the most important foreigners to serve the American cause was Baron von Steuben, a forty-seven-year-old Prussian junker who had been on the staff of Frederick the Great. Drilling soldiers was Steuben's specialty, and one of Washington's main sources of trouble. There was no standard manual of arms, and colonial lads were not used to prompt obedience of crisp orders. Steuben drew up a manual of arms, formed a model company, drilled it himself, and in a few weeks made such smart soldiers of these men that the whole army became drill-conscious. At Washington's recommendation he was promoted major general and appointed inspector general of the Continental army. He also brought about an important reorganization. Owing to the differing responses to recruiting, some line regiments then had their full strength of 500 men, while others were down to as few as thirty. So Steuben created a new unit, the battalion of 200 men, so that the army could be maneuvered accurately. The Battle of Monmouth was the first test of this reorganized Continental army; thenceforth the Continentals were equal to the best British regulars.

3. The Weapons

Colonel von Steuben, when he reported to Washington at Valley Forge, ascertained that one infantry company might be armed with a mixture of muskets, carbines, shotguns, and rifles. He used his influence to have all foot soldiers armed with the standard infantry weapon, the smooth-bore, muzzle-loading musket with an 11-gauge (¾-in.) bore. Trained soldiers could fire a musket twice or thrice a minute; but after a few rounds they had to check to let the barrel cool off. Steuben found the bayonet unknown to Americans, and they had no defense drill against the enemy's use of that arm. British infantry frequently scored because they carried bayonets as standard equipment, and if they got near enough for a bayonet charge, usually won. And in stretches of wet weather, muskets misfired. General Washington, concerned over British superiority with the bayonet, made every effort to equip his army with them; and American bayonet tactics improved as the war progressed. Stony Point was captured in 1779 by a brilliant assault of Continental light infantry with muskets unloaded and bayonets fixed.

The rifle, introduced into the colonies by Germans and Swiss, had by 1775 become the American frontiersman's favorite weapon. It was far more accurate than the smooth-bore musket. A fair rifleman could make 40 per cent hits on a standing man at 100 yards. Morgan's Rifles, recruited from the back country of Pennsylvania, Maryland, and Virginia, formed a part of Washington's first army. But rifle never replaced musket as the standard infantry weapon, because loading the heavy, six-foot barrel required a full minute; and fighting in those days was at such close range that the enemy could bayonet a rifleman before he had a chance to reload. General Peter Muhlenberg wrote to Washington that he wanted his regiment of riflemen converted to musketry, because rifles were "of little use," on a march in wet weather. And Anthony Wayne wrote that he "would almost as soon face an Enemy with a good musket and bayonet without ammunition," as with a rifle. Nevertheless, riflemen were useful if posted on the flanks, especially on rough ground and under cover, to fire on the enemy at long range. On the British side, Major Patrick Ferguson invented a light, breech-loading rifle to which a bayonet could be fixed and which, had it gone into production, might have changed the course of the war. But the conservatism of the war office prevented that, and Ferguson, ironically enough, was killed by an American rifle ball at Kings Mountain.

Nowadays the United States Marine Corps is the elite American fighting force; but in this war the "leathernecks," as the sailors called them, were stationed on shipboard to pick off enemy gunners in close combat. The elite of Washington's army, as of the British army, was the light infantry. General Washington organized a light infantry corps in 1777, for which he selected young, agile, and dependable lads who were good shots. They wore a dashing leather helmet with horsehair crest and carried less equipment than the line. Lafayette commanded a corps of 2000 light infantry which acquired such a reputation that every ambitious young officer wished to transfer to this corps. Alexander Hamilton left Washington's staff to be a light infantry captain; Colonel Alexander Scammell left his post of adjutant general to command a light infantry corps organized shortly before the Yorktown campaign, and lost his life in the assault. Lafayette later maintained that his American light infantry were the finest troops he ever commanded, whether in America or France.

The artillery of the Continental army was commanded by General Henry Knox, a former Boston bookseller whom Washington considered the ablest and most dependable of his generals. It consisted of brass or iron muzzle-loaders, the best being captured English cannon or those imported from France, and was limited in size to what men, not horses, could pull over bad roads. A "12-pounder," a cannon that shot a round iron ball of that weight, was the caliber that all gunners wanted but did not always obtain. One- or two-gun companies of artillery, posted among the infantry or on the flanks with the riflemen, usually withheld fire until the enemy was about 400 yards distant and then let go with small balls called grapeshot; solid balls were used at shorter range. Siege artillery included howitzers to throw "carcasses" (incendiary shells) and mortars which fired exploding bombshells with slow fuzes.

Cavalry was not much used by either side, largely because of the rough, wooded nature of the country. The British found that horses and their forage took up too much room on transports, and sent home from New York in 1778 one of the two cavalry regiments they had brought over. Washington, however, was able to procure enough horses to form a cavalry corps, and enough uniforms to clothe the troopers properly. The most useful mounted units were the "legions," organized in the Southern campaign under leaders such as Pulaski and "Light Horse Harry" Lee; these troopers generally fought on foot, using horses merely for quick movement, like the European dragoons.

4. The Navies

Britain's most striking military superiority over the Thirteen Colonies lay in her navy, which might have been decisive, had France not intervened. A tight blockade of the North American coast was impossible in days of sail, but the Royal Navy, which at the onset of hostilities had 28 warships with over 500 guns and 4000 men in ports between Halifax and Florida, was strong enough to keep regular trade routes open, to operate from its Halifax and New York bases throughout the war, and from Chesapeake Bay, Boston, Newport, Charleston, and Savannah for limited periods. This meant that the British could shift troops by sea from England to America, or from one American port to another almost at will, and could deny the sea to all enemy ships except nimble privateers and frigates. And Britain had plenty of ships for patrolling the narrow seas and the Mediterranean, and escorting convoys to the West Indies, Canada, and the ports she held in the United States.

American efforts to diminish British naval superiority were divided and largely ineffective. General Washington commissioned what we might call the army's salt-water navy during the siege of Boston; and some of these little armed schooners operated into the year 1777. The army also had a fresh-water navy on Lake Champlain, organized by Benedict Arnold, which prevented the British from invading New York in 1776. No fewer than six states — Massachusetts, Pennsylvania, Maryland, Virginia, and the Carolinas — had navies of their own, to guard inland waters or prowl off shore in search of prizes. Congress, and most of the states too, commissioned privateers — about 1500 all told — to prey on enemy commerce; and, on top of all that, there was the Continental navy.

Congress, it must be admitted, had nerve to found a navy, as it did on 13 October 1775, not without opposition. Samuel Chase of Maryland said it was "the maddest idea in the world to think of building an American fleet"; but a Virginia delegate, Professor George Wythe, silenced him with an appeal to history. The Romans, he observed, built a fleet from scratch and managed to destroy Carthage. The first Continental fleet, which raided Nassau before the Declaration of Independence, consisted of converted merchantmen. Congress, in the meantime, had authorized the building of thirteen frigates, which it hopefully expected to be ready for sea in three months. These were three-masted square-riggers, about 125 feet long on an average, carrying a main battery of 12-pounders and a second battery of 4-, 6-, and 9-pounders. Their construction was given to several shipyards between Portsmouth and Baltimore, and former masters in the merchant marine were appointed to command them. The fate of this fleet is a sad example of what happens to an inferior sea power. Four of the frigates were destroyed on the stocks to prevent their falling into enemy hands. Frigates *Warren* and *Raleigh* were actually launched and ready for sea in the spring of 1776, but the former, together with *Providence*, was bottled up in Narragansett Bay by the British for two years; and *Raleigh*, which for want of men and guns never left port until mid-1777, was captured within a year.

Virginia, built in Baltimore and commanded by the senior American naval captain, James Nicholson, was captured even before leaving the Chesapeake; Nicholson was then given command of *Trumbull* and lost her when, after two years, she was trying to elude the British blockade of the Connecticut river. Frigate *Randolph*, commanded by Nicholas Biddle, remained inactive at Charleston for months because her crew deserted; in her next fight she blew up, killing all hands. *Hancock* was captured by the British in 1777 and renamed *Iris*; it was she that took *Trumbull* in 1781. All the earlier converted navy had been captured or destroyed by the end of 1779, and most of the officers not languishing in British jails had turned to privateering for want of another command. By the end of the war the United States Navy consisted of only one or two ships larger than an armed schooner.

Captain John Paul Jones and Robert Morris, who in addition to his financial burdens became Congress's first secretary of the navy, wished to organize the Continental navy in task forces to make diversionary raids on the British Isles or the West Indies. This was actually done only by exceptional leaders like Jones; for the British broke up most attempts of American warships to assemble, and, owing to the competition of privateers, naval ratings had to be kept happy by taking prizes. A privateersman had little discipline and not much danger, since these ships were built for speed and could escape any enemy that looked powerful. On the other hand, they had ample opportunity to get rich out of prize money — or rather, only thought they did, for most of them were eventually captured and the sailors spent the rest of the war in English prisons. Nevertheless, few men could be recruited for the Continental navy unless the captain made it clear that his major job was to capture prizes. There was no money in raiding British ports, as John Paul Jones found out to his sorrow.

Thus the only results effected by these private, state, and Continental navies were to annoy British commerce and supply the American war market with consumer goods at enemy expense. The real naval accomplishments of the war, for America, were effected by the royal navy of France.

5. *The Loyalists*

The War of American Independence was a true civil war. In America itself a strong minority who called themselves Loyalists, and by their enemies were called Tories, supported the mother country; and there was much fighting between Loyalist and Patriot partisan (guerrilla) bands. In England itself there was no fighting, apart from the exploits of John Paul Jones in coastal waters; yet sympathy with the American cause was widespread. Vice Admiral Augustus Keppel and General Sir Jeffrey Amherst refused to serve against America; General Harry Conway refused to "draw his sword in that cause"; the Earl of Effingham, colonel of a regiment ordered to America, turned in his commission because "the duties of a soldier and a citizen" had become "inconsistent." He was publicly congratulated on his stand by the city corporations of Dublin and London. Charles James Fox adopted blue and buff for the colors of the Whig opposition because they were those of General Washington's uniform.

The Loyalist party in America persisted throughout the war, although it never managed to get properly organized outside New York City. Socially, it was top-heavy. The royal officeholders, about half the councillors in the royal and proprietary colonies, and many wealthy merchants, went Tory. The pacifist sects — Quakers, Moravians, and Mennonites — stayed neutral if they could. Most of the Anglican ministers in New England and the Middle colonies remained loyal to the king, the head of their church; and when British troops evacuated New York, the rector of Trinity Church and his entire congregation went with them. Families everywhere were divided. Almost every leading American — Adams, Otis, Lee, Washington, Franklin, Jefferson, Randolph, and Rutledge — had Loyalist kinsmen. But there were also many thousand farmers, artisans and shopkeepers, on the king's side; and it is probable that a majority of the back countrymen in the Carolinas, initially, at least, were loyal, since the Regulator troubles had created bitter enmity toward local Whigs. Many who started as good Whigs could not swallow the Declaration of Independence, and others were so outraged by mob action as to repudiate it.

The number of the Loyalists varied from colony to colony. They were strongest in New York, partly because the city was occupied by the British after the Battle of Long Island and held by them throughout the war; partly because New York had an aristocratic social structure. They were weakest in Connecticut, Massachusetts, and Virginia, where the radical leaders were talented, respectable men and good organizers. Governor Dunmore of Virginia drove to the Patriot side many who otherwise would have been Tory, by a proclamation inviting slaves to desert their masters. Estimates of as high as 50 per cent of the total population have been made for New York and as low as 8 per cent for Connecticut. My guess is that not more than 10 per cent of the white population of the United States was actively Loyalist; that about 40 per cent was actively Patriot, and about 50 per cent indifferent or neutral. The significant fact is that nowhere, except in Georgia and in occupied seaports, were the British able to organize a Loyalist civil government.

One factor that had no visible effect on a man's choice was race and language. The Negroes in general remained faithful to their masters, and many served in the Continental army and navy. German-Americans contributed their share to George III who, after all, was a German king; and the only place during the war where German was recognized as a second official language was in New York City under British rule. Even the Irish were far from unanimous on the Patriot side. Loyal Irish volunteers were organized during the siege of Boston to help defend that town against Washington; and a big Loyalist corps, Lord Rawdon's Volunteers of Ireland, did valiant work for several years. The first New York St. Patrick's Day parade on record was staged by 500 members of this corps in 1779. Conversely, many English, Irish, and Scots who had been but a short time in America became ardent Patriots and fought for the cause. Among these were Generals Montgomery, Gates, and St. Clair, and Captains Barry and Paul Jones.

Wherever a British army held firm, Loyalists flocked to its protection; but when the troops evacuated, they had to leave too or suffer vengeance from the Patriots. But by far the greater number of Loyalists stayed in the United States. There was no general purge, concentration camp, gas chamber, forced-labor battalion, or other cruelty with which we are recently familiar. If a Loyalist was discreet, kept his mouth shut, paid his taxes, refrained from spying or enlisting in partisan raids, it was possible for him to stay at home with no damage other than to his pride; and thousands did. But Loyalists afforded aid and comfort to the enemy. Scattered thoughout the country, they acted as secret service for the king. After Sir Henry Clinton had consolidated his army in New York City, he began enrolling special Tory units; New York State furnished more troops to the king than she did to Congress.

The persecution that Loyalists suffered early in the war aroused the liveliest resentment; and their tactics when they were enrolled in military units were to wage war with the utmost severity. The massacre of the garrison of Fort Griswold, New London, in 1781, was the work of Loyalist battalions from New York and New Jersey, led by Benedict Arnold. Colonel John Butler's Tory Rangers and Sir John Johnson's Loyal Greens, with 500 Seneca auxiliaries, perpetrated the Wyoming Valley massacre of peaceful farmers. Loyalist units directed by former Governor Tryon would dash over to the New Jersey or Connecticut shore, burn houses and crops, and seize booty and prisoners. In the Carolinas the civil war between Patriots and Loyalists was most severe and prolonged. Oaths and tests were applied by both sides, only to be violated at the first opportunity. Prisoners were hanged by one side for treachery, and the other side retaliated in kind. Thus the War of Independence was a civil war in which the contending parties were not mainly sectional, as in the war of 1861–65; they lived side by side throughout the length and breadth of the land, and, naturally, they fought tough.

6. The Commander in Chief

Although the Thirteen States lacked a great political leader to call forth a spirit of sacrifice, Washington did his best to fill the political as well as the military role. He was more than a general: the embodiment of everything fine in the American character. With no illusions about his own grandeur, no thought of the future except an intense longing to return to Mount Vernon, he assumed every responsibility thrust upon him, and fulfilled it. He not only had to lead an army but constantly to write letters to Congress, state leaders, and state governments, begging them for the wherewithal to maintain his army. He had to compose quarrels among his officers and placate cold, hungry, unpaid troops. Intrigues against his authority he ignored, and the intriguers came to grief. In his relations with French officers he proved to be a diplomat second only to Franklin. Refusing to accept a salary, he dipped into his modest fortune to buy comforts for the soldiers and to help destitute families of his companions in battle. Thus Washington brought something more important to the cause than military ability and statesmanship: the priceless gift of character.

Although Washington was scrupulous in his respect for the civil power, there was a certain jealousy of him in Congress and the state governments, largely from fear that he would be too successful and become a dictator. Yet, inconsistently, several members, especially Richard Henry Lee of his own state, and James Lovell of Massachusetts, thought he was not successful enough and played with the idea of relieving him by Charles Lee, or Gates, or the French Duc de Broglie. Just how far the "Conway cabal" of 1777 intended to go; whether it was an officers' plot to supersede Washington, or mere grumbling by ambitious malcontents, is still a mystery. But it is certain that the commander in chief was regarded by the rank and file, and by people in all parts of the country, with deep respect and affection. He did not have the personality of a Napoleon, a Nelson, or a Stonewall Jackson to arouse men to fanatical loyalty; but the soldiers knew that they could depend on him for valor, for military wisdom, and for justice.

WAR AND WASHINGTON

Vain Bri-tons boast no lon-ger with proud in-dig-ni-ty, By land your con-q'ring le-gions, Your match-less strength at sea. Since we, your brav-er sons in-cens'd, Our swords have gird-ed on. Huz-za, huz-za, huz-za, For War and Wash-ing-ton!

XVI

The Northern Campaigns

1776-1778

1. *Long Island and New York City*

NEW YORK CITY, with about 22,000 inhabitants, was second only to Philadelphia as an American town and port of entry. If the British could hold it and the Hudson valley, they could cut off New England from the rest of the rebel colonies.

If General Sir William Howe had lifted his army from Boston directly to New York City, he could doubtless have held both city and colony for the king. But Sir Billy was one of the greatest bus-missers in British military history. After evacuating Boston on 17 March 1776, his army was escorted by the fleet of his brother Admiral Lord Howe to Halifax, to await reinforcements. Not until 7 June did the Howe brothers sail from Nova Scotia to New York, and their first transports arrived in the Narrows on 2 July. Washington had transferred his Continental army to New York directly after the siege of Boston, so Sir Billy had to fight for New York instead of having it fall into his lap.

Washington now had 18,000 men in and around Manhattan, almost the top strength attained by the Continental army during the war. General Howe landed 25,000 men on Staten Island without opposition, and the British fleet acquired complete control of New York harbor, the East river, and the Hudson.

Washington transferred most of his army to Brooklyn and fortified the Heights, hoping that he could force the enemy to evacuate. But Sir Billy, in an unusual spasm of energy, shifted a large part of his army by ships' boats across the bay and challenged Washington on 27 August 1776 in the Battle of Long Island. That battle very nearly crushed both Washington and the cause. Instead of taking a stand on the Heights, Washington drew up his forces on the plain, where the British had the advantage. They were used to European methods of open-field fighting, which Americans were not; and Howe fought his army skillfully. The American commander in chief's dispositions were defective, the New England militia panicked, and the result was a bad defeat for the Americans. They lost over 1000 men killed, wounded, and captured, including two general officers. But Howe's failure to pursue enabled Washington to execute a strategic retirement. Nine thousand men, with field artillery, provisions, cattle, horses and wagons, were transferred across the East river to Manhattan in thirteen hours. Skillful retirements do not win wars; but this one, like that of the British from Dunkerque in 1940, saved an army from annihilation and allowed the war to continue.

Washington's situation on Manhattan was still bad. He now had fewer than 15,000 effectives, constantly diminishing by desertion and expiring enlistments, against 20,000 to 25,000 British regulars and German mercenaries, constantly augmented by reinforcements from England and supported by a naval force unopposed by anything Congress could set afloat. Manhattan was impossible to defend without Brooklyn Heights. The most sensible military measure would have been to burn the city and retire, which Washington proposed to do; but Congress forbade. So he withdrew to Harlem Heights in the north end of Manhattan. In the meantime, Admiral Howe sailed his warships up both flanks of the island, threw a cordon across it at the site of 34th Street, and took possession of the city.

New York remained in British hands throughout the war. This was a tremendous asset. By concentrating their main military force in New York, the British were able to strike out in three directions — into New England, up the Hudson, and down through the Jersies. And since the Royal Navy commanded the Atlantic except for a few months in 1778 and 1781, troops could be shifted from New York to any part of the Atlantic coast by sea. The food problem was not serious, because the British also held Staten Island, parts of Long Island, and most of Westchester County, and were able to bring in army rations from Europe.

Washington did not immediately give up Manhattan. At the upper end, near where 180th Street meets the Hudson, he built Fort Washington, and Fort Lee across the river on the Palisades. After beating off an attack on his left flank at White Plains, he decided to retire further up the Hudson and establish stronger lines behind the Croton river. General Howe now forced his hand by moving the British army up to Dobbs Ferry, which placed it between Washington's army and the two forts, and in a position to march across New Jersey to Philadelphia.

Washington countered by sending 5000 men under General Israel Putnam into New Jersey, leaving 7000 under General Charles Lee at North Castle, where the Croton flows into the Hudson. Before so doing he advised General Nathanael Greene, commander at Forts Washington and Lee, to abandon them as useless enclaves inside the British lines. Greene made the valiant but unwise decision to defend Fort Washington and lost it, together with 2500 men taken prisoner. Howe's subordinate, General Lord Cornwallis, then transferred 5000 men across the Hudson, mounted cannon on the Palisades, and forced Greene to abandon Fort Lee too; but this time the garrison made a successful retreat. Fort Washington was renamed Fort Knyphausen, after the Hessian general who led the assault; it was, in fact, a German victory on

American soil. "This sort of glory, won by German mercenaries against free-born English subjects has no charms for me," said Edmund Burke.

2. The Campaign of the Jersies

Washington with 5000 men had crossed into New Jersey before Corn-wallis. The first phase of this Campaign of 1776 in the Jersies was a race for the bridge over the Raritan at New Brunswick. Washington won, getting there on 1 December. His immediate objectives were to preserve the Continental army intact and to cover and defend Philadelphia. Howe's objective should have been to destroy Washington's divided army. It was the time of times for a British commander to go all out, while Washington's small army was split three ways. Yet, at this juncture, Howe chose to send a large part of his force, in 70 transports, escorted by 11 warships, to Newport, Rhode Island. Not until 7 December did Howe himself cross into New Jersey and take personal command of Cornwallis's force in hope of bringing Washington to decisive action.

New Jersey was a problem for Washington. The Jerseymen waited to see who would win before committing themselves. When the British entered the state, they encountered no countryside in arms; rather, a countryside that took to the cellar. General Howe offered British protection papers to all and sundry who would come in and take an oath of allegiance; and so many did so that the blanks gave out. "The conduct of the Jerseys has been most infamous," wrote Washington to his brother Augustine. "Instead of turning out to defend their country, and affording aid to our army, they are making their submissions as fast as they can. If they had given us any support, we might have made a stand at Hackensack and after that at Brunswick, but the few militia that were in arms, disbanded themselves . . . and left the poor remains of our army to make the best we could of it."

So Washington's little army, with no help from Charles Lee's division, plodded wearily across wintry New Jersey, keeping one jump ahead of Howe. On 7–8 December they first crossed the Delaware river. There were no bridges above Philadelphia, which made the river an excellent defense; but it was a difficult stream for an army to cross. Foreseeing everything, Washington sent men and officers ahead from as far back as New Brunswick, to collect every boat within twenty miles of Trenton. General Lord Stirling [1] held up Howe at Princeton, then made a forced march to Trenton and got his last man on board just as a Hessian brigade entered Trenton with brass bands playing.

Naturally the Americans kept all the boats on the Pennsylvania side of the river, so there were none for the British to use. And Howe on 13 December

1. William Alexander, son of a New York lawyer who defended John Peter Zenger, and a claimant to the earldom of Stirling.

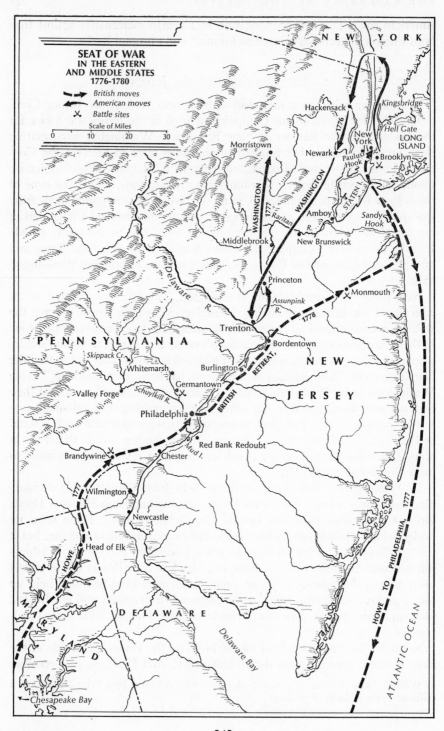

SEAT OF WAR
IN THE EASTERN
AND MIDDLE STATES
1776-1780

- - ➤ British moves
- - ➤ American moves
✗ Battle sites

Scale of Miles
0   10   20   30

NEW YORK

Hackensack

Kingsbridge

Hell Gate

Morristown

Newark

New York

LONG ISLAND

Paulus Hook

Brooklyn

WASHINGTON 1776

WASHINGTON

Raritan R.

Amboy

STATEN I.

Sandy Hook

Middlebrook

New Brunswick

WASHINGTON 1777

Princeton

Monmouth

Assunpink R.

1778

Trenton

PENNSYLVANIA

Skippack Cr.

Bordentown

Whitemarsh

Burlington

NEW

Germantown

BRITISH RETREAT

Valley Forge

Schuylkill R.

JERSEY

Philadelphia

Red Bank Redoubt

Brandywine

Chester

Mud I.

1777

Wilmington

HOWE TO PHILADELPHIA, 1777

Newcastle

HOWE

Head of Elk

MARYLAND

DELAWARE

Delaware Bay

ATLANTIC OCEAN

Chesapeake Bay

242

decided to call off the campaign for that year. The Jersies were very cold and wet, he had a charming mistress in New York City, and, gentlemen did not wage war in winter. Washington's ragged army might melt away before spring; surely the Americans now realized that Britain was invincible? So Howe distributed his army in houses and cantonments all the way from Burlington to Hackensack.

General Howe, by wintering in New Jersey, succeeded in curing the Jersey-men of their neutralist attitude. About half the forces strung from Burlington to Hackensack were German mercenaries, and Germans have been notorious looters from the days of Tacitus to those of Hitler. Protection papers issued to loyal Jerseymen did them no good because the Germans couldn't read; even so, they stole books out of the Princeton library and ransacked shops and houses indiscriminately. So many trains of army wagons moved into New York laden with plate, furniture, and clothing that it looked as though all Jersey were moving to town. The officers were generous in letting their men have a piece of every load. Those not so fortunate stole horses and saddlebags and loaded them with valuables; one Hessian private even got a grandfather clock into New York on horseback.

So far as General Howe was concerned, the campaign of 1776 was over. But Washington had different ideas. He had a touch of the gambler in him, as have all great military leaders. He had been retreating for almost six months; to do nothing all winter but watch the ice cakes float down the Delaware would about finish his army. "You can form no idea," he wrote to his brother Augustine on 18 December, "of the perplexity of my situation. No man, I believe, ever had a greater choice of difficulties, and less means to extricate himself from them . . . under a full persuasion of the justice of our cause I cannot entertain an idea that it will finally sink."

He had to do something, and that soon, because the enlistments of half his army would expire with the year 1776, and few replacements were coming. To protect his position on the west bank of the Delaware, he had spread his line regiments thin along 25 miles of the river. A Hessian brigade was in Trenton; if it were allowed to take the offensive it might crash through and march into Philadelphia. So Washington took the offensive, with 2400 men whom he led nine miles upstream to cross at McKonkey's Ferry, where most of the boats were assembled. Pan ice was floating down the river. For landing craft Washington had a fleet of Durham boats, 30 to 40 feet long, whose peace-time employment was to carry freight on the Delaware. Each was manned by four or five men of Colonel Glover's webfooted Marblehead regiment.

The crossing started at 7:00 p.m. Christmas Day. By 3:00 a.m. all the men and 18 fieldpieces were across. It took an hour to form the regiments on the east bank. At 4:00 o'clock December 26, the advance began in two columns through snow and in a biting wind. Sunrise found the columns a mile from Trenton, where Colonel Rall's Hessians were sleeping off Christmas. They were completely surprised, their retreat cut off, and when General Knox's artillery fired briskly down the two main streets of the village, the German officers decided to surrender. At a cost of none killed, four wounded, but two frozen to death, Washington captured over 900 prisoners, 1200 small arms, 6 brass cannon and the colors of the Hessian brigade.

"All our hopes," wrote Lord George Germain the British secretary at war, "were blasted by the unhappy affair at Trenton." American enlistments at once increased. Pennsylvania militia swarmed into Washington's camp, delighted at an opportunity to invade New Jersey. Three New England line regiments, whose enlistments had expired, were persuaded by a personal appeal from the General to remain six weeks longer.

Washington now established headquarters at Newtown, hoping to advance before New Year's and drive the enemy from New Jersey. Congress responded by granting him — for six months, — the authority to raise a new army and to appoint all officers under rank of brigadier general. He now had 5000 men, partly new recruits but including many veterans. Lord Cornwallis, leaving strong rear guards at Princeton and Lawrenceville, took up a position with about 5500 men before Trenton on the left bank of Assumpinck Creek. Washington evaded this main enemy force and on the night of 1–2 January 1777 advanced on Princeton. At dawn an advance column under General Hugh Mercer encountered a small British force marching south to reinforce Cornwallis, and the Battle of Princeton took place. General Mercer was killed, and the battle almost became an American rout; but Washington personally rallied his men within thirty paces of the enemy and held them in check until Pennsylvania riflemen and veteran New England troops could deploy. Once again Washington proved that he was as good a field commander as he was a planner and strategist. The British were routed and chased into the college town, where one of the regiments barricaded itself in Nassau Hall but surrendered after Washington's artillery fired a few cannon balls into the building.

Washington wished to march on to New Brunswick, but his men were dog-tired, falling asleep by the roadside, and Cornwallis was on his trail. So, five miles out of Princeton, he marched by the left flank, again eluded Cornwallis, and by the end of the first week of January took up winter quarters at Morristown. Cornwallis retired to the New Brunswick-Perth Amboy-Paulus Hook triangle. From Morristown, Washington could maintain communications with Philadelphia, Albany, and New England; and by sending out raids he captured Hackensack, Elizabethtown, and Newark in the course of the winter. In a campaign lasting only three weeks, at a time of year when gentlemen were not supposed to fight, the military genius of America's greatest gentleman, and the fortitude of some five thousand of his men, had undone everything Howe accomplished, recovered the Jersies, and saved the American cause.

Thomas Paine struck the keynote, not only for that day but for every time of tribulation, in his *Crisis* paper which appeared 19 January 1777:

These are the times that try men's souls. The summer soldier and the sunshine patriot will, in this crisis, shrink from the service of their country; but he that stands it now deserves the love and thanks of man and woman. Tyranny, like hell, is not easily conquered; yet we have this consolation with us, that the harder the conflict, the more glorious the triumph. What we obtain too cheap, we esteem too lightly; it is dearness only that gives everything its value. Heaven knows how to put a proper price upon its goods; and it would be strange indeed if so celestial an article as freedom should not be highly rated.

3. The Saratoga Campaign

The small Northern American army under Benedict Arnold, after failing to capture Quebec, fought a series of stubborn retiring actions from the St. Lawrence to Lake Champlain that consumed most of the summer of 1776. Arnold's opponent, Governor Sir Guy Carleton, was a capable officer; but Arnold's energy in building a fleet on Lake Champlain, and his skill in handling it in the Battle of Valcour Island (11 October 1776) delayed the British long enough to keep them off Washington's neck in the critical summer of 1776.

The season for gentlemanly campaigning closed earlier in Canada than in the Jersies. Carleton, after recovering Crown Point, retired on 2 November to winter quarters in the loyal Province of Quebec. Major General John Burgoyne now sold the North ministry a plan for invading New York and New England by way of Lake Champlain and the Hudson, under his command. This sounded good because the same route had so often served during the colonial wars; and Sir Guy supported it, even though "Gentleman Johnny" Burgoyne would reap the glory. Sir John Johnson, son of old Sir William of the Mohawks, promised to bring in thousands of Mohawk valley Loyalists and Iroquois braves to support any British army that marched thither.

Nevertheless, the plan made very little sense, owing to the existence of another potential countryside in arms. Since the conquest of Canada, the "Hampshire Grants," the future State of Vermont, had been settled by thousands of New England farmers and frontiersmen. They organized a de facto independent state which was not represented in the Continental Congress, owing to the opposition of New York. The British government appears not to have heard of these Green Mountain Boys, or else assumed them to be of the same breed as the amiable Jerseymen.

General Howe had no fewer than 27,000 men in and near New York City in the spring of 1777, doing nothing. Admiral Howe had a sizable fleet; and the sensible way for the British to secure the line of the Hudson and Lake Champlain would have been to thrust up the Hudson. But this sound strategy was not adopted, because Sir Billy wished to retrieve his poor performance in the Jersies by taking Philadelphia, which he imagined would put an end to the war. The British war department ordered Howe to send a substantial force up the Hudson and rendezvous with Burgoyne near Albany, but it approved his sending the bigger force to Philadelphia, and left him the choice of route.[1] He selected the longest ocean route, via Chesapeake Bay, because his brother's fleet could escort him, and Congress had set up strong points on the Delaware below Philadelphia. He was uncommonly slow in getting started, wasting May and June in marches and countermarches between Hoboken and New Brunswick, hoping to draw Washington into a pitched battle; Washington, with an army greatly inferior in numbers, naturally declined. On the first anniversary of the Declaration of Independence, General Howe loaded in transports all the troops he could spare from holding down New York. There ensued one of those long spells of July calm that are the despair of Long Island yachtsmen, and not until the 23rd did a fair wind enable the fleet to sail through the Narrows.

Leaving Sir Billy's army, miserable and seasick as the transports rolled in a heavy ground swell off the Jersey coast, let us follow Burgoyne. Around the first of June he jumped off from the St. Lawrence with about 4000 British regulars, 3000 Germans, and 1000 Canadian militia and Indians. These Indians, Burgoyne expected, would put the fear of God and King George into any rebel frontier settlements they might encounter, and he amused himself by making grandiloquent speeches to them: — "Warriors! Go forth in the might and valor of your cause!" etc. Burgoyne so relished his own oratory that he sent copies of these speeches to the London papers. Horace Walpole wrote to a friend, "Have you read Burgoyne's rhodomontade, in which he almost promises to cross America in a hop, step and jump? He has sent over, too, a copy of his 'talk' with the Indians, which they say is still more supernatural. I own I prefer General Howe's taciturnity who, at least, if he does nothing, does not break his word." The "talks" may have amused the Indians, but they made the Green Mountain Boys grimly determined to stop Gentleman Johnny at first opportunity.

Burgoyne's campaign opened well for him and ill for the Americans. Fort Ticonderoga was held by a small garrison under Major General Arthur St. Clair. Assaulted by an overwhelming force of redcoats, Indians, and the Canadian freshwater navy, St. Clair evacuated Ticonderoga in good order on 6 July and marched his men by forest trail to Fort Edward on the Hudson, where they reinforced the American Northern army under General Philip Schuyler.

At this juncture the morale of the American Northern army was jeopardized by congressional shillyshallying about the command. A controversy over

1. The story was current in England that the dispatch ordering Howe to help Burgoyne failed to reach him in time because the war minister had to enjoy his Christmas holidays before signing it. This was not true, but George Bernard Shaw used it effectively in his play *The Devil's Disciple*. In defense of Howe, when he first received word from London to help Burgoyne, on 16 August, he ordered Sir Henry Clinton, in command at New York City, to start north; but Clinton, too, got the slows and did not start until 3 October.

the respective merits of Generals Schuyler, Arnold, and Gates, which their partisans have continued to this day, has obscured the events of the campaign. In the promotions of general officers by Congress in the spring of 1777, Brigadier Benedict Arnold, who deserved a second star for his brilliant work in the Canadian campaign, missed out because New England's allowance of major generals was already filled. Consequently he could not command the Northern army, which should then have been placed under General Philip Schuyler of Albany, who had done very well under Arnold in the retreat. But the New England troops refused to serve under Schuyler. An aristocrat like Washington, he was not a great enough gentleman to be effective as a leader of plain people, and had made himself unpopular by insisting on excessive military punctilio. Moreover, Schuyler belonged to the class of New York patroons who had opposed the settlement of Vermont by New Englanders, contested their titles, and endeavored to have them ejected. So the leaders of the Green Mountain Boys threatened to do nothing to stop Burgoyne if General Schuyler were given the command. Congress, on 4 August, then gave command of the Northern army to General Gates.

Horatio Gates, as a man and a soldier, is something of an enigma. He seems to have been pushed by circumstances and an ambitious wife into positions too great for his merits. He had served in the British army in America during the French and Indian War, after which he bought a plantation in Virginia, raised thoroughbred horses, and reflected the politics of his neighbors. Washington made him adjutant general of the Continental army, an administrative command similar to that of a modern chief of staff. His brother officers never liked him, and soldiers observed that, unlike Washington, he never exposed his person to bullets. But he had a way with politicians, especially those of New England, who, when disappointed in Charles Lee, made Gates their favorite son.

It took Burgoyne's army, encumbered by officers' wives and children and enormous quantities of baggage, nearly a month to reach Fort Edward, which Schuyler had abandoned. The problem of logistic supply was insoluble. To carry one month's provisions to the army at Fort Edward required 180 Canadian batteaux, hauled by relays of oxen and horses over the portages between the two lakes and the Hudson, a job that required five weeks. While waiting for food to arrive from Canada, Burgoyne made two diversions, each of which ran into a countryside in arms.

Colonel Barry St. Leger commanded the first. He moved up the St. Lawrence to Oswego, then across country to Fort Stanwix, the Mohawk country where Sir John Johnson had promised a big turnout of Loyalist militia and Mohawk braves. But there was a bigger turnout of Patriot militia under General Nicholas Herkimer. On 7 August St. Leger reached Fort Stanwix. Herkimer, marching to relieve the garrison, was ambushed by the Mohawks at Oriskany and badly cut up. A small force under Benedict Arnold now marched up the Mohawk to relieve Fort Stanwix. He managed, by spreading false rumors, to panic the Mohawks. St. Leger then gave up the siege of Fort Stanwix on 22 August, and retired through the woods to Canada.

Burgoyne's second diversion went into Vermont in search of food. The general's ideas of American geography were so hazy that he imagined his raiders in two weeks could march across Vermont to Bellows Falls, down the Connecticut to Brattleboro and back by the Albany road, collecting hundreds of horses and cattle and wagonloads of grain. For this incursion he chose 375 dismounted German heavy dragoons under Colonel Baum, and 300 Canadians and Indians. They did not even reach the Vermont line; for, as Burgoyne complained, "Wherever the King's forces point, militia to the number of three or four thousand assemble in a few hours." General John Stark, hero of the rail fence at Bunker Hill, led a force of Green Mountain Boys out from Bennington to meet them, and on 16 August captured or killed the entire raiding force.

In militia warfare, nothing succeeds like success. The Battle of Bennington brought Vermont militia by the hundreds to the headquarters of General Gates, who took command of the Northern American army on 19 August. And the British delay at Fort Edward gave Washington time to send important reinforcements from New Jersey, in the shape of Morgan's Rifles. General Burgoyne, still jaunty despite the failure of his two diversions (which cost him a good 1000 men), marched south and crossed to the west bank of the Hudson. He was now in a rich farming country where ripe wheat and corn were available for men and horses. The Americans felled trees across the roads and destroyed bridges, slowing his advance to about one mile a day.

Although Gates's army now outnumbered Burgoyne's almost two to one, Gates almost lost the campaign by constructing a strong entrenched camp on Bemis Heights (12 September) and refusing to budge, even when it became evident that Burgoyne was about to occupy a hill commanding his position. Arnold begged to lead an attack with Morgan's brigade and a New England regiment, and Gates grudgingly consented. Through leadership, audacity, and tactical skill, Arnold beat Burgoyne badly in the First Battle of Freeman's Farm, 19 September. One Yankee soldier said of Arnold, "There wa'n't no waste timber in him. It was 'Come on, boys!' not 'Go on, boys!' He didn't care for nothin'. He'd ride right in." He rode right in on Gates, too, when the commanding general neglected to mention his name in the official report of the action. Gates then suspended Arnold from command.

Burgoyne's situation worsened daily. General Benjamin Lincoln, with a force of New England militia, cut his communications with Canada. Burgoyne could no longer retreat, his Indian allies were slipping away, his foraging parties were being bushwhacked by militia, his field hospital was crowded with the sick and wounded. On 7 October Burgoyne made a bold attempt to turn the Americans' left. During this Second Battle of Freeman's Farm,[1]

1. Also called Battle of Bemis Heights, or Stillwater.

Arnold, without Gates's permission, rushed into the fray, took command of the New England regiments, turned a British defeat into a rout, and was badly wounded. One week later, when his force had fallen to less than 6000, Burgoyne sent a flag of truce to American headquarters and asked for terms. On 17 October Gates granted Burgoyne very favorable terms of surrender. His army was allowed to return to England, on the promise not to serve again.

This was a turning point in the war. Burgoyne surrendered six generals and 300 other officers, and about 5500 enlisted men. Gates, as top commander, received credit which should have gone to Benedict Arnold, who now began to think that his talents would be better appreciated by the king than by Congress.

4. From the Brandywine to Monmouth

Shortly before Burgoyne marched south from Fort Edward, General Howe disembarked 18,000 troops at Elkton near the head of Chesapeake Bay, 50 miles from Philadelphia. To oppose his advance, Washington had 12,000 men, including militia. So few had uniforms that he ordered each man to wear on his tattered jacket a sprig of green, as a symbol of hope. Since Philadelphia could not be abandoned without a fight, the best Washington could do was to delay the enemy, whose navy commanded all sea approaches.

Washington made his first stand, on 9 September 1777, at a ford of Brandywine creek, which flows into Delaware Bay at Wilmington. Howe used excellent tactics. The Americans lost 1000 men killed and wounded, and Congress had to retire to Lancaster. On 26 September Howe occupied Philadelphia. He made no move to pursue Washington, but decided to take the two American forts on the Delaware. While so engaged, Washington attempted to exploit Howe's temporary weakness in Philadelphia by attacking his main encampment at Germantown (5 October). Everything that can go wrong in an attack, went wrong in that one; and Washington lost over 1000 more men. He then retired to Valley Forge.

Two weeks after Washington's defeat at Germantown came the triumphant news of Burgoyne's surrender. It is not surprising that a movement (the Conway cabal) began, to replace retreating Washington by victorious Gates. Members of Congress and a few general officers were involved, but the whole thing fizzled out and nobody thereafter would admit having had anything to do with it. The fact that the country and the army stood by Washington is a tribute to their appreciation of a really great man. In no other major revolution has a loser of so many battles been supported to the point where he could win.

Sir Billy Howe now settled down for the winter in Philadelphia. He cared not to risk arousing another countryside to arms. The British army, numbering on 1 April 1778 some 19,500 men in Philadelphia, 10,500 in New York, and 3700 in Newport, Rhode Island, was completely stymied by the example of what had happened to Burgoyne.

Capture of the "rebel capital" brought the war's end no nearer. Shortly there arrived news of the French alliance with the United States. The North ministry relieved Howe on 8 May by Sir Henry Clinton whose instructions were to evacuate Philadelphia, concentrate on New York, and prepare to fight a French expeditionary force. He decided to retire across New Jersey. Washington followed on a parallel line, watching for an opportunity to attack. It came on 28 June 1778 when Clinton was at Monmouth County Court House. There followed one of those battles that are difficult to untangle. The essential thing is that Charles Lee (who had been exchanged and commanded the van) was ordered by Washington to attack. He disobeyed, and retreated with so little reason as to be suspected of treason. Washington brought up the main body and prevented the retreat from becoming a rout, but could not prevent Clinton's reaching New York.

The Commander in Chief then did the only thing he could do; he half encircled the city on the north side, hoping that a French fleet would appear to break the stalemate. He had to wait almost three years for that.

THE BATTLE OF THE KEGS

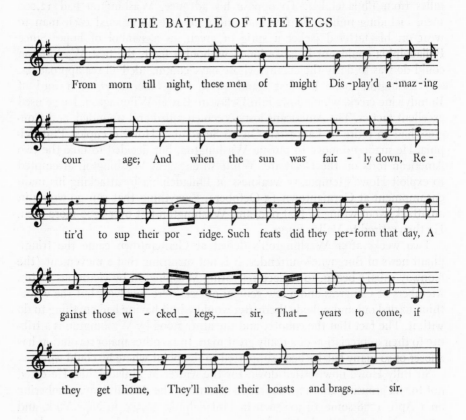

From morn till night, these men of might Dis-play'd a-maz-ing cour - age; And when the sun was fair - ly down, Re-tir'd to sup their por - ridge. Such feats did they per-form that day, A-gainst those wi - cked_ kegs,___ sir, That_ years to come, if they get home, They'll make their boasts and brags,___ sir.

Diplomacy, Carolinas, Yorktown, and Peace

1778-1783

1. The French Alliance

THE CONTINENTAL CONGRESS began fishing for foreign aid even before declaring independence. In November 1775 it appointed a committee to correspond secretly with Great Britain, Ireland, "and other parts of the world," meaning France. Thither Silas Deane, Arthur Lee, and Franklin were sent to buy munitions and hold out the advantages of direct support. In a debate on the advisability of asking for a French alliance, John Adams, our original isolationist, said, "We ought not to enter into any alliance with her, which would entangle us in any future wars in Europe." He wanted only something equivalent to the lend-lease of 1940. His view prevailed for a time, but before long the military situation became so desperate that Congress instructed the commissioners to conclude alliances with France and Spain, if necessary to obtain their participation in the war.

Lousi XVI, amiable but stupid, and even younger than George III, was then king of France. His able foreign minister, the Comte de Vergennes, had been following American revolutionary movements with the keenest interest, and showed his approval of Thomas Paine's *Common Sense* by putting its author on a secret French payroll. All France approved the American Revolution. The government saw in it a means of weakening the British empire and restoring the balance of power which had been upset by the previous war. Rising French industrialists craved more direct access to the American market than they could obtain under the taut imperial system inaugurated by Charles Townshend. The bourgeoisie wished to get even with "perfidious Albion," and the intelligentsia admired America on idealistic grounds.

For a generation the dominant intellectual movement in France had been directed toward the reconstruction of society. Everyone was talking about scrapping feudalism, disestablishing the church, and starting fresh on the basis of liberty and "reason." The *philosophes* found inspiration in Pennsylvania, where one could lead the good life without a nobility or an established church. Voltaire admired the Quakers, who really meant peace when they talked peace; Rousseau regarded American Indians as unspoiled "children of nature"; Condorcet was so charmed with what he read about Connecticut that he signed one of his tracts "Un Bourgeois de New Haven." The *écon-*

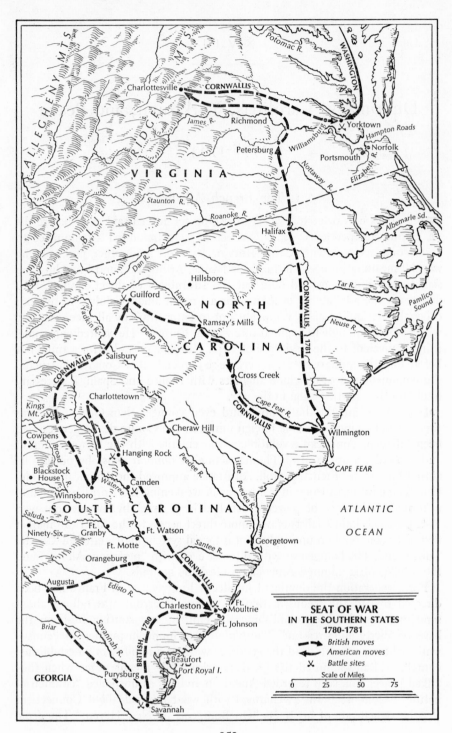

ALLEGHENY MTS.

BLUE RIDGE MTS.

Potomac R.

WASHINGTON

Charlottesville

CORNWALLIS

James R.

Richmond

Yorktown

Hampton Roads

VIRGINIA

Williamsburg

Norfolk

Petersburg

Portsmouth

Nottaway R.

Elizabeth R.

Staunton R.

Roanoke R.

Halifax

Albemarle Sd.

Dan R.

Tar R.

Pamlico Sound

Hillsboro

Guilford

Haw R.

NORTH

Neuse R.

Yadkin R.

Deep R.

Ramsay's Mills

CAROLINA

CORNWALLIS, 1781

Salisbury

CORNWALLIS

Cross Creek

Charlottetown

Cape Fear R.

CORNWALLIS

Kings Mt.

Cheraw Hill

Wilmington

Cowpens

Hanging Rock

Peedee R.

CAPE FEAR

Broad R.

Blackstock House

Camden

Little Peedee R.

Winnsboro

Wateree R.

ATLANTIC

SOUTH   CAROLINA

OCEAN

Saluda R.

Ft. Granby

Ft. Watson

Santee R.

Georgetown

Ninety-Six

Ft. Motte

Orangeburg

CORNWALLIS

Augusta

Edisto R.

BRITISH, 1780

Charleston

Ft. Moultrie

Briar Cr.

Savannah R.

Ft. Johnson

Beaufort

GEORGIA

Purysburg

Port Royal I.

Savannah

SEAT OF WAR
IN THE SOUTHERN STATES
1780-1781

British moves
American moves
Battle sites

Scale of Miles

0   25   50   75

252

omistes, especially Dupont de Nemours whose sons established an industrial empire in Delaware, found Virginia an illustration of their theory that agriculture is the sole source of wealth; that commerce, manufacturing, and finance are so many parasites on the farmer's back. Turgot, finance minister of Louis XVI, wrote that Americans were "the hope of the world. They may become its model."

All these generous, hopeful people boiled over with enthusiasm for America. The Virginia Declaration of Rights and the state constitutions embodied eternal principles of liberty; Washington was a modern Cincinnatus, with a volunteer army of free and virtuous republicans. Instead of fearing that royalist France might be contaminated by the radical example of America, the French intellectuals warned America not to let French opulence undermine republican simplicity.

This atmosphere explains the remarkable success of our republican commissioners in monarchical Paris. Thomas Carlyle describes the amusing spectacle of those sons of the Puritans, "sleek Silas, sleek Benjamin," consorting with the gay, sophisticated, Roman Catholic society of the French court. Ben Franklin, wilier than the cleverest diplomat of Europe, was a brilliant choice. The homely quips from his *Way to Wealth*, translated as *La Science du Bonhomme Richard*, won acclaim from liberal Catholics as evidence that a scientist could have sound moral principles. His inventions proved that science was not negative and destructive but offered a positive program to a better life. As a freemason, he was welcomed to French lodges where liberals congregated, and his contributions to the knowledge of electricity won him admission to the Academy of Sciences. At the same time his suit, unadorned by gold lace because he hadn't the money for court dress, and his unpowdered hair, in which he appeared before Louis XVI because the hired wig didn't arrive, made a great hit as the embodiment of republican simplicity. Franklin took care to play up to this image. He did not drive about Paris waving his arms and soliciting cheers; he held receptions at his lodgings in Passy, dined with courtiers, and became almost a legend in his lifetime. But he could not have accomplished this but for his genuine love of people. Of the French he later wrote, "I have spent several years in the sweet society of a people whose conversation is instructive, whose manners are highly pleasing, and who above all the nations of the world, had in the greatest perfection the art of making themselves beloved by strangers."

Franklin's difficulties in France came not from the French, but from fellow Americans. Deane and John Adams, who came over in 1777, were jealous of him; Arthur Lee jumped to the conclusion that he was a thief, and through Richard Henry Lee and Samuel Adams, tried to undermine Franklin in Congress. Often without funds, Franklin had to borrow money from the French to feed his staff; his first loan for the colonies was raised against future deliveries of Virginia tobacco. But he kept a constant eye on his main mission, to obtain French military aid and, if possible, an alliance. And he returned to Philadelphia poorer than when he left home.

For France to recognize American independence would have meant instant war with England, for which Louis XVI was not prepared. But his government, through the intermediary of the playwright Beaumarchais (author of *Le Mariage de Figaro*), sent valuable cargoes of munitions and clothing to Congress, and allowed American privateers and naval vessels to use French ports while the country was still officially neutral.

The surrender of Burgoyne at Saratoga on 17 October 1777 brought a change in French policy. Vergennes, subtly steered by Franklin, became fearful that this signal defeat might persuade Lord North to offer generous terms which Congress would accept, and the empire be restored. North very nearly did so. He introduced a new conciliatory bill in November 1777 which, if passed promptly, might have changed our entire history; but the country M.P.s had to have their Christmas holidays and Parliament adjourned without passing it. In the meantime, Franklin so worked on French fears of an accommodation with Britain that on 6 February 1778 Vergennes signed two treaties with the United States, one of amity and commerce, and one of alliance.

Vergennes allowed Franklin to write his own terms, which consequently were very liberal. The main thing was a promise that neither nation would lay down arms until Great Britain recognized American independence. France renounced designs on Canada, so the way was still open to making that British possession the fourteenth state. In return, the United States guaranteed French possession of those West Indian colonies which she then held. And commerce was to be on the basis of most favored nation.

Eleven days later, on 17 February, Lord North's conciliatory bill passed Parliament. It offered even more than the Second Continental Congress had demanded; as much as Adams, Wilson, and Jefferson had suggested in their dominion proposals of 1774–75. A royal commission headed by the Earl of Carlisle was sent over to negotiate with Congress on this basis. It was authorized to conclude an armistice, to promise repeal of the Coercive acts and all revenue acts since 1763, to cancel overdue quitrents, taxes, and claims arising from the war; even to renounce parliamentary regulation of imperial trade. It could concede any other insistent American demands "short of open and avowed Independence." These terms were to be secured by an intra-imperial treaty like that, over a century later, which recognized the Irish Free State. Had this plan gone through, the revolted colonies would have returned to British allegiance, leaving only war and foreign relations to the crown.

It was too late. News of the French treaties, which reached New York on 2 May 1778, engaged the honor of the country to France. Washington even earlier advised Congress in vigorous terms to pay no attention to the Carlisle mission, and Congress refused to meet it unless American independence were first recognized, the one thing that the commissioners were forbidden to do.

They tarried in New York until late in the year, hoping that a change in the military situation might soften up Congress, and even offered £10,500 and a fat job to a congressman if he would help them. But they got exactly nowhere.

The French treaties said nothing about the amount or kind of warlike aid to be furnished to the United States. At the time they were signed, John Paul Jones's plan for a French fleet to attack Lord Howe's fleet in Delaware Bay and then recapture New York was adopted by the French minister of marine, but executed so slowly that the fleet, under Rear Admiral the Count d'Estaing, only reached the Delaware on 8 July, after Howe had left for New York. D'Estaing followed him thither, but the local pilots were so unnerved by the sight of the British fleet drawn up in line, ready to rake the French ships fore and aft, that they refused to pilot them through the Narrows. D'Estaing then sailed to Newport, where Washington arranged for a detachment of his army to co-operate in wresting that base from the British. Just as the French marines were about to land, a summer gale blew down Narragansett Bay and the fleet put out to sea. There they encountered Lord Howe's fleet, reinforced by that of Commodore Byron, which had just arrived from England. The summer gale became a line storm, and both fleets were kept so busy cutting away masts and avoiding collision, that no battle developed. The British ships returned to New York; the French put in at Boston, where their sailors on liberty were beaten up by Sam Adams's waterfront mobsters. D'Estaing then sailed for the West Indies, a more profitable theater for a winter campaign than the coast of New England.

Georgia in the meantime had been reconquered by the British. General Robert Howe, in command of the American Southern army at Savannah, had only 700 Continentals and 150 militia under him. In November 1778 a British amphibious operation under Colonel Sir Archibald Campbell, mounted in New York, landed some 3500 men unopposed on Tybee Island, advanced on Savannah, routed Howe's force and took the Georgia capital. Campbell then pressed inland to Augusta, while Sir George Prevost, advancing overland with the garrison of loyal East Florida, occupied Sunbury. Loyalists flocked to the British colors, the royal governor was reinstated, an assembly summoned; and by the spring of 1779 it looked as though Georgia were back in the empire.

Congress relieved Robert Howe by General Benjamin Lincoln, who brought reinforcements south by land and took command at Charleston. Prevost then advanced on the South Carolina capital. That expedition, for looting, vandalism, and savagery by Tories and Cherokee Indians, makes Sherman's march through Georgia in 1864 seem a picnic in comparison. Charleston was only protected from capture by the prompt arrival of Pulaski's Legion, which helped Generals Lincoln and Moultrie to win an engagement. Prevost then retired to Savannah.

At this juncture appeared Admiral d'Estaing, gallantly answering a call for help. The French fleet of 20 ships of the line, 13 frigates, and transports carrying 6000 troops, arrived off Tybee Island on 8 September 1779. The British had only 3200 men to defend Savannah. It was just such a situation that led to the surrender of Cornwallis at Yorktown. But, with no safe anchorage for his big ships, and autumn gales threatening, D'Estaing insisted on launching a premature assault on 9 October. Casualties were heavy, Pulaski was killed, and the Admiral wounded. The French re-embarked and returned to France without anything to show for fifteen months in American waters. The Bailli de Suffren, who served under D'Estaing, summed him up in a phrase — "Had only his seamanship equalled his courage!"

2. Hit-and-Run Raids

A year and a half had elapsed since the conclusion of the French alliance, and victory still seemed far away. The war had reached a stalemate. Washington, without sea power, could not force the British out of New York City; Sir Henry Clinton dared not invade the interior for fear of running into another Bennington. So each side resorted to raids and to desultory, haphazard operations that had no useful military result but aroused bitterness and hatred.

The British did most of it, to employ the thousands of soldiers and scores of ships that were idling at New York. Sir Henry Clinton was instructed by the war office, on 8 March 1778, to make no offensive land operations into the interior (a tribute to the "countryside in arms") but to raid seaports and destroy rebel property, especially ships. That year there were British raids on Egg Harbor in New Jersey, New Bedford and Fairhaven in Massachusetts, and Vineyard Haven on Martha's Vineyard. Commodore Sir George Collier in May 1779 ravaged the shores of Chesapeake Bay, capturing many American merchant ships and burning Portsmouth; he then returned to New York, sailed up the Hudson, and attacked Stony Point. Having secured that good military objective, Sir George resumed the pitiful strategy of burning defenseless villages. Commanding a fleet of 50 vessels, carrying 2600 troops (mainly Loyalists and Germans), he sailed through Hell Gate into Long Island Sound and on 4 July issued a proclamation to the people of Connecticut who, he hoped, had "recovered from the phrensy which has distracted this unhappy country," and were about to "blush at their delusions." Next day, the soldiers landed to attack New Haven; but the unblushing countryside rallied and forced the troops to re-embark without indulging in their anticipated pleasure of burning Yale College. On 8 July the village of Fairfield was looted and completely destroyed, and on the 11th, Norwalk received similar treatment. There was no military purpose in these exploits except to terrify the Yankees. Congress, in retaliation, discussed ordering Franklin to hire incendiaries to burn London, starting with Buckingham Palace; but they thought better of it and left retaliation in the able hands of Captain John Paul Jones.

That accomplished officer, in sloop-of-war *Ranger*, raided the English port of Whitehaven to burn shipping, tried to kidnap his former Scots neighbor

Lord Selkirk, and captured H.M.S. *Drake*. In 1779, Franklin and the French admiralty fitted out for him a task force consisting of an old East Indiaman which Jones renamed *Bonhomme Richard*, the new Continental frigate *Alliance*, French frigate *Pallas*, and two smaller French vessels, all under the American flag. Eleven different nationalities were represented in *Bonhomme's* crew of 380, but the officers were almost all Americans; and Jones's genius whipped this motley collection of professional sailors, beachcombers, and peasants into as stout a force as ever served under the Stars and Stripes.

Jones sailed around the British Isles, took many prizes, scared the daylights out of Edinburgh and Newcastle, and on 23 September 1779 in the North Sea fought his greatest fight, against H.M.S. *Serapis* off Flamborough Head. In a hot ship-to-ship battle between *Bonhomme Richard* and *Serapis*, lasting from 6:30 to 10:30 p.m., Jones fought his almost disabled ship long after any other captain would have struck, and had the satisfaction of receiving the British captain's surrender. *Bonhomme Richard* was so badly shot up that she went down; but Jones, transferring his flag to *Serapis*, sailed her and the rest of the squadron, including a sloop-of-war captured by *Pallas*, into the neutral Dutch port of the Texel.

3. *Fall of Charleston; Carolinas Campaign*

Paul Jones's victory shone the brighter because the years 1779–80 were very dark for his cause. The Massachusetts state navy was wiped out in an abortive attack on the British base at Castine, Maine. And the worst American defeat of the entire war was the loss of Charleston, South Carolina.

Charleston has always been a hard nut for an enemy to crack, as General Lord Cornwallis had found in June 1776; but he was eager to try again. Cornwallis despised the hit-and-run strategy that Sir Henry Clinton had been employing. In the fall of 1779 he sold Sir Henry the plan of an amphibious expedition against Charleston, to be followed by the conquest of the Carolinas with the help of local Loyalists, and a joint military and naval campaign in Virginia to secure that state and Chesapeake Bay. There was nothing wrong with this strategy, but two unexpected factors wrecked it. The Carolina Loyalists were neither numerous nor strong enough to counteract the local Patriots, and the French navy intervened at a crucial point.

The campaign opened brilliantly for Britain. General Benjamin Lincoln, after failing to recapture Savannah, was now based on Charleston, commanding about 1200 men of the South Carolina and Virginia Lines, and some 2000 militia. Clinton organized a formidable expedition against Charleston, with Cornwallis as second in command. Some 8500 troops, about one-third of them American Loyalists, were embarked in 90 transports and escorted by 14 men-of-war. To meet this overwhelming naval force, Congress dispatched to Charleston the only available vessels of the Continental navy, three frigates and sloop-of-war *Ranger*, under Commodore Abraham Whipple USN. Whipple adopted the fatuous plan of anchoring his ships close to the city, in the hope that their guns might sink British landing craft. But Clinton and Cornwallis were much too smart to try a frontal assault. They landed most of their troops south of Charleston and advanced against its land side, which Lincoln had left almost undefended, while the British light-draft frigates crashed through the fire of Fort Moultrie and anchored off the city (8 April 1780). Clinton then summoned the Americans to surrender. Lincoln might have cut his way out; but too long he hesitated, and on 12 May he surrendered unconditionally. The British took the town, with about 5500 prisoners, captured the three Continental ships which had not been scuttled, and set up a Loyalist government.

Clinton now returned to New York and left Cornwallis in charge. Using mainly his Loyalist units, especially Colonel Banastre Tarleton's Legion, which seldom gave quarter, he overran almost the whole of South Carolina within three months. The Patriot militia under General Sumter were overwhelmed. Cornwallis set up a line of fortified posts between Camden and Ninety-six to protect the state from attack from the north, and placed garrisons at Savannah, Port Royal, and Charleston to protect the coast. Expedient Charleston merchants resumed trade with England, the former royal governor took over, and to all appearances the Palmetto State was back in the empire along with Georgia.

American reinforcements, however, were coming. In April 1780 Washington dispatched the Maryland and Delaware line regiments southward under General de Kalb, to succor the Carolinas. These veteran outfits had fought in every northern campaign, but took their new and difficult mission without a murmur. On 22 June they reached Hillsboro, North Carolina, after incredible hardships owing to the failure of the states through which they passed to furnish supplies. Soldiers went without food for days, then gorged on peaches, green corn, and raw beef, with devastating results to their digestive tracts. When news of the fall of Charleston reached Congress, it appointed Horatio Gates, the politicians' favorite general, to command the Southern Department, over De Kalb's head and against Washington's advice. Gates, when he took command at Hillsboro, decided to advance on Camden; and, against everyone's advice, insisted on taking the direct route through the pine barrens where there wasn't enough food to support a hog, instead of following the longer wagon road along which were many farms and well-affected people. This march, too, was attended by hunger and dysentery.

Near Camden, Gates's army with between 2600 and 3000 men fit for duty (only 1000 of them Continentals) was attacked by Cornwallis. The British were inferior in numbers, but all were regulars except the Royal North Carolinians and Rawdon's Volunteers of Ireland. And Cornwallis was an outstanding leader, beloved by his men, which Gates was not. The Battle of Camden, 16 August 1780, was one of the fiercest fights of the war. American militia panicked at the first British bayonet charge; De Kalb, mortally wounded, held

the field with the Maryland and Delaware Line. These famished but courageous soldiers stood their ground until all, except Major John Eager Howard's
threescore who cut their way out, were killed or captured. General Gates,
mounted on one of his Virginia thoroughbreds, galloped at the head of the
fleeing militia and never stopped until he reached Charlotte, North Carolina,
sixty miles from the battlefield. This battle finished his army career and
scattered most of his troops to the woods and swamps.

Bad news indeed for America; and worse was to come. On 25 September
1780, Benedict Arnold went over to the enemy. For over a year he had been
providing Sir Henry Clinton with military intelligence and dickering for the
price of treason. Only the capture of their go-between, the unfortunate Major
André, prevented Arnold from delivering West Point to the enemy.

North Carolina now lay open to Cornwallis. He marched deliberately into
that state, hampered only by attacks of Colonel William R. Davie's dragoons
and other hastily organized volunteer units. At the same time, Major Patrick
Ferguson, who had organized and armed 4000 South Carolina Loyalists was
ordered by Cornwallis to march north on a route parallel to his own. Ferguson, a gallant Scots veteran, uttered a foolish threat that brought out a countryside in arms. He sent word to the frontiersmen of the Watauga country
that in retaliation for their having taken part in the South Carolina fighting
he would soon lay waste their settlements and hang their leaders to the
nearest tree. So they decided to get him first; and in this enterprise they were
joined by rangy militia from western Virginia.

Major Ferguson, with a force of 1400 Loyalists, took his stand on the top of
a wooded ridge called Kings Mountain and sent word that "he defied God
Almighty and all the rebels out of hell to overcome him." There then took
place (7 October) a Bunker Hill in reverse. Frontier militia swarmed up the
forested slopes. Twice they were driven down by bayonet charges; but their
long rifles, fired from behind trees, forced the Tories into a huddled mass,
killed Ferguson, and slaughtered everyone who did not surrender.

Kings Mountain was the Trenton of the Southern campaign, giving new life
to an apparently lost cause. Since Cornwallis's advanced position at Charlotte
was now untenable, he hurriedly retreated to Winnsboro, South Carolina.
There he remained all winter while his dashing cavalry officers, Tarleton and
Wemyss, indulged in a series of skirmishes with the Patriot partisan leaders
Pickens, Marion, and Sumter.

Congress, thrice having failed to pick winning generals in the South, now
allowed Washington to choose a successor to galloper Gates. He appointed
Nathanael Greene, who took command of the Southern Department at Charlotte in December 1780. Greene's army comprised fewer than 950 Continental infantry, 150 Continental gunners and troopers, and about 530 militia.
"The appearance of the troops," wrote Greene early in January 1781, "was
wretched beyond description, and their distress, on account of lack of provisions, was little less than their suffering for want of clothing and other neces-

sities." But Greene, who like Knox had been selected from the ruck of New England militia officers by the discerning eye of Washington, was a great strategist. Only thirty-eight years old, mild and serene in manner, there was something about him that inspired confidence in troops.

He not only reorganized the army but adopted the audacious strategy of dividing his inferior force into two columns, one under General Daniel Morgan, the other under himself, in order to harass Cornwallis and live off the country. Washington managed to send reinforcements, notably "Light Horse Harry" Lee's elite cavalry legion, every man a disciplined scout and raider. Cornwallis, too, had been reinforced from New York. He now divided his army into three parts, hoping to knock out both Morgan and Greene with a swift left-and-right, then march north with the third division. On an open plain at a place near Kings Mountain called the Cowpens, Morgan took his stand and awaited attack by Tarleton's Tory troopers and a Scots infantry regiment. Morgan's tactics were so sound and his men, both militia and Continentals, fought so well that, at a minimum cost, they killed or captured nine-tenths of the British force.

Victory at the Cowpens gave Greene opportunity to show his strategic skill in a shifty campaign that puzzled Cornwallis. The Englishman was too stubborn to do the prudent thing, retire to Charleston; pride led him again to invade North Carolina. Morgan and Greene kept well ahead of him, hauling boats on wheels to expedite the crossing of rivers. Greene crossed the Dan river into Virginia, leaving Cornwallis momentarily elated, since he imagined that both Carolinas were now in the royal bag. But Greene, without even waiting for reinforcements, struck back across the Dan, chose his ground at Guilford Courthouse, and awaited attack. On 15 March 1781 it came: one of the bloodiest and most bitterly contested battles of the war. Cornwallis forced Greene to retreat after all his militia and one line regiment had panicked. But it proved to be an empty and barren victory. British casualties were almost 30 per cent, whilst Greene saved the bulk of his army. Cornwallis, having outrun his supplies, and unable to live off the country, had to retire to the coast, at Wilmington. Logistics won when arms failed.

Already Greene had profited by the retreat of Cornwallis to lash back into South Carolina. This general had an amazing record of losing battles but winning campaigns. Although beaten in a number of small engagements during the summer of 1781 and in the Battle of Eutaw Springs on 8 September, Greene always inflicted greater losses on the enemy than he suffered himself. And in the fall he drove all British and Loyalist units back into Charleston.

Cornwallis on the day of the Guilford battle wrote to General William Phillips, then operating in Virginia, "If we mean an offensive war in America, we must abandon New York, and bring our whole force into Virginia; we then have a stake to fight for, and a successful battle may give us America. If our plan is defensive, mixed with desultory expeditions, let us quit the Carolinas (which cannot be held defensively while Virginia can be so easily armed against us) and stick to our salt pork at New York, sending now and then a detachment to steal tobacco, etc."

Sound strategy indeed; but cautious Clinton could not be persuaded to abandon comfortable New York. The most he would allow Cornwallis to do was to march north into Virginia.

The Old Dominion was now in almost as unhappy a condition as Carolina. Benedict Arnold, now a British general, invaded Virginia with a force of about 1700 Tory volunteers in January 1781. No countryside rose in arms against him, partly because so many militia had already been sent south, but mostly owing to the incompetent administration of Governor Thomas Jefferson, whom Arnold had the satisfaction of chasing out of Richmond. Washington detached Lafayette's light infantry corps to handle Arnold; but the Marquis, lacking naval support, could accomplish nothing in that land of many and deep rivers. Arnold and his relief, General Phillips, made a particular point of burning tobacco, as the only export which paid for military supplies in France and Spain. That was the reason for Cornwallis's gibe about "a detachment to steal tobacco."

Cornwallis, with fresh supplies obtained by sea, started north from Wilmington, North Carolina, on 25 April 1781. He marched unopposed to Petersburg, Virginia, where he was joined by Phillips's force and by reinforcements from New York. These brought his numbers up to 7200, including a fair number of cavalry under the redoubtable Tarleton, who raided the interior as far as Charlottesville, where he nearly captured Jefferson. On 6 July Lafayette fought a brisk engagement with Cornwallis at Greenspring (old Governor Berkeley's plantation) and was defeated, but saved his little army by a timely retreat to Malvern Hill — scene of a greater battle in 1862. Cornwallis now brought his entire force into Yorktown and began turning that little town into a naval and military base.

There we shall leave Cornwallis, while we describe the mighty events by sea and land which forced him within three months to surrender.

4. Sea Power and Yorktown

The winter of 1780–81 marked the nadir of the American cause. England, controlling the sea, could throw in troops anywhere she chose. If Cornwallis managed to establish another military and naval base on Chesapeake Bay, she would possess every major American seaport except Boston. On the other side, the French alliance had proved a bitter disappointment. Congress seemed impotent to raise men or money. Many Americans began to accept the probability of defeat. Desperate diplomatic deals were proposed in Congress: to cede Spain everything west of the Appalachians in return for an alliance; to offer Catherine II of Russia a slice of Western territory if she would attack England! Rochambeau's French expeditionary force had been in Newport since the summer of 1780, but for want of sea power Washington knew not how or where to employ these 6700 French regulars. He was more discouraged than at any other period of the war.

In his diary for 1 May 1781 Washington thus summarized the situation:

Instead of having magazines filled with provisions, we have a scanty pittance scattered here and there in the different States. Instead of having our arsenals well supplied with military stores, they are poorly provided, and the workmen all leaving them. Instead of having the various articles of field equipage in readiness to deliver, the Quartermaster General (as the denier resort) . . . is but now applying to the several States to provide these things for the troops. . . . Instead of having a regular system of transportation . . . all that business, or a great part of it, being done by military impress. We are daily and hourly oppressing the people — souring their tempers — and alienating the affections. Instead of having the regiments compleated to the new establishment and which ought to have been so by the 1st of February . . . scarce any State in the Union has, at this hour, an eighth part of its quota in the field and little prospect, that I can see, of ever getting more than half. In a word — instead of having everything in readiness to take the field, we have nothing; and instead of having the prospect of a glorious offensive campaign before us, we have a bewildered and gloomy defensive one — unless we should receive a powerful aid of ships, land troops, and money from our generous allies; and these, at present, are too contingent to build upon.

Yet presently a new and radiant light shone from France. Louis XVI decided to commit the major part of his navy to support Washington and Rochambeau. Twenty line-of-battle ships under a great fighting sailor, Rear Admiral the Count de Grasse, departed Brest in March 1781 for the West Indies. There he drove off a British blockading squadron, captured an island or two, and escorted a convoy of 200 merchantmen to Cap Haitien, Hispaniola, where four more battleships joined, and the combined fleet took on board 3000 soldiers of the Saint-Domingue garrison commanded by General the Marquis de Saint-Simon. It was now July, time to "stand by" for hurricanes, and the French fleet must make haste.

It did, and Washington was expecting it. On 21 May he held a conference with Rochambeau at Wethersfield, Connecticut, to decide on their objective. Washington was eager for a combined attack on New York City; but, as he wrote to Rochambeau in a letter that shows his strategic savvy, "In any operation, and under all circumstances a decisive Naval superiority is to be considered as a fundamental principle, and the basis upon which every hope of success must ultimately depend." He agreed with Rochambeau that they move against whatever target Admiral de Grasse chose, assuming it would be Yorktown if not New York.

There followed a faultless pattern of co-operation between two allied armies on the continent, and two French fleets, at Newport and the West Indies. Rochambeau sent word by frigate *La Concorde* to De Grasse of his and Washington's intentions, and begged the French admiral to inform them promptly of where he decided to strike. He chose the Chesapeake rather than New York, because of D'Estaing's failure to break through the Narrows three years earlier, whilst within the Chesapeake his ships would have room to maneuver. *La Concorde* on 12 August brought this dispatch to Newport, whence it was forwarded to Rochambeau, who had already pulled up stakes and marched his army across Connecticut to join Washington at White Plains.

Thus, all allied forces converged on Cornwallis's army at Yorktown, not on Clinton's at New York. On 19 August Washington and Rochambeau broke camp at White Plains and ferried 6000 men across the Hudson at King's Ferry. Commodore the Count Barras de Saint-Laurent, stationed at Newport, loaded his ships with Rochambeau's siege artillery, too heavy for overland haulage, and prepared to pop into the Chesapeake as soon as De Grasse had cleared the ocean lanes. By this time the big French fleet was off Cape Hatteras, sailing north before prosperous southwest winds.

In contrast to this beautiful co-ordination between the allied armies and fleets, the British were making a mess of their communications. Rear Admiral Thomas Graves was in command at New York. Rear Admiral Sir Samuel Hood's fleet sailed north from the West Indies to reinforce him, but the frigate that should have brought the word got into a fight, and not until 28 August, when Hood's flagship entered New York, did the British there know that De Grasse was coming north.

Two days later De Grasse's fleet anchored in Lynnhaven Bay within the Chesapeake Capes. On 1 September Graves and Hood sailed from New York for the same destination. Washington, who had long since lived down his alleged disinclination to tell a lie, set up an elaborate deception to make Clinton believe that he and De Grasse were planning to attack New York City via Staten Island. He left 4000 men at White Plains, gave out a series of false intelligence to British spies, and even constructed fake hardtack bakeries in New Jersey to make Clinton think that this would be his most advanced base. Clinton was completely fooled; he never sent one man to reinforce Cornwallis.

On 31 August Washington's and Rochambeau's armies began marching through Philadelphia. Everything now depended on whether De Grasse could keep the British fleet out of the Chesapeake long enough to allow the Franco-American army, and Lafayette's contingent, to surround Cornwallis at Yorktown. Washington was very, very anxious. On 2 September he wrote to Lafayette, "I am distressed beyond expression, to know what is become of the Count de Grasse, and for fear the English Fleet, by occupying the Chesapeake . . . should frustrate all our flattering prospects in that quarter." Three days later, when he reached Chester, Pennsylvania, he received news that De Grasse had arrived at Lynnhaven Bay. The French officer who brought the word said that he had never seen a man express such joy. "Washington acted like a child whose every wish had been gratified."

At that very moment the decisive naval battle was being fought off the Capes. At 8:00 a.m. 5 September, a picket frigate off Cape Charles sighted a fleet of 19 ships bearing down before the wind, and identified it as that of

Admiral Graves. De Grasse was in a critical situation. About 2000 sailors were absent in landing craft, engaged in setting ashore Saint-Simon's troops near Jamestown. The tide was on the flood, and he had to get his cumbersome ships under way, beat out against both wind and tide, and form line of battle. Graves missed the opportunity (which Jones or Nelson would have grasped) to attack the French while their ships were in confusion. He wore ship (turned every vessel on the other tack), waited for the French to sortie, and bore down on a course diagonal to that of De Grasse, to deliver a classic line-of-battle attack.

The wind was so light that not until 4:15 p.m. did the two fleets clash. The British had so poor a system of flag signals — the only method, except shouting, to send orders ship-to-ship — that Hood, in command of the British rear, did not understand what Graves wanted of him, and sheered off. De Grasse maneuvered his fleet so expertly that when the two came together, sixteen of his ships engaged eleven of the British. For over two hours it was "Fire-away-Flanagan" between these units. By the time darkness fell and gunfire ceased, the British had suffered heavy casualties and two ships were in a sinking condition, but all French vessels were in good shape. The decisive Battle off the Capes of the Chesapeake was over, and the French had won.

For four days, 6–9 December, De Grasse steered southerly, luring the British away so as to give Barras a chance to enter with the siege artillery. He then broke visual contact with the British and squared away for the Capes, and found Barras's ships within, while Graves's fleet limped down-wind to New York for repairs. These took over a month; and when Graves next arrived off the Capes, all was over.

Washington and Rochambeau conferred with De Grasse on board his 110-gun flagship *Ville de Paris* in Lynnhaven Bay on 17 September, to make plans for the investment of Yorktown. The small French vessels — for every fleet in those days was accompanied by a squadron of frigates, corvettes, and light craft — helped ferry the Allied troops down the Bay from Elkton and Annapolis, and delivered naval gunfire support during the siege of Yorktown which began on 28 September. De Grasse was eager to depart for the West Indies. These were his orders from France, and he was apprehensive of hurricanes. But Washington persuaded him to stay, and wrote to him (27 September), "The resolution that your Excellency has taken in our circumstances proves that a great mind knows how to make personal sacrifices to secure an important general good."

The siege of Yorktown was conducted according to the book, with redoubts, trenches, horn-works, saps, mines, and countermines. Cornwallis had about 8000 men in the little town on the York river, which French ships patrolled so that he could not break away. The armies of Rochambeau and Saint-Simon were almost as numerous as his, and in addition Washington had 5645 regulars and 3200 Virginia militia. The commander in chief, profiting by D'Estaing's error at Savannah, wasted no men in premature assaults. There were gallant sorties and counterattacks, one led by Lieutenant Colonel Alexander Hamilton. Casualties were light on both sides, fewer than in the naval battle; but Cornwallis, a good professional soldier, knew when he was beaten. On 17 October he sent out a white flag, and on the 19th surrendered his entire force. Pleading illness, he sent his second in command, Brigadier Charles O'Hara, to make the formal surrender to General Lincoln, whom Washington appointed to receive him. One by one, the British regiments, after laying down their arms, marched back to camp between two lines, one of American soldiers, the other of French, while the military bands played a series of melancholy tunes, including one which all recognized as "The World Turned Upside Down."

Lafayette announced the surrender to Monsieur de Maurepas of the French government, in terms of the classic French drama: "The play is over; the fifth act has come to an end." Lieutenant Colonel Tench Tilghman carried Washington's dispatch to Congress at Philadelphia, announcing the great event. Arriving at 3:00 a.m. on 22 October, he tipped off an old German night watchman, who awoke the slumbering Philadelphians by stumping though the streets with his lantern, bellowing, "Basht dree o'glock und Gornvallis ist gedaken!"

Windows flew open, candles were lighted, citizens poured into the streets and embraced each other; and after day broke, Congress assembled and attended a service of thanksgiving.

5. Conclusion of the War

When Lord North heard the news of Yorktown at 10 Downing Street, on 25 November, he threw up his arms as though hit in the breast by a musket ball and cried, "O God! it is all over!" But it took more than a year and a half to end a war that had extended to almost every part of the world, and in which Britain was fighting not only the United States but France, Spain, and the Netherlands.

Washington was keen to follow up his Yorktown victory by a combined attack on Wilmington or Charleston, but De Grasse obeyed orders from his government to return to the West Indies with the French troops. Early in 1782 he recaptured several islands from the English. England then reinforced her West Indies fleet with a dozen ships of the line under Admiral Rodney, who on 12 April beat the French badly in the Battle of the Saints, capturing De Grasse in his flagship.

Rodney's victory prevented France from sending another fleet to North America for months. In the meantime, British warships and privateers based on New York and Halifax were sweeping American coastal waters, capturing most of the few merchantmen still at sea, and wiping out the New England privateering and fishing fleets. General Washington, who had been vainly urging the states to reinforce his army, on 18 July wrote to James McHenry, "At present, we are inveloped in darkness . . . Providence has done much for us in this contest, but we must do something for ourselves." But the British will to victory, feeble at best, had completely evaporated.

The only fighting on American soil in 1782 was in the West. By that time the British there were in the ascendant, owing largely to better treatment of the Indians. Colonel William Crawford, Washington's old associate in land speculation, was ambushed and killed by a force of Loyalists and Indians at the site of Sandusky, Ohio, on 4 June 1782. This brought into the war many more Indians, who began raiding deep into Pennsylvania, western Virginia, and Kentucky. It was a situation much like that after Braddock's defeat, or during Pontiac's rebellion. Bryan's Station, a fort near Lexington, Kentucky, was besieged in August by Tories and Indians, who routed a relieving force of frontier militia at the Lower Blue Licks. George Rogers Clark then collected 1100 mounted riflemen and on 10 November 1782 routed the Shawnee and burned their villages near Chillicothe, Ohio. That was the last land battle of the War of American Independence.

Lord North had long been in favor of ending the war by recognizing American independence. Rockingham was willing to form a ministry with that end is view; but George III said he would rather lose his crown than call in "a set of men" who would make him "a slave." It took several months' tearful pleading by Lord North to persuade the king to do just that. In March 1782 George had to let his favorite resign and accept an Old Whig ministry, including Shelburne and Charles James Fox. That opened the way to peace negotiations.

The Count de Vergennes, the French foreign minister, wished to keep these negotiations under French control. He persuaded Congress, in 1781, to order the American envoys in Paris to negotiate with England only under French direction, and to conclude nothing without his consent. At the same time Congress appointed John Jay and John Adams, together with Franklin, who was already minister to France, as the peace commission.

Formal negotiations began at Paris in April 1782 between Franklin (since the other two had not arrived) and Richard Oswald, a liberal Scots merchant sent over by Shelburne. John Jay, arriving on 23 June, raised objections to the wording of Oswald's commission, "To treat with the Thirteen Colonies . . . or any parts thereof." He insisted on Oswald's obtaining a new commission to treat with "The United States of America." This wasted time, during which the British position grew stronger by winning the Battle of the Saints and raising the Franco-Spanish siege of Gibraltar. But for this quibbling over words, the United States might have obtained preliminary articles making no mention of Loyalists or debts, and giving her the Canada boundary of 1763. Shelburne, the prime minister, was anxious to conclude peace at almost any terms.

Shelburne now sent Oswald new instructions, authorizing him to treat with "Commissioners of the Thirteen United States," thus acknowledging independence before the negotiations began. These were received in September 1782. John Adams, the third commissioner, arrived in Paris in October after obtaining a commercial treaty from the Netherlands. In the end, Britain consented to the present northern boundary because Shelburne had the good sense to see that it would allow the United States and Canada to expand on parallel lines. The United States promised nothing for the Loyalists, except to "earnestly recommend" that the states restore their property, and that "no future confiscations" be made. American debts, owed to British subjects before the war, would be paid; and, at Yankee Adams's insistence, Britain conceded that American fishermen enjoy their ancient liberty to land and dry fish on the coast of Newfoundland.

The preliminary treaty of peace was signed on 30 November 1782, more than thirteen months after Cornwallis's surrender; the definitive treaty on 3 February 1783, the same day as the treaties between Great Britain and France, Spain, and the Netherlands. The entire transaction was called the Peace of Paris. Britain kept Gibraltar, which she had successfully defended, but ceded Minorca and the Floridas to Spain. France got nothing but Tobago in the West Indies and Senegal in Africa. The United States won the West to the Mississippi, north to Canada, and south to the Floridas. This was more territory than she actually controlled at the war's end, when Britain still had garrisons on the Atlantic coast at Castine, New York City, Wilmington, Charleston, and Savannah; and six different points on the northern border. And Spain still controlled the east bank of the Mississippi up to the Walnut Hills at the site of Vicksburg.

Franklin now wrote to the English ambassador at Paris, "What would you say to a proposition of a family compact between England, France, and America? America would be as happy as the Sabine girl if she could be the means of uniting in perpetual peace her father and her husband." That was too much to expect. An effort to conclude a commercial treaty failed, owing to the resignation of Shelburne and the formation of a less liberal ministry, who wished to prove that the Americans had been foolish to attempt independence. In the French government there was a feeling that the Americans had let them down by signing a preliminary treaty without French consent. Thus, on the morrow of achieving independence, the United States was a lone lamb in the society of nations.

The new republic, however, was hailed with enthusiasm by all liberal elements of England and Europe. The Old Whigs felt that Washington's valor had saved them from a royal despotism; and no later British monarch ever aspired to the power that George III exercised between 1774 and 1781. The French intelligentsia hailed the triumph of liberty and reason over tradition and autocracy; they looked forward to doing the same thing for their own

country, and had not long to wait. European liberals everywhere, filled with
an unsatisfied longing for liberty, equality, and the rule of reason, felt that the
triumph of the American Republic portended a new order for old Europe.

They were right. As the English historian Lord Acton stated, "It was from
America that the plain ideas that men ought to mind their own business, and
that the nation is responsible to Heaven for the acts of the State — ideas long
locked in the breast of solitary thinkers, and hidden among Latin folios —
burst forth like a conqueror upon the world they were destined to transform,
under the title of the Rights of Man . . . and the principle gained ground,
that a *nation can never abandon its fate to an authority it cannot control.*"
Many, alas, have done so, but their people have aways suffered for it.

News of the preliminary treaty of 30 November 1782 did not reach America until 12 March 1783. Since the treaty included an armistice, the war in
America ended then and there, to the "inexpressible satisfaction" of General
Washington. Recently, by a personal appeal, the General had dissuaded his
officers from presenting a rude ultimatum to Congress about pay and pensions. The Continental treasury was so empty that the soldiers had to be sent
home with no pay, only chits for three months' arrears, signed by Robert
Morris; and with their muskets as a gift.

General Sir Guy Carleton, now British commander in New York City,
completed the evacuation of his garrison on 25 November 1783. General
Washington marched in, his ill-clad troops a contrast to the smart, scarlet-
uniformed regulars who had departed. But, as a spectator remarked, "They
were *our* troops . . . and I admired and gloried in them the more, because
they were weather-beaten and forlorn."

At the Fraunces Tavern on 4 December, the commander in chief and the
few remaining officers of his vanishing army dined together for the last time.
Filling a wineglass, he held it up and said, "With a heart full of love and gratitude, I now take my leave of you. I most devoutly wish that your later days
may be as prosperous and happy as your former ones have been glorious and
honorable." With tears in his eyes, Washington invited each officer to come
forward and shake his hand. First to do so, because nearest to the commander
in chief (as he had been throughout the war), was Henry Knox, the one general officer who in eight years' service had never given Washington a moment's trouble. When Knox held out his hand, the commander in chief not
only grasped it but embraced him and kissed him on the cheek, both shedding
copious tears; for in those days strong and brave men were not ashamed to
weep on suitable occasions. Washington passed between the ranks of a guard
of honor and then past throngs of citizens, to a wharf on the North river,
whence a barge rowed him to Paulus Hook. There he mounted a horse to
ride south and resign his commission to Congress.

Hurrying on, in the hope of keeping Christmas at Mount Vernon, Washington reached Annapolis, where Congress was sitting, on 19 December.
The Marylanders, true to form, insisted on giving the General a ball before he

retired, so Congress set the public ceremony in the State House for the 23rd. Congress's address was written by James McHenry, who described the moving scene in a letter to his fiancée, Peggy Caldwell:

It was a solemn and affecting spectacle. . . . The spectators all wept, and there was hardly a member of Congress who did not drop tears. The General's hand which held the address shook as he read it. When he spoke of the officers who had composed his family, and recommended those who had continued in it to the present moment to the favorable notice of Congress he was obliged to support the paper with both hands. But when he commended the interests of his dearest country to almighty God . . . his voice faultered and sunk, and the whole house felt his agitations. After the pause which was necessary for him to recover himself, he proceeded to say in the most penetrating manner, "Having now finished the work assigned me I retire from the great theatre of action, and bidding an affectionate farewell to this august body under whose orders I have so long acted I here offer my commission and take my leave of all the employments of public life." So saying he drew out from his bosom his commission and delivered it up to the president of Congress. He then returned to his station, when the president read the reply that had been prepared.

By very hard riding, which meant little to a man of his splendid physique, George Washington reached Mount Vernon in time to keep Christmas Eve with Martha and her grandchildren.

THE WORLD TURNED UPSIDE DOWN

X V I I I

Revolutionary Constitution Making

1775-1781

1. *The Bills of Rights*

ONE OF THE MOST REMARKABLE things about the American Revolution is the fact that the radicals of 1774–76 who started it, also saw it through to a point — that point being 1787, when younger men took over to put a capstone on the edifice. All modern history proves that it is easy enough for a determined minority to pull down a government, but exceedingly difficult to reconstruct, to re-establish law and order on new foundations. And in no other great revolution have the initial agitators long survived liquidation by their successors. Dozens of nations since World War II have won independence — but how many have secured liberty?

According to the natural history of revolutions, we would expect the American Confederation to fall apart, or that the army or some outstanding leader would set up a military despotism. What actually happened was the establishment of government under law. The reasons for this noteworthy outcome lie, first, in the political experience of Americans. As Emerson wrote, "We began with freedom." Secondly, they believed in the importance of political institutions as a guarantee of liberty. Thomas Jefferson, for instance, wrote to a member of the Virginia assembly on 16 May 1776 that constitution making "is the whole subject of the present controversy; for should a bad government be instituted for us in future, it had been as well to have accepted . . . the bad one offered to us from beyond the water, without the risk and expense of conflict." Moreover, the principles of the American Revolution were essentially conservative; the leaders were thinking of preserving and securing the freedom they already enjoyed rather than, like the Russians, building something new and different. As John Dickinson said in the Federal Convention, "Experience must be our only guide, reason may mislead us." One cannot imagine such a thing being said by a French or a Russian revolutionist.

Thus, when the Americans risked law and order to attain liberty, they made every effort to win them back. Their political experience before 1775 set the pattern for their new institutions. Unlike the French, who had little or no experience with representative government when their revolution opened in 1789, Americans needed merely to maintain, develop, and correct the state of things political and religious, which already existed. Americans had enjoyed

270

more freedom than any other people in the world, and so large a measure of self-government that they were competent to make it complete. Certain conservative patriots feared lest the people take up revolutionary slogans with such enthusiasm that all government would be threatened. But there was really very little danger of that. The typical feeling was expressed by the Massachusetts farming town of Medfield: "While we profess ourselves advocates for Rational Constitutional Liberty we don't mean to patrionise Libertinesm and Licenteousness we are sensible of the necessety of Government for the Security of Life Liberty and property." That tiny community had grasped the principle that the rule of law is perhaps the greatest achievement in the long struggle for liberty, and that if it is lost, liberty is lost; that the use of orderly, "due process" to change the law is essential for an orderly society.

Most of the American state and federal constitutions were the work of college-educated men who had studied political theory in Aristotle, Plato, Cicero, Polybius, and other ancient writers, and had given deep thought to problems of political reconstruction. Men such as George Mason and Thomas Jefferson, James Madison, John Adams, and James Bowdoin knew exactly what they were doing. And most of these were relatively young men. Jefferson was thirty-three years old and Madison twenty-seven when they helped draft the Virginia constitution. John Adams, when he did the same for Massachusetts, was a mature forty-four; of the same age was John Dickinson when he drew up the Articles of Confederation. The New York constitution was drafted by three graduates of King's College (now Columbia): Gouverneur Morris, Robert R. Livingston, and John Jay, aged respectively twenty-four, thirty, and thirty-two. These men were familiar with what ancient and modern publicists had written on government; yet they were no mere doctrinaires. Every one had had political experience in colonial assemblies, local conventions, or the Continental Congress. This synthesis of classical discipline with practical politics accounts for the striking success of the Americans at constitution making. Their efforts won the admiration of the Old World, and from them the New World still benefits today.

Everyone assumed that the new states must have written constitutions, limiting and defining the powers of government. They were used to colonial charters, had felt the want of a written British constitution defining the respective powers of Parliament and the colonial assemblies. The objects of these state constitutions were, to establish the rule of law which they believed that George III had violated, to secure life, liberty, and prosperity, and to set up a practical frame of government.

Liberty was no vague term with our revolutionary forebears. It had not yet acquired the fuzzy overtones of economic choice and social welfare that have accrued in the course of a century and a half. To the Americans of 1776, liberty meant, first, freedom under laws of their own making; and, second, the right to do anything that did not harm another. One of the crisp sayings of John Locke, with whom all reading Americans were familiar, was, "Where law ends, tyranny begins." The proper way, they felt, to secure liberty to posterity was to set up a representative government, limited in scope by a statement of natural rights with which no government may meddle. Consequently, every state constitution included a bill of rights. The first, Virginia's, was drafted by George Mason and adopted by the Virginia convention on 12 June 1776.

This Virginia Declaration of Rights is one of the great liberty documents of all time. It applied the past experience of free-born Englishmen, and parented not only all other American bills of rights, but the French *Déclaration des droits de l'homme et du citoyen* of 1789 and, the Universal Declaration of Human Rights adopted in 1948 by the General Assembly of the United Nations. Virginia begins by asserting, "That all men are by nature equally free and independent, and have certain inherent rights of which, when they enter into a state of society, they cannot . . . deprive or divest their posterity; namely, the enjoyment of life and liberty, with the means of acquiring and possessing property, and pursuing and obtaining happiness and safety."

Certain clauses of the Virginia Declaration came down from the Magna Carta of 1215 — the right to a jury trial, the right not to be deprived of liberty except by the law of the land or the judgment of one's peers. Others are derived from the Petition of Right with which Charles I was confronted in 1628: that a man cannot be compelled to give evidence against himself, that standing armies in peace time should be avoided as dangerous to liberty, "and that in all cases the military should be under strict subordination to and governed by the civil power." The prohibition of excessive bail and of cruel or unusual punishments was derived from the English Bill of Rights of 1689 which concluded the Glorious Revolution. Others were developments from principles merely hinted at before, such as freedom of the press, and religious liberty.

These rights were valid, not only as derived from American and English experience, but because they were based on the ancient theory of natural law; the principle of Western civilization that laws must have divine sanction. Blackstone, the English legal writer most widely read in America, in his *Commentaries* declared, "This law of nature, being coëval with mankind and dictated by God himself, is of course superior in obligation to any other . . . no human laws are of any validity if contrary to this." These "unchangeable, unwritten laws of Heaven," as Sophocles called them in the *Antigone*, twenty-one centuries before Blackstone, must be the foundation of human enactments which are to endure. They became the basis of the American constitutional system.

The other states, in general, followed Virginia in their bills of rights. Pennsylvania had stronger statements than Virginia on religious liberty, added freedom of speech to Virginia's freedom of the press, protected conscientious objectors to military service, and gave foreigners "of good character" the right to buy land and to become citizens. An amusing difference between the two constitutions was Virginia's declaration that no government separate from

Virginia's should be erected or established within the limits thereof; whilst Pennsylvania declared, "All men have a natural inherent right . . . to form a new state in vacant countries." For Virginia then claimed the future Kentucky and Northwest Territory, whilst Pennsylvania had a definite western boundary.

The Massachusetts Declaration of Rights, declaring "All men are born free and equal," was construed by the courts of that commonwealth as freeing all slaves from bondage. And a separation of powers between the legislative, executive, and judicial departments was enjoined, "to the end it may be a government of laws and not of men."

2. The Frames of Government

Most of the state constitutions were drafted by legislative bodies and placed in effect without consulting the voters. John Adams felt that this was not the right way to do it. In the Congress he urged that we "invite the people to erect the whole building with their own hands, upon the broadest foundation . . . by conventions of representatives chosen by the people." The first instance in which he managed to have a specially elected convention and popular ratification was in his own commonwealth in 1780.

State governments during this era followed three main types: the Virginian or legislative supremacy, the Pennsylvanian unicameral, and the Massachusetts "mixed" types. Virginia, impressed by John Locke's dictum that the legislative should be the chief power in a commonwealth, gave hers most of the power. The governor, chosen by joint ballot of both houses, could do nothing without the advice and consent of a council, which was elected by joint ballot of the legislature, as were the judges. This constitution was a bad example of seeking political guarantees against past dangers, in this instance the arrogant royal governors; and Virginia suffered from that mistake during the war. Owing, however, to the prestige of Virginia, her constitution was imitated by a majority of the Thirteen States.

Pennsylvania adopted a different type of constitution, reflecting an internal revolution; the Philadelphia artisans, the Scots-Irish frontiersmen, and the German-speaking farmers were now on top. George Bryan and Dr. Thomas Young, a former leader of the Boston Sons of Liberty, drafted this constitution, with the blessing of Benjamin Franklin who presided over the provincial congress that adopted it. It was the most democratic of American revolutionary constitutions, except that of Vermont, which was a copy. Every male taxpayer and his adult sons could vote. Rotation in office was enjoined; none could serve as representative for more than four years in every seven. A single-chamber legislature was set up, the only qualification for membership being that one must be a Christian. Membership was apportioned according to population, as the back-country people had always wanted. Instead of a single governor, this constitution provided an elective executive council, with rota-

tion of office to prevent "the danger of establishing an inconvenient aristocracy." The president of the council, chosen annually by joint ballot of council
and assembly, acted as chief executive. A peculiar feature of the Pennsylvania
and Vermont constitutions was the election every seven years of a Council of
Censors, whose duty was "to enquire whether the Constitution has been
preserved inviolate in every part," to order impeachments, and to summon a
constitutional convention if necessary.

This type of constitution worked well enough in the homogeneous frontier
community of Vermont; but in Pennsylvania, where there were deep class,
racial, and religious divisions, it established the nearest thing to a dictatorship
of the proletariat that we have had in North America. A Pennsylvanian wrote
to Thomas Jefferson, "You would execrate this state if you were in it. . . .
The supporters of this government are a set of workmen without any weight
of character." The legislature managed to disfranchise Quakers by a loyalty
test oath to which they could not subscribe; and the assembly, controlled by
the leather-aproned boys, frontiersmen, and the less prosperous Germans,
expended more energy during the war in plundering Tories, jailing profiteers,
and persecuting conscientious objectors than in supporting the army. Eventually Pennsylvania turned against this "popular front" government, and in
1790 elected a convention which drafted a new constitution with a bicameral
legislature and a proper governor.

Nevertheless, the Pennsylvania constitution, introduced by Franklin to the
French intelligentsia, was hailed in Europe as well-nigh perfect, because it was
"rational." If the people were to rule, there was no logic in a second chamber
or in checking a legislative power by a governor or judges. Turgot wrote a
treatise attacking the American state constitutions for compromising with
custom and privilege, and for adopting "mixed" forms; but he gave that of
Pennsylvania a clean bill of health. John Adams replied in a more lengthy
treatise, defending the bicameral system as necessary to protect the people
against unwise, hasty, and proscriptive legislation, and defending a strong
executive as necessary to enforce the laws and give the government leadership.
The events of the American Revolution period showed unmistakably that
John Adams was right and Turgot wrong; yet, in 1791, the very year after the
"rational" Pennsylvania constitution had been superseded, the French Constituent Assembly adopted a unicameral constitution for France.

Around 1780 a mildly conservative reaction set in throughout the United
States. It was reflected in some of the early radicals being dropped out of the
Continental Congress, in giving greater authority to General Washington and
to Franklin, in appointing Robert Morris superintendent of finance, and
creating the office of secretary of foreign affairs for Robert R. Livingston. And
the reaction was reflected in the constitution of Massachusetts.

This most conservative of the state constitutions was adopted through a
completely democratic process. A constitutional convention, elected by man-

hood suffrage, met in the fall of 1779, appointed a committee to prepare a draft, and adjourned. The committee of three — James Bowdoin and both Adamses — wisely let John Adams do it. His draft was submitted to the convention in 1780, amended, and then tossed back to the town meetings. They voted on the constitution clause by clause, and stated their objections. A surprising popular interest was shown; many town meetings debated the constitution clause by clause, and some made original proposals such as the popular initiative and referendum, which were adopted many years later. But the people did ratify the constitution as a whole, as an adjourned session of the convention, after counting the votes, declared on 15 June 1780.

John Adams's Massachusetts constitution was based, not on Locke's principle of legislative supremacy, but on Polybius' theory of "mixed government" (which Governor Winthrop pointed to in the seventeenth century), which by this time had been renamed "checks and balances." The theory was this: any "pure" governmental form degenerated into something else — pure democracy into class tyranny or anarchy, pure aristocracy into a selfish oligarchy, pure monarchy into absolutism. Hence, to secure the happiness of the people, a government must be a mixture of the three: a strong chief executive to represent the principle of authority, a senate to represent property, and a lower house to represent the multitude. These "mutually keep each other from exceeding their proper limits," as Blackstone wrote in his *Commentaries*. Finally — John Adams's own contribution — you needed an independent judiciary as a balance wheel. Thus, Massachusetts was given a popularly elected house of representatives; an "aristocratic" senate apportioned according to taxable wealth, not population; and a governor, re-eligible indefinitely, with a veto (which only one other state governor enjoyed) over legislation, and power to appoint most of the state officials. The governor of Massachusetts was intended to assume leadership, and to that end he too was chosen by popular vote, as were the governors of only three other states.

Connecticut and Rhode Island, which had popularly elected governors under their old royal charters, made the transition from colony to state simply by altering the name of the body politic, declaring that the "excellent constitutions of government" derived from their "pious ancestors" were still in force, and tacking on a bill of rights. These amended colonial charters served Connecticut until 1818, and Rhode Island until 1842. The Massachusetts constitution of 1780, though never formally superseded, has been so amended from time to time as to make it more democratic, supporting one of the least efficient and most corrupt of modern state governments.

Other features were common to all state constitutions. Several forbade the granting of titles of nobility. One-year terms for governors and assemblymen were the rule in every state except South Carolina; since it was a common American belief that "where annual elections end, tyranny begins." In seven states, every male taxpayer could vote; elsewhere there were moderate property qualifications. Women could vote in New Jersey, if they could meet the property requirement, and free Negroes in general had the same political privileges as white men.

In most states there was a high property qualification, about $4000 in New Jersey and Maryland, for membership in the upper house. In all states, judges were appointed for long terms, or during good behavior — no more "pleasure" tenure for free-born Americans. Test oaths of allegiance, designed to exclude from office Loyalists and (in some instances) Roman Catholics, were common. And, whilst the principle of freedom of worship for all religions was generally adopted, church and state were not completely separated. The Church of England was not disestablished in Virginia until 1785, and in Connecticut and Massachussetts a modified official preference to the Congregational churches continued until 1818 and 1833, respectively.

In addition to the Old Thirteen and Vermont, several American communities beyond the mountains established temporary states during or shortly after the war. Transylvania was organized in 1775 by pioneers of Kentucky who had emigrated to the blue-grass country or had been brought there by a land company organized by Judge Henderson of North Carolina.

The several thousand settlers scattered along the banks of the Watauga, Holston, and other tributaries of the Tennessee river took care of themselves throughout the war and, as we have seen, "took care" of Major Ferguson at the Battle of Kings Mountain. But in 1784, owing partly to the Cherokee going on the warpath, frontier leaders called a convention at Jonesboro which adopted the constitution of the State of Franklin. Taxes were payable in beaver skins, well-cured bacon, clean tallow, rye whisky, peach and apple brandy. After a few years North Carolina asserted her jurisdiction, and Franklin eventually became part of Tennessee. Another isolated group in central Tennessee formed in 1780 the Cumberland County Compact for self-government and protection from Indian attack.

Thus, political maturity was common to every section and class. The people had a genius for self-government. They followed leaders who were political scientists, not with docility but critically. And even the rough frontiersmen realized that liberty could only be secured under law.

3. The Articles of Confederation

While framers of state constitutions were wrestling with that perennial problem of government, balancing liberty with authority, the Continental Congress grappled with a vital question which colonials and British had long been squabbling about — federalism. This, another aspect of the *libertas* vs. *imperium* problem, is to find a balance between a central government and the rights of member states. The federal question has bedeviled American history to the present day.

The central problem of federalism is to distribute sovereign powers in layers, as it were, between a central government and member states. A federal constitution should draw the line, but it is impossible to make a clean-cut distinction. Before 1763, the government of the British empire was *de facto* federal. But the colonies found that they had no security for their rights in this informal arrangement unless it became *de jure* as well; if Parliament had the sovereign power that it asserted in the Declaratory Act and applied in the Coercive Acts, colonial reserved rights were worthless. That is why Adams, Jefferson, and Wilson suggested a federal constitution for the British empire; but nobody in England except Camden and Shelburne seemed to understand what they were talking about. Now the controversy was transferred to Philadelphia. All the old problems: war and peace, taxation, Indians, the West, commerce, were crying for solution in an expanding continental area.

The Articles of Confederation were another American attempt, following the New England Confederation and the Albany Plan, to grapple with this central problem of government. It is no wonder that the Articles were imperfect; even so, they were the best instrument of federal government adopted anywhere up to that time. The Articles would have secured American union for many years but for unfavorable circumstances and certain defects, which could not be removed because only a unanimous vote of the member states could carry an amendment.

John Dickinson, chairman of a congressional committee to draft a confederation, reported it to Congress in July 1776. Congress, in the meantime, had assumed sovereign powers and was in no hurry to confirm by law what it had assumed of necessity. Dickinson's draft provided representation of the states in Congress in proportion to their population, but the small states would have none of that. So it was agreed that each state have one vote. But, as Congress was too busy directing the war to spend much time debating federal union, it was not until 15 November 1777 that it adopted the Articles in their final form and submitted them to state legislatures for ratification. These also took their time; but by February 1779 all states had ratified except Maryland, which held out until 1 March 1781. Consequently, the United States fought the war almost to the Yorktown campaign with no federal constitution, only an informal union. The Continental Congress simply exercised powers that by common consent seemed necessary to wage war and conduct foreign affairs.

The essential reason for the long delay in ratifying the Articles of Confederation was land-grabbing. Virginia claimed the entire West north of her southern boundary and west of Maryland and Pennsylvania. The land companies that were lobbying at London for enormous grants in the 1760's, now transferred their activities to Philadelphia. The Indiana Company (formerly the Vandalia) tried to persuade Congress to insist on Virginia's ceding her Western land claims to the Confederation, which they hoped to get. Franklin wrote a tract for this company, and Tom Paine wrote an attack on Virginia's land claims which was published under the persuasive title *The Public Good*. But the old Ohio Company of Virginia, in which Washington was mildly interested, naturally blocked any cession of land to the Confederation until its claims were honored.

Most powerful, however, of the land companies was the Illinois-Wabash, which before the Revolution, in defiance of royal proclamations, purchased land from the Indians both north and south of the Ohio. Among influential stockholders were Robert Morris, James Wilson, four Maryland signers of the Declaration of Independence, and the first two French ministers to the United States. The Wabash Company engaged in tortuous negotiations with Congress, with Maryland and with France and Spain; an intrigue which, could it be unraveled, might prove more fascinating than the story of Arnold's treason or Burr's conspiracy. The influence of this group at Annapolis caused Maryland to declare that she would never ratify the Articles of Confederation until the states with Western lands, especially Virginia, ceded all land claims west of the mountains to the Confederation, which the Wabash-Illinois Company hoped would then validate its purchases from the Indians. The Virginia speculators countered by inducing their state to set on foot the George Rogers Clark expedition of 1778, a patriotic version of Governor Dunmore's War. Colonel Clark floated his Virginia force down the Ohio to the mouth of the Cumberland, then made a bold march across the wilderness to the British post of Kaskaskia in the Illinois country, and in February 1779 bagged Vincennes too. Thus Virginia implemented her old charter claims to the whole Northwest.

The next move of the Illinois-Wabash Company was to turn to Spain. In 1780 one of its stockholders, the French minister at Philadelphia, urged Congress to cede all territory between the Appalachians, the Ohio and Mississippi rivers to Spain, in return for a Spanish alliance. The most prominent member of Congress to support this proposal was another stockholder, Daniel of St. Thomas Jenifer, The Company felt they would get a better land deal from Spain than from Virginia or Congress.

This particular intrigue was defeated in Congress, and about the same time the states, starting with New York, began ceding their western land claims to Congress. A congressional resolution of 10 October 1780 promised that any western lands ceded to the United States would be "settled and formed into distinct republican States, which shall become members of the Federal Union, and shall have the same rights of sovereignty, freedom and independence, as the other States." Here was the beginning of a new federal colonial policy.

Virginia was first to respond. The assembly on 2 January 1781 offered to cede claims north of the Ohio, under several conditions — that the state be repaid expenses of Colonel Clark's expedition; that 150,000 acres north of the Ohio river be reserved for Clark and his soldiers; and that all other purchases from the Indians be considered null and void — a slap at the Illinois-Wabash crowd. This was too much for Congress to accept. Nevertheless, Maryland voted to ratify the Articles of Confederation, because her assembly had become tired of playing the speculators' game.

Consequently, this first Constitution of the United States, the Articles of Confederation, went into effect on 1 March 1781. The church bells of Philadelphia pealed the good news; sloop-of-war *Ariel*, commanded by John Paul Jones, dressed ship and fired a 21-gun salute; Samuel Huntington, president of Congress, gave a reception and "the evening was ushered in by an elegant exhibition of fireworks."

Actually the adoption of the Articles made no perceptible change in the federal government, because it did little more than legalize what the Continental Congress had been doing. That body was now taken over as the Congress of the Confederation; but Americans continued to call it the Continental Congress, since its organization remained the same. Each state was represented by not less than two or more than seven members, as it preferred, but each state had one vote. The new provisions were: (1) assent of nine out of thirteen states was required for decisions on important matters such as making war or concluding treaties, borrowing money, raising armed force, and appointing a commander in chief. (2) Congress acquired the power to appoint executive departments, and shortly created five: foreign affairs with Robert R. Livingston as secretary; finance with Robert Morris as superintendent; war with General Lincoln as secretary; a board of admiralty of which Robert Morris was the only effective member, and a post office department. (3) A committee consisting of one delegate from each state sat between sessions of Congress to exercise all powers except those that required the consent of nine out of the thirteen.

A guiding principle of the Articles of Confederation was to preserve the independence and sovereignty of the states. The federal government received only those powers which the colonies had recognized as belonging to king and parliament. Thus, Congress was given all powers connected with war and peace, except the important one of taxation to support a war. It could conclude no commercial treaty limiting the states' rights to collect customs duties. It had power to establish post offices and charge postage (the only taxing power it possessed), to set standards of weights and measures, and to coin money. It had power to regulate the trade and manage all affairs with "Indians, not members of any of the states," a recognition that Western Indian affairs must be under federal control. In view of the land cessions by the states to Congress, a strange oversight was the failure to give the new government power over federal territory; but as somebody had to do that, Congress went ahead and did, and the greatest permanent success of the Confederation was in working out a new territorial policy.

The only colony outside the Thirteen expressly invited to join the Confederation was Canada, and Canada declined. None other could be admitted unless agreed to by nine states. Vermont, whose war record entitled her to admission, never got into the Confederation because New York and New Hampshire claimed her territory.

Of powers that the Articles did not make federal, the most important was the touchy one of taxation. Congress was not even allowed to tax imports, since colonial experience had shown that customs duties could be used against liberty. The colonial system of requisitions continued; all expenses of the federal government were to be assessed "in proportion to the value of all land within each state"; but the taxes to pay these requisitions had to be laid by the states. Congress had no power to regulate domestic and foreign commerce, because it was felt that Parliament's power to pass the Acts of Trade and Navigation had been abused. No federal judiciary was set up. Instead, a complicated machinery was provided to determine boundary and other controversies between the states. And finally, its greatest weakness, the Confederation was given no means to enforce such powers as were granted; it rested on the good will of the states. In his "Vices of the Political System of the United States" (1786) James Madison wrote: "A Sanction is essential to the idea of law, as coercion is to that of Government. The federal system being destitute of both, wants the great vital principles of a political constitution. Under form of such a constitution, it is in fact nothing more than a treaty of amity and of alliance between independent and sovereign states."

For all that, the Confederation might have met the needs of the Union for many years, could its powers have been increased by amendment. The unanimous consent of the member states was required for amendment, and that wrecked it.

Congress hoped that the Articles would constitute a "perpetual union"; and in a sense they did. The Great Seal of the United States, adopted on 20 June 1782, continues as the official seal to this day. Although some members wished to adopt a distinctly American bird like the wild turkey, or a dove of peace, Congress chose the eagle, symbol of imperial Rome. Over his head is a "glory" of thirteen stars, a new constellation in the galaxy of nations. In one talon the eagle grasps an olive branch and in the other a sheaf of arrows, to represent peace and war. In his beak is a ribbon inscribed *E Pluribus Unum*, and on his breast a shield with thirteen vertical stripes for the states, surmounted by a horizontal "chief" for Congress. On the reverse of the seal is a pyramid of thirteen courses of stone, to indicate permanence, with room for a few more at the top; and over it, in another "glory," the all-seeing eye of Divine Providence. On this reverse are two Latin mottoes: ANNUIT COEPTIS, meaning, "He has favored our undertakings"; and NOVUS ORDO SECULORUM, "A New Cycle of Centuries." Both were suggested by the poetry of Virgil: *Aeneid*, ix.625 and *Eclogues*, iv.5–7, best known by Shelley's paraphrase:

The World's great age begins anew,
The golden years return.

The classically trained leaders of the American Revolution were very fond of this prophecy. They believed that the Declaration of Independence had inaugurated a new order; and they hoped that they themselves were the *nova progenies*, the new Heaven-born generation predicted by the Latin poet.

ODE TO THE FOURTH OF JULY

'Tis done, the e - dict past, by Hea - ven de-

creed,__ And Han - cock's_____ name con - firms the

glo - rious deed. On this au - spi - cious morn was__

In - de - pen - dence born: Pro - pi - tious day!

Hail the U - ni - ted_ States of_ blest A - mer - i - ca!

The Creative Period in Commerce and the Arts

1782-1789

1. *The Revival of Commerce*

JOHN ADAMS IN PARIS was overwhelmed by the painting, the statuary, the architecture, and the gardens of Versailles. But to his "dear Portia" Abigail he wrote a prophetic letter to the effect that, for America, political problems must long take precedence over the arts and sciences. He predicted that two generations must elapse before Americans would have opportunity to study poetry, music, and the fine arts.

John's countrymen were not so patient. Peace and independence, they felt, should bring prosperity at once, and cultivation of the arts would soon follow. Americans were now free to develop their own arts and industries. They hoped to enjoy free trade with the world; and with that end in view, Congress concluded commercial treaties with four European countries. But for several years the results were disappointing. The main trouble was the double adjustment that the country had to make — from a war to a peace economy, and from a favored position within the British empire to an independent status in a competitive world. A secondary cause of slow recovery was the right of each state to set up its own customs service. This not only deprived the Confederation of bargaining power with Europe, but permitted local protective tariffs.

Jefferson, who succeeded Franklin as American minister to France in 1784, wished to strengthen economic relations with our ally in order to free America from the commercial domination of Great Britain. During the war, France enjoyed a favorable trade balance with the United States, and intended to keep it. But, after a few years, the French realized that the American profits from selling to France were being used to pay their bills for English manufactures. Official France became vexed with American "ingratitude." But the real reasons for this situation were the lack of credit facilities in France, a natural preference of Americans for English consumer goods, and French protective tariffs. The only United States products that France wanted in large quantities were rice and tobacco. A French corporation which had the monopoly of importing tobacco made a contract with Robert Morris at such a low price that he could not meet his quota, and the French had to buy American tobacco in the English market.

It was much the same with rice. Before the Revolution, Britain had been the entrepôt for American rice, as for tobacco. During the British occupation of Charleston and Savannah, British and Loyalist export firms sent almost the entire rice crop to England, whence it was re-exported to the continent of Europe. Jefferson exerted himself to send seeds of an improved strain of rice to South Carolina, and persuaded French commercial houses to pay in advance for shipments; but he could not loosen the hold that British merchants had acquired on the Carolina trade through their credit facilities.

French efforts to persuade Americans to alter their drinking habits in favor of French wines likewise failed. Shortly after the war, the French consul at Boston entertained leading citizens in a champagne party. The Boston gentry, thinking champagne to be a sort of sparkling cider, got merrily drunk; but the experience did not change their preference for sherry and madeira. And the common people continued to drink rum. Consequently, the only commercial advantage France obtained from American independence was the facility to export directly, instead of through England, silks and other articles of feminine adornment.

Although England got back most of her trade with the United States, she recovered little good will with it. John Adams, when received by George III as the first American minister in 1785, expressed his hope that "the old good nature and the old good humor" between the two countries would be restored; and the king appeared to agree. But British shipping interests prevented the admission of American ships to the British West Indies, and the government refused to conclude a commercial treaty, feeling that it could get back all the American trade it wanted without making concessions. That is about what happened. New Jersey, Connecticut, and New Hampshire, trying to steal foreign trade from New York, Rhode Island, and Boston, conceded more favorable rights of entry to British ships and goods than to those of their sister states.

The South recovered prosperity earlier than the North, since she produced tobacco, indigo, rice, and naval stores which Britain could buy nowhere else so cheap. Virginia's prewar exports, in value, were restored by 1786; but in the same year the exports of Massachusetts were only one-quarter of what they had been in 1774. New England's West Indies trade, deep-sea whaling, and offshore fishing had been almost completely wiped out; Nantucketers emigrated to Milford Haven and Dunkerque to build up a whaling industry for England and France. Under the old Navigation Act, the Northern colonies had built hundreds of ships for British owners; now they no longer had this privilege. Here, as in other ways, Americans learned too late that the old imperial system had not been so oppressive as their political leaders loudly asserted.

To compensate for lost imperial trade, America showed enterprise in establishing new lines of business and commerce. Before the Revolution there was not a single bank in the Thirteen Colonies. If a man wanted capital, he borrowed from an individual. Robert Morris established the Bank of North America at Philadelphia in 1781; Boston and New York followed suit in 1784. Local paper factories prospered, and farmers made nails out of rod iron imported from Sweden. The Cabot family set up a small cotton-spinning factory at Beverly in 1784, and the same year began to trade with the Baltic, exporting tobacco, flour, and rum, and bringing back Swedish iron and Russian duck and hemp for ships' sails and cordage.

The boldest new trade to be established was with the Orient. Robert Morris and a number of New York merchants built the ship *Empress of China* and sent her to Canton in 1784. She was laden largely with borrowed silver and ginseng, an herb which the Chinese believed to be a restorative for male virility. She brought back a valuable cargo of tea, porcelain, silk, and nankeen, the cotton cloth which gentlemen of that period favored for their breeches. The difficulty about trading with China was to find a product that the Chinese wanted. Silver was scarce, and American ginseng did not produce the desired results. New England solved the problem by the Northwest Coast-Hawaii-China trade. In 1787 Bostonians fitted out ship *Columbia* and sloop *Washington*, each less than 100 feet long, and sent them around Cape Horn laden with iron tools, looking-glasses, and all manner of knickknacks, to trade with the Indians of Vancouver Island for sea-otter fur, then in great demand among Chinese mandarins. The outward passage took eleven months. After spending a winter trading on the Northwest Coast, the *Columbia*, Captain Robert Gray, proceeded to Canton where she exchanged her cargo for China goods, and returned to Boston around the world, the first American ship to do so. This curiously complicated trade, which usually included a call at the Hawaiian Islands to pick up sandalwood for the China market, continued to be profitable for some thirty years. On her second voyage, in 1792, the *Columbia* sailed into the mouth of the great river named after her, and established the United States claim to the Oregon country.

In the meantime the merchants of Salem, Massachusetts, had been approaching the Canton market by way of the Cape of Good Hope, trading also with India and Indonesia. Salem, through her Oriental, Baltic, and West Indies trade, became a worthy rival to Boston, New York, and Philadelphia before the turn of the century. During a period of twenty days in 1790, the Salem custom house (where, 50 years later, Nathaniel Hawthorne could spend whole days dreaming) entered from Canton three ships, paying more than $53,000 customs duties; seven from the West Indies, and seven from Lisbon and Cadiz.

By that time the West Indies trade was in a measure restored because France, owing to Jefferson's efforts, admitted American ships and products to her Antilles; and because the people of the British islands badly needed North American produce. Local authorities were always ready to certify that a Yankee schooner put in "under distress." Captain Horatio Nelson of H.M.S. *Boreas* on the West Indies station, gave up in despair his attempts to enforce the British Acts of Trade. The islanders, he said, were "as great rebels as ever were in America," and Yankee skippers would "swear through a nine-inch plank" for permission to sell cargoes illegally.

Even the horse kind contributed to the postwar revival. "Royal Gift," a big jackass sent to General Washington by the king of Spain, was a slow starter; and (wrote the General to Lafayette), performed with a "majestic solemnity supposed to be the example of his late Royal Master." But, having become "a little better acquainted with republican enjoyment," Royal Gift decided to "amend his manners" and began covering mares not only locally but on tours all the way to Charleston, siring strong, heavy mules which proved a boon to American farmers and to the army.

In England during the war, several of the new classics of the turf, such as, the Derby, the St. Leger and the Oaks, began; and after the war some of the winning stallions were imported into the United States. Messenger, a gray thoroughbred descended from the Darley Arabian, landed at Philadelphia in 1788, and sired the Hambletonian race of trotters. Ten years later Diomed, in whose veins ran the blood of all three of England's Oriental stallions, began serving mares in Virginia. Toward the end of his life he begot Sir Archie, whom General Davie bought for the then unprecedented sum of $5000, and whose stud fees made a fortune for his subsequent owners.

These imported thoroughbreds imparted a magic touch to American mares. but the all-American sire of the period was a horse of unknown ancestry named Justin Morgan. This stallion, named after his first owner, a school-teacher who brought him as a two-year-old to Randolph, Vermont, was better known for a quarter-century than any two-legged citizen of the Green Mountain State. He was a dark red bay with black points, 14 hands tall, with a compact body, small, fine ears, a large bright eye, long, thick mane and tail, and a sweet disposition. Justin Morgan transmitted both conformation and characteristics to his descendants for a century and a half. No American horse ever began to touch the Morgan breed as the people's choice; they could win quarter-mile running races, pull stone boats, work in wagon teams, carry the children to school and the family to church — anything that a horse could do except compete with thoroughbreds in four-mile races or with hunters timber-topping. Justin Morgan came on the scene just in time for his get to replace the Narragansett pacers, no longer in demand for road work.

2. Debts, Loyalists, and Western Posts

The resumption of friendship with Great Britain that both John Adams and George III wished, did not come about; and Adams left London in 1788 feeling frustrated. There were several bones of contention. Congress recom-mended the states to restore Loyalist property, as the treaty required, but few states complied, except Pennsylvania which paid the heirs of William Penn $650,000; and Maryland, which generously compensated the Calverts for the loss of their proprietary rights. The treaty also provided that "no future confiscations" be made. Except in New York and South Carolina, where the civil war between Whigs and Tories had been particularly vicious, this was complied with. A New York confiscatory law was invalidated by a decision of the state supreme court, after a trial in which Alexander Hamilton defended the Loyalists; a similar law in South Carolina was repealed in 1786.

Although British historians such as Arnold Toynbee continue to assert that Loyalists "were expelled bag and baggage, men, women, and children, from their homes after the war was over," this is incorrect. None were expelled after the war, and only a few royal officials were exiled during the war. Tory migration was almost completely voluntary; about 80,000 departed with the British garrisons to which they had flocked for protection. The loss to the United States was the British empire's gain, since most of these exiles settled in New Brunswick, Nova Scotia, or Ontario, where they became leaders in their communities and helped to keep them loyal to England. The great majority of Loyalists never left the states, but became good American citizens; and a surprisingly large number who did leave, drifted back. Cadwalader Colden returned from self-imposed exile and was elected mayor of New York City. Henry Cruger, a member of Parliament during the war, came back and was elected to the New York state senate. Dr. John Jeffries of Boston, a surgeon in the British army during the war, made the pioneer balloon crossing of the English Channel; he then returned to Boston and built up a large practice. Philip B. Key, uncle of the author of *The Star Spangled Banner*, served as officer in a Maryland Loyalist regiment; after the war he was admitted to the Maryland bar and received an appointment to the federal bench while still receiving his British pension. Isaac Coffin of Boston, an officer of the Royal Navy when the war began, remained in the king's senior service and rose to be Admiral Sir Isaac Coffin, but he founded a school at his ancestral home, Nantucket, and exported English thoroughbreds to improve the breed of horses in New England. In general, the only Loyalists who were not allowed to return to their homes after the war were those who had indulged in partisan warfare and Indian raids.

In the matter of prewar debts owed by American citizens to British subjects, Britain had good reason to complain. The treaty of peace required that "no legal impediment" be placed in the way of recovering such debts. Most states complied, but Virginia, whose citizens owed the most, insisted that those debts had been cancelled by state legislation during the war, and no longer existed. This subject was not settled until 1802, when the United States paid to the British government the lump sum of £600,000 as compensation to individual creditors. The amount would have been greater, but for deducting the value of hundreds of Negro slaves that the British armies either sold in the West Indies or carried off when evacuating, which was also contrary to the treaty of peace.

Canadian border posts on territory ceded to the United States in the peace treaty caused the most ill feeling. British garrisons of Atlantic coast ports from Castine to Savannah were evacuated "with all convenient speed," as the treaty required; but those on the northern border, at two points on Lake Champlain; at Ogdensburg, Oswego, and Niagara; and at Detroit and Michilimackinac, refused to budge. At the request of the governor of Canada, his superiors held these posts "to secure the fur traders in the Interior Country." Several Scots firms had built up a fur trading empire in the Old Northwest, producing peltry to the value of a million dollars a year; and the Western posts were the keys to keeping the Indians quiet and loyal; or, from the United States point of view, warlike and hostile. Although this retention of the posts was originally conceived as a temporary measure to help the fur traders to wind up their affairs, the longer they were retained, the more reluctant Canadians became to give them up. So, under the convenient excuse that Americans broke the treaty first in the matters of debts and Loyalists, the British government held on until 1796, narrowly escaping a war on that issue.

Equally troublesome to the infant republic was the attitude of Spain, whose government was determined to check American expansion to the south or west. As a result of the war, Spain recovered both Floridas and posted garrisons at Natchez and the Walnut Hills (Vicksburg), denying Britain's right to cede the east bank of the Mississippi to the United States. In 1784 the Creek, Choctaw, and Cherokee nations, or parts of them, made treaties placing themselves under Spanish protection. With ammunition obtained from former Loyalists at Pensacola, these Indians began raiding American settlements on the Cumberland and Tennessee rivers.

Possession of New Orleans and posts on the Mississippi enabled Spain to put pressure on Western pioneers. Without any better system than the pack mule to cross the Appalachians, Western farmers had to send their bulky products down the Mississippi and its tributaries to reach the sea and foreign markets. A surprising number of American backwoods politicians, notably General James Wilkinson of Kentucky, accepted pensions from Spain in return for a promise to promote the secession of trans-Appalachia and make it a satellite to the Spanish empire. This movement became especially strong after 1786 when John Jay, the Confederation's secretary for foreign affairs, failed to persuade Spain to recognize the "right of deposit," which meant the privilege to transit New Orleans, where the Spanish empire straddled both banks of the Mississippi. And this Western secession movement continued even after the federal government was established in 1789. We shall later find a former Vice President of the United States fishing in these troubled waters — the lagoons of Louisiana and the Gulf of Mexico.

Vermont, too, was threatening secession because denied a place in the Confederation. Levi Allen, Ethan's brother, journeyed to London to seek a treaty with Great Britain. With suitable encouragement, which he did not obtain, he might have persuaded the veterans of Bennington and Saratoga to vote for annexation to Canada.

Thus, the War of the American Revolution settled American independence, but little else. Unless American statesmen played their cards cannily and well, the United States might long be confined to a comparatively narrow strip between Canada, the Appalachians, the Floridas, and the Atlantic. And the indications were that it would be a very poor country at that.

3. Literature and Education

This was the bright dayspring of republican culture. Many young Americans, despite John Adams's prediction, turned to arts, letters, and science as soon as the war was over. They accomplished nothing great; but we now look on their efforts with tolerant appreciation.

The keynote was struck in 1778 by Noah Webster, a twenty-five-year-old schoolmaster at Hartford: "America must be as independent in *literature* as she is in politics, as famous for *arts* as for *arms.*" He did his best to make her so with his famous bluebacked speller, his first American reader, and the monthly *American Magazine,* which he edited. That failed within a year, but the books were astounding successes. *The American Spelling-Book,* which simplified the king's English by omitting the *u* from words like *labour* and *colour,* and spelling *wagon* with one g, became an all-time best seller, and remained in print for over a century. Webster's *American Dictionary,* first to record colloquial words and Americanisms, is still being published in both enlarged and condensed editions not far from Noah's old home. His reader, *An American Selection of Lessons in Reading and Speaking* (1785), was compiled "to Improve the minds and refine the Taste of Youth." It is a true anthology, culled from American orations, American history and politics, as well as from classic English literature. These are interspersed with amusing bits such as a recommendation of square dancing to "excite a cheerfulness of mind, and producing copious perspiration," and "a Dialogue between Mr. Hunks and Mr. Blithe," representing the older generation and the new. Mr. Hunks complains, "There's no living in this prodigal age — the young people must have their bottles, their tavern dinners, and dice, while the old ones are made perfect drudges to support their luxury."

Similar works were Caleb Bingham's *The Young Lady's Accidence; or, A Short and Easy Introduction to English Grammar* (Boston, 1785); *The Sister's Gift; or, The Naughty Boy Reformed* (Worcester, 1786), an attempt to cure juvenile delinquency; and Eleazar Moody's *The School of Good Manners, Composed for the Help of Parents Teaching Children How To Behave* (Portland, 1786).

The Reverend Jedediah Morse (father of the artist who invented the electric telegraph) brought out the first edition of his *Geography Made Easy* in 1789, the year following his graduation from Yale; it became almost as popular as Webster's speller. Most agreeably, Morse did not confine his book to mere facts and statistics. For instance, "The refreshing sea breezes . . . render

Charleston more healthy than any part of the low country in the southern states. On this account it is the resort of great numbers of gentlemen . . . who come here to spend the *sickly months*, as they are called, in quest of health and of the social enjoyments which the city affords." One Yankee product Morse refused to promote. "New England rum is by no means a wholesome liquor," he observed. "It has killed more Indians than their wars and sicknesses. It does not spare white people, especially when made into flip, which is rum mixed with small beer, and muscovado sugar."

American schoolboys needed new arithmetic books, now that they had to reckon in dollars and cents, even though the dollars were still Spanish "pieces of eight," and the copper cents hard to come by. Nicholas Pike brought out *A New and Complete System* of that science at Newburyport in 1788. It ran through many editions and became the standard American text.

These works were intended as schoolbooks or manuals; but creative literature was not altogether wanting. Joel Barlow, Noah Webster's Yale classmate, was no sooner out of college than he began an epic poem which eventually ran to over 5000 lines and was printed at Hartford in 1787 as *The Vision of Columbus*. Timothy Dwight, tutor of both these young poets at Yale, sparked off a group called the "Hartford Wits" who contributed squibs to the newspapers, of which the best known are Barlow's *Anarchiad* (1786–87), a satire on Shays's Rebellion; and John Trumbull's *McFingal*, a lengthy and heavily humorous attack on the Tories. Royall Tyler, after serving as a major in the war, brought out in 1787 *The Contrast*, the second play to be produced by a native American,[1] and in which Jonathan, the first stage Yankee, provided most of the laughs.

Philip Freneau, a Princeton graduate, was the first poet of the American Revolution. In 1786 he brought out a sizable volume of his collected poems, including the humorous doggerel *Sketches of American History* containing amusing cracks at the New England Puritans and Dutch Knickerbockers. But the public neglected Freneau's *Sketches* while enthusing over his odes to heroes of the Revolution, and his poem on an Indian Burying Ground.

The girl wonder of this age was Phillis Wheatley, a Negro slave born in Africa and owned by a Boston tailor. Before the war she exhibited such versifying talent that her master took her to London where her *Poems on Various Subjects* was published. Returning to Boston free, she married a member of her race and celebrated her country's emancipation and her own with *Liberty and Peace, A Poem* (1784), ending:

> Auspicious Heaven shall fill with fav'ring Gales,
> Where e'er *Columbia* spreads her swelling Sails:
> To every Realm shall *Peace* her Charms display,
> And Heavenly *Freedom* spread her golden Ray.

1. The first was Thomas Godfrey's *The Prince of Parthia*, produced at Philadelphia in 1767.

There was soon enough native poetry by this time to fill an anthology — *American Poems, Selected and Original*, which appeared at Litchfield, Connecticut in 1793.

John Trumbull, cousin to the like-named poet, aspired to be a painter, but was packed off to Harvard by an unsympathetic father, the governor of Connecticut. He served for two years in the Continental army, then resigned his commission and set up a studio in Boston. Finding neither teacher nor customers there, he obtained a safe conduct from the British to London, where he studied under Benjamin West, an expatriate artist from Philadelphia. There Trumbull painted his "Battle of Bunker Hill" and "Death of Montgomery," and began his famous "Declaration of Independence."

Another American pupil of Benjamin West was the prolific Charles Willson Peale of Annapolis, who lived in Philadelphia during the war, and as captain of Pennsylvania militia fought at Trenton and Princeton. During the war he undertook to paint all the distinguished generals and naval officers from life; Washington sat for him at least seven times, and from these sittings Peale produced no fewer than sixty portraits of the commander in chief. This artist depicted the Continental uniform in careful detail, but unfortunately used a standard face so that his portraits of Washington and Lafayette, who differed greatly in physiognomy, look like father and son; and even John Paul Jones looks like a member of the same family.

After the good start made by Franklin and the colonial *cognoscenti*, this period became fruitful in natural science. David Rittenhouse, a self-educated Philadelphian, became the first American professor of astronomy, at the University of Pennsylvania. A practical science in great demand in a growing country was surveying. For want of competent American surveyors, Mason and Dixon had come from England to survey the line that has made their names immortal; but Rittenhouse and Andrew Ellicott continued the line from the spot where the two Englishmen dropped it in 1767. Ellicott, with the aid of an amateur Negro astronomer named Benjamin Banneker, surveyed the ten-mile square for the District of Columbia. Manasseh Cutler, one of many scientifically inclined New England ministers, compiled the first flora of New England, and measured the height of Mount Washington — very inaccurately — by carrying a huge mercury barometer to the summit on his back. Dr. Benjamin Rush of Philadelphia began lecturing on medicine at the University of Pennsylvania in 1780, and six years later established the first free medical dispensary in the United States. And he devoted a large part of his energy and fortune to promoting the abolition of slavery, and better education for women.

Franklin's colonial Junto of Philadelphia was reorganized in 1780 as a learned academy, the American Philosophical Society. The same year, Harvard professors and several New England parsons founded the American Academy of Arts and Sciences at Boston; and the same group founded the first American historical society, that of Massachusetts, ten years later. Several valuable histories of the American states were written, and one, the Reverend

Jeremy Belknap's *History of New Hampshire* (1784), has literary merit. George Richards Minot, extravagantly called "the American Sallust" by his admirers, picked up the history of Massachusetts where Governor Hutchinson had been forced to leave off, and brought out a *History of Shays's Rebellion* in 1788. Mrs. Mercy Warren, gifted sister of James Otis, after writing satires on Tories during the war, now began a fresh and original *History of the Rise, Progress and Termination of the American Revolution*, which finally appeared in 1805. This lively presentation of the "pure republican" and antifederalist point of view delighted Thomas Jefferson but infuriated John Adams. Equally unorthodox was *A History of New England, with Particular Reference to the Baptists* (3 vols., 1777–96) by a robust minister of that denomination, the Reverend Isaac Backus, who had led the movement for religious liberty in Massachusetts.

This creative activity resulted from a feeling that Americans could know and love their country better through scientific investigation of her natural resources, by studying her past, and by writing poetry on native themes. Even those writers who began with something imitative turned "American." For instance, Peter Markoe of Philadelphia, after writing *The Patriot Chief*, a tragedy of ancient Lydia which he had printed in 1784 but never managed to produce, wrote a pungent satire on American affairs, *The Algerine Spy* (1787), in the form of "Letters Written by a Native of Algiers." The Reverend Timothy Dwight, after producing a dreary Old Testament epic, *The Conquest of Canaan* (1785), wrote a charming pastoral about the Connecticut countryside, *Litchfield Hill*, printed in 1794. By contrast, during the subsequent Federalist and Jeffersonian periods, the leading American literary men, Joseph Dennie and his circle, abandoned local themes in favor of pallid imitations of *The Spectator* and "Gothic" novels of mystery and horror.

After the war, when paper became more available, newspapers and periodicals increased in number. The *Pennsylvania Packet and General Advertiser* of Philadelphia, which started in 1784, was the first daily newspaper to last more than a few weeks; and by 1789 over eighty weekly or bi-weekly gazettes and a few monthly magazines were being published.

In education, this period was marked by the founding of new colleges in the South, and privately endowed secondary schools such as the two Phillips academies of Andover and Exeter. All Northern colleges suffered from the war, but Yale forged ahead with a graduating class of seventy in 1785, more than twice Harvard's. In William and Mary College, where the first intercollegiate fraternity, Phi Beta Kappa, was founded during the war, two chairs of theology were converted to law and history by Governor Jefferson, and by 1787 this college was offering an excellent liberal arts course.

Impressive is the list of colleges and universities founded in the South shortly after the war, in some cases before it was over. Religious bodies were responsible for most of them. Presbyterians founded four colleges in 1782–87: Hampden-Sydney, Liberty Hall which has been renamed Washington and

Lee, Transylvania in the frontier state of Kentucky, and Dickinson at Carlisle, Pennsylvania. The Episcopalians founded three colleges in 1782–85: Washington at Chesterton, Maryland, St. John's at Annapolis, and Charleston College, South Carolina. The first Roman Catholic college in the United States was Georgetown, founded in 1789 by Bishop Carroll. It was typical of the liberal spirit of the South in this era that she pioneered in state universities free from sectarian control. The University of North Carolina, first state university to be established, was chartered in 1789 and opened in 1795.

Even in music this era was far from silent. William Billings, the Boston psalm singer who had written patriotic odes during the war, was still producing hymns and choruses which have been revived in the present century. Secular song and dance books were Daniel Bayley's *Essex Harmony* (Newburyport, 1785), John Griffiths's *Collection of the Newest and Most Fashionable Country Dances and Cotillions* (Providence, 1788), William Brown's *Three Rondos for the Piano Forte* (Philadelphia, 1787), and the *Charms of Melody, A New Collection of Songs* (Philadelphia, 1788). Oliver Holden of South Carolina wrote hymn tunes of which the best known is *Coronation*, to which is sung "All Hail the Power of Jesus' Name." The Moravians of Bethlehem, Pennsylvania, had already established their festivals devoted to Johann Sebastian Bach. Francis Hopkinson, signer of the Declaration of Independence, judge, poet, painter, and organist of Christ Church, Philadelphia, composed an oratorio *The Temple of Minerva*, which was performed before General and Mrs. Washington in 1781. And the German Reformed Church of Philadelphia, in 1784, sold over 2000 tickets to a concert by 50 instruments and 250 choristers, at which works of American composers were performed. The concert concluded with a lusty rendering of Handel's Hallelujah Chorus, an appropriate celebration for achieving American independence.

4. Religion and Reform

Throughout the country one encountered the same complaints that are heard after every war, that moral and religious standards had declined; and frequent advertisements in the newspapers of quack cures for social diseases indicate that they had indeed. But independence was a distinct gain for the institutional aspect of religion, since it put many sects on their own resources. And a general spirit of mutual tolerance and religious liberty was in the air. Least affected were the Congregational churches of New England, and the Quaker meetings, which had always been independent of those in the old country. The Presbyterians, who had numbers, wealth, and a great leader in Dr. John Witherspoon, held a series of synods between 1785 and 1788 which drew up a confession of faith and a form of government and discipline for the Presbyterian Church of America. The Dutch Reformed, the Lutherans, and the German evangelical sects broke loose from their old-world organizations.

The French alliance led to a favorable attitude toward the Roman Catholic church on the part of American Protestants, and this was encouraged by Washington, Franklin, and other leading men. The Roman communion in 1785 counted only 24 priests and about 25,000 souls, mostly in Maryland and Philadelphia. The first mass to be celebrated openly in Boston was on 2 November 1788 by a former chaplain in the French navy; the first Catholic church in New York was St. Peter's, consecrated in 1785. The small number of Roman Catholics in the English colonies had been under the jurisdiction of a vicar apostolic in London. Now that that bond was broken, Pope Pius VI in 1784 appointed the Reverend John Carroll of Baltimore his apostolic prefect. Upon hearing that the Gallican church was endeavoring to have him replaced by a Frenchman, the Maryland clergy petitioned to have Carroll made a bishop; and as such he was consecrated in 1790, by a Roman Catholic bishop in England. His see covered the entire United States until 1804. During that era, the Catholic churches in the United States usually presented their own priests for ordination, almost as if they had been Congregational.

Two important developments took place among the Anglicans. The Methodists or Wesleyans, who had never formally separated from the Anglican communion, did so in 1784 when the Reverend Francis Asbury of Delaware, John Wesley's superintendent, called a conference at Baltimore. It chose him and the Reverend Thomas Coke joint superintendents, and organized the Methodist Episcopal Church in the United States. Asbury, who styled himself "The Bishop," and apparently was accepted as such by the brethren, gave an example of his church's favorite method of proselytizing, by circuit riding far and wide. "My horse trots stiff," he complained, "and no wonder when I have ridden him upon an average of 5000 miles a year for five years."

Before 1776 the Anglican church was supported by taxation, and enjoyed a monopoly of performing marriages in all Southern colonies and in parts of New York. It was disestablished in New York, Maryland, and the Carolinas, and complete religious liberty adopted in those states, during the war. In Virginia, however, it took a ten-year contest, which Jefferson called the severest of his life, to separate church from state. Finally the Virginia Statute of Religious Liberty, drafted by Jefferson, passed the assembly on 16 January 1786. The exercise of religion, it declares, is a "natural right" which has been infringed by "the impious presumption of legislators and rulers" to set up their own "modes of thinking as the only true and infallible"; and "to compel a man to furnish contributions of money for the propagation of opinions which he disbelieves," which "is sinful and tyrannical." The statute roundly declares, "No man shall be compelled to frequent or support any religious worship, place or ministry whatsoever." It even warns later assemblies that any attempt on their part to tamper with this law "will be an infringement of natural right." None, to this day, have ventured to do so; the statute is still in force.

At the close of the War of Independence the Anglican church reached its all-time low in America, partly owing to loss of support from taxes, partly because many Anglican clergymen went Tory. But there were enough patriotic laity left to demand an independent episcopate. The Reverend Samuel Seabury, former rector of Westchester, New York, was elected bishop of Connecticut and sent abroad in 1784 to obtain consecration. This was no easy matter, since the Archbishop of Canterbury still regarded the Americans as rebels and traitors; but the Scots bishops were more liberal, and through them Bishop Seabury transmitted apostolic succession to the American episcopate. The Protestant Episcopal Church of America was organized at a series of conventions between 1784 and 1789. These conventions adopted the Book of Common Prayer, omitting prayers for the royal family, and gave more power to the laity than churchmen enjoyed in England.

In the meantime John Adams, as American minister to the Court of St. James's, obtained an act of Parliament allowing bishops to be consecrated without taking an oath of allegiance to the king. Consequently the Reverend Samuel Prevoost and the Reverend William White, elected respectively bishops of New York and Pennsylvania, were consecrated by the Archbishops of Canterbury and York at Lambeth in 1787. Shortly after the Reverend James Madison, president of William and Mary College, was consecrated bishop of Virginia. The Reverend Edward Bass, elected bishop of Massachusetts, missed out on this occasion because he remarried within six months of the death of his first wife, which was thought to be a bit brisk for a sixty-three-year-old bishop; but he finally obtained his consecration from Bishop White in Philadelphia in 1797.

Just as Noah Webster maintained that there should be an American language and literature, so there were freethinkers who aimed at a republican religion. The apostle of this group was Colonel Ethan Allen, leader of the Green Mountain Boys of Vermont. In 1784 he brought out a long, dreary tract entitled, *Reason the only Oracle of Man, or a Compendious System of Natural Religion.* Therein he denied that the Bible was the Word of God, and attempted to substitute a vague deism for Christianity. When relighted by Thomas Paine's *Age of Reason* this cult shot up into a flame that for a time frightened the clergy, but died out when the French Reign of Terror seemed to point out the consequences of abandoning the Christian religion.

Although a political revolution, like war, may speed things up socially — "Revolution is the locomotive of history," said Karl Marx — this does not necessarily occur, and did not happen here. American patriots wanted no social upheaval. No flaming demagogues, no radical reformers, emerged from the revolutionary ferment. The abolition of primogeniture (leaving one's entire property to the eldest son) and entails (making it illegal for an heir to sell his estate) in Virginia and other states has been cited as social reform; but in reality amounted to little. Primogeniture was abolished for the heirs of people who died intestate — without making a will; and entails, in a country expanding westward with wide economic opportunities, were a burden rather than a privilege.

The confiscation of Loyalists' estates has been called a social revolution. Loyalist patroonships in New York were divided up, but not excessively; and in North Carolina the purchasers of Henry McCulloh's 40,000 acres acquired up to 5000 each, and the 3600-acre estate of Tom Hooper, Tory, passed intact to John McKinsey, Patriot. But for the most part, Loyalists' estates were of average size, and the result of confiscation was simply to substitute new owners for the old.

A social revolution indeed was the abolition of slavery, but this did not extend to any state where slaves were numerous or slavery was considered essential to the economy. In Rhode Island, a participant in the African slave trade, the assembly of 1774 resolved that, whereas Americans were now contending for rights and liberties, all slaves henceforth imported into that colony would be free. In Massachusetts a Negro named Quork Walker won his freedom in 1781 on the ground that the state constitution said "All men are born free and equal"; and that ended slavery in Massachusetts. The other New England states and Pennsylvania did not free existing slaves, fearing lest their support fall on the taxpayer, but gave freedom to all children thenceforward born of slave parents. New York and New Jersey, where slavery was more of an economic factor than in New England, did not begin gradual abolition until 1799 and 1804, respectively.

South of Mason and Dixon's line, the efforts of liberals such as Jefferson and George Mason to put slavery on the way to extinction were defeated, precisely because this would have meant a social revolution. Many Southern leaders declared publicly that slavery was morally wrong and contrary to Revolutionary principles, but they could not convert the voters. The Virginia assembly in 1783 freed slaves who had served in the armed forces. Two years later, when Methodists petitioned the Virginia assembly to begin a general emancipation on the ground that slavery was "contrary to the fundamental principles of the Christian religion" and a violation of the Declaration of Rights, their petition was unanimously rejected. Had it been acted upon, there might have been no American civil war.

The African slave trade, however, was prohibited by Delaware, Maryland, Virginia, and all Northern states by 1783. North Carolina placed a heavy tax on slave imports, and in South Carolina the trade was prohibited between 1787 and 1803, when the act was repealed as unenforceable. But abolishing the direct trade from Africa merely shifted it to the border slave states as source of supply for plantations of the lower South.

Discussion of slavery was still completely free and every Southern state nourished one or more abolition societies. The general American expectation seems to have been that slavery would fade away in competition with immigrant white labor. Oliver Ellsworth of Connecticut predicted in the Federal Convention that "as population increases, our laborers will be so plenty as to render slaves useless. Slavery in time will be a speck in our country." Alas, if only it had turned out that way! But for the coming convulsions in Europe, indentured labor from Ireland and the Continent might have come in such numbers as to fulfill Ellsworth's prophecy. There were fewer than 700,000 slaves in the United States in 1790. The emancipation of these Negroes, their becoming domestic servants, common laborers and small farmers, even the return of many to Africa, would then have been possible. But the Revolutionary generation lacked the imagination to foresee the tragic consequences of perpetuating an institution which denied the very premises upon which American independence was based.

X X

The Creative Period in Politics

1785-1788

1. *Some Western Problems Solved*

ALMOST EVERY WESTERN SETTLEMENT that we have described suffered during the war from Indian raids and cattle thieves. Nevertheless, the attraction of blue-grass and hardwood, and desire to escape the war, brought in thousands from Virginia and the Carolinas. When in 1780 Virginia set up a land office in Kentucky, it was flooded with prospective settlers and speculators, and the movement increased after news of peace arrived. Congress now became eager to obtain control of the West north of the Ohio (it never had any chance to get anything south of that river), in order to sell land and put something into the empty Confederation treasury.

When Virginia again offered to cede her land claims north of the Ohio, with reserves for veterans but no other strings, Congress accepted (1 March 1784). Massachusetts and Connecticut followed two years later. Connecticut retained a tract of land on Lake Erie, known to this day as the Western Reserve. She had agreed with Pennsylvania to give up her claim to the Wyoming valley, where there had been clashes between rival settlers, if Pennsylvania would support her claim to this section of Ohio. William Grayson of Virginia cynically remarked that the Connecticut cession was "nothing but a state juggle contrived by old Roger Sherman to get a sidewind confirmation to a thing they had no right to." Anyway, Connecticut got it, and the Western Reserve was governed as an integral part of that state (like Maine by Massachusetts) until Ohio was admitted to the Union in 1802.

Through these state cessions north of the Ohio in 1784–86, the United States became a colonial power; or, to use another word which has recently been denigrated, an imperial power. John Paul Jones referred to his adopted country as an "imperial republic"; and Joel Barlow, in his Fourth of July Oration of 1787 remarked, "Every free citizen of the American empire ought now to consider himself the legislator of half mankind."

But before going that far, the new "Empire" had its own problems. Congress was confronted with Western questions which had been debated or decided in London before the war. Should white settlement in the Indian country be encouraged or discouraged, and how? Should Congress anticipate a long-term colonial status for the West to protect Indians and fur traders, or encourage

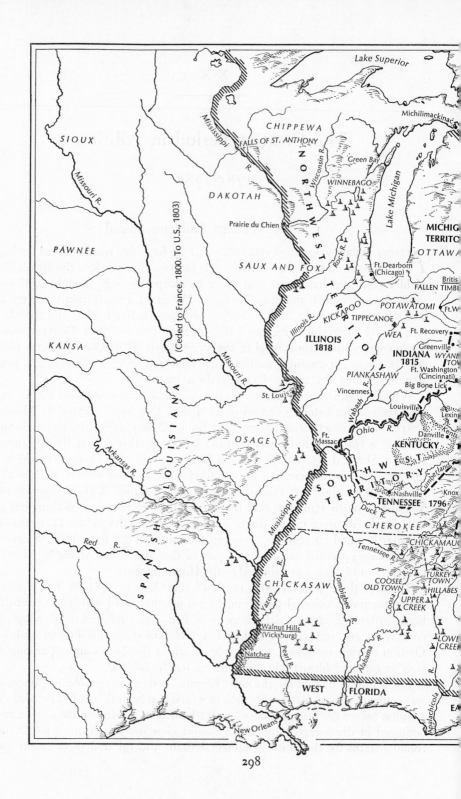

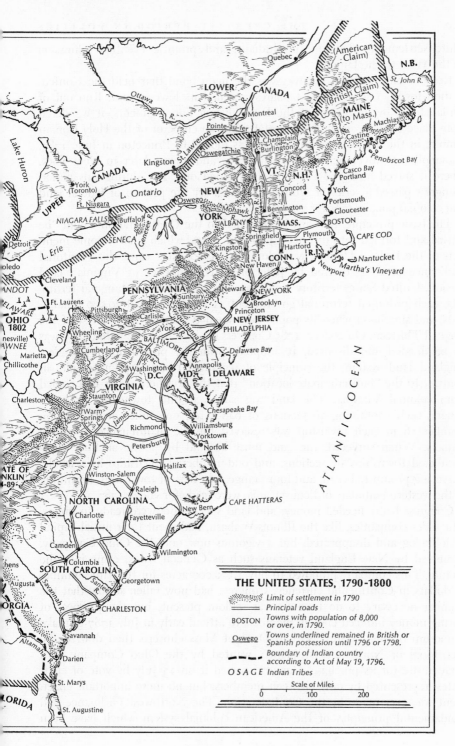

Lake Huron

Ottawa R.

LOWER CANADA

Quebec

(American Claim)

N.B.

St. John R.

(British Claim)

MAINE
(to Mass.)

Montreal

Pointe-au-fer

Machias

Castine

Penobscot Bay

St. Lawrence R.

Oswegatchie

Champlain

Burlington

CANADA

Kingston

L. Ontario

York
(Toronto)

Ft. Niagara

UPPER

NIAGARA FALLS

Buffalo

Oswego

Casco Bay
Portland

VT.

N.H.

Concord

York

Portsmouth

Gloucester

BOSTON

MASS.

Plymouth

CAPE COD

Nantucket

Martha's Vineyard

Newport

CONN.

R.I.

Hartford

New Haven

NEW
YORK

Mohawk R.

ALBANY

Springfield

Kingston

SENECA

Genesee R.

Hudson R.

Bennington

Detroit

L. Erie

oledo

ANDOT

Cleveland

Ft. Laurens

ELAWARE

OHIO
1802

nesville)

AWNEE

Marietta

Chillicothe

PENNSYLVANIA

Sunbury

Pittsburgh

Carlisle

Ohio R.

Wheeling

York

Susquehanna R.

Cumberland

BALTIMORE

Potomac R.

Newark

NEW YORK

Brooklyn

Princeton

NEW JERSEY

PHILADELPHIA

Delaware Bay

Washington
D.C.

MD.

Annapolis

DELAWARE

VIRGINIA

Staunton

Charleston

Warm
Springs

James R.

Richmond

Petersburg

Chesapeake Bay

Williamsburg

Yorktown

Norfolk

ATE OF
FRANKLIN
4-89

Winston-Salem

Halifax

Raleigh

New Bern

CAPE HATTERAS

NORTH CAROLINA

Charlotte

Fayetteville

Camden

Wilmington

hens

Augusta

ORGIA

SOUTH CAROLINA

Columbia

Santee R.

Georgetown

CHARLESTON

Savannah

Altamaha R.

Darien

St. Marys

LORIDA

St. Augustine

Savannah R.

ATLANTIC OCEAN

THE UNITED STATES, 1790-1800

Limit of settlement in 1790

Principal roads

BOSTON — Towns with population of 8,000 or over, in 1790.

Oswego — Towns underlined remained in British or Spanish possession until 1796 or 1798.

— — — Boundary of Indian country according to Act of May 19, 1796.

O S A G E Indian Tribes

Scale of Miles

0   100   200

white settlement, abandon the Indians, and promise eventual admission of the West to the Union?

Responsibility for this territory was the main bond that held the Confederation together. In 1783–84 Congress reached its lowest point. Run out of Philadelphia by mutineers of the Pennsylvania line regiments, it wandered from place to place in the Middle states like an emperor of the Holy Roman Empire in the fifteenth century. Congress moved to Princeton in June 1783, Annapolis in November, Trenton in 1784, and a year later to New York, where it stayed until the Confederation faded out. Yet, during this period Congress passed a series of ordinances which set the pattern of federal land and colonial policies for over a century.

The basic principle, that any lands ceded to the Confederation would "be settled and formed into distinct republican states, which shall become members of the Federal Union," was adopted in 1780. Next came the Territorial Ordinance of 1784, drafted by Jefferson in consequence of Virginia's land cession. United States territory would be divided into ten rectangular territories, each promised territorial government as soon as it had 20,000 inhabitants, and statehood when its population equaled that of the smallest of the original Thirteen. On 20 May 1785 Congress decided how the public land was to be divided and disposed. It adopted, from the precedent of the New England land system, the principle of rectangular survey prior to sale, in contrast to the "indiscriminate location" that the Southern states had copied from colonial Virginia. The land was surveyed into townships six miles square, each containing 36 sections of 640 acres, one mile square. Section number 16 in each township was reserved for the maintenance of public schools. When surveyed, the land must be sold by public auction; even-numbered townships by sections, and odd-numbered townships as a whole. Surveying promptly began, and four "ranges" or tiers of townships, beginning at the western boundary of Pennsylvania, were ready for sale in 1787.

Congress badly needed money, and land speculators were ready to oblige. The older companies, like the Illinois-Wabash, had spent their initial capital in lobbying and disappeared; but a vigorous new one, the Ohio Company, organized by New England veterans such as General Knox, came into the picture. This company proposed to buy 1,500,000 acres for the same number of dollars in Continental currency. Congress had now fallen so low that the number necessary to do business was seldom present, but the prospect of raising money induced enough members to attend early in July 1787 to make a quorum of eight states. Nathan Dane of Massachusetts then drafted the Territorial or Northwest Ordinance, wanted by the Ohio Company as a prerequisite for its purchase. Congress passed it on 13 July by vote of eight states, represented by only eighteen members; but no more important enactment was ever made by the Confederation. The Northwest Ordinance laid fundamental principles of the American colonial system which have been followed, even through the admission of Alaska and Hawaii. A territorial assembly, under a governor appointed by Congress, was promised as soon as a "district" had a population of 5000 free males. Statehood was promised as soon as any one of three districts attained 60,000 people. A bill of rights was established "as articles of compact between the original States and the people and States in the said territory," forever to remain inalterable. And one of the articles in this bill of rights stated, "There shall be neither slavery nor involuntary servitude in said territory."

This was the greatest triumph for antislavery in the Creative Period. It dedicated the entire West north of the Ohio and east of the Mississippi to free soil. And, although the authority of Congress to legislate for the West was doubtful, both state and federal courts have held that the Northwest Ordinance is still superior to all constitutions and laws subsequently adopted by the five states — Ohio, Indiana, Illinois, Michigan, and Wisconsin — carved out of the Northwest Territory.

Thus the main lines of federal land and territorial policy were adopted by the Congress of the Confederation before the Federal Constitution was adopted. These were: the principle of future statehood after an intermediary stage as a partly self-governing territory, and division into six-mile-square townships and one-mile-square sections, reserving a portion for education.

So wrote Philip Freneau in his contemporary poem "On the Emigration to America and Peopling the Western Country."

> Far brighter scenes a future age,
> The muse predicts, these States will hail,
> Whose genius may the world engage,
> Whose deeds may over death prevail,
> And happier systems bring to view.
> Than all the eastern sages knew.

2. Shays's Rebellion and the Movement Toward Stronger Union

> My name is Shays; in former days
> In Pelham I did dwell, Sir.
> But now I'm forced to leave the place
> Because I did rebel, Sir.
>
> Within the State I lived of late,
> By Satan's foul invention,
> In Pluto's cause against the laws
> I raised an insurrection.

So runs a ballad about Shays's Rebellion in Massachusetts, which stimulated local bards, as the War of the Regulation had inspired those of North Carolina. There was much in common between these movements, and Shays's followers were often called Regulators. Both were revolts of poor farmers against intolerable conditions; both were relatively bloodless, and both were put down in the name of law and order. Shays's Rebellion, moreover, gave an emotional fillip to the movement for stronger union.

There were "combustibles" of revolt, as Washington put it, in almost every state; but only in Massachusetts did they catch fire. The basic causes were the postwar readjustment and consequent poverty, which made the poor and discontented seek relief from their state governments. As John Jay wrote, "New governments have not the aid of habit and hereditary respect, and being generally the result of preceding tumult and confusion do not immediately acquire stability and strength."

In states where conditions were better than in Massachusetts, legislatures relieved debtors and poor farmers by unorthodox financial expedients which had earlier been quashed by the British government. A favorite device was the old land bank scheme in which the state lent script to farmers up to the value of their real estate, and made it legal tender for taxes, sometimes for all payments. Another was the stay law, postponing the collection of all debts and mortgages for a number of years. The Rhode Island assembly, worst offender against sound finance, provided that if a creditor refused to accept state paper currency at par, the debtor could discharge his debt simply by depositing the scrip with the nearest judge. The reverse of the usual situation took place — harassed creditors were pursued by implacable debtors eager to tender a wad of depreciated paper for the full value of their debts! Rather than sell goods for worthless paper, merchants shut up shop, hid their stock, or loaded it on a vessel and escaped to New York or the West Indies.

In Massachusetts, where the farmers' situation was worse, the political setup brought about an explosion. In the state constitution, as we have seen, the senate represented property, so that the maritime counties had a majority and were able to defeat all relief measures passed by the lower house. Mercantile influence had been strong enough to put the state on a specie basis in 1782, which meant a rapid deflation. Following the old Puritan adage, "A bargain's a bargain and must be made good," the commonwealth paid off old bills and notes in specie at the market value of the time of issue, instead of following Virginia's example of discharging state debts at the depreciated value of a thousand to one. Heavy taxes had to be laid to support this sound money policy, and the taxes were not justly apportioned; 40 per cent of the total was collected by poll taxes, which fell equally on rich and poor.

Merchants in the seaports, pressed by foreign creditors to pay for imported goods, tried to collect from country storekeepers and they from the farmers. A situation was created somewhat like the old nursery tale which begins, "The stick began to beat the dog." With trade at a standstill, farm produce a drug in the market, no employment for common labor, and little specie in circulation, court judgments for debts or overdue taxes could in most cases be enforced only by stripping a farmer of his real estate, his cattle, and his furniture. In Worcester County alone, 92 persons were imprisoned for debt in 1785. The situation was very bad, and rumor made it seem worse; stories flew about that the wealthy men of Boston and Salem were trying to get all the land into their hands and convert the free farmers of Massachusetts into a dependent peasantry.

The people now resorted to the measures which they had employed against the Coercive Acts. They prevented the county courts from sitting, so that there would be no more judgments for debts; they held county conventions to state grievances and draft petitions, and appointed committees of correspondence between counties. This was a grim joke on the leaders of the American Revolution who were now running the state government. Samuel Adams, now a respectable member of the state council, proposed to hang anyone who used the methods he had employed in 1774.

In the fall in 1786, mobs of farmers prevented the courts from sitting in the four western counties of Massachusetts, and in Middlesex County at Concord. Annual state elections at that time came in the spring; and the main object of the insurgents was to stop executions for debt and taxes until they could elect a new legislature to grant legal relief, as had been obtained in other states. James Bowdoin, a staunch conservative, was now governor of Massachusetts. In September 1786 he issued a proclamation against unlawful assemblies and called out the militia to disperse them. This made the insurgents desperate. Daniel Shays was now thrust forward as a leader, against his will. He had served with distinction as captain in a Massachusetts line regiment, and settled at Pelham after the war. He was a poor man; a few years earlier he had been unable to raise twelve dollars to pay a debt. He now served as chairman of a committee which resolved to prevent the sitting of the state supreme court at Springfield, fearing lest it indict their leaders for treason. Major General Shepherd, at the head of loyal militia, undertook to defend both the courthouse and the federal arsenal where the insurgents hoped to get arms. He defeated an attack on Springfield by 1100 men led by Shays, with Luke Day and Eli Parsons as lieutenants. Shepherd had artillery and they none, so it is not surprising that after one volley the insurgents broke and ran (25 January 1787). A fresh militia army from the eastern counties then arrived on the scene, impressively led by General Benjamin Lincoln, and pursued the rebels through the snow to Petersham, where their force was scattered, and many prisoners taken. A few skirmishes occurred elsewhere, but the rout of Shays's main force at Petersham on 4 February broke the back of the rebellion. Shays escaped to Vermont.

Massachusetts, fortunately, reacted with wisdom and mercy. Fourteen leaders were captured and sentenced to death, but all were either pardoned or let off with short prison terms. The newly elected legislature, in which a majority sympathized with the rebels, granted some of their demands, such as allowing soldiers' notes to be tendered for taxes. And the return of prosperity in 1787 caused the eruption to subside, leaving no bitter slag. Law and order had been maintained without the mass murders which have characterized the suppression of revolts by desperate people in our day.

Shays's Rebellion had a great influence on public opinion. News of it delighted the English Tories, as proof that Americans were incapable of self-government. It alarmed all American leaders except Jefferson, who, from his snug retreat in the Paris legation, remarked, "A little rebellion now and then is a good thing; the tree of liberty must be refreshed from time to time with the blood of patriots and tyrants." When Massachusetts appealed to the Confederation for help, Congress was unable to do a thing. That was the final argument to sway many Americans in favor of a stronger federal government.

Washington and almost all military leaders of the war, and many civilians as well, had long felt that the Confederation could never become a respectable government without the power to tax. It could not even apportion requisitions as the Articles required, according to the assessed value of real estate in each state, because it had no money to make a survey. Congress could only obtain taxing power by amendment, which required unanimous consent of the member states. The first attempt, the impost amendment of 1781 which granted Congress power to levy an import duty of not more than 5 per cent, failed because Rhode Island refused to ratify, and Virginia reneged on her ratification. In 1783 a second attempt, limited in operation to twenty-five years, was ruined by the selfishness of New York landowners who feared higher land taxes if their state gave up customs revenue. An amendment proposed in 1784, to give the Confederation limited power to regulate domestic and foreign commerce, did not even pass Congress. The prospect of getting money by any means, except selling Western land to speculators, seemed hopeless. Only New Jersey refused absolutely to pay her annual requisition, but other states did so in fact, by applying their shares to pay interest on federal debts owed to their own citizens.

There were enough interstate brawls to cause great disquiet. The New York assembly in 1787 assessed heavy entrance and clearance fees on all vessels coming from or bound to New Jersey and Connecticut; New Jersey retaliated by taxing the lighthouse on Sandy Hook £30 a month. But another interstate conflict furthered the cause of more perfect union. Virginia and Maryland, long at loggerheads over the oyster fishery, made a settlement at a joint conference in Alexandria. Pennsylvania and Delaware were also concerned, because some of their commerce had to pass through Virginia's territorial waters. Virginia's assembly, which at this juncture was in a nationalist mood, invited all the states to send delegates to a convention at Annapolis, "to take into consideration the trade of the United States."

This Annapolis Convention, which met in September 1786, was attended by delegates from only five states. Two of its youngest members, Alexander Hamilton and James Madison, took the lead in persuading the delegates that nothing could be accomplished by so slim a body, and in adopting a report which Hamilton drafted. This report pointed up the critical situation of the Confederation, and proposed that all thirteen states choose delegates to a convention, "to devise such further provisions as shall appear to them necessary to render the constitution of the federal government adequate to the exigencies of the Union." This was the genesis of the Convention of 1787.

Congress took its time to consider the Annapolis invitation. On 21 February 1787 it invited the states to send delegates to a convention at Philadelphia in May, "for the sole and express purpose of revising the Articles of Confederation," to "render the federal constitution adequate to the exigencies of government, and the preservation of the Union."

3. The Federal Convention of 1787

The Federal Convention, which sat in Philadelphia from 25 May to 17 September 1787, drafted the most successful constitution in history, now covering fifty instead of thirteen states, and a population approaching 200 million as compared with fewer than four million enrolled in the census of 1790.

At Philadelphia twelve states (Rhode Island having sulkily declined the invitation) were represented by fifty-five delegates. Two (William S. Johnson and Abraham Baldwin) were college presidents; three (George Wythe, James Wilson, and William C. Houston) were or had been professors; twenty-six others were college graduates. Four delegates had read law at the Inns of Court in London; nine were foreign-born. Twenty-eight had served in Congress, and most of the others in state legislatures. The most surprising thing about the delegates is their youth. Five, including Charles Pinckney, were under thirty years old; Alexander Hamilton was thirty-two; in the next oldest group James Madison, Gouverneur Morris and Edmund Randolph were within a year of thirty-five. Wilson, Luther Martin, Oliver Ellsworth, and William Paterson were between forty-one and forty-five. General Washington who, much against his desire, had been "drafted" for the Convention, was now fifty-five, the same age as Dickinson and Wythe. Only four members had reached or passed the age of sixty; and Benjamin Franklin at eighty-one was the oldest member by fifteen years. Practically every American who had useful ideas on political science was there except John Adams and Thomas Jefferson on foreign missions and John Jay, busy with the foreign relations of the Confederation. Jefferson contributed indirectly by shipping to Madison and Wythe from Paris sets of Polybius and other ancient publicists who discoursed on the theory of "mixed government" on which the Constitution was based. The political literature of Greece and Rome was a positive and quickening influence on the Convention debates.

The Convention had been summoned to meet on 14 May, but not until the 25th did enough delegates report at the place of sessions, the State House next to Independence Hall, to enable it to organize. George Washington was chosen president of the Convention, and it was decided to keep all proceedings secret until the results were known.

In the meantime, the national-minded Virginia delegation, led by young Randolph and Madison, who arrived in mid-May, held several informal mettings with Robert Morris and other Philadelphia nationalists. At these caucuses the important decision was made not to try to amend the Articles of Confederation but to start fresh. An outline plan for a new nationalist government was presented by Edmund Randolph of Virginia on the third day of the Convention's sessions, 29 May. The essential principles of these Virginia resolutions, as they were called, were a "national legislature" of two houses, members of both to be apportioned according to population, and those of the upper house to be elected by the lower; a "national executive" and a "national judiciary," both to be appointed by the national legislature; provision for amendment, and for binding members of state governments by oath to support the new constitution.

The Convention immediately resolved itself into a committee of the whole to debate this national plan. Roger Sherman and Elbridge Gerry, still trembling over the recent Shays's Rebellion, opposed popular elections. "The evils we experience flow from the excess of democracy," said Gerry. But George Mason, with the serenity of a liberal Southern gentleman, "argued strongly for an election of the larger branch by the people," and was supported by Madison and by James Wilson, who "was for raising the federal pyramid to a considerable altitude, and for that reason wished to give it as broad a basis as possible." Popular election "of the first branch of the National Legislature" was adopted by a vote of six states to two, with two divided.

The Convention then debated whether the national executive power should be vested in one man or several. Wilson argued for "a single magistrate, as giving most energy, dispatch and responsibility to the office." Randolph opposed it as "the foetus of Monarchy." Oliver Cromwell, Julius Caesar and every "man on horseback" of ancient and modern history were prancing in the members' minds.

The Convention then debated the method of election and apportionment of the second branch, which it agreed to call the Senate, following Roman precedent. Madison made a great speech on "the use of the Senate" — to proceed "with more coolness, with more system, and with more wisdom, than the popular branch." He wished to have the Senate, too, elected by the people (as it has been since 1913); but Gerry insisted that the commercial and monied interests would be more secure in the hands of the state legislatures than of the people at large; and Mason agreed that to have senators elected by the states would be the best way to make these "a constituent part of the national establishment." The Convention so voted, unanimously.

This realistic appreciation of distinct economic but sectional interests in the United States was shared by many members. How were the rival interests of seaboard merchants and back-country farmers (expressing the age-old antagonism between town and country), creditors and debtors, produce-exporting Southerners and trading Yankees, to be reconciled? Madison observed that the larger the political unit, the less likelihood of class or sectional injustice; he pointed out that Rhode Island was the place where one class had been riding roughshod over every other. "All civilized societies," he said, were "divided into different sects, fashions, and interests, as they happened to consist of rich and poor, debtors and creditors, the landed, the manufacturing, the commercial interests, the inhabitants of this district or that district. . . . Why was America so justly apprehensive of Parliamentary injustice? Because Great Britain had a separate interest. The only remedy is to enlarge the sphere, and thereby divide the community into so great a number of interests and parties, that a majority will not be likely to have a common interest separate from that of the whole or of the minority."

Enlarge the sphere, and balance the interests: has not American history proved Madison's wisdom? And has not the completely contrary communist theory, of recognizing no interests except those of the "workers" and the state, brought an end to personal liberty wherever put into effect?

The Convention was still happily debating the Virginia national plan when William Paterson of New Jersey exploded a bomb in the form of the New Jersey plan. The essential feature of it was one state, one vote; it was little more than an amended Articles of Confederation. The New Jersey plan naturally appealed to delegates from smaller states, who feared having their interests overridden by majorities formed out of big ones. Paterson introduced it with a long speech on state sovereignty, to which young Charles Pinckney retorted, "Give New Jersey an equal vote, and she will dismiss her scruples, and concur in the National system." And Hamilton remarked, "It is a contest for power, not for liberty."

Delegates from the four larger states, Massachusetts, Pennsylvania, Virginia, and Connecticut, in alliance with the Carolinas, defeated the New Jersey plan on 19 June and brought the national plan back as order of the day. But the wisest members reflected that their task was not to draft a theoretically best constitution, but as good a one as could probably get ratified; that they must make concessions to state rights. So, as a starter, the words "national government" in the Virginia plan were replaced by "Government of the United States."

Hot weather now set in, tempers flared, and the Convention seemed to be getting nowhere. So, on 28 June, Benjamin Franklin made his famous speech recommending that sessions be opened with prayer:

The small progress we have made after four or five weeks . . . is methinks a melancholy proof of the imperfection of Human Understanding. We indeed seem to feel our own Want of political wisdom, since we have been running about in search of it. . . . In this situation . . . groping as it were in the dark to find political truth . . . how has it happened, Sir, that we have not hitherto once thought of humbly applying to the Father of lights to illuminate our understanding? . . . I have lived, Sir, a long time, and the longer I live, the more convincing proofs I see of this truth, *that God governs in the affairs of men.* And if a sparrow cannot fall to the ground without his notice, is it probable that an empire can rise without his aid?

Franklin's motion was lost, not because the delegates disbelieved in prayer, but because they had no money to pay a chaplain. The states which elected them provided neither salary nor expense account.

The deadlock was broken on 16 July when the Convention adopted the great compromise of the Constitution, by some called the Connecticut compromise because it was suggested by Roger Sherman. The House of Representatives would be popularly elected, and apportioned according to the number of free inhabitants, plus three-fifths of the slaves (the so-called federal ratio); but the Senate would consist of two members from each state, elected by the state legislatures.

All decided points were now turned over to a large committee, which reported on 6 August a series of propositions which the Convention debated one by one. Franklin spoke in favor of a liberal admission of foreigners. Irish-born Pierce Butler of Georgia opposed this, as did Gouverneur Morris, who wanted no "philosophical gentlemen, those citizens of the world as they call themselves . . . in our public councils." He would not be polite to foreigners at the expense of prudence. "He would not carry the complaisance so far as to bed them with his wife," as the hospitable Indians did with strangers. Gouverneur Morris was the "bad boy" of the Convention. Hamilton once bet him a dinner if he would slap Washington on the back and say, "How are you today, my dear General?" Morris took him up; but declared that after the look Washington gave him, he wouldn't do it again for a thousand dinners. Morris was a wit but no clown; it was his pen that put the final, taut touch to the language of the Constitution, and on 5 July he made one of the most eloquent and prophetic speeches of the session. As reported by Madison, Gouverneur Morris said, "He came here as a representative of America; he flattered himself he came here in some degree as a Representative of the whole human race; for the whole human race will be affected by the proceedings of this Convention. He wished gentlemen to extend their views beyond the present moment of time; beyond the narrow limits of place. . . . Much has been said of the sentiments of the people. They were unknown, they could not be known. All that we can infer is that if the plan we recommend be reasonable and right; all who have reasonable minds and sound intentions will embrace it. . . . This country must be united. If persuasion does not unite it, the sword will."

Elbridge Gerry, seconded by Luther Martin, wished to restrict the members of the United States Army to 3000 in time of peace, and made a humorous comparison (transmitted by oral tradition) of a standing army to a standing member — "an excellent assurance of domestic tranquillity, but a dangerous temptation to foreign adventure." But he got no support; it was agreed that the President be commander in chief of the army and navy, and that the size of each be left to Congress.

As the debates continued, the proposed constitution lost the legislative supremacy character of the original Virginia resolutions, and became more and more a "mixed government," in which the democratic, aristocratic, and authoritarian elements were balanced, as John Adams had done in the constitution of Massachusetts. Luther Martin even sneered at the Federal Constitution as "a perfect medley."

It is not, however, correct to say that the sentiment of the Convention was undemocratic. Members did not propose to set up an unlimited democracy like the Pennsylvania constitution; but they insisted on giving democracy its share in what they intended to be a balanced government. Apart from using the Senate "to protect the minority of the opulent against the majority," there were no built-in safeguards to property in the Constitution. Certain confiscatory practices of the states during the last few years, such as breaking contracts and issuing paper money, were forbidden to them, but not to the federal government — as the Civil War period and our own have learned. The Constitution gave Congress power to pay the national debt but did not require it to do so, as Gerry and other members of the Convention demanded it should. And in one respect the Constitution was more democratic than that of any state except Pennsylvania. No property qualifications were imposed for any federal office, although several Southern delegates argued that not only officials but voters should be men of property. George Mason, whose alleged democratic principles did not go very deep, wished congressmen to have the same landed requirements as those imposed on members of the House of Commons in the reign of Queen Anne. Charles Pinckney wanted a property qualification of at least $100,000 for the President, and $50,000 for federal judges, congressmen, and senators. But Gouverneur Morris hinted that any such requirement would exclude George Washington from high office; and John Dickinson, reverting to his original character as the Pennsylvania Farmer, "doubted the policy of interweaving into a Republican constitution a Veneration for wealth." Franklin, consistently democratic, expressed his dislike of everything that tended "to debase the spirit of the common people," or to discourage the emigration of such to America. Thus, a proposal to make the federal government "high-toned" was emphatically defeated.

The odd method of choosing a President of the United States was the result of several compromises. It was assumed that Washington would be the first President, and the number of terms was not limited; but the Convention, not anticipating the rise of a two-party system, expected a free-for-all after the General, each state voting for a "favorite son," and none obtaining a majority of electoral votes. Hence it provided for a final election by the House of Representatives where the voting would be by states, a majority of states being necessary to elect.

An interesting sectional struggle took place over three subjects that had no logical connection: the African slave trade, export taxes, and the power to pass a navigation act. George Mason made a prophetic speech against continuing the slave trade: "Slavery discourages arts and manufactures. The poor despise labor when performed by slaves. They prevent the immigration of whites, who really enrich and strengthen a country. They produce the most pernicious effect on manners. Every master of slaves is born a petty tyrant. They bring the judgment of Heaven on a country." General Charles Cotesworth Pinckney, however, insisted that his state and Georgia could not "do without slaves"; and John Rutledge threatened that the three states of the lower South would secede unless permitted to continue this traffic. The Southern states, since their main profits came from exporting agricultural products, also insisted that export taxes be outlawed; and they wanted free competition in freight rates, having very little shipping of their own. Thus, they demanded the exceptional requirement of a two-thirds majority in Congress for passing a navigation act restricting shipping to the American flag. These three proposals on exports, slave-trading, and shipping were then committed and compromised. There could be no federal interference with the slave trade for twenty years. A navigation act could be passed like any other law by a bare majority; but federal taxes on exports were absolutely forbidden. That is why the United States today is almost the only nation that cannot impose export duties.

Finally, all agreed propositions were embodied in twenty-three resolutions and submitted to a committee on detail, of which Gouverneur Morris was chairman. Their report contained the significant Article VI on sanctions, which may be traced to the New Jersey plan. Paterson proposed that if any state ignored or failed to enforce an act of Congress, the executive should have power "to call forth the power of the Confederate States . . . to enforce and compel an obedience." Hamilton and Madison objected: "The larger states will be impregnable, the smaller only can feel the vengeance of it. . . . It was the cobweb which would entangle the weak, but would be the sport of the strong." One of the signal achievements of the Convention was to reject this "coercion by force," as Ellsworth called it, and substitute "coercion by law."

That principle is embodied in two key clauses of the Constitution. In Article VI, section 2, we find: "This Constitution, and the laws of the United States, which shall be made in pursuance thereof; and all treaties made, or which shall be made, under the authority of the United States, shall be the Supreme Law of the land; and the judges in every State shall be bound thereby, any thing in the Constitution or laws of any State to the contrary notwithstanding." And Article III, section 2, gives federal judges jurisdiction over "all cases, in law and equity, arising under this Constitution, the laws of the United States, and treaties made . . . under their authority."

These clauses give the Constitution a different character from that of earlier federal governments. They afforded the new federal government, in contrast to that of the Confederation, "complete and compulsive operation" on the individual citizen. State officials are expressly bound to enforce acts of Congress; and, as Madison pointed out, the federal judiciary may declare null and void any law "violating a constitution established by the people themselves."

Luther Martin objected, in a speech lasting over three hours, with "arguments too diffuse, and in many cases desultory." "The General Government," he said, "was meant merely to preserve the State Governments, not to govern individuals." That was true of the Confederation, as it is now true of the United Nations. But the genius of the Convention of 1787, its greatest contribution to political science, was to get away from this horizontal separation between the state governments and federal government, and give the latter a direct line to each individual citizen. Nevertheless, events in the South as recently as 1964 have proved that if a state government is firmly opposed to a federal measure, it becomes almost unenforceable.

By mid-September the work of the Convention neared its end. The New York members, except Hamilton, had already withdrawn in disgust; others, for various reasons, declared they would never sign. Gouverneur Morris cleverly devised a form to make it seem unanimous: "Done in Convention, by the unanimous consent of the States present the 17 September." At 4:00 p.m., 17 September 1787, "The Members adjourned to the City Tavern, dined together, and took cordial leave of each other."

During the four months of sessions in a muggy Philadelphia summer, they had thrashed out great issues in political theory and practical politics, and produced a constitution which has gathered prestige with age. When the Convention adjourned, most members felt that the compromises had vitiated the result. Alexander Hamilton called the Constitution a "weak and worthless fabric," certain to be superseded. Luther Martin regarded it as a stab in the back of the goddess of liberty. Daniel Carroll called it "the Continental Congress in two volumes instead of one." Madison accepted Carroll's criticism as a factor in the new government's strength; it was not a clean break with the Confederation. "The change which it proposes consists much less in the addition of *New Powers* to the *Union*, than in the invigoration of its Original Powers." The most that Madison and the majority of delegates hoped, was that this practical, workable constitution, planned to meet the immediate needs of Thirteen States with approximately four million people, would last a generation.

The Federal Constitution gave new meaning to the term "federal," by setting up a "sovereign union of sovereign states." This federal government is supreme and sovereign within its sphere; but that sphere is defined and limited by the Constitution. Explicit in the Constitution is the statement (Article VI, section 2) that laws "which shall be made in pursuance thereof," and none other, are the supreme law of the land; and implicit is the principle that the Tenth Amendment of 1791 made clear: "Powers not delegated to the United States by the Constitution, nor prohibited by it to the States, are reserved to the States respectively or to the people." The states are co-equally sovereign within the sphere of their reserved powers; in no sense are they subordinate corporations as the British insisted that the colonies must be. Both federal and state governments rest on the same broad bottom of popular sovereignty.

The balance that the Constitution created has been upset by time and circumstances, and other successful federal constitutions have been adopted — notably that of Canada. But the Constitution of 1787 is still unique in many respects; above all, in meeting the test of over 175 years. It is still imperfect, creaky in vital spots, as the segregation struggle has recently proved; but Ben Franklin's prophecy that, with all its faults, no better one could be obtained, has proved to be correct. The philosopher Alfred North Whitehead well said:

> The men who founded your republic had an uncommonly clear grasp of the general ideas that they wanted to put in here, then left the working out of the details to later interpreters, which has been, on the whole, remarkably successful. I know of only three times in the Western world when statesmen consciously took control of historic destinies: Periclean Athens, Rome under Augustus, and the founding of your American republic.[1]

4. The Ratification Contest

The Convention, anticipating that the influence of many state politicians would be Antifederalist, provided for ratification of the Constitution by popularly elected conventions in each state. Suspecting that Rhode Island, at least, would prove recalcitrant, it declared that the Constitution would go into effect as soon as nine states ratified. The convention method had the further advantage that judges, ministers, and others ineligible to state legislatures, could be elected to a convention. The nine-state provision was, of course, mildly revolutionary. But the Congress of the Confederation, still sitting in New York to carry on federal government until relieved, formally submitted the new constitution to the states and politely faded out before the first presidential inauguration.

In the contest for ratification the Federalists (as the supporters of the new government called themselves) had the assets of youth, intelligence, something positive to offer, and the support of Washington and Franklin. Everyone knew that the General favored the Constitution, and the Philosopher promptly made it clear that he did too. This was unexpected, since Franklin believed in unicameral constitutions like that of Pennsylvania. But on the last day of the Convention he made his famous harmony speech, saying,

1. Lucien Price, ed., *The Dialogues of Alfred North Whitehead* (Reprinted by permission of Atlantic-Little, Brown & Co., 1954), p. 203.

"The older I grow, the more apt I am to doubt my own judgment." Not only was he astonished that a constitution the result of so many compromises could be as good as this one but, he predicted, "It will astonish our enemies, who are waiting with confidence to hear that our councils are confounded. . . . Thus I consent, Sir, to this Constitution *because I expect no better, and because I am not sure that it is not the best.*" He hoped that every member who disliked the Constitution would do the same, and keep his mouth shut.

Nevertheless, only thirty-nine of the fifty-five delegates signed the Constitution. A few non-signers, such as Martin, Yates, and Lansing, were completely opposed to it. Mason, Randolph, and Gerry abstained largely from wounded vanity, since their pet projects were not adopted. All delegates who opposed, except Randolph, who saw the light, worked hard against the Constitution. This Federalist-Antifederalist contest was largely personal; it was not a class, a sectional, or an economic cleavage. Some of the wealthiest men in the country were Antis. George Mason, who looked down his nose on Washington as an "upstart surveyor," and James Winthrop, scion of New England's most aristocratic family, wrote pamphlets against the Constitution. Delegates to the Virginia ratifying convention from the old tidewater region were mostly Antifederalist; those from the recently settled valley, Federalist. And so it went, all over the country. The only generalization that can stand the test of fact is that the cleavage was one of age against youth. Old political war horses such as Gadsden and Willie Jones of the Carolinas, Henry and the Lees of Virginia, Martin of Maryland, George Bryan of Pennsylvania, George Clinton of New York, and (for a time) Samuel Adams and John Hancock of Massachusetts, were Antifederalist; but the warmest advocates of the Constitution were eager young men such as Madison, Morris, and McHenry, all within a year of thirty-five, Rufus King and Hamilton who were thirty-two, and Charles Pinckney who was twenty-nine.

Antifederalists appealed to Tom Paine's sentiment, "That government is best which governs least." They viewed with alarm the omission of annual elections and rotation in office. And there is little doubt that the Antifederalists would have won a Gallup poll. Elderly radicals such as General James Warren and his gifted wife Mercy, who believed that the states were the true guardians of "Republican Virtue," predicted that the new Constitution would encourage vice and speculation, and that under it America would soon go the way of imperial Rome. This prediction is repeated every four years.

The Federalists were the realists. They had learned from experience that the natural rights philosophy, taken straight, would go to the nation's head and make it totter, or fall. Had not half the commonwealth of Massachusetts gone on a terrific binge? Federalists believed that the slogans of 1776 were outmoded; that America needed more national power, that the immediate peril was not tyranny but dissolution, that certain political powers such as foreign affairs, war and commerce were national by nature, that the right to tax was essential to any government, and that powers wrested from king and parliament should not be divided among thirteen states.

Supporters of the Constitution promptly opened a campaign of education through pamphlets and newspaper articles. Most famous and effective were the essays that appeared in a New York newspaper, written by Madison, Hamilton, and John Jay over the common signature "Publius," later repub- lished under the title *The Federalist.* Numerous editions of this collection have been published in many languages, and it has been a mine of arguments as to the nature of the Constitution and what the founding fathers thought of it. Important as these essays were, the knowledge that Washington and Franklin were in favor of the new Constitution probably did more to affect public opinion than all the pamphlets and oratory.

Even so, the struggle for ratification was tough. Only in a few small states was there no contest, since their leaders knew that with an equal vote in the Senate and two extra votes for presidential electors they were getting more than their share of power. Delaware ratified unanimously in December 1787. Pennsylvania, second state in population, was second to ratify since the Fed- eralist policy there was to rush things through before the Antis could organize. Next came Massachusetts, where the situation was critical; since a rebellion had just been suppressed. Shortly after the ratifying convention met on 9 January 1788, a straw vote polled 192 members against the Constitution and 144 in favor. John Hancock, elected president of the convention, refused to take his seat, pleading "indisposition" until the three leading Federalists promised to support him for Vice President if the Constitution were ratified — a promise that they never fulfilled. Samuel Adams, so far Anti, was reached through a backfire kindled by the Federalists among his old cronies, the shipwrights of Boston. After leading merchants had promised to build new ships when and if the Constitution was ratified, these and other artisans passed strong Federalist resolutions, and Sam listened to *vox pop.*

The most important strategy by the Bay State Federalists was to propose a bill of rights to supplement the Constitution. This had not been provided by the Federal Convention, partly because the Constitution set forth limited and specific powers for which no bill of rights was logically necessary; but mostly because members were worn out and wanted to go home when they got around to the subject. Lack of a bill of rights, however, was a strong Antifederalist talking point. So the Massachusetts Federalists agreed to support a set of amendments, to be recommended to the states, and Hancock presented these as a bill of rights. That settled it; the Massachusetts convention ratified on 6 February 1788, 187 for to 168 against.

The Maryland convention, also proposing a bill of rights, ratified on 28 April by an emphatic vote; partly, it seems, because the members grew weary of listening to Luther Martin's three-hour Antifederalist speeches. South Carolina came next. Charles Pinckney made strong arguments in favor of union, which he lived long enough to repudiate; and on 23 May his state ratified the Constitution by a strong majority. New Hampshire had the honor of being the ninth state, whose ratification put the Constitution into force.

But four states, with about 40 per cent of the population, were still undecided. In Virginia, the most important, there took place a bitterly contested struggle. On the Federalist side were Washington, Madison, Colonel Henry Lee, John Marshall, and Edmund Randolph, who had been converted. Antifederalists leaders were Mason, Richard Henry Lee, and Patrick Henry, who disliked the entire Constitution. It was too consolidated. It "squints toward monarchy." The President will "make one push for the American throne." Congress, with power of taxation will "clutch the purse with one hand and wave the sword with the other." The time-honored system of requisitions would be abolished. "Never will I give up that darling word requisitions!" These withering blasts of oratory were patiently met with unanswerable logic by Madison and Edmund Pendleton, and the objections were disposed of, point by point. John Marshall, thirty-two years old in 1788, defended the federal judiciary which he was later to adorn. Someone brought in a "red herring" proposal to ratify on condition that a bill of rights be adopted; it was voted down, and the convention ratified unconditionally on 23 June by the close vote of 89 to 79.

Immediately before this vote was taken, Patrick Henry, seeing that his cause was lost, set a fine example of the good loser: "I will be a peaceable citizen. My head, and my heart, shall be at liberty to retrieve the loss of liberty, and remove the defects of the system in a constitutional way." Antifederalist leaders without exception followed his example. There was no attempt to sabotage the new government, or to set up a "Confederation in Exile" in Providence or Quebec.

Three states were still outside. In New York, as Washington remarked, there was "more wickedness than ignorance" in Antifederalism. Governor Clinton opposed the Constitution, as did most of the big landowners, who feared heavier taxation if the state lost her right to levy customs duties. John Jay and Hamilton led the Federalist forces in the state convention with great skill, and the convention ratified by a vote of 30 to 27. Willie Jones, who dominated the North Carolina convention, prevented a vote at the first session, but it met again in November 1789 and decided to go along. Rhode Island, still controlled by the debtor element, called no convention until 1790, and then came in.

Congress Confederation declared the new Constitution duly ratified, arranged for the first presidential and congressional elections, and appointed 4 March 1789 for the first presidential term to begin. But this had to be postponed. The new House of Representatives, which had no quorum until 1 April, counted the electoral ballots on the 6th. It took another week for Washington to learn officially that he had been chosen. The old Congress selected New York as the first capital of the new government.

Thus ended happily the most active and tumultuous quarter-century in the entire history of the United States. It was a period of little social change, but of a violent war and a turnover from a dependent colonial status to that of an independent federal union. The Federal Constitution was the capital achievement of this creative period; a work of genius, since it set up what every earlier political scientist had thought impossible, a sovereign union of sovereign states. This reconciling of unity with diversity, this practical application of the federal principle, is undoubtedly the most original contribution of the United States to the history and technique of human liberty.

But, would the Constitution work? Nobody then knew the answer. This question was a major challenge to the age that was waiting before.

ODE ON SCIENCE

So Sci - ence spreads her light - ed ray O'er

lands which long in dark - ness lay; Fair

Free - dom, her at - ten - dant waits, To crown the young and

ris - ing States With lau - rels of im - mor - tal day! The

Brit - ish yoke, the Gal - lic chain, Was urg'd u - pon our

necks in vain; All pet - ty ty - rants we dis - dain, And

shout, "Long live A - mer - i - ca!"

Washington's First Administration

1789-1793

1. Organizing the Federal Government

WASHINGTON'S ADMINISTRATIONS were no less creative, and even more critical, than the six previous years. A proper organization of the new government could not be taken for granted. No federal or republican government had ever worked on so large a scale. The Dutch and Swiss Republics
were federal, but covered no more area than a single state of the American
Union; the unified Roman Republic was followed by an autocratic empire.
But our new federal show opened with fair weather and before expectant
spectators. Defeated Antifederalists were ready to "play ball," but they were
so prone to cry "Foul!" at any hit close to the constitutional base line as to
cramp the style of Federalist batters.

George Washington made so triumphant a progress from Mount Vernon
to New York that a lesser man might have thought himself a god. But the
President had no illusions about himself or the situation. He wrote to General
Knox that he faced "an ocean of difficulties, without that competency of
political skill, abilities, and inclinations which is necessary to manage the
helm." Prospects seemed bright on the morning of 30 April 1789 when Washington, a fine figure of a man, stepped out onto the balcony of Federal Hall
overlooking Wall Street and took the oath: "I do solemnly swear that I will
faithfully execute the office of President of the United States and will, to the
best of my ability, preserve, protect, and defend the Constitution of the United States." But "an ocean of difficulties" did lie ahead. The Federal Constitution was so flexible and open to such varied interpretation that the solution of those difficulties it had been created to overcome, depended more
upon precedents created, traditions begun, and policy followed during the
ensuing years, than upon the actual words of the document. Gouverneur
Morris wrote wisely when urging Washington to accept the presidency:
"No constitution is the same on paper and in life. The exercise of authority depends on personal character. Your cool, steady temper is *indispen-
sably necessary* to give firm and manly tone to the new government."

This new government had to create its own machinery. Every revolutionary
regime of Europe and Asia, and most of those in Africa, took over a corps of

officials, an administrative system, and a treasury; but the American Confederation left nothing but a dozen clerks with their pay in arrears, an empty treasury, and a burden of debt. The American army consisted of 672 officers and men; the navy had ceased to exist. No successful leader of a revolution has been so naked before the world as Washington was in 1789. There were no taxes or requisitions coming in, and no machinery for collecting taxes. The new Congress quickly imposed a customs tariff; but months elapsed before officials could be appointed to collect it, in a loose-jointed country 2000 miles long. Until a federal judiciary were set up, there would be no means of enforcing any federal law. The country itself was just beginning to experience the return of prosperity; but free capital was exceedingly scarce. Washington, reputed to be a man of great wealth, had to borrow $3000 to meet pressing debts and the expense of his removal to New York.

Fortunately, there were many saving elements. By 1790 a time of easy money had returned. Virginia and the Carolinas had recovered their prewar volume of exports. Crop failures in Europe profited the grain growers of the Middle states. The West Indies trade, mainstay of New England, was now almost normal, and new markets had been opened in China, India, and Russia. All this had been effected by individual enterprise before the new government came into operation; but the Federalists were quick to claim credit for the tide on which their ship was launched.

The federal government could count on good newspaper support, but also hostility; journals which had opposed ratification soon began sniping at Washington's administration, and later became out-and-out opponents. Antifederalists continued to regard the federal government with deep suspicion, despite Washington's essential simplicity and his appearing at his inauguration in brown homespun instead of English broadcloth or a military uniform. The excessive adulation poured on him by *The Gazette of the United States*, and his custom of driving about New York in a coach and six, like royal George, were regarded by some as very sinister. So were the fortnightly "levees" and more select "drawing rooms" by which the new President and his lady tried to solve one of the social problems that has bedeviled their successors. Aping the British court, hissed the Antifederalists! Everything that the Washingtons said was repeated; everything they did was watched. No subsequent President of the United States has lived in such a glare of publicity.

In describing himself as one who had inherited "inferior endowments from nature," Washington was too modest; but his superiority lay in character, not talents. He had the power of inspiring respect, but no gift of popularity. He was direct, not adroit; stubborn rather than flexible; slow to reach a decision rather than a man of quick perception. The mask of dignity and reserve that concealed his inner life came from humility, and stern self-control. A warm heart was revealed by innumerable kindly acts to his dependents and subordinates. Some men, especially unreconstructed Antifederalists such as Senator Maclay of Pennsylvania, found him dull and stiff; but the ladies never did. He talked with them charmingly and danced with gusto. Fifty years later there were dowagers in every town from Portsmouth to Savannah who cherished memories of presidential persiflage when he danced with them as young girls, on his tours of North and South.

In his inaugural address Washington hinted that Congress should promptly add a bill of rights to the Constitution, in order to appease the Antifederalists. Madison took the lead in the movement, and Jefferson wrote to him prophetically from Paris that the best argument for it was "the legal check which it puts into the hands of the judiciary." After much discussion in both houses, and a going-over by a committee composed of Madison, Ellsworth, Carroll, and Paterson, Congress approved twelve amendments on 25 September and submitted them to the states.

Although several leading Antifederalists continued to scream for a new Federal Convention and sneered at the bill of rights (William Grayson said they were "good for nothing," and Henry wanted an amendment hamstringing the taxing power), there is no doubt that they converted most of those who still opposed the Constitution. Virginia was only the eleventh among the states to ratify the bill of rights, on 15 December 1791; but eleven were sufficient to put Amendments I through X into effect.[1] But Massachusetts, whose convention had started this whole movement, never did ratify until the 150th anniversary of the bill of rights, when someone discovered the omission!

Virginian aristocrat that he was, in the proper sense of the word, Washington was more nationalist and less provincial than any other American of his generation. His army experience had given him intimate knowledge of men from all parts of the country and the ability to size them up, and get along with them. Like some of his ablest successors, he wisely used the qualities of able men while ignoring their faults. Thus, he could put up with Hamilton's insolence and Jefferson's indirectness, because he needed their virtues and capacities to help run the government.

Heads of departments had to be appointed by the President with the consent of the Senate, but Congress, in organizing executive departments, might have made their heads responsible to and removable by itself. Instead, it made the secretaries of state and of war responsible to the President alone, and subject to his direction within their legal competence. Moreover, when the first question of dismissal from office came up, the Senate admitted that the President could remove officials without its consent. The effect of this precedent was to make the entire administrative force and foreign service responsible to the chief executive, as he, by his independent tenure, was responsible to the people.

For heads of the three departments, there was no large field of choice, as

1. Two amendments submitted to the States but never ratified determined the size of the House of Representatives, and forbade congressmen and senators from raising their own salaries. Connecticut and Georgia also delayed ratification until 1941.

the Confederation had given small scope for civil administration. For secretary of state someone with diplomatic experience was needed. Franklin was too old and feeble, John Adams had been elected Vice President, and John Jay had made enemies by negotiating an unfortunate treaty with Spain. So Washington's choice fell on Thomas Jefferson, who as minister to France had shown himself to be an excellent diplomat. Robert Morris declined the treasury department but suggested Alexander Hamilton, which fell in perfectly with Washington's inclinations. General Knox, Washington's reliable chief of artillery, continued as secretary of war, which he had been for the Confederation; Edmund Randolph, whose term as governor of Virginia had expired, was appointed attorney general.

The making of minor appointments turned out to be, as Washington feared, the "most difficult and delicate part of his duty." He wished to reward war service, but to avoid any suspicion of personal or sectional partiality. He appointed no prominent Antifederalists — since there were plenty of deserving Federalists available — and rather conspicuously refused office to Benjamin Franklin's progeny, who were somewhat disreputable. He scrutinized applications carefully, asked the advice of senators and representatives from the applicant's state, and sought out able men when none applied. The federal civil service began under principles of efficiency and honesty that were in sharp contrast to the jobbery and corruption in contemporary European governments, and even in some of the state governments.

A Vice President was created by the Federal Constitution in order to provide an acting chief magistrate in the event of the death or disability of the President, without the need of a special election. In order to give him something to do, he was made president of the Senate, with a casting vote in case of tie. John Adams, the first Vice President, received only 34 out of the 69 second votes of the presidential electors, the others going to a variety of favorite sons. It was generally felt that if the President were a Virginian the Vice President should be a New Englander; and John unquestionably was the most eminent New Englander for character, ability, and experience. His one fault was vanity. Unfortunately, during his residence in the Dutch Republic where every top government official was addressed as "His Highmightiness," Adams acquired the notion that no republic could be "respectable" without titles. Senator Maclay was shocked at Adams's referring to the President's inaugural address as "His Most Gracious Speech," and reminded the Senate that the removal of royal trappings was an object of the Revolution. The Vice President "expressed the greatest surprise that anything should be objected to on account of its being taken from the practice of that government under which we had lived so long and happily formerly; that he was for a dignified and respectable government"; but the phrase was struck out. Later a committee of the Senate reported that the President should be addressed as "His Highness the President of the United States of America and the Protector of the Rights of the Same." The House refused to agree; and Washington and his successors have remained plain "Mr. President."

Although this first Senate was friendly to the administration (about half the senators had been delegates to the Federal Convention), it early developed that club spirit which has been the bane of willful Presidents. "Senatorial courtesy," the practice of rejecting any nomination not approved by the senators from the nominee's own state, soon began. In the matter of treaties, however, the Senate's sense of its own dignity defeated its ambition. The Constitution grants the President power, "by and with the advice and consent of the Senate, to make treaties, provided two-thirds of the senators present concur." On one memorable occasion Washington appeared before the Senate with Secretary Knox to explain a negotiation pending with the Creek Indians. Hampered in freedom of debate by the august presence, the Senate voted to refer the papers in question to a select committee. The President declared, "This defeats every purpose of my coming here," and stalked out, irritated. On two other occasions Washington sent a message requesting senatorial advice on a current negotiation, but in later and more important matters he dispensed with advice until a treaty was ready for ratification. This practice has been followed by his successors.

"Impressed with a conviction that the due administration of justice is the firmest pillar of good government," wrote Washington in 1789, "I have considered the first arrangement of the judicial department as essential to the happiness of our country and the stability of its political system." The Constitution left this branch more vague than the other two. It defined the scope of federal judicial power, settled the mode of appointing judges, and fixed their tenure during good behavior. But Congress had to create and organize the federal courts, determine their procedure, and provide a bridge between state and federal jurisdiction.

All this was done by the Judiciary Act of 24 September 1789, the better part of which is still in force today. It provided for a Supreme Court consisting of a Chief Justice and five associates, for thirteen district courts, and three circuit courts. The problem of getting cases that involved jurisdictional disputes out of state courts and into federal courts, in order that the Constitution, laws, and treaties of the United States might indeed be "the supreme law of the land," was solved in the twenty-fifth section of this Act. A final judgment in the highest court of a state, in any case involving a conflict between federal and state power, may be re-examined in the Supreme Court of the United States upon a writ of error. This section is as essential to the peaceful working of the federal system as the Constitution itself. Without it, every state judiciary could put its own construction on the Constitution, laws, and treaties of the Union.

John Jay having been appointed Chief Justice, the Supreme Court opened its first session at New York on 2 February 1790. The judges wore gowns of black and scarlet, but honored Jefferson's appeal to "discard the monstrous wig which makes the English judges look like rats peeping though bunches of oakum." Under Chief Justice Jay the federal judiciary assumed its place as the keystone to the federal arch. As early as 1791, in a case involving British debts, one of the circuit courts declared invalid a law of Connecticut which infringed Article VI of the treaty of peace. In 1792 a state law of Rhode Island was held unconstitutional, as impairing the obligation of contracts. The same year another circuit court refused to execute an act of Congress that required the federal courts to pass on veterans' pension claims on the ground that this was a non-judicial function, beyond the constitutional power of Congress to impose, or of the court to assert. Thus was asserted the power of judicial review over both state and federal laws. Later, and even in our time, judicial review has been vehemently attacked behind the cover of state rights and democracy; but in the early years of the Republic it went almost unchallenged.

Washington was unwilling to make any vital decision without taking the advice of people in whom he had confidence; hence the extra-constitutional cabinet. There had been talk in the Federal Convention of providing the President with a "council of state," but it went no further. Shortly after the Convention adjourned, Charles Pinckney wrote that the President was expected to call upon such heads of departments as Congress might create, for informal consultation; and that is what he did. The secretaries of state, war, and treasury, and the attorney general, began meeting at the President's house in 1791; two years later they met almost weekly. These officials were already known collectively as the President's cabinet; but not until 1907 was the cabinet officially recognized as such by law.

The American cabinet, unlike the British, has no connection with the legislature, and this lack of co-ordination between executive and legislature is one of the distinctive features of American federal government. It came as a reaction against George III's very intimate relations with the House of Commons. The Constitution guarded against executive control through "placemen" by disqualifying federal officials, whether civil or military, for membership in Congress, and by forbidding the appointment of members, during the term of their election, to an office created, or increased in profit, during that term. There was nothing, however, to prevent a cabinet official's appearing in person before either house. And the important section requiring the President to recommend measures to Congress, and to keep them informed as to "the state of the Union," reflected a desire that the executive should take the lead in legislation.

Washington had not the temperament to do this alone. He wanted a young and energetic man to give the impulse, and attend to his relations with the Congress. Fortunately, the right man, Alexander Hamilton, was appointed to the right office, the treasury. For the primary problems of Washington's first administration were fiscal.

2. Alexander Hamilton

If the character of Washington fortified the new government, the genius of his secretary of the treasury enabled it to function successfully. Alexander Hamilton was thirty-four years old in 1789 when Washington appointed him to the post.[1] As a student at King's College, he had brilliantly defended the rights of the colonies. At twenty-two he had earned a place on Washington's staff. At twenty-six he had published articles showing the defects of the Confederation, written a remarkable treatise on public finance, and as colonel of light infantry led the assault on a British redoubt at Yorktown. Admitted to the New York bar at the conclusion of peace, he quickly rose to eminence in the law. His contributions to *The Federalist* helped to obtain the ratification of a constitution in which he did not strongly believe. One of the greatest of Americans, he was the least American of his generation: a statesman rather of the type of the younger Pitt, whose innate love of order and system was strengthened by the lack of those qualities among his fellow citizens. Self-disciplined, Hamilton was eager to discipline his countrymen. He had a keen and quick perception of means, and a steady eye on remote ends. He produced bold plans and definite policies where others had cautious notions and vague principles. When Congress was thinking of what the people would say, Hamilton told it and the people what they ought to do. He had untiring energy, and accepted responsibility with gusto.

The treasury department was the creation of Congress, not of the Constitution; and the Organic Act of 1789, still in force, gave it so many duties as to make it the most important and powerful federal department for many years. The secretary had the duty "to digest and prepare plans for the improvement and management of the revenue and for the support of the public credit," as well as estimate of the same, "to receive, keep, and disburse the monies of the United States," to collect customs duties and excise taxes, to run the lighthouse service, set up aids to navigation, and start a land survey of the United States. Until 1792, when the post-office department was established by Congress, the treasury ran the mails. Other duties, such as providing medical care for seamen, were added by Congress from time to time, until, by the turn of the century, the treasury included over half the total federal civil service. This was little enough in comparison with the present horde of civil officials, although compared by jealous Jeffersonians to the "swarms of officers" sent by George III "to harass our people and eat up their substance."[2]

1. Recent research has established that Hamilton was born in Nevis, 11 January 1755, not 1757 as had earlier been assumed.
2. The treasury department, according to L. D. White, *The Federalists* (1948), in 1801 had 78 employees in the central offices, 1615 in the field services. The post-office department was run by the postmaster general and seven clerks, and the local postmasters numbered about 900.

Hamilton's financial policy was determined by his conception of the governmental problem in 1789; and that, in turn, by his political philosophy. As he remarked in the Federal Convention, "All communities divide themselves into the few and the many. The first are the rich and well-born; the other the mass of the people . . . turbulent and changing, they seldom judge or determine right. Give therefore to the first class a distinct, permanent share in the Government." The Federal Constitution, leaving too many powers to the states, could only be made an instrument for good by "increasing the number of ligaments between the government and interests of individuals." The old families, merchant-shipowners, public creditors, and financiers must be made a loyal governing class by a straightforward policy favoring their interest. That was the object of Hamilton's domestic and foreign policy. His conscious purpose was to use that class to strengthen the federal government. He would clothe the Constitution with the sword of sovereignty and the armor of loyalty by giving the people who then controlled America's wealth a distinct interest in its permanence. The rest, he assumed, would go along, as they always had.

The House of Representatives called upon Hamilton, ten days after he took office, to prepare and report a plan for the "adequate support of public credit." The report was laid before the House at its next session, on 14 January 1790. Based on the tried expedients of English finance, it was worthy of an experienced minister of a long-established government.

Hamilton first laid down principles of public economy and then adduced arguments in support of them. America must have credit for government, industrial development, and commercial activity. Her future credit would depend on how she met her present obligations. The United States debt, foreign and domestic, "was the price of liberty. The faith of America has been repeatedly pledged for it . . . Among ourselves, the most enlightened friends of good government are those whose expectations [of prompt payment] are the highest. To justify and preserve their confidence; to promote the increasing respectability of the American name; to answer the calls of justice; to restore landed property to its due value; to furnish new resources, both to agriculture and commerce; to cement more closely the Union of the States; to add to their security against foreign attack; to establish public order on the basis of an upright and liberal policy; these are the great and invaluable ends to be secured by a proper and adequate provision, at the present period, for the support of public credit."

Next, Hamilton made precise recommendations of ways and means. The foreign debt and floating domestic debt, with arrears of interest, should be funded [1] at par, and due provision should be made by import duties and excise taxes to pay the interest and gradually repay the principal. The war

1. To fund, in government finance, means to pay off one debt by creating another; in this instance to issue 6 per cent bonds in exchange for various securities and certificates of indebtedness which had survived the war.

Algonkin Queen and Child, by John White, *c.* 1588

Conjectural model of the *Santa Maria*, by R. C. Anderson

The Virginia fleet of 1607: *Godspeed, Discovery, Susan Constant*

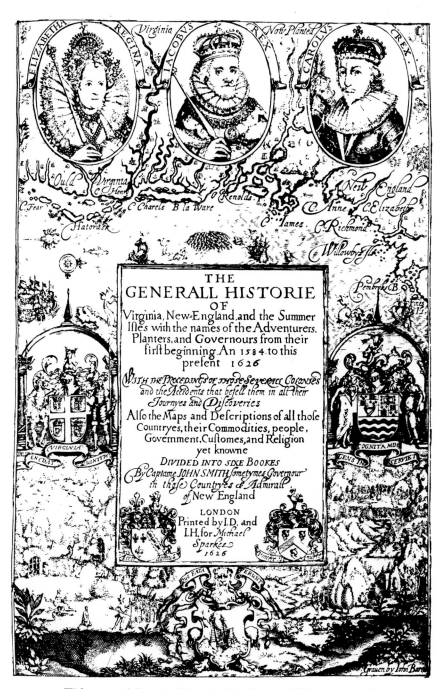

Title page of Captain John Smith's *Generall Historie* (1626)

Cecilius Calvert, 2nd Baron Baltimore,
with his grandson Cecil and a Negro attendant. By Gerard Soest, 1670

One of the four Mohawk chiefs who called on Queen Anne, 1710.
Contemporary mezzotint by I. Verelst

Paul Revere Liberty bowl, 1769

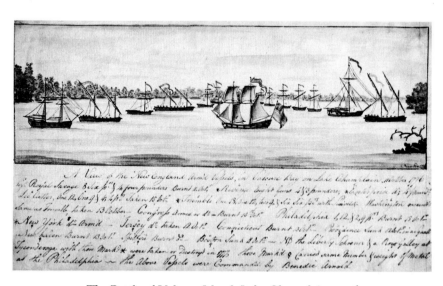

The Battle of Valcour Island, Lake Champlain, 1776.
Drawing by C. Randle, 1776

THOMAS JEFFERSON, by Houdon, *c.* 1785

JOHN ADAMS, by Mather Brown, 1785

General George Washington at the Battle of Princeton, by Charles Willson Peale

The battle is raging in the background. Nassau Hall is visible.
General Mercer, mortally wounded, lies at Washington's feet.

"The Tory Editor and his Apes"
Caricature by William Charles, 1808, illustrating American
sailors as dressed in 1812 period.

President Washington reviewing the Western Army at Fort Cumberland, 1795,
by Frederick Kemmelmeyer

Riding behind him are Generals Morgan and Henry Lee, and Colonel Alexander Hamilton.

"AMERICA GUIDED BY WISDOM"
Allegorical print by B. Tanner, published in England about 1800

Minerva points to the shield, upheld by the Genius of America.
At her feet is a Horn of Plenty, symbolizing Prosperity. General
Washington's statue is placed in front of the triumphal arch, "indicating the progress of the liberal arts." At the left, Mercury, representing Commerce, stands on "bales of American Manufactures,"
and points to the ships as a lesson in "the advantage of encouraging
and protecting Navigation," for the benefit of Ceres, who holds
wheat sheaves. Behind her is a beehive, symbolizing Industry, a
plow, flail, and harrow for Husbandry, and a "female spinning," to
indicate another useful occupation.

PRESIDENT ANDREW JACKSON in 1829, by Thomas Sully

ANTI-JACKSON TOKENS AND TEMPORARY MONEY, 1832-37

Obverse and reverse of a pro-Bank token

Obverse: Jackson removing the deposits; *reverse:* first appearance of the Democratic donkey. The "LL.D." alludes to Jackson's being granted that degree by Harvard.

One cent tokens. The building is the Merchants' Exchange in New York.

Traveling by Coach, *c.* 1836, by George Tattershall

Waiting for the Stage, by Richard Catton Woodville

Flying Cloud

Two American Clipper Ships

Young America

Blue Sulphur Springs, Greenbrier, Virginia.
From a lithograph by Ritchie and Dunnavant of Richmond, 1859.

Penn Steam Marble Mantel Factory, Philadelphia, *c.* 1859

debts of the states should be assumed by the federal government in order to bind state creditors to the national interest. A sinking fund should be created in order to stabilize the price of government securities by buying them in whenever they fell much below par. The want of banking facilities should be filled by a Bank of the United States, on the model of the Bank of England, but with the right to establish branches in different parts of the country.

This daring policy could not have been carried out by Hamilton alone. Every proposal was matured by the cool judgment of the President; and in both House and Senate he found eager co-operation. Congress had already passed a customs tariff, with tonnage duties discriminating in favor of American shipping — essential parts of Hamilton's system. The foreign and domestic debt was funded at par; the former was entirely paid off by the end of 1795, the latter, despite another war, in 1835. Most of the states' debts were assumed by Congress after a bitter struggle not unmixed with intrigue. The Bank of the United States was chartered, and its capital subscribed within four hours after the books were open. By August 1791 United States 6 per cents were selling above par in London and Amsterdam, and a wave of development and speculation had begun.

At the end of 1791, Hamilton presented to Congress a Report on Manufactures. Alone of his state papers, this report fell flat; yet it became an arsenal of protectionist arguments on both sides of the Atlantic. He wished the government to protect infant industries in order to increase national wealth, induce artisans to immigrate, cause machinery to be invented, and employ women and children. Hamilton's aim here, as with his funding system, was "to increase the number of ligaments between the government and the interest of individuals." He perceived that merchants and public creditors were too narrow a basis for a national governing class. He believed that manufactures might prosper in the South as well as in the North. The report was a distinct bid for Southern support over the heads of Jefferson and Madison. The South, however, regarded protection as another tax for Northern interests. Hamilton's argument would have been sound, had not Eli Whitney's invention of the cotton gin, the following year, made the culture of upland cotton a far more profitable employment for slave labor than manufactures.

Nobody in fact showed any enthusiasm for protection, because the Northern merchant-shipowners had a stake in free trade, and Congress took no action on the Report. Twenty-five years later it was resurrected by the new manufacturing interest built up during the War of 1812, and never since have Hamilton's arguments been allowed to grow cold. They were imported into Germany by Friedrich List, into England by Joseph Chamberlain. Hamilton, far ahead of his time, grasped the nineteenth-century compromise between paternalism and laissez faire: protection to property interests valuable to the state; free competition for labor.

Hamilton's other plans were adopted. He turned dead paper into marketable securities, and provided for their redemption by taxes that the nation was well able to bear. He set standards of honesty and punctuality that were invaluable for a people with somewhat loose financial conceptions. His youthful country, so lately on the verge of bankruptcy, acquired a credit such as few nations of Europe enjoyed. Yet Hamilton failed to achieve his ultimate end of consolidating the Union. His measures, sound though they were, stimulated a dangerous opposition.

To understand wherein Hamilton failed, we have only to glance at the effect of his measures on two states: Massachusetts and Virginia. Massachusetts was the second state of the Union in population. Her premier interests were maritime; her fishing villages benefited by new bounties on dried codfish; her foreign trade and shipyards by the low tariff and the discriminating tonnage duties. Good business men themselves, the merchants knew the value of sound credit and honest finance. Their wartime gains were partly invested in government paper, worthless but for the funding system. Maritime prosperity, percolating from the coastal towns to the interior, raised the price of country produce and healed the wounds of Shays's Rebellion. Washington's foreign policy completed the process; and Boston, once the home of radical mobs, became safe for the new Federalist party. The "junto" of leaders from Essex County — Cabots, Higginsons, Lowells, and Jacksons — who had been to sea in their youth and viewed politics as from a quarterdeck, hailed Hamilton as their master. With them, in general, were the solid men of Rhode Island and Connecticut, of New York City and the seaports southward. Charleston, South Carolina, until 1800 was as solidly Federalist as Boston.

But the great mass of the American people was untouched, either in imagination or in pocket, by Hamilton's policy. It would have been otherwise had the public debt remained in the hands of its original possessors. But farmers, discharged soldiers, small shopkeepers, and the like who held government securities representing services rendered, goods supplied or money advanced during the war, had been forced to part with them at a ruinous discount during the hard times that followed. By 1789 the bulk of the public debt was in the hands of the "right people" at Philadelphia, New York, Charleston, and Boston; and the nation was taxed to pay off at par, securities which they had purchased at a few cents on the dollar.[1]

By the same economic test, a system that appeared sound and statesmanlike in Massachusetts seemed unwarranted and unconstitutional in Virginia. The Old Dominion was the most populous state in the Union, and easily the proudest. Although well provided with a long sea frontage, Virginia owned few seagoing ships; Yankees and foreigners carried her wheat and tobacco to market. Virginia planters knew little of business, and less of finance. A gentle-

1. In 1795 the federal government disbursed $309,500 in interest to citizens of Massachusetts as against $62,300 to natives of Virginia; $367,000 to New York, as against $6800 to Georgia.

man inherited his debts with his plantation, and not infrequently bequeathed them to his eldest son; why then should debt trouble the United States? Why not pay it off at market value, as a gentleman compounds with his creditors? Most Virginians had sold their government I.O.U.s at a loss; why should they be taxed to pay off the New York purchaser at par? Virginia had wiped off the larger part of her state debt; why should she be taxed to assume the debts of other states? Toward Hamilton's Bank of the United States, the opposition of the Virginia planters was as natural and spontaneous as that of the English Tories, a century before, toward the Bank of England; they felt that it was a scheme to make monied men richer and depress the landed interest. The confusing paraphernalia of Hamilton's system seemed to portend colossal taxation as in England, jobbery and corruption as in England; perhaps monarchy as in England.

Patrick Henry drafted a remonstrance against the federal assumption of state debts which the Virginia assembly adopted. Therein, on 23 December 1790, were expressed the misgivings of plain folk throughout the country, as well as those of the Virginia gentry:

In an agricultural country like this . . . to erect, and concentrate, and perpetuate a large monied interest, is a measure which your memorialists apprehend must in the course of human events produce one or other of two evils, the prostration of agriculture at the feet of commerce, or a change in the present form of federal government, fatal to the existence of American liberty . . . Your memorialists can find no clause in the constitution authorizing Congress to assume the debts of the States.

A vision of future civil war flashed across Hamilton's mind as he read this remonstrance. "This is the first symptom," he wrote, "of a spirit which must either be killed, or will kill the Constitution of the United States."

Hamilton was making new enemies for the administration. The Federalists of 1790 were no longer the Federalists of 1788. But Virginia could hardly form an opposition party without aid from some of her citizens highly placed in the federal government. Washington, national in his outlook, and convinced that Hamilton's policy was honest and right, signed every bill based on his recommendations. Richard Henry Lee, elected to the Senate as an Antifederalist, became a convert to Hamilton's views. Thomas Jefferson, secretary of state, and James Madison, leader of the House of Representatives, wavered — but found the Virginia candle stronger than the Hamiltonian star.

The breach between Jefferson and Hamilton was not personal. The Republican and Federalist parties that they helped to found were not mere projections of rival personalities; only in a limited sense were they a division between democracy and aristocracy, or between radicalism and conservatism. They were the political expressions of a deep-lying antagonism between two great sectional interests — the planting-slaveholding interest which was mainly rural-Southern, and the mercantile-shipping-financial interest of seaport cities from Salem to Charleston. These interests, a century older than Washington's administration, found in the federal government a stake worth fighting for; and in Hamilton and Jefferson they found natural leaders. American political history until 1865 is largely the story of these rival interests, capitalist and agrarian, Northern and Southern, contending for the control of the federal government — using government to help themselves and starve their rivals, undermining each other's vote, interfering with each other's laboring force, bidding for Western support, gambling with petty wars, and finally staking everything on civil war. Principle also divided the parties, particularly in their infancy; but principles were both changed and exchanged, whilst Massachusetts and Virginia remained the intellectual foci after they ceased to be the economic nuclei of the two systems.

3. Thomas Jefferson and the Opposition

When Thomas Jefferson returned to Virginia in November 1789, he was surprised to learn of his nomination to the department of state; only Washington's urgency persuaded him to accept. He had no intention of founding a political party. "If I could not go to heaven but with a party, I would not go there at all," he wrote that very year. But, beneath his bland exterior Jefferson was ambitious for the highest office, and the presidency (if not heaven) could be attained only through a party, which he was the first to lead.

Jefferson, twelve years older than Hamilton, had had much more experience. As the author of the Declaration of Independence and *Notes on Virginia*, he was famous in both continents. As United States minister to France he had become a consulting attorney on revolution. Science, literature, and the fine arts interested Jefferson as much as they had Franklin; and he was the first American architect of his generation. His Virginia mansion "Monticello," superbly situated on a hilltop facing the Blue Ridge, was admirably designed and landscaped. "Bremo," the mansion that he built for a friend in Fluvanna County, is one of the most beautiful country houses in America; and for the University of Virginia he designed a beautiful and symmetrical group of buildings. Jefferson wrote upon Neo-Platonism, the pronunciation of Greek, the Anglo-Saxon language, the future of steam engines, archaeology; even on theology. In France he had assiduously promoted American business interests. But on one subject he was as ignorant as any Virginia planter, yet as self-confident as a French economist. That was Hamilton's specialty, finance.

Hamilton's political theories had more validity for the future America than for the simple country with whose common mind and condition Jefferson's ideas agreed. Yet if America has outgrown Jefferson's principles, she is still indebted to them for the ideals that she has preserved in an industrial society. Hamilton wished to concentrate power; Jefferson to diffuse power. Hamilton feared anarchy and thought in terms of order; Jefferson feared tyranny and thought in terms of liberty. Hamilton believed republican government could only succeed if directed by a governing elite; Jefferson that a republic must be based on an agrarian democracy. The people, according to Jefferson, were the safest and most virtuous, though not always the most wise, depository of power, and education would perfect their wisdom. Hamilton would diversify American economic life, encouraging shipping and creating manufactures by legislative enactment; Jefferson would have America remain a nation of farmers. All those differences in temper, theory, and policy were bracketed by two opposed conceptions of what America was and might be. Jefferson inherited the idealistic conception of the new world to which the French *philosophes* paid homage — a republic of mild laws and equal opportunity, asylum to the oppressed and beacon-light of freedom, renouncing wealth and power to preserve simplicity and equality. To Hamilton, this was sentimental nonsense. Having assimilated the traditions of the New York gentry into which he had married, Hamilton believed that the only choice for America lay between a stratified society on the English model and a squalid "mobocracy." Jefferson, who knew Europe, wished America to be as unlike it as possible; Hamilton, who had never left America, wished to make his country a new Europe.

Their appearances were as much of a contrast as their habits of mind. Hamilton's neat, lithe, dapper figure, and air of brisk energy, went with his tight, compact, disciplined brain. Yet Hamilton's written style was heavy; he could not have composed a state paper such as the Declaration of Independence. Jefferson's mind in comparison was somewhat untidy, constantly gathering new facts and making fresh syntheses. "His whole figure has a loose, shackling air," wrote friendly Senator Maclay in 1790. "I looked for gravity, but a laxity of manner seemed shed about him." His sandy hair, hazel eyes, and ill-fitting, much-worn clothes played up this impression of careless ease; whilst Hamilton radiated energy as well as charm. Women found him irresistible, but they did not care much for Jefferson; he wooed them or wrote to them in the stilted phrases of eighteenth-century literature.

Jefferson approved payment of the domestic and foreign debt at par, but not the assumption of the state debts. Nevertheless, he arranged with Hamilton a deal by which the capital was transferred from New York to Philadelphia in 1790 for ten years, pending removal to the new federal city of Washington on the Potomac.[1] Jefferson persuaded two Virginia congressmen to vote for assumption, and Hamilton rounded up Yankee votes for the Potomac capital. As late as November of 1790, Jefferson regarded the pending Virginia remonstrance against assumption as a mere afterclap of Antifederalism. But from the date of Hamilton's report recommending a national bank (13 December 1790), Jefferson's attitude toward him and his policies began to change. To George Mason, on 7 February 1791, he mentioned a "sect" high in office who believed the British constitution to be the goal of perfec-

1. Congress adjourned at New York 12 August 1790 and met next at Congress Hall, Philadelphia, on 6 December.

tion; and intimated that Congress was under the control of "stock-jobbers."

Madison, principal architect of the Federal Constitution, and fellow author with Hamilton of *The Federalist*, opposed the bank bill in the House on the ground that the chartering of such an institution transcended the powers of Congress. The President called for opinions on that point from his cabinet. Jefferson declared that the congressional power "to make all laws necessary and proper" for executing its delegated powers did not include laws merely convenient for such purposes. A national bank was not strictly necessary — the existing state bank at Philadelphia could be used for government funds. It was a clear case, he thought, for the presidential veto.

Hamilton replied with a nationalistic, "loose construction" interpretation of the Constitution:

Every power vested in a government is in its nature sovereign, and includes by force of the term, a right to employ all the means requisite . . . to the attainment of the ends of such power . . . If the end be clearly comprehended within any of the specified powers, and if the measure have an obvious relation to that end, and is not forbidden by any particular provision of the Constitution, it may safely be deemed to come within the compass of the national authority.

Congress, he pointed out, had already acted upon that theory in providing lighthouses, necessary and proper to the regulation of commerce. A bank has a similar relation to the specified powers of collecting taxes, paying salaries, and servicing the debt. This opinion satisfied the President. He signed the bank bill; but it was not until 1819 that Chief Justice Marshall's opinion in the case of *McCulloch* v. *Maryland* read the doctrine of implied powers into the Constitution.

Jefferson was neither silenced nor convinced. The Federal Constitution, from his point of view, now also Madison's, was being perverted into a consolidated, national government, building up through financial favors a corrupt control of Congress with an "ultimate object" of introducing monarchy. That belief remained a fixed tenet of Jefferson for the rest of his life. Completely innocent as Hamilton was of any such intention, he had laid himself open to suspicion. For Hamilton, although he knew that monarchy would never do for America, often expressed his admiration for it, and avowed his belief that corruption was a necessary engine of government. Complicated projects in federal finance he arrogantly refused to explain to those (Jefferson among others) who did not understand them.

The suspicions of plain people were deepened by the brisk speculation in lands, bank stock, and government funds that began in 1790. No sooner did Hamilton's financial reports appear than Northern speculators began combing the countryside for depreciated government paper which they anticipated would be redeemed at par. William Duer, Hamilton's first assistant secretary, and Henry Knox, secretary of war, floated the Scioto Company, a colossal speculation in Ohio lands. Duer and Macomb, an associate of Hamilton's father-in-law, formed a blind pool to speculate in government bonds; an operation which produced a financial flurry in New York and landed Duer in jail. Hamilton sincerely deprecated all this, and his own hands were clean — but some of the speculators were very close to him.

Political parties were in bad odor at the end of the eighteenth century. No provision for party government had been made in the Constitution. Washington hoped to get along without one, and when organized opposition began to appear, nobody knew what to do about it. Should Jefferson resign as secretary of state, leaving Hamilton in control of the cabinet? Was it proper for a minister to oppose policies that the President had accepted? Washington, believing that every month and year the government endured was so much gained for stability, endeavored to keep the smoldering fires from bursting forth, preaching charity to Jefferson and forbearance to Hamilton. He entreated both men to remain in office, and both consented. But Jefferson, believing Hamilton's policy to be dangerous, used every means short of open opposition to check it; whilst Hamilton, when Jefferson's management of foreign affairs appeared to be mischievous, spared no effort to thwart him, even going over his head to the British minister at Philadelphia.

The most important step toward forming a nation-wide opposition party was for Virginia malcontents to come to an understanding with Antifederalists and other discontented elements in the North. This was effected in the course of a summer visit by Jefferson and Madison to New York in 1791 — which they called "botanizing." New York politics were still largely determined by family connections and hunger for the sweets of office. One faction was led by Governor George Clinton, whose political lieutenant, Colonel Aaron Burr, had discovered the value of a city benevolent society called the "Sons of St. Tammany." But the old aristocratic faction, including the Schuylers into which Alexander Hamilton had married, having supported the Constitution in 1788, obtained all federal appointments in New York; no plums went to the Clintons. We may be certain that promises were made on both sides in the course of this "botanizing" tour. It was then that the visitors from Virginia persuaded Philip Freneau, Madison's Princeton classmate and the poet of the Revolution, to come to Philadelphia and start an opposition newspaper. The inducement was a job in Jefferson's department as "translating clerk" — although Freneau knew no foreign language but French, and not much of that.

This alliance set the pattern of the Jeffersonian Republican party and its successors. Until 1964 the "solid South," Tammany Hall, and other big-city political machines have been the principal supporters of the Democratic party.

4. Washington's Foreign Policy

Washington's foreign policy may be summed up in three words: peace, union, and justice. Peace, to give the country time to recover from the Revolutionary War, and to permit the slow work of national integration to continue.

But justice could not be done, nor the Federal Union maintained, without a vigorous foreign policy.

It was certain that Westerners would not long remain in the Union unless Washington could secure the navigation of the Mississippi; that the support of the trading classes would be lost if their commerce were not protected; that there would be a demand for war with Britain if the Northwest posts were not surrendered. The federal government had to satisfy all parts of the country that their essential interests were being promoted. To obtain these ends peaceably would require years of patient and skillful diplomacy. But Washington seemed to have absorbed in his person all the patience and serenity in America. War clouds were hanging over Europe, and if they broke it would be difficult to prevent their deluging the new world as well as the old.

Jefferson and Hamilton agreed with Washington's objects, but disagreed as to means. The polestar of Jefferson's policy was to cement commercial and diplomatic ties with France. And his love for France had been strengthened by the revolution, whose early and hopeful stages he had observed. Jefferson hated England, because English society, government, and manners were of a kind that he wished his country to avoid, and he believed it to be Hamilton's object to make the United States a transatlantic copy of the mother country.

Hamilton believed that the essential interest of Great Britain and the United States were complementary, not competitive. He never attempted to graft the British constitution onto the federal one, but believed that Americans had many political lessons to learn of their mother country. England, for him, had found the just balance between liberty and order. Her friendship would be wholesome for a young nation which needed above all things integration and stability. Hamilton, partly French in blood, liked individual Frenchmen, who in turn found him more *sympathique* than Jefferson; but on the French Revolution, Hamilton saw eye to eye with Edmund Burke, whose *Considerations* on that great upheaval are an arsenal of conservative arguments to this day. It was most disconcerting, just when there seemed some hope of America settling down, to have her favorite nation blow up and invite everyone else to follow her example.

Hamilton knew that Anglo-American commerce was valuable for England, but vital for America — and he knew that England knew it. Three-quarters of the foreign commerce of the United States was with Great Britain. Ninety per cent of American imports came from Britain, and Hamilton planned to finance his new fiscal system with customs duties, the only large source of revenue then open to the federal government. England could better afford to play the game of commercial retaliation than America; and retaliate she would if Congress began it. Commercial warfare, even if it did not lead to hot war, would destroy every calculation on which Hamilton's funding scheme was based; would "cut out credit by the roots." Without credit, Hamilton could see the federal government's becoming impotent as the Confederation, and the Federal Constitution discarded as another failure. Not on sentimental

Anglophilism, but on this keen perception of the essential facts in relation to his domestic policy, was Hamilton's foreign policy based.

At Hamilton's suggestion the first Tariff Act, of 1789, levied higher duties on foreign than an American vessels, but placed English and French vessels in the same class. The effect was threefold. The British government perceived that Washington's administration was friendly, and American shipping recovered more than its fair share of the Anglo-American carrying trade. France complained of being placed in the same category as Britain in spite of her repeated favors to America. The French minister to the United States advised his government to press for the recovery of Louisiana from Spain, to keep America in hand. Within three years the French Republic acted upon this pregnant suggestion, and in 1800 Bonaparte put it through.

Britain's retention of the seven Northwest posts was serious. In 1791, when Parliament set off Upper Canada (the future Ontario) from Quebec, the seat of the new provincial government was placed at Fort Niagara on the United States side of the border, suggesting that Canada intended to hold that place forever. Posts on the Great Lakes, especially Detroit, enabled Canadian fur traders to preserve influence over the Indians of the American Northwest Territory, with whom Congress on 1 June 1789 concluded the first of 371 formal treaties with Indian nations. It became the firm belief of American frontiersmen that British garrisons incited the Indians to harass the American frontier. That was untrue; but the British did supply the redskins with arms and ammunition for hunting "game," which could be and occasionally was human.

Washington and Congress were as deeply concerned over Indian as over European relations. In a number of presidential messages and congressional laws, certain basic principles for dealing with the Indians, inherited from the old colonial system, were laid down: (1) The Indians' lands should be guaranteed to them by solemn treaties, and land purchases therefrom prohibited, except by the federal government; (2) promotion of federally regulated and controlled Indian trade; (3) white people to be punished for abusing Indians, and they for attacking whites; (4) Indians living on their own lands not to be taxed or considered citizens of the United States, to govern themselves by tribal law but to be welcomed as citizens if they chose to settle among white people. As early as the treaty of 7 August 1790 with the Creek nation, the United States was to furnish "useful domestic animals and implements of husbandry," in the hope that they would become "herdsmen and cultivators instead of remaining hunters." Few of these high-minded principles, except the exemption from taxation, were enforced in practice, owing to the weakness of the federal government and the rapacity of frontiersmen; in them we may discern the ambiguity that has been characteristic of our Indian relations from the seventeenth century almost to this day. Protect their rights, yes; but pressure them into becoming good Christian farmers, just like us.

The President, it must be admitted, first broke his own principles by attempting, without Indian consent, to build a fort at the principal village of the Maumee, in order to counteract British influence. This task was entrusted to General Arthur St. Clair, governor of the Northwest Territory. At the head of some 2000 troops, including the entire regular army, St. Clair jumped off from Fort Washington at the site of Cincinnati in the fall of 1791. On 4 November, when only a few miles short of his destination (the site of Fort Wayne, Indiana) his force was surprised and routed by the Indians, and suffered over 900 casualties. Washington, who from his experience under Braddock had warned St. Clair to "beware of surprise," burst into one of his rare explosions of wrath when he heard the bad news. He did not attempt to gloss it over. Knowing (what some of his successors have forgotten) that it pays to be candid with the American people, the President communicated the devastating facts to Congress. The House established a precedent in ordering an inquiry; but, more honest than some twentieth-century investigating committees, did not try to pin the blame on anyone.

In comparison with the nearby Indian menace, Algerian pirates attracted little attention in Congress, but gave Washington's administration almost as much trouble. Seamen taken prisoner by Barbary corsairs, who had discovered that the Stars and Stripes carried no naval protection, were still languishing in the dungeons of Algiers or chained to the thwarts of the Dey's war galleys; and it was only under the protection of the Portuguese navy patrolling the Strait of Gibraltar, that American vessels were able to sail to and from Lisbon and Cadiz. Jefferson reported the facts to Congress, leaving it to choose "between war, tribute and ransom." The Senate piously resolved that a naval force was the answer, but did nothing to provide one; and the matter dragged along until 1792, when survivors of the American sailors captured seven years earlier sent Congress a petition threatening that if something were not done for them promptly they would be forced to abandon Christ and country and turn Moslem. This horrid prospect moved Congress to appropriate $54,000 for ransoming the captives at $2000 a head, and for a tribute treaty with Algiers. John Paul Jones, charged with carrying out this ignominious mission, died before he could undertake it. So the American prisoners stayed in jail or on board the galleys for several years more.

"Tranquillity has smoothed the surface," wrote a congressman after the Bill of Rights was adopted; but "faction glows within like a coalpit." Washington was eager to retire in 1793. Both Hamilton and Jefferson urged him to accept another term; the one because the President had constantly supported his measures, the other because he wanted more time to nurse an opposition party. Washington consented, reluctantly. Again he received the unanimous vote of the electoral college, and John Adams was re-elected Vice President, but by a reduced margin. First fruits of the Virginia-New York alliance were gathered when those two states and North Carolina threw their second electoral votes to George Clinton.

Americans have long argued and will continue to argue over the respective merits of Hamilton and Jefferson. The Republic was fortunate to have the services of both; for in a sense they were complementary. Hamilton, the man of action, grasping political and economic realities, promoted basic policies which enabled the new nation to attain unity and strength; and the best tribute to those principles is that when Jefferson became President, he accepted them as the basis of federal power. Jefferson's theories make a seductive appeal to all democrats and liberals, and he managed to impress an image of himself which makes him the protagonist of American idealism. He was probably right in resisting Hamilton's plan to base government on an aristocracy of wealth and talents, but no country can afford to disregard talents, and wealth has been a greater factor in the federal equation during the last half-century than ever it was under the Federalists. Jefferson's foreign policy of disentanglement from European affairs suited the new nation far better than Hamilton's desire to be junior partner to Great Britain.

These opposing principles of foreign policy were now to come to a test, for Washington's second term opened in March 1793 in the shadow of a European war, which precipitated all floating elements of political dissension into two national parties: — the Federalists led by Hamilton, and the Republicans led by Jefferson. These parties held the national stage for a generation; and with few intervals the two-party system has lasted to this day.

HAIL COLUMBIA!

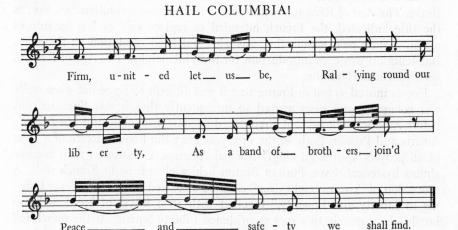

Firm, u-nit-ed let us be, Ral-'ying round our

lib-er-ty, As a band of broth-ers join'd

Peace and safe-ty we shall find.

Broils with England and France

1793-1801

1. The French Revolution and American Politics

EVENTS OF THE FRENCH REVOLUTION, beginning with the capture of the Bastille on 14 July 1789, were followed in America with the keenest interest and, up to a point, with universal sympathy. The French Constituent Assembly, in which Lafayette and Tom Paine were playing leading roles, abolished titles of nobility and other special privileges, and adopted a bill of rights modeled on those of the American states. Edmund Burke's *Considerations* on the course of events in France, by the most beloved English friend to the American Revolution, shook many leading Americans including Washington, Adams and Hamilton, out of their complacency; and Tom Paine's answer to Burke, *The Age of Reason*, confirmed them as counter-revolutionaries. For, as the title indicated, the French intended to replace rule of law by rule of reason — their own reason; that was what put their revolution on the skids. But Jefferson wrote an introduction for the Philadelphia *The Age of Reason*, with a sneer at Hamilton.

Events moved so fast in France that it was difficult to figure out what really was going on, and news arrived so infrequently that it was three months before Americans heard that France had become a republic and was fighting Austria and Prussia. Early in the new year 1793 the French decree of a "war of all peoples against all kings" reached America. Enthusiasm then became almost hysterical. Even Puritan Boston held a civic feast in French style. A procession of "citizens eight deep" escorted a roasted ox labeled "Peace Offering to Liberty and Equality," together with 1600 loaves of bread and two hogsheads of punch, to a spot rechristened Liberty Square. As the punch fell lower in the hogsheads, the ardor of the citizens rose; and if anyone had been so tactless as to suggest that all was not well in France, he would probably have been ducked in the Frog Pond.

For three months there was no news from Europe. Then, in April 1793, one month after Washington's second inauguration at Philadelphia, came word that brought war to the Delaware Capes and made the French Revolution an issue in American politics. France had declared war on Great Britain and Spain; Louis XVI, our good friend, had been guillotined; the Girondin party was in power, and Citizen Genet was coming over as minister plenipotentiary of the French Republic.

A cabinet meeting was promptly held at Philadelphia. Hamilton, loathing the French Revolution, wished to declare the alliance of 1778, which required us to defend the French Antilles, suspended by the change. Jefferson considered the cause of France "the most sacred cause that ever man was engaged in," but was eager to keep America out of the war; Washington still wished the French well, but thought of his own country first. Accordingly, on 22 April 1793, the President issued a neutrality proclamation declaring the "disposition of the United States" to "pursue a conduct friendly and impartial toward the belligerent powers," and warning citizens that "aiding or abetting hostilities" or carrying contraband would render them liable to prosecution in the federal courts. Congress implemented the proclamation by passing a Neutrality Act next session. Whether these could be enforced, when the great majority of Americans were eager to help France, was another matter.

In the meantime Citizen Genet, quaintest of many curious diplomats sent by European governments to the United States, had landed at Charleston, South Carolina. Before presenting his credentials he presumed to fit out privateers against British commerce and to recruit soldiers. His progress to Philadelphia was a continual ovation, in comparison with which the President's formal and dignified reception seemed cold and unfriendly. But the minister needed more than that to cool his revolutionary ardor.

Genet's instructions ordered him to use the United States as a base for privateering on the ocean and filibustering Spanish Florida and Louisiana, with the addition of Canada to the American Union as bait. Several land speculators like George Rogers Clark, who had corruptly obtained from the Georgia legislature an immense land grant on the Mississippi near the mouth of the Yazoo, eagerly accepted commissions from Genet as officers in a "French army of the Mississippi." The minister expected to finance these unneutral enterprises from advances on the American debt to France. Hamilton naturally refused to anticipate installments, and Genet's warriors had to return empty-handed to their frontier farms.

The popular reception of Genet turned his head. "I live in a round of parties," he wrote to his government. "Old man Washington can't forgive my success." Like many later heroes, he mistook the applause of curious crowds for approval. When he found he could not move the American government, he conceived the notion of turning it out. His progress through the states was marked by founding Jacobin clubs, corresponding roughly to the Communist cells of our own time. Jefferson, who at first welcomed Genet as a fillip to the opposition, concluded after a few weeks that he was likely to become a Jonah, and supported Washington in requesting his recall. Robespierre gladly consented, and in return asked for the recall of Gouverneur Morris, whose intrigues in Paris had been more frivolous than Genet's in Philadelphia, though hardly as mischievous. A new French minister arrived in the United

States early in 1794 with an order to send his predecessor home under arrest. Instead of returning to feed the guillotine, Genet married the daughter of Governor Clinton and settled down to the life of a country gentleman on the Hudson.

That year, 1794, saw the crystallization of unstable political elements into national parties. European issues are apt to reach America without shadings, all black and white. Thus the French Revolution seemed to some a clean-cut contest between monarchy and republicanism, oppression and liberty; to others it was a fresh breaking-out of the eternal strife between anarchy and order, atheism and religion, poverty and prosperity. Americans of the first way of thinking joined the Republican party; others, the Federalist. Sectional and economic groups were polar to the completed parties; but in the reverse order to general expectation. Formerly democratic New England, especially the seaports, became the headquarters of the pro-British Federalists; whilst the landed interest, particularly in slaveholding communities, was swept by Gallomania.

The explanation is largely social and economic. In New England the clergy had been worrying over the younger generation: students preferred to read Voltaire and Gibbon rather than Jonathan Edwards. Tom Paine's scurrilous *Age of Reason* caused the sincerely religious to repudiate the party that supported France. Paine himself, by a nasty attack on Washington, identified Jeffersonianism with Jabcobinism in the mind of the average Northerner. But the planters of Virginia seem to have been immune to religious panic and so certain of the loyalty of their own slaves that the massacre of white people in Haiti when "liberty, equality and fraternity" were applied in that French colony did not alarm them. Virginia's opposition to British capital and sea power was part of her hatred for Northern capital and Hamiltonian finance schemes. The writings of the French *philosophes and économistes* enabled country gentlemen to rationalize their instincts that land was the unique source of wealth, that trade and finance were parasites. Chief local philosopher was Colonel John Taylor "of Caroline" a Virginia county. His pamphlets declared that every dollar made by merchants came out of the farmer's pocket, that England through her disregard of "true economic principles" was a "sinking nation," and that trade with her was draining America of her wealth. These absurd notions became doctrine in the South; and it took them long to die.

To the merchant-shipowners, on the contrary, British capital was an indispensable credit instrument necessary for American trade with Britain. Like Hamilton, they did not care to risk a quarrel with the power that could give or withhold. British spoliations on neutral trade might annoy American shipowners, but the British admiralty gave compensation whilst the French Republic did not. During the entire period of the Anglo-French war, as in 1914–17 and 1939–41, there was no time when American shipowners could not make immense profits by accepting British regulations, whilst the French

privateers' attacks on neutral commerce, like those of the German submarines, were a net loss.

Around these two poles American opinion crystallized in 1793–95. You
were either for the Republicans and France, or for the Federalists and Britain.
Emotion for a principle, and for the kind of country you wanted America to be,
joined interest and policy. This was not Britain and France corrupting American opinion, but Americans seeking both practical and ideological support in
Europe. "Each party will use foreign influence as it needs, to dominate,"
predicted Volney, a French scholar traveling in America. The Republicans
(ancestors of the Democrats of today) [1] and the Federalists (of whom the
present Republicans are residuary legatees) supported the Federal Constitution, although each accused the other of trying to subvert it. Their basic
principles, to 1815, were agrarianism and the French Revolution against capitalism and Britain. If the one in 1794 stood for state rights, and the other for
a strong federal government, it was only because the one was out and the
other in. Each party attempted to undercut the other on its home field by
appealing to some local interest contrary to the dominant one. Thus, in
Virginia the wheat-growing Shenandoah valley, which hated the slave-owning
aristocracy, remained Federalist; whilst the South Carolina back country,
which hated Charleston, went Republican. Jefferson reached out to the
underdog in New England, where Baptists and other sects of inferior status
generally went Republican, as did poor fishing ports such as Marblehead,
jealous of Federalist Salem. These are early illustrations of a side to American
politics so puzzling to outsiders — the fact that national parties are always to
a great extent local. Thousands of votes in every presidential election are
dictated by state issues, local rivalries, and racial or religious feuds.

Polar also to the economic and section cleavage was the ideological. Jefferson believed that a government could be based on, and its official policy
dictated by, "reason," as the French Republic was attempting to do, with dire
results. John Adams and Edmund Burke, who warned France that this would
happen, believed, as John Dickinson had said, "Let Experience be our guide.
Reason may mislead us." And long has it continued to mislead people — notably the Communists. Over a century after Jefferson's day, Elihu Root
said, "The great difficulty in the application of pure reason to practical affairs
is that never . . . does the reasoner get all the premises which should affect
the conclusions; so it frequently happens that the practical man . . . who
feels the effect of conditions which the reasoner overlooks, goes right, while
the superior intelligence of the reasoning man goes wrong."

1. Jefferson began referring to his friends as "the Republicans" in 1791, in order to imply
that all others were monarchists; the Hamiltonians kept the name Federalist in order to
imply that all others were Antifederal. Their favorite names for the Republicans were
"Jacobins" or "Democrats." The latter name, sometimes used by the Northern wing of the
Republican party, was distasteful to the Southerners. Jefferson tried calling the Federalists
"monocrats" but it did not catch on.

Jefferson was no pure reasoner, and Hamilton no pure empiricist; but the one wished to make a fresh start based on reason; and the other, to build on tried ways and habits. In their approach to life and its problems, these two typified Goethe's dichotomy: the spirit that creates and the spirit that denies; the hope that man is perfectible and the belief that he is irremediably stupid and evil. We shall find these two poles constant while our political globe spins. There was no clean-cut difference between the two parties that Hamilton and Jefferson organized. The Republicans had the greater share of optimism, and the Federalists of pessimism; but each had something to give the country, and both were equally guilty of appealing to men's fears and appetites. Jefferson's "botanical excursion" of 1791 began the substitution of expediency for idealism; whilst the character of Washington, the genius of Hamilton and the intellect of Marshall transcended reaction by maintaining principles of national integrity and international justice that were vital to an enduring Union.

2. The Crucial Year 1794

If Victor Hugo's "1793," year of the Reign of Terror, was crucial in the French Revolution, 1794 was the most critical in America's federal experiment. The Supreme Court suffered a setback, but the executive won a signal victory in putting down a rebellion of Western "moonshiners" against Federal "revenooers." Outrages by Barbary corsairs induced Congress to reestablish the United States Navy. A new governor of Upper Canada tried to cash in on St. Clair's defeat by converting the Northwest Territory into an Indian satellite state, but General Wayne avenged St. Clair at the Fallen Timbers. The United States teetered on the brink of war with England, but Washington sent Jay to negotiate at London; and his treaty, viciously attacked by the Republicans as a base capitulation, not only prevented war but swung open the gate to the West.

The setback was a refusal of the State of Georgia to obey a decision of the Supreme Court of the United States, in a suit to recover debts, brought by a citizen of another state. Not only did Georgia get away with virtual nullification; the other states became so alarmed at the prospect of being forced by the Supreme Court to pay old war claims, that Congress passed (5 March 1799), and the states ratified, Amendment XI to the Constitution, forbidding the federal judiciary to entertain any suit brought against a state of the Union by a citizen of another state or nation. Thus the states recovered a traditional royal prerogative, to be sued only with their consent.

Congress's act of 1791 levying a moderate excise tax on distilleries seemed as unjust and tyrannical to mountain men as the British Stamp Act had to all Americans. In the Appalachians and beyond, distilling was a practical method of using surplus corn. Whisky could bear the cost of transportation and kegs of it were even used as currency. Congress modified the law so that there was less snooping, and opposition quieted down except in Washington County, the westernmost part of Pennsylvania. There a frontier lawyer named David Bradford and old Herman Husband, who had led the North Carolina Regulators before the war, organized resistance to the law. Covenants were signed never to pay the tax, law-abiding distillers were terrorized, federal marshals at Pittsburgh were roughly handled, a mass meeting appointed a "committee of safety," and citizens were conjured to rise and fight for their spirituous liberties. But for the moderating influence of Hugh H. Brackenridge and Albert Gallatin, a recent immigrant from Geneva, Washington County might have seceded from Pennsylvania and the Union. This movement became jocularly known as the Whisky Rebellion.

Governor Thomas Mifflin of Pennsylvania, now a Jeffersonian Republican, refused to do anything to enforce the law lest it hurt his popularity. But President Washington and his secretary of the treasury accepted this challenge as a test whether the federal government could really enforce the law without the help of the states. Congress had been given power "to provide for calling forth the militia to execute the laws of the Union." Congress so authorized the President, and on 7 August 1794 he called out 15,000 militiamen from four states. Most of them responded. The President, accompanied by Generals Daniel Morgan and Henry Lee, and Alexander Hamilton in uniform, led them in a stiff hike over the Alleghenies. Upon the approach of the army, most of the rebel leaders fled and the rank and file quit. Two ringleaders were caught and convicted of treason, but pardoned by the President.

This was a severe but successful test of the new government in its domestic relations. Henceforth, persons and interests who had a grievance against the federal government had to carry at least one state and evolve the doctrine of state rights as a defense. That form of resistance was supposedly ended in 1865; yet, almost a century later, it has been possible for several states to defy Congress and the Supreme Court on the racial question.

Washington's cool, serene temper had all it could do to quench a hot demand for war with England. In her war against the French Republic, England applied her ancient doctrine that enemy property on the high seas was good prize, even if in a neutral vessel. France and the United States, as the weaker sea powers, contended for the principle "Free ships make free goods"; meaning that a neutral flag protected enemy property except contraband of war, arms, and munitions. Britain now declared good prize any neutral ship carrying provisions to the French West Indies. When this order in council of 6 November 1793 reached British naval officers abroad, the Caribbean was swarming with small American vessels eager to profit by neutral trade. A number of them were captured and roughly treated in British vice-admiralty courts, since naval officers were eager for prize money and judges took a cut on condemnations. News of these captures brought consternation to the American trading community, backbone of the Federalist party. Even Hamilton was exasperated. Congress began war preparations and clapped an embargo on the seaports. In the midst of the crisis, news leaked into American newspapers of a truculent speech by Lord Dorchester to an Indian delegation, encouraging them to look for British aid in driving the Yankees across the Ohio river for good and all.

In Congress the opposition party was not prepared for war, but demanded commercial retaliation which would certainly have led to war, as it did in 1812 when Jefferson and Madison tried it, and in 1941 when Franklin D. Roosevelt tried it. A timely gesture of friendship from the British foreign minister prevented matters from going farther. He revoked the provision-capture order. In April 1794, shortly after this news reached Philadelphia, Washington nominated Chief Justice Jay envoy extraordinary to Great Britain. "My objects are, to prevent a war," he wrote, "if justice can be obtained." Jay's nomination was confirmed by the Senate on 19 April. "The day is a good omen," said John Adams. His casting vote as Vice President defeated a bill to suspend commercial intercourse with Great Britain, and the embargo on exports was allowed to lapse because the French minister wanted it so, in order to get food to France. An enormous convoy of American provision ships sailed from the Chesapeake under escort of French men-of-war, which Admiral Lord Howe defeated on "the Glorious First of June" 1794, thus winning the fame that he had sought in vain during the War of Independence. But the convoy of over a hundred sail slipped safely into Brest in time to relieve a famine which followed the Reign of Terror.

A main object of Jay's mission was to obtain British evacuation of the Northwest posts. General St. Clair's defeat had encouraged both the Indians and the government to retain them, and in 1792 the governor of Canada proposed that the entire territory between the Great Lakes and the Ohio river, together with a strip of New York and Vermont, be erected into a satellite Indian state. Although the British government did not take this up, it informed the United States government that the Northwest posts would be retained, whether or not America paid her contested debts, and Lieutenant Governor Simcoe of Upper Canada set up a new garrison at the rapids of the Maumee river about 100 miles southwest of Detroit.

The United States Army, reorganized after St. Clair's defeat and recruited to 2000 men, was now placed under the command of Major General Anthony Wayne. In the fall of 1793 he established winter quarters at the site of Greenville, Ohio. "Mad Anthony," as his men called Wayne for his reckless courage, really had a cool head. His communications were assured by six fortified posts, and by constant vigilance. An admirable disciplinarian, he trained his troops in the tactics of forest warfare, and the redskins gave them plenty of practice. Several hundred Kentucky mounted riflemen joined him in the spring of 1794.

Simcoe strengthened his new fort on the Maumee and bent all his energy to mobilizing the Indians. Provisions, blankets, muskets, powder and ball, and vermilion warpaint were dispensed from Canadian depots and arsenals.

When the oak leaves were fully out, completing nature's ambush, the Indians attacked. Wayne beat them off and took the offensive. Advancing cautiously through the hardwood forest and protected by a screen of scouts, he debouched into the Erie plain, the Indians' granary. Along the Maumee and the Glaize there were log cabins, fruit trees, and cornfields. In the midst of these savage gardens, Wayne built Fort Defiance, a stockade with blockhouse bastions. There he offered peace once more, and again it was rejected. The Indians retreated to the vicinity of the new British fort and took cover behind a natural stockade of fallen trees. There were 1500 to 2000 of them: Miami under Chief Little Turtle; Black Wolf with his Shawnee; the "three fires" of the Ottawa, Chippewa, and Potawotomi under Blue Jacket; Sauk and Fox from Lake Superior; a few Iroquois diehards, and 70 white Canadian rangers under an old Loyalist. On 20 August Wayne marched forth to meet them. A squadron of dragoons charged on the Indians' left flank. Both the American captains were picked off, but a lieutenant took command, and the troopers, jumping their horses over the fallen timber as in a steeplechase, burst in on the redskins and gave them cold steel. The infantry and riflemen then poured in a volley of hot stuff and charged with bayonets before the Indians had time to reload. In forty minutes it was all over. The Battle of the Fallen Timbers sent all tribesmen from distant parts scampering home and enabled Wayne to destroy the Indian villages, lay waste their cornfields, and build Fort Wayne at the forks of the Maumee. His army returned to Greenville, to await envoys of peace.

On 16 June 1795 a peace conference was summoned in a forest clearing at Greenville. Delegates of tribes between the Great Lakes, the Mississippi, and the Ohio assembled to the number of 1130. The conferences lasted for six weeks. The patience of General Wayne was rewarded on 3 August 1795 with the Treaty of Greenville, between the assembled tribes and the "Fifteen Fires" of the States. The Indians ceded the southeastern corner of the Northwest Territory together with several enclaves such as Vincennes, Detroit, and the site of Chicago, in return for annuities to the value of some $10,000.

So ended almost twenty years of fighting: the last phase of the War of Independence. Peace came to the border from the Genesee country to the Mississippi. Pioneers began to swarm up the valleys of the Scioto and the Muskingum; but within ten years their greed for land made the Treaty of Greenville a scrap of paper.

This same year 1794 witnessed an overdue rebirth of the United States Navy, with Barbary corsairs acting as midwives. By February, 126 American sailors were enslaved at Algiers, and more were coming in weekly. A navy, rather than an indefinite payment of tribute, was the obvious remedy. Despite Republican opposition (Senators Maclay and Monroe accusing the Federalists of wanting patronage, not protection), Congress passed and the President signed a law authorizing the building of six warships, and a modest establishment of 54 officers and 2000 ratings. In accordance with this law, Joseph

Humphreys designed the first three frigates of the new navy: U.S.S. *Constitution*, *United States*, and *Constellation*. But, as the limited appropriation made it impossible to complete these ships within three years, Washington had to buy peace with Algiers in 1796 and ransom the prisoners at a cost of almost a million dollars.

3. Jay's Treaty and the Election of 1796

Jay's treaty, signed in London on 19 November 1794, obtained the prime objects of his mission — a promise to evacuate the Northwest posts by 1796, and a limited right of American vessels to trade with the British West Indies. It preserved the peace, secured America's territorial integrity, and established a basis for Western expansion. Other unsettled questions were referred to mixed commissions, one of which made a beginning of settling the Maine-New Brunswick boundary. Some £600,000 was eventually paid by the United States in satisfaction of prewar debts, and £1,317,000 by Great Britain for illegal captures of American ships.

Yet, when the terms of this treaty were printed in Philadelphia (2 November 1795), a howl of rage went up that Jay had betrayed his country. This clamor was completely unjustified. Jay had refused even to discuss the proposed Indian satellite state. He resisted a British demand to rectify the frontier in the Northwest so as to give Canada a corridor to the site of St. Paul, and which would eventually have made lat. 45° N instead of 49° N the international boundary. He declined to make any concessions on the navigation of the Mississippi. He procured the desired evacuation of the posts. A good part of the rage against the treaty was due to the French "party line" being repeated by Republican newspapers; for it prevented a war which the French government wanted. A bare two-thirds majority for the treaty was obtained in the Senate, and Washington ratified it in 25 June 1795 — a wise and brave act which made him the target for vicious party attacks. Six months later, the House of Representatives threatened to nullify the treaty by withholding supply for the mixed commissions, and a powerful speech by Fisher Ames just prevented the mischief.

All Northwest posts were evacuated before the end of the year. Lord Shelburne, who had been responsible for the treaty line so long withheld, wrote to Major William Jackson in 1797, "I cannot express to you the satisfaction I have felt in seeing the forts given up. . . . The deed is done, and a strong foundation laid for eternal amity between England and America. General Washington's conduct is above all praise. He has left a noble example to sovereigns and nations, present and to come."

Jay's treaty also gave America the unexpected dividend of a settlement with Spain that included the right of transit at New Orleans. Baron de Carondelet, governor of Louisiana, endeavoring to establish an Indian satellite state in the Southwest, built a new fort on United States territory at Chickasaw Bluffs

(Memphis) and persuaded the Creek and Cherokee nations to denounce their earlier treaties with the United States. Thomas Pinckney, whom Washington sent to Madrid, found the Spanish government in a favorable frame of mind because it suspected that Jay's treaty included a secret Anglo-American alliance, and feared losing Louisiana to American filibusters. Accordingly, in the Treaty of San Lorenzo (27 October 1795), His Catholic Majesty conceded the right to navigate the lower Mississippi, and the transit rights at New Orleans so ardently desired by the West. Spain then evacuated her posts on the east bank of the Mississippi, north of the southern boundary of the United States, which now had full control of her own territory.

When Jefferson retired from the department of state on the last day of 1793, Washington appointed in his place Edmund Randolph, whom his acidulous kinsman John Randolph of Roanoke compared to "the chameleon on the aspen, always trembling, always changing." Officially approving Washington's policy, he secretly worked against it; and his downfall was brought about through an indiscretion of Citizen Fauchet. A giveaway dispatch from this envoy of the French Republic to his government was captured at sea by the British, who passed it along to Washington. It referred to certain "precious confessions" by Randolph and hinted that the secretary had asked him for money at the time of the Whisky Rebellion. "Thus, a few thousand dollars would have decided between war and peace! So the consciences of the so-called American patriots already have their price!" observed Fauchet. Washington, like a Roman father, confronted Randolph with this dispatch in a cabinet meeting and demanded an explanation. Randolph promptly resigned. What really passed between him and Fauchet will never be known; the most probable explanation is that he tried to obtain secret service money from the French to procure evidence implicating England in the Whisky Rebellion.

Randolph's disgrace ended Washington's attempt to govern with a bipartisan cabinet. The premier secretaryship was now conferred on Timothy Pickering, a New England Federalist of the most pronounced type, a Puritan who hated the French Republic as the incarnation of evil. Hamilton, who had resigned from the treasury department after the Whisky Rebellion, had been replaced by the first auditor of the treasury, Oliver Wolcott, and James McHenry became secretary of war. All three were disciples of Hamilton.

Washington had made the mistake of appointing James Monroe, a pronounced Anglophobe, to the Paris legation while Jay was negotiating in London; and he made a greater mistake by recalling Monroe in 1796 when he was doing his best to appease the injured feelings of the French government. The Executive Directory of France, now regarding America as a British satellite, suspended diplomatic relations but retained its minister in Philadelphia as a political agent in the presidential election.

This situation Washington thankfully left to a successor. By refusing to stand for a third term he established the two-term tradition in American politics, which became constitutional in 1951 by virtue of Amendment XXII. Through correspondence and private consultation the Republicans decided to support Jefferson and Aaron Burr for President and Vice President; the Federalists, John Adams and Thomas Pinckney. Jay's treaty was the central issue of the campaign, to which the French minister contributed a political pamphlet, together with much intrigue. The result was a narrow Federalist victory. Adams obtained the presidency with 71 votes in the electoral college. Jefferson's 68 votes made him Vice President by the constitutional method that was changed by Amendment XII in 1804.

"I now compare myself," wrote Washington on 2 March 1797, "to the wearied traveller who seeks a resting place, and is bending his body to lean thereon. But to be suffered to do *this* in peace is too much to be endured by *some*." During his last year in office the President was assailed with a virulence such as few of his successors have suffered. Jefferson, in a letter to Filippo Mazzei, an Italian friend, which found its way into print, referred to "men who were Samsons in the field and Solomons in the Council," whose heads had been "shorn by the harlot England." Everyone knew that he meant Washington, Hamilton, and Adams. The Philadelphia *Aurora*, on the morrow of Washington's retirement, proclaimed that "this day ought to be a Jubilee in the United States . . . for the man who is the source of all the misfortunes of our country, is this day reduced to a level with his fellow citizens."

Six months previously, on 17 September 1796, Washington summed up his political experience in a farewell address of permanent value. An eloquent plea for union is followed by a pointed exposition of disruptive tendencies. Politicians, he said, misrepresent "the opinions and aims of other districts" in order to acquire influence within their own; pressure groups are formed to override or control the constitutional authorities; the "baneful effects of the spirit of party" hamstring a President's efforts to promote the national interest. As to foreign policy, the Father of his Country enjoined citizens to "Observe good faith and justice towards all nations; cultivate peace and harmony with all. . . . The Nation which indulges towards another an habitual hatred or an habitual fondness is in some degree a slave."

Washington's famous doctrine of isolation is contained in the following sentences:

Europe has a set of primary interests, which to us have none, or a very remote relation. Hence she must be engaged in frequent controversies, the causes of which are essentially foreign to our concerns. . . . Our detached and distant situation invites us to pursue a different course. . . . 'Tis our true policy to steer clear of permanent alliances, with any portion of the foreign world. . . . Taking care always to keep ourselves, by suitable establishments, on a respectable defensive posture, we may safely trust to temporary alliances for extraordinary emergencies.

This farewell address fell on deaf ears in a Europe that was ringing with the exploits of a new hero, General Bonaparte. But there it was written, for whosoever cared to read, that a new power in the West considered herself outside the European system. Nor was it much heeded in America, where the leading politicians believed that the dearest interests of their respective parties were bound up with England or with France.

Washington's services in time of peace have never been adequately appreciated. His unique place in history rests not only on his superb leadership in war, and on his wise administration of the federal government; but even more on his integrity, good judgment, and magnanimity. As Samuel T. Coleridge, one of his many English admirers, wrote shortly after Washington's death:

Tranquil and firm he moved with one pace in one path, and neither vaulted nor tottered. . . . Among a people eminently querulous and already impregnated with the germs of discordant parties, he directed the executive power firmly and unostentatiously. He had no vain conceit of being himself all; and did those things only which he only could do.

4. John Adams and the Naval War with France

John Adams, now sixty-one years old, was "always honest, often great, but sometimes mad," remarked Franklin. Even after eight years' experience as Vice President, he was by temperament unsuited for the presidency. He did know more than any other American, even Madison, about political science; but as an administrator he was uneasy. He did not attract personal loyalty and had few close friends in the political world; that probably explains his initial error of continuing Washington's entire cabinet in office. The three key members, Pickering, Wolcott, and McHenry, devoted to Hamilton, secretly referred every major question to him in New York, acted on his recommendations, and persuaded the President to adopt them. Thus Hamilton, whom Adams distrusted, really ran his administration until 1799 when he discovered what was going on and sent the triumvirate packing.

Adams paid less attention to his duties than any of this successors. Whilst Washington was absent from the seat of government 181 days in eight years, Adams stayed away for 385 days in four years. He did so mainly because he loved his home and farm at Quincy, but partly because both he and his excellent wife disliked Philadelphia society which insulted them (so Abigail felt) by continuing to celebrate George's birthday instead of John's. And when the federal government moved to the District of Columbia in 1800, life in the uncompleted White House was too much like camping out for an aging couple who liked comfort.

Adams's attitude toward his predecessor may be gathered from a remark he made while being painted by Gilbert Stuart: "Washington got the reputation of being a great man," he told the painter, "because he kept his mouth shut." That was one thing John could never do. But the foreign situation he faced in 1797 was more difficult than Washington's. Jay's treaty had embroiled the

United States with the aggressive and subversive French Directory, and American Republicans seemed determined to follow the French party line, no matter what. They even advised the next French move, to let privateers loose against the American merchant fleet. The ensuing French spoliations on commerce made those of Britain in 1793 seem mild in comparison. Red-bonneted ruffians who represented France in the West Indies made an open traffic of blank letters of marque. Frenchmen at Charleston secretly armed American vessels to prey upon American commerce under the authority of forged commissions. In June 1797 the secretary of state reported that more than 300 American vessels had been captured under color of French authority.

The Directory refused to receive Monroe's successor at Paris, and its official language toward the United States became truculent and threatening. President Adams declared that he would submit to no indignities but hoped to maintain Washington's policy of neutrality. Following the Jay precedent, he made another effort to obtain justice through diplomacy. In order to satisfy the Republicans that he was not seeking a quarrel, Adams appointed a Jeffersonian, Elbridge Gerry; and in order to keep Gerry out of mischief, joined with him in the mission two sound Federalists, John Marshall and Charles Cotesworth Pinckney.

The first year of Adams's administration passed without news from the mission. In the meantime, the party cleavage deepened. The Republicans, refusing to believe that the French government had changed character since 1792, stoutly defended the spoliations as a natural answer to Jay's treaty, and opposed every effort of the Federalists to build up national defense. Congress now hastened to complete the three frigates under construction. But, when the *United States* was launched at Philadelphia in 1797, with such speed that she smacked the opposite shore, and at Boston the *Constitution* stuck on the ways, Jeffersonian papers shouted with glee and expressed the hope that these fine ships would never get to sea. Philip Freneau, the kept poet of the party, even published a poem to that effect: "O frigate *Constitution!* Stay on shore!"

To the Federalists, on the other hand, France had become just such a menace to American independence as certain communist powers became in 1946. The European situation was a small-scale portent of the world situation of our own era, when the free world has had to defend itself both against the Nazis and the Reds. For the French Republic had invented the political strategy that Hitler and Stalin imitated: an ideological offensive implemented by armies and the replacing of established governments by puppet regimes. Thus, Holland became the Batavian Republic in 1795, and the Cisalpine, Parthenopean, and Helvetian Republics followed. United Ireland received encouragement from Paris, and in 1798 British radicals were toasting the day when a French army would proclaim Tom Paine president of an English Republic. Would America's turn come next?

The Western world was being divided into countries which had made terms with France, and those which had not; and by 1797 Britain, the United States, and Russia were the only three important ones which had not. "If England will persevere," wrote Senator George Cabot," she will save Europe and save us; if she yields, all will be lost. . . . She is now the only barrier between us and the deathly embraces of universal irreligion, immorality and plunder." Better to fight France by England's side, rather than be forced to fight her alone later.

So reasoned the Federalists — as Democrats and others did in 1917 and 1941. Fears of a French invasion were not unreasonable, since we now know that French designs on Canada, the West, and Florida were definite and dangerous. General George Rogers Clark and other prominent Westerners were on the payroll of the French Republic, which was pressuring Spain to cede Florida and Louisiana to France. That would have semi-circled the United States with French territory and thrust her western boundary back to the Appalachians. General Victor Collot in 1796 traveled down the Ohio and the Mississippi to select strong points for this scheme. Quebec habitants were being worked on by secret agents to declare a Canadian Republic under French protection. Relations were renewed with Genet's unpaid warriors; and Milfort, a halfbreed chief of the Creek nation, was commissioned a French brigadier general.

The American mission arrived in Paris at an unpropitious moment, in October 1797, after Bonaparte had beaten Austria, and the Directory was at the height of power and arrogance. The Directors, at least one of whom had a pecuniary interest in privateering, felt they could with impunity continue "a little clandestine war" against the United States. A comic, if one-sided, bit of bargaining ensued. Talleyrand, the French minister of foreign affairs, sent some hangers-on (referred to in the dispatches as X, Y, and Z) to play on the fears of the American envoys, and sound their pockets. A bribe of some $250,000 for the minister, and a loan of $10 million as compensation for President Adams's "insults," were the prerequisites to negotiation. Pressed for an alternative, Monsieur Y hinted at the power of the French party in America, and lightly touched upon the fate of recalcitrant European states. Gerry was alarmed by these suggestions, but Pinckney and Marshall were unshaken. "Our case is different from that of the minor nations of Europe," the Virginian informed Monsieur Y. "They were unable to maintain their independence, and did not expect to do so. America is a great, and, so far as concerns her self-defence, a powerful nation." After several months of fruitless palaver, Marshall and Pinckney took their leave. Gerry, fatuously believing his presence necessary to avert war, remained for a time in Paris.

The envoys' dispatches, recording in detail their strange experiences, reached America early in 1798, and were sent to Congress by the President. These "X Y Z despatches" were printed; and the public was deeply moved by its first-hand view of French diplomacy. On Republicans the effect was stupefying. "Trimmers dropt off from the party like windfalls from an apple tree in

September," wrote Fisher Ames. Jefferson "thought it his duty to be silent." Loyal addresses poured in on President and Congress, indignation meetings were held, reams of patriotic poetry (including one national anthem that has endured — Joseph Hopkinson's *Hail Columbia!*) were produced, and "Millions for Defense, but Not One Cent for Tribute" became the slogan.

President Adams and the Federalists adopted a policy of armed neutrality, expecting a declaration of war by France to unite all honest men to their standard. Congress created a navy department, a vast improvement over having the navy treated as an adjunct to the army. Under the new secretary, Benjamin Stoddert, and the senior naval officer, Commodore John Barry, the United States Navy became an efficient fighting force. Congress also revived the Marine Corps. Frigates *United States, Constitution,* and *Constellation* were fitted for sea; *President, Congress* and *Chesapeake* were completed; five more frigates were built by groups of merchants and sold to the government; many smaller vessels were purchased and converted; navy yards were purchased, and an ambitious program of naval construction undertaken. Privateers were fitted out, and both they and the warships were authorized to capture French armed vessels wherever found. But they were not allowed to take unarmed merchant ships, as in a declared war. Since almost every French ship that they encountered was armed, that prohibition did not matter.

By the close of 1798 there were fourteen American men-of-war at sea, and some two hundred merchant vessels had taken out letters of marque and reprisal. By arrangement with Great Britain, her navy protected American transatlantic shipping, and the United States Navy took care of the merchant ships of both nations in the Caribbean. Organized in four task forces of three to ten ships each, it combed the Caribbean from Caracas to Cuba, and from the Straits of Florida to the Gulf of Paria, sweeping the French picaroons out of those waters, protecting property worth millions of dollars from spoliation. On 9 February 1799 the navy received its first battle test off Nevis, where U.S.S. *Constellation* (Commodore Thomas Truxton) fought for an hour and, owing to superior gunnery, captured the crack French frigate *L'Insurgente.* A year later, off Guadeloupe, *Constellation* (38 guns) chased *Vengeance* (54 guns) all day, brought her to action at eight in the evening, and fought her within pistol shot until one in the morning. The French commander struck his colors twice during the action but Truxton did not perceive it in the smoke and darkness, and *Vengeance* managed to escape. Frigate *Boston* (28 guns, Captain Little) had a terrific fight with the French corvette *Le Berceau* (24 guns) in the open ocean on 12 October 1800, and captured her. The only United States ship to be defeated during this war was schooner *Retaliation* (14 guns), by two frigates which together mounted 80 guns.

The effect of this quasi-war on the United States Army was less happy. In 1798, when its total strength amounted to only 3500 officers and men, Congress ordered the immediate enlistment of 10,000 more; and the creation, on paper, of a "provisional army" of 50,000. George Washington, who wholeheartedly supported the Adams administration, accepted an appointment as lieutenant general to command this new army, and insisted on Hamilton receiving the senior major generalship, so that he could command in the field. President Adams growled over these preparations, which he considered excessive, and postponed active recruiting until the spring of 1799, when most of the anti-French fire had died down. By that time the British navy, by bottling up Bonaparte's army in Egypt, had rendered France incapable of invading America. Consequently, only about 3000 men, whom Washington described as "the riff-raff of the country and the scape-gallows of the large cities," could be persuaded to enlist in the new army, and the provisional force existed only on paper. But one permanent benefit was derived from this army which never fought. The secretary of war promoted the formation of a school for gunners and sappers. West Point was selected as the location, and on his last day of office President Adams appointed the first faculty of the United States Military Academy.

In the congressional elections of 1798–99 the Federalists won a strong majority, destined to be their last. Jefferson and his party appeared to be discredited by their excuses for French aggression and for treating the exploits of the United States Navy with sneers and jeers. But time was preparing the Republicans' revenge. A rift appeared in the Federalist party between the President and Hamilton, and into this rift Talleyrand insinuated a wedge.

A difference in objective caused the trouble. Adams's was to protect American commerce and force the French Republic to respect our flag. He was willing to accept war if declared by France, but hoped to avoid it; and most Federalists agreed. Hamilton and the New England Federalist leaders regarded the French imbroglio not as an affair to be wound up but as an occasion to be improved. It was to be a starting point for spirited measures that would strengthen the federal government, discipline the American people, and "crush the French canker that feeds on our vitals." Talleyrand, although annoyed by the exposure of his venality to the amused laughter of all Europe, refused to play into their hands, as Jefferson assured him a declaration of war would do. "The maintenance of republican principles," added the Vice President, "depends entirely on French prudence." Talleyrand cared nothing for republican principles, but he respected the new United States Navy. Accordingly, he used every available channel to communicate peaceful intentions to America. Any minister the President might send would be received, and no questions asked. The French embargo on American vessels was lifted, letters of marque issued in the West Indies were annulled, and French officials were ordered to respect neutral ships and property. An official explanation of the X Y Z episode was issued, in a tone of injured dignity. The American ministers, it appeared, had been imposed upon by charlatans. The Directory had intended to treat with the Americans, but they shut themselves up in their hotel and went off in a huff before they could be received. For just such a cue the discomfited opposition had been waiting in America. It

became the Republican party line that the X Y Z affair was a hoax by Federalist warmongers.

French conciliatory advances were treated by the bent-on-war Federalists as
insincere. In the President's absence the cabinet, advised as usual by Hamilton, decided to continue war preparations and to declare war on France as
soon as Congress convened. Hamilton had the outlines of a grandiose plan.
Since Spain was a French ally he, as senior major general, would lead the new
American army overland, and with naval support would capture New Orleans
and the Floridas. If that worked well, the next operation would be an invasion of Mexico while the British, in concert with the South American patriot
Miranda, liberated New Granada. Anglo-American friendship would be cemented by dividing the spoils of Spanish America, Hamilton would return
laurel-crowned at the head of his victorious legion, to become the first citizen
of America as Napoleon Bonaparte was already the first citizen of France.

President Adams now made a decision which knocked these ambitions on
the head. Without consulting a single person, on 18 March 1799 he nominated a new minister to France. The strongly Federalist Senate would have
rejected the nomination, but dared not meet the Republican charge of prolonging hostilities after the President had initiated peace. So it compromised by
asking for a commission of three instead of a single envoy, to which the
President consented; but while Adams enjoyed one of his prolonged vacations
at Quincy, Secretary Pickering held up the mission. In October 1799 the
President hastened back to Philadelphia and hustled the peace commission on
board an American frigate. It reached Paris in time to deal with Bonaparte,
who had kicked out the Directory and set himself up as First Consul. For
seven months the negotiations dragged, while Napoleon crossed the Alps to
thrash the Austrians again. He would admit no liability for the French spoliations, unless the United States recognized the treaties of 1778, which Congress
had denounced at the height of anti-Gallican feeling. No alliance, no money!
The American mission, fearing to bring home a renewed entangling alliance,
signed on 30 September 1800 a mere commercial convention, each party reserving its rights as to treaties and indemnities. Captured French warships had
to be returned, but not captured privateers.

On the very next day, 1 October 1800, France secretly obtained the retrocession of Louisiana from Spain. Hamilton would have been proved right,
after all, had not Napoleon tossed Louisiana to Jefferson in 1803.

Substantial gains to the nation from this quasi-war were protection of American commerce, and the virtual rebirth of the United States Navy. Fifty-four
American warships were afloat at the end of hostilities, as compared with
about ten at the beginning; and they had captured ninety-three French armed
vessels. An officers' corps and thousands of seamen and marines received
training that would bear fruit later. The total cost of operating the navy in
this war was only $6 million. Unfortunately, peace with France and the
election of Jefferson caused the navy to be radically reduced.

5. Federalist Intolerance and the Election of 1800–1801

While organizing defense and drumming up war enthusiasm, the Federalists did not neglect enemies at home. The Naturalization, Alien, and Sedition Acts of 1798 were aimed at domestic disaffection as much as foreign danger. These laws provoked the first organized state rights movement under the Constitution, and promoted the election of Jefferson to the presidency. They afford a striking instance of political intolerance. But provocation was not lacking.

The events of the 1790's sent many radical Europeans to America; and one who came earlier, Albert Gallatin, was now the Republican minority leader in Congress. Dr. Priestley, accused of trying "to decompose both Church and State" with his chemical formulas, had found refuge in Pennsylvania after a "patriotic mob" had gutted his house in England. There he was joined by another English radical, Thomas Cooper, who edited a violently Republican newspaper; both men were very much "wanted" by the Federalists. Adet, the French minister who worked for Jefferson in the election of 1796, was also a chemist by profession, and the French botanist Michaux did espionage for his government. By French consular estimates, there were 25,000 French refugees in the United States in 1798. Many were aristocratic émigrés, but most were proscribed Jacobins who wished to stand in well with the Directory. Refugees from the Irish rebellion of 1798 were also pouring in. A Federalist congressman wrote that in a journey through Pennsylvania he had seen very many Irishmen who, with few exceptions, were "United Irishmen, Free Masons, and the most God-provoking Democrats this side of Hell." Thus, as has happened twice in the twentieth century, the fear of political refugees engaging in treasonable activities against the United States, produced legislation against them. The Naturalization Act of 1798 extended the required period of residence for citizenship from five to fourteen years. The Alien Act, passed for two years only, gave the President power to expel suspected foreigners by executive decree. Adams, although frequently urged by Pickering to sign warrants for expulsion, did so only in the case of two Irish journalists, but over a dozen shiploads of Frenchmen left the country in anticipation of trouble.

For the Sedition Act of 1798 there was a legitimate need. There being no common law of the United States, the federal courts required statutory authority before taking cognizance of conspiracies against the government, or libels on high officials. One section of the new law, however, made it a misdemeanor punishable by fine or imprisonment to speak or write against President or Congress "with the intent to defame" or to bring them "into contempt or disrepute." The act made proof of the truth of the libel a sufficient defense, and required a jury trial, which was more than similar laws did in European countries. But the Sedition Act was foolishly enforced, so as to confound political opposition with sedition. About twenty-five men were arrested and ten convicted, including one member of Congress and several Republican editors who were silenced by heavy fines or jail sentences. David Brown, a wandering "apostle of sedition" who persuaded the Jacobins of a Massachusetts village to erect a liberty pole (French version of the liberty tree), got the longest sentence, four years in jail. All this seems mild in comparison with the killings and torturings that nowadays are inflicted on critics of petty tyrants the world over, but it was too strong meat for American taste in 1800.

Two startling protests by state legislatures: the Virginia resolves drafted by Madison, and those of Kentucky drafted by Jefferson, rallied the opposition. Both declared the Alien and Sedition Acts unconstitutional. As to the Alien Act, there is no getting around the fact that the power of expelling aliens belongs to the federal government, not to the states. The Sedition Act, however, stands in a different light; for Amendment I of the Constitution forbids Congress to pass any law abridging the freedom of speech, or of the press. Federalist lawyers, like many American lawyers of late, attempted to extract all meaning from this clause by assuming that freedom of the press meant freedom merely from censorship; or by asserting that it was not meant to apply in time of war. A much more drastic sedition law (the Espionage Act) was passed in 1917 and enforced by sentences far more severe than those of 1798. But the American Revolution was too near in 1798 for an American government to punish opinion with impunity.

The "compact" or "state rights" theory embodied in the Virginia and Kentucky resolves is significant. Kentucky declared that whenever Congress palpably transcends its powers, as in the Sedition Act, each state "has an equal right to judge for itself, as well of infractions as of the mode and measure of redress." She calls upon her "co-states" to "concur . . . in declaring these acts" void, and to unite "in requesting their repeal." Virginia hinted at "interposing" state authority between the persecuted citizen and his government.

Both state legislatures had their eyes on the coming presidential election and were really engaged in lighting a fiery cross to rally the Republican clans. Yet the principles of the Virginia and Kentucky resolves of 1798 became a platform to all later movements in state rights. Within ten years the New England Federalists were flinging them back at Jefferson and Madison; to the Southern particularists of a later generation they became an indispensable gloss on the Constitution.

In any true federal government there will be conflicts between powers of the nation and powers of the states. A minority party, or minority sectional combination, if ridden too hard or too proud to be ridden at all, will try to escape the consequences of a minority position by raising the banner of state rights. In American history the doctrine of state rights has not been a cause, but an effect of this condition. Almost every man in public life between 1798 and 1860 spurned it when his section was in the saddle, and embraced it when his constituents deemed themselves oppressed. Almost every state in turn declared its absolute sovereignty, only to denounce as treasonable similar declarations by other states. The Virginia doctrine of "interposition" has been invoked by the states of Alabama and Mississippi as recently as 1962 to justify illegal exclusion of Negroes from public schools and colleges.

The "Federalist Reign of Terror," [1] as the Republicans called the second half of Adams's administration, alarmed a nation which had strong notions of personal liberty. Vice President Jefferson, however, remained hopeful and serene. Strong in his faith that the people would "recover their true sight," he presided impeccably over the Senate, writing letters far and wide to his political lieutenants, and enjoying the spectacle of Federalists hanging themselves on their own ropes. "Hold on then, like a good and faithful seaman," he wrote a discouraged congressman, "till our brother sailors can rouse from their intoxication and right the vessel." But it was John Adams who drove the drunken sailors from the quarterdeck, only to bring the ship into port for Thomas Jefferson.

If the French had been so obliging as to land even a party of saboteurs on American soil, the election of 1800 might have gone very differently. But, as time went on and no enemy appeared, the patriotic fervor of 1798 damped down. In the meantime, unwise sedition prosecutions and the direct tax were having their effect. There was even a flare-up in Pennsylvania, the "Fries Rebellion," a minor Whisky Insurrection in Bucks County. When federal assessors invaded this rural paradise to survey houses and lands for the direct tax on real estate, they were attacked by irate housewives with broomsticks and boiling water, and a popular auctioneer named David Fries put himself at the head of a rabble which drummed the officials out of the county. Fries, arrested by troops of the regular army, was tried for treason, found guilty, and sentenced to death in 1799, but pardoned by President Adams.

Presidential candidates for the election of 1800 were selected by party caucuses in Congress. The Republicans respected the original understanding between Virginia and New York by supporting Jefferson and Aaron Burr; Federalists renominated John Adams, with Charles Cotesworth Pinckney of the X Y Z mission for Vice President. The Hamiltonian faction then intrigued to bring in Pinckney over Adams's head, by persuading one or two presidential electors to vote for the South Carolinian. Adams undoubtedly gained popularity by his peace move, but the "high Federalists" threw it away by their publicly expressed rage at having no war declared.

Neither in this, nor in any presidential or state election prior to the Jacksonian era, did candidates make speeches or issue statements. They were

1. The use of this term by the opposition is understandable, but for historians to apply it is unpardonable, after the real reigns of terror that the world has survived. In Adams's administration nobody was hanged, nobody sent before a firing squad, nobody tortured; the writ of habeas corpus was not suspended, the rule of law operated, public discussion remained free. Only a few persons obnoxious to the Federalists were imprisoned for short periods.

supposed to play coy, obeying a call to service from their country, saving their energies for the task of government. Electioneering was done by newspapers, pamphlets, and occasional public meetings. Even so, the politicians managed to make the campaign of 1800 very scurrilous. Jefferson was accused of being a Jacobin, an atheist, and a French agent; Adams was asserted to be an autocrat and a slavish admirer of the British monarchy. The Jonathan Robbins affair was typical. Thomas Nash, an Irish boatswain in the Royal Navy, had led a successful mutiny and killed an officer. Two years later, having changed his name to Jonathan Robbins, he indiscreetly boasted at Charleston of these exploits. On the British consul's application, in accordance with Jay's treaty, President Adams granted Nash's extradition to Jamaica, where he was tried, found guilty, and hanged. Nash and his lawyers claimed that he was a native-born citizen of Danbury, Connecticut; the Republicans played him up as a victim to Federalist tyranny; and his alleged martyrdom was the subject of a popular ballad, *Robbins's Lament*, one stanza of which, at least, is worth rescuing from the old songbooks:

> To his blood-thirsty foes, given up as a prey,
> When his claims were refuséd, he cry'd,
> "Tis thus" (his tobacco quid throwing away,)
> "Tis thus many brave men have died."

The Republicans in Congress forced an investigation, in the course of which it was proved that nobody named Robbins had ever lived in Danbury, and that Nash had confessed the crime before his execution. But the harm had been done. Jefferson, who was in a position to know, wrote that this false story "affected the popular mind more" than any "circumstance" in ten years — more even than the sedition prosecutions and the heavy taxes.

It was a close election. Seventy-three Republican and 65 Federalist electors were chosen. As no Republican elector dared throw away his second vote, Jefferson and Burr tied for first place. Until the Twelfth Amendment to the Constitution (1804) removed the possibility of a tie between two candidates on the same ticket, the House of Representatives, voting by states, had to make the final choice, a majority of one state being necessary for election. Federalists in the House saw an opportunity to thwart their enemies by voting for Burr, a cynical and pliant politician whom they preferred to a "dangerous Jacobin." But Burr refused to promise them anything, whilst Jefferson promised not to scuttle the new navy or dismiss Federalists from subordinate offices. Party division was so close that during 35 ballots, one all-night session, and until 17 February 1801, the House was deadlocked. There was talk of preventing an election, and of civil war. Virginia militia were preparing to march on Washington, D.C., where the federal government had finally settled in the summer of 1800. Finally, three Federalists cast blank ballots, permitting Jefferson to be elected President by a majority of two states.

This presidential election cannot fairly be called a popular verdict, since over half the electors were chosen by state legislatures. But in congressional elections the Republicans obtained an emphatic majority, and most of the newly elected senators were Republicans. This meant that the Federalists lost every branch of government except the judiciary, which Jefferson soon attempted to purge by impeachment.

So passed into minority the party that contained more talent and virtue, with less political common sense, than any of its successors. The Federalists went down with colors flying, content "that in the fall of laws a loyal man should die"; but their usefulness had gone. It had been their task to tame the wild forces set loose by the American Revolution, to integrate discordant elements, to lead an inchoate nation to enduring union. And they succeeded to a remarkable degree. But their chosen basis, an oligarchy of wealth and talent, was not sufficiently broad or deep. Neither their patience nor their vision was adequate for their task. Their old-world precepts of vigor, energy, and suppression had become fixed ideas, enclosing them in a network of delusion that set them in antagonism to deep-rooted popular feelings. The expanding forces of American life enveloped and overwhelmed them.

Jefferson's Administrations

1801-1809

1. The "Revolution of 1800"

THOMAS JEFFERSON, having proclaimed the proper goal of government to be preservation of "life, liberty and the pursuit of happiness," was now President of the one country in which there was reasonable likelihood of reaching those objectives. What did his followers expect, and his opponents fear? And what did he think about it?

Jefferson believed that his election saved the country from militarism and monarchy; that his mission was to get the ship of state on an even keel of peace and republican simplicity. But there never had been any danger of monarchy — that was just the Republican "big lie" about the Federalists, repeated so often that Jefferson came to believe it himself. And John Adams, if anyone, saved the country from militarism. In the other camp, the Federalists were victims of their own lies about Jefferson. Everyone who knew him personally believed that there was little or nothing to fear, but the New England parsons and local Federalist editors who had been denouncing Jefferson as an "atheist," "Jacobin," and the like, expected America under him to become a French satellite — guillotines, conscription and all. Now, when nothing of that kind happened, they hardly knew what to say. At the same time, thousands of plain people throughout the country felt that with Jefferson's election the federal government had been returned to them. Dr. Nathaniel Ames of Dedham, Fisher Ames's Republican brother, saluted the dawn of the nineteenth century as inaugurating "the irresistible propagation of the Rights of Man, the eradication of hierarchy, oppression, superstition, and tyranny all over the world."

Actually, the election of 1800–1801 brought more change in men than in measures. Jefferson liquidated the misnamed "reign of terror" by letting victims of the Sedition Act out of jail, completing army demobilization, and dismantling most of the navy. But, in essence, his inauguration meant a transfer of the center of federal power from the Boston-Hartford-Philadelphia axis to the New York-Richmond-Raleigh axis. And as for "monarchy," it was Jefferson who founded the "Virginia Dynasty" which reigned for almost a third of a century. He was succeeded by his close friend and secretary of state, James Madison of Virginia; he, after two presidential terms, by his secretary of state and Jefferson's friend James Monroe of Virginia; and Monroe, after two terms, by his secretary of state John Quincy Adams who had been allied with this dynasty for twenty years. But when Andrew Jackson, whom Jefferson regarded as a menace, won the presidency in 1829, the dynastic pattern was broken and a mild revolution did occur.

Thomas Jefferson was no social democrat but a slave-holding country gentleman of exquisite taste, lively curiosity, and a belief in the perfectibility of man. His kind really belonged to the eighteenth rather than the nineteenth century. A Christian but no churchman, he had the serenity of one to whom now and then the Spirit has not disdained to speak. He held the hearts of plain people without speech-making, military service, or pretending to be anything he was not. The secret of his power lay in the fact that he appealed to and expressed America's idealism, simplicity, and hopeful outlook, rather than the material and imperial ambitions which Hamilton represented. Jefferson's political object, as he wrote in a letter of 1802, was to prove that Americans were ripe for "a government founded not on the fears and follies of man, but in his reason; on the predominance of his social over his dissocial passions."

The government that he took over answered this description better than any of its European contemporaries; but it is questionable whether Jefferson led it any further toward perfection than Washington and Adams had done. In order to gain support he was forced to give men offices; he acquired an empire in Louisiana, which Hamilton had dreamed of conquering by arms, but it was no less an empire for that. In the midst of Napoleonic wars, Jefferson attempted to carry to its logical conclusion the neutrality policy that he had supported as Washington's secretary of state in 1793. And he aspired to an almost Chinese isolation — social and economic as well as political.

Jefferson's first inaugural address was eighteenth-century idealism rubbed through the sieve of practical politics. Instead of denouncing his opponents as villains or heretics, he invited them to join the true republican church: "We are all Republicans — we are all Federalists. If there be any among us who would wish to dissolve this Union, or to change its republican form, let them stand undisturbed as monuments of the safety with which error of opinion may be tolerated where reason is left free to combat it." This government, "the world's best hope," must not be abandoned "on the theoretic and visionary fear" that it is not strong enough. "Sometimes it is said that man cannot be trusted with the government of himself. Can he then be trusted with the government of others?" The only thing "necessary to close the circle of our felicities" is "a wise and frugal government, which shall restrain men from injuring one another, shall leave them otherwise free to regulate their own pursuits of industry and improvement, and shall not take from the mouth of labor the bread it has earned."

If a government of that nature was ever attainable, the time and place were in the simple, rural America at the turn of the nineteenth century. And if the net result of Jefferson's and Madison's administrations was to bring Hamilton's dream of a warlike and industrial nation nearer fulfillment, that was due to world forces beyond their control.

Jefferson could well afford to be frugal because his administration opened during a brief truce in the European wars, Indians on the frontier were quiet, and the American public had not yet got the habit of looking to Washington for pensions, bounties, and handouts. Washington, D.C., was a perfect scenario for an experiment in republican simplicity. The federal city had been laid out according to plans of a French engineer, Major Pierre L'Enfant who (to the subsequent confusion of motor traffic) imposed a series of avenues radiating from circles on a grid of numbered and lettered streets. Jefferson himself, when secretary of state, had determined the sites for the Capitol and the White House after L'Enfant quit in a huff. William Thornton, a West Indies physician turned architect, won a competition for the design of the Capitol; and by 1801 the north wing, containing the "old" Senate chamber (now the "old" Supreme Court), was ready for occupancy.[1] The city itself was little more than a scattering of new buildings between a forest and the Potomac and Anacostia rivers. Pennsylvania Avenue, studded with stumps and alder bushes, led from the Capitol through a morass to the White House; for whose design Dublin-born James Hoban received a fee of $500 and a city lot. Two miles further west lay Georgetown, a comfortable little Maryland town that afforded officials an agreeable change from each other's society. The red clay soil of the District became dust in dry weather and liquid cement in every rain, after which swarms of mosquitoes spread malaria. Several fine groves of tulip trees were the only features of natural beauty within the city site; Jefferson's one recorded wish for despotic power was to save these trees from the inhabitants, who proceeded to fell them for firewood. Except for scornful Federalists and a complaining diplomatic corps (one of whom named the capital "The City of Magnificent Distances") everyone made light of the difficulties and looked forward to some magic transmutation of this backwoods settlement into a new republican Rome. It was a city of great expectations, much like Brasilia, the new capital of our sister republic to the south.

Washington, therefore, was a fit setting for an experiment in frugal government. Members of Congress, forced to leave their wives at home and live in boarding houses, finished the public business as quickly as possible. The President, a widower, was free to establish a new code of republican etiquette. Every morning the White House was open to all comers. Invitations to dine were issued in the name of "Mr. Jefferson" instead of "The President of the United States." White House dinners were well prepared by a French chef, and Jefferson's wine bill for one year was $2800; but his attempt to abolish

1. The south wing was completed in 1803–9 under the superintendency of Benjamin H. Latrobe, a recent immigrant from England. These two wings, with the rotunda between, were the entire Capitol until 1851, when work was begun on the present House and Senate wings and the great dome.

precedence of diners, leaving each guest to choose his own chair, resulted in so much pushing and shoving among wives of officials that a protocol had to be drawn up. And Washington has never been able to get rid of protocol.

Jefferson's inaugural pledge to pay the public debt, and preserve "the general government in its whole constitutional vigor" caused Hamilton to predict "that the new president will not lend himself to dangerous innovations, but in essential points will tread in the steps of his predecessors." That, in the main, was what Jefferson did. He took over the Federalist administrative machine, but fed a slightly different material into it.

Madison became secretary of state. For the treasury he chose Albert Gallatin, an offshoot of aristocratic Geneva who had risen to leadership in Congress. Gallatin had already proved himself in the Pennsylvania assembly to be a "wizard of finance," a branch of statesmanship in which Jefferson was woefully deficient. He agreed with the President in wishing to pay the national debt as quickly as possible. Gallatin would even have retained the excise on whisky, which his former constituents had resisted; but Jefferson insisted on removing that detested relic of federalism, and so made his name immortal in the mountains. Although "executive influence" over Congress had been a party cry of the Republicans when in opposition, Gallatin worked as cozily with the Republican majorities in Congress as Hamilton had with the Federalists, and he managed to reduce the national debt from $80 million to $45 million in ten years.

Under Washington and Adams, Congress had often appropriated lump sums to the different departments to spend at their discretion. The Republicans always opposed this practice as violating the sacred principle of separation of powers. Jefferson and Gallatin, with unusual self-denial, now recommended a change, but Congress moved very slowly toward the modern practice and slight detail was applied to the three basic appropriations for army, navy, and the civil list. The navy, for instance, was granted lump sums for pay, provisions, repairs, and maintenance of yards and docks, giving it a discretion that the navy department now regards somewhat wistfully, when its budget is over a hundred times as great.

Jefferson's remark, "We are all republicans — we are all federalists," caused no little dismay in his own camp. Commodore James Nicholson, Gallatin's father-in-law, asked if enemies were to be kept "in office to trample on us." William B. Giles, the loud-mouthed bully of the Virginia delegation, reminded the President that "a pretty general purgation of office, has been one of the benefits expected by the friends of the new order of things." No one seriously charged the federal civil service with inefficiency or corruption, but it was almost completely Federalist, since Washington and Adams never knowingly appointed an Antifederalist or a Republican. Offices were regarded as proper rewards for public service, and Jefferson's followers were hungry There was then no such thing as a retirement pension, and Jefferson complained that officials seldom die, and never resign. He had to create vacancies by the presidential prerogative of removal. There was no general purge, only a mild bloodletting; but even that did not square with the bland professions of the inaugural discourse. It was a good instance of what Hamilton called Jefferson's "ineradicable duplicity" — seeming to say one thing while meaning another. But neither Jefferson nor his three immediate successors tried to buy votes in Congress with patronage; and Jefferson's appointments, in the main, were excellent.

Other features of the Federalist establishment were retained, such as discriminatory tonnage duties, fishing bounties, and the mixed commissions set up under Jay's treaty. The army was reduced by a "chaste reformation," as Jefferson called it, from 4000 to 2500 men; but Congress in 1802 enlarged President Adams's school for army gunners and sappers at West Point to create the Military Academy. The Republican press having viciously attacked the navy as a sink of waste and corruption, and a vile imitation of England's, Jefferson, who knew nothing about ships, felt he must cut it down radically. An act of the last Federalist Congress allowed the President to reduce by about two-thirds the respectable navy that had been built up during the hostilities with France. Jefferson not only did that, selling naval vessels to become merchantmen, but stopped new construction, discharged every naval constructor, and had most of the retained frigates dismantled to save expense. Naturally they disintegrated; wooden ships cannot be "put up in mothballs" like modern steel warships. Yet, paradoxically, the most brilliant achievements of Jefferson's first administration were in war and diplomacy!

The only Federalist creation that Jefferson really tried to destroy was the judiciary, where the Federalists had invited attack. In January 1801 President Adams made his most fortunate appointment, that of John Marshall as Chief Justice of the United States. Toward Marshall his kinsman Jefferson entertained an implacable hatred because he had shown him up and broken the sentimental French bubble in the X Y Z affair. The last Federalist Congress passed a new judiciary act (February 1801) creating sixteen circuit courts to relieve Supreme Court justices of the arduous duty of riding circuit. Had President Adams left it to Jefferson to make the new appointments, the law might have stood; but he filled up every newly established judicial office by "midnight appointments" on the evening of 3 March. Consequently, Jefferson hammered at Congress until he got this law replaced by a new judiciary act which added one more justice to the Supreme Court but abolished the new circuit courts and required all federal judges to resume their wide-ranging horseback exercise. A peculiar item in this act postponed the next session of the Supreme Court to February 1803.

At that session Chief Justice Marshall defied the executive in the case of *Marbury* v. *Madison*. William Marbury was one of forty-two justices of the peace for the District of Columbia, included among President Adams's "midnight appointments." Madison, the new secretary of state, refused to deliver his commission to Marbury, who then sued him for it before the Supreme

Court. By a legal twist, which the Jeffersonians considered mere chicanery, the Chief Justice managed to deliver an opinion which has become classic, on the superiority of the Constitution over acts of Congress: "The particular phraseology of the Constitution of the United States confirms and strengthens the principle, supposed to be essential to all written constitutions, that a law repugnant to the Constitution is void; and that *courts*, as well as other departments, are bound by that instrument."

Jefferson now incited some of his henchmen in the House to move against certain federal judges. A district judge who had become intemperate to the point of insanity was removed by impeachment. The next victim was to be Justice Samuel Chase of the Supreme Court, a signer of the Declaration of Independence, who on the bench had made himself peculiarly obnoxious to the Republicans, predicting that under Jefferson "our republican constitution will sink into a mobocracy, the worst of all possible governments." The House of Representatives presented him for impeachment on several counts of malfeasance and misfeasance in office. Strange to relate, after all that had been said about the danger of following British precedents, the Senate was fitted up in imitation of the House of Lords at the impeachment of Warren Hastings. Vice President Burr, who a few months earlier had killed Alexander Hamilton in a duel, presided; and the eloquent John Randolph of Roanoke prosecuted. There was no evidence to substantiate the serious charges against Justice Chase, although his manners on the bench were bad; and when it came to a vote on 1 March 1805 the impeachment failed.

Had Chase been found guilty on the flimsy evidence presented, there is good reason to believe that the entire Supreme Court would have been impeached and purged. As it was, this trial proved to be the highwater mark of Jefferson's radicalism. Under Chief Justice Marshall conservatism rallied, and from the Supreme Court there developed a subtle offensive of ideas — the supremacy of the nation, the rule of law, and the sanctity of property.

2. Pirates Punished and an Empire Acquired

By the time Jefferson became President, almost $2 million, one-fifth of the annual revenue, had been paid to the Moslem states of Morocco, Algiers, Tunis, and Tripoli, either to ransom prisoners or in return for permitting American merchant ships to sail the Mediterranean. Jefferson, after reducing the navy somewhat further than the Act of 3 March 1801 permitted, looked around for profitable employment of warships remaining afloat. He found it against the bashaw of Tripoli who, feeling he was not receiving enough tribute money, declared war on the United States in May 1801. This naval war dribbled along in desultory fashion until 1804, when Commodore Edward Preble appeared off Tripoli in command of a respectable task force, U.S.S. *Constitution* flagship, and dished out a series of bombardments. Before his arrival, frigate *Philadelphia* had grounded on a reef off Tripoli, from which the enemy floated her free. The bashaw imprisoned Captain Bainbridge and his crew, and would have equipped the frigate for his own navy had not Lieutenant Stephen Decatur, in captured schooner *Intrepid*, entered the harbor at night, boarded and captured *Philadelphia* and, after setting fire to her, made a safe getaway. Decatur performed other dashing feats in this war, but the most extraordinary exploit in it was that of a former army officer named William Eaton, American consul at Tunis.

Eaton, who had acquired a deep disgust for the pirate prince of Tripoli, and believed that blockade and bombardment would never defeat him, persuaded the American naval commander on the Mediterranean station to espouse the cause of a pretender to the Tripolitan "throne," then in exile in Egypt. At Alexandria he collected a force composed of sixteen members of the United States Navy and Marine Corps, forty Greeks, a squadron of Arab cavalry, a hundred nondescripts, and a fleet of camels. Under his command this motley expeditionary force marched over 500 miles across the Libyan desert, the terrain made famous in World War II by the exploits of Rommel and Montgomery, to Derna. Eaton then led an attack on that town, in which three American man-of-war brigs co-operated, and captured it. His exploit led to a favorable treaty with Tripoli, negotiated by the captured Captain Bainbridge. Eaton's efforts went for nought, he and the rival bashaw were repudiated, and he became an embittered enemy of the Jefferson administration.

While Tripoli was being taught a lesson, the boundary of the United States advanced to the Rocky Mountains. Louisiana, comprising all territory between the Mississippi and the Rockies, had been in Spanish possession since 1769. Less than one per cent of it was settled. The Creoles, numbering with their slaves about 40,000 in 1800, were concentrated on both banks of the lower Mississippi. There were a few garrisons and trading posts on the west bank of the river up to St. Louis, and a few more on the Red river; the rest was in undisputed Indian possession. Sugar cane and cotton had recently been introduced from the West Indies, and the commercial importance of the Mississippi river to the American West was greater than ever.

The retrocession of this great province from Spain to France, by a secret treaty on 1 October 1800, completed the policy of successive French governments to replace the loss of Canada by a more profitable base in North America. Bonaparte, as soon as his hands were free in Europe, proposed to make France the first power in the New World as in the Old. As it was inconvenient to take immediate possession of Louisiana, he kept the treaty secret until late in 1801, when another event revealed its implications. Bonaparte dispatched an expeditionary force to Hispaniola with orders to suppress Toussaint L'Ouverture's Negro republic and then take possession of New Orleans and Louisiana. The prospect of a veteran French army at America's back door was very unpleasant. On 18 April 1802 Jefferson wrote to the American minister at Paris, "The day that France takes possession of New Orleans . . . we must marry ourselves to the British fleet and nation." He was ready to adopt Washington's formula of "temporary alliances for extraordinary emergencies."

Late in 1802 the Spanish governor of Louisiana withdrew the right of transit at New Orleans from American traders. The West exploded with indignation, and the Federalists, delighted at an opportunity to divide Jefferson from his Western admirers, fanned the flame and clamored for war.

Jefferson remained serene and imperturbable. His annual message, in December 1802, breathed platitudes of peace, friendship, and economy. In the meantime, some of his friends pushed through Congress an appropriation of $2 million for "expenses in relation to the intercourse between the United States and foreign nations." And in March 1803 the President commissioned James Monroe as envoy extraordinary to France, with an interesting set of instructions to himself and to the resident minister Robert Livingston.

First they were to offer anything up to $10 million for New Orleans and the Floridas. That would give the United States the whole left bank of the Mississippi, and the Gulf coast. If France refused, $7.5 million should be offered for the Island of New Orleans alone. Failing there, they must press for a perpetual guarantee of the right of transit. If that were refused, Monroe and Livingston were ordered to "open a confidential communication with ministers of the British government," with a view to "candid understanding, and a closer connection with Great Britain."

Livingston began the negotiations before Monroe sailed, and at first made little progress. Fortunately for us, Bonaparte, who was about to renew war with England and make himself emperor, was becoming disgusted with the Hispaniola campaign. Troops had been poured into that island to the number of 35,000, and yellow fever swept away those that the Haitians did not kill. Without Hispaniola, Louisiana lost half its value to France; and when war came, Louisiana, for want of French sea power to keep up communications, would be Britain's for the plucking. So, why not sell it to the United States?

On 11 April 1803, the day that France broke diplomatic relations with England, Talleyrand suddenly remarked to Livingston, "What will you give for the *whole* of Louisiana?" Livingston gasped that he supposed the United States would not object to paying $4 million. "Too low!" said Talleyrand. "Reflect and see me tomorrow." Napoleon had already determined to sell the whole. On 30 April 1803 the treaty of cession was signed; $12 million was paid for the province of Louisiana as acquired by France from Spain, and the United States assumed the claims of citizens against France for the naval spoliations of 1797–98. Inhabitants of Louisiana were guaranteed the rights of American citizens, and eventual admission to the Union.

The Louisiana purchase turned out to be the greatest bargain in American history; but in 1803 it seemed likely that the United States was paying $12 million for a scrap of paper. Her title was defective on several points. The province was still in the hands of Spain. Bonaparte had promised never to dispose of Louisiana to a third power. The French constitution allowed no alienation of national territory without a vote of the legislature. The boundaries were indefinite; how far north Louisiana extended, and whether it included West Florida or Texas, or neither, was uncertain. Finally, according to the "strict construction" of the Virginia Republicans, the treaty itself was unconstitutional! If the federal government, as Jefferson had always claimed, possessed no power not expressly granted, the President had no right to increase the national domain by treaty, much less to promise incorporation in the Union to people outside its original limits.

Jefferson's constitutional scruples vanished when a letter arrived from Livingston, urging immediate ratification before Napoleon changed his mind. The President's friends furnished him with some good Hamiltonian arguments, and the treaty was ratified by the Senate. On 30 November 1803 Louisiana was formally handed over by the Spanish governor to a French prefect, who promptly established the *code Napoléon,* and as many other French institutions as he could think up. Three weeks later he transferred it to the United States.

Even before the purchase, Jefferson had ordered Meriwether Lewis and William Clark, officers of the regular army, to conduct an overland exploring expedition in the hope of finding a water route from the headwaters of the Missouri river to the Pacific. Lewis and Clark left St. Louis 14 May 1804 with thirty-two soldiers and ten civilians, embarked in a 55-foot keel boat and two "periaguas." These, propelled by sails and oars, took them up the Missouri into North Dakota, where they wintered among the Mandan near the site of Bismarck, and the following spring pushed on into Montana. A fleet of dugout canoes, built above the Great Falls, took them to the foothills of the Rocky Mountains in what is now Idaho. Here their interpreter Sacajawea made friendly contact with the Shoshone, who furnished horses for the men, and women to tote the baggage. Crossing the Lemhi pass over the Rockies, the expedition moved north down the Bitter Root valley and in the Nez Percé country reached a branch of the westward-flowing Snake. In newly built boats they rowed down-stream to the Columbia, reaching tidewater on 7 November 1805. There, within sound of the Pacific breakers, the party built Fort Clatsop. Lewis and Clark expected to hail a ship and sail home, since through the coastal Indians' use of such elegant phrases as "son-of-a-pitch" they guessed that Yankee fur traders had been frequenting this region.

Months passed with no ship, so the leaders decided to return overland. Lewis and half the party took the shorter route to the Great Falls, while the other half cut overland from the forks of the Missouri to the Yellowstone, and floated down to its junction with the Missouri at the site of Fort Union. There the leaders met, and the expedition reached St. Louis 23 September 1806 intact, having avoided fights with the Indians.

Jefferson was delighted with Lewis and Clark's reports, their conduct toward the natives, and the specimens that they brought to Washington; and their journals are still a valuable source of information on the Far West in the early nineteenth century.

"Never was there an administration more brilliant than that of Mr. Jefferson up to this period," said John Randolph in later years. "We were indeed in the 'full tide of successful experiment.' Taxes repealed; the public debt amply provided for, both principal and interest; sinecures abolished; Louisiana acquired; public confidence unbounded."

3. *Plots and Conspiracies*

Jefferson yearned to convert New England from her perverse conservatism. He appreciated the danger of attempting to govern a loose federal union by a sectional party, and hoped by moderation to persuade the Yankees that their mercantile and shipping interests were safe in Republican hands. Gains in the congressional elections of 1802–3 showed that he was succeeding; but the Federalist leaders grew bitter and desperate as their power waned.

To the clergy and party leaders of New England, Jefferson's victory was a triumph of democracy, which to them meant terror, atheism, and free love. "The principles of democracy are everywhere what they have been in France," wrote Fisher Ames. "Our country is too big for union, too sordid for patriotism, too democratic for liberty." New England was yet pure; but the barricades to her virtue were falling. "And must we with folded hands wait the result?" asked Senator Pickering of Massachusetts. "The principles of our Revolution point to the remedy — a separation."

Thus Virginians like John Taylor had reasoned in 1798 when Virginia was hag-ridden by the Federalists. Jefferson then had calmed them with a promise of victory, but no such hope could console New England Federalists for the Louisiana purchase. Their minority was dwindling, and they knew it. Ohio, admitted to the Union in 1803, looked to Virginia for guidance, although largely settled by Yankees. In all probability the new states to be formed from Louisiana would follow the same light. New England Federalists reasoned that the annexation of that vast province, upsetting the balance of power within the Union, absolved all original states from their allegiance. Before 1803 was out, Timothy Pickering, Roger Griswold, and other leaders in Massachusetts and Connecticut, began to plan a Northern Confederacy of New England and New York, "exempt from the corrupt and corrupting influence and oppression of the aristocratic democrats of the South." New England conservatives in 1804, like Southern conservatives in 1861, assumed that a political boundary could protect them from ideas.

Knowledge of this conspiracy was confined to a very few Federalists, and the British minister at Washington in whom they confided. Hamilton would have none of it. Intrigue was repulsive to his character, and reasoning such as Pickering's to his intellect. Secession was a futile cure for democracy, he pointed out, since the democratic "poison" was already present in every Northern state.

The conspirators then turned to Aaron Burr. He had carried New York for Jefferson in 1800, and without that state's vote Jefferson could not have been elected. Once safe in office, Jefferson ignored Burr in distributing New York patronage, and his party dropped Burr from the presidential ticket in 1804 in favor of George Clinton. The Vice President then decided to contest the governorship of New York with the regular Republican candidate. In return for Federalist aid in this election he agreed, if successful, to swing New York into the Northern Confederacy and become its president. Hamilton, on hearing of this deal, advised his friends to vote against Burr, and defeated him. The Federalist conspiracy then dissolved. How remote its chance of success the election of 1804 proved; Jefferson and Clinton carried all New England except Connecticut, and every other state except Delaware.

Burr was a ruined politician at the age of forty-eight, but far from finished. He had broken with the Republicans and failed the Federalists. Hamilton was responsible. This was not the first time that Hamilton had crossed his path, but it must be the last. In June 1804, six weeks after the New York election, Burr wrote to his enemy, demanding retraction of a slur upon his character reported in the press. Hamilton refused, Burr challenged him to a duel, Hamilton accepted. He had no business to accept, for he did not believe in dueling and he did not need to prove his courage. But Hamilton expected the Jefferson regime to end in anarchy like the French Republic. America would then demand a Bonaparte, and he intended to fill that role; but no one suspected of cowardice could do that. So Hamilton went to his doom, resolved to prove his courage, yet not kill; to throw away his fire in the hope that his adversary would miss and honor be satisfied. Aaron Burr, in the duel on 11 July 1804 under the Palisades, took deliberate aim and hit Hamilton just below his chest. Death relieved him after thirty hours of intense suffering.

So perished one of the greatest men of the age, for his little faith in the government he had helped to form, and in the people he had served so well.

Before leaving Washington at the expiration of his term as Vice President (4 March 1805), Burr approached the British minister with an offer to detach Louisiana from the Union for half a million dollars and the loan of a naval force. The minister thought well of the offer and urged his government to buy, but received no reply. Britain was not interested in promoting American secession. Burr then proceeded to the headwaters of the Ohio, and sailed down-river in a luxury flatboat, stopping over to visit prominent people and to promote some project — a different one to each. The Westerners, duellers themselves, were charmed by the polished gentleman from New York. Harman Blennerhasset, a romantic Irish exile, was fascinated by a plan to conquer Mexico and make Burr emperor, and himself grand chamberlain. In Tennessee, Burr met and won the friendship of Andrew Jackson, who proposed getting him into the Senate if he would make his home in Tennessee. James Wilkinson, an old friend of Burr, still in Spanish pay while federal governor of Louisiana Territory and commanding general of the United States Army, had already, in Washington, discussed with him a secret project. They would "liberate" Mexico from Spain, and at the same time make Louisiana an independent republic, which Mississippi Territory would surely decide to join. At New Orleans Burr got in touch with Creoles who disliked being annexed to the United States, and with American filibusters who were eager to invade Mexico. The Catholic bishop of New Orleans and the Mother Superior of the Ursuline convent gave Burr their support and blessing. Returning overland to Washington, Burr obtained $2500 from the Spanish minister, ostensibly to promote the independence of Louisiana and the West.

In the summer of 1806 the former Vice President established his headquarters at Lexington, Kentucky, and began active recruiting for his expedition. His public pretext was to take up a dubious claim to 400,000 acres of land in western Louisiana which he had purchased. Evidence is strong that Burr intended to wait at Natchez until his supporters at New Orleans had declared the independence of Louisiana, and offered him the presidency; he would then build up his army and on some pretext invade Mexico. By the end of the year, Burr and Blennerhasset, commanding an advance guard in ten flatboats, had reached the mouth of the Cumberland river. At this juncture General Wilkinson, deciding that Burr was worth more to betray than to befriend, wrote a lurid letter to President Jefferson denouncing "a deep, dark, wicked, and widespread conspiracy" on Burr's part to dismember the Union. Jefferson issued a proclamation offering a reward for Burr's arrest. He was apprehended and brought to Richmond for trial on the charge of treason against the United States.

The President left no stone unturned to obtain a conviction. Chief Justice Marshall presided at the trial and took care that the constitutional definition of treason, "levying war against the United States or adhering to their enemies," with the safeguard of "two witnesses to the same overt act," was strictly observed. Hence it followed that the mere gathering of forces with intent to promote secession was not treason if the expedition collapsed. Burr was acquitted. Regretting, no doubt, that he had not killed Jefferson instead of Hamilton, he sought exile in Europe. Wilkinson, a traitor to every cause he embraced, retained his command and the confidence of the President.

This was the most formidable secession conspiracy prior to 1860, one which probably would have succeeded had not Wilkinson ratted on Burr. Not adventurers only but hundreds of respectable people in many parts of the country were behind Burr, although most of these supporters, including Andrew Jackson, were duped by the public explanation that he intended a mere filibustering expedition.

Burr continued his schemes in Europe. His charm was such that he obtained money from influential people in England and France for wild schemes such as restoring Canada to France, and enlisting unemployed sailors during Jefferson's embargo to march on Washington and set up himself as dictator. By some means he obtained a passport and returned to the United States in 1812, built up a law business in New York, and, at the age of seventy-seven, married the beautiful widow Jumel, who used to boast that she was the only woman in the world who had slept both with George Washington and Napoleon Bonaparte. After he had run through her property she divorced him, shortly before his death in 1836.

4. Foreign Complications and the Embargo

The acquittal of Justice Chase, and of Aaron Burr, marked a turning point in Jefferson's fortune and popularity. His second term, which began on 4

March 1805, was compared by Bible readers to Pharaoh's dream of the seven lean kine that ate up the seven fat kine. Many old Virginia Republicans felt that Jefferson had deserted his own principles with the acquisition of Louisiana; as he certainly did when, in his second innaugural address, he recommended spending federal money on roads and other internal improvements. As John Randolph put it, Jefferson spelled Federalism backward for four years, and now began spelling it forward again, by adopting policies that he had formerly condemned. The President began to rely for support in Congress on Republicans from the Northern states, who for the most part were a sad lot, interested mainly in patronage. Randolph called one of them, Barnabas Bidwell of Massachusetts (who later fled to Canada to excape the consequences of stealing public money), "The President's clerk of the water-closet."

To do Jefferson justice, he built up the federal government (what Randolph meant by "spelling Federalism forward") to cope with the European situation. Peace in Europe had been the condition of his earlier success; but there was to be no peace in Europe for many years. By the end of 1805 Napoleon had become supreme on land, and Britain on the ocean. Each sought to strangle or starve the other by continental or maritime blockade. Washington and Adams dealt with one belligerent at a time; Jefferson was confronted with both at once. A clever diplomat might conceivably have played off one country against another, with an armed force as stake in the game. But neither Jefferson nor Madison could grasp the realities of Napoleonic Europe, and the President began a further reduction of the United States Navy even before concluding peace with Tripoli.

During Mediterranean hostilities, American naval officers had felt the need of small gunboats for use in shoal water and light wind. Jefferson snapped at this suggestion for more than it was worth, "believing," as he wrote, "that gunboats are the only *water* defence which can be useful to us, and protect us from the ruinous folly of a navy." Gunboats were cheap, they could be hauled out when not in use, and contracts for their construction by numerous small shipbuilders could be used to reward the faithful.[1] Congress did provide a useful class of 119-foot sloops of war (*Hornet* and *Wasp*) and 80-foot brigs (*Nautilus*, *Vixen*, *Viper*). But instead of the frigates that the leading naval officers wanted, Congress caused 69 gunboats to be built by 1807. None sailed to Europe in time for the Tripolitan war; not one proved useful in the next war. These little vessels, averaging 60 feet in length and costing about $10,000 each, were equipped with a battery of one or two guns, which in foul weather had to be stowed below to prevent the vessel's capsizing. When one gunboat, torn from her moorings by a spring tide and heavy gale, was deposited in a cornfield, a Federalist wit offered the toast: "Gunboat No. 3: If our gunboats are no use on the water, may they at least be the best on earth!"

1. For instance, Matthew Lyon, hero of the first fist-fight in Congress, jailed under the Sedition Act, and returned to Congress in time to cast the vote of his state for Jefferson, was given a contract for five gunboats at Eddyville, Ky., on the Ohio river.

For two years Jefferson's principal foreign problems were connected with British sea power. For the Royal Navy in 1805 resumed its disagreeable practice of impressing sailors from American vessels on the high seas. Britain never claimed the right to impress native-born Americans; but until other means were found to recruit the Royal Navy, she insisted on impressing the king's subjects from foreign vessels wherever encountered. As Britain did not then recognize expatriation — nor did the United States — American naturalization was no protection to British-born seamen. And it was notorious that the comparatively high wages in the United States Navy and merchant marine stimulated desertion from the Royal Navy; the *Constitution* in 1807 carried 149 British subjects and 29 other foreigners in her crew of 419.

British frigates began operating off New York in 1805, stopping every passing vessel and stripping her of seamen whom the captain supposed to be British subjects. American merchants and shipowners, making big profits in neutral trade, remained silent under these indignities until Sir William Scott announced in the *Essex* case the doctrine of continuous voyages. This meant that the voyage of a neutral ship from an enemy port, calling at a neutral country and then going on to another enemy port, was in effect one continuous voyage, which rendered both ship and cargo good prize. The United States enforced the same principle against blockade runners during the Civil War.

James Madison, secretary of state, now sent a set of unrealistic instructions to James Monroe and William Pinkney, joint ministers to Great Britain: England must stop impressment, scrap the continuous voyage doctrine, and pay for confiscations under the *Essex* decision. Monroe and Pinkney soon realized that without a strong navy to back them up, these demands were a joke. So, at the end of 1806, they accepted the best terms they could get. Britain offered to moderate her maritime practices without abandoning any principle, and to improve the situation of American commerce without granting complete reciprocity. But this smelled so of Jay's hated treaty against which the Republicans had screamed "Treason!" that Jefferson did not even submit the Monroe-Pinkney treaty to the Senate.

In June 1807 there occurred an impressment outrage that brought the two countries to the verge of war. A British squadron, stationed within the Capes of the Chesapeake to blockade two French warships which were being repaired at Annapolis, was losing men by desertion. The officers had reason to believe that many had enlisted in the United States Navy, which was true. On 22 June U.S.S. *Chesapeake*, flying the broad pennant of Commodore James Barron, got under way from Norfolk, and among her crew were a number of these deserters. Ten miles outside the Capes, H.M.S. *Leopard* drew alongside and demanded the right to examine *Chesapeake*'s crew and impress deserters and, when Barron refused, poured three broadsides into the American warship and rendered her helpless. Barron's crew was then mustered by *Leopard*'s officers, who impressed a British-born deserter, an American Negro, an Indian, and a native of Maryland.

News of this insult to the flag brought the first united expression of American feeling since 1798. Even the Federalists, who hitherto defended every move of the British, went along. If Jefferson had summoned Congress to a special session, he could have had war at the drop of a hat, and a more popular and successful war than the one finally declared in 1812. But Jefferson's serenity was undisturbed. He instructed Monroe to demand apology and reparation in London, and ordered British warships out of American territorial waters. When Congress met in late October, the President obtained an appropriation of $850,000 for building 188 more gunboats, and ordered three of the largest vessels of the seagoing navy to be hauled out. No suggestion of war, or war preparations.

For Jefferson imagined he could strangle England by economic sanctions. For years he had been wanting an opportunity to try commercial exclusion as a substitute for war. The moment had arrived. A private word to the faithful in Congress, and in one day, 22 December 1807, it passed the Embargo Act. American or other vessels were forbidden to sail foreign; all exports from the United States whether by sea or land were prohibited; certain specified articles of British manufacture were refused entrance. The embargo went into effect immediately; and for fourteen months all American ships that were not already abroad, and could not escape, lay in port or went coasting.

From what particular egg in Jefferson's clutch of theories this chick was hatched it is difficult to say. Probably he was merely carrying out a favorite Republican theory that American trade was so vital to Great Britain that she would collapse if it were stopped. But the embargo was not directed against England alone. Napoleon had issued drastic decrees against neutral trade, confiscating any neutral ship which had touched at a British port. The Republicans defended the embargo as a protection to American shipowners, who wanted no part of it. For they were thriving on trade with England under a system of licensing and inspection far less rigorous than the methods adopted by the United States and her allies in both world wars.

There were plenty of leaks in the embargo. Smuggling of British goods and American products went on over the Canadian frontier, on the Great Lakes, and from Spanish Florida. But there was much suffering in the seaports. Unemployed seamen and shipwrights emigrated in large numbers to the British provinces. The great shipowners who already had fleets abroad survived the embargo well enough; but many others were ruined, and certain small seaports such as Newburyport and New Haven never recovered their earlier prosperity. Agricultural produce fell, and the interior had to live on its own fat; but cotton, tobacco, and wheat could bear storage better than ships. Consequently, the embargo bore most heavily on New England and New York; and it was there that its political effects were felt by the administration.

One of these leaks became legendary. John Jacob Astor, who had branched out from fur trading to the China trade, managed to get his 427-ton ship *Beaver* out and home through the embargo by playing a trick on Jefferson. A character describing himself as "The Honorable Punqua Wingchong, a Chinese mandarin," requested permission to charter a ship to return from New York to China, "where the affairs of his family and particularly the funeral obsequies of his grandfather, require his solemn attention." Jefferson, thinking this might strengthen American relations with China, ordered Gallatin, who knew John Jacob Astor, to issue the necessary papers. Gallatin not only did so but allowed Hon. Punqua to take numerous "attendants" and $45,000 worth of specie or merchandise, and permitted the *Beaver* to bring a return cargo from China. As it turned out, the alleged mandarin was a petty clerk in Astor's employ, the cargoes were Astor's speculations; and the *Beaver*, returning to New York crammed with China goods while the embargo was still in effect, put her owner well on his way to becoming the richest man in America.

As a successful diplomatic weapon, commercial retaliation requires an unusual combination of circumstances, such as actually occurred four years later, but not in 1808. The embargo created a shortage of provisions in the French islands and of colonial produce in France; but Napoleon, tongue in cheek, confiscated every American vessel that arrived at a French port, on the ground that he was enforcing Jefferson's wishes. British shipowners were delighted with Jefferson's policy. When the American minister in London offered to lift the embargo if Britain would withdraw her antineutral orders, George Canning replied that His Majesty's government "would gladly have facilitated its removal as a measure of inconvenient restriction upon the American people." As John Quincy Adams once remarked, Canning "had a little too much wit for a minister of state."

Jefferson's mistake was the Federalists' opportunity. Their strength had been dwindling steadily; in 1807 every state government except Connecticut had gone Republican. Senator Pickering, the secession conspirator of 1804, rallied Yankee opinion in a public letter, asserting that the embargo was dictated by Napoleon and adopted by Jefferson in hope of helping him and impoverishing New England. Northern Republicans were restive under a measure that turned their constituents Federalist; and in New York City the embargo produced a schism in the Republican party. When Madison was nominated for the presidential succession by a congressional caucus, the New York legislature placed George Clinton in nomination as an anti-embargo Republican. In Virginia, a group of dissident Republicans nominated Monroe, disaffected by Jefferson's treatment of his English draft treaty. If a union could have been effected between this faction and the Federalists, Madison might have been defeated; as it was, the Federalist candidate carried little but New England, and Madison was elected President by a comfortable majority.

Jefferson intended to maintain the embargo until the British orders or the French decrees were repealed. In January 1809 Congress passed a Force Act, permitting federal officials without warrant to seize goods under suspicion of foreign destination, and protecting them from legal liability for their actions. George III and Lord North had been tender in comparison! The New England people, now in their second winter of privation, began to look to their state governments for protection, and by this time every state government in New England was Federalist. The state legislatures hurled back in the teeth of Jefferson and Madison the doctrines of the Kentucky and Virginia resolves of 1798. A proposal to summon a New England convention for nullification of the embargo was under serious discussion in February 1809. But by that time the embargo had been in force fourteen months, the Northern Republicans revolted, and Jefferson was shaken by a battery of resolutions from New England town meetings, some threatening secession. A bill for the repeal of the embargo was rushed through Congress, and on 1 March 1809 Jefferson signed it. Three days later his term ended, and he retired to Monticello.

The embargo was intended to be the crowning glory of Jefferson's second administration, as Louisiana had been of his first. It proved to be his greatest mistake. It altered the policy of Britain or of Napoleon not by one hair, it failed to protect the American merchant marine, and it convinced many good people that the Virginia Dynasty was bound to the Napoleonic. Pro-British leanings of the Federalist party were confirmed and strengthened; and whatever President Madison might do, he would never have such united support as Jefferson had enjoyed in 1807.

Of all ironies in American history, the career and influence of Thomas Jefferson are the greatest. This Virginia aristocrat and slave-owner proclaimed the "self-evident" truth "that all men are created equal." In so doing he undermined and overthrew both Tories and Federalists, who believed that man was created highly unequal and that the best, not the most, should govern. The Federalists, but for Jefferson — and their own folly — might have continued for another generation to direct the government along conservative and national lines; might even have settled the Negro question without war, which Jefferson's disciples were unable to do. His Southern supporters accepted Jefferson's principles with the reservation that they applied only to white men, and used them mainly as a stick to beat the Federalists and win power. But the Northerners whom Jefferson converted to his views took him seriously and literally. They came to believe that political equality meant all Americans, no matter what race or color; that democracy meant rule of the majority, not by a cultivated minority of merchants and landowners. Long did the art of politicians ignore or muffle this ambiguity; but when the issue became really acute in 1860–61, the society which Jefferson loved, and which still worshipped his name, repudiated both his basic principles; and in so doing was overthrown by the society which had taken those principles to heart. If Jefferson anticipated the end product of his "glittering generalities," he was a humbug; if not, he lacked intelligence.

Still, the gift of prophecy is given to few men. We should judge Jefferson by his acts rather than his words; and still more by what he refrained from doing when he had the power. Of all revolutionists (taking him at his own word that he was one), Jefferson was the most tolerant. He never "brayed humanity in a mortar to bring the savor from the bruised root." [1] Accustomed as we now are to revolutionary leaders imposing their policies by rigid tyranny and cruel oppression, we may take inspiration from one who deliberately preferred the slow process of reason to the short way of force. By his forbearance, even more than by his acts, Jefferson kept alive the flame of liberty that Napoleon had almost snuffed out in Europe.

1. Robinson Jeffers, *Apology for Bad Dreams.*

The Second War with Great Britain

1809-1815

1. *Diplomacy and Drift*

J AMES MADISON must be accounted a great statesman, owing to his labors on
the Federal Constitution, but he was a very poor politician; and we have
learned by experience that to be a successful President one has to be a good
politician. Slight in stature and unimpressive in personality, eager to please but
always looking puzzled, as if people were too much for him, "Jemmy" Madison had few intimate friends, and among the people at large he inspired little
affection and no enthusiasm. He had a talent for writing logical diplomatic
notes; but logic was of little use in dealing with Europeans locked in a deadly
struggle. Negative in his dealings with Congress, he allowed Jefferson's personal "strings" for influencing House and Senate to rot from disuse. And he
was stubborn to the point of stupidity.

Yet, within six weeks of his inauguration on 4 March 1809, Madison was
being greeted as a great peacemaker. Congress, when repealing Jefferson's
embargo, substituted a non-intercourse act aimed at both Britain and France,
with the promise that the President would restore commercial relations with
either nation, if and when it repealed its decrees injuring American commerce. Madison, almost too eager to reach an understanding with England,
arranged a treaty with Erskine, the British minister in Washington, by virtue
of which His Majesty's government would rescind its orders in council against
neutral shipping, and the United States would resume normal trading relations with Britain but maintain non-intercourse with France. Touchy subjects
such as impressment and the *Chesapeake* affair were postponed.

Had this draft been accepted by George Canning, the British foreign minister, there would have been no second war with England. But Canning
brutally and inexplicably repudiated both Erskine and the treaty, and Anglo-
American relations returned to a state of mutual recrimination. The Congress
that assembled in December 1809 had no idea what to do, and received no
lead from Madison. On 16 April 1810 it voted to reduce both the army and the
navy, weak as they already were. And on 1 May it passed the so-called
Macon's Bill No. 2, reversing the principle of the Non-Intercourse Act of
1809. This law restored intercourse with both Britain and France, but promised to the first power which recognized neutral rights, to stop trading with its

enemy. American shipping soon engaged in making profits under British licenses, and merchant tonnage reached figures that were not attained for another twenty years.

Madison took advantage of this interlude in commercial warfare to take a bite of West Florida. The Republican administrations claimed it to be part of Louisiana, but forbore to insist while there was hope of inducing the Spanish government to recognize the claim. In 1810 the Spanish empire appeared to be breaking up. Accordingly, the inhabitants of that portion of West Florida bordering on the Mississippi "self-determined" for the United States, seized Baton Rouge, and were incorporated by presidential proclamation into the Territory of Orleans, which two years later became the State of Louisiana. In May 1812 a second bite was taken when the district between the Pearl and Perdido rivers was annexed by Act of Congress to Mississippi Territory.

Napoleon found time between campaigns, and divorcing Josephine and marrying Marie Louise, to cast his eye over Macon's Act and observe an opportunity to incorporate the United States in his continental system. That system was strikingly similar to Hitler's scheme for bringing England to her knees without winning control of the sea. It meant getting the European continent under his control, in order to impoverish the country which he, like Hitler, considered "a nation of shopkeepers." America could help this strategy by adding a seapower component, as she actually did in 1812, too late to help Napoleon.

For five years Napoleon had treated American shipping harshly and arbitrarily. In the summer of 1810 our merchantmen in the Bay of Naples were seized by his command and sold. But on the same day Napoleon's foreign minister informed the American minister to France that "His Majesty loves the Americans," and as proof of his solicitude had declared that his decrees against neutral shipping after 1 November would be revoked, "it being understood that the English are to revoke their orders in council."

John Quincy Adams, then minister to Russia, warned Madison that this note was "a trap to catch us into a war with England." But the guileless President snapped at the bait. By proclamation on 2 November 1810 he announced that France had rescinded her antineutral system and that nonintercourse would be revived against Britain, if in three months' time she did not repeal her orders in council. Almost every mail, for the next two years, brought news of fresh seizures and scuttlings of American vessels by French port authorities, warships and privateers. But Madison, having taken his stand, obstinately insisted that "the national faith was pledged to France." On 2 March 1811 he forbade intercourse with Great Britain, under authority of Macon's Act. That was a diplomatic victory for Napoleon; it brought the United States within his continental system. And at this, the third attempt, economic sanctions really worked on England, but too late to preserve the peace.

The winter of 1811–12 was the bitterest that the English people experienced between the Great Plague and 1940–41. Napoleon's continental system had now closed all western Europe except Portugal to British goods. American non-intercourse shut off the only important market still open except Russia, which Napoleon was about to try to force into his cordon. A crop failure drove up the price of wheat, warehouses were crammed with goods for which there was no market, factories were closing, workmen rioting. Deputations from the manufacturing cities besought Parliament to repeal the orders in council, hoping to recover their American market.

During these critical months several accidents postponed the repeal too long to maintain peace with America. On 16 May 1811 there took place an off-the-record fight between U.S. frigate *President* and H.M. corvette *Little Belt*, the results of which seemed to prove that the United States Navy was not to be feared. The American legation at London was vacant, except for a silly young chargé d'affaires, when the conciliatory Lord Castlereagh entered the foreign office. Spencer Perceval, the prime minister, was assassinated just after he had made up his mind to repeal the orders in council, and the business of finding a successor brought another and fatal delay. Finally on 16 June 1812 Castlereagh announced that the orders in council would be suspended immediately. If there had been a transatlantic cable, this would not have been too late. For Congress, without word of the concession, declared war against Great Britain two days later.

2. War Fever Rises

Congress so acted in response to a message from President Madison recommending war with Britain on four grounds — impressment of seamen, repeated violations of American territorial waters by the Royal Navy, declaring an enemy coast blockaded when it was not blockaded in fact, and the orders in council against neutral trade. Yet eight senators, a large majority of the congressmen from the New England states, and a majority in both houses from New York, New Jersey, and Maryland voted against the declaration of war; whilst representatives of the inland and Western states from Vermont to Tennessee, and of the states from Virginia south, were almost solid for war. New England, where three-quarters of American shipping was owned, and which supplied more than that proportion of American seamen, wanted no war and agitated against it to the brink of treason; whilst back-country congressmen who had never smelt salt water (unless in the Potomac) and whose constituents would as soon have thought of flying to the moon as enlisting in the United States Navy, screamed for "Free Trade and Sailors' Rights." And, still more curious, one-quarter of the Republicans abstained.

What is the explanation?

In the first place, a new generation of Americans which had grown to maturity since the Revolution was "feeling its oats." Nearly half the inept House that passed Macon's Act No. 2 failed of re-election in 1810–11, and new members became leaders. There were thirty-four-year-old Henry Clay and Richard M. Johnson from Kentucky, young Felix Grundy and the aged but bellicose John Sevier from Tennessee; Peter B. Porter, also in his thirties, from Buffalo, New York, and twenty-nine-year-old John C. Calhoun from the back country of South Carolina. These men, collectively dubbed the "war hawks" by John Randolph, combined with other new members to brush aside old Nathaniel Macon and elect Henry Clay speaker of the House; and Clay named his friends chairmen of the important committees. The war hawks wished to scuttle diplomacy and economic sanctions and declare war against Great Britain, using arguments that reminded old hands of the Hamiltonian reasons for war with France in 1798. They passed a bill to raise a regular army of 25,000 but did nothing for the navy; it was still Republican doctrine that navies were evil. Some of the war hawks wished also to declare war on France, but Madison used his influence to stop that. Stubbornly, against cumulative evidence of Napoleon's bad faith, the President insisted that France had repealed her antineutral decrees.

The war hawks were disgusted with the wordy diplomacy of Madison and his secretary of state Monroe; they felt that national honor demanded a fight. In vain the Federalist minority urged that if we must fight someone, we should fight France, since Napoleon had become the Number 1 enemy to the free world and an autocrat. But the war hawks had very good reasons for wanting to fight England, if they must fight someone. War with Great Britain, if successful, would conquer Canada, end the Indian menace on the western frontier and throw open more forest land for settlement by United States pioneers. These motives were open and avowed. John Randolph of Roanoke, leader of the old-fashioned "pure" Republicans who wished to keep the peace, poured his scorn on this "cant of patriotism," this "agrarian cupidity," this chanting "like the whippoorwill, but one monotonous tone — Canada! Canada! Canada! Not a syllable about Halifax, which unquestionably should be our great object in a war for maritime security." Land-hungry pioneers of the Old Northwest coveted the fertile, wooded peninsula of Upper Canada between Lakes Huron, Erie, and Ontario. Actually, several thousand emigrants from the United States had already infiltrated this country. They lived easy under the "British yoke," but the war hawks in Congress expected them to "rise as one man" and rally to the Stars and Stripes.

And there was the Indian question. The Treaty of Greenville (1795) put the Northwest Indians on the defensive. Jefferson professed benevolent principles toward them, but coveted their lands in order to encourage western migration and keep the United States agricultural. He looked forward to removing all Indians across the Mississippi. Such a policy could be squared with humanity and justice only by protecting the red men from the whites during the process; and that was not done. Although the Indians faithfully fulfilled their treaty stipulations, white pioneers in the Northwest committed the most wanton and cruel murders of them, for which it was almost impossible to obtain a conviction from a pioneer jury. From time to time a few hungry and desperate chiefs were rounded up by government officials and plied with oratory and whisky until they signed a treaty alienating the hunting grounds of their tribe; sometimes of other nations as well. Jefferson encouraged this process, and William Henry Harrison, superintendent of the Northwest Indians and governor of Indiana Territory, pushed it so successfully that between 1795 and 1809 the Indians parted with some 48 million acres.

The process then came to a temporary halt, owing largely to the formation of an Indian league or confederacy by two really noble savages, the twin brothers Tecumseh and Tenskwatawa, sons of a Shawnee chief. The former, a lithe, handsome, and stately warrior, had been one of those who defeated St. Clair in 1791; Tenskwatawa, better known as The Prophet, was a half-blind medicine man. These undertook the task of saving their people. They sought to reform their habits, stop the alienation of their land, keep them apart from the whites, and weld all tribes on United States soil into a confederacy. It was a movement of regeneration and defense; a menace indeed to the expansion of the West, but in no sense to its existence. The Indians had so decreased in the last decade that scarcely 4000 warriors were counted in the space between the Lakes, the Mississippi, and the Ohio. Opposed to them were at least 100,000 white men of fighting age in the Ohio valley.

For a time the partnership of warrior and priest was irresistible. The Prophet kindled a religious revival among the tribes of the Northwest and even induced them to give up intoxicating liquor. All intercourse with white men, except for trade, ceased; rum and whisky were refused with disdain. In 1808 the two leaders, forced from their old settlement by the palefaces, established headquarters at a great clearing in Indiana where Tippecanoe creek empties into the Wabash river. The entire frontier was alarmed; Indian prohibitionists were something new to backwoods experience.

Governor Harrison met the situation with an act that Tecumseh could only regard as a challenge. Rounding up a few score survivors of tribes whom he frankly described as "the most depraved wretches on earth," the governor obtained from them several enormous tracts, to the amount of some three million acres, cutting into the heart of Tecumseh's country up both banks of the Wabash. This deprived Tecumseh of his remaining hunting grounds and brought the white border within 50 miles of the Tippecanoe.

With justice, Tecumseh declared this treaty null and void. He called on the British authorities at Amherstburg in November 1810, and declared that he was ready for war; but Canada was not. More Western nations joined his confederacy, and in July 1811, assuring Governor Harrison that his object was defensive, he journeyed south to obtain the allegiance of the Creek nation. Harrison decided to force the issue. With the tacit approval of the war department, he collected about 1100 soldiers, marched up the Wabash valley and encamped hard by Tecumseh's village. The Prophet allowed himself to be maneuvered into battle by a few reckless young braves, who raised the war-whoop and pierced the first line of American tents. The engagement then became general, the Americans were almost surrounded; but after two hours' fighting Harrison drove the Indians into a swamp and destroyed their village. The general brought his army safely back to Vincennes and was hailed throughout the West as their savior. This Battle of Tippecanoe (7 November 1811) elected him President, thirty years later.

Throughout the West it was believed that Britain was behind Tecumseh's confederacy. That was not true; the confederacy would have been formed if there had been no white men in Canada. After Tippecanoe, however, the new governor general, Sir George Prevost, decided that war with the United States was inevitable, and his agents welcomed Tecumseh with his warriors at Amherstburg in June 1812.

These events explain why Western and many other patriots were keen for war with England. It would, they hoped, absorb Canada and wipe out the assumed source of Indian troubles. The Carolinians and Georgians went along because they hoped to do the same to the troublesome Creek nation and Spanish Florida, Spain being an ally of England. John Sevier, in the long debate on Madison's war message, said that "fire and sword" should be carried into the Creek country where "British emissaries" were supposed to be lurking, and that Florida should be annexed along with Canada. Henry Clay boasted, "The militia of Kentucky are alone competent to place Montreal and Upper Canada at your feet."

Shortly after the declaration of war, the Republican organ of Boston printed a gallant exhortation to the local citizenry:

> Since war is the word, let us strain every nerve
> To save our America, her glory increase;
> So, shoulder your firelock, your country preserve,
> For the hotter the war, boys, the quicker the peace.

But New England, now that an end had come to Indian raids on her frontier, showed very little sympathy with other frontiers.

3. The War of 1812: Aggressive Phase

Everyone knew, well before the declaration of 18 June 1812, that this war for "Free Trade and Sailors' Rights" would be fought largely on land, preferably in Canada. That made strategic sense, just as England's attacking Napoleon in Spain made sense; Canada was the only part of the British Empire that Americans could get at dryshod. But Canada was a very long, strung-out country, and a good deal depended on where she was attacked.

The population of British North America was less than half a million; that of the United States, by the census of 1810, seven and a quarter million. In the States, by the time the war broke out, the regular army had been recruited to about 7000 officers and men. There were fewer than 5000 British regulars in North America at that time, and little chance that Britain, heavily engaged in the Peninsular campaign, could spare reinforcements. Upper Canada (Ontario) had been, as we have seen, largely settled from the States, and the French Canadians in Quebec were not expected to do much to help Britain. The former American Loyalists who had peopled the Maritimes were ready to fight for King George, but the war never swung their way.

Canada, however, could count on Tecumseh's braves, and the war was far from popular in the United States. Not only Federalists but old-school Republicans were against it. Congress adjourned 6 July 1812 without making any provision to increase the navy, whose total strength until the spring of 1813 was six frigates, three sloops-of-war, and seven smaller vessels, not counting the fleet of completely useless gunboats. To refuse to increase one's naval force in a war with the world's greatest sea power for "Free Trade and Sailors' Rights" seemed gross hypocrisy to the Federalists. And the President, instead of trying to rally them to the flag, drove them to fury by publishing, three months before his war message, the purchased letters of a British spy in an attempt to incriminate them as British agents. This attempt backfired. At the time the letters came out the Massachusetts state government was Republican, as a result of the first "gerrymander" signed by Governor Gerry; but in the spring elections the Bay State went Federalist again. The lower house issued a manifesto urging the country to "organize a peace party" and "let there be no volunteers." The new governor, as well as his colleagues in Rhode Island and Connecticut, refused to call state militia into national service, and Federalist merchants refused to subscribe to war bonds or fit out privateers.

Although New England was the most solid section against the war, merchant-shipowners everywhere disliked it. At Baltimore the plant of a Federalist newspaper which came out for peace was demolished by a mob. The friends of Alexander C. Hanson, the editor, lodged for safety in the city jail, were dragged out of it by a waterfront mob led by a Frenchman, and beaten to a pulp. Hanson and General Henry Lee were badly injured, and General J. M. Lingan was killed. Federalists throughout the country shuddered over this episode, recalling as it did the cowardly massacres of prisoners in the French Revolution; and it turned Maryland Federalist for the duration.

Robert Smith, a former secretary of state, issued a public address against the war; Chief Justice Marshall wrote to him that he was mortified at his country's base submission to Napoleon; that the only party division henceforth should be between the friends of peace and the advocates of war. That was indeed the division in the presidential election of 1812. The Federalists supported De Witt Clinton, who had been placed in nomination by an antiwar faction of the New York Republicans and carried every state north of the Potomac except two. But Madison was re-elected.

The administration's military strategy was as stupid as its diplomacy. The settled portions of Canada (excluding the Maritimes) may be compared to a tree, of which the St. Lawrence river was the trunk, the Great Lakes and their tributaries the branches, and the sea lanes to England the roots. Britain had conquered Canada in 1759–60 by grasping the roots and grappling the trunk. Madison had no proper navy to attempt the former; but he might well have tried to hew the trunk by a sharp stroke at Montreal or Quebec. Instead, he attempted several feeble and unsystematic loppings at the branches.

Three weeks before war was declared, Governor William Hull of Michigan Territory, a sixty-year-old veteran of the War of Independence, was given a brigadier's commission. In command of 1500 troops, he was ordered to march to Detroit from Dayton, Ohio, cutting his own road through the wilderness, and thence to invade Upper Canada. Hull begged the war department first to obtain control of Lake Erie, in order to secure his communications and hamper those of General Isaac Brock, the British commander in Upper Canada. But nothing was done. Hull led his force, now stiffened by a regiment of regulars, to Detroit, and on 12 July crossed the river. The Canadian inhabitants of that thinly settled area were little impressed by the General's proclamation offering them liberty under the American flag, and their militia gave a good account of itself.

In the meantime, a small military encounter in the far Northwest made Hull's situation precarious. The commander of the British post at St. Joseph's on the Sault forced the American garrison at Michilimackinac to surrender (17 July). General Hull then fell back on Detroit, and ordered the American commander at Fort Dearborn (Chicago) to come to his assistance; but the Indians captured a part of that small force and massacred the rest. General Brock, having transported to Detroit the few troops he could spare from the Niagara front, paraded them in sight of General Hull and summoned him to surrender. A broad hint in Brock's note, that the Indians would be beyond his control the moment fighting began, completely unnerved the elderly general. Dreading a general massacre, deserted by some of his militia, cut off from his base, Hull surrendered his army on 16 August 1812.

So ended the first invasion of Canada. The effective military frontier of the United States was thrown back to the Wabash and the Ohio.

Major General Samuel Hopkins, another veteran of Hull's vintage, was now ordered to lead 4000 Kentucky militiamen, mobilized at Vincennes, on a punitive expedition against the Indians who had massacred the Fort Dearborn garrison. Henry Clay boasted he could conquer Canada with Kentucky militia alone; declared that his problem was to quench, rather than blow up, the ardor of his native state. In this instance, ardor cooled so quickly that after five days the Kentucky militia became mutinous and unmanageable. A council of officers advised the General to retreat. Hopkins made the militia an eloquent address, asking for 500 volunteers to press forward. Not one man offered himself.

One week after Hull's surrender, General Brock was back at Niagara, eager to attack his enemy on the New York side of the Niagara river. Governor Prevost restrained him, letting the Americans take the initiative on 13 October 1812. Captain John E. Wool led a small detachment of regulars across the river, to an attack on Queenston heights, and General Brock was killed; but the tide of battle soon turned. Several thousand New York militia under General Stephen Van Rensselaer who were there to support Wool, refused to budge. They had turned out to defend their homes, not to invade Canada. In vain the Patroon exhorted them. They calmly watched their countrymen on the other bank being enveloped and forced to surrender.

Command of the American troops on the Niagara front was now given to a curious character named Alexander Smyth, known as "Apocalypse Smyth" because he wrote an explanation of the Book of Revelation. He owed his brigadier's commission to a reputation in the Virginia House of Delegates for oratory, a gift which he proceeded to employ in speeches to his army. These orations were studded with such gems as, "Be strong! Be brave! and let the ruffian power of the British king cease on this continent!" On a sleety November evening Smyth tumbled his army into boats to cross the Niagara, consoling them for spending the night embarked with this message: "Hearts of War! Tomorrow will be memorable in the annals of the United States!" But on the morrow, not liking the looks of the Canadians on the further bank, Smyth called off the campaign. The soldiers joyfully discharged their muskets in every direction, showing a preference for the general's tent as a target. Smyth followed Hull and Van Rensselaer into retirement and got himself elected to Congress, where he continued to bray for many years.

There still remained a considerable force at Plattsburg on Lake Champlain, under the immediate command of Major General Henry Dearborn, a sixty-two-year-old veteran of Bunker Hill. He was supposed to strike the Canadian trunk at Montreal. On 19 November he marched his troops twenty miles north of Plattsburg. The militia then refused to go further, and Dearborn marched them back to Plattsburg.

On the ocean there is a different story to tell. The United States Navy was vastly outnumbered, but the Royal Navy was so deeply engaged in war with France that it could spare only one ship of the line, seven frigates, and a number of smaller warships to operate off the American coast. The pride of the United States Navy were frigates *Constitution, United States,* and *President,* designed to outclass all other two-deckers and outrun ships of the line. They threw a heavier broadside than the British frigates, and were so heavily timbered and planked as to deserve the name "Old Ironsides"; yet with such fine, clean lines and great spread of canvas that they could outsail anything afloat. The crews were volunteers; and the officers, young and tried by experience against France and Tripoli, were burning to avenge the *Chesapeake.* On the other hand, the compatriots of Nelson, conquerors at Cape St. Vincent, Trafalgar, and the Nile, were the spoiled children of victory, confident of beating any vessel not more than twice their size. Hence, when U.S.S. *Constitution,* Captain Isaac Hull, knocked H.M.S. *Guerrière* helpless in two hours and a half on 19 August 1812, and on 29 December, under Captain Bainbridge, reduced H.M. frigate *Java* to a useless hulk; when sloop-of-war *Wasp* mastered H.M.S. *Frolic* in 43 minutes on 17 October, and U.S.S. *Hornet*, Captain James Lawrence, in a hot fight off the Demerara river, sank H.M.S. *Peacock* in fifteen minutes; and when frigate *United States*, Captain Stephen Decatur, entered New London harbor with H.M. frigate *Macedonian* as prize on 4 December 1812, there were amazement and indignation in England, and rejoicing the the United States.

The moral value of these victories to the American people, following disaster on the Canadian border, was beyond calculation. They even converted Jeffersonian Republicans from their anti-navy doctrine, as may be read in a report of the House committee on naval affairs on 27 November 1812. "It is a bright attribute in the history of the tar," it says, "that he has never destroyed the rights of the nation. Thus, aided by economy and fortified by republican principle, your committee think they ought strongly to recommend that the fostering care of the nation be extended to the Naval Establishment." Congress accordingly made generous appropriations to increase the navy by four ships-of-the-line and six heavy frigates. "Frigates and seventy-fours," sighed Thomas Jefferson, "are a sacrifice we must make, heavy as it is, to the prejudices of a part of our citizens." None of this new construction got to sea during the war; but after Madison had obtained a competent secretary of the navy, William Jones of Philadelphia, important reforms were effected in naval administration.

Unfortunately, the military value of these naval victories was slight. Most of the American men-of-war that put into harbor during the winter of 1812–13 never got out again. The British blockaded Delaware Bay and Chesapeake Bay from the fall of 1812, extended the blockade in the spring of 1813 to New York and the seaports south of Norfolk, and to New England in the spring of 1814. This blockade stifled the operations of the small American high-seas fleet. Frigate *United States* and her prize *Macedonian* stayed in New London harbor for the duration. Frigate *President*, after crossing the Atlantic and capturing twelve small prizes, put into New York in the fall of 1813, and Captain Decatur lost her when trying to elude the blockading squadron. Captain Lawrence of unlucky *Chesapeake*, with a green and mutinous crew, unwisely accepted a challenge from Captain Broke of H.M.S. *Shannon* and sortied from Boston to defeat and glorious death on 1 June 1813. U.S.S. *Essex* eluded the blockade, rounded Cape Horn, and, after clearing British privateers from the South Pacific, was captured (28 March 1814) by two British frigates off the coast of Chile. *Constitution* entered Boston for repairs after sinking *Java*, and never got out until December 1814. Under Captain Charles Stewart she again distinguished herself by capturing *Cyane* and *Levant* off the African coast on 20 February 1815 — almost two months after peace had been signed.

Thus, the situation at sea for the United States in 1813–14 was much as it had been during the War of Independence in 1779–80, but with no help from France; the British were able to move troops by water at will. And their base at Halifax was almost effective as their loyalist base had been at New York.

During 1813 the Royal Navy was too busy in Europe to lay anything better than hit-and-run raids on the Atlantic seaboard. Randolph of Roanoke, in one of his imprecatory orations against the war, declared, "Go march to Canada! Leave the broad bosom of the Chesapeake and her hundred tributary rivers unprotected!" Which is exactly what happened. From Bermuda a powerful raiding force under Admiral John Borlase Warren, with Rear Admiral Sir George Cockburn second in command, was sent to spread terror and destruction in Chesapeake Bay. It was prevented from attacking Norfolk by a navy- and militia-manned battery on Craney Island, which drove off the landing force and sank the admiral's barge. Cockburn, a tough and ruthless old salt, then devastated the country around Lynnhaven Bay, sailed to the upper part of the Chesapeake, and within one week in April-May 1813 raided Havre de Grace, destroyed a cannon foundry up the Susquehanna and a munitions store on the Elk, and two villages on the Sassafras river; all without the loss of a man on either side. During the rest of the year, Warren and Cockburn cruised around Chesapeake Bay and off the Delaware Capes, landing frequently to burn buildings and replenish provisions.

In the meantime naval history was being made on the Great Lakes. Hull's surrender at Detroit convinced President Madison that command of the Lakes was essential. The Canadian authorities naturally determined to retain the supremacy they already enjoyed. It was comparatively easy for them to bring in more guns and fresh supplies up the St. Lawrence river to Lake Ontario. The Americans surmounted greater difficulties through the energy and resourcefulness of Captain Isaac Chauncey, with headquarters at Sackets Harbor on Lake Ontario, and Captain Oliver H. Perry, with headquarters at Presqu'ile (Erie), Pennsylvania. Here the Americans had a logistic advantage, since Pittsburgh, not far from Erie, was already a manufacturing town. And an American raid on York (Toronto) obtained some valuable cannon for this fresh-water United States Navy. Captain Perry managed to construct a fleet of stout little vessels during the winter of 1812–13.

General Harrison, victor of Tippecanoe, advanced from the Ohio river toward Detroit in three divisions, during the winter of 1812–13. British General Proctor did not wait for them to unite, but beat both separately at Frenchtown on the Raisin river (22 January 1813) and Fort Meigs at the rapids of the Maumee (5 May). Harrison then decided to await a naval decision on Lake Erie. Perry got his fleet over the Presqu'ile bar on 4 August and sought out the British Lake squadron. He found it on 10 September at Put In Bay among the islands at the western end of the lake. A strange naval battle ensued between vessels hastily built of green wood, manned largely by militiamen, Negroes, frontier scouts, and Canadian canal men. The fight was a matter of banging away until one or the other fleet went down; and it was

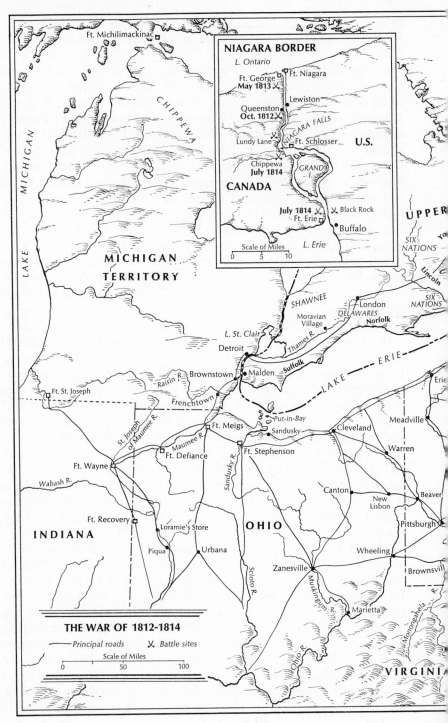

NIAGARA BORDER

L. Ontario

Ft. George
May 1813 ✗ — Ft. Niagara

Lewiston

Queenston
Oct. 1812 ✗

NIAGARA FALLS

Lundy Lane ✗ — Ft. Schlosser

U.S.

Chippewa
July 1814

GRAND I.

CANADA

July 1814 ✗ — ✗ Black Rock
Ft. Erie

● Buffalo

Scale of Miles
0   5   10

L. Erie

Ft. Michilimackinac

CHIPPEWA

MICHIGAN

LAKE

MICHIGAN
TERRITORY

SHAWNEE

London
Moravian
Village

DELAWARES
Norfolk

L. St. Clair
Detroit

Thames R.

SIX
NATIONS

Lincoln

SIX
NATIONS

UPPER

Brownstown ● Malden — Suffolk

Raisin R.

LAKE   ERIE

Erie

Ft. St. Joseph

Frenchtown

Put-in-Bay

Ft. Meigs
Sandusky

Cleveland

Meadville

St. Joseph
of Maumee R.

Maumee R.
Ft. Defiance

Ft. Stephenson

Sandusky R.

Warren

Ft. Wayne

Wabash R.

Canton

New
Lisbon

Beaver

Pittsburgh

Ft. Recovery

Loramie's Store

OHIO

INDIANA

Piqua   Urbana

Scioto R.

Wheeling

Brownsvill

Zanesville

Muskingum R.

Marietta

THE WAR OF 1812-1814

— Principal roads   ✗ Battle sites

Scale of Miles
0   50   100

Ohio R.

Monongahela R.

VIRGINIA

388

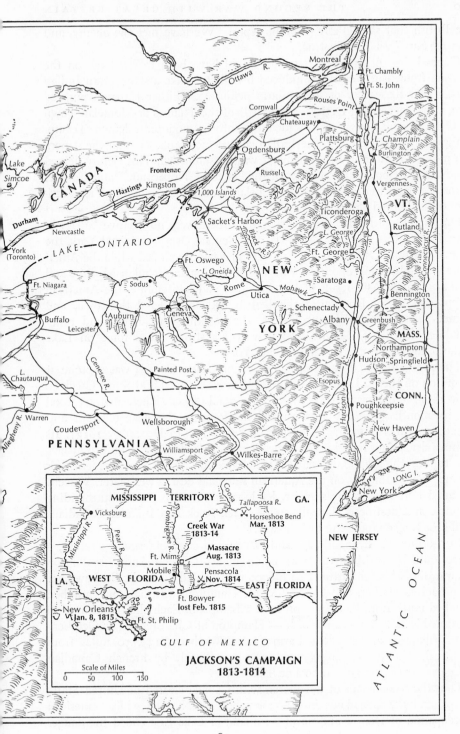

Montreal

Ottawa R.

Ft. Chambly

Ft. St. John

Cornwall

Rouses Point

Chateaugay

Plattsburg

Ogdensburg

L. Champlain

Burlington

Lake Simcoe

Frontenac

Russel

Vergennes

CANADA

Hastings Kingston

1,000 Islands

Ticonderoga

VT.

Durham

Sacket's Harbor

L. George

Rutland

Newcastle

LAKE — ONTARIO

Black R.

Ft. George

Connecticut R.

York (Toronto)

Ft. Oswego

NEW

Saratoga

Ft. Niagara

Sodus

L. Oneida

Rome

Mohawk R.

Bennington

Buffalo

Auburn

Geneva

Utica

Schenectady

Leicester

YORK

Albany

Greenbush

MASS.

Northampton

Genesee R.

Painted Post

Hudson

Springfield

L. Chautauqua

Esopus

CONN.

Warren

Poughkeepsie

Coudersport

Wellsborough

New Haven

PENNSYLVANIA

Williamsport

Wilkes-Barre

LONG I.

New York

MISSISSIPPI TERRITORY

Coosa

Tallapoosa R.

GA.

Vicksburg

Horseshoe Bend
Mar. 1813

Mississippi R.

Tombigbee R.

Creek War
1813-14

Pearl R.

Massacre
Aug. 1813

NEW JERSEY

Ft. Mims

LA.

WEST FLORIDA

Mobile

Pensacola
Nov. 1814

Pensacola

EAST FLORIDA

ATLANTIC OCEAN

New Orleans
Jan. 8, 1815

Ft. Bowyer
lost Feb. 1815

Ft. St. Philip

GULF OF MEXICO

JACKSON'S CAMPAIGN
1813-1814

Scale of Miles

0   50   100   150

the British that sank. Perry's laconic report "We have met the enemy, and they are ours," was literally true.

General Proctor's prudent strategy would have been to fall back on the Niagara front. But Tecumseh induced his ally to make a stand at an Indian village near the center of the Ontario peninsula. Thither Harrison pursued him, after reoccupying Detroit. The Battle of the Thames or Moravian Town (5 October 1813) was a victory for the Kentucky mounted riflemen. Tecumseh was killed, Proctor fled, the Indian confederacy broke up, and the American military frontier in the Northwest was re-established. This victory helped to advance the political ambitions of the "Hero of Tippecanoe," and Colonel Johnson's claim that he personally had slain Tecumseh made him Vice President of the United States.

On Lake Ontario and the Niagara front there were no decisive battles in 1813. On 27 April Captain Chauncey and General Dearborn raided York, the capital of Upper Canada. A large powder magazine exploded while the Americans were advancing upon the village, killing General Zebulon M. Pike and about 300 men. As a result of this incident, and indiscipline, the American troops got out of hand after the British had surrendered the town, and burned two brick parliament houses, the governor's residence, and other buildings. But, as Sir James Yeo now had a strong naval force on Lake Ontario, the Americans had to evacuate York.

The next attempted American invasion of Upper Canada was a probe at Hamilton on the St. Lawrence. General Vincent stopped it at Stony Creek (6 June 1813) and captured two American general officers. There matters stood for six months. Vincent than shifted his force to the Niagara front and pushed an American garrison out of Fort George (10 December 1813). Its commander, on retiring, burned Newark and as much as he could of Queenston, turning the inhabitants out of their houses on a cold winter's night. For this act the inhabitants on the American side paid dear, a week later. Vincent captured Fort Niagara by surprise, let loose his Indians on the surrounding country, and destroyed the villages of Black Rock and Buffalo. Canadians held Fort Niagara for the rest of the war.

In the meantime, an unsuccessful attempt to carry out sound strategy, a pincer attack on Montreal, was being made. General James Wilkinson (Aaron Burr's former partner) with 8000 men floated down the St. Lawrence from Sackets Harbor; and General Wade Hampton, with half that number, marched north from Plattsburg on Lake Champlain. Each allowed himself to be turned back by a mere skirmish — Hampton at Chateaugay (25 October) and Wilkinson at Chrysler's Farm (11 November 1813), 70 miles from Montreal. The former engagement was won largely by French Canadian militia under Lieutenant Colonel de Salaberry.

Thus the second year of war closed with Canada cleared of United States troops, and the Canadians in possession of Fort Niagara; whilst American reoccupation of Detroit and naval command of Lake Erie ended the danger of flanking movements from the Northwest. So far, the British forces in Canada had waged defensive warfare; but the tables were turned in 1814.

American lack of success in the initial phase was later blamed by Republicans on the New England Federalists. But a sober look at the facts proves that the entire country was responsible. The war department was never able to build up the regular army to half its authorized strength, and the President obtained only 10,000 one-year volunteers out of 50,000 authorized. The loyal minority in New England more than made up for the disloyal stand of the state governments; her five states provided the regular army with nineteen regiments, the Middle states with fifteen, the Southern states with only ten. The war was unpopular everywhere, after Hull's surrender had shown that it would be no pushover. One reason, no doubt, was the uninspiring leadership of Madison and his cabinet ministers, who, with the exception of Monroe and Gallatin (who resigned in 1813), were political hacks. The navy's sea-going command was excellent; but the general officers of the army, with the exception of Jacob Brown and Andrew Jackson, who only came into the picture in 1813, were the worst military leaders of any war in which the United States has ever been engaged. Jackson had been eager for service at the start, and it was typical of the way this war was run, that Madison refused him a federal commission because he had supported Monroe for President in 1808.

4. The War of 1812: Defensive Phase

After Napoleon's abdication on April 1814, Britain was able to provide Canada with an adequate army to carry the war into the United States, and to extend and intensify the naval blockade of the Atlantic coast. The war office planned to invade the United States from three points successively: Niagara, Lake Champlain, and New Orleans, and simultaneously to raid the Chesapeake.

On the Niagara front America took the initiative before British reinforcements arrived. The army had learned much from two years of adversity. Incompetent officers had been weeded out, and promising young men were promoted; more reliance was placed on regulars, less on militia. On 3 July 1814 General Jacob Brown floated his army of about 5000 men across the Niagara river and forced Fort Erie to capitulate. On the 5th, his subordinate Winfield Scott was about to hold a holiday parade when three regiments of British regulars broke up the celebration and the Battle of Chippewa was joined. This was a European-style stand-up fight in open country. Both lines advanced in close order, stopping alternately to load and fire; the British broke when they were about 60 paces away. On 25 July, hard by Niagara Falls, occurred the Battle of Lundy's Lane, the most stubbornly contested fight of the war. Fighting was begun in the late afternoon by Winfield Scott's brigade, which crossed bayonets with the enemy four times before being reinforced by General Brown's brigade. The battle continued until midnight. General Brown ordered Colonel James Miller to capture the artillery which protected the enemy's position. "I'll try, Sir," said the colonel, and did; his infantrymen rushed the British guns and bayoneted the cannoneers in the act of loading. Both American generals were badly wounded, and the casualties were very heavy for a battle of that era: 43 to 45 per cent. The British later recovered their guns, but these actions prevented an invasion of the United States from the Niagara front and gave the United States Army a new pride and character. British officers who had fought in the Peninsular War said they had never seen anything to equal Colonel Miller's charge.

By mid-August General Sir George Prevost commanded some 10,000 British veterans encamped near Montreal, ready to invade the United States by the classic route of Lake Champlain and the Hudson. It was the strongest, best disciplined, and most completely equipped army that had ever been sent to North America. Prospects were very bleak for the United States, particularly as the war department had lately transferred most of the regulars from Plattsburg to Niagara. Early in September, Sir George moved down the western shore of Lake Champlain, synchronizing his movements with that of a fresh-water flotilla, and forcing the Americans back to a strong position behind the river that empties into Plattsburg Bay. There they were protected by a line of forts, and by the American lake squadron, Captain Thomas Macdonough, anchored inside the entrance.

Prevost's army reached Plattsburg on 6 September 1814. Facing him were only 1500 American regulars and a few thousand militia. The American forts were formidable, and Prevost wished to secure control of the lake before advancing further. Early in the morning of 11 September the British fleet hove to off Cumberland Head. There followed a murderous engagement. Small vessels, without bulwarks to protect their crews, anchored side by side at pistol range, attempted to pound each other to pieces. After British flagship *Confiance* had silenced the starboard battery of American flagship *Saratoga* and killed one-fifth of her crew, Captain Macdonough "wound ship" — turned *Saratoga* completely around while at anchor — brought his port battery to bear and forced H.M.S. *Confiance* and three other vessels to surrender. The British commodore lost his life, and Prevost was so discouraged by the loss of the fleet that he retreated to Canada. "Macdonough's Victory," the naval Battle of Plattsburg, proved to be decisive. But it was not the last battle of the war.

In June 1814 a British expeditionary force was mounted at Bordeaux to make a diversion in the Chesapeake. The campaign that followed reflected little credit to the one side, and considerable disgrace to the other. General Robert Ross, commander of the land forces, was instructed by Admiral Cochrane "to destroy and lay waste such towns and districts upon the coast" as he might find assailable. A fleet of Jeffersonian gunboats, retreating up the Patuxent river, led Ross's army from Chesapeake Bay to the back door of

Washington. For five days the British army marched along the banks of the Patuxent, approaching the capital of the United States without seeing an enemy or firing a shot. In the meantime, Washington was in a fever of preparation. About 7000 militia, all that turned out of 95,000 summoned, were placed under an unusually incompetent general and hurried to a strong position behind the village of Bladensburg, five miles from the capital. After the militia had suffered only 66 casualties, they broke and ran, leaving Commodore Joshua Barney with 400 seamen and five naval cannon to dispute the field. Their resistance was soon overcome, and Ross pressed on to Washington that evening (24 August). Some of the officers arrived in time to eat a dinner at the White House that had been prepared for President and Mrs. Madison.

All public buildings of the capital were deliberately burned, partly in retaliation for the American burning of York and Newark, partly to impress the administration with the uselessness of further resistance. General Ross personally superintended the piling up of furniture in the White House before it was given to the flames, and Admiral Sir George Cockburn gave orders to burn the department buildings; but the troops, under good discipline, were not allowed to indulge in looting or destruction of private property.

This was a dark period for Madison's fugitive administration. Discouraging news only had arrived from the peace commission at Ghent. Sir George Prevost was expected to march south again; and a new British expeditionary force was on its way to New Orleans. The last war loan had failed, and all banks south of New England had suspended specie payments. John Jacob Astor, who had received many favors from the government since his "mandarin" hoax, combined with two Philadelphia bankers to buy the unsubscribed part of the federal loan at 80, paying in such depreciated bank notes that they really got the bonds for 40 cents on the dollar.

Fortunately the destruction of Washington illustrated the strategic truth that hit-and-run raids accomplish nothing except to amuse the aggressors and infuriate the victims. On the night of 25–26 August 1814 the British army withdrew to its transports, and proceeded to the next objective, Baltimore. Here the inhabitants were prepared, and Maryland militia showed a very different spirit from that of their Virginia countrymen. Naval bombardment of Fort McHenry accomplished nothing for the British, but gave us a stirring national anthem. Francis Scott Key, a prisoner on board one of the bombarding vessels, gained his inspiration for "The Star Spangled Banner" from seeing the flag still flying over Fort McHenry "by the dawn's early light." General Ross was killed at the head of a landing party (12 September), and that ended the Chesapeake campaign.

Before the third British expeditionary force reached New Orleans, the West had produced a great military leader, General Andrew Jackson. He had emigrated to Tennessee as a young man, grown up with that state, represented it in the United States Senate, and as commander of its militia had been winning laurels in warfare against the "Red Sticks," the Upper Creeks.

That Indian nation endeavored to remain neutral, but Tecumseh's emissaries stirred up the younger braves. The result was a series of raids on the frontier and the capture of Fort Mims above Mobile, together with some 260 white scalps. This news found Andrew Jackson in bed at Nashville, recovering from a pistol shot received in a street brawl with Thomas H. Benton, the future senator from Missouri. Within a month, Jackson at the head of 2500 militia and a band of Choctaw and Lower Creek auxiliaries was in the Upper Creek country. Five engagements, fought between November 1813 and January 1814, accomplished little; and the Tennessee militia showed the same disposition to panic as their brethren on the Canadian border. But after Jackson had executed a few militiamen to encourage the others, the spring campaign of 1814 went very well. At the Tohopeka or Horseshoe Bend of the Tallapoosa river (27 March 1814), the military power of the Creek nation was broken; they left 557 warriors dead on the battlefield, and Jackson lost only 26 of his men and 23 Indian allies. This campaign deprived the British of a powerful ally. And a subsequent treaty with the Upper Creeks opened about two-thirds of Alabama, the heart of the future cotton kingdom, to white settlement and Negro slavery.

In early August, a small British force landed at Pensacola in Spanish Florida. Its leader, an impetuous Irishman named Edward Nicholls, proceeded to organize and drill Creek refugees, and the "maroons," Negro slaves who had escaped from the United States, with a view to renewing the war in that quarter. Jackson invaded Florida on his own authority and crushed this diversion by capturing Pensacola on 7 November 1814.

The most formidable British expedition of this war was already under way. The Cochrane-Ross force which had captured Washington and been repulsed before Baltimore, retired for refit and rendezvous at Negril Bay, Jamaica. There this assault force of 3000 men, now under command of Major General Sir Edward Pakenham, was reinforced by fresh troops from England and a fleet under Admiral Cochrane, consisting of 6 ships of the line, 14 frigates, dozens of smaller ships, and 11 transports capable of carrying 7450 troops. The objective was to occupy New Orleans and as much Gulf territory as possible, to be used as bargaining pawns in the peace. Louisiana was to be encouraged to secede from the United States, and either annex herself to the Spanish empire or become a British satellite state.

To meet this threat Jackson had about 5000 men, three-quarters of them militia; and for naval support, two 15-gun sloops-of-war at New Orleans, and seven gunboats on Lake Borgne. And he made the bad guess that the British would attack Mobile first. He wished all naval forces to be moved to Mobile Bay, which their senior officer refused to do, recalling what had happened to Commodore Hopkins at Charleston in 1780. The two sloops remained at New Orleans (and later lent Jackson's army valuable gunfire support), while the gunboats were drawn up across Lake Borgne, by which the British elected to approach the back door of New Orleans. These 5-gun craft, under Lieutenant Ap Catesby Jones, were overwhelmed and sunk by an advance force of British in 40 armed boats, on 14 December. Only then did General Jackson realize that New Orleans was the British objective.

The boating of an amphibious force in that era took days instead of hours, so that it was not until 23 December that the British assault force could be floated up the bayou that almost connects Lake Borgne with the Mississippi. It then occupied the Villeré plantation on the left (north) bank of the great river, only a few miles from the city. Up to that moment it looked as if General Jackson were in a class with Hull and Smyth; and he might have been, if Pakenham had promptly advanced on New Orleans. But delay was fatal to anyone facing Andrew Jackson. This lank, long-haired general in his "well-worn leather cap, a short Spanish cloak of old blue cloth, and great unpolished boots whose vast tops swayed uneasily around his bony knees," was master of the situation the moment an enemy was in sight.

In a sharp night attack on the British, 23–24 December, Jackson checked their advance, then retired to the Maccarty plantation five miles below New Orleans, and entrenched. In an artillery duel on New Year's Day 1815, the British were again repulsed. While General Pakenham waited a week for reinforcements, Jackson strengthened his main position behind a canal and high mud breastworks, reinforced by sugar barrels.

At dawn 8 January began the main Battle of New Orleans. On the south bank of the river the Kentucky militia "ingloriously fled" before a British brigade which included a regiment of West Indies Negroes. This gave the enemy a chance to attack the main American army on the north bank, from the rear. But General Pakenham threw away the chance. Instead, he chose, at 6:00 a.m., to direct a foolhardy frontal assault of some 5300 men in close column formation, against Jackson's 3500 men on the parapet, so well protected that the British, without ladders or fascines, could not get at them. The result was more of a massacre than a battle. General Pakenham and over 2000 of all ranks were killed, wounded, or missing; the second and third generals in line of command were fatally wounded. Only 13 Americans were killed and 58 wounded before the attacking columns melted. For ten days the two armies maintained their respective positions. Then the only surviving British general officer withdrew the army to its transports.

This Battle of New Orleans had no military value since peace had already been signed at Ghent on Christmas Eve; but it made a future President of the United States, and in folklore wiped out all previous American defeats, ending the "Second War of Independence" in a blaze of glory.

5. Disaffection and Peace

One of the many anomalies in this war was bitter opposition by the New England States, despite the fact that war built up their economy. Since the

British blockade was not extended to the New England coast until May 1814, that section of the country traded freely with the enemy in the Maritime Provinces and Quebec, and legitimate foreign trade passed through New England seaports, whence it was distributed to the Middle states and the South by ox wagons and sleds. Permanently important for New England was the stimulus to manufacturing; by 1815 half a million spindles were in operation.

Although this war enriched New England, the Federalists claimed that their section was being ruined. Their leaders, and many followers too, got themselves into just such a state of emotional frustration over Republican "Jacobins" and "that Little Man in the Palace," as Republican leaders did in the 1930's about "dangerous radicals" and "that man in the White House." [1] Federalist press and pamphlets spread the notion that the real objects of the war were to help Napoleon, and to lay open Eastern seaports to devastation by the Royal Navy while the American army pranced into Upper Canada. Allied victories in Europe were celebrated, and a vote of thanks to a naval hero was rejected in the Massachusetts legislature as "not becoming a moral and religious people." However justified these stern Puritans may have been in refusing to support a war of conquest against a kindred people, there was no excuse for stiffening this attitude after Napoleon had been disposed of and the character of the war had changed. It was now a matter of defending national integrity against an overwhelming land and sea power.

For some years there had been talk of holding a New England convention to make a concerted protest against Republican policy. Events of the summer of 1814 conspired to bring it about. Massachusetts was thrown upon her own resources for defense, with no protection from Washington. The British occupied Maine east of the Penobscot, and the Royal Navy raided various parts of the coast. This was largely the fault of Federalist governors in refusing to place state militia under the war department, for fear that they would be marched off to Canada; but New England was past reasoning on such matters. On 6 October 1814 Massachusetts summoned a New England Convention at Hartford, for the express purpose of conferring upon "their public grievances and concerns," upon "defence against the enemy . . . and also to take measures, if they shall think proper, for procuring a convention of delegates from all the United States, in order to revise the Constitution thereof."

This language showed a compromise between the moderate and the extreme Federalists. The former, led by Harrison Gray Otis, were not disunionists, but wished to take advantage of the situation to obtain concessions for their section. Alarmed at the rising tide of secession sentiment, they hoped the Convention would act as a safety valve to let it off; and their desire to concert defensive measures against the enemy was sincere. But the violent wing of the Federalist party, led by Timothy Pickering and John Lowell, had other objects in view. It was their belief that the British invasion of New

1. The White House was generally called "The Palace" until around 1820.

Orleans would succeed and that Aaron Burr's secession plot for Louisiana and the West would then bear fruit. They wished the Hartford Convention to draft a new Federal constitution, with clauses to protect New England interests, and present it as to the original Thirteen States only. If these accepted, well and good; if not, New England would make a separate peace and go it alone. In answering echo, the London *Times* declared on 26 December, "New England allied with Old England would form a dignified and manly union well deserving the name of Peace."

The New England Convention, representing mainly Massachusetts, Rhode Island, and Connecticut, with scattered delegates from New Hampshire and Vermont, met in secret session at Hartford on 15 December 1814. Fortunately the moderates gained control and issued a calm and statesmanlike report on 5 January 1815. An element of their caution was the strength of the Republican party in New England; the Federalists controlled all five states, but only by small majorities, and there would certainly have been civil war had the extremists put through an ordinance of secession. Madison's administration and the war were severely arraigned by the Hartford Convention; "but to attempt upon every abuse of power to change the Constitution, would be to perpetuate the evils of revolution." Secession was squarely faced, and ruled out as inexpedient and unnecessary since the causes of New England's calamities were not deep and permanent but the result of bad administration, and of partisanship in the European war. A suggestion was thrown out that the administration permit this section to assume their own defense, applying to that purpose the federal taxes collected within their borders. A few constitutional amendments were proposed. But there was no threat of a separate peace.

Secession agitation in New England now calmed down. Presently the good news from Ghent and New Orleans put Madison's administration on a high horse, and made New England the scapegoat for government mismanagement of the war. A stigma of unpatriotism, from which it never recovered, was attached to the Federalist party. Yet no stigma was attached to the doctrine of state rights; and within a few years it was revived by states like Virginia, which had denounced the Hartford Convention as treasonable.

Peace negotiations began almost as soon as the war did, but time was wasted over an attempted mediation by the emperor of Russia. When Lord Castlereagh finally offered to treat directly with the United States, Madison replied favorably (January 1814) and Ghent in Belgium was selected as the place of negotiation. By the time the American commissioners arrived there in June, the British government was in no hurry for peace. It shortly expected news of decisive victories on the Canadian border, which would place it in position to dictate instead of negotiate.

To the astonishment and distress of the American peace commissioners (John Quincy Adams, Albert Gallatin, Henry Clay, Jonathan Russell, and James A. Bayard), their opposite numbers were instructed to admit neither impressment nor neutral rights even as subjects of discussion. The United States must abandon all claims to the Newfoundland fisheries, the northeastern boundary must be revised to provide a direct British road between St. John, N.B., and Quebec; and the northwest boundary must also be rectified to give Canada access to the upper Mississippi. Finally, the old project of an Indian satellite state north of the Ohio river was revived. Adams, an experienced diplomat, expected the negotiations to terminate on this point, and prepared to go home. Henry Clay, untrained in diplomacy but an expert poker player, was confident the British would recede, as they did. On 16 September, the British commissioners were instructed to drop the Indian project. The next obstacle was a British proposal to settle the boundary on the basis of what each side held when the war was over, which would mean the cession of eastern Maine and of any territory that Generals Prevost and Pakenham might conquer. The Americans refused to entertain any other basis than the 1783 boundary. This deadlock was broken in mid-October by news of the British repulses at Baltimore and on Lake Champlain, which the London *Times* described as a "lamentable event to the civilized world." But to the American peace commission the news from Plattsburg had "the effect of a reprieve from execution."

The British premier now turned to the Duke of Wellington, since Napoleon had been temporarily disposed of. The Iron Duke was invited, on 4 November, to take over the top command in America, with full powers "to make peace, or to continue the war with renewed vigor." He promptly replied in terms that showed a sound grasp of strategy. "That which appears to me to be wanting in America is not a general, or general officers and troops, but a naval superiority on the Lakes," he wrote. "The question is, whether we can acquire this. If we can't, I shall do you but little good in America, and I shall go there only to prove the truth of Prevost's defence; and to sign a peace which might as well be signed now. I think you have no right from the state of the war to demand any concession of territory from America."

Thus, Macdonough's victory at Plattsburg proved to be the decisive action.

By this time, the British public was sick of war, and the ministry was eager to wind it up and conclude peace all around. So, in the end, nothing much was said about anything in the Treaty of Ghent, signed on Christmas Eve 1814. Both sides agreed to disagree on everything important except the conclusion of hostilities and restoring prewar boundaries. Nothing was said about Madison's declared reason for the war — impressment and neutral rights. Yet the treaty did bear good fruit. Four boundary commissions were created to settle the boundary between Canada and the United States. Claims, commercial relations, naval forces on the Lakes, and the Oregon question were postponed to future negotiations. And, before the next maritime war broke out, impressment had been given up as a means of manning the Royal Navy.

So ended a futile and unnecessary war which might have been prevented by a little more imagination of the one side, and a broader vision on the other.

At least it was a cheap one, in terms of money and casualties; only 1877 American soldiers and sailors were killed in action. On relations between the two governments, however, the war had a good effect. The fighters and the diplomats learned to respect one another. The United States was never again denied the treatment due to an independent nation, and Americans began to grasp the basic fact that whatever Canada's future, she would never join the United States. At the same time, Jackson's incursion into Florida indicated that the Spanish empire in North America was ready to fall apart.

Internally, the conduct of this conflict offered many lessons in how not to fight a war and how not to organize and lead armies. Practically none of these were heeded. The myth of "citizen soldiery" being a sufficient defense, and of self-taught generals being superior to West Pointers, persisted for a century. But the gallant record of the navy wrought a change of public opinion toward that fighting force. Most of the wartime fleet was maintained after peace, and within three months of the Treaty of Ghent it found profitable employment in punishing three Barbary States for piracy.

THE CONSTITUTION AND THE GUERRIERE

It oft-times has been told—— how the Brit-ish sea-men bold—— Could—— flog the tars of France so neat and han-dy O! But they ne-ver found their match till the Yan-kees did them catch, Oh, the Yan-kee boys for fight-ing are the dan-dy O!

Good Feelings and Bad

1815-1823

1. A Nationalist Era

A<small>N</small> "ERA OF GOOD FEELINGS," as contemporaries called it, followed the second war with England and the quarter-century of struggle between Federalists and Republicans. Relations with Great Britain became friendly, and a permanent basis for peace with Canada was furnished through partial disarmament. President Madison and his party adopted the nationalism of Washington and Hamilton as if they had been born to it, and Federalist enmity did not long survive Republican conversion. A Congress in which Republicans were dominant resurrected Hamilton's Report on Manufactures, passed the first protective tariff, and in the same year, 1816, chartered a second Bank of the United States, on the model of Hamilton's. James Monroe, legitimate heir of the Virginia dynasty, succeeded to the Presidency in 1817 almost unopposed, and in 1821 he obtained every electoral vote but one; two years later, with unanimous approval, he issued a momentous declaration of American foreign policy.

The United States was tired of party and sectional strife, as Europe was weary of war and revolution. New forces were transforming the country, and while this readjustment was taking place, Americans acquiesced in nationalism. That is the key to the Era of Good Feelings. Manufacturing was displacing shipping as the premier interest of New England and Pennsylvania. Society and politics were being democratized in New York. Virginia was declining as an agricultural state, but finding no other interest than slave-breeding to take the place of tobacco. King Cotton's domain was advancing from South Carolina and Georgia into the new Gulf states. The Northwest, rapidly expanding in population and influence, was acquiring new wants and aspirations. A series of sharp and bitter sectional conflicts brought out the underlying antagonism, and by 1830 sections had again become articulate, defining the stand they were to take until the Civil War. It became a major problem of politics to form combinations and alliances between sections whose interests were complementary, in the hope of achieving their common wants through the federal government; the task of statesmanship was to reconcile rival interests and sections through national party organizations.

These new interests brought a change in the attitude of different parts of the country toward the Constitution, reversing the similar change that had taken place during Jefferson's administration. As soon as nationalist legislation, in appearance at least, began to cramp the economic life of certain states and sections, their public men adopted the state rights theories of New England Federalists, which they in turn had taken over from Jefferson. Daniel Webster, who in 1814 warned Congress that Massachusetts would nullify a conscription law, by 1830 was intoning hymns to the Union. John C. Calhoun, leader of the war hawks of 1812 and promoter of nationalist legislation thereafter, began in 1828 to write textbooks on state rights. Of prominent American publicists and statesmen whose careers bridged the War of 1812, only five were consistent, and three were Virginians. John Taylor went on writing, and John Randolph talking, as if nothing had happened since 1791. Henry Clay and John Quincy Adams hewed to the nationalist line that they had long followed, and Chief Justice Marshall intensified the nationalism that he had learned from Washington.

Except for the Monroe Doctrine, Marshall's Supreme Court opinions were the only enduring feature of the new nationalism of 1815. The first, *McCulloch* v. *Maryland*, defended the constitutionality of the new Bank of the United States against the State of Maryland, which in taxing the bank's Baltimore branch, denied the power of Congress to charter it. Marshall met this argument with an historical survey of the origin of the Constitution, and concluded: "The government of the Union . . . is emphatically and truly a government of the people. In form and substance it emanates from them. Its powers are granted by them, and are to be exercised directly on them, and for their benefit." Here is the classic definition of national sovereignty, undercutting the ground of state rights. On a second point, that the power to charter corporations is not expressly granted to Congress by the Constitution, and cannot be inferred from the "necessary and proper" clause, Marshall remarked:

The government of the Union, though limited in its powers, is supreme within its sphere of action . . . We admit, as all must admit, that the powers of the government are limited, and that its limits are not to be transcended. But we think the sound construction of the Constitution must allow to the national legislature that discretion, with respect to the means by which the powers it confers are to be carried into execution, which will enable that body to perform the high duties assigned to it, in the manner most beneficial to the people. Let the end be legitimate, let it be within the scope of the Constitution, and all means which are appropriate, which are plainly adapted to that end, which are not prohibited, but consist with the letter and spirit of the Constitution, are constitutional.

"A deadly blow has been struck at the Sovereignty of the States," declared a Baltimore newspaper in printing this opinion. Pennsylvania proposed a constitutional amendment prohibiting Congress from erecting a "moneyed institution" outside the District of Columbia; Ohio, Indiana, and Illinois concurred. The legislature of South Carolina, on the contrary, declared that "Congress is constitutionally vested with the right to incorporate a bank," and "they apprehend no danger from the exercise of the powers which the people of the United States have confided to Congress." South Carolina would not speak this language much longer; Pennsylvania and the Old Northwest would shortly speak no other.

The Supreme Court was not deterred by local opposition, or influenced by public opinion, as long as Marshall was Chief Justice. To mention only four cases: in *Martin* v. *Hunter's Lessee* (1817) and *Cohens* v. *Virginia* (1821) the Court reasserted its right to review any final judgment of a state supreme court that affected treaties or laws of the United States. In *Martin* v. *Mott* (1827) the Court denied to a state the right to withhold militia from national service when demanded by the President. In *Gibbons* v. *Ogden* (1824) it not only smashed a state-chartered monopoly of steamboat traffic but mapped out the course that Congress followed in regulating interstate commerce.

Henry Clay and John C. Calhoun were the nationalist leaders in Congress during the Era of Good Feelings. Both feared growing sectionalism. Their formula, which Clay christened the "American System," was a protective tariff for manufacturers, a home market, and better transportation for the farmers. "Let us," said Calhoun in 1817, "bind the Republic together with a perfect system of roads and canals." And, he added, a protective tariff "would form a new and most powerful cement." It was a propitious moment. "Infant" industries, some of them born during the war, were crying for protection, from which almost every section of the country expected to benefit. Pittsburgh, a center for the iron deposits of the Alleghenies, was eager to sell its charcoal-smelted pigs and bars in the coastal region, in place of British and Swedish iron. In Kentucky there was a new industry of weaving local hemp into cotton bagging, menaced by the Scots jute industry. All Western centers wanted roads and canals. Vermont and Ohio shepherds demanded protection against English wool; the grain producers of central New York, excluded from England by the corn laws, were attracted by the "home market" argument that manufactures increase local purchases of farm produce. Even this early, vineyards which would eventually rival those of Europe were being planted in New York. Congressmen from states which a generation later preferred secession to protection, eagerly voted for the tariff of 1816; maritime New Englanders, destined to pocket great benefits from protection, voted against it.

Internal improvements, meaning roads and canals, were the complement to protection. Immediately after the War of 1812, people eager to exploit the lands conquered from Tecumseh and the Creek nation, began a new westward movement. Between 1810 and 1820 the population of states and territories west of the Appalachians more than doubled. Four new states — Indiana (1816), Mississippi (1817), Illinois (1818), and Alabama (1819) — were admitted to the Union. Steam traffic increased on the Western rivers. In 1817 a steamboat chugged up the Mississippi to Cincinnati; within two years 60 light-draught stern-wheelers, of the type familiar to readers of Mark Twain, were plying between New Orleans and Louisville. Their freight charges to the upper Ohio valley were less than half the cost of wagon transport thither from Philadelphia and Baltimore. For selfish reasons, Eastern cities would not promote the Western desire for federal roads and canals. Pennsylvania built her own roads, and later her own canals, and New York in 1817 began the construction of the Erie Canal, which was destined to make New York City outstrip all rival seaports.

Clay and Calhoun persuaded Congress to build a national road from old Fort Cumberland to Wheeling in western Virginia.[1] Connected with Baltimore by a state road, this "national pike" became the most important westward route for emigrants, who traveled on foot, on horseback, and in Conestoga wagons. Congress proposed in 1817 to earmark certain federal revenues for bolder projects of the same sort. President Madison so far had accepted every item in the nationalist program, but here he drew the line and vetoed that internal improvements bill.

2. Western Panic and Missouri Compromise

The usual postwar panic and depression, caused by too great optimism and overextension of credit, began in 1819. The Bank of the United States, which might have put a brake on inflation, was second to none in the scramble for profits. Late in 1818 the directors took overdue steps to curtail credit. Branches were ordered to accept no bills but their own, to present all state bank notes for payment at once, and to renew no personal notes or mortages. The result was to hasten the inevitable panic; and in 1819 it broke. Many state banks collapsed, and enormous amounts of Western real estate were foreclosed by the B. U. S. At this juncture came the decision in *McCulloch* v. *Maryland*, forbidding states to tax the "monster," as Westerners began to call it. "All the flourishing cities of the West are mortgaged to this money power," declared Senator Benton of Missouri. "They may be devoured by it at any moment. They are in the jaws of the Monster. A lump of butter in the mouth of a dog — one gulp, one swallow, and all is gone!"

Would the panic and the McCulloch case turn the West against nationalism, and some new leader arise to plot secession? Or would West and South shake hands, control the federal government by votes, and turn it against the "money power"? Or would North and West combine? That was anyone's guess.

Up to 1820 the basic law for the sale of public land was that of 1796. This required alternate townships to be sold in blocks of eight sections, intervening townships in single sections (640 acres), all at auction for an upset price of two dollars an acre, which could be paid by installments within three years.

1. The National or Cumberland road was later pushed across Ohio and Indiana to Vandalia, Illinois, by successive appropriations between 1822 and 1838; but the federal government relinquished each section, upon its completion, to the state within which it lay. It is now part of national route 40.

The only important change in this law, in 1800, was to lower the unit of sale to a quarter-section. When Ohio, first state to be hewn out of the national domain, was admitted to the Union in 1803, two important precedents were adopted: the federal government retained all ungranted land within the new state's borders, but donated one section of each township still unsold to a state education fund. Under the Act of 1796, the United States sold, to 1 July 1820, 19.4 million acres for $47.7 million; but some 5.7 million acres were recovered for non-payment of installments, especially during the depression. By the Public Land Act of 1820 credit was stopped, the upset price was lowered to $1.25 an acre, and the minimum unit of sale to 80 acres. This made it easier for a poor man to acquire land, but the West was not satisfied. The panic of 1819 was brief and mild in the East, but hard times lasted in the West until 1824, affording an ideal culture-bed for state rights.

While debt and deflation were producing preliminary symptoms of a vertical cleavage between East and West, the question of slavery extension threatened to cut the Union horizontally into North and South. Ever since the Federal Convention of 1787 there had been a tacit political balance between these two sections, along the old Mason and Dixon's line and the Ohio river. This boundary divided slave-holding states and territories from those in which slavery had been abolished, or was in process of extinction. In 1789 North and South were approximately equal in numbers, but in 1820 the Northern or free states had a population of 5,152,000 with 105 members in the House; whilst the Southern or slave states had 4,485,000 people with 81 congressmen. An even balance had been maintained in the Senate by the admission of free and slave states alternately, and after the admission of Alabama in 1819 there were eleven of each.

Congress had done nothing to disturb slavery in the territory of the Louisiana purchase, where it existed by French law, and Louisiana entered the Union in 1812 as a slave state. During the westward rush after the war, several thousand slave-owners with their human property moved into the Territory of Upper Louisiana. There they established corn and cotton plantations in the rich bottom lands of the lower Missouri river, or on the west bank of the Mississippi near the old fur-trading town of St. Louis. Thus, when the people of this region claimed admission to the Union as the State of Missouri, slavery was permitted by their proposed state constitution.

In February 1819, a bill admitting Missouri as a state came before the House of Representatives. To the surprise and indignation of Southern members, James Tallmadge of New York offered an amendment prohibiting the further introduction of slaves into Missouri, and requiring that all children subsequently born therein of slave parents should be free at the age of twenty-five. Thus amended, the bill passed the House, but was lost in the Senate.

After Congress adjourned in March, the question of slavery or freedom in Missouri went to the people. In state legislatures, in the newspapers, and in popular mass meetings it was discussed and agitated — not so much as a moral question but as one of sectional power and prestige, yet no less bitterly for that. Northerners had long been dissatisfied with the "federal ratio" which gave the slave states, it was estimated, twenty seats in Congress and twenty electoral votes, based on enumerating human chattels, who could not vote. Northern leaders regarded the admission of Missouri, which lay almost wholly north of the then dividing line between freedom and slavery, as an aggressive move toward increasing the voting power of the South. Southerners were not yet prepared to defend the rightfulness of slavery, but asserted their right to carry their property across the Mississippi. Both sides uttered threats of secession. Surviving Federalist politicians and Republicans of the Middle states saw an opportunity to create a solid North; to "snatch the sceptre from Virginia," as Harrison Gray Otis put it. Thomas Jefferson, who reverted to sectional and proslavery feelings as he grew older, was outraged over what he regarded as an attempted revival of Federalism.

When Congress took up the question again in January 1820, fear of a Federalist renaissance caused enough Northern Republicans to defect from antislavery to pass a compromise measure. Missouri was admitted as a slave-holding state, but slavery was prohibited in the territory of the United States north of Missouri's southern boundary, latitude 36° 30'. At the same time, Maine, which had just detached herself from Massachusetts, was admitted to the Union, making twelve free and twelve slave states. This was the famous Missouri Compromise, which put the question of slavery extension at rest for almost a generation. It was a fair solution. The South obtained her immediate object, with the prospect of Arkansas and Florida entering as slave states in the near future; the North secured the greater expanse of unsettled territory, and maintained the principle of 1787, that Congress could keep slavery out of the Territories if it chose.

Angry passions quickly subsided, the sectional alignment dissolved, and politics resumed their delusive tranquillity. But for a moment the veil had been lifted, and some saw the bloody prospect ahead. "This momentous question, like a fire bell in the night, awakened and filled me with terror," wrote Jefferson. "I considered it at once as the knell of the Union." And John Quincy Adams recorded in his diary, "I take it for granted the the present question is a mere preamble — a title-page to a great, tragic volume."

3. Anglo-American Adjustments

In 1815 there seemed slight hope of a lasting Anglo-American peace. John Quincy Adams considered the treaty that he had negotiated a mere truce because "nothing was adjusted, nothing was settled." Canada's long and vague boundary, rival fur and fishing interests, and fresh-water navies, provided so many points of friction that a leading English banker with American investments wished his government would give Canada back to the Indians. It "was fit for nothing but to breed quarrels."

A good beginning was made by an Anglo-American commercial treaty in 1815, which ended discriminating duties in Britain against United States ships, and vice versa. But the postwar attitude in Britain toward America was defiant, even truculent. Governing classes in England no longer regarded America as a jest, but as a menace to British institutions. That uneasy feeling was largely responsible for sneering strictures upon American life, character, and letters with which English literature abounded during the generation following 1815; an attitude which prevented the common ties of blood and language from having their natural effect.

The three statesmen who did most to preserve peace were President Madison, his successor President Monroe, and Lord Castlereagh, who had done his best, though too late, to prevent the War of 1812. Castlereagh was the first British statesman since Shelburne to regard friendship with America as a permanent interest. His policy was to treat the United States in every respect as an equal, "to smooth all asperities between the two nations, and to unite them in sentiments of good will as well as of substantial interest, with each other." Madison and Monroe met him halfway, but not John Quincy Adams. He, too, hoped to preserve the peace, but he had a suspicious nature. Harsh and irascible in personal intercourse, Adams made a poor diplomat and as Monroe's secretary of state his notes needed pruning and softening by the now kindly and mellow President. But Adams's perception was abnormally keen, and he alone of contemporaries in either hemisphere foresaw America's future place in the world.

The Treaty of Ghent provided that the contracting parties "use their best endeavors" to abolish the African slave trade. Congress had outlawed the traffic in 1808, and in 1820 declared it to be piracy, punishable by death. But the United States refused to enter any international agreement for joint suppression, because, owing to recent memories of impressment, Adams refused to allow American ships to be searched for slaves by British men-of-war. A squadron of the United States Navy was maintained off the African coast, to watch for slavers flying the American flag; but plenty of enslaved Negroes got by under the flag of freedom, into Cuba or the Southern states.

Disarmament on the Great Lakes was the first and most lasting fruit of Anglo-American diplomacy after the war. Peace found each side "armed to the teeth" on the Lakes, especially on Lake Ontario, and building more ships. Two American and two British 74s were on the stocks; and at Kingston, Ontario, a fresh-water battleship designed to carry 110 guns was nearing completion. The Canadians, apprehensive of further American aggression, frustrated in their hope of an Indian satellite state to give them control of the Lakes, expected the British treasury to complete this building program.

It is a national trait to prepare for war only when war comes; and when war is over to disarm. Congress in February 1815 authorized the President to sell or haul out each unit of the Lake fleet not necessary for enforcing the revenue laws, which he promptly did. At the same time the army was reduced to

10,000, and in 1820 to 6000 officers and men. During the summer and fall of 1815 there occurred several "right of search" incidents on the Lakes, and from London came a disquieting rumor that the British government had decided to complete its naval construction program. President Madison then made a momentous proposal. On 16 November 1815 he instructed Adams (then minister to Great Britain) to point out that if each side began competitive building on the Lakes, "vast expense will be incurred and the danger of collision augmented in like degree." He therefore authorized Adams to propose a limitation of naval forces on the Lakes, to "demonstrate their pacific policy." Considering that only fifteen months before President Madison had been a refugee from devastated Washington, this was a rare example of magnanimity.

Castlereagh, after sounding the British cabinet, transferred the formal negotiation to Washington, and on 28 and 29 April 1817 an agreement was effected by an exchange of notes between Charles Bagot, the British minister, and Richard Rush, acting secretary of state. This agreement, which the Senate approved though not a formal treaty, limited the naval force of each country on the Lakes to four single-gun vessels of 100 tons each; one on Lake Ontario, one on Lake Champlain, and two on the upper Lakes; and forbade further naval construction on any of the Lakes. The Rush-Bagot agreement is still in force, modified as to details by mutual agreement, in order to meet newer types of warships.[1]

Disarmament, to be successful, must be a symptom of underlying friendliness, as happened here; though not immediately. The development of mutual respect and good will have been the main forces in keeping this long boundary undefended and unfortified.

First, one had to settle the boundary. Only a scant 200 miles of the easternmost section, from the Bay of Fundy north, had been determined. Several joint commissions for this purpose were provided in the Treaty of Ghent. The first ran the eastern end of the boundary between Eastport, Maine, and Campobello, New Brunswick. The second commission was unable to discover what the treaty of 1783 meant by the "highlands between the St. Lawrence and the Atlantic Ocean." So this major part of the northeastern boundary was referred to the arbitrament of the king of the Netherlands who, pleading similar inability to locate non-existent highlands, recommended a compromise that the United States refused to accept. The matter was then postponed to the Webster-Ashburton negotiation of 1842. A third joint commission drew the long part of the boundary from latitude 45° up the St. Lawrence and

1. In 1838 both sides began to replace sailing revenue cutters by steamers; U.S.S. *Michigan*, an iron paddle-wheel gunboat completed in 1844, remained in commission until 1926. In 1939, when the U.S. Navy had five ships on the Lakes, only one armed and the newest 34 years old, it was agreed by exchange of notes with the Canadian foreign minister that both navies could build vessels on the Lakes for oceanic service and maintain a few ships armed with 4-inch guns for training naval reserves. This was extended in 1946 to allow any warships to be sent to the Lakes for training purposes.

through the Great Lakes, to the Sault Ste. Marie between Huron and Superior; Webster and Ashburton continued it as far as the Lake of the Woods.

At that point the international frontier had been left hanging in mid-air by the treaty of 1783. No line could be drawn "from the Lake of the Woods westerly to the Mississippi," because the source of the Mississippi lay to the eastward and southward of that lake. This problem was dealt with in a fresh Anglo-American treaty of 1818; it extended the boundary along 49° N, latitude of the Lake of the Woods, to the "Stony Mountains."

West of the Rockies, between Spanish California and Russian Alaska, lay a region vaguely known as Oregon. Britain had challenged Spain's exclusive claim to this territory in 1790, but Captain Gray's discovery of the Columbia river mouth in 1792 gave the United States a claim. No real settlements had yet been made, but the Canadian Northwest Company (absorbed by the Hudson's Bay Company in 1821) and J. J. Astor's American Fur Company established trading posts near the mouth of the Columbia. During the War of 1812 the Canadian company purchased Astoria. America's rights were recognized by the Treaty of Ghent, but no agreement could be reached in 1818 as to partition. So Oregon was left open for ten years to the vessels and nationals of the two powers. Before that period ended, the United States had extinguished the claims of Russia and Spain, and in 1827 the agreement for joint Anglo-American occupation was renewed. A final partition was effected in 1846.

The Newfoundland fisheries question was also dealt with in 1818. Although the broad provisions of the treaty of 1783 were not renewed, American fishermen were conceded the right to take, dry, and cure fish, and obtain wood and water, within the three-mile limit on definite parts of the Newfoundland and Labrador coasts. Unfortunately, since diplomats had very slight knowledge of codfishing, certain privileges which American fishermen considered essential, such as purchasing bait, were not accorded; and the efforts of the Newfoundland government strictly to enforce the treaty produced a series of brawls and an almost continual diplomatic controversy until 1910. The Hague tribunal then gave an arbitral decision which put that question to sleep.

The dreary subject of American trade with the British West Indies still caused friction, despite the fact that this line of commerce was becoming less and less important. It remained for Andrew Jackson's administration to settle that question. But there was no bar to American sailing vessels in other parts of the world. They went everywhere. Edward Trelawny, Shelley's friend, describes a visit that he and the poet made to the waterfront of Leghorn in 1822. Ships of almost every nation were at the docks. The two friends first visited a Greek coaster, so ill-kept that Shelley said she suggested hell rather than Hellenism. They then boarded an American clipper schooner, of so graceful a model that they thought a poet must have designed her. Let Trelawney describe the visit, and what the Yankee mate said.

I said we wished to build a boat after her model. "Then I calculate you must go to Baltimore or Boston to get one; there is no one on this side the water who can do the job. We have our freight all ready, and are homeward-bound; we have elegant accommodation, and you will be across before your young friend's beard is ripe for a razor. Come down, and take an observation of the state cabin." It was about seven and a half feet by five; "plenty of room to live or die comfortably in," he observed, and then pressed us to have a chaw of real old Virginian cake, *i.e.* tobacco, and a cool drink of peach brandy. . . . I seduced Shelley into drinking a wine-glass of weak grog, the first and last he ever drank. The Yankee would not let us go until we had drunk, under the star-spangled banner, to the memory of Washington, and the prosperity of the American commonwealth. "As a warrior and statesman," said Shelley, "he was righteous in all he did, unlike all who lived before or since; he never used his power but for the benefit of his fellow-creatures."

"Stranger," said the Yankee, "truer words were never spoken; there is dry rot in all the main timbers of the Old World, and none of you will do any good till you are docked, refitted, and annexed to the New."

Those Yankee ships took no back wind from anyone. Lord Byron, sailing near the Dardanelles in H.M.S. *Salsette,* was on deck when the frigate almost fouled an American trader. Captain Walter Bathurst RN hailed her "and with the dignity of a lord, asked him where he came from, and the name of his ship." Byron was delighted with the reply: "You copper-bottomed sarpent, I guess you'll know when I've reported you to Congress!"

On the southeastern border, Anglo-American peace was gravely endangered. Florida was still a Spanish province, but Spanish authority was little exercised beyond the three fortified posts of Pensacola, St. Marks, and St. Augustine. There a situation developed not unlike that of 1811 in the Northwest. There was meddling with the Indians on the American side of the boundary, not by Spaniards but by individual British traders. The Seminole were cultivated by an elderly Scot named Arbuthnot, who owned a trading schooner named *Chance.* He gained the Indians' friendship, became their informal protector, and suggested the dangerous notion that Andrew Jackson's treaty of 1814 with the Upper Creeks was voided by the Treaty of Ghent. And Arbuthnot's companion, a young adventurer named Ambrister, joined a group of Seminoles and maroons on the Suwannee river, under a chief called Bowlegs. Independent of English activities, frontier hostilities broke out in the fall of 1817, owing largely to Indian resentment of the United States Army's pretension to hunt runaway slaves on the Spanish side of the border. In the course of these brawls, some white settlers on the American side were scalped, and a detachment of forty officers and men on their way to reinforce Fort Scott were ambushed on the Apalachicola river and killed. General Andrew Jackson and a force of Tennessee militia, under federal orders, now burst into Spanish Florida like avenging demons, marched into St. Marks (7 April 1818) and hauled down the Spanish flag. Jackson arrested Arbuthnot, and had the two Seminole chiefs who had refuged there, hanged. Next he pushed through a gloomy forest festooned with Spanish moss to surprise Bowlegs at the Suwannee river. The Indians escaped to the Everglades. Jackson, furious and baffled, learned the cause of their escape when Ambrister blundered into his camp with a letter from Arbuthnot warning Bowlegs of Jackson's approach, and offering him ten kegs of gunpowder. The General promptly set up a court-martial to try Arbuthnot for espionage and Ambrister for actively leading Indians in war against the United States. Both were found guilty and executed.

The Seminoles' power was broken for the time being, but Jackson was not through. After another quick march through the jungle, Pensacola was taken (25 May), the Spanish governor ejected, and the fortress garrisoned with Americans. Jackson then returned to Tennessee, acclaimed a hero by Westerners. But in Washington, senators thought of Roman history and trembled; Henry Clay reminded Congress that "it was in the provinces that were laid the seeds of the ambitious projects that overturned the liberties of Rome." Calhoun, the secretary of war, and an excellent one (it was he who revived the moribund military academy at West Point by appointing Major Sylvanus Thayer superintendent in 1817), wanted the aggressive general to be court-martialed, or at least reprimanded. John Quincy Adams alone of the cabinet ministers took the ground that Jackson's acts were justified by the incompetence of Spanish authority to police its own territory, and Adams had his way.

When the news reached London, the press rang with denunciation of the "ruffian" who had murdered two "peaceful British traders." Public opinion demanded instant apology and reparation, or war. "The firmness of Lord Castlereagh under the emergency," wrote the American minister, Richard Rush, was the main reason why no war occurred. Unmoved by public clamor, the foreign secretary calmly examined the documents from Washington, and decided that the "unfortunate sufferers" had been engaged in such practices "as to have deprived them of any claim on their own government for interference."

There was no need to repeat Jackson's warning. His invasion of Florida convinced Madrid that this province, which it had neglected for three centuries, had better be sold before it was seized. Accordingly, Spain ceded all her lands east of the Mississippi, together with her claims to the Oregon country, in return for $5 million on 22 February 1819. In addition, the boundary between the United States and Mexico, which lasted until 1846, was determined.

Castlereagh's life ended in September 1822. He did more for Anglo-American friendship than any other statesman of the century. George Canning, his successor, was spoiling for another round with the same adversary he had beaten in 1809. Five new American nations had come into existence. Let them be linked up with British America, and the United States stew in their vaunted isolation!

4. The Monroe Doctrine

There were only two independent nations in the New World in 1815, the United States and Haiti. The next seven years saw an eruption of new republics in South America, a revolution comparable only to what has happened in Africa since 1957. An unstable situation, rich in possibilities of trouble, had been created. Anything might happen — armed intervention by the European Holy Alliance, new balance of power, an Anglo-American entente, or a Pan-American alliance. Out of the confusion of voices came one clear note: the Monroe Doctrine, to which the policy of the United States respecting Latin America has ever since been tuned, although redefined from time to time to meet new conditions or Latin American susceptibilities.

The Latin-American nations, excepting Brazil,[1] acquired their independence under unfortunate circumstances which rendered almost impossible their union on the United States model. Spanish America began to enjoy preparation for self-government in the enlightened reign of Carlos III (1759-88). Then the French Revolution spoiled everything; and Ferdinand VII, the monarch restored in 1814, was such an imbecile that the colonies had to strike for independence. Since there had been no prior movement for colonial union, as in North America, all Spanish provinces became de facto independent, their commerce was thrown open to the world and their intellect to modern ideas. Ferdinand demanded unconditional submission from all South American leaders, which they refused. The king, however, had an army and a fleet. By 1816 he had reduced all the de facto states but La Plata (the Argentine) and had restored the Spanish colonial system. José de San Martín kept the revolutionary flame alive in a remote province of La Plata, among a population not unlike the North American frontiersmen. In January 1817 he began his famous march across the Andes with 3500 men, to defeat a royalist army at Chacabuco on the Pacific slope. Chile now organized as a republic under Bernardo O'Higgins, son of an Irish officer in the Spanish service. In the meantime, Simón Bolívar had spread revolution up the Orinoco valley and created the Republic of Great Colombia, comprising the present Colombia, Panama, Ecuador and Venezuela.

Recognition of their independence at Washington was naturally expected by the new republics. Henry Clay, in an oration describing the "glorious spectacle of eighteen millions of people struggling to burst their chains and be free," gave the lead to North American opinion. Yet Clay's eloquence had slight effect on Monroe's administration, especially on John Quincy Adams, who "wished well" to the new republics, but saw "no prospect that they

1. Portugal may be said to have seceded from Brazil, rather than the contrary; after Portugal had gone liberal, a senior branch of the House of Braganza continued to rule in Brazil, 1822-89.

would establish free or liberal institutions of government. Arbitrary power, military and ecclesiastical, was stamped upon their habits, and upon all their institutions. Civil dissension was infused into all their seminal principles."

This attitude, together with fear of offending Spain while the Florida treaty was pending, explains the cautious policy of Monroe's administration toward the Latin Americans. Their independence was desired as an additional bulwark for American isolation, but not with sufficient ardor to risk a European war. Monroe and Adams did not entertain the remotest idea of forming a Pan-American league with the United States at the head. As long as Europe did not actively intervene, they were content to stand aside and let Spain fight it out with her former colonies; but they would certainly oppose any general European attempt to interfere. So Gallatin, now American minister at Paris, informed the French foreign minister in June 1823.

Castlereagh, and after him Canning, were at one with the American government in that feeling, but at variance in every other aspect of policy toward Latin America. British exports to South America in 1822 surpassed those to the United States. British commercial houses were established in South American ports, mining concessions were obtained by British subjects in several countries, and loans of the new republics were floated in London.

In 1821, events in Spanish America began to march with a rapidity that forced the North American hand. The Argentine and Chile, having established their independence, went to the aid of Peru, San Martín leading an army, the Chilean navy co-operating under Admiral Cochrane. Bolívar, at the same time, was rolling up Spanish armies westward from the Orinoco, consolidating liberated territory in the Great Colombian Republic. In 1822, when Bolívar and San Martín met in Guayaquil, only one Spanish army was left in the field, and that surrendered after the battle of Ayacucho. A mutiny in the Spanish garrison at Vera Cruz forced the Spanish viceroy to accept a provisional treaty for the independence of Mexico, including Central America. Thus, by the autumn of 1822, continental America from Great Lakes to Cape Horn was independent, and all except Mexico and Brazil were republican. Europeans retained control only in Belize, Bolivia, and the Guianas.

In his message of 8 March 1822, President Monroe declared that the new governments of La Plata, Chile, Peru, Colombia, and Mexico were "in the full enjoyment of their independence," of which there was "not the most remote prospect of their being deprived," and that they had "a claim to recognition by other powers." Congress then appropriated money to defray the expenses of "such missions to the independent nations on the American continent as the President might deem proper." Diplomatic relations were shortly after established with these five nations.

France invaded Spain in 1823, with the object of delivering Ferdinand VII from a liberal constitution that he had been forced to accept. It was a matter of common talk that a Franco-Spanish expeditionary force to South America would follow this military promenade. The possibility that this, too, would succeed, made the British government apprehensive. So it happened that on 16 August 1823, Canning at the foreign office put a question to Richard Rush, the American minister at London, that started wheels revolving in the United States. What did Mr. Rush think his government would say to going hand in hand with England to bar France from South America? Rush's dispatches embodying the conversation arrived in Washington in October 1823. President Monroe sent copies to Jefferson and Madison. The covering letter stated his own opinion that Canning's overture should be accepted.

Jefferson, then eighty years old, was in placid retirement at Monticello. Horace and Tacitus, he wrote to the President, were so much more interesting than the newspapers that he was out of touch with public affairs. But this question of co-operation with Great Britain was "the most momentous which has ever been offered to my contemplation since that of Independence. . . . America, North and South, has a set of interests distinct from those of Europe, and peculiarly her own. . . . One nation, most of all, could disturb us in this pursuit; she now offers to lead, aid and accompany us in it. . . . With her then, we should most sedulously cherish a cordial friendship." And Madison, from Montpelier, gave similar advice, adding that he was in favor of an additional Anglo-American declaration to support Greek independence.

Three white-haired statesmen, each on his Virginia hilltop (for Monroe was now at Oak Hill), pondering a vital question of foreign policy: what a delightful aroma of antique republicanism! Hard-boiled Adams, however, came up with a different idea. Strongly nationalist, ever suspicious of England, at the next cabinet meeting in Washington (7 November 1823) he declared, "It would be more candid, as well as more dignified, to avow our principles explicitly to Great Britain and France, than to come in as a cockboat in the wake of the British man-of-war." For Adams, moreover, the big question transcended Latin America. Russia in 1821 claimed that Alaska extended to latitude 51° N, well within the Oregon country, and closed to foreigners the waters thence to Bering Strait. Adams believed that colonial establishments were immoral and destined to fall, and that the New World should now be considered closed to further colonization by European powers. On 17 July 1823 he told the Russian minister so, explicitly. Then, in October, the Russian minister at Washington communicated to Adams a note that contained remarks on "expiring republicanism" which were as offensive to the American government then as were Khrushchev's remarks about "burying" us, over a century later.

As Adams saw it, his government had been challenged on four points, which could be answered at once: (1) the proposal of Anglo-American co-operation; (2) rumored European intervention in Latin America; (3) Russian extension of her colonial establishments, and (4) the czar's denunciation of republican principles. "I remarked," Adams wrote of the cabinet meeting of 7 November, "that the communications lately received from the Russian Minister afforded, as I thought, a very suitable and convenient opportunity for us to take our stand against the Holy Alliance, and at the same time to decline the overture of Great Britain."

Monroe agreed in principle, but vacillated between doing nothing in fear of the Holy Alliance, and carrying the war into Turkey, to aid the Greeks. Their struggle for independence had aroused immense interest, because the Greek language and literature were then basic in the education of American gentlemen. South Carolina petitioned Congress to acknowledge Greek independence; Albert Gallatin proposed to lend Greece a fleet; William Cullen Bryant wrote *The Greek Partisan;* the martyrs of Chios and the exploits of Ypsilanti were commemorated in the names of frontier hamlets; classic colonnades were added to modest farm-houses. All this struck a chord in Monroe's kindly heart; in his annual message to Congress of 1822 he remarked, "The mention of Greece fills the mind with the most exalted sentiments and arouses in our bosoms the best feelings of which our nature is susceptible." In the first draft of his epoch-making message, the President proposed to acknowledge the independence of Greece, and to ask Congress to provide for a diplomatic mission to Athens. Against this meddling in European affairs Adams argued vehemently. He wished "to make an *American* cause and adhere inflexibly to that."

In the end Adams had his own way. Monroe consented to omit all but a pious wish for the success of Greece, but he forced Adams to delete a high-pitched exposition of republican principles. The passages on foreign relations in Monroe's annual message of 2 December 1823, although written in more concise language than Adams would have used, expressed the basic conception of his secretary of state. We may summarize this original Monroe Doctrine in the President's own words:

1. Positive principles: (a) "The American continents, by the free and independent condition which they have assumed and maintain, are henceforth not to be considered as subjects for future colonization by any European powers." (b) "The political system of the allied powers is essentially different . . . from that of America . . . We should consider any attempt on their part to extend their system to any portion of this hemisphere as dangerous to our peace and safety."

2. Negative principles: (a) "With the existing colonies or dependencies of any European power we have not interfered and shall not interfere." (b) "In the wars of the European powers in matters relating to themselves we have never taken any part, nor does it comport with our policy so to do."

Therein is the whole of President Monroe's doctrine, whatever later developments may be included under the name of the Monroe Doctrine. Critics of Monroe have pointed out that his message was a mere declaration, which in itself could not prevent an intervention which had already been given up; that in view of the exclusive power of Congress to declare war, a mere presidential announcement could not guarantee Latin-American independence. That may be true, but is irrelevant. What Adams was trying to do, and what he and

Monroe accomplished, was to raise a standard of American foreign policy for all the world to see; and to plant it so firmly in the national consciousness that no later President would dare to pull it down.

By this time the Era of Good Feelings was over. When the year 1824 dawned, no fewer than five candidates who claimed to represent the Jeffersonian tradition were jockeying for the presidency. John Quincy Adams who, more than any other man, was responsible for the Monroe Doctrine, won; but his presidential administration was the unhappiest in history for the incumbent.

HUNTERS OF KENTUCKY

You've heard, I s'pose, how New Or-leans is fam'd for wealth and beau-ty, So Pack-en-ham he made his brags, if he in fight was luck-y, He'd have their girls and cot-ton bags, In spite of old Ken-tuck-y.

There's girls of ev'-ry hue, it seems, from snow-y white to soot-y.

Oh, Ken-tuck-y! the hunt-ers of Ken-tuck-y.

Second Adams and First Jackson Administrations

1825-1833

1. A Minority President

AMERICA WAS FAR MORE INTERESTED in the coming presidential election of 1824 than in the Monroe Doctrine or the Holy Alliance. The Jeffersonian Republican party was breaking up into factions, and it was anyone's guess how they would divide or blend to make new parties. Three members of President Monroe's cabinet and two others aspired to the succession. John Quincy Adams, secretary of state, qualified by faithful and efficient public service for thirty years, wanted it. William H. Crawford of Georgia, secretary of the treasury, wanted it very much, and thought that he should have it since his nomination by a congressional caucus made him officially the party candidate; but this hardly counted, since the caucus was attended by only one-quarter of the Republican senators and congressmen. Henry Clay, speaker of the House, placed in nomination by the legislature of his native Kentucky, once said that he would "rather be right than be president," but now he wanted to be President. As advocate of the "American System" he made a wide appeal, and his charming personality made him everyone's second choice. But Clay had a Western rival, General Andrew Jackson, senator from Tennessee, whose legislature nominated him for the presidency. John C. Calhoun, secretary of war, was the favorite son of South Carolina; but after Jackson's strength in the Southwest became evident, Calhoun consented to be nominated for the vice presidency, expecting to be next in line for the top.

The presidential campaign of 1824 was quiet and seemly. All four candidates stood for about the same thing, none electioneered actively, and the newspapers were decent. But no one obtained a majority in the electoral college. The framers of the Constitution expected this situation to occur more often than not; but it has never happened again in a century and a half.

Adams carried New England, received 26 of New York's 36 votes, and picked up a few elsewhere, making a total of 84. Crawford carried only Virginia and his native Georgia, but obtained a few scattered electoral votes which put him ahead of Henry Clay for third place; and, according to the Constitution, only the first three could be candidates for the final election by the House. Jackson showed surprising strength. He ran away with Pennsylvania, New Jersey, the Carolinas, and most of the South and West, with a total of 99, still short of a majority but an impressive plurality; and in states where electors were chosen by the voters he had three votes to Clay's one. Politicians all asked each other, what did this mean? They would soon learn.

The election of a President now had to be made by the House of Representatives, voting by states, a majority of states being necessary for choice. So when Congress convened in January 1825, the corridors of the Capitol, and the streets, barrooms, and boardinghouses of Washington became scenes of personal conferences, sly offers, and noncommittal replies, as backers of Jackson and Adams tried to work up a majority for their respective candidates. Crawford, who had suffered a paralytic stroke, was no longer considered. Jackson had eleven states in the bag, but needed two more. Adams had seven states, and needed six more. Clay, no longer a candidate himself, controlled the votes of three states; and, after it was half understood, half promised that if Adams were elected Clay would be secretary of state, he threw all three for the New Englander. James Buchanan of Pennsylvania had already tried to make a similar deal between Clay and Jackson but failed. Adams still needed three more. Missouri and Illinois, which had voted for Jackson, were now represented each by one congressman, who were "conciliated" (Jackson men said "bought") by Adams. Doubtful Maryland members who still called themselves Federalists were assured that Adams, if elected, would not take revenge on that dying party for what it had done to him and his father. And so it happened that on 9 February 1825 the House on its first ballot elected John Quincy Adams President of the United States, by a majority of one state.

It was a barren victory, although perfectly legal and constitutional. The cry "We was robbed!" at once went up from the Jackson forces, and active electioneering for 1828 began.

John Quincy Adams had shown signal ability in political finagling, but he was a lonely, inarticulate person unable to express his burning love of country in any manner to kindle the popular imagination. Short, thick-set, with a massive bald head and rheumy eyes, his port was stern and his manners unconciliatory. His concessions were ungraceful, and his refusals were harsh. A lonely walk before dawn, or an early morning swim in summer, fitted him for the day's toil, which he concluded by writing his perennial diary. Even in his own New England Adams was respected rather than loved, and other sections resented his election over favorite sons. Senator Benton of Missouri, with a wild plunge into what he believed to be Greek, said it violated the *demos krateo* principle. When Adams defiantly gave Clay the state department, the cry "Corrupt bargain!" was raised; Randolph of Roanoke called it "the combination unheard of till then, of the puritan with the blackleg." There followed a duel between Randolph and Clay; fortunately both were bad shots.

Woodrow Wilson, another stern President elected by a minority, built up a personal following by appointments as well as oratory. But Adams was no orator, and he refused to make appointments to cultivate the support of journalists; and in that day, before highly developed ward politics (not to speak of radio and TV) newspapers could make or break a President. Although Crawford had opened the way to the spoils system in the four-year tenure-of-office act of 1820, Adams would have none of it; he reappointed men who had worked against him, and, when vacancies occurred, appointed Jackson men to prove his public virtue. That was the road to political suicide.

President Adams's major mistake was to trim his sails to nationalism after the wind had changed, and to refuse to come about. A sentence in his first annual message: "The great object of the institution of civil government is the improvement of those who are parties to the social compact," is the keynote of his domestic policy. To "slumber in indolence" would be "to cast away the bounties of Providence and doom ourselves to perpetual inferiority." He would use the ample federal revenue to increase the navy, build national roads and canals, send out scientific expeditions, establish institutions of learning and research, and make Washington the national cultural center. All these things were to come; Adams was a true prophet; but he urged them in the midst of a state rights reaction. If, asked the cotton states, we admit federal powers of this scope, will not some future administration claim the power to emancipate slaves?

In foreign affairs, the outstanding conflict in Adams's administration was the pulling and hauling between him and George Canning the British foreign minister for the favor of new Latin American republics. We had got the jump on England with the Monroe Doctrine; Canning made the next move by recognizing all the new republics early in 1825. The United States had already recognized six of them, but they accepted that as a right from a sister republic; from the king of Great Britain it was an honor, an accolade. Canning wrote jubilantly, "Spanish America is free, and if we do not mismanage our affairs sadly, she is English, and *novus saeculorum nascitur ordo*," a new era is born — quoting the very motto on the Great Seal of the United States.

President Adams's policy toward Latin America was honest and cautious. He wished to obtain commercial treaties on the basis of most-favored-nation, to encourage the new nations to observe republican principles and live at peace among themselves, and to discourage them from provoking Spain by attacking the *sempre fidel isla* of Cuba.

Mexico, largest and most conservative of the new republics, having many points of possible friction with the United States and a pressing need for capital and markets that England could best supply, was the most promising ground for British influence. President Adams appointed as the first United States minister to Mexico Joel R. Poinsett, an accomplished gentleman from South Carolina who spoke fluent Spanish, had visited Mexico, and written a short book about it. He appeared to be the ideal choice, but made a mess of his mission for want of judgment and superfluity of zeal, that quality fatal to diplomatists. The Republican party in Mexico, eager to establish York rite

Masonic lodges in opposition to Scottish rite lodges then being used by the British and the monarchists, persuaded Poinsett to obtain York rite charters for new lodges. All Mexico became divided into *Escoceses* and *Yorkinos;* civil war broke out, and Poinsett's name became the rallying point for one party and the target for the other. The Scots won, and Poinsett was recalled under a cloud. But his mission was not wholly fruitless, for he brought home cuttings of the scarlet flower which botanists named *Poinsettia pulcherrima* after him.

At the Panama Congress of 1826, Canning scored again. Bolívar the Liberator summoned this meeting to promote the unity of Latin America and to work out a common policy toward Spain. He disliked the United States and intended to leave her out, but to invite England in the hope that she might become leader of a Latin-American league. Mexico and Colombia, however, invited President Adams to send delegates, and he accepted. He hoped to convince the new republics of North American friendship, to dissuade them from "liberating" Cuba and Puerto Rico, and to adopt his favorite principles of most-favored-nation and freedom of the seas. To cover the cost of sending delegates, he appealed for an appropriation to Congress, where vehement opposition developed. Jackson supporters regarded the Panama Congress as a gala performance invented by Henry Clay to dazzle the public mind and enhance the administration's prestige. Congress finally voted the money and the Senate confirmed the President's appointments, but too late for the two American delegates to arrive in time. The Congress accomplished nothing, to be sure; but the British delegate who attended made the United States, in comparison, appear coldly indifferent. Fortunately this dangerous rivalry, which might have made Central America the Balkans of the New World, ended with the death of Canning in 1827.

Many things recommended by President Adams were thus rudely rejected by Congress but adopted years later. For instance, he wanted, as a beginning to making Washington a cultural center, a national astronomical observatory; and, hoping to give it constitutional grounds, he described observatories as "lighthouses of the sky." That phrase was kicked about in Congress as if uttered by a halfwit. He recommended the establishment of a naval academy, and that touched off old Jeffersonian prejudices. Representative Lemuel Sawyer of North Carolina predicted that the glamor of a naval education would "produce degeneracy and corruption of the public morality and change our simple Republican habits"; Senator William Smith of South Carolina, after pointing out that neither Julius Caesar nor Lord Nelson attended a naval academy, predicted that American bluejackets "would look with contempt upon trifling or effeminate leaders," such as a naval school might produce. Not until the eve of the Mexican War did Congress create the United States Naval Academy at Annapolis.

Watchers from afar can discern the shadow of things to come in 1826, midway in President Adams's term of office. The Erie Canal, completed the

previous year, made New York the Empire State and New York City the
world's most populous urban center. Yet the doom of the canal as a principal
means of heavy transportation was sounded in 1826 by a little horse-drawn
line, first railroad in the United States, built near the home of the Adamses in
Quincy; and shortly the Baltimore & Ohio steam railway would be chartered.
In 1826 J. Fenimore Cooper published *The Last of the Mohicans*, which
strengthened the "noble red man" theme in literature, without helping the
Indians. The same year an obscure preacher named Charles G. Finney was
conducting a religious revival in the Mohawk valley which eventually fed the
antislavery movement. In 1826 Josiah Holbrook founded the American
lyceum, a scheme for "the public diffusion of knowledge" through lectures by
experts in scientific and cultural subjects; this fathered the Chautauquas,
forums and adult education movements. The American Home Missionary
Society was organized in 1826 to carry the gospel to the frontier and the
immigrant. George Bancroft, destined to become America's favorite historian, spoke on the Fourth of July in favor of "a determined, uncompromising democracy." And on that same Glorious Fourth, there occurred an
event which for a moment fused the jarring factions of American life into one
great, loving family.

The lives of Thomas Jefferson and John Adams the one eighty-three and the
other ninety years old, were flickering to a close. Could they live until the
Fourth, fiftieth anniversary of the adoption of that great Declaration for
which they were jointly responsible? All America was praying that they would.
As midnight of 3–4 July approached, Jefferson at Monticello returned to
consciousness for the last time. He murmured to a kinsman at his bedside,
"This is the Fourth?" The young man nodded assent, Jefferson heaved a
sigh of content that proved to be his last utterance, and at noon breathed his
last. At that moment the house of John Adams at Quincy was shaken by the
blasts of saluting cannon, and watchers by his bedside could hear the roar of
approval in the town square when an orator flung out the sentiment given to
him by the old gentleman — "Independence forever!" The dying patriot
seemed trying to speak; and his granddaughter who bent her ear close, caught
between gasps the whispered words, "Thomas — Jefferson — still — surv —."
He lingered until the tide turned, and crossed the bar at sunset.

Forgotten for a time were party struggles and rivalries of other days. Americans thought of Saul and Jonathan, "Lovely and pleasant in their lives; and
in their death they were not divided; they were swifter than eagles, they were
stronger than lions."

2. Election of 1828

John Quincy Adams's campaign for re-election began even before he was
inaugurated President, and there was little let-up during the next four years.
The election of 1828 was simpler than that of 1824 because there were only

two candidates. Just as the Jeffersonian and Hamilton factions of 1791 were
the nuclei of the Republican and Federalist parties, so the Jackson-Calhoun
and Adams-Clay factions of 1823–28 were developing into the Democratic
and Whig parties that occupied the political stage until the eve of the Civil
War.

National political parties in the United States are generally of local origin,
and never completely lose their basic character as a bundle of local factions
and interests. In this instance, the impulse for the election of Jackson came
largely from state politicians seeking national power. During the Era of Good
Feelings, the Republican party within each state was breaking up into conservative and democratic factions. Generally speaking, the democratic group
wished to level down such political inequalities as still remained, especially
property qualifications for the franchise, thus diluting the electorate with
elements susceptible to a more emotional appeal than those of the Jeffersonian school. Another effect was to breed a new litter of professional politicians, among whom enjoyment of state office and patronage created a brisk
appetite for the more luscious emoluments of federal power. The best of
these men represented some genuine aspiration toward equality, the worst
were mere demagogues; but at the head of them were able men of lowly origin
but ingratiating form and phrase, such as Martin Van Buren of New York and
James Buchanan of Pennsylvania. Their political strategy was to join hands
with democratic factions in other states, under some national figure who
would reflect glory on themselves and lead them to victory. Adams, stiff and
scrupulous, was no leader for such as these; Calhoun, the Carolina highbrow,
was little better; and Clay's lot was now cast with the President. General
Jackson, hero of New Orleans and subjugator of the Creek nation, was a man
who could be counted on to reward friends and punish enemies, a heaven-
sent leader for this new democracy.

It did not matter that there was no national issue or popular grievance; the
politicians would see to that, and principles could be attended to after victory.
Adams must be discredited. The "corrupt bargain" charge, engineered by
Buchanan, was the opening gun of the Jackson campaign. Next came the
attack on Adams's motives for promoting the Panama Congress. Pro-Jackson
men won a majority in mid-term congressional elections. Investigations of
alleged presidential corruption were started but not pushed home, so that the
victim had no chance to clear himself. Van Buren admits in his *Autobiography*, "Adams was an honest man, not only incorruptible himself, but an
enemy to venality in every department of the public service." Yet Van Buren
was the first to prefer charges of outrageous corruption against the President.
The South, now in full tide of reaction against nationalism, was assured that
Jackson would defend state rights. The West's loyalty to Henry Clay was
impaired by Adams's professed intention to administer the public lands on
business principles, rather than squander them on shiftless squatters. Richard
Rush, who became Adams's secretary of the treasury after his return from

London, reported that the low price of government land was a "bounty in favor of agricultural pursuits." That sort of talk won no votes in the West. Adams counted on income from the sale of public land to finance far-reaching plans for exploring expeditions and scientific research. The West cared for none of that, but cheap land it must have.

This election of 1828 was the first presidential one that really smelled. The most absurd lies were spread. Adams had furnished the White House at his own expense with a billiard table and a set of chessmen; in the mouth of a Jackson orator these became "gaming tables and gambling furniture" purchased from public funds. He was even accused of playing pimp to the emperor of Russia. Newspapers that supported Adams, however, were not idle; there was a "coffin hand-bill" on the shooting of six militiamen by Jackson for insubordination; and the General's frontier brawls and alleged premarital relations with Mrs. Jackson were described in detail. Altogether, it was the most degrading presidential election the United States had ever experienced. Worse, however, were to come.

Jackson polled 56 per cent of the popular vote, carried the Southern and Western states, Pennsylvania, and most of New York, winning 178 electoral votes to Adams's 83. Virginia held her aristocratic nose and voted for Jackson, believing him the lesser evil; South Carolina voted for him as a state rights man, which she soon had reason to regret. But in the last instance it was classes rather than sections that elected Jackson: The Southern hunters and backwoods farmers whom he had led to glory, and the Northern democracy, tired of respectable, gentlemanly promotions from cabinet to White House. They cared little for policies, but much for personality, and they voted for Jackson because he was their sort of man. After all, the most sophisticated among us have often no better reason for voting as we do than had the American democracy of 1828, in exalting a man of their own sort; ill-educated, intolerant, yet professing the immortal principles of the Declaration of Independence and, though a state rights man, completely devoted to the Union. Nor was the democracy disappointed.

John Quincy Adams never understood why he was spurned by the country he loved with silent passion, rejected by the people he had served so faithfully. In the four sad months between election and the end of his term, there kept running through his head the refrain of an old song he had first heard at the court of Versailles: *Richard O mon Roi, l'univers t'abandonne* — "The whole wide world has abandoned thee."

Yet this was not the end for Adams. The noblest part of his long career lay ahead.

3. Jacksonian Democracy

We are now in an age of great political figures. Adams, Clay, Webster, Van Buren, and Calhoun were statesmen of whom any age or country could be proud; and the man who towered above them in popularity and gave his name to an era was Major General Andrew Jackson. "Old Hickory" as he was nicknamed by the press, "The Gineral," as his intimates called him, "reigned," as his enemies called his occupancy of the White House, for two terms. He practically appointed his successor, Martin Van Buren; and, after one term of Whig opposition, Democracy returned to the saddle in the person of James K. Polk, "Young Hickory," who was followed by Zachary Taylor, a tired old general who died in office, and a colorless vice president. Then came two Democratic Presidents who had been spoon-fed by Jackson — Franklin Pierce and James Buchanan. And that brings us to the great American tragedy.

Thus, Andrew Jackson and the brand of democracy associated with him dominated the political scene from 1828 to the Civil War. And they set a pattern of American politics which, with surprisingly few changes, has persisted into the second half of the twentieth century. People with long memories frequently compared Franklin D. Roosevelt and Harry Truman to Andrew Jackson, and both Presidents regarded this as a compliment. So, what was Jacksonian Democracy, and what manner of man was Andrew Jackson?

Jacksonian Democracy was the upsurge of a new generation of recently enfranchised voters against a somewhat ossified Jeffersonian Republican party. It was a national movement in that it opposed disunion and knew no geographical limits; Jackson men in Maine and Louisiana uttered the same clichés in spell-binding oratory and deplored the same largely imaginary sins of their opponents. But it was antinational in rejecting Henry Clay's "American System." That is, it wanted roads, canals, and (in a few years) railroads to be chartered and aided by the states, but no federal government messing into them or sharing the expected profits. Jacksonian Democracy believed in equality only for white men; it was far less charitable toward the Indian and the Negro than its "aristocratic" opponents. It was not "leveling" in the European sense, having no desire to pull down men of wealth to a common level; but it wanted a fair chance for every man to rise. In the states, Jackson Democrats sometimes, but not invariably, favored free public education and a somewhat cautious humanitarianism, but dissociated themselves from most of the "isms" of the period, such as abolition, feminism, and Mormonism. In general, they shared that contempt for intellect which is one of the unlovely traits of democracy everywhere. There was no contact between the political democracy of Jackson and the philosophical democracy of such men as Emerson; and the efforts of a few intellectuals (such as Theodore Sedgwick III and Robert Rantoul Jr.) to bridge the gap were ineffective. Of the greater literary figures of this era, only Nathaniel Hawthorne and in a half-hearted way, James Fenimore Cooper were Democrats, and President Jackson could not have cared less. His attitude toward literature may be gauged by a letter he wrote late in life to President Polk, urging that his old crony Amos Kendall be appointed to the Madrid legation, then held by an eminent American author. "There can be no delicacy in recalling Erwin," he wrote; "he is only fit to write a book and scarcely that." He could not even remember Washington Irving's correct name! The jackass as symbol of the Democratic party was first used by the Whigs as a satire on the supposed ignorance of Old Hickory, and it is significant that the party not only joyfully accepted this emblem but has retained it to this day.

With that bland inconsistency so characteristic of politicians, Jackson cultivated the old Federalists, whom Adams had always kept at arm's length, and even won over the sons of Alexander Hamilton. Alexis de Tocqueville, an observant young Frenchman who toured the United States in 1831, had a talk with Charles Carroll of Carrollton, last survivor of the signers of the Declaration of Independence. He then reflected, "This race of men is disappearing, after providing America with her greatest men. With them is lost the tradition of cultivated manners. The people become educated, knowledge extends, a middling ability becomes common. Outstanding talents and great characters are more rare. Society is less brilliant and more prosperous." But there was a good side to all this. The common man gained active participation in government at all but the highest levels, and public education was provided for his children — if he were white and free.

One amusing sign of the times was a new appetite for political and military titles. Before Jackson came to Washington, nobody thought of addressing officials under the President as anything but plain "Mr." But from now on, every man had to be "Senator" this, "Mr. Secretary" or "Governor" that; or, if he had nothing better, his rank in the state militia. As W. S. Gilbert parodied this phenomenon,

> When everybody's somebody,
> Nobody's anybody.

Jacksonian Democracy catered to mediocrity, diluted politics with the incompetent and the corrupt, and made conditions increasingly unpleasant for gentlemen in public life. The party caucus, the stump speech, the herding and mass-voting of drunks and helpless immigrants by city bosses, became standard practices in Jackson's time, although curious students can find a few earlier instances. But there was nothing low or vulgar about Jackson himself; he was one of nature's gentlemen. And although we think of him as peculiarly and exclusively American, his friend Martin Van Buren, when minister to Great Britain, found Jackson's likeness in the "Iron Duke," Wellington.

"Old Hickory," rough-hewn out of live-oak, accustomed to command and to be obeyed, quick to anger and slow to forgive, had a fine sense of honor, and a gallant attitude toward "the fair," as he called the other sex. Born on the Carolina frontier in 1767 to immigrant parents from Northern Ireland, he had risen to be a successful lawyer in Tennessee and acquired lands, slaves, and blooded horses. But he had none of the touchiness about slavery that was common among the Southern politicians of his era. He had sufficient knowledge of the Bible and Shakespeare to write good, forcible English and to express himself well. Jackson was no champion of the poor, or even of the "common man"; but they loved him because he proved that a man born in a log cabin could become rich, win battles, and be elected President of the United States. Incidentally, once Jackson was in, it became difficult for anyone *not* born in a log cabin to reach the presidency.

The President-elect, sixty-two years old, was an impressive figure. Six feet one in height and weighing 145 pounds, slim and straight as a ramrod, his lean, strong face lit up by hawk-like eyes and surmounted by a mane of thick gray hair, he could never melt unseen into a crowd, as J. Q. Adams did all too easily. Leaving his Hermitage near Nashville in deep mourning because his beloved wife Rachel had lately died, he traveled by steamboat to Pittsburgh and thence by horseback over the Alleghenies to Washington. At the capital, where he put up at Gadsby's Indian Queen Tavern near the northwest corner of Pennsylvania Avenue and 6th Street, he became the center of attention, while Adams quietly and sadly prepared to move out of the White House. On the day of inauguration Washington (population about 18,000) was crowded to suffocation with an estimated 10,000 visitors, some of whom had come from very distant parts to see their idol. Jackson could have had an imposing parade of military companies and Old Hickory clubs, but he declined all such honors, and in republican simplicity walked with a few friends the half mile from Gadsby's to the Capitol. After taking the oath of office, administered by Chief Justice Marshall, and delivering his inaugural address, he mounted his saddle horse and rode to the White House. An informal and unplanned inaugural parade, people in carriages, wagons, and carts, mounted and on foot, followed the President up Pennsylvania Avenue, parked their horses in Lafayette Square, and surged into the White House almost on his coattails. No police arrangements had been made, and the press of well wishers forced the President to escape by a rear window and take refuge in Gadsby's. Glasses were broken and trodden under foot, punch was spilled, and damask chairs soiled by muddy boots. Conservatives shuddered over what they feared to be the opening scene of another French Revolution; the pastor of the Unitarian church preached a sermon on Luke xix.41, Jesus "beheld the city and wept over it." But the Jacksonian Revolution, if it may so be called, was marked neither by class war nor persecution of "aristocrats"; the only victims of mobs were unpopular minorities, such as Negroes, abolitionists, Catholics, and Mormons. Washington's and Jefferson's principles of toleration declined as the power of the common man rose.

No President of the United States suffered from so many continued and painful illnesses as Jackson, and his pain was augmented by never ending sorrow for his wife. At the time of his inauguration he carried in his body two bullets which poisoned his system. He suffered from headaches, chronic dysentery, nephritis, and bronchiectasis. In the eight years of office he had at least two severe pulmonary hemorrhages and several attacks of dropsy. Numerous doctors, including the celebrated Philadelphia surgeon Philip S. Physick, who had saved the life of Chief Justice Marshall by a bladder operation, did their best for "Old Hickory," and a stout will and iron constitution pulled him through.

4. *The Spoils System and the Cabinet*

A simple way of thinking — everything black or white — and a habit of command are keynotes to Jackson's policy, which he well summed up in a short note to Van Buren in 1830, after vetoing the Maysville Road bill:

The people expected reform, retrenchment and economy in the administration of this Government. . . . The great object of Congress, *it would seem*, is to make mine one of the most extravagant administrations since the commencement of this Government. This must not be; The Federal Constitution must be obeyed, state-rights preserved, our national debt *must be paid, direct taxes and loans avoided*, and the Federal union preserved. These are the objects I have in view, and regardless of all consequences, will carry into effect.

Note the emphasis on reform. The pro-Jackson editors and politicians, by persistent lying about the "extravagance and corruption" of the honest, efficient and economical Adams administration, had persuaded both President and people that his first task was to "cleanse the Augean stables" of accumulated filth; in other words, to fire enough office-holders to make way for deserving Democrats. Rotation in office and the spoils system had long been in vogue in New York, Pennsylvania, and other Northern states. Many members of the civil service came out for Jackson in time to save their jobs, but others did not. Jackson removed only 252 out of 612 presidential appointees and, like Warren Hastings, was "surprised at his own moderation." Even this 40 per cent purge entailed much hardship, as there were then no pensions for aged or retired civil officials, many of whom had been appointed for charitable reasons. A few cases of overdrawn or careless accounts by earlier appointees were unearthed and held up to public scorn; but these were nothing in comparison with the scandals created by Jackson appointees. The most notorious was Samuel Swartwout, a participant in the Burr conspiracy who became a speculator in New York and worked hard to elect Jackson. Rewarded with the juiciest plum at the President's disposal, the collectorship of the port of New York, he managed in less than ten years of office to steal more than a million dollars of public money.

It is a fair statement that Jackson introduced the spoils system into the federal government, and that he never regretted it. His theory, stated in his first annual message, was that "the duties of all public offices" were so "plain and simple" that any man of average intelligence was qualified; and that more would be lost by continuing men in office than could be gained by experience. Naturally, when the Whigs won in 1840 they threw the Jackson men out, and when the Democrats came back under Polk, they threw the Whigs out; and so on. The consequences were more power to party organizations, diminishing prestige of the federal civil service, and decreasing efficiency. This sort of thing became so engrained in the American political system that, despite repeated reform legislation, it still continues. As recently as 1959 Senator Herbert H. Lehman of New York "called for the eradication of the spoils system in politics," especially the removal of the judiciary from "the control of party bosses."

Jackson's first cabinet was a collection of mediocrities, with the exception of Martin Van Buren, secretary of state. Noteworthy was the lack of anyone from Virginia or New England, the first time that had occurred. Jackson's choices registered, rather neatly, the rise of the Western and Middle states' democracy to federal power, and a brush-off to the Virginia dynasty and the Yankees. But he had to call on them in the end.

For two years the simple political issue of the Jackson administration was, who would be the next President? For Jackson, like many others in that exalted office, had let it be known that he intended to retire after one term. Vice President Calhoun was the heir presumptive. There had been some sort of gentlemen's agreement to that effect between his followers and Jackson's that if Calhoun, fifteen years younger than the General, should accept the vice presidency, Jackson would go all out for him in 1832. But Old Hickory was already beginning to feel cool toward Calhoun, and his appointment of Martin Van Buren as secretary of state, instead of the man whom Calhoun wanted, showed how the wind blew. Van Buren was much too astute to ask the President for an official accolade. He simply allowed events to take their course, and came out on top as he always knew he would.

An ill wind that helped to waft "Little Van" into the White House and blow Calhoun back to South Carolina, arose over the wife of Secretary Eaton. Born Peggy O'Neale, daughter of the principal tavern keeper at the Georgetown end of Washington, she was a luscious brunette with a perfect figure and a come-hither look in her blue eyes that drove the young men of Washington wild, and some of the old ones too. Married at an early age to a purser in the navy, she became during his long absences at sea the mistress of her father's star boarder, John H. Eaton, bachelor senator from Tennessee. At least so "all Washington," except Jackson, believed. Eaton bought the tavern when Papa O'Neale went broke, in order to continue this pleasant arrangement, and persuaded the navy department to give the purser plenty of sea duty. About the time of the presidential election, the complaisant husband, caught short in his accounts, died or committed suicide — nobody knew which; and shortly after the news arrived, on New Year's Day 1829, his bonny widow, now thirty-two years old, married Eaton. All except the President-elect tried to stop it, but Jackson practically commanded him to marry her in order (as he thought) to stop the gossip and make her an honest woman. And Jackson appointed Eaton his war secretary.

Mrs. Calhoun refused to receive the "hussy," and the other cabinet wives followed suit. They declined to call, and at official receptions or White House dinners, refused to speak. Neither would the ladies of the diplomatic corps or the wives of most of the senators and congressmen. Van Buren, however, was a widower, and Charles Vaughan the British minister and Baron Krudener the Russian minister were bachelors. They could afford to show the lady marked attention, which was not difficult since she had wit as well as beauty. The crisis came at a Jackson birthday ball in January 1830. All the secretaries' ladies ignored Peggy and tempers rose so high that cabinet meetings had to be postponed. But the President refused to surrender. He actually held a cabinet meeting *re* Mrs. Eaton, whom he pronounced "as chaste as a virgin." Henry Clay, hearing this, quipped "Age cannot wither nor time stale her infinite virginity!"

This "Eaton malaria" as the gossips called it was catching, and no laughing matter for the Jackson men. It was not only making a breach between the administration and respectable society, but making a fool of the President. The opposition was jubilant; for if the American people can once be got to laugh at instead of with a national figure, it is all up with him.

Still, there was use to be made of the affair by Van Buren. The sly fox from New York was wrapping himself around the heart of the old hero. It was "Little Van" who bound up the wounds of disappointed office-seekers and directed the negotiations which brought prestige to the administration. His tiny figure could be seen riding horseback beside the tall President on his daily constitutionals. Many a time they must have discussed the Eaton affair. That gave Van Buren the opportunity gently and discreetly to eliminate one possible anti-Peggy plotter after another, until Jackson inevitably reached the conclusion that Calhoun had put up his wife to start the snubbing.

At the same time, the President was moving toward a breach with Calhoun on other grounds. From our present point of view, American politicians of that period were highly vindictive. Jackson's hostility to Adams stemmed in part from the assumption that in President Monroe's cabinet he had been the one who wanted him recalled and court-martialed for his unauthorized invasion of Spanish territory. William H. Crawford, one of the defeated candidates of 1824, was the real mischief-maker in that case, and this. Animated by an implacable hatred of Calhoun, he caused letters to be placed in the "right" hands to prove that the South Carolinian was the cabinet member who had wanted the General punished. Jackson demanded an explanation. Calhoun was really out on a limb, since for years he had encouraged Jackson to believe that he had been the General's ardent supporter in Monroe's cabinet. He answered with a lengthy and unconvincing letter which the President endorsed: "This is full evidence of the duplicity and insincerity of the man."

These two controversies, Peggy Eaton's virtue and the Vice President's lack of candor, trivial and personal as they were, combined to deprive Calhoun of his expected succession, with dire results. Once it was clear that Jackson would never support him, Calhoun embraced the separatist doctrine that his native state was assuming. And Van Buren stepped into his shoes. "Little

Van" used to point out the spot on the Tenallytown road where, after Jackson had sounded off about the Calhoun men in the cabinet, he, Van Buren, offered to resign; how Jackson wouldn't hear of it, but was finally brought to see that if the secretary of state resigned, the small fry would have to follow, and that the President could then reconstruct his cabinet. This was done, and the whole lot resigned except the postmaster general, who had offended nobody. Van Buren was nominated minister to the Court of St. James's and exercised that function very capably for seven months, when the Senate by a majority of one (Calhoun's casting vote) rejected his nomination. Eaton was consoled by an appointment as American minister to Spain.

Thus, in 1830–31, Jackson's cabinet was completely reconstructed. Edward Livingston of Louisiana, a capable lawyer who had been on the General's staff at the Battle of New Orleans, became secretary of state; Louis McLane received the treasury; General Lewis Cass, a rising Democratic politician of Michigan, stepped into the war department; Levi Woodbury, who had helped swing New Hampshire into the Democratic column, became secretary of the navy; and Roger B Taney, later a great chief justice of the United States, succeeded an obscure attorney general. With a strong and distinguished cabinet, "Eaton malaria" cured, "Calhoun the traitor" eliminated for the time being, Andrew Jackson decided to run for a second term.

Nullification and the Bank War

1833-1837

1. The Tariff, the South, and Calhoun

AFTER ANDREW JACKSON had been in the saddle about two years, riding nowhere in particular, events began to give him direction. He had become
President with no other policy than "reform," by which he meant reviving
the republican simplicity of Jefferson's first term. But by the time he left
office, republican simplicity was out, never to return. The country had moved,
and the new Democratic party moved with it.

The two vital issues of Jackson's presidency were nullification and the Bank
of the United States. Neither figured in the campaign of 1828, neither had
been anticipated, and Jackson did not ask for them. They were presented to
him in a form that one of his wishy-washy successors might have evaded but
that he, brave and conscientious, chose to face. And it was the manner in
which he faced these issues that gave Jackson his place in history. But for
them, he might have gone down as one of several military men who made
undistinguished chief magistrates.

The first issue with which Jackson had to deal was South Carolina. That
state evolved politically between 1820 and 1830 (as Massachusetts between
1790 and 1812) from ardent nationalism to a state of economic flux in which
everything bad was blamed on the federal government. The protective tariff
of 1816 was largely the work of two South Carolinians, Lowndes and Calhoun. Although national in outlook, they expected their state to share the
benefit. Their state had water power and cotton; so why not cotton mills?
And was it wise for planters to be so dependent on outside markets for selling
cotton? The next few years disproved these expectations. Competent managers were rare in the South, and Yankee mill superintendents were unable to
handle Negro labor, which could be employed with more immediate profit in
growing cotton. Thus, the benefits of a protective tariff appeared to be going
to Northern manufacturers, whilst Southern planters bore the burden of
higher prices for consumer goods. As tariff schedules rose by successive acts of
Congress, and the country as a whole grew richer, South Carolina remained
stationary in population and declined in wealth. Many of her more enterprising planters emigrated to the newly opened black belts of Alabama and
Mississippi, where their bumper crops enriched Mobile and New Orleans

instead of swelling the exports of Charleston. And, as the area of cotton growing increased, the price declined. Soon it reached a point so low that planters on worn-out land in the older states were impoverished.

Actually, the protective tariff merely aggravated a situation for which the wasteful, land-destroying system of cotton culture was responsible, but the South Carolina planters could not see it. By 1825 there had been created among them just that atmosphere of pride, poverty, and resentment which, in our time, has favored the growth of Arab nationalism. In South Carolina this took the form of a local state rights party, propagating a doctrine that the protective tariff and "internal improvements" were wicked devices for taxing the South for the benefit of the North. The New England Federalists had taken the same line not long before, but that ended in talk at Hartford. Charleston, however, lay ten degrees of latitude south of Boston, and the South Carolina aristocracy was beginning to squirm over race relations. Behind all the heat and fury was the fear lest nationalism, in any form, lead to congressional tampering with slavery. Jackson saw that, and so did Calhoun.

Northern manufacturers were not satisfied with the tariff of 1824, and in 1828 when J. Q. Adams was still President, a new bill was passed. It was a politicians' tariff, drafted with an eye on the presidential election. Pro-Jackson congressmen wished to present their candidate to the South as a free trader, and to the North as a protectionist; they therefore introduced a bill with higher duties on raw materials than on manufactures, hoping that New England votes would help defeat it, and Adams be blamed. As Webster said, "Its enemies spiced it with whatever they thought would help render it distasteful; its friends took it, drugged as it was."

In July 1828, two months after this "tariff of abominations" passed Congress, William Huskisson made a speech in the British House of Commons the object of which, he later admitted, "was to alarm the Southern States in respect to the means within our power, of drawing from other countries the articles with which we are now supplied principally from those States." And, he added, if the tariff be not lowered, "it will expedite an event inevitable, I think, at no distant period — the separation of the Southern States." That speech probably found more readers in South Carolina than in England. Senator McDuffie cleverly popularized the British free trader's views in the "forty-bale theory." The protective tariff, according to him, so decreased English purchasing power for American cotton, and enhanced the price of consumers' goods to the South, that forty out of every hundred bales of cotton there produced were, in effect, stolen by Northern manufacturers. John Randolph went back even further, asserting again and again that the capital which built up manufactures in the North had been plundered from the South through Alexander Hamilton's financial measures. Progress in the North was not due to skill, thrift, or know-how, but to battening on the South. Harriet Martineau observed a few years later, in the course of her sojourn at Charleston, "The high spirit of South Carolina is of that kind

which accompanies fallen, or inferior fortunes . . . When they see the flourishing villages of New England they cry, 'We pay for all this!' " At a great
anti-tariff meeting in Columbia, S.C., in 1827, President Thomas Cooper of
South Carolina College asked, "Is it worth our while to continue this Union
of States, where the North demands to be our masters and we are required to
be their tributaries?"

Calhoun, aloof in the vice presidential office, was not indifferent to this
local turmoil. He had always been alive to the danger of disunion in a country
so rapidly expanding. Like Hamilton, Adams, and Clay, he had sought to
prevent disintegration by the cement of national legislation. Now he admitted
his mistake. Protection, instead of a binding force, had proved an instrument
of class and sectional plunder. So he came up with the doctrine of nullification.

First set forth in a document called the Exposition of 1828, it was approved
that summer by the legislature of South Carolina. Nullification was based on
two postulates: the common assertion that the Federal Constitution was a
compact between states, and the theory of indestructible sovereignty. If the
Constitution was established, not by the American people but by thirteen
sovereign states, they must still be sovereign in 1828; and as such, each had
the right to judge when its "agent," the federal government, exceeded its
powers. A state convention, the immediate organ of state sovereignty, may
then determine whether a given act of Congress be constitutional or not; and,
in the latter event, take measures to prevent enforcement within state limits.

Such was the doctrine of nullification. It was not wholly new or original.
The Kentucky and Virginia resolves of 1798 asserted the same state sovereignty; but the remedies which they demanded against the Sedition Act were
a collective "interposition," followed by nullification of the law by all the
states. Nullification by a single state, disobeying the laws of the Union while
claiming its privileges, was a different matter. As the aged Madison declared,
"For this preposterous and anarchical pretension there is not a shadow of
countenance in the Constitution."

Calhoun was a tiresome person. One wearies of his dry, humorless, logical
writings as of the Noble Roman pose of his portraits, hand resting on heart,
handsome features, and glaring eyes. But we must admit his intelligence and
his sincerity. His political switch was not entirely caused by thwarted ambition. Confronted, like John Adams in 1775, with an accepted constitutional
theory that supported what he considered tyranny, he sought a new one to
preserve liberty, within the existing body politic. The South, constantly growing away from the rest of the country — or, if you will, left behind by it —
could not afford to remain in the Union unless some constitutional check
were applied to majority rule. So Calhoun sought in the Federal Constitution
an implicit theory to provide that check, and discovered nullification. But,
unless the other side would yield, the only possible result, as in 1776, must be
disunion. And Calhoun's conception of liberty, which he held more dear than

union, was the liberty of the slave-owner to the full product of his slave's labor, and his right to full protection by the federal government. He admitted in 1830 that "the real cause of the present unhappy state of things" was "the peculiar domestic institution of the Southern States."

Calhoun's authorship of the Exposition of 1828 was secret, since as Vice President he was supposed to be loyal to the administration. He advised South Carolina to stay quiet, hoping that Jackson would insist upon a reduction of the tariff. But, as months stretched into years and the "tariff of abominations" remained on the statute books, it became clear to the Southerners that they could obtain no reduction without Western votes. And Western votes against nationalism could only be purchased by conceding something that the West wanted more than protection.

2. The West and Daniel Webster

The West, as we have seen, looked to Jackson to reform certain features of the national land system. The poorer public lands, unsalable at the minimum price of $1.25 per acre, made large blocks of untaxable wilderness between settled areas. To remedy this, Senator Benton of Missouri proposed a device called "graduation," which was the bargain-basement principle, reducing the price of unsold public land after a given period. Frontiersmen who squatted on the public domain before it was placed on sale disliked having their illegal holdings sold to outsiders. The squatters, better men with fist or rifle than the settlers who bought the lands they occupied, could usually make the latter pay handsomely for "improvements," and move further West. Prospective buyers were sometimes frightened away by squatter eloquence, of which this is a specimen: "My name, sir, is Simeon Cragin. I own fourteen claims, and if any man jumps one of them, I will shoot him down at once, sir. I am a gentleman, sir, and a scholar. I was educated at Bangor, have been in the United States Army, and served my country faithfully — am the discoverer of the Wopsey — can ride a grizzly bear, or whip any *human* that ever crossed the Mississippi, and if you dare to jump one of my claims, die you must!" But the Westerners preferred, or politicians thought they preferred, to legalize their position by a pre-emption act, giving them an option to purchase at a minimum price the quarter-section (160 acres) where they had squatted, whenever it was offered for sale by the government.

Older communities, both North and South, were opposed to encouraging westward migration, since by making labor scarce, it supposedly kept up wages; but if tariff schedules were to be maintained, some way must be found to get rid of the surplus revenue coming in from public lands. In order to catch Western votes for protection, Henry Clay proposed a clever scheme known as "distribution." The proceeds from land sales would be distributed among the states for use in public works and education, giving a special bonus to those states wherein the lands lay.

This was all a game of balance between North, South, and West, each section offering to compromise a secondary interest, in order to get votes for a primary interest. The South would permit the West to plunder the public domain in return for reduction of the tariff. The North offered the sop of "pre-emption" and the bait of "distribution" in order to maintain protection. On the outcome of this sectional balance depended the alignment of parties in the future; even of the Civil War itself. Was it to be North and West against South, or South and West against North and East?

On 29 December 1829 Senator Foot of Connecticut proposed that Congress inquire into the expediency of putting a brake on the sale of public lands. Senator Benton of Missouri denounced this as a barefaced attempt of Eastern capitalists to keep laborers from settling "the blooming regions of the West." He summoned the gallant South to the rescue of the Western Dulcinea, and Senator Hayne of South Carolina was the first to play Don Quixote. One after another the giants of the Senate rushed into the fray, and there took place one of those classic debates that America used to love — speeches hours long, each consuming a whole day's session, yet delivered from mere scraps of notes held in the palm of the hand, and every word reported in the newspapers; one of those contests of eloquence that seemed to typify the manliness and shrewdness of the nation.

As the debate progressed, less was said about the public land, more on the subject of whether North or South was the West's best friend, and most of all on constitutional theory. The acme came on 26 January 1830, when Daniel Webster replied for the second time to Robert Y. Hayne. Webster was the most commanding figure in the Senate, a swarthy Olympian with a crag-like face, and eyes that seemed to glow like dull coals under a precipice of brows. It has been said that no man was ever so great as Daniel Webster looked. His magnificent presence and deep, melodious voice gave distinction to the most common platitudes; but his orations were seldom commonplace. He carried to perfection the dramatic, rotund style of oratory that America then loved. The South Carolinian's attack on the patriotism of New England, and his bold challenge to the Union, called forth all Webster's intellectual power. His reply is the greatest recorded American oration, thrilling to read even today in cold print, when the issues with which it deals are long since settled by men who followed in 1861 the standard that Webster raised in 1830.

Imagine, then, the small semicircular senate chamber in the Capitol, the gallery and every bit of floor space behind the desks of the forty-eight senators packed with visitors; Vice President Calhoun in the chair, his handsome, mobile face gazing into that of the orator, and reflecting every point; Daniel Webster, in bluetailed coat with brass buttons and buff waistcoat getting under way slowly and deliberately like a man-of-war, then clapping on sail after sail until he moved with seemingly effortless speed and power. Hour after hour the speech flowed on, always in good taste and temper, relieving the high tone and tension with a happy allusion or turn of phrase that provoked laughter, thrilling his audience with rich imagery, crushing his opponents with a barrage of facts, passing from defense of his state and section to a devastating criticism of the "South Carolina doctrine," and concluding with an immortal peroration on the Union:

I have not allowed myself, Sir, to look beyond the Union, to see what might lie hidden in the dark recess behind. I have not coolly weighed the chances of preserving liberty when the bonds that unite us together shall be broken asunder. I have not accustomed myself to hang over the precipice of disunion, to see whether, with my short sight, I can fathom the depth of the abyss below; nor could I regard him as a safe counselor in the affairs of this government, whose thoughts should be mainly bent on considering, not how the Union may be best preserved, but how tolerable might be the condition of the people when it should be broken up and destroyed. While the Union lasts we have high, exciting, gratifying prospects spread out before us, for us and our children. Beyond that I seek not to penetrate the veil. God grant that in my day at least that curtain may not rise! God grant that on my vision never may be opened what lies behind! When my eyes shall be turned to behold for the last time the sun in heaven, may I not see him shining on the broken and dishonored fragments of a once glorious Union; on States dissevered, discordant, belligerent; on a land rent with civil feuds, or drenched, it may be, in fraternal blood! Let their last feeble and lingering glance rather behold the gorgeous ensign of the republic, now known and honored throughout the earth, still full high advanced, its arms and trophies streaming in their original lustre, not a stripe erased or polluted, nor a single star obscured, bearing for its motto, no such miserable interrogatory as "What is all this worth?" nor those other words of delusion and folly, "Liberty first and Union afterwards"; but everywhere, spread all over in characters of living light, blazing on all its ample folds, as they float over the sea and over the land, and in every wind under the whole heavens, that other sentiment, dear to every true American heart, — Liberty *and* Union, now and forever, one and inseparable!

That peroration, declaimed from thousands of school platforms by the lads of the coming generation, established in the hearts of the Northern and Western people an emotional, almost religious conception of the Union. It became something that men were willing to fight for. One of its earliest readers was a dreamy youth on the Indiana frontier named Abraham Lincoln.

Time only could reveal the full import of Webster's reply to Hayne; but it went home instantly to the honest old patriot in the White House. Jackson counted himself a state rights man, but he never doubted the sovereignty of the nation. State rights could never justify disobedience to the laws of the Union. Calhoun and the nullification group, at a dinner on the anniversary of Jefferson's birthday in 1830, foolishly attempted to trap Jackson into endorsing their cause. The formal toasts were worded to prove a connection between nullification and Republican orthodoxy. Jackson sat silently through them, but when his turn came, the old soldier rose to his full height, fixed his eye on Calhoun, and flung out a challenge:

"Our Federal Union — it *must* be preserved!"

Calhoun may, as Van Buren asserts, have drunk the toast with trembling hand; but he took up the challenge with another:

"The Union — next to our liberty, the most dear!"

3. Nullification Attempted

For two years after that famous dinner, the South Carolina nullifiers were held in check by the unionists of their own state, and by Calhoun's reluctance to break with the President and lose hope of reducing the tariff. As time went on the Carolinian hotheads grew hotter, and the rise of abolition sentiment inflamed them still more. Henry Clay forced their hands in 1832. With the aid of Western votes, attracted by "distribution," Clay pushed a new tariff bill through Congress on 14 July, and Jackson signed it. Some of the abominations of the 1828 tariff were removed, but high duties on iron and textiles were maintained; and the new law had an air of permanence which acted upon South Carolina as a challenge.

In the state election that autumn, the state rights party, the "pinks of chivalry and fire-and-brimstone eaters," carried all before them. The new legislature summoned a convention, which on 24 November 1832 declared in the name of the sovereign people of South Carolina that the tariff act was "unauthorized by the Constitution of the United States, null, void, and no law, nor binding upon this State, its officers or citizens." This ordinance of nullification forbade federal officers to collect customs duties within the state after 1 February 1833, and threatened instant secession if the federal government attempted to blockade Charleston or to use force.

President Jackson took precautions to maintain the law of the land. Forts Moultrie and Sumter were reinforced, revenue cutters were ordered to collect duties if customs officials were resisted, and close touch was maintained with the South Carolina unionists. On 10 December he issued a ringing proclamation to the people of South Carolina. Their nullification ordinance, he said, was founded on the strange proposition that a state might retain her place in the Union and yet be bound only by those laws that she might choose to obey. He then faced the "right of secession" which Calhoun inferred from the compact method of forming the Constitution: "Whether it be formed by compact between the States, or in any other manner," he said, "it is a government in which all the people are represented, which operates directly on the people individually, not upon the States. Each State having parted with so many powers as to constitute, jointly with the other States, a single nation, cannot possess any right to secede, because such secession does not break a league but destroys the unity of a nation." Such was the doctrine upon which Abraham Lincoln acted in 1861.

South Carolina could not be cowed by proclamation. Her legislature hurled defiance at "King Jackson" and raised a volunteer force to defend the state from "invasion." The President, encouraged by loyal addresses that poured in from all parts, wished to throw an army into South Carolina at the first show of resistance to customs officers. But could he afford to? It was no question of suppressing a mere local insurrection, as Washington had done in 1794, but of coercing a state of the Union. Virginia regarded nullification as a caricature of her resolves of 1798, Georgia "abhorred the doctrine," and Alabama denounced it as "unsound in theory and dangerous in practice"; but Georgia had made the dangerous proposal of a Southern Convention. Thus, Jackson's friends feared that coercion would disrupt their party; and the nullifiers did not want bloodshed, but to reduce the tariff. Within three weeks of the President's proclamation, the House committee of ways and means proposed to lower the duties. Concession and compulsion went hand in hand. On the same day (2 March 1833) Jackson signed a force bill, authorizing him to use the army and navy to collect customs duties if judicial process were obstructed; and Clay's compromise tariff, providing a gradual scaling down of schedules until they reached 20 per cent ad valorem in ten years' time. The South Carolina convention then re-assembled and repealed the nullification ordinance.

Each party marched from the field with colors flying, claiming victory. Both seemed to have derived fresh strength from the contest. The Union was strengthened by Jackson's firm stand, but South Carolina had proved that a single determined state could force her will on Congress. Jackson would have preferred to have conceded nothing until Calhoun and his party had passed under the Caudine forks; for beyond nullification he saw secession. The "next pretext," he predicted, "will be the Negro, or slavery question." He counted on Calhoun, whom he now described as "one of the most base, hypocritical and unprincipled villains in the United States," to bring that up later.

4. Jackson, Re-elected, Fights the Bank

In the midst of these alarums and excursions came the presidential election of 1832, memorable in the history of political organization. Jackson men from all parts of the Union, now organized as the Democratic party, sent delegates to a national convention at Baltimore. It resolved that a two-thirds majority was necessary for nomination, a rule which Democratic national conventions did not abandon until 1936. The 1832 convention renominated Jackson for the presidency by acclamation, and Van Buren for the vice presidency with somewhat less enthusiasm. The opposition, organized as the National Republican party (for which the name Whig, of happy memory, was shortly substituted), nominated Henry Clay. And there was a third party in the field, the Anti-Masons.

That a party of so strange a title should contend for national power was of social rather than political significance. Americans of the nineteenth century were so in love with the methods of democracy, that no sooner did a few earnest men capture a bit of what they took to be eternal truth, than they proceeded to organize it politically. If local success proved the scent good, it brought politicians hotfoot to the hunt, that they might partake of the kill or lead off the field in pursuit of bigger game. The Anti-Mason party arose in 1826 out of the disappearance of a New York bricklayer named Morgan, who had divulged the secrets of his masonic lodge. A corpse was found floating in the Niagara river. It could not be proved to be Morgan's; but, as a politician said, it was "good enough Morgan until after election." Both the event and the freemasons' efforts to hush it up revived an old prejudice against secret societies. Several young politicians such as William H. Seward, Thurlow Weed, and Thaddeus Stevens threw themselves into the Anti-Masonic movement, which became strong enough to elect a couple of state governors. In 1831 it held a national convention and nominated presidential candidates, who took thousands of Northern votes away from Clay. In a few years' time this party faded out; but the sort of people who were attracted by it easily took up with others such as the Liberty party, the Free-Soil, the Know-Nothing and, finally, the Republican party.

This presidential election decided the case of Andrew Jackson v. the Bank of the United States. Since 1819 the B.U.S. had been well managed. In the Eastern states it had become a necessary part of business mechanism; Pennsylvania Democrats and Carolina nullifiers had no quarrel with it and even Calhoun had no constitutional qualms on the subject.[1] But the Bank was still unpopular in the West because it kept local banks within bounds by presenting their notes promptly for payment, thus reducing the amount of paper credit for speculation. Jackson shared this prejudice, together with a vague feeling that the "money power" was an enemy to democracy. As the B. U. S. charter would expire in 1836, if not earlier renewed by Congress, Jackson's opinion was of some importance. "I do not dislike your bank more than all banks," he informed Nicholas Biddle, president of the B.U.S., "but ever since I read the history of the South Sea Bubble, I have been afraid of banks." What he wanted was a bank of deposit attached to the treasury department under officials appointed by himself.

Biddle was no mean antagonist. Precursor of a race of energetic and autocratic financiers, he had the same dislike of democracy that Jackson had of banking, but was anxious to keep his bank out of politics. Unfortunately, his social and business relations were largely with Jackson's opponents. Daniel Webster was at the same time a bank director, its leading counsel, it debtor to the sum of many thousand dollars, and senator from Massachusetts. Congressmen were often paid their salaries by the Bank in advance of the annual appropriation bill, without interest charges. Journalists like James Gordon Bennett, the Scots-born father of the American yellow press, obtained loans on very favorable terms in return for favorable publicity in their columns.

1. In January 1832 the bank stock was distributed as follows (in round numbers): New York, 31,000; Pennsylvania, 51,000; Maryland, 34,000; South Carolina, 40,000; New England, 15,000; the West, 3000; Europe, 84,000.

Henry Clay was responsible for the financial war. He insisted on making the rechartering of the B.U.S. a major issue in the campaign of 1832; a most inadvisable move, as it aroused Jackson's pugnacity. Congress, led by Clay, passed a recharter bill on 3 July 1832, and most of Calhoun's partisans voted for it. Jackson vetoed it, with a message that smacked of demagoguery. The bank recharter was not only an unconstitutional invasion of state rights; it would continue a monopoly and exclusive privilege, the profits of which must come "out of the earnings of the American people," in favor of foreign stockholders and "a few hundred of our own citizens, chiefly of the richest class." He could not permit the "prostitution of our Government to the advancement of the few at the expense of the many." The logic of this veto message was defective, but as a popular appeal it was irresistible, and it helped to re-elect Jackson, together with a House of Representatives upon which he could depend. Nicholas Biddle took up the challenge. "This worthy President," he boasted, "thinks that because he has scalped Indians and imprisoned judges, he is to have his own way with the Bank. He is mistaken."

So the fight was on. Instead of waiting for the Bank to die a natural death in 1836, Jackson decided at once to deprive it of government deposits. One Secretary, McLane, had to be "kicked upstairs" from the treasury to the state department, and his successor dismissed, before a third, Levi Woodbury, could be found to obey orders. Government receipts were then (1833) deposited in local banks — the so-called "pet banks" — which Jackson believed to be safer than the expiring "monster."

This financial war came in the midst of a period of speculative activity, coincident with improved transportation, a brisk demand for cotton, and heavy westward migration. The death of the B.U.S., with its wholesome policy of keeping local banks in line, took off the last brake. The currency was already chaotic, when an Act of 1834 made matters worse by establishing the coinage ratio of 16 to 1 between silver and gold, which drove silver from the country. Yet the Treasury's main embarrassment was a surplus! After January 1835, when the national debt was completely paid off, the tariff and public land sales began to bring in more money than the federal government could use in those frugal days before foreign aid, cold wars, welfare, and price supports. Jackson considered this a great triumph, but surplus proved to be a greater curse than deficit.

From Jackson's veto of the Maysville road bill, it was evident he could never be induced to spend the surplus on internal improvements. So Clay, fearing lest Jackson blow it in, got through Congress a "distribution" scheme in 1836. About $28 million was theoretically lent, but really given by the treasury to state governments. Some states used the money for public works, others turned it into educational funds, many of which were badly invested and fed the speculative movement. Jackson countered with a severe astringent, the "specie circular" of 1836, ordering the treasury to receive nothing but hard money for public lands. For he had always hated "folding" money, and many of his supporters believed that metallic coinage would cure all the country's financial ills.

Shortly after, the panic of 1837 burst upon the country, and the federal surplus disappeared overnight. Short-term treasury notes tided over the crisis, but the whole of Van Buren's administration (1837–41) was spent in seeking a substitute for the B.U.S. None comparable with it for service and efficiency was found until 1913, when the Federal Reserve system was adopted.

Jackson's war on the bank was not wholly personal, but an aspect of that fundamental hostility to monopoly and special privilege which the colonists had brought from England, and which had broken out in the Boston Tea-Party. It would break out again in the populist and progressive movements, and in the New Deal. But rarely to this day has a bank in the United States been permitted to have branches outside the locality or county where it is established. In every other Western country the important banks are nation-wide or (as in the case of the Bank of Nova Scotia) spread throughout the British Commonwealth.

After the lapse of over a century, it is clear that although democracy won the battle with the Bank, it lost the war. The bankers of New York City, almost splitting their sides laughing over the discomfiture of rivals on Chestnut Street, Philadelphia, promptly picked up the pieces of the B.U.S. and on Wall Street constructed a vastly bigger money power than anything ever dreamed of by Mr. Biddle. Poor farmers, mechanics, and frontiersmen gained nothing by this bank war; the net result was to move the financial capital of the United States from Philadelphia to New York.

XXVIII

Foreign Affairs and Removal of the Indians

1830-1838

1. Peace with England, Fight with France?

ANDREW JACKSON was unpredictable. One would suppose him to have been the sort of person who would enjoy "twisting the British lion's tail," but he inaugurated the most friendly period of Anglo-American relations in the nineteenth century. When in 1830 Louis Philippe, who as an exile had taught school in America, was made king of the French by liberal elements, led by Lafayette, one would suppose that Franco-American relations would reach an all-time high; but the contrary happened. In view of Jackson's strong republican sentiments, it was assumed that he would maintain the Monroe Doctrine and cultivate the new republics of Latin America. But he and Van Buren never invoked or even mentioned the Monroe Doctrine, regarding it apparently as an Adams shirt to be discarded; and their Latin American policy gravely offended Argentina and Mexico.

Jackson and Van Buren entertained the most friendly feelings toward the British and reversed the policy of Adams and Clay who, even after the Rush-Bagot agreements, had been querulous and complaining. Minor issues on which Clay would have written waspish notes to the British government, were now settled as man to man between Sir Charles Vaughan and Van Buren, with an "assist" from Peggy Eaton, whom they both admired. Adams had made stiff and impossible demands in respect to the West Indies; Van Buren made haste to accept British concessions, removing all restrictions there upon American produce and ships — much to the dismay of Canada's Maritime Provinces. It was not Jackson's fault that Dutch arbitration in 1831 of the Maine-New Brunswick boundary question was not accepted. The State of Maine insisted that no treaty could deprive her of territory without her consent — precisely what Georgia was contending respecting the Cherokee. The President, consistent with his attitude in that case, refused to press the Dutch compromise, which allotted the United States a greater share of the disputed territory than Webster later obtained from Lord Ashburton.

Jackson's dealings with Great Britain were in marked contrast to his handling of a controversy with France. He and the "Citizen King" bristled at each other like a couple of gamecocks, and war was narrowly averted. The dispute was over claims. The United States demanded about $23 million for

French depredations on American ships and property during the Napoleonic wars. France had a smaller claim for supplies furnished to the United Colonies at the beginning of the Revolution. Adams and Clay had worked on these claims for twelve years with no success. Old Senator Samuel Smith, uncle of Madame Jerome Bonaparte, reminded Van Buren of what Ben Franklin did not need to be told: "It is not well-written notes — that can succeed in France; it is sociability, intercourse, pleasantry — in fine what the French call 'les maniers.' The man must make himself acceptable to the ladies as well as to the gentlemen."

William Cabell Rives, Jackson's minister to France, followed this advice to such good purpose as to negotiate a treaty on 4 July 1831 by which France promised to pay the United States $5 million, less $300,000 for French claims against the United States. In return, Rives agreed to reduce American customs duties on French wines by about one-third. This treaty was ratified in France and unanimously approved by the United States Senate; and the House, disregarding complaints from New York vintners, duly knocked down the wine duties. So, when the first payment of a million dollars fell due, the treasury hopefully wrote a draft on the French minister of finance for that sum.

Alas, that check bounced! The French government refused to honor it because the Chamber of Deputies had not yet appropriated the money; and the United States Treasury had the further mortification of having to pay Nicholas Biddles's B.U.S. 15 per cent damages on the "rubber" draft. Jackson was furious with the Bank and still more so with Louis Philippe. Nevertheless, he appointed the best possible man, secretary of state Edward Livingston, to relieve Rives as American minister at Paris. Livingston, although his "maniers" were better than his predecessor's, could get nowhere; the French legislature repeatedly stalled. Jackson, in his annual message of December 1834, recommended that Congress pass "a law authorizing reprisals upon French property," if the debt were not paid at the next session.

At that era there was nothing unusual in this procedure — France herself had recently done it vis-à-vis Portugal — but for the United States to threaten France was denounced as barbaric, Red Indian diplomacy. A French fleet was dispatched to the West Indies; Jackson alerted the United States Navy; ministers to both countries were recalled; mass meetings were held in seaboard cities to back up the President. John Quincy Adams came out strongly in his favor; only Calhoun made snide remarks to the effect that if war came it would be Jackson's fault.

The French legislature now voted the money, with the proviso that nothing should be paid until the king had received *des explications satisfaisantes* of the President's message of 1834. This demand for "satisfactory explanations" sounded so like the preliminaries to a duel, of which Jackson had plenty of experience, that he flew into a passion. He disclaimed any intention to insult France, but refused to "explain" his threat of reprisals. Matters were at a deadlock and the two countries on the brink of war when the British foreign secretary, Lord Palmerston, miraculously mediated. "Pam" had a reputation as quarrelsome as Jackson's but he did not wish to see England's ally involved in an unprofitable war with the United States. A formula was found that satisfied wounded honor on both sides, and the treaty was executed some five years after it had been signed.

An important though unseen element in preventing war was the United States Navy. The French minister of marine warned the foreign office that his navy, with heavy commitments in the Mediterranean, would find it difficult to operate profitably against the United States. The American West Indies Squadron might well capture Guadeloupe and Martinique before France could come to their assistance.

2. The Navy and Latin American Relations

Andrew Jackson was land-minded rather than sea-minded. His calls on Congress to build shore installations and coast-defense forts, which created more jobs than did shipbuilding, were better heeded than his recommendations to lay down new warships. But he used the navy, as his predecessors had done, to protect American commerce on the high seas, especially in the Pacific, where whaling ships from New England had become very active. Sloop-of-war *Vincennes* made the first voyage around the world by any American warship in 1829–31, presenting letters from the President to King Kamehameha III of Hawaii and showing the flag at Guam, Macao, and Capetown. On a subsequent cruise she called at the Fijis, the Marquesas, and Tahiti (affording Queen Pomaré an inter-island cruise), rescued American merchant seamen held prisoner by the king of Babelthuap in the Palaus, and burned a Samoan village where American whalers had been murdered.

President Jackson would stand for no more "nonsense" on the part of Orientals, than of the French. Upon complaint that ship *Friendship* of Salem had been ambushed and plundered and her crew slaughtered by the sultan of Quallah Battoo on the coast of Sumatra, the President sent U.S. frigate *Potomac* to retaliate. She did that very successfully, in a one-ship amphibious operation of 1832. But Sumatra had not yet been taken over by the Dutch, and another local sultan, at Mukkee, had to be given the same treatment before American ships could trade safely with Indonesia. A Yankee pioneer in Far Eastern trade and diplomacy named Edmund Roberts, appointed "special agent of the United States" and embarked in sloop-of-war *Peacock*, negotiated treaties with the king of Siam and the sultan of Muscat in 1833.

The most important official overseas project in this era was an exploring expedition. This brain child of John Quincy Adams, turned down by the congresses of his administration, was picked up by Senator Southard of New Jersey in 1836 and supported by memorials from men interested in the China trade. Van Buren's literary secretary of the navy, James K. Paulding, got the expedition off to sea in the summer of 1838. Under command of Captain Charles Wilkes USN, it comprised three warships (*Vincennes*, flag) and three auxiliaries, with surveyors, botanists, geologists, and other scientists. In a cruise lasting four years, the Wilkes expedition sailed as far north as Alaska and as far south as Antarctica (where Wilkes Land records the visit), made charts of Polynesia and Micronesia (which we used when invading Tarawa in 1943), and prepared other data of inestimable value to commerce and science.

Another naval incident of the period had unhappy consequences for relations with Latin America. Spanish claims to the Falkland Islands in the South Atlantic, off the southern tip of Argentina, had been ceded in 1771 to England. She had never bothered to take possession, but the islands were frequented by ships from Stonington, Connecticut, whose crews slaughtered, for the skins, the great herds of seal that bred there. Around 1820 the Argentine Republic put in a claim for the Falklands and appointed as governor Louis Vernet, who imported cattle and *gauchos* and established a flourishing ranch. As the American seal-skinners showed a propensity to slay and eat his cattle, Vernet caused two of their vessels to be seized, plundered, and sent to Buenos Aires. Jackson's secretary of the navy, Levi Woodbury, then ordered sloop-of-war *Lexington*, Captain Silas Duncan, to sail to the Falklands and protect American interests. Duncan did this very effectively by rounding up the not unwilling *gauchos*, long unpaid and heartily sick of the Falklands, and sailing them 1000 miles to Buenos Aires and Montevideo.

Unknown to Secretary Woodbury, the British government had decided to take possession of the Falklands, and did so without opposition in 1833 since nobody was there — thanks to Captain Duncan. The Argentine government protested both to Britain and the United States, alleging that but for Captain Duncan the "invaders" would have been driven off by Vernet's forty cowboys. Naturally the Monroe Doctrine was invoked and the argument made that it was a mere sham if Britain were allowed to get away with the Falklands. The United States maintained the view that these islands were legally a British colony with which, as the Doctrine expressly stated, we "shall not interfere"; and that Duncan's act was a suppression of piracy. But the Duncan incident has never been forgotten or forgiven at Buenos Aires.

"Van Buren observed to me," wrote Sir Charles Vaughan to the British foreign secretary in 1830, "that the present administration of the United States was not disposed to assume the high tone in their relations with the States of Spanish America which had been assumed by President Adams and Mr. Clay." This resolution was not observed with respect to Mexico, since Jackson wanted Texas. To further this end, he replaced Poinsett as minister to Mexico by an old crony, Colonel Anthony Butler, a vain and ignorant swindler who thought that if he greased the right palms in Mexico City he could buy anything. Jackson finally got wind of Butler's behavior and recalled him. The Texas Revolution, toward which Jackson's neutrality was benevolent, now broke out and succeeded. That gave a new and bad twist to United States-Mexican relations.

3. Removal of the Eastern Indians

An American journalist who had spent several years in India, and whose small children had come to love the Indians, came home in 1958. Shortly thereafter he found the boys crying as they watched a TV "Western" because, as one moaned, "They're killing *Indians!*" Papa had to explain that these were not Indians of India but Red Indians, and that to kill them was part of the American Way of Life.

The only extenuation of American policy toward the natives of North America is that it continued an old-world process of one race or people pushing a weaker one out of an area that it wanted. Almost every European today is a descendant of Asiatic intruders into Europe; almost every North African the descendant of Arab intruders. "The country is a land for cattle," said the children of Reuben to Moses when they saw the land of Gilead, "and thy servants have cattle; wherefore, said they, if we have found grace in thy sight, let this land be given unto thy servants for a possession." In the United States, as elsewhere in the nineteenth century, this process of conquest and expansion took the form of a relatively highly developed civilization pushing out a backward people who could not or would not be absorbed, and who were too few in number and weak in technique long to resist. But some of the Indians put up a very good fight.

The problem of United States-Indian relations, which for many years had involved international rivalries, became localized after the Florida treaty was ratified in 1821. "Foreign interference" could no longer be used as an excuse for abusing the Indians. And there was no more need to placate them to prevent their siding with the British, French, or Spanish.

Efforts to maintain Indian reservations within the Eastern states were generally unsuccessful, although a few small ones, such as that of the Abnaki in Oldtown, Maine, and the Tuscarora reservation near Niagara Falls, still endure, menaced or sliced away by the bulldozer. Conditions for a reservation's lasting were a partial adoption by Indians of the American Way of Life, and a strong government service to protect them from the white man's trickery and alcohol. But, for fifty years after American independence, the Indians did not wish to conform, many federal agents were political hacks, government trading posts were unable to compete with unauthorized private traders who supplied the Indians with liquor, and frontiersmen everywhere coveted the Indians' land.

Monroe's administration bowed to demands of the West by adopting a removal policy. Plans for concentrating the tribes west of the Mississippi now began to take shape, and piecemeal removal began in the 1820's from the Old Northwest and the lower South, to segments of what had been the domains of the Caddo, the Quapaw, and the Osage. Tribesmen with well-developed farms, especially influential halfbreeds, were given the choice of removal, or staying put and becoming American citizens. Those who preferred to leave, exchanged their property for new lands in the West and were promised payment for travel expenses and the value of improvements on their relinquished property. The assent of the Indians was often merely nominal; federal commissioners bribed important chiefs and, if necessary, got them drunk enough to sign anything. "Persuasion" often took the form of urging the Indians to sell improvements for cash with which to pay off debts to white traders. This removal policy slowed down during the administration of John Quincy Adams, whose attitude toward the Indians was humane and paternal, but picked up momentum and was carried to a successful conclusion (from the white point of view) under Jackson. The President, having negotiated several removal treaties during his military career, knew very well the hardships involved, but regarded this as the only possible way to save the Indians from extinction. They were faced with the irresistible force of a white expansion which the Democrats had no intention of checking.

Soon after Jackson's inauguration, Georgia, Alabama, and Mississippi asserted jurisdiction over Indian reservations, in contemptuous disregard of federal treaties, and even set up county governments to be put in operation as soon as the rightful owners of the soil were expelled. Congress then passed an Indian Removal Act (1830), appropriating half a million dollars for this purpose. The President was authorized to grant lands in the unorganized part of the Louisiana Purchase in exchange for those relinquished in the East, to protect the Indians in their new reservations, to pay expenses of removal and one year's subsistence, and compensate them for improvements on the relinquished land.

The liquidation of Indian reservations in the Old Northwest was largely accomplished between 1829 and 1843. Mixed bands of Shawnee, Delaware, Wyandot, and others were persuaded to accept new reservations west of Missouri. Their numbers were drastically reduced by disease on the journey. Theft by federal officials of what was due to the Indians, and funeral rites for those who died en route, exhausted their resources long before this "trail of tears," as it was aptly called by later writers sympathetic to the Indians, came to an end. Many groups were unable to make the journey in one season and suffered intensely at improvised winter quarters. A cholera epidemic broke out in 1832; measles took hundreds of lives. Further trials awaited the survivors, especially those who hoped to till the soil; the cost of equipment reduced them to penury or debt long before they could raise a crop or draw upon tribal annuities. Money from the sale of improvements at the old village ordinarily went into the expenses of travel, if it did not stick in the pockets of federal agents.

At one point during these removals, hostilities broke out. Black Hawk, chief of the Sauk and Fox, who had fought on the British side in 1812, tried to retain his ancient tribal seat at the mouth of Rock river, Illinois, opposite Davenport, Iowa. White squatters encroached on the village and enclosed the Indians' cornfields. After the governor of Illinois had threatened him, Black Hawk agreed that after crossing the Mississippi for his annual winter hunt, he would never return. But his people, threatened by hostile Sioux, ran out of food. Hoping to find a vacant prairie in which to plant a corn crop, Black Hawk recrossed the Mississippi in the spring of 1832 with about 1000 members of his tribe. The governor of Illinois, assuming this to be a hostile expedition, called out the militia (Abraham Lincoln commanding a company) and pursued the starving Indians up the Rock river into the Wisconsin wilderness. It was a disgraceful frontier frolic, stained by wanton massacre of Indians, including women and children. The only redeeming feature was the chivalrous consideration of Black Hawk by Lieutenant Jefferson Davis of the regular army, when the captured chief was placed in his charge; forty years later, Davis referred to Black Hawk's rear-guard action at Wisconsin Heights as the most gallant fight he had ever witnessed. Black Hawk subsequently visited the "Great White Father" in Washington and was presented with a sword and a medal by President Jackson. But he lost his tribal lands.

The four great Indian nations of the Old Southwest, the Chickasaw, Creek, Choctaw, and Cherokee, were Jackson's particular problem. In 1830 the Choctaw of Mississippi signed a treaty providing for their removal within three years. As with others, this migration brought death, suffering, and poverty. In 1832 a treaty was signed with the Creek nation to wind up their large reservation in Alabama. Some members kept individual allotments and faced the cunning of new white neighbors who poured into their reservation before they could leave. Many died on the journey. By 1860 the Creek nation had lost about 40 per cent of its population. The rest settled in the Indian Territory, near the Choctaw. The Chickasaw of Mississippi, a fairly small group, fared better and obtained fairly good prices for their improvements, since their land was desirable for cotton plantations.

These three nations were agricultural and sedentary; some even held Negro slaves. The Cherokee, whose nation spread over northwest Georgia into Alabama and around Chickamauga, Tennessee, were even more advanced, by European standards. It had always been a white grievance against the Indians that they rejected "civilization." The Cherokee, unfortunately for themselves, took the palefaces at their word. George Gist, a halfbreed whose Indian name was anglicized as Sequoyah, provided the necessary spark. Convinced that literacy was the key to Indian survival, Sequoyah invented a simple form of writing and printing the Cherokee language; Bibles, other books and even a weekly newspaper *The Cherokee Phoenix* were printed. These Indians welcomed Christian missionaries, built roads, houses, and churches, adopted a constitution for the Cherokee nation and elected a legislature. They became more civilized than the Georgia "crackers" and "hill-billies" who coveted their lands. Nor, for that matter, do the inhabitants of Faulkner's Yoknapa-

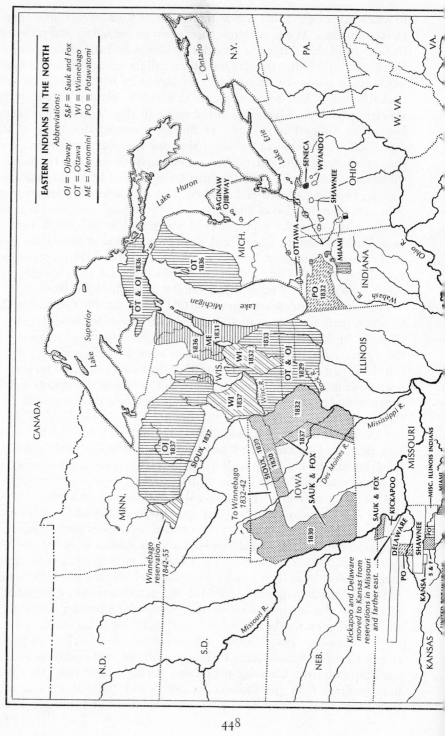

EASTERN INDIANS IN THE NORTH

Abbreviations:

OJ = Ojibway   S&F = Sauk and Fox
OT = Ottawa   WI = Winnebago
ME = Menomini   PO = Potawatomi

Winnebago reservation, 1842-55

To Winnebago 1832-42

Kickapoo and Delaware moved to Kansas from reservations in Missouri and farther east.

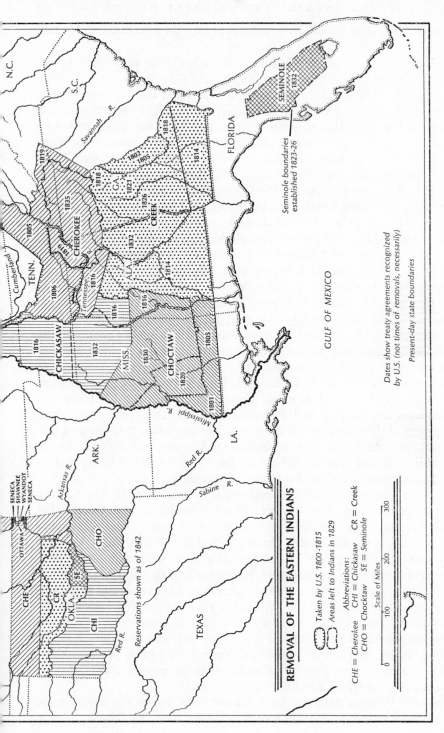

REMOVAL OF THE EASTERN INDIANS

Taken by U.S. 1800-1815

Areas left to Indians in 1829

Abbreviations:
CHE = Cherokee   CHI = Chickasaw   CR = Creek
CHO = Chocktaw   SE = Seminole

Reservations shown as of 1842

Dates show treaty agreements recognized by U.S. (not times of removals, necessarily)

Present-day state boundaries

Seminole boundaries established 1823-26

Scale of Miles
0   100   200   300

GULF OF MEXICO

tawoha County appear to be an improvement over the Chickasaw whom they replaced.

The independence of the Cherokee nation had been guaranteed by the United States in a treaty of 1791, but the State of Georgia had been chopping away at their lands for over thirty years, and regarded the treaty as obsolete. Discovery of gold in the Cherokee country in 1828 brought this controversy to a head, and a rough class of whites to the spot. Here was a case of federal supremacy against state rights, as clear as that of South Carolina; but President Jackson let Georgia have her own way. His secretary of war, Peggy Eaton's husband, informed the Cherokee that they were mere tenants at will. The federal troops sent by President Adams to protect the Indians were withdrawn, and Major Ethan Allen Hitchcock, sent by the war department to investigate frauds against them, made so devastating a report that the department suppressed it. Chief Justice Marshall decided, in a test case brought by a missionary (the Reverend Samuel C. Worcester of Vermont), that the laws of Georgia rightly had no force within Cherokee territory. Jackson commented, "John Marshall has made his decision. Now let him enforce it."

As Georgia held a lottery to dispose of their lands, and no friends in power appeared to help them, the Cherokee were forced to accept removal. Agents of the Indian administration negotiated a treaty with a small minority of the chiefs in 1835, but most of them refused to attend the negotiations, and few departed within the three-year limit set by the treaty. A protest to President Van Buren, signed by 15,665 Indians, was blandly ignored. So, in 1838, regular troops under General Winfield Scott rounded up the Cherokee and started them on the long trail to Indian Territory. This journey cost them one-quarter of their number, but the remainder reorganized their national government, prospered, and have retained their language and alphabet to the present day. Several hundred diehards in the Great Smokies, who resisted removal, were eventually given the Qualla reservation in North Carolina.

A similar controversy with the Seminole of Florida ended in war. A tricky treaty of removal, negotiated in 1832 with a few chiefs, was repudiated by the greater portion of the tribe, led by a brave chieftain named Osceola. Secure in the fastnesses of the Everglades, Osceola baffled the United States Army for years, and was only captured by treachery at a truce conference. Many Seminoles were rounded up and sent west, but others kept up the fight until 1842. By that time they had cost the United States some $20 million and 1500 lives. A few thousand remained in the Everglades. Their descendants, known as the Miccosukee Seminoles, are the only occupants of some 200,000 acres of swampland north of the Tamiami trail. They live, like their ancestors, by hunting, fishing, and a little agriculture. Never having made peace with the United States, they are currently threatened by drainage and development projects, and a "progress" which they do not want.

The only Western statesman to denounce these shabby and dishonorable proceedings was Henry Clay. His speech in the Senate on 14 February 1835 is the more praiseworthy because the Indians had no votes, and because his Kentucky constituents cared nothing for them. He quoted the long list of treaties guaranteeing to the Cherokee their lands, and the still longer list of acts of the State of Georgia which violated not only these treaties, but the most elementary principles of justice and decency. He drew tears from the eyes of the senators, but they did nothing for the Cherokee except to expedite their removal.

President Jackson seems to have kept a good conscience about all this, and several friends of the Indians, such as Lewis Cass and Thomas L. McKenney, head of the war department's bureau of Indian affairs, supported removal as the only alternative to extermination. Jackson's rationale of Indian removal appears in his Farewell Address of March 1837: "The states which had so long been retarded in their improvement by the Indian tribes residing in the midst of them are at length relieved from the evil, and this unhappy race — the original dwellers in our land — are now placed in a situation where we may well hope that they will share in the blessings of civilization." Lewis Cass went the General one better, piously invoking the theory that God intended the earth to be cultivated. Cherokee cultivation evidently did not count.

By the end of Van Buren's presidential term, it was assumed, at least by the Democrats, that the Indian question had been solved. All important Eastern tribes — those who, in Jackson's phrase, had "retarded improvement" (i.e. resisted white land grabbers) — had been provided for behind a barrier that ran from Lake Superior through Wisconsin and Iowa Territories, thence along the western boundaries of Missouri and Arkansas to the Red river on the Texas border. Behind this line the tribes were guaranteed possession "as long as grass grows and water runs"; and thence most of them were eventually ousted, when the tide of white settlement lapped around them and slaughtered their game. But, in a sense, the removal policy was justified by the later history of the "five civilized Indian Nations" — Creek, Cherokee, Choctaw, Chickasaw, and Seminole — in Oklahoma. Removal gave them the necessary respite to recover their morale, and until the Civil War they succeeded in keeping white men out.

Looking backward, it is now evident that, in view of the irresistible push of the westward movement, Indian removal was the lesser evil. It had to be, but, the process was carried out with unnecessary hardship to the victims.

In many instances missionaries and other individuals managed to protect the Indians. The Ojibway or Chippewa had a reservation along the Bad river of Wisconsin, which was taken under the protection of the Reverend L. H. Wheeler, a Protestant missionary at La Pointe. When, in 1850, white pioneers began lobbying Congress to remove these Indians west of the Mississippi and acquire their lands, Wheeler visited the proposed site of the resettlement and reported that it would be a deed of mercy to shoot every Ojibway rather than send them there. Congress reconsidered, and in 1854 guaranteed these Indians three small reservations on the south shore of Lake Superior, which they still hold in 1964. Other tribes were not so fortunate. Between 1853 and 1856 the United States negotiated no fewer than fifty-two treaties, mostly with nations in the Mississippi valley or west of the great river, by virtue of which it added 174 million more acres to the public domain.

Remnants of the Six Nations who had been guaranteed possession of reservations in New York State, by treaties concluded as far back as 1784, have been fighting a losing battle. Chief Red Jacket of the Seneca long managed to preserve the integrity of his people in their reservation, which is now covered by the city of Buffalo. After his death in 1830, a group of New York speculators known as the Ogden Land Company began an intensive drive to get possession of the Seneca reservation. By bribing greedy individuals to act as "chiefs" and sign away land, this company managed to rob the tribe of almost their entire heritage. President Van Buren, to his credit, denounced the subsequent "treaty" as a steal, but it passed the Senate, by the casting vote of Vice President Johnson, the reputed slayer of Tecumseh.

As recently as 1960, the Tuscarora, in the sacred name of progress, lost a case to preserve their reservation against the Niagara Power Project's bulldozers. They carried the case to the Supreme Court of the United States, which decided against them. Mr. Justice Black, in his dissenting opinion, in which Chief Justice Warren and Justice Douglas joined, said: "The record does not leave the impression that the lands of their reservation are the most fertile, the landscape the most beautiful or their homes the most splendid specimens of architecture. But this is their home — their ancestral home. There they, their children and their forebears were born. They, too, have their memories and their loves. Some things are worth more than money and the costs of a new enterprise. I regret that this court is the governmental agency that breaks faith with this dependent people. Great nations like great men, should keep their word." [1]

Thus, unjust treatment of the Indians was not confined to the Jackson era, or to the South, or to the Democrats. Some day an American historian of Indian blood may pen a devastating indictment of the United States.

4. Conclusion on Jackson

The fourth of March 1837 marked the passing of a vital personality and the arrival of Number Two in a new presidential dynasty. Up Pennsylvania Avenue wound a military procession, escorting a small phaeton (built from the wood of U.S.S. *Constitution*) drawn by four gray horses. The President, though emaciated by illness and feeling his seventy years, sat erect wth his white hair bared to the sunshine, the old indomitable spirit flashing from his eyes. Beside him, and a head lower, sat Martin Van Buren with the bland aspect of a cat who had swallowed the canary. Chief Justice Taney administered the inaugural oath and there followed a more seemly reception at the

1. *Federal Power Commission and New York Power Authority* v. *Tuscarora Indian Nation.*

White House than that of 1829. Andrew Jackson then returned by easy stages to his home in Tennessee. He was not expected to live long, but he survived another eight years and continued to dictate party decisions and appointments. The Hermitage became a sort of Mecca where Democratic aspirants had to do homage.

President Jackson had so many limitations that it is doubtful whether he should be included in the ranks of the really great Presidents. His approach to problems was too personal and instinctive, his choice of men, at times, lamentably mistaken; and, unlike the Roosevelts, he had little perception of underlying popular movements, or of the ferment that was going on in the United States. His modern counterpart for pugnacity, chivalry, and capacity for quick but correct decisions is Harry Truman. But one cannot help but love old Jackson. His simplicity and forthrightness, his refusal to equivocate or compromise, his gentleness where women were concerned, are admirable. And he dealt swiftly and severely with the one disruptive movement whose significance he did perceive. In 1861 men of good will were saying, "O for one hour of Andrew Jackson!"

Of all the Presidents, only Lincoln and the second Roosevelt have made as great an appeal as Jackson to the popular imagination. In his person he proved that the average American of sound character and common sense could win, and was fit to administer, the powerful office of the presidency. He left a mass of unsolved problems for his successors, and the ground swell of the slavery question was beginning to break along the political coast. Yet he is, and always should be, a popular hero; so with Vachel Lindsay let us sing:

> A natural king with a raven wing;
> Cold no more, weary no more —
> Old, old, old, old Andrew Jackson.

XXIX

Van Buren and Our Northern Neighbors

1837-1858

1. Democrats, Whigs, and the Panic of 1837

MARTIN VAN BUREN, nominated unanimously at Jackson's behest, and elected by 170 votes out of 294, made a shrewd, able, and dignified President. After, to a great extent, inventing the game of democratic politics in New York, he had obtained a firm grip on the federal administration as Vice President, and learned about foreign affairs both as secretary of state and minister to Great Britain. After seeing his predecessor off by the new Baltimore & Ohio Railway — first presidential patronage of a railroad — Van Buren announced his cabinet appointments. He kept John Forsyth as secretary of state, gave the unlucky but capable Poinsett the war department, and appropriately left in office Jackson's wire-pulling crony Amos Kendall as postmaster general. Democratic (and some Republican) Presidents seem to require one of these "twilight personages" on whom they can rely — Woodrow Wilson's Colonel House, Franklin D. Roosevelt's Harry Hopkins, and Dwight Eisenhower's Sherman Adams are recent examples. Amos Kendall, "A puny, sickly-looking man with a weak voice, a wheezing cough, narrow and stooping shoulders, a sallow complexion, slovenly dress and a seedy appearance generally," could never have been a leader himself; but he enjoyed the power of being the leader's confidential adviser, and for two Presidents he acted as sifter of patronage demands and liaison to the press.

One of the strangest characters ever to serve as Vice President was Richard M. Johnson, congressman from Kentucky, a favorite of Jackson's, and his errand boy during the Peggy Eaton affair. Colonel Johnson was a hero of the War of 1812, and claimed to have killed Tecumseh at the Battle of the Thames. Since William H. Harrison, one of the several Whig candidates for the presidency, was campaigning as the Hero of Tippecanoe, Johnson's friends countered with:

> Rumpsey dumpsey, rumpsey dumpsey,
> Colonel Johnson killed Tecumseh!

But this slogan, never surpassed for electioneering imbecility, failed to give him a majority in the electoral college. So the election of Vice President had to be made by the Senate, voting by states according to Amendment XII of the Constitution; the only time that has happened. Johnson was then elected.

The Whig party, on the losing end, was a regrouping, under a new name, of Republican factions which refused to follow Jackson, and of surviving Federalists. It inherited from Jefferson a humanitarian attitude toward the poor and helpless; and from Hamilton, a tender regard for finance, commerce, and manufacturing. If the Democrats had the "best principles," as Ralph Waldo Emerson wrote, the Whigs had the "best men," with Clay of Kentucky, Webster and Everett of Massachusetts, John Bell and Hugh L. White of Tennessee, Reverdy Johnson of Maryland, Hugh S. Legaré and James L. Petigru of South Carolina, and a dozen others of intelligence and integrity. Had they not been overwhelmed by the rising tide of democracy, these men might have saved the Union. But the Whigs, with too many prima donnas jostling one another for the big spot, could not agree upon one candidate in 1836, so the election became a tryout of "favorite sons." General Harrison won the most electoral votes; and when the *Boston Atlas*, which affected to carry the whole Eastern business world on its shoulders, came out solemnly for his nomination in 1840, all other contenders withdrew.

The "Little Magician" (as people called Van Buren) might turn political dross into precious metal, but he was unable to cope with the panic of 1837. It was blamed on the Democrats, as panics always are on the party in power. Speculation was the basic cause. The boom in Western land, manufacturing, transportation, banking and all other business enterprises that began about 1825, resulted in overextension of credit, to which Jackson unwittingly contributed by withdrawing government deposits from the conservative B.U.S. in favor of "pet banks," which used them to promote further speculation. In pursuance of Jackson's specie circular, millions in hard money were withdrawn from deposit banks to pay for purchases of government land in the West; at the same time, the price of cotton fell by one-half, and the wheat crop of 1836 failed. The same thing, in a smaller way, was happening in Europe; and American enterprises were then largely dependent on European capital. Thus, when continental Europe put pressure on English banks, they demanded the repayment of their short-term loans to American enterprises. Demands for gold from English creditors reached the banks at the very time they were depleted to pay for Western lands; and the failure of three English banking houses early in 1837 precipitated the crisis, much as the Austrian Kreditanstalt failure precipitated the crash of 1931.

Van Buren was no sooner seated in the White House than American mercantile houses and banks began to fail, and there were riots in New York over the high cost of flour. In May, after almost every bank in the country had suspended specie payments, and the government had lost $9 million through the collapse of pet banks, the President summoned Congress for a special session. In the meantime, there was widespread suffering; less probably than in later depressions, because the majority of Americans were farmers, and industrial workers in many cases could return to a parental farm. On the other hand, there was no social security or government assistance of any kind for the desperate other than town and county poorhouses. Cold and hungry people in the cities had to depend on private charity for fuel and food. And a promising labor movement collapsed; the estimated 300,000 trade unionists of 1837, about half the total number of skilled workers, could no longer pay their dues.

The special session of Congress accomplished nothing except to authorize a large issue of temporary treasury notes, which began a new national debt. As a permanent fiscal measure, Van Buren proposed an independent treasury, essentially a government bank; but that was too much for state banking interests to swallow, and an alliance of conservative Democrats with the Whigs prevented it from becoming law until 1840. Thus, the next presidential election was held in the midst of a depression, which has always meant woe for the party in power.

2. The Log Cabin Campaign of 1840

"Little Van" deserved re-election, and he might have been re-elected had he chosen to play politics with the Canadian rebellion, which we shall consider presently. He lost his own state, where sympathy with the Canadian rebels was strongest, by only 13,293 out of 441,139 votes; and New York's 42 electoral votes would have gone far toward giving him the decision.

The reason why the 1840 campaign became the jolliest and most idiotic presidential contest in our history is that the Whigs beat the Democrats by their own methods. They adopted no platform, nominated a military hero, ignored real issues, and appealed to the emotions rather than the brains of voters. Expectations of profit and patronage were employed to "get out the vote," and the people were given a big show. Democratic politicians, even Jackson himself, now complained of Whig demagoguery.

Who were the Whigs in 1840? The only really accurate answer is, everyone who was not a Democrat. Everyone, that is, except a few rabid abolitionists at one end of the political spectrum, and sullen nullifiers at the other. The party included people hard-hit by the depression and the war on the Bank, old-fashioned state-righters offended by Jackson's nationalist stand; New England and Middle-state Yankees who disliked all Democrats, factory owners who wanted more protection, and Westerners who had discovered that Clay's "distribution" and "pre-emption" did more for them than Jackson's and Van Buren's promises. Yet Clay, the logical candidate and the most fit man living to be President, did not get the nomination. For Henry had made many enemies; whilst old General Harrison, the Hero of Tippecanoe, had proved to be a good vote-getter and could be "built up." Harrison was not politically inexperienced, having served as congressman and senator from Indiana, but he was not associated with any particular measures. As American minister to Colombia (appointed by Adams and recalled by Jackson) he had incurred the enmity of Bolívar by lecturing the Liberator on the duties of a republican president. But that did not hurt him with the North American public.

Harrison's nomination set the pattern that Jackson's had begun — a nationally known figure, uncommitted on controversial issues. The Whig convention even appointed a committee to supervise the General's correspondence lest he write something incautious and be quoted! In order to capture the state rights vote in the South, the convention, to its members' subsequent regret, nominated a very positive and rambunctious character, John Tyler. This old-fashioned Virginia Republican resigned his seat in the Senate rather than vote to expunge a resolution of censure on Jackson, as the state legislature had instructed him to do. That made him a hero to the Whigs, but failed to change his views or even make him a Whig. He had just turned fifty years of age, whilst Harrison was already pushing seventy.

For principle the Whigs substituted mass enthusiasm. "Tippecanoe and Tyler Too!" was the slogan. Van Buren, unfortunately for himself, had acquired luxurious tastes on his brief diplomatic mission and transferred them to the White House; this gave the Whigs a chance to repeat Jackson's tactics against Adams. Charles Ogle, a Pennsylvania congressman otherwise unknown to fame, made a famous and widely circulated speech on "The Royal Splendor of the President's Palace." Maine lumberjacks, Buckeye farmers, and Cajans in the bayou country were shocked to learn that under Little Van the White House had become a palace "as splendid as that of the Caesars"; that the President doused his whiskers with French *eau de cologne*, slept in a Louis XV bedstead, sipped *soupe à la reine* with a gold spoon, ate *paté de foie gras* from a silver plate, and rode abroad in a gilded British-made coach, wearing a haughty sneer on his aristocratic countenance. What a contrast to old hero Harrison, the Cincinnatus of the West, the plain dirt farmer of North Bend, Indiana!

> No ruffled shirt, no silken hose,
> No airs does Tip display;
> But like "the pith of worth" he goes
> In homespun "hodden-grey."
>
> Upon his board there ne'er appeared
> The costly "sparkling wine,"
> But plain hard cider such as cheered
> In days of old lang syne.

What really turned the tide, however, was the unlucky sneer of a Democratic journalist in Baltimore to the effect that if Old Tip were given a barrel of hard cider and a pension of $2000 he would prefer his log cabin to the White House. It then became the log-cabin, hard-cider campaign. There were log-cabin badges and log-cabin songs, a *Log Cabin* newspaper and log-cabin clubs, big log cabins where the thirsty were regaled with hard cider that jealous Democrats alleged to be stiffened with whisky; little log cabins borne on floats in procession, with latchstring out, cider barrel by the door, coonskin nailed up beside, and real smoke coming out of the chimney, while lusty voices bawled:

> Let Van from his coolers of silver drink wine,
>   And lounge on his cushioned settee;
> Our man on his buckeye bench can recline,
>   Content with hard cider is he.
> Then a shout from each freeman — a shout from each State,
>   To the plain, honest husbandman true,
> And this be our motto — the motto of Fate —
>   "Hurrah for Old Tippecanoe!"

In vain the Democrats worked a counter-line of campaign lies, to the effect that Harrison was an abolitionist and a "Hartford Convention Federalist"; in vain did "Rumpsey-dumpsey" Johnson try to take the curse off dandy Van by clowning in a red jacket he claimed to have stripped off Tecumseh. In vain James Buchanan, in his nasal Pennsylvania twang, stuffily "endeavored, without giving personal offense, to carry the war into Africa."

In those days some states, notably Maine (which continued the practice until 1958), held their elections in late summer; and from the 1840 Maine election, which Edward Kent the Whig candidate for governor won easily, it was clear that a landslide had started. After the Maine returns were in, it became the custom for one Whig, meeting another on the street, to ask: How did old Maine went?" To which the other would answer: "She went hell bent for Governor Kent!" And, together with sympathetic bystanders, they roared the chorus,

> And Tippecanoe and Tyler too!

By mid-November it was clear that "Tip and Ty" had won. They carried Clay's Kentucky, Jackson's Tennessee, and the entire West except Illinois and Missouri which were salvaged for Little Van by the stentorian voice and bad grammar of "Old Bullion" Benton. They carried all the populous Middle states, all New England except Isaac Hill's bailiwick New Hampshire, and the solid South except Virginia and South Carolina. The result was 234 electoral votes against 60. But the popular vote was very close — Harrison 1,269,763; VanBuren 1,126,137. A few thousand votes in New York, Pennsylvania, and Ohio could have turned the tide.

General Harrison, an honest, simple old soldier, was expected by Whig politicians to place himself in the hands of such men as Clay and Webster. The latter had the impudence to offer him a ready-made inaugural address of his own composition. But the General had already compiled from schoolboy memories of Plutarch a turgid address of which he was very proud. With some difficulty he was persuaded to let Webster revise it. After one day's work the "god-like Daniel" arrived late to a dinner party, looking so haggard that his hostess was alarmed. She hoped that nothing had happened?

"Madam," replied Webster, "you would think something had happened, if you knew what I have done. I have killed seventeen Roman proconsuls as dead as smelts!"

The fourth of March 1841 was the coldest inauguration day in history. The old soldier disdained the protection of hat or overcoat, and his expurgated address took an hour and forty minutes to deliver. John Quincy Adams, who had supported Tip and Ty somewhat wryly, remarked in his diary, "Harrison comes in upon a hurricane; God grant he may not go out upon a wreck!" Worse than that, he went out in a hearse. In the damp, unheated White House the cold that Harrison caught at the inauguration developed into pneumonia, complicated by congestion of the liver. The doctors, after blistering and "cupping" him, administered violent emetics and cathartics; then switched to opium, camphor, and brandy; finally, in desperation, administered Indian medicine men's remedies such as crude petroleum and snakeweed. These finished him — Tecumseh's revenge, perhaps! On 4 April 1841, the hero of Tippecanoe gave up the ghost. John Tyler succeeded to his office, and title, too.

Tyler declared Sunday, 14 May, a day of national fasting and prayer in honor of the departed President. This gave the ministers a chance to preach hortatory sermons, no fewer than 138 of which were printed. The death of Harrison, after only one month in office, was assumed to be a divine castigation for national sins. There was complete disagreement, however, as to what sins the Almighty intended to rebuke. Immorality and sabbath-breaking were the choices of most; but some Northern preachers thought that the Lord was delivering a warning to free the slaves, whilst the Reverend Mr. Gadsden of St. Philip's, Charleston, believed that "current wild notions of equality" and "organized movements to break down distinctions among men" had aroused the divine wrath.

It was soon demonstrated that lust for office was the only binding force in the Whig party. Henry Clay expected to be "mayor of the palace" as well as leader of the Senate; but Tyler was an obstinate man with a mind of his own. Clay's immediate object was to charter a new Bank of the United States. Tyler believed it to be his mission to assert Virginia state rights principles of 1798, and to strip the federal government of its "usurped" powers. He took over Harrison's cabinet, carried through a purgation of the civil service that Harrison had begun, and signed a "distribution-pre-emption" bill of Clay's to discharge the party's debt to the West. This law gave the squatters what they had long wanted, the right to pre-empt a quarter-section of public land at the minimum price. Tyler accepted an upward revision of tariff schedules as a measure necessary to raise revenue, but vetoed all bills for internal improvements and harbor works, and refused to accept any fiscal device that bore the remotest resemblance to the B.U.S. of detestable memory. Clay's bill for a new national bank was returned with the President's veto, as was a second bill specially drafted to meet his constitutional scruples.

From that date, 9 September 1841, there was open warfare between Tyler and Clay. Four days later the entire cabinet, excepting Webster, resigned and the President was practically read out of the Whig party. Here was Calhoun's chance to count in the sectional balance of power. For three years (1841–43) he played a waiting game, intriguing to obtain the Democratic nomination for the presidency in 1844. Webster left the cabinet in 1843; and the following March Calhoun became secretary of state.

This meant that Tyler had gone over to the Democrats, and that Calhoun had returned to the fold. Calhoun's purpose was to "reform" the Democratic party on the basis of state rights; to adopt the formula which he believed to be necessary to preserve the Union. This formula at bottom was a theoretic cover for the main purpose of his devoted followers, to perpetuate slavery where it existed, and extend it into regions where it was not. Calhoun tipped the internal balance of the Democratic party very definitely southward; the defection of Tyler inclined the internal balance of the Whig party no less definitely northward.

The important question of which side the West would take was decided when the Democrats nominated James K. Polk for the presidency in 1844, on a platform of westward expansion, which proved to be an even more potent appeal to the voters than "Tippecanoe and Tyler too." But it was ominous that in the same platform the Democrats neglected to reaffirm their faith, as had been their wont, in the principles of the Declaration of Independence.

The same declining faith in "the right of the people to alter or to abolish" a government which has become destructive of "inalienable rights," became evident in the attitude of the Tyler administration, and the American public generally, toward the so-called Dorr Rebellion in Rhode Island. That state was still using its seventeenth-century charter, unamendable by due process, as a constitution. Landed property was still a requirement for voting, and the apportionment of seats in the legislature virtually disfranchised Providence and other rising cities. Thomas H. Dorr, a young Harvard graduate and manufacturer who for years had been agitating political reforms which the legislatures rejected, organized the People's Party, which called a constitutional convention in 1841 without the legislature's permission. This convention drafted a new constitution embodying manhood suffrage and reapportionment which, submitted to popular vote, was ratified by a huge majority. Dorr was elected governor in April 1842 and a new slate of state officials was chosen. But another state government, elected under the colonial charter, defied Dorr's. President Tyler, appealed to by both, declared that only the old government was legal and that he would support it by force if necessary — a somewhat startling conclusion for a man who had supported South Carolina's nullification. Encouraged by this promise, the old government issued warrants for the arrest of Dorr, who was actually convicted of treason to Rhode Island and sentenced to life imprisonment at hard labor. But the old government was frightened by the threat of civil war into calling a new constitutional convention which extended the franchise to all native-born white citizens. This was adopted by popular vote before the end of the year. Governor Dorr was pardoned, but the Supreme Court of the United States, in the case of *Luther* v. *Borden*, branded his entire movement as an extralegal rebellion.

The effect of that decision, to this day, has been to deny constitutional reform in certain states, including Massachusetts, unless by permission of the government which needs to be reformed.

3. Canada Boils Over

During the quarter-century from 1815 to 1840 the development of British North America ran parallel to that of the United States in some respects, and in others was dissimilar as if on a separate continent. It is fascinating to follow Canadian history during this period because it indicates what might have happened to the Thirteen Colonies if the American Revolution had ended in a suppressed rebellion.

Canada, as we may for short call the whole of British North America, although it had no union until 1867, consisted in 1825 of six settled provinces: Newfoundland, the three Maritimes (Prince Edward Island, Nova Scotia, and New Brunswick); Lower Canada, which at the time of federation became the Province of Quebec; and Upper Canada, which at the same time became the Province of Ontario.[1] The Hudson's Bay Company continued to own the watershed around the bay of that name, and with the Northwest Company divided control of all western Canada to the Pacific. In these vast regions the natives still hunted and fished with no European contacts other than a few trappers and missionaries.

The five provinces south of Newfoundland received a large stream of immigrants from Great Britain and Ireland, and the Ontario peninsula, thrusting down between New York, Pennsylvania, and Michigan, attracted a good share of westward-moving pioneers from the United States. Canada was increasing about as fast as her big neighbor. Of the three most populous provinces, Nova Scotia counted 202,600 people in 1838; Quebec, 625,000 in 1841; and Ontario in the same year 455,700; about the same as Michigan, Indiana, and Maryland respectively. The total population of British North America in 1840, about 1,450,000, was roughly the same as that of the white population in the Thirteen Colonies around 1765. Apart from the Indians, who were not counted in this enumeration, the Canadians were practically all white; the few hundred Negro slaves owned by the French in Quebec, and those brought in by American Loyalists, were all liberated in 1833.

Relations between Canada and the United States during this period may be described as warily friendly. The strong Loyalist element in the population tended to be anti-American, and everyone remembered the aggressive War of 1812. But the Rush-Bagot agreement for naval disarmament on the Great

1. The later names Quebec and Ontario are used here for the sake of clarity.

Lakes was faithfully maintained, and prevented border incidents — up to a point. That point was reached in 1837 when the political lid blew off in Quebec and Ontario; the lack of armed forces on the border then became a handicap to enforcing neutrality laws. There was nothing in the Rush-Bagot agreement, however, against building forts. During this period the British government strengthened the citadels at Halifax and Quebec, built a new strongpoint at Kingston, near old Fort Frontenac; and kept more than 5000 regular troops in Canada.

Although Canada had enjoyed since 1791 a measure of representative government in the shape of a lower house elected on a fairly broad franchise, the British government had ample means of control in order to defeat inconvenient expressions of popular will. As in the royal provinces among the Old Thirteen before 1775, the crown appointed and removed at pleasure the governor, most of the high officials, the judges, and a legislative council which acted as upper house of the legislature. The governor not only could veto a bill; he could send any act of the legislature to England for disallowance. Moreover, the governor and other high officials were paid out of crown revenue instead of being dependent on the lower house, as the royal governors in the Old Thirteen had been. In other words, the British government had the same set-up in the Canadian provinces that Lord North was aiming for in Massachusetts Bay in 1774: an element of authority strong enough to keep popular movements in check.

Each province was in fact ruled by a local Tory oligarchy which supported the governor. In Quebec it was the "château clique" led by Chief Justice Jonathan Sewall, son of an old Massachusetts Tory; in Ontario it was the "family compact," led by Archdeacon Strachan of the Anglican Church and John Beverley Robinson, of Virginia and New York loyalist background. The result was a feeling of frustration on the part of a large number, perhaps a majority, of the voters. They saw the United States advancing rapidly in power and wealth, with representative government responsible to the people. This proved that democracy worked, for aught the Tories might say. But every attempt to express popular wants was quashed by the ruling oligarchy. A serious blow-up resulted.

In Quebec, the dominant French population had few aspirations toward progress. Their ideal was to preserve l'ancien régime as of 1760; but the Scots merchants of the château clique wanted improvement and development. Paradoxically, it was a Canadian gentleman of the old regime, Louis-Joseph Papineau, speaker of the assembly since 1815, who combined with John Neilson, a sturdy Scots liberal, and Edmund B. O'Callaghan, an emotional Irishman, to agitate for responsible government in Quebec. Papineau, a student of the French and American revolutions, appeared to be leading Quebec in their footsteps, with himself in the combined roles of Samuel Adams and Mirabeau. A cholera epidemic of 1832 was blamed on the British; the same year there was a "Montreal massacre" to parallel the Boston massacre of 1770;

patriotic demands were incorporated in ninety-two resolutions (the mystic Massachusetts number); non-importation agreements followed, and patriots ostentatiously wore homespun. The government rejected Papineau's minimum proposal, to let the voters choose the legislative council. Young men began organizing as *Fils de la liberté*, the countryside armed secretly and displayed the tricolor, and called extralegal conventions. One of some 5000 people met at Saint-Charles on 23–24 October 1837, rallying around a liberty pole topped by the Phrygian liberty cap. It looked as if the "Spirit of '76" had entered Canada.

But the same combustible materials were not present in Canada as in the earlier Boston. As the Canadian historian Creighton well says, "The radicals in both provinces sought to persuade a people whose grandfathers had rejected the gospel of Thomas Jefferson, to accept the revised version of Andrew Jackson. They tried to induce the Canadians to re-enact the American Revolution sixty years after their ancestors had failed to take part in the original performance."

Papineau's fatal error, in contrast to Sam Adams's cultivation of the Protestant clergy, was to alienate Catholic priests by anticlerical outbursts. After the Bishop of Montreal had pronounced against him, few French Canadians would follow his lead. Warrants were issued for the arrest of O'Callaghan and Papineau. At Saint-Denis and Saint-Charles on the Richelieu river, cast for the roles of Lexington and Concord, a few armed men defied British regulars. But the repeat performance ended then and there. The "rebels" did "disperse," and their leaders fled to Vermont. And at Saint-Eustache north of Montreal, a loyal rabble chased the patriots into a church and then smoked them out. The entire rebellion would have ended as a farce but for refugees in the United States.

President Van Buren issued a neutrality proclamation on 5 January 1838, and the governors of New York and Vermont forbade citizens to help refugee rebels. Nevertheless, between December and February there took place three or four raids on Quebec by bands of Canadian patriots who had organized on American soil. The most serious, led by two Quebec physicians, Robert Nelson and Cyrille Coté, crossed Lake Champlain, invaded Canada from Vermont, and issued a declaration of independence. There was no response; no "embattled farmers" flocked to the tricolored banner. The rebels retreated to Plattsburg, where General Wool disarmed them. Nelson maintained a republican government of Quebec in exile, with a secret society of refugees and American sympathizers called the *Frères Chasseurs*, or Hunters' Lodges. Those at one time had an estimated 50,000 members, but only 3000, of whom barely one-third were armed, accompanied "President" Nelson to a grand encampment at Napierville, P.Q., in November 1838. Loyal volunteers and regular British troops dispersed them and took 750 prisoners, of whom 99 were sentenced to death for treason, and a dozen were executed.

In Ontario, the uprising came much nearer success. Here the social rift was religious rather than racial. Methodists, Presbyterians, and Baptists, mostly recent immigrants from the British Isles and the United States, were pressing for a share of public money from the dominant old-Tory Anglicans and North of Ireland Presbyterians, and for an overhaul of the public land system. The provincial government, not wanting a rowdy West of the American type, reserved one-seventh of every 640-acre township for the crown, and one-seventh for the church; these reserves obstructed roads, retarded settlement, and were generally a nuisance. In addition, there were immense private grants to government favorites, untaxed but held for future profit, like the proprietary lands in provincial Pennsylvania. Rural Ontario was full of poor people from Britain who had hoped to better their condition by emigration but found themselves as poor as ever, together with a substantial middle class of whom a witty Irishman remarked, "All had money, but few of them had any sinse, and none of them knew how to work." Outside the "family compact" and snug little groups of officials and professional men in towns like Kingston and Toronto, Ontario was a scene of frustration and blighted hopes.

The principal leaders of opposition in Ontario, fundamentally conservative men who wanted only a fair deal, were Egerton Ryerson, son of a New Jersey Loyalist who founded a Methodist newspaper in 1829; William Lyon Mackenzie, a fiery Scots journalist, editor of a newspaper published in Toronto and mayor of that city; and Marshall S. Bidwell, son of Jefferson's "clerk of the water-closet" who had fled to Ontario when the Federalists found his accounts to be $10,000 short. Five times Mackenzie was elected to the assembly, five times he was ejected from that body for a supposed libel on the government, a procedure recalling that of the House of Commons with Jack Wilkes in the 1770's. On the sixth re-election, Mackenzie was allowed to keep his seat and became the opposition leader, with a program of political and land reform which was more moderate and constructive than Papineau's ninety-two resolutions. The Ontario reform party was largely inspired by American example, especially that of New York. Mackenzie aimed to give the people more control over their provincial and local governments, and to unlock the land reserves; but he too became anticlerical, which lost him the support of the Methodists and Orangemen.

The explosion occurred in Ontario at the same time as in Quebec, but for different reasons. It was precipitated by the appointment as lieutenant governor of Upper Canada of a stupid retired soldier named Francis Head, apparently by mistake — the colonial office in London thought it was appointing his gifted cousin Sir Edmund Head. The new governor, after a brief flirtation with the reformers, decided that they were a pack of traitors, and embarked on a policy of autocracy and repression. He vetoed all bills for roads, schools, and public works, dissolved the assembly dominated by Mackenzie, and orated for the Tories in a new election. With the aid of the Orangemen, who provided strong-arm work at the polls similar to what their Catholic fellow countrymen were doing in New York, Head won a majority of seats.

Mackenzie, defeated in his Ottawa constituency, now took the road to rebellion, drafted a declaration of independence on 31 July 1836, armed and drilled thousands of settlers, and set a date, 7 December 1837, for the patriots to capture Toronto. The panic of 1837, in the meantime, had hit Ontario. It was not so severe as in the United States, because the "family compact" had checked speculation and inflation. Nevertheless, it created unemployment and discontent, which the rebels exploited. Under Mackenzie's vacillating and incompetent leadership, the rebels were defeated in their march on Toronto by one volley delivered by a loyal sheriff and 27 militiamen from behind a rail fence. The embattled farmers of York County duly rallied on 7 December, several hundred strong, but were routed by loyal militia in a field outside the town. Mackenzie then fled to Buffalo and set up a "Republican Government of Upper Canada" at Navy Island in the Niagara river but on the Canadian side of the border. He made active preparations, with the aid of the Hunters' Lodges and American sympathizers, to invade Ontario from three points at once.

Here is where the United States almost became involved. American sympathies, naturally, were for the rebels; it was expected that "history would repeat itself" (which it never does), and that the Canadian provinces would be freed from British tyranny by Mackenzie's and Nelson's patriots.

President Van Buren, friendly to the British empire and anxious to avoid trouble, endeavored to maintain strict neutrality. On the long, unfortified boundary his means were few and feeble, whilst the state governments of New York and Vermont were weak in will and not much stronger in means. Hence Mackenzie and his followers were able to obtain money, supplies, and recruits in the United States to invade Canada. It was a scandalous situation; within a year (1837–38) some dozen to fifteen raids on Canada were launched from American soil. Some of them, to be sure, were only two men in a rowboat, but all defied the neutrality laws.

After Mackenzie had recruited 200 or 300 "liberators" at Buffalo among unemployed bargees, lake sailors, and stevedores, President Van Buren sent thither a force of regulars under General Winfield Scott. Rebel headquarters on Navy Island were supplied from the New York shore by the small American paddle steamer *Caroline*. On the night of 29 December 1837, as she lay at her wharf on the United States side, a picked band of Canadian volunteers performed the hazardous feat of rowing across the Niagara river where its current rushes toward the falls, capturing the *Caroline*, and sinking her. In the brawl an American named Durfee was killed. It was a violation of neutrality analogous to that of General Jackson's in Florida; but New York was not a Spanish province, and England now had a pugnacious foreign minister, Lord Palmerston.

This affair created a tremendous uproar along the border; the Rochester *Democrat* called for revenge "not by simpering diplomacy but by blood." Van Buren, however, relied on diplomacy, both internal and external. He protested to Palmerston about the "outrage," but also prosecuted Mackenzie and "General" Rensselaer Van Rensselaer of his American volunteers. He jailed them both, sent more troops to the border, and kept General Scott's men busy disarming volunteers. But the President was unable to prevent the Hunters' Lodges from organizing an attack on Prescott, across the St. Lawrence, in November 1838. That was the last serious raid. The Hunters surrendered to Canadian troops, and a number of them were hanged.

In the meantime, another danger point had developed in the disputed territory on the Maine-New Brunswick frontier. Canadian lumberjacks entered the region claimed by the United States on the Aroostook river in 1838 and seized a protesting state senator from Maine. The governors of New Brunswick and Maine called out the militia, but this " 'Roostook War," as it was called, ended in bloody noses and mutual invective. General Scott arranged a truce in March 1839; and three years later Daniel Webster and Lord Ashburton concluded the treaty that settled this troublesome boundary question.

But there was no peace for Van Buren. In November 1840, before the President could persuade Palmerston to admit that the attack on the *Caroline* had been deliberate and official, a Canadian named McLeod boasted in a New York barroom that he had killed Durfee, the American in the affray. McLeod was promptly arrested and indicted for murder. Palmerston demanded his immediate release. The execution of McLeod, so he informed the British minister at Washington, "would produce war, war immediate and frightful in its character, because it would be a war of retaliation and vengeance." By the time this barroom boaster came to trial at Utica, Tyler was President and Daniel Webster, secretary of state. Although anxious as Van Buren to preserve the peace, they were equally hampered by the limitations of federal government. Governor Seward of New York insisted that his state's justice should take its course, and Webster could do no more than provide counsel for the prisoner. Fortunately, McLeod sober managed to find an alibi for McLeod drunk, and was acquitted.

Nova Scotia, which was not subjected to the religious and racial stresses of the Canadas, obtained responsible government in 1848 without a rebellion. This peaceful solution came about largely through the statesmanship of her native son Joseph Howe, son of a Boston Loyalist. The governments of New Brunswick and Prince Edward Island underwent a similar peaceful evolution.

The outcome of the Canadian rebellion was happy for both countries. Queen Victoria appointed the young and energetic Earl of Durham commissioner for British North America, with power to suspend provincial legislatures and the duty to make recommendations. "Radical Jack," as he was called, arrived at Quebec in May 1838. He adopted a policy of clemency toward captured rebels, traveled about the settled regions of the Canadas, sent his brother-in-law Charles Grey to talk to President Van Buren; and, although forced to resign in the fall, owing to the English political situation, wrote his "Report on the Affairs of British North America." This Durham

Report, one of the finest state papers in the English language, laid down the principles which have guided British colonial policy ever since. He advised a union of Upper and Lower Canada as a step toward federation of all Canada. He made many recommendations in advance of his time (such as the Canadian Pacific Railway); he cited devastating statistics on the land reserves, and recommended that the American public land system be adopted. But the crux of his advice was to give Canada responsible government in the English sense; i.e. a ministry responsible to an elective assembly. His union of the two Canadas was immediately adopted, but that turned out to be a false step, as the French of Quebec hated it. But his federation and responsible government projects bore fruit in the British North America Act of 1867, which brought the Dominion of Canada into existence.

Thus the rebellions of 1837–38, tragi-comic failures though they were, started the British government on a course of colonial reform, because Durham and the British liberals learned the right lessons from them.

TIPPECANOE AND TYLER TOO

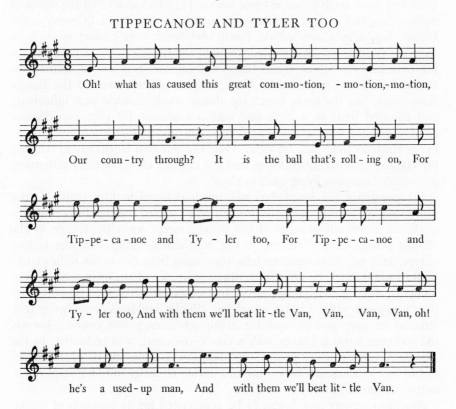

Oh! what has caused this great com-mo-tion, - mo-tion,-mo-tion,

Our coun-try through? It is the ball that's roll-ing on, For

Tip-pe-ca-noe and Ty - ler too, For Tip-pe-ca-noe and

Ty - ler too, And with them we'll beat lit-tle Van, Van, Van, Van, oh!

he's a used-up man, And with them we'll beat lit-tle Van.

X X X

Society and Business in the North

1820-1860

1. America Finding Herself

NOW LET US TAKE a look at the material and moral forces that were pulsing through the United States in this crucial generation, and which in so many ways set the pattern of the America to come. Statesmen and politicians had done much to shape those forces. They had weathered the storm of nullification and created two national parties, both pledged to preserve the Union. Yet, despite their efforts, North and South were pulling apart. Both were progressing, but divergently. Northern society was being transformed by the industrial revolution, cheap transportation, and educational, humanitarian, and migratory movements. These, to some extent, touched the Border slave states; but the lower South lay almost wholly outside such influences, and adjusted itself to a slave and cotton economy. By 1850 two distinct civilizations had been evolved, as different in material basis and outlook on life as England and Spain are today. Only the common language and religion, the common political institutions, and the devoted efforts of elder statesmen, prevented them from flying apart in 1850.

In appearance the North had not much changed in fifty years. Harriet Martineau, an intelligent Englishwoman who traveled through the country in 1836, was never out of sight of the woods, except for a short time in the Illinois prairies. A new feature in the Northern landscape was the factory village, built near river rapids or falls, containing from two to ten mills plainly built of wood, brick, or stone, pretentious mansions of the owners or superintendents, and hundreds of operatives' houses, exactly alike. Georgian architecture had given place to the neo-classic. Public buildings were being constructed of gray granite, and the wealthier farmers and country lawyers masked their wooden houses with a classic colonnade and pediment. In the Middle West the white painted farmhouse was beginning to predominate; but in new settlements, log cabins and untidy clearings full of stumps dominated the landscape.

American scenery now began to be appreciated for its contrasts of mountain with valley, sand beach or rocky coast with island-studded sea, gorges and cataracts. Every foreign visitor had to see Niagara Falls, the Hudson river, and the Natural Bridge of Virginia. Big wooden hotels with long, covered piazzas were being put up at places like Saratoga Springs, Niagara Falls, Newport, and Nahant, to accommodate sightseers and provide for the brief vacations of professional and business men and the longer ones of their wives. Country houses imitated from Italian villas or the "Gothic" cottages of England multiplied near the larger cities, portending a new class of city-bred gentleman farmer.

As at the time of the American Revolution, liberal elements in Europe looked to America with admiration and hope. The aged Madame de Staël told young George Ticknor, "Vous êtes l'avant garde du genre humain, vous êtes l'avenir du monde." Ten years later Goethe, who loved to talk with any American who came to Weimar, wrote a poem to the United States:

> America, thou hast it better
> Than our old continent; . . .
> Within, naught restrains thee
> From a livelier era;
> No useless memories
> Of unforgotten strife.
> Face thy future with happiness!

And Achille Murat, liberal offspring of the Napoleonic dynasty, wrote home from Florida in 1826, "You should see the calm, majestic advance of this Republic. You can form no idea of it, you who have only known Liberty amid the tempest and under attack by subversive parties. Here her principles are imperishably established both in minds and in hearts. The people are unanimous in support of the government."

True enough, and what's more, republicanism and democracy did work, and the resources of a new country, exploited by the people under laws of their own making and breaking, had brought a degree of comfort and security to the common man that his forebears in Europe had never known. It is not surprising that Americans were full of bounce and bluster, contemptuous of Old-World monarchies. They had many unpleasant habits, particularly in connection with tobacco. "Spitting and swearing are nearly out of fashion in Philadelphia," says the writer of A Pleasant Peregrination in Pennsylvania (1836); "at this moment we cannot recall more than two or three gentlemen who would think of such a thing as spitting on the carpet of a lady's drawing room." Obeisance was not to be had of the white American at any price; but those who addressed him as an equal discovered a natural civility and kindness that took the place of manners. Intercourse between man and man (providing both were white and not too recent immigrants) was easy because there was no assumption of social superiority on the one side, or acknowledged inferiority on the other.[1] It was not so much the freedom, simplicity,

1. One aspect of this attitude that has disappeared was dislike of uniforms. The first New York City police force in 1844 struck at wearing a uniform blue coat as servile. Railroad conductors and postmen refused to wear uniforms until some time after the Civil War; academic gowns were revived about the same time.

and good humor of the people that endeared them to Harriet Martineau as the "sweet temper diffused like sunshine over the land," and "the practice of forbearance requisite in a republic."

Forbearance the Americans carried to excess in their uncritical attitude toward their own books, customs, institutions, and abuses. Almost every foreign traveler of the period remarked the patience of Americans under the afflictions of contemporary travel, denounced their deference to majority opinion, and deplored their fear of expressing unpopular views. This meant that Americans were becoming less independent and more gregarious, deference to the opinions of others being a condition of social intercourse on a democratic level. Yet so complex was the American character that the excess of one quality was balanced by the reverse. Intolerance appeared in the persecution of unpopular groups such as Negroes, immigrants, abolitionists, and Catholics; and in hot resentment of unfavorable criticism. But we find these unattractive qualities in some of the countries that have became independent since World War II, as also in those with ancient traditions.

Nor was distinction wanting in a country that produced in one generation Clay, Jackson, Calhoun, and Webster; Poe, Bryant, and Washington Irving; and in the next, Emerson, Longfellow, Whitman, Lee, and Lincoln. There was merely a lack of those differences in dress, manner, and mode of living by which Europeans were accustomed to recognize the distinguished person. Clerks dressed almost as well as their employers, and factory girls copied the latest Paris fashions. Scarcity of good servants, since Americans regarded domestic service as a badge of inferiority, made it impossible for all but the wealthiest to keep up a large establishment. Young married couples in the cities often had to live in a hotel or boarding house for lack of "help" to perform the heavy domestic tasks that modern gadgets have to some extent superseded.

It was America's busy age, or one of them. Eighteenth-century travelers scolded Americans for their indolence; nineteenth-century travelers criticized their activity. Each Northern community was an anthill, intensely active within and constantly exchanging with other hills. Every man worked, or at least made a semblance of it; the few who wished to be idle and could afford it, fled to Europe and dabbled in the arts or pursued some pallid branch of scholarship — the type of American expatriate immortalized by Henry James. Nothing struck European travelers more forcibly than the total want of public parks and pleasure resorts, of games and sports, or of simple pleasures like country walking. For the Northern American had not learned how to employ leisure. His pleasure came from doing; and as almost everyone worked for long hours six days a week, and (except in New Orleans) the Puritan sabbath prevailed, there was not much time for recreation, and very few holidays other than Thanksgiving (still confined to the Yankee area), Christmas, and the Glorious Fourth. Farmers enjoyed county fairs with their agricultural exhibits, trotting races, and sideshows. Country boys found time for shooting and fishing; Henry Thoreau in *Walden* remarked, "Almost every New England boy among my contemporaries shouldered a fowling-piece between the ages of ten and fourteen, and his hunting and fishing grounds were not limited, like the preserves of an English nobleman." But the average adult American regarded games as a waste of time. Oliver Wendell Holmes described the college students of 1832 as "soft-muscled, pasty-complectioned youth." Francis Parkman found it difficult to find a friend to go camping with him in the northern wilderness, and his classmates thought him odd to follow the Oregon trail. As early as 1840 there were informal sculling and 6- to 8-oar rowing races on the Schuylkill and in the Eastern harbors, and by college crews; rowing was the only competitive sport to be organized before the Civil War.

Country gentlemen both North and South, and many plain farmers too, took a deep interest in horse breeding, and horse racing was the most popular sport of this era. A memorable event on the turf was the running race on 27 May 1823 at Union Park, Long Island. Colonel William R. Johnson, the "Napoleon of the Turf," brought north from Virginia and Kentucky five horses to challenge nine-year-old Eclipse, descendant both of Diomed and Messenger, for the thoroughbred crown. Some 60,000 people viewed this race, in which four-year-old Sir Henry, by Sir Archie out of a daughter of Diomed, won the first four-mile heat, but lost the next two and the championship to Eclipse. At least $200,000 changed hands on this intersectional race, which was several times repeated in the next twenty years. Even more popular than running races were the harness races, trotters driven from a spindly sulky (four-wheeled at this era), a sport exclusively North American. Justin Morgan's breed dominated the trotting world, especially after it was crossed with that of the New York stallion Hambletonian, a famous name in American equine annals. He was foaled in 1849 in Orange County, New York, by Abdallah, grandson of Messenger, out of a lame mare. A farm hand bought Hambletonian and his dam for $125, and in 24 years made $300,000 in stud fees. Hambletonian blood revitalized the American quarter horse and is now considered the leading family in Standard Bred.[1] And the Morgan breed was still prominent. Ethan Allen, foaled in 1849, a descendant of Justin Morgan, won countless trotting races in the 1850's and reduced the mile record to 2:25½ in 1858. As early as 1856 there were 38 trotting courses of national repute in the Northern states, and five in the South; and every agricultural fair included a one-mile track where local sports tried the paces of their horses. "Never was such horseflesh as in those days on Long Island or in the City," wrote Walt Whitman. Folks look'd for spirit and mettle in a nag, not tame speed merely." In this era, too, we have the first American sporting books, by "Frank Forester" (H. W. Herbert) of New Jersey. His *Warwick Woodlands*, *Field Sports*, and *Horse and Horsemanship* have become classics.

1. Greyhound, who established a trotting harness record of 1:55¼ for the mile in 1938, came from four generations of Hambletonians, as did Adios Butler, who lowered the pacing record to 1:54⅗ in 1960.

The only completely professional sports of this era were cock-fighting and boxing. The *New York Herald* of 1850 devoted only two inches of small print, on an average, to "Sporting Intelligence," mostly local harness races and to such contests as: "A Rat Match, at no. 72 Prince Street will take place at 9 o'clock This Evening, for $50 a side, between Mr. Tibley's dog and John Walker's to kill 25 Rats each, against time." Boxing matches, a traditional Anglo-American sport, were also reported, but the "manly art" took a black eye in 1842 when two welterweights, Chris Lilly and Tom McCoy, fought 120 rounds with bare knuckles to a finish which involved the death of McCoy.

Respectable forms of public entertainment were the theater, the concert, and grand opera. There were choral societies in the larger cities, and German immigrants carried their love for Bach and Beethoven to the frontier; but apart from folk ballads, sentimental songs, and minstrel shows there was little native music.

Most famous of ballad singers were the Hutchinson quintet from New Hampshire, who toured the North and West for over thirty years. The Hutchinsons "packed 'em in" to hear jolly and sentimental songs, some of their own composition, and many with a definite antislavery slant. Every principal city had a stock company, and traveling companies brought theater to the smallest towns. Edwin Forrest of Philadelphia, William Warren of Boston, Junius Brutus Booth of Maryland and his sons Edwin and John Wilkes (the assassin) were the most famous American actors of this era. Charlotte Cushman, who graced the boards for forty years from 1835, was one of the most powerful actresses in tragic and melodramatic roles that America has ever produced. They frequently toured England; and the best English actors of the day, such as Charles Matthews, Edmund Kean, and William Macready, played to crowded houses in America. Cultural exchanges of this sort were not always happy. Kean was egged off the stage in Boston in 1825; Macready's friends countered by hissing Forrest's performance of *Macbeth* in London; and when Macready returned to New York in 1849 to act *Macbeth*, Forrest's partisans, mustered by "Captain Rynders" the Tammany brave, mobbed the theater, broke all the windows, battled a militia company, and the riot ended only after 22 people had been killed and the Astor Place Opera House completely gutted.

Although small-town "opry houses" seldom entertained grand opera, that art was imported. A company from Havana played Italian opera, including Verdi's *Ernani* and Bellini's *Norma* to crowded houses at the gas-lighted Howard Athenaeum in Boston for six consecutive weeks in the spring of 1847. Owing to old Puritan prejudice, almost every theater in New England was disguised under the name of "Museum" or "Athenaeum." So, too, was Phineas T. Barnum's American Museum of New York, a collection of oddities, freaks, fakes, and midgets, including the famous "General Tom Thumb." Barnum was the impresario for the concert tour of Jenny Lind, "The Swedish Nightingale," in 1850.

Another form of entertainment was the panorama, a painting on continuous strips of cloth arranged around a circular auditorium. John Rowson Smith, a painter of theatrical scenery in Philadelphia, made a panorama of Burning Moscow which, accompanied by bells, cannon shots, and explosions, thrilled audiences throughout the country. John Banvard traveled up and down the Mississippi to paint a panorama of the Father of Waters which was shown all over the United States and Great Britain. Benjamin Russell, a self-taught painter of New Bedford, sailed around the world in a whaleship between 1841 and 1845, making notes; and the quarter-mile panorama which he and a local house painter produced on muslin not only has considerable artistic merit but is a precious document for the ships and seaports of that era. During the infancy of photography, panoramas had an enormous vogue and were never wholly superseded until colored moving pictures were invented.

American cooking at this period was generally bad, and the diet worse. Senator Beveridge of Indiana once described to me the breakfasting habits of the people in his native village before the Civil War. Shortly after dawn the men might be seen issuing from their cabins and houses, converging on the village butcher's, where each purchased a beefsteak cut from an animal slaughtered the previous evening. Coming and going, they stopped at the village store for a dram of corn whisky. Returning, their wives prepared a breakfast of black coffee, fried beefsteak, and hot cornbread.

This regimen, and lack of outdoor exercise, made the "females" of this period somewhat "delicate"; and the robust constitutions of frontiersmen were undermined by fevers and agues, particularly in the river bottoms or alluvial plains of the Mississippi and its tributaries. "We was sick every fall regular," reminisced the mother of President Garfield. Medicine was still relatively primitive, and a lad who wanted a good medical education had to go to Austria or France, where Louis Pasteur was beginning the experiments which founded the science of bacteriology. Nobody knew how to cure tuberculosis, diphtheria, or a dozen other diseases; cholera, typhus, and yellow fever killed thousands of adults, and puerperal fever thousands of mothers every year, but nobody knew what to do about them. Dr. Oliver Wendell Holmes did indeed anticipate bacteriology by his paper on the causes of puerperal fever in 1842, but most obstetricians considered him a quack. A few other Americans at this period made notable contributions to medical knowledge. Dr. William W. Gerhard of Philadelphia made a careful study of cerebral meningitis in 1834 and, three years later, first distinguished typhus from typhoid fever; but he could not cure either. In searching for some better anesthetic than the old method of getting the patient dead drunk, Dr. Crawford W. Long of Georgia in 1842 and Dr. William T. G. Morton of Massachusetts in 1846, successfully applied ether, with gratifying effects on the alleviation of human suffering. On the whole, the quality of American physicians declined after 1830, owing to small, inefficient private schools of medicine supplanting the old apprentice system of training, and a complete lack of medical regulation, despite the efforts of the American Medical Association, founded in 1847.

Since America has become as famous for plumbing as for liberty, it is astonishing to find how little progress had been made in sanitary engineering before the Civil War. The lack of city water systems, and a crude system of sewers were responsible. Philadelphia, generally reckoned the cleanest North American city, set up the Fairmount waterworks, pumping water from the Schuylkill river with wooden pipes bored out of solid logs, as early as 1801; it was gradually improved to a point when, in 1830, six million gallons could be delivered daily. Low-lying New Orleans followed, of necessity, in 1833. But New York City did not complete her Croton aqueduct until 1842, and prior to the present century the principal city reservoir was on the site of the Public Library at Fifth Avenue and 42nd Street. Boston tapped Lake Cochituate, whose water was introduced with a great display of fountains in the Frog Pond in 1848. Until a town or city obtained municipal water, residents drew their supplies for cooking and drinking from wells in their back yards (cozily adjacent to the privies), or from rainwater cisterns which were breeding places for mosquitoes, or patronized tank wagons which peddled country water from door to door. Boston's four-story Tremont House, built in 1829 of native granite in the Greek revival style, with columns, capitals, and other details faithfully copied from James Stuart's *Antiquities of Attica*, had numerous public rooms and private parlors, 170 guest rooms, and eight "bathing rooms" in the basement, supplied with cold water only from rainwater cisterns. The Tremont House's rival for "America's best hotel" was the Astor House in City Hall Square in New York, built in 1836. This had 309 guest rooms and was the first building to have running water laid on above the ground floor. Chicago, owing to difficulty of drainage, had practically no plumbing until 1861. In towns and cities, waste water from baths and sinks was commonly discharged into adjacent street gutters.

The worst pests in this era of cesspools, manure piles, and the like were flies, mosquitoes, and other insect life. Although "wire cloth" had been made since the end of the previous century, and housewives used sieves made of it, not until after the Civil War did the better houses get window screens. Cotton mosquito net was commonly draped over four-poster beds in summer, but the only way to keep flies from the food was to cover everything and wave a fan over the table.

The humble watercloset, which European humorists consider an emblem of American civilization, came in slowly, and only where city water and sewerage made it possible. Boston, with a population of 165,000 in 1857, had only 6500 W.C.s of which eight, in the basement of the Tremont House, served 200 to 300 guests. New York City had 10,384 W.C.s but only 1361 set bathtubs in 1855, when the population was 630,000. At that time, very few American bathrooms had hot water laid on. The standard bathtub was a wooden box lined with copper or zinc, filled with water brought up in buckets from the kitchen stove.

Central heating was rare, even in the cities. About a million "parlor stoves" in thousands of different designs were manufactured in 1860; but many large houses were still heated by wood or coal in open fireplaces, inadequate to keep interior plumbing from freezing in zero weather. Foreigners traveling in America, who now complain of being roasted by steam heat in winter and chilled by air-conditioning in summer, in those days could never keep warm in winter or cool in summer. Cooking stoves were being improved, but all used coal and wood fuel. Illuminating gas was fairly common by 1860 — 337 cities and towns in the North and 44 in the South had it piped in from central plants using coal fuel. Whale-oil lamps and tallow or spermaceti candles were universally used in country districts, and in many city houses as well, since the gas was both smelly and dangerous. Successful drilling of mineral oil wells in Pennsylvania, starting in 1859, led to a brisk development of kerosene for lighting purposes.

All in all, the United States was a pretty crude country in 1850 by present standards, or European standards of that era. Yet, with all their drawbacks, the Northern and Western states were a land where dreams of youth came true; where the vast majority of men were doing what they wished to do, without restraint by class or administration. "We were hardly conscious of the existence of a government," wrote a Scandinavian immigrant in New York. The fun of building, inventing, creating, in an atmosphere where one man's success did not mean another's failure, gave American life that peculiar gusto that Walt Whitman caught in his poetry. Half the population were engaged in realizing the ambition of frustrated peasant ancestors for a farm of their very own, clear of rent. The other half, having achieved the farm, had tired of it; and like the boy who loses interest in his completed toy boat, had turned to some other occupation or taken up pioneering again.

2. Land and Sea Transportation

The westward movement recovered momentum after the hard times of 1837–41. New Englanders, who a generation before had settled the interior of New York and Ohio, now pressed into the smaller prairies of Indiana and Illinois, where the tough sod taxed their strength but repaid it with bountiful crops of grain; where shoulder-high prairie grass afforded rich pasturage for cattle, and groves of buckeye, oak, walnut, and hickory furnished wood and timber. A favorite objective for Yankee settlement was southern Michigan, a rolling country of "oak openings," where stately trees stood well spaced as in a park. Others were hewing farms from the forests of southern Wisconsin, and venturing across the Missisippi into land vacated by Black Hawk's warriors — to Minnesota and

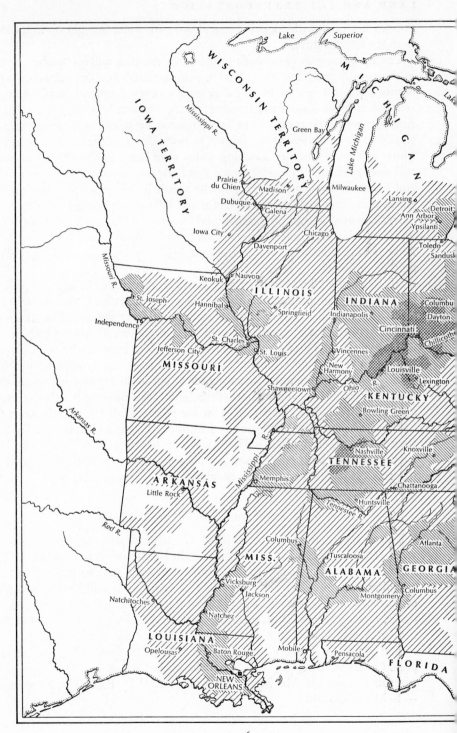

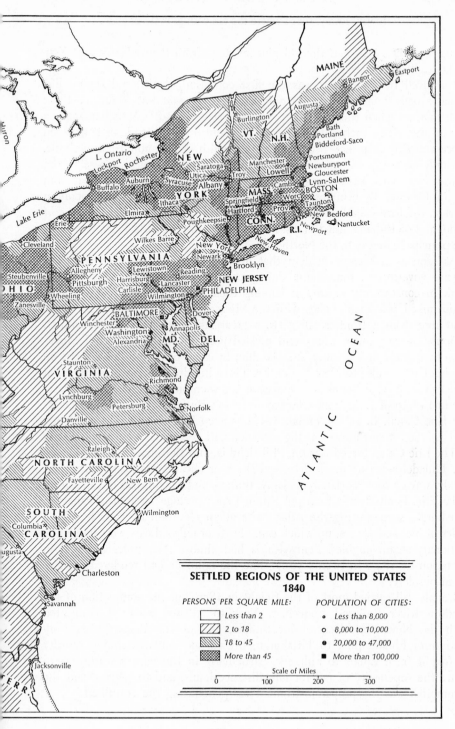

SETTLED REGIONS OF THE UNITED STATES
1840

PERSONS PER SQUARE MILE:

- Less than 2
- 2 to 18
- 18 to 45
- More than 45

POPULATION OF CITIES:

- Less than 8,000
- 8,000 to 10,000
- 20,000 to 47,000
- More than 100,000

Scale of Miles

0   100   200   300

477

Ioway, Ioway, that's where the tall corn grows!

German immigrants, and the old pioneer stock from Pennsylvania and Kentucky swelled the stream.

Improved transportation was the first condition of this quickening life. Canals, roads, and railroads not only took people west but connected them with markets when they got there. In 1826, when Charles Vaughan made a trip on the newly opened Erie Canal, the country on each side of it between Utica and Rochester had been cleared to a width of not more than one mile. Yet only next year the governor of Georgia was complaining that wheat from central New York was being sold at Savannah more cheaply than wheat from central Georgia. By bringing the Great Lakes within reach of a metropolitan market, the Erie Canal opened up the hitherto neglected northern regions of Ohio, and of Indiana and Illinois. At the same time it made New York City the principal gateway to the Northwest.

As soon as it became evident that no help could be expected from the federal government for internal improvements, other states followed New York in constructing canals, or lending their credit to canal corporations. Ohio linked the Great Lakes with the Mississippi valley in 1833–34. Cleveland rose from a frontier village to a great lake port by 1850; Cincinnati (population 115,000 in 1850) sent pickled pork down the Ohio and Mississippi by flatboat and steamer, shipped flour by canal boat, and drove cattle on the hoof 1000 miles to New York City. Three hundred lake vessels arrived at Chicago in 1833, although its population was then only 350. Three years later the first cargo of grain from Chicago arrived at Buffalo for trans-shipment by the Erie Canal. In 1856 Chicago was connected by railway with New York, and by 1860 it was almost as big as Cincinnati and about to pass St. Louis.

The Erie Canal forced Boston, Philadelphia, and Baltimore into rival activity. Philadelphia was shocked to find that her cheapest route to Pittsburgh was by way of New York City, Albany, Buffalo, and wagon road or canal from Lake Erie. Pennsylvania then put through the "portage" system of canals to Pittsburgh, surmounting the Alleghenies at an elevation of 2300 feet by a series of inclined planes, up which canal boats or railroad cars were hauled by stationary steam engines. Pennsylvania had almost 1000 miles of canal in operation by 1840. In twenty years' time the railroads had rendered most of them obsolete.

Canals still carried most of the freight in 1850, but the completion of the Hudson River Railroad from New York to Albany, where it connected with the New York Central for Buffalo, and of the Pennsylvania Railroad from Philadelphia to Pittsburgh, caused such an astounding transfer of freight from canals to railroads, particularly in the winter season, as to prove the superiority of rail for long-distance hauls, and to suggest that the locomotive was the proper instrument for penetrating the continent.

America, the first country to make practical use of steam navigation, lagged behind England in applying steam to the deep-sea merchant marine. The wooden paddlewheel steamboat was an ideal type for rivers, or for protected tidal waters like Long Island Sound and Chesapeake Bay, but the ocean steamer was born in the tempestuous waters about the British Isles. American shipbuilders concentrated their skill and energy on sailing vessels, which largely captured the freight and passenger traffic between Liverpool and New York. "The reason will be evident to anyone who will walk through the docks at Liverpool," wrote an Englishman in 1824. "He will see the American ships, long, sharp built, beautifully painted and rigged, and remarkable for their fine appearance and white canvas. He will see the English vessels, short, round and dirty, resembling great black tubs." The former were the flash packets of the American marine, the famous Swallow Tail and Black Ball liners, that were driven by their dandy captains, bucko mates, and Liverpool Irish crews, across the Western Ocean, winter and summer, blow high blow low, in little more than half the average time taken by the British vessels.

THE BLACK BALL LINE

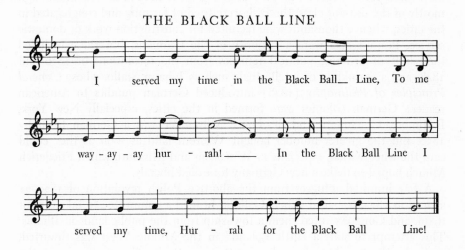

I served my time in the Black Ball Line, To me way - ay - ay hur - rah! In the Black Ball Line I served my time, Hur - rah for the Black Ball Line!

3. Immigration

Canal and railway construction created a demand for cheap labor, and made it easier for people to reach the West. During the decade of the 1820's, only 129,000 "alien passengers" entered the United States from foreign countries; in the 1830's the number swelled to 540,000, of whom 44 per cent were Irish, 30 per cent German, and 15 per cent English; this figure was almost tripled for the 1840's, and rose to 2,814,554 for the 1850's. Roughly half of the immigrants from 1840 were Irish, with Germans a close second.[1]

Liverpool, Le Havre, and Hamburg were the principal ports of embarkation. European governments attempted without much success to mitigate the hardships of the passage by requiring a minimum of space, rations, and decent treatment on shipboard. Congress did not legislate on the subject until 1855; prior to that neither the federal nor the state governments attempted to protect the immigrant. Many arrived penniless, having exhausted their savings on the journey; and those who did not, often fell prey to waterfront sharpers. But, as soon as they recovered their shore legs, the immigrants were well able to defend themselves. As early as 1835 we hear of Irishmen driving the Whigs from the polls in New York, and putting the mayor and sheriff's posse to flight with showers of "Irish confetti," — brickbats. Despite the dark picture of suffering, homesickness, and difficult adjustment painted in those days by Charles Dickens, and in ours by Oscar Handlin, most of the newcomers prospered and helped their friends and relatives to come over.

All but a small fraction of the newcomers landed in seaports between Boston and Baltimore, and remained in the northern half of the country. Irish immigration reached its peak after the great famine of 1846. Although mostly of the peasant class, the Irish were tired of farming and congregated in the cities, whence thousands were recruited for construction work or domestic service. Peasant also were a majority of the Germans, but these included thousands of artisans, political refugees from the revolutions of 1830 and 1848, and a sprinkling of intellectuals such as Johann Stallo, whose *General Principles of Philosophy* (1848) introduced German pundits to American readers. German colonies were formed in the cities, especially New York, Baltimore, Cincinnati, and St. Louis; Milwaukee was a German town by 1850. But the greater number bought Western land as soon as they could earn the wherewithal, especially in Wisconsin and Missouri, which Friederich Münch hoped to make a new Germany for exiled liberals.

A few hundred refugees from the abortive Polish revolution of 1830–31 arrived in 1834, the aged Albert Gallatin headed a committee to take care of them, and Congress voted them a township from the public lands in Illinois. This attempt to start a "little Poland" in the Middle West was thwarted, partly by the hostility of nearby squatters, partly by dissensions among the Poles themselves. But this settlement did start Polish emigration to America; "Big Mike" Goldwasser, grandfather of Senator Goldwater, was one who came over in 1848.

Sloop *Restaurationen*, which sailed from Stavanger in 1825 with 53 pilgrims from the northern kingdoms, was the Scandinavian *Mayflower*. Her passen-

1. To appreciate what this influx meant, the total population of the United States in millions was 9.6 in 1820, 12.9 in 1830, 17 in 1840, 23.2 in 1850, and 31.5 in 1860. The number of immigrants arriving in the 1930's was only 699,315, when the total population rose to 131.7 million.

gers, bound for western New York, were precursors of many thousands who before the Civil War settled among the forests and lakes of Wisconsin and Minnesota, similar to those of their native land; and many more followed.

Almost every immigrant of the period 1820–60 came from northern Europe. They were naturalized, and those in the cities became Jackson Democrats, largely because the politicians of that party were the first to cultivate them, to see that they got jobs, and to help them when in trouble. This wave of immigration enhanced the wealth and progress of the country, yet encountered bitter opposition, as did Asiatics half a century later. Sudden influxes of foreigners with strange ways and attitudes always do that, everywhere. In part, the antagonism was religious, since most of the Irish and many of the Germans were Roman Catholics. In part it was due to the widespread belief among native Americans that the immigrants were paupers. It is true that European authorities, in order to relieve their taxpayers, paid for thousands of their poor to go to the United States, and some of these became public charges the moment they landed. The greater number of immigrants, however, only wanted an opportunity to work; but their need for work was so desperate that they cut wages at a time when native-born mechanics were trying to raise their standard of living through the labor unions. Natives often refused to work with the newcomers. In the depression of 1837–40, wages for common laborers fell to between 50 and 75 cents a day. "A dollar a day is a white man's pay" was an ideal rather than a fact. The only people who took much interest in the immigrants were the contractors who used their labor, the politicians who wanted their votes, and the priests who preferred ghetto-like isolation for their flocks as protection from Protestant influence. Irish immigrants of the first generation comprised 34 per cent of all voters in New York City in 1855. Yet they added surprisingly little to American economic life, and almost nothing to American intellectual life. The reform movements of the age met the determined opposition of the Irish Catholic population of the cities. Their hostility to abolitionists and hatred of free Negroes became proverbial; and as the Democratic party swung into that attitude, Irish loyalty to the party of Jackson became firmer. German immigrants, even though a majority were Catholics, took the same position as native Americans on all reform issues except Prohibition. The German refused to give up his beer; instead, he made Milwaukee famous.

Protestant Irish fitted easily into American communities because they were free from the influence of the Catholic clergy, most of whose leaders had been afraid of liberalism since the French Revolution. The Irish-American press not only reflected this hostility, but expressed it in the angry tones of Dublin journalism. Orestes Brownson, a New England reformer who became a Catholic convert, attempted to acquaint Irish Catholics with the main currents of American thought but gave it up in despair. Father Isaac Hecker, converted like Brownson after a brief flirtation with transcendentalism, made a successful bridge to the German immigrants; but he became posthumously the center of a conflict within the church, in which his ideas, very similar to those of Pope John XXIII, were repudiated by Leo XIII.

Ugly racial and religious riots arose in the Eastern cities at least once every decade. These were not only the result of inherited "no popery," but also of Irish provocation. The American states had accorded to Catholic immigrants complete religious and political liberty, far more than Spain and several other Catholic countries have accorded Protestants to this day. Native-born Americans disliked having their heads broken by the "bhoys" when they attempted to vote Whig in the cities, and resented Catholic agitation against the use of the King James Bible in the public schools. The Irish, on the other hand, resented having Protestant-slanted textbooks crammed down their children's throats, and regarded as Protestant bigotry the understandable reluctance of employers to give "genteel" jobs to newly arrived uncouth peasants.

In 1843, nativist resentment against immigrants, mostly Irish in the East and German in the West, boiled over into politics. A shortlived "American Republican party" was founded, pledged to obtain a new naturalization law requiring a residence of 21 years. In the midst of this agitation occurred the worst religious riot of the century in the "City of Brotherly Love."

The Philadelphia school board in 1843 conceded the Catholic bishop's reasonable request that pupils of his faith be allowed to use the Douay version of the Bible, and be exempted from other religious exercises. This sparked a campaign of vilification — "The Pope reigns in Philadelphia," etc. — by local anti-Catholics and their weekly newspaper. In the spring municipal election of 1844, "American Republican" voters were assaulted and driven from the polls in Irish Catholic districts. This and other incidents aroused the "Americans," who around 1 May provocatively held mass meetings in the heart of Kensington, the principal Irish district. They were driven out with clubs, stones, and shots, one of which killed a Protestant boy. The "Americans" rallied, advanced armed into Kensington, and burned down about thirty houses, together with St. Michael's and St. Augustine's churches. Some 200 Irish families were rendered homeless, militia had to be called out to restore order, and rioting again flared when the "Americans" staged an anti-Catholic parade. A third Catholic church was then attacked, and bluejackets from U.S.S. *Princeton* helped the militia to defend the church and disperse the rioters. Order finally was restored, but casualties in the two sets of riots amounted to 30 killed and 150 wounded.

These riots had the effect of discrediting the "American Republicans" as "church burners," and the movement went underground, except in Baltimore. That lusty, growing city, which had acquired a sinister reputation for mobbing as early as 1812, was dominated on the low level by white native American workmen, who were equally hostile to Negroes and to the Irish, and intimidated Irish Catholics from voting. Edgar Allan Poe died a victim to Baltimore political practices. Arriving from Richmond by steamer just before the fall election of 1849, in a state of advanced inebriation, he was seized and hustled into one of the "coops," where local Whig politicians kept down-and-outs "on ice" for repeated voting. He was rescued after five days' detention, but in such condition that he died in a hospital.

4. Manufacturing

New methods of transportation not only helped to people the North and West; by extending the domestic market they hastened industrialization, and attracted rural boys and girls to urban communities. Between 1820 and 1850 the combined population of New York, Philadelphia, Baltimore, and Boston rose from 343,000 to 1,162,000. During the 1840's the population of the United States went up 36 per cent, but the growth of towns and cities of 8000 or more people showed a phenomenal 90 per cent increase. Measured by numbers, the urban movement was stronger than westward migration; and its effect on the American character has been equally important.

The factory system for cotton spinning and weaving became firmly established in New England as a result of the War of 1812. In Europe, textile machinery destroyed domestic industries in which the worker owned his tools and implements; but in America there was so little domestic weaving that the factory was introduced without friction. By 1840 there were 1200 cotton factories in the United States, operating 2,250,000 spindles, two-thirds of them in New England. Ring or frame spinning had been invented, power looms were being manufactured in large numbers, and even exported.

Francis C. Lowell, inventor of the first American power loom, was a man of social vision. At Robert Owen's model town in Scotland, he learned to run a factory without degrading labor. Farmers' daughters were attracted to the new factory city of Lowell, Massachusetts, by relatively high wages; the scruples of their parents were overcome by the provision of strictly chaperoned boarding-houses. For a generation the Lowell factory girls, with their neat dresses, correct deportment, and literary weekly, were one of the wonders of America. Never, unfortunately, were they typical of America; but, owing to wide opportunities in a rapidly developing country, no permanent proletariat was created. Factory girls left the mills to marry after three or four years, and child laborers elsewhere usually managed to find some other occupation by the time they reached their majority.

Woolen manufactures developed more slowly, and although protected by higher tariff schedules than those of cotton, were less successful in capturing the domestic market. Lawrence, Massachusetts, a woolen counterpart to Lowell, was established on the same river in 1845. Rhode Island, with Woonsocket and Pawtucket, became another important textile center. By 1850 there were over 1500 woolen mills in the Northern states; most of them small, individually owned establishments with a few sets of machinery, employing country people of the neighborhood, and producing blankets, flannel, and coarse worsteds.

In England the industrial revolution depended largely on coal and iron, but not in the United States. Textile and other mills were operated largely by water power, and the iron industry developed very slowly. Suitable coal for coking was not found east of the Appalachians, and Pennsylvanian ironmasters were more skillful in obtaining tariff protection than in improving their methods. Cort's puddling process, invented in 1783, was not introduced to America until 1830, and then on a small scale. Even Pittsburgh, "the Birmingham of America," used charcoal for smelting prior to 1840, rather than the bituminous coal which was plentiful in the neighborhood. American production of pig iron, only 54,000 tons in 1810, increased tenfold in 40 years; but by 1850 Great Britain's production was almost 3 million tons, and the United States was importing iron and steel to almost twice the value of the domestic product. Almost every waterfall in Connecticut was harnessed to a small factory for making machine tools, firearms, furniture (the famous Hitchcock chairs), wooden clocks, and all manner of oddments. Connecticut tin ware and wooden ware were carried by Yankee peddlers far and wide; and one of the standard jokes of this era was the Yankee peddler who sold wooden nutmegs and basswood hams to unsuspecting Southerners.

Most American industries developed locally, as a result of some person's enterprise, but others were imported directly from Europe. The pottery towns of England, for instance, sent scores of entrepreneurs and thousands of potters to various towns of the Middle West, where clay suitable for making domestic crockery was found. Viticulture was begun by Nicholas Longworth of Cincinnati, who after much experimentation settled on the native Catawba grape as a base; and by 1830 wine making had become a leading industry of southwestern Ohio. Although Longworth and his compeers never succeeded in making America a nation of wine drinkers, their enterprise extended profitably into central New York, and eventually to California. And the introduction of American *porte-greffes*, grafted vine stalks, rescued European vineyards from the devastation of the phylloxera rot in the last third of the century.

The most important American industry that remained in the domestic stage until after the Civil War was boot and shoe making, for which no machine process of any importance had been invented. In New England it was a winter occupation of farmers and fishermen who, when the harvest was gathered or the vessel hauled out for the winter, formed a "crew" to make shoes in a neighborhood workshop, from stock put out by some local merchant. Every man was master of his own time, and had something to fall back on when demand slackened; there was no clatter of machinery to drown discussion. A boy was often hired to read to the workers. It was said that "Every Lynn shoemaker was fit to be a United States Senator"; and Henry Wilson, "the cordwainer of Natick," became Vice President.

The Empire State, Citadel of Democracy

1820-1860

1. New York State and City in Mid-Century

THE DEMOCRATIC PARTY's solidarity from 1828 to 1860 to a great extent was the work of the New York wing. From Martin Van Buren's up-state machine the "Albany Regency," and Tammany Hall in New York City, emanated the political methods and tactics that were copied by both parties throughout the Union, as well as the objectives that held Democrats together. In New York, too, lived most of the few intellectuals who supported the party with brain and pen.

The "Empire State" — a sobriquet which at this time replaced the plain old "York State" — was justly so called. With 1,372,812 inhabitants in 1820, New York, which had been one of the smaller states at the time of the Revolution, reached first place. And she held that distinction through all subsequent censuses, although probably passed by California in 1964. In 1880 New York was the first state to count more than 5 million inhabitants; in 1920, first to have more than 10 million; in 1951, first to reach 15 million; and in 1960, still first with 16.8 million. Between 1830 and 1860 New York contained about one-seventh of the population of the United States, which made her electoral vote top prize in a presidential contest. And a galaxy of brilliant politicians exploited this advantage to the full.

New York City, first in the United States since 1820, grew even faster than the state, partly because of the Western commerce that came to it via river, and railroad, but also through the skill of its financiers and merchants in handling Southern and European trade. President Jackson, in his war on the Bank of the United States, was not trying to build up Wall Street at the expense of Chestnut Street, Philadelphia; but that is precisely what he accomplished. An ambitious state program of public works created thousands of jobs and attracted hordes of immigrants, especially Irish. There were 343,000 Irish-born in New York State in 1850, thrice the number of the next nationality, the Germans. Most of them stayed in or near the city, but many settled along the line of the Erie Canal, for the digging of which they supplied much of the labor.

The city's increase in population was phenomenal; there has been nothing like it since, even in California. It passed the 100,000 mark about 1815;

300,000 in 1840; and in 1850 counted 515,547 souls, to which should be added 96,838 living in Brooklyn. The 1960 population was 7,781,984. New York City was a bustling metropolis with no distinction except that of its magnificent site and harbor. The masts of squareriggers at the wharves topped the highest buildings, except a few church steeples; City Hall was the finest structure; shops and office buildings with cast-iron fronts and frames, precursors of the steel skyscraper, were just beginning to rise, and A. T. Stewart's, the first big department store, was opened in 1845 on Broadway between Read and Chambers Streets. At the time the city had only one restaurant, Delmonico's at 2 South William Street, but plenty of "eating-houses." Visiting foreigners admired the monuments of Baltimore, the rows of imposing stone public buildings in Philadelphia, the lush gardens of New Orleans, and the literary society of Boston; but they found nothing to praise in New York except the bustle.

The built-up part of Manhattan extended only to 14th Street in 1820, and to 42nd Street in 1850. Everything north of 44th Street was then country; Edgar Allan Poe and his wife boarded with a farmer at Broadway and 84th Street in 1844 and lived in a cottage at the rural village of Fordham in 1846. Central Park was laid out in 1856, just in time to save that rocky central spine of Manhattan for the people. Downtown New York had no public parks, only a few open squares restricted to residents.

Fortunes were being accumulated by the Astors and others simply by holding onto real estate in a growing city; and also by the bankers, merchants, and shipbuilders. The New York Yacht Club, founded in 1844, put on a "voyage" to Newport under Commodore Stevens that year. New York society was easygoing and flexible in comparison with the top social circles of Boston, Philadelphia, Baltimore, and Charleston. As a cultural center, however, the city fell short of her competitors, largely for want of institutions of higher education. Columbia University, the only college in the city until 1831 when New York University was founded, graduated on an average only 24 bachelors of arts each year between 1835 and the Civil War; N.Y.U. added a bare 21 to the list, and Fordham a few more after 1841. New York business men, unlike those of other cities, did not send their sons to college. The boys went straight into business from school or read law by the apprentice system in a lawyer's office, or attended a medical school or theological seminary. People raising money for New England and Western colleges never bothered to apply to the rich men of New York; it was no use.

An integral part of the American political picture from 1820 to the present has been the "foreign vote," that of recent immigrants and their children. After manhood suffrage went into effect in New York in 1827, Tammany Hall developed a system of recruiting aliens, in contrast to the indifferent or hostile attitude of Federalists and Whigs. Immigrants, especially the Irish, were met at the dock, assisted in finding jobs, and rushed through naturalization, sometimes in a few days, although five years were required by federal law. Chief hatchet man of "The Wigwam" (Tammany Hall) was "Captain" Isaiah Rynders, a former New Orleans gambler of uncertain origin. His henchmen were mostly Irish — John Morrissey, a popular prizefighter; "Honest John" Kelly, "Slippery Dick" Connolly, and "Mike" Walsh.

Saloons and volunteer fire companies, social organizations such as the "chowder and marching clubs," were organized by Democratic politicians. By 1855 over 300 of the city's 1100 policemen were Irish. The immigrants were slow to obtain clerical positions for want of education (New York's schools were unable to keep up with the flow of newcomers); and not until after the Civil War were any appreciable number of them elected alderman or state assemblyman. Immigrants in general gave their votes for the satisfaction of immediate needs — shelter, jobs, relief, and friendship. An alliance between urban politicians, the underworld of gambling and prostitution, and the foreign vote was already cemented in 1850.

In New York State at large, especially along the colonial highway of the Hudson river and in western Long Island, descendants of Dutch colonists were still the ruling class, socially and financially. Martin Van Buren, though not of the elite, attracted a large part of it, including the Livingstons and Roosevelts, into his party. But in the great seaport and the interior, the Yankees, as Washington Irving wrote in his delightful *Knickerbocker's History*, were still disproving the ancient adage that a rolling stone gathers no moss. Merchants and shipowners, with a keen scent for new opportunities, deserted decaying seaports of New England for New York City. Farmers for whom the hills of New Hampshire and Vermont offered little attraction, flocked into the Mohawk valley to provide a body of thrifty husbandmen and a top layer of ambitious citizens eager for a chance to get rich from a country store or bank, handling produce, selling land, floating stock of a canal or turnpike company. These were the men who broke the rural, semi-feudal pattern of the Dutch patroons. As early as 1840 one-quarter of the population of the state, and two-thirds in New York City, were engaged in trades and manufacturing; mostly in small, widely scattered establishments run by water power.

Albany was the upstate metropolis as well as the capital; Rochester, Schenectady, Syracuse, Utica, and Buffalo had not yet caught up. A few miles from Albany lay Saratoga Springs, the leading American spa, with enormous firetrap hotels where for a modest room-and-board of two dollars a day you could meet everybody who was anybody. Into Albany poured Hudson river steamboats and schooners, the railway that became (under Commodore Vanderbilt's manipulation in the 1850's) the New York Central, and the Western Railroad from Boston which eventually the N.Y.C. swallowed. Westward-bound passengers crossed the Hudson by horsepower ferry in summer or sleigh in winter, and there entrained on a railroad which, with several changes took them to Buffalo, the gateway through which freight and people streamed westward. By 1845 almost 100,000 westward-bound people were passing annually through Buffalo.

Upstate New York, owing to the predominantly New England population, was well provided with secondary academies and colleges. As people pushed up the Mohawk valley, Protestant sects saw to it that they obtained the proper facilities. Union College at Schenectady (Presbyterian) came early under the presidency of a celebrated academic czar the Reverend Eliphalet Nott, who outlasted all critics and hung up an all-time record of 62 years for a college presidential term. Hamilton College (Congregationalist) at Clinton was founded in 1812; Hobart (Episcopalian) at Geneva in 1826, Colgate (Baptist) at Hamilton in 1835, the University of Rochester (Baptist) in 1850. These were denominational colleges of the familiar New England pattern, which in time developed into non-sectarian universities. New York's most original contribution to higher education was Rensselaer Polytechnic Institute, founded at Troy in 1824. This was the precursor of M.I.T., California Tech, and a host of engineering and technical universities. It was at Rensselaer that Amos Eaton, an expert botanist and geologist who had studied under Benjamin Silliman at Yale, initiated scientific training by individual laboratory work and field trips.

2. The Albany Regency and National Party Organization

Martin Van Buren was not only responsible for bringing order, discipline and cohesion to the forces that followed the Jackson banner; he may be considered the principal architect of the modern American political party. When he entered the United States Senate in 1821 he left control of New York politics in charge of a coterie of his friends who were first known as the "Holy Alliance," and then as the "Albany Regency." With uncanny instinct for a winner, Van Buren won them for Andrew Jackson in 1824, and they became the backbone of the new Democratic party.

All members of the "Regency" were transplanted New Englanders; the most important being William L. Marcy who, when defending Van Buren in the United States Senate, added to our political vocabulary by stating that he could see "nothing wrong in the rule that to the victor belongs the spoils of the enemy." John A. Dix, Silas Wright "the Cato of the Senate," a confidant of Van Buren as Van had been of Jackson; Benjamin Franklin Butler, Van Buren's law partner,[1] and Samuel A. Talcott, editor of the Regency's mouthpiece, the Albany *Argus*, were also of New England origin. These were not faceless local "pols," but well-educated, public-spirited men of character. Their views on social and economic questions varied between left center and extreme right, but they agreed that the Democratic party in New York must

1. Jackson's attorney general and secretary of war, not to be confused with the Civil War general and Massachusetts politician (1818–93) of the same name.

be a united center party. This they effected by a system of rewards and punishments, through control of the state senate and so (under the constitution of 1821) of appointive offices. They extended their organization into every town and county, which afforded them an unparalleled political intelligence service. By supporting winning presidential candidates in 1828, 1832, and 1836, they got a stranglehold on the federal patronage as well. Van Buren and his friends, regarding themselves as champions of "the people" against "special interests," advocated making former appointive offices elective since they could select the candidates in party conventions. They honestly believed that "the people," to prevail against organized wealth, must be led by bosses and kept in line by the spoils system.

The Albany Regency was embarrassed by Jackson's war on the Bank of the United States, which upstate Democrats interpreted as a war on all paper-issuing banks, and insistence on hard-money currency. That did not suit the city financiers at all; they were delighted with Jackson's downing the Philadelphia bank, but a prohibition on issuing bank notes would have spoiled the juicy prospect of making Wall Street the nation's financial center. Democratic politicians, fearing lest their new friends the city bankers go Whig, resisted the upstate hard-money program. The result was a temporary schism in Democratic ranks. And in 1835 there was a radical rebellion in the usually solid Tammany organization over the subject of "monopolies," as the dissidents called chartered turnpikes, railroads, banks, and manufacturing corporations. The rebels had the majority in a nominating caucus but the regulars turned off the gas. Undaunted, the rebels found candles, struck a light with a new brand of safety match called "locofoco," and continued the meeting. They organized as the Equal Rights party, won the support of the *Evening Post* while editor Bryant was in Europe, and drew up their own slate of candidates. Playing the political game according to the accepted rules, they dickered with Whigs and other possible allies for mutual exchange of endorsements. That was one reason why the thirty-seven-year-old Whig candidate William H. Seward was elected governor in 1838. But the "Locofocos," as their rivals named them, really wished to control the Democratic party in order to establish hard money, abolish charter privileges, and enforce strict accountability of representatives to their constituents. Believing they were in line with national Democratic policies, they sought to organize on a state-wide basis, taking in a local third party called the Workingmen's, which wanted free schools and other reforms.

Despite these internal stresses between doctrinaire radicals and the expedient, anything-to-win politicians, the New York Democratic party held together well enough to give Van Buren the state's electoral votes for president in 1837. After his election the President, by a judicious use of patronage, pulled the dissidents back into regularity, undercut the Locofocos, and apparently restored the former solidarity. But in 1842 the Democrats split again over the issue of expanding the state canal network by public loans. The two wings of the party, the conservative "Hunkers" and the radical "Barnburners" (as the Locofocos were now called) became clearly defined. In 1845 the latter, disappointed because President Polk gave none of them a cabinet office, moved toward the Free-Soil opposition, which attained national importance in 1848.

The Albany Regency's political system in New York spread throughout the Union, although issues differed from state to state. Party organization in the Jackson era settled into a pattern that has changed little since. In contrast to its British prototype, which exists normally on the one level for electing members of Parliament, the American party existed in three layers, federal, state, and municipal. Analysis of the Whig and Democratic parties and their successors reveals a bundle of local, sectional, and class interests. Their cross sections, instead of displaying a few simple colors, were a jigsaw puzzle of radicalism and conservatism, nationalism and state rights, personal loyalties and local issues. Party strategy was directed toward accumulating as many bundles as possible, and statesmanship was the art of finding some person or principle common to all factions that would make them sink their differences and in union find strength.

Constitutional developments in the states were quickly reflected in the national party organizations. State constitutional changes between 1830 and 1850, in most instances effected by constitutional conventions and popular referendums, tended toward government of, for, and by the people. Religious tests and property qualifications for office were swept away, and manhood suffrage adopted. The newer state constitutions, beginning with that of Mississippi in 1832, transferred many offices from the appointive to the elective class. County officials such as sheriffs and justices of the peace, heads of executive departments such as state treasurer and attorney general, even judges of the higher courts, were henceforth elected by the people; and the democratic principle of rotation limited both the number and the length of their terms. As the urban movement gathered volume, new municipalities with elective mayors and bicameral city councils were established. Political partisanship extended down from the federal to the state and municipal governments: a good Democrat would no more think of voting for a Whig governor or a Whig sheriff than for a Whig congressman or President. Federal, state, and local politics were so closely articulated that the misconduct of a state treasurer might turn a presidential election, and the attitude of a President on the tariff or the public lands might embarrass his party's candidates for municipal office. State legislatures consumed much time in drafting resolutions on federal subjects outside their competence, for the purpose of attracting voters and influencing Congress.

The convention method of nominating candidates for elective office, if not invented by the Albany Regency, was perfected by it, spread nation-wide, and was adopted by the Whigs. Local caucuses sent delegates to county conventions which nominated candidates for county offices and elected the delegates to state conventions for nominating state candidates, and to district conventions for nominating congressional candidates. State conventions chose delegates to the quadrennial national convention for nominating presidential candidates and drafting the platform. Few but professional politicians managed to survive these successive winnowings. Every state had its captains of tens, hundreds, and thousands working for the party every day in the year, and looking for reward to the spoils of victory. Annual or biennial state and local elections kept interest from flagging during a presidential term, and were regarded as portents of the next general election. Innumerable local rallies, often synchronized with an anniversary, a county fair, or a barbecue, gave the leaders an occasion for inspiring the faithful, "spellbinding" the doubtful, and confounding the enemy. Steamboats and railways now carried political orators long distances without undue expenditure of time, enabling them to speak in many parts of the country. In 1840, for instance, Senator Rives of Virginia addressed a vast outdoor gathering at Auburn, New York, for three and a half hours, after which Legaré of South Carolina carried on for two and a half hours more. Clay addressed 12,000 men in a tobacco factory, Webster stumped from Vermont to Virginia, attracting audiences of 15,000. On one occasion, so many favorite sons preceded Webster at an evening rally that he did not come on until 2:00 a.m.; he talked for over an hour, "and you could have heard a pin drop," the audience was so entranced. Seargent Prentiss, whom many regarded as the greatest American orator, in the same campaign made speeches in Portland, New Orleans, Chicago, and fifty other places.

This was a good system for socially democratic regions where politics still offered the most attractive career to talented and ambitious men, and where the people, for want of other diversions, took a keen interest in government. Men like Abraham Lincoln rose through the caucus and convention to heights that they could hardly have attained otherwise. But in the cities and manufacturing districts of the North, and wherever social inequality prevailed, property went in search of political power and the politicians in search of property. The multiplicity of elective offices and the spoils system led to corruption. The rough-and-tumble of politics repelled good men from public life, and the civil service was degraded in America when it was improving in England. As Emerson jotted in his Journal in 1845 after the election of Polk, the Whigs, "The real life and strength of the American people, find themselves paralyzed and defeated everywhere by the hordes of ignorant and deceivable natives and the armies of foreign voters who fill Pennsylvania, New York and New Orleans. . . . The creators of wealth, and conscientious, rational and responsible persons, . . . find themselves degraded into observers, and violently turned out of all share in the actions and counsels of the nation." Yet these political methods, insofar as they aroused the active interest of the average voter and stimulated party loyalty, strengthened the Federal Union. They brought humble men forward and rewarded ability.

3. The Anti-Rent War

Most political parties start radical but turn conservative after they reach power. This principle is well illustrated by the Democratic party in New York. It took a popular rebellion and a constitutional convention to bring about a reform which should have been dealt with in the early years of the Republic.

Rensselaerswyck and Livingston Manor on the Hudson, covering respectively 24 by 48 miles and 10 by 18 miles of good agricultural land, as well as smaller manors like Scarsdale, Pelham, and Fordham which covered most of Westchester County, were the principal targets. Land in these manors was not held by the occupants in absolute ownership but by perpetual lease from the lord of the manor, in return for a bewildering variety of feudal dues. These were more irksome than onerous — such as ten bushels of wheat per 100 acres, one day's labor of a man and yoke of oxen and, inevitably, "four fat hens." (One wonders what the Van Rensselaers and Livingstons did with so many hens, lacking deep freeze.) The really burdensome thing to the tenant was "quarter money." This meant that if he sold out, at least 25 per cent of the sum he received went to the landlord. And the tenant paid state and local taxes, and for all improvements to his farm. From time to time popular discontent with these outmoded charges broke out in local riots; but the influence of the old families was still so pervasive that nothing was done about it until the death of Stephen Van Rensselaer, "the last patroon," in 1839. That sparked off a rebellion. As a contemporary ballad puts it,

> A great revolution has happened of late,
> And the pride-fallen landlord laments his sad fate;
> The cry has gone out through the nine counties o'er,
> Our landlord is falling to rise nevermore.

Since America became independent, Van Rensselaer had let out the hitherto untilled part of his enormous domain to thousands of immigrants from New England and elsewhere, on the same old feudal terms. But he had been so easygoing about collecting the rent that at the time of his death the tenants owed his estate some hundreds of thousands of dollars and about a million fat hens; and when the Patroon's sons tried to collect, trouble arose. Farmers in the western, hilly part of Albany County forcibly resisted the serving of writs. Governor Seward called out the militia and put down the embattled farmers by force. He did appoint a commission to look into the whole matter; but before it reported, the "anti-rent war," as these disturbances were called, broke out in the Livingston and other manors.

These affairs usually took the form of men crudely disguised as Indians [1] who tarred, feathered, or otherwise maltreated sheriffs when trying to serve

1. J. Fenimore Cooper's sneers at these "Injins" and vents his indignation over the anti-rent movement in his novel *The Redskins*.

writs for overdue rent. The New York legislature, on recommendation of Seward's Democratic successor Governor Silas Wright, passed a law punishing men who appeared in disguise carrying arms. After a body of 200 "Injins" in Delaware County had opened fire on a sheriff's posse and killed one of his deputies, the governor declared that county to be in "a state of insurrection." Sixty of the rebels were imprisoned, and two of them convicted of murder. Next, a convention of anti-rent delegates from eleven counties was held at Berne, birthplace of the movement; a weekly paper, *The Anti-Renter,* was published at Albany; ballads were written and songbooks published, and candidates for the state assembly were required to declare themselves pro- or anti-rent. The issue was thus forced into politics; but the politicians cannily passed the buck to the state constitutional convention of 1846.

This convention, to which a majority of Democrats, but no leading politician, was elected, drafted a new and democratic constitution. All judges were to be popularly elected for definite terms, white adult male suffrage was adopted, one-year terms for assemblymen and two years for state senators were set. On the anti-rent question, the bill of rights was augmented by declaring "feudal tenures of every description with all their incidents to be abolished"; and, "no lease or grant of agricultural land for a longer period than twelve years" should thereafter be legal.

Actually, the system was already on the way out, because the anti-rent agitation had forced most landlords to cancel or modify their leases. But the constitutional convention of 1846 put a seal on the process, leaving the Province of Quebec the only place in North America where feudal dues and services persisted. Henceforth the Van Rensselaers and Livingstons had to raise their own poultry.

The New York Whigs, despite their respect for vested rights, showed more sympathy for the anti-renters than did the Democrats. Walt Whitman, editor of the Democratic *Brooklyn Eagle,* denounced the anti-renters as a "violent faction which had disgraced the state." The Whig candidate for governor, said Walt, was counting on the spirit of rebellion to win. "Let the people judge," he added smugly, "whether the Indians shall again raise their fiendish cries." The Whigs won, nevertheless. The reason for this party line is clear. Democratic politicians, who once had been radical, were now trying to shake off the curse. Since the Whigs liked to accuse them of flirting with various "isms," they were eager to appear respectable and conservative, so that the Democratic party could pose as the nation-wide defender of the Union and of Property. In this aim they were very successful until a fire that they were unable to quench — antislavery — blew them apart.

In the Democratic state convention of 1847 a so-called "cornerstone resolution" expressing "uncompromising hostility" to slavery extension was adopted. That really split the party, causing the formation of the Free-Soilers, whose presidential nomination was accepted by Van Buren, smarting from his defeat by "dark horse" Polk. David Dudley Field, who drafted this cornerstone resolution, was one of the party's reformers. Almost singlehanded he carried on against the New York bench and bar (notably against Chancellor Kent) a campaign for codification of the common law. This reform, which Daniel Webster called "the wildest and weakest argument of the age," was conceived as a protection of the people from lawyers. Field's code of civil procedure, rejected by New York, was adopted in whole or part by 24 states; and since (as has well been said), substantive law has been "gradually secreted in the interstices of procedure," Field may be considered one of the great law reformers of the century.

4. *The Intellectuals*

In New York State, American democracy found most of its intellectual supporters. Van Buren appointed as secretary of the navy James Kirke Paulding, who had done more than anyone except Washington Irving to make popular the traditions and folkways of the old Dutch. Although Irving never pretended to be a Democrat, President Jackson gave him his first diplomatic appointment, secretary of the American legation in London, where he was already famous for his *Sketch Book* and *Life of Columbus*. Irving met Van Buren in London, and they became lifelong friends; in return for the author's introducing him to English country life, Van Buren took him on a two-week tour of the Hudson valley in 1833, to gather more Dutch legends. But Irving "ratted" on the Democrats after he had become a country gentleman near Tarrytown, and accepted an appointment by President Tyler as minister to Spain. Nominally a Democrat, J. Fenimore Cooper, after returning from Europe in 1833 devoted himself to berating democratic aspects of American life. He continued to produce novels, but became as stodgy and contemptuous of the American scene as Irving.

The most fruitful of President Van Buren's diplomatic ventures was to send John Lloyd Stephens, a New York lawyer and Tammany Hall orator, on a somewhat hazy mission to the Federal Republic of Central America. Intrigued by previous hints from Europeans of jungle-covered ruins, Stephens traveled in company with an English artist named Frederick Catherwood, to sketch them. The *Incidents of Travel in Central America, Chiapas, and Yucatán*, which they published jointly in 1841, introduced Palenque, Chichen Itzá, Copan, Uxmal, and other forgotten Mayan cities to an astonished world, and founded the science of American archaeology.

Nathaniel P. Willis, who wrote, "The shadows lay along Broadway, 'Twas near the twilight tide," was one of thirty or more poets who lived in New York City. They formed little self-conscious coteries, oases of culture in a desert of commerce, meeting at a bookshop on the corner of Broadway and Pine Street. The most famous, Fitz-Greene Halleck, is remembered for his lyric "Marco Bozzaris." But he also wrote mildly amusing satires on city politics and society. Halleck and his pals would have been greatly astonished to learn that the fame of one whom they never recognized as a poet has outlasted them all. This was Clement C. Moore, professor of Hebrew and Greek at the General Theological Seminary, forever famous for the poem that he tossed off at Christmastide 1821:

'Twas the night before Christmas, and all through the house . . .

Santa Claus, hitherto a tutelary deity of the New York Dutch, reached every child in America through that poem. Moore's other claim to fame is his success in procuring a Columbia College professorship in Italian for Lorenzo da Ponte, a talented scamp from Venezia, who in his youth had written the librettos for Mozart's *Le Nozze di Figaro, Don Giovanni,* and *Cosi Fan Tutte.* Da Ponte may claim to have been the herald of Italian culture in North America; he taught the first classes on Dante at Columbia, promoted Italian opera, and, supported by other Italian immigrants who had made money, built the first opera house in New York in 1833. It was a dismal failure, and Da Ponte died poor and forgotten in 1838, wishing he had cast his lot in Athenian Paris rather than Boeotian New York.

All these people were on the fringe, as it were, of democratic culture in New York City. The core consisted of a series of literary periodicals of which the most notable was *The Literary World,* edited by Evert Augustus Duyckinck. He held a salon at 10 Clinton Place, where American writers whom he appreciated were welcomed and distinguished foreigners were entertained. Duyckinck, a fastidious gentleman, edited the best anthology of American literature published in the nineteenth century, and contributed to *The Democratic Review.* John Louis O'Sullivan, the editor of that monthly, coined the phrase "manifest destiny" in 1845, founded the "Young America" movement, and dedicated his periodical "to strike the hitherto silent string of the democratic genius of the age and the country." He and his contributors, whose names are now known only to graduate students writing dissertations on American literature, were a pretty sad lot. They were always shouting for a national literature free from contamination by decadent Europe; but whenever a writer of national scope appeared, such as Emerson, they failed to recognize him. They objected to Parkman's *Oregon Trail* because his Indians did not resemble Cooper's Indians, and sneered at Melville's *White Jacket* as manufactured for the English market by a traitor to his country.

The Whigs, too, had their organ, *The American Review,* which in 1845 thus challenged the Democrats: "If they want something really native, let them consider the Ethiopian Minstrels; let them hold up as the national symbol, Jim Crow." This really went home, for the minstrel show was a native folk art which blossomed in New York City out of Negro dancing, singing, and banjo-playing. After a New York "ham" actor named Thomas Rice had made an astounding success with his character "Jim Crow," Edwin P. Christy in 1842 put on the first full evening of his "Virginia Minstrels" in a pattern that endured into the twentieth century. In the first act the performers, most of them white men in blackface, sat in a semicircle around the interlocutor, a dignified colored gentleman in dress suit who acted both as master of ceremonies and butt for the jokes of the end men — "Mistah Tambo" who banged a tambourine, and "Mistah Bones" who rattled castanets. Besides repartee and horseplay, the cast played banjo melodies and sang comic or sentimental songs. The second act, known as the olio, included a "hoe-down" dance, comic parodies of grand opera, and a "walk-around," in which the players one by one took the center of the stage for individual songs or dances while the rest clapped time to the music. Minstrel shows were immensely popular. Christy's played continuously in New York City for nine years and made a triumphal tour of England; in the 1850's ten theaters were presenting minstrel shows in New York alone.

The Democratic literati despised the minstrel show as unworthy of "Young America"; but, though unable to comprehend Melville's *Mardi* or *Moby-Dick*, they inadvertently helped to launch him on a literary career. When Louis McLane accepted the London legation in 1845 to help President Polk solve the Oregon question, he was given as first secretary a young man from Albany named Gansevoort Melville, who was looked upon as the coming Democratic orator to rival Webster; and it was Gansevoort who sold *Typee*, the first book by his younger brother Herman, to a London publisher. Herman roamed the seas to very good purpose, when he might have been picking political plums in New York; and his masterpiece, *Moby Dick*, came out in 1851. No second edition was needed for over sixty years, and *Billy Budd*, now the basis for a movie, two plays, and an opera, he could never get published. He showed no interest in politics and received his first political appointment, that of a customs inspector on the New York wharves, after the Civil War.

William Cullen Bryant, whose position as America's greatest poet was disputed only by Poe (and in the next two decades by Longfellow), maintained a loose connection between the Democratic party and the intellectuals by virtue of his long editorship of the New York *Evening Post*. Bryant supported the workers' right to strike at a time when judges called strikes conspiracies, and endeavored to counteract Democracy's pro-slavery tendencies. He followed Van Buren into the Free-Soil party, returned to the fold with Franklin Pierce, but went Republican with Frémont. President Pierce obtained for his Bowdoin College classmate Nathaniel Hawthorne, in return for writing the campaign biography, two custom house jobs, the meager income from which enabled the "Locofoco surveyor," as he humorously described himself, to write *The Scarlet Letter*.

Almost every member of the Democratic literary coterie enjoyed at one period or another a clerkship in the New York Custom House, as reward for hewing to the party line. Thus the party "took care" of its intellectuals. But the attempt of these literati to create a democratic literature was a dismal failure; and when Walt Whitman, who had taken their admonitions to heart, published his first book, he got nothing from them but contumely.

Walt could have occurred nowhere else but in New York. He edited or contributed to twelve or fifteen different newspapers and magazines; he wandered through the streets of "the Manhatoes" and along the then deserted beaches of "Paumanok" (Long Island); he rubbed shoulders with wildcat journalists, reformers, Tammany braves, Irish workingmen, saloon keepers, ferryboat sailors, drunks, and bawds. Especially he loved the theater, for which this was a golden era in New York City; [1] and at Da Ponte's opera house he became fairly intoxicated with the "vocalism of sun-bright Italy." Walt's genius, applied to this hotchpot of experience, produced his *Leaves of Grass* (1855). After losing his job on the *Eagle* for refusing to follow the party line in 1848, Whitman became independent of clique or party; but always, after his brief attack on the anti-renters, on the side of "liberdad" and the "comerados" of equality and fraternity. For word pictures of mid-century New York there is nothing to compare with the poetry and prose of Walt Whitman. Take this, for instance, on the ferry-boats between Brooklyn and Manhattan:

The river and bay scenery, all about New York island, any time of a fine day — the hurrying, splashing sea tides — the changing panorama of steamers, all sizes, often a string of big ones outward bound to distant ports — the myriads of white-sailed schooners, sloops, skiffs, and the marvelously beautiful yachts — the majestic Sound boats as they rounded the Battery and came along toward 5, afternoon, eastward bound — the prospect off toward Staten Island, or down the Narrows, or the other way up the Hudson — what refreshment of spirit such sights and experiences gave me years ago (and many a time since).

5. *The Hudson River School of Painting*

Although the *Democratic Review* literati were pitifully unsuccessful in making New York the literary center of the nation, New York City, with no help from them, became the North American center of the fine arts. Colonel John Trumbull of Connecticut, painter of the famous "Declaration of Independence" and "Battle of Bunker Hill," established a pathetic little American Academy of Fine Arts in City Hall Square around 1817. This, after his death in 1843, was absorbed by the National Academy of Design founded by Trumbull's rival Samuel F. B. Morse. Thomas Sully remained faithful to Philadelphia, but other portrait painters, such as John Wesley Jarvis, came to New York where merchants and bankers were eager to immortalize their features in oil at $100 a head. As there were not enough of them to support an artist, Jarvis, like Sully, toured the South every winter, doing six portraits a week with the aid of an assistant. There was a sufficient number of American artists by 1834 to provide material for William Dunlap of New York to publish his *History of the Rise and Progress of the Arts of Design in the United States*. That book accomplished for early American fine arts what Vasari did for *cinquecento* Florence.

1. See Chapter XXX, above.

Hitherto the few American artists who went beyond portraits painted "edifying" scenes from the Bible and ancient history; anything but what they could see in their own country. But there presently arose in New York the Hudson River School of artists, first to paint American scenery with its violent contrasts, wild cataracts, brilliant autumn scenery, and long white beaches. Their instigators were Thomas Cole and Asher B. Durand.

Durand, an engraver from New Jersey, became teacher of painting at the National Academy of Design. Around 1825–30 he formed a "Sketch Club" with other local artists and the poet Bryant, who had already struck a keynote for the future in his *Thanatopisis:* — "Go forth, under the open sky, and list to Nature's teachings." Thomas Cole, English-born, emigrated to Philadelphia in order to see the "romantic" American scenery for which Shelley had yearned in vain. After years as an itinerant painter, doing portraits at $5 and $10 a head, he came to New York in 1825, visited the Catskills, and became a devotee of Hudson valley scenery. Cole persuaded Durand to drop the heroics and historicals and paint landscape. He too fell in love with American scenery and the Hudson River School was born.

Of other members of this school, one may name Frederick E. Church (Cole's favorite pupil) of Hartford; Christopher P. Cranch, who had connections with the New England transcendentalists; and George Inness of New Jersey, who studied for several years in France. Most of these men had studios in New York but traveled in search of subjects as far east as Mount Desert Island, Maine, and as far west as California. There were dozens of artists of this school, many of their names now unknown; but their paintings are now eagerly sought by galleries and collectors. From them it was but a step to Winslow Homer (who had his first drawing lessons at the National Academy of Design in the 1850's) and the great American painters of the second half of the century. But the spark came from Cole, Durand, and Bryant in New York.

Two New York organizations which did excellent missionary work for the fine arts were the Apollo Association, which became the American Art Union; and the International Art Union, founded in 1848, which acquired over 5000 subscribers in two years, imported annually over a hundred paintings, and sent them on a traveling exhibition to the principal American cities, including Chicago, Charleston, and New Orleans. After that they were raffled off to the subscribers. The American Art Union published a bulletin, the first American periodical devoted to the fine arts, and held annual exhibits of the work of American artists.

While the Hudson River School limned the wilder beauties of American scenery, Andrew Jackson Downing of Newburgh on the Hudson, son of a nurseryman from Lexington, Massachusetts, cultivated landscape architecture and the building of country estates. His *Treatise on Landscape Gardening* (1841) led to his being employed by President Fillmore to lay out the grounds of the Capitol, the White House, and the Smithsonian in Washington.

His *Architecture for Country Houses* (1850) dictated the designs of gentle-men's country residences for the next twenty or thirty years, long after he had perished in one of those tragic and not infrequent burnings of Hudson river steamboats.

Thus New York City, in spite of the absorption of leading citizens in politics and business, and the futility of its literati, became a real cultural center, and remained the principal center of the fine arts in America for another thirty or forty years.

All this proved to the satisfaction of Americans and the astonishment of foreigners that the finer things of life could be attained in a democratic medium, even though the general trend of democracy was toward uniformity and mediocrity.

THE ERIE CANAL

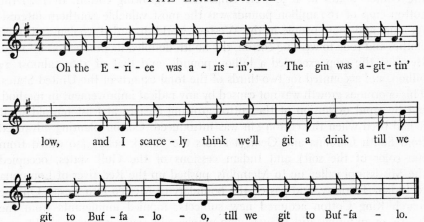

Oh the E - ri - ee was a - ris - in', ___ The gin was a-git-tin'
low, and I scarce - ly think we'll git a drink till we
git to Buf - fa - lo - o, till we git to Buf-fa - lo.

The Southern States

1820-1850

1. *The Cotton Kingdom*

COTTON WAS KING in the South from 1815 to 1861; and the principal bulwark of his throne was Negro slavery. Almost 60 per cent of the slaves in the United States in 1850 were employed in growing cotton. In 1820 the cotton crop of 160 million pounds was the most valuable Southern interest. As more and more people in the Western world discarded woolen and linen clothes and took to wearing cotton, the South doubled its production by 1830. By 1850 the crop exceeded a billion pounds, and that of 1860, almost 2⅓ billion, and accounted for two-thirds of the total exports of the United States. This enormous growth was not caused by any radical improvement in method, but by rapid expansion of the cotton-growing area to at least tenfold what it had been when the cotton gin was introduced. Cotton planting advanced from South Carolina and Georgia across the "black belts" (so called from the color of the soil) and Indian cessions of the Gulf states, occupied the Mississippi valley up to Memphis, pushed up the Red river of Louisiana to Indian Territory, and passed the boundary of Mexico into Texas. On the march King Cotton acquired new subjects: monied immigrants from the North, or ambitious dirt farmers who purchased a slave or two on credit, and with good luck became magnates. In every region fit for cotton, the richest lands were absorbed by plantations during the first generation of settlement. Hunter folk moved westward and poor whites closed in on the gullied hillsides and abandoned fields. Some of the best minds of the South endeavored to arrest this process by scientific methods of agriculture; but as long as good land remained plentiful and cheap, whether within the United States or adjacent under the feeble sovereignty of Mexico, the cotton growers preferred their old ways.

On a first-class plantation, with improved implements, healthy Negroes, strong mules, and a competent overseer, ten acres of cotton or corn could be cultivated per able-bodied field hand. On rich soil, with a proper division of labor, five bales (2000 pounds) or more of cotton per field hand could be produced; but a more nearly average figure, in the Carolina and Georgia piedmont, would be 1200 pounds. The average annual price of upland cotton at Liverpool fluctuated between 11 and 19 cents a pound from 1820 to 1840, fell to 8 cents in 1845–48, rose to 14 cents in 1850, and averaged about 12 cents until the Civil War. A planter was lucky to get half the Liverpool price for himself; the rest was consumed by transportation, brokerage, and interest on advances. One of the puzzles of the old Southern economy was its dependence on New York for money to move the cotton crop to market. Southerners frequently threatened to establish shipping lines and banks of their own; but the capital that might have done these things was poured into more land and more slaves.

Sugar planters of Louisiana and tobacco growers of Virginia and Kentucky were allies of the cotton kingdom. Border slave states acted as tributary provinces, supplying labor, food, and mules. Northern centers of banking, shipping, and manufacturing profited as the cotton kingdom prospered. North Carolina, where little cotton was grown, remained an enclave of antique republicanism in the new monarchy; western Virginia and the mountainous regions of Kentucky and Tennessee were Northern salients. Virginia, with a surplus of labor, could maintain her economy only through hiring out the surplus to tobacco factories and ironworks or selling it to the Lower South. The economic decrepitude of the Old Dominion was a spiritual loss to the nation. Once she had led American progressive thought and statesmanship; now she devoted herself to sustaining a hopeless cause.

Kentucky had the most varied agriculture of any slave state, and largely replaced Virginia as the home of the American Thoroughbred. The blue-grass country around Lexington, where limestone soil promoted bone and stamina, and nearby parts of Tennessee, were ideal for breeding blood horses. General Jackson started his stud as far back as 1806, and on his deathbed confessed that he regretted only two things; that no horse of his had ever beaten a Diomed filly named Haynie's Maria — and that he had not hanged John C. Calhoun! Boston, a chestnut sired by Timoleon, son of Sir Archie foaled in 1833, reigned king of the turf for nine years; he won 35 out of 38 two-, three-and four-mile races which he contested as far north as Long Island and as far south as Georgia, winning purses of $50,000 for his owners. Boston at stud produced blood-bay Lexington, the most famous American Thoroughbred prior to Man O'War, and a chestnut named Lecompte. These two sons of the same sire contested a race at New Orleans in 1854, the most brilliant event in prewar annals of the American turf. Lexington won, covering the four miles in 7:19¾, a record unbroken for 40 years. The Kentuckians "came back from New Orleans with a boatload of money," and Lexington, who had now gone blind, continued for 21 seasons to sire the fastest-running horses of the next generation.

The human thoroughbred of the plantation regime was the Southern gentleman. Although few in number, he ruled the older Southern states by virtue of his personality even more than his property, and governed them honorably and efficiently. States like Mississippi, which engaged in wildcat banking enterprises and repudiated debts, were under the control of middle-class and poorer planters, not the gentry. Discriminately hospitable, invariably gracious to women, endowed with a high sense of personal honor and civic virtue, the Southern aristocrat, had he not succumbed to democratic pressure, might have kept his beloved Southland from suffering one of the worst debacles in modern history. His way of life, as related in postwar memoirs and fluffed up by novelists, makes a sentimental appeal to a democratic age just as, in Europe, people like to read about France of the Old Regime or Victorian England.

Of this class, only a small fraction were descended from the colonial aristocracy. Washington's type appeared undiminished in his Lee kinsmen, the old Huguenot families of South Carolina had a large share in promoting Southern culture, and wealthy descendants of the French creoles of Louisiana were fairly numerous. But the mass of the wealthier planters, by 1860, were self-made men like Jefferson Davis, whose parents had lived in log cabins. If not well educated themselves, their sons and daughters would be.

One of the really great gentlemen of the Lower South was John Hampden Randolph, who in 1841 purchased a plantation in Iberville Parish, Louisiana, for $30,000 — the down payment being only $863. For several years he planted cotton, but by the time the debt was paid he turned to sugar, increased his land holdings to several thousand acres, and his labor force from 23 to 195 slaves. He maintained a resident physician to care for their health, employed white Arkansans to help process the sugar, and hired Irish immigrants to dig the drainage ditches. For his children's education he employed a Northern college graduate as tutor as well as itinerant music and dancing masters. The older boys entered the University of Virginia or Rensselaer Polytechnic, and the girls attended a fashionable school in Baltimore. In 1858 Randolph built the fifty-one-room mansion Nottoway which has successfully weathered a century. After the Civil War, with free Negro labor, his plantation proved to be more profitable than it had been with slaves, a thing that no Southerner before 1860 would have thought possible.

The average upper-class cotton or sugar plantation was not nearly as splendid as Randolph's. The mansion house, seated on rising ground, was usually a well-proportioned wooden building with a columned portico that gave dignity to the front elevation and afforded shade to the ground floor and first story. The rooms were high-studded and simply furnished. There were plenty of flowers and masses of native flowering shrubs and creepers, in which the Southland was rich. Simplicity rather than ostentation was the dominant note in the Southern gentleman's life. His recreations were largely field sports, but he enjoyed little leisure. On a Virginia plantation visited by Frederick Law Olmstead, not ten consecutive minutes elapsed, even during dinner, when the owner was not interrupted by a servant. He had to lock his stables every night as the alternative to finding his horses hagridden in the morning. Even if an overseer were employed to direct the field force, the owner's wife had to keep linen, silver, food, and household supplies under lock and key, serve out supplies with economy, and admonition with tact; had to bind up wounds and nurse the sick. Mrs. Ann R. Page of Virginia devoted her life to the welfare of her slaves, and when the property had to be divided after her husband's death, she prayed that none might fall into alien hands. Yet even Mrs. Page had to put up with late meals, tasks unfinished, and orders forgotten — to say nothing of the cockroaches, centipedes, and other insect life against which the Southern housewife waged perpetual war.

Such a life was a continuous exercise of tact, self-control and firmness; yet the condition of unlimited power over a race with exasperating habits was a constant temptation to passion. The Southern gentleman had the same conflicting character as an old regime Russian or Hungarian landlord. He could tolerate an amount of shirking and evasion that would drive any Northern or British employer frantic; but to cross his will, question his authority, or impugn his honor was to ask for serious trouble. The descendants of "Cavaliers" were so afraid of being thought afraid that they were apt to see insult where none was intended, and to respond in a manner that forced a fight. Governor John L. Wilson of South Carolina published a textbook on dueling in 1838, but most disputes between white men were settled by less honorable forms of conflict. Alexander H. Stephens, future vice president of the Confederacy, was unable to take part in a political campaign because he had been disabled by stabs received in an "affray" with Judge Cone. Items in the press such as the following are revealing:

The Hon. Edward P. Pitts, late state senator from Accomac Co., Va., was attacked by John C. Wise Esq. at a public vendue on December 27 last and horsewhipped by him. Mr. Wise was inflamed by a remark made by Pitts at a political meeting during a recent campaign, at which the Hon. James W. Custis knocked Mr. Wise off the stand, while speaking, for some disrespectful remark.

Although the gentry gave the tone to Southern white society, there were relatively few of them, probably not more than 15,000 families. The typical Southerner was a farmer who owned his land and buildings, and with his own labor and that of half a dozen slaves cultivated the cash crop — sugar, tobacco, or cotton — which seemed most profitable. He also raised cattle, swine, and a large part of his own food; and there were several hundred thousand Southern families who owned no slaves. These were the backbone of the country, who proved so difficult for Union armies to defeat. Small slave-owners and non-slaveholding yeomen lived in a double log cabin or bare frame house without conveniences, on a diet largely of "hog and hominy," read no literature but the Bible and a weekly paper, enjoyed no diversions but hunting, fishing, and visits to the county seat. Such people belonged to the governing class in Alabama, Mississippi, and Arkansas.

About half the cotton crop was made by those who owned from one to half a dozen slaves. Mark Twain describes "one of those little one-horse cotton plantations" in *Huckleberry Finn*:

A rail fence around a two-acre yard . . . big double log house for the white folks — hewed logs, with the chinks stopped up with mud or mortar, and these mud-stripes had been white-washed some time or another; round-log kitchen, with a big, broad, open but roofed passage joining it to the house; log smoke-house back of the kitchen; three little log nigger-cabins in a row t'other side the smoke-house . . . outside of the fence a garden and a water-melon patch; then the cotton fields begin; and after the fields, the woods.

Below these yeomen farmers came a class known as "pore white trash," "crackers," "peckerwoods," and other opprobrious nicknames. These dwellers on numerous antebellum "tobacco roads" constituted less than 10 per cent of the white population. They appear to have been largely frontiersmen stranded on worn-out land by the westward march of the cotton kingdom. A sallow, undernourished, and illiterate class, envious of successful white men and bitter haters of the Negro, their only pride was their color. Twentieth-century biologists, notably Charles W. Stiles, discovered that the principal causes of the poor whites' indolence were improper diet and the hookworm, which they contracted by going barefoot. Very different were the mountain men, the "hillbillies" who lived in the secluded valleys and on the steep slopes of the Appalachians and the Ozarks. These were a proud, upstanding, and inde-pendent people, expert hunters and fishermen, almost completely isolated from the rest of the South, which knew them only when they drove ox teams to market to sell moonshine whisky that they made in illicit stills, and the pork that they cured from acorn-fed pigs.

The white urban population of the South was small; fewer than 8 per cent lived in towns of over 4000 inhabitants. And small-town dwellers were so closely integrated with the plantation aristocracy as to exercise no liberal influence on public opinion, as the burghers of European towns had on feudal society. James L. Petigru, the leading lawyer of Charleston, "engaged in the ordinary and legitimate proceeding of investing his professional profits in a plantation and negroes," according to his contemporary biographer. "It was the approved Carolina custom in closing every kind of career. No matter how one might begin, as lawyer, physician, clergyman, mechanic, or merchant, he ended, if prosperous, as proprietor of a rice or cotton plantation."

2. Slavery and the Slave

Although cotton growing was the most profitable employment for slaves, slave labor was an uneconomical method of growing cotton. Once entangled in the system, no planter could escape it, and few wished to. Slaves were the only available labor for large-scale production, and slaves cost only $15 to $60 a year (according to various estimates), to keep; but the purchase absorbed a large amount of capital. The most expensive, a "prime field hand" 18 to 25 years old, was worth $500 in 1832 and $1300 just before the panic of 1837. The price of this class of slave reached $1800 on the eve of the Civil War.

Negro women on cotton plantations were such poor breeders that the labor supply had to be replenished by purchase, and the land was always wearing out; hence the profits that on a Northern farm would have been put into better buildings and equipment, in the South went into more land and more slaves. Even planters opulent in nominal wealth found it difficult to keep out of debt, and probably a majority of them depended on loans from cotton factors to carry them between crops.

What did the Negro himself think of this system? Here we have inferences that are poles apart. On the one hand (as stated by Jefferson Davis in his reply to Lincoln's Emancipation Proclamation), these "several millions of human beings of an inferior race" were "peaceful and contented laborers in their sphere." The pampered domestic servant, the happy, carefree, banjo-playing "darkey," theme of countless post-Civil War novels, were all that many upper-class travelers saw of the South's "peculiar institution," as her statesmen like to call it. On the other hand, it is the fashion for Negro intellectuals to describe their forebears as the most oppressed and exploited labor force in modern history, held down by fear and force, constantly striving for escape from slavery. It has often been said that the Negro understands the white man much better than the other way around; but it is also possible that the colored intellectual of the 1960's knows less about the plantation Negro of the 1840's than did many white masters of that era.

It should not be forgotten that the African slave trade began among the Negroes themselves in Africa; that to be reduced to slavery was a common expectation in the Dark Continent, and that victims of the system who were shipped to America, provided they survived the passage, were better off than those who remained in bondage in Africa; [1] better off, in fact, than many thousand poor workers and peasants in Europe. John Randolph's slave valet who accompanied his master to Ireland in 1827, "looked with horror upon the mud hovels and miserable food" of the Irish peasantry. But these "white slaves," as the scornful Virginian called them, could emigrate to America as free men; their sons could become congressmen and bishops, and their grandsons, governors and even President; whilst the great majority of Negroes in America were slaves, and their children were born into bondage, despite the proud statement in the Declaration of Independence, "All men are created equal." And their descendants are still struggling for equality.

The Negro was expedient. He accepted his slave status because he had to, and got as much fun out of life as he could, consoled by belief in a Heaven where no color line would be drawn. When converted to Christianity, he observed the parallel between his own bondage and that of the Israelites, and derived his most poignant spiritual hymns from the Book of Exodus. Owing to his capacity for hard work, in addition to his adaptive qualities and cheer-

1. Compare Saint-Exupéry's account in *Wind, Sand and Stars* (1939) of an old and useless slave being turned out into the desert by his Moslem master to die of starvation, around 1928.

ful spirit, the Negro made an excellent slave. He did not mope and die, like the Indians enslaved by the colonists, and his color prevented him from infiltrating his master's society as the Greeks and Asiatics enslaved by the Romans had done. Between him and his "white folks" there often developed mutual affection; and for the Southland itself he acquired so firm a love that it was long after the Civil War before any appreciable number would move to other places where they could enjoy more opportunity and encounter less prejudice.

Southern Negroes as a whole cannot fairly be described by sweeping generalizations. There were social gradations among them even before they landed. The social gap between a colored Virginian majordomo, whose ancestors had been American for two centuries, and a "Gullah" (Angola) Negro recently smuggled into South Carolina, was equal to that between prince and pauper in the Old World. Domestic slaves, the favored class, became completely assimilated to American civilization. Many an aged butler or nurse enjoyed a position similar to that of the household slaves one encounters in Greek and Roman literature. Negroes had an uncanny flair for recognizing "quality" or lack of it; their observations on the characters of young men who courted master's daughters were freely offered and often respected.

Field hands constituted the majority of slaves. A third and intermediate class were slaves who learned a trade such as carpenter, millwright, blacksmith, or barber; many of these were hired out by their masters and some were allowed to purchase their freedom out of their wages, but state laws made that increasingly difficult. Free Negroes were anathema to the whites; their "very virtues became objects of suspicion, and the instinct of [white] self-preservation would nip in the bud the first development of superior intellect," wrote in 1828 William Blackford, a public-spirited Virginian.

In the decade of the 1840s, slaves increased more than twice as fast as free Negroes. In antiquity, the Romans usually freed a talented slave, and in any case his progeny were free. But America offered no legal escape to the talented or intellectual Negro slave. It subjected a writer like Frederick Douglass or a born leader of men like Booker T. Washington to the caprice of a white owner who might be his inferior in every respect. And one drop of African blood made a person a Negro. Thirteen per cent of all Negroes in the United States in 1860 were mulattoes. The beautiful octoroons of New Orleans, equal in their profession to the most talented courtesans of old France, were bought and sold like field hands — but at far higher prices, and for a different purpose.

Whilst the average Englishman or free-state American disliked the Negro as such, Southern slave-owners understood and loved him as a slave; Southern gentlefolk still love him "in his place." There was no physical repulsion from color in the South. White children were suckled by black "mammies" and played with their children. In a stagecoach or railroad car, as a squeamish English visitor observed, "A lady makes no objection to ride next a fat Negro woman, even when the thermometer is at ninety degrees; provided always that her fellow travellers understand she is her property." In the treatment of field hands, there was an immense difference between one plantation and another. Olmsted passed a plantation in central Mississippi owned by a "very religious" lady who had the reputation of working her slaves from 3:30 every weekday morning until 9:00 at night, and alternately catechizing and whipping them every Sunday. A few days earlier, however, he had stayed with the jolly owner of twenty slaves who had "not been licked in five year," who taught one another to read, languidly swung master's hoes, and shared his dinner "right out of the same frying-pan." In every part of the South the small slave-owner worked side by side with his men in the field, and treated them like his own children, as indeed they sometimes were. But if he rose to planter's estate, that sort of thing became *infra dig*.

Flogging with a rawhide or blacksnake whip was the usual method of punishing slaves. Imprisonment lost the master their time, and short rations impaired their health. Most Southern towns had a public flogger with a regular tariff for laying on the number of lashes prescribed by the culprit's owner. Although the laws forbade cruelty, a master or overseer was not often brought to book for it, since even a free Negro's testimony was not received against a white man, and the feeling rose that for prestige reasons the white must be right. Severity pushed too far was apt to maim a slave or force him to run away, thus destroying or losing a valuable piece of property. Yet the most civilized communities today need societies for the prevention of cruelty to children and animals. It was an old plantation maxim, "Never threaten a Negro, or he will run." Consequently, little time elapsed between detection and a punishment which was not softened by reflection. Instances of sadistic cruelty to slaves are so numerous in the records that they cannot be dismissed as mere abolitionist propaganda. These were extreme cases; no doubt the majority of masters were kind and humane; but should not a system be judged by the extremes that it tolerates? May we not judge Hitler's regime by the gas chambers, or Stalin's by purges, forced-labor camps, and firing squads?

The feature of slavery that most outraged human sympathy was the separation of families by private sale or auction. The laws of two states forbade this, but only for children under ten. It was often asserted that Negroes had very slight family attachment; that Whittier's "Farewell of a Virginia Slave Mother," with its haunting refrain:

> Gone, gone, — sold and gone
> To the rice-swamps dank and lone,

was mere abolitionist cant. Yet, when a young Northerner asked Randolph of Roanoke, who had listened to the speeches of English and American statesmen, to name the greatest orator he had ever heard, the old Virginian snapped out: "A slave. She was a mother, and her rostrum was the auction-block."

The years 1822–32 are a watershed in the history of Southern ideas about slavery. Before that, the general attitude of the planter class was to apologize for slavery as a bad system they could not get rid of. Beginning around 1822 there was a gradual tightening up of the "black codes" in the slave states to keep the Negroes in order, and the defiant adoption of a theory that slavery was not only the one possible means of keeping Negroes subordinated, but a positive good in itself, sanctioned by the Bible.

The starting point for this change of sentiment was Denmark Vesey's insurrection at Charleston in 1822, the first serious one in the United States since colonial days. Vesey was a free Negro who enlisted slaves in an attempt to capture the city of Charleston, although what he intended to do if he succeeded is a mystery. Betrayed by one of the conspirators, who could not bear to kill a kind master, Vesey's revolt was nipped in the bud and thirty-seven Negroes were executed for participation. A system of control was then adopted in the lower South and gradually spread to Virginia and the border states. Negroes were forbidden to assemble or circulate after curfew, and nightly road patrols were set up. Whites were forbidden to teach slaves to read and write in every Southern state except Maryland, Kentucky, and Tennessee.

On the assumption that the majority of slaves were happy and contented, Vesey's and subsequent insurrections were blamed on outside agitators — as, after the two world wars, domestic discontents were blamed on communist agitation. In accordance with this theory, free colored sailors on Northern or European ships calling at Charleston or Savannah were by law haled ashore and confined to the local calaboose until the ship sailed. Justice William Johnson of the Supreme Court, a native of Charleston, ruled that this was unconstitutional,[1] but gave no relief to the imprisoned Negro plaintiff, and South Carolina successfully defied his dictum. A distinguished Massachusetts lawyer and former member of Congress sent to Charleston in 1844 to try to get the law relaxed (it being inconvenient for a shipmaster to have his colored cook impounded while in port), was accused by the South Carolina legislature of attempting to incite a slave insurrection, threatened with violence, and hustled on board ship.

A very serious insurrection took place in tidewater Virginia in 1831. A pious slave named Nat Turner enlisted a number of others who ran wild in August and killed 57 whites before they were rounded up, with the help of regular troops from Fortress Monroe and sailors from the navy. Between 40 and 100 Negroes were killed, and Turner was hanged. This outbreak was blamed by Southern opinion on William Lloyd Garrison's new abolitionist newspaper *The Liberator*, although there is not the slightest evidence that even one copy of it had reached any Southern Negro. Harrison Gray Otis, mayor of Boston where *The Liberator* was published, received an appeal from General Washington's niece, Mrs. Lawrence Lewis of Woodlawn, to suppress the paper. She gave an eloquent description of the terror created in Virginia: — "It is

1. *Elkison* v. *Deliesseline* (*U.S. Federal Cases*, No. 4366, p. 493).

like a smothered volcano — we know not when, or where, the flame will burst forth, but we know that death in the most repulsive forms awaits us." Otis answered that he had no power to suppress the journal, and that in his opinion any attempt to do so would drive moderate men "to make common cause with the fanatics." In a letter to a friend in Philadelphia he observed that nothing could satisfy the Southerners. "The force of opinion in favor of emancipation throughout the world must blow upon them like a perpetual tradewind, and keep them in a constant state of agitation and discomfort."

That is exactly what happened. Sentiment for the abolition of slavery was not brewed in the "obscure hole" (as Otis described it) where Garrison printed his "incendiary" sheet. Abolition had already gone far in England, where slave revolts in the West Indies had an effect contrary to that in the United States, creating a feeling that slavery must go, and soon. Under the leadership of Wilberforce and Clarkson, Parliament in 1833 passed an act emancipating all slaves in the British colonies, with compensation to their owners. The Second Republic did the same for the French Antilles in 1848. The Spanish American republics, starting with Argentina (1813), Central America (1824), and Mexico (1829), abolished slavery shortly after they became independent; and by the time President Ramón Castilla issued his emancipation proclamation for Peru in 1854, slavery was legal in the New World only in the Spanish and Dutch islands, the United States, and Brazil. Nevertheless the white South refused to admit that anything had to be done about it in the United States. Rufus King in 1825, Otis in 1832, Henry Clay in 1849, proposed gradual compensated emancipation financed by the sale of public lands, and removing the freedmen. These and other suggestions of the sort received only abuse in the South. Lincoln, as late as 1862, presented a gradual emancipation plan to the representatives of loyal slave states, with the bait of an appropriation of $100 million, but they would have none of it.

Every scheme for gradual emancipation, to be acceptable even in the border states, had to include a return of the freed slaves to Africa. This had been going on, in a small way, since 1817 when the American Colonization Society was founded. That society, supported largely by private contributions in Maryland, Virginia, and Kentucky, by 1855 had returned to Africa only 3600 Negroes. But its efforts had one concrete result, the Republic of Liberia which became independent in 1857 with a constitution patterned on that of the United States. Liberia attracted very little voluntary emigration, since the American Negroes had assimilated the civilization of their white masters and did not wish to return to Africa; and the return of hundreds of thousands of them to Africa against their will would have been disastrous to them and ruinous in cost. Any practical scheme of compensated emancipation would have left the Negroes on the spot, as had happened in the Northern states and British West Indies; and that was unacceptable to the white South.

Although there were no slave insurrections comparable to Nat Turner's during the next 30 years, it was the strict patrol and control system which prevented anything getting started. But a number of spontaneous and unsuccessful strikes for freedom were recorded in the Southern press. In 1845, for instance, about 75 unarmed slaves from southeastern Maryland attempted to fight their way through to Pennsylvania and freedom. They were rounded up about 20 miles north of Washington and shot, hanged, or sold "down the river." However docile the majority of slaves may have been, unrest was so widespread as to keep the master class in a constant state of apprehension. And evidence is wanting that any of these outbreaks were caused by Northern abolitionist influence.[1]

The cold war between pro- and antislavery was waged largely between white extremists on both sides. For thirty years the politicians of both political parties tried to ignore or suppress this conflict, or find some way to compromise. They failed utterly and completely, and emancipation was achieved the hard way, and in the worst way.

3. The Literature of Chivalry

A Southern chivalry tradition arose during the generation following 1820. Readers of Walter Scott's *Ivanhoe* and the flood of imitative literature that followed found a romantic mirror of their life and ideals. William A. Caruthers's novel *The Cavaliers of Virginia* (1832) set the tradition. Michel Chevalier, in his *Lettres sur l'Amérique du Nord* (1836) asserted that Northerners were descended from Cromwell's Roundheads, and Southerners from King Charles's Cavaliers; this explained their differences in a manner very comforting to the South. Every owner of two Negroes, however dubious his origin or squalid his existence, became a "cavalier," entitled to despise the low-bred shopkeepers, artisans, and clerks of the North. The rage to establish *Mayflower* or Knickerbocker ancestry in the North, fifty years later, was a compensation of the same sort for old families being crowded by immigrants.

To comprehend the Southern planter, we must remember that his social system was on the defensive against the rest of the civilized world. His com-

1. It is sometimes said that Virginia was within an ace of emancipation in 1831–32 when Garrison's intemperate attitude stiffened the slaveholders and defeated the movement. What actually happened is this: The Nat Turner insurrection aroused public opinion in two opposite directions: abolition, and a more stringent slave code. Some members of the old liberal families combined with western Virginians in the state legislature of 1831–32 to push for the principle of gradual emancipation. A committee to which petitions in that sense had been referred, reported that action thereon was inexpedient. W. B. Preston, a westerner, then moved, "It is expedient to adopt some legislative amendment for the abolition of slavery." This motion was defeated, 73 to 58; the ayes coming almost exclusively from members from the Shenandoah valley and the western counties. Subsequently, in January 1832, a bill was brought in for the colonization in Africa of free Negroes, and of such as might subsequently be freed by their owners. This passed the house, but was lost by a single vote in the senate. The assumption that this defeat was due to Garrison finds no support in contemporary reports of the debates.

mon sense, too, made him indifferent or hostile to the multiple "isms" which were trying to put all crooked ways straight in England and the Northern states. Just as New England in 1800 refused every quickening current from France or Virginia lest it bear the seeds of Jacobinism, so the South, a generation later, rejected literature and philosophy which might conceal abolition. The enthusiasm for compulsory free popular education that swept over the North hardly got under way in the South prior to the 1850's, when Calvin H. Wiley of North Carolina and William L. Yancey of Alabama began improvements that were interrupted by the Civil War. At that time, the percentage of illiteracy among native-born Southern whites was about 20 per cent, compared with 0.42 per cent among native-born New Englanders. The University of Virginia, which Jefferson had intended to be the crown of a free public school system, became instead the seminary of a privileged class. At a time when Bryant, Emerson, Longfellow, and Whittier were redeeming Northern materialism with cheerful song, Southern silence was broken only by the gloomy and romantic notes of Edgar Allan Poe. Stephen C. Foster, who attuned the beauty and pathos of the Old South to the human heart in "Uncle Ned," "Old Black Joe," and "My Old Kentucky Home," was a Pennsylvanian.

The intellectual barrenness of the antebellum South has been ascribed by her apologists to the want of urban centers where creative spirits could meet and talk, whence literature and the arts have usually sprung. There were at least five urban centers in the slave states bigger than Athens, Jerusalem, or Florence at their prime, yet none seemed capable of supporting a literary, artistic, or scientific group. William Gilmore Simms of Charleston, the most distinguished Southern man of letters, had to publish in New York the ten romances that he wrote between 1834 and 1842, including *The Yemassee*, one of the best American historical novels; and at a time when Northern men of letters had become shining figures in their communities, Simms went unrecognized in his. He wrote in 1858, "All that I have done has been poured to waste in Charleston." And his biographer wrote that a Southerner "had to think in certain grooves." These grooves were glorification of the Southern way of life, and defense of slavery. The abolition agitation, instead of making converts in the South, engendered a closing of minds. Not immediately, however; at least not in Virginia. In 1832 the Richmond *Enquirer* could still call slavery "a dark and growing evil"; but twenty-three years later, when it was still darker and still growing, the same newspaper was calling for a revival of the African slave trade.

Public criticism of slavery was suppressed in the South by the force of public opinion, even where laws were lacking. Mails from the North and England were examined and "purified" of any matter which might suggest to the slaves that they were not the world's happiest working people. Ministers, teachers, professional men, and politicians who would not bow down to

mumbo-jumbo were eliminated. Laws were even passed against criticism outside the South of Southern institutions, and a price was placed on the heads
of prominent abolitionists. Bishop Moore of Virginia, in conversation with
Dr. Daubeny of Oxford, "spoke of the certainty of an abolitionist being
lynched, not indeed as a thing he approved, but without any expression of
moral indignation."

Yet who are we, having lately weathered a hurricane of unreasoning intolerance to scorn the antebellum South? Southern whites were not by nature
less tolerant than their Northern counterparts whose attitude toward Catholics, Mormons, and other minorities we have had occasion to notice. The presence of Negro slavery subjected Southern white people to a constant emotional pressure which led them to do many wrong and foolish things. And the
result of their efforts to smother discussion is the strongest warning in all
American history against attempts to suppress free speech.

A positive proslavery theory of society, corresponding to the political doctrine of state rights, was provided by Thomas R. Dew, a bright young Virginian who returned from study in Germany to a chair at William and Mary
College. In pamphlet of 1832 he argued that slavery had been the fertilizer of
classical culture, that the Hebrew prophets and St. Paul admitted its moral
validity, that civilization required the many to work and the few to think.
George Fitzhugh, in a tract entitled, *Cannibals All!* argued that the Negro
was something less than human; and in his *Sociology for the South* provided a
new set of principles to replace the "glittering generalities" of a century of
enlightenment. John C. Calhoun gave proslavery doctrine the sanction of his
name and character, and so cunningly combined it with American preposses-
sions that slavery appeared no longer the antithesis but an essential condition
of democracy.

Calhoun began with the axiom that no wealthy or civilized society could
exist unless one portion of the community lived upon the labor of another.
White labor, class-conscious in England and enfranchised in the Northern
states, threatened property and civilization. Social stability could not be maintained where labor was free. It was too late to re-establish serfdom in Europe
or extend it to the North; but a beneficent providence had brought to the
South a race created by God to be hewers of wood and drawers of water for
His chosen people. In return, kind masters provided for all reasonable wants
of their slaves and saved them from the fear of misery and destitution that
haunted the white proletariat. The masters, themselves, relieved from manual
labor and sordid competition, would attain that intellectual and spiritual
eminence of which the founders of the Republic had dreamed. "Many in the
South once believed that slavery was a moral and political evil. That folly and
delusion are gone. We see it now in its true light, and regard it as the most
safe and stable basis for free institutions in the world."

This nonsense became orthodox in the South by 1850; but how wide or
deep it really went we shall never know. It was not accepted by the great

Virginians who fought so valiantly for the Confederacy.[1] There was no place in the system for the poor whites, from one of whom, Hinton R. Helper, came *The Impending Crisis* (1857), a prophecy of disaster which was suppressed. Calhoun, more humane than his doctrine, refused privately to condone the domestic slave trade, although he might publicly threaten that the South would secede rather than allow it to be excluded from Washington. Many non-slaveholding, illiterate whites disliked slavery, but they agreed with the planters that it would never do to emancipate the Negro, and fought bravely to maintain an institution that bore more heavily upon them than upon any other class.

4. Science and Religion

Scientific culture in the South followed in general the genial eighteenth-century tradition, exemplified by Jefferson, of liberally educated gentlemen pursuing natural science for their own amusement and edification. The South had many amateur botanists, mineralogists, and geologists who were intent on finding out more about the nature that they loved. John James Audubon, America's most popular naturalist, born in French Saint-Domingue, lived for a time in Louisiana and Kentucky. He ranged America from the Labrador to Texas in search of material; but he had to journey to London and Edinburgh to find a publisher for his famous *Birds of America*. Upon his return to America in 1831, Audubon met at Charleston the Reverend John Bachman, who helped him write *The Quadrupeds of North America*, his second classic. He was entertained by Dr. Edmund Ravenel, who had already become the leading American authority on shells, both living and fossil; and he may have met the Doctor's young cousin Henry W. Ravenel, who in 1853 would start publishing the first American work on fungi. A nearby Georgia planter, Louis Le Conte, maintained a botanical garden at his plantation, where his two famous sons John and Joseph were born. Edmund Ruffin published a work on soil chemistry in 1832 and kept up a continual agitation for better methods, which did much to bring back to fruitfulness the "old fields" of tidewater Virginia; but he was also a violent agitator for secession. Commander Matthew Fontaine Maury USN, also of Virginia, became the world's greatest oceanographer, charting the ocean winds and currents, and publishing *The Physical Geography of the Sea* (1855) which helped navigators to cut down the time and increase the safety of ocean voyages. This scientific achievement was the fairest cultural flower of the South before the Civil War.

Organized religion, which had declined in the South when that section was

1. Robert E. Lee emancipated the few slaves he inherited from his mother, and owned no others. Stonewall Jackson purchased two slaves at their own request, and allowed them to earn their freedom. J. E. Johnston and A. P. Hill never owned slaves and disliked slavery. J. E. B. Stuart owned but two slaves, and disposed of them, long before the war. M. F. Maury, who called slavery a "curse," never owned but one, a family servant.

liberal and antislavery, recovered after it became conservative and proslavery. The influence of the evangelical sects increased in proportion as their ministers claimed arguments for slavery in the Bible. The Catholic and Episcopalian churches remained neutral on the subject, and stationary in numbers. Thomas Jefferson, dying, saluted the rising sun of Unitarianism as destined to enlighten the South; but it sent only a few feeble rays beyond Baltimore. Horace Holley, the gifted young Unitarian who had made of Transylvania University in Kentucky a Southern Oxford, was driven from his post by Jackson Democrats and Presbyterians. Thomas Cooper, a chemist who had taken refuge in the South from persecutions under the Federalist Sedition Act, was forced to resign both from the University of Virginia and the College of South Carolina, as a Unitarian.

For a time the Protestant churches were a bond of union between North and South; but when in 1842 the Methodist Church insisted that a Southern bishop emancipate his slaves, the Southerners seceded and formed the Methodist Church South on a proslavery basis. The Baptists followed, and doubled their membership in fifteen years. While these Southern evangelicals defended slavery, they banned card-playing and dancing; by 1860 the neo-puritanism of the age was more prevalent in Alabama and Mississippi than in Massachusetts and Connecticut.

One religious manifestation that drew both sections and races together was the revival, or camp meeting, as it was generally called, because no one building was big enough to hold the crowds. These were equally popular with middle class and poor whites, and with the Negroes. The camp meeting and the "spirituals" that went with it gave people who led drab lives an outlet for their emotions. Despite all the fun poked at them by sophisticated sects, they did much to elevate the moral and religious tone of thousands of rural communities.

The years following 1831 were crucial for the future relations of the two major sections. In the United States the peaceful process of slave emancipation stopped with New Jersey's law of 1804. Why did not Americans follow the example of Britain's emancipation of 1833? One reason, doubtless, was the invention of the cotton gin, which made the cultivation of upland cotton by slaves immensely profitable. We can make that concession to economics; yet slavery seemed no less necessary to maintain the sugar industry of the West Indies. The difference in part was constitutional. The West Indian planter had no representatives in Parliament, where the abolitionists, gathering public opinion like a snowball, proved to be irresistible. Yet there was another factor in causing the South to dig in her heels and resist emancipation to the death — Jacksonian Democracy.

The old Federalist and Jeffersonian leaders in the South were well educated and thoughtful men, in close touch with English and European currents of thought. They looked forward to eventual emancipation of the slaves, and might have put it across, at least in Virginia and the Border states, but for the horrible example of the massacres that followed emancipation in Haiti. If they and their kind had been left in control of the Southern press, the legislatures and the congressional delegation, it is possible that gradual compensated emancipation would have been worked out. But the growth of democracy and the rise of the common man overwhelmed the old governing aristocracy (most of whose survivors went Whig) with a tide of provincial, ill-educated politicians who catered to the prejudices of the middle class and poor whites. Only a minority of the middle class, as we have seen, were slave-owners; but for the most part they were "nigger haters" who did not imagine it possible to keep Negroes in order except as slaves. This new race of Southern politicians, instead of preparing the South to face inevitable emancipation and seek a peaceful way out, flattered people into a fatal belief in the righteousness of slavery and their own ability to protect the "peculiar institution" perpetually. Southern policy then came to be based on two principles which were assumed to have divine sanction; (1) Negroes are an inferior race and must be kept subordinate, like children who cannot take care of themselves. (2) The only way to do this is to keep them in a slave status.

The second axiom was blown up at Appomattox. But the first, after the lapse of another century, is still believed by middle- and lower-class whites whom democracy has brought into power. And, at the time of writing, this dominant white South is displaying exactly the same ostrich-like attitude toward the world-wide movement for equality as its ancestors did toward the world-wide movement for emancipation.

MOBILE BAY

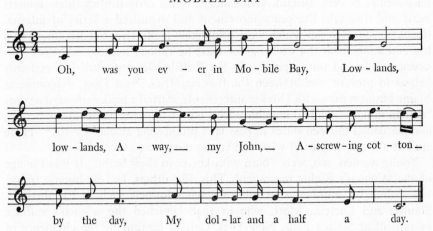

Oh, was you ev - er in Mo - bile Bay, Low - lands, low - lands, A - way,— my John,— A - screw - ing cot - ton by the day, My dol - lar and a half a day.

Ferment and Culture in the North

1820-1850

1. Reformers and Revivalists

"THE ANCIENT MANNERS were giving way. There grew a certain tenderness on the people, not before remarked," wrote Emerson of his America. "It seemed a war between intellect and affection; a crack in Nature, which split every church in Christendom. . . . The key to the period appeared to be that the mind had become aware of itself. . . . The young men were born with knives in their brain."

One of the young men was Thomas H. Gallaudet, son of a Philadelphia merchant, who studied the education of deaf-mutes under Abbé Sicard in Paris and, before he was thirty, established the first American school for the deaf at Hartford, Connecticut. Samuel Gridley Howe of Boston fought for Greek independence in his early twenties and returned with Michael Anagnos, one of his comrades in arms, to found the Perkins Institute for the Blind, a searchlight for those deprived of sight. Elihu Burritt, the "learned blacksmith" of New Britain, Connecticut, in his early thirties threw himself heart and soul into the peace movement and organized a series of international peace congresses which were completely ineffective; but his efforts in a less ambitious field, the exchange of what he called "friendly addresses" between people and municipalities in the British Isles and America, certainly helped to prevent war between the two countries. Neal Dow, a prominent Maine business man with Quaker antecedents, started a brisk campaign against "demon rum," which had tangible effects on the drinking habits of the people, and persuaded thirteen states to pass laws prohibiting alcohol by 1857. These are but a few examples of what the young men were accomplishing.

Young women, too, were "born with knives in their brain." It was the age of the Women's Rights movement. This, like others, had its lunatic fringe, but included a number of sensible women reformers such as Elizabeth C. Stanton and Lucretia Mott, who in 1848 launched the women's suffrage movement at Seneca Falls, New York. Carried forward by the eloquence of Lucy Stone and the energy of Susan B. Anthony, this finally bore fruit in Amendment XIX to the Constitution (1920). One of Miss Stanton's early converts, Amelia Bloomer the dress reformer, should not be blamed for the baggy gym pants formerly associated with her name; her "bloomers" were well cut slacks, adopted by thousands of women for housework, although only the bravest could face the jeers and insults to which wearers of them were subjected in public.

Most remarkable of all was Dorothea Lynde Dix, a New England gentlewoman who, after teaching for several years in a fashionable girls' school, at the age of thirty-three began a life-long crusade in favor of intelligent and humane treatment of the mentally afflicted. Most of these unfortunates were then treated as criminals, "chained, naked, beaten with rods and lashed into obedience," as she described their plight in her memorial of 1843 to the Massachusetts legislature. This beautiful young woman, naturally timid and diffident, visited every part of the United States investigating conditions and lobbying to better them. She persuaded Congress to establish St. Elizabeth's Hospital. She was the first New England reformer to penetrate the South, where chivalry gave her a hearing; and, at her urging, public hospitals for the insane were established in nine Southern states between 1845 and 1852. Off then she went to Europe, where the situation was almost equally appalling. Dorothea enlisted the support of Queen Victoria, and in Rome told Pope Pius IX that the local insane asylum was "a scandal and disgrace"; the Pope listened to her, and even did something about it.

The great breeding ground of mid-century "isms" was not New England itself, but the area peopled by Yankees in the rolling hills of central New York and along the Erie Canal. These folk were so susceptible to religious revivals and Pentecostal beliefs that their region was called "The Burned-over District." There antimasonry began and the temperance movement gathered strength. Joseph Smith published The Book of Mormon at Palmyra, New York, in 1830, and there converted Brigham Young. Charles G. Finney, probably the greatest American evangelist, stumped up and down the state bringing souls to Christ. William Miller, a veteran of the War of 1812, worked out at Hampton, New York, the theory that the second coming of Christ would take place on 22 October 1843. He founded the Millerite or Adventist sect which persuaded thousands to sell their goods and, clothed in suitable robes, await the Second Coming on roofs, hilltops, and haystacks, which they believed would shorten their ascent to Heaven. Mother Ann Lee at New Lebanon, New York, and Jemima Wilkinson at Jerusalem, New York, attempted to sublimate the sexual urges of mankind by founding celibate Shaker and "Universal Friend" communities. John H. Noyes, on the contrary, sought perfection as well as catharsis in sexual indulgence at his Oneida Community, which ended as an arts-and-crafts organization. Spirits from the other world seeking means to communicate with this, appropriately chose Rochester, New York, the burned-over metropolis, where the Fox sisters' spirit-rappings and table-turnings had the whole country agog in 1848. From their performances issued the cult of Spiritism, which within ten years had sixty-seven newspapers and periodicals devoted to culling messages from "angel spheres." And from central New York a vast swarm of Yankee "isms" descended on the West like a flight of grasshoppers.

2. Abolition, Antislavery, and Utopia

Southern chivalry was no protection to lady abolitionists. The Grimké sisters, Sarah and Angelina, pretty blonde daughters of a wealthy Charleston lawyer, grew up hating slavery, but had to leave home and confine their work to the North. And that was no easy matter in the early years of the abolition movement. Advocates of Negro emancipation were attacked furiously in the free states. Whether in city or country, in New England, New York or the Middle West, devoted men and women addressing an abolition meeting were assailed by rotten eggs and stones, and their voices were drowned by tin horns, drums, and sleighbells. Charles Stuart, son of a British army officer who, after observing slavery in Jamaica, hoped to destroy it in the United States, was whipped out of Plainfield, Connecticut, by angry farmers. A philanthropist who built a school for Negro children in a Maine village found it one day in the middle of a swamp, hauled there by local ox teams. Elijah Lovejoy, who persisted in printing an abolitionist paper at Alton, Illinois, had his press twice thrown into the river, and he was murdered by a mob in 1837. Philadelphia abolitionists held a protest meeting in Pennsylvania Hall, which they and their reformer friends had just built; but a mob burned it down. All that summer there were outbursts of mob violence against Negroes in the City of Brotherly Love; in 1842 a particularly bad one, when many homes of colored residents were burned.

Philadelphia was far from unique in violence. On 21 October 1835 William Lloyd Garrison was paraded around Boston with a rope around his neck, by what was called a "broadcloth mob"; and on the same day delegates who met at Utica to organize an antislavery society were dispersed by a mob of "very respectable gentlemen" led by a congressman and a judge. Yet the abolition movement grew, and made converts at every mobbing: — of Gerrit Smith, for instance, at the Utica affair; of Wendell Phillips in Boston; of Cassius M. Clay, a cousin of Henry Clay, in Kentucky. By 1840 the membership of the abolition and antislavery societies in the Northern states was over 150,000. The pen of James G. Whittier was already consecrated to the movement, and presently James Russell Lowell would lend his gift of biting satire.

The abolitionists were not single-minded; they supported many other reforms as well. Their general starting point was the Puritan conscience, stirred up by an evangelical preacher. They made slight appeal to politicians of either national party (although the Northern ones, in the end, had to pay them some attention) or to financiers, manufacturers, and others who were making money. They had no support from any immigrant group except, shortly before the Civil War, from the rural Germans. But they slowly captured the native farmers and middle classes by appealing to their Jeffersonian liberalism, and making them reflect that if monarchical England could do it, the Land of the Free could and should liberate its slaves.

Theodore Dwight Weld, the most effective abolitionist, was typical for his many reform interests. A Connecticut boy who attended Hamilton College, New York, he was converted to evangelical Christianity by Finney. He then became interested in a "Society for Promoting Manual Labor in Literary Institutions," which proposed to cure the physical flabbiness of college students by making them do their own chores and learn an honest trade. A great bear of a man himself, Weld was capable of cowing a mob or whipping an assailant, which he often had to do. He took up with another Yankee reformer, the Reverend Sylvester Graham, who was waging a one-man war against white bread, for which he was mobbed by the bakers of Boston.[1] The South was wont to charge abolitionists with knowing nothing of slavery at first-hand; but Weld really studied it, traveling to the Gulf of Mexico in 1831-32, and observing social conditions very closely. On that trip he recruited James G. Birney, an upstanding young blood of Kentucky who owned a big plantation in Alabama, and Birney became the first antislavery candidate for President of the United States, polling 3000 votes in 1840.

Weld and two wealthy New York City merchants, Arthur and Lewis Tappan, organized the American Anti-Slavery Society in 1833. Weld then tried teaching at Lane Seminary, Cincinnati, so close to the slave area and so dependent on Southern trade that the trustees forbade discussion of slavery by the students. He and his student converts — many of them Southerners — seceded to Oberlin, which became the first college in the United States to admit both women and Negroes. In the meantime the Grimké sisters, after many hesitations, had taken the public platform for abolition; and Angelina, the younger and comelier, was wooed and won by Theodore Weld.

In the South, everyone not for slavery was called an abolitionist, but opponents of slavery in the North were divided into a number of sects. At the extreme left was William Lloyd Garrison the Boston firebrand, who demanded emancipation immediate and uncompensated, or else secession of the free states from the Union. In the center were Theodore Weld, the Tappans, and their friends, who demanded a beginning of emancipation, compensated or otherwise, and who became an expert pressure group for their cause. Their weekly journal *The Emancipator* had the largest circulation of any antislavery paper; on its staff were Elizur Wright and the poet Whittier. Weld wrote *Slavery As It Is*, concentrating on the inhumanity of the system through telling extracts from Southern newspapers; over 100,000 copies were sold the first year. He also brought out a careful study, *Emancipation in the British*

1. Hence the name graham bread. Sylvester Graham was also responsible for the regimen of cold showers and sleeping with wide-open windows in zero weather, which took about 50 years to become popular, and another 50 years to be proved the cause of pulmonary disorders.

West Indies (1838), to prove that it did work well there and to assure Southern whites that British masters' throats had not been cut by the freed Negroes.

Abolitionists took every opportunity to bring test cases into the courts. As a matter of interstate comity, slaveholders had always been allowed to bring slaves with them in and out of the free states; but this became difficult after the Nancy Jackson case. She was a young domestic owned by a Presbyterian parson in Georgia. When he moved to Hartford, Connecticut, he brought her along and kept her there for two years. Weld brought suit to show cause why Nancy should be kept in bondage in a free state, and freed she was in 1837 in a decision which became a precedent.

The most famous case involving slavery, until eclipsed by Dred Scott's, was that of the *Amistad* in 1839. She was a Spanish slave ship carrying 53 newly imported Negroes who were being moved from Havana to another Cuban port. Under the leadership of an upstanding Negro named Cinqué, they mutinied and killed captain and crew. Then, ignorant of navigation, they had to rely on a white man whom they spared to sail the ship. He stealthily steered north, the *Amistad* was picked up off Long Island by a United States warship, taken into New Haven, and with her cargo placed in charge of the federal marshal. Then what a legal hassle! Spain demanded that the slaves be given up to be tried for piracy, and President Van Buren attempted to do so but did not quite dare. Lewis Tappan and Roger Sherman Baldwin, a Connecticut abolitionist, undertook to free them by legal process, and the case was appealed to the Supreme Court. John Quincy Adams, persuaded to act as their attorney, argued that the Negroes be freed, on the ground that the slave trade was illegal both by American and Spanish law, and that mankind had a natural right to freedom. The court, with a majority of Southerners, was so impressed by the old statesman's eloquence that it ordered Cinqué and the other Negroes set free, and they were returned to Africa. The ironic epilogue is that Cinqué, once home, set himself up as a slave trader.

At the right wing of the emancipators were people who spurned the name abolitionist (just as socialists hate to be confused with communists), and called themselves antislavery men. They opposed the extension of slavery into more United States territory, but did not propose to interfere with slavery in the states. The antislavery wing included many evangelists such as Finney, who warned "Brother Weld," his proselyte, that extremist sentiment would "roll a wave of blood over the land." Similarly, Francis Wayland, president of Brown University, warned the abolitionists that their agitation had "rendered any open and calm decision of this subject in the slaveholding states utterly impossible"; that abolition "would be a great calamity were it to terminate by violence, or without previous moral and social preparation." Emerson took a similar position. But most of these moderate antislavery men were eventually forced by Southern intransigence into more radical views.

The South made tactical errors in combating abolition. It assumed that every antislavery person was a firebrand, an inciter of Negro insurrection. Southern legislatures passed laws making it increasingly difficult for masters to liberate slaves, or for free Negroes to exist. And by frantic attempts to suppress discussion of the subject, and to buttress, protect, and expand slavery, the spokesmen of the South ended in convincing the North that every man's liberty was at stake. Birney, one of the first to see this aspect of the problem, wrote from Kentucky to Gerrit Smith in 1835, "It has now become absolutely necessary that slavery should cease in order that freedom may be preserved in any portion of the land." William Jay, son of the Chief Justice, pointed out the next year, "We commenced the present struggle to obtain the freedom of the slave; *we are compelled to continue it to preserve our own.*"

Excepting that lonely fanatic John Brown, no abolitionist attempted to incite a slave insurrection, but many took part in a conspiracy of evasion. The "grapevine telegraph" carried news south of an "underground railroad" to liberty. Slaves who had the courage to strike for freedom would take cover in woods or swamps near their master's plantation until the hue and cry was over, then follow the North Star to the free states. The most dangerous part of the escape route was in the South itself, where slaves helped one another. Harriet Tubman, an illiterate field hand, not only escaped herself, but returned repeatedly and guided more than 300 slaves from bondage to freedom, taking some as far as Canada. In the Northern states, fugitives were transferred from one abolitionist or free Negro household to another, sometimes driven in a Friend's carriage, disguised in women's clothes and wearing a deep Quaker bonnet.

Efforts have recently been made to pooh-pooh the underground as a myth, and it never rescued more than a tiny fraction of the slave population. But it was real enough to the Negroes whom it helped, and to the masters whom it robbed. Here, for instance, is what Moncure D. Conway, a young antislavery Virginian, observed at a Concord home in 1853:

I found the Thoreaus agitated by the arrival of a coloured fugitive from Virginia, who had come to their door at daybreak. Thoreau took me to a room where his excellent sister Sophia was ministering to the fugitive, who recognized me as one he had seen. . . . I observed the tender and lowly devotion of Thoreau to the African. He now and then drew near to the trembling man, and with a cheerful voice bade him feel at home, and have no fear that any power should again wrong him. That whole day he mounted guard over the fugitive, for it was a slave-hunting time. Next day the fugitive was got off to Canada.

By a federal law, any master or his agent who caught a runaway in a free state could forcibly repatriate him after swearing to his identity before a magistrate. Owing to the employment of professional slave-catchers who were not particular about identification, the kidnapping of free Northern Negroes became so frequent that Pennsylvania in 1825 and other states later passed personal liberty laws to protect their free colored citizens. Local resentment against kidnapping fed public opinion against the return of genuine fugitives, and the tightening up of the personal liberty laws which made a runaway's identity almost impossible to establish. A fugitive was forcibly rescued from his captors in Boston in 1843, and his freedom purchased by popular subscription. The abolitionists for the first time voiced a popular sentiment when Whittier declared:

> No slave-hunt in our borders — no pirate on our strand!
> No fetters in the Bay State — no slave upon our land!

Southerners played into the abolitionists' hands not only by stifling criticism of slavery when they had the power, but by demanding its suppression in places where they had no power. Thousands of Northerners who were indifferent to slavery valued freedom of speech, of the press, and of petition. In 1835 the abolitionists began sending petitions to Congress to abolish slavery and the slave trade in the District of Columbia, over which Congress had exclusive jurisdiction, and which had become a shipping point for slaves from Virginia and Maryland to the cotton states. Even from the windows of the Capitol one could see coffles of chained Negroes marching by, guarded by armed men. Slave auctions were frequently held in the District. Why, as Henry Clay inquired, should members be continually "outraged" by scenes "so inexcusable and detestable?" The answer was that members from slave states felt that Washington was a strategic outpost, a prestige point to be held at all costs. John C. Calhoun, now back in the Senate, declared that any intermeddling with slavery in Washington would be "a foul slander on nearly one-half the States of the Union." All such petitions were rejected unread and forgotten; but that was not enough for the Southern members. In 1836, at their behest, the House voted the first of the so-called "gag resolutions," declaring that all petitions or papers "relating in any way" to slavery or the abolition thereof, should be "laid on the table."

John Quincy Adams, now a congressman from Massachusetts, was no abolitionist, but the gag rule awakened ancestral memories of royal tyranny; a thing to be resisted in its prime, like taxation without representation. He denounced it as "a direct violation of the Constitution of the United States, of the rules of the House, and the rights of my constituents." The gag actually stimulated abolitionists to greater efforts. During the session of 1837–38, tens of thousands of petitions on the forbidden subject were sent to Congress. The flood continued unchecked until it reached this Congressional dam. Session after session, Adams fought against the gag, using his knowledge of parliamentary practice and rich resource in harsh and bitter eloquence. Theodore Weld came to Washington to participate, and from one of his letters to his wife we have a lively description of a debate when the seventy-five-year-old Adams defended himself and clawed his assailants, like a bear at bay:

Old Nestor lifted up his voice like a trumpet; till slave-holding, slave trading and slave breeding absolutely quailed and howled under his dissecting knife. Mr.

Adams had said the day before that he should present some petitions that would set them in a blaze, so I took care to be in the house at the time, and such a scene I never witnessed. Lord Morpeth, the English abolitionist of whom you have heard, was present and sat within a few feet of Mr. Adams, his fine intelligent face beaming with delight as the old man breasted the storm and dealt his blows upon the head of the monster. Wise of Virginia, Rayner of North Carolina, W. C. Johnson of Maryland, and scores more of slaveholders, striving constantly to stop him by starting questions of order and by every now and then screaming at the top of their voices: "That is false!" "I *demand*, Mr. Speaker, that you shut the mouth of that old harlequin!" A perfect uproar like Babel would burst forth every two or three minutes as Mr. Adams with his bold surgery would smite his cleaver into the very bones. At least half of the slaveholding members of the house left their seats and gathered in the quarter of the Hall where Mr. Adams stood. Whenever any of them broke out upon him, Mr. Adams would say, "I see where the shoe pinches, Mr. Speaker, it will pinch *more* yet!" "If before I get through every slaveholder, slave trader and slave breeder on this floor does not get materials for bitter reflection it shall be no fault of mine."

Every attempt short of personal violence was made to silence, to censure, or to expel Adams; but the tough old Puritan persisted. Public opinion in the Northern states finally forced their representatives to support him, and in 1844 the gag rule was repealed. It made no difference to the slaves, but the eight-year controversy had educated opinion on both sides of the cold war as nothing else could. The South learned that she needed more weight in the councils of the nation by annexing Texas certainly, Cuba probably, and Mexico perhaps; that slavery's banners must fly not only over the Capitol but on the high seas and even in the free states, where discussion of the subject must be stifled. The North began to see that the price of union would be surrender all along the line to the "slaveocracy," as Adams called it, and that this surrender would involve rights for which their fathers fought.

That same curious reversal of values which argues that resistance to Hitler was the cause of the Second World War, or that unilateral disarmament on our part will exorcise the communist menace, has been applied to the whole antislavery movement. The abolitionists, we are told, were nasty, power-hungry men and sex-starved women seeking notoriety; everything would have worked out all right and slavery have died a "natural death" if they had been shut up. But it is perfectly clear that slavery was too firmly rooted in Southern society to die otherwise than by violence. The abolitionists are also accused of hypocrisy because they did so little for free Negroes in the free states. Actually, they did a great deal, such as getting public schools legally desegregated; but, sharing the laissez-faire philosophy of that era, they assumed that the Negro, once free, could compete on equal terms with white people. Time has proved them wrong in this confident expectation, but the antislavery people were right in concentrating on freedom as the essential first step.

Abolition was an irresistible power in a world awakening to new concepts of humanity. It could no more be kept down in Boston and Indianapolis than in London and Paris. Orators such as Weld, Garrison, the Grimkés, Charles

Sumner, and Wendell Phillips, spoke with voices to which America was obliged to listen. "They were members of a family of minds that had appeared in all the Western countries, in Italy, in Germany, in France, to defend the religion of liberty, poets militant, intellectual men who were glad to fight and die for their beliefs, figures that were appearing in flesh and blood on battlefields and barricades in Europe. Brothers of Mazzini, heirs of William Tell, men of the world themselves and men of culture, they roused the indifferent minds of the thinking masses and made the American antislavery movement a part of the great world-struggle of darkness and light." [1]

The abolitionists, as we can now see, expended so much compassion on the slave that they had no pity left for the owner who was equally involved in the system and could see no way to get rid of it. But in view of Southern resistance to any form of gradual, compensated emancipation, and of Southern insistence on acquiring more territory and more federal protection for slavery, violence was the only way left. Yet the freedmen were not really free in 1865, nor are most of their descendants really free in 1965. Slavery was but one aspect of a race and color problem that is still far from solution here, or anywhere. In America particularly, the grapes of wrath have not yet yielded all their bitter vintage.

The American artisan now began to question the value of his vote. Jacksonian Democracy killed Monster Bank, but supplied no bread. As they were searching for the root of the trouble, American laborers were approached by earnest idealists, each with his peculiar vision of a new society in which people might lead free and happy lives. Robert Owen in 1845 summoned a "World Convention to Emancipate the Human Race from Ignorance, Poverty, Division, Sin and Misery." Instead of trying to assimilate and humanize the new industrial order, these well-meaning people dissipated their energy in efforts to escape it.

Almost every known panacea was applied, with the same meager results as in Europe. Josiah Warren, the first American anarchist, devised a system of "time stores" and "labor notes," which were no cure. The typical experiment of the period was a community. Brook Farm, the transcendentalist group so happily described in Hawthorne's *Blithedale Romance*, was one of forty Fourierite phalanxes in the Northern states, of which Owen's New Harmony, Indiana, was the most long-lived and successful. The one at Ripon, Wisconsin, was almost too successful — its land became so valuable that the brethren decided to sell out and become individual farmers. These communities solved no problem, but for a time they gave friendship and a sense of "belonging" to thousands of sanguine souls. The one positive gain was the co-operative movement, which emerged phoenix-like from the ruins of little producers' and consumers' co-operatives set up by labor unions during the depression of 1837–40.

1. Van Wyck Brooks, *The Flowering of New England*, pp. 393–4.

Horace Greeley kept the columns of his New York *Tribune* hospitable to all these movements; but his best advice to the worker was, "Go West, young man, go West!" Here was a point of contact with national politics. Public land at $200 the quarter-section was not for those who needed it most, but for those who had the price, or for squatters who defied all comers to dislodge them. George Henry Evans and Horace Greeley insisted that every man had the same natural right to a piece of land as to air and sunlight. "Equality, inalienability, indivisibility" were Evans's three points: a free homestead from the public domain to every settler, limitation of individual holdings, no alienation of the homestead, voluntary or otherwise. "Vote yourself a farm" was his slogan. The first free homestead bill was introduced in 1846 by Andrew Johnson of Tennessee. Northern Whigs and Southern Democrats combined to defeat it. In 1851 an agrarian law limiting inheritance of land to 320 acres passed a second reading in the Wisconsin legislature, but did not become law, for the Western farmer was a land speculator by nature.

In the field of labor relations, a landmark is the decision by Lemuel Shaw, Chief Justice of Massachusetts, in the case of *Commonwealth* v. *Hunt* (1842), that a trade union was a lawful organization whose members were not collectively responsible for illegal acts committed by individuals, and that a strike for a closed shop was legal.

All this ferment was little reflected in legislative acts. A typical first child labor law was that of Massachusetts in 1836, which forbade the employment of children under fifteen in *incorporated* factories, *unless* they had attended school at least three months the year before. Jefferson had so firmly grounded his ideal of a simple agrarian society that Americans did not know how to check the abuses that arose in the new industrial order. Farmers could see no reason why factory operatives should work shorter hours than they did; reformers were much too busy with diet, demon rum, and their dark brethren to look into child labor in the cotton mills; evangelicals were generally persuaded that if everyone would come to Jesus, everything would work out all right.

It must have been a stimulating if somewhat exhausting experience to live among those young men and women "with knives in their brain." As Wordsworth wrote of the French Revolution, so we may say of America between 1820 and 1850:

> Bliss was it in that dawn to be alive,
> But to be young was very heaven.

3. The Renaissance of New England

Just as the Virginia galaxy of political theorists flickered to its close, the same revolutionary spirit that inspired them ignited a new constellation in a higher latitude. The year 1836, when Emerson published his *Essay on Nature*, may be taken as opening a period in American literary culture, corresponding to 1775 in American politics.

Transcendentalism is the name generally given to this spirit in the Northern states between 1820 and 1860. It may be defined as an intellectual overtone to democracy, a belief in the divinity of human nature. It appeared in some men as intense individualism, in others as a passionate sympathy for the poor and oppressed. It gave to Hawthorne his perception of the beauty and tragedy of life, to Walt Whitman his robust joy in living. Transcendentalism inspired many of the American men of letters who flourished between 1820 and 1860; and almost every aspect of it may be found in Emerson, who embodied the essence of it, a belief in the soul's inherent power to grasp the truth. Historically speaking, transcendentalism was an attempt to make Americans worthy of their independence, and elevate them to a new stature among the mortals.

It may have been mere accident that this outburst of intellectual activity occurred largely within a fifty-mile radius of Boston during a single generation. Transcendentalism has been called the inevitable flowering of the Puritan spirit. But Puritanism does not necessarily bear blossoms, and the fruit thereof is often gnarled and bitter. In New England, however, the soil was conserved by a bedrock of character, mellowed by two centuries of cultivation, and prepared by Unitarianism. New England Federalism checked the flow of sap, fearful lest it feed flowers of Jacobin red. There was just time for a gorgeous show of blossom and a harvest of wine-red fruit, between this late frost and the early autumn blight of the Civil War.

Unitarianism and her sister Universalism took a great weight off the soul of New England. Yet something was lacking in Unitarianism. Faith in the essential goodness of human nature might be a theological counterpart to democracy; but it failed to supply the note of mysticism that democrats, no less than subjects of a monarchical state, seek in religion. The historical function of Unitarianism in America was to liberate the minds of the well-to-do and to provide a church for rationalists. Unitarianism became prolific in men of letters and reformers, but did not extend far from the New England settlements, or even deep within them. Holmes's "One-Hoss Shay" was a symbol of the sudden crumbling of Calvinism; but that happened only in eastern Massachusetts. Congregationalists, Presbyterians, Methodists, and Baptists howled down the Unitarians as atheists and maintained their hold on the native-born masses. Most immigrants remained loyal to Catholicism and other old-country faiths. The reform movements that we have described were inspired by evangelical sects rather than by liberal religion. But the influence of liberalism went far beyond those who embraced it as a faith.

The Reverend Theodore Parker began as a Unitarian, but, as Lowell wrote in his *Fable for Critics*, "from their orthodox kind of dissent he dissented." Parker became a fiery preacher for prison reform, the rights of factory workers, and the slave; Lincoln remembered and treasured his definition of democracy as "the government of all, by all, for all." His scholarship in law, philosophy, and German literature was impeccable. When he died in Florence in 1860, Parker was mourned by Emerson as "my brave brother," whose "place cannot be supplied."

Ralph Waldo Emerson in 1832, at the age of twenty-nine, laid down his pastoral office in the Unitarian church because it no longer interested him. In his next four years of reading and travel he found God again in nature, and settled down a "lay preacher to the world" in a Concord which harbored during one generation Emerson, Hawthorne, Thoreau, and the Alcotts. The atmosphere of that placid village is preserved in *Little Men* and *Little Women*, which Louisa Alcott wrote in order to maintain her transcendental father and family after the failure of his "Fruitlands" community. And at the same time Nathaniel Hawthorne was writing tragedies of New England life that penetrate to the core of all human life.

If Jefferson was the prophet of democracy and Jackson its hero, Emerson was its high priest. Like Jefferson, he believed ardently in the perfectibility of man, but the philosopher knew what the soldier and the statesman never learned, that free institutions could not liberate men not themselves free. His task was to induce Americans to cleanse their minds of hatred and prejudice, to make them think out the consequences of democracy instead of merely repeating its catchwords, and to seek the same eminence in spirit that they had reached in material things.

Henry Thoreau, whose *Week on the Concord and Merrimack Rivers* came out in 1849, was the best classical scholar of the Concord group, and the most independent of classic modes of thought. Concord for him was a microcosm of the world. His revolt was directed against a society so confident and vigorous that it could afford to ignore him. His genius was little appreciated in his own country until the twentieth century. W. H. Hudson called Thoreau's *Walden* (1854) "the one golden book in any century of best books." Marcel Proust hailed Thoreau as a brother; and in France, Germany, Holland, Scandinavia, South America, and Russia, his works were translated. Tolstoy in 1901 sent a "Message to the American People," inquiring why they paid so little attention to the voices of Emerson, Thoreau, and Theodore Parker. On the Orient Thoreau has had an even greater impact. Mahatma Gandhi was inspired by the *Essay on Civil Disobedience*; Pandit Nehru sponsored translations of *Walden* into the principal languages of India. When bumbling county commissioners in 1959 tried to turn the shores of Walden Pond into a beach resort protests world-wide halted the desecration.

In Hawthorne, Emerson, and Thoreau, in half-Yankee Herman Melville, and in Emily Dickinson of the next generation, the New England that had slowly matured since the seventeenth century justified herself. Excellence is the binding quality of these five. Longfellow, Bryant, Poe, and Whitman wrote bad poetry as well as good; Cooper, Irving, and the New York Democratic group were responsible for much wretched, pretentious prose; but every word that the three Concordians, Melville, and Dickinson wrote, whether published in their lifetimes or later, is a treasure. They had this too in common, that they recognized no law save that of their own nature. They obeyed Sir Philip Sidney's injunction, echoed by Longfellow in his *Voices of the Night*: "Look in thy heart and write."

If Walt Whitman was the poet of democracy, Longfellow was democracy's favorite poet. The American people, when they read poetry, wished to be lifted out of themselves by verses that rhymed or scanned into a world of romance and beauty. Hawthorne, Whittier, and Longfellow felt that craving themselves, deriving many themes from American folklore and colonial history: Hawthorne's *Scarlet Letter*, his masterpiece; Whittier's "Skipper Ireson's Ride"; Longfellow's "Song of Hiawatha" and "Evangeline." Longfellow, "poet of the mellow twilight of the past," as Whitman called him, "poet of all sympathetic gentleness — and universal poet of woman and young people" — had an influence on his generation second only to Emerson's. And no poem had a greater effect in creating that love of the Union which made young men fight to preserve it, than the peroration to Longfellow's "Building of the Ship":

> Thou, too, sail on, O Ship of State!
> Sail on, O Union, strong and great!
> Humanity with all its fears,
> With all the hopes of future years,
> Is hanging breathless on thy fate!

Energy was a binding quality of New England men of letters — excepting Hawthorne, who always "lived like a ghost," and shy Emily of Amherst. These writers were in a sense provincial, but they were intensely aware of what was going on in the world. Whittier and Lowell were energetic editors; George Ticknor, Longfellow, and Lowell taught college students; and Dr. Oliver Wendell Holmes, "The Autocrat of the Breakfast Table," lectured at the Harvard Medical School. Emerson toured the lyceums of the North and West; but he was a philosopher who founded no cult and gathered disciples, since what he said came from no wish to bring men to himself, but to themselves.

In the art of painting, Gilbert Stuart monopolized the field until his death in 1828. He was succeeded as portraitist of merchants, statesmen, and current belles by Chester Harding, a York State country boy who, after painting eighty portraits in six months, made a triumphant tour of England. Alvan Fisher, who set up a studio in Boston as early as the War of 1812, began to paint American landscapes even earlier than did the Hudson River School and, unlike them, depicted country scenes such as corn husking, punging, children swinging, and barn interiors. Fitz-Hugh Lane of Gloucester, crippled in early life so that he could not be a sailor, more than compensated by painting ships, harbors, and coastal scenes.

Whilst these artists lived aloof from the New England intellectuals, the sculptors were in the main stream. They did live in Italy during the greater part of their careers; not, however, as escapists but for the good reason that in America it was difficult to find a young girl to pose nude, and impossible to have plaster statues executed in marble or bronze. Fortunately for the American sculptors, it had become fashionable to augment family portraits by portrait busts, and for public buildings to be adorned with statues of celebrities (usually in Roman togas), and battle groups, pioneers, and Indians. First among American sculptors were three remarkable Greenough brothers of Boston, Horatio, Henry, and Richard. Horatio, after graduating from Harvard, went to Rome to study sculpture under Thorwalsden, and later settled in Florence, where he became the center of an artistic-literary circle. In 1833 he obtained a commission for the heroic statue of Washington at the Capitol, which after many vicissitudes has found a resting place in the new Smithsonian. In 1843 he published *American Architecture*, in which he had the wit to declare that nothing constructed in the New World gave a better example of a practical design producing true beauty, than did the squarerigged sailing ship. Henry and Richard Greenough joined their brother in Florence; Richard made an equestrian statue of Washington for West Point and also executed classic subjects such as "Circe" and "The Carthaginian girl," which Henry James scornfully but not unjustly said were characterized by a "senseless fluency."

Hiram Powers, son of a Vermont farmer, self-educated in Ohio, made busts of statesmen in Washington, which attracted such admiration that friends subscribed to send him to Florence to study under Horatio Greenough. There he executed the most famous piece of American statuary of that era, "The Greek Slave," to which Mrs. Browning dedicated a sonnet. The first nude statue to be exhibited in America, it aroused hostility as well as admiration, but served to make the country sculpture-conscious and shattered a Puritan prejudice against the nude in art.

Parallel to the career of Powers was that of Thomas Crawford, a poor Irish boy of New York City whose artistic ability so impressed his employer, a maker of gravestones, that he sent him in 1835 to study with Thorwalsden in Rome. There, after almost starving to death, he attracted the interest of Charles Sumner who found him the money to complete "Orpheus," his first great group of statuary. This made Crawford famous, orders flowed in from all parts of America, and in 1849 he won a competition for the equestrian statue of Washington at Richmond. In the 1850's he executed the sculptures on "The Past and Present of America" for the Capitol at Washington; and his death in Rome at the age of thirty-four, in 1857, was regarded as a national calamity.

Youngest of the New England sculptors who made a career in Italy was William Wetmore Story. For ten years after graduating from Harvard he labored in the legal groove set by his father, Justice Joseph Story, but yearned to be a sculptor; and to Italy he went in 1847. His statue "Cleopatra," described by Hawthorne in *The Marble Faun,* made his fame. He also won distinction as a poet and descriptive writer, and in Rome he resided, center of an artistic circle, until his death in 1895.

4. *Popular and Higher Education*

The most tangible social gain during this period of ferment was in education. Since the War of Independence, education had been left largely to private initiative and benevolence. Secondary academies and colleges had been founded, and in this the South was ahead of the North. But almost all these institutions charged fees. Elementary education was then the most neglected branch. Most of the Northern states had some sort of public primary school system, but only in New England was it free and open to all. In some instances a child had to be taught his letters before he was admitted to one of these schools, and in others only parents pleading poverty were exempted from paying fees. In addition, the Quakers and other philanthropic bodies maintained charity schools for the poor, which had the effect of fastening a stigma on free schools. In New York City, around 1820, nearly half the children went uneducated because their parents were too poor to pay fees, or too proud or indifferent to accept charity.

Opposition to free public education came from the people of property, who thought it intolerable that they should be taxed to support common schools to which they would not dream of sending their children. To this argument the poor replied with votes, and reformers with the tempting argument that education was insurance against radicalism.

In New England the first problem was to make efficient the colonial system of free elementary schools, maintained by townships and taught by birch-wielding pedagogues or muscular college students during their vacations. Horace Mann sought efficient methods in Europe, and found them in Germany. Victor Cousin's report on Prussian education, which he had translated, became widely known in the United States and was adapted to American needs when, in 1837, Horace Mann became chairman of the new Massachusetts board of education. He and his colleagues combined enthusiasm with an intellectual balance that brought permanent results. Under their influence the first American teachers' college was established in 1839. After a struggle with the older teachers, who insisted that mental discipline would be lost if studies were made attractive, the elementary school ceased to be a place of terror for the young; but there was no "permissiveness" — children still had to learn the fundamentals. Boston set the pace in free public high schools (English High School 1821, Girls' High School 1828); and Massachusetts in 1852 passed a truancy law that had teeth. The argument against compulsory school attendance, which time and experience gradually overcame, now sounds odd; it was then compared with compulsory church attendance, infringing on the rights of parents to the use of all their children's time.

Outside New England, public schools generally were supported by interest on a fund set up out of the proceeds of the sale of public lands, or earmarked taxes, administered by a specially appointed state board. The Board of Regents of the University of New York, which still has oversight of all public education in the Empire State, is a survival of this system. In Pennsylvania there was a terrific fight for free schools, because not only the well-to-do but the Germans did not want them, fearing the loss of their language and culture. The Pennsylvania public school law of 1834, although optional in the school districts, was bitterly attacked, and the eloquence of Thaddeus Stevens is credited with preventing its repeal the following year. By 1837, about 42 per cent of the children in the Keystone State were in free schools.

Ohio was well provided with free public elementary schools by 1830, and six years later the state sent Calvin E. Stowe, professor of Biblical literature in Lane Theological Seminary at Cincinnati (better known as husband of the author of *Uncle Tom's Cabin*), to Europe to investigate public school systems. His *Report on Elementary Instruction in Europe* had an influence only less than the reports of Horace Mann, and among other things was responsible for dividing Ohio public education into elementary, grammar, and high school grades. By 1850 the modern system of grades one through twelve had been adopted in every place where there were enough pupils.

Indiana adopted a free public school system by a narrow majority in 1848. Several years passed before it was enforced, and court decisions adverse to the right of local authorities to raise taxes for their maintenance, in the 1850s, closed most of the high schools that had been started and almost wrecked the system. Illinois used its state educational fund to subsidize private schools. Orville H. Browning, a Whig friend of Abraham Lincoln, pleaded in the state assembly for a public school law in 1843, alleging the benefits conferred on Connecticut by her public schools; to which a Democratic member replied that taxing one class for the benefit of another was unjust, and Connecticut had inundated the West with clock peddlers and others who lived by their wits! A state-wide public school law, passed by representatives of the northern part of the state against the opposition of the river counties, was not adopted until 1855.

Many years elapsed before free Negroes of the North derived any benefit from free public education. In Philadelphia, the controller of public schools opened the first school for colored children in 1822, apologizing to the public for doing something for "this friendless and degraded portion of society." In northern New England, where Negroes were few, they were admitted to the public schools without question; but in urban centers both reformers and the Negroes themselves favored separate schools to give the children more congenial companionship. The move against segregation began with the antislavery agitation of the 1830s. Massachusetts in 1855 was the first state to enforce integration of all colors, races, and religions in her public schools. None of the feared consequences, still used as arguments against integration, occurred. Other Northern states where there was a considerable colored population followed very slowly; segregation was not legally ended in New York City schools until 1900.

By 1850, then, there had been formulated and, to some extent established, the basic principles of American education: (1) that free public primary and secondary schools should be available for all children; (2) that teachers should be given professional training; (3) that all children be required to attend school up to a certain age, but not necessarily the free public school; religious and other bodies having complete liberty to establish their own educational systems at their own cost. These privileges as yet were only imperfectly extended to women, and even less to Negroes. Quality had not been sacrificed to quantity; yet the public elementary schools of 1850 were generally superior to the private schools thirty years earlier, and the public high schools, small according to twentieth-century standards and mostly taught by a few scholarly and enthusiastic men and women, gave a far better training in the fundamentals of mathematics, the classics, modern languages, and history than do most of the bloated and diluted central high schools of today.

The Old Northwest in general, and Ohio in particular, were as prolific in founding colleges at this period as New York State. New settlers were eager to reproduce institutions of higher education, and their motives were largely religious. The Methodists were very energetic, opening instruction of college grade at De Pauw (1837), Ohio Wesleyan (1841), Illinois Wesleyan (1850), Lawrence (1847), and Northwestern University (1855). Presbyterians were responsible for Muskingum (1837) and Knox (1842); the Disciples of Christ for Antioch (1853). Congregationalists from Yale founded Western Reserve (1826), Wabash (1832), Oberlin (1833), Beloit (1846), and Ripon (1855). Baptist colleges included Denison (1837), Shurtleff (1831), Bucknell (1846), and the first University of Chicago (1859), of which Stephen A. Douglas was a founder. German Lutherans founded Wittenberg (1845); the Episcopalians, Kenyon (1824), and the Catholics, with help from Europe, St. Xavier in Cincinnati (1831) and Notre Dame (1842).

In New England there were founded Amherst College (1821, Congregational), to preserve country boys from the wickedness of Harvard; Trinity (Episcopalian, 1823), located in Hartford for the same reason respecting Yale; Colby (1818, Baptist); Wesleyan (1831, Methodist), and Holy Cross (1843, Catholic). In 1835 Wheaton Female Seminary, now Wheaton College, was founded at Norton, Massachusetts. A temporary member of the teaching staff was Mary Lyon, who in 1836 established the first American women's college, Mount Holyoke. But few opportunities for women in higher education were offered before 1880.

It was typical of America that nobody thought of founding a new college in the same town where one already existed; local and sectarian feelings were too strong to follow the example of Oxford and Cambridge. By 1840, over 150 small denominational colleges, each located as far distant as possible from the others, were in existence. The driving impulse for secondary and higher education in the United States prior to the Civil War, and a principal motive to this day, has been religious, not secular; and these slenderly endowed sectarian colleges educated the whole man and maintained a standard of excellence in the liberal arts that has seldom been attained in wealthy, tax-supported state universities.

The older colonial and early federal colleges were now being transformed into proper universities by adding faculties of law, medicine, theology, and science to the original arts and letters. George Ticknor and others who followed postgraduate studies in Germany persuaded Harvard to make the course for the bachelor's degree more flexible and varied, to establish professorial chairs, and make a greater use of lectures. But the idea of a university being a center for scholarly and scientific research lay far in the future. Michigan established a state university in 1837, Missouri two years later, and the University of Wisconsin was founded at Madison in 1849 at a wilderness site crossed by Black Hawk's warriors only fifteen years before.

Adults were not neglected in this educational awakening. In all cities and larger towns, mechanics' institutes provided vocational courses and night schools. Free public libraries, supported by taxation, were generally established, the first being that of Peterborough, New Hampshire, in 1833. In towns and even villages the lyceum offered popular lectures, scientific demonstrations, debates, and entertainment. Under their influence, Americans of the Northern states acquired the habit of attending lectures. Reading was furthered by mechanical improvements in printing, which made possible the penny press. The New York *Tribune*, Baltimore *Sun*, and Philadelphia *Ledger* started as penny newspapers in the 'forties. These, and the mildly sensational New York *Herald* of James Gordon Bennett, were journals of information, with abundant domestic and foreign news and serialized English novels. Under Horace Greeley's editorship, the *Tribune* became a liberal power of the first magnitude. English visitors of the period invariably remarked, and usually deplored, the fact that shop clerks, mechanics, and even common laborers subscribed to daily newspapers.

5. *Science and Technology*

American science, like everything else, now became specialized. Benjamin Franklin had made stoves and lightning rods as well as pursuing original research in electricity. But it was typical of our era that Joseph Henry, who discovered the electromagnet, handed over to Samuel F. B. Morse the problem of adapting it to the telegraph.

Joseph Henry, son of a Scots day laborer in Albany, began to experiment with electricity in 1826 when, at the age of twenty-nine, he was appointed professor of natural philosophy in the local academy which he had attended. After inventing the electromagnet, he devised means to increase the intensity of attraction produced by the same source of current, and by reversing the current he produced a rudimentary motor which he regarded as "a philosophical toy." His studies of induced currents, begun independently of his English contemporary Michael Faraday, who first announced the discovery, led Henry to discover step-up and step-down transformers, formulate theories of intensity (voltage) and quantity (amperage) of currents, and make some of the earliest observations of oscillating energy discharged by electricity in a spiral coil. Outside that field he worked on solar radiation and capillary action of liquids.

Henry came as near to being a "pure" scientist as any American prior to the 1870's. The stress in the United States always had been on "useful knowledge" — the declared purpose of the eighteenth-century American Philosophical Society and the American Academy of Arts and Sciences. Tocqueville devoted a chapter of his *Democracy in America* (1835) to the subject, "Why Americans Prefer the Practice Rather than the Theory of Science." He pointed out that there were few calm spots in America for meditation, which is necessary for the cultivation of pure science; democracy wanted results and American scientists were afraid of losing themselves in abstractions. The sapient Frenchman observed that in a democratic society short-cuts to wealth, labor-saving gadgets, and inventions which add to the comfort or pleasure of life, "seem the most magnificent effort of human intelligence." And this on the whole remained true of America until after World War II. Almost all the great and fruitful scientific ideas were hatched in Europe; but the widest applications of them to common life, or to destruction in war, were made in America. "Mind, acting through the *useful* arts, is the vital principle of modern civilized society," pontificated Edward Everett in 1857. "The mechanician, not the magician, is now the master of life." Everett was premature; but in due time the scientist occupied a position in American society analogous to that of the medicine man among the Indians.

The machine-tool industry with interchangeable parts was already entrenched in the Naugatuck valley of Connecticut by 1836, the year that Samuel Colt patented the revolving pistol, "equalizer" of the frontier. Charles Goodyear in 1844 patented the vulcanization of rubber, which eventually enabled all America to roll or fly. Two years later, Elias Howe invented the sewing machine, which took the making of clothes out of the home and tailor's shop into the factory. Cyrus McCormick of Virginia in 1834 invented the reaper, which made possible prairie farming on a grand scale. More spectacular and far-reaching was Samuel F. B. Morse's invention of the electric telegraph in 1832. Morse worked it out while teaching painting and sculpture at New York University. His friends in Congress got him an appropriation of $30,000 in 1843 to establish between Baltimore and Washington the first telegraph line, built by Ezra Cornell who later founded Cornell University. The first message sent over this line in dots and dashes on 24 May 1844 between Morse himself and a friend in Baltimore, was "What hath God wrought!"

John Goffe Rand, an assistant to Morse, invented in 1841, to hold paints, the collapsible metal tube, the use of which has extended to thousands of other products. At the Crystal Palace Exposition in London in 1851, the cheap clocks, reapers, ranges, machine-made buckets, and other "Yankee notions" exhibited by Americans gave notice that the tide of invention had risen higher in the United States than in the Old World. The preserving of food by canning was invented in time to be put to limited use in the Civil War.

Noteworthy was the popularity of science on lyceum platforms. One of the greatest teachers and scientists of the era was Benjamin Silliman, for 51 years professor of chemistry and natural history at Yale. It was he, more than any other, who grafted the new natural science onto the old liberal education. His popular lectures on geology and chemistry, delivered all the way from New England to New Orleans and St. Louis, were as important in spreading knowledge of the fast-growing body of natural science, as Emerson's for thought and literature. *The American Journal of Science and Arts* which Silliman founded in 1818 became a leading vehicle of information. In 1847 at the age of sixty-eight when, according to modern ideas, he should have retired, Silliman founded the Sheffield Scientific School of Yale University. The central idea was to supplement lectures and readings in the current topics of scientific education (mainly physics, chemistry, geology, and mineralogy) by laboratory research as the core of a college scientific department. At the same time, Amos Eaton at Rensselaer Polytechnic was using the Erie Canal as a practical training ground for civil engineering, even setting up a traveling summer school on a canal boat.

At Amherst College one of Silliman's lifelong friends, the Reverend Edward Hitchcock, made his mark as a professor of geology and natural theology. As promoter and director of the first state geological survey to be completed, he set standards which made his advice and assistance sought for similar projects, North and South. He published a popular textbook on geology and exhibited to a wondering public the footprints left by dinosaurs in sandstone along the Connecticut river.

In 1848, when Louis Agassiz from Switzerland accepted the chair of natural history at the Lawrence Scientific School (Harvard's bid to equal Yale's "Sheff"), the Cambridge college began to rival Yale in science. Agassiz, renowned as paleontologist and propounder of the glacier theory, became a famous personality and helped to bring government aid to scientific investigation. Asa Gray, who had taken a chair at Harvard a few years earlier, wrote a *Manual of the Botany of the Northern United States* (1848) which became a classic. And he became America's first great exponent of Darwin's theory of evolution. All leading American scientists of this period were devout men, presenting scientific discoveries as unfolding the wonderful works of God. It was otherwise with the later disciples of Darwin and Huxley, who repudiated the Biblical account of creation.

Organized religion, however, was partly responsible for the slow development of astronomy in America as compared with other Western countries or even Russia. To probe the starry firmament with a telescope was considered mildly blasphemous; Democrats defeated President Adams's suggestion of a government observatory. Nevertheless, Professor Denison Olmsted of Yale studied the Leonids, the great meteoric shower of 1833, which the superstitious thought heralded the world's end, and proved that they were particles from comets passing through the earth's atmosphere. Harvard College, stimulated by Benjamin Peirce, built an observatory for its 15-inch refracting telescope (as big as any then in the world), which was imported and assembled in 1847. The work of this observatory was largely practical, such as plotting the latitude and longitude of places on earth, and the orbits of planets and the visible stars, and computing the annual *American Nautical Almanac*. Through the new telescope William C. Bond and a Boston daguerreotypist made the first stellar photograph in 1850.

Why did Congress never establish a national university at Washington as every President of the United States through John Quincy Adams recommended? State rights and the distaste of older colleges for competition are the probable answer. The nearest thing to the "national institution of learning" which the Father of his Country hoped for, was the Smithsonian Institution, founded by a bequest of £100,000 to the United States in 1835 "for the increase and diffusion of knowledge among men," by an English man of science, James Smithson. President Jackson ignored it; several senators, including Calhoun, declared it to be unconstitutional; but John Quincy Adams finally argued Congress into accepting it.

Then came a ten-year wrangle over what to do with Smithson's bounty. Congress incorporated the Smithsonian Institution and set up a Board of Regents who first met in 1846. They persuaded Joseph Henry to leave his chair of natural philosophy at Princeton to be the first director; and, as such, he made the Smithsonian the first institution for pure scientific research in the New World. Originally he was required by law to promote practically every branch of knowledge. He persuaded Congress and the regents to slough off several arts and sciences to other institutions in the District, such as the Corcoran Gallery of Fine Arts, the National Museum, the Congressional Library, the Weather Bureau, and the Bureau of Standards, leaving a central core of scientific research that has functioned admirably. Samuel P. Langley, secretary of the Smithsonian, wrote *Experiments in Aërodynamics* (1891) which became the take-off for heavier-than-air aviation.

American archaeology and ethnology languished, despite the good start given by Stephens's books on Central America. In 1847 George Catlin's remarkable collection of life portraits of American Indians, which had been displayed in the Louvre to the admiration of French critics, was offered for sale to the Smithsonian. Congress refused to appropriate the money, one senator remarking that he would rather acquire portraits of American citizens murdered by the Indians. But eventually the collection became one of the glories of the National Museum.

XXXIV

Pacific Empire Beckons

1766-1860

1. *Oregon and the "Mountainy Men"*

LIEUTENANT JONATHAN CARVER, on a Western journey in 1766–67, learned from Cree and Sioux Indians that the sources of the four biggest rivers in North America lay close together. These were the St. Lawrence, the Mississippi, the Red river of the North, and a great westward-flowing stream which they called the Oregon. William Cullen Bryant picked up that euphonious name and ensured its place on the map of North America in his *Thanatopsis* (1817):

> Where rolls the Oregon, and hears no sound
> Save his own dashings.

That concept of a "Great River of the West" flowing majestically to the Pacific long dominated geographic thought and Western ambitions.

Shortly after the end of the War of 1812, Great Britain and the United States agreed to a joint occupation of the Oregon country, which included the present states of Oregon, Washington, Idaho, and the province of British Columbia. John Quincy Adams, one of those

> Stern men with empires in their brains
> Who saw in vision their young Ishmael strain
> In each hard hand a vassal ocean's mane

kept the American claim to the Oregon country alive through decades of national indifference. His diplomacy persuaded Spain to limit her claims to the present northern boundary of California, and Russia to limit hers to latitude 54° 40′ North, the present southern tip of Alaska. But the Yankee fur trade dwindled, while the Hudson's Bay Company in 1824 set up a great trading "factory" at Fort Vancouver on the Columbia river opposite the site of Portland. Four times did Adams, as secretary of state and President, offer to divide Oregon with Canada by extending the northern boundary of the United States along latitude 49° to the Pacific. Four times England refused, demanding everything north of the Columbia. Adams declined to make that concession because he envisaged a naval base and trading city on Puget Sound. He wished to open a window to the Pacific, and shorten the sea route

538

to China. That was the ancient dream of Columbus; again the reality surpassed the dream.

In the meantime, the west coast from San Diego to Queen Charlotte Island was being visited by Boston fur traders and "hide droghers." Many of these vessels also traded with Hawaii, where the American Board of Foreign Missions had established a native Congregational church in 1820 under the Reverend Hiram Bingham. California belonged to Mexico and to the Roman Catholic church, but Bingham kept urging his Boston backers to do something about the free-for-all Oregon country. This appealed to an odd Yankee named Hall J. Kelley, who in 1830 founded "The American Society for Encouraging the Settlement of the Oregon Territory." Kelley stirred up Nathaniel J. Wyeth, whose zest for oceanic trade had been whetted by successfully exporting ice from Fresh Pond, Cambridge, to South America.

Since even seagoing Yankees could not send large numbers of settlers to Oregon by the 200-day voyage around Cape Horn, they would have to come overland. And that leads us to the third element which contributed to the securing of Oregon, the fur traders and trappers of the Great Plains and Rocky Mountains. These "mountainy men" were indispensable to land-trailing immigrants. Once the pioneers had crossed the Great Plains, which covered the present states of Oklahoma, Kansas, Nebraska, the Dakotas, most of Montana, and large parts of Wyoming and Colorado, the mountainy men guided them across the Rocky Mountains to the Snake and Columbia rivers, which floated them to the Pacific.

The smooth or gently rolling surface of the Great Plains, rising gradually or by step-like escarpments to an elevation of 6000 feet, was covered with a carpet of grass which grew rank and thick in the eastern parts, but gave way to tufts of short buffalo grass and sagebrush in the parched High Plains. An occasional rocky dome, butte, or mesa made a welcome landmark, like a lighthouse to a mariner. The Platte and Missouri rivers, with their short tributaries, cut deep gashes in the soil and watered a thin line of willow, cottonwood, and wild plum trees. A short summer of blistering heat, with fierce thunderstorms and frequent cyclones, followed hard on a long winter of bitter northwest winds and heavy snow. Over this area roamed the Kansa, Pawnee, Sioux, Cheyenne, Blackfoot, Crow, Arapaho, and other tribes. Countless herds of buffalo grazed on the plains and supplied the redskins with every necessity of life: meat for immediate use, or, dried and pounded into pemmican, for winter subsistence; skins for clothing, harness, vessels, and the tipi or tent; sinews for thread, cordage, and bowstrings; bone for arrowheads and implements; peltry to sell to the traders; even fuel. These Indians had long since domesticated the wild mustang, offspring of those set free by Spainards in Texas, and had become expert at killing buffalo with bow and arrow while riding bareback.

The Plains Indians seldom practised agriculture or other primitive arts, but they were fine physical specimens; and in warfare, once they had learned the use of the rifle, much more formidable than the Eastern tribes who had slowly yielded to the white man. Tribe warred with tribe, and a highly developed sign language was the only means of intertribal communication. The effective unit was the band or village of a few hundred souls, which might be seen in the course of its wanderings encamped by a watercourse with tipis erected; or pouring over the plain, women and children leading dogs and packhorses with their trailing travois, while gaily dressed braves loped ahead on horseback. They lived only for the day, recognized no rights of property, robbed or killed anyone if they thought they could get away with it, inflicted cruelty without a qualm, and endured torture without flinching.

The "mountainy men" who, save for an occasional soldier or explorer, were the only whites to penetrate this region prior to 1832, were for the most part as savage and ruthless as Indians — they had to be, to survive. The thing that brought them into the High Plains and Rockies was beaver — that industrious little animal whose fur had kept the Pilgrim colony alive and made the Iroquois Confederacy arbiters of international rivalry. Beaver fur was more in demand than ever, to make the extravagantly tall hats then worn by gentlemen, while less valuable furs went into felt hats for the common people. Mountainy men, buckskin-clad, lean, bearded, and usually very dirty, were of all races and origins. Many had Indian wives, a valuable asset for a white trapper not only as a drudge, but because her Indian relatives were bound to avenge him if he were "rubbed out," a phrase first used here. Some were lone operators, others employees of General William H. Ashley's American Fur Company or other less important companies. Annually an autumn rendezvous between trappers and buyers was set on the upper Platte, the Sweetwater, the Big Horn, or in the Teton Mountains farther west. Supplies and trading goods were sent thither from St. Louis in the spring floods, at first by 50-foot keel boats towed by 15 to 20 men trudging along the bank, and in shoal water by "bull boats" made of buffalo hide stretched on a wicker frame. To this rendezvous converged Indians and mountainy men, with their women and their season's take of beaver, "hairy banknotes" which they swapped for raw alcohol from the Cincinnati distilleries, and for arms and munitions, coffee, sugar, tobacco, and blankets. After this "blowout," as they called it, had lasted a few days or a couple of weeks and the liquor had been drunk and the goods gambled away, the mountainy men, poor as before, staggered off into the wilderness to get ready for next year's trapping. When the beaver hibernated they too holed up with their wives, trapped again as soon as the ice melted, and in the fall attended another rendezvous. By 1840 they had almost exterminated beaver in the Rockies; but in their hunting had discovered and mentally mapped every stream and mountain in that region. Jed Smith in 1823 discovered the South Pass of the Rockies in Wyoming, a wide valley of rolling hills that takes one to the transcontinental divide by easy gradients, and which later became the most practical route for wagons. Without such men as guides, most of the emigrants to the Oregon country, Utah, and California would have perished.

Among these guides were the Sublettes who guided Wyeth on his first transcontinental journey; James Bridger, first white man to report the Great Salt Lake; "Kit" Carson and Thomas Fitzpatrick, who indicated a path to the misnamed "pathfinder" Frémont; Henry Chatillon, who guided Francis Parkman over the Oregon Trail. These men could neither read nor write but they were simple-minded, courageous nature's gentlemen, carrying in their heads an encyclopedic knowledge of Indians and the West. Bridger in 1843 established as a way station Fort Bridger, Wyoming, where the Oregon trail swings south to avoid the Yellowstone Mountains, and where his hospitality saved thousands of emigrants' lives. Fitzpatrick's influence with the Plains Indians was largely responsible for the important treaties of Fort Laramie (1851) and Fort Atkinson (1853) which kept them quiet while the transcontinental movement was at its height. Carson became a valuable army scout in the Mexican War and managed the Navajo during the Civil War.

2. Pioneers and the Oregon Trail

So much for the background: trappers swarming over the Great Plains and into the Rockies, missionaries trying to whip up interest in settling the Oregon country, and a Hudson's Bay trading post on the lower Columbia. If Nathaniel Wyeth the Cambridge iceman needed another stimulus, he got it when trading brig *Owhyhee* of Boston returned from the Northwest Coast in 1831, carrying the first shipment of pickled Columbia river salmon. The fish sold readily, but President Jackson's treasury department made the importer pay duty on it as "foreign-caught fish." Clearly it was time to prove that Oregon was part of the United States.

Wyeth raised capital to put a Yankee pincer on Oregon, and recruited 24 men and boys for the overland route. He constructed three vehicles that he called "amphibia" — ancestors of the World War II "dukws" — which could be drawn on wheels or sailed on the water. On 1 March 1832 he dispatched brig *Ida*, loaded with trade goods for the projected colony, around Cape Horn. Wyeth's own party proceeded by railway, road, and river steamboat to St. Louis. There William Sublette offered to guide him to a trappers' rendezvous provided he dropped the amphibia, and Wyeth accepted. Sublette's brother Milton eventually took over and guided the emigrants to the Snake river, whence Wyeth with a dozen men and boys pressed on. By mid-September they were in the wooded country that the French had named Boisé, and saw their first forests of tall western conifers. At Fort Walla Walla, a Hudson's Bay Company outpost, he hired a boat to take him down the Columbia, carrying around the Dalles, and on 29 October 1832, 233 days from Boston and 190 from St. Louis, he reached Fort Vancouver. There he learned that brig *Ida* had been lost at sea, and his plans for a colony were ruined. So Wyeth returned overland, joining Captain Bonneville en route.

Wyeth's backers, who still had faith in him and in Oregon, now put up the money for a second trip, in 1834. Again he dispatched a brig around the Horn, laden with supplies and hundreds of knocked-down barrels which he hoped to fill with pickled salmon for the Boston market. With him on the overland journey were Thomas Nuttall and John K. Townsend, ornithologists, the Reverend Jason Lee, and four other missionaries who had been recruited to convert the Flathead Indians. This party made Fort Vancouver on 15 September 1834, — 160 days from St. Louis. Another failure. The fur company refused to accept Wyeth's trade goods, the ship arrived too late for the salmon fishing; and in 1836, at the age of thirty-four, Wyeth returned empty-handed to Boston and went back into the ice business.

Yet, from the long view, Wyeth's project did more than any other to win Oregon for the United States. The ornithologists helped to make that country known. Jason Lee and his fellow missionaries settled in the Willamette valley near the present Salem, Oregon, and combined with former employees of the Hudson's Bay Company to raise wheat and cattle. Lee's backers published a periodical called *The Oregonian and Indians' Advocate*, packed with luscious sales-talk on the Oregon country.

One could hardly exaggerate the beauty of this country. The majestic Columbia river, teeming with salmon, breaks through the Cascade range, where snowcapped peaks (Hood, St. Helena, Adams, Rainier) soar like serene white souls above virgin fir forests. Here are the fertile valleys of the Clackamas, the Willamette, and the Umatilla, ripe for grain fields and orchards, and a mild, moist climate more like Old England's than New England's. And the continent is rimmed by an ironbound coast, with an occasional sand beach on which the long Pacific surges eternally tumble and roar.

Fort Vancouver offered a market for all the grain and livestock the settlers could raise; the difficulties were in getting there, and settling the question of what flag you were under when you arrived. Presidents Jackson, Van Buren, Harrison, and Tyler paid no attention to Oregon. Nothing was done to extend American law to this region, or to settle the question of sovereignty. Nevertheless, Lee and his neighbors, following the same instinct for self-government that had produced the Mayflower Compact and the State of Franklin, called a meeting at Champoeg in the Willamette valley and drew up a compact for governing Oregon country on 5 July 1843. The laws of Iowa were adopted, and arrangements were made to settle land titles, that fruitful subject of frontier disputes.

In the meantime the American Board of Foreign Missions had sent religious and medical missionaries to the eastern part of the Oregon country, especially the future state of Idaho. In response to a plea from four Flatheads who had visited St. Louis, the Board sent out young Dr. Marcus Whitman with his twenty-year-old bride in the spring of 1836. It took them five months from St. Louis to reach Fort Walla Walla. Narcissa Whitman, first white woman to pass the Rockies, had to discard one article after another from their hand-drawn cart; even her bridal trunk.

This Whitman party and others that soon followed, established missions to the Cayuse Indians, to the Nez Percé, and to the Flathead, this last near the site of Spokane. For a decade these missions flourished and part of the New Testament was printed in Nez Percé. But the Cayuse became estranged when tough characters of the heavy migration of 1845–47 harassed them and brought in measles. Owing to an unfounded rumor that Dr. Whitman's measles medicine was poison, he and most of the mission group were massacred in November 1847. This provoked the first of Oregon's Indian conflicts, the Cayuse War, in which 250 armed men punished the guilty Indians.

Nor did the Catholic church neglect this mission field; by 1847 there were fourteen Jesuit missionaries in the Northwest. Father Pierre-Jean de Smet from the Catholic University of St. Louis, "Blackrobe" to the Indians, founded the Sacré Coeur Mission in the Coeur d'Alene country.

In 1842 "Oregon fever" struck the frontier folk of Iowa, Missouri, Illinois, and Kentucky. By temperament and tradition these were backwoodsmen who had no use for treeless prairies or arid high plains; they wanted wood, water, and game, which the Oregon country had in abundance, and to slough off the fevers and agues that afflicted them in the lowlands bordering the Mississippi. Independence, Missouri, was their jumping-off place. "Prairie schooners," as the canvas-covered Conestoga wagons were nicknamed, assembled there in May when the grass of the plains was fresh and green. Parties were organized, a captain appointed, an experienced mountaineer engaged as guide; and with blowing of bugles and cracking of long whips, the caravan, 100 wagons strong with a herd of cattle on the hoof, moved up the west bank of the Missouri. At Fort Leavenworth, bastion of the Indian frontier, the emigrants broke contact with their flag and its protection.

At first there was neither road nor trail. Near Council Bluffs, where the Missouri is joined by the Platte river, the route to Oregon turned west to follow the Platte over the Great Plains. Until wagon wheels had ground ruts into the sod, it was easy to lose the way. Numerous tributaries, swollen and turbid in the spring of the year, had to be forded or swum, to the damage of stores and baggage. Every night the caravan formed a hollow square of wagons around a campfire, the horses and mules inside; cattle were allowed to graze outside, as no Indians wanted them. Sentries stood guard and the howling of prairie wolves was drowned by a chorus of hymns and old ballads. At dawn the horses and mules were let out to browse for an hour or two; then

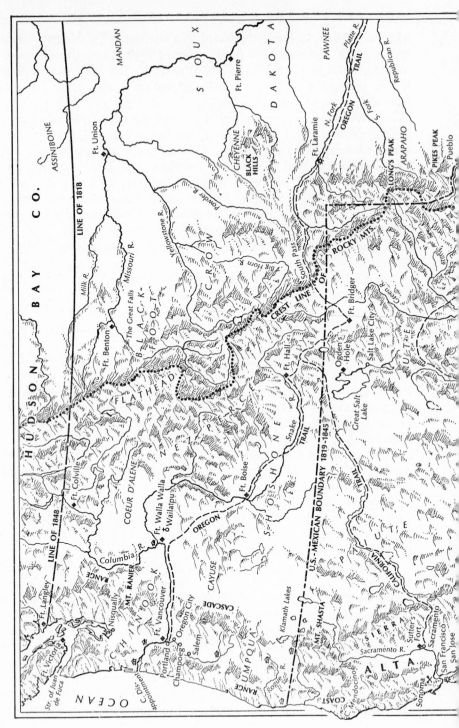

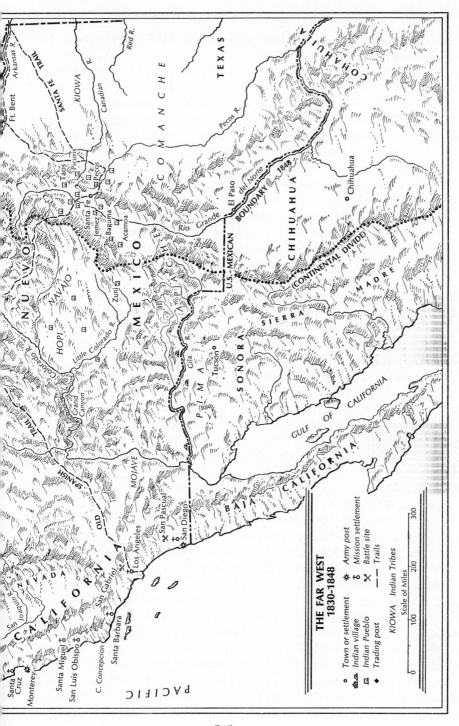

THE FAR WEST
1830-1848

° Town or settlement   ☆ Army post
▲ Indian village   ✝ Mission settlement
▣ Indian Pueblo   ✕ Battle site
◆ Trading post   — Trails

KIOWA   Indian Tribes

Scale of Miles

0   100   200   300

the oxen were rounded up and hitched to the wagons, bugles blew gaily, and another start was made down-sun.

Following the north fork of the Platte, the trail became hilly, then mountainous as one turned aside to avoid the Laramie spur of the Rockies. Beyond South Pass came the worst part of the journey — a long, hard pull across the arid Wyoming basin where the grass was scanty and alkali deposits made the water almost undrinkable. Between the Gros Ventre and Teton ranges of the Rockies the Oregon-bound emigrant found westward-flowing waters and took heart; but there were still 800 miles more to go to the lower Columbia, following the meanderings of the Snake river. Wagons were often rafted down the stream; and with fair luck a party that left Independence in May might celebrate Thanksgiving Day in the Willamette valley. But it was a lucky caravan indeed that arrived with the same number of souls that started, and some of the weaker parties completely disappeared — whether by starvation after losing the trail, or at the hands of Indians, no one ever knew.

Hitherto there had been no law in the Oregon country except that of the Champoeg provisional government. The heavy immigration of the next three years, some 5000 strong, strained this organization and convinced Congress that something must be done to provide a legal government. First, however, the federal government wished to reach a settlement with Great Britain.

Webster and Ashburton discussed the Oregon question in 1842 but reached no conclusion. Next year, agitation for annexing the whole of Oregon up to the border of Russian Alaska, 54° 40′ N, started in the Western states. President Tyler opened negotiations on the subject in 1844, repeating the proposal formerly made by J. Q. Adams, to divide the territory along latitude 49°. Lord Aberdeen, like his predecessors, refused to lower the Union Jack from the right bank of the Columbia.

If the question were decided by actual occupation, that British claim was fair. Over 700 British subjects but only half a dozen American citizens had settled north of the Columbia. The United States, however, could afford to wait. A decline in the fur trade was making Fort Vancouver unprofitable, and the increasing number of American immigrants threatened its security. The Hudson's Bay Company abandoned this fort in 1845 and erected a new post at Victoria on Vancouver Island.

By this time an expansionist, James K. Polk, had become President of the United States. The Democratic platform called for "re-occupation of Oregon, re-annexation of Texas." In his annual message of December 1845 Polk asserted that the American title up to latitude 54° 40′ N was "clear and unquestionable." He asked for authority to terminate the joint occupation agreement of 1818, and Congress gave it. Polk never intended to risk war over Oregon, since he expected shortly to be fighting Mexico for California. So, when Lord Aberdeen proposed to extend the international boundary along latitude 49° N to Puget Sound, thence to the ocean through Juan de Fuca Strait, leaving Vancouver Island to Canada, Polk accepted. He submitted this offer to his cabinet on 6 June 1846, when the war with Mexico was but three weeks old, and to the Senate immediately after. It was during this debate that a Western expansionist coined the slogan, "Fifty-four Forty or Fight!" Nevertheless, the Senate on 15 June consented to a treaty accepting Aberdeen's boundary. It took five months for the news to reach the settlements on the Willamette.

Thus Canada, as well as the United States, obtained an outlet to the Pacific. Except for a minor controversy over the islands of Puget Sound, this western end of the lengthy frontier between Canada and the United States gave no further trouble.

3. The Mormons

The Church of Jesus Christ of the Latter-day Saints, commonly called the Mormons, was responsible for settling Utah.

Joseph Smith came of a New England family which, after ten moves in less than twenty years, settled at Palmyra, New York, in the midst of the "burned-over district." An Angel of the Lord, so Joseph claimed, showed him the hiding place of inscribed gold plates, together with a pair of magic spectacles which enabled him to read the characters. The resulting Book of Mormon, first printed in 1830, described the history of allegedly lost tribes of Israel (the Indians), whom the Saints were commanded to redeem from paganism. Joseph Smith, a shrewd, able Yankee, organized his church as a co-operative theocracy, all power emanating from himself as "Prophet." The hostility of "gentile" neighbors forced the Saints to remove first to Kirtland, Ohio, then to Missouri; and again, in 1839, to a place in Illinois which the Prophet named Nauvoo. There Smith received a "revelation" in favor of polygamy.

In Illinois the Mormons were courted by both political parties and Nauvoo was given a city charter. But the settlement grew so rapidly — faster, even, than Chicago — that the Illinois "gentiles" (as the Mormons called other Christians) became alarmed, and a group of them in 1844 murdered Smith. Brigham Young, who succeeded to the Prophet's mantle and took over five of his twenty-seven widows, directed retaliation on the gentiles by a corps of "avenging angels," and for two years terror reigned in western Illinois. It was clearly time for another move.

Yet the Mormons had made an astonishing gain in numbers. Their missionaries had been raking in converts from the Northern states since 1831; and in 1840, when Brigham Young visited Liverpool, England became one of their principal harvest fields. Thousands of poor workers and tenant farmers were charmed by the prospect of decent living and the promise of heavenly "thrones, kingdoms, principalities and powers." Almost 4000 English converts reached Nauvoo between 1840 and 1846, and 40 or 50 churches of Latter-day Saints in the old country contributed modest tithes to the Prophet's bulging treasury.

Under their new Moses, Brigham Young, a ruthless autocrat but a leader of energy and vision, the Mormons abandoned Nauvoo in 1846 and began their great westward journey, several thousand strong. After wintering near Council Bluffs, Brigham Young pushed ahead with a pioneer band along a new trail on the north bank of the Platte. In July 1847 he reached the promised land, the basin of the Great Salt Lake. By the end of 1848, 5000 people had arrived in the future State of Utah, which Brigham Young called Deseret.

This new Canaan was an inhospitable land. Young chose it in the hope that his Saints would no longer be molested by gentiles, and because it was Mexican territory; but the Mexican War changed that. Arid wastes, where salt and alkali deposits glistened among sagebrush thickets, sloped down from the Rocky Mountains to the Great Salt Lake, desolate as another Dead Sea. But in the mountains lay natural reservoirs of rain and snow, the means of quickening life.

For such unfamiliar conditions the experience of English-speaking pioneers was inadequate, but the community sense of the Mormons proved competent to cope with them. Brigham Young caused irrigation canals and ditches to be dug, appointed committees to control water for the public benefit, discarding the common-law doctrine of riparian rights. He set up a system of small farms, intensively cultivated and carefully fertilized. He forbade speculation in land, but respected private property and accumulated a large fortune for himself. He kept the Indians quiet by a judicious mixture of firmness and justice. He repressed heresy and schism with a heavy hand. He organized foreign and domestic missions and financed both transatlantic and transcontinental immigration. By means of a complicated hierarchy he controlled both civil and spiritual affairs with Yankee shrewdness, rough humor, and substantial justice, holding himself responsible only to God.

For ten years there was intermittent want and starvation in Deseret, and the gold rush of 1849 to California caused unrest. Brigham Young announced in the Tabernacle at Salt Lake City, "If you Elders of Israel want to go to the gold mines, go and be damned!" The wiser Saints found it more profitable to sell corn and potatoes to passing Argonauts. Yearly the community grew in numbers and wealth, a polygamous theocracy within a monogamous and democratic nation. Congress organized Deseret as Utah Territory in 1850, and President Fillmore appointed Brigham Young territorial governor. Federal judges were driven from Utah when they refused to do his will; and when President Buchanan in 1857–58 sent an army of regulars under Colonel Albert Sidney Johnston to support a new territorial governor, the United States forces, defeated by Young's scorched-earth strategy, obtained only nominal submission. In the Civil War, Utah was practically neutral. After the Civil War, Utah and the Mormons profited by prosperity and the influx of new elements. Polygamy, forbidden by federal law in 1862, gradually died out. The Latter-day Saints brought comfort, happiness, and self-respect to thousands of humble folk; and Brigham Young must be included among the most successful commonwealth builders of the English-speaking world.

THE MORMON HAND–CART SONG

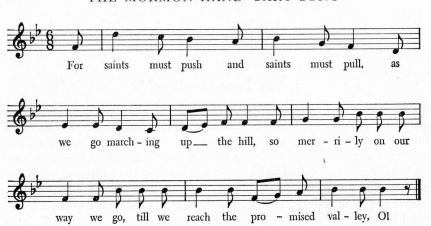

For saints must push and saints must pull, as we go march-ing up__ the hill, so mer-ri-ly on our way we go, till we reach the pro-mised val-ley, O!

X X X V

Texas and the Mexican War

1820-1848

1. *The Lone Star Republic*

LONG BEFORE the Oregon question was settled, even before it arose, another problem of power and expansion was rising in the Southwest. While one column of pioneers deployed into the prairies of Illinois and Iowa, and another was preparing to wind over the Oregon Trail, a third from Louisiana and the Mississippi valley had crossed into Mexican territory and taken possession of the coastal plain of Texas. Expansion in that direction was no simple matter of endurance or of driving back redskins. In Texas the English-speaking pioneer came into contact with a proud and ancient civilization, represented by the Republic of Mexico. Who could tell whether Mexico might develop the same expansive force as the United States?

In 1820 Upper California (the present state of California), New Mexico (including Arizona), and Texas, frontier provinces of Mexico as of New Spain, spread out toward the United States and were attached to the parent trunk by the frailest of stems. Explored as early as the sixteenth century by the Spaniards, they had been thinly colonized after a long interval, and in the Roman rather than the English sense. Missions had been planted among the Indians as centers of civilization and exploitation; frontier garrisons were established to protect the fathers in their work; and such few colonists as could be persuaded to venture so far were generously endowed by the Spanish government with lands and Indian serfs. Although a constant drain on the mother country, these frontier provinces were maintained mostly as protection against westward-pushing Anglo-Americans. The new Republic of Mexico, weak, distracted, and lacking expansive energy, knew not how to use them, but was too proud to dispose of them. Garrisons were withdrawn, the missions secularized, and the Indians allowed to relapse into their old folkways.

Santa Fe, capital and only town of New Mexico, was the gateway to a country of marvels and enchantments, shimmering plains with no vegetation but strange cacti, mesas striped with ochre and vermilion, aboriginal cliff dwellings, and the stupendous canyon of the Colorado river. Annually from 1824, an armed caravan of American traders assembled at Independence, Missouri, and followed the Sante Fe trail with pack mule and wagon through the country of the Osage and Comanche to this lonely emporium, returning with silver and peltry.

In 1823 a wedge of North Americans thrust across Mexico's borders into Texas. That province, 750 miles long from the Sabine river to El Paso, and of equal depth from the tip of the "panhandle" to the mouth of the Rio Grande, is larger than France and almost as varied in climate and natural resources. The pioneers found moist gulf plains studded with cane-brakes, and cold, arid plateaus; dense forests of pine and hardwood; prairies of a deep, black, waxy loam perfect for cotton growing, and others of lighter soil, adapted for grain; sagebrush and yucca deserts; and the Llano Estacado or High Plains where roamed immense herds of buffalo and mustang. Texas had never formed part of Louisiana, and the American claim to it, renounced in the Florida Treaty of 1819, was based on nothing better than the supposition that Napoleon was about to seize it before he decided to sell Louisiana to the United States. Nevertheless, no sooner had President Monroe agreed upon the Sabine and Red rivers as the southwestern boundary of the United States, than he was attacked for giving away something for nothing. Presidents Adams and Jackson, as we have seen, pressed the Mexican government to sell Texas. The first offer was received as an insult and the repetition created resentment.

Inexplicably, Mexico encouraged emigration from the United States to Texas. An important grant was given in 1821 to Moses Austin of Connecticut, successively dry-goods merchant in Philadelphia and Richmond, owner of the Chiswell lead mines in Virginia, pioneer lead miner in Missouri, and banker in St. Louis. He died six months after obtaining this Texan grant, but the Mexican Congress confirmed it to his son in 1823. This gave Stephen F. Austin the privilege of settling 300 American families in one of the most fertile regions of Texas; later, the number was increased. Each family received free 177 acres of rich tillage, together with 13,000 acres of prairie pasture, Austin taking a bonus of 65,000 acres. By 1834 Austin's colony comprised 20,000 white colonists and 2000 slaves, outnumbering the native Mexicans in Texas four to one. Austin, a grave and gentle young man, chose recruits for his colony with care, and ruled it with autocratic power until 1829. In social structure it resembled an English proprietary colony like Maryland; and Texas was more law-abiding and better governed than any nineteenth-century American frontier.

Although antislavery by preference, Austin found himself in the same dilemma as every colonist with capital: the choice btween pioneer poverty and using some form of forced labor. There were no Indians who could be made peons, and the soil offered such rich opportunities for cotton and sugar culture that Southern planters would not come unless permitted to bring slaves, and could not prosper without them. The Mexican Congress in 1831 declared slavery abolished throughout the Republic. But Austin was always able to obtain some "explanation" of the decree which allowed his people to hold slaves in fact, if not by law. Similarly, it was a condition of his grant that all settlers should be Roman Catholics, but very few were.

Many factors pulled Texas away from Mexico. Austin and the older American *empresarios* tried to be good Mexicans; but it was difficult to respect a government in constant turmoil and revolution. The North American colonist admired the horsemanship of his Mexican neighbor, adopted his saddle and trappings and some of his vocabulary; but his general attitude toward him was condescending. There was trouble about the tariff, representation, immigration, and with Mexican army garrisons. And in the early 1830's Austin's law-abiding pioneers began to be outnumbered by men of another type — swashbucklers like Sam Houston of Tennessee, a former subordinate of General Jackson; David G. Burnet of Ohio, who had followed Miranda to Caracas in 1806; Branch T. Archer "of stalwart form and Cato-like look," who had fled from Virginia after a successful duel; the Bowie brothers of Louisiana, slave smugglers who designed the long knife that bears their name; Davy Crockett, a professional backwoodsman; others of restless ambition and pungent personality, who had left their country for their country's good.

President Santa Anna's proclamation in 1835 of a unified constitution, which made a clean sweep of state rights, caused the secession of Texas. The North American settlers set up a provisional government and expelled the Mexican garrison from San Antonio de Bexar. Santa Anna with 3000 men then crossed the Rio Grande and besieged the Alamo, the fortress of San Antonio, garrisoned by fewer than 200 Texans. They refused to retreat or to surrender. On 5 March 1836 Santa Anna assaulted the Alamo, captured it after every Texan had been killed or wounded, and killed the wounded.

Already a convention elected by North American colonists had proclaimed the independent Republic of Texas, elected Burnet president, and adopted a flag. Santa Anna's army advanced eastward, settlers and President Burnet fleeing before him; but Generalissimo Sam Houston managed to keep an army together and awaited the Mexicans in a grove of live oak by the ferry of the San Jacinto river, not far from the site of the city that bears his name. On 21 April, shouting "Remember the Alamo!" the Texas cavalry led by a gallant Georgian with the conquering name of Mirabeau Buonaparte Lamar, attacked Santa Anna's army. Infantry followed and put the Mexicans to flight, taking the general prisoner. The Texans ratified their new constitution, legalized Negro slavery, elected Sam Houston president, and sent an envoy to Washington to demand annexation to the United States or recognition as an independent republic.

Enthusiasm over the defense of the Alamo, as well as liberal land offers, drew hundreds of North American adventurers into the Texas army. President Jackson made no attempt to prevent this unneutral aid, but on questions of recognition and annexation his attitude was diplomatically correct. Only on his last full day of office (3 March 1837), after Congress had approved, did he recognize the Lone Star Republic.

Texas would have preferred outright annexation, but that was a year of agitation in Congress over the domestic slave trade and the gag resolution. On 23 May 1836 Calhoun remarked in the Senate that "there were powerful reasons why Texas should be a part of this Union. The Southern States, owning a slave population, were deeply interested in preventing that country from having the power to annoy them." The same year a Quaker abolitionist named Benjamin Lundy, who had been to Texas, brought out a pamphlet called *The War in Texas; a Crusade against the Government set on foot by Slaveholders*. His theory was simple: the Texas revolution was a conspiracy to gain new territory for slave-grown cotton. This appealed to that widespread Northern sentiment opposed to the political dominance of the South and to the extension of slavery. Everyone realized that the annexation of Texas would affect the balance of power between North and South. On 1 November 1837 the Vermont legislature "solemnly protested" against the admission of any state "whose constitution tolerates domestic slavery." That, naturally, aroused a contrary feeling in the South. Calhoun solemnly announced that any attempt to exclude a state on account of its "peculiar institution" would be a virtual dissolution of the Union.

The slave states were beginning to realize that they had got the thin end of the Missouri Compromise of 1820, prohibiting slavery in territories north of 36° 30'. Arkansas and Michigan had just been admitted to the Union, making thirteen free and thirteen slave states. Florida was the only slave territory left; but three free territories — Wisconsin, Iowa, and Minnesota — would be demanding admission shortly, and more would follow if the Indian barrier to the Great Plains were broken. The Alabama legislature, on Christmas Day 1837, resolved: "It needs but a glance at the map to satisfy the most superficial observer that an overbalance is produced by the extreme northeast, which as regards territory would be happily corrected and counterbalanced by the annexation of Texas." It might be carved into several slave states, a New Slavonia to balance New England.

A resolution for the annexation of Texas was promptly introduced in Congress. President Van Buren, engaged at the time in delicate negotiations with Mexico and anxious to keep slavery out of politics, used his influence against the resolution, which was finally smothered by a speech of J. Q. Adams that took three weeks to deliver in July 1838.

The politicians were content to let so explosive a question rest. In the meantime, thousands of petty planters, ruined by the panic of 1837, left their debts at home and started life anew across the Sabine.

2. President Tyler Annexes Texas

Texas built a navy, accumulated a national debt, and received British and French recognition. The Lone Star Republic now belonged to the family of nations, but for how long? Her white population was barely 50,000, and

Mexico had 6 or 7 million people. Texan finances were even shakier than Mexico's — a debt of $7 million, and currency that depreciated to the vanishing point. Mexico made no attempt to reconquer Texas except for a fantastic raid in 1842. Next year Charles Elliot, British minister to Texas, negotiated a truce; but at any turn of the political wheel in Mexico City the truce might be denounced and hostilities renewed. Political conditions in Texas were chaotic. President Mirabeau Buonaparte Lamar aimed to annex New Mexico, California and the northern tier of Mexican states to the new republic, and himself led an expedition against Santa Fe, which the Mexicans easily defeated. Sam Houston, who succeeded Lamar after that imperialist incursion, felt that Texas needed protection and security, not enlargement. He preferred annexation to the United States, but if the United States refused, the best bet would be a dual mediation by Britain and France to obtain Mexican recognition of Texas independence, and a guarantee to maintain it.

Lord Aberdeen in the foreign office toyed with the idea; Louis-Philippe, the French king, still smarting from his bout with President Jackson, was ready to go along. For here was a ready-made wedge between the United States and Latin America, and an independent source of supply for cotton, sugar, and tobacco. There was little doubt of Texan acceptance if the offer were made in time; but this mediation scheme required the consent of Mexico, and no Mexican cabinet dared accept Texan independence. More sense of reality and less of prestige at Mexico City in 1844 might have changed the entire course of American expansion.

Amid the cross-currents of notes, suggestions and conversations between London, Paris, Washington, Austin, and Mexico City, another fact stands out clearly: the fear of Southern statesmen that Texas might abolish slavery. Duff Green, Calhoun's journalist son-in-law, picked up in London the alarming gossip that Aberdeen had agreed to guarantee Texan independence if the Lone Star Republic would do just that; he would even lend money to compensate Texas slaveholders, as England had done for her West Indian subjects. The prospect of Texas becoming a refuge for fugitive slaves from the Gulf states, even a springboard for abolition propaganda, alarmed Southern leaders to the point of panic. Abel P. Upshur, President Tyler's secretary of state, at once began negotiating a treaty of annexation with the Texas minister at Washington, and informed him that the English abolition project was inadmissible.

At this juncture a fatal accident on a United States warship influenced political history. Captain Robert F. Stockton had persuaded Congress to build U.S.S. *Princeton*, a 950-ton auxiliary screw frigate. Her architect was John Ericsson, a young Swedish engineer who had invented the propeller, and whom Stockton had persuaded to visit the United States. Equally revolutionary was *Princeton*'s main battery, consisting of two smooth-bore 12-inch wrought-iron guns, one called "Oregon" which Ericsson had brought from England; the other "Peacemaker," designed by Stockton and cast in an American foundry. Both were tested successfully; but on a gala excursion down the

Potomac on 28 February 1844, with President Tyler, cabinet ministers, diplomats, senators, and numerous ladies on board, Peacemaker burst. Secretary Upshur, navy secretary Gilmer, and a New York state senator were killed; Senator Thomas H. Benton and nineteen others were severely wounded.

The explosion virtually threw into President Tyler's arms the fair Julia Gardiner, daughter of the slaughtered state senator; she became the second Mrs. Tyler and mistress of the White House. And the loss of the two secretaries gave the President an opportunity to reconstruct his cabinet, without a single Northerner or even a Whig. John C. Calhoun returned to power as secretary of state. Tyler's compass needle no longer vacillated; it pointed southwest, to Texas.

Calhoun was appointed for two main purposes, to get Texas into the Union and to obtain for Tyler the Democratic nomination for the presidency in 1844. Like several later Vice Presidents who have succeeded through death, "Tyler too" dearly wanted to be elected President "in his own right." Calhoun accepted the state department because he hoped to be the blacksmith to link Texas with Oregon, forging a chain of South and West, and so reach the coveted presidency.

Lord Aberdeen, as soon as the gossip about his intention to emancipate slaves in Texas reached London, sent a dignified denial to Secretary Calhoun: "Great Britain desires, and is constantly exerting herself to procure, the general abolition of slavery throughout the world. But the means which she has adopted, and will continue to adopt, for this humane and virtuous purpose, are open and undisguised." Calhoun replied by reading the British government a lesson on the beauties of Negro slavery. He also observed that the "threatened danger" to the "safety and prosperity of the Union" justified American annexation of Texas. In other words, the mere prospect of abolition in a neighboring republic was sufficient reason to absorb it.

To Northern Whigs there seemed to be no more danger to the United States in leaving Texas independent than in Canada remaining British; the only things threatened were slavery, and the dominance of the Democratic party. Four Northern state legislatures, and those of Delaware and Maryland, all under Whig control, resolved that the annexation of a foreign country was unconstitutional and "an alarming encroachment upon the rights of the freemen of the Union." On the other hand, six Southern state legislatures, together with Democratic Maine, New Hampshire, and Illinois, memorialized Congress for annexation; and the extremist party in South Carolina made the fantastic proposal that, if annexation failed, the Southern states should secede and join the Republic of Texas.

A second annexation treaty, which Calhoun negotiated with some difficulty (since Sam Houston was playing coy and beginning to think that Texas would be a better theater for his talents than the United States Senate), failed to obtain ratification. But Tyler had another card up his sleeve. After the presidential election of 1844 he recommended that Texas be admitted to the Union by joint resolution of both houses, which did not require a two-thirds vote. This deed of questionable constitutionality was done on 28 February 1845. President Tyler on his last day of office had the satisfaction of sending a courier to inform President Houston that only the consent of the Lone Star Republic was necessary to make Texas the twenty-eighth state of the Union. That she gave promptly.

This indecent haste to annex Texas, in marked contrast to the administration's indifference to Oregon, was occasioned by fear on the part of influential Southern editors and politicians that the Republic of Texas would abolish slavery.

President Tyler was regarded by Whigs as a renegade, and the Democrats would have none of him. Yet, on the whole, Tyler was a good second-rate President. To his credit are the Maine boundary negotiations with England, and a reorganization and partial rebuilding of the navy. Socially, his administration was brilliant. Slim, gracious, and handsome, he and his charming young wife led capital society. He was the last Virginian in the White House. But by the end of his term he had incurred the dislike or hatred of Whigs and Democrats alike; and the country roared with laughter over his literally missing the boat — the day steamer from Washington to Norfolk — on the day after Polk's inauguration. It took so long to organize the ex-presidential cavalcade that by the time it arrived at the wharf, the steamboat had cast off. Someone shouted, "Hold on — the President is coming!" To which the skipper, a stout Whig, replied, "Tyler be damned — let him stay!" And the ex-President had to wait for the night boat.

3. President Polk and the Road to War

While Tyler and Calhoun were plotting to pull Texas into the Union, wiser men were trying to keep the subject out of politics. Martin Van Buren, who expected to receive the next Democratic presidential nomination, discussed Texas in 1842 with Henry Clay, equally confident of being the Whig choice. Each agreed to publish a letter opposing the immediate annexation of Texas, and did so; Van Buren predicting that to rush the affair would mean war with Mexico, Clay declaring that he would welcome Texas only if she could be annexed "without dishonor, without war, with the common consent of the Union, and upon just and fair terms."

These praiseworthy efforts to preserve the peace lost Van Buren the nomination and Clay the election. For "manifest destiny" was in the air. When the Democratic nominating convention met at Baltimore in May 1844, a majority wanted Van Buren. But the Southern and expansionist delegates, led by Robert J. Walker of Mississippi, put over the two-thirds rule,[1] which Little Van had not votes enough to surmount. After playing

1. First adopted in 1836, but not used in 1840; after this it continued in Democratic national conventions until 1936.

around with several candidates (even old "Rumpsey Dumpsey" Johnson), the expansionists trotted out the first "dark horse" in presidential history. His name, new to most of the country, was James K. Polk.

By holding firmly to "Old Hickory's" coattails, Polk had become speaker of the house and governor of Tennessee; now, with support of the aged and ailing Jackson, he won the presidential nomination. To appease Northern Democrats, "Re-occupation of Oregon" was given equal honors on the platform with "Re-annexation of Texas"; but Oregon was a minor factor in the campaign. Clay, now sixty-seven years old, received the Whig nomination by acclamation. He had recently made a triumphal progress through the South, speaking to "vast concourses of people," and felt confident of election. But his letter on Texas offended the annexationists, and enough antislavery Whigs voted for Birney, the abolitionist candidate in New York, to give Polk a slight edge in that state, whose electoral vote proved decisive. The popular vote was very close — 1,337,000 for Polk; 1,299,000 for Clay.

Nobody really knows why Americans vote the way they do, and often they don't understand it themselves. But, in this instance, a growing conviction of America's "manifest destiny" to expand west to the Pacific and south to at least the Rio Grande brought victory to obscure Polk over radiant Clay. America was on the move, and anyone who objected, be he Mexican, European, or Whig, had better get out of the way! The prospect of acquiring Texas, Oregon, and California appealed to simple folk who were recovering confidence after the hard times of 1837–41. They wanted all three, and Polk got them. If *vox populi* be *vox dei*, Polk was the Almighty's choice; and the Almighty must have willed a good, stiff bloodletting for America. Had Henry Clay become President in 1845, he would undoubtedly have managed to placate Mexico; and with no Mexican War there would have been no Civil War, at least not in 1861.

But would Clay have acquired California?

California! The very name connoted mystery and romance. It had been given to a mythical kingdom "near the terrestrial paradise," in a Spanish novel of chivalry written in the lifetime of Columbus. President Polk did not read novels, but he wanted California much as Don Quixote wooed Dulcinea, without ever having seen her, and knowing very little about her. The future Golden State, with forests of giant pines and sequoias, broad valleys suited for wheat, and narrow vales where the vine flourishes, extensive grazing grounds, mountains abounding in superb scenery and mineral wealth, was then a Mexican province, ripe for the picking. Barely 6000 white men lived there; and the Indians, a strangely feeble lot, were not to be feared. Oregon had been well advertised for years, but in 1845 almost nothing was known in the United States about California, except two descriptions — R. H. Dana's *Two Years Before the Mast*, and J. C. Frémont's *Report of the Exploring Expedition to . . . Oregon and North California*.

When Mexico opened her trade to foreigners, ships which rounded the

Horn both ways began a profitable exchange of consumer goods from Boston for California hides, and several hundred New Englanders settled there, speaking Spanish with a down-east twang and marrying California heiresses. Dana wrote an unforgettable description of ships anchored off Santa Barbara, swaying in the long Pacific swell, sailors "droghing" hides on their heads out to the ship's longboat or hurling them over the cliff at San Juan Capistrano, and the relaxed life of the Spanish Californians, soon to be overwhelmed by energetic *Yanquis*.

About this time John C. Frémont, a twenty-eight-year-old second lieutenant in the United States Army's topographical corps, wooed and won sixteen-year-old Jessie, daughter of Senator Thomas H. Benton of Missouri. Papa Benton, equally devoted to daughter, hard money, and Western expansion, conceived the plan of sending his son-in-law exploring, with competent guides to take care of him. On his second trip, Frémont struck political pay dirt. Turning south from Oregon into the future Nevada and then into the Sacramento valley, he passed through central and southern California and returned via Santa Fe. His *Report* of this journey (largely written by Jessie), published in the fall of 1845, gave Washington its first detailed knowledge of the rich, luscious possibilities of California and the feeble bonds by which Mexico held that romantic land. And it made Frémont a presidential candidate.

Even though President Polk knew little about California except what Frémont related, he wished desperately to acquire it for the United States because he feared lest England or France get it first. First he tried to buy it, but Mexico refused to sell. Next, he tried to stir up revolution in California. When that failed to come off on time, he baited Mexico into a war with the United States in which California was the big pile of blue chips.

The country knew hardly more of James K. Polk than Polk knew of California. A stiff, angular person not yet fifty years of age, he already looked like an old man. Sharp gray eyes and a prim mouth set off a sad, lean face. Secretive, unhumorous, and prejudiced; to him, Whigs, Englishmen, abolitionists, and even many Democrats were villains. But Polk dominated a cabinet of able men, half of them his seniors; and in a single term he accomplished all his aims — to reduce the tariff (which a Whig congress had jacked up again in 1842), to re-establish Van Buren's independent treasury which the Whigs had destroyed, to settle the Oregon question, and to acquire California. All this with the handicap of chronic ill health, which the situation of the White House on the edge of "foggy bottom" made worse. Those swamps bordering the Potomac were breeding grounds of mosquitoes and flies which (completely undetected by science) carried the germs of malaria, dysentery, and typhoid to Presidents and garbage collectors alike; and the White House as yet was innocent of plumbing, or even a fixed bathtub.

Polk's apprehensions about California were not unfounded, in an era when England and France were picking up Pacific empires in New Zealand and the Marquesas, and King Kamehameha III of Hawaii even offered to place the

Islands under the protection of Queen Victoria. She was not interested; but her Admiralty had an eye on San Francisco Bay, and there was talk of canceling Mexico's debt to Britain in exchange for California. Polk would have preferred to buy California from Mexico, rather than take it, but similar propositions respecting Texas had been turned down.

Any chance of Mexico's selling California was spoiled by the surprising attempt of Commodore Thomas Ap Catesby Jones to beat the gun. He was at Callao in 1842, in command of the Pacific Squadron, when he read in the newspapers a peppery note from the Mexican government to President Tyler, from which he assumed that war with Mexico was inevitable. He set sail, arrived off Monterey on 19 October and forced the astonished Mexican governor to surrender to him. Then, upon receiving later newspapers which showed that no war had been declared, Commodore Jones returned Monterey to the Mexicans and sailed away. This premature "conquest of California" by Ap Catesby Jones occurred before Polk became President, but it convinced Mexican officials that North Americans were aggressive men of bad faith.

In October 1845 Polk's secretary of war wrote a significant dispatch to the American consul at Monterey, suggesting that the Californians follow the Texans' example. "If the people should desire to unite their destiny with ours, they would be received as brethren. . . . Their true policy for the present is to let events take their course, unless an attempt should be made to transfer them without their consent either to Great Britain or France." And Frémont was on his way to California with a third exploring expedition designed to support any revolt that might erupt.

Shortly after Polk entered office, Mexico protested against the annexation of Texas and broke diplomatic relations with the United States. In July 1845, after Texas had formally accepted annexation, Polk ordered a detachment of the regular army under General Zachary Taylor to take position on the Nueces river, the southwestern border of Texas, to protect the new state against possible Mexican assault. Polk's apologists make much of the sophistry that as soon as Taylor crossed the Sabine river into Texas he was invading Mexico from the Mexican point of view, hence war was inevitable. This argument makes no allowance for Latin disinclination to acknowledge a disagreeable *fait accompli*. In 1845 Spain was still technically at war with most of Spanish America, although there had been no hostilities between them for over twenty years; but no Latin American state would have thought itself thereby justified in attacking Cuba. If Polk had been content with Texas and had not reached for California, there is no reason to suppose that Mexico would have initiated hostilities, although she would long have delayed acknowledging the loss of Texas.

While Polk was priming revolt in California, he made another attempt to buy it, in exchange for writing off claims. These claims were for repudiated bonds, revoked concessions and damage to American property during the civil wars that broke out every few months. Hitherto, America had been forbearing, in comparison with the French government which sent a squadron to collect by bombarding San Juan de Ulúa in 1839. Mexico and the United States in 1843 ratified a convention by virtue of which Mexico was to pay about $4.5 million in twenty quarterly installments. After three installments, Mexico suspended payment — as several states of the Union had done on their bonds — but did not repudiate the debt, as Michigan and Mississippi had done with theirs. Torn by civil dissension and virtually bankrupt, she could then do no better.

Here was the President's opportunity. On 10 November 1845 he commissioned John Slidell minister to Mexico, with instructions to assume unpaid claims of American citizens against Mexico, in return for Mexican recognition of the Rio Grande as the southern boundary of the United States. Another $5 million was to be offered for the cession of New Mexico, and "money would be no object" for California. This was a sincere offer from a practical man who hoped to put through a business deal with a government that lacked business sense. Slidell was refused reception by President Herrera. Then, General Paredes raised the standard of rebellion on the ground that Herrera was proposing a treasonable bargain with the United States! His revolution succeeded, as most Mexican revolutions did; and by New Year's Day 1846 the government was in the hands of a military faction spoiling for a fight with the United States.

Polk did not give them long to wait. On 13 January 1846, the day after he received word of Herrera's refusal to receive Slidell, but before he knew of the Paredes revolution, Polk ordered General Taylor to cross the Nueces river and occupy the left bank of the Rio Grande del Norte. That was an act of war, since the Nueces had been the southern boundary of Texas for a century. The barren region between it and the Rio Grande, east of longitude 100°, belonged to the State of Tamaulipas. The authority of the Lone Star Republic had never been exercised beyond the Nueces. One of the best exposés of the falseness of Polk's claim that both banks of the Rio Grande were American soil was made by a freshman congressman from Illinois named Abraham Lincoln.

4. *Glory and Conquest*

General Taylor on 23 March 1846 occupied the left bank of the Rio Grande, his guns bearing on the Mexican town of Matamoras. The Mexican general there in command ordered him back to the Nueces. Taylor replied by blockading Matamoras. The Paredes government had made no military dispositions threatening Texas or occupying the disputed territory. But more than Mexican caution was needed to stop Polk now.

On 12 March 1846 the Mexican foreign minister informed Slidell definitely that he would not be received, that Mexico still regarded the annexation of Texas as just cause of war, which would be inevitable if the United States persisted in its present course of adding injury to insult. Having thus asserted his own and his country's dignity, the minister intimated a willingness to negotiate with a commissioner *ad hoc* the question of the annexation of Texas. This distinction without a difference, dear to the Latin American mind, was dismissed by Polk as insincere and treacherous. On 25 April he began to prepare a message to Congress urging war on the sole grounds of Slidell's rejection and the unpaid claims — which amounted to exactly $3,208, 314.96 when adjudicated by a United States commission in 1851. On the evening of Saturday, 9 May, dispatches from General Taylor gave the President a more plausible *casus belli*. On 25 April, Taylor having blockaded Matamoras, a Mexican force crossed the Rio Grande, engaged in a cavalry skirmish with a troop of United States dragoons and inflicted several casualties. Polk promptly called a cabinet meeting. All agreed that a war message, with documents proving the "wrongs and injuries" the United States had suffered from Mexico, should be laid before Congress on Monday. All day Sunday, except for two hours spent at church, Polk labored with his secretaries preparing the war message. "It was a day of great anxiety to me," wrote the President in his diary, "and I regretted the necessity which had existed to make it necessary for me to spend the Sabbath in the manner I have."

At noon on Monday 11 May 1846 the war message was sent to Congress. "The cup of forbearance has been exhausted," declared the President. "After reiterated menaces, Mexico has passed the boundary of the United States, has invaded our territory and shed American blood upon the American soil." Congress then declared, "By act of the Republic of Mexico, a state of war exists between that Government and the United States."

That evening, Secretary Buchanan almost upset the presidential war chariot. He proposed to send a circular letter to American ministers and consuls stating, "In going to war we did not do so with a view to acquire either California or New Mexico or any other portion of the Mexican territory." The President remarked coldly that California was our own business, and ordered him to cut it out. This completes the proof that Polk baited Mexico into war over the Texas boundary question in order to get California, after concluding that Mexico would not sell California.

In the Mississippi valley this war was popular. Texas and states bordering on the Mississippi furnished 49,000 volunteers, eager to "revel in the halls of the Montezumas," but in the older states there was little enthusiasm and much opposition; the original Thirteen sent only 13,000 volunteers. Most of the elder statesmen of the South were content with Texas; Calhoun's clear vision foresaw that the conquest of more territory would upset the sectional balance and revive the question of slavery in the territories. The Whig party opposed, but voted for war credits and supplies in the hope that the Democrats would make a mess of the war, which they did. Antislavery men and abolitionists regarded the war as a conspiracy for more slave territory.

> They just want this Californy
> So's to lug new slave-states in
> To abuse ye, an' to scorn ye,
> An' to plunder ye like sin.

Thus James Russell Lowell castigated the Mexican War, in his *Biglow Papers*. The legislature of Massachusetts declared it to be a war to strengthen the "slave power," a war against the free states, unconstitutional, insupportable by honest men, to be concluded without delay, and to be followed by "all constitutional efforts for the abolition of slavery within the United States." But that was all talk; even the Northern "conscience Whigs," as the antislavery wing of the party was called, flinched before actually obstructing the war; remembering what had happened to the Federalists after the War of 1812.

Henry Thoreau made his private protest against the war by refusing to pay the state poll tax. After he had spent a night in the Concord lock-up, his aunt paid the tax and he went back to his cabin on Walden Pond. It sounds petty and futile, as one tells it. Yet, the ripples from that Concord pebble, like the shot of 19 April 1775, went around the world. Thoreau's *Essay on Civil Disobedience*, which he wrote to justify his action, became the best known work of American literature to the peoples of Asia and Africa struggling to be free, and it has earned the honor of being suppressed in communist countries.

Americans expected a quick and easy victory, for which 20,000 volunteers, in addition to the regular army of 7500, would suffice. In Europe, however, many doubted whether the United States could beat Mexico. Disparity in population and resources was admitted, but it was no greater than in the War of 1812, when the American offensive against Canada failed. Could soft, untrained American volunteers cope with the hardbitten, wiry Mexicans? Mexico was confident enough. An officer boasted that his cavalry could break lines of infantry with the lasso. There was wild talk of breaking into Louisiana, arming the slaves, loosing the Comanche and Sioux on the American frontier. And the unsettled Oregon question suggested that Mexico might soon have a powerful ally.

But Polk was too smart for them there. As we have seen, he compromised on Oregon in the treaty of 15 June 1846.

California, the President's main objective, became the scene of amusing if confusing conflicts. Frémont, supposedly on another exploring expedition, rushed about distractedly. A few dozen American settlers in the Sacramento valley pulled off the "Bear Flag Revolt" on 14 June 1846, taking possession of Sonoma and hoisting a white flag with a bear painted on it. Commodore Sloat of the Pacific Squadron, having heard of the outbreak of hostilities, hoisted the Stars and Stripes at Monterey on 7 July and declared California annexed to the United States. Spanish-speaking Californians, not relishing these proceedings, rose in arms, reoccupied Monterey, and tangled with Colonel Kearny, who had led 150 troopers overland from Independence by the

Santa Fe trail. But by the end of 1846 California was completely in the hands of the North Americans.

In the Rio Grande theater of war, General Taylor won two minor engagements but refused to move forward until he received reinforcements and supplies, since Polk originally assumed that he ought to live off the country! After a few men and some munitions had been sent, Taylor advanced and captured the town of Monterrey (Nuevo Leon) after a three-day battle (21–23 September 1846). Polk was not too pleased with this victory. "Old Rough and Ready" Taylor, an outspoken soldier of the Jackson breed, was becoming dangerously popular and was writing letters to the newspapers. When a general starts doing that, you may be certain that he has designs on the presidency. To bypass him, Polk conceived the brilliant stroke of creating Thomas H. Benton, sixty-four-year-old senator from Missouri, lieutenant general in command of the United States Army. Unfortunately for Mexico, Congress refused to create this new grade. The President then turned to Major General Winfield Scott of the regular army, a Whig indeed but a dandy swashbuckler whose airs and foibles were unlikely to make him popular. Scott's plan to win the war by marching on Mexico City from Vera Cruz, earlier rejected by the Washington strategists, was now adopted. Taylor, starved of reinforcements and supplies, could not move beyond Monterrey, but the navy enabled Scott to strike from Vera Cruz.

Congress was within an ace of abolishing "undemocratic" West Point when war was declared, and the army was as unprepared for war as in 1812. But the United States Navy performed efficiently on 9 March 1847, landing within 24 hours General Scott's entire army of 12,000 men with artillery, horses, vehicles, and supplies on a beach three miles from Vera Cruz, using 65 "surf boats" shipped in the holds of transports. Siege guns manned by sailors were then sited to bombard Vera Cruz, which surrendered on 27 March.

General Scott's campaign was brilliant. With little more than half the troops he asked for, hampered by jealous subordinates and volunteer officers who had been appointed for political reasons, thwarted by the administration's incompetence, often forced to live off the country and to fight with captured ammunition, he yet accomplished his ends. Scott's army marched to Mexico City along the road Hernando Cortés had followed three centuries earlier. In two weeks' time it reached the fortified pass of Cerro Gordo. Captain Robert E. Lee found a way to outflank the Mexicans by a mountain slope, a brilliant operation in which Captain George B. McClellan and Lieutenant Ulysses S. Grant also took part. The army pushed on to Puebla and remained there for three months, receiving replacements for volunteers whose terms of enlistment had expired. On 10 August the army reached the continental divide, 10,000 feet above sea level, with the beautiful valley of Mexico below and the towers of Mexico City rising through the mist. A stiff battle was fought at Churubusco on 20 August, the American forces losing 177 killed or missing and 879 wounded, or about one in seven. Most of these casualties were inflicted by artillery of the San Patricio battalion, a Mexican outfit made up of Irish and other deserters from the United States Army. But 3000 Mexican prisoners (including eight generals) were captured, and the enemy was overwhelmed.

In the meantime, President Polk had provided Mexico with a new president. General Santa Anna, in exile at Havana, persuaded Polk that, once in possession of the Mexican government, he would sign the sort of treaty that the President wanted. He was then allowed to pass through the lines, enter Mexico City in triumph in September 1846, and assume the presidency. General Taylor beat him badly at Buena Vista (22–23 February 1847) near Monterrey, a picture-book battle on a sunsoaked plain. That battle made two American Presidents — Taylor and his son-in-law Colonel Jefferson Davis who distinguished himself by so disposing his regiment (uniformed in red shirts, white pants, and slouch hats) as to break up a Mexican cavalry charge. Santa Anna then raised more troops and marched south to oppose Scott's advance from Cerro Gordo.

General Scott did not push on to the capital after his Churubusco victory of 20 August, because he did not wish to drive Santa Anna to desperation. Instead, he accorded Mexico an armistice. Polk had attached to the American army as peace commissioner Nicholas Trist, chief clerk of the department of state. Trist's instructions were to obtain the Rio Grande boundary for Texas, together with New Mexico, California, and the right of transit across the Isthmus of Tehuantepec, one of the proposed interocean canal routes. Mexican officials raised such a row on hearing these terms that Santa Anna decided to try another throw of the dice with Scott. The American army, refreshed by a fortnight among the orchards and orange groves of the valley of Mexico, marched to a blood bath at Molina del Rey (8 September), and five days later stormed its last obstacle, the fortified hill of Chapultepec, which was heroically defended by the boy cadets of the Mexican military school. On pushed Scott's troops, taking cover under the arches of the aqueducts, Lieutenants Raphael Semmes and U. S. Grant mounting howitzers on roofs and belfries. At dawn 17 September a white flag came out from Mexico City.

Mexicans crowded windows and rooftops of the city while a vanguard of battered, mud-stained doughboys [1] and marines, led by Brigadier General Quitman who had lost a boot in the latest fight, swung into the main plaza. There the conquerors gazed with wonder on the great baroque cathedral and the lofty pink-walled palace, the "Halls of the Montezumas." Presently a clatter of hoofs was heard on the stone-paved streets; and as the weary veterans snapped into "Atten-*shun!* Present — *arms!* General Scott, splendidly uniformed and superbly mounted, escorted by a squadron of dragoons with gleaming swords, dashed into the plaza.

1. This term for infantrymen began in the Mexican War and lasted until World War II, when it was replaced by "GI."

Santa Anna abdicated, and months elapsed before any Mexican government was willing to negotiate. In the meantime, Trist had been recalled by Polk, who held him responsible for the broken armistice. Instead of obeying orders, he remained, and by dint of his remarkable ability to deal with Mexicans, negotiated the Treaty of Guadalupe Hidalgo (2 February 1848). Mexico ceded Texas with the Rio Grande boundary, New Mexico (including Arizona), and Upper California (including San Diego) to the United States. The victor assumed the unpaid claims and paid $15 million to boot — three-fifths of the amount Slidell had been instructed to offer for the same territory in 1846.

In the meantime Democratic expansionists, intoxicated with success, were beginning to demand the whole of Mexico. Polk set his face sternly against this. He sent Trist's treaty to the Senate, which ratified it after the usual bitter debate. Then the President did his best to humiliate Scott who had won the war, and Trist who had won the peace. He relieved the former by a Democratic major general, and dismissed the latter from the department of state.

The United States at minimal cost — 1721 killed in battle or died of wounds; 11,550 deaths from "other causes," mainly disease — had rounded out her continental area, excepting Alaska. It remained to be seen whether these valuable acquisitions would be added to "Freedom's airy," or provide "bigger pens to cram with slaves."

GREEN GROWS THE LAUREL

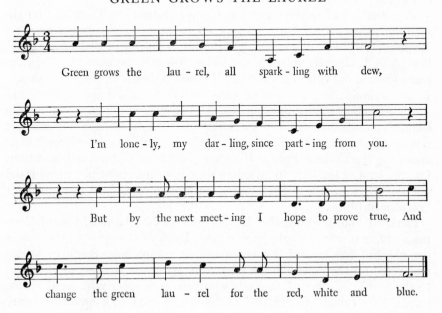

Compromise and Calm

1846-1854

1. The Wilmot Proviso

JOHN C. CALHOUN well predicted that acquisition of new territory would re-open the question of slavery expansion. The man who opened the door was an obscure Democratic congressman from Pennsylvania named David Wilmot. On 8 August 1846, about twelve weeks after the war began, the President asked Congress for a secret appropriation of $2 million as a down payment to bribe Santa Anna into ceding California. Wilmot remarked that although it was all right with him to buy California, Mexican territory was free territory, and he did not think it compatible with democratic principles to extend slavery therein. He therefore proposed as an amendment to the $2 million bill that in any territory so acquired, "Neither slavery nor involuntary servitude shall ever exist." This phrase, copied from the Northwest Ordinance of 1787, became the famous "Wilmot Proviso."

The question of slavery extension was no abstraction. There was no climatic or other natural bar to slavery extension, or to the Negro race — a Negro accompanied Admiral Peary to the North Pole in 1909. If slavery could flourish in Texas, why not in New Mexico, Arizona, and points west? In the warm climate and rich soil of southern California, Negro slaves, if introduced, would undoubtedly have thrived and multiplied, as did the Chinese and Mexicans who later filled the demands of ranchers and fruit growers for cheap labor. The question was not immediately practical, to be sure; but principle was involved. Every Northern state legislature but one passed resolutions approving the Wilmot Proviso. To many Northerners it seemed monstrous for "the land of the free" to introduce slavery, even in principle, where it did not already exist. But to Southerners the Proviso seemed an insult to their "peculiar institution."

President Polk proposed that latitude 36° 30′ N (the old Missouri Compromise line of 1820) divide freedom and slavery in the new territories as in the old; but few favored this commonsense compromise. Southern Whigs who voted for the Proviso in the interest of peace were denounced as traitors to the South; Northern Democrats who voted the other way, for the same reason, were called "doughfaces" or "Northern men with Southern principles." The Wilmot Proviso did not pass, nor did any measure to organize the newly acquired territory. American settlers in the Far West went without law and government, because Congress could not decide whether or not they could have slaves. Oregon in 1848 was finally organized as a Territory without slavery because two Southern senators voted with their Northern colleagues; but Polk's presidential term ended on 4 March 1849 before anything had been done about California, New Mexico (including Arizona), or Utah.

Hitherto everyone assumed that Congress could legislate slavery in or out of territories, since the Constitution gave it the power to "make all needful rules and regulations respecting the territory or other property belonging to the United States." Congress had admitted slavery to some territories and banned it from others. Now, from the Wilmot Proviso debates new theories emerged: (1) Congress has the moral duty to prohibit slavery wheresoever its jurisdiction extends; freedom should be national, slavery sectional. Presently the Free-Soil and Republican parties would be founded to enforce this doctrine. (2) Congress has no power to prohibit slavery in the territories, but a duty to protect it there. Presently the South would insist on this doctrine, and the Supreme Court give it a supposedly final endorsement.

Calhoun was equal to the task of sustaining this extreme Southern view, upsetting a constitutional practice of sixty years. Territories, he argued, belonged to the States United, not to the United States. Congress was merely the attorney of a partnership, and every partner has an equal right to protection for his property anywhere in the United States. Slaves were common-law property like cattle; consequently Mexican laws against slavery ceased to have effect in Mexican territory annexed to the United States. Congress in 1820 had prohibited slavery in territories north of 36° 30', but that Act was unconstitutional and void. Slavery should follow the American flag, wherever firmly planted. Calhoun's doctrine, embodied in resolutions by the Virginia legislature in 1847, became the "platform of the South"; and in the Dred Scott case of 1857 it was read into the Federal Constitution. Only one more step, said many Northerners, and slave-owning would come to be regarded as a natural right which not even a state legislature could impair.

It is idle to debate whether Wilmot or Calhoun, North or South, was the aggressor in this matter. All depends on the moral standpoint. If slavery was a positive good or a practical necessity, any attempt to restrict or to pinch it out by degrees justified Southern opposition to the point of secession. If slavery was an evil and a curse, any attempt to establish it in virgin territory, even nominally, was an affront to the public opinion of the Western world. Motives on both sides were fundamentally defensive. Even when Calhoun wrote of forcing the slavery issue in the North, his motive was to protect the domestic institutions of the slave states. Even when Seward and Chase asserted that every inch of the new territory must be free soil, their object was to defend Northern farmers, wage-earners, and lovers of liberty against further wars and encroachments of the "slave power." To yield on this issue of the Territories, it was feared, would encourage Southern extremists to demand protection for their property throughout the United States as their price for staying in it. It is just such matters of prestige and strategic advantage that bring on great wars.

The state of the American Union in 1848 may be compared with that of Europe in 1913 and 1938. Political and diplomatic moves become frequent and startling. Integrating forces win apparent victories, but in reality grow feebler. The tension increases until some event that, in ordinary times, would have little consequence, precipitates a bloody conflict.

2. Gold Rush and Compromise

President Polk, sick and exhausted by the labors of his eventful term, refused to stand for re-election in 1848. Lewis Cass of Michigan, an expansionist who had always tried to placate the South, received the Democratic nomination. The Whigs again passed over Henry Clay and, following the lucky precedent of Tippecanoe, nominated "Old Rough and Ready" Taylor of Louisiana, hero of Buena Vista, with Millard Fillmore, a colorless lawyer of Buffalo who had played with splinter parties like the Anti-Masons, for second place. A third party, the Free-Soil, was formed in the North by a coalition of three hitherto separate and hostile elements — the abolitionist Liberty party, the radical "locofoco" or "barnburner" faction of the New York Democrats, and the "conscience" or antislavery Whigs of Northern states, especially New England. Their first object was to pass the Wilmot Proviso; their platform was comprised in the phrase "Free soil, free speech, free labor and free men." Martin Van Buren, snubbed in 1844 and convinced that only slavery restriction could save the Union, accepted the Free-Soil nomination for the presidency. He carried no state, but his personal popularity robbed Cass of so many votes in New York that the Whigs won that state; and as New York went, so went the election.

Nathaniel Hawthorne now lost his place in the Salem Custom House and proceeded to write The Scarlet Letter. Walt Whitman, through writing an editorial in favor of Van Buren, was fired from the Brooklyn Eagle and wrote Leaves of Grass. These were literary by-products of Zachary Taylor's election, and of the clean sweep that followed in the civil service. He was a simple, honest soldier who detested the sophistries of politicians and regarded the slavery question as an artificial abstraction. He was ready to sign any bill that Congress might pass for organizing the new territories; but before Congress could resolve the deadlock, California proposed to skip the territorial stage and become a free state of the Union.

On 24 January 1848, shortly before peace was concluded with Mexico, a workman in the Sacramento valley discovered gold in Sutter's mill-race. In a few weeks the news spread along the Pacific coast; and in a few months all America was repeating tales of fortunes made from the stream-beds of the

Sierra Nevada merely by separating golden grains from the sand in a common washbowl. Farmers mortgaged their farms, pioneers deserted their clearings, workmen dropped their tools, clerks left their stools and even ministers their pulpits, for the California gold-washings. Young men organized companies with elaborate equipment and by-laws and were "grubstaked" by local capitalists. Any and every route was taken by the "forty-niners": around Cape Horn in the slowest and craziest vessels, across the continent by the Oregon or California trails; or, if pressed for time and well fixed for money, by the Isthmus of Panama. So, by the end of 1849, thousands of Argonauts from every region of Europe, North America and the antipodes were jumping each other's claims, drinking, gambling, and fighting in ramshackle mining villages such as Red Dog, Grub Gulch, and Poker Flat.

San Francisco rose in a few months from a squalid village to a city of 20,000 to 25,000 people, where eggs laid on the other side of Cape Horn sold for ten dollars a dozen, and a drink of whisky cost a pinch of gold; where Englishmen and Frenchmen, Yankees and Yorkers, Indiana "Hoosiers," Georgia "Crackers," Michigan "Wolverines," Illinois "Suckers," and Missouri "Pukes" rubbed shoulders with Indians, Mexicans, Sydney "Ducks," and the "Heathen Chinee." Fortunes were made in the gold-diggings, only to be lost overnight in a 'Frisco faro palace; even more was made by speculation in goods and land.

Owing to neglect by Congress, the government of California was still military in theory but impotent in fact; alcaldes appointed by the military governor administered any sort of law they pleased — the code of Mexico or of Napoleon, common law, or lynch law. So California went ahead and made herself a state, with the blessing of President Taylor. His military governor issued writs of election for a convention which met at Monterey in September 1849 and drafted a constitution prohibiting slavery. This was ratified by a popular vote of over 12,000 to 800. Without waiting for congressional sanction, the people chose a governor and legislature which began to function in 1850. Only formal admission to the Union was wanting.

This indecent haste shown in the admission of California balanced that of Texas. Besides the desire to establish law and order in a swarming country which had neither, there was the political motive of adding to the Whig contingent in the United States Senate. And California, like Texas, precipitated a crisis which almost split the Union.

Up to this time the most extreme Southerners had admitted the right of a state to prohibit slavery, slavery being a state matter. But if California were admitted to the Union with its "Wilmot Proviso" constitution, the most valuable American conquest from Mexico would be closed to slavery. During 1849 the temper of the South had been steadily rising. The governor and legislature of South Carolina hesitated from secession only because they hoped to persuade the rest of the South to go along. Calhoun wrote to his daughter, "I trust we shall persist in our resistance [to the admission of

California] until the restoration of all our rights, or disunion, one or the other, is the consequence. We have borne the wrongs and insults of the North long enough." California's demand for admission to the Union when Congress convened in December 1849 started a movement for a Southern Convention. Like the Hartford Convention of 1814, this was intended by extremists to be a stepping stone toward a new confederacy.

It is now difficult to grasp the real reason for all this sound and fury. After all, as Henry Clay pointed out, the Southern states had an equal vote in the Senate, a majority in the cabinet and the Supreme Court, and a President who was Virginia-born and Louisiana-bred. Since 1801 the South had obtained from the Union all that she really wanted — free trade (Polk's Congress had reduced the tariff again in 1846), protection to slavery in the national capital, vast theaters for slavery extension such as Louisiana, Florida, the Indian Territory, and Texas. Only extreme abolitionists threatened to interfere with slavery where it already existed, and Garrison had come out openly for separation of North from South — secession would be playing his game.

Probably we need a psychotherapist to unravel the Southern complexes of that day. "Cavaliers" were tired of hearing their form of society denounced by Northern "mongrels and mudsills" who, according to popular Southern economics, fattened upon tribute forced from the South. From every side — England and New England, Jamaica and Mexico, Ohio and the Northwest, and now Oregon and California — abolition seemed to be pointing daggers at the South's heart. It is under circumstances such as these that fear, the worst of political counselors, supersedes thought. But there was a positive, almost a utopian aspect to secession. A vision of a great slaveholding republic stretching from the Potomac to the Pacific, governed by gentlemen and affording perfect security to their property in human beings, monopolizing the production of cotton and so dictating to the world, was beginning to lift up the hearts of the younger and more radical Southern leaders.

Zachary Taylor, the fourth distinguished soldier to be elected President of the United States, was the first to have had no political experience whatsoever; he had been in the army for over forty years, during which he had never cast his vote in a presidential election. His cabinet, with the exception of John M. Clayton of Delaware, secretary of state, was weak; he exerted no leadership, and had no knack for dealing with Congress. But he was straightforward, sincere, and although a large slaveholder, devoid of proslavery sentiment. He saw no reason why the South should be bribed to admit California as a free state if California rejected slavery.

The House of Representatives that met in December 1849 was so factional that 63 ballots were taken before it could elect a speaker, and even the opinions on slavery of candidates for the post of doorkeeper were subjected to careful scrutiny. President Taylor recommended the immediate admission of

California with her free constitution, and the organization of New Mexico and Utah Territories without reference to slavery. To protesting senators from Georgia, the old soldier declared his determination to crush secession wherever and whenever it might appear, if he had to lead the army personally.

In the Senate, leaders of the new generation, such as Jefferson Davis, Stephen A. Douglas, William H. Seward, and Salmon P. Chase, sat with giants of other days, such as Webster, Clay, and Calhoun. It was Henry Clay who divined the high strategy of the moment. The Union was not ripe to meet the issue of secession. Concessions must be made to stop the movement now; time might be trusted to deal with it later. On 27 January 1850 he brought forward the compromise resolutions that kept an uneasy peace for eleven years. The gist of them was (1) immediate admission of California; (2) organization of territorial governments in New Mexico and Utah without mention of slavery; (3) a new and stringent fugitive slave law; (4) abolition of the domestic slave trade in the District of Columbia. Such was the Compromise of 1850.

These resolutions brought on one of those superb Senate debates that moulded public opinion. Clay defended them in a speech that lasted the better part of two days. Haggard in aspect and faltering in voice as he rose to speak, his passionate devotion to the Union seemed to bring back all the charm and fire of "Young Harry of the West," and to lift him and his audience to high levels. He appealed to the North for concession, and to the South for peace. He asked the North to accept the substance of the Wilmot Proviso without the principle, and honestly to fulfill her obligation to return fugitive slaves. He reminded the South of the great benefits she derived from the Union, and warned her against the delusion that secession was constitutional, or could be peaceful, or would be acquiesced in by the Middle West. For Clay was old enough to remember the excitement in Kentucky when Spain and France had threatened to close her outlet to the sea. "My life upon it," he declared, "that the vast population which has already concentrated . . . on the headwaters and the tributaries of the Mississippi, will never give their consent that the mouth of that river shall be held subject to the power of any foreign state."

Calhoun, grim and emaciated, his voice stifled by the catarrh that shortly led to his death, sat silent, glaring defiance from his hawk-like eyes, while his ultimatum was voiced for him by Senator Mason of Virginia (4 March 1850). "I have, Senators, believed from the first that the agitation of the subject of slavery would, if not prevented by some timely and effective measure, end in disunion." "The cords that bind the States together" are snapping one by one. Three great evangelical churches are now divided. The Federal Union can be saved only by satisfying the South that she can remain within it in safety, that it is not "being permanently and hopelessly converted into the means of oppressing instead of protecting" her. The senator from Kentucky cannot save the Union with his compromise. The North must "do justice by conceding to the South an equal right in the acquired territory" — admitting slavery to California and New Mexico — by doing her duty as to fugitive slaves, by restoring to the South, through constitutional amendment, the equilibrium of power she once possessed in the federal government; and she must "cease the agitation of the slave question." Note well that imperative — silence on slavery.

Three days later Webster rose for his last great speech. His voice had lost its deep resonance, his massive frame was shrunk, and his face was lined with suffering and sorrow. But in his heart glowed the ancient love of country, and the spell of his personality fell on Senate and galleries with his opening words: "I speak to-day for the preservation of the Union. Hear me for my cause." Viewing the situation eye-to-eye with Clay, Webster merely restated in richer language the points made by his old-time rival. The North could never have been induced to swallow a new fugitive slave law, had not Webster held the spoon; and, even so, it gagged and vomited. Just as his reply to Hayne in 1830 stimulated the growth of Union sentiment, so the Seventh of March Speech of 1850 permitted that sentiment to ripen, until it became irresistible.

Senator Seward of New York, in opposing the compromise from the opposite angle, spoke for the yet unborn Republican party. He admitted that Congress had the constitutional power to establish slavery in the territories. "But there is a higher law than the Constitution which regulates our authority over the domain": the law of God, whence alone the laws of man can derive their sanction. The fugitive slave bill would endanger the Union far more than any antislavery measure. "All measures which fortify slavery or extend it, tend to the consummation of violence; all that check its extension and abate its strength, tend to its peaceful extirpation."

As the debate progressed, compromise sentiment developed. The Nashville convention of delegates from nine Southern states adjourned in June after passing harmless resolutions. Yet much parliamentary maneuvering, and the steady support of Southern Whigs, both in and out of Congress, were necessary to get the compromise through. In early September 1850 the essential bills passed. Their passage was greased by Congress assuming the national debt of Texas. This obtained for Texas bondholders, mainly Northern bankers, 77 per cent of the par value of bonds that had cost them 5 to 15 per cent. Principal measures passed were the admission of California, a fugitive slave law, the organization of New Mexico and Utah as territories free to enter the Union without reference to slavery, and abolition of the domestic slave trade in Washington.

It was a fair compromise, this of 1850, for which Henry Clay deserves the chief credit; but he had powerful assistance from Stephen A. Douglas and other Democrats. Both North and South obtained something that they badly wanted, and the New Mexico-Utah bills avoided both the Wilmot Proviso "stigma" and the forcible introduction of slaves to regions which had none.

Once more the Union was preserved by the same spirit of compromise that created it; but for the last time.

President Taylor did not like the compromise; he saw no reason why California should be included in a package deal. But he did not live long enough to be faced with the hard decision whether to sign or to veto the bills. "Old Rough and Ready," now sixty-five years old, succumbed to a combination of official scandals, Washington heat, and doctors. The scandal he knew nothing about until it broke, for like certain other military Presidents he trusted too many rascals. Governor G. W. Crawford of Georgia, Taylor's secretary of war, had taken over, on a fifty-fifty basis, the settlement of a pre-revolutionary claim which originally amounted to less than $45,000. With the help of friends he got a bill appropriating that amount through Congress. Then, by a smart triple play with the attorney general and secretary of the treasury, Crawford got an additional payment of $191,353 for 73 years' interest, the half of which made him a neat little fortune. As ventilated by Congress, this Galphin claim affair, as it was called, smelled worse than anything of the sort prior to the Credit Mobilier scandals in the administration of the next soldier president, U. S. Grant.

On 4 July 1850, already depressed by the Galphin revelations, the President was subjected to two hours' oratory by Senator Foote in the broiling sun, and then tried to cool off by consuming an excessive quantity of cucumbers, washed down with copious draughts of iced milk. Washington, with its open sewers and flies, was always unhealthy in the summer, and the President came down with acute gastroenteritis, then called cholera morbus. He would probably have recovered if left alone, but no President ever has that chance. The physicians of the capital, assisted by a quack from Baltimore, rallied around his bedside, drugged him with ipecac, calomel, opium, and quinine (at 40 grains a whack), and bled and blistered him too. On 9 July he gave up the ghost. Millard Fillmore now became President of the United States and signed all compromise acts before Congress adjourned on 30 September 1850, after a record session of 302 days.

In the North the Democrats accepted the Compromise. Free-Soilers and abolitionists denounced it in the most frenzied terms, Whigs were divided. The Fugitive Slave Act really stuck in Northern throats. The one hope for preserving slavery was to let the Northerners forget about it, instead of rubbing it in by hunting runaways in their streets and countryside. Even Emerson, the philosopher who had serenely advised the abolitionists to love their neighbors more and their colored brethren less, wrote in his journal, "This filthy enactment was made in the nineteenth century, by people who could read and write. I will not obey it, by God!" In the South, another year elapsed before it was certain that the secession movement could be halted. In state elections Whigs and Democrats disappeared; the contest was between a Union party and a Southern Rights or immediate secession party. The Union-

ists met the secessionists on their own ground, squarely denying the existence
of a constitutional right of secession, and in every cotton state but South
Carolina the unionists won.

Already two of the principal antagonists had passed away. Calhoun died 31
March 1850. His coffin made a triumphal progress through the Southern
states to Charleston, where friends and followers pledged devotion to his
principles by the marble tombstone over his grave in St. Philip's churchyard.
His real monument, Walt Whitman heard a soldier say in 1865, was Southern society torn up by the roots, and servants become masters.

Andrew Jackson ended his long life of pain at the Hermitage in 1845; John
Quincy Adams, stricken at his seat in the House, survived his old rival less
than three years. "Old Bullion" Benton was defeated for re-election to the
Senate in 1851; his sturdy nationalism had grown too old-fashioned for Missouri. Clay and Webster, the one denounced as traitor by Southern hotspurs,
the other compared with Lucifer by New England reformers, had two years
only to live; time enough to give them grave doubts whether their compromise could long be maintained. With their death the second generation of
independent Americans may be said to have gone. Of all statesmen born
during the last century and brought up in the generous atmosphere of the
American Revolution and Jeffersonian Republicanism, only Van Buren was
alive, fuming at home over the "half-baked politicians" of the 1850's; and the
limp Buchanan. There seemed nobody left to lead the nation but weak,
twofaced trimmers and angry young men, radical or reactionary.

3. Prosperity, Pierce, and "Young America"

The early 1850's shed a warm glow of hope and satisfaction over the American scene. A writer in the United States Review in 1853 predicted that
electricity and automatic machinery would so transform life and relieve mankind of drudgery that, within half a century, "Machinery will perform all
work — automata will direct them. The only task of the human race will be to
make love, study and be happy."

Industrial development continued apace, railroads reached out into the
West, supplanting the canals as freight carriers, immigration from Europe
reached a new high level, yet wages rose, and in the labor movement talk gave
way to action. Unions of the later American type were concluding trade
agreements with their employers, federating nationally on craft lines, but
avoiding politics. The National Typographic Union (1852), the United Hat-
ters (1856), and the Iron Moulders' Union of North America (1859) were
the first permanent federations. Marxian socialism arrived with the German
immigrants, but the Proletarierbund that one of them founded soon expired;
American workingmen discarded utopia for two dollars a day and roast beef.
Neal Dow won an apparent victory for cold water with the Maine prohibition
law; humanitarian reform and education marched hand in hand. Baseball first

became popular, schooner yacht *America* won a race against all comers at Cowes in 1850 which gave a fillip to yacht racing. Intercollegiate rowing began, and the clipper ship gave the American eagle another exploit to scream about.

A promising beginning of orchestral music — which the Civil War diverted into brass bands — opened in 1853 when a Frenchman, Louis Jullien, started a school of music in New York. Theodore Thomas, the German-born boy wonder, became first violin of an orchestra that Jullien organized on the side. And when we consider the great American books of this decade, it is evident that culture was no laggard. In 1850–51 appeared Hawthorne's *Scarlet Letter* and *House of the Seven Gables*, Whittier's *Songs of Labor*, Melville's *White Jacket* and *Moby-Dick*, Emerson's *Representative Men* and *English Traits*. The following year Harriet Beecher Stowe's *Uncle Tom's Cabin* reminded the public that the slavery question could not be ignored. Thoreau's *Walden*, Whitman's *Leaves of Grass*, and Melville's *Piazza Tales* appeared in 1854–56. Elisha Kent, helped by the navy and a New York shipowner, completed his northern voyages and published his fascinating *Arctic Explorations* in 1856. The *Atlantic Monthly* was founded in 1857 with James Russell Lowell as editor, and Longfellow, Whittier, and Dr. Holmes (whose *Autocrat* appeared in 1858) as contributors. This was Longfellow's most productive decade, with *The Golden Legend, Hiawatha*, and *The Courtship of Myles Standish*. Parkman's *Conspiracy of Pontiac* (1851) opened a noble historical series that required 40 years to complete, and Prescott had almost finished his when he died in 1859.

All these were Northern writers. In the South, Poe was dead, John P. Kennedy had become President Fillmore's secretary of the navy; William Gilmore Simms, still writing historical novels, was still neglected in his native Charleston. Materially, however, the cotton kingdom was stronger and more self-conscious. Kentucky backwoodsmen who in the 1830s had taken up land in the black belts, were now gentlemen planters mingling on equal terms with the first families of Virginia in the thermal stations of the mountains. Their elder sons, after leading volunteers in the Mexican War, had become lawyers or planters; their younger sons were attending the newer colleges of the lower South, or the University of Virginia, with hounds and hunters and black servants. Dread of abolition, with its implication of Negro equality, was binding the yeomen and poor whites more closely to their slaveholding neighbors. There seemed to be no limit to cotton production. The annual crop rose from 1000 million to 2300 million pounds in this decade, but never wanted purchasers. De Bow's progressive *Review* was preaching the use of guano, conservation of soil, diversification of crops, and local manufactures; also, ominously, a revival of the African slave trade. If only the South had dared lift the ban on creative thought, the late 'fifties might well have brought an outburst of literature surpassing that of New England. Instead, she produced little but proslavery propaganda.

Another "might have been" is suggested by the progress of manufactures in the South at this period, owing to the enterprise of William Gregg, a Charleston jeweler, and Edwin M. Holt of North Carolina. In the 1850's the value of the product of Southern cotton mills almost doubled. A good start; and had it continued without the interruption of war, it might have aligned the old South with the Northeastern states in favor of a protective tariff, as finally happened in the present century.

There was also progress in processing another raw material, tobacco. In 1860 Virginia and North Carolina factories were producing most of the chewing, smoking, and snuffing tobacco in the United States. Cigars, if not imported from Cuba, were made in Connecticut (out of cabbage leaves, the envious said); Cuban cigarettes had not yet invaded the North American market; but Richmond plug tobacco, especially a brand with the seductive name "Wedding Cake," was reaching even the California gold diggings. The Tredegar Iron Works of Richmond, employing slave labor, were doing well and would do better with war orders.

The Southern railway network, encouraged by financial aid from states, counties, and towns, was greatly extended. Georgia built a railroad across the southern end of the Appalachians, which helped to make Atlanta and Chattanooga great cities; Charleston planned a railway to the Ohio river to siphon off Western trade from New York, with a connecting steamship line to Europe; and by 1860 there was through rail connection between New York and New Orleans. Several other promising efforts were made toward bringing the South in line with dynamic America, but there was too little time. Southern liberals and industrialists for the most part were lonely individuals, socially looked down upon by aristocratic planters, neglected by politicians, and scolded by journalists.

Although extremists on both sides disliked the Compromise of 1850, the presidential election of 1852 proved that an overwhelming majority were disposed to regard it as final. As such it was proclaimed in the platform of the Democratic national convention at Baltimore. Owing to the operation of the two-thirds rule, all strong men of the party — Lewis Cass, Stephen A. Douglas, William L. Marcy, and Buchanan who, though a waverer, was a political veteran — killed each other off, so that on the forty-ninth ballot a dark horse won. This was Franklin Pierce of New Hampshire, whose only qualifications were a handsome face and figure, a creditable military record in the Mexican War, and an almost blank, hence blameless, political record. He was introduced to the public, who knew practically nothing about him, as "Young Hickory of the Granite State." It is a great pity that Cass, who had a touch of Old Hickory in him, or Douglas, the "Little Giant" of Illinois, was not nominated. What the presidential office then needed was backbone; and Pierce had the backbone of a jellyfish.

Any Democrat could have won in 1852. The New York "barnburners," starved by four lean years with the Free-Soil party, returned to their former allegiance; thousands of Southern Whigs, disgusted by the antislavery tendencies of Northern Whigs, went Democratic. General Winfield Scott, the Whig presidential candidate, made himself somewhat ridiculous in the campaign; and, although a Virginian by birth, that asset was canceled by a nationalist career. The result was a landslide for Pierce, 254 electoral votes to 42. Scott carried only Vermont, Massachusetts, Kentucky, and Tennessee.

The Whig party never recovered. Wanting organic unity, it had no chance when its rival undertook to maintain the great Compromise, and the great silence. The Democratic party, purged of democracy, became a national conservative party directed by Southern planters and maintained by Northern votes. It controlled the federal government for the next eight years.

A diversion of this period was the "Young America" movement, a grouping of the younger men in the Democratic party, originally intended to create new ideals of civic duty and to support democratic movements overseas. The first object faded out, and the second ended in loud talk and bad diplomatic maneuvers. The Young Americans in 1848 had talked wildly of annexing Ireland and Sicily, as certain revolutionists in those countries suggested; and when the news came that Hungary had fallen before a Russian invasion and had been forcibly incorporated with Austria, the legislatures of New York, Ohio, and Indiana called for action. Daniel Webster, as Fillmore's secretary of state, insulted the House of Hapsburg in a diplomatic note declaring, "The power of this republic at the present moment is spread over a region, one of the richest and most fertile on the globe, and of an extent in comparison with which the possessions of the House of Hapsburg are but as a patch on the earth's surface." Louis Kossuth, brought to New York as guest of the nation in 1851, was given an overwhelming ovation. "Europe is antiquated, decrepit, tottering on the verge of dissolution," declared Senator Douglas. "It is a vast graveyard." Young America wanted thirty-nine-year-old Stephen Douglas for President, but it got Pierce who, though at forty-eight the youngest man yet elected President, wanted no part of Young America, except the bad manners. He followed the Adams-Clay precedent (which continued to 1923) of appointing as secretary of state his chief rival for the nomination. This was William L. Marcy, the veteran New York spoilsman. Buchanan, who thought he should have had it, grudgingly accepted the London legation for which, since it spared him the contentions over Kansas, he later became very grateful.

Marcy, sixty-six years old when appointed, saw eye to eye with Young America in truculent diplomacy. Universally approved by the Democracy was his circular on the official costume of American diplomats and consuls abroad. These had been accustomed to provide themselves with fancy uniforms covered with gold lace, a *chapeau-bras* (the "fore'n 'aft hat" recently discarded by the navy), knee breeches, and silver-buckled shoes. Secretary Marcy issued positive orders that members of the foreign service "appear in the simple dress of an American citizen." This created consternation, as no gentleman could attend a European official ball or reception except in court dress, complete with breeches and sword. James Buchanan after (fortunately) rejecting the notion that he dress like President Washington in Stuart's portrait, conformed by wearing the usual dark frock coat and trousers of that era with a black dress sword, which got by Queen Victoria's chamberlain. But John Y. Mason, minister to France, after ascertaining that the parvenu court of Napoleon III required more fixings, appeared in a fancy uniform which his envious first secretary described as having been designed by a Dutch tailor, following the livery of a minor German diplomat's lackey. For that, the minister received a strong reprimand from Marcy.

"Manifest destiny" under Pierce was directed by Southern gentlemen who wanted new slave territory as compensation for their "loss" of California. Cuba, during these eventful years, was in her normal state of unrest. There was fear lest the island fall to England or become a black republic like Haiti. President Polk proposed to buy Cuba in 1848 for $100 million, but Spain rejected the offer with contempt. There were filibustering expeditions, frowned upon by President Taylor, tolerated by Pierce, and consequent interference by Spanish authorities with suspicious-looking Yankee ships. One such case, that of the *Black Warrior* (1854), almost provoked Spain into war. The secretary of war, Jefferson Davis, egged President Pierce on; but Secretary Marcy kept his head, and Spain disappointed the annexationists by apologizing.

The next move of the Pierce-Marcy team was exceedingly odd. At their suggestion the American ministers to Spain (Pierre Soulé of Louisiana), France (Mason), and Great Britain (Buchanan) met at Ostend and on 18 October 1854 drafted a pompous recommendation to Secretary Marcy of how to settle the Cuban question. "In the progress of human events," they observed, "the time has arrived when the vital interests of Spain are as seriously involved in the sale as those of the United States in the purchase of the island. . . . The Union can never enjoy repose, nor possess reliable security," as long as Cuba is not embraced within its boundaries. With the purchase money Spain might build railroads, "become a centre of attraction for the travelling world," and "her vineyards would bring forth a vastly increased quantity of choice wines." Should she refuse, then, "By every law, human and divine, we shall be justified in wresting it from Spain if we possess the power." The New York *Herald* obtained a "scoop" of this document — largely a product of Buchanan's muddled brain — and published it under the catchy title "The Ostend Manifesto," creating a furor at home and abroad. It seemed to indicate that the Pierce administration was ready to fight Spain to get Cuba, as a slave-state balance to California. Pierce had no intention of doing that, but he sent Soulé to Madrid with orders to buy Cuba. Democratic statesmen never seemed to learn that such offers were insulting. A Latin nation might cede to force, but it could not be bought.

4. Japan Opened

Not only trouble but much good flowed from the territorial acquisitions of 1846–48. The difficulty of communicating overland with Oregon and California led to the project of an interoceanic canal, the perfection of the sailing ship, and plans for transcontinental railways. And the United States, as a new Pacific Ocean power, was instrumental in ending the isolation of Japan. American diplomacy followed by almost fifty years the first American merchant ship to cross the Pacific. Caleb Cushing negotiated with China in 1844 a treaty by which American ships obtained access to ports already open to Europeans, and extraterritorial privileges for merchants. China for fifteen years was torn apart by the Taiping rebellion, and the China trade suffered. That was one reason for American interest in Japan, but not the only one.

Japan had been closed for two centuries to foreign intercourse except a strictly regulated trade with the Dutch and Chinese at Nagasaki. Foreign sailors wrecked on the shores of Japan were not allowed to leave, and Japanese sailors wrecked on the west coast of the United States were not permitted to return. U.S.S. *Preble*, Commander James Glynn, boldly entered Nagasaki harbor in 1849 and by a show of firmness recovered twelve American sailors. En route she called at Okinawa in the Ryukyus (then called the Great Lew Chew), where the crew "went ashore and rambled all about the country, visiting the king's palace, a privilege never before granted to any stranger." The same palace, at Shuri, was occupied by United States Marines in 1945.

After this knock at the outer door, President Fillmore decided to try the main entrance. He entrusted the mission to Commodore Matthew Calbraith Perry, brother of the hero of Lake Erie and commander of a squadron that had won two amphibious operations in the Mexican War. The Commodore was somewhat ostentatious, which helped him to deal with Orientals, but he had studied every available book on Japan. On 8 July 1853 his armed squadron, including steam frigates *Mississippi* and *Susquehanna*, anchored in the mouth of Tokyo Bay. Perry's orders forbade him to use force, except as a last resort; but the Kanagawa Shogun who then ruled Japan was so impressed by this display that, contrary to precedent, he consented to transmit the President's letter to the Emperor. Perry tactfully sailed away in order to give the elder statesmen time to make up their minds, and by the time he returned (February 1854) with an even more impressive squadron, they had decided to yield. Conferences were held at the little village of Yokohama where gifts were exchanged: lacquers and bronzes, porcelain and brocades, for a set of telegraph instruments, a quarter-size steam locomotive complete with track and cars, Audubon's *Birds* and *Quadrupeds of America*, an assortment of farming implements and firearms, a barrel of whisky, and several cases of champagne. Thus old Japan first tasted the blessings of Western civilization.

Japanese progressives who wished to end isolation persuaded the Emperor to sign an agreement allowing the United States to establish a consulate, and permitting American vessels to visit certain Japanese ports for supplies and a limited trade.

Such was the famous "opening" of Japan. It was followed by an exploring expedition, successively under Commanders Ringgold and Rogers, which in 1855 charted some of the Ryukyus, the east coast of Japan, and the Kamchatka peninsula. Next year, President Buchanan sent Townsend Harris, a New York merchant, to Japan as the first American consul and to negotiate a formal treaty. The fine character of Townsend Harris and his genuine appreciation of the Japanese founded that traditional friendship between the two countries, roughly but temporarily broken in the 1940s.

In the 1850's the Ryukyu and Bonin Islands were virtually independent of Japan. Commodore Perry was eager to obtain a coaling station to serve the navy, which was being converted to steam, and merchant steamships, too. He bought land for one at Chichi Jima from a group of New Englanders and Hawaiians who had settled there many years earlier, and instructed them to set up a local government under American protection. But the navy department and Congress, unprepared for such "imperialism," disavowed both actions, and a few years later Japan formally annexed both island groups. Ninety years later, Okinawa and Iwo Jima were conquered by the United States after heavy loss of life.

5. Isthmian Brawls

For shortening travel time between the older states and those on the Pacific coast, an interoceanic canal was badly needed. Three different routes were considered: the Isthmus of Panama, the Isthmus of Tehuantepec, and the Nicaraguan. President Polk obtained right of transit across Panama in 1840 by treaty with Colombia, and in return guaranteed that republic her sovereignty over the Isthmus. American capital then built the Panama railway, completed in 1855. The Tehuantepec route was too long for a canal, but Mexico granted to the United States a right of way over it in 1855. Jockeying for control of the Nicaragua route brought on controversies with Central America and Great Britain.

At the time the Monroe Doctrine was declared, Britain had two bases in Central America: the old logwood establishment of Belize, the Bay Islands crown colony off Honduras, and a protectorate over the Miskito Indians along the coast of Nicaragua. Owing to the weakness of the Central American republics, the enterprise of British agents, and Washington's lack of interest in Latin America after the J. Q. Adams administration, British influence increased in Central America. "Mosquitia" became an Indian satellite state, with a flag incorporating the Union Jack; and Lord Palmerston, who believed it high time to check "manifest destiny" in that quarter, in 1848 declared the sovereignty of Mosquitia over Greytown or San Juan del Norte, eastern terminus of the proposed Nicaragua ship canal. A milestone in Isthmian diplomacy was planted when John Clayton, President Taylor's secretary of state, negotiated with Lytton Bulwer, British minister at Washington, the Clayton-Bulwer treaty of 15 April 1850. Therein it was agreed that neither government would fortify, or obtain exclusive control over, any Isthmian canal. Each guaranteed its neutrality, when and if built, and invited other nations to do likewise. This was a fair compromise of the responsibilities that Britain had undertaken in the political vacuum of Central America, and the new United States interest in Isthmian communication.

Unfortunately, like other Anglo-American treaties, the Clayton-Bulwer one was ambiguous. The United States assumed that it required the British to withdraw from the Bay Islands, Greytown, and the Miskito coast; the British government, insisting that it merely forbade future territorial acquisitions, held what it had. This dispute became acrid in 1854 when President Pierce and the Democrats were looking for an issue to distract the country from the slavery question, and virtual anarchy in Nicaragua led to dangerous jostling on the spot between rivals.

An incident at Greytown might have triggered off an Anglo-American war. Solon Borland, minister to Central America, when about to sail home from Greytown, got involved in a local political brawl and was hit on the head with a bottle. President Pierce sent U.S.S. *Cyane* to the scene to demand an apology; and, when none was forthcoming, her commander gave the population time to retire, bombarded Greytown 13 July 1854, and destroyed the town. The British government demanded reparation and didn't get it; the London press blustered and threatened war, but by this time England was involved in the Crimea and her government let the matter drop.

Incident followed incident in Nicaragua. During the California gold rush, "Commodore" Cornelius Vanderbilt of the Hudson river steamboat fleet organized a company to compete with the Panama railway. He ran steamers up the San Juan del Norte to Lake Nicaragua, whence freight was forwarded to the Pacific coast by muleback. Since Nicaragua was troubled by frequent revolutions as well as earthquakes, Vanderbilt hired William Walker, a professional filibuster, to set up a stable government. Walker, who had already tried to filibuster Lower California into a new slave state, succeeded in 1855 in making himself president of Nicaragua. "The gray-eyed man of destiny," as his friends called him, was preparing, with the approval of Secretary Jefferson Davis, to re-establish Negro slavery and to conquer the rest of Central America, when he had the bad judgment to quarrel with Vanderbilt. The Commodore then supported a Central American coalition that invaded Nicaragua, and threw Walker out. Walker tried twice again, finally meeting his death from a Honduran firing squad.

England's cession of the Bay Islands to Honduras and of Mosquitia to Nicaragua in 1859–60, ended this conflict in Central America. But *Cyane's* bombardment and Walker's filibustering left the Latins suspicious of and hostile to the United States.

6. Relations with Canada

The union of Ontario and Quebec as the Province of Canada, first fruit of Lord Durham's mission, did not work well. People of British stock mixed with the French habitants no better than oil with water. But the union did have a large degree of self-government: an elected assembly with a responsible ministry.

Hitherto, demands for the annexation of British North America to the United States had come from the southern side of the border, but now annexation propaganda came from Canada, even from Tories who hitherto had been vociferously loyal to the Queen. English merchants of Quebec were disgusted with the British government for repealing the corn laws, which had favored Canadian grain. So a group of leading Montrealers in 1849 issued the "Annexation Manifesto," pointing out advantages for Canada in joining the American Union. This movement fell flat. French Canadians would have none of it, knowing that their church could not maintain its special privileges under the American system; and the mass of British Canadians held loyalty to England above any economic advantage. The annexationists received no encouragement from the other side of the border, where the mere prospect of two or three more free states would have aroused Southern resentment.

The sensible alternative to annexation was reciprocity in customs duties, suggested in 1846 by William H. Merritt, promoter of the Welland Canal around Niagara Falls, first link in the St. Lawrence Seaway of a century later. But the moving factor was a dispute between the New England states and the Maritime provinces about fishing rights. Yankee fishermen claimed the right to pursue the sportive mackerel within the Canadian three-mile limit, which Newfoundland and Nova Scotia flatly denied. It was high time that such petty quarrels be composed.

The foreign office and the state department had no trouble in concluding a reciprocity treaty (5 June 1854), but this treaty required concurrent acts of Parliament and Congress, and of four Canadian provincial legislatures. Secretary Marcy is said to have greased the way at Halifax, Fredericton, and St. John; and Lord Elgin, a hardheaded but genial Scot, was accused of floating the treaty through the United States Senate on "oceans of champagne." If true, both men served their respective countries well. The treaty, renewable after ten years, opened the United States to Canadian coal, farm produce, lumber, and fish; and Canada to American turpentine, rice and tobacco, and Yankee fishermen. The navigation of the Lakes, the St. Lawrence, and their connecting canals became common to both nations. Thus Britain maintained her political dominion over Canada by sanctioning a partial economic union with the United States.

7. Noble Ships

While governments wrangled over future canals to the Pacific, the ship-wrights of New York and New England were engaged in cutting down the time of ocean passage around Cape Horn. In one month of 1850, thirty-three sailing vessels from New York and Boston entered San Francisco Bay after an average passage of 159 days. Then there came booming through the Golden Gate the clipper ship *Sea Witch* of New York, 97 days out. At once the cry went up for more clippers.

This type of full-rigged sailing vessel was characterized by great length in proportion to breadth of beam, an enormous sail area, and long concave bows ending in a gracefully curved cutwater. *Sea Witch*, designed by John W. Griffith and built for the China-New York tea trade, now proved the new type's value for the California trade. Her record was broken by *Surprise*, designed by a twenty-three-year-old Bostonian, Samuel H. Pook. Well named was she, since her owners — the Lows of New York — cleared a profit of $650,000 over total cost from her first round voyage to California. Donald McKay of Boston now entered the scene as ship designer and builder. His *Flying Cloud* in 1851 made San Francisco in 89 days from New York, a record never surpassed, and only twice equaled, once by herself.

As California then afforded no return cargo except gold dust (the export of wheat did not begin before 1855), the Yankee clippers sailed in ballast from San Francisco to the treaty ports of China, where they came into competition with the British merchant marine; and the result was more impressive than *America*'s victory over the English yachting fleet. Crack British East India-men waited for a cargo weeks on end, while one American clipper after another sailed with a cargo of tea at double the ordinary freight. When the Lows' *Oriental* arrived in London 97 days from Hong Kong, crowds thronged the docks to admire her, and *The Times* challenged British shipbuilders to set their "long practised skill, steady industry, and dogged determination" against the "youth, ingenuity and ardour" of the United States.

In 1852 Donald McKay launched *Sovereign of the Seas*, largest merchant vessel yet built and the boldest in design; stately as a cathedral, beautiful as a terraced cloud. Lieutenant Matthew F. Maury USN having discovered that strong and steady westerly gales blew in the "roaring forties" south latitude, the *Sovereign* followed his sailing directions and on her homeward passage made a day's run of 411 nautical miles, surpassed only seven times in the history of sailing vessels, all but two of them by products of McKay's drafting board and shipyard.

Talk about races! The 15,000-mile course from New York or Boston to California, around Cape Horn, was the longest and toughest in the world, trying the skill and energy of navigator and crew to the utmost. Over it, McKay's *Flying Fish*, in the winter of 1851–52 raced *Sword Fish* of New

York. They left their respective home ports the same day. The Bostonian led to the equator, the New Yorker caught up at lat. 50° S, and they raced around the Horn within sight of one another. *Sword Fish* drew steadily ahead and won, making San Francisco in less than 91 days from New York.

By this time the British Navigation Act had been repealed, and gold had been discovered in Australia. For that destination four clippers were ordered to be built by Donald McKay for the Australian Black Ball Line. These proved to be the world's fastest sailing ships. *James Baines*, with skysail, studdingsails, and main moonsail, established the record transatlantic sailing passage — 12¼ days Boston to Liverpool — and another from Liverpool to Melbourne — 63 days — that still holds. *Champion of the Seas*, combining the imposing majesty of a man-of-war with the airy grace of a yacht, from noon to noon, 11–12 December 1854, fulfilled the challenge of her name by hanging up the greatest day's run of all time made by a sailing vessel — 465 nautical miles.

These clipper ships of the early 1850's were built of wood in shipyards from Rockland in Maine to Baltimore. Their architects, like poets who transmute nature's message into song, obeyed what wind and wave had taught them, to create the noblest of all sailing vessels, and the most beautiful creations of man in America. With no extraneous ornament except a figurehead, a bit of carving and a few lines of gold leaf, their one purpose of speed over the great ocean routes was achieved by perfect balance of spars and sails to the curving lines of the smooth black hull; and this harmony of mass, form and color was practised to the music of dancing waves and of brave winds whistling in the rigging. These were our Gothic cathedrals, our Parthenon; but monuments carved from snow. For a few brief years they flashed their splendor around the world, then disappeared with the finality of the wild pigeon.

For the clipper ship fulfilled a very limited purpose: speed to the gold fields at any price or risk. When that was no longer an object, no more were built.

World-wide whaling out of Sag Harbor, New Bedford, and other New England ports reached its apogee in the 1850's; the discovery of oil in Pennsylvania in 1859 sounded its knell. The whale ships, mostly built locally, were low-bred compared with the clippers, as they had to be, in order to "try out" the blubber on board and bring home a cargo of full oil casks after a voyage lasting three years or more. Officers and petty officers were generally native New Bedfordites, Vineyarders, or Nantucketers. Gay Head Indians were preferred as harpooners; the crews were of all races and colors — Yankee country boys lured to the sea for adventure; Portuguese from the Azores and Cape Verde Islands; Fijians like Melville's Queequeg. Although a green hand's "lay" or proportion of the catch (no wages were paid in the whaling industry) netted him little enough for a three-year yoyage, there were other compensations — seeing the world, and the sport. *"Thar she blows! — thar she breaches!"* from a masthead lookout was the pistol shot that started an inspiring race to the quarry, each of the four mates exhorting his boat crew with slogans such as "Roar and pull, my thunderbolts! Lay me on — lay me on!" As the oarsmen's backs are to the whale, they know not how near they are until the mate shouts to the harpooner, "Stand up and let him have it!" A shock as bow grounds on blubber, a frantic "Starn all!" and the death duel begins. Anything may happen then. At best, a "Nantucket sleighride" as the harpooned whale tows the boat at tremendous speed, then slows down, exhausted, the crew closes, dispatches him with a few well-directed thrusts, and pulls quickly out of his death-flurry. At worst, a canny old sperm whale sinks out of sight, rises with open jaws directly under the boat, and shoots with it twenty feet into the air, crushing its sides like an eggshell while the crew jump for their lives into seething, bloodstreaked foam.

Whalemen enjoyed a variety of adventures such as no other calling approached, such as no big-game hunter of today can command.

BLOW, YE WINDS

XXXVII

Kansas, Nebraska, and New Parties

1854-1859

1. *Prairie Settlement and Railroad Routes*

DOWN TO 1850, American agricultural settlement, owing to the pioneer's
dependence on timber and running water, had been largely confined to
woodland and to small prairies with oak groves. The vast, treeless prairies of
Illinois and Iowa were not wanted, for lack of fuel. As late as 1849 one could
look northward from a knoll near Peoria, Illinois, over an undulating plain
unbroken by house or tree as far as the eye could reach. The earliest prairie
settlers had to live in sod cabins and contend with wolves, fires, and locusts.
Many of the old breed of pioneers preferred the long journey to Oregon, where
they could renew the forest environment that they loved. But by the mid-
1850's the typical American pioneer had become a prairie farmer, owing in part
to new agricultural machinery: — Cyrus McCormick's mechanical reaper,
Marsh's harvester, Appleby's self-knotting binder, the steel-toothed cultivator,
an improved form of plow with a steel mould-board, steel wire fencing. Yet
the greatest impetus to prairie farming came from the rising price of
wheat — from 93 cents a bushel in 1851 to $2.50 in 1855 — and a rapid
building of railroads from lake and river ports like Chicago, Milwaukee, and
St. Louis into the prairie country. Railroads had hardly penetrated the Middle
West by 1850; in the next ten years it was covered by their network. The
prairie farmer, hitherto dependent on long wagon hauls to a canal or river,
was now able to market his grain and livestock. Most important of prairie
railways was the Illinois Central, financed and managed by capitalists of New
York and Boston, and endowed by Act of Congress with alternate sections
(640 acres) of public land in a checkerboard pattern in a strip six miles wide
on each side of its right of way. The completion of this line from Chicago to
Cairo in 1856 opened the central prairies to profitable settlement.

A struggle over the route of a transcontinental railway had severe political
consequences. Of many different schemes projected since 1845, the four most
important were (1) the Northern, from the upper Mississippi to the upper
Missouri, and by the Oregon trail to the Columbia river; (2) the Central
from St. Louis up the Kansas and Arkansas rivers, across the Rockies to the
Great Salt Lake and by the California trail to San Francisco; (3) the "Thirty-
fifth Parallel" route from Memphis, up the Arkansas and Canadian rivers,

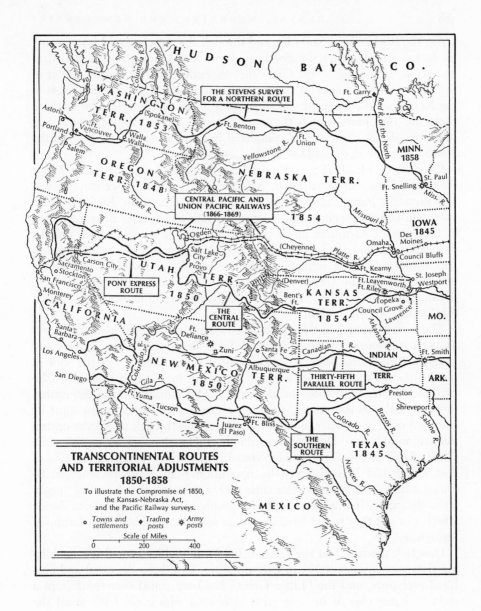

THE STEVENS SURVEY
FOR A NORTHERN ROUTE

CENTRAL PACIFIC AND
UNION PACIFIC RAILWAYS
(1866-1869)

PONY EXPRESS
ROUTE

THE
CENTRAL
ROUTE

THIRTY-FIFTH
PARALLEL ROUTE

THE
SOUTHERN
ROUTE

HUDSON BAY CO.

WASHINGTON
TERR. 1853

Astoria
Portland
Ft. Vancouver
Salem
Walla
Walla
(Spokane)

Ft. Garry

Ft. Benton

Yellowstone R.

Ft.
Union

Red R. of the North

MINN.
1858

St. Paul

OREGON
TERR. 1848

Snake R.

NEBRASKA TERR.

1854

Missouri R.

Ft. Snelling

Miss. R.

IOWA
1845

Ogden

(Cheyenne)

Platte R.

Omaha

Des
Moines

Council Bluffs

Carson City
Sacramento
Stockton
San Francisco
Monterey

Salt Lake
City
Provo

UTAH
TERR.
1850

(Denver)

Ft. Kearny

Ft. Leavenworth
Ft. Riley

St. Joseph
Westport

CALIFORNIA

Santa
Barbara

Bent's
Ft.

KANSAS
TERR.
1854

Topeka
Council Grove
Lawrence

Arkansas R.

MO.

Los Angeles

San Diego

Ft.
Defiance

Zuni

Santa Fe

Canadian R.

INDIAN

Ft. Smith

Colorado R.

Gila R.

NEW MEXICO TERR.
1850

Albuquerque

TERR.

ARK.

Ft. Yuma

Tucson

Juarez
(El Paso)

Ft. Bliss

Preston

Shreveport

Colorado R.

Brazos R.

Sabine R.

TEXAS
1845

MEXICO

Nueces R.

Rio Grande

**TRANSCONTINENTAL ROUTES
AND TERRITORIAL ADJUSTMENTS
1850-1858**

To illustrate the Compromise of 1850,
the Kansas-Nebraska Act,
and the Pacific Railway surveys.

○ Towns and
settlements
♦ Trading
posts
❋ Army
posts

Scale of Miles

0   200   400

across the Rockies near Santa Fe, and through the Apache and Mojave country to Los Angeles; (4) the Southern, from New Orleans up the Red river and across Texas, and by the Gila valley to Yuma and San Diego.[1] Either of the first two would follow an existing trail, and bind Oregon and California to the North, but the unorganized Indian country was an obstacle. The southern route was the shortest, with the best contours, and led through states and territories already organized. If completed in time, it might have enabled the South to recover all she had lost by the Compromise of 1850.

Congress, in March 1853, authorized surveys of these four routes under the direction of the war department. Jefferson Davis was then secretary of war and President Pierce's mentor. Although a state rights man, his keen desire for a Southern transcontinental railway led him to advocate its construction by the federal government under the war power — a policy justified only by nationalist theories. As soon as it became clear that this line would have to pass through Mexican territory, Davis persuaded the President to buy the necessary land — the Gadsden purchase of the Gila river valley in southern Arizona; and, as the Mexican government badly needed money, it swallowed this "insult" for $10 million.

The scene was now set for Congress to sanction the southern route, but Stephen A. Douglas stole the show. A lively five-footer, full of bounce and swagger, this "Little Giant," senior senator from Illinois, was the idol of the Northern Democracy. As a heavy speculator in Western lands and Chicago real estate, he wished the transcontinental railway to take the central route. In order to contest the southern route, law and government must be extended over, and settlers invited into, the region through which the central railroad would pass. Douglas, accordingly, reported a bill to organize the Great Plains as the Territory of Nebraska, in January 1854. Earlier bills of that nature had been defeated by opposition from Southern senators. So Douglas baited this one for their votes with a principle that he called "popular sovereignty." It would rest with the people of the new territory to decide whether or not they would have slavery, as soon as they obtained a territorial legislature.

Douglas's motives, and the forces behind a bill which caused the smoldering slavery-extension conflict to flare up again, have been discussed and analyzed ever since, and the "Little Giant" has been called everything from a reckless demagogue to the one great statesman who could have saved the Union. It is probable that his motives were not only economic but political. Old parties were breaking up, old issues were worn thin, politicians were feeling insecure and looking about for some powerful issue to keep themselves in power. Douglas and a group of Democratic politicians in Washington,

1. These worked out as (1) Northern Pacific, (2) Missouri Pacific, Denver & Rio Grande and Southern Pacific; (3) Rock Island and Santa Fe; (4) Texas & Pacific and Southern Pacific.

known as the "F Street Mess" from the boardinghouse where they lived, were seeking an explosive political issue for 1856. The Kansas-Nebraska bill was their big idea. It was explosive enough to blow up the Union.

Popular sovereignty, or squatter sovereignty as it was contemptuously called, pleased nobody. As Nebraska lay north of 36° 30', slavery therein would be prohibited by the Missouri Compromise of 1820. Douglas's bill would have repealed that Act implicitly; but Senator Dixon of Kentucky and Senator Atchison of Missouri insisted on repealing it explictly. Douglas made a fatal mistake in consenting. He also agreed to divide the new territory into Kansas and Nebraska, so that the Missourians might secure the one and the Iowans the other. There was a touching scene when Senator Dixon told him, "Sir, I once recognized you as a demagogue, a mere manager, selfish and intriguing. I now find you a warm-hearted and sterling patriot."

2. Kansas-Nebraska Act and a Strange Interlude

The fat was in the fire. At this proposal to repeal the Missouri Compromise the angry passions of pro- and anti-slavery flared up; and there was no Henry Clay to quench them. Everyone forgot about the railroad. The South had not asked for Kansas, did not want Kansas; but "Southern rights" were involved. Few slaveholders planned to carry Negroes further west, but Southern honor demanded that slavery follow the flag. Northerners, on the other hand, were alarmed at a proposed extension of slave territory, and the breach of a sectional compromise of over thirty years' standing. People could hardly have been more startled at a proposition to repeal habeas corpus and trial by jury. Stephen Douglas, morally obtuse, could not see that principles were involved; he never appreciated the strong sentiment in the North against opening virgin territory to the "peculiar institution." The North, in Lincoln's picturesque phrase, was determined to give her pioneers "a clean bed, with no snakes in it." Nor did he realize how passionate the South had become over prestige.

For three months the bitter debate dragged on. President Pierce tried to whip his party into line, and all but a few of the Northern Democrats obeyed. Old Sam Houston of Texas reminded the Senate in vain that by solemn treaties it had confirmed most of Kansas and Nebraska to the Indians "as long as grass shall grow and water run." Nobody else cared for the aborigines. Hordes of emigrants to Oregon and California had killed their game and thinned their numbers by spreading disease. Federal agents were already bullying them into selling their "perpetual" land titles. The once powerful Delaware or Leni-Lenape accepted a small reservation with an annual bounty. Others, like the Shawnee and the Miami, who had once terrorized the Old Northwest, were removed to the Indian Territory, which fortunately lay between the rival railway routes.

Democratic discipline triumphed. On 25 May 1854 the Kansas-Nebraska Bill passed the Senate by a comfortable majority and received President Pierce's signature.

As a sample of the effect on Northern opinion, one may quote the Reverend Francis Wayland, president of Brown University. He had always been a moderate antislavery man, declaring in 1844 that to terminate slavery "by violence, or without previous moral and social preparation," would be a calamity. But in 1854 he denounced this new extension of slave area as a violation of moral law, "giving just cause for a dissolution of the Union."

"If the Nebraska Bill should be passed, the Fugitive Slave Law is a dead letter throughout New England," wrote a Southerner from Boston. "As easily could a law prohibiting the eating of codfish and pumpkin pies be enforced." The day after it passed, a Boston mob led by a Unitarian minister tried to rescue a fugitive slave from the courthouse where he had been detained for examination. Anthony Burns, the slave, was identified by his master and escorted to the wharf by a battalion of United States artillery and four platoons of marines, through streets lined with hissing and groaning spectators who were kept back by twenty-two companies of state militia. It cost the United States about $40,000 to return that slave to his master; and he was the last returned from Massachusetts.

The Northwest, seething with indignation over the Kansas-Nebraska Act, was ripe to form a new antislavery party. A meeting in a little schoolhouse at Ripon, Wisconsin on 28 February 1854 resolved to oppose the extension of slavery, and recommended that a new "Republican party" be formed to do it. Later in the year, similar meetings were held in other states, to the same purpose. Outside the Northwest the new party slowly gathered momentum. Seward sulked in his Whig tent; the "Anti-Nebraska Democrats" were loath to cut all connection with their party; the Free-Soilers could not see why a new party was needed; and the people were distracted by a new gospel of ignorance.

Know-Nothingism was a flare-up of the anti-Catholic and anti-foreign sentiment which had led to riots in the 1840's. The visit of a tactless papal nuncio appears to have convinced many that the Republic was in danger from Rome; and the activities of German radicals, who had begun to preach the gospel according to St. Marx, alarmed the pious. Accordingly a secret "Order of the Star-Spangled Banner," with elaborate ritual and rigid discipline, was formed by native-born Protestants. Members, when questioned by outsiders, answered, "I know nothing." Candidates secretly nominated developed surprising strength at the polls, and many minor politicians joined up, thinking that this was the wave of the future. In the state elections of 1854, the Know-Nothings almost won New York, and did win Massachusetts, electing a completely new legislature that passed some reform legislation but also conducted clownish investigations of Catholic schools and convents. At Baltimore they organized "plug-uglies," gangs of hoodlums who attended the polls armed with carpenters' awls, to "plug" voters who did not give the pass-word. In some Baltimore wards loaded swivel-guns were stationed at the polls to intimidate the Democrats, and bands of "native American" rowdies drove through the streets on election day, firing pistols and insulting women. St. Louis, in August 1854, was the scene of a series of pitched battles between native Americans and Irish Catholics — the Germans staying carefully aloof. Police and militia were helpless, many lives were lost, and order was restored only after the mayor, Edward Bates (later Lincoln's attorney general) organized a force of 700 armed citizens to cow the rival mobs.

In the summer of 1855 the American party, as the Know-Nothings now called themselves, held a national convention at which the Southern members obtained control, passed proslavery resolutions, and nominated for the presidency old Millard Fillmore. The Northerners then lost interest; and except in Maryland, which voted for Fillmore in 1856, the movement collapsed. Rufus Choate wrote their epitaph: "Any thing more low, obscene, feculent the manifold heavings of history have not cast up." He could not have said that a century later.

3. Kansas and a New Party

"Bleeding Kansas" soon diverted attention from the "Popish Peril." Since popular sovereignty was to settle the status of slavery in Kansas, pro- and antislavery people scrambled to get there first. The federal government opened a land office in Kansas in July 1854, before the Indian titles had been extinguished; and even earlier, Missourians began to flock across the border and stake out claims. In the meantime, enterprising Yankees had formed a company to finance emigration to Kansas, as they already had to Oregon. This effort aroused savage indignation among the Missourians, who proceeded to blockade the Missouri river against immigrants from the Northeast, and to sack their first settlement at Lawrence. The Emigrant Aid Company then decided to arm free-state settlers with a new breechloading weapon of precision, the Sharps rifle. These were merry times in Kansas for men who enjoyed fighting. Parties of Northern "Jayhawkers" battled "Kickapoo Rangers," "Doniphan Tigers," and other organizations from Missouri and points south, whom the Northerners called "border ruffians." Senator Atchison of Missouri boasted, "We had at least 7000 men in the Territory on the day of the election, and one-third of them will remain there. The proslavery ticket prevailed everywhere. Now let the Southern men come on with their slaves. . . . We are playing for a mighty stake; if we win, we carry slavery to the Pacific Ocean."

Few Southerners, however, cared to risk valuable property in such a region, and free-staters poured in with the spirit of crusaders. One, a fanatic named John Brown, killed a number of innocent people at the "Pottawotami massacre." Such were the workings of Douglas's "popular sovereignty." Kansas had become the theater of cold (and not so cold) war that led to the Civil War. It was one of those contests preliminary to major wars, like the Balkan Wars of 1912–13 to World War I, and the Spanish Civil War to World War II.

Could nothing be done to prevent a head-on collision? The abolitionists were no help. Garrison, who had long since denounced the Constitution as "a covenant with death and an agreement with hell," accented this odd theory by publicly burning a copy of it. The only constructive proposal came from the Sage of Concord. Before the Anti-Slavery Society of New York on 6 February 1855, Emerson proposed that slavery be extinguished by granting full compensation to the owners. He recognized that the slaveholder was caught in a trap from which emancipation on the British model offered the only peaceful escape. The federal government and the states could give the proceeds of public lands. "The churches will melt their plate," wealthy bene-factors will give their thousands, and school children their pennies; "every man in the land would give a week's work to dig away this accursed mountain of sorrow once and forever out of the world."

Nobody seconded the motion. The South was determined not to give up slavery, and the North was unwilling to pay them to do it. Emerson's estimate of the cost, $2 billion, would have been cheap enough in comparison with that of the Civil War.

Charles Sumner, a scholar and a radical lawyer, senator from Massachu-setts as the result of a political deal, had begun to rival William H. Seward as the spokesman of antislavery sentiment. His handsome features and oratorical talent caused him to be compared with Calhoun; but he had none of Cal-houn's restraint. He was one of those fortunately rare and rarely fortunate persons who are not only thick-skinned themselves but assume that everyone else is. In a turgid oration on 19 May 1856, "The Crime against Kansas," he exhausted the vocabulary of vituperation. The elderly and moderate Senator Butler of South Carolina he described as a Don Quixote whose Dulcinea was "the harlot slavery," and Stephen A. Douglas as Sancho Panza, "the squire of slavery, ready to do its humiliating offices." The tone of this speech was so nasty that it would probably have ended Sumner's political career, had not "Southern chivalry" demanded physical chastisement. Three days after its delivery a South Carolina congressman, a distant cousin of Senator Butler, passed up the opportunity to attack Sumner on the steps of the Capitol when able to defend himself; then, with a stout stick, beat him senseless when sitting helplessly at his desk in the Senate chamber. The assailant was praised by the Southern press and presented by admirers with suitably inscribed sticks. Sumner, badly injured, returned to his seat only at intervals for the next three years; but he was now a hero and martyr in the North.

A few days after this disgraceful affair, the new Republican party held a national nominating convention at Philadelphia. It was a mass meeting of earnest men from all Northern states, who were convinced that the cause of freedom in self-defense must support the new party. The name of John C. Frémont, "The Pathfinder," whose career (except for a few months as senator from California) had been devoted to exploration of the Far West, stampeded the convention. Apparently the politicians thought that they needed a "glamour boy." The Republican platform took a swipe at the Mormons and the South by declaring it to be "both the right and the duty of Congress to prohibit in the Territories these twin relics of barbarism, polygamy and slavery."

Flabby James Buchanan, long an aspirant for the Democratic presidential nomination, now easily obtained it. The "Black Republicans," as their enemies called them, made a lively campaign. "Free soil, free speech, and Frémont" was the slogan, but slavery in the territories was the only real issue. Many Southern leaders warned the country that if Frémont were elected the South would secede; and when John M. Botts, an independent Virginia Whig, called this an idle threat, the Richmond *Enquirer* advised him to leave the state lest he "provoke the disgrace of lynching." A sectional showdown in 1856 was prevented by Buchanan's carrying every slave state except Maryland, together with Pennsylvania, Illinois, and Indiana, which gave him 174 electoral votes to Frémont's 114. But the "Pathfinder" polled an impressive popular vote, 1,340,000 to Buchanan's 1,838,000. Ominous figures, because all but 1200 of Frémont's votes came from the non-slaveholding states.

4. *Dred Scott*

Dred Scott was a slave who had been taken by his master, an army officer, to Illinois, thence to unorganized territory north of 36° 30′ where slavery had been forbidden by the Missouri Compromise, then back to Missouri, where he sued for his freedom as having been a resident of free soil. The case reached the Supreme Court, which published its decision on 6 March 1857.

Chief Justice Taney and the four Southerners among the associate justices saw in this case an opportunity to settle the question of slavery in the territories by extending it legally to all United States territory. President-elect Buchanan put them up to it, hoping thus to restore harmony to the Democratic party. Two justices tipped him off on the decision in advance. So Buchanan slipped a clause into his inaugural address declaring that the Supreme Court was about to decide "at what point of time" the people of a territory could decide for or against slavery. To their decision he pledged his support and urged "all good citizens" to do likewise.

Poor, foolish Buchanan! He had hoped for a peaceful term of office, but the Dred Scott case unleashed the worst passions of pro- and anti-slavery when his administration was less than a week old.

The opinion of the court decided against Scott's claim for freedom on three grounds: (1) as a Negro he could not be a citizen of the United States, and therefore had no right to sue in a federal court; (2) as a resident of Missouri the laws of Illinois had no longer any effect on his status; (3) as a resident of the territory north of 36° 30′ he had not been emancipated because Congress had no right to derpive citizens of their property without due process of law. The Missouri Compromise of 1820, therefore, was unconstitutional and void.

None of the Chief Justice's opinion was *obiter dictum*, but only on the second point was it sound. As Justice Curtis proved in his vigorous dissenting opinion. Negroes had been considered citizens in all Northern states, even though few had possessed the vote, and as citizens had frequently sued in federal courts. "Due process of law" in the Constitution referred to the method of a law's enforcement, not to the substance of a law itself. Only once before, in *Marbury* v. *Madison* had the Supreme Court declared an Act of Congress unconstitutional. In that case the law directly concerned the federal judiciary; but the Missouri Compromise was a general law which had been in force for 36 years, and had been regarded as hardly less sacred than the Constitution itself.

In this decision the Court sanctioned Calhoun's doctrine that slavery was national, freedom sectional. Oregon and Nebraska, as well as Kansas, were now opened to slavery. Squatter sovereignty thenceforth was no sovereignty; slavery was theoretically legal in every territory of the United States.

Federal troops were now keeping order in Kansas, but the free-state and proslavery men refused to co-operate. Each group held a convention, one at Topeka and one at Lecompton, drafted a state constitution and under it appealed to Washington for statehood. The antislavery Topeka constitution was rejected by the Senate in 1856; the Lecompton constitution, an out-and-out proslavery charter, was accepted by the Senate. Douglas, however, insisted that the people of Kansas be allowed to vote, and they rejected it by an overwhelming majority. For his honest adherence to principle, and for standing by the result, Douglas was now denounced as a "traitor to the South," and lost his chance to be elected President in 1860.

5. *The Lincoln-Douglas Debate*

Abraham Lincoln, prior to the Kansas struggle, stood out from hundreds of Midwestern lawyer-politicians only by a reputation for complete honesty, and a habit of prolonged, abstracted contemplation. He had played the usual game of Illinois politics, and not too well. Elected to Congress as a Whig, he was defeated for a second term owing to his opposition to the Mexican War. Slavery he regarded as an evil thing from his first contact with it on a raft trip down the Mississippi; but the abolitionist agitation seemed to him mischievous and unrealistic. He was an antislavery man, but willing to let slavery alone where it was established.

About the time of the Kansas-Nebraska Act, some new force began to work in Lincoln's soul. He began to preach a new testament of antislavery, without malice or hatred toward the slave-owners.

I surely will not blame them for not doing what I should not know how to do myself. If all earthly power were given me, I should not know what to do, as to the existing instituiton. . . . When they remind us of their constitutional rights, I acknowledge them, not grudgingly, but fully, and fairly; and I would give them any legislation for the reclaiming of their fugitives, which should not, in its stringency, be more likely to carry a free man into slavery, than our ordinary criminal laws are to hang an innocent one. . . . But all this, to my judgment, furnishes no more excuse for permitting slavery to go into our own free territory, than it would for reviving the African slave trade by law.

Slavery is founded in the selfishness of man's nature — opposition to it, in his love of justice. These principles are an eternal antagonism; and when brought into collision so fiercely, as slavery extension brings them, shocks, and throes, and convulsions must ceaselessly follow.

These quotations are from Lincoln's Peoria speech of 16 October 1854. It made him known throughout the Northwest. Four years later he became a rival candidate to Douglas for election as United States Senator from Illinois. The first paragraphs of his opening speech in the campaign (16 June 1858) gave the ripe conclusion to his meditations during the last four years; and struck the keynote of American history for the seven years to come:

We are now far into the *fifth* year, since a policy was initiated, with the *avowed* object, and *confident* promise, of putting an end to slavery agitation.

Under the operation of that policy, that agitation has not only, *not ceased,* but has *constantly augmented.*

In *my* opinion, it *will* not cease, until a crisis shall have been reached, and passed.

A house divided against itself cannot stand.

I believe this government cannot endure, permanently half *slave* and half *free.*

I do not expect the Union to be *dissolved* — I do not expect the house to *fall* — but I *do* expect it will cease to be divided.

It will become *all* one thing, or *all* the other.

Either the opponents of slavery, will arrest the further spread of it, and place it where the public mind shall rest in the belief that it is in the course of ultimate extinction; or its *advocates* will push it forward, till it shall become alike lawful in *all* the States, *old* as well as *new* — *North* as well as *South.*

William H. Seward echoed this sentiment in his speech of 25 October 1858. "It is an irrepressible conflict between opposing and enduring forces, and it means that the United States must and will, sooner or later, become either entirely a slaveholding nation, or entirely a free-labor nation."

Lincoln and Douglas engaged in a series of joint debates, covering every section of the state, through the summer and autumn of 1858. Imagine a parched little prairie town of central Illinois, set in fields of rustling corn; a dusty courthouse square, surrounded by low wooden houses and shops blistering in the August sunshine, decked with flags and party emblems; shirtsleeved farmers and their families in wagons and buggies and on foot, brass bands blaring out "Hail! Columbia" and "Oh! Susanna"; wooden platform with railing, a perspiring semicircle of local dignitaries in black frock coats and immense beaver hats. The Douglas special train (provided by George B.

McClellan, superintendent of the Illinois Central) pulls into the "deepo" and fires a salute from the twelve-pounder cannon bolted to a flatcar at the rear. Senator Douglas, escorted by the local Democratic club in columns of fours, drives up in an open carriage, and aggressively mounts the platform. His short, stocky figure is clothed in the best that Washington tailors can produce. Every feature of his face bespeaks confidence and mastery; every gesture of his body, vigor and combativeness. Abe Lincoln, having arrived by ordinary passenger train, approaches on foot, his furrowed face and long neck conspicuous above the crowd. Wearing a rusty frock coat, the sleeves of which stop several inches short of his wrists, and well-worn trousers that show similar reluctance to approach a pair of enormous feet, he shambles onto the platform. His face, as he turns to the crowd, has an air of settled melancholy. But no recorded debate in the English language has surpassed those between Lincoln and Douglas for keen give and take, crisp, sinewy language, and clear exposition of vital issues.

Although the Dred Scott decision was a stunning blow to the "gur-reat pur-rinciple of popular sovereignty," Douglas had stuck to it courageously, and defied Buchanan and the Southern Democrats when they attempted to impose the Lecompton constitution on Kansas. In the debate at Freeport, Lincoln attempted to place Douglas in a dilemma by asking whether the people of a territory could, in any lawful way, exclude slavery from their limits. Apparently, Douglas must either accept the Dred Scott decision and admit popular sovereignty to be a farce, or separate from his party by repudiating a dictum of the Supreme Court. Very neatly Douglas found a way out. "Slavery cannot exist a day or an hour anywhere, unless it is supported by local police regulations." If a territorial legislature fail to pass a black code, slavery will effectually be kept out. This "Freeport doctrine," as it was called, won Douglas his re-election to the Senate; and he deserved it. Kansas was safe for freedom; and if slavery were theoretically legal in the territories, there was slight chance of any except New Mexico and Arizona becoming slaveholding states. The main political justification for Lincoln's stand, forbidding slavery in the territories, was the extreme unlikelihood that the South would rest content with the Dred Scott principle, any more than she had rested content with the compromises of 1820 and 1850.

Lincoln furnished an even deeper justification in his Quincy speech of 13 October 1858. This controversy over strategic positions, he pointed out, was an effort to dominate the fundamental moral issue; it was

The difference between the men who think slavery a wrong and those who do not think it wrong. The Republican party think it wrong — we think it is a moral, a social and a political wrong. We think it is a wrong not confining itself merely to the persons or the states where it exists, but that it is a wrong in its tendency, to say the least, that extends itself to the existence of the whole nation. Because we think it wrong, we propose a course of policy that shall deal with it as a wrong. We deal with it as with any other wrong, in so far as we can prevent its growing any larger, and so deal with it that in the run of time there may be some promise of an end to it . . .

I will add this, that if there be any man who does not believe that slavery is wrong in the three aspects which I have mentioned, or in any one of them, that man is misplaced, and ought to leave us. While, on the other hand, if there be any man in the Republican party who is impatient . . . of the constitutional guarantees thrown around it, and would act in disregard of these, he too is misplaced standing with us.

In his reply Douglas took the ground that the rights and wrongs of slavery were nobody's business outside the slave states. "If each state will only agree to mind its own business, and let its neighbors alone, . . . this republic can exist forever divided into free and slave states, as our fathers made it and the people of each state have decided."

Lincoln, in rejoinder, thanked his opponent for the admission that slavery must exist forever.

6. The African Slave Trade

Ominous was a growing insistence by spokesmen of the lower South that new territory must be acquired for slavery, no matter where, and that a fresh supply of Africans be imported to work it.

Laws of the United States and of almost every Western nation declared the African slave trade to be piracy, punishable by death; but, prior to the Lincoln administration, no American citizen was executed for this offense. Laws against it either were not enforced, or were so construed that traffic in human flesh was protected by the American flag. The British navy was the only force seriously trying to suppress the trade; but successive presidential administrations, faithful to the obsolete issue of visit and search, refused permission to the British to search American vessels. A slave ship only had to raise the "proud banner of freedom" to evade search, and escape. Conversely an American slaver when sighted by a United States warship could escape by displaying a foreign flag.

A United States naval squadron was supposed to help the Royal Navy police the African coast, but it consisted entirely of sailing vessels, slower than most of the slavers, and accomplished very little. In 1849, for instance, the four American warships which were engaged in "suppressing the slave trade" spent most of their time at a temporary naval base in the Cape Verde Islands, 1000 miles from the nearest barracoon. "No one thinks of catching slavers," wrote a participant, "nor do I believe the officers of the squadron . . . wish to catch them." One reason for this attitude was the navy department's warning to these officers that they would be personally liable for damages if they made any mistakes. Several captured slavers sent into an American port for adjudication had been freed for "want of evidence" (chains and fetters on board being mere trade goods, apparently), and the officers who captured them were sued for damages by the shipowner. So it is not surprising that between 1843 and 1857 the United States Navy's score of captures was 19 slavers, only 6 of which were condemned; a period when the Royal Navy made almost 600 seizures and all but 38 were condemned. Even so, British cruisers were unable altogether to stop the trade. An estimated 440,000 slaves were illicitly exported from the West Coast of Africa in the years 1840–47 to the United States, Cuba, and Brazil, and the number rose annually; but only 31,180 were freed and returned to Africa. Of the residue, it is anyone's guess how many reached the United States. President Buchanan and navy secretary Toucey, ashamed of the monstrous proportions that the traffic had attained under their flag, really attempted to suppress it in 1858–60. Four steam warships were joined to the Africa squadron, the supply base was brought nearer to the coast, and in 1860 it captured seven slavers in addition to five taken by the home squadron off the coast of Cuba.

Ironically enough, profits of the trade in "black ivory" mostly went north. During eighteen months of 1859–60, some 85 slave ships were fitted out in New York City alone. Many, but not all, were owned by Cuban or Brazilian firms, and most of them carried slaves to the Latin American countries where slavery was still legal, rather than to the United States. Every Northern seaport, as well as Mobile, Charleston, and New Orleans, took part. Charles A. L. Lamar, scion of one of the first families of Georgia, was a leader in this inhuman traffic. He figured on a profit of 60 per cent per voyage, and another slave trader boasted that he had landed 1300 slaves in Cuba at $1000 a head. According to several estimates, the total number imported into the United States in the 1850s ran well into five figures and was greater than it had been half a century earlier when the trade was legal. In 1858, for instance, U.S.S. *Dolphin* captured off the coast of Cuba and sent into Charleston slave ship *Echo*, with 300 Congo Negroes on board. Charleston and Richmond papers then started an agitation to have "these useless barbarians" given "good masters" and put to work. They had reached the "threshhold of civilization"; why return them to dark Africa? President Buchanan enforced the law and sent them to Liberia.

Open advertisements of fresh slave imports in Southern newspapers showed how the wind blew. At the annual Southern commercial conventions, speeches and resolutions favoring the legal reopening of the trade occupied much of the delegates' time after 1856. These conventions reflected the views of the Southern middle class, who could not afford to buy slaves at the prevailing high prices — more than $2000 for a prime field hand. They were commonly attended by radical "fire-eaters" who could not get elected to Congress or to state legislatures, and who stirred up this new issue just as rabblerousers operate today on various "patriotic" conventions. A committee report of the Montgomery commercial convention of 1858 pointed out that the South could only regain power in the Union by obtaining more slaves to take into Kansas and other territories opened by the Dred Scott decision. Governor James H. Adams of South Carolina in 1856 recommended his legislature to press for a reopening.

William L. Yancey declared that it was unjust for the North to enjoy free immigration of European labor while the South was forbidden access to the vast pool of African labor. "If it is right to buy slaves in Virginia and carry them to New Orleans," he said, "why is it not right to buy them in Cuba, Brazil, or Africa?" A Charleston gentleman named L. W. Spratt became a persistent advocate of reopening, and made a powerful speech in favor of it before the South Carolina legislature in 1858, painting an attractive picture of the "prosperity to be poured upon us by the teeming thousands from the plains of Africa," promising that every white man could then afford to own a slave. An "African Labor Supply Association" was formed at Vicksburg in 1859, and J. D. B. De Bow, whose *Review* supported the movement, was elected president.

Reopening the African slave trade was opposed in the border slave states, whose surplus Negroes were exported southward; hence the lower South, needing their support in a crisis, refrained from pressing such proposals in Congress; and the Confederate Constitution, as a bait for the border states, forbade it. But Spratt promptly started a movement to have this prohibition removed by constitutional amendment. There was no denying Yancey's logic if it was right to buy slaves in Virginia, why was it wrong to buy them in Africa? This movement was growing, and reopening the African slave trade might well have become a Southern ultimatum if Douglas instead of Lincoln had been elected in 1860.

The African slave trade had always emitted a disagreeable odor; but no such stench emanated from Southern desire to acquire more slave territory at the expense of Spain or Mexico — a promising method to acquire new sources of "black ivory," and of political power.

President Buchanan, whose ministry in London had gained him valuable friendships there, conducted foreign relations himself, disregarding his aged and querulous secretary of state, Lewis Cass. A détente of all irritating questions between the two countries was signaled by a visit of the nineteen-year-old Prince of Wales (later Edward VII) to the United States. He was the first royal personage, except exiles, to visit this republic. Balls in his honor were given in several Eastern cities; and the prince managed to pass through Baltimore without falling in love, unlike his grandson Edward VIII, with a local belle. His warm reception paid dividends later in the friendliness of his parents, Victoria and Albert, to the Union.

There were no filibustering expeditions against Cuba at this time because Narciso Lopez, leader of the *Cuba libre* rebels, was bent on abolishing slavery. But the hope of buying or conquering Cuba from Spain burned high in many a Southern breast, as well as in President Buchanan's. He urged measures to acquire Cuba in at least three of his annual messages, and both Democratic platforms of 1860 demanded that Cuba be annexed by fair means or foul.

Buchanan was equally zealous in trying to secure more Southern slave territory from distracted Mexico. During his administration Benito Juárez, a full-blooded Indian and by any standards a great statesman, was constitutional president of Mexico; but a reactionary regime ruled Mexico City and states bordering on the Rio Grande. Buchanan in messages of 1858–59 to Congress proposed that he be authorized to establish military posts in Sonora and Chihuahua to "restore order." He recognized the Juárez government, but attempted to extort from it, in return for paying several million dollars, the state of Baja California, obviously as a sop to the Southern expansionists who were still complaining of having been robbed by the State of California's outlawing slavery. That was a bit too much for Juárez to swallow, but he or his foreign minister did sign a draft treaty giving the United States a perpetual right of transit from the Gulf to the Pacific across the northern tier of Mexican states. Buchanan, who regarded this as a useful entering wedge for more annexation, submitted the treaty to the Senate in January 1860, but the Senate rejected it, hands down. Presently the American Civil War would give European powers an opportunity to intervene in Mexico far more deeply than Buchanan ever thought of doing; but in the meantime, the image of Uncle Sam as an intriguing imperialist had been created in Central America.

XXXVIII

The Approach to War

1859-1861

1. Booth, Brown, and the Election of 1860

NORTHERN AGGRESSIVENESS was not wanting. In 1859 came two startling portents of the irrepressible conflict. A certain Booth, convicted in a federal court of having forcibly rescued a runaway slave, was released by the supreme court of Wisconsin on the ground that the Fugitive Slave Act of 1850 was unconstitutional. After the Supreme Court of the United States had reversed this decision, the Wisconsin legislature, citing the Kentucky resolutions of 1798 which Southerners considered almost a part of the Constitution, declared "That this assumption of jurisdiction by the federal judiciary . . . is an act of undelegated power, void, and of no force." The federal government rearrested and imprisoned Booth; but that did not lessen the effect on Southern sentiment. The deeper significance lies in the fact that the slavery issue had transcended constitutional theory and each side turned to nationalism or state rights as best suited its supposed interest.

If the Booth case aroused bitterness, the next episode of 1859 brought the deep anger that comes from fear. John Brown, perpetrator of the Pottawatomi massacre in Kansas, was a belated Puritan who would have found congenial work in Cromwell's invasion of Ireland. A madman with a method, he formed a vague project to establish a republic of fugitive slaves in the Appalachians, whence to wage war on the slave states. From Canadian and New England abolitionists he obtained money and support, although none were informed as to his exact intentions, and he seems to have had no definite plan. On the night of 16 October 1859, leading an armed troop of thirteen white men and five Negroes, John Brown seized the federal arsenal at Harper's Ferry, killed the mayor of the town, and took prisoner some of the leading people. By daybreak the telegraph was spreading consternation throughout the country.

Governor Wise called out the Virginia militia and implored the federal government for aid. John Brown retreated to a locomotive roundhouse, knocked portholes through the brick wall, and defended himself. Lewis Washington, one of his prisoners, has left us a graphic description of the scene: "Brown was the coolest and firmest man I ever saw in defying danger and death. With one son dead by his side, and another shot through, he felt the pulse of his dying son with one hand and held his rifle with the other, and commanded his men with the utmost composure, encouraging them to be firm and to sell their lives as dearly as they could." In the evening, when Colonel Robert E. Lee arrived with a company of marines from Washington, only Brown and four men were alive and unwounded. Next day the marines forced an entrance and took all five prisoner.

Eight days after his capture the trial of John Brown began in the court-house of Charles Town, Virginia. From the pallet where he lay wounded the bearded old fighter rejected his counsel's plea of insanity. There could be no doubt of the result. On 31 October the jury brought in a verdict of murder, criminal conspiracy, and treason against Virginia. John Brown, content (as he wrote to his children) "to die for God's eternal truth on the scaffold as in any other way," was hanged on 2 December 1859.

He had played into the hands of extremists on both sides. Southern Union-ists were silenced by secessionists saying, "There—you see? That's what the North wants to do to us!" Keenly the South watched for indications of Northern opinion. That almost every Northern newspaper, as well as Lincoln, Douglas, and Seward, condemned Brown they did not heed, so much as the admiration for a brave man that Northern opinion could not conceal. And the babble of shocked repudiation by politicians and public men was dimmed by one bell-like note from Emerson: "That new saint, than whom nothing purer or more brave was ever led by love of men into conflict and death . . . will make the gallows glorious like the cross."

The Republican party, having won the congressional elections of 1858, had good reason to hope for victory in 1860, although the leaders of the lower South let it clearly be understood that they would not submit to the rule of a "Black Republican" President. Only six years old, the new party was already more united than the Whigs had ever been; and the platform of its national nominating convention, adopted at Chicago on 18 May 1860, showed that it was no longer a party of one idea, but a Northern party. It had lost the first flush of radicalism, and was beginning that evolution to the right which made it eventually the party of big business and finance. In 1860 Republicanism combined the solid policies of Hamiltonian Federalism with the hopeful and humanitarian outlook of its namesake, the party of Jefferson.

On the slavery question the platform was clear enough, though less trucu-lent than in 1856. No more slavery in the territories; but no interference with slavery in the states. So there was no place for abolitionists, who denounced the Republicans as no better than Cotton Whigs; Wendell Phillips called Lincoln "the slave-hound of Illinois." The Chicago platform repudiated John Brown, along with the border ruffians of Missouri, promised settlers a free quarter-section of public land, and revived Henry Clay's American system of internal improvements and protective tariff, Northern desires which had been balked by Southern interests. The tariff of 1857, passed by a Democratic

congress and lowest since 1790, was blamed by Northern bankers and manufacturers for the shortlived panic of 1857, and for low prices that followed.
Everything that the North had wanted in recent years — subsidies for transatlantic cables and steamship lines, dredging Western rivers, improvement of
Great Lakes harbors, overland mail route, telegraph line to California — had
been blocked by Southern votes or President Buchanan's vetoes.

Abraham Lincoln received the presidential nomination on the third ballot,
not for his transcendent merits, which no one yet suspected, but as a matter
of political strategy. His humble birth, homely wit, and skill in debate would
attract the same sort of Northerner who had once voted for Andrew Jackson,
and no one but he could carry Indiana and Illinois. William H. Seward, the
most distinguished and experienced candidate, had too long and vulnerable a
record; Salmon P. Chase was little known outside Ohio. As Lincoln's running
mate the convention chose Senator Hannibal Hamlin of Maine, an old Jackson Democrat.

The Democratic nominating convention at Charleston split on the issue of
popular sovereignty in the territories. Southern Democrats believed that they
had been duped by Douglas. They had "bought" popular sovereignty in 1854,
expecting to get Kansas; but Kansas eluded them and its territorial legislature
was now in the hands of antislavery men, encouraged by Douglas's Freeport
Doctrine to flout the Dred Scott decision. Nothing less than active protection
to slavery in every territory, present or future, would satisfy the Southerners.
Jefferson Davis demanded a plank in the platform requiring Congress to
apply a "black code" to all territories. William L. Yancey of Alabama insisted
that the Democratic party declare flatly "that slavery was right." "Gentlemen
of the South," replied Senator Pugh of Ohio, "you mistake us — you mistake
us — we will not do it." Nor did they; and on 30 April 1860, after the
convention had rejected an extreme proslavery platform with the Davis plank,
the delegations of eight cotton states withdrew.

After this secession, since no candidate was able to win the two-thirds
majority required by Democratic tradition, the convention adjourned to Baltimore, where in June it made Douglas the official nominee of the Democratic party. The seceders held a rival convention presided over by Caleb
Cushing of Massachusetts, which nominated for the presidency the then Vice
President, John C. Breckinridge of Kentucky, with Senator Joseph Lane of
Oregon, and adopted the Charleston minority platform that the extremists
wanted.

In retrospect, the symbolic secession at Charleston on an issue partly emotional, partly semantic, seems even more rash and foolish than the state
secession which inevitably developed from it, like vinegar from cider. For the
only possible way for the South to protect her "peculiar institution" was to
elect a Democrat to the presidency, which this sectional split made impossible. Jefferson Davis, more than any other, was responsible for it. His object,
apparently, was to throw the election of President, for want of a majority in

the electoral college, into Congress. The House was then so evenly divided that it would have been deadlocked, but in the Senate the Democrats had a majority. They were expected to nominate Senator Joseph Lane of Oregon, who had proved himself a consistent proslavery man, Vice President; then, if the House could not agree, Lane would become President. Devious indeed, but legal.

John Bell of Tennessee and Edward Everett of Massachusetts were placed in nomination by the National Constitutional Union, a party freshly formed for this campaign, avowing no political principle other than the Constitution, the Union, and law enforcement. This was a praiseworthy attempt to build a middle-of-the-road party dedicated to solving the sectional issue by reason and compromise. Conservatives, North and South, declared it to be the only party "a gentleman could vote for." But passions had been too much aroused for a gentleman's party to win.

Although the Union was at stake, the campaign followed the pattern begun in 1840: torchlight parades, the Republicans carrying sections of rail fences, Bell-and-Everett processions featuring the ringing of a great bell as an alarm to the Union, fat boys recruited as "Little Giants" parading for Douglas; ballads, jokes, and songs, one of the most popular being a minstrel show "walkaround" called "Dixie's Land," which the Southern Confederacy later took over. There was plenty of serious argument, too. The Republicans managed to convince the plain people of the Northwest that if slavery extension continued, the Great Plains would be carved into slave plantations instead of free homesteads. Recent immigrants and native-born artisans disliked the Negro, but were repelled by the sneers of Southern Democrats at wage earners, and by deadly quotations from Southern literature on the evils of a free society. Republican orators posed a rhetorical question: "Can a free laboring man expect to get two dollars a day when a slave costs his master but ten cents?" Or, as Senator Ben Wade put it when a Southern colleague called the Homestead Bill a sop to Northern paupers, "Is it to be lands for the landless, or niggers for the niggerless?" In some obscure way the Northern laborer had come to look upon slavery as an ally of the capitalists who were doing their best to exploit him. He wished to break up what Charles Sumner called the alliance between the "lords of the lash and the lords of the loom."

As Minnesota and Oregon had been admitted to the Union in 1858 and 1859, there were now eighteen free and fifteen slave states. Breckinridge carried every cotton state, together with North Carolina, Delaware, and Maryland. Douglas, though a close second to Lincoln in the popular vote, carried only Missouri. Virginia, Kentucky, and Tennessee went for Bell although his popular vote was the least. Lincoln carried every free state, and rolled up a large majority in the electoral college, although his combined opponents polled almost a million more votes than he. Here are the results: [1]

1. These figures include no popular vote in South Carolina, where Breckinridge electors were chosen by the legislature.

	Popular Vote	Electoral Vote
Lincoln	1,866,452	180
Douglas	1,376,957	12
Breckinridge	849,781	72
Bell	588,879	39

Although it is difficult to argue that the election of Lincoln to the presidency was a mistake, it may well have been if one believes that postponement of the Civil War might have prevented it altogether. An examination of the election returns shows that moderate elements were still strong in the South, where important people were pointing out, as the Whigs had always done, that slavery extension into the territories was impractical, even if the Dred Scott case had made it legal; that there was no sense pressing for something which nobody really wanted. Even Breckinridge hoped that no slave-owners would go to the territories. But (one asks), if there was so much moderate sentiment in the South, why did it not rally to Douglas?

The answer is, politics. There had been a factional breach between the Douglas men and the Buchanan men. There was the feeling that Douglas was a fourflusher who had promised Kansas to the South and then let her down; and one of the politicians who did the most to foment that mischievous notion was Jefferson Davis. Douglas did his best to placate the South — he was the only candidate to go there on a speaking tour, but it was no use. The John Brown raid had jangled Southern nerves fatally. It started a chain of hysteria like the "great fear" of 1789 in the French Revolution. Rumors of slave insurrection popped up on every side; stories were spread of poisoned wells and the like, creating a feeling that nothing short of Breckinridge or secession could protect Southern society from subversion at the hands of vicious agitators.

Extremists on both sides whipped up hostile sentiment between the sections. Charles Sumner, returning to the Senate after a three-year attempt to cure the injuries inflicted by Preston Brooks, on 4 June 1860 delivered a four-hour oration on "The Barbarism of Slavery" which was no less offensive than the Kansas speech which provoked the beating. Southerners in general assumed that Sumner "spoke for the North"; they did not know that, for all his social graces and noble English friends, Sumner was ostracized by Boston society. Far closer to Northern sentiment was a letter of Francis Parkman the historian: "I would see every slave knocked on the head before I would see the Union go to pieces, and would include in the sacrifice as many abolitionists as could conveniently be brought together." That was pretty much Lincoln's feeling too.

On the other hand there were conciliatory pro-Union speeches by Senators Douglas, Crittenden, and many others. But Daniel C. DeJarnette, a "freshman" congressman from Caroline County, Virginia, countered Sumner with an extraordinary oration on the evils of free society and the beauties of slavery from which these are a few extracts:

The free suffrage and free labor of the North . . . has so shattered the framework of society, that society itself exists only in an inverted order.

African slavery furnishes the only basis upon which republican liberty can be preserved.

There is more humanity, there is more unalloyed contentment and happiness, among the slaves of the South, than any laboring population on the globe.

For every master who cruelly treats his slave, there are two white men at the North who torture and murder their wives.

More significant were the dithyrambic prophecies by Southern leaders of a Southern Confederacy's world prospects. Robert Barnwell Rhett, addressing the South Carolina assembly on 10 November 1860, predicted that historians in A.D. 2000 would praise the brave Southerners for "extending their Empire . . . down through Mexico to the other side of the great Gulf," establishing "a civilization teeming with orators, poets, philosophers, statesmen and historians, equal to those of Greece and Rome." Lucius H. Minor, a conservative Virginian, added that a Southern Confederacy, thus expanding, would command not only "the whole trade of South America with Europe," but the transit trade between Atlantic and Pacific. Henry Timrod, in his rapturous *Ethnogenesis*, predicted that a Southern Confederacy would not only extend from sea to sea, but would solve the problem of poverty throughout the world. This, he declared,

Is one among the many ends for which
God makes us great and rich!

Here indeed was the "purple dream," as Stephen Vincent Benét called it; the dream of a tropical empire based on Negro slavery. That enticing thought, recalling the wild ambitions of Hitler, permeated deeper than anyone in the North suspected. President Lincoln, in March 1861, sounded out James L. Petigru, a stout Unionist at the head of the South Carolina bar. Petigru told him that "no attachment to the Union" any longer existed there; Charleston merchants were looking forward to a "golden era" when their city would be the New York of a Southern empire. Foreign observers wondered at the landslide of secession, in contrast to the calm deliberations of the Continental Congress extending over a period of almost two years before cutting loose from Britain. Richard Cobden could not understand the "passionate haste and unreasoning arrogance of the secessionists." He had not heard of the purple dream. It had become so brilliant a dream that no possible concession from the North could have prevented an attempt to realize it. As the New Orleans *Bee* editorialized on 14 December 1860, the South could stay in the Union only after "a change of heart, radical and thorough" of Northern opinion "in relation to slavery." Or, as Lowell put it the following month, "What they demand of us is nothing less than that we should abolish the spirit of the age. Our very thoughts are a menace."

He did not exaggerate. South Carolina's Declaration of Independence, passed on Christmas Eve 1860, declared among the causes of her action, that the Northern states "have denounced as sinful the institution of Slavery," and that their public opinion had "invested a great political error with the sanctions of a more erroneous religious belief."

2. Secession Landslide in the Cotton States

The full-fledged secessionists chose South Carolina as their launching pad because of the prestige of Calhoun and the nullification tradition, and they chose well. Leaders of opinion in that state had long been waiting for an occasion to unite the South in a new confederacy. As soon as the election of Lincoln was certain, the South Carolina legislature summoned a state convention. On 20 December 1860 it met at Charleston and unanimously, after only a shadow of debate, declared "that the union now subsisting between South Carolina and other States, under the name of 'The United States of America' is hereby dissolved."

In other cotton states a strong Unionist party still existed. Men like Jefferson Davis, who had served in Washington and traveled in the North, wished to give Lincoln's administration a fair trial. Outside South Carolina, secession was largely the work of petty planters, provincial lawyer-politicians, journalists, and clergymen. Alexander H. Stephens waged a hopeless struggle in Georgia. "All efforts to save the Union will be unavailing," he predicted on 30 November 1860. "The truth is, our leaders and public men . . . do not desire to continue it on any terms. They do not wish any redress of wrongs; they are disunionists *per se*." And, on 3 December, "The people run mad. They are wild with passion and frenzy, doing they know not what." Howell Cobb of Georgia, who resigned as Buchanan's secretary of the treasury to agitate secession, convinced waverers with the meretricious argument "We can make better terms out of the Union than in it"; and Georgia took him at his word on 19 January 1861. Alabama, Florida, and Mississippi had already done so. Louisiana and Texas, where old Sam Houston the Jackson nationalist pled in vain for delay, were out of the Union by 1 February 1861. On the 8th, delegates from these seven states met at Montgomery, Alabama, and formed the Confederate States of America. Next day the congress elected Jefferson Davis president, and Alexander H. Stephens vice president of the Southern Confederacy.

Henry Timrod, unofficial laureate of the Confederacy, was there, and in honor of the occasion wrote one of his best poems:

> At last, we are
> A nation among nations; and the world
> Shall soon behold in many a distant port
>   Another flag unfurled!
> Now, come what may, whose favor need we court?
> And, under God, whose thunder need we fear?

The Constitution of the Confederate States of America, as Jefferson Davis said, differed from that of 1787 only insofar as it was "explanatory of their well known intent," as expounded in the South during the previous thirty years. It was based on the twin foundations of state rights and slavery. Congress was forbidden to grant bounties, pass protective tariffs, or appropriate money for internal improvements. No supreme court was provided and any federal judge could be impeached by the legislature of a state in which his functions were exercised. Congress could pass no law "denying or impairing the right of property in Negro slaves," and in any territory acquired by the Confederacy, or new state admitted to it, "the institution of Negro slavery, as it now exists in the Confederate States, shall be recognized and protected by Congress and by the territorial government." Vice President Stephens declared in a speech of 21 March 1861 on the new government, "Its foundations are laid, its cornerstone rests, upon the great truth that the Negro is not equal to the white man; that slavery . . . is his natural and moral condition." The fragile nature of the one foundation and the rottenness of the other doomed the Southern experiment to defeat. No federal government based on state rights could wage war efficiently; and the slavery underpinning lost the Confederacy all chance of winning a foreign ally.

It is true that many Southerners disliked slavery and believed it to be wrong; but they had to go along with their neighbors or fight them. And nobody who has read the letters, state papers, newspapers, and other surviving literature of the generation before 1861 can honestly deny that the one main, fundamental reason for secession of the original states which formed the Southern Confederacy was to protect, expand, and perpetuate the slavery of the Negro race. In the official declarations by the seceding conventions in states which formed the Confederacy, there is no mention of any grievance unconnected with slavery. The tariff figured prominently as a cause in Confederate propaganda abroad, to win support in England and France; but most of the Southern congressmen, including the entire South Carolina delegation, voted for the tariff of 1857, which the Confederate congress re-enacted.

After the war began, the higher motive of winning independence prevailed over the lower one of protecting slavery, and the white men who fought so gallantly for the Confederacy regarded their cause, as many a monument to the Confederate dead declares, as just and even holy.

3. The Contest for the Border States

When the Confederate States of America were organized, on 8 February 1861, the Democratic administration at Washington had almost a month more of life. President Buchanan possessed the same power that Jackson had asserted to enforce federal law, and General Winfield Scott begged him to exert it; but the seventy-year-old President, timid by nature and fearful of offending Virginia, prayed and twittered and did nothing. We shall be the more tolerant of him when we find his successor doing nothing for six weeks.

In the meantime, two sincere attempts were made to compromise. The essence of one, called after its principal proponent the Crittenden compromise, was, by constitutional amendment, to declare slavery inviolate except by state law, to compensate owners for fugitive slaves not recovered, and extend to the Pacific the old Missouri Compromise 36° 30′ line between free and slave territories. Lincoln, when President-elect, promised to support the first two if Southern senators would issue an appeal against secession, which they refused to do; but on slavery extension he held "firm, as with a chain of steel." These measures were discussed in Congress, mostly in committee, for two months.

A second, eleventh-hour attempt to compromise was made by the Peace Convention of 133 delegates appointed by the legislatures of 21 states, which met in Washington for two weeks in February 1861. It had been initiated by the Virginia legislature in the hope of producing a set of constitutional amendments that would attract the seceding states back and satisfy the border slave states to stay in. Ex-President Tyler presided, and many distinguished men such as David Dudley Field of New York, James B. Clay of Kentucky, and Salmon P. Chase of Ohio took part. This convention adopted, and submitted to Congress, seven constitutional amendments similar to Senator Crittenden's, which were passed by narrow majorities. The most important was a "never-never" constitutional amendment on slavery, to the effect that Congress never by law, and the country never by further amendment, would presume to interfere with slavery in any state. That was passed by the House of Representatives on 27 February by a two-to-one majority, submitted to the states, and promptly ratified by Ohio. But this armor-plated assurance failed to budge the determination of the Confederate States to be independent, or to satisfy all the border slave states.

These were not the only evidences of the Republican and Northern desire to compromise. A Boston petition for the passage of the Crittenden compromise, with 22,313 signatures, was rolled into Congress on 12 February, and an equally imposing one followed from New York. Charles Francis Adams was working in Congress for the admission of New Mexico as a slave state if the people of that territory so chose. Wisconsin and other Northern states repealed their personal liberty laws favoring fugitive slaves. In Boston a well-dressed mob broke up an attempt to hold a memorial meeting in honor of John Brown, and howled Emerson down when he tried to speak. Nothing worked. The mind of the lower South was made up; the purple dream had now come too near reality to be abandoned. But the mind of Virginia was not yet made up.

On 4 March 1861, when Abraham Lincoln was inaugurated President of the United States, Washington nervously expected trouble. It was rumored that secessionists from Virginia or "plug-uglies" from Baltimore would raid the capital and prevent the inauguration. General Scott took every possible precaution, but the soldiers at his disposal were too few even to color the black-coated somberness of the crowd. The inaugural procession, as it moved up Pennsylvania Avenue under the harsh glare of a March sun, while a blustery wind blew the dust roof-high, might have been a funeral procession. The Capitol, with its uncompleted dome supporting an unkempt fringe of derricks, suggested a Piranesi engraving of Roman ruins. President Buchanan, urbane and white-haired, and old, bowed Chief Justice Taney, seemed symbols of a departed golden age of the Republic. President Lincoln, uncouth and ill at ease, inspired little confidence until his high-pitched, determined voice was heard delivering the solemn phrases of the inaugural address.

After a brief review of the constitutional issues involved in secession, Lincoln renewed the pledge of his party to respect slavery in the states, and to enforce any fugitive slave law that had proper safeguards for the colored people of the free states. But he made it perfectly clear that he was not going to acquiesce in secession.

I hold that, in contemplation of the universal law and of the Constitution, the Union of these States is perpetual. . . . No state, upon its own mere motion, can lawfully get out of the Union. . . . I shall take care, as the Constitution itself expressly enjoins upon me, that the laws of the Union be faithfully executed in all the States. . . . The power confided to me will be used to hold, occupy, and possess the property and places belonging to the government, and to collect the duties and imposts. . . .
In your hands, my dissatisfied fellow-countrymen, and not in mine, is the momentous issue of civil war. The government will not assail you. You can have no conflict without yourselves being the aggressors. You have no oath registered in heaven to destroy the government, while I shall have the most solemn one to "preserve, protect, and defend" it.

By this time, all forts and navy yards in the seceded states, except Fort Pickens at Pensacola and Fort Sumter at Charleston, had been seized by the Confederates. From the Southern point of view, jurisdiction over such places passed with secession to the states; their retention by the federal government was illegal. A few days after Lincoln's inauguration, Confederate commissioners came to Washington to treat for their surrender. Although Seward refused to receive the gentlemen, he assured them indirectly that no supplies or provisions would be sent to the forts without due notice, and led them to expect a speedy evacuation. Fumbling and bumbling on both sides in this unprecedented situation was natural. Secretary Welles on 28 March ordered U.S.S. *Powhatan*, just returned from sea, to be decommissioned, and her crew discharged from the navy! Four days later the President ordered her to be recommissioned as flagship of a relief expedition to the forts.

Lincoln had reached the conviction that to yield Forts Sumter and Pickens would bring no "wayward sisters" back, and that even though Virginia would probably secede the moment he struck a blow for the Union, strike he must. Against the advice of General Scott and of five out of seven members of the cabinet, he ordered a relief expedition to be prepared for Fort Sumter. Attempting to play fair with the Confederacy, he had a telegraphic warning sent to Montgomery that an attempt would be made "to supply Fort Sumter with provisions only."

The Confederate congress on 15 February had resolved "that immediate steps should be taken to obtain possession of Forts Sumter and Pickens, either by negotiation or force, as early as practicable." President Davis, having to do something, sent a group of staff officers to demand the surrender of Fort Sumter. Major Anderson, commander of the garrison, had no desire for the sort of fame that would come from starting a civil war. But, as no word got through to him of the relief expedition, he offered to surrender in two days' time, when his food supply would be exhausted. The Confederate staff officers refused to allow this slight delay, and on their own responsibility gave orders to the shore batteries that commanded the fort, to open fire. For, as one of them admitted in later life, they feared that Davis and Lincoln would shake hands and the chance of war would slip away forever.

On 12 April 1861, at 4:30 a.m., the first gun of the Civil War was fired against Fort Sumter. The relief expedition shortly appeared but was unable to get within range. All day Sumter replied to a concentric fire from four or five Confederate forts and batteries, while the beauty and fashion of Charleston flocked to the waterfront as to a gala. Next day, his ammunition exhausted, Major Anderson accepted terms of surrender and the garrison marched out with drums beating and colors flying.

Lincoln's patience during the first six weeks of his term was now rewarded. The rebels had fired on the flag; that was enough to arouse "a whirlwind of patriotism," as Emerson described it, in the Northern states. "Now we have a country again," he wrote. "Sometimes gunpowder smells good."

For a brief — too brief — time, until they realized what sacrifice a civil war would require, almost everyone in the North backed the President, and had only one word for the act of firing on the flag — treason.

Events now moved as swift as the telegraph. On 15 April Lincoln issued a call for 75,000 volunteers to put down combinations "too powerful to be suppressed by the ordinary course of judicial proceedings," and "to cause the laws to be duly executed." On the 17th the Virginia convention passed an ordinance of secession. On the same day Jefferson Davis invited ships in Southern ports to take out letters of marque and reprisal to prey on American commerce. Two days later Lincoln declared the ports of all seceded states under blockade. On the 20th, Virginia militia captured the important United States navy yard at Norfolk, which the navy department had neglected to reinforce for fear of offending that state.

Virginia alone of the Confederate states left the Union after due deliberation. In the state convention which met at Richmond on 13 February 1861 more than half the 158 delegates were sober and conservative men who had voted for Bell and Everett, and only about thirty were secessionists at the beginning; these decided to wait and see what Lincoln would do. But the

President's call for volunteers — "coercion of a state" — fired latent localism in most of the Unionists' hearts. An ordinance of secession then passed by a vote of 88 to 53; and without waiting for popular ratification, Virginia organized for war and (25 April) joined the Confederacy. There then took place a secession from the seceders; the western delegates, long discontented with a state government that undertaxed slaveholders and denied them free public education, organized their trans-Appalachian region as a loyal Virginia, and in 1863 that part of the Old Dominion was admitted to the Union as the State of West Virginia.

The attitude of Maryland was crucial, for control of her by secessionists would have isolated Washington. The first Northern troops on their way to the capital were mobbed as they passed through Baltimore (19 April); and Lincoln wisely permitted the rest to be marched around the city until he could spare enough soldiers to occupy it and enforce martial law. The Maryland legislature protested against "coercion" of the Southern Confederacy but refused to summon a state convention. The government of Kentucky, where opinion was evenly divided, refused to obey the call for volunteers and endeavored in vain to remain neutral, but by the end of the year threw in its lot with the Union. Missouri was practically under a dual regime throughout the war; Delaware's loyalty never wavered. In California there was a fierce struggle between Southern sympathizers and Unionists, which the latter won; but California was too remote to give the Union cause other than pecuniary aid, in which she was generous. Most of the five civilized tribes of the Indian Territory, many of them slaveholders, cast their lot with the South.

Undoubtedly the principle of state sovereignty strongly affected the attitude of Virginia, and of three more states (Arkansas, North Carolina, Tennessee) which elected to follow her out of the Union. If the states were sovereign, and the federal government a mere loose compact terminable at will by any member, a state had the right to secede; and any attempt to restore the Union by force was unjust and unconstitutional. This doctrine had been consistently drummed into the electorate for thirty years. Southerners, it is true, had been inconsistent in raising the nationalist banner to cover anything that their section wanted, such as the acquisition of new territory and the return of fugitive slaves. But the steady obligato had been the Virginia and Kentucky resolutions of 1798, state sovereignty, and the writings of Calhoun. The bright flame of devotion to the Union, kindled in the North by the words and acts of men like Webster, Jackson, and Clay, had so little penetrated the South that hardly anyone there expected the North to fight for the Union, and everyone felt cheated when it did. The Northern states, too, had been inconsistent; they had tried by state action to defeat the annexation of Texas and the fugitive slave law; but in the North state rights were mere sticks in the woodpile to pull out occasionally and flourish, not a settled backlog of doctrine; and none had threatened secession since 1814.

The Union of twenty-three states and the Confederacy of eleven were now arrayed against each other. But the lines were not strictly drawn between the people of states that seceded and of those that did not. The majority went with their neighborhood leaders, as majorities usually do. But there were thousands who made their decision from high motives of sentiment and ideology. One might express the problem of "Which side shall I take?" in a pair of medieval dichotomies:

> The Union must be preserved.
> The Confederacy has a perfect right to Independence.

> Democracy cannot survive the breakup of the Union.
> Democracy is played out; the Southern social system is superior.

Thus, the Confederate army contained men from every Northern state who preferred the Southern type of civilization to their own; and the United States army and navy included men from every seceded state who felt that the breakup of the Union would be a fatal blow to self-government, republicanism, and democracy. Admiral Farragut was from Alabama; Caleb Huse, the most efficient Confederate agent in Europe, was from Massachusetts; Samuel P. Lee commanded the Union naval forces in the James river while his cousin Robert E. Lee was resisting Grant in the Wilderness; two sons of Commodore Porter USN fought under Stonewall Jackson; Major General T. L. Crittenden USA was brother to Major General G. B. Crittenden CSA. Three grandsons of Henry Clay fought for the Union, and four for the Confederacy. Three brothers of Mrs. Lincoln died for the South; several kinsmen of Mrs. Davis were in the Union army. In a house in West 20th Street, New York, a little boy named Theodore Roosevelt prayed for the Union armies at the knee of his Georgian mother whose brothers were in the Confederate navy. At the same moment, in the Presbyterian parsonage of Augusta, Georgia, another little boy named Thomas Woodrow Wilson knelt in the family circle while his Ohio-born father invoked the God of Battles for the Southern cause.

Colonel Robert E. Lee USA was stationed at a frontier post near San Antonio in January 1861. To one of his sons he wrote that he could anticipate no greater calamity than a dissolution of the Union.

Secession [he wrote,] is nothing but revolution. The framers of our Constitution never exhausted so much labour, wisdom and forbearance in its formation, and surrounded it with so many guards and securities, if it was intended to be broken by any member of the Confederacy at will. . . . In 1808, when the New England States resisted Mr. Jefferson's Embargo law, and [when] the Hartford Convention assembled, secession was termed treason by Virginian statesmen; what can it be now? Still, a Union that can only be maintained by swords and bayonets, and in which strife and civil war are to take the place of brotherly love and kindness, has no charm for me. If the Union is dissolved, the government disrupted, I shall return to my native state and share the miseries of my people. Save in her defense, I will draw my sword no more.

Herein we see the distress of a noble mind. For such as he, and for thousands of others in Virginia, North Carolina, Kentucky, and Tennessee, making a decision was agonizing, as it had been for their grandfathers in 1775–76 to choose between king and congress, or for their remote ancestors in 1641 to choose between king and parliament. Two great Virginians in the United States Army, Generals Winfield Scott and George H. Thomas, remained loyal to the United States. For Thomas, "Whichever way he turned the matter over in his mind, his oath of allegiance always came uppermost." And to still another Virginian, Senator James M. Mason, we are indebted for the most accurate definition of the great struggle that was about to begin. "I look upon it then, Sir, as a war of sentiment and opinion by one form of society against another form of society."

Thus it was a true civil war,[1] as much ideological as sectional. By May 1861 everyone had taken his stand. Once having done so, everyone was steadfast in his loyalty; there was no switching sides in mid-war as had taken place in the American Revolution; no defection; but plenty of desertion by soldiers of both sides.

1. The earlier official title, War of the Rebellion, has been dropped, out of deference to Southern wishes; and the cumbrous title "The War Between the States" is grossly inaccurate. "The War for Southern Independence" suggested by the historian Channing is well enough; but why change "The American Civil War," which it was? During the war it was generally called "The Second American Revolution" or "The War for Separation" in the South.

DIXIE'S LAND

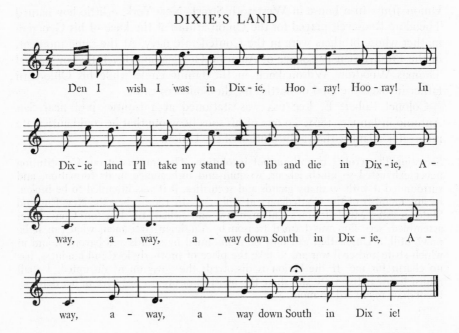

Den I wish I was in Dix-ie, Hoo-ray! Hoo-ray! In Dix-ie land I'll take my stand to lib and die in Dix-ie, A-way, a-way, a-way down South in Dix-ie, A-way, a-way, a-way down South in Dix-ie!

The War in 1861

1. A Brothers' War

So, THERE IT WAS. The "great tragic volume," of which John Quincy Adams had glimpsed the title page in 1820, now opened. As the philosopher William James put it, "What law and reason were unable to accomplish, had now to be done by that uncertain and dreadful dispenser of God's judgments, war. War, with its abominably casual, inaccurate methods of destroying good and bad together, but at last unquestionably able to hew a way out of intolerable situations, when through man's delusion or perversity every better way is blocked."

As always, one could have kept the peace, had one been willing to pay the price, which in this case would have been a permanent division of the Union and the prospect of an interminable series of internecine wars. Suppose Lincoln, on his accession, had recognized the Confederacy as of March 1861. The pulling and hauling of Virginia and the Border states would have gone on, the Confederacy would have insisted on a share of the territories and southern California, and dissension would have sprung up over fugitive slaves, reopening the African slave trade, the transit trade of the Mississippi, and aggression at the expense of Spain or Mexico. This war to preserve the Union, long and bloody though it was, prevented many more wars, and a probable fracturing of the United States into several confederacies, reducing North America to something approaching the present status of Central America.

The white South almost unanimously, a strong minority in the Northern states, and almost every thinking European, expected the Confederacy to achieve independence. Numbers and wealth, to be sure, were against the South; comparison of her white population of 5.5 million with that of the nineteen free states, 18.9 million, is not entirely fair, since, with Negroes to cultivate the soil, more white men could be spared to fight. The four non-seceding slave states (Delaware, Maryland, Kentucky, Missouri), with 2.6 million people, contributed about the same number of soldiers to each side. But determined secessions had generally been successful against even greater odds: the United Netherlands against Spain, the Thirteen Colonies against Britain, Latin America against Spain, the Italian states against Austria, Greece against Turkey. In the realm of high strategy, the Southern Confederacy, to win, needed only to defend her own territory long enough to weary the Northerners; but the United States, to win, had to conquer an empire and crush a people. Any less emphatic result than unconditional surrender of the Confederate armies and collapse of the government, would have been a Southern victory. Nor were material advantages all in favor of the Union. To offset Northern superiority in numbers, wealth, industry, and sea power, the Confederacy had the advantage of interior lines, and a social organization better fitted for creating an efficient fighting force. On the emotional scale, the Confederacy had a definite advantage, since the white Southerners, from their point of view, were fighting for everything that men hold most dear: liberty and self-government, hearth and home, racial superiority. But the Northern people could have stopped the war at any moment, at the mere cost of recognizing what to many seemed an accomplished fact, and without any sacrifice of the social and material factors that closely touch the life of the individual.

Every European military expert thought that Lincoln had taken on an impossible task to "conquer" the South, and two leading English military writers of the last generation, Fuller and Henderson, never seemed to understand how he did. But they ignored three vital factors: — sea power, Union sentiment, and the Emancipation Proclamation. Yet, in the first years of trial, the prospect of freeing slaves sent no blood leaping through Northern veins. It was the simple sentiment of "The Union forever!" Lincoln made this crystal clear in his famous Letter to Horace Greeley of 22 August 1862: "My paramount object in this struggle is to save the Union, and is not either to save or to destroy slavery."

Union sentiment alone made it possible for the superior strength of the North to prevail. Even today one feels that there was something miraculous in the extent to which the common people came to share the vision of Abraham Lincoln, that the whole future of their country and of democracy everywhere was bound up with the Union of the States. Robert Frost has brought this out in his poem about the widow of one and the mother of two Union soldiers killed in this war: [1]

> One wan't long in learning that she thought
> Whatever else the Civil War was for,
> It wasn't just to keep the States together,
> Nor just to free the slaves, though it did both.
> She wouldn't have believed those ends enough
> To have given outright for them all she gave.
> Her giving somehow touched the principle
> That all men are created free and equal.
>
> *   *   *
>
> White was the only race she ever knew,
> Black she had scarcely seen, and yellow never.
> But how could they be made so very unlike
> By the same hand working in the same stuff?
> She had supposed the war decided that.

1. "The Black Cottage," *Complete Poems of Robert Frost*, Copyright 1930, 1939 by Holt, Rinehart and Winston, Inc. Reprinted by permission of the publishers.

But it did not; and, as I write, white men in the states where the Confederacy was proclaimed, and in South Africa too, are desperately striving to hold back a rising tide of the race to which they so long have denied equality. Nevertheless, may not the future regard this American Civil War as a war of emancipation which brought a little nearer the realization of Jefferson's dream?

2. The Presidents and Their Cabinets

During the war both Davis and Lincoln were regarded by their enemies as fiends incarnate, and by many of their own people were accused of everything from incompetence to tyranny. In 1861 few on either side doubted that the Southerner was the abler, as he appeared more dignified. Successively lieutenant of dragoons, colonel of volunteers, congressman, senator, and secretary of war, Davis brought experience such as Lincoln had never had, and talents that he never claimed, to the Confederate presidency. Courage, sincerity, patience, and integrity were his; only tact, perception, and inner harmony were wanting to make him a great man. He moved (said his wife) in an atmosphere of high thought and settled conviction, and "could not understand any other man coming to a different conclusion after his premises were stated." Isolated from the Southern democracy out of which he had sprung, Davis moved as to the manner born among the whispering aristocracy of Richmond; yet he had a perverse knack of infuriating the gentlemen who tried to work with him. In four years he had five secretaries of war, and he worked less in harmony with the Confederate congress than had any President of the United States with the federal Congress. Davis vetoed no fewer than 38 bills, all but one of which were passed over his veto; Lincoln exercised the veto power only thrice. Davis's military experience led to his cardinal error of attempting to direct military operations. His health and nerves gave way under self-assumed responsibilities, and his state papers show increasing querulousness and bitterness, in contrast to the sustained dignity and magnanimity of everything that Lincoln wrote.

Davis selected his cabinet for work, not for politics. It contained only two members of the governing class, Robert Toombs and Pope Walker, and they soon quarreled with him and resigned. The others exerted little political influence and inspired slight public confidence. Secretary Memminger of the treasury was a Charleston lawyer who knew nothing of public finance, and learned less. Judah P. Benjamin (successively war and state), of whom it has been said that no one served the Confederacy with better brain and less heart, was a British subject by birth and a Jew. Secretary Mallory of the navy, a West Indian, proved to be the ablest of the group, creating a navy from almost nothing. John H. Regan, the Texan postmaster general, was so devoted to Davis as to put his face on Confederate postage stamps, which has never been done before or since for a living American.

Lincoln's cabinet carried more weight than that of Davis, but had even less cohesion. Not one member was a personal friend or follower of the President. William H. Seward as secretary of state brought the administration confidence, and eventually strength, but not until he had almost wrecked it by an overaggressive foreign policy. Simon Cameron, secretary of war, a Pennsylvania manufacturer who proved to be criminally careless in the management of his department, had to resign under a cloud. Salmon P. Chase, an imposing college graduate, Cincinnati lawyer, antislavery leader, and governor of Ohio, received the treasury, for which he had no preparation; but the business men from whom the government had to borrow money trusted Chase, and he initiated the national banking system which lasted until 1917. Chase's aspirations were whetted by office, and he never really appreciated Lincoln, especially his sense of humor; once saying to a friend, "I can't treat this war as a joke." Gideon Welles, secretary of the navy, formerly a bureau chief in the navy department, latterly a small-town newspaper editor, was a recent convert from the Democratic party; he proved to be an excellent navy secretary. Edward Bates and Montgomery Blair, attorney general and postmaster general, were good sound men who represented the loyal states.

At the beginning of Lincoln's administration the cabinet members distrusted one another, Blair alone had much respect for the President, and several months elapsed before Lincoln was really master in his own house. The change of scene, the hurly-burly of war preparations, the pressure of patronage, seemed for a time to cut his contact with that unseen force which lifted him from the common herd. Yet his feeling for the democratic medium in which he had to work, for its possibilities, limitations, and imperfections, was akin to that of a great artist for the medium of sculpture or painting. He could capture the imagination of the common soldier and citizen, and at the same time make the outstanding quality of an ill-balanced character such as McClellan or Stanton the instrument of a great purpose. This railsplitter, this prairie lawyer with his droll stories and his few, crude social devices, had an innate tact and delicacy that carried conviction of his moral and intellectual greatness to all but the most obtuse, and a humanity that has opened the hearts of all men to him in the end.

If Lincoln was slow to direct the conduct of the war, he never faltered in his conception of the purpose of the war. From Sumter to Appomattox, it was for him a war to preserve the Union. The power that lay in that word came less from an instinct of nationality than from the passionate desire of a youthful people to prove its worth by the only test that the world accepted. The Union, which for Washington was a justification for the American Revolution, and for Hamilton a panoply of social order, had become, in the hands of Jackson, Clay, and Webster, a symbol of popular government. Lincoln drove home this conception in his every utterance, and gave it classical expression in the Gettysburg address. He made the average American feel that his dignity as citizen of the republic was bound up with the fate of the Union, whose destruction would be a victory for the enemies of freedom everywhere.

Lincoln could not bring everyone to this conception. Many leaders of the Democratic party still looked upon the states as the guardians of democracy. The abolitionists would support the Union only on the condition of its serving their immediate purpose. Nor did Lincoln completely dominate his own group. Many Republicans regarded the war as a mere assertion of Northern superiority, for their party in 1861 was essentially a Northern party. Because Lincoln, ignoring every appeal to hatred, sectionalism, and humanitarianism, raised the standard of Union at the beginning and kept it paramount, the Union was preserved. Prominent Democrats such as Stephen Douglas rallied the best elements of their party to the colors; and in a few months the entire Ohio valley, half slaveholding in fact and largely proslavery in sentiment, was secure. His enemies sneered, "Lincoln would like to have God on his side, but he must have Kentucky." His friends doubted whether even God could preserve the Union without Kentucky. Nor did he ever forget that those whom he liked to call "our late friends, now adversaries" must, if his object were attained, become fellow citizens once more. The frantic appeals of Davis to class and sectional hatred found no answering echo in the words of Lincoln, who could never bring himself to contemplate the South with feeling other than regret for her rebellion and compassion for her plight.

3. The Two Armies

In military preparation the Confederacy had a start of several months over the United States. As early as 6 March 1861 President Davis called for and quickly obtained 100,000 volunteers for a year. Virginia's secession on 17 April gave the Confederacy many of the ablest officers of the United States Army; no new nation has ever had commanders of the caliber of Lee, both Johnstons, both Hills, Beauregard, and Jackson at its birth. The Union, on the contrary, found her proper military leaders only through the costly method of trial and error. McClellan, Grant, Sherman, indeed most of the West Pointers who rose to prominence in the Union army, were in civil life when war began. The regular army of the United States — 16,257 officers and men — was kept intact instead of being broken up to leaven the volunteers; thus brilliant junior officers like Philip Sheridan were confined to small regular units until late in the war.

The forty United States naval vessels in commission were scattered over the seven seas. Until mid-April no attempt was made to enlarge or even to concentrate these slender forces, for fear of offending Virginia. In the meantime the Confederate States had seized upon the United States arsenals and navy yards within their limits and obtained munitions from the North and from Europe.

Winfield Scott, General in Chief of the United States Army, infirm in body but robust in mind, advised the President that at least 300,000 men, a first-rate general, and two or three years' time would be required to conquer even the lower South. No one else dared place the estimate so high; and

Seward believed with the man in the street that one vigorous thrust would overthrow the Confederacy within 90 days. The President, in his proclamation of 15 April 1861, called for 75,000 volunteers, for three months. The response was heartening. Within two weeks 35,000 troops were in Washington or on their way thither, and 20,000 were waiting for transportation. The government should have taken advantage of this patriotic outburst to create a national army for the duration of the war. Instead, Lincoln on 3 May called for forty more volunteer regiments of an average of 1050 officers and men each, and 40,000 three-year enlistments in the regular army and navy, leaving the recruiting, organization and equipment of volunteer regiments to the states. Overzealous states were coldly admonished, "It is important to reduce rather than enlarge this number."

As a basis for the new army, every Northern state had a volunteer militia force, neither well officered nor properly drilled. Company officers were elected by the men, regimental and general officers were appointed by the state governor. There were also many semi-social, semi-military companies such as the Fire Zouaves,[1] the Garibaldi Guards with red shirts and *Bersaglieri* plumes, the New York Highlanders in kilt and sporran, and the Irish Sarsfield Guards. Many of these volunteered en masse and marched to glory without delay or change of uniform. But for the most part, the volunteer regiments that made up the bulk of the United States Army during the war, were regiments *ad hoc*. A patriotic citizen would receive a colonel's commission from his governor, then raise a regiment by his own efforts and those of men who expected majorities under him. Units of 50 to 100, recruited by some youth of local popularity whom they would elect lieutenant or captain, were incorporated as companies. When the regiment was reasonably complete and at least partially equipped, it was forwarded to a training camp and placed under federal control. Examining boards were appointed to remove incompetent officers, but in practice the federal government had to respect state appointments until they were found wanting in action. And its own were scarcely better. Prominent politicians such as Frémont, Banks, and Butler received major generals' commissions from the President, outranking seasoned officers of the regular army. For giving the whole country a stake in the war, for using community pride and attracting to the colors the greatest number of men in the shortest possible time, no better method could then have been devised; but it was continued too long.

By much the same system was the first Southern army raised, but with less

1. Zouaves were originally Moslem auxiliaries to the French army in Algeria. Their precise close-order drill, quick-step (preserved by the French *chasseurs alpins*), and showy uniforms, with baggy red breeches, red tasseled fez, and blue tunic, appealed to the urge for a little more color in life, North and South. The Louisiana "Tigers" and "Pelicans" were Zouave outfits. An entire regiment of New York Zouaves, red pants and all, was captured by Dick Taylor's Texans in the Battle of Pleasant Hill, April 1864. The Texans were disgusted — swore they hadn't enlisted to fight women!

baneful results, and the Confederacy adopted conscription a year earlier than the Union did. Southern respect for rank and family meant prompt recognition of natural leaders. General Joseph E. Johnston CSA observed that familiarity with firearms, and zeal, gave the Confederates superiority in 1861, but that "the thorough system of instruction introduced into the United States army gradually established equality in the use of firearms; and our greater zeal finally encountered better discipline." Straggling and desertion impaired the strength of both armies, particularly the Confederate. "Stragglers cover the country, and Richmond is no doubt filled with the absent without leave," wrote General Johnston in the midst of the peninsular campaign. "The men are full of spirit when near the enemy, but at other times to avoid restraint leave their regiments in crowds."

If the Confederates won more battles, it was owing to better leadership, which gave them tactical superiority on the field of battle, against the superiority of their enemies on the field of operations. Frequently we shall find a numerically inferior Confederate force defeating its enemy in detail; or a Union commander failing to deploy superior forces to influence an action. Since the North had the greater immigrant population, it had a larger proportion of foreign-born soldiers; but the average Union soldier was a farmer's son. And there were considerable numbers of Irish, Germans, and foreign soldiers of fortune in the Confederate army.

Mostly boys fought this war. No age statistics are available, but it is certain that the majority on both sides were under twenty-one. Walt Whitman, who visited thousands of the wounded in hospitals and heard their stories, found many as young as fifteen. It was so, too, with the officers. Major General S. D. Ramseur CSA, just out of West Point, won his first star at the age of twenty-five, and his second at twenty-seven. Francis Channing Barlow, who entered the war as a private, fought as a major general at Gettysburg, when he had just turned twenty-eight. His division was one of those driven from the knoll on the first day, and he fell, pierced by a minié bullet. General John B. Gordon CSA, seeing this youthful officer lying among the Union dead, dismounted, gave him water from his canteen and received a message to his wife, that his deepest regret was to be about to die without looking on her face again. But die he did not; carried to the Confederate rear, unconscious Barlow was viewed by General Early, who remarked that obviously nothing could be done to save his life. At which Barlow came to and responded, "General Early, I will live to whip you yet!" In a letter to his mother a week later, Barlow says, "Several Confederate officers were very kind and attentive." Abandoned when the Confederates retreated, Barlow fully recovered and distinguished himself in several later actions.

This is but one of many instances of humanity on both sides, which support the dictum of one who survived over half a century, Major Randolph Barton CSA: "This was the last gentlemen's war."

Throughout the war the "Federals," as the more polite Southerners called the Union army, were better equipped in shoes and clothing, and more abundantly supplied with rations and munitions. War department red tape, and the prejudice of elderly officers, prevented the adoption of the breech-loading rifle. Both in artillery and small arms it was largely a war of the muzzle-loader, and to a great extent, of the smooth-bore. Although the blockade stopped big shipments from Europe in 1862, the Confederate ordnance service, under a resourceful Pennsylvanian named Josiah Gorgas, was able to keep the army so well supplied that the South never lost a battle for want of ammunition. Richmond was one of the principal coal- and iron-producing centers in the United States, and her Tredegar Iron Works were well equipped for the manufacture of heavy castings and ordnance. It was there that the armor of C.S.S. *Virginia* (ex-*Merrimack*) was rolled and her rifled guns cast. These were the only works in the Confederacy so equipped until 1863, when a newly established plant at Selma, Alabama, began to turn out cannon. Great enterprise was also shown by the Confederate government in organizing woolen mills to weave cloth for uniforms, and the Confederate bluish-gray was less conspicuous than the Union dark blue. Southern regiments from frontier districts preferred homespun jackets and trousers dyed brown with the butternut or white walnut, and officers indulged them in that preference. The Confederate army was never properly supplied with shoes; many of those it did obtain came from Lynn, Massachusetts, via Bermuda and the blockade runners, or off Federal dead and wounded. And Confederate wants were often relieved by supplies abandoned by Union armies in their frequent retreats, or captured from wagon trains by cavalry raids.

Many of the general and flag officers of this war were "characters" who blazoned their individualities in diverse ways, especially tonsorially. Generals Pickett and Custer allowed their curly hair to grow long, and indulged in other sartorial whimsies suggesting the cavalier. Older officers who had served in the War of 1812, such as Admirals Farragut and Generals Scott and Wool, remained clean-shaven; but beards had returned to fashion during the Crimean War, and our Civil War heroes exhibited a greater luxuriance of whiskerage than any of their profession since Alexander the Great set the fashion of shaving. McClellan, Beauregard, and Joe Johnston, who fancied themselves successors to Napoleon, went in for the mustache and *impérial*, then fashionable in the Tuileries; Hooker, who probably had been told that he resembled Alexander, went clean-shaven; Don Carlos Buell trimmed his hair and beard to resemble portraits of Don Carlos I of Spain; Burnside cultivated a style of whisker extending from ear to ear which was named "burnsides" after him. Most of the others grew beards of varying lengths, but none could match those of John Pope, J. B. Hood, or Fitzhugh Lee, which extended well below the breastbone. Naval officers, not prevented (as their British compeers had been) by royal command from vying with the soldiers, matched the generals in whiskerage. Admiral Dupont, in particular, grew a complete hairy frame for his face, in the style later associated with "Oom Paul" Kruger, the Boer president.

Leonidas Polk, who had left West Point to enter the church and served as bishop of Louisiana for the past twenty years, returned to his namesake's profession as major general CSA, but retained the hairdo of a Victorian bishop until his death in action. He was the most eminent man of God in either army; but there were many others of lesser rank, such as the Rev. Thomas Wentworth Higginson, colonel of the first Negro regiment in the Federal service, and the Rev. William B. Greene, colonel of a coast artillery regiment that defended Washington, who posted a sign outside his headquarters tent, "Dogs and Congressmen Keep Out!"

Hardly less remarkable than the generals' whiskers was their ill health, probably the result of constant exposure, lack of sleep, and bolted meals. George H. Thomas was the only general on either side who attempted to maintain a mess commensurate with his rank; but Thomas, like Jubal A. Early, suffered from arthritis, never mounted a horse without a wrench, and suffered agonies when riding rapidly. General Grant suffered from splitting headaches; D. H. Hill from dyspepsia and a spinal ailment; I. R. Trimble from erysipelas and osteomyelitis. Dick Ewell, described at the age of forty-six as an "old soldier with a bald head, a prominent nose and a haggard, sickly face," had only one leg, suffered from stomach ulcers and malaria, and lived largely on boiled rice and frumenty. A. P. Hill "took sick" on the first day of Gettysburg; Lee became very ill at a most critical time on the North Anna river. Braxton Bragg's chronic dyspepsia, coupled with a mean disposition, made him the most unpopular general in either army. After reading about the aches and pains of the Confederate generals, one feels that very few could have passed the "physical" for their rank in World War II.

Few generals on either side cared for guard mounts, dress parades, or other military pomp and circumstance. And, in contrast to the liberally decorated uniforms in the two world wars, those of the Civil War bore neither medals nor ribbons. Congress authorized the Medal of Honor in 1862, but it was awarded both sparingly and captiously, and the recipients do not appear to have worn it.[1] The Confederacy issued no medals. Judging from their photographs, the generals were averse to being buttoned up, and a wide variety in headgear was permitted. General "Jeb" Stuart, the dashing Confederate cavalryman, wore a plume in his felt hat to suggest that he belonged to the royal house of his name, and his chargers were frequently encumbered by floral decorations from admiring ladies.

Toward the end of the war the Union army, to ease the logistics problem involved in moving herds of live cattle and wagonloads of flour, tried canned

1. After the war, distinguishing badges of the Army of the Cumberland, Army of the Potomac, etc., were informally adopted; these look like medals on the tunics of the officers but were really only badges, like those issued for marksmanhip.

rations on Sherman's army as it advanced into the Carolinas. The soldiers disliked them, and the General referred to the canned goods as "desecrated vegetables" and "consecrated milk."

Each army took an unprecedented amount of punishment; casualties in our Civil War were greater, in proportion to the population, than those even of the British and French in World War I. The official Union casualties were 93,443 killed in action or died of wounds; 210,400 from disease — the latter being broken down into 29,336 from typhoid, 15,570 from other "fevers," 44,558 from dysentery, and 26,468 from pulmonary diseases, mainly tuberculosis. There are no statistics of Confederate losses, and estimates vary widely. Deaths from battle were probably around 80,000 or 90,000. If losses from disease ran proportionately as high as in the Union ranks — and there is no reason to suppose that they were any lower — they must have reached 160,000 to 180,000. We may safely say that at least 540,000 Americans, in a total population of over 31 million (1860), lost their lives in, or as a result of, this war. Yet, so fecund is nature that the population increased over eight million between 1860 and 1870.

The average soldier, whether in blue or in gray, was sick enough twice or thrice a year to be sent to a hospital, which often proved more dangerous than the battlefield. Poor sanitation, infected water, wretched cooking, dirt and sheer carelessness were largely responsible for this sad state of affairs, repeated in every war of the nineteenth century. Medical services were inadequate and inefficient, hospitals often primitive, care for the wounded haphazard and callous. Behind the lines, overworked doctors labored desperately in improvised field hospitals. Antisepsis was unknown, and anesthetics were not always available; abdominal wounds and major amputations meant probable death. Out of a total of 580 amputations in Richmond during two months of 1862, there were 245 deaths; no wonder a Confederate officer wrote that in every regiment, "There were not less than a dozen doctors from whom our men had as much to fear as from their Northern enemies."

It was still thought not quite respectable for women to nurse soldiers at the front, and the armies at first relied on untrained male nurses like Walt Whitman. Dorothea Dix was appointed superintendent of Union nurses at the beginning of the war, and over 3000 women volunteered to work in hospitals. Much of the medical care on both sides was voluntary. The United States Sanitary Commission inspected camps and hospitals and provided nursing and relief both at the front and behind the lines, combining the work which the Red Cross and the United Services Organization carried out in the two world wars. The Young Men's Christian Association did similar work in both North and South, but many of the Confederate sick and wounded were tenderly nursed in nearby homes. Confederate medical skill was no worse than that of the Union; but lack of drugs, anesthetics, and surgical instruments imposed heavy losses.

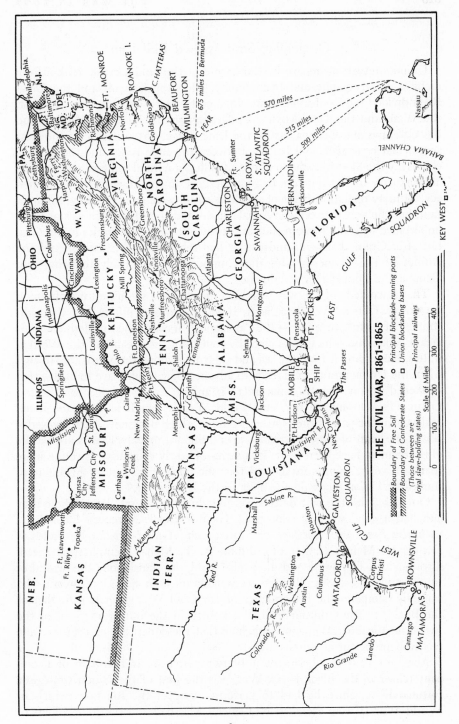

THE CIVIL WAR, 1861-1865

Boundary of Free Soil
Boundary of Confederate States
(Those between are
loyal slave-holding states)

o Principal blockade-running ports
□ Union blockading bases
— Principal railways

Scale of Miles

0   100   200   300   400

NEB.

KANSAS

Ft. Leavenworth
Ft. Riley
Topeka

INDIAN
TERR.

MISSOURI
Kansas City
Jefferson City
St. Louis
Springfield
Carthage
Wilson's Creek

ILLINOIS
Springfield

INDIANA
Indianapolis

OHIO
Columbus
Cincinnati

KENTUCKY
Louisville
Lexington
Mill Spring

Cairo
New Madrid
Ft. Donelson
Ft. Henry
Nashville
Murfreesboro
Knoxville
Chattanooga

TENN.
Shiloh
Corinth
Memphis

MISS.
Jackson

ARKANSAS

LOUISIANA

TEXAS

Marshall
Sabine R.
Washington
Austin
Columbus
Houston
Corpus Christi
MATAGORDA
GALVESTON

Red R.
Arkansas R.
Colorado R.

Rio Grande
Laredo
Camargo
MATAMORAS
BROWNSVILLE

GULF WEST SQUADRON

The Passes
New Orleans
Ft. Hudson
Vicksburg
Mississippi R.
SHIP I.
MOBILE
Selma
Montgomery

ALABAMA

GEORGIA
Atlanta
Savannah

FLORIDA
Jacksonville
FERNANDINA

KEY WEST
EAST GULF SQUADRON

FT. PICKENS
Pensacola

SOUTH CAROLINA
Charleston
Ft. Sumter
PT. ROYAL
S. ATLANTIC SQUADRON

NORTH CAROLINA
Goldsboro
C. FEAR
WILMINGTON
BEAUFORT
C. HATTERAS
ROANOKE I.
FT. MONROE

VIRGINIA
Norfolk
Richmond

W. VA.
Prestonsburg
Harper's Ferry

MD.
DEL.
N.J.
Washington
Baltimore
Philadelphia

PA.
Gettysburg
Pittsburg

Ohio R.
Tennessee R.
Mississippi R.

BAHAMA CHANNEL
Nassau

500 miles
515 miles
570 miles
675 miles to Bermuda

625

4. Geography, Strategy, and Bull Run

Union strategy, aggressive by the nature of the Union cause, took a form dictated by geography and hydrography. The Appalachians and the Great River divided the Confederacy into three parts, nearly equal in area: the East, the West, and the Trans-Mississippi theaters of war. The first, Virginia and the Carolinas and Georgia east of the Blue Ridge, was the scene of the most spectacular campaigns and battles. Between the Blue Ridge and the Appalachians lay the Shenandoah-Cumberland valley, a natural military road leading northeasterly to Washington, or southwesterly to the heart of the Confederacy. Military operations west of the Mississippi were comparatively unimportant, but the area between the Appalachians and the Mississippi was of equal importance with the Eastern theater. Lee might perform miracles in Virginia; but after Grant, Farragut, and Porter had secured the Mississippi, and the Armies of the Tennessee and the Cumberland were ready to swing into Georgia, the Confederacy was doomed.

That it worked out this way was due primarily to a significant use of Union sea power. General Winfield Scott, though aged and infirm, had the right strategy of victory in mind — the "anaconda" it was called in derision. This meant constricting the Confederacy by control of the ocean and the Western waters, blockading it from the sea and splitting it along the Mississippi so that when the Union armies were ready to advance they would have to deal with a weakened enemy. Scott's "anaconda" is an interesting parallel to Winston Churchill's "closing the ring" in World War II, but it required too much patience on the part of the Northern public, which demanded swift, powerful jabs at the heart of the Confederacy to end the war quickly. Events proved the old veteran to have been right. In a series of costly campaigns covering more than two years, the South showed that she could take care of herself until starved by Union blockade and split by the Mississippi.

On both sides the best officers were graduates of West Point, where they had had a good military education. Their textbook *Advanced Guard . . . with the Essential Principles of Strategy and Grand Tactics* by Professor Dennis H. Mahan (father of Admiral A. T. Mahan) emphasized speed, surprise, and firepower; and they also read, in translation, the works of Jomini and Clausewitz. Blunders were made on both sides; but anyone who candidly compares the performance of our Civil War generals with that of the British in the Crimean War, the French in the war of 1870–71, or the British in the Boer War must conclude that the Americans of 1861–65 were relatively proficient in military art.

Abraham Lincoln, whose only military experience had been that of a company officer in the Black Hawk War, was the best of the Union strategists; fortunately so, since he had to perform many of the functions which in World War II were exercised by General Marshall and the Joint Chiefs of

Staff. He, too, "boned up" on Jomini. Lincoln saw the whole strategic picture from the start, made very few mistakes, grasped immediately the advantages of superior numbers and sea power, and urged the generals to keep tightening the squeeze on the Confederacy until time and circumstance invited a break-through. And he saw that the main objective should be the surrender of the Confederate armies, rather than the occupation of territory. Clausewitz was right when he wrote that the best qualifications for a commander in chief, whether king, emperor, or president, were not military knowledge but "a remarkable, superior mind and strength of character." Lincoln had both. But Jefferson Davis, from supposedly expert knowledge, frequently overrode generals like Joseph Johnston and Lee, who were better strategists than he, and relied heavily on incompetents like Braxton Bragg, or blowhards like Beauregard.

Lincoln and Scott's plan of campaign for 1861 was to blockade the Southern coast and occupy strategic points both there and on Western rivers, while the big volunteer army was being trained. Since Kentucky had to be nursed out of neutrality, and Confederate sympathizers in Missouri threatened the Union right flank, and western Virginia was at stake, the first forward movements were diverted into those border states. George B. McClellan, commanding volunteers raised in Ohio, beat a small Confederate force, saving West Virginia for the Union and making himself the man of the hour. In Missouri, Nathaniel Lyon fought a skillful campaign against local Confederates, prevented the fall of Missouri into enemy control, and lost his life in action (10 August).[1] Kentucky was saved for the Union, largely through the energy of Ulysses S. Grant. The "sacred soil of Virginia" was first "polluted" by the "abolition hosts" of a "reckless and unprincipled tyrant" (so General Beauregard declared) on 24 May 1861, when Union troops occupied the Lee mansion at Arlington Heights.

By July 1861 the Confederacy had almost 60,000 men under arms in Virginia, and 22,000 of them, commanded by General Beauregard, hero of the bloodless battle of Fort Sumter, concentrated near Centerville. There was another strong force at Harper's Ferry under General Joseph Johnston; and under him in the chain of command was Brigadier General Thomas J. Jackson, one of the most extraordinary characters of this or any other war. A thirty-seven-year-old West Pointer and Mexican War veteran, Jackson for the past nine years had been professor of mathematics and science at the Virginia Military Institute, which has educated more great soldiers than any other independent college. At "V.M.I.," recorded one of his pupils, "He was simply a silent, unobtrusive man, doing his duty, regarded as a quiet, harmless eccentric." Unknown to the boys, he was earnestly studying the art of war, and by

1. In southern and western Missouri there was partisan warfare of the bitterest kind during almost the entire war. I once asked President Truman, whose forebears were on the Confederate side, to recommend an accurate and impartial history of the Civil War in Missouri. "There's no such thing;" he replied, "they're all liars!"

1861 probably knew more of strategy and tactics than any general on either side. In appearance he was unprepossessing. Colonel Dick Taylor, bringing up Louisiana troops to join Jackson's brigade in the Shenandoah valley, found the general seated on a rail fence sucking a lemon — his method of keeping healthy — and noted his "mangy cap with visor drawn low, a heavy, dark beard and weary eyes," and enormous hands and feet. Mounted, Jackson would usually be set on Little Sorrel, a short, thick-set, barrel-chested gelding of unknown ancestry, chosen from a load of captured Union army remounts. Little Sorrel had marvelous endurance, subsisted on corncobs if necessary, and could go without water like a camel.

The Confederate army was the most pious army since Cromwell's New Model, and Jackson's brigade was the "prayin'est" in the Confederacy. If possible, no day passed without divine service, and officers who visited Jackson's tent were apt to find the general on his knees "wrestling with the Lord." He wrestled to very good purpose on 20 July 1861.

The United States Congress, convened in special session on 4 July, authorized the President to recruit half a million men for the duration of the war. Already there were some 25,000 three-months volunteers in Washington, spoiling for a fight. The Northern press and people were vociferous for action. Against General Scott's advice, Lincoln yielded to the cry, "On to Richmond!" So General McDowell crossed the Potomac to seek out Beauregard's army near Manassas Junction, Virginia. A throng of newspaper correspondents, sightseers on horse and foot, and congressmen in carriages with ladies and picnic hampers, came out to see the sport.

This was on 20 July, when the two armies clashed on a plateau behind a small stream called Bull Run. Troops on both sides were so ill trained, the officers so unused to handling large numbers, the opposing flags so similar, and the uniforms so varied, that a scene of extraordinary confusion took place. For hours it was anyone's battle. Union victory was averted by Johnston sending reinforcements by railroad in the nick of time, the "stone wall" stand of Jackson, and the charge of Colonel Arthur C. Cummings's 33rd Virginia Regiment. The Union lines began to retreat, and the retreat became a rout. All next day soldiers were straggling into Washington without order or formation, dropping down to sleep in the streets; rumors flying about that Beauregard was in hot pursuit, that the Capitol would be blown up if not abandoned. "One bitter, bitter hour — perhaps proud America will never again know such an hour," wrote Walt Whitman, who lived through it all. But Lincoln never flinched and Beauregard did not pursue; his army was more disorganized by victory than McDowell's by defeat. There was no more talk of a 90-day war. The Union was nerved to make adequate preparations for a long war; while the South, believing her proved superiority would dissolve the Northern "hordes" and procure foreign recognition, indulged in an orgy of self-applause.

Had the South but known it, the second half of 1861 gave her the best chance of victory. Cotton should have been rushed to Europe, arms and munitions imported, and Confederate finances put on a sound basis before the Union blockade closed in. Instead, the Southern states, faithful to the old Jefferson embargo theory, withheld cotton, fatuously believing that this would force Europe to break the blockade, and no taxes were levied by the Confederate congress in 1861! Joe Johnston urged an invasion of Pennsylvania before the Union had time to organize and train a great army, but Jefferson Davis thought he knew better; the South must stay on the defensive. Perhaps he was right, we never can know; but the folly of the cotton embargo, the tardy buildup in arms, and timid finance, are obvious.

5. Terrain and Tactics

Most actions of the Civil War were fought in rough, forested country with occasional clearings, and amid a scattered population. Antietam, Gettysburg, and Fredericksburg were the only important battles in open country. Standard tactics were, roughly, these: the defending infantry was drawn up in double line, the men firing erect or from a kneeling posture or from field entrenchments if there was time to dig them. The attacking force, also in two lines, moved forward by brigade units of 2000 to 2500 men,[1] covering a front of 800 to 1000 yards. Captains, and often colonels and majors, marched in front of their men, to encourage them with voice and sword; the other officers and non-coms were in the rear to discourage straggling. Normally the attacking troops moved forward in cadenced step to the beat of drum, halting at intervals to fire and reload. The defending force returned fire until one or the other gave ground. Occasionally the boys in blue, more often those in gray, advanced on the double, the former shouting a deep-chested *hurrah!*, the latter giving vent to their famous rebel yell, a shrill staccato yelp, derived perhaps from the view-halloo of the hunting field. As the two lines closed, swords flashed, colors glowed, bugles blew, drums beat, mounted aides dashed back and forth carrying messages. Since smokeless powder had not been invented, the battlefield soon became so thickly shrouded in smoke that the commanders had no idea of what was going on.

Standard books on tactics prescribed that an attack of this sort should be concluded with the bayonet, but that seldom happened because fire power had improved much faster than tactics. The conical minié bullet (invented by

---

1. In general, 10 companies = 1 regiment; 4 regiments = 1 brigade; 4 brigades = 1 division, 2 or 3 divisions = 1 army corps. In six important battles, average regimental strength was only 500. The regiment at full strength numbered 1050 officers and men, but they were allowed to waste away to almost nothing; new regiments were organized, instead of providing replacements for the old ones.

a French officer of that name in 1848) made infantry fire about twice as deadly as it had been in the Mexican War, and led to the earliest use of field entrenchments as the only way to prevent the defense being slaughtered. Fire directed from these improvised earth bulwarks, as at Fredericksburg and Kenesaw Mountain, made a shambles of the attack before it closed near enough to use bayonets. But Lee persistently underestimated the effect of rifle fire over open ground; that is why his attacks failed at Antietam and Gettysburg.

Not only in field entrenchments, but in skirmishing did the fighting in the Civil War foreshadow World War I. This description of General Barlow's skirmishers at Spottsylvania might apply equally well to the standard tactics of an infantry attack on the western front in 1918; or in Sicily in 1943:

To Barlow's brigades the very life of military service was a widely extended formation, flexible yet firm, where the soldiers were largely thrown on their individual resources, but remained in a high degree under the control of resolute, sagacious, keen-eyed officers, who urged them forward or drew them back as the exigency of the case required, where every advantage was taken of the nature of the ground, of fences, trees, stones, and prostrate logs; where manhood rose to its maximum and mechanism sank to its minimum, and where almost anything seemed possible to vigilance, audacity, and cool self-possession.

Although over 80 different types of shoulder arms were used in the Union army alone, the muzzle-loading .58 caliber rifle, 4 feet 8 inches long, weighing 9 pounds, and fired by a percussion cap, was standard. A trained infantryman could get off 3 rounds per minute, and with the minié-ball cartridge he could stop an attack at 200 to 250 yards, and kill at over half a mile. Good breech-loading repeating rifles were on the market, but the chief of Union ordnance James W. Ripley, (nicknamed "Ripley Van Winkle") disapproved of them — as did General Lee — and only by Lincoln's intervention were enough made for issue to Union cavalry. The mounted service, as of old, enjoyed top prestige. Cavalry in the Civil War was used mainly for reconnaissance or hit-and-run raids; not, as in Europe, for shock tactics. The romantic exploits of the great Confederate cavalrymen Stuart, Forrest, Morgan, and Shelby, contributed little to their cause; but Thomas and Sheridan, by turning troopers into dragoons (using horses to get there but fighting on foot), captured fortified lines at Nashville and cleared the Shenandoah valley of Confederate forces.

Union field artillery for the most part was muzzle-loading; either the "Napoleon" smooth-bore bronze cannon, firing a 12-pound ball, or the Parrott cast-iron 3-inch rifled cannon. The latter, an invention of Robert P. Parrott, a former United States Army officer, was guaranteed against bursting like the old "Peacemaker" by a wrought-iron hoop welded into the breech. Parrotts of larger caliber, firing projectiles up to 300 pounds' weight, were supplied in large numbers both to army and navy. Mortars up to 13-inch caliber were used in siege operations and on specially converted vessels; and Captain John

A. Dahlgren USN invented a bottle-shaped 9-inch rifled cannon, which was also much in evidence. He also designed the 15-inch smooth-bores for the monitors. Confederate artillery, composed of a hodgepodge of imported and captured cannon, together with many pieces from the federal ordnance depots in the South, was well handled, especially in wooded terrain at very short range, to stop an infantry assault; but it was no match for the more powerful Union guns. This placed the Southern troops at no great disadvantage, because cannonfire never became an effective killer like the minié bullet; artillery then had neither the range nor the precision to give assaulting infantry valuable support. On the other hand, massed artillery as a defense, as on Malvern Hill in the peninsular campaign, could be decisive; and General O. O. Howard in the Atlanta campaign once held 12,000 Confederates at bay with 29 cannon.

Moments of actual combat were more deadly than modern battles to infantry officers and men, but as soon as contact was broken the men were comparatively safe, since there was no continued harassment by enemy artillery. A common feature of the Civil War was the fraternizing of picket guards, and even of whole units, during intervals between battles; the Southerners swapping tobacco, of which they had plenty, for coffee, of which they were always short.

Other important tactical innovations in the Civil War, on the naval side, were the armored ironclad, and the mine and submarine for defense in shoal waters; some 40 warships were sunk or badly damaged by mines during the war. On the land side, the extensive use of field entrenchments, railways and telegraph, and air observation from balloons, was new. An efficient field telegraph system would have been of great assistance to military commanders, enabling them to dispense with mounted messengers, as well as to keep distant commands promptly informed. But the Union telegraph service was controlled by a superintendent in Washington, who would allow no interference with his personnel by field commanders. General Grant was driven almost frantic by lazy, cowardly, or venal telegraphers who ran to the rear when most wanted, or let messages from speculators take precedence over military orders. General Schofield almost lost the Battle of Franklin, because his headquarters telegraph operator took fright and ran away with the code so that urgent messages to General Thomas had to be sent by messenger.

Exactly the contrary took place with the balloon corps; enthusiastic pioneer aviators were consistently snubbed by the military and their organizer was denied military rank. Balloons had been used for observation of enemy troop movements in Europe as early as the French Revolution. A native of Jefferson Mills, New Hampshire, with the impressive name Thaddeus Sobieski Coulincourt Lowe, the leading American balloonist, obtained the support of Joseph Henry to investigate currents of the stratosphere, and made a record ascent of 23,000 feet in 1860. After war broke out he was allowed to organize and direct a civilian balloon corps attached to the army's signal corps. Lowe's organization at one time had six lighter-than-air ships costing only $1500 each.

Two of them, with pongee silk envelopes, inflated with hydrogen gas from portable generators, were employed by the Army of the Potomac in the peninsular campaign. They were used both for observation and artillery spotting, and Lowe himself was in the balloon at Chancellorsville which reported Stonewall Jackson's flanking movement; but General Hooker was too stupid to profit by this intelligence. General Joe Johnston wanted balloons for his army, but apparently the technical difficulties were too much for the Confederates. So much friction was created by a civilian organization operating within the Union army, so many difficulties attended the inflating, launching, and handling of these big gasbags with four-man baskets and mile-long manila cables in the wooded terrain of the Civil War, that the Union balloon corps was disbanded in June 1863.

6. Europe, Canada, and the War

Southern hopes of a quick victory were based on the expectation that the North would not fight, and the delusion that the Lord Chancellor of England sat on a cotton bale instead of a woolsack. Southerners were as certain that England would go to war, if need be, to get cotton, as they were of the justice of their cause. The European textile industry did largely depend on American cotton, but two important factors were overlooked by plantation economists. In April 1861 there was a 50 per cent oversupply both of the fiber and of cotton cloth in the English market; and the bumper cotton crop of 1860, largely exported before the blockade, added to the glut. The war enabled European cotton brokers to work off surplus stock at inflated prices, and later they found new sources of supply in Egypt and India.

Both North and South felt that they were entitled to the sympathy and support of the British and Canadian people, and were bitter when they didn't get it, as the British and Canadians were about American neutrality in 1914 and 1939. A chain of events threatened international complications. First, Jefferson Davis on 17 April 1861 invited Southern shipowners to take out letters of marque and prey on Northern merchant vessels. This forced Lincoln's hand, and two days later he declared a blockade of all ports and coasts of the seceded states. A blockade had to be publicly declared before neutral ships would submit to visit and search, but implicit in the proclamation was the recognition of the Confederacy as a belligerent. Hence it is not surprising that on 13 May Lord Palmerston's government, in recognizing the blockade and ordering British ships to respect it, declared England's "determination to maintain a strict and impartial neutrality in the contest . . . between the Government of the United States of America and certain States styling themselves the Confederate States of America." To the Northern people this seemed grossly unfriendly, and Seward took occasion to draft an intemperate protest which Lincoln toned down. In the excitement over this neutrality proclamation, almost everyone overlooked an order of 1 June forbidding British and imperial port authorities to admit prize ships. That British order killed Confederate privateering and resulted in the *Alabama* and her sister raiders having to destroy almost all the prizes that they captured. Thus, the British doctrine of naval warfare worked for the North. As Earl Russell, the foreign minister, observed, the Union blockade of Southern ports was a real blockade satisfying all the rules of international law, and in view of England's interest as the dominant sea power, he dared not insist on any stricter standard. The reiterated Southern complaints that the blockade was a mere "paper" one he shrewdly suspected to be indications to the contrary, as indeed they were.

Canada, Britain, and France were keenly interested in the Civil War. Opinions divided ideologically: restoration of the Union would mean a new triumph for democracy; destruction of the Union a possibly mortal wound to democracy. The United States had long been obnoxious to European ruling classes and to Canadian Tories for the encouragement that it afforded to liberal and radical elements. An "all-powerful and unconquerable" instinct, wrote the Comte de Montalembert, "at once arrayed on the side of the proslavery people all the open or secret partisans of the fanaticism and absolutism of Europe." Many liberals, however, could see no difference between the Southern struggle for independence and the nationalist movements in Europe which they had supported. Humanitarians, who would have welcomed a war against slavery, were put off by the repeated declarations of Lincoln and Seward that slavery was not an issue. The commercial classes marked the return of the United States in 1861 to a high protective tariff, which the Confederate constitution forbade, and Southern propaganda made much of the contrast. Shipping interests hoped for the ruin of their most formidable competitor, and approved a new cotton kingdom for which they might do the carrying trade. Under the circumstances it is not surprising that the Union had few articulate partisans in the England of 1861. And there was grave danger lest some untoward incident precipitate hostilities between the Union and the Empire.

Such an incident was the *Trent* affair. A British mail steamer of that name was conveying from Havana to Southampton two Confederate diplomatic agents, Senators James M. Mason and John Slidell, when on 8 November 1861 she was boarded from U.S.S. *San Jacinto*, Captain Charles Wilkes, and deprived of her two distinguished passengers and their secretaries, who were then confined in a federal fortress. Wilkes, who should have sent the *Trent* into port for adjudication instead of removing the two envoys, became a hero of the hour in the North and was promoted. But in England the incident was rightly considered an insult to the British flag — a reverse impressment, 1807 style. The London press shouted for apology or war, and Russell, for the cabinet, drafted a peremptory demand for apology and release of the envoys. Fortunately Prince Albert, Queen Victoria's ailing consort (he had only a fortnight to live), toned down the dispatch; and by a notable dispensation of

Providence the Atlantic cable had ceased to function, so that mutual insults were not immediately reprinted in the newspapers. By 19 December, when Russell's dispatch reached Secretary Seward, the Northern public had begun to weigh the consequence of antagonizing England, but Lincoln feared the political effect of yielding to British menace. Senator Sumner argued before the cabinet for four hours on Christmas Day before the President yielded. Seward then told the British minister, "The four persons . . . will be cheerfully liberated." That was promptly done. In the end, the *Trent* episode cleared the air.

American-Canadian relations had been friendly since the adoption of the reciprocity treaty in 1854. The Rush-Bagot agreement was still in force, and the fresh-water navies hauled out in 1819 had rotted away. All phases of Canadian opinion, except for some descendants of 1776 Tories, were pro-Union at the start of the Civil War. Canada, having got rid of Negro slavery in 1833, had received some 20,000 fugitive slaves in the past decade. Friendliness quickly changed to resentment and apprehension in the latter half of 1861, owing to a number of factors. The British declaration of neutrality, and still more the *Trent* affair, unleashed a nasty jingoism in the Northern American press, with threats of invading Canada which recalled 1812.

During the *Trent* crisis, Britain strengthened her Canadian garrison of 6400 regulars by over 14,000 men. Many of these reinforcements were glad to avail themselves of Seward's tactful offer to be landed at Portland, Maine, instead of Halifax, and proceed to Quebec over the recently built Grand Trunk Railway. Thus the *Trent* affair cleared the air in Canada too.

THE BATTLE CRY OF FREEDOM

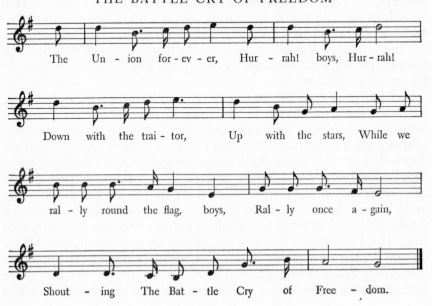

Eighteen Sixty-two, the Crucial Year

1. McClellan, the Radicals, and Stanton

O N 24 JULY 1861, four days after Bull Run, President Lincoln summoned General George B. McClellan to Washington and gave him command of the Army of the Potomac. McClellan was thirty-four years old. A graduate of West Point on the eve of the Mexican War, in which he performed distinguished service as a lieutenant of engineers, he later served as American military attaché to the allied armies in the Crimea and wrote a report that showed unusual powers of observation. Subsequent business experience accustomed him to deal with large affairs and won him the confidence of men of property; personal magnetism and success in West Virginia made him a popular idol. The Northern states provided him with plenty of three-year volunteers. Congress was generous with money and equipment, and the President gave him full support. No untried general in modern times has had such abundant means as McClellan enjoyed during the nine months that followed Bull Run.

This general proved to be a great organizer. His methodical mind, appetite for detail, vivid personality, and genuine interest in his men were exactly the qualities needed to form an army from a mob. But defects in conduct and character impaired his usefulness and weakened his support when the time came for action. There can no longer be any reasonable doubt of his technical military ability; General Lee, after the war, said that he was the ablest of his opponents. McClellan's position, however, required not only military ability but some perception of the democratic medium in which he must work; and that perception, which was given to Grant and Lincoln, he decidedly lacked. The note of self-laudation and contempt for the President that runs through McClellan's confidential letters, and his acceptance of the presidential nomination on a defeatist platform in 1864, make it difficult to do him justice today. Yet no Union general was so beloved as "Little Mac" was by the untrained volunteers whom he turned into a superb instrument of war, the Army of the Potomac.

McClellan's admirers called him, and he liked to be called, the "Young Napoleon," but apart from being adept at inspiring troops (even using Napoleon's own phrases, badly translated), his resemblance to the great Emperor was superficial. Napoleon was a master of audacity and celerity in maneuver, whilst McClellan excelled in careful preparation and methodical planning. So far as he resembled any French general, "Little Mac" may be compared with Bazaine or Pétain, who carried political ambitions in their marshal's batons and fancied that politicians were scheming against them. McClellan fully expected to "crush the rebels in one campaign," as he wrote to his adoring wife; he then would persuade the Confederate government to surrender by guaranteeing security to slavery. This arrangement, he expected, would be ratified by popular acclaim, and he would be elected to the presidency of a reunited country — still half slave and half free — in 1864.

Weeks stretched into months, and the newspapers had nothing to report but drills and reviews. "All quiet along the Potomac" appeared so often in the headlines as to become a jest.

Lincoln long resisted efforts of the politicians to worry him into forcing McClellan into action. When General Scott got in McClellan's way, the President allowed him to resign; and on 1 November 1861 he appointed McClellan general in chief of all the armies of the Republic. Yet the General persistently snubbed the President, and on one occasion — going to bed when Lincoln came to his headquarters for a conference — affronted him in a manner that no other head of state would have pardoned. "Never mind," said Lincoln, "I will hold McClellan's horse if he will only bring us success." December came, and the General began to play with plans for an oblique instead of a direct advance on Richmond. "If something is not done soon, the bottom will be out of the whole affair," said the President. "If General McClellan does not want to use the army I would like to *borrow* it." Lincoln knew what Churchill and Roosevelt learned in World War II, that the people and politicians in a democratic country will not stand for a "phony war," that they must have action. Yet McClellan's strategy of careful preparation and delay was correct. It was the true policy of the Union to postpone offensive movements until the blockade began to pinch, and superior Northern resources were organized for offensive war.

Walt Whitman shrewdly evaluated McClellan as a straddler, a soft hitter, one who "felt that the man who dealt the softest blows all around would be the great man, the general idol, the savior." The virtue of this defect was that McClellan kept the war clean; in Virginia he did his best to restrain soldiers from looting or committing outrages on civilians.

The new year 1862 opened gloomily in both capitals. President Davis was flattered by unanimous re-election to the presidency, but troubled by a new and factious Congress. The *Trent* affair had fizzled, the blockade was beginning to be felt, Confederate paper money had depreciated 50 per cent, and prices were soaring. But the Southern people still trusted in the potency of cotton and the impotence of Northern men.

In the North, McClellan's inaction enhanced Lincoln's political embarrassment. The unity forged by the guns that fired on Fort Sumter was falling to pieces; and from the Republican party a faction emerged to challenge Lincoln's leadership. This was led by "Bluff Ben" Wade, "Zach" Chandler, Western senators with a fine talent for politics, and "Thad" Stevens, a congressman from Pennsylvania. From their point of view the war was one of revenge on an insolent slave power; the policy they wished to force upon the President was immediate emancipation and arming of the slaves. That, if adopted in 1861, would have driven the border slave states into secession, alienated the Northern Democrats, and narrowed the war party to a faction.

Those violent elements which war inevitably releases were arousing a new and nasty temper in the Union, and to this temper the Radicals appealed by voice and pen during the recess of Congress, August-December 1861. To their standard surged the bitter-ender, unconditional-surrender sort of people, sincere in their desire to win the war yet certain to lose it for any government that yielded to their misguided zeal. In his first annual message to Congress Lincoln said, "I have been anxious and careful that the inevitable conflict . . . shall not degenerate into a violent and remorseless revolutionary struggle." To Radicals this was a sign of weakness.

The first product of this complex of hatred and zeal, suspicion and super-patriotism, was the appointment by Congress of a Joint Committee on the Conduct of the War, on 20 December 1861. Radical Republicans dominated this committee. Throughout the war their inquisitorial activities, *ex parte* investigations, and missions to the front hampered the executive and the best generals — and undermined army discipline. Frémont, Butler, Banks, and Hooker, the four most incompetent generals on the Union side, were, in the opinion of this committee, peerless leaders who could do no wrong.

Owing to the efforts of a House committee, corruption on a gigantic scale was uncovered in the war department, and the scandal smirched Secretary Cameron. Lincoln let him down easily into the St. Petersburg legation and appointed a Democrat, Edwin M. Stanton, secretary of war. Gloomy, ill-mannered, and vituperative, Stanton was another cross for Lincoln to bear. Intolerant of delay and harsh to subordinates, he was hated by almost every officer with whom he came in contact, and to several he did cruel injustice. Yet for all that, Stanton's honesty, determination and system made him a fit instrument for Lincoln's purpose. He stood for discipline against the President's desire to pardon all deserters. He browbeat state governors and other politicians and got things done. As Lincoln remarked at a dark period for the Union cause, "Folks come up here and tell me that there are a great many men in the country who have all Stanton's excellent qualities without his defects. All I have to say is, I haven't met 'em! I don't know 'em! I wish I did!"

When Stanton took office (15 January 1862), McClellan had already prepared, and the President approved, the general outline of a plan of operations for 1862: (1) in the Eastern theater of war, McClellan to advance against Richmond, but by what route was still undecided. (2) In the Western theater Don Carlos Buell, commanding the Union Army of the Ohio, to rescue the beleaguered Unionists of eastern Tennessee and to cut the Richmond-Memphis railway. Albert Sidney Johnston, commanding the Confederate Department of the West, was there to prevent him. (3) In a military department which embraced both banks of the Mississippi, Henry W. Halleck, then occupied with an isolated war in Missouri, was usefully constructing a fleet of armored river gunboats. This should support the army pushing down the Mississippi valley and join with a naval expedition under Farragut, which would force a passage from the Gulf to New Orleans and Vicksburg. The Confederacy was improvising an armored naval force to repel this invasion and break the blockade.

Action began in the Western theater. Colonel James A. Garfield marked a stage in his progress "from Log Cabin to White House" by defeating a body of Confederate mountaineers at Prestonburg in eastern Kentucky (10 January 1862), but went no farther. General George H. Thomas was attacked at Mill Springs on 19 January by General Zolicoffer, who lost both the battle and his life. Thick and sticky mud stopped a further advance, and almost smothered Thomas's communications. Lincoln, desperate for action, then issued (27 January) his pathetic General War Order No. 1, designating Washington's birthday as "the day for a general movement of all the land and naval forces of the United States against the insurgent forces."

February 22 passed before even a definite plan for the Army of the Potomac had been agreed upon. The first substantial victory for the Union came in an unsuspected quarter by an almost unknown general.

2. Grant and Farragut

Captain Ulysses S. Grant, an officer who disliked war and loathed army routine, had fallen on evil days since his proud moment before Mexico City. He was forced to resign from the army to avoid a court-martial for drunkenness. Unable to extract a living from "Hardscrabble Farm" near St. Louis, he attempted to sell real estate, and failed again. His father bestowed a clerkship in the family leather store at Galena, Illinois. Brothers condescended, fellow townsmen sneered. Only his wife had faith; and the most ill-tempered horses were docile to his voice and hands.

Shortly after the war broke out Grant, now thirty-nine years old, obtained a colonelcy of volunteers. His regiment was promptly ordered into Missouri to dislodge a Confederate regiment under a Colonel Harris. Approaching the reported position, so Grant relates, fear gripped his heart; but he had not the moral courage to halt and consider what to do. Suddenly there opened a view of the enemy's encampment — abandoned! "It occurred to me at once that Harris had been as much afraid of me as I had been of him. This was a new view of the question I had never taken before; but it was one I never forgot afterwards."

This brief and bloodless engagement earned Grant a brigadier's commission. In the fall of 1861 he was assigned to Halleck's department and stationed at Cairo, the important junction of the Ohio with the Mississippi. In the summer of 1861 the Confederates began to throw up earthworks at various points along the Mississippi where the old Spanish forts used to choke down-river trade. In order to force a passage past them, J. B. Eads, an engineer of St. Louis, constructed a fleet of river gunboats, each with a partially armored casemate shaped like a mansard roof, and a flat-bottomed hull.

Less than 50 miles up the Ohio from Cairo the Tennessee and Cumberland rivers offered parallel routes into Tennessee, Alabama, and Mississippi. Grant observed that Forts Henry and Donelson, the Confederate earthworks which closed these rivers, were the twin keys to the rebel West. Their capture would open a navigable waterway into the enemy's center and drive in his flanks. On 30 January 1862 Grant, after consulting with Commodore Andrew H. Foote, commanding the gunboat flotilla, obtained Halleck's reluctant consent to try, and was furnished with the necessary transports and gunboats. On 6 February Fort Henry, feebly garrisoned, was reduced by the gunboats before Grant's army arrived. And a three-gunboat raid up the Tennessee river to Cerro Gordo near the Mississippi border, captured a big river steamer which the Confederates were converting to an ironclad.

Fifteen miles across country from Fort Henry, on the high left bank of the Cumberland, lay a much stronger entrenched camp, Fort Donelson. There Albert Sidney Johnston had stationed 20,000 men, over half his army. Grant, after a quick midwinter march, disposed his troops in a semicircle about this fort on the land side. Foote's gunboats steamed down the Tennessee, up the Cumberland, and on 13 February attacked the fort at a range of 200 yards. They were driven back, disabled. It seemed that a siege would be necessary. But General John B. Floyd (President Buchanan's secretary of war), commanding the Confederate garrison, decided to fight his way out, and almost did. Grant arrived in the thick of the battle to find his right in disorder and his center in danger. Deducing from the three days' rations in a captured Confederate's haversack that the enemy was trying to escape, Grant made the right tactical dispositions to drive him back into the entrenchments. It was a fierce, blind battle in the forest but the result justified Grant in demanding and General Simon Bolivar Buckner (Floyd having escaped by boat) in consenting to "unconditional surrender" of garrison and fortress. The phrase gave new meaning to Grant's initials.

The results of this surrender were spectacular. Nashville was no longer tenable by the enemy, and A. S. Johnston retreated to the Memphis-Chattanooga Railway. Grant had practically restored Tennessee to the Union. Equally important was the moral gain to the then dispirited North. The prairie boys of the new Northwest had tested their mettle against rangy foresters of the old Southwest, and the legend of Southern invincibility began to fade.

Grant understood that momentum, keeping unremitting pressure on the enemy, is a first requisite in the art of war; but his jealous and pedantic superior, Halleck, instead of allowing him to pursue Johnston, diverted troops to attack the northernmost Confederate strongholds on the Mississippi. The capture of New Madrid and Island No. 10, with the aid of Foote's gunboats (7 April 1862), was a pretty operation, in which General John Pope unfortunately acquired fame; but it wasted time. Grant's way, up the Tennessee river, was the right method to open the Mississippi; Halleck's way gave Johnston time to concentrate some 50,000 men with Beauregard and Polk at Corinth.

Halleck, after subjecting Grant to unnecessary humiliation, finally ordered him, after waiting for Buell's Army of the Ohio to join, to lead against the enemy. Buell was a slow-motion general, and before he arrived Grant was caught napping. His Army of the Tennessee, encamped in an ill-chosen position at Pittsburg Landing, its front unprotected by entrenchments, was attacked on 6 April by Johnston and Beauregard. The Battle of Shiloh, or Pittsburg Landing, began. For twelve hours there was confused fighting between detached portions of the Union lines and the dashing Confederates, superbly led. Grant's steadfast coolness, the fiery valor of divisional commanders like William Tecumseh Sherman and B. M. Prentiss, and the pluck of individual soldiers, prevented a rout. By the end of that terrible Sunday the Confederates had captured the key position at Shiloh church, Union lines were dangerously near the river, and some 5000 refugees were cowering panic-stricken under the bluffs at Pittsburg Landing. It was a spectacle of complete defeat, and any ordinary general would have settled for saving the rest of his army by retreat. But Grant was no ordinary general. Reinforced by the van of Buell's Army of the Ohio and by Lew Wallace's division, he counterattacked Monday morning. Albert Sidney Johnston was killed, and Beauregard, after ten hours' desperate fighting, withdrew the Confederate army to Corinth. Grant hadn't the heart to call on his own exhausted troops to fight further, and Buell refused to move.

Shiloh was a Union victory at doleful cost. Out of 55,000 Union troops engaged the loss was over 13,000; the Confederates lost about 11,000 out of 42,000. A storm of controversy arose. Grant's lack of precaution was magnified by the newspapers into gross incompetence, even drunkenness. Buell's friends claimed all the credit for him. Political pressure was put upon the President to remove Grant, but Lincoln replied, "I can't spare this man; he fights."

Immediately after Shiloh, two Union jabs were made deep into the Confederate West. Ormsby MacKnight Mitchel, America's leading astronomer, was now a divisional commander under Buell. On his own initiative he led his division in a rapid march from Shelbyville, Tennessee, to Huntsville, Alabama, captured the city, and would have captured Chattanooga, too, had the "Great Locomotive Chase" succeeded. James J. Andrews, a Union sympathizer, stole a railroad train near Marietta, Tennessee, and with 20 soldier volunteers, started full speed for Chattanooga, hotly pursued by a Confederate train. The Southerners won, captured the locomotive crew, and executed them as spies.

Although Lincoln couldn't spare Grant, Halleck could and did, by personally taking over command of the Army of the Tennessee on 11 April. After assembling 100,000 men at Pittsburg Landing, Halleck took a month to cover 23 miles thence to Corinth, giving Beauregard plenty of time to withdraw the Confederate army intact.

Union gunboats continued their descent of the Mississippi, breaking up a Confederate flotilla off Memphis on 6 June, running up the White river into the heart of Arkansas, forcing the enemy to evacuate Missouri, and on 1 July 1862 joining Farragut's fleet above Vicksburg.

Commodore Farragut had to sail up the Mississippi from the Gulf without a single ironclad, but his old wooden walls were manned by stout hearts. At Plaquemines Bend, 90 miles below New Orleans, the river was protected by forts Jackson and St. Philip, sunken hulks supporting a boom, a fleet of rams and armed steamers, and a 3- to 4-knot current. A flotilla of small Union mortar schooners fired continuously on Fort Jackson for three days, without much effect. In the small hours of 24 April, Farragut's fleet of eight steam sloops of war and fifteen wooden gunboats, with chain cables secured as a coat of mail abreast the engines, crashed the boom and ran the gantlet of armored rams, fire rafts, river-defense fleet, and the two forts.

In the gay creole city of New Orleans, largest and wealthiest of the Confederacy, there had been little business since the blockade closed down, and no laughter since the news of Shiloh. When Farragut's fleet anchored off the levee on 25 April, so near that the crowd could see the grinning Jack Tars as they fondled the breeches of their Dahlgren guns, New Orleans was already abandoned by Confederate armed forces and the United States took over. The Union troops of occupation were commanded by a tough character, General B. F. Butler. Repeated insults to his men by the creole wenches were put a stop to by his order of 15 May 1862, rendering such a person "liable to be treated as a woman of the town plying her avocation"; or in other words to be lodged in the common jail. Butler was declared a felon and an outlaw by President Davis, denounced in Parliament, and finally removed from his post in consequence of diplomatic protest. But, alas, this was not the end to his military career.

Farragut, after landing the army, proceeded upriver, received the surrender of Baton Rouge and Natchez and ran past Vicksburg to join the upstream gunboat fleet (1 July). But as General Halleck could not be induced to provide troops for a joint attack on Vicksburg, that "Gibraltar of the Mississippi" held out for a year longer, enabling the Confederacy to maintain communication with Arkansas, Missouri, and Texas. Thus the Union army and navy offensive in the West failed to attain its major objective, yet accomplished much. By July 1862 the enemy had been driven south of the Memphis-Chattanooga Railway, and the greater part of the Mississippi was under Union control. "Anaconda" tightly pinched the Confederacy along her waistline; but her blood still circulated.

3. *Sea Power and the War*

No big modern war has been won without preponderant sea power; and, conversely, very few rebellions of maritime provinces have succeeded without acquiring sea power. The Thirteen Colonies, as we have seen, could not have won independence but for the help of the French navy; the South American republics employed retired British naval officers to build up fleets which challenged Spain's; even the Dutch rebels of the sixteenth century had their "sea beggars" who played hob with Spanish communications. Similarly, in the Civil War, control of the sea was a priceless asset to the Union. The navy maintained communications with the outside world, severed those of the South, captured important points on the coast, and on the Western rivers co-operated with the army like the other blade to a pair of shears.

Gideon Welles's somewhat meager knowledge of the service was supplemented by a capable assistant secretary, Gustavus V. Fox. By them the navy was much more efficiently directed than the army, because Congress did not try to interfere or to make admirals out of politicians. But the problem of blockading 3350 miles of coastline from Washington to Matamoras, with the vessels and seamen available, seemed insoluble. The 42 ships of the navy in commission, mostly steam-propelled but none armored, could not cope with the problem. Only twelve ships were in the home squadron; the rest were dispersed among various foreign stations, and it took time to recall them and refit for blockade duty. The American merchant marine had a limited supply of screw steamers suitable for conversion to men of war, and a few machine shops capable of turning out good marine engines. But a large construction program was immediately undertaken — Ericsson's *Monitor* being the most spectacular example — and sidewheelers, clipper ships, tugboats, and even ferry boats were purchased in wholesale quantities at retail prices. Time and legislation were required to build ironclads, to retire aged officers, and to establish promotion by merit.

The blockade was largely a "paper" one for about three months, and did not become really effective until 1862. How effective it ever became is still a matter of controversy. The Richmond government declared loudly and frequently that it never did, and that England should never have recognized it as a proper blockade; but the scarcity of consumer goods in the Confederacy, and soaring prices, proved the contrary. No ships could cover so long a coast-line without bases, which the Union navy lost no time in obtaining.

Hatteras Inlet, back door to Virginia, was captured by a small amphibious operation under General Burnside on 26 August 1861. Ship Island in the Gulf of Mexico, an important staging point for Farragut's assault on New Orleans, was taken on 17 September. An amphibious operation of 17,000 men under Commodore Samuel F. Du Pont, beat down the fort on Hilton Head at the entrance to Port Royal Sound, South Carolina, on 7 November, forcing a gunboat flotilla under Commodore Tattnall csn to retire. To these, by April 1862, were added Roanoke Island (the site of the first Virginia colony), New Bern, and Fort Macon, North Carolina, and Fort Pulaski commanding the approaches to Savannah. The Confederate commander in the South Carolina department, General Robert E. Lee, here had his first experience of sea power. To his children, in December 1861, he wrote describing the "big black ships like foul blots on the surface of the water miles from shore," and the "Yankee gunboats" steaming up the Edisto river and shelling the houses of prominent secessionists.

Once provided with these bases, the United States blockading squadron put a tighter and tighter squeeze on the Confederacy until it was practically eating its own tail. Few officers and still fewer sailors who kept this ceaseless vigil became known to fame. They deserve a tribute like that which Mahan paid to Nelson's two-year blockade of the coast of France in the Napoleonic wars: "Those far distant, storm-beaten ships, upon which the Grand Army never looked, stood between it and the dominion of the world." The blockading squadrons under Commodores Du Pont. Melancton Smith, John A. Dahlgren, and David D. Porter, a motley collection of sailing frigates, converted paddlewheel steamers, tugboats, ferry boats, and even stranger craft, which few leaders of the Confederacy even sighted, stood between them and the independence of the South.

Owing to the character of the Southern coast, it was impossible for blockading squadrons to close Confederate ports completely. Private firms in Nova Scotia and the British Isles built a fleet of low-freeboard blockade runners, powered by the best steam engines of the day and capable of turning up 14 knots' speed. Cargoes from Europe or Canada would be trans-shipped to the runners at St. George, Bermuda, from which it was only 674 miles to Wilmington, North Carolina; or at Nassau in the Bahamas whence it was 500 miles to Charleston; or at Havana, about the same distance to Mobile. Tampico and Vera Cruz were the jumping-off places for the Rio Grande. The runners, choosing the dark of the moon, would steal through a blockading squadron to a short distance off the coast, steam in shoal water at low speed, blacked-out, until off an inlet or harbor; then pile on coal and dash in, often under cover of a Confederate fort. If pursued and shelled, they could be run ashore and the cargo salvaged; for profits were so immense that one successful voyage paid for the ship. Bermuda and the Bahamas acquired an importance they had not known since the days of the buccaneers, and a prosperity they did not recover until they became winter playgrounds for the rich.

Richard King of Texas, who had founded the fabulous King Ranch in 1853, owned a fleet of river steamboats which he promptly put under the Mexican flag; and as both sides respected neutral flags in this war, the King fleet ferried thousands of bales of cotton to Tampico and Vera Cruz with impunity; for the Confederacy in 1862 changed its "hold back cotton" policy to an "export it all" policy. At times there were over 100 merchant ships in the roadstead off the mouth of the Rio Grande, waiting to land goods and load cotton, transported thither by ox wagon over distances as great as 500 miles. The Union did not even partly close this leak until November 1863 when General Banks, in his one successful military operation, landed 7000 troops at the mouth of the Rio Grande and forced the Mexico-Texas trade upriver to Laredo. By the end of 1863 the Union had occupied every principal Gulf port of Texas except Sabine City, an attack on which by Union gunboats was gallantly defeated by one company of Texas heavy artillery; and Galveston, where a small amphibious operation was similarly routed. This Texas-Mexico border would have been a very serious leak in the blockade, but for the insoluble problem of distributing goods imported there, and corruption in getting the cotton out; Texas profiteers were enriched, but the Confederate treasury profited very little.

Although blockade running gained the South both arms and consumer goods, it never did enough, as the runners had small cargo capacity, a large part of which was taken up by expensive luxuries which could stand the freights of $300 to $1000 a ton. A runner's life was gay but short; captains were paid up to $5000 in gold for a single round trip, but on an average only four and a half trips were made before capture or running aground. The Confederate treasury department issued some phony statistics — for instance, that half a million pounds of coffee were run into Wilmington in the last ten week of 1864 — to prove that the blockade was ineffective. Actually it was efficient enough to weaken the Southern will to victory. Almost 100 steamships were engaged in blockade running in 1864, but early next year the number dropped to 24. The Union navy captured or destroyed 295 steamers and about 1100 row- and sail-boats trying to run the blockade, and some 40 of the fast captured steamers were armed and converted to blockaders.

The Confederacy naturally had more difficulty in improvising a navy than building an army. Secession secured it about 20 per cent of the United States naval officers, but they couldn't bring their ships with them, and outside Norfolk, which she captured on 20 April 1861, the South had no great shipbuilding center. Secretary Mallory, who had been chairman of the naval affairs committee in the United States Senate, showed great energy and ingenuity, but could not get army-minded President Davis to support him in time to count. He did build a fleet of armored gunboats, but it took eleven months to get the first (Virginia, ex-Merrimack) to sea, and she fought her famous but inconclusive Battle of Hampton Roads with U.S.S. Monitor (9 March 1862) too late to influence the peninsular campaign. The Confederacy was energetic and ingenious in building armored rams and gunboats to defend Southern rivers and harbors, and produced the first submarine in history to make a kill. R. L. Hunley, a 35-foot boat built in Mobile and requiring eight men to turn the propeller shaft, poked her single torpedo's 95-pound warhead into U.S.S. Housatonic off Charleston after dark on 17 February 1864, and disappeared with all hands when the Union frigate blew up and sank.

These suicide tactics were not repeated. The South never managed to create an oceanic fleet, or to break the Union blockade at any point.

Owing to negligence on the part of the British government (for which it later paid dear), powerful steam raiders were built for the Confederacy in England and, manned largely by British crews, embarked on commerce-destroying cruises. C.S.S. *Alabama* and *Florida*, counterparts to Jones's *Ranger* and Barry's *Alliance* in the War of Independence, wrought relatively greater damage than those heroes did on enemy merchant vessels; but no more than Jones and Barry did they affect the outcome of a war. The Confederacy wanted what the infant United States had from 1778 on — an ally powerful on the ocean. That, she had high hopes of obtaining from England; but after the *Trent* crisis passed, the chance of the Royal Navy supporting the Confederacy became slim indeed.

The naval war on the Mississippi and its tributaries was as important as the maritime blockade in putting the squeeze on the Confederacy. Here, Gideon Welles put the Union fleet of river gunboats under the army, and the close co-operation between Grant and Foote won the important victory of Fort Donelson early in 1862. That same year the Union navy co-operated closely with General McClellan in the peninsular campaign and got his army out; after this campaign General Lee forced the Union armies to give battle well inland, where naval guns could not support them.

Naval blockade alone has never won a war; it was the armies of Grant, Sherman, and Thomas that delivered the knockout blows to the Confederacy. But they were only able to do that after the South had been materially weakened by the blockade. Again, the similarity to Winston Churchill's strategy for defeating Germany is striking. The Civil War well illustrated Mahan's dictum, "Not by rambling operations, or naval duels, are wars decided, but by force massed and handled in skillful combination."

4. The Peninsular Campaign, March–July 1862

We must now return to the biggest campaign of 1862, waged on the peninsula between the York and James rivers, between the Army of the Potomac (General McClellan) and the Army of Northern Virginia (Generals Joseph Johnston, Jackson, and Lee).

"In ten days I shall be in Richmond," boasted McClellan on 13 February. He was planning a frontal advance on the Confederate capital via Fredericksburg, but when Joe Johnston anticipated him by occupying that town, he demanded another delay. This was the last straw for Lincoln. He gave the general the choice between carrying out the frontal advance, and a wide flanking movement, supported by the Union navy, to the James. McClellan wisely chose the latter, which *Monitor*'s victory in the Battle of Hampton Roads (8 March) made practicable, even though *Virginia* still closed the mouth of the James. The President then stripped McClellan of his supreme command over all armies of the Republic, leaving him only the Army of the Potomac; and within the next few weeks Lincoln detached McDowell's corps from that army to protect Washington, and gave Frémont more troops in West Virginia than he knew how to handle. Thus McClellan was no longer a theater commander.

The Army of the Potomac, 110,000 strong, clothed in dark-blue tunics, light-blue trousers, and blunted cloth képis, was the most formidable military force yet seen on American soil. The men were well armed, equipped, and disciplined, eager for action, devoted to their glamorous commander. At the end of March they were floated down the Potomac in 100 or more transports and landed at or near Old Point Comfort, on the York peninsula. Here they were on a classic ground of American History: Jamestown, the Chickahominy river (first explored by Captain John Smith), Williamsburg, and Yorktown. The greater part of the peninsula had reverted to forest, and even the environs of Richmond were a wilderness, broken by occasional farms and clearings. Maps were unreliable, roads few. McClellan's best chance to win Richmond was to press forward at the best speed of marching men, before summer heat set in; audacity above all was wanted. Instead, he wasted a month on siege operations against Yorktown, where there were only 16,000 rebels.

That was exactly what Joe Johnston, a cautious thrust-and-parry, mine-and-sap strategist like McClellan, wanted the Union leader to do. General Lee, now "general in charge of military operations," liked it equally well, but for another reason — to gain time to build up the Confederate army by conscription, and to get Stonewall Jackson's army down from the Shenandoah. Johnston pulled his garrison secretly out of Yorktown 4 May, covering the retreat by a rear-guard action near the old capital of Williamsburg. And for the next three weeks he and "Little Mac" played classic tactics of maneuver on the peninsula while Stonewall Jackson executed a series of swift marches and smashing victories that have secured him a place among war's immortals. He beat Frémont at MacDowell in Virginia on 8 May, and then sent Banks reeling back to Winchester. Secretary Stanton, in a blue funk, recalled General McDowell's corps to defend the capital; Jackson inflicted two more defeats on Frémont and Banks on 8 and 9 June, then hastened south to join Johnston and Lee before Richmond.

In the meantime the Army of the Potomac was proceeding slowly up the York river side of the peninsula, while the Union navy under Commodore Louis M. Goldsborough USN was seizing control of the James. On 10 May Goldsborough pinched the rebels out of Norfolk and forced Commodore Tattnall CSN to destroy ironclad *Virginia*. The *Monitor* and a second ironclad now steamed up the James but were rudely checked by a Confederate battery at Drewry's Bluff, eight miles below Richmond. Goldsborough begged McClellan to shift at least part of his army James-side to help the navy silence this battery, and open a water route to Richmond; but McClellan refused to alter his set plan.

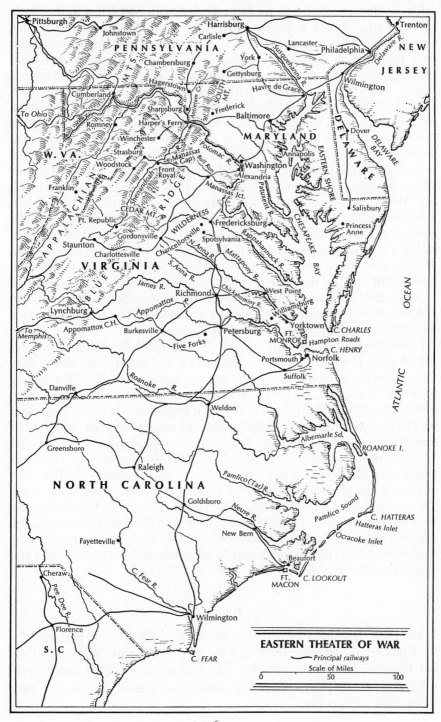

EASTERN THEATER OF WAR

—— Principal railways

Scale of Miles

0   50   100

On 31 May, Johnston had his first real clash with McClellan in the Battle of Fair Oaks. It was a drawn battle, and the Confederate commander, wounded, was relieved next day by Lee, who promptly and happily named his army the Army of Northern Virginia. McClellan, still cautious, took up a strong position and waited for fair weather to advance. In the meantime Jackson was sweeping down from the Shenandoah valley, threatening McClellan's York river base at White House. On 25 June, too late, the Union commander decided to accept Goldsborough's invitation to shift base to the James. Next day Lee took the initiative and the series of actions known as the Seven Days' Battles [1] began. Therein McClellan proved himself a tactical commander second to none. "Throughout this campaign we attacked just when and where the enemy wished us to attack," wrote General D. H. Hill csa. McClellan, outnumbered after Jackson joined Lee, conducted his left-flank maneuver with the precision of a review, inflicted superior losses on the enemy (20,614 Confederates, 15,849 Federals killed, wounded or missing), and in a chosen position on Malvern Hill, stood at bay while Lee hurled his divisions one ofter another over wheatfields swept by artillery and fire from Union gunboats. By the close of 2 July, while Lee withdrew his decimated legions toward Richmond, the Army of the Potomac, with wagon trains intact and morale unimpaired, was safe under the guns of the Union navy in a fortified base at Harrison's Landing on the James.

It was magnificent, and not a retreat. The Army of the Potomac was still full of fight, ready to resume the advance on Richmond when and if reinforced. The Union navy in the James was now so formidable that Lee refused to attack McClellan at Harrison's Landing. The summer was still young. McClellan entreated Lincoln to give him an opportunity to attack Richmond via Petersburg. But General Halleck (who had replaced Stanton in control of operations) placed his clammy hand on this sound plan (which Grant adopted two years later), and Lincoln feared that the administration could no longer carry McClellan. It was not merely that performance had fallen short of promise; his dispatches during the campaign had been querulous, sometimes insolent, and once hysterical. The Committee on the Conduct of the War was clamoring for his scalp, and the autumn elections were coming up. Accordingly, on 3 August, Halleck ordered the Army of the Potomac by driblets back to its cantonments near Washington, and the navy covered and escorted its retirement by sea.

5. Interlude

The eight weeks that followed the Seven Days' Battles were pure gold for the Confederacy. Jefferson Davis and the people of Richmond enjoyed their last happy summer, confident that they had proved that the South could

1. Mechanicsville (26 June), Gaines's Mill (27th), Savage Station (29th), Frayser's Farm (30th), Malvern Hill (1 July).

never be conquered. They had found a leader, Robert E. Lee — and what a leader! Fifty-five years old, tall, handsome, with graying hair and deep, expressive brown eyes which could convey with a glance a stronger reproof than any other general's oath-laden castigation; kind at heart and courteous even to those who failed him, he inspired and deserved confidence. No military leader since Napoleon has aroused such enthusiastic devotion among troops as did Lee when he reviewed them on his horse Traveller. And, what a horse!

— An iron-gray, sixteen hands high,
Short back, deep chest, strong haunch, flat legs, small head,
Delicate ear, quick eye, black mane and tail,
Wise brain, obedient mouth.[1]

Davis and Lee were masters of the situation. Thousands of replacements came pouring into Richmond. Although New Orleans was gone, Vicksburg kept Richmond in touch with the Far West; delegates from Arizona and the Indian Territory sat in the Confederate congress. Morgan's brilliant cavalry raid through Kentucky in July seemed to prove that state ripe for the plucking. There was that pesky blockade, to be sure, and prices rose daily, but four powerful ironclad rams were being built in Britain to break the blockade, and British-built C.S.S. *Alabama* now left port on a cruise that proved equally costly for the American merchant marine and the British taxpayer. The sunshine of victory was partly shaded by bickerings, characteristic of touchy "cavaliers." Robert Toombs challenged General D. H. Hill to a duel; A. P. Hill and Longstreet were not on speaking terms; there was even a cabal against Lee, who wrote to his wife before the end of July, "In the prospect before me I cannot see a single ray of pleasure during this war."

But the prospects for the Union being restored were really dim. "There is an all but unanimous belief that you *cannot* subject the South," Richard Cobden wrote to Senator Sumner when news of the Seven Days' Battles reached England. On 11 July an English M.P. introduced a motion for Franco-British mediation. It did not pass, but Napoleon III was ready to go along if Palmerston recognized the Confederacy. That summer there was a panic in Wall Street. The gold dollar reached a 17 per cent premium over paper when Congress authorized a second issue of $150 million in greenbacks. Lincoln called upon the states for 300,000 volunteers for nine months. There were patriotic rallies at which "John Brown's Body" was set to new words: "We are coming, Father Abraham, three hundred thousand more"; but fewer than 80,000 actually enlisted, and they were organized in new nine-months' regiments instead of being used like Confederate conscripts as permanent replacements.

1. Stephen Vincent Benét *John Brown's Body*, book 4, based on the General's own description. Traveller, foaled near Blue Sulphur in 1857, probably a descendant of the great Diomed, was purchased by Lee in 1861, and served as his principal mount throughout the war. He had amazing speed, frequently tiring out the horses of the staff, remarkable endurance, and only twice became frightened by bursting shells. On the second occasion, at Spotsylvania, he reared just in time for a cannon ball to pass harmlessly under his girth.

"Old Brains" Halleck, now Lee's opposite number, decided to try the original plan for 1862, a frontal advance from Washington on Richmond. To execute this, General John Pope, hero of Island No. 10, was summoned from the West to command a new army, composed in part of the veterans of the peninsula. Pope, with a stern countenance and great black beard, looked more like a great general than anyone in either army, but had slight military ability and less common sense. His first act on taking command was to issue an extraordinary set of orders to his men, contrasting their lack of success with his in the West, "where we have always seen the backs of our enemies." To the press he proclaimed, "My headquarters will be in the saddle!" Lincoln, on reading this, remarked, "A better place for his hindquarters."

Pope in mid-August began to concentrate along the Rappahannock, covering both Washington and the point on the Potomac to which McClellan's army was being rapidly transferred. Lee adopted a plan amazing in its audacity: to divide his army in the face of a far more numerous enemy, send Jackson by a circuitous route round Pope's right to attack the Union base at Manassas Junction, draw Pope away from his line of concentration, and fall upon him in the open.

On 26 August Jackson's "foot cavalry," having marched 50 miles in 36 hours, were between Pope and Washington, reveling in the Union stores at Manassas. Halleck and Pope, unprepared for this bold maneuver, made one blunder after another. Pope won the race with Lee to the old Bull Run battlefield, but, incapable of handling large numbers of men, and bewildered by attacks from unexpected quarters, was badly defeated in the Second Battle of Bull Run, or Manassas (29–30 August 1862). It was the neatest, cleanest piece of work that Lee and Jackson ever performed. Their irresistible combination of audacious strategy and perfect tactics had undone the Union gains of an entire year in the Virginia theater of the war. "Dark days are upon us. Pope, a lying braggart — has been driven into Washington. . . . The rebels again look upon the dome of the capitol," wrote Gustavus Fox at this crisis, "and the flag of disunion can be seen on the neighboring hills."

General Halleck, confounded by the rapid movements of the last few days, sat in the war department, perpetually rubbing his elbows and gazing with watery eyes at a mounting pile of dispatches. One bright thought came, to bring back McClellan, to his old command. On 1 September, as the news from the front became more and more alarming, McClellan conferred with Halleck and the President. Early next morning Lincoln, without consulting anyone, placed McClellan in "command of the fortifications of Washington, and of all the troops for the defense of the capital." The general at once rode out to meet Pope's retreating army, and to witness the wild enthusiasm that his presence always inspired among the troops.

In the meantime Lincoln had faced a tough cabinet meeting. Stanton and Chase vehemently opposed McClellan, and all but Seward and Blair concurred. Lincoln admitted most of their allegations but pointed out that no one else had the confidence of officers and men, or the ability to cope with so desperate a situation. "In stating what he had done," wrote Gideon Welles, "the President was deliberate, but firm and decisive. His language and manner were kind and affectionate, especially toward two of the members who were greatly disturbed; but every person present felt that he was truly the chief, and every one knew his decision, though mildly expressed, was as fixed and unalterable as if given out with the imperious command and determined will of Andrew Jackson."

Lincoln had attained new stature. Resolute in purpose and sure of vision he had always been; yet often vacillating and uncertain in performance. From those anxious vigils at the White House during the terrible summer of 1862 the perplexed, overadvised, and humble Lincoln emerged humble before God, but the master of men. He seemed to have captured all the greater qualities of the great Americans who preceded him, without their defects: the poise of Washington without his aloofness, the mental audacity of Hamilton without his insolence, the astuteness of Jefferson without his indirection, the conscience of John Quincy Adams without his harshness, the courage of Jackson without his irascibility, the magnetism of Clay without his vanity, the lucidity of Webster without his ponderousness; and fused them with a sincerity and magnanimity that were peculiarly his.

When, on 5 September, news reached Washington that Lee was crossing the Potomac at Sharpsburg above Harper's Ferry, Lincoln orally gave McClellan "command of the forces in the field."

6. Antietam and Emancipation

Of many crises for the Union, this was the most acute. General Lee, having persuaded President Davis to countenance a bold offensive, had decided to invade Maryland and Pennsylvania. If he could capture Harrisburg, there would be no railroad communication between Eastern cities and the West; he would cut the loyal states in two, as Burgoyne had attempted to do with the rebel states when he marched south from Canada in 1777. Additional objectives were food, shoes, clothing, of which northern Virginia had been swept clean, and to persuade Maryland, whose "dalliance does thee wrong," as the sentimental war song charged, to clothe her "beauteous limbs with steel" and "be the battle queen of yore."

Lee, counting on McClellan taking weeks to reorganize, ventured to divide the Army of Northern Virginia, sending Jackson to capture Harper's Ferry while he moved into Pennsylvania. But, within a week of Manassas, McClellan was marching on Frederick Town with 70,000 men, followed by frantic telegrams from Halleck to turn back and protect Washington. But McClellan kept on, reassured by picking up on 13 September a copy of Lee's plan of the campaign, dropped by some careless aide.

South Mountain, as the Blue Ridge is called where it crosses Maryland, now separated the hostile armies. Sending his van to force the passes, McClellan sat his horse Dan as in review by the roadside, pointing to where clouds of smoke showed that the Battle of South Mountain had begun. Men and officers as they passed cheered themselves hoarse, falling out of ranks to touch his leg, pat his charger and cry, "God bless you, Little Mac!" That day (14 September) South Mountain was carried. "I thought I knew McClellan, but this movement of his puzzles me," exclaimed his West Point classmate, Stonewall Jackson. Lee knew exactly what it meant, and hastened south just in time to prevent McClellan's interposing between his great lieutenant and himself. They joined on 16 September, but even so the Army of Northern Virginia was not only outnumbered but caught in a cramped position between Antietam Creek and the Potomac, where Lee had no room to perform those brilliant maneuvers that were his delight and the enemy's confusion. He had no alternative but to fight or to retreat, and he chose to fight.

The Battle of the Antietam, or Sharpsburg (17 September 1862) was a series of desperate, unco-ordinated attacks and equally desperate but skillful counterattacks that exhausted Lee's army but did not force it to retire. It was one of the bloodiest battles of the war. Of about 36,000 Confederates engaged, 10,700 were casualties, and three general officers were among the killed; of 87,000 troops under McClellan, only about half of whom were engaged, he lost 12,410. Although fresh reserves were available, McClellan refused to renew the battle next day, as Grant or Sherman would certainly have done. So Lee recrossed the Potomac into Virginia on the night of 18 September. The crisis was ended. Nevertheless, "Antietam's cannon long shall boom," as Herman Melville prophesied. The Union victory averted foreign recognition of Confederate independence; and by giving Lincoln the opportunity he sought to issue the Emancipation Proclamation, it brought the liberal opinion of the world to his side.

During the summer of 1862 the British government moved fast, impelled by many motives — desire to relieve unemployment before winter, a humane wish to stop the carnage, upper-class dislike of democracy, belief that the Confederacy was invincible. Napoleon III was eager to join. The British government's failure to prevent *Alabama* slipping out to sea from Liverpool in July was a hint of this change of policy. Palmerston wrote to his foreign minister on 14 September, "Washington or Baltimore may fall into the hands of the Confederates"; and Russell replied on the very day of Antietam, "I agree with you that the time is come for offering mediation to the United States government with a view to the recognition of the independence of the Confederates. I agree, further, that in the case of failure, we ought ourselves to recognize the Southern States as an independent state."

The news of Antietam caused Palmerston to cool off; and although Gladstone, chancellor of the exchequer, in a speech on 7 October (which later he took great pains to explain away) declared that Jefferson Davis had "made a nation," and that the Northern people "have not yet drunk of the cup which the rest of the world sees they nevertheless must drink," Britain moved not.

On the heels of the news that Lee had retreated into Virginia came the Emancipation Proclamation. Lincoln, with his uncanny sense of timing, chose the week after Antietam to issue this famous document. His policy as to the Negro had been stated in his famous Letter to Horace Greeley; but only a delicate perception of public opinion, and an accurate weighing of imponderabilia, could decide what action respecting the Negro would serve the Union best at a given time. Steps had been taken before Antietam. From the first advance into Confederate territory, slaves of rebel owners flocked into the Union lines, embarrassing both government and commanders, until the irrespressible Benjamin F. Butler declared them "contraband of war." The "contrabands" were then organized in labor battalions, and welfare workers were provided to look after them in the several occupied portions of the Southern coast where they congregated.

Loyal slave states had to be considered. Delaware, Maryland, Kentucky, West Virginia, and Missouri, sensitive on the subject, blocked proposals for compensated emancipation on which the President had set his heart. In April and June 1862 Congress carried out a Republican party pledge by abolishing slavery in the District of Columbia and the territories. Another long step was taken in the Confiscation Act of 12 July 1862 declaring "contrabands" and slaves of convicted rebels to be forever free, and authorizing the President to recruit Negroes for the army. Lincoln signed this bill only after it had been so modified as to make its application discretionary with him; for the President's war powers were involved. Lincoln rightly insisted on his exclusive power, as commander in chief of the army and navy, to decree a general emancipation in enemy territory. If Congress were able to wrest this power from him it might also dictate his war policy, and — what he feared most of all — impose a vindictive peace.

An even larger question intruded: of what avail to restore the Union if slavery, the original cause of disruption, remained? "The moment came," said Lincoln, "when I felt that slavery must die that the nation might live," when he hearkened to "the groaning of the children of Israel, whom the Egyptians keep in bondage" (Exodus vi.5). In the cabinet meeting of 22 July he proposed to proclaim that on next New Year's Day all slaves in rebel territory would be free. Seward pointed out that such a declaration at that time would be interpreted as "our last shriek on the retreat" from Richmond. Lincoln saw the point, and put aside the proclamation, on which he had been working nights, to be a crown to the next Union victory. Then, on 22 September, five days after Antietam, Lincoln opened a cabinet meeting by reading a completely irrelevant passage from the humorist Artemus Ward — his method of putting the cabinet in a receptive mind. He then turned serious. He had not summoned them for their advice. He had made a covenant with God to free the slaves as soon as the rebels were driven out of Maryland; God had decided on the field of Antietam. His mind was fixed, his decision made. In the preliminary Emancipation Proclamation, published next day, the President, by virtue of his power as commander in chief of the army and navy, declared that upon 1 January 1863 all slaves within any state then in rebellion against the United States, "shall be, then, thenceforward, and forever free."

This proclamation, more revolutionary in human relationships than any event in American history since 1776, lifted the Civil War to the dignity of a crusade. Yet it actually freed not one slave, since it applied only to rebel states where it could not be enforced. The loyal slave states, occupied New Orleans, and occupied parts of Virginia were excepted.[1] The South, indignant at what she considered an invitation to the slaves to cut their masters' throats, was nerved to greater effort; for it meant that only a Southern victory would prevent unconditional surrender. The Northern armies received from it no new impetus. The Democratic party, presenting it to the Northern people as proof that abolitionists were responsible for the duration of the war, gained seats in the autumn elections. A large section of the press, in the United States and Canada, adopted a cynical and sneering attitude toward the Proclamation. It remained for Emerson, as usual, to strike the tuning fork of the future, when at a celebration in Boston of Emancipation Day he declaimed:

> Today unbind the captive
> So only are ye unbound;
> Lift up a people from the dust,
> Trump of their rescue, sound!

In England and Europe generally, the Proclamation was hailed with joy by liberals and radicals. By degrees public opinion at home and abroad came to perceive that the Union cause had been definitely fused with that of human liberty. Pro-Union meetings were held in several English cities. One meeting of 6000 workingmen at Manchester resolved:

The erasure of that foul blot upon civilization and Christianity — chattel slavery — during your Presidency will cause the name of Abraham Lincoln to be honoured and revered by posterity. Accept our high admiration of your firmness in upholding the proclamation of freedom.

To which Lincoln replied:

I know and deeply deplore the sufferings which the working men at Manchester, and in all Europe are called to endure in this crisis. . . . I cannot but regard your decisive utterances upon the question as an instance of sublime Christian heroism which has not been surpassed in any age or in any country. . . . I hail this interchange of sentiment, therefore, as an augury that whatever else may happen, whatever misfortune may befall your country or my own, the peace and friendship which now exist between the two nations will be, as it shall be my desire to make them, perpetual.

1. Slavery was abolished by state action in West Virginia in 1863, in Maryland and Missouri in 1864, in Tennessee in 1865, and in Delaware and Kentucky the same year by Amendment XIII to the Constitution.

Emancipation created so strong a feeling abroad in favor of the North that neither England nor France dared take a step toward recognizing Confederate independence; and those elements who dearly wished for it had to admit that Antietam rendered the winning of that independence very unlikely — unless (a big "if") the North grew tired of the struggle.

7. Fredericksburg

After the Battle of Antietam the Army of Northern Virginia retreated up the Shenandoah valley. "The absent are scattered broadcast over the land," Lee wrote to the secretary of war on 23 September. "Unless something is done, the army will melt away." And the invasion of Kentucky, too, had proved disappointing; "We must abandon the garden spot of Kentucky to its cupidity," wrote General Braxton Bragg on 25 September. Two weeks later, Don Carlos Buell won a Western Antietam, at Perryville, and Bragg abandoned not only Kentucky but most of Tennessee.

General McClellan now reverted to "the slows." Instead of pursuing Lee, or following Lincoln's good advice to try to beat Lee to Richmond "on the inside track," the general demanded more supplies, clothing, and remounts before he would move. The prospect of another winter of bickering and procrastination was more than Lincoln thought the Union cause could bear. He decided that if McClellan permitted Lee to get between himself and Richmond, McClellan must go. On 26 October the Army of the Potomac began to invade Virginia. Lee promptly moved Longstreet's corps athwart its path, and on 7 November the President relieved McClellan, this time for keeps. It may well be argued that this was a mistake; that "Young Napoleon" was growing up at last, that nothing could have been worse than sending the Army of the Potomac to fruitless sacrifice under its new commander, General Ambrose E. Burnside.

But nobody could have imagined how incompetent Burnside would prove to be. A handsome West Pointer and Mexican War veteran, he had handled the Hatteras Inlet invasion well, and his corps at Antietam had rushed the bloody "Burnside bridge" against Hill, one of the crucial attacks in that battle. It is not unusual in war for an officer competent on one echelon to be a failure on the one next higher. The captain of a battleship may prove to be incapable of handling a task force, a division commander may be no good when placed over an army corps, and so on. Burnside, to do him justice, didn't want the new command, felt inadequate; but he went in and did his best, which unfortunately was very bad indeed.

Burnside decided to mass his army behind the Rappahannock opposite Fredericksburg, and thence advance on Richmond. Lee and Jackson hastened across northern Virginia and had some 75,000 men posted on the south bank before Burnside had obtained pontoons to cross the river. "The luxurious

Army of the Potomac, petted to bursting, is no match in celerity of movement to the famished freezing soldiers of Lee," wrote Gustavus V. Fox. Lee
took his stand on the wooded heights above Fredericksburg. There, on 13
December, he met an attack by Burnside's army of 113,000 that presented the
most inspiring spectacle and the most useless slaughter of the Civil War.
With insane stupidity Burnside refused to make flank attacks through the
forest, but delivered a frontal attack across open ground. Six times the Union
infantry — long double lines of blue, bright national and regimental colors,
bayonets gleaming in the sun — pressed on across a bare plain, completely
swept by the Confederate artillery and entrenched infantry, to the stone wall
at the foot of Marye's Heights. Six times the survivors were hurled back,
leaving thousands of killed and wounded lying literally in heaps. "It is well
that war is so terrible," said Lee as he watched the battle, "or we should grow
too fond of it."

On 15 December Lee consented to a brief truce to bury the dead and
relieve such wounded as had survived the day. Here the horror of the Brothers' War could be seen at its most horrible. According to an eye-witness,
Randolph A. Shotwell:

Eleven hundred dead bodies — perfectly naked — swollen to twice the natural
size — black as Negroes in most cases — lying in every conceivable posture —
some on their backs with gaping jaws — some with eyes large as walnuts, protrud-
ing with glassy stare — some doubled up like a contortionist — here one without a
head — there one without legs — yonder a head and legs without a trunk —
everywhere horrible expressions — fear, rage, agony, madness, torture — lying in
pools of blood — lying with heads half buried in mud — with fragments of shell
sticking in the oozing brain — with bullet holes all over the puffed limbs.

Four-fifths of them were victims of the deadly minié bullet; the rest, of the
Confederate artillery. Total losses were 12,653 for the Union, 5309 for the
Confederacy. On almost any other continent, to any European or Asiatic
army, Fredericksburg would have been a knockout; but not here. Burnside
retired beyond the Rappahannock and Lee wrote to his wife, "The battle did
not go far enough to satisfy me. . . . The contest will have now to be renewed, but on what field I cannot say." That was the dispiriting thing about
the Southern cause — no matter how often or how badly the Confederates
whipped a Union army, Lincoln refused to admit defeat.

Walt Whitman, who too was there, recorded,

That never did mortal man in an aggregate fight better than our troops at Fredericksburg. In the highest sense it was no failure. The main body troops descending the hills on the Falmouth side to cross the pontoon bridge could plainly see,
over back of Fredericksburg, the Secesh batteries rising in tremendous force and
plenty on the terrace required to our men's crossing . . . . and also the flats thick
with their rifle pits. . . . Nearer view on Saturday, the day of the fight, made
everything still more ominous to our side. But still the men advanced with unsur-
passed gallantry — and would have gone further, if ordered.

Thus the year 1862 closed for the Union in gloom, and for thinking men in the Confederacy, without much hope. The Northern congressional elections increased the Democratic delegation; defeatist Democrats were elected governors of New York and Pennsylvania. Lincoln confided to a friend on 19 December, "We are now on the brink of destruction."

Yet, looking back, one can see that the Union cause had come out of its slough. The year 1862 in the Civil War corresponded to 1942 in World War II — "the end of the beginning," to use Winston Churchill's phrase. The danger of foreign intervention had passed; the Confederacy would never have a maritime ally; the anaconda squeezed ever tighter. Numbers, immigration (84,000 from Europe alone in 1862, double next year), industrial organization, were beginning to count. The Union army had been tried in battle and found not wanting in valor; only generals competent to match wits and skill with Lee and Jackson had not yet been found. Lincoln was master in his own house. If the Northern will to victory and devotion to union could endure, the end could not longer be in doubt. People might sneer at the Emancipation Proclamation, but it gave the cause the dignity of a crusade. Julia Ward Howe, in the darkness of her tent after viewing "the watchfires of a hundred circling camps," scribbled down the words in which she caught the new spirit, and which were to be sung to the stirring cadence of "John Brown's Body":

BATTLE HYMN OF THE REPUBLIC

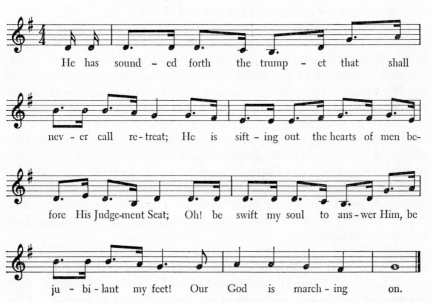

He has sound – ed forth the trump – et that shall nev – er call re – treat; He is sift – ing out the hearts of men be- fore His Judge-ment Seat; Oh! be swift my soul to ans - wer Him, be ju - bi - lant my feet! Our God is march - ing on.

At Home and Abroad

1861-1865

1. *Internal Politics, North and South*

LINCOLN WIELDED a greater power throughout the war than any other President of the United States prior to Franklin D. Roosevelt; a wider authority than any British ruler between Cromwell and Churchill. Contemporary accusations against him of tyranny and despotism read strangely to those who know his character, but not to students of his administration. Lincoln came near to being the ideal tyrant of whom Plato dreamed, yet nonetheless he was a dictator from the standpoint of American constitutional law. Jefferson Davis is open to the same charge. And on both sides there were many men of high standing who preferred to risk defeat at the hands of the enemy rather than submit to arbitrary government.

At the beginning of the war, Lincoln as commander in chief of the army and navy called for enlistments not yet sanctioned by Congress, declared a blockade, and suspended the writ of habeas corpus in parts of Maryland. The first assumption of power was quickly made legal by Congress and the second by the Supreme Court; but Chief Justice Taney protested in vain against executive suspension of the famous writ (ex parte *Merryman*). Lincoln refused to indulge a meticulous reverence for the Constitution when the Union was crumbling. As he put it in his message of 4 July 1861, "Are all the laws but one to go unexecuted, and the government itself go to pieces, lest that one be violated?" But the power he asserted was grossly abused by some army officers. A loyal mayor of Baltimore, suspected of Southern sympathies, was arrested and confined in a fortress for over a year; a Maryland judge who had charged a grand jury to inquire into illegal acts of government officials was set upon by a provost marshal's guard while his court was in session, beaten, dragged bleeding from the bench, and imprisoned for six months; and there were many like incidents.

Simultaneously with the Emancipation Proclamation, Lincoln issued an order that seemed to deny white citizens the liberty that he proposed to accord to Negro slaves. He proclaimed that all persons resisting the draft, discouraging enlistment, or "guilty of any disloyal practice affording aid and comfort to rebels" would be subject to martial law, tried by the military, and denied the writ of habeas corpus. Under this proclamation, over 13,000 persons were arrested and confined by military authority, for offenses ranging from theft of government property to treason. Earlier in 1862, and only a few days after he had denounced Lincoln's tyranny, President Davis obtained from his congress the power to suspend the writ of habeas corpus, and promptly did so in Richmond and other places, where equally arbitrary and unjust proceedings occurred.

Undoubtedly the provocation was great, especially in the North, where opposition to the war was open, organized, and active. For instance, the Laconia (New Hampshire) *Democrat* attacked Lincoln and the war with a virulence equal to that of the most rabid Southern newspaper. This journal urged that Democratic Northern states combine with the Southern, toss out Lincoln with the Constitution, and adopt that of the Confederacy, "rather than submit to have the country divided and ruined to carry out the . . . selfrighteous nigger abstractions of a set of ignorant and hypocritical fanatics of New England." A religious sect, the Osgoodites, regarded the Lincoln administration as the Beast of the Book of Revelation, and sang a hymn beginning, "The Lincoln party made the war, we know."

One of the most delicate and difficult subjects with which both presidents had to deal was the peace movement. Many sincere people on both sides believed that the Union could be restored, or Southern independence established, by negotiation; that only the obstinacy of Lincoln or the ambition of Davis stood in the way of peace. The "copperheads," as the Northern defeatists were called, held a mass meeting in Lincoln's home town on 17 June 1863, which resolved "that a further offensive prosecution of this war tends to subvert the Constitution and the Government." In North Carolina over 100 peace meetings were held within two months after Gettysburg, to promote negotiations for reunion. On both sides the defeatists organized secret societies. In the Middle West "Knights of the Golden Circle" harassed loyal households by midnight raids and barn-burnings; in the South "Heroes of America" gave aid and comfort to the Union. Neither government made any systematic effort to suppress these organizations: they were too formidable.

In Ohio, Indiana, and Illinois, where treason flourished side by side with the most stalwart loyalty, General Burnside attempted repression in 1863 with slight success. In a general order he declared, "The habit of declaring sympathy for the enemy will not be allowed in this department." For violating this order in a campaign speech, the most prominent copperhead, Clement L. Vallandigham, was arrested, tried by a military tribunal, and sentenced to confinement for the duration of the war. Lincoln humorously altered the sentence to banishment within the military lines of the Confederacy, whither Vallandigham was escorted in May 1863.[1] But it took more than that to

1. Vallandigham's declaration that "he did not want to belong to the United States" prompted Edward Everett Hale to write *The Man Without a Country*. This piece of fiction, which appeared in the *Atlantic* in December 1863, was widely republished, and did more to stimulate patriotism than any other wartime writing.

silence Vallandigham. After assuring Jefferson Davis that if the South could hold out another year the Northern Democrats "would sweep the Lincoln dynasty out of political existence," he made his way to Canada, received *in absentia* the Democratic nomination for governor of Ohio, conducted a peace campaign from Canadian soil, and returned in time to draft the defeatist plank in the Democratic platform of 1864.

After the war was over the Supreme Court took cognizance of a case of arbitrary arrest and court-martial (ex parte *Milligan*), and declared that neither the Constitution nor any stretch of the President's war powers sanctioned the military trial of a civilian in districts where civil courts were open. This decision came too late to help anybody. Yet, on the whole, defeatists, conscientious objectors, the hostile press, and violent critics of the government, fared better under the Lincoln regime than under those of Woodrow Wilson and Franklin D. Roosevelt. Throughout the Civil War active disloyalty was effectively dealt with wherever it raised its head; but there was no general censorship of the press, no "relocation" of suspects; and discussion of leaders and war aims remained open, unrestrained and often ill-informed, libelous, and nasty. Sentences of courts-martial were comparatively mild, and offenders were pardoned with the coming of peace.

In the Confederacy there were no organized political parties, but Vice President Alexander H. Stephens of Georgia came very close to an opposition leader. Endowed with a superior mind, Stephens made several wise statements about the war; but in his loyalty to political abstractions he resembled John Randolph of Roanoke, and his thin body, falsetto voice, and waspish speech suggested that he suffered under a similar disability. Stephens hated the war, hated Davis, and hated Richmond, so much so that he absented himself for 18 months from his official post as president of the senate. Stephens conducted a campaign against the government for subverting the liberty it was supposed to protect, and encouraged state governors to resist conscription. This sniping campaign was directed by Linton Stephens, a member of the Georgia house of representatives, who went so far as to write to his brother in October 1863 that President Davis was "a little conceited, hypocritical, sniveling, canting, malicious, ambitious, dogged knave and fool." The Stephenses worked hand-in-glove with Governor Joseph E. Brown of Georgia, who obstructed the Confederate conscription laws in many ways and by 1864 had brought his state to a mental condition akin to open revolt. Barnwell Rhett of South Carolina, the original secessionist, even planned a convention of the states to depose Davis.

Governor Zebulon B. Vance of North Carolina was another sharp thorn in Davis's side. He not only withheld troops from the Confederate service but did his best to retain for the North Carolina regiments all the uniforms manufactured in his state, and to take the pick of all supplies that entered Wilmington through the blockade. He had a bitter controversy with Davis over C.S.S. *Tallahassee,* a converted blockade runner which slipped in and out of Wilmington in 1864 to destroy merchant vessels. On one of her visits to her home port, the captain of *Tallahassee* filled his bunkers with steam coal which Vance wanted for a state-owned blockade runner. Vance accused Davis of hamstringing operations which would have relieved his people of their misery, in order to fuel a Confederate raider that only destroyed "a few smacks." Davis, when the Confederacy was on its last legs, had to report this silly controversy to the Confederate congress, and explain that the "insignificant smacks" were forty-six ships, nineteen of them square-rigged.

General Bragg, a few other Confederate commanders, and the governor of Texas, declared martial law in 1862, but President Davis revoked these orders as unwarranted assumptions of power. Nevertheless provost marshals infested the South, demanding passports, credentials, and loyalty oaths from all who excited their attention or suspicion. A more general subject of Southern discontent was the impressment of supplies for the army by the commissary department, when farmers refused to sell for Confederate money. This practice stripped many a Southern farm of corn and livestock; then Sherman's "bummers" came along and took the poultry too.

In the face of frequent, acrid, and unreasonable attacks, Davis maintained an admirable patience. He could be acid and querulous when commenting on Union acts and policies; but to his own people, no matter how great the provocation, he was always the high-minded, courteous gentleman.

2. *Troubled Waters*

In Europe the movement for mediation in the Civil War, which implied recognition of the Confederacy, raised its head again in the first half of 1863, before Gettysburg and Vicksburg. Recognition of the Southern Confederacy would have made no practical difference, since all maritime powers respected the Union blockade. The United States and Great Britain in the last fifty years have recognized many small nations in Europe, Asia, and Africa, which have been snuffed out without either country doing anything to protect them. But a *de jure* recognition of Southern independence would have been a prestige victory of immense value, and the two principal Confederate agents in Europe, Mason, and Slidell, pursued it vigorously by press subvention, personal interviews, and by selling Confederate bonds, which established a financial interest in Southern victory.[1] Mason, a provincial Virginian, made little headway in London, partly owing to his constant chewing of tobacco and letting the juice slobber over his chin and shirt. Slidell, a clever and subtle manipulator of men and money, found a sympathetic milieu in the somewhat raffish group which surrounded Napoleon III, and was even invited to dine at the Tuileries. But one needed a longer spoon than Slidell possessed

1. In Britain a Confederate loan of over £2 million, and in France an even bigger one, was floated, with cotton (to be delivered after the war) as security; and a large part of the domestic Confederate loan also was taken up by British investors.

to sup with "Napoleon the Little." He would gladly have recognized the South, but owing to many European commitments, and his wish to cultivate liberal opinion in France, he dared not do so without British support. And of that there was never a chance after the Emancipation Proclamation. So the Emperor's note to his ambassador in London in June 1863, to the effect that the time had come to recognize the Confederacy if the Union refused mediation, fell on barren ground.

Napoleon's Mexican adventure dictated his favoring the Confederacy as much as he dared. This adventure stemmed from a joint British, French, and Spanish naval demonstration before Vera Cruz to force the Juárez government to pay its foreign debts. Britain and Spain withdrew in April 1862 after discovering that Napoleon III intended to make the debts an excuse for taking over the country. Napoleon then poured some 30,000 troops into Mexico, who entered Mexico City in June 1863 and set up a puppet government which chose Maximilian, a young Austrian archduke as emperor.

Here was a new problem for Lincoln and Seward. Napoleon's intrusion of monarchy into Mexico was obnoxious in 1863 as, a century later, the intrusion of communism into Cuba, and equally a violation of the Monroe Doctrine; but they could do nothing about it but protest. Napoleon III was trying to do what Talleyrand and George Canning had attempted unsuccessfully, to extend the European balance-of-power system to America. Before Maximilian left Europe to assume his uneasy crown, he became the focus of a series of odd intrigues and shady deals. Napoleon persuaded him to turn over the Mexican states of Sonora and Lower California to France to exploit, retaining only nominal Mexican sovereignty, in return for more French aid; but Maximilian, after arriving in Mexico (May 1864), found this proposition so distasteful to his new subjects that he refused to honor it. Former Senator Gwin of California, who had defected to the South, tried to sell Napoleon a project to set up under his protection a colony of Confederate refugees and sympathizers in the states of Sonora, Chihuahua, Durango, and Taumalipas. The French emperor was favorable, but the Mexican emperor would have none of it. There is also a tradition (for which no substantial evidence can be found) that when the Confederacy was *in extremis* a Southern agent, claiming to act for President Davis, offered to cede Texas to France in return for recognition. However that may be, something equally crazy was seriously proposed to Jefferson Davis by the veteran journalist Francis Preston Blair in January 1865. He would reunite North and South on the basis of a joint crusade, spearheaded by the Confederate army under Davis's personal command, to overthrow Maximilian and restore the Republic of Mexico.

Spain's attitude, too, was important, as she still held Cuba and Puerto Rico, and had a respectable navy. The Spanish government at the outset of the Civil War was in the hands of an ambitious premier, General Don Leopold O'Donnell, duke of Tetuan. Although he followed England and

France in declaring neutrality and closing Spanish ports to prize ships, O'Donnell did a little fishing for Spain in the troubled waters of the Caribbean. Shortly before the firing on Fort Sumter, General Don Pedro Santana of the Dominican Republic endeavored to end the civil war in that unhappy land by offering to return it to Spain; O'Donnell accepted for his queen (and mistress) Isabella II, who made Santana her viceroy and awarded him a Spanish marquisate. Here was an even more spectacular violation of the Monroe Doctrine, about which Lincoln's government was unable to do anything but protest. In Santo Domingo the harshness and stupidity of Spanish rule defeated itself, a republican rebellion against the Spaniards erupted in 1863, O'Donnell's ministry fell, Spain agreed to withdraw her garrison early in 1865, and by the time Lee surrendered the Dominican Republic was restored.

One curious semi-diplomatic incident of the war was the simultaneous appearance of two Imperial Russian fleets in New York and San Francisco. Northerners took this to be a pro-Union demonstration, earnest of the Czar's intention to fight on their side if England or France helped the South. The Russian naval officers (one of whom was the composer Rimsky-Korsakoff) were entertained to capacity; but all that this visit signified was the Russian government's desire to have fleets at sea in case England went to war to help Poland, then in the midst of one of her many tragic rebellions.

A far greater menace to the Union than recognition, or fishing in American waters, was the building of warships for the Confederacy in British and French ports. After James D. Bulloch, Confederate navy agent in England, had hoodwinked the British foreign office and got C.S.S. *Alabama* and *Florida* out to sea, he made contracts with the Laird shipyard at Liverpool for two powerful double-turret seagoing ironclads, which were to be hurled against the Union blockading fleet. Charles Francis Adams, American minister at the Court of St. James's, frequently called Lord Russell's attention to the un-neutral destination of the Laird rams (as these vessels were called), but not until 3 September 1863, after the meaning of Gettysburg and Vicksburg had sunk in, were they detained. The Royal Navy subsequently purchased them, and they became H.M.S. *Scorpion* and *Wyvern*. Another ironclad fleet was being constructed for the Confederacy at Nantes and Bordeaux, Slidell having been given the official wink that Napoleon III would not interfere provided the destination were kept secret. A clerk whom the shipbuilders had fired tipped off the United States legation, which protested vehemently; and in February 1864, when the Emperor's confidence in Confederate victory had been shaken, he compelled the sale of these six ironclads to foreign powers. Bulloch succeeded in buying back one from Denmark, but as C.S.S. *Stonewall* she had only reached Cuba when the war ended.

In the meantime, *Florida* and *Alabama* had been romping around the Atlantic destroying almost every American merchantman they encountered. *Alabama* (Captain Raphael Semmes), most famous and successful of the Confederate commerce destroyers, with Southern officers and a British crew, even made an incursion into the Indian Ocean and sank a number of American ships pursuing the India and China trade. Her total score was 64 vessels, all but ten burned. The Union navy finally caught up with her in the shape of U.S.S. *Kearsage*, Captain John S. Winslow, who took station outside the port of Cherbourg, waiting for the raider to sortie, as Semmes had threatened to do. On a beautiful Sunday in June, as Captain Winslow was reading divine service on the quarterdeck, a lookout reported the *Alabama*'s masts pricking up over the horizon. Winslow with prayerbook in hand ordered his men to battle stations, closed to half a mile, and opened fire. The two ships fought broadside to broadside for 90 minutes. They were evenly matched in weight of metal, but Winslow's superior gunnery sank the Confederate cruiser before *Kearsage* was seriously damaged.

Florida (Captain J. N. Maffitt) managed to run the blockade in and out of Mobile, and converted a couple of her prizes to armed cruisers which, in June 1863, raised havoc among fishing vessels in the Gulf of Maine. They burned all their captures except the Gloucester fisherman *Archer*, to which Lieutenant C. W. Read csn transferred his armament and crew. Entering Portland, Maine, at night, Read surprised, boarded, and captured U.S. revenue cutter *Caleb Cushing* and in her put to sea. Before the cutter had a chance to operate under the Stars and Bars, she was cornered by a couple of sidewheel passenger boats commanded by the mayor of Portland, with soldiers and fieldpieces on board. Read abandoned and burned *Caleb*, surrendering to the mayor in steamer *Chesapeake*, whose adventurous war career had just begun.

An Indiana copperhead named Braine, with about fifteen fellow conspirators, some of them Canadian, took passage in *Chesapeake* on her regular New York-Portland run in December 1863, overpowered the crew and captured the ship, intending to take her to Bermuda for conversion to a Confederate privateer. After a game of hide-and-seek with Union patrol vessels along the Nova Scotia coast, she was captured inside the three-mile limit and towed by U.S.S. *Dacotah* into Halifax harbor. This "Second *Chesapeake* Affair" (with reference to 1807) was potentially as explosive as the *Trent* business, but Secretary Seward and the British minister in Washington handled it admirably, and the steamer was awarded by the vice-admiralty court at Halifax to her proper owner. Braine tried several similar exploits in the Caribbean, and his career as an international pirate continued for another half-century.

As the destruction of fishing schooners by *Florida*'s prizes indicates, the Confederate navy had adopted a policy similar to Grossadmiral Doenitz's integral tonnage doctrine in World War II. It mattered not what enemy ships you destroyed or where, so long as you made a score; if pursuit became too hot in one area, you moved to another. In pursuance of this dubious naval strategy, C.S.S. *Florida* was ordered to the Pacific Ocean in 1864, to prey on American whale ships. When she was coaling at Bahia, that port was raided by U.S.S. *Wachusett* (Commander Napoleon Collins), who captured *Florida* and towed her to Hampton Roads. Brazil protested and Secretary Welles

promised to return the raider; but before he could do so, she was "accidentally" rammed and sunk. C.S.S. *Shenandoah*, last of the raiders, now performed *Florida*'s original mission around Cape Horn, and continued (for
want of orders to the contrary) to destroy defenseless whale ships for several
months after the war was over.

The Confederate navy, with only a handful of commerce raiders, destroyed
257 vessels, about 5 per cent of the Union merchant fleet — only two of them
steamers — but caused over 100 more to be transferred to neutral flags. It
probably inflicted more relative damage than the German surface raiders in
the two world wars. All this destruction, however, was senseless, and the
Confederacy could have used its limited resources to better advantage elsewhere. There is no more striking example in history of the uselessness of a
third-rate navy, and the folly of trying to beat a maritime nation by mere
commerce destroying.

Relations between Canada and the United States became touchy again in
1863. "Skedadlers," as Union draft dodgers were called, took refuge in
Canada, Confederate prisoners escaped thither from prisons along the northern border, and Davis sent several well-heeled Confederate agents to Montreal and Quebec, seeking opportunities for mischief. On the other hand,
about 5000 Canadians were recruited for the Union army. With some 15,000
Confederates and active Southern sympathizers in Canada, a tense situation
arose, the reverse of that during the Canadian rebellion of 1837. A Confederate plot to seize U.S.S. *Michigan*, the single-gun American warship on Lake
Erie, and liberate Confederate prisoners in a camp on Johnson Island off
Sandusky, was thwarted in November 1863 by the vigilance of the governor-
general. But the most explosive incident in our Canadian relations came late
in 1864.

During October a score of young Confederate soldiers, passing as Canadian
sportsmen, infiltrated the town of St. Albans, Vermont, about fifty miles from
Montreal. After their leader had announced the annexation of St. Albans to
the Southern Confederacy, these merry raiders robbed the local banks of
some $200,000 in greenbacks, attempted to burn the town, and retired to
British territory where, hotly pursued by a sheriff's posse, all but five of them
were captured and handed over to Canadian authorities. This comic affair
came close to creating a serious breach, which perhaps was its real purpose;
Senator Clement C. Clay of Alabama, a Confederate agent in Canada, was
the organizer. If so, the United States very nearly fell into the trap. Abroga-
tion of the Rush-Bagot agreement and a naval building program on the Lakes
almost passed Congress. General John A. Dix USA, commanding the military
district to which Vermont belonged, ordered his troops, in the event of
another such raid, to pursue the culprits into Canada "and destroy them."
Dix's order set Canadian nerves jangling, and indignation was aroused on the
American side when the Montreal police magistrate before whom the captured raiders were arraigned, discharged them. In the end, Lincoln counter-

manded Dix, Canada stiffened her frontier guard, the complacent police magistrate was reproved, five of the raiders were rearrested (the rest escaped), and the incident caused a reaction in Canada in favor of the Union.

3. Conscription, Commerce, and Culture

During the winter of 1862–63 it became evident in Washington that unless old scruples against conscription were forgotten, the war would be lost. Congress on 3 March 1863 passed the first conscription act. It was a most imperfect law, a travesty of conscription. All men between the ages of twenty and forty-five had to register as liable to military service. As soldiers were needed, the number was divided among the states in proportion to their population, and subdivided among districts, giving credit for previous enlistments. In the first draft, credits wiped out the liability of most of the Western states, which had been forward in volunteering. Between each subsequent call and the actual draft, every state and district had fifty days' grace to reduce its quota by volunteering, after which the balance was obtained by drafting names by lot from the registered list. No attempt was made to levy first on younger men or bachelors; and instead of exempting specified classes such as ministers and heads of families, money payment was made the basis of exemption. One could commute service in a particular draft upon payment of $300, or evade service during the entire war by procuring a substitute to enlist for three years — no matter if the substitute died or deserted next day. The system was inequitable to the poor, and in the working-class quarters of New York the first drawing of names in 1863 was the signal for terrible riots.

The hatred of Irish-Americans for Negroes, which we have already noted, broke out viciously. Archbishop John Hughes, who later visited Europe to argue the Union cause with leading Catholics, warned the war department in 1861 that his Roman Catholic flock was "willing to fight to the death for the support of the constitution, the government, and the laws of the country," but not "for the abolition of slavery." The Emancipation Proclamation and the importation of Negroes to break a stevedores' strike caused Irish resentment to boil up into riot. On 13 July, while the names of draftees were being drawn from the urns, the provost marshal was driven from his office by a mob. Rioters controlled the streets during the better part of four days and nights, sacking shops and the homes of antislavery leaders, gutting saloons, lynching or torturing Negroes who fell into their clutches, burning mansions and a colored orphan asylum. Only the pleas of Catholic priests dissuaded them from burning the presidential lodge and other buildings of Columbia College. When the mob could find no more Negroes, they vented their rage on Chinese and Germans, or anyone who would not go along. Priests and the police (also mainly Irish) did their best, but it was not until troops were poured into the city that order was restored, after the loss of several hundred people killed and wounded, and a million dollars in property damage. This was equivalent to a Confederate victory, for Meade's army was so weakened by detachments for guard duty in Northern cities that he was unable to resume the offensive after Gettysburg.

Although there were three more drafts in 1864, a very small proportion of the Union army was furnished by direct conscription.[1] Every fresh draft began an ignoble competition between districts to reduce their quotas by credits, and to fill the residue by bounty-bought volunteers. As recruits were credited to the district where they enlisted, and not to that of their residence, several wealthy communities escaped the draft altogether. State agents scoured occupied portions of the South for Negro soldiers and even obtained men from the poorhouses of Belgium and the slums of Europe. Federal officials were bribed to admit cripples, idiots, and criminals as recruits. One can easily imagine the effect on the morale of a veteran regiment which received replacements of this sort.

War was the Confederacy's only business. Fighting for independence and race supremacy, the Southerners gave their government more, and asked less, than did the Northern people. Yet the latest generation of Southern historians has proved that selfishness, indifference, and defeatism played a great part in losing the "lost cause." And there was a shrewd instinct on the part of poor whites that it was "a rich man's war and a poor man's fight."

Confederate conscription, adopted in April 1862, was in theory a mass levy of Southern manhood between the ages of 18 and 35. Yet, instead of promoting solidarity, it fomented class antagonism. Although the law exempted conscientious objectors, railway employees, teachers, and the like, South Carolina of her own "sovereign" authority proceeded to extend the privilege and to assert the right of nullification in 1862 as roundly as in 1832. Congress was frightened into adding to the already numerous exempts, editors, printers, and plantation overseers at the rate of one to every twenty slaves. This "twenty-nigger law" created a mighty clamor from the poorer whites. Buying a substitute was allowed, as in the North, until the close of 1863, when the price of a substitute had reached $600. Shortly thereafter the Congress cut down exemptions and extended the age bracket to 17-50 years.

In June 1863, when the proportion of absentees from the Confederate army was approaching one-third, President Davis proclaimed an amnesty to deserters who would return to the colors. So few came in that the offer was repeated shortly after Gettysburg. The president may well have been right in his contention that the South would have been invincible had every white man done his duty.

1. From the draft of July 1863, and the three drafts of 1864, there were 776,829 names drawn; 402,723 were exempted for physical disability or paying the $300 commutation, 200,921 substitutes were bought, and the quotas were further diminished by 834,692 voluntary enlistments, so that the net number of draftees obtained amounted to only 46,347. The principal effect of the draft was to stimulate volunteering, because volunteers got bounties and draftees did not.

It was an article of faith in the Confederacy that Northern industry would collapse when cut off from its Southern markets and its supply of cotton. Northern industry, on the contrary, grew fat and saucy during the war. Union sea power, despite Confederate raiders, protected freight and passenger service to foreign markets. War's demands stimulated production: in Philadelphia alone 180 new factories were built during the years 1862–64. A government generous in contracts and lavish in expenditure helped to create a new aristocracy of profiteers, who became masters of capital after the war.[1] Paper money and the high protective tariff that Congress imposed as a counterweight to internal taxation brought a sharp rise of prices, which the government made no effort to control. Owing to the relatively slight development of labor unions, wages did not rise in the same proportion; average prices rose 117 per cent, average wages 43 per cent in 1860–65, and teachers' salaries even less. There was unemployment in cotton mills, but American factory operatives, more mobile and less dependent than their English fellows, returned to the farms whence many of them had come, or shifted into woolen and other industries; and after mid-1862 enough cotton was obtained from occupied parts of the South to reopen many closed cotton mills. The only important Northern industry that suffered permanently from the war was shipping, and during the war neutral shipping took its place.

In several ways the drain of men into the army and navy was compensated. Immigration during the five war years amounted to almost 800,000 people. Many labor-saving devices, invented earlier, were now generally applied. The Howe sewing machine proved a boon to clothing manufacturers, and a curse to poor seamstresses, whose wages dropped to eight cents an hour in 1864. The Gordon McKay shoe machine for sewing uppers to soles speeded up that process one hundredfold. Petroleum, discovered in Pennsylvania in 1859, was so rapidly extracted that production increased from 84,000 to 128 million gallons in three years, and exports of it to Great Britain in the year prior to October 1862 were valued at over £500,000. Refining methods were so rapidly improved that kerosene in cheap glass lamps began to replace candles and whale-oil lamps for lighting American farmhouses and English cottages.

Like causes speeded a revolution in Northern agriculture. The mechanical reaper, hitherto confined to the better prairie farms, came into general use, giving every harvest hand fivefold his former capacity with scythe and cradle. Westward migration and the opening up of new prairie cornlands were greatly stimulated by the passage of the Homestead Act in 1862, after almost forty years' agitation by agrarians and pioneers. Under this law the federal government presented a quarter section of public land (160 acres) to any

---

1. The foundations of fortunes laid during the war were: Armour (meat packing), Havemeyer (sugar), Weyerhaeuser (lumber), Huntington (merchandise and railroads), Remington (guns), Rockefeller (oil), Carnegie (iron and steel), Borden (milk), Marshall Field (merchandise), and Stillman (contraband cotton). There were even a few such in the South — the King Ranch of Texas, for instance.

bona fide settler for a nominal fee. Fifteen thousand homesteads,[1] including 25 million acres, were thus given away during the war. The annual pork-pack almost doubled, the annual wool-clip more than tripled between 1860 and 1865. Every autumn brought bumper crops of wheat and corn, and since England and Europe suffered a series of poor harvests, they turned to the United States, whence over 40 million bushels of wheat and flour were exported in 1862, as compared with less than 100,000 in 1859. Although the lack of cotton threw many English factory operatives out of work, it was evident that any attempt to break the blockade, and consequently fight the United States, would bring the British Isles face to face with famine. "Old King Cotton's dead and buried, brave young Corn is King," went the refrain of a popular song.

The Far West continued to grow throughout the Civil War. Colorado, the goal of "Pike's Peak or Bust" gold rush in 1859, was organized as a territory in 1861; Dakota and Nevada became territories the same year. Kansas became a state in 1861, as soon as Congress lost its Southern delegation; and Nevada was admitted prematurely in 1864 because the Republicans thought they needed her electoral vote. At least 300,000 emigrants crossed the plains to California, Oregon, and the new territories during the war — some to farm or dig gold, many to escape the draft. Mark Twain was one of those who went west after a few weeks' inglorious service in the Confederate army.

In the North generally, normal activities continued throughout the war. Social functions were held as usual in the cities in winter; in Newport, Long Island, and Saratoga Springs in summer. New York City in September 1862 was less interested in the Battle of Antietam than in the trotting match for a purse of $5000 at a Long Island racecourse between the thirteen-year-old stallion Ethan Allen, great-grandson of Justin Morgan, and six-year-old George Wilkes, son of Hambletonian, who won. The Saratoga track opened in 1863. Kentucky gentlemen did not allow the war to interrupt their favorite sport, except in 1862 when General Kirby-Smith, with singular want of taste, encamped his Confederate army on the Lexington racecourse.

One of P. T. Barnum's greatest triumphs was staged at Grace Church, New York, on 10 February 1863 when "General Tom Thumb," his two-foot-five-inch midget, married the equally tiny Mercy Lavinia Warren Bump. It took two hours for carriages to deliver guests, who were described by the New York *Times* as "the elite, the creme de la creme, the upper ten, the bonton, the select few, the very FF's of the City, nay of the Country."

Enrollment in Northern colleges and universities dropped slightly, and fifteen new colleges were established in wartime, including Vassar, the Massa-

1. Over 10,000 were in Minnesota, although there was a serious outbreak of Sioux Indians there in 1862; 5000 in Wisconsin, Kansas, and Nebraska. In addition, these states sold hundreds of thousands of acres from their educational grants, and the Illinois Central Railroad sold in wartime almost one-third of the 2.6 million acres granted to it by the federal government.

chusetts Institute of Technology, LaSalle, Bates, Swarthmore, Cornell, and the University of Maine. Many bequests were obtained by the older institutions; Louis Agassiz even got a generous grant from the Massachusetts legislature for his new museum of zoology. The Harvard-Yale boat races, interrupted in 1861, were resumed in 1864, while Grant was besieging Petersburg.

Most of the Northern authors who were active before the war continued to write. Henry Thoreau, after a valiant defense of John Brown, succumbed to tuberculosis, and prematurely ended his quest for the lost hound, the turtledove, and the bay horse. His *Cape Cod* was published posthumously in 1864. Hawthorne lived just long enough to salute Longfellow's *Tales of a Wayside Inn* (1863) "with great comfort and delight." Every Northern man of letters except George Ticknor supported the administration and the war, "infernal" though most of them thought war to be. One of the youngest and most promising, Theodore Winthrop, was killed at Big Bethel, first of many battles lost by Ben Butler. Longfellow sought shelter from his private griefs and "the tumult of the times disconsolate" by translating Dante and writing a superb sonnet sequence on *The Divine Comedy*; the first volume appeared a month before Lee's surrender. Emerson, suffering poverty from falling royalties and lecture fees, turned his "serene, unflinching look" on anyone who proposed "any peace restoring the old rottenness," and enjoyed serving on the visiting board of West Point, where he concluded that "war is not the greatest calamity." Charles Eliot Norton ran the Loyal Publication Society (precursor of the syndicated column), which printed poems, articles, and opinions on the war, and sent them to 1000 different newspapers in the North.

Thomas Ball, a New England-born sculptor trained in Florence, spent the entire war working in Boston on his spirited equestrian statue of Washington, which was erected in the Public Garden in 1869. George Perkins Marsh, Vermont lawyer, congressman, and diplomat, composed, while American minister to Italy, his *Man and Nature* (1864), the bible of the conservation movement, pointing out from his observations at home and abroad the wasteful folly of destroying forests, making "the face of the earth . . . no longer a sponge, but a dust heap."

Walt Whitman wrote his incomparable sketches of the war while in active service as an army nurse. James Russell Lowell's second series of *Biglow Papers* had the merit of making people laugh at themselves, at England, and at the Rebels. Bancroft went ahead with his *History of the United States*; and Parkman, deeply chagrined that bad eyesight kept him out of the army, struggled along with his series on New France. Whittier continued to write poetry and to do war work, such as collecting money to relieve the unemployed English workers who had so nobly supported the Union. His purely fictitious "Barbara Frietchie" created a kindly feeling in the North toward Stonewall Jackson, and he was invited to visit the Army of the Potomac early in 1864 since (in the words of his host, Brigadier General Rice), "Your loyal verse has made us all your friends, lightening the wearisomeness of our march, brightening our lonely campfires, and cheering our hearts in battle when 'the flags of war like storm-birds fly.' " When a fellow Quaker confessed qualms of conscience to Whittier about supplying timber for U.S.S. *Kearsage*, then building at Kittery, the bard remarked, "My friend, if thee does furnish any of that timber thee spoke of, be sure that it is all sound!" Bryant, who sturdily and elegantly edited the New York *Evening Post* throughout the war, published another *Thirty Poems* in 1864, more than half a century after his first imprint. The Northern magazines, especially *The Atlantic Monthly* (edited by James B. Fields), *The North American Review* (edited by Lowell and Norton), *Scientific American, Harper's Monthly* and *Weekly* (edited by George William Curtis) maintained their already high standards; and before the war ended a fund of $100,000 was raised to start the weekly *Nation*, with Edwin L. Godkin as editor.

In the South the war effort absorbed everything; the only Confederate literature that has endured are a few poems by Timrod, Sidney Lanier, and Paul Hamilton Hayne, and an excellent *Life of Stonewall Jackson* (Richmond 1863) by John Esten Cooke. The one original novel of the Confederacy, by Augusta Jane Wilson, *Macaria, or Altars of Sacrifice* (Richmond 1864), gives an idealized picture of Virginia society before the war; the hero, mortally wounded in the peninsular campaign, dies happy when he hears that McClellan is whipped. Numerous reprints of English novels, mostly of "high life" (*East Lynne, or the Earl's Daughter; Lady Audley's Secret,* etc.), were published, and a few translations of French works, notably Victor Hugo's *Les Miserables*, which became so popular that the soldiers of the Army of Northern Virginia jokingly called themselves "Lee's Miserables." Two periodicals lived a precarious existence. De Bow's *Commercial Review* catered to Southern self-esteem with articles on "The Puritan and the Cavalier," and Timrod's "There's Life in the Old Land Yet." *The Southern Literary Messenger* kept a fairly high standard in articles of a general nature, giving its readers an opportunity to escape from the war by reading on Life in Japan, and Faraday's Experiments in Science. Both expired in the summer of 1864. Confederate literary output consisted largely of sermons on the death in battle of sundry "Christian soldiers," sentimental war poems and songs, paperback accounts of the war, and schoolbooks, largely reprints of those which Southern schools had been buying from Northern publishers. An original exception is *The New Texas Primary Reader* (Houston, 1863), which declares Texas to be "an empire of itself," has a table of pronunciation of difficult Spanish and Indian place names (Guadalupe = "Warloop"), and promises "little reader" that if he is a good boy he may some day be governor of Texas.

Texas could afford to be smug. Distant from the scene of conflict, uninvaded until 1865 (except by the Comanche on her western frontier), she always had plenty to eat, and many luxuries imported via Mexico. East of the Mississippi, and in Missouri where local vendettas were most vicious, the people began to feel the pinch of poverty and undernourishment in 1863–64.

This requires explanation, since the Confederacy was primarily an agricultural country, food production rose as an increasing proportion of cotton fields were planted with corn and wheat, and there was no lack of labor. The slaves generally remained loyal and at work until a Union army appeared in the neighborhood.

But transportation was wanting. That was the weakest point in the Confederate economic organization; yet the South in 1860 was as well provided with railroads as the North. Through traffic encountered many bottlenecks and even breaks, where goods had to be transported by wagon from one station to another. Congress appropriated money to construct missing links, but little was accomplished, and the few rolling mills and foundries were too busy with government work to replace outworn railway equipment. Main lines could be kept going only by cannibalizing branch lines; junctions became congested with supplies, and breakdowns were frequent. That is why a women's bread riot occurred in Richmond in 1863 when the barns of the Shenandoah valley were bursting with wheat, and why government clerks had to pay $15 a bushel for corn that was bringing the farmer only a dollar in southwestern Georgia. Blockade-run coffee cost $5 a pound in Richmond.

As an example of plenty in parts of Virginia, one may recount the experience of young Randolph Barton, who enlisted in the Stonewall Brigade at the age of seventeen (bringing two horses and a Negro groom with him) and ended the war as a major. Furloughed after receiving his sixth wound, in the Wilderness campaign, he first convalesces with friends at Staunton; then, owing to Sheridan's advance up the valley, seeks refuge with Colonel Massie in the highlands of Albemarle County:

This establishment was typical of Southern life. It had never been visited by either army. It was a beautiful farm just at the foot of the mountain, which rose with some grandeur back of it or to the west, protecting it from the cold blasts of winter. All varieties of cultivation were to be seen on the rolling hills and fertile meadow bottoms. . . . The Negroes were around in the usual large numbers, docile and attentive. Gardens, lawns and orchards surrounded the house, and on all sides were evidences of peace and plenty. And to crown all was the unbounded hospitality of Colonel and Mrs. Massie and their family, the chief ornament of which was their pretty daughter, Miss Florence. Think of a tiresome day's journey crowned by such a reception, a bountiful Virginia supper and a spotlessly clean and far-retired chamber, and one can understand into what luxurious oblivion I sank about nine o'clock. I remember so well the beauty of the next morning. Dew, sunlight, shadows, sparkling water, a full feeling of refreshment, safety, an incomparable breakfast and three exceedingly pretty girls all to myself; and the enjoyment of all justified by a painlessly-healing, honorable wound! I record these incidents to show that the dark clouds of war sometimes lifted and we basked once in a while in glorious sunlight.

Nor was this the first, or the last, of such happy interludes enjoyed by this gallant youngster during the war.

At the end of the war General Johnston obtained ample supplies in the Carolinas and Georgia for his retreating army, and President and Mrs. Davis, on their pathetic retreat from Richmond south, never wanted food or hospitality in regions that Sherman had not ravaged. But Lee's army, on the eve of Appomattox, was at the point of starvation because a whole trainload of supplies never reached it. The General himself had meat only twice a week and lived largely on corn bread and cabbage. Once, having invited a number of his officers to dine, he ordered his cook to prepare the best meal he could. The piece de resistance turned out to be a mess of cabbage, in the midst of which was a small piece of "middling," pork off the side of a hog. The guests, with noble self-restraint, declined the meat, so the General did too. Next day he ordered his man to produce it. The cook admitted, "Marse Robert, de fac' is, dat ar middlin' was borrowed middlin'. We-all didn't have none, and I done paid it back to de place where I got it!" So General Lee, with a sigh, pitched into another meal of cabbage.

The ruling class in the South, which had most at stake, gave all it had to the cause. In the North able-bodied young men of means and position could remain in civvies without incurring social stigma; in the South the women saw to it that there were no gentlemen slackers. The patriotism of the Southern ladies was only equalled by their devotion. Left in charge of plantations, they had to direct the necessary change from cotton-raising to food production, to revive household industries such as spinning, weaving, and dyeing, to extract nitrates from the earth of cellars and smokehouses, to care for wounded soldiers, and feed passing armies. Yet those who remained on their plantations fared well in comparison with refugees and government clerks at Richmond, where the speculators and their wives, dressed in the latest Parisian fashions and drinking expensive wines imported in blockade runners, offered as great a contrast to their own penurious lives as the more bloated profiteers of New York did to the Northern wage-earner. For, as Rhett Butler remarked in *Gone With the Wind*, there is as much money to be made out of a losing cause as from a winning one.

Richmond society remained gay and hospitable despite high prices. "You can always buy an egg for a dollar," wrote the editor of the *Examiner*. Baron von Borcke, a volunteer on Jeb Stuart's staff, introduced the German cotillion. Vizetelly, war correspondent for the *London Illustrated News*, helped the ladies plan charades and private theatricals; officers from the Army of Northern Virginia would gallop into town night after night, to attend dances and dinners, and get back to camp in time for reveille. General Lee encouraged all this: "Go on, look your prettiest," he wrote to a committee of Richmond ladies, "and be as nice to them as ever you can be."

Although many, many instances of selfishness, indifference, incompetence, and defeatism on both sides, can be quoted, one main fact stands out: — no earlier war in history drew out so much sacrifice, energy, and heroism as this. Vice President Stephens divined the situation at the beginning of 1863 when he wrote: "The great majority of the masses both North and South are true to the cause of their side. . . . A large majority on both sides are tired of the war; want peace. But as we do not want peace without independence, so they do not want peace without union." Remember, too, that the average American then, as now, loathed army life, and only accepted it because of social and patriotic compulsion. Both Union and Confederate soldiers sang, "When This Cruel War Is Over," and both rejected the "fighting" ballads printed by patriots behind the lines. Yet both fought vigorously to the end.

"War, when you are at it, is horrible and dull," wrote thrice-wounded Captain Oliver Wendell Holmes, Jr. "It is only when time has passed that you see that its message was divine. I hope it may be long before we are called again to sit at that master's feet. But some teacher of the kind we all need. In this snug, over-safe corner of the world we need it, that we may realize that our comfortable routine is no eternal necessity of things, but merely a little space of calm in the midst of the tempestuous untamed streaming of the world, and in order that we may be ready for danger." Of his generation he wrote, twenty years after the war, "Through our great good fortune, in our youth our hearts were touched with fire." Alas that for so many, many thousands on both sides that fire was snuffed out with life itself; but in Holmes it burned bright and high for a long lifetime, so that young men who went to war in 1917 and even in 1941, were able to catch the flame from this noble master.

4. The Negro and the War

The attitude both of the Union and the Confederacy toward Negroes was ambiguous, inconsistent and even hypocritical, reflecting the unfortunate fact that the average Northern soldier, hardly less that the Southern, disliked any contact with a colored man which implied equality. Congress at first refused to allow free Negroes of the North to enlist in the Union army, and the influx of fugitive slaves into Union lines was an embarrassment. Benjamin F. Butler returned runaways to their masters when he invaded Louisiana in 1862, provided the masters were loyal. An effort was made to settle the "contrabands" on land deserted by its owners, but little land was available under Union control. Many were organized as labor troops, but most were simply kept alive in concentration camps.

After the Emancipation Proclamation it was only logical to allow Negroes to fight for their own freedom, and efforts were made to organize Negro regiments, not only from Northern freemen but from able-bodied contrabands. Butler mustered the first colored army corps in Louisiana in 1862; and, with the imagination that is a redeeming feature of that old rogue, called it Le Corps d'Afrique. This corps, with Negro officers, took part in the assaults on Port Hudson in 1863 and fought well. With incredible meanness, the Federal Congress for over a year set the colored private's pay at $7 per month, when white soldiers received $13.

One of the first states to organize colored regiments was Massachusetts; her

54th and 55th Infantry were recruited from all over New England, and in Philadelphia, and St. Louis. Longfellow found it an "imposing sight, with something wild and strange about it," to see the 54th swinging down the flag-decked streets of Boston on 28 May 1863, commanded by Colonel Robert Gould Shaw. They embarked for the South on the very wharf whence less than ten years earlier the fugitive Anthony Burns had been returned to slav-ery. Seven weeks later, while a foreign-born mob was lynching Negroes in New York City, Colonel Shaw's regiment had the place of honor in the five-regiment assault on Fort Wagner near Charleston, losing its commander, two-thirds of the officers, and nearly half the men. "Together," as the inscription on St. Gaudens's monument to Colonel Shaw in Boston reads, "they gave . . . undying proof that Americans of African descent possess the pride, courage and devotion of the patriot soldier."

To the Confederates, the use of Negro troops by the Union was a crowning indignity. Congress, on 1 May 1863, resolved that any white officer of colored troops, if captured, should be executed. Threats of retaliation prevented this from being carried out. The Confederacy, however, was just as ambiguous in its attitude as the Union. From the beginning of the war, both slaves and free Negroes were employed in the Southern army as cooks, body servants, team-sters, and labor troops, in war industries such as the Tredegar and Selma Iron Works. Many of these were enlisted in the army and drew army pay. (Gen-eral Lee was much amused by an enlisted cook explaining his absence of wounds: " 'Cause I stays back wid de ginerals!") In 1862 several Southern states, and next year the Confederate government, authorized the impress-ment of slaves for war work; and in February 1865 Secretary Mallory reported to Congress that out of 2225 workers employed in the Confederate navy's shore establishments, 1143 were Negroes. But the rulers of the South gagged at allowing Negroes to bear arms for the Confederacy.

General Lee on 10 March 1865 wrote to the president urging the enlist-ment of slave soldiers, provided both slave and owner volunteered. Davis then signed a bill calling on the states to provide 300,000 more troops irrespective of color, but including a certain proportion of slaves between the ages of eighteen and forty-five. Even these were not to be emancipated; and, except for two companies organized in Richmond, none had been recruited before Lee's surrender.

As one of Davis's adoring biographers has admitted, he did everything too late. In 1865 he sent a special envoy to London with power to promise abolition in return for British recognition. An amazing offer, considering that the Confederate constitution embalmed slavery! Could even Davis have per-suaded his people to give up the basis of their society? But he did not have to ask, since the British government never contemplated the recognition of a tottering Confederacy to further an emancipation which Lincoln had already announced, if not effected.

The Campaigns of 1863-1864

1. *Chancellorsville and Gettysburg*

AFTER FREDERICKSBURG, beaten Burnside was relieved as commander of the Army of the Potomac by "brave, handsome, vain, insubordinate, plausible, untrustworthy" General Joseph Hooker, another good corps commander who failed higher up. Plenty of valor had "Fighting Joe" — thrice promoted for bravery on the battlefield in the Mexican War. Since Fredericksburg he had been so outspoken in criticism of brother officers and the government that the President, upon appointing him to the new command, read him a little lecture on conduct: "I have heard of your recently saying that both the army and the government needed a dictator. Of course it was not for this but in spite of it that I have given you the command. Only those generals who gain successes can set up as dictators. What I ask of you is military success, and I will risk the dictatorship." Hooker took in good part this reproof, surely one of the most singular ever sent by a chief of state to a general. He did much to restore the morale and improve the organization of the Army of the Potomac, but he began boasting of what he would do to Lee. What Lee did to him is history.

This was at the Battle of Chancellorsville, scenario for Stephen Crane's *The Red Badge of Courage*, and subject of John Bigelow's great battle monograph. It was fought largely in a wilderness a few miles west of Fredericksburg. Hooker's sound plan for a double envelopment of Lee's army was checked by stout Confederate defense on 1 May, and this seemed to take all the wind out of his sails. While he reformed defensively, Lee adopted the brilliant strategy of dividing his army, inferior in numbers to Hooker's, and sending Stonewall Jackson, with more than half of it, by circuitous roads to attack General O. O. Howard's XI Corps on the Union right flank. Cavalry under the General's nephew Fitzhugh Lee had reconnoitered this flank and found it to be "hanging in the air," with no defenses or natural obstacles to the west or south. At 4:00 a.m., 2 May, this bold movement began, and it took all of a hot and dusty day to complete. Although observed by the Union balloonists and others, Hooker fatuously estimated it to be a retreat. At 4:00 p.m. Jackson's 25,000 men began to deploy in the forest within a mile, and across a clearing, from Howard's unsuspecting troops who were cooking supper, playing cards, or lounging.

General Jackson sat on Little Sorrel, watch in hand. At 6:00 p.m. he gave

676

the word. The woods rang with bugle calls and the skirmishers in gray sprang forward, followed by the battle lines. So rapid was the advance, so complete the surprise, that the first intimation Howard's troops had of Stonewall's forward surge was a flurry of rabbits, foxes, and deer, driven from the forest ahead of the Confederates. In ten minutes' time the whole Union right was in panic-stricken rout. Earlier in the war, this would have led to complete disaster, and only individual valor now saved the Army of the Potomac. Hooker seemed to forget the very rudiments of strategy, while Lee chose time and place of attack. After two days of it, Hooker retreated across the Rappahannock with some 37,000 troops still uncommitted.

The Chancellorsville victory, however, was too dearly won. During the moonlit night that followed the surprise, Jackson and his staff, returning to their lines after a reconnaissance, were mistaken for Union cavalry by a trigger-happy regiment, and swept with a deadly volley. Jackson received two bullets in the left arm near the shoulder, crushing the main artery. In an improvised field hospital the arm was amputated, the general was removed to a house at Guiney's Station, attended by his wife and a Richmond surgeon, and prayed for by the entire army — General Lee "wrestled in prayer" all night for Jackson's life. But pneumonia set in, followed by pulmonary embolism, and the intrepid commander sank into death, and deathless fame. His last words were, "Let us cross over the river and rest under the shade of the trees."

Above the pompous official obituaries Jackson himself would probably have preferred the impromptu tribute by General Grant when, a year later, he rested in the very house where Stonewall had died :"He was a gallant soldier, and a Christian gentleman."

Lee was soon ready for another spring at the Keystone State, Pennsylvania. Others high in Confederate councils doubted the wisdom of an offensive at that juncture, when Vicksburg and the entire West were hanging in the bight, but political considerations forced Davis's hand. Victory in Pennsylvania might undermine Union morale, encourage (as Lee wrote) "the rising peace party in the North," even gain European recognition. It was a bold game for the highest stake, but Davis was not a bold player. He could not make up his mind to weaken Bragg's or Johnston's armies, or to strip Richmond and the Carolinas. So Lee moved northward (3 June 1863) with only 76,000 men, while 190,000 Confederate troops were deployed between the Mississippi and the Rappahannock.

General Hooker on 28 June, the day after Lee had the entire Army of Northern Virginia in Pennsylvania, conferred a benefit on the Union cause by resigning. Lincoln turned over the army to another corps commander, General George Gordon Meade. For once, "swapping horses in midstream," as Lincoln called it, was justified. Meade was the very type of good working-horse general, sound in judgment, realistic, certain to do nothing foolish if unlikely to perform anything brilliant. An irascible disciplinarian, he "made people jump around," recorded a member of his staff; and his good eye for terrain, and power to make a quick decision in a fluid tactical situation, saved the day at Gettysburg.

Davis may have hoped that the mere presence of Lee's army in Pennsylvania would force Lincoln to negotiate on the basis of independence; for Davis entertained some peculiar ideas at this time. He told a visiting guards officer from the British army, that "most of the intelligent people" in the State of Maine were planning to secede and join Canada, in order to get out from "under the thumb" of Massachusetts! But the North showed no sign of flinching. Democratic as well as Republican governors promoted volunteering; state militia and even civilians turned out in large numbers to protect the Pennsylvania cities. Grave anxiety was felt, but no panic; and Lincoln did not recall a single unit from the West.

On 29 June, when the Army of Northern Virginia was spread over a wide arc between Chambersburg and Harrisburg, Lee still had no clear idea of where his enemy was — "Jeb" Stuart having gone off on one of his stunt rides. So Lee ordered the Army of Northern Virginia to concentrate on the eastern slope of South Mountain, near Cashtown. There, in a strong defensive position, he proposed to await attack. Meade intended to take a defensive position and let Lee attack him. But chance placed the great battle where neither general wanted it. On 30 June a unit of A. P. Hill's corps, covering Lee's concentration, marched toward Gettysburg in search of shoes, of which the Confederate troops were always short. Boots and saddles were there — on one brigade of General John Buford's cavalry division, which held up the Confederates two miles outside the town. Gettysburg commanded important roads, and each army was so eager for action that this chance contact drew both as to a magnet, into the quiet little town. There, on 1 July, the great three-day battle began, each unit joining in the fray as it arrived.

The first day went ill for the Union. A. P. Hill and Ewell drove the Union I Corps, General Winfield Scott Hancock, through the town. In the nick of time, Hancock rallied the fugitives on Cemetery Hill, where Howard had had the foresight to plant his XI Corps. This position, with its like-named Ridge, proved to be admirable for defense: a limestone outcrop shaped like a fish-hook, with the convex side turned west and north, toward the Confederates. Along it Meade placed the Union army as rapidly as it arrived from the south and east, while the Confederates took up an encircling position, the right on the partly wooded Seminary Ridge parallel to the Cemetery.

Lee decided to attack the following day, 2 July. His great opportunity for a double envelopment of the enemy came that morning. Before half the Union army was in position, Ewell captured a part of Culp's Hill, on the Union right — the barb of the hook — but Longstreet's corps arrived too late (it always did) to do much against the Union left. It drove in Sickles's III Corps which had incautiously occupied a knoll in advance of Cemetery Ridge, but III Corps retired to Little Round Top — the eye of the hook — possession of which would have enabled Confederate artillery to enfilade the entire Union

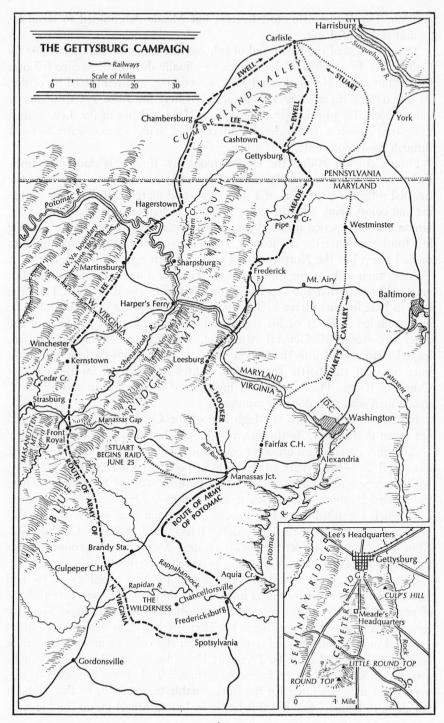

THE GETTYSBURG CAMPAIGN

Railways

Scale of Miles

0   10   20   30

Harrisburg

Carlisle

Susquehanna R.

EWELL

STUART

CUMBERLAND VALLEY

Chambersburg

LEE

EWELL

York

Cashtown

Gettysburg

PENNSYLVANIA

MARYLAND

MEADE

Hagerstown

Antietam Cr.

SOUTH

Pipe Cr.

Westminster

Potomac R.

W. Va. boundary June 1863

Martinsburg

Sharpsburg

Frederick

Mt. Airy

STUART'S CAVALRY

Baltimore

LEE

Harper's Ferry

W. VIRGINIA

MTS.

Shenandoah R.

Nov. 1863

Winchester

Leesburg

Kernstown

MARYLAND

Patuxent R.

Cedar Cr.

VIRGINIA

RIDGE

HOOKER

Strasburg

D.C.

Manassas Gap

BLUE

Washington

Front Royal

Fairfax C.H.

MASANUTTEN MT.

Bull Run

Alexandria

STUART BEGINS RAID JUNE 25

Manassas Jct.

ROUTE OF ARMY OF POTOMAC

Potomac R.

ROUTE OF ARMY OF

Brandy Sta.

Rappahannock R.

Culpeper C.H.

Aquia Cr.

N. VIRGINIA

Rapidan R.

Chancellorsville

THE WILDERNESS

Fredericksburg

R.

Gordonsville

Spotsylvania

Lee's Headquarters

SEMINARY RIDGE

Gettysburg

CULP'S HILL

CEMETERY RIDGE

Meade's Headquarters

Rock Cr.

LITTLE ROUND TOP

ROUND TOP

0   1 Mile

679

position. The Union army lost heavily; but Meade determined to stand his ground and fight it out.

The third day of the battle and of July opened with a desperate struggle for Culp's Hill, from which Ewell's corps was finally dislodged. Silence fell over the field at noon. Meade guessed what was coming, and reinforced his center. At one o'clock there came a preparatory artillery fire from 172 Confederate guns, which did surprisingly little damage. Deep silence again. Lee, against Longstreet's protest, had ordered a direct attack across open country to break through the Union center.

From Cemetery Ridge, the Union troops saw three gray-clad battle lines, Pickett's, Pettigrew's, and Trimble's divisions, 15,000 strong, issue from the wooded ridge three-quarters of a mile away, and march with bayonets glittering and colors flying into the valley between. When less than halfway across, Union artillery opened up on them. A little nearer they came under a raking fire from the batteries on Round Top. The Confederates' flank divisions melted away; but the Northern troops, peering through the smoke, could see Pickett's men still coming on the double. Lost for a moment in a swale, they emerged so near that the expressions on their faces could be seen. Then the boys in blue let them have it. Two of Pickett's brigadiers were killed and he was wounded. Fifteen of his regimental commanders were killed, and the other five wounded. General Armistead, with cap raised on sword-point, leaped a stone wall into the Union lines; 100 men followed him, and for a brief moment the battle flag of the Confederacy floated on the crest of Cemetery Ridge. Then the Union lines closed in relentlessly and all Armistead's men were shot down or captured.

Pickett's charge marked the high tide of the Confederacy, but defeat did not mean destruction. As the survivors limped back to Seminary Ridge, the Union army expected an order for counterattack; but Meade refused. All next day — 4 July — Lee remained defiantly in position. That evening his army, with baggage and prisoners, retired to a position west of Sharpsburg. There the flooded Potomac stopped his retreat, and gave Meade a second opportunity, which Lincoln begged him to seize. "Act upon your own judgment and make your generals execute your orders," telegraphed Halleck. "Call no council of war. . . . Do not let the enemy escape." Meade called a council of war (12 July), the Potomac subsided, and two days later the enemy escaped.

Lee was too candid to congratulate himself for having got away. He had seen the flower of his army wither under the Union fire. He knew that all hope of peace that summer was gone, and he must have felt that slight hope for Southern independence remained. Yet after the battle, as before, his soldiers gathered only confidence and resolution from the calm countenance of their beloved "Marse Robert." To President Davis he wrote, "No blame can be attached to the army for its failure to accomplish what was projected by me, nor should it be censured for the unreasonable expectations of the public. I am alone to blame." Lee lost this battle by letting Stuart go on the loose, by not seizing opportunities that opened during the fighting, and by hurling his men to certain death across an open field covered by rifle and artillery fire. Burnside at Fredericksburg had not done much worse. Meade, placed in command of an army thrice whipped within a twelvemonth, on the eve of battle with the hitherto invincible Lee, fairly won the greatest battle of the war, even though he failed to deliver a knockout blow to a staggering enemy. And from the Wilderness to Appomattox he was the right arm of Grant.

On 19 November 1863, at the national cemetery on the battlefield of Gettysburg, Lincoln delivered his immortal address:

Fourscore and seven years ago our fathers brought forth on this continent a new nation, conceived in liberty, and dedicated to the proposition that all men are created equal.

Now we are engaged in a great civil war, testing whether that nation, or any nation so conceived and so dedicated, can long endure. We are met on a great battle-field of that war. We have come to dedicate a portion of that field as a final resting-place for those who here gave their lives that the nation might live. It is altogether fitting and proper that we should do this.

But, in a larger sense, we cannot dedicate — we cannot consecrate — we cannot hallow — this ground. The brave men, living and dead, who struggled here, have consecrated it far above our poor power to add or detract. The world will little note nor long remember what we say here, but it can never forget what they did here. It is for us, the living, rather, to be dedicated here to the unfinished work which they who fought here have thus far so nobly advanced. It is rather for us to be here dedicated to the great task remaining before us — that from these honored dead we take increased devotion to that cause for which they gave the last full measure of devotion; that we here highly resolve that these dead shall not have died in vain; that this nation, under God, shall have a new birth of freedom; and that government of the people, by the people, for the people, shall not perish from the earth.

2. Vicksburg

Let us now turn to great events in the Western theater of war, for these affected the eventual outcome even more than did the deadly battles in the East. Here was the situation on New Year's Day 1863: General Rosecrans's Army of the Cumberland had concluded the drawn battle of Murfreesboro or Stone River in middle Tennessee, with Braxton Bragg, after which both armies were too badly mauled to do anything for several months. Grant's Army of the Tennessee covered the important east-west railway from Memphis to a point beyond Corinth, Mississippi. His purpose was to open the Great River to New Orleans. Although both banks of it below Memphis were under Confederate control, there was nothing to oppose the passage of a Union fleet downstream until it reached Vicksburg, or upstream from New Orleans until it reached Port Hudson, Louisiana. At both points the line of bluffs that borders the valley touches the river itself. The Confederates fortified both ends of this natural defense which enabled troops and supplies from Arkansas, Louisiana, and Texas to cross the river.

Vicksburg was the most difficult nut to crack. Strongly fortified on a high bluff, the river front was impregnable to assault, and on the east the town was protected by the valley of the Yazoo river, intersected by countless backwaters and bayous. The Confederate commander here, with 56,000 troops at his disposal, was General John C. Pemberton, a Pennsylvania Quaker who unaccountably chose the United States Army for his career and, even less understandably, defected to the Confederacy, which he served very ill.

General Grant, after one check in December 1862, concentrated the Army of the Tennessee on the west bank of the Mississippi about twenty miles north of Vicksburg, and spent the wet months of the new year in fruitless attempts to outflank Pemberton in the slimy jungle of the lower Yazoo. There was no lack of amphibious activity, much of it of a confusing nature bordering on the burlesque — Confederates capturing ram *Queen of the West*, and Admiral Porter floating a dummy monitor past the Vicksburg batteries to draw their fire. Never a dull moment on the Western waters when Grant and Porter were in command!

Any other general would now have retired to Memphis with "baffled and defeated forces," as Jefferson Davis predicted Grant would do, but Grant was not that kind of general. In his judgment, "There was nothing left to be done but to go forward to a decisive victory." In order to advance he must cut loose from his base of supplies, march his army along the west bank of the Mississippi, cross over below Vicksburg to dry ground, and attack Pemberton from the rear. A bold plan, resembling Wolfe's strategy that won Quebec.

Grant's reputation was still under the cloud of Shiloh. He had failed to take Vicksburg. He was reported to be a drunkard. There was a vicious campaign against him in the Eastern press. Owing to this controversy, important people and busybodies visited Grant's simple headquarters to size him up. Everyone was impressed by his rough natural dignity despite his sloppy military *tenue*; they noted his strong, quick eye, square jaw, and quiet way of handling men. The Army of the Tennessee worked in perfect concert with the fresh-water navy. "Grant and Sherman are on board almost every day. Dine and tea with me often; we agree in everything," wrote Porter.

Grant's plan was audacious as any of Lee's, and he had difficulties such as Lee never encountered. The Army of the Tennessee marched along the west bank of the Mississippi to Bruinsburg, south of Grand Gulf, where there was an easy crossing. Porter's gunboat fleet had to run the Vicksburg gantlet on the night of 16–17 April 1863, to support Grant's crossing. With lights dowsed and engines stopped, the gunboats floated downstream until discovered by a Confederate sentry. Then, what a torrent of shot and shell from the fortress, and what a cracking-on of steam in the fleet, and what a magnificent spectacle, lighted by flashing guns and burning cotton bales, as the casemated gunboats, turtlebacked rams, and river steamboats with tall flaring funnels, dashed by the batteries! "Their heavy shot walked right through us," wrote

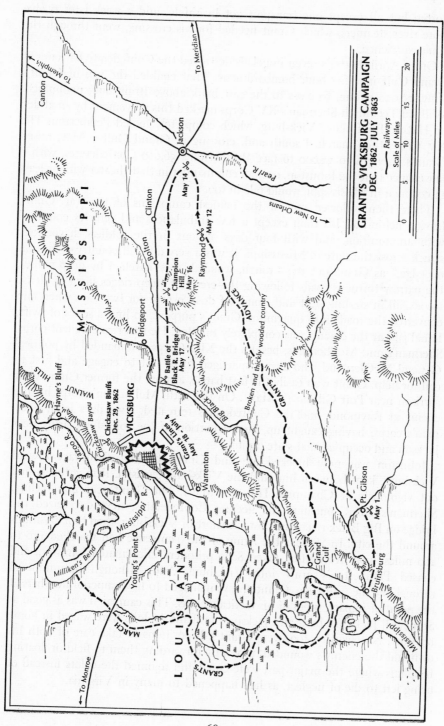

GRANT'S VICKSBURG CAMPAIGN
DEC. 1862 - JULY 1863

Railways

Scale of Miles

0   5   10   15   20

To Memphis

Canton

To Meridian

Jackson

Pearl R.

To New Orleans

Clinton

Bolton

May 14

Champion Hill May 16

May 12

Raymond

Bridgeport

MISSISSIPPI

ADVANCE

Broken and thickly wooded country

GRANT'S

Battle of Black R. Bridge May 17

Big Black R.

Haynes Bluff

WALNUT HILLS

Yazoo R.

Chickasaw Bayou

Chickasaw Bluffs Dec. 29, 1862

VICKSBURG

Grant's Lines May 18 - July 4

Warrenton

Milliken's Bend

Young's Point

Mississippi R.

Pt. Gibson May 1

Grand Gulf

Bruinsburg

Mississippi R.

LOUISIANA

MARCH

GRANT'S

To Monroe

Porter; but all except one transport got by safely, and a week later twelve more river steamers, which Grant needed for his crossing, went through the same experience.

On 29 April, Porter's seven ironclads destroyed the Confederate batteries at Grand Gulf in a five-hour bombardment. That enabled the van of Grant's army, 20,000 strong, to cross to the east bank above Bruinsburg unopposed. William Tecumseh Sherman's XV Corps masked this movement by an attack on Haynes Bluff above Vicksburg, which completely fooled Pemberton. The XV Corps then marched south and, crossing at Grand Gulf 7 May, raised Grant's strength to 33,000 to face Pemberton's 56,000 Confederates, with a fair chance that Joe Johnston, over-all commander in that theater with at least 11,000 men in Mississippi, would pile in too.

There then followed one of the boldest campaigns of the war. Grant, leaving behind all his train except a few ambulances and vehicles crammed with ammunition, and with four days' rations in the soldiers' haversacks, struck across the state of Mississippi. It was a very difficult country — "stands on edge," as Grant put it: — rough, wooded, cross-hatched by deep gullies, the narrow tortuous roads following the crests of steep ridges lined by dense woods, all in sizzling heat and clouds of dust, except for two days when rain converted the roads into quagmires. Grant's purpose, to hurl a series of swift, lethal jabs at the enemy, was completely fulfilled. He had two excellent corps, Sherman's and McPherson's, besides the XIII Corps commanded by political General McClernand who always managed to be last to engage and first to call for help. Grant won easily the first battle, against the former Grand Gulf garrison near Port Gibson (1 May). On the 12th, McPherson's corps hit the enemy at Raymond, and the Confederates retreated. Two days later, Sherman's corps, having caught up, beat a portion of Joe Johnston's army near Jackson and occupied that state capital.

Johnston was now blocked off; and Grant, turning about-face toward Vicksburg, kept between him and the Vicksburg garrison. Pemberton lashed out vigorously at Champion Hill (16 May), but Grant sent him reeling. Sherman's corps, pursuing the fleeting Confederates, next day seized the bridge on Big Black river, last obstacle short of Vicksburg, then took positions around the city. In 18 days the Army of the Tennessee had marched 150 to 200 miles, won five battles, taken 8000 prisoners, checkmated Johnston, and chased Pemberton's army into Vicksburg. And, although outnumbered throughout the campaign, Grant always managed to have superior numbers at the point of impact, proof of his tactical genius. This campaign was as good as Stonewall Jackson's best, and Jackson's brilliant exploits were waged in home territory. Noteworthy, too, were Grant's dispositions to take care of both his own and the enemy's wounded, promptly forwarding them to field or floating hospitals where the major part were cured and rejoined the colors instead of being left to die of neglect, as had happened to many in Virginia.

Grant now sent Sherman north to take Haynes Bluff and the enemy forts on the Yazoo from the rear. After a couple of probes at the defenses of Vicksburg, he sat down to besiege the city, with the help of Porter's fleet. Pemberton surrendered the city and his army, now reduced to 30,000 men, on 4 July 1863, the last day of Gettysburg, which made it "the best Fourth of July since 1776."

Lincoln, thanking Grant in a characteristic letter, did something which few politicians and still fewer Presidents ever do — he admitted a mistake. He had thought that when Grant crossed the Mississippi on 29 April he should have marched downstream to join General Banks. "I now wish to make the personal acknowledgment that you were right and I was wrong." Banks at that time was besieging Port Hudson on the east bank, about 24 miles upstream from Baton Rouge. He had naval gunfire support from Farragut's Gulf Squadron, and from Porter's gunboats. After two costly and fruitless attempts to take Port Hudson by assault, Banks sat down for a siege. But the Confederate commander there was so discouraged by the fall of Vicksburg that he, too, surrendered on 9 July with over 30,000 prisoners.

Lincoln could now announce, "The Father of Waters flows unvexed to the sea." The loss of Vicksburg and Port Hudson was a far more deadly blow to the Confederacy than Gettysburg. And a nasty, three-cornered controversy broke out between Jefferson Davis, Johnston, and Pemberton as to who was to blame. It never seemed to occur to them that Grant and his army were responsible.

3. The Chattanooga, Red River, and Atlanta Campaigns

"It was not until after both Gettysburg and Vicksburg that the war professionally began," wrote General Sherman, twenty years later. "Then our men had learned in the dearest school on earth the simple lessons of war. Then we had brigades, divisions and corps which could be handled professionally, and it was then that we as professional soldiers could rightly be held to a just responsibility."

Now that a watery ring, fresh and salt, had been flung around the Confederacy, the time was ripe for a lethal thrust from Tennessee to Savannah. Now began the campaign that led to Sherman's march to the sea. Initial target was Chattanooga, where the Tennessee river breaks through parallel ridges of the southern Appalachians, and an important junction on the Richmond-Knoxville-Memphis railway. Union armies, once in possession of Chattanooga, could swing round the Great Smoky Mountains and advance on Atlanta.

The opening phase of the Chattanooga campaign was conducted on both sides by second-raters; Rosecrans, who had most of McClellan's faults without his ability, and Braxton Bragg, a dyspeptic martinet whose actions were completely unpredictable. But from the first battle of the campaign, at Chickamauga (19 September), there emerged a great commander, the loyal Virginian George H. Thomas. After Bragg had swept the Union right and center into Chattanooga, General Thomas for six hours held his left against repeated assaults; and when nightfall found him stripped of ammunition, he retired unmolested to a safe position. "The *élan* of the Southern soldier was never seen after Chickamauga," wrote D. H. Hill. "That brilliant dash which had distinguished him was gone forever." It broke against the lines of Thomas, "the rock of Chickamauga."

Rosecrans now allowed his army to be penned up and besieged in Chattanooga. He was approaching a state of imbecility when Lincoln sent Grant to the rescue, as supreme commander in the West. Grant placed Thomas in command of the Army of the Cumberland, and ordered him to hold Chattanooga at all hazards. "I will hold the town till we starve," said Thomas.

There was no more accomplished horseman in either army than General Grant, but he had bad luck with his war horses. A handsome bay named Charlie shied at a locomotive's whistle in New Orleans and fell on Grant, causing him intense pain and confining him to bed for three weeks. He was still suffering from the effects when he received Lincoln's order; during the last part of the journey, over washouts and swollen creeks, he had sometimes to be lifted from his horse and carried in men's arms. Once in command, resolute and tireless, he ordered his army to take the offensive.

On 22–23 November opened the great battle for Chattanooga. Simultaneous attacks delivered by Hooker, Sherman, and Thomas drove the enemy from steep wooded ridges across the river. The capture of Missionary Ridge was the most gallant action of the war. As General H. V. Boynton, who was there, describes it:

Eighty-nine regiments rushed for the earthworks at the base of the ridge — every soldier like an arrow shot from a string which had been drawn to its full tension. . . . Riflemen in the Confederate earth-works and belching batteries above pelted them with the varied hail of battle. The sun swung low over the ridge. It never looked in all its shining over battle-fields upon a more imposing rush. Two miles and a half of gleaming rifle-barrels, line after line of them, and more than a hundred and fifty banners, state and national, blossoming along the advance. Not a straggler, only the killed and wounded, dropped from the ranks. They swept over the lower earthworks, capturing many prisoners, and . . . swarmed up the slopes. The colors rushed in advance, and the men crowded towards the banners. Each regiment became a wedge-shaped mass, the flags at the cutting edge cleaving the way to the summit. Without faltering, without a stay, the flags went on, — not long, it is sadly true, in the same hands, but always in willing hands, and in an hour from the sounding of the signal guns for starting, the crest for three miles was crowned with the stars and stripes, Bragg's whole centre was in flight, and forty of his guns and two thousand prisoners were in the hands of Thomas's victorious army.

This battle finished Bragg and placed the combined armies of the Tennessee and the Cumberland (Sherman and Thomas) in position to advance into

Georgia in the early spring. The center of gravity had now shifted to the West. And the West had provided the Union with two great generals.

One more Union fiasco was yet to take place, the Red river campaign of the spring of 1864. After the fall of Vicksburg, all Confederate forces west of the Mississippi, including several thousand Indians, were under the command of General Edmund Kirby-Smith. Someone at Washington conceived the idea of using Porter's gunboat fleet to escort Banks's Army of the Mississippi, augmented by a corps from Sherman's army, up the Red river to Shreveport, whence the doughboys should be able to march into the heart of Texas. The gunboats did their part, but on 8 April 1864 Banks was jumped by Kirby-Smith at Pleasant Hill and badly defeated, leaving the fresh-water navy grounded and the river falling. Army engineers had to construct a dam to build up a head of water and float out the fleet.

Sherman's drive on Atlanta opened on 5 May, in accordance with typical orders from Grant: "You I propose to move against Johnston's army, to break it up and get into the interior of the enemy's country as far as you can, inflicting all the damage you can against their war resources." Sherman, the most trusted corps commander under Grant, resembled him physically — cropped rusty beard, disheveled appearance — and in an indomitable will to victory. But Sherman was loquacious when Grant was taciturn, and he loved dancing and pretty women. He proved himself even more skillful than the victor of Vicksburg, having learned from that campaign that surprise and mobility are the master keys to strategy. Sherman, too, glimpsed the concept of total war — war on the enemy's will to fight and capacity to support fighting men, as much as on the soldiers themselves. Robert E. Lee was the finest general of a Napoleonic age that was passing; Sherman was the first general of an age that was coming, and whose end we have not yet seen.

Sherman now commanded a group of three armies some 100,000 strong — the Cumberland (Thomas), Tennessee (McPherson), and Ohio (Schofield). Opposed to him was Joe Johnston with only 60,000 in his Army of the Tennessee, but three excellent corps commanders — Hood, Hardee, and Bishop Polk — with the rich logistic resources of Georgia, and home-guard manpower and Negro labor troops to draw upon. Sherman jumped off from Chattanooga 5 May 1864, his army stripped to barest essentials in food and equipment; no tents even for senior officers. His base lay 150 miles north, at Nashville, over a one-track railroad that had to be protected from Confederate cavalry raids.

The four months' campaign for Atlanta that followed was professional war at its best. Johnston adopted Fabian strategy: to hold up Sherman by delaying actions, hoping to catch him "with his neck out" and, anyway, to produce war weariness in the North. "The whole country is one vast fort," wrote Sherman on 23 June. "As fast as we gain one position the enemy has another all ready." Sherman endeavored to outflank Johnston and get between him and Atlanta, but "Old Joe" showed as great skill and versatility in retiring actions as Marshal Kesselring was to exhibit in Italy some eighty years later, and the terrain was not dissimilar. On the 26th Sherman wrote, "We have devoured the land and our animals eat up the wheat and corn fields close. All the people retire before us and desolation is behind. To realize what war is one should follow our tracks." Next day Sherman, feeling that he had done enough marching and maneuvering, assaulted Johnston's entrenched line on Kenesaw Mountain, failed, and lost heavily; but this one mistake was followed by three weeks of brilliant maneuvering which took the Union army across the Chattahoochee river, eight miles from Atlanta. On that day (17 July) Jefferson Davis, in an insulting letter, relieved Johnston of his command and placed both theater and army under his impetuous corps commander, John B. Hood.

That was an ill-deserved cut to "Old Joe"; but retreats, however well conducted, do not win wars, and he had been outwitted. Again and again, in the 130-mile advance, Sherman lured the Confederates into vain attacks, and from each action gained a fresh vantage point. "To force an opponent acting on the strategic defensive into such a succession of costly tactical offensives was an example of strategic artistry rarely seen in history," writes Captain Liddell Hart.

Now, unwilling to decimate his army in frontal assaults on Atlanta's static defenses, Sherman tricked Hood into a series of reckless attacks. In one of these, at Allatoona Pass, Hood pushed some 1500 Union troops under General John M. Corse into earthworks at the crest of a hill. Here Corse, by flag signaling to Kenesaw Mountain, 20 miles away, asked for help; Sherman replied, "Hold the Fort. I am coming." Come he did, in time to drive the Confederates off, and his cheery signal became the theme of a popular hymn. Sherman now maneuvered the greater part of his army in a wide wheel about Atlanta and forced the Confederates to evacuate it on 1 September 1864.

"Atlanta is ours," reported Sherman. It had been a costly campaign for both sides; but so firmly had Sherman guarded communications, and so well had he been reinforced, that his army, despite a loss of some 27,000 killed and wounded, was stronger than it had been four months earlier. And the enemy's loss, which could not be wholly replaced, was only about 1000 less.

4. The Wilderness Campaign

The first of January 1864 was the brightest New Year's day for the Union since the war began. Volunteering was going on rapidly, the danger of foreign intervention was over, the copperheads seemed cowed by recent victories, and nothing but the armies of Lee and Johnston stood between the Union and victory. A considerable "but." Lee's Wilderness campaign came measurably close to destroying the Northern will to victory.

On 9 March 1864 Grant was appointed general in chief of the armies of the United States. Summoned to Washington, where he had never been, to confer with Lincoln, whom he had never seen, the scrubby-looking general with his "slightly seedy look" caused misgivings among those who were used to the glittering commanders of the Army of the Potomac. But Lincoln knew that now he had a general "who would take the responsibility and act." And Grant never doubted the greatness and wisdom of his President.

Grant's plan for the Virginia campaign against Lee appeared to be as inexorable as a nutcracker. With Meade commanding the Army of the Potomac, he would move toward Richmond, forcing the Confederates to give battle or abandon their capital. General Franz Sigel (a veteran of the war of '48 in Germany who had helped to save Missouri for the Union) now commanded the Army of the Shenandoah, whose mission was to push up the valley to Lynchburg and prevent any Stonewall Jackson shenanigans. That old rascal B. F. Butler was given command of the Army of the James, apparently in order to keep him out of politics. His mission was to march up the south bank of the James, take Petersburg, and cut Lee's communications with the lower South. Both diversions miscarried. Sigel, beaten by Breckenridge at Newmarket on 15 May, was superseded, and Jubal A. Early later drove his army across the Appalachians. The Army of the James, after being convoyed upriver by monitors and gunboats under Rear Admiral Samuel P. Lee, got itself, through Butler's fumbling ineptitude, "bottled up" (in Grant's words) by Beauregard in Bermuda Hundred at a loop of the river.

Thus, upon Grant fell the entire burden of the offensive. He chose the direct approach in which superior numbers would count, and he had as strong a will to victory as Marshal Foch, who employed similar strategy in 1918. "I determined," wrote Grant himself, "to hammer continuously against the armed force of the enemy and his resources, until by mere attrition, if in no other way, the military power of the rebellion was entirely broken."

On 4 May 1864 Grant crossed the Rapidan without opposition, and began to march his army of over 100,000 men through the same tangled Wilderness from which Jackson had fallen upon Hooker's flank at Chancellorsville. When he was halfway through, Lee repeated Jackson's maneuver. Grant accepted the challenge and promptly changed front, but his army maneuvered with great difficulty in that dense undergrowth, and in two days' fierce fighting he lost 17,700 men; Lee, less than half that number. A bad beginning for Grant; he now faced a general of different metal from those whom he had beaten in the West.

Grant next tried to outflank the enemy. Clouds of dust from his marching columns warned Lee of his intention, and by the time his van had reached the crossroads at Spottsylvania Court House, the Army of Northern Virginia was there to check him. Both armies threw up field entrenchments, and the five days' battle that followed (Spottsylvania, 8–12 May, the battle of the "Bloody Angle") opened a long and terrible chapter of trench warfare, result of the increasing deadliness of firearms.

Having lost 12,227 more men at Spottsylvania, the indomitable Grant proposed "to fight it out on this line if it takes all summer." He moved by his left flank in the hope of outflanking Lee's right. Again the Army of Northern Virginia was there to receive him, and in a position so well chosen and entrenched that Grant needed all his adroitness to withdraw in safety and continue his flanking march (26 May). Lee swung with him to McClellan's old battlefield of Gaines's Mill. Both armies entrenched. Then came the Battle of Cold Harbor, costly and futile — an assault upon the entire line of Lee's trenches with no adequate preparation to improve any temporary success. About 12,000 men were sacrificed, but hardly a dent was made on the Confederate lines.

During ten more days the armies faced one another. War had now acquired the horrors associated with World War I. The wounded, unattended between the lines, died of thirst and loss of blood. Corpses rotted on the ground. Sharpshooters kept up their deadly work. Officers and men fought mechanically, hopelessly. The war had begun so long ago that one could hardly remember a state of peace. Would it continue until everyone on both sides was dead?

In one month Grant had advanced to the Chickahominy, the exact spot where McClellan had stood two years before; and he had suffered severe losses, though no more, proportionally, than Lee.[1] But Grant never flinched. On 12 June he carried out McClellan's old plan — a change of base to the James, and an attempt to cut the communications of Richmond at Petersburg. The maneuver was skillfully executed, but an opportunity to push into undefended Petersburg was lost, owing to Butler's check on the James. Lee slipped into Petersburg, entrenched in time, and three general assaults of 15-18 June cost the Union 8000 more men.

A war of positions had arrived in the Virginia theater. Grant's army besieged Petersburg for nine months. He never had enough men or artillery to carry the enemy lines by assault, and one attempt to do so, by mining under them and blowing them up by dynamite — the Battle of the Crater — ended in costly defeat. But he was right in pinning Lee down while Sherman reduced the effective area of the Confederacy; for Lee unable to maneuver was not dangerous.

Such, in brief, was the most desperately fought campaign of the war. Lee, with inferior forces, had saved his army and saved Richmond. Grant, after making mistakes and suffering losses that would have broken any of his predecessors, was still indefatigable. But how long would the country suffer such stupendous losses, with no apparent result?

Lincoln, too, was indefatigable. In a speech on 16 June he said:

1. The oft-repeated statement (e.g. Freeman's, *Lee*, III, p. 446) that Grant lost more men in this campaign than Lee's entire army at the outset, is shown by Channing, *United States*, VI, p. 571n. to be false. Actually, Lee's losses were proportionally greater than Grant's.

We accepted this war for an object, a worthy object, and the war will end when that object is attained. Under God, I hope it never will end until that time. . . . This war has taken three years; it was begun or accepted upon the line of restoring the national authority over the whole national domain, and for the American people; as far as my knowledge enables me to speak, I say we are going through on this line if it takes three years more.

Within a month his fortitude would be severely tested by Early's raid and by peace intrigues.

TENTING TONIGHT

Man-y are the hearts that are wea-ry to-night,

Wish-ing for the war to cease;

Man-y are the hearts that are look-ing for the right To

see the dawn of peace. Tent-ing to-night,

Tent-ing to-night, Tent-ing on the old camp ground.

Victory and Death

1864-1865

1. Early's Raid and the Election of 1864

JUBAL A. EARLY, "Old Jube" to his troops, was a snarling misanthrope, bent by arthritis contracted in the Mexican War, but eager and aggressive. He now pulled off a spectacular raid. On 2 July 1864 his 15,000 veterans were at Winchester, marching north by the classic valley route. A few days later he was across the Potomac, laying Hagerstown and Frederick under contribution, and at noon on 11 July his van passed through Silver Spring and reached Fort Stevens in the District of Columbia. Fortunately, his advance had been held up for two days at the Monocacy river by General Lew Wallace, so that on the same day that Early sighted the dome of the Capitol, a Union corps which Grant had hurriedly diverted from the Army of the Potomac, disembarked at Washington. It went right into action, President Lincoln watching the engagement from the parapet of Fort Stevens, rebel bullets whistling past his tall hat. The Confederates were driven back, and on 13 July made good their escape to the Shenandoah valley, gorged with loot and provisions.

Early's raid, in combination with Grant's check before Petersburg and Sherman's halt before Atlanta, provided fodder for the peace movement in the North; even for a change of administration. A considerable section of the public had lost confidence in Grant and in Lincoln. The appalling toll of casualties seemed to have brought the war no nearer conclusion. Paper dollars fell to one-third their value in gold on the day that Early appeared before Washington. And the cost of living had soared far beyond the rise of wages or salaries. Unable to look beyond their own troubles to the far greater ills of their enemy, many people in the North began to ask whether further prosecution of the war would profit anyone but the profiteers. This undercurrent of doubt and despair induced some strange developments in the presidential campaign that was already under way.

Alone of modern governments prior to World War II, the United States faced a general election in wartime. For, as Lincoln said, "We cannot have free government without elections; and if the rebellion could force us to forego or postpone a national election, it might fairly claim to have already conquered and ruined us." On 7 June 1864 Lincoln was renominated for the presidency by a National Union convention representing both Republicans and War Democrats, with Democrat Andrew Johnson, the stout Union war governor of Tennessee, for the vice presidency. The New York *World*, organ of "high-toned" Democrats, declared the nomination of these "two ignorant, boorish, third-rate backwoods lawyers" to be "an insult to the common sense of the people."

There now developed a movement against Lincoln within his own party. Salmon P. Chase, hoping to be President himself, resigned from the cabinet and struck an alliance with political adventurers and marplots such as General Butler, Roscoe Conkling a New York congressman, and Horace Greeley, editor of the New York *Tribune*. This noted journalist, suffering from one of his not infrequent brainstorms, believed that the Confederacy could be wheedled back into the Union by diplomacy, and that Lincoln was a liability. On the subject of peace, Lincoln wrote to Greeley on 9 July, "If you can find any person anywhere professing to have any proposition of Jefferson Davis, in writing, for peace, embracing the restoration of the Union and abandonment of slavery, say to him he may come to me." Greeley met on Canadian soil two men who claimed to have a peace offer, only to find that they were charlatans; but his ardor for negotiation was not dampened.

As if this were not enough, a breach opened between the President and the Radicals over reconstructing the Union after the war. When on 8 July Lincoln pocket-vetoed a bill embodying Radical views of reconstruction, Senator Ben Wade of Ohio and Representative Henry Winter Davis of Maryland issued a public manifesto accusing the President of a "studied outrage on the legislative authority of the people" from the basest motives of personal ambition. Greeley published this Wade-Davis Manifesto in the *Tribune* on 5 August; and two weeks later he and the Radicals began to circulate among other politicians a "call" for a new Republican convention to reconsider Lincoln and nominate General Butler, or anyone. Diehards and defeatists in alliance, to elevate to the presidency a general who had never won a battle! The executive committee of the Republican party even implored Lincoln to make peace overtures to Jefferson Davis, as a sop to defeatist sentiment.

This panic of the politicians — fortunately it went no further — was dangerous. What Lincoln really thought of the situation is clear from the paper he wrote and sealed on 23 August, to be opened only after the election: "It seems exceedingly probable that this administration will not be re-elected. Then it will be my duty to so co-operate with the President-elect as to save the Union between the election and the inauguration, as he will have secured his election on such ground that he cannot possibly save it afterward."

If Jefferson Davis had been adroit, he could have completed the distraction of Union councils by proposing an armistice or peace conference on any terms. For, had the fighting once been halted, it is doubtful whether it could ever have been renewed. But the Southern president was still living in a dream world, certain that his cause was invincible. "Say to Mr. Lincoln from me," he told a volunteer peacemaker, "that I shall at any time be pleased to receive proposals for peace on the basis of our Independence. It will be useless to approach me with any other."

In the face of this honest statement, published on 20 August 1864, the Democratic national convention on the 29th adopted a resolution drafted by the copperhead Vallandigham: "After four years of failure to restore the Union by the experiment of war . . . justice, humanity, liberty, and the public welfare demand that immediate efforts be made for a cessation of hostilities . . . to the end that, at the earliest practicable moment, peace may be restored on the basis of the federal Union of the States." General McClellan accepted the Democratic nomination for President; the vice-presidential nomination went to "Gentleman George" Pendleton, an Ohio congressman who had been vilifying the Lincoln administration throughout the war. McClellan repudiated the peace plank in the platform, but was not unwilling to ride on it to the White House.

Jefferson Davis by his frankness, the Democrats by their shameless defeatism, and Sherman by capturing Atlanta on 2 September, knocked the bottom out of this "reconsider Lincoln" conspiracy. On 6 September a new army draft went quietly into effect and, marvelous to relate, Wade and Chase took the stump for the President. A smashing military victory in an old theater of Union frustration undoubtedly helped.

Dashing, thirty-three-year-old, five-foot-two-inch Philip Sheridan, one of the heroes of Chickamauga and Lookout Mountain, had reorganized the mounted service of the Army of the Potomac so that it became tactically equal if not superior to the Southern *beaux-sabreurs*. In August 1864 Grant gave him command over the Army of the Shenandoah, with the objective of destroying the Shenandoah valley as a base of enemy operations or supplies. After beating Early twice on 19 and 22 September, Sheridan began a systematic devastation of the valley. Leaving his army encamped at Cedar Creek near Strasburg, Sheridan, returning from a conference at Washington, had reached Winchester when he heard firing to the southward. Mounting his charger Rienzi, a magnificent jet-black Morgan gelding, Sheridan rode down the valley pike and presently met panic-stricken units of his army. Early had routed them in a brilliant surprise attack. Rallying the men and turning them right-about, Sheridan rode the 20 miles to Cedar Creek, galloped along the lines to hearten wavering troops who had not retreated, and did what few generals have done since Napoleon. He transformed a defeated, panic-stricken mob into an army again, and ended by completely routing Early's Confederates.[1]

Another victory that helped re-elect Lincoln was Admiral Farragut's at Mobile Bay. The Confederate navy there, under Admiral Buchanan, had

---

1. Rienzi is estimated to have covered 75 miles that day, and mostly on the gallop. The poem "Sheridan's Ride," a favorite subject of school declamations for half a century, was composed a few days after the event by the painter-poet Thomas B. Read, then a major on General Lew Wallace's staff.

constructed its most powerful ship, the 209-foot ironclad ram *Tennessee*, armed with 6- and 7-inch guns. Stupidly enough, she was given so much draught that she could not steam across the bar in normal tides to get at the blockading fleet; but she was strong enough to be a "fleet in being" that had to be eliminated. The Confederates had planted the channel into Mobile Bay with anchored mines (in that era called torpedoes), and the entrance was further protected by Fort Morgan. Admiral Farragut's seven wooden sloops-of-war, *Brooklyn* leading and flagship *Hartford* next, with a parallel column of four monitors and ten gunboats in two groups, opened fire at 6:30 a.m. August 5. C.S.S. *Tennessee* and three gunboats steamed out to challenge. The lookouts in U.S.S. *Hartford* sighted what surely were mines, but Farragut the invincible, perched high in the rigging to get a better view, ordered, "Damn the torpedoes, full speed ahead!" He evaded *Tennessee*'s attempt to ram, but his round shot rolled off the rebel's six-inch armor like marbles off a tin roof. Buchanan's gunboats, however, were knocked off in one-two-three order. U.S.S. *Monongahela*, *Lackawanna*, and *Hartford* in succession rammed the rebel, scraping along her topsides so close that sailors could fight each other through the portholes. Finally the 11-inch bullets of U.S. monitor *Chickasaw*, by pounding on the after side of the casemate like a dentist's hammer on a sore tooth, made a breach and shot away the ram's tiller chains so that she became helpless. She surrendered at 10:00 a.m., and Admiral Buchanan with a broken leg became a prisoner of war. This was the greatest naval action of the Civil War. Fort Morgan surrendered 23 August to a troop assault, supported by a heavy naval bombardment. Mobile city was now sealed off, and the Union navy's control of the Gulf of Mexico became complete.

On 8 November 1864, the Northern voters chose 212 electors for Lincoln and Johnson, only 21 for McClellan and Pendleton, representing Delaware, Kentucky, and New Jersey. The popular vote was not so emphatic — roughly 2.2 million to 1.8 million, and in the three pivotal states of New York, Pennsylvania, and Ohio, Lincoln had a margin of only 86,400. This strong minority vote did not all represent defeatism; many thousands voted for McClellan because they regarded him as a possible Napoleon or De Gaulle who would save the country, and Lincoln as a country bumpkin who knew not how to end a war he had started. No presidential election better illustrated P. T. Barnum's adage that you can fool some of the people for some of the time, but not all the people all the time.

2. *From Atlanta to Appomattox*

President Davis assured his people on 28 September that Sherman must sooner or later retreat from Atlanta, "and when that day comes the fate that befell the army of the French empire in its retreat from Moscow will be reacted." On 17 October Sherman cut loose from Atlanta in the opposite direction, toward the sea. Abandoning his logistics line, and breaking all communications so he could not be recalled, he led 62,000 men and 2500 six-mule teams laden with supplies into enemy country, leaving two army corps to deal with Hood in Tennessee. Amazing as it seems, Washington had no news of Sherman's army for an entire month, except what it could glean from Richmond newspapers.

The march to the sea, like Sheridan's Shenandoah campaign, was one of deliberate destruction, in order to ruin a main source of provisions for Lee's and Hood's armies. Sheridan cut a swath 60 miles wide through "the garden spot of the Confederacy," destroying stores of provisions, standing crops and cattle, cotton gins and mills, railways beyond possibility of repair; in fact, everything that could be useful to the Confederacy and much that was not. The indiscriminate looting of private houses, although forbidden by orders, was largely the work of the "bummers" — stragglers from both sides; and also of Joe Wheeler's Confederate cavalry which hung on the flanks. Outrages on persons were surprisingly few, and on women, none. It was the sort of campaign that soldiers love — maximum of looting and destruction, minimum of discipline and fighting: splendid weather, few impediments, plenty of broiled turkey and fried chicken and roast pork, swarms of Negroes eager to pillage their former masters, tagging joyfully along. As Herman Melville wrote,

> It was glorious glad marching
> For every man was free;

and the song "Marching Through Georgia" composed shortly after by Henry C. Work, has become a part of Negro folklore, in the West Indies and even Africa. Sherman emerged at the seacoast near Savannah on 10 December, and was able to offer Lincoln the city as a Christmas present.

Sherman's ignoring Hood and going off in a contrary direction, perhaps the biggest gamble of the war, paid off handsomely. Hood, with 40,000 veterans, moved into central Tennessee, hoping to catch Thomas's and Schofield's corps and whip them separately. At the end of November he caught up with Schofield at Franklin, and sacrificed 6000 men in a series of gallant but futile attacks. Schofield slipped away to Nashville, where Thomas, "the rock of Chickamauga," was in command. Disregarding frantic telegrams from Stanton and Grant, Thomas bided his time, and on 27 December 1864 inflicted on Hood at Nashville the most smashing defeat of the war, capturing over 10,000 men and 72 guns. Grant made prompt amends to Thomas for his impatience; but this great Virginian, who had forsaken home and kindred out of loyalty to the Union, and to whom no military critic today would deny a place among the immortals, was neglected in the distribution of postwar honors.

There were still leaks in the blockade that needed caulking, and the Confederate navy was constructing ironclads to bust through — notably *Albemarle*, built on the Roanoke river. Lieutenant William B. Cushing USN, a handsome, intrepid youth, commanding a 30-foot steam launch fitted with a torpedo at the end of a spar, sneaked upstream on the night of 27–28 October

1864 to find *Albemarle* moored to a wharf at Plymouth, N.C., and protected by a log boom. Cushing turned up full speed, crashed through the boom under hot fire from the ironclad, and poked his torpedo under her bottom just as one of her big guns opened on him at a range of 12 feet. The ironclad blew up and sank, and so did the launch; but Cushing and most of his crew escaped by swimming. Subsequent capture of Plymouth by Union gunboats stopped that leak in the blockade.

The biggest leak, through the Cape Fear river to Wilmington, whence a railway forwarded supplies to Richmond, was a difficult one to cork. The twin entrances to the river were dominated by forts; and one, 75-gun Fort Fisher, could only be taken by amphibious assault. Secretary Welles had been trying for over a year to get troops to do it, but the army insisted first on attacking Charleston, and wasted time and strength on that futile operation. General Grant, however, saw the strategic value of sealing off Richmond's back door, and provided a landing force. Unfortunately he placed these troops under General Butler, who here "goofed" for the last time. His big idea, to explode a dynamite-filled hulk under the sea face of the fort while he landed troops on a nearby beach, fizzled; Butler then quit cold, leaving the navy to extricate his men. Rear Admiral Porter, commanding the Union blockading squadron, begged Grant to let him try again, and Grant did. After the hottest naval bombardment of the war by Porter's 44 ships, on 13–14 January 1865, a landing force under General Alfred H. Terry attacked Fort Fisher from the rear, while 2000 bluejackets and marines of the fleet assaulted it directly from the sea. The sailors and leathernecks (Lieutenant Cushing leading)were driven back after heavy loss, but by throwing the defense off balance they enabled the doughboys to gain a foothold within the fort. The following night it surrendered, with 2100 Confederates. This, the most successful amphibious operation of the Civil War, ended blockade running.

Next day, in Washington, General Butler was testifying to his pals of the Congressional committee on the conduct of the war, that Fort Fisher was impregnable, when newsboys were heard shouting an extra — "Fort Fisher Surrendered!" Everyone, including Ben, roared with laughter.

Five days before the fall of Fort Fisher, Sherman's army broke loose from the sea and began marching into the Carolinas, as Cornwallis had done; but what a difference from 1780! Country from which the redcoats could not find food for one meal a day was now glutted with grain and livestock, and Sherman saw to it that only scorched earth was left. He had about 60,000 men at the start; Johnston (reluctantly restored by Davis to command over Hood on 23 February 1865) had about 40,000. Sherman adopted tactics which portended those of the German panzer forces that swarmed over northern France in 1940. Moving on a wide, irregular front in four to six columns, each one of which could push on if others were blocked, he kept the enemy guessing as to his next objective. Would it be Columbia or Charleston and, next, Charlotte or Fayetteville? and, after that, Raleigh or Goldsboro? Sherman himself never decided which it would be until his cavalry reported enemy dispositions. On 17 February he seized Columbia and pinched the Confederates out of Charleston. On 11 March he was in Fayetteville; on the 23rd, after pushing Johnston out of his way, Sherman arrived at Goldsboro, 425 miles from Savannah.

The sun of the Confederacy was setting fast, though gloriously; yet the civilian leaders looked the other way. Lee, they hoped, would break contact with Grant, unite with Johnston's 35,000 men, and pull off a counteroffensive against Sherman — like Rundstedt's Battle of the Bulge 80 years later. There were still enough white men of fighting age in the Confederacy to provide her army with half a million men.[1] The Confederate munitions service was now independent of foreign supplies; its producing center at Selma, Alabama, was not captured until 2 April. Despite Sherman, there was still plenty of cattle and corn in the Carolinas, and the latest Confederate war secretary, General John Breckenridge, reported 8 million rations to be en route from the deep South to Richmond. Every material factor seemed to justify protracted resistance; only morale was wanting. The re-election of Lincoln, the hopeless prospect of foreign aid, Union victories by land and sea, Grant's strategy of attrition, and the increasing pinch of the blockade, took the heart out of the South. "Two-thirds of our men are absent . . . most of them absent without leave," admitted President Davis in September 1864. Joe Johnston wrote that he did not blame his men for going A.W.O.L.; they were getting letters from home telling how their farms had been stripped of food and animals by the Confederate commissary; they had to desert to save their families. Senator Benjamin H. Hill of Georgia, who wrote to President Davis on 25 March 1865, "We shall conquer all enemies yet," admitted nine years later, "All physical advantages are insufficient to account for our failure. The truth is, we failed because too many of our people were not determined to win."

Davis could see only the outer reality — so many men and rifles and cannon, so much food and gunpowder. To the deeper reality in the hearts of the people he was insensible as any European dictator. Pressure by some of his top advisers persuaded him to ask for a peace conference, in the hope of obtaining from Lincoln a statement of Union war aims to "fire the Southern heart." The statement came out of a four-hour conference on board steamer *River Queen* in Hampton Roads, between President Lincoln and Vice President Stephens, who had been Lincoln's friend in Congress sixteen years earlier. Stephens had credentials to negotiate peace as the envoy of an independent republic. Lincoln patiently repeated his refusal to negotiate on that basis. Senator Hunter, who accompanied Stephens, alleged as precedent the negotiations during the English Civil War. Lincoln replied, "I do not profess to be posted in history. On all such matters I will turn you over to Seward. All I

1. Actually, 174,223 Confederate troops surrendered in April and May 1865. Comparing the number of desertions during the previous four months, and the white population of fighting age, the estimate of 500,000 possible fighting men is not excessive. But the Union armies on 1 May numbered 1,052,038 officers and men.

distinctly recollect about the case of Charles I is that he lost his head." But, he added, "The war will cease on the part of the Government, whenever it shall have ceased on the part of those who began it." And that was that.

As Lincoln predicted, Davis "cannot voluntarily re-accept the Union; we cannot voluntarily yield it." Lee might with honor surrender his army to irresistible force; Davis could not with honor surrender his nation. The inherent dignity of his refusal was marred by a silly boast at a public meeting in Richmond that he would compel the Yankees in less than twelve months to petition him for peace on his own terms.

It was now the eighth day of February 1865, and the Confederacy was sinking fast. Even slavery was jettisoned in principle. Sherman, as he marched northward, was proving his sulphurous definition of war. Joe Johnston fought his last battle at Bentonville, North Carolina, on 19 March. On the 23rd Sherman marched into Goldsboro and made rendezvous with Thomas, the victor of Nashville. Reunited, this great Army of the West had 90,000 men; Johnston a scant 25,000. Sherman nevertheless passed some anxious hours when he learned that Lee and his grim veterans were on the loose again.

For nine months the two armies in Virginia had faced one another across long lines of entrenchment running through the suburbs of Petersburg. At the beginning of the siege their forces were not disparate; but by the middle of March 1865 Grant had 115,000 effectives to Lee's 54,000. If Lee did not move out of his trenches, Grant would envelop him; but if Petersburg were abandoned, Richmond must fall. Lee first tried moving forward, but his assault on the Union left was a costly failure. He must make up his mind to retreat, or it would soon be too late even for that. Sheridan, having disposed of Early, marched his Army of the Shenandoah across Virginia, thrust back Lee's right at the Battle of Five Forks (1 April), and next day Grant penetrated the center of the Confederate defenses. Lee's only hope was to retire and unite with Johnston.

On the night of 2–3 April, Lee's army slipped out of the Petersburg lines; next evening the Union forces entered Richmond. Without pause, Grant pursued. Rations failed to reach Lee, through fumbling at Richmond; his 30,000 men had to live on a thinly populated country in springtime. By 9 April Sheridan had closed the only avenues of retirement west or south. Possibly Lee could have cut his way through to the mountains and waged guerrilla warfare, but he had too great a sense of responsibility to take any such course, or to ride into a volley of Union bullets. So he ordered a white flag (the Confederates had no such thing, so used a towel) to be carried through the lines, to request an interview with General Grant.

The scene that followed, in the McLean house of the tiny village of Appomattox Court House, has become a part of American folklore: Lee, in a new full-dress uniform with sash and jewel-studded sword, Grant in his usual unbuttoned private's blouse, "his feelings sad and depressed at the downfall of a foe who had fought so long and valiantly." Small talk of other days, in the old army. Grant wrote the terms of surrender in his own hand. "Officers and men paroled . . . arms and matériel surrendered . . . officers to keep their side arms, and let all the men who claim to own a horse or mule take the animals home with them to work their little farms." "This will do much toward conciliating our people," said Lee. The conference over, the Confederate leader paused a moment in the doorway, looking out over a field blossoming with the Stars and Stripes. Thrice, and slowly, he struck a fist into the palm of his gauntleted hand. He mounted Traveller and returned to his field headquarters.

A sound of cheering spread along the Union lines. "The soldiers rushed, perfectly crazy, to the roadside, and shouted, screamed, yelled, threw up their hats and hopped madly up and down! The batteries were run out and began firing, the bands played, the flags waved." As soon as this clamor reached his ears. General Grant ordered it to cease, in these words: "The war is over; the rebels are our countrymen again."

"Over the carnage rose prophetic a voice," wrote Walt Whitman, catching the spirit of that great moment. "Affection shall solve the problems of freedom yet."

Could his prophecy have been fulfilled but for the insane assassination on 14 April? It certainly might have been, had things been left to the fighting officers and men. Commissioners appointed by Lee and Grant to arrange practical details of the surrender had no difficulty reaching an agreement. Grant not only rushed rations to the half-starved Confederates but allowed them free transportation home on government ships and railways. As General Gordon, one of the commissioners, said, courtesy and even deference was shown to the defeated officers; everyone looked forward to "a liberal, generous, magnanimous policy" toward the South. A Confederate cannoneer, who had expected to be "paraded through Northern cities for the benefit of jeering crowds" (as had been done to Union prisoners in Richmond), was relieved to learn that he could go home. There was good-humored chaffing between officers of both sides. General Meade, who had superbly commanded the Army of the Potomac through this last campaign, rode out to meet the Confederate commander, doffed his cap (the old-fashioned army salute), and said, "Good morning, General." Lee remarked, "What are you doing with all that gray in your beard?" To which Meade replied, "You have to answer for most of it!"

On 12 April came the formal laying down of arms. Two Union brigades were drawn up on each side of the road near Appomattox Court House. At the right of the line, mounted, was Major General Joshua L. Chamberlain, former colonel of the 20th Maine, chosen by Grant for this honorable post since he had fought nobly in the last campaign. At the head of the tattered, mud-caked Confederate column rode General Gordon, one of Jackson's old captains; and by his choice the Stonewall Brigade, now down to 210 officers and men, marched in the van. Then came the other regiments, now so decimated that their massed colors formed a ruddy crown to the marching men. As the column approached the Union lines, a bugle spoke; General Chamberlain had given the order "Carry *Arms!*" — the marching salute. General Gordon raised his downcast eyes when he heard the familiar snap and rattle of the muskets, gave Chamberlain the cavalryman's sword salute, and passed the word to his own men, "Carry *Arms!*" In complete, awed silence the Confederate column passed at the salute; then, in perfect order, the men stacked arms and cartridge boxes and laid down their flags. At that final symbol of defeat, many broke ranks and, sobbing, pressed the beloved colors to their lips. General Gordon, with moist eyes, addressed the men from horseback, urging them to depart in peace, to obey the laws and work for the future of a reunited nation.

The remaining history of the Confederacy is quickly told. President Davis slipped away from Richmond in a special train ahead of the Union troops on 2 April, together with several members of his cabinet and about $500,000 in specie. Davis did not feel that he was retreating, only looking for a new capital. On 4 April he issued a proclamation that the Southern people had "now entered upon a new phase of the struggle, the memory of which is to endure for all ages"; that nothing but "unquenchable resolve" was needed to make victory certain. Even the news of Lee's surrender affected Davis's resolve not a whit; he was still living in the purple dream, hero of an historic drama, blind to the raw fact of utter defeat. At Greensboro, North Carolina, he summoned Generals Johnston and Beauregard to attend a Confederate cabinet meeting and vainly endeavored to persuade them to continue the war. Secretaries Benjamin, Mallory, and Breckenridge urged Davis to throw in the sponge, but still he refused.

On 16 April the presidential party took to the road, with what was left of the treasury in a carriage. Ten days later, Johnston surrendered his army to Sherman. When Jefferson Davis reached Abbeville, South Carolina, on 3 May, he implored a group of faithful cavalry officers to stand firm: — "Three thousand brave men" he said, "are enough for a nucleus around which the whole people will rally." After the troopers had sadly told him the truth, he admitted "All is indeed lost." The cabinet ministers now took off to save themselves. On 10 May a troop of Union cavalry captured President and Mrs. Davis near Irwinsville, Georgia, and the Confederacy as a government flickered out.

General Richard Taylor had already surrendered all remaining Confederate forces east of the Mississippi; General Simon Bolivar Buckner, Kirby-Smith's chief of staff, negotiated at New Orleans on 26 May a surrender of all west of the Great River. While these negotiations were going on, the last land battle of the war was fought on 12–13 May at Palmetto Ranch near the Rio Grande — and, ironically enough, it was a Confederate victory. The Confederacy's Indian allies held out a month longer; Colonels Stand Watie of the Cherokee and Peter B. Pitchlynn of the Chocktaw did not surrender their armed men until 23 June. Most of the vessels of the Confederate navy still in port were scuttled or burned, and their crews scattered. One-sided hostilities continued in the Pacific Ocean, where C.S.S. *Shenandoah* was engaged in destroying Yankee whale ships. Her commander pursued this inglorious occupation into August, then sailed back to England and surrendered his ship to British authorities on 6 November 1865. Her ensign was the last war flag of the Confederacy to be lowered.

3. The Last Days of Lincoln

With malice toward none; with charity for all; with firmness in the right, as God gives us to see the right, let us strive on to finish the work we are in; to bind up the nation's wounds; to care for him who shall have borne the battle, and for his widow, and his orphan — to do all which may achieve and cherish a just and lasting peace among ourselves, and with all nations.

Thus closed the second inaugural address of President Lincoln. The struggle over reconstruction was already on, but when Congress next met in December, it might be confronted with the established fact of a restored nation, if the South were wise, and nothing happened to Lincoln.

Toward the end of March, the President and Mrs. Lincoln, on steamer *River Queen*, visited General and Mrs. Grant at the general's rear headquarters at City Point on the James. On the 26th Lincoln accompanied Grant on an inspection of General Ord's division, and Grant paid the President a compliment he had given to no other man, lending him his thoroughbred Cincinnati. Lincoln rode Cincinnati, it is said, like a professional, although he presented a rather odd figure in his tall stovepipe hat, flapping coattails, and trousers inching up toward his knees. On 3 April Lincoln met Grant again in liberated Petersburg, and next day, with a guard of under twenty officers and men, he visited burned Richmond. Then back to City Point. That evening a military band gave a concert on board the *River Queen*, and at the President's request played "The Marseillaise" in honor of Lafayette's grandson, the Marquis de Chambrun, who was a guest; and "Dixie," which Lincoln quaintly remarked, "is Federal property" now. On the 9th, as the party steamed up the Potomac to Washington, Lincoln read aloud passages from Shakespeare; and Chambrun later recalled with what solemnity he pronounced a passage from *Macbeth*:

> Duncan is in his grave;
> After life's fitful fever he sleeps well;
> Treason has done his worst: nor steel, nor poison,
> Malice domestic, foreign levy, nothing
> Can touch him further.

Driving from the Washington wharf to the White House, Mrs. Lincoln remarked, "That city is full of enemies," to which the President retorted with an impatient gesture, "Enemies — never again must we repeat that word!" Mary, alas, was right. An assassination plot was coming to a head.

Everywhere in Washington, wrote Chambrun, "the words peace, pardon and clemency can be heard." On 11 April, the day after Lee's surrender was announced, Lincoln delivered his last public address, from a window in the White House to a crowd on the lawn. After a brief allusion to Appomattox and the hope of a speedy peace, he unfolded his reconstruction policy — the most magnanimous terms toward a helpless opponent ever offered by a victor. For Lincoln did not consider himself a conqueror. He was, and had been since 1861, President of the United States. The rebellion must be forgotten; and every Southern state be readmitted to full privileges in the Union as soon as 10 per cent of its citizens had taken the oath of allegiance and organized a state government.

On Thursday night, 13 April, Washington was illuminated on account of Lee's surrender, and crowds paraded the streets. A general lightheartedness was in the air; everyone felt that the war was practically over. On Good Friday, the 14th, at breakfast Lincoln's son Robert showed the President a photograph of General Lee. "It is a good face," said the President. "I am glad the war is over at last." That morning he held his last cabinet meeting, with General Grant present. He had decided to lift the blockade. He urged his ministers to turn their thoughts to peace. There must be no more bloodshed, no persecution. Grant was asked for late news from Sherman, but had none. Lincoln remarked that it would come soon, and be favorable, for last night he had dreamed a familiar dream. In a strange, indescribable ship he seemed to be moving with great rapidity toward a far, indefinite shore. He had had this same dream before Antietam, Mufreesboro, Vicksburg, and Wilmington. Matter-of-fact Grant remarked that Murfreesboro was no victory; "a few such fights would have ruined us." Lincoln looked at him curiously and said, however that might be, his dream preceded that battle.

That evening Lincoln, who loved the theater, took his wife and two friends to Ford's Theater to see Laura Keene in a play called "Our American Cousin." This was exactly what the principal assassin wanted. As an actor, his face and presence were familiar to the theater employees, and he knew all the doors and passageways. The secret service man who should have guarded the entrance to the President's box moved to the balcony so he could follow the play better.

At about 10:13 p.m. a pistol shot rang out, the President slumped in his seat, Booth leaped from the box to the stage, paused a moment to brandish his gun and shout *Sic semper tyrannis!*, rushed through the rear exit, and was off and away on horseback.

Let Secretary Welles be our guide to the doleful events of that night. He had gone early to bed and was just falling asleep when someone shouted from the street that the President had been shot and the secretary of state and his son assassinated by another member of the murder gang. Welles dressed and crossed Lafayette Square to Seward's house on 15th Street. The lower hall was full of excited people. Welles rushed upstairs to a room where Seward was lying on a bed saturated with blood, his lower jaw sagging as if in death. In the next room lay Frederick Seward, unconscious from the injuries he had received while defending his father.

Welles, joined by Stanton, hurried downtown in a carriage. The President had been carried from Ford's Theater across 10th Street to a lodging-house, and laid on a bed in a narrow back room. He never recovered consciousness. "The giant sufferer," writes Welles, "lay extended diagonally across the bed, which was not long enough for him. . . . His slow, full respiration lifted the clothes with each breath that he took. His features were calm and striking." It was a dark and gloomy night, and rain fell at dawn. Crowds remained in the street, looking in vain for hope from the watchers who came out for a breath of air. "About once an hour Mrs. Lincoln would repair to the bedside of her dying husband and with lamentation and tears remain until overcome by emotion." At 7:22 a.m. April 15 the President's breathing stopped and his heart ceased to beat. Dr. Gurley, the Lincolns' pastor, made a short prayer. Then silence, broken only by Stanton's calm sentence: "Now he belongs to the ages."

In a parlor of the lodging-house the cabinet assembled without Seward, and wrote a letter to Vice President Johnson, "informing him of the event, and that the government devolved upon him."

Welles continues, "I went after breakfast to the Executive Mansion. There was a cheerless cold rain and everything seemed gloomy. On the Avenue in front of the White House were several hundred colored people, mostly women and children, weeping and wailing their loss. This crowd did not appear to diminish through the whole of that cold, wet day; they seemed not to know what was to be their fate since their great benefactor was dead, and their hopeless grief affected me more than almost anything else, although strong and brave men wept when I met them."

Reconstruction

1865-1877

1. War's Aftermath

TEN THOUSAND CURSES on the memory of that foulest of assassins, J. Wilkes Booth! Not only did he kill a great and good President; he gave fresh life to the very forces of hate and vengeance which Lincoln himself was trying to kill. Had Lincoln lived, there is every likelihood that his magnanimous policy toward the South would have prevailed; for, even after his death, it almost went through despite the Radicals. Never has a murderer wrought so much evil.

Lincoln himself had said, "Blood cannot restore blood, and government should not act for revenge." But for weeks after the assassination there was a petty reign of terror directed by Secretary Stanton. Only the stern intervention of General Grant prevented the arrest of Lee and other Confederate generals as "conspirators." Colossal rewards for Davis and his cabinet, as alleged promoters of the assassination, resulted in the capture of several, and "Hang Jeff Davis!" became a popular cry like "Hang the Kaiser!" after World War I. But the charge of official complicity in the crime was soon seen to be preposterous; and that of treason, though pressed for a time, was wisely directed to the circumlocution office. Almost every civil or military leader of the Confederacy expressed regret over the murder of Lincoln; the nastiest recorded remark about it was made by a mid-western copperhead journalist known as "Brick" Pomeroy: "The shameless tyrant, justly felled by an avenging hand, rots in his grave, while his soul is consumed by eternal fire at the bottom of the blackest hole in hell."

Popular thirst for revenge appeared to be slaked by shooting Lincoln's assassin and hanging three accomplices and the wretched woman who had harbored them, after trial by a military tribunal. Jefferson Davis was incarcerated in Fortress Monroe for two years and then released; [1] Stephens and a few members of the Confederate cabinet were confined for shorter periods. The only war criminal executed was Captain Henry Wirz for his cruelties to Union prisoners in the stockade at Andersonville. Many more Canadians

---

1. General Nelson A. Miles, governor of the fortress, put Davis in irons for five days because he hurled the first rations issued to him in the face of the corporal who brought them.

were executed for their uprising of 1837 than were Confederates for a more costly rebellion.

European observers were astonished at the quick demobilization of the Union army and the almost universal acceptance of the war's verdict in the South. With a celerity that surprised everyone, the Union Army was reduced from a million men at the time of Appomattox to 183,000 on 10 November 1865, and by the end of 1866 to about 25,000, a number that remained constant for thirty years. Most of the navy's ships were sold; only a few wooden sloops-of-war and ironclad monitors were retained. Discharged soldiers and sailors were quickly absorbed into civilian life. Goldwin Smith, the British publicist, regarded American disarmament as "the most truly magnanimous and wisest thing in history." It was assumed in Europe that President Johnson, with a big army at his disposal, would grab Canada as "compensation" for war losses, or invade Mexico to oust Maximilian. But, beyond sending an army of observation to the Mexican border to give moral support to Juárez, he did nothing in either quarter; and a few years later, Congress refused to buy a naval base in the West Indies, indicating that "manifest destiny" had come to a full stop. The United States, to be sure, bought Alaska from Russia in 1867, but here the seller was more eager than the buyer, the transaction was denounced as "Seward's folly," and there is at least a strong suspicion that Russian gold eased the passage of the treaty through the Senate.

Equally astonishing to a Europe accustomed to persistence of Irish, Polish, and other national grievances was Southern acceptance of the result. No guerrilla operations, no Confederate "government in exile," but young Southerners entering West Point and Annapolis to be trained as officers of the United States. Lee, Johnston, and almost every Southern leader except Davis advised their people to accept the verdict of battle and endeavor to be good citizens in a reunited country. The great majority did so, with important reservations on the freedom of the Negro.

Of the several thousand who refused to return to their former allegiance, a large proportion went to Texas, where this postwar ditty started:

> Oh, I'm a good old rebel, that's what I am;
> And for this land of freedom I don't care a damn,
> I'm glad I fought agin' her, I only wish we'd won,
> And I don't axe any pardon for anything I've done.

A few hundred went abroad, where some of the leaders, who had built up bank accounts in Europe during the war — notably Slidell, Toombs, Breckenridge, and Benjamin — lived in luxury. A Confederate colony was planted in the state of São Paolo, Brazil, where slavery still prevailed; but abolition eventually caught up with it. General Jo Shelby, a dashing cavalry leader, refused to surrender his Iron Brigade; with "Prince John" Magruder and 1000 troopers he marched to Mexico City in August 1865. Shelby offered to enroll them in the Mexican foreign legion and to recruit 40,000 ex-Confederates to uphold the empire. Maximilian declined; his throne already rested on French bayonets and he did not propose to affront his subjects further by shifting the support to *gringos*. The Emperor, however, encouraged immigration with generous land grants in a fertile coastal plain near Vera Cruz. About 500 people, some with faithful slaves, arrived within a year at Carlota, as Shelby named the new town in honor of the beautiful Empress of Mexico. But the French army evacuated, Indian soldiers of Juárez moved in, and this last pathetic attempt to fulfill the Confederacy's "purple dream" was rudely liquidated.

The vast majority of Southern white people returned to their former allegiance, retaining only a nostalgic loyalty to the Stars and Bars. Nevertheless, something much more powerful and pervasive than a Confederate government in exile took place. This was the firm and almost unanimous resolve by Southerners of European descent to keep the South a "white man's country." That conviction, observed a Southern historian, "whether expressed with the frenzy of a demagogue or maintained with a patrician's quietude, is the cardinal test of a Southerner and the central theme of Southern history." It implied, primarily, keeping the emancipated Negro subservient, like the helots in ancient Sparta. This Confederate "underground," as we may call it, has been highly successful in a formally reunited country. In the British and French West Indies, descendants of Negro slaves now rule unchallenged; but the American South has remained "white man's country" to this day.

This deep determination and nourished resentment never exploded into violent nationalism, because the Southerner had a long training in representative government and democratic politics. He applied violence locally and sporadically to keep the Negro down, but in general he had the patience to wait, knowing that under a federal system he would eventually get his own way; no federal government could maintain a squad of soldiers on every plantation. The North may have won the war, but the white South won the peace. It preserved the essence of slavery: — a pool of cheap, subservient labor — but escaped the capital outlays and social obligations that slavery imposed on the masters. So, what difference did it make whether terms imposed on the defeated South, under the name reconstruction, were tender or severe? It made a vast deal of difference. Lincoln's plan for immediate reentrance to the Union "as it was" would have made possible a policy of gradualism toward the Negro. It was wrecked by a combination of Southern folly and Radical malevolence.

The economic plight of the South in 1865 was deplorable; far worse than that of central Europe in 1919 or 1945. Unfortunately, the Southern sufferings of that era entered into the reconstruction myth as something deliberately imposed by the North, not the natural result of war and secession. The country had neither capital or currency. Where Sherman and Sheridan had passed, almost the entire apparatus of civilized life had been destroyed. In many parts, the white rural underworld swarmed out of swamps and hills to loot the planters whom it envied, and kill the Negroes whom it hated. These probably did as much damage as had the Union armies. No Southern bank was solvent, no shop had much to sell. Few schools were left for white children, and none for Negroes. Young men of family, who had interrupted their education to fight for Southern independence, had to labor in the fields to keep their families from starving; and a planter's family which still had young men was deemed fortunate. "Pretty much the whole of life has been merely not dying," wrote the poet Sidney Lanier. But the landed basis of Southern wealth was still there, and in regions where the invading armies had not penetrated, Negroes continued to work for their former masters and life went on as before the war. Texas, uninvaded by the Union army until the end of the war, and whose manpower losses had been relatively small, was back to normal by the fall of 1865, and her population increased 35 per cent in that decade. But the Carolinas, Georgia, and the Gulf states gained only 4.4 per cent between 1860 and 1870.

Adversity brought many fine qualities to the fore. One Confederate who refused to be defeated was Washington Duke, who returned from army service to his little farm near Durham Station, North Carolina, with total assets of one log cabin, two blind mules, half a dollar, and a barn full of local-grown bright tobacco. Sherman's army, quartered nearby while waiting for Joe Johnston to surrender, found this tobacco to its liking and carried a demand for it north. This encouraged Duke and his young sons to set up a small factory, whence "Bull Durham" in muslin bags began to furnish the "makings" for cigarettes all over the country. Similarly, the Reynolds family built up Winston, North Carolina, and pipe and cigarette smoking began to replace the traditional "chaw" as the favorite American method of taking tobacco.

Normal trading relations with the North and the world were promptly restored to the South; and the victorious Union, unlike the Germans and Russians after suppressing Polish, Hungarian, and other rebellions, did not systematically confiscate private property. All Confederate and state property — which amounted to very little — was confiscated, but President Johnson's attorney general ruled that peace turned wartime confiscation of personal property into mere sequestration until the owner established his claim and took the oath of allegiance. Lands abandoned in occupied parts of the South, such as Louisiana and the sea islands of South Carolina, were in many instances sold for unpaid taxes, bought in by the government and parceled out to freedmen, but the balance of the purchase price was paid to the original owners. General Lee was compensated for his Arlington estate being taken as a national cemetery; and Richard L. Cox, whose valuable estate in Georgetown, District of Columbia, was turned over to a colored orphans' home when he defected to the Confederacy, got it back after the war and the orphans were ousted.

A large segment of the Confederate officer class, especially in the upper

South, sought better opportunities in the cities of the border states or in Philadelphia and New York. Baltimore for many years was jocosely nicknamed "the poorhouse of the Confederacy"; during the rest of the century many of Baltimore's prominent business and professional men were from Virginia and further south. Some of the most eminent Americans in arts and letters in the postwar generation were Southerners — Frederick Barnard, Joseph LeConte, H. H. Richardson, Basil Gildersleeve, George W. Cable, for example — but their careers were made outside the former Confederacy.

2. Presidential Reconstruction

Reconstruction is still a controversial subject in American history, distorted by emotion. A proud people led by a warrior caste who believed themselves to be invincible were badly whipped; and on top of the resulting emotional trauma, reconstruction was imposed by the victors. Naturally, a fabulous theory about the war and reconstruction was built up, as in Germany about World War I; and as Hitler used the Jews and the Allies as scapegoats, so the white South used Negroes and Republicans. This Reconstruction stereotype, already generally accepted in 1890, was promoted by David W. Griffith's film *The Birth of a Nation* (1915), and reinforced by Margaret Mitchell's novel *Gone With the Wind* (1936). It has now taken so strong a hold on the American mind, North as well as South, that it seems hopeless for a mere historian to deflate it.

The accepted fable represents reconstruction as the ruthless attempt of Northern politicians to subject the white South, starving and helpless, to an abominable rule by ex-slaves which, as the Bible says, is a thing the earth cannot bear,[1] and from which it was rescued by white-hooded knights on horseback who put the Negro "back where he belonged." There is some truth in this, but it is far from being the whole truth; and only recently have Southern as well as Northern historians endeavored to bring out facts on the other side. Yet, even after that is known, reconstruction was a deplorable and tragic episode in our history.

One basic fact, ignored by the Griffith-Mitchell stereotype, is this: The white people of the former Confederacy were masters in their own states for a period of one to three years, when no compulsion was put upon them to enfranchise the Negro. During that period, when no Negro was allowed to vote, nothing was done to prepare him for responsible citizenship; on the contrary, the whites did everything conceivable to humiliate him and keep him down. In the South there were half a million free Negroes — mechanics, truck farmers, barbers, small business men, and the like; the literate third-generation free colored of New Orleans collectively owned property worth $15 million. These could have been used as a nucleus to educate the ex-slaves; but the white South would have none of that, or of them. And no counsel

1. Proverbs xxx.2. Compare Kipling's poem "The Servant When He Reigneth."

was taken of Maryland and Kentucky, whose freed slave population quietly took its place in society without violence or repression.

Nor does the reconstruction stereotype mention the streams of private benevolence which poured in from the North immediately after the war. Hodding Carter has estimated that $4 million in food, besides what the government distributed, was donated by Northerners to relieve hunger by the end of 1867. George Peabody, a Massachussets-born financier, set up a trust fund of $3.5 million to promote primary education in the "suffering South," and with no racial strings. Grant, Farragut, and Hamilton Fish were on the board of trustees, and Barnas Sears, a former president of Brown University who administered this and Peabody's other Southern charities, saw to it that the money was well spent.

General Samuel C. Armstrong, colonel of a Negro regiment in the war, was so moved by the plight of the freedmen at Hampton, Virginia, in 1886, that he raised funds to found the Hampton Normal and Industrial Institute. His object, which the Institute admirably served, was to afford the Negroes both mental and manual training, to fit them for freedom. Booker T. Washington was an early alumnus. Other "damyankees" who helped the South to rise again were General Clinton B. Fisk who founded Fisk University at Nashville, in 1865; Paul Tulane who revived the moribund university in Lousiana which now bears his name; and Edward Atkinson, an economist who promoted diversified agriculture and cotton manufacture in the South. Massachusetts-born William Marsh Rice of Houston, a Texas Unionist, was so badly treated during the war that he left Texas never to return but, like Loyalist Count Rumford, he remembered his old home in his will and founded Rice Institute, now Rice University. In New York City in 1868 a financial drive headed by the Rev. Henry Ward Beecher and Bishop Potter was launched for support of Washington College in Lexington, Virginia, of which Robert E. Lee had become president. For the General had captured all well-disposed hearts in the North by his innate nobility and his advice to all Southerners to accept war's verdict.

The political aspects of reconstruction were discussed in Congress during the war. Were the seceded states to be considered in or out of the Union after the rebellion had been crushed? If secession was illegal, the Southern states would still be states of the Union. But if secession was constitutional, the Confederacy might consistently be treated as a conquered country. Yet each side adopted the proper deduction from the other's premise! Radical Republicans managed to prove to their satisfaction that the Southern states had forfeited their rights, whilst former secessionists clamored for privileges in the Union which they had made every effort to destroy.

Lincoln in his last speech, on 11 April 1865, declared that the question whether the Southern states were in or out of the Union was a "pernicious abstraction." Obviously they were not "in their proper practical relation with the Union"; hence everyone's object should be to restore that relation. The

President himself had already pursued that policy, and at the time of his death loyal state governments, organized by virtue of his proclamation of 1863 that these could be organized as soon as 10 per cent of the 1860 voters had taken an oath of allegiance, controlled almost the whole of Tennessee, and a large part of Arkansas and Louisiana.

The Negro was the central figure in reconstruction. Lincoln, who anticipated the difficulty of making large numbers of free Negroes live amicably with whites, believed that colonization of that race offered the best solution, and made several fruitless efforts to start it. Lincoln was probably right; a wholesale colonization of the freedmen in, say, Arizona, as had been done with the five civilized Indian tribes in Oklahoma, might have solved the problem of fitting people of African origin into a predominantly European society without amalgamation. That, one must admit, has never been done anywhere, either in North or South Africa, Britain or the West Indies. And in many countries where Negroes have won complete control, as in Haiti and the Congo, they have killed or expelled the whites. Colonization was impractical in postwar America because the Negro did not wish to leave and the Southern whites wanted him to stay and work for them. Thus the freedman became temporarily a ward of the Union with undetermined status and a dubious future. The Union victory and Amendment XIII to the Constitution set him free but made no provision for his livelihood. Many Negroes, assuming that freedom meant leisure, took to the woods or clustered about army posts, living on doles and dying of camp diseases.

Congress recognized this new responsibility by creating the Freedmen's Bureau of the war department in March 1865, with general powers of relief and guardianship over all refugees. It performed wonders in relief but not in racial readjustment, largely because of Southern white obstruction to its efforts. Staffed largely by civilians and headed by General O. O. Howard, the Freedmen's Bureau issued emergency rations, established more than 40 hospitals, urged Negroes to return to their former masters and work for agreed wages, restored thousands of white refugees to their homes, set up courts to adjust disputes between employers and employees, and founded the first schools that the Southern Negro ever had, besides helping to support four colleges for his higher education — Howard, Hampton, Atlanta, and Fisk. The Bureau's work was not confined to Negroes; out of 21 million rations distributed in two years, 5.5 million were issued to white people. The usual mistakes were made that always occur when an army of "do-gooders" is turned loose; but the work of the Freedman's Bureau compares favorably with that of lush, overstaffed UNRRA in Europe after World War II.

Lincoln's reconstruction plan progressed smoothly during the year 1865. President Johnson appointed provisional civil governors in every former Confederate state where Lincoln had not already done so. Each governor summoned a state constitutional convention, elected by former citizens of the Confederacy who took the oath of allegiance to the United States. Fourteen specified classes, assumed to be impenitent rebels, were not allowed to vote: civil officials of the Confederacy, state governors, general officers of the Confederate army and senior officers of the navy, former U.S. Army or Navy officers or congressmen who had defected, and all other Confederates worth over $20,000. These, however, could be pardoned by the President if they asked for it and swore allegiance; and almost 14,000, starting with General Lee, did just that. Thus, there was no general proscription, but the immediate effect was to exclude many natural leaders and experienced statesmen from the new state governments. No Negroes were allowed to vote for delegates to the conventions, or in the state governments that they set up. These conventions declared invalid the ordinances of secession, repudiated state war debts, admitted the abolition of slavery, and amended the state constitutions. Elections were promptly held, and by January 1866 civil administrations were functioning in every former Confederate state except Texas. President Johnson restored the writ of habeas corpus, and on 20 August 1866 declared the "insurrection" at an end, "and that peace, order, tranquility and civil authority now exist in and throughout the whole of the United States."

Such was the fact; yet within a few months this promising work was undone, and the former Confederate states were once more thrown into the melting pot. Radicals in Congress had vowed to do this even before Lincoln's death, but they never could have got away with it but for the provocation given by the restored state governments.

This provocation consisted, partly, in what seemed an excessive participation of former Confederate officers in the new governments, their occasional acts of defiance, such as the governor of Mississippi refusing to display the national flag on the state capitol, insulting speeches about "Yankee vandals," and the like. But mostly it was the new black codes, implementing a determination of middle- and lower-class whites to keep the Negro "in his place," that fed ammunition to the Radicals. Many leaders of the Confederacy such as Generals Lee and Wade Hampton, and Vice President Stephens, deplored this trend and even advised that respectable, property-owning Negroes be given the vote on the same terms as white men; but their words of wisdom were not heeded. The white South felt that security required all Negroes to be kept down. This was not all prejudice. No benefit was derived from British experience of emancipation because a revolt of landless Negroes in Jamaica erupted in October 1865 and had to be violently suppressed. The only two nations that had long been controlled by Negroes, Liberia and Haiti, did not offer promising examples of that race's capacity for self-government. In Haiti a burlesque imitation of Napoleon III, "L'Empereur Faustin I," had recently been overthrown by violence.

Every Southern state gave the freedmen essential rights to contract, sue and be sued, to own and inherit some forms of property. Their marriages, which under slavery had no more significance than the mating of cattle, were legalized. But in no instance were they accorded the vote or made eligible for juries; nor could they be witnesses in a lawsuit unless a Negro were involved, or possess firearms, bowie knives, or liquor. In some states the freedmen were forbidden to engage in any occupation other than domestic service or agriculture, or were required to pay prohibitive license fees to do anything else. Certain Negro children were forcibly bound out as apprentices to white people in Mississippi. That state even forbade Negroes to own or lease rural real estate, and re-enacted the old slave code for cases not covered by the new laws. Municipal regulations were devised to impress inferiority on the Negro. Faulkner's Mayor Sartoris's forbidding a Negro woman to appear on the street without an apron may have been fiction, but in some places a Negro was forbidden to come to town without an employer's permission, or he was required to prove that he had some acceptable occupation as an alternative to being hired out to a white man. These black codes of 1865–66 in many ways resemble Hitler's laws against the Jews, but they were not conceived as a prelude to extermination. The white South wanted the Negro to stay, as a valuable worker; but he must be compelled to labor for a stable economy; and for social security he must be prevented from getting "uppity," a word still common in the South. Elsewhere in the United States it was deemed a virtue for a poor man to rise; in the South, for a Negro to better his condition aroused suspicion and invited violence from his poor white neighbors.

Southern whites, who had never dreamed it possible to live side by side with large numbers of free Negroes, believed their new laws to be liberal and generous; they were passed by people who "understood the colored." But from the Negro and Radical point of view they were a palpable attempt to evade the Emancipation Proclamation. The more objectionable laws, nullified by the Freedmen's Bureau (which had power to regulate labor contracts and take jurisdiction over conflicts involving Negroes) were both futile and injudicious; but equally futile in the long run was Northern opposition. The essential principle of the black codes, making the Negro a second-class citizen, is defiantly maintained by the white public of the lower South a century after the war ended.

Little was done by the new state governments to protect Negroes from white hoodlums. Efforts of the Freedmen's Bureau to help the former slaves were bitterly resented as the "outside interference" of "nigger lovers" and were often nullified by violence such as burning schools set up by the Bureau, persecuting or running white teachers from the North out of town. The Southern white yeomanry firmly believed that education "spoiled" the Negro, that he must forever be required to be the hewer of wood and drawer of water for a superior race. The black codes, as Hodding Carter writes, were "a backward-looking effort to deal with a desperately new problem." And the sad thing is that they need never have been, had the old planter aristocracy not forfeited its leadership to "poor white trash."

3. Congress Takes a Hand, 1866–1868

That was the situation when the Congress elected in November 1864 assembled in December 1865. Lincoln and Johnson had refrained from calling a special session, hoping to carry out their reconstruction program without interference. Every former Confederate state except Texas now had a government elected under the presidential plan; the Freedmen's Bureau had successfully wrestled with Negro vagrancy and the destitution of both races, and agriculture was returing to normal; but black codes of varying severity were on the statute books. Reconstruction appeared to be an accomplished fact.

Accomplished facts, however, bore no terrors for the Radical leaders, who were determined to set up new state governments based on manhood (including Negro) suffrage, governments which they assumed would be run by the Republican party. Congress refused to allow any member-elect from the reconstructed states to take his seat, and set up a joint committee on reconstruction, a revival of that wartime pest, the committee on the conduct of the war. This committee promptly opened hearings on conditions in the Southern states, largely from witnesses who spread on the record tales of defiant rebels and oppressed Negroes and Unionists.

Congressional opposition to the Lincoln-Johnson policy was due in large part to legislative *esprit de corps.* That has happened after each of our great wars; Congress feels frustrated by the executive calling the tunes and winning all the glory, and is mad to get back "into the act." Hatred engendered by the war and the assassination of Lincoln, and tales of horror spread about by the human wrecks released from Andersonville, also played their part. But the fundamental reason for the forthcoming appeal to passion seems to have been political. If the Southern states returned a solid Democratic contingent to Congress, the reunited Democratic party would have a majority in both houses and be able to repeal the fiscal, homestead, and other legislation passed by Republican congresses. As Thaddeus Stevens put it, the states of the South "ought never to be recognized as valid states, until the Constitution shall have been so amended . . . as to secure perpetual ascendancy" to the Republican party. The amendment that Stevens had in mind was Negro suffrage. By this device, selfish and cynical politicians obtained the support of humanitarians and doctrinaires who believed the vote to be necessary to protect and uplift the Negro.

Thaddeus Stevens, a sour and angry congressman, really loved the Negroes; at least he lived with one, and had himself buried among them. The destruction of his property at Chambersburg by Lee's soldiers in 1863 had made him at the age of seventy-four harsh and bitter in his hatred, which now encompassed the memory of Lincoln with the living Johnson. Former slaves he would exalt to political and social equality; the former masters he would disfranchise and expropriate, distributing their landed property among the freedmen. Stevens was a finished parliamentarian, with a talent for controlled invective and devastating sarcasm. Charles Sumner, Republican leader in the Senate, vain, pedantic, and irritable, was a doctrinaire. Against the ex-Confederates he cherished no vindictive feelings; but, with little personal knowledge of former slaves, he believed that they only wanted the vote to prove themselves worthy of sharing the duties and privileges of citizenship. While Sumner, who loved the sound of his own voice, declaimed in polished periods on the rights and wrongs of the colored, Stevens played for time. It would not do to make an issue of Negro suffrage on its merits, for few of the Northern states outside New England allowed their Negroes to vote; and the reaction of the average Union veteran to his contacts with the freedmen bordered on contempt.

In April 1866 the joint committee reported a congressional plan for reconstruction, in its essence a denial of the right of statehood to the South until Negro equality should be incorporated in their laws. Since even the Radicals doubted the constitutionality of any act of Congress to that effect, their plan was embodied in what subsequently became Amendments XIV and XV to the Constitution. These guaranteed to Negroes civil rights and the vote, disqualified ex-Confederates who had formerly held federal office, and forbade the states to pay Confederate war debts. Southern representatives would be admitted to Congress, it was announced, only on condition of their states ratifying the XIV Amendment. In July 1866 Congress passed over the President's veto an act giving the Freedmen's Bureau a new lease on life, at a time when its legitimate relief work was almost completed; and this worthy organization degenerated into a political machine.

The issue was now joined between President Johnson and the Radicals. Everything turned on the election of a new House of Representatives in November 1866. Politically astute Lincoln might have out-maneuvered the sharp-witted Radical leaders, but Johnson played into their hands. Of origin as humble as Lincoln's, in early life a tailor in a Tennessee mountain village and unable to write until taught by his wife, he had honesty and courage, but wanted tact and the art of winning men's minds and hearts. His policy was identical with Lincoln's, but he was unable to connect with Northern sentiment. And Johnson was in a far more difficult situation than Lincoln had been on the morrow of victory and the eve of death. He had taken over Lincoln's cabinet, and both Seward and Welles were loyal to him, but Stanton sneaked out cabinet secrets to the Radicals and they, including most of the professional Republican politicians, controlled the party machinery and the civil service. Johnson's pugnacious personality antagonized people, and by undignified acts and foolish speeches he lost the support of the Northern pulpit, press, and business.

In the congressional campaign of 1866, the most important off-presidential election in our history, the issue was clearly drawn; in most districts the voters had to choose between a Radical Republican and a Copperhead Democrat.

Johnson openly supported the Democrats but managed the campaign very ill. Incapable of advocating a tolerant policy in a tolerant manner, his "swing around the circle," a stumping tour of the Middle West, became an undignified contest of vituperation. Instead of appealing to the memory of Lincoln, and to the Christian virtue of forgiveness, he called names and rattled the dry bones of state rights. The Radicals, on the other hand, soft-pedaling Negro suffrage, made the issue one of "patriotism" against "rebellion." Reiterated tales of Southern defiance and race riots at Memphis and New Orleans in which hundreds of Negroes were murdered by white hoodlums, were played up for even more than they were worth. "Jefferson Davis is in the casemate at Fortress Monroe, but Andrew Johnson is doing his work," declared Sumner. "Witness Memphis, witness New Orleans." Under such circumstances it is not surprising that the Northern people returned a sufficient Republican majority to override any presidential veto.

The newly elected Congress met on 7 March 1867 in a vindictive temper. There is nothing to equal the kindness of the American heart when touched, except the bad judgment of Americans when irritated; and although the truth about the Southern states was enough to annoy men of good will, Radical propaganda had so enlarged on the facts as to make it seem that a defiantly disloyal South was planning to revive the Confederacy. One heard no more in Washington "the words peace, pardon and clemency" as Chambrun did in April 1865; now, barely eighteen months later, all one heard spoken of was armed force, punishment, retaliation. Photographs of the Radical leaders of this period, and of Johnson too, show visages glowering balefully like a Mussolini or a Hitler, in contrast to the calm and dignified war leaders, or the conventional smiles of latter-day politicians.

Lincoln had grasped a great truth which other Western statesmen never realized until 1945: that reconstruction of a shattered empire must be approached with wisdom rather than strict justice; the defeated foe must be helped to his feet and treated more like the prodigal son than a convicted felon. Lincoln and Johnson had tried this Christian policy on the South; the South (so it seemed) had contemptuously declined the friendly hand and defied the victors. Woe, then, to the South!

4. Reconstruction Reconstructed, 1867–1875

In March 1867 military rule by virtue of act of Congress replaced the civil administrations which had been operating in the South for one or two years. The first Reconstruction Act divided the South into five military districts under general officers who were to take orders from General Grant, not the President, and whose first duties were to protect persons and property, create a new electorate based on male suffrage, and supervise the election of conventions to draft new state constitutions on the same basis. They were also given the right to replace civil officials elected by fraud or violence, and to purge legislatures of "disloyal" members.

The five military governors, known in Southern literature as the "satraps" or "despots," [1] ruled with a firm hand, though sometimes with flagrant disregard of civil rights. Confederate veterans' organizations, parades, and even historical societies were suppressed. Thousands of local officials and the governors of six states were removed. Civil courts were superseded by military tribunals, when the courts could not be depended on to punish violence against Negroes. The legislatures of Georgia, Alabama, and Louisiana were purged in the Cromwellian sense; state laws were set aside or modified. An army of occupation, some 20,000 strong and aided by Negro militia, enforced this military rule, harsh indeed but with the merits of honesty and efficiency. Great efforts were made by the military to cope with economic disorganization and to regulate social life. Thus, in South Carolina General Dan Sickles, the most hated of the "satraps," stayed foreclosures on property, made the wages of farm laborers a first lien on crops, prohibited the manufacture of whisky, and forbade discrimination against Negroes. The troops were mostly confined in forts, army posts, and barracks; they were not quartered on the people in traditional army of occupation fashion, and not called out except to supervise elections and quell disorder.

In each of the ten states over which they had jurisdiction, the Union military enrolled a new electorate. In South Carolina, Alabama, Florida, Mississippi, and Louisiana the Negro voters outnumbered the white. This electorate chose in every state a constitutional convention which drafted a new constitution enfranchising Negroes, disqualifying former Confederate leaders, and guaranteeing civil and political equality to the freedmen.

The new constitutions were more democratic than those they superseded. South Carolina's, for example, abolished property qualifications for officeholding, drew up a new bill of rights, reformed local government and judicial administration, abolished imprisonment for debt, protected homesteads from foreclosure, enlarged the rights of women, and established the state's first system of universal public education. By the summer of 1868 reconstructed governments had been set up in eight of the Southern states; the other three — Mississippi, Texas, and Virginia — were reconstructed in 1870. After their legislatures had ratified Amendments XIV and XV, Congress formally readmitted them to the Union, seated their elected representatives and senators, and, as soon as the supremacy of the new governments appeared reasonably secure, withdrew or greatly diminished the army garrisons.

Both conventions and legislatures might have been of higher quality if thousands of whites had not boycotted the elections, or if they had conde-

1. The initial appointees were Generals Schofield, Thomas, Ord, Sickles, and Sheridan. The last two (and Pope who relieved Thomas) were replaced by President Grant after they had made themselves obnoxious to the white population through arbitrary acts.

scended to organize the Negro vote and play on the Negro's basic trust in his old master class and not left that field to the "carpetbaggers" and "scalawags." President Johnson pardoned 13,500 Confederates excluded by earlier acts, and his "universal" proclamation at Christmastide 1868 left only 300 persons unpardoned and ineligible to vote, in the entire South. But congressional reconstruction acts annulled the benefits of executive clemency by denying political privileges to those pardoned by the two Presidents.

The "carpetbagger" was supposed to be a Northern adventurer who came South after the war with all his possessions in a carpetbag — a satchel made of two squares of carpeting held together by cloth or leather. A "scalawag" meant any Southern white who joined the Republican party or took a job under the Freedmen's Bureau. Some carpetbaggers were indeed adventurers — H. C. Warmouth, a notoriously corrupt governor of Louisiana, had been a Union officer with a bad war record — but many were Northerners who came South after the war to promote new industries. John T. Wilder and Willard Warner of Ohio, both Union general officers, were largely responsible for starting the iron works at Birmingham and Chattanooga. And some of the alleged scalawags, such as General Longstreet and Colonels J. A. Alcorn and R. W. Flournoy, were former Confederate officers who joined the Republican party in hope of moderating Radical zeal.

Although some illiterate Negroes were elected to state conventions and legislatures, many of the colored leaders were men of education who showed ability equal to the ordinary run of state legislators anywhere. For instance, Jonathan J. Wright, state senator and associate justice of the supreme court of South Carolina, had been a member of the Pennsylvania bar before the war; Robert B. Elliott, member of the lower house of South Carolina and later representative in Congress, had been educated at Eton College in England. Hiram R. Revels, educated at Knox College, pastor of a Baltimore church before the war and chaplain to a Negro regiment, was elected in 1870 to Jefferson Davis's former seat in the United States Senate; John R. Lynch, a self-educated former slave of Louisiana, later a professional photographer, became speaker of his state house of representatives and a congressman. Of those whom he observed in Congress, Speaker Blaine wrote, "They were as a rule studious, earnest, ambitious men, whose public conduct . . . would be honorable to any race." Black faces in the newly elected legislatures were naturally conspicuous, and obnoxious to the average Southern white; but it is inaccurate to describe the state system under reconstruction as Negro rule. The colored controlled no state government at any time, and only in South Carolina did they ever have a majority in either house. Owing to their inexperience, they were manipulated by carpetbaggers and scalawags, on whom most of the blame for the corruption of these states should be placed, and who alone profited by it. Negroes did not attempt to domineer over or pass vindictive legislation against their former masters; in Mississippi the colored members of the legislature even petitioned Congress to restore the political abilities of former Confederates. Unlike the Congolese Africans who went on a vicious rampage in 1960 when Belgian rule was withdrawn, the Southern Negro of 1865–75 behaved like a civilized and responsible citizen. He made no attempt to repeal laws against mixed marriages or to force his way into white society; on the contrary, he formed hundreds of "African" Methodist, Baptist, and other Protestant churches.

Although the white South was willing to tolerate colored clowns in office, it bitterly resented any Negro who showed political intelligence or ability, since he disproved the theory that his race was incapable of improvement. James Pike, on his way south in 1873, looked in at the lower house of the Virginia assembly where a "member three-quarters black" was speaking ably against a certain tax bill. He was "listened to with a good deal of interest after it was found that he could not be drowned out by rustlings and loud talk," although "the venerable old Virginia gentlemen on the Democratic benches looked on with a mixture of surprise and chagrin at the spectacle." That was typical: surprise that the Negro could do it, chagrin that he was in a position to do it; and, had these been poor whites instead of gentlemen, there would have been a note of hatred.

Although the Radical governments that flourished for periods of two years (in North Carolina) to eight years (in Louisiana, Florida, and Texas) are famous for picturesque and flagrant forms of corruption, such as a free restaurant-bar for the Palmetto State "solons," and Governor Warmouth's stealing half a million dollars from Louisiana school funds, they were also responsible for much good legislation. War damage to public buildings, bridges, and roads was repaired; railroad building — a principal source of graft — was encouraged; efforts were made to obtain capital and settlers from the North and Europe; and, most of all, free public education for all children, although in racially separate schools, was established throughout the South by 1870. The black codes, naturally, were repealed, and laws against vagrancy were applied equally to both races. Penal systems were modified, though not always improved; public works were undertaken. All this cost money, still a scarce commodity in the South, and as the people could not bear heavy taxation, deficit financing was the order of the day. It may be said in excuse, though not in defense, of the reconstructed state governments, that their "lily-white" successors and may of their Northern contemporaries were no better; and that major operations such as those of the Whisky Ring and Boss Tweed's steal of over $100 million from New York City threw the operations of Southern carpetbaggers and scalawags into the shade.

A curious feature of reconstruction is the rival expectations that were built up. The former slaves believed that each Negro family was to be given "forty acres and a mule" by Uncle Sam; and Thaddeus Stevens, had he lived, would have pressed for just that, but nothing of the sort was attempted. Nor is it likely that giving land to former slaves would have helped them much. Attempts to set up peasant proprieties out of large landed estates, in Mexico and elsewhere, have mostly failed, as the small landowner cannot maintain him-self without seed, stock, implements, and training to tide him over the first years of independence. And if he does not get these, as he certainly would not have done in the United States, he drifts back to serfdom.

On the other side, many Southern whites indulged the wild notion that if they could only elect a solid Democratic contingent to Congress, these would join with Northern Democrats to pay compensation for the freed slaves, and discharge the Confederate debt. A bill to indemnify former slaves for their years of servitude would have had a better chance in Congress.

After all that can be said in their favor, the congressionally reconstructed state governments were a disgrace, and in the end neither the freedmen nor the Republican party profited. The Negroes, thrown into politics without preparation or experience, under conditions which would have tried the wisest statesmanship, were abandoned by the best men of the South and deceived by the worst; their innocence exposed them to temptation and their ignorance betrayed them into the hands of astute and mischievous spoilsmen. Some of the wisest men in the North predicted this. Even old abolitionist Garrison wished the Negroes to be given more education before they were accorded the vote.

Worse disgrace was to come — the impeachment of President Johnson and the hooded violence of the Ku Klux Klan.

5. Impeachment of Johnson and End of Reconstruction

The Radical leaders of the Republican party, not content with establishing party ascendancy in the South, aimed at capturing the federal government under guise of putting the presidency under wraps. By a series of usurpations they intended to make the majority in Congress the ultimate judge of its own powers, and the President a mere chairman of a cabinet responsible to Con-gress, as the British cabinet is to the House of Commons. An opening move in this game was the Tenure of Office Act of March 1867 which made it impossible for the President to control his administration, by requiring him to obtain the advice and consent of the Senate for removals as well as appoint-ments to office. The next move was to dispose of Johnson by impeachment, so that Radical Ben Wade, president pro tem of the Senate, would succeed to his office and title.

Johnson, convinced that the Tenure of Office Act was unconstitutional — an attitude later vindicated by the Supreme Court in *Myers* v. *United States* — countered in August 1867 by ordering Secretary Stanton, who had long been playing with the Radicals, to resign. Stanton refused and barricaded himself in the war department. On 24 February 1868 the House of Representatives impeached the President before the Senate, "for high crimes and misdemean-ors," as the Constitution provides. Ten of the eleven articles of impeachment rang changes on the removal of Stanton, the other consisted of garbled newspaper reports of the President's speeches.

Although a monstrous charge preferred by George S. Boutwell, that Johnson was accessory to the murder of Lincoln, was not included, the impeachment of Johnson was one of the most disgraceful episodes in our history. It was managed by a committee led by Benjamin F. Butler and Thaddeus Stevens, who exhausted every device, appealed to every prejudice and passion, and rode roughshod, when they could, over legal obstacles in their ruthless attempt to punish the President for his opposition to their plans. Ben Butler, now uglier and paunchier than ever, employed a device borrowed from Jenkins's ear in 1739: he illustrated an oration on the horrors of presidential reconstruction by waving a bloody shirt which allegedly belonged to an Ohio carpetbagger flogged by Klansmen in Mississippi.

Johnson was defended by able counsel including William Maxwell Evarts, leader of the American bar, and Benjamin R. Curtis, formerly a justice of the Supreme Court. They tore the prosecution's case to shreds. No valid grounds, legal or otherwise, existed for impeachment. Yet the Radicals would have succeeded in their object but for Chief Justice Chase's insistence on legal procedure, and for seven courageous Republican senators who sacrificed their political future by voting for acquittal: Grimes of Iowa, Trumbull of Illinois, Ross of Kansas, Fessenden of Maine, Van Winkle of West Virginia, Fowler of Tennessee, and Henderson of Missouri.[1] One more affirmative vote, and Ben Wade, president of the Senate, would have been installed in the White House. Then, in all probability, the Supreme Court would have been battered into submission and the Radicals would have triumphed over the Constitution as completely as over the South.

After the trial was over, President Johnson had less than ten months to serve, and the Republican national nominating convention met shortly after his acquittal. There was no longer any effective opposition to the Radicals within party ranks, and the reconstructed states gave them plenty of docile delegates. General Grant, who, to his discredit and subsequent sorrow, had been brought into the Radical camp by arousing an ambition to be President, obtained the nomination by acclamation, with Schuyler Colfax of Indiana for Vice President. The Democrats, regarding Johnson as a liability, nominated Horatio Seymour, the war governor of New York who had skated close to copperheadism. Grant won 214 electoral votes to Seymour's 80, but his plurality in the popular vote was only 300,000; three Southern states which would certainly have voted for Seymour took no part in the election. It would have been better for the country had that elderly lawyer and politician of the Jackson-Van Buren line been President for the next eight years, instead of General Grant.

1. President Kennedy told the story of Senator Edmund G. Ross in his *Profiles of Courage*. All seven were denounced as Benedict Arnolds, Judas Iscariots, etc., and all but Grimes and Fessenden, who died shortly, were defeated when next they came up for election.

Social revolutions such as Congress intended the reconstruction of the South to be, cannot be accomplished except by overwhelming force applied mercilessly and over a long period of time. That is how fascist and communist governments operate, but no Christian government could be merciless; and the South succeeded in wearing down Northern willingness to apply even limited force.

Thaddeus Stevens had the wit to see that political equality would avail the Negroes little, as long as the whites owned the land. His death in 1868 cost Radicalism its fighting edge, and his program of confiscation was not carried out. Thenceforth congressional reconstruction was on the defensive. Of several attempts to hold ground already won, the most notable was Amendment XV to the Constitution, ratified in 1870, forbidding the states to deny anyone the vote "on account of race, color, or previous condition of servitude." To the time of writing this has proved a mere paper guarantee.

Even if the congressionally reconstructed states had been as pure as Jeffersonian Virginia, the Southern whites would have overthrown them by fair means or foul, because of racial animosity and excessive taxation. Poor-white animosity was directed primarily against Negro schools and militia. Northern teachers who came South to teach the freedmen were ostracized, forced to board with colored families (and then accused of miscegenation), whipped, even murdered. The black militia companies organized by the carpetbag governors to preserve law and order were bitterly hated, and some of their officers were murdered. To the Southern gentry, the carpetbag governments were rendered intolerable by a crushing burden of taxation on real estate, forcing thousands of farms which the owners were painfully trying to bring back into production, to be sold for unpaid taxes. And the situation became worse after the panic of 1873, which depressed agricultural prices. The planter class was being strangled.

Even before Grant's election the white South was preparing to recover supremacy by the only means left: a combination of tomfoolery and terror. The methods of Radicals who had organized the Negro vote were turned against them and life became very uncomfortable for carpetbaggers, who were apt to find themselves "accidental" targets for the bullets of participants in a shooting affray. The Negroes were dealt with largely by secret societies, of which the most famous, though not the most powerful, was the Ku Klux Klan. It began with a group of wild young men in Pulaski, Tennessee, who discovered that their initiation garb of sheets and pillowcases made them authentic spirits from another world to the superstitious. Realizing political possibilities, they formed other groups which in 1867 organized as "The Invisible Empire of the South." This was before congressional reconstruction began. When it did begin, this and other secret societies, such as the Knights of the White Camellia, became an "invisible empire," policing unruly or allegedly impudent Negroes, delivering spectral warnings against using the ballot, and whipping or even murdering some of those who did. Thus Radical power was paralyzed at its source. Although apologists for the South decry the crimes of the K.K.K. (163 Negroes murdered in one Florida county in 1871, 300 murdered in a few parishes outside New Orleans), they were led by "the flower of Southern manhood," who cannot escape responsibility for acts in the same class with those of Hitler's storm troopers. The "Grand Wizard" of the K.K.K. was General Nathaniel B. Forrest CSA; General Gordon was "Grand Dragon" for Georgia, and former Governor Vance had the same "exalted" rank in North Carolina. The Klan was formally disbanded in 1869 and the Knights the following year; but under one or another guise the intimidation of Negroes went on.

The Radical answer was renewed military occupation of districts formerly evacuated, and a new crop of supervisory acts of Congress authorizing the President to suspend the writ of habeas corpus and suppress disturbances by military force. Some 7400 indictments were found under these acts, but there were relatively few convictions, and only once did President Grant find it expedient to re-establish military rule on a large scale. And he withdrew all Negro units of the regular army.

Grant was re-elected in 1872, but two years later the Democrats captured the House of Representatives, marking Northern repudiation of Radicalism. In the meantime all Southern states had been "readmitted" to representation in Congress, and by the Amnesty Act of 1872 all white men still disfranchised were restored to full political privilege. An immense impact on Northern opinion was exerted through *The Prostrate State* (1873) by a former abolitionist, James S. Pike of Maine. This *Uncle Tom's Cabin* in reverse, an exaggerated description of conditions in South Carolina, has become a classic document of the reconstruction stereotype. During the centennial celebrations of 1875–76 Southern orators like Henry W. Grady and Lucius Quintus Cincinnatus Lamar played on the "mystic chords of memory" to which Lincoln had vainly appealed in 1861, and paid moving tributes to the Great Emancipator himself. In this sentimental meeting of hearts the cause of the freedman was forgotten; and whatever solicitude for him survived in the North was conveniently overlaid by the picture of the "happy darkey" presented by Joel Chandler Harris the creator of Uncle Remus, and Thomas Nelson Page the creator of "Marse Chan's" Sam. In Congress, Ben Butler proposed an amendment to a civil rights bill in 1875 which would have compelled racial integration of all schools in the South, but President Grant had the amendment stricken out on a plea from Barnas Sears, Yankee almoner of the Peabody fund.

By this time the Radicals were in full retreat in the South. Factional struggles between carpetbaggers and scalawags split the Republican party; and the Negroes, finding that their vote produced no "forty acres and a mule," began to desert the Republicans and vote for members of the old master class in whom they had confidence. It was becoming evident that Radical rule could only be maintained by a much stronger army of occupation, but Congress was becoming so tired of reconstruction that the garrisons were progressively weakened. In state after state the white people organized as "Conservatives" or "Redeemers," and recaptured control of the political machinery. This occurred between 1869 and 1871 in Tennessee, Virginia, North Carolina, and Georgia; in 1874–75 in Alabama, Arkansas, Texas, and Mississippi.

What happened in Mississippi is instructive. There the carpetbag Republican governor was Adelbert Ames, a West Pointer from Maine who had fought brilliantly in the Union army and had come to Mississippi hoping to be a conciliator. But the conduct of white men toward Negroes impelled him to champion that race. Even Ames's enemies admitted him to have been an honest and courteous gentleman who did his best to build up the state's economy. Appointed provisional governor by General Grant in 1868 and elected United States Senator in 1870, he resigned to be elected governor of Mississippi in 1873 for a four-year term. Unable to control his more voracious supporters, he alienated some of the best, such as Senator Revels. When elections for the state legislature were coming up in 1875, Ames agreed with the Democratic leaders to disband the Negro militia which, they claimed, were the principal inciters of election riots, in return for a promise to restrain white people from violence. This promise the local Democrats either could not or would not keep, and they had as their leader L. Q. C. Lamar, the silver-tongued orator. Any meeting of Negro voters was apt to be set upon by armed white men; and in these clashes Negroes, still timid and unresourceful, were invariably worsted. Governor Ames appealed to President Grant for federal troops, but was told by the attorney general, "The whole public are tired of these annual autumnal outbreaks in the South." With most of the Republicans intimidated from voting (only four Republican votes cast in one county where there was a Negro majority), the Democrats won a majority in both houses and threatened to impeach Ames. He resigned, since his position was hopeless, and the president of the newly elected senate became governor. A United States Senate committee which investigated this election reported it to be "one of the darkest chapters in American history," but nothing was done about it; the Northern public was sick of the subject.

By 4 March 1877, when Rutherford B. Hayes was inaugurated President, carpetbag regimes had been overthrown in every Southern state except South Carolina and Louisiana. In the Palmetto State two rival governors were elected: General Wade Hampton CSA as champion of the Redeemers, and General Daniel H. Chamberlain USA as candidate of the Republicans. President Hayes broke this deadlock by withdrawing federal troops from Columbia on 10 April 1877, when the Redeemers peaceably took possession. Two weeks later, when the troops were evacuated from New Orleans, white rule was completely restored in Louisiana.

These Redeemer governments did not entirely undo the work of their predecessors. The most prominent and respected of the new governors, such as Wade Hampton and George F. Drew of Florida, had promised to respect the civil rights of the colored, and made their promises good. In every former Confederate state except Texas, which fell into the hands of spoilsmen and crooks, the government was now in the hands of the old officer class. For two decades, Negroes continued to vote in large numbers, and a few were elected to state legislatures. Even more important than laws were good racial relations. Booker T. Washington, a former slave who founded Tuskegee Institute in Alabama, dedicated himself to making his people better farmers and artisans, and discouraged any effort toward political or social equality. Thomas Wentworth Higginson, former colonel of a Negro regiment, found race relations to be just and friendly when he revisited the South. The editor of a Negro newspaper in New York, who went South looking for trouble, found none. In general, white and colored mingled on railroad and street cars, at lunch counters, theaters, circuses, and public parks. But the disgruntled "white supremacists" had only gone underground, as numerous lynchings of Negroes in rural districts indicated; and presently "Jim Crow" would emerge and the lot of the Southern Negro become worse than before.

Thus, by 1877 all former Confederate states were back in the Union and in charge of their domestic affairs, subject only to the requirements of two constitutional amendments to protect the freedmen's civil rights.

Looking back over the whole episode of reconstruction, one must regret that the magnanimous policy of Lincoln was not long followed. Yet, all in all, considering what it cost the Union to preserve itself, the victors treated the vanquished pretty well. A recent European historian of our Civil War remarked wryly that the Poles who were overrun in World War II, the central Europeans subjected to one totalitarian regime after another, the defeated Hungarian rebels of 1956, and the expropriated landowners and middle class in every communist state, including Cuba, would have considered the sufferings of the Southern white people a heavenly dispensation in comparison with theirs.

X L V

The Republican Dynasty

1869-1893

1. *The United States, Great Britain, and Canada*

IT WOULD HAVE BEEN well for Grant's reputation had he retired from public life after his great gesture at Appomattox. He was unfitted for the presidency by temperament, and less equipped for it than any predecessor or successor. The simplicity of character which had shielded him from intrigues during the Civil War exposed him to the wiles of those whose loyalty to himself he mistook for devotion to the public weal; he could never understand that a good soldier did not necessarily make an honest public servant. The death in 1869 of his faithful chief of staff and first war minister, John A. Rawlins, left him with no intimate adviser, and his choice of cabinet members fell, with one or two exceptions, on mediocrities. Of the complex forces that were shaping the United States anew, he was completely unaware.

"Let us have peace," said Grant, when accepting the Republican nomination for the presidency. But internal peace between North and South, which is what he meant, could not be obtained by merely wishing it. Grant had been maneuvered, in part by Southern intransigence, in part by politicians, into the Radical position; but his doubts about that policy were voiced in his first inaugural: "I know no method to secure the repeal of bad or obnoxious laws as effective as their stringent execution." Grant became a fairly consistent supporter of congressional reconstruction.

Foreign affairs, where Grant's innate sense of justice was enforced by a competent secretary of state, Hamilton Fish, show his two administrations in their fairest light. There was much to be done. Seward, by allowing the French (who needed little persuasion) to retire peaceably from Mexico, and by purchasing Alaska from Russia, had eliminated these nations from the American continent. But Earl Russell's peremptory refusal to submit the *Alabama* claims to arbitration prevented any prompt settlement with Great Britain. Postponement of these claims was dangerous. There was a deep feeling of resentment in America that was likely to flare up into war if not satisfied through law. One strong bond, the Canadian reciprocity treaty of 1854, expired in 1866 and was not renewed, largely owing to the rising tide of protectionist policy in the Republican party. When Albert J. Smith, premier of New Brunswick, went to Washington to see what could be done about renewing the treaty, the best offer he could get from the chairman of the ways and means committee was that in return for access to the inshore fisheries of Canada the United States would admit free Canadian firewood, grindstones, old rags, and gypsum.

During the war Canada had been the base for Confederate raids on the United States. The Irish Revolutionary Brotherhood, better known as the Fenians, now took similar liberties from the other side of the border. Two rival Irish Republics were organized in New York City, each with president, cabinet, and general staff in glittering uniforms of green and gold. Each shook down Irish-American business men, congressmen, servant girls, and hod-carriers, for "loans." Each planned to invade Canada, largely with Irish veterans of the Union army, and hold it as hostage for Irish freedom. In 1866 each Irish Republic of New York attempted to execute its plan. In April an invasion of Campobello, future summer home of Franklin D. Roosevelt, was promptly nipped by federal authorities at Eastport, Maine. But the ensuing howl from the Irish vote, with congressional elections only six months away, frightened President Johnson and his cabinet. Before the attorney general and the secretaries of war and of the navy could decide who should take the onus of stopping him, "General" John O'Neil ferried 1500 armed Irishmen across the Niagara river and raised the green flag on old Fort Erie. Next day (2 June 1866) the Canadian militia gave battle, and fled; but the Fenians, too, fled back to New York where they were arrested and promptly released. Ridiculous and futile as they were, these Fenian forays caused Canada much trouble and expense, for which she was never reimbursed by the United States. And the distrust that they aroused was a leading factor in pushing the Canadian federation movement to its consummation in 1867.

The Dominion of Canada was mainly the product of three forces: — the rise of Canadian nationalism, a desire of British liberals to slough off colonial responsibilities, and the ambition of certain elements in the United States to annex Canada. Both Sumner and Seward adhered to the old Ben Franklin doctrine that a division of North America was "unnatural"; that there could never be lasting peace between Britain and the United States while Canada remained British. Most of the Radical Republicans, and Presidents Johnson and Grant, had the same point of view. Without countenancing aggression against Canada, they hoped that the British provinces would join the American Union voluntarily. They played with a suggestion that Britain hand over all her North American possessions to the United States as payment for the *Alabama* claims. And in Britain an important segment of public opinion, the "little Englanders" or "Manchester school," were bored with Canada and her problems and eager to pull out.

Fortunately it was the Canadians themselves who called the tune in this unharmonious trio. In 1866 Confederationists won the provincial elections in New Brunswick and Nova Scotia, which sent delegates to London to discuss a plan of union with the two Canadas (Quebec and Ontario) and with representatives of the British Parliament. Out of this conference came the British North American Act of 1867, to which Queen Victoria gave her assent, and which established the Dominion of Canada.

Dominion government went into effect 1 July 1867 with Sir John Macdonald, one of its principal architects, as premier. The frame of government was parliamentary, like that of Great Britain. It would have been called the Monarchy of Canada but for fear of offending the United States. Even so, Congress passed a joint resolution to the effect that they "viewed with extreme solicitude" the formation of this Confederation on a monarchical basis, hinting that it contravened the Monroe Doctrine, ignoring the statement in Monroe's original message that "with existing European colonies we have not interfered and will not interfere." President Johnson paid no attention to this piece of bad manners, but neither did he extend the hand of fellowship to Premier Macdonald.

According to the British North American Act the British government controlled foreign affairs, war and peace, and appointed the governor general of Canada; but in all other essentials the Canadian Parliament was sovereign. It had plenary powers of taxation and the ministry was responsible to it. On paper, the new Canadian federal government enjoyed more power than the one across the border. It not only appointed governors of the member provinces but could disallow acts of provincial legislatures. All residuary powers rested in parliament, not in the provinces or the people, although it was understood that the traditional civil rights of British subjects were still in force. Thus, sovereignty extended from the top down, not from the people up. Warned by the trouble that state rights had made in the United States, provincial rights were, in theory, ruled out in Canada; but that, as we shall see, did not prevent loud cries of outraged localism and the recovery of many powers by the provinces in practice. Canada bought out the Hudson's Bay Company's territorial rights in 1869, adding a big Northwest Territory to the Dominion. British Columbia joined in 1871; and with the entrance of Prince Edward Island two years later, the Dominion of Canada extended north of the United States boundary from sea to sea and to the Arctic Ocean — excluding only Newfoundland which remained a crown colony, and Alaska which Seward had purchased for the United States.

The organization of this Dominion was an achievement equal to that of the Federal Constitution eighty years earlier. The United States now had a northern neighbor of growing power which could no longer be ignored, trifled with or considered a region for territorial aggrandizement.

President Grant now made a positive contribution to Anglo-American amity by settling the *Alabama* business. After one agreement to submit these claims to arbitration had been rejected by the Senate in 1869, Sir John Rose, finance minister of Canada, staged with Secretary Hamilton Fish a diplomatic play of wooing and yielding that threw dust in the eyes of extremists on both sides. The covenant thus secretly arrived at, the Treaty of Washington of 8

May 1871, provided for submission to arbitration of boundary disputes, the fisheries question, and the *Alabama* claims, and agreed upon rules of neutrality to govern the arbitral tribunal.

In presenting their case to this tribunal at Geneva in December 1871, the United States claimed compensation not only for actual damage inflicted by the Confederate cruisers, but for the numerous transfers of registry occasioned by fear of capture. Hamilton Fish had no intention of pressing these "indirect" claims, but English opinion was outraged by their presentation, and an ill-tempered press discussion ensued. William E. Gladstone, the "Grand Old Man" of British politics, would have withdrawn from the arbitration on that issue had not Charles Francis Adams, the American member, who never forgot that he was a judge, not an advocate, proposed that the Geneva tribunal rule out indirect claims in advance. It was done, and the arbitration proceeded smoothly to its conclusion on 14 September 1872, an award of $15.5 million for depredations committed by C.S.S. *Alabama, Florida,* and *Shenandoah.*

The greater victory was for peace and arbitration. Never before had disputes involving such touchy questions of national honor been submitted to the majority vote of an international tribunal; and England accepted the verdict with good grace. The Treaty of Washington also began a better era in Canadian-American relations. Controversies over the international boundary through Puget Sound, and the rights of American fishermen in Newfoundland waters, were settled peaceably by negotiation and arbitration.

President Grant, by his unwavering support of peaceful methods, showed a quality not unusual in statesmen who know war at first hand. In a later message to a group in Birmingham, England, the soldier President avowed his guiding principle: "Nothing would afford me greater happiness than to know that, as I believe will be the case, at some future day, the nations of the earth will agree upon some sort of congress which will take cognizance of international questions of difficulty and whose decisions will be as binding as the decisions of our Supreme Court are upon us. It is a dream of mine that some such solution may be."

2. The "Gilded Age"

In his handling of domestic questions, Grant was the most unfortunate chief magistrate in American history, and the scandals of his administration were only equaled by those of Harding's. In his first administration, the fluctuations of "greenback" currency, a hold-over from Civil War finance, gave some smart operators an opportunity. Uncertainty as to whether Congress would redeem them in gold or keep them in circulation as farmers and debtors wanted, caused their value to fluctuate. In September 1869 two notorious New York stock gamblers, Jay Gould and Jim Fisk, took advantage of this situation to organize a corner in gold; and, with the connivance of persons high in the confidence of the President and the treasury, almost pulled it off. On "Black Friday," 24 September 1869, the premium on gold rose to 162, and scores of Wall Street brokers faced ruin. The government then dumped $4 million in gold on the market, and the corner collapsed; but Grant was blamed for permitting himself to be enmeshed in the sordid affair. "The worst scandals of the 18th century," wrote Henry Adams, "were relatively harmless by the side of this which smirched executive, judiciary, banks, corporate systems, professions, and people, all the great active forces of society."

Senator James W. Grimes of Iowa wrote to Senator Lyman Trumbull of Illinois in 1870 that the Republican party was "going to the dogs"; that it had become "the most corrupt and debauched political party that has ever existed." This then sounded extravagant; but within ten years it was seen to be true. Weak cabinet appointments, intimacy with New York financiers of bad reputation, failure to obtain any substantial reduction in the wartime customs duties, failure to take even one step toward civil service reform, and the notorious failure in reconstruction, raised opposition to Grant's re-election within his own party.

A Liberal Republican convention met in May 1872 and erected a platform that included withdrawal of garrisons from the South, civil service reform, and the resumption of specie payments. Candidates for the nomination were Salmon P. Chase, whose lust for the presidency increased year by year, Charles Francis Adams the diplomat, and several others. After they had killed each other off, the convention was stampeded for Horace Greeley, and this nomination was endorsed by the Democrats.

As a "headliner," Horace Greeley could not have been bettered. In his thirty years' editorship of the New York *Tribune* he had built it up to be the country's leading newspaper, whose articles and editorials were quoted nationwide. His personal integrity and moral earnestness were unquestioned. But he was also something of a crackpot (recall his needling Lincoln during the war?) and at one time or another he had espoused unpopular causes such as socialism, temperance, spiritism, and women's rights. Greeley made a strong speaking campaign, but the Republicans had the money and the organization; and the average citizen, having to choose between an old soldier whose very name stood for patriotism, and a journalist who had been as often wrong as right, voted for Grant. The President carried all but six states with a popular vote of 3.6 million as against 2.8 million for his opponent. Greeley, exhausted, broken-hearted, and at the age of sixty-one turned out of his editorial chair by the *Tribune*'s owner, Whitelaw Reid, went out of his mind and died before the end of November.

Of the public scandals during Grant's second term, the Credit Mobilier attracted the most attention. This was a company organized by promoters of the Union Pacific in order to divert the profits of railway construction to themselves. Fearing lest Congress intervene, the directors placed large blocks of stock "where they would do the most good"; that is, in the hands of congressmen. Vice President Schuyler Colfax and several Republican senators were also favored. These operations brought the Union Pacific to the verge of bankruptcy but paid the promoters over threefold their investment. After this affair, together with maladministration in several executive departments, had been exposed, the Democrats won the congressional elections of 1874 and plied the muckrake in earnest. A "Whisky Ring" in St. Louis was found to have defrauded the government of millions in taxes, with the collusion of treasury officials and the President's private secretary, General Orville E. Babcock. Despite Grant's honest zeal to "let no guilty man escape," most of them did, Babcock included. Even the Indians, who had little to lose, were victimized; General William W. Belknap, Grant's second-term secretary of war, received a "kickback" of almost $25,000 from the post trader whom he had appointed at Fort Sill. Corruption in the post office and interior departments stopped just short of the President who, though surrounded by crooks, would never believe anything against a friend. Navy yards, regarded by spoilsmen as part of their patronage, were riddled with graft; payrolls were padded before election with the connivance of Grant's navy secretary. Commander Alfred T. Mahan testified in a congressional investigation that a million feet of lumber purchased by the Boston navy yard had simply disappeared, and that the famous yacht *America* had been remodeled for Benjamin F. Butler at the taxpayers' expense.

Until Amendment XVII to the Constitution required popular election, United States senators were chosen by state legislatures, and it was much cheaper to "buy" members than to have to cultivate the entire electorate. Consequently, few reached the Senate without financial support from one or more of the leading "interests," such as railroading, oil, textiles, iron and steel, mining, and sugar refining. Of able senators who made and unmade Presidents, James G. Blaine was easily first; others in the power group who governed the United States until 1910 were Chauncey Depew, Thomas C. Platt, and David B. Hill of New York, William B. Allison of Iowa, Matthew S. Quay of Pennsylvania, Mark Hanna and Joseph B. Foraker of Ohio, Arthur P. Gorman of Maryland, Nelson W. Aldrich of Rhode Island, and William A. Clark of Montana. These were no faceless puppets of bloated business but men of pungent personality: Depew, perhaps the wittiest impromptu speaker in our history; Blaine, the "Plumed Knight" to his devoted followers; Quay and Foraker, ruthless to political dissidents. All became very rich, some were gentlemen, most were not. No more than any municipal boss are they remembered for any act of generosity or disinterested statesmanship; and their orations, once listened to by enraptured audiences, now seem but sounding brass and tinkling cymbal. But, to do them justice, these men were not simply greedy (though most of them were that); they fancied they were renewing the Hamiltonian policies, binding the great financial and commercial interests to the federal government through mutual favors.

There were still men of integrity in the Senate — Hoar of Massachusetts,

Lamar of Georgia, Sherman of Ohio, Trumbull of Illinois, for instance; but nobody of the towering stature of Clay, Calhoun, and Webster. It is also remarkable that all were of colonial or revolutionary stock. The Irish, German, and Italian immigrants of 1830–70 had not yet risen above local and municipal politics.

The federal government was at the summit of a pyramid of corruption in the Northern states. "Boss" Tweed's gang stealing $100 million from New York City; Jim Fisk and Jay Gould looting the Erie Railroad by stock-watering, and their rival, Cornelius Vanderbilt, doing the same, somewhat more respectably, to the New York Central; Collis P. Huntington buying the California legislature and bribing congressmen to promote transcontinental railroad interests; Peter Widener obtaining street railway franchises by bribing aldermen; John D. Rockefeller using strong-arm methods when chicanery failed, to build his Standard Oil empire. These were conspicuous examples in the middle tier of this indecent pyramid, the lower courses of which were built by a sordid alliance between liquor, prostitution, and city police; by the "shell game" at country fairs, "city slickers" selling gold bricks and shares in Boston Common to country bumpkins, and recruiting country girls for prostitution. Well did Mark Twain call this the Gilded Age, for when the gilt wore off one found only base brass; everyone was trying to make a "fast buck." The Civil War, like every other great war, broke down morals, and although Puritan standards for women held up fairly well until after World War I, gambling, heavy drinking, and whoring were prevalent among men of every social class.

Stock speculation, over-rapid expansion of the agricultural West, and a world-wide drop in prices brought on the panic of 1873 and a depression which lasted three years. Before economic recovery took place the centennial of independence was celebrated by the first American world's fair, at Philadelphia. Sidney Lanier symbolized reunion by contributing the words for a Centennial Cantata on a high note of optimism; but James Russell Lowell, who eleven years earlier had sung, "O Beautiful! My Country! Ours once more!" wrote a sarcastic ode on the end products of a century of freedom:

> Show your State Legislatures; show your Rings;
> And challenge Europe to produce such things
> As high officials sitting half in sight
> To share the plunder and to fix things right;
> If that don't fetch her, why you only need
> To show your latest style in martyrs, — Tweed!

And the concerts at the Philadelphia centennial, conducted by Theodore Thomas, were so poorly attended that the sheriff closed them and sold Thomas's music library to pay the performers. Walt Whitman, too, scored the materialism of the age; and even the genial, smiling Longfellow broke forth in 1872:

Ah, woe is me!
I hoped to see my country rise to heights
Of happiness and freedom yet unreached
By other nations, but the climbing wave
Pauses, lets go its hold, and slides again
Back to the common level, with a hoarse
Death-rattle in its throat. I am too old
To hope for better days.

3. *The Disputed Election and President Hayes*

Republican defeat seemed certain in 1876 as the Grant administration approached political bankruptcy. The Republican convention nominated Rutherford B. Hayes over James G. Blaine. Hayes, a lawyer old enough to have studied under Joseph Story at Harvard, had won a brigadier's commission under Sheridan and served three terms as governor of Ohio. In that office he became so noted for integrity as to earn the contemptuous nickname "Old Granny" from the professional "pols." He was acceptable to liberal Repulicans, and the Stalwarts, as the Radicals now called themselves, had no alternative to supporting him.

The Democrats, determined to make reform the issue of the campaign, chose Governor Samuel J. Tilden, a wealthy but honest lawyer of Albany Regency background who had exposed the Tweed and similar political rings battening on the canal system of New York. Every paragraph of the Democratic platform began with "Reform is necessary in . . ." and indeed it was. So much dirt was exposed in the campaign of 1876 that it seemed impossible for the Republicans to win again. But "waving the bloody shirt" was still effective. "Every man that shot Union soldiers was a Democrat!" screamed Robert G. Ingersoll, now remembered largely for his militant atheism. "The man that assassinated Lincoln was a Democrat. Soldiers, every scar you have got on your heroic bodies was given you by a Democrat!" Tilden refused to make a vigorous campaign, partly because of bad health, mostly because he did not really want the presidency. Nevertheless, when the first returns came in it seemed that he had won, but the votes of three Southern states and Oregon were doubtful, and without them Tilden had only 184 electoral votes; if the Republicans carried those four states, Hayes would have 185.

From all four disputed states came two sets of electoral votes. In South Carolina, Florida, and Louisiana, still under carpetbag rule, the election boards had thrown out thousands of Democratic votes on the ground of fraud or intimidation. Congress met the problem by setting up an electoral commission of thirteen members, eight Republicans and five Democrats; from House, Senate, and Supreme Court, "Visiting statesmen" were sent to the disputed Southern states; and there seems no doubt that a deal was made by the Republicans with Southern Democratic leaders, by virtue of which, in return for their acquiescence in Hayes's election, they promised on his behalf to withdraw the garrison and to wink at non-enforcement of Amendment XV, guaranteeing civil rights to the freedmen. The bargain was kept on both sides. On 2 March 1877 the electoral commission by a strict party vote rejected the Democratic returns from doubtful states and declared Hayes the winner by a majority of one electoral vote. And virtually no attempt was made by the federal government to enforce Amendment XV until the Franklin D. Roosevelt administration.

Even with the disputed states counted as Republican, Tilden had a plurality of 250,000 votes over Hayes. There is no longer any doubt that this election was "stolen."

Grant spent two years touring Europe, returning in the fall of 1879 in the hope of being nominated by the Republicans for a third term. The former President and general, who had nothing to live on but income from the gifts of old friends, now formed a brokerage firm with an incompetent partner, and that firm went bankrupt. He was already afflicted with cancer of the throat; but in order to pay his creditors he moved to a small cottage on Mount McGregor, New York, to write his own account of the Civil War. There, suffering intense pain but indomitable to the end, he finished in bed the last page of his great military memoirs on 19 July 1885, four days before death claimed him.

President Hayes appointed a strong cabinet: William Maxwell Evarts, one of the country's greatest lawyers, as secretary of state; Senator John Sherman (principal "fixer" with the Southern Democrats) to the treasury; Carl Schurz, German-American leader, to the interior; and he made the first ex-Confederate cabinet appointment, Senator David M. Key of Tennessee, as postmaster general. The first thing he did about reconstruction was to end the deadlock in South Carolina in favor of Governor Wade Hampton, and his withdrawal of troops from Louisiana allowed the conservatives to take over that state too.

Questions of finance were important in all postwar administrations. The desire of debt-ridden farmers for cheap money was the principal obstacle to redeeming the greenbacks, as big business wanted. Congress, at President Grant's instance, passed an act in January 1875 requiring the treasury four years later to redeem the paper dollars in gold. In protest, farmers organized the Greenback party, pledged to redeem the national debt in depreciated paper, and polled a small vote in the election of 1876. President Hayes insisted that payment of the debt and redemption of paper currency in specie be resumed on 1 January 1879, the date fixed by the Act of 1875. But the Bland-Allison Act for the "free" coinage of silver, an inflationist measure which profited the mining barons of Nevada, was passed over his veto and made mischief later. He took a strong and, on the whole, successful stand against the various acts of congressional usurpation that had taken place under Johnson and Grant, removed some of his predecessor's worst appointees, and began civil service reform. Nevertheless, both houses of Congress went Democratic in 1878, and that party looked forward to a sure-thing election in 1880.

Hayes was an upright, conscientious, and better-than-average President, but the professional politicians of the Republican party disliked him, and his wife's refusal to serve wine at White House dinners brought ridicule from Washington society. He was uneasy in the presidency, and, alone of Presidents since Polk, absolutely refused to be considered for a second term.

4. The Garfield-Arthur Administration

In consequence of Hayes's refusal to run in 1880 there was a free-for-all in the Republican convention. Grant's friends entered his name for a third term and he led Blaine for several ballots but could never obtain a majority. On the 36th ballot a liberal "dark horse," General James A. Garfield, ran away from the field. As a sop to the Stalwarts, Chester A. Arthur, a favorite of Roscoe Conkling's Republican machine in New York State, was given the vice presidential nomination. Garfield had a good record in the war and as governor of Ohio, but the Republicans made more of his birth in a log cabin, the last time that that venerable cliché was dragged out. At the same time the "bloody shirt" was buried; this was the first presidential election when reconstruction questions were not seriously discussed. The Democrats, hoping to cash in on military renown, nominated General Winfield Scott Hancock of Pennsylvania, whom Grant considered the best of his corps commanders. As one of the reconstruction "satraps" he had ruled with a moderation that pleased the South. But Hancock, with no experience in politics, made as lame and lazy a campaign as had his namesake General Scott in 1852. His popular vote was only 9500 less than Garfield's, but even with the solid South in his favor he won only 155 electoral votes to Garfield's 214. The Greenback vote of over 300,000 for General James B. Weaver of Iowa, if thrown to Hancock, might well have elected him.

Four months after Garfield's inauguration, while still struggling with questions of patronage, the President was shot by a disappointed office seeker, screaming, "I am a Stalwart! Arthur is now President!" After a gallant struggle for life, Garfield died on 19 September 1881, and the Vice President succeeded.

Chester A. Arthur was a prominent lawyer whose sole political position had been that of collector of the port of New York City, to which Grant had appointed him and from which Hayes had tried to remove him. Handsome and affable, a fifty-one-year-old widower, he and his White House hostess, a charming married daughter, gave Washington its only fashionable administration since Tyler's. Champagne returned to White House dinners, and whisky to the sideboard. Whether receiving guests in an East Room reception or dining out with senators, or driving his pair of bay horses in an open landau, Chester A. Arthur was always the gentleman.

Unexpectedly, and to the dismay of his Stalwart supporters, he also became somewhat of a reformer. The manner of Garfield's death gave popular sanction to what the Civil Service Reform League had been advocating for years. Every President since Polk complained of the demands that patronage made on his time, energy, and judgment. Scandal had followed scandal in the civil service; yet the spoils system had been extended even to scrubwomen in the public offices. Rotation in office was never complete, and a large residuum of trained public servants remained in office; but in general the federal service had become permeated with a class of men who were tempted to anticipate future removal by present corruption. Federal officials, regularly assessed for campaign contributions, were expected to spend much of their time in political activity. For the President it was no simple matter of turning out the vanquished and putting in the victors. There were usually several applicants for every vacancy, representing different factions of the party. If the congressional delegation from a state could agree upon federal appointments within their state, the President generally took their advice; but often they disagreed, and by so-called senatorial courtesy no nomination to which the senators from the nominee's state objected, could be confirmed. And the Tenure of Office Act, which limited the presidential power of removal, was not repealed until 1886. Congress, since the Civil War, had so largely eaten into presidential prerogative that the chief executive was by way of becoming a mere figurehead, like the presidents of the Third French Republic. President Garfield, just before the assassin's bullet struck him down, declared, "I'm going to find out whether I am merely a recording clerk for the Senate or chief executive of the United States." The situation was exposed by a book entitled *Congressional Government* published in 1885 by young Professor Woodrow Wilson, who later attained the power to reverse it.

A landmark in civil service reform is a law of 1883 sponsored by "Gentleman George" Pendleton, who had been McClellan's running mate in 1864. This set up a civil service commission to administer a new set of rules, required appointments to be made as the result of open competitive examinations, and forbade political assessments on, or "kickbacks" by, federal officials. These rules were initially applied to some 14,000 positions, about 12 per cent of the total; but the President was empowered to extend them at his discretion. Presidents Cleveland, Wilson, and both Roosevelts made large additions to the merit lists, and in 1940 some 727,000 out of over one million federal employees were in the classified civil service. At the same time, some of the states began to pass civil service laws of their own, but they never went so far as those of the federal government.

It would be idle to pretend that civil service reform fulfilled the expectations of its advocates. Neither the emoluments nor the prestige have been sufficiently high to attract the best men, and too often civil service rules have prevented lazy and incompetent people from being discharged. There has, however, been a great improvement in morale and efficiency; and it was fortunate indeed that the merit principle was adopted before the twentieth century, when administrative expansion greatly enhanced the need for honest and expert service. But a large part of this expansion has not been put under civil service rules; the "pols" still control most of it. Pennsylvania, for instance, had 81,000 jobs at her new governor's disposal in 1963, and only 13,000 were under civil service. The 1962 figures for federal employees in the classified civil service are 1,058,485 out of a total of 2,515,870. Thus, the federal patronage has increased both relatively and absolutely to a height that would have been envied by all nineteenth-century spoilsmen.

James Bryce, visiting the United States in the 1880's to write his *American Commonwealth*, found reformers everywhere fighting corruption and boss rule. Except for civil service reform and the Australian ballot, they accomplished little until the next century. Organized wealth and professional politicians had too strong an interest in keeping things as they were. Periodicals like Godkin's *Nation* and *The Forum*, of which Walter Hines Page became editor in 1890, did much to arouse public opinion and to prepare for the happy day when Theodore Roosevelt became President.

The War of the Pacific of 1879–84, won by Chile against Peru and Bolivia, awakened the United States to the decrepitude of her navy. Twenty years after building the *Monitor* it was inferior to the Chilean navy as well as to that of every principal European country. Not one rifled cannon had been mounted, the capital ships were fourteen small ironclads, mostly monitors, each mounting two 5-inch smooth-bores. After long discussion, Congress on 5 August 1882 authorized the construction of two "steam cruising vessels of war . . . to be constructed of steel of domestic manufacture . . . said vessels to be provided with full sail power and full steam power," and two more in 1883. These were cruisers *Chicago*, *Atlanta*, and *Boston*, and "dispatch boat" *Dolphin*, which joined the fleet in 1887. That began a new era in American naval history.

5. Mugwumps, Democrats, and the Second Harrison

Henry Adams, who had left Cambridge ("a social desert which would have starved a polar bear") for metropolitan Washington, snarled at President Arthur as "a creature for whose skin the romancist ought to go with a carving-knife," and sneered at his administration as "the centre for every element of corruption." What Henry Adams found in Washington society is a mystery. His wife wrote that the "moral miasma" was worse than the fogs of "foggy bottom," location of many of the government buildings. There was no opera, little theater, no good university, and only the Smithsonian Institution to attract men of intellect. The legations were staffed with the riffraff of European and South American foreign services. Most of the conversation between men was about who was to get what, or carry which. Apart from a core of old families who had come to the capital in the early years of the Republic, and retired army and navy officers, Washington was a bloated middle-class American town, rootless because few expected to be there long. But Henry Adams, like his creation Mrs. Lightfoot Lee in his novel *Democracy*, wanted to see the wheels go 'round; he was "bent upon getting to the heart of the great American mystery of democracy and government." That, for all his perceptiveness, he never did because nobody in Washington thought about what they were doing; they simply took it for granted. Adams's *Democracy*, nevertheless, is the best mirror of Washington society under Arthur, as Mark Twain's *Gilded Age* is of the Hayes administration.

From the viewpoint of the 1960's, Arthur's administration stands up as the best Republican one between Lincoln and Theodore Roosevelt. He had the courage to veto a Chinese exclusion bill which conflicted with a treaty, and a river and harbor bill which was a monument of logrolling and jobbery. This offended the Stalwarts, and the reformers never felt sure of Arthur, so he had no chance to succeed himself in the election of 1884, the most exciting since the Civil War.

The Republicans nominated James G. Blaine, a man of great talents and fascinating personality, long in public life and a leader in party councils. Of all politicians between Henry Clay and Theodore Roosevelt, Blaine had the most devoted personal following; but he had a heavy load to carry. The principal charge against him was prostitution of the speakership to personal gain. In that connection he had acted as broker for the bonds of a subsequently bankrupt railroad, the Little Rock & Fort Smith, and made some $100,000 in the transaction. When Congress earlier investigated this affair, Blaine triumphantly vindicated himself. But the reformers now produced an incriminating letter on the same business by Blaine, which concluded, "Burn this letter," which the recipient had not done. There is no longer any doubt that Blaine corruptly profited from his political position. When, as secretary of state for a few months under Garfield and Arthur, he ordered the American ministers at Lima and Santiago de Chile to mediate peace in the War of the Pacific, he also instructed them to include in the settlement the payment of a dubious claim in which one of his friends was interested. His official salaries were never enough for his luxurious tastes, and he had not enough moral stamina to resist temptation. But his friends would never believe a word against the "Plumed Knight," as they dubbed this able, charming, sophisticated, but morally obtuse politician.

Blaine's nomination was more than conscientious Republicans could take. Under the lead of Carl Schurz and George William Curtis the reform wing of the party "bolted" from the convention, promised to support any decent nominee of the Democrats, and proudly assumed the name "Mugwump," which was first given them in derision. As bolting is the great offense in American political ethics, few Mugwumps managed to resume a public career; younger delegates like Henry Cabot Lodge and Theodore Roosevelt, who continued to support Blaine while admitting the worst, had their reward. The Democrats nominated Grover Cleveland, a self-made man who as governor of New York had distinguished himself for firmness and integrity, to the disgust of Tammany Hall. "We love him for the enemies he has made," said a prominent Mugwump.

An amusing feature of the 1884 campaign was furnished by the now aged and disreputable Benjamin F. Butler who had attended the Democratic convention hoping the presidential "lightning" would strike him. He was, however, nominated for the presidency by two minor parties, the Antimonopolists and the Greenbackers. The Republicans paid for Ben Butler to go on a speaking tour in a private railroad car, hoping he would take votes from Cleveland; but this attempt backfired and left the national Republican committee with a pretty bill to pay for Butler's junket.

As the campaign proceeded, it became noisy and nasty. Cleveland's supporters were taken aback by his honest admission of the fact that he had fathered an illegitimate child; but, as one of them concluded philosophically, "We should elect Mr. Cleveland to the public office which he is so admirably qualified to fill, and remand Mr. Blaine to the private life which he is so eminently fitted to adorn."

Blaine, profiting by several anti-British orations, had a strong following among Irish-Americans, but lost it at the eleventh hour through the tactless remark of a clerical supporter. In his presence a hapless parson named Burchard described the Democrats as the party of "Rum, Romanism, and Rebellion." At the same time the new Prohibition party's nominee, Governor John P. St. John of the dry state of Kansas, was directing a fiery campaign against Blaine and demon rum from a New York attic. Cleveland carried New York State by a plurality of only 1149; and New York's 36 electoral votes, thanks to St. John's efforts and Burchard's bloopers, won him the presidency.

For a person of such generous bulk, Grover Cleveland was remarkably austere, unbending, and ungenial. Elected at a period when subservience to the popular will was supposed to be the first political virtue, this President remained inflexible in the right as he saw it, modified very slightly his preconceived ideas on any subject, and made little or no attempt to please. He selected a strong cabinet, with William A. Bayard of Delaware secretary of state, and Lucius Quintus Cincinnatus Lamar secretary of the interior, but alienated the Irish vote by appointing a Mugwump, William Crowninshield Endicott, secretary of war instead of Mayor Patrick A. Collins of Boston. Cleveland was a bachelor of forty-eight years upon entering the White House (5 March 1885), but he promptly wooed and won Frances Folsom, a beautiful debutante of half his age — and barely half his weight. An amusing instance of the affectionate irreverence with which Americans regard their chief magistrate occurred on Decoration Day 1886 at a military review before the President. Gilbert and Sullivan's *Mikado* was then the rage; and when the President appeared, the bands struck up "He's going to marry Yum-Yum — Yum-Yum!" They were married in the White House three days later, and a very happy marriage it proved to be.

Deserving Democrats, deprived of the sweets of office for twenty-five years, now demanded as clean a sweep as the law would allow — 88 per cent clean; virtuous Mugwumps insisted on no sweep at all. Since the Tenure of Office Act had been repealed, the President was free to remove incumbents without senatorial advice and consent; and by the end of his term Cleveland had replaced nearly every postmaster and about half the other federal officials. The Democrats were not satisfied, and the Mugwumps were not pleased.

Cleveland continued to make enemies. He was rude to the press, resenting its interest in his private affairs. He deeply offended Union veterans — at least so their spokesmen, the G.A.R., insisted — by giving two "rebels," Lamar and Garland, cabinet positions and proposing to return the captured Confederate battle flags to their states. He vetoed hundreds of private pension bills by means of which Congress tried to put deserters, skedadlers, and soldiers dishonorably discharged from the army, on the already bloated pension roll. There was a roar of protest from cattle ranchers when the President nullified their illegal leases of grass lands from the Indians. Congress and the President endeavored to do justice to these wards of the nation in the Dawes Act of 1886, but as we shall see in due course, this made the redskins' situation worse than before. Cleveland endeavored, without success, to stop the "free coinage" of silver under the Bland-Allison Act. Warned not to touch so explosive a subject as the tariff, he nevertheless urged Congress to reduce it. The Interstate Commerce Act of 1887 opened a new volume of federal regulation that is not yet ended; but Cleveland as a protest against this trend vetoed a $10,000 appropriation for distributing seed grain in Texas counties suffering from a drought, declaring, "Federal aid in such cases encourages the expectation of paternal care on the part of the government and weakens the sturdiness of our national character." Nevertheless, American farmers have obtained "paternal care" to the tune of billions of dollars. His administration showed slight positive achievement; but Cleveland dared say "No!" And merely to say "No!" in that era of political favoritism became a prime virtue.

Cleveland was renominated by the Democrats in 1888 without enthusiasm. The Republicans nominated Benjamin Harrison of Indiana, grandson of "Old Tippecanoe," with Levi P. Morton of Indiana for Vice President. Harrison, an able brigadier general in the Union army, a middle-of-the-road Republican and former senator from Indiana, had such a cold personality that the efforts of Republican politicians to call him "Young Tippecanoe" and wage a rickety-rackety campaign like that of 1840, had to be abandoned. The Republicans carried New York State by 14,000 and again New York was decisive; in the popular vote, however, Cleveland polled a plurality of 100,000.

Harrison made a dignified but ineffective President. With a Republican majority in both houses,[1] and autocratic Thomas B. Reed as speaker, the President urged constructive legislation. But Congress was led by men who wanted no legislation other than raids on the treasury and hold-ups of the consumer. Senators from the Far West, where silver mining interests were strong, obtained in return for their support of protection the Sherman Silver-Purchase Act (1890), increasing the monthly coinage of that metal by 125 per cent. Manufacturers who had contributed liberally to the Republican campaign fund were rewarded by an upward revision of duties, the McKinley tariff of 1890. Civil service reform languished, although the President promoted it by appointing as civil service commissioner a young Harvard graduate, amateur historian and Western rancher named Theodore Roosevelt. He "brought a glare of happy publicity" into that office as he did to everything that he undertook.

Harrison's administration might well have been called the Maine administration. The State of Maine, having attained prosperity through farming, lumbering, fishing, and wooden shipbuilding, hatched a clutch of Republican politicians who occupied key positions in the federal government. Speaker Reed's private secretary illustrates this by a droll story which must have happened in 1889.

John Sergeant Wise, a New York financier, was shown into the Speaker's office. "Who's running this government, anyway?" he blustered.

"The great and the good, John, of course. Be calm!" said the Speaker in his Down-East twang, with a twinkle in his eye.

"Well the great and the good must all live in Maine, then. I come up here on business with the secretary of state — Mr. Blaine of Maine. I call to pay my respects to the acting vice president — Mr. Frye from Maine. I wish to consult the leader of the United States Senate — Mr. Hale from Maine. I would talk over a tariff matter with the chairman of the ways and means committee — Mr. Dingley from Maine. There is a naval bill in the house in which I am greatly interested — Chairman Boutelle from Maine. I wish an addition to the public building in Richmond — Chairman Milliken from Maine. And here I am in the august presence of the great speaker of the greatest parliamentary body in the world — Mr. Reed from Maine!"

"Yes, John, the great, and the good — and the wise. The country is safe."

And out they went, laughing, to lunch with the Chief Justice of the United States — Mr. Fuller from Maine.

Blaine as secretary of state took up with more zeal than tact the formation of a Pan American Union. But the new McKinley tariff on hides, passed to please the cattle barons of the West, infuriated South Americans and rendered abortive the Pan American Congress that the President summoned to Washington.

The McKinley tariff on manufactures also occasioned a sharp rise in prices,

1. Substantially increased in the Senate by the admission of four new states: North Dakota, South Dakota, Montana, and Washington, on 22 February 1889. To these were added Wyoming and Idaho in 1890. All six were then Republican in politics.

which is probably the main reason for an overturn in the congressional elections of 1890. Only 88 Republicans were returned to the new House, as against 235 Democrats; and the Republican majority in the Senate was reduced to eight unstable votes from the Far West. The same trend continued in the presidential election of 1892. Harrison had alienated many Republican leaders, but it was an accepted principle that if a party did not renominate a President for a second term, it confessed failure. So Harrison won the nomination on the first ballot; and for the same reason Cleveland obtained the Democratic nomination. His running-mate was Adlai E. Stevenson of Illinois, grandfather of the like-named statesman who twice ran against General Eisenhower and became United States representative to the United Nations. The new Populist party with James B. Weaver, a former Greenbacker, as standard bearer, polled over a million votes and carried six states west of the Mississippi; but Cleveland and Stevenson, again supported by the Mugwumps, won a safe majority in the electoral college and polled some 365,000 more votes than Harrison. There was more to this verdict, however, than revulsion from the tariff or disgust at Republican chicanery and corruption. It registered a deep lying unrest that would presently break forth and carry William Jennings Bryan to prominence, Theodore Roosevelt to achievement, and Woodrow Wilson to the presidency.

So, before telling briefly the story of Cleveland's second term, we must survey the winds of change that had been blowing through the nation since reconstruction.

HAIL, HAIL, THE GANG'S ALL HERE!

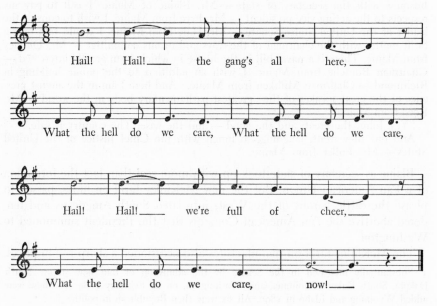

Expansion and Development

1870-1900

1. Railroads, "Electrics," and Shipping

DURING THE LAST third of the nineteenth century, American society began to reflect the economic transformations that began during the Civil War or earlier, but underwent no profound change such as that which followed a general adoption of the internal combustion engine. There was merely an expansion and extension of the first industrial revolution, marked by the application of machine power, in constantly enlarged units, to new processes and in new regions.

Transportation was the key. There were 35,000 miles of steam railroad in the United States in 1865; more than five times as much in 1900, more than in all Europe. Among inventions which diminished the discomfort of long-distance travel were the Pullman sleeping car, the safety coupler and the Westinghouse air brake. In the 1870's the refrigerator car, first used to carry freshly slaughtered beef from Chicago to the Eastern cities, was adapted for the carriage of fruit and vegetables, which eventually enabled the products of California to undersell those of Eastern truck gardeners. After the turn of the century the Pennsylvania Railroad built the first all-steel passenger coaches, and the American Locomotive Company brought out the magnificent Pacific type, which dominated railroading for a quarter-century.

Transcontinental railroads were the most spectacular postwar achievements. The Union Pacific thrust westerly through Nebraska and Wyoming Territory, near the line of the old Oregon and California trails and across the Wasatch Range of the Rockies into the basin of the Great Salt Lake. The Central Pacific, in the meantime, climbed eastward from Sacramento over the difficult grades of the Sierras, then through the arid valleys of Nevada. When the two joined rails with a golden spike near the Great Salt Lake on 10 May 1869, the Union Pacific was regarded as the winner; but the Central Pacific promoters had made enough to enable them to buy the state government of California.

Congress in the meantime had granted charters to three other lines: (1) the Northern Pacific — from Lake Superior across Minnesota, through the Bad Lands of Dakota, up the valley of the Yellowstone, across the continental divide at Bozeman to the headwaters of the Missouri, and by an intricate route through the Rockies to the Columbia river and Portland; (2) the Southern Pacific — from New Orleans across Texas to the Rio Grande, across the *llano estacado* to El Paso, through the territory of the Gadsden Purchase to Los Angeles, and up the San Joaquin valley to San Francisco; (3) the Santa Fe — from Atchison, Kansas, up the Arkansas river to Trinidad, Colorado, across the Raton spur of the Rockies to Santa Fe and Albuquerque, through the country of the Apache and the Navajo parallel to the Grand Canyon of the Colorado, and across the Mojave desert to San Bernardino and San Diego. All three were aided by government land grants — twenty square miles to every mile of track — and by 1884, after numerous bankruptcies and reorganizations, all three had reached the coast. At the same time the Canadian Pacific, aided by even more generous subsidies from the Dominion, was pushing through to the Pacific and reached it on 7 November 1885.

These transcontinental lines were promoted largely with a view to profit, but the peopling of a vast region proved to be their most valuable function. In this respect they performed a work comparable with that of the Virginia Company of 1612 and the Ohio Company of 1785.

At the end of the Civil War the great plains west of eastern Kansas and Nebraska, the high plains, and the Rocky Mountain region, were uninhabited by white men excepting the mining towns in Colorado and Nevada and the Mormon settlements in Utah. Mail coaches of the Overland Stage Line required at least five days to carry passengers and mails from the Missouri river to Denver. Silver ore extracted in Nevada had to be freighted by wagon to San Francisco, thence transported around Cape Horn to the East Coast and Great Britain. Transcontinental railroads pushed out into the plains in advance of settlers, advertised for immigrants in the Eastern states and Europe, transported them at reduced rates to the prairie railhead, and sold them land on credit. Thousands of construction workers became farm hands, obtained free homesteads from the federal government, and bought tools, horses, and cattle with their savings. The termini and junction points of these lines — places like Omaha, Kansas City, Missouri, hard by Independence (old jumping-off place for the Oregon trail), Duluth the "Zenith City of the Unsalted Seas," Oakland on San Francisco Bay, Portland in Oregon, Seattle and Tacoma in Washington — places non-existent or mere villages before the Civil War, became metropolitan cities in thirty years' time.

Railroading was the biggest business of a big era, and the railway builders were of the mettle that in Europe made Napoleons and Von Moltkes. The Northwest was the domain of James J. Hill, greatest of our railroad builders. St. Paul was a small town on the edge of the frontier when he emigrated thither from eastern Canada just before the Civil War, and Minneapolis a mere village at the St. Anthony falls of the Mississippi. There, the "Twin Cities" were located at the end of a trail which connected Winnipeg with the outside world. In the winter of 1870 Donald A. Smith, the future Lord Strathcona, then resident governor of the Hudson's Bay Company, started south from Winnipeg, and James J. Hill started north from St. Paul, both in dogsleds. They met on the prairie and made camp in a storm, and from that meeting sprang the Canadian Pacific and Great Northern railways.

During the panic of 1873 the St. Paul & Pacific railroad went bankrupt. Hill watched it as a prairie wolf watches a weakening buffalo, and in 1878, in association with Donald Smith and George Stephen (the future Lord Mount Stephen), wrested it from Dutch bondholders by floating new securities.

The day of land grants and federal subsidies was past, and Hill saw that the Great Northern Railway, as he renamed his purchase, could reach the Pacific only by developing the country as it progressed; and that took time. He struck due west across the Dakota plains, sending out branches to people the region and carry wheat to market. In the summer of 1887 his construction made a record stride, 643 miles of grading, bridging, and rail-laying from Minot, North Dakota, to the Great Falls of the Missouri. Two years later, the Rockies yielded their last secret, the Marias pass, to a young engineer, John F. Stevens. In 1893 the trains of the Great Northern reached tidewater at Tacoma. Within ten years Hill acquired partial control of the Northern Pacific Railway, purchased joint control of the Chicago, Burlington & Quincy, connecting his eastern termini with Chicago, and was running steamship lines from Duluth to Buffalo and from Seattle to Japan and China.

The Great Northern, the Northern Pacific, and the Union Pacific (which sent a taproot northwesterly) were responsible for opening the great inland empire between the Cascades and the Rockies, and for an astounding development of the entire Northwest. This once isolated Oregon country, with its rich and varied natural resources, magnificent scenery, and thriving seaports, has become as distinct and self-conscious a section of the Union as New England. The three states into which it was divided — Washington, Oregon, and Idaho — increased in population from 282,000 in 1880 to 2 million in 1910 and 5.3 million in 1960; whilst California, which contained only half a million people when the golden spike was driven in 1869, kept well in front, rising to 15.7 million in 1960. The population of Kansas, Nebraska, and the Dakotas, starting at the same level in 1870, increased sixfold in two decades; Utah and Colorado, where there was a great mining boom in the 'seventies, tripled their population in the same period. Oklahoma and the Indian Territory, where not one white man was enrolled in 1880, had over 2 million palefaces and 55,000 Indians in 1960; and Texas, with the aid of a network of railways, doubled its population of 1.5 million between 1880 and 1900, and by 1960 had almost 10 million people. By 1890 the last serious Indian outbreak had been suppressed, and the surviving redskins confined to reservations; the last great area of public lands had been thrown open to settlement.

There were still great unexplored regions in the Far West in 1865 which the railroad only reached later, if ever. Four men who combined a zest for exploration with skill as naturalists, geologists, and writers were largely responsible for the conservation of some of America's greatest natural wonders.

Clarence King, who headed a congressional survey of the region between eastern Colorado and California, published the results in his seven-volume *Exploration of the Fortieth Parallel* (1870–80), which has become a classic. In 1878 King was made head of the newly established United States Geological Survey. He was largely responsible for establishing the wondrous Sequoia National Park in the high Sierras.

John Muir began in 1867 a 1000-mile walk from Wisconsin to the Gulf of Mexico, visited and studied the Yosemite valley and, aided by writing articles in Eastern magazines, labored successfully to have the Yosemite made a national park. Muir was also an apostle of conservation, and it was on the basis of reports by a national forestry commission of which he was a member that President Cleveland, just before the end of his second term, created thirteen forest reserves comprising 21 million acres. The McKinley administration threw most of them back to the loggers, but Muir captured the ear of the public in a series of brilliant articles, and aroused the interest of Theodore Roosevelt in conservation.

John Wesley Powell, who lost an arm at Shiloh and became a professor of geology after the war, led a 900-mile descent of the Colorado river in boats through the Grand Canyon in 1869. He described this and later adventurous surveys in the Southwest in his *Canyons of the Colorado*, and did effective work under King in the Geological Survey; his interest in the Indians found an outlet as head of the Smithsonian's Bureau of Ethnology. Ferdinand V. Hayden, whose career as a soldier and paleontologist paralleled that of Powell, was largely responsible for Congress's creating the Yellowstone National Park in 1872. These four men deserve to be kept in fond remembrance, and not only for their discoveries; they were the lions whose boldness and determination prevented the jackals of exploitation from consuming the whole of America's most glorious natural heritage. But after they died the jackals, armed with the bulldozer, got away with a good part of it, owing, as Bernard DeVoto wrote, to the West's "historic willingness to hold itself cheap and its eagerness to sell out." The end result almost justifies DeVoto's description of the Far West as "the plundered province."

This disappearance of the frontier was hailed by Frederick J. Turner, a great American historian, as the close of a movement that began in 1607; and the Spanish-American War of 1898 was interpreted as the beginning of a new phase of imperialism. After the lapse of years, it is difficult to discern any break in the rhythm of American life in the year 1890. The settlement of the Great West had not then been completed; in areas covering thousands of square miles it had not even begun. The westward movement of population continued. Even outside the national parks and forest reserves there are still areas of virgin wilderness in the Rocky Mountains, the Sierra Nevada and the high plains. There has, to be sure, been a gradual assimilation of the West to Eastern modes of living and thinking; but that, too, had been going on since the seventeenth century. Barely two generations separate the male vigor of Bret Harte's *Roaring Camp* and *Poker Flat* (1870) from the insipid society portrayed by Sinclair Lewis's *Main Street* (1920). Yet even today there is a marked difference between East and West. The transcontinental tourist, whether by train or car, as he leaves the settled farms of Dakota or Kansas for the broad sweep of the high plains, has the feeling of a land still young to the white man's tread.

Rail penetration of the far Northwest, improved agricultural machinery, the handling of grain in carload lots, trans-shipment to lake or ocean steamers by grain elevators, and a new milling process which ground the Northern spring wheat into superfine flour (much too superfine), were factors which combined to move the center of wheat production north and west from Illinois and Iowa into Minnesota, the Dakotas, Montana, Oregon, and the Canadian Northwest. In this new wheat belt the "bonanza" wheat farms, veritable factories for wheat production, were well established by 1890. The wheat crop increased from 152 to 612 million bushels between 1866 and 1891. With the low prices that prevailed after the panic of 1873, this meant disaster to competing farmers in the Middle West and the Eastern states; and, even more completely, to England. The silo which enabled dairy farmers to turn corn into milk, poultry raising, and the breeding of horses and cattle, saved Eastern farming from ruin; but enormous areas within a few hours of the great industrial centers on the Atlantic coast have reverted to forest.

Wool production remained almost constant in this period; and cotton, owing to the dislocation of Southern society, did not attain its high prewar figure until 1878. As the corn belt extended into Kansas and Nebraska, the crop, already 868 million bushels in 1866, passed 2000 million bushels in 1891. The greater part of the corn was converted into meat, cured at thousands of local bacon factories and at the great packing plants in Chicago. And we have yet to record the revolution in meat production which took place between 1865 and 1880.

Richmond, Virginia, has the credit of making the first successful experiment with electric streetcars in 1888, a mode of urban and suburban transportation which reached its zenith around 1920 and has since almost completely disappeared. Other cities at once began replacing horsecars by trolley cars. (Oliver Wendell Holmes saluted the "broomstick train" as the Salem witches' revenge), or cars that obtained electric power from underground conduits. Before the end of the century, interurban electric railways were taking passenger traffic away from steam railroads, and it was possible to travel from northern New England to the Middle West by "electrics," if one could spare the time — as few Americans felt they could afford to do.

Nor did rail have a monopoly of long-distance freight transportation. A large part of the nation's traffic, and all foreign trade except with Canada and Mexico, was carried by ships, sail or steam. This was the heyday of the sternwheeler on the Mississippi and its tributaries — incidentally producing a galaxy of songs, such as "Waiting on the Levee . . . for the *Robert E. Lee*," a steamboat which beat the *Natchez* in a famous river race. On the Great Lakes were fleets of ore carriers, tankers, and grain ships, with a dying fleet of local sailing craft like the *Jolie Plante* in which poor Marie, fresh-water counterpart to that golden-haired damsel who perished in Longfellow's "Wreck of the Hesperus," lost her life. Hard by the "reef of Norman's Woe" lies the snug haven, Gloucester, home port for hundreds of sailing fishermen; stubby "bankers" or "hand-liners" immortalized by Kipling's *Captain Courageous* (1886), and the tall mackerel seiners, which James B. Connolly described in *Out of Gloucester*. Hundreds of schooners, two-, three-, and even six-masted, plied between ports of the Maritime Provinces, the East Coast, the Caribbean, and South America, carrying fish, coal, lumber, granite, and even general cargoes in competition with the coastal steamboats. Of these there were literally hundreds: deep-water runs several times weekly from New York to Norfolk, Baltimore, Charleston, Halifax, and New Orleans; night runs of sound steamers to Hartford, Stonington, New London, and Fall River. Every evening in Boston, weather permitting, saw departures to sundry Maine and Nova Scotia ports. Traffic "down east" as yet had no Cape Cod Canal (completed in 1914), but the inland waterways from Norfolk south were being improved for tug and barge traffic. By 1894 the Fall River Line's *Puritan* and *Priscilla*, "queen of all steamboats," were carrying 300,000 passengers annually between New York and New England. These Long Island Sound lines carried on into the great depression of the 1930's, when they were killed by the competition of trucks and the exactions of the Seamen's Union.

River and coastal traffic had been protected from foreign competition by navigation laws ever since 1789. But America's foreign trade had to meet foreign competition, and thereby suffered. Before the war, two-thirds of the value of American imports and exports had been carried in American-flag ships. By 1870 the proportion had dropped to one-third; and by 1880 to one-sixth. The initial drop has often been ascribed to the depredations of Confederate cruisers; but they could hardly be blamed for the 1870–80 slump. Captain John Codman of Boston testified before a congressional committee in 1882, "We have lost our prestige and experience; we are no longer a maritime nation; our shipowners have been wearied and disgusted; they have gone into other business, forced by their government to abandon their old calling. Our ship-masters, the pride of the ocean in the old packet days, are dead, and they have no successors."

A congressional investigation of 1882 reported that the basic cause of this decline was the superior attraction for American investors of railroads, Western land, manufacturing, and mining, when the merchant navies of several European powers and Japan were earning only 4 or 5 per cent. Congress could have made up the difference by ship subsidies; but Congress, in contrast to its lavish support of transcontinental railroads, let the merchant marine decline nearly to the vanishing point. Almost all the sound, river, and coastal steamers of this era were built of wood, and bad fire hazards they were. Owing to the backwardness of American builders and designers in steel hulls and marine engines, and the laws against placing foreign-built vessels under the American flag, the United States never regained a place in fast transatlantic traffic until after World War II. The American Line, a combine of several, was enabled to compete only by virtue of a special act of Congress allowing it to acquire two foreign-built liners, *City of Paris* and *City of New York*. These two, in 1889–92, were the first to make a transatlantic passage between New York and Queenstown, Ireland, in less than six days. *Deutschland* of the North German Lloyd captured the "blue riband of the Atlantic" in 1900 and held it for seven years, when the ill-fated *Lusitania* made the crossing in less than four days, twenty hours.

Another exception made by Congress after the Civil War was a liberal subsidy of the Pacific Mail Line to carry mail from San Francisco to Hawaii and the Orient. Pacific Mail long held its own in competition with the Canadian Pacific steamship line, and Japan's Toyo Kisen Kaisha. Its 5000-ton, iron-screw steamers *City of Peking* and *City of Tokio*, built at Chester, Pennsylvania, with auxiliary four-masted barque rig, lowered the record from San Francisco to Yokohama to sixteen days. Collis Huntington of the Southern Pacific Railroad got control of this line in 1893, and built five new ships. It carried on until 1915, when killed by a law requiring the Oriental crews to be replaced by Americans.

Despite Captain Codman, the American sailing marine did pretty well. Square-riggers, built largely in Maine or on Puget Sound, officered by Americans and manned by sailors of every nation, race, and color, continued to carry bulk cargoes to European ports, around the Horn to the West Coast, Japan, China, and Hawaii, and around the Cape of Good Hope to Australia and India. As late as 1892 there was more tonnage under the American flag in sail than in steam. In this final phase of deep-water sail, the wooden square-rigger was perfected. "These splendid ships, each with her grace, her glory," as John Masefield wrote, were not so fast as the clippers, but carried more cargo for their size and, with labor-saving devices (but no auxiliary propulsion) were more economical to operate on long voyages than steamers, a large part of whose cargo space had to be given to coal bunkers. Among the famous ships of this era was Donald McKay's last creation, *Glory of the Seas*, launched in 1869, 2000 tons burthen, 240 feet long. In 1875 she hung up a record from San Francisco to Sydney, 35 days, which still stands. The slightly smaller *Grand Admiral*, also built in 1869, carried the black horse flag of the Weld family for 28 years, during which she logged 727,000 miles in 5360 sailing days — an amazing record, considering that many of those days must have been windless. Last full-rigged three-skysail yarder to be built in the United States was *Aryan*, 1939 tons, 248 feet long, designed locally and built on the Kennebec in 1893. Her owners kept her sailing out of sentiment until 1918, long after the competition of steamers had made her unprofitable. The adoption of high-pressure, triple-expansion marine engines in the 1890's, requiring less than one-tenth of the coal per horsepower of the old compound engines, doomed the sailing ship on round-the-world trading routes. They hung on for carrying bulk cargoes on protected coastal routes until the 1930's.

2. Indians, Cattle, and Cowboys

The dismal story of relations between white Americans and the American Indian continued with little change. In contrast to the Negroes who were denied their ambition to participate on equal terms in American civilization, the Indians, who desired above all to continue their own way of life, were deprived of hunting grounds which would have made that possible, and were pressured to "settle down" and become "good" farmers and citizens.

Before that pressure could be exerted, the redskins had to be defeated in battle. Indians of the Great Plains and the Rocky Mountains, about 225,000 in number, presented a formidable obstacle to white settlement. The strongest and most warlike were the Sioux, Blackfoot, Crow, Cheyenne, Arapaho, and Nez Percé in the north; the Comanche, Apache, Ute, Kiowa, Southern Cheyenne, and Southern Arapaho in the south and center. Mounted on swift horses, well armed for plains warfare, and living on the herds of buffalo that roamed the open range, these tribes long maintained a stubborn resistance to white penetration of their hunting grounds.

The first serious invasion of these hunting grounds came with the great migration of the 1840's. In 1850 there were approximately 100,000 Indians in California; in 1860 there were barely 35,000 "despoiled by irresistible forces of the land of their fathers; with no country on earth to which they can migrate; in the midst of a people with whom they cannot assimilate," as Congress's committee on Indian affairs reported. The advance of miners into the mountains, the building of transcontinental railroads, and the invasion of the grasslands by cattlemen, threatened every other Indian nation of the West with the same fate. Wanton destruction of the buffalo, indispensable not only for food but for housing, bowstrings, lariats, and fuel; the Colt six-shooter, fearfully efficient in the hands of palefaces, and the spread of white men's diseases among the Indians; all were lethal.

Until 1861 the Indians of the Great Plains had been relatively peaceful, but in that year the invasion of Colorado by thousands of miners, and the advance of white settlers along the upper Mississippi and Missouri, began a series of armed clashes. Sioux of the Dakotas went on the warpath in 1862, devastated the Minnesota frontier, and massacred or captured almost 1000 white people. Retribution was swift and terrible, but for the next 25 years Indian warfare was a constant of Western history. Each new influx of settlers and of railroad gangs who carelessly destroyed the buffalo, drove the redskins to raid settlements in search of food, and to acts of desperation which brought on punitive expeditions by the United States Army. There were some

200 pitched battles between soldiers and Indians in the years 1869–76. The contest was not unequal, for the Indians had become excellent shots. They could attack or flee from the heavy United States cavalry at will, and they were not troubled by logistic problems. Had they been able to unite, they might have tired out the United States (as white resistance to reconstruction was doing in the South); but no Tecumseh, no Prophet appeared. The army could always recruit Indian scouts, and the redskins were defeated piecemeal.

It was not that nobody did anything about it. Congress in 1867 set up an Indian Peace Commission, which included Generals Sherman and Terry, to stop the fighting, and it did that for about two years. This commission recommended an end to the farce of making treaties with Indian nations — there were roughly 370 of them in the archives — and in 1871 Congress did so. General Francis A. Walker (future president of M.I.T.), whom Grant appointed commissioner of Indian affairs that year, did his best to carry out a paternalistic policy. He placed defeated tribes on new reservations, set up schools for their children, and issued rations to those who had no more game; but his best was not good enough. In his report of 1872 he remarked cogently, "Every year's advance of our frontier takes in a territory as large as some of the kingdoms of Europe. We are richer by hundreds of millions, the Indian is poorer by a large part of the little that he has. This growth is bringing imperial greatness to the nation; to the Indian it brings wretchedness, destitution, beggary."

For ten years after the Civil War the Sioux, in particular, fought desperately to preserve their hunting grounds on the Great Plains. In December 1866 Captain William J. Fetterman USA, stationed at Fort Phil Kearny, Wyoming, was ambushed by Red Cloud, and his command of eighty men were killed. Fort Buford, on the Missouri just across the Montana line, was sniped at by Sioux in 1867. The American public was stirred up by a report of a "horrible massacre" there which actually never took place, a report which the commissioner of Indian affairs attributed to "the rapacity and rascality of frontier settlers, whose interests are to bring on a war and supply our armies . . . at exorbitant prices." For several years there were occasional skirmishes with the Sioux, but their knell of doom struck in 1875 when prospectors discovered gold in the Black Hills — "them thar hills" — of South Dakota and founded fabulous Deadwood, where "Wild Bill" Hickok, hero of many a border brawl, died with his boots on. These hills, to the Sioux, were holy ground which the government had promised to retain for them inviolate. For one summer General Sheridan was able to hold back the greedy gold seekers, but in the following spring they broke through. Under Sitting Bull and Crazy Horse the Sioux struck back.

Colonel George A. Custer of the 7th Cavalry, a distinguished veteran of the Civil War who had been fighting Indians off and on for the last nine years, had come to like and respect them. "If I were an Indian," he wrote in an article about an earlier battle with the Sioux, "I would certainly prefer to cast my lot . . . to the free open plains rather than submit to the confined limits of a reservation, there to be the recipient of the blessed benefits of civilization with its vices thrown in." In June of 1876 he led a column west from Bismarck to disperse the Sioux and Northern Cheyenne, who had left their Black Hills reservation. Custer found them encamped by the Little Big Horn river in Montana. Rashly the officer in tactical command, Brigadier General Alfred Terry, divided the regiment into three columns, one of which, Custer's, was surrounded by some 2500 braves under Crazy Horse. Custer and his entire command of 265 officers and men were killed. Colonel Nelson A. Miles in January 1877 caught up with and defeated Crazy Horse, whose enemies gave him the compliment of calling him "one of the bravest of the brave and one of the subtlest and most capable of captains." Custer became a hero to the boys who grew up in that era, and his bright and joyous figure, his long yellow locks, and trooper's swagger shine through the murk of controversy over who was to blame for the massacre on the Little Big Horn.

More Indians were now driven from their ancient homes. In Montana the Crow and Blackfoot were ejected from their reservations; in Colorado the vast holdings of the Ute were confiscated and opened to settlement. The discovery of gold on the Salmon river in western Idaho precipitated an invasion of the peaceful Nez Percé. They refused to surrender lands guaranteed to them, and the federal government in 1877 decided to drive them out. Chief Joseph struck back, but in vain, and then conducted 200 braves and 600 squaws and papooses on a fighting retreat over 1500 miles of mountain and plain, a memorable feat in the annals of Indian warfare; and for strategic and tactical skill in a class with Marshal Kesselring's Italian campaigns of 1944–45. In the end, when just short of asylum in Canada, Chief Joseph surrendered (5 October 1877), saying, "Hear me, my chiefs. I am tired; my heart is sick and sad. From where the sun now stands I will fight no more, forever." Joseph then devoted himself to the peaceful betterment of his people, part of whom returned to their ancestral lands, and part settled in Oklahoma.

In the Southwest, twenty years of intermittent warfare with various branches of the Apache ended in 1886 with the surrender of their chief Geronimo and the subjugation of his tribe. Geronimo became a Christian convert and lived both to write his autobiography and to take part in the inaugural procession of President Roosevelt in 1905.

In 1881 President Arthur declared, "We have to deal with the appalling fact that though thousands of lives have been sacrificed and hundreds of millions of dollars expended in the attempt to solve the Indian problem, it has until within the past few years seemed scarcely nearer a solution than it was half a century ago." Federal authority over Indian affairs was divided between the war and interior departments, both of which pursued a vacillating and uncertain policy, and each failed to live up to treaty obligations or to protect the Indians on their reservations from white settlers' aggressions.

These aggressions often took the form of alienating by fraud and chicanery large areas of Indian lands to railroads and other speculators. One railroad acquired 800,000 acres of Cherokee land in southern Kansas, an operation that the governor of that state denounced as "a cheat and a fraud in every particular," but nothing was done to cancel it, and the railroad resold the lands to settlers at a vast profit. Only the intervention of the secretary of the interior prevented a particularly crass deal whereby the Osage were to sell 8 million acres to a railroad for 20 cents an acre.

American frontiersmen in general still subscribed to their traditional feeling that the only good Indian was a dead Indian; but in the East, churchmen and reformers urged a humane policy toward the nation's wards. Statesmen like Carl Schurz, religious leaders like Bishop Henry B. Whipple, literary figures like Helen Hunt Jackson, whose *Century of Dishonor* (1881) stirred the nation's conscience, were loud in their criticism of the government's treatment of the Indian, and their attitude was effective in bringing about important changes in policy.

Paternalism culminated in the passage of the Dawes Act of 1887, which established the policy of breaking up reservations into individual homesteads. This was an attempt to "civilize" the Indian by folding him into the body politic of the nation. Passage of this law was promoted by Indian Rights and other societies who wished the redskins well; it was based on the "Protestant ethic" premise that ownership of real estate was a moral good, fostering thrift, industry, and providing the spark of energy or ambition that leads to wealth and prestige. But the "do-gooders" overlooked the fact that the Western Indian, by habit and heredity, was a hunter rather than a cultivator; that his ideas of land ownership were communal, not individual; that the last thing he wanted was to become a homesteader. By persuading Indians to be individual land-owners as an alternative to living on government rations on a reservation, pressuring them to try homesteading before they had acquired the technique and values that alone make "the American way of life" viable, the Dawes Act was certain to be a very partial success. It overlooked a trait of the Indian character: that he literally takes "no thought for the morrow," and is easily tempted to sell his birthright to go on a big binge. Thus, it was taken advantage of by landgrabbers and speculators.

The act, in general, provided that the President of the United States should direct that a reservation be broken up when and if he had evidence that the Indians wanted it; then a homestead of 160 acres would be granted to each family, and the unallotted remainder of the reservation would be purchased by the government for sale to white men, the money to be put in trust for the tribe. After allotment began, in 1891, the acreage of Indian reservations was reduced 12 per cent in a single year. Congress then speeded up the process by passing another law which allowed the allottees to lease their lands. That really doomed the system. Indians living on a reservation lapped about by white men's farms, faced with the alternative of becoming a tribal slum on the prairie or unwilling homesteaders, snapped hungrily at the allotment bait, knowing that individual farms could now be leased, and hoping to live well on the rent. In 1894 it was ascertained that the Omaha and Winnebago in Nebraska had leased lands to a real estate syndicate for 8 to 10 cents an acre, which the syndicate released to white farmers for $1 to $2 an acre, per annum. Out of 140,000 acres allotted by 1898 to these two nations, 112,000 had been leased, mostly illegally, and the wretched lessors were living in squalor on their meager rents, drifting into the towns and cities, unable to fit into the white man's civilization. The Indian allottee did not know what to do with his land. Now for the first time he was subject to state taxes, and if he did not succumb to the temptation to lease, and held his allottment for the required 25 years, he generally sold it as soon as a fee simple patent was issued, squandered the proceeds, and became a pauper. In the half-century after 1887, Indian holdings decreased from 138 to 48 million acres. Indian timberlands, too, were acquired by speculators; the Indian commissioner blandly declared in 1917 that "as the Indian tribes were being liquidated anyway, it was only sensible to liquidate their forest holdings as well." Tribal funds amounting to more than $100 million were diverted from their proper use to meet the costs of the Indian Bureau — including the costs of despoiling the Indians of their lands.

Fortunately for the Five Civilized Tribes, the Dawes Act did not apply to them, or to a few others such as the Osage, Miami, Sauk and Fox who had located in the Indian Territory. These were given special treatment. As punishment for their support of the Confederacy, the Five Civilized Tribes were compelled in 1866 to accept new treaties relinquishing the western half of the Indian Territory, where some twenty tribes from Kansas and Nebraska were settled in thirteen new reservations. Two million acres of this western half, called Oklahoma Territory, were bought from the Indians and thrown open to settlement in 1889, with the consequent land rush which is well described in Edna Ferber's *Cimarron*. It was an extraordinary spectacle, a *reductio ad absurdum* of laissez-faire. Some 20,000 "boomers," as they were called, lined up on both the Kansas and Texas borders of Oklahoma. Here, wrote an eyewitness, James Morgan, was the chronically moving family in its covered wagon, beaten on a dozen frontiers for half a century but always hopeful that the next would prove a bonanza; Texans who were finding Texas too tame; lawyers and doctors with their diplomas and instruments; gamblers and fancy men; "all the elements of western life — a wonderful mixture of thrift and unthrift, of innocence and guile, of lambs and wolves." Shepherded by United States cavalry, they lined up on the two borders in wagons, on horseback, and afoot, and at the shot of a pistol, raced to grab one of the 6000 homestead lots. In many instances the "boomers" found the "sooners," those who had jumped the gun, ahead of them; claims staked out had to be defended — or lost — by gunfire, and it took years to straighten out the mess of land titles. Altogether the most inefficient and wasteful way of settling a new country that anyone could have imagined.

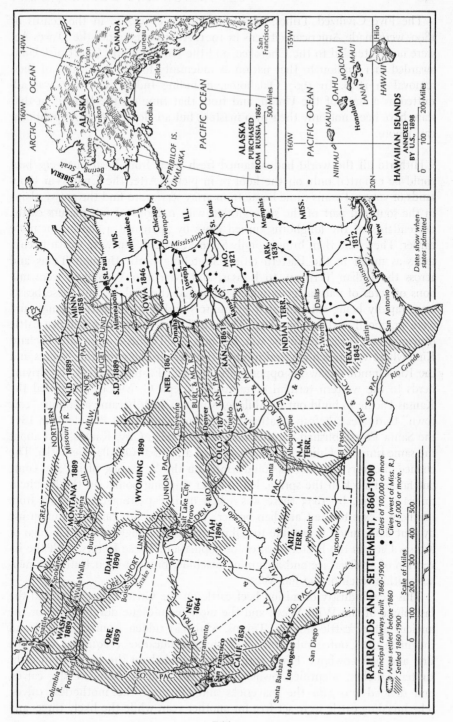

RAILROADS AND SETTLEMENT, 1860-1900

—— Principal railways built 1860-1900
● Cities of 100,000 or more
● Cities (west of Miss. R.) of 5,000 or more.
⌒⌒ Areas settled before 1860
///// Settled 1860-1900

Scale of Miles
0   100   200   300   400   500

Dates show when states admitted

ALASKA
PURCHASED FROM RUSSIA, 1867

ARCTIC OCEAN
SIBERIA
Bering Strait
Nome
UNALASKA
PRIBILOF IS.
Kodiak
ALASKA
Yukon R.
Ft. Yukon
Sitka
Juneau
CANADA
PACIFIC OCEAN
San Francisco

0   500 Miles

HAWAIIAN ISLANDS
ANNEXED BY U.S., 1898

PACIFIC OCEAN
NIIHAU
KAUAI
OAHU
Honolulu
MOLOKAI
LANAI
MAUI
HAWAII
Hilo

0   100   200 Miles

The Five Civilized Tribes, who numbered over 51,000 in the census of 1890, were made American citizens in 1901. Allotments under the Dawes Act were now extended to the Cherokee, and the United States Court of Claims awarded $1.1 million to that nation as indemnity for the hardships of their removal in 1838. In 1907 Oklahoma, including Indian Territory, was admitted as a state of the Union, and from that time on the Indians in that state have been not only their own masters, but an element that no politician can ignore.

Hitherto all the world had obtained fresh meat from local butchers; beef could be exported only on the hoof or in pickle. After the Civil War thousands of young Texans came home from army service, to find the grassy plains in the southern part of the state glutted with millions of fat, mature cattle, descendants of the longhorns turned loose by Spaniards a century or more earlier. They were then bringing only $1 to $5 a head, but were worth twenty times as much in the Eastern cities. Stretching north through Texas and across the Indian Territory to Kansas, and even into Wyoming, were millions of acres of natural grass which supported the buffalo; but these beasts were rapidly being exterminated by hunters and railroad section gangs, and were practically extinct by 1884. There had been some long-distance cattle droving from Texas before the war, but now the Texans — especially Richard King whose vast ranch covered most of the territory between the Nueces and the Rio Grande — saw an opportunity to reach Eastern markets by driving herds to the western termini of railroads. Joseph G. McCoy persuaded the Kansas Pacific to build out to Abilene, Kansas, which became a famous "cow town" thirty years before it fathered a famous general and President; in 1871 the Santa Fe established another railhead at Dodge City, Kansas, and about the same time the Union Pacific established a third at Oglalla, Nebraska. The chance discovery that beeves could winter on the Wyoming plains and come out fat and sleek in the spring, led to other shipping points on the Northern railways. Thus, by 1875 there was a belt of free pasturage extending from southern Texas to the Canadian border. The refrigerator car, in common use by that date, made it possible to sell dressed beef, slaughtered at Chicago or Kansas City, in the Eastern centers of population. These factors, with the invention of artificial ice and a canning machine, brought even European markets within reach of the Far West.

This new industry of raising beef cattle on the Great Plains produced the last phase of the Wild West, and the most picturesque development of the ancient art of cattle-droving. Texans, who had ridden from childhood and fought in the Confederate army, and Mexican bucaroos (*vaqueros*) were the first and best cowboys. Every spring they rounded up the herds from eight to ten ranches, identified ownership by the brands, branded the calves, and divided *pro rata* the mavericks and "dogies," the motherless calves. The breeding cattle were set free for another year, while the likely three- and four-year-olds were conducted on the long drive. There were three principal trails, all of which crossed the Indian Territory; but the Indians did not object to palefaces and cattle who passed through instead of settling down; the Cherokee even issued grazier licenses for a small fee. In 1871, peak year of the long drive, some 600,000 head were driven north.

A typical herd on the long drive of 1200 to 1500 miles consisted of 2500 longhorns. This required about twelve cowboys with a *remuda* (remount) of from five to six horses each, controlled by a "horse wrangler," and a "chuck wagon" drawn by mules for the men's food and camp equipment. The cattle walked slowly, making ten to twenty miles a day, swam rivers, and, if properly driven and prevented from stampeding, would even gain weight en route. They were allowed to browse all night, for an hour or two every morning, and again at noon. At the end of the drive the cattle were sold to buyers from Chicago and Kansas City, and the cowboys, after being paid off and "blowing in" most of their wages in the cow town, returned by the same trail.

While the long line of cattle moved slowly, the cowboys were continually riding up and down, urging stragglers along, and on the lookout for raiding "bad men," wild Indians, or prairie-grass fires. They had to continue riding around the herd at night lest it be stampeded by a thunderstorm or by steers simply getting the notion to bolt. The cowboy's high-horned Mexican saddle, lariat, broad-brimmed sombrero, high-heeled boots, and leather "chaps" and six-shooter were perfectly adapted to his work. His bronco — a short-legged, varicolored mustang of Spanish origin, hardy as a donkey and fleet as an Arab, and which he broke with unnecessary cruelty — made an ideal cow pony. The authentic cowboy was spare of frame, pithy and profane in speech, a superb rider although a bowlegged walker; alert with the sort of courage needed to rope steers, fight cattle rustlers, or stop a stampede; hardworking and enduring, asking no better end than to die with his boots on. His life is recorded in ballads which are now nation-wide favorites. These ballads record the freedom and discipline, the violence and friendship of the Far West; one can almost smell the odor of sun on saddle leather, and of the buffalo-chip fire over which cookie prepared the evening meal; a hard, challenging open-air life that attracted young men, knights of the long trail. The cowboy of the long drive flourished for a brief score of years, fading into legend with the passing of the open range.

By 1885 the range had become too heavily pastured to support the long drive, and was beginning to be crisscrossed by railroads and by the barbed-wire fences of homesteaders. Then came the terrible winter of 1886–87, when thousands of animals perished in the open. Cattle owners began to stake out homestead claims in the names of their employees and to fence off areas to which they had no claim. Almost in a moment cattle and sheep ranches replaced the open range, and the cowboy of the long drive became a domesticated ranch hand.

So much for the cowboy of history. But why did this ephemeral type capture the nation's, almost the world's, imagination rather than the earlier trapper of the Far West, the lumberjack of the northern forests, the river man who rode logs down rapids, or the sailor in blue water? These, too, had their ballads or chanties; their lives were not lacking in beauty, and they too experienced the same violent contrast between long periods of exceedingly hard, dangerous work and brief, bawdy blowouts. One answer is that the cowboy was a horseman, and since the dawn of history the rider has seemed more glamorous than the sailor or footman — witness the gay cavalcade of Athenian knights on the frieze of the Parthenon. And the cowboy was rendered famous by three gifted "tenderfeet" or "dudes," [1] Eastern college graduates who sojourned briefly in the Far West produced souped-up versions in prose, painting, and sculpture of Life in the Raw for the effete East. Frederic Remington, after playing football with Walter Camp at Yale, became a cowboy and rancher in Kansas for about two years but devoted the rest of his life (at New Rochelle, New York) to drawing, painting, and sculpturing cowpunchers, Indians, and trappers in action, partly as illustrations to his own books. Theodore Roosevelt invested half his patrimony in a cattle ranch in the Bad Lands of Dakota Territory in 1883, lived there for less than three years, doing the hardest work and acquiring a taste for the "great open spaces" which produced the Rough Riders of 1898, and fed the Rooseveltian conception of Strenuous Life. "In that land," he wrote in his *Autobiography*, "we led a free and hardy life, with horse and with rifle. . . . We knew toil and hardship and hunger and thirst; and we saw men die violent deaths as they worked among the horses and cattle, or fought in evil feuds with one another; but we felt the beat of hardy life in our veins, and ours was the glory of work and the joy of living."

Roosevelt's love for the Far West was deep and genuine; but the man who contributed most to the cowboy legend was a literary cowboy, Owen Wister, a Philadelphia patrician who reached Wyoming in time to witness the so-called Johnson County War between cattle barons and the homesteaders. Many young Easterners and Englishmen of wealth, eager to combine sportsmanship with profit, had begun cattle-raising in Wyoming, taking advantage of the free open range. Wister found their society, which centered upon the Cheyenne Club, as congenial as that of the Porcellian, although the members wore a different costume. It so happened that Johnson County had been thrown open by the Land Office to homesteaders, and many — mostly from the Ozarks — had located there, built barbed-wire fences around their 160-acre lots, and in other ways hindered the operations of the gentlemen who had organized the powerful Wyoming Stock Growers' Association. Wister

1. "Tenderfoot" first meant a yard-raised cow turned out on the range; "dude" (pronounced "dood"), a word of unknown origin which appeared around 1881, was first applied to the New York "young men about town" glorified in Richard Harding Davis's *Van Bibber* books, who dressed in the latest London fashion and were caricatured as wearing a monocle and a topper and sucking the handle of a walking stick. In the Far West it meant any well-heeled Easterner, and there it survives in the term "dude ranch."

regarded the "grangers" or "nesters" as the settlers were called locally, as low fellows of the baser sort, and in several short stories, combined in the popular novel *The Virginian* (1902), glorified the cowboy and condoned the murderous onslaughts on homesteaders by the gentlemen's hired killers. Wister created the literary cliché of the gentle cowpuncher who respected virtuous womanhood (and eventually married a schoolteacher from New England), defending the free open life of the range against homesteaders and other bad men who were trying to destroy it. He was the progenitor of standardized "Western" literature, of the rodeos for which horses are trained to buck, and the so-called "horse opera" on radio and in the movies, which have made the fortunes of hundreds of hack and script writers. This distorted image of the American Far West has traveled around the world; small boys in Europe, Asia and Africa are still listening to these impossible tales of the Wild West and sporting imitations of Levi overalls, spurs, colt revolvers, and "tengallon hats."

3. The Farming Country

There was no essential change in Northern farm life between the Civil War and the coming of the automobile.[1] From Maine westward through Nebraska and the Dakotas, country folk lived in wooden frame houses such as those depicted by Grant Wood and Grandma Moses. The kitchen served as family living room; the parlor, with horsehair-covered furniture, Prang chromos, and crayon enlargements of family photos on the walls, perhaps a Rogers group on the table, was used mostly for the daughters' courting, and for weddings and funerals. The carpenter who built a farmer's house differentiated it from the barn by putting scroll work under the eaves and by building at the front a porch with carved posts. These houses were heated in winter by cast-iron stoves, lighted by kerosene lamps and protected from flying insects by iron-meshed screens. The farmer's wife cooked for her own family and the hired hands on a wood or coal stove and hauled or pumped her water from a nearby well, unless she lived in a region where a windmill could do it. Fewer than 10 per cent of American farm houses before 1900 had plumbing; a wooden washtub served for the weekly bath, and the back-house, whose passing James Whitcomb Riley celebrated in a famous unpublished poem, served other basic human needs.

The cow barn, always larger than the house, doubled as horse stable and afforded plenty of storage space for root crops as well as hay; its well-worn floor of wide boards was perfect for country dances. Daily Bible reading and Sunday "goin' to meetin'" were the rule, and much of the farm family's

1. Alexander Graham Bell invented the telephone in 1876, and Thomas A. Edison the incandescent light bulb in 1879; but it was long before either spread to country districts. In 1885 the Bell Telephone Company had over 134,000 subscribers in the United States as compared with about 13,500 in the United Kingdom; but most of the telephones were in towns and cities.

recreation turned around church socials. The farmer did not invite neighbors to dinner — "swapping meals" made no sense to him. The horse served as pet, transportation, and sport to all country-bred Americans, and to many in the cities. It was a poor farmer who hadn't a team of Clydesdales or Percherons for heavy hauling, a fast trotter for his buggy, and a saddle horse or two for his children; nobody walked if he could help it. Breeding horses, raising and training the colts, were part of a farmer's education and afforded him and his children infinite pleasure and profit, especially in horse trading. And it was a rare farmer who did not take the time to go fishing with his boys, or to shoot quail, duck, and partridge; or, if he lived on the edge of the northern wilderness, to hunt deer and moose.

This horse-centered economy created a vast market for hay and feed grains, and supported such handicraft industries as blacksmithing, saddlery, and harness making, and the construction of wagons, carriages, buggies, and sleighs. These were generally lighter than European models, but fashioned to last; beautifully functional, with a different kind of wood for each part, as Dr. Holmes described in "The Wonderful One-Hoss Shay." Winter and snow were a blessing in those days. Roads were tramped down by pooling the community's ox teams as Whittier described in "Snow-Bound," or, later, by great wooden horse-drawn rollers. The farmer and his boys put away their wheeled vehicles and let down by tackles from the barn loft their steel-runnered pungs and sledges which had been gathering dust and rust since spring. Heavy hauling of timber and the like now began, local sportsmen organized trotting races in their cutters (two-seater one-horse sleighs) painted gay colors. A swain who had taken his girl buggy-riding in the fall now tucked her into a smart cutter with a buffalo robe; and away they went at a fast clip over the snowy roads, to the merry jingle of sleigh bells.

The hired man on the average farm was not the pathetic type whose death Robert Frost recorded, but a stout youth. He had the right to keep a horse at his employer's expense, and every Saturday afternoon he dressed up, slicked down his hair, put on a derby hat, and drove to town in his own buggy to call on a girl, or have fun generally. For in all Northern and Western farm country there was almost always a small town within driving distance to which the farmer could haul his cash crop for shipment by rail, and where he could make his purchases. Here would be a new high school, several general stores, and (if the temperance movement had not reached it) a hotel built around a bar; two or three Protestant churches, a lawyer or two, and a doctor who also acted as dentist and veterinarian; possibly an "opera house" where strolling actors played. The barber shop was the center for sporting intelligence and smut, where waiting customers sang close-harmony in "barber-shop chords." If Germans were about there was an amateur string orchestra, brass band, or *Singverein*; possibly also a *Turnverein* for the boys to practice simple gymnastics. Smart farmers' sons went from high school or endowed academy to one of the little hilltop colleges scattered throughout the land, even to a state university to prepare for business or the professions. There were bleak and narrow aspects to this way of life, well described in Edgar Howe's grim novel of Kansas, *The Story of a Country Town* (1883), but it was active and robust. The insipidity portrayed in Sinclair Lewis's *Main Street* (1920) did not, in general, enter the life of the Northern American countryside or small town until its more enterprising people had been lured away by big industry. Many farmers' boys grew up hating this rustic routine and drudgery; Henry Ford and Frank Lloyd Wright admit in their autobiographies that revulsion against life on the farm impelled them, respectively, into automobile manufacture and architecture.

After this life had passed away forever, many became sentimental about it, and some of the best novels in American literature describe nostalgically the rural society of those days: — Mary M. Wilkins Freeman for northern New England; Willa Cather's *My Ántonia* for Nebraska; Hamlin Garland for the Middle Border; O. E. Rölvaag (who wrote in Norwegian but whose *Giants in the Earth* was translated by Lincoln Colcord) for Scandinavian pioneers in Minnesota. James Whitcomb Riley recorded Hoosier child life in verse; but nobody has better depicted this way of living in which most of our Presidents from Lincoln to Coolidge were raised, and the impact on it of big industry, than Sherwood Anderson in his *Poor White* (1920).

4. *Iron and Steel, Big Business and Politics*

A good index of the industrial development of the Middle West is the rise of ship tonnage passing through the "Soo" (Saulte Ste. Marie) canal between Lakes Superior and Huron. Roughly 100,000 tons in 1860, the burthen rose to half a million in 1869 and 25 million in 1901. Wheat and iron ore formed the bulk of these cargoes. The iron came from new orefields of Michigan and Minnesota, to which the application of the Bessemer smelting process gave America cheap steel, an essential factor of industrial development. These orefields on Lake Superior are distant hundreds of miles from coal deposits, but cheap lake and rail transport brought them together in the smelters of Chicago, where the first American steel rails were rolled in 1865, and in Cleveland, Toledo, Ashtabula, and Milwaukee. Much ore was transported to Pittsburgh, center of the northern Appalachian coalfields where native and Irish labor, revolting against the twelve-hour shifts imposed by the iron masters, was replaced by sturdy Hungarians and Slavs. In the 1880's the iron and coal beds of the southern Appalachians began to be exploited, and Birmingham, Alabama, became a Southern rival to Pittsburgh and Cleveland. American steel production, a mere 20,000 tons in 1867, passed the British output with 6 million tons in 1895 and reached 10 million before 1900.

In world economy the United States in 1879 was still a country of extractive industries; by 1900 it had become one of the greater manufacturing nations of the world. Yet the value of farm products still greatly exceeded those of industry, and the expanding home market precluded serious competition with England and Germany for export markets. In 1869 there were two million wage earners in factories and small industries, producing goods to the value of $3,385 million; in 1899 there were 4.7 million wage earners in factories alone, producing goods to the value of $11,407 million. In 1870 there were 6.8 million workers on farms, and the value of farm productions was $2.4 billion; in 1900 the number of farm workers was 10.9 million, and the value of their products, $8.5 billion. The number of horses and mules "on farms" (apparently those in towns were not counted) rose from 7.8 million in 1867 to 25 million in 1920. Then began the long decline, as more and more farmers relied on gasoline-powered vehicles and machinery.

In New England and the North generally, small waterpower factories declined in favor of concentrated manufacturing cities such as Fall River, Bridgeport, Paterson, Scranton, Troy, Schenectady, Youngstown, and Akron. Chicago rose triumphantly from the ashes of the great fire started by Mrs. O'Leary's cow in 1871, became the most populous American city after New York, and in 1893 staged the World's Columbian Exposition.

This development was neither steady nor orderly. Overproduction of goods and raw materials, overcapitalization of railroads, and feverish speculation in securities brought financial panics in 1873 and 1893. During the hard times that followed, labor expressed its dissatisfaction by strikes of unparalleled violence, and the farmers sought solution for their troubles in political panaceas. It was a period of cutthroat competition in which the big fish swallowed the little fish and then tried to eat one another. Competing railroads cut freight rates between important points, in the hope of obtaining the lion's share of business, until dividends ceased and the bonds became a drug in the market. The downward trend of prices from 1865 to 1900, especially marked after 1873, put a premium on labor-saving machinery, on new processes of manufacture, and on greater units for mass production. "Gentlemen's agreements" between rival producers to maintain prices and divide business, or even to pro-rate profits, were characteristic of the period after 1872. But it was found so difficult to enforce these pools that a gentlemen's agreement came to mean one that was certain to be violated. About 1880 the pool began to be superseded by the trust, a form of combination in which the affiliated companies handed over their securities and their power to a central board of trustees. John D. Rockefeller organized the first and most successful, the Standard Oil Trust, in 1879. A large measure of his success was due to improvements, economies, and original methods of marketing; but his monopoly was secured by methods condemned even by the tolerant business ethics of his day, and pronounced criminal by the courts. By playing competing railroads against each other, Standard Oil obtained rebates from their published freight rates and even forced them to pay over rebates from its competitors' freight bills to Standard Oil. If competing oil companies managed to stagger along under such handicaps, they were "frozen out" by cutting prices below cost in their selling territory, until Standard had all the business.

Thomas W. Lawson, author of *Frenzied Finance* (1905), a plunger and speculator who acquired great wealth during this period, wrote of it cynically: "At this period Americans found they could, by the exercise of a daring and cunning of a peculiar, reckless and low order, so take advantage of the laws of the land and its economic customs as to create for themselves wealth, or the equivalent, money, to practically an unlimited extent, without the aid of time or labor or the possession of any unusual ability coming through birth or education."

The trust as a method of combination was outlawed by most of the states in the early 'eighties; but the holding company, a corporation owning the shares of other corporations, proved to be a legitimate and more efficient financial device. In popular usage, however, the term "trust" was applied to combinations of any structure, provided they had sufficient power to dictate prices. These were the trusts which became targets of popular indignation in the early twentieth century. Not until the late 1880's did the American public demand regulation of trusts, and that problem was greatly complicated by a federal form of government. The states, not the federal government, issue corporate charters (excepting transcontinental railways); and a corporation chartered by one state has the right to do business in every other. Gas, electric lighting, and water companies and street railways depended for their very existence on municipalities. Hence the corrupt alliance cemented after the Civil War between politics and business. Plain bribery was often practiced with municipal councils, which gave away for nothing franchises worth millions, while cities remained unpaved, ill-lit, and inadequately policed.

Greatest in power, and most notorious for their abuse of it, were the great railway corporations. The power of an American transcontinental railway over its exclusive territory approached the absolute; for until the automobile age people in the Far West had no alternate means of transportation. A railroad could make an industry or ruin a community merely by juggling freight rates. The funds at their disposal, often created by financial manipulation and stock-watering, were so colossal as to overshadow the budgets of state governments. Railway builders and owners, like James J. Hill, had the point of view of a feudal chieftain. Members of state legislatures were their vassals, to be coerced or bribed into voting "right" if persuasion would not serve. In their opinion, railroading was a private business, no more a fit subject for government regulation than a tailor's shop. They were unable to recognize any public interest distinct from their own. In many instances the despotism was benevolent; and if a few men became multimillionaires, their subjects also prospered. But Collis P. Huntington, Leland Stanford, and their associates who built the Central and controlled the Southern Pacific were indifferent to all save considerations of private gain. By distributing free passes to state representatives, paying their campaign expenses and giving "presents" to their wives, they evaded taxation as well as regulation. By discriminating freight charges between localities and individuals, they terrorized merchants, farmers, and communities "until matters had reached such a pass," states a government report of 1887, "that no man dared engage in any business in which transportation largely entered without first obtaining the permission of a railroad manager." Through the press and the professions they wielded a power over public opinion comparable to that of slave-owners over the old South. Their methods were imitated by Eastern and Midwestern railroads, so far as they dared. In New Hampshire as in California, the railroad lobby, entrenched in an office near the state capitol, acted as a third chamber of initiative and revision; and few could succeed in politics unless by grace of the railroad overlord. Winston Churchill's *Coniston* (1906) and Frank Norris's *Octopus* (1901) accurately portray the social and political effects of railroad domination in these two states.

These exactions and abuses were long tolerated by Americans, so imbued were they with laissez-faire doctrine, so proud of progress, improvement, and development, and so averse from increasing the power of government. Thus it was not until 1887 that the federal government first attempted to regulate railroads and break up trusts. Congress then passed the first Interstate Commerce Act, declaring "unreasonable" rates, pooling and other unfair practices to be illegal. Enforcement was vested in the first modern American administrative board, the Interstate Commerce Commission. But administrative regulations were so foreign to the American conception of government that the federal courts insisted on their right to review orders of the Commission, and by denying its power to fix rates, emasculated the Act. So the railroads continued to charge "all the traffic would bear." Equally futile was the Sherman Anti-trust Act of 1890, which declared illegal any monopoly or combination in restraint of interstate trade. When the Supreme Court in 1895 held that purchase by the sugar trust of a controlling interest in 98 per cent of the sugar refining business of the country was not a violation of the law because not an act of interstate commerce, the Sherman Act became temporarily dead letter.

Theodore Roosevelt well summed up this last quarter of the nineteenth century in his *Autobiography*: "A riot of individualistic materialism, under which complete freedom for the individual . . . turned out in practice to mean perfect freedom for the strong to wrong the weak. . . . The power of the mighty industrial overlords . . . had increased with giant strides, while the methods of controlling them, . . . through the Government, remained archaic and therefore practically impotent." Roosevelt also had the wit to see that merely breaking up the trusts into smaller units was no answer; that was merely a futile attempt to remedy by more individualism the evils that were the result of unfettered individualism.

5. Canada Comes of Age

Canadian development lagged behind that of the United States. Sir John Macdonald and other founders of the Dominion hoped that federation would solve everything, but the reality fell far short of their expectations. Geography and race offered the greatest difficulties. The Dominion, stretching from the Strait of Belle Isle north of Newfoundland to Dawson in the Klondike, covered 15 more degrees of longitude than the United States; yet the depth of country north of the border habitable by people of European stock was in no place over 400 miles wide and in many, not half that. For five months every year the St. Lawrence was closed by ice. Under Canada's constitution — the British North American Act of 1867 — the Dominion Parliament at Ottawa retained all reserved powers of government. But this failed to quench provincialism in a country whose seven provinces had very diverse interests, and whose French population considered itself a nation apart. Enterprising, go-ahead Canadians of British stock found themselves hampered at sundry points by the French of Quebec, whose values were still largely those of Norman peasants of the Old Regime, and whose leaders, not content with their provincial privileges under the Quebec Act of 1774, demanded their extension to every other part of the Dominion. Macdonald, they claimed, had persuaded the French to federate by promising to make all Canada bilingual.

Canada even had her own civil war five years after the one in the United States ended. The *métis*, French-speaking half-breeds of the Red River Colony, under the lead of Louis Riel, seized control of that region in 1869, demanded special rights in the Dominion, and executed some people who objected. The *métis* were put down by British regulars, and that colony became the Province of Manitoba in 1870. One result of this rebellion was the formation of the Royal Canadian Mounted Police, who proved to be more successful than the United States Army in preserving law and order in the West. But the *métis*, although given separate schools in Manitoba with French equal to English, were not satisfied. Racial minorities, as the history of the last century shows, are seldom satisfied because their leaders, to keep in power, are always stirring up fresh resentments.

Other issues, too, disturbed the Dominion. The first was the depression of 1873 which lasted a good twenty years in Canada, and slowed the growth of the country. Population increased only from 3.7 to 4.8 million between 1871 and 1891, when that of the United States rose from 38.6 to 63 million. A mild degree of protection was added to the tariff, but this seemed to do no good; and in 1874 a proposal to revive reciprocity with the United States resulted only in another snub from President Grant, and the rejection of a draft treaty by the Senate. The other big issue was the Canadian Pacific Railway. It had no sooner been chartered in 1873 than word got out, in a series of letters that rivaled James G. Blaine's for sensationalism, that the promoters had contributed $350,000 to campaign funds of the Conservative party. Sir John Macdonald's telegram, "Must have another $10,000," almost broke him, as Blaine's "Burn this letter" had lost him the presidency. And it did ruin the railway corporation. Parliament, shocked at the revelations, cut off government subsidies.

A new Liberal government under Alexander Mackenzie, a dour, self-made Scot, now tried to build the transcontinental railway piecemeal, and by 1878 had completed it as far west as Winnipeg. This was not nearly fast enough for the public, especially in British Columbia, which threatened secession if the line were not promptly pushed through. This situation, and the depression, led to a return of Macdonald and the Conservatives to power the same year. Macdonald now lent his support to a group of promoters led by George Stephen, a Montreal banker, and the Canadian Pacific Railway was rechartered on terms so liberal as to make mouths water across the border: a cash grant of $25 million, 30 million acres of land tax-exempt for 20 years, a gift of the 700 miles of railway already built, no rival road for 20 years, no rate regulation until the company was making 10 per cent on its capital! Even these were not enough; every few years the C.P.R. directors emitted cries of distress and obtained additional government loans up to $27.5 million.

George Stephen was raised to the peerage for his completion of the C.P.R., but the man who really put it through was a Yankee railroader, William C. Van Horne who, on the recommendation of James J. Hill, became general manager in 1881. The road was now vigorously pushed westward from Winnipeg, and eastward from Vancouver. Forward went the steel rails across the prairies of Manitoba and Saskatchewan, into the great plains of Alberta, spawning towns and cities like Moose Jaw, Medicine Hat, and Calgary en route; past superb Lake Louise, crossing the Selkirk range of the Rockies at Kicking Horse Pass, an elevation of over 5000 feet, while the Vancouver group worked up the valley of the Fraser river. When the last spike was driven where the two met, at Eagle Pass on 7 November 1885, less than five years had elapsed since the work had been resumed, and in that time almost half of this 2881-mile transcontinental railway had been constructed. And another 500 miles were added when the C.P.R. acquired the Intercolonial Railway from Montreal to the ice-free port of St. John, New Brunswick.

The completion of the C.P.R. coincided with the end of Louis Riel. He returned from exile to Manitoba in 1884 to head a full-fledged rebellion of *métis* and Indians. After a brief war with the Canadian army and the "Mounties," he was captured, tried for treason, and hanged, as he well deserved. This provoked an emotional explosion in Quebec, where the French population for the first time deserted the conservative guidance of their clergy, swept the provincial elections, made Sir Wilfrid Laurier leader of the Liberal party, and with the aid of discontented elements in the Maritimes and elsewhere, almost defeated the Conservatives in the general election of 1891. Sir John Macdonald won again, but the hardships of winter campaigning brought on a shock, of which this "Grand Old Man of Canada" died. A bitter controversy over sectarian schools in Ontario and Manitoba followed; the Liberals won the general election of 1896, and Laurier became premier. He rode into power on a wave of prosperity, of which the principal ingredient was a rapid development of the prairie provinces, first fruit of completing the railway. And he continued premier until defeated in 1911 on the issue of reciprocity with the United States.

Sir Wilfrid was a remarkable French Canadian gentlemen, a lawyer descended from a colonel of the Carignan-Salières regiment. In his nature the energy of Theodore Roosevelt was combined with the finesse of Franklin D. Roosevelt. Loyal to the British crown and friendly to the United States, he consistently advocated Canadian nationalism. At the conference of colonial and dominion prime ministers with the British colonial secretary on the occasion of Queen Victoria's diamond jubilee, Sir Wilfrid took the lead in thwarting Joseph Chamberlain's effort to replace the loose imperial tie by a centralized system resembling the European Common Market of the 1960's.

Canada contributed 7300 volunteers to the British army in the South Africa War of 1899–1901. Her foreign relations were still conducted from London, and the Royal Canadian Navy had not yet been launched; but the Dominion entered the new century with her march toward independence almost 90 per cent achieved.

THE OLD CHISHOLM TRAIL

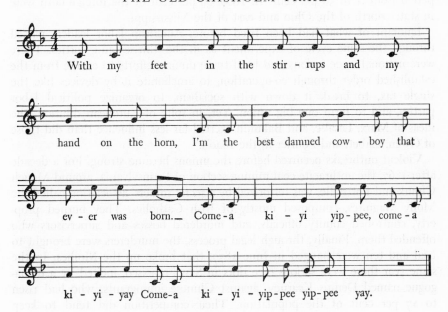

With my feet in the stir - rups and my hand on the horn, I'm the best damned cow - boy that ev - er was born.__ Come-a ki - yi yip-pee, come-a ki - yi - yay Come-a ki - yi - yip-pee yip-pee yay.

Social and Cultural Developments

1870-1900

1. *The Rise of Organized Labor*

ORGANIZED LABOR passed through phases of bewildering complexity before it won the power to meet organized capital on equal terms. There was little continuity with the antebellum period. Wage earners of the 1840's had largely become farmers, shopkeepers, and petty capitalists by the 1870's. Their places were taken by farmers' sons, discharged soldiers lured by the attractions of urban life, and a new wave of immigrants, European rather than British, who were not interested in unions and were willing to work for low wages. Annual immigration passed 300,000 in 1866 and rose to 789,000 in 1882, the highest for any year of the nineteenth century. The proportion of British and Irish immigrants fell from 45 per cent in 1861–70 to 18 per cent in 1891–1900; that of Russians, Italians, and other southern Europeans, rose in the same period from .1 to 50 per cent. In 1900, 86 per cent of the foreign-born were in states north of the Ohio and east of the Mississippi.

Ignorant of what had been tried before, American labor leaders passed through the same cycle of experiment as in the 'thirties and 'forties. There were national trade unions and local trade unions, efforts to escape from the established order through co-operation, to ameliorate it by devices like the single tax, to break it down with socialism, to organize political labor parties, and to form one big union. Yet, in spite of European dilution, the ideas of Marx, Lasalle, and Bakunin exerted far less influence than did those of Owen, Cabet, and Fourier in the 1840's.

Violent outbreaks occurred before the unions became strong. For a decade after 1867, the anthracite coal mining section of Pennsylvania, around Mauch Chunk and Pottsville, was terrorized by a secret miners' association called the Molly Maguires, composed mostly of Irish Catholics. They burned property, controlled county officials, and murdered bosses and supervisors who offended them. Finally, through legal process, the murderers were brought to trial and ten were hanged in June 1877; that broke up the Mollies. In the same year there were serious race riots in San Francisco, incited by a demagogue named Dennis Kearney, against Chinese immigrants, who had risen to 17 per cent of the population. Their competition did tend to keep wages down. This problem was solved by a series of Chinese exclusion acts, starting in 1882, which obtained support in Congress because a stupid shoe manufacturer tried to break a strike in North Adams, Massachusetts, by importing coolies.

The year 1877 was very rough. When the four Eastern trunk lines (the through railroads) jauntily announced a wage cut of 10 per cent, second since the panic of 1873, the unorganized railroad employees struck and were supported by a huge army of hungry and desperate unemployed. During one week in July, traffic was suspended on the trunk lines, and every industrial center was in a turmoil. In Pittsburgh, Martinsburg, and Chicago there were pitched battles between militia and the mob; order had to be restored by federal troops. Unfortunately the reported presence of German and French socialists led the public to the easy conclusion that imported agitators were alone responsible. (Compare the South's conviction that abolitionists and other outsiders have been responsible for Negro unrest.) Few Americans realized that their country had reached a stage of industrial development which created a labor problem, or that the "Great Strike of '77" would be the first of a long series of battles between labor and capital.

Two years later, when good times and full employment were back, the labor movement developed into a contest for leadership between organizations representing labor unionism, craft unionism, and socialism. The Order of the Knights of Labor (founded 1869), native-American in leadership and largely in personnel, was an attempt to unite workers into one big union under centralized control. Its professed object was to escape from the wage system through producers' co-operation, popular education, and the union of all workers by hand or brain. Terence V. Powderly, a Pennsylvania machinist who became grand master in 1878, was an idealist who disliked the tactics of combative unionism; but the order first become powerful in 1884 by winning a railroad strike in the Southwest. Capital met labor on equal terms, for the first time in America, when the financier Jay Gould conferred with the Knights' executive board and conceded their demands. The Knights were largely responsible for a congressional act of 1885 which forbade the importation of contract labor.

Parallel with the rise of the Knights of Labor, trade unions of skilled workers grew and multiplied, while others affiliated with Marx's International or with the "Black" (anarchist) International. Knights, trade unions, socialist unions, and anarchists simultaneously struck for the eight-hour day at Chicago in 1886, when the country was prosperous and business was booming. The spectacular event of this strike was the Haymarket Square riot in Chicago on 4 May. After an English anarchist had begun inciting a mob of about 1000 strikers to violence, the police ordered them to disperse. Someone threw a dynamite bomb which, with subsequent pistol shooting, killed eight policemen and wounded sixty-seven. Eight anarchists were tried for murder and found guilty, although the bomb thrower was never identified. The verdict was sustained by the Supreme Court of the United States and four men were hanged. The horror of the crime was matched by the injustice of the punishment; and, as in the later Sacco-Vanzetti case, many Americans prominent in literature and the arts protested. In 1893, when the German-born Governor John P. Altgeld pardoned the three survivors then in jail because convinced of their innocence, he was widely denounced as an abettor of anarchy, and his political career was ruined.

As champions of the unskilled, the Knights attained a membership of about 700,000 around 1886, as compared with 250,000 in the national trade unions. Powderly, however, so mismanaged matters that the Knights lost their grip, and the van of the labor movement was usurped by an organization of skilled workers on craft lines, the American Federation of Labor.

In the late 'sixties a bullet-headed young fellow named Samuel Gompers, a British subject of mixed Hebrew and Flemish ancestry, was working in a highly unsanitary cigar-making shop in New York's lower east side, and speaking at the meetings of a local union. Cigar-making was then a sociable handicraft. The men talked or read aloud while they worked, and Gompers learned to concentrate on the economic struggle and to fight shy of intellectuals who would ride union labor to some personal utopia. He determined to divorce unionism from politics which dissipated its energy, and from radicalism which aroused public apprehension. In the hard times of the 1870's he experienced cold and hunger, the futility of charity, and the cowardice of politicians. By 1881 he and other local leaders had thought their way through to a national federation of craft unions, economic in purpose, evolutionary in method, and contending for immediate objects such as shorter hours and higher wages. Five years later the American Federation of Labor was born, and as the Knights of Labor declined it became the fighting spearhead of the American labor movement.

It is perhaps a contradiction to include the "hoboes" among the workers; but no picture of America in that era is complete without these "knights of the road" who roamed the northern part of the country, catching rides on freight trains, stealing or begging their food, and spending cold winters in local jails. The first lot were discharged soldiers of the Union army who refused to settle down. These "Weary Willies," "Tired Tims," and "Happy Hooligans" added a picturesque feature to the countryside like the Gypsies of old, and afforded cartoonists and journalists infinite material for amusement. Some were criminals, but most of them were harmless vagrants.

During this period, when England reached her nadir of unpopularity in the United States, and "twisting the British lion's tail" always won votes, the three writers who had the most influence on the American mind were English — Charles Darwin, Thomas Huxley, and Herbert Spencer. Spencer's *Social Statics* (1865) raised laissez-faire to a dogma among American business men. He had picked up a phrase of Tom Paine, "That government is best which governs least," and taught that the functions of the state should be limited to internal police and foreign protection — no public education, no limitation of hours of labor, no welfare legislation. To this he added in his *Principles of Biology* (presenting the theories of his friend Darwin) the phrase "survival of the fittest," which exactly suited the winners in the dog-eat-dog competition of that day. So deep did Spencer's theories penetrate American thought that Justice Holmes, in a dissenting opinion of 1905, felt obliged to remind his fellow jurists that *Social Statics* was not embodied in the Constitution of the United States.

Spencer's influence undoubtedly delayed factory inspection, limitation of hours, and the like. The first state labor law to be adequately enforced was the Massachusetts Ten-Hour Act of 1874 for women and children in factories. The need to provide administrative machinery for the enforcement of labor laws was generally overlooked, and even if it were, the courts were apt to declare such laws unconstitutional. The New York act of 1883 prohibiting the manufacture of cigars in tenement houses, which Gompers persuaded young Theodore Roosevelt to sponsor and Governor Cleveland to sign, was intended as an entering wedge to break up sweatshops in the cities, a rapidly growing menace. The constitutionality of this law, brought before the highest state court, was invalidated on the ground that it interfered with the profitable use of real estate, without any compensating public advantage. "It cannot be perceived how the cigar-maker is to be improved in his health or his morals by forcing him from his home and its hallowed associations and beneficent influences to ply his trade elsewhere," declared the court. Roosevelt, who had personally inspected these one-room "homes" where whole families and their lodgers ate, slept, and rolled cigars, then began to revise his conception of justice; and Gompers renewed the fight against the sweatshop.

Most state constitutions, and Amendment XIV to the Federal Constitution, forbid the government to deprive citizens of property without due process of law. As no reform can be effected without depriving someone of something that he may deem to be a property right, American courts early invented the doctrine of a superior police power, the reserved right of any state to protect the people's health, safety, and welfare. This police power had been held to justify even confiscatory reforms, such as the prohibition of lotteries, or the manufacture and sale of alcohol; but when labor and factory laws appeared on the statute books, judges began to draw the line. Corporations, securing the best lawyers, found it easy to convince courts that such laws were not a proper and reasonable exercise of the police power, and to point out conflicts with Amendment XIV or other clauses of the Federal Constitution. The Supreme Court in 1873 declined to intervene between the state of Louisiana and the New Orleans butchers, who alleged that state regulations were confiscatory. The Court explained that Amendment XIV had been adopted to protect the freed slaves, not to make the federal judiciary "a perpetual censor upon all legislation of the states . . . with authority to nullify such as it did not approve." But this was before the judges began reading Herbert Spencer.

Where a conflict with the Constitution could not be discovered, judges around 1886 began to postulate a theoretical liberty of contract, "the right of a person to sell his labor upon such terms as he deems proper." [1] A Pennsylvania statute forbidding payment of miners' wages in orders on the company store was judicially nullified by a decision declaring such a law "degrading and insulting to the laborer," and "subversive of his rights as a citizen." An Illinois court declared unconstitutional a statute limiting the hours of labor for women in sweatshops, on the ground that they had the same liberty of contract as men. In 1905 the Supreme Court of the United States took a similar view of a New York statute limiting the hours of labor in bakeries; the bakers, declared the court in effect, were sufficiently intelligent to make their own labor contracts in their own interest. Justice Holmes, whom Theodore Roosevelt had translated from the supreme judicial court of Massachusetts to the Supreme Court of the United States in 1902, dissented from 43 out of the 171 decisions in which the Supreme Court invalidated state laws in the name of due process between 1905 and 1932, when he retired. But the appointees of Presidents Taft and Wilson to the Supreme bench, with the notable exception of Justice Brandeis, continued to act as a chamber of revision on state regulatory and welfare legislation, into the first administration of Franklin D. Roosevelt.

Thus, ironically, laissez-faire as a social concept reached its logical development in American courts just as it was breaking down as a social structure before modern industrialism.

These were some of the many difficulties that labor in general encountered, the A. F. of L. in particular. Despite the loss of the great Homestead strike against the Carnegie Steel Company in 1892 (during which pacifist Andy Carnegie bawled loudly for troops), the A. F. of L. weathered the hard times of 1893–97 and turned the century with a membership of over half a million. Each national union has had to struggle for recognition, higher wages, the closed shop, and a shorter work week. The Federation carried on the struggle for a square deal from the courts, and battled socialists and other doctrinaires in its own ranks. Yet Gompers always managed to keep the A. F. of L. true to its first principles. The American unions, dealing with a body of labor divided by race and, until after World War I, constantly diluted by immigration, were slow to attain significant power. Gompers through the A. F. of L. accomplished more than any other to raise the material standards of American labor. But neither he nor any other American trade union leader did anything

1. Justice Harlan, in *Adair* v. *U.S.* (1908). This theory was given the blessing of Herbert Spencer in his *Justice* (1891), a book which, together with the writings of William Graham Sumner the Yale economist, became the sacred scriptures of conservatives who wished government to keep hands off business.

to help the Negro; all were as "lily-white" in preventing the entry into unions of colored men, as the most prejudiced group in the South.

2. The State of Religion

For all the corruption and pitiful politics of the Gilded Age, it was a robust, fearless, generous era, full of gusto and joy of living, affording wide scope to individual energy and material creation. And although not one of the greatest eras in American arts and letters, it was far from barren in these, or in spiritual forces.

The Roman Catholic Church, which already had 12 million members in 1890, was faced with many problems in accommodating itself to a predominantly Protestant country wedded to the concept of separation of church and state. Apart from small upper-class groups, descendants of Lord Baltimore's friends in eastern Maryland and of French Creoles in St. Louis and Louisiana, the Catholic Church in the United States was one of recent immigrants, and therefore of the poor. Despite the Latin language of the liturgy, the different ethnic groups which composed members of that faith balked at worshipping together, and demanded priests of their own nationality who could preach and hear confession in their own old-world tongue. Italians and French Canadians in particular disliked belonging to Irish parishes; even Poles and Lithuanians demanded separate churches in the manufacturing cities of New England. This situation worked itself out in time with new native-born generations, but created so many difficulties that Peter P. Cahensly, a layman of St. Louis, started a movement to have bishops appointed on the basis of language groups instead of geography. This, with some difficulty, was prevented by James Cardinal Gibbons, Archbishop of Baltimore, and John Ireland, Archbishop of St. Paul. The Cahensly movement is understandable, because the Germans brought over the European tradition of Catholic scholarship, whilst the Irish, sons of peasants or small shopkeepers and clever in ecclesiastical as in local and state politics, obtained most of the bishoprics.

A plenary council at Baltimore in 1884, comprising over seventy bishops, monsignori, and professors of theology, did a great deal to secure uniformity in worship, to set up parochial schools and diocesan seminaries, and to found the Catholic University of America in Washington. The impulse for this came from Rome, where many members of the papal curia looked down their long noses at all things American. Rome, in general, regarded American democracy, as did the old Federalists, as a bastard brat of French Jacobinism and was concerned to protect her transatlantic faithful from Protestant influence. She had been deeply impressed by the wild guess of one prelate that a million and a half Catholics had defected to Protestantism since 1820. Consequently, Rome supported what is now called by Catholics themselves the "ghetto complex" — trying to keep Catholics living together and forbidding them to take part with Protestants even in secular American activities other than politics. Archbishop Ireland of St. Paul openly declined to go along, and in his diocese Catholics and Protestants mingled amicably. Cardinal Gibbons felt likewise; but the archbishops of Boston and New York followed the Roman line.

Liberal Catholic discontent came to a head with the publication in 1897 of a badly translated biography of Father Isaac Hecker, one of the liberals of the antebellum era. Conservative Catholics in Europe picked on this and on certain acts of American Catholics which seem insignificant enough today — the rector of the Catholic University of America accepting an honorary degree from Harvard, and priests attending a Congress of Religion at the Chicago World's Fair — as expressions of undesirable "Americanism." Their influence procured from Leo XIII in 1899 a papal letter condemning certain "American" doctrines, especially Hecker's idea that the church relax her doctrinal rigor and glorify virtue in the Roman sense rather than passive morality and monastic vows. In other words, that she favor those English Puritan values which had created the American Protestant ethic. Cardinal Gibbons and other American prelates hastened to declare that no such heresies were current in America; and in 1902 Leo XIII congratulated the American hierarchy on their people's "perfect docility of mind and alacrity of disposition."

Whether or not by "alacrity of disposition" the Holy Father meant the increasing take by Catholic charities, it is probable that the swelling stream of Peter's pence from America to the Vatican brought about a more favorable disposition in Rome. Pope Pius X in 1908 removed the American church from the jurisdiction of the Propaganda Fidei and placed it on equality with the ancient churches of France and Spain. After another half-century, it became obvious that Popes John XXIII and Paul VI were moving toward the "Americanism" condemned by Leo XIII.

The Roman Catholic Church, through emphasis on sacraments rather than sacred Scriptures, escaped the controversy over Darwinism that rocked most of the Protestant churches to their foundations. And it successfully rode out the storm of German "higher criticism" of the Bible because most of the German theologians were unintelligible. Darwin's *Origin of Species* (1859), however, was read by almost every literate American sooner or later. It inculcated the doctrine of evolution through natural selection and taught that man was the end process of development from lower forms of life. Asa Gray of Harvard begged Darwin to postulate some Grand Design, some Beneficient Deity in all this; but Darwin could not persuade himself "that a beneficent and omnipotent God would have designedly created the *Ichneumonidae* with the express intention of their feeding within the living bodies of caterpillars, or . . . that the eye was expressly designed." Thomas Huxley's *Man's Place in Nature* and Charles Lyell's *Geological Evidences of the Antiquity of Man* (both 1863) were ready for Americans to read after the Civil War; and pretty soon Herbert Spencer's *Principles of Biology* (1867) and John Fiske's *Outlines of Cosmic Philosophy* (1874) carried the word still further. Henry Adams could make superior fun of evolution (which he pointed out would make U. S. Grant a better man than George Washington), and indignant preachers might quote Disraeli's quip, "Is man an ape or an angel? I, my Lord, am on the side of the angels." But the more intellectual and prominent Protestant clergy, such as Henry Ward Beecher, James Freeman Clarke, Phillips Brooks, and James McCosh, unable to refute Darwin's facts or challenge his conclusions, conceded that the Book of Genesis could not be taken literally. This was no embarrassment to the Unitarians, who already regarded the Bible as symbolical. But the evangelical churches in general rejected the Darwinian view of the cosmos as blasphemous and even persuaded several Southern states to pass laws against the teaching of evolution in the schools. In support of the law in Tennessee, William Jennings Bryan won the case but lost his last battle in 1925; and in 1964 that law is still on the books.

The Mormons, whose sacred book had been revealed to Joseph Smith, and the new sect of Christian Scientists, which picked up the slack of disillusioned Christians with Mary Baker Eddy's *Science and Health* (1875), were not greatly affected by this controversy. But there is no doubt that it weakened the hold of religion on the average American. He stopped reading the Bible when it no longer could be considered divine truth; and in so doing his character suffered. For, as Romain Rolland's Jean Christophe says, "The Bible is the marrow of lions. Strong hearts have they who feed on it. . . . The Bible is the backbone for people who have the will to live." Darwin may have killed Adam as an historical figure, but the old Adam in man survives; and if his intellect fails to control the fell forces he has wrested from nature, the few, if any, who survive the holocaust will tardily bear witness to the realism of the Biblical portrait of mankind.

3. Arts, Letters, and Education

Owing to a series of devastating fires in the early 1870's, the growth of urban population,[1] and the increase of wealth, the Eastern cities and Chicago were largely rebuilt between 1870 and 1900. In the process some distinguished buildings were designed by architects such as H. H. Richardson, Louis Henri Sullivan, Richard Morris Hunt, and the firm of McKim, Mead and White; but the general run of residential buildings was tiresome. Brownstone-front row houses of New York, brick rows of Philadelphia and Baltimore, and the wooden "three-deckers" of Boston were uninteresting as the outside of a shelf of books, but they met the needs of the time. Around 1890, late colonial and federal styles were revised to make satisfactory homes for the middle class. Some elaborate private residences were built for the rich — such as the Ro-

1. New York City remained ahead, increasing from 1.36 million to 2.05 million, 1870–1900). Chicago's growth was spectacular, 443,534 to 1.7 million. Brooklyn (not yet part of New York City), Boston, Philadelphia, Baltimore, Richmond, New Orleans, Cleveland and St. Louis, combined, grew from 2.9 million to 4.86 million; San Francisco from 223,000 to 342,782. The sprawling growth of Los Angeles was yet to come.

manesque Adams and Hay houses in Washington, the French-chateau Vanderbilt mansions on Fifth Avenue, New York, and many Ruskin-inspired
combinations of brick and stone in the Back Bay of Boston. It became the
fashion in the twentieth century to sneer at America's "Victorian" architecture (and, it must be admitted, some very strange buildings were constructed); but in general the urban construction of this era was so sound that
its destruction in favor of glass-and-chromium rectangles is regretted. Herbert
Spencer, a well-traveled critic, was "astonished by the grandeur of New York"
in 1882 in comparison with London, and in Baltimore he admired the classic
front of the Peabody Institute, concealing a functional cast-iron "cathedral of
books," designed by Edmund G. Lind.

Church architecture in general followed the modes of Europe, examples
being St. Patrick's (Gothic) and St. Bartholomew's (Byzantine) in New
York; Trinity Church, Boston (Provençal Romanesque), and numerous stone
churches, imitating Venetian Gothic, English Perpendicular, and other medieval styles. Some excellent public buildings in the French Palais du Louvre
style, such as the State-Army-Navy building in Washington, were constructed
in the 1870's. But the Capitol at Washington continued to exercise an unfortunate influence on public buildings, especially state capitols, each of
which had to have a dome and colonnade. The Chicago World's Fair of 1893,
designed in part by Richard Morris Hunt and McKim, Mead and White,
started the revival of a purer classicism.

In the meantime there arose a distinctively American urban form, which
has had world-wide influence. The combination of rising land values, cheap
structural steel, and the gregarious habits of American business men, produced the skyscraper. Hitherto the height of buildings had been restricted by
the need for impossibly thick walls to support more than eight or ten floors,
and by slow pneumatic elevators. Now, in one of the most revolutionary
processes in the history of architecture, both walls and floors could be supported by a steel frame, and electric elevators could whisk one up thirty
stories faster than walking up three. The first all-steel skeleton structure to be
called a skyscraper was L. H. Sullivan's ten-story Auditorium Building of
Chicago, finished in 1889, and the new mode reached New York in the
375-feet-high, 26-story World Building, completed in 1890. New York City's
skyline, hitherto dominated by church spires and the masts of ships, by 1900
showed every variety of skyscraper; for architects were wrestling with the problem of giving the façades, with their necessarily monotonous fenestration,
individuality and distinction. Today they appear to have given up the attempt. It was also in Chicago that Frank Lloyd Wright, Sullivan's favorite
helper, began in 1893 to design the public and private buildings that gave him
world fame.

The extension of railroads, the cheapness of iron and steel, and the public's
impatience at having to shift from car to ferryboat and back for crossing
rivers, led to important bridge-building. The iron bridge of the Erie Railroad

over the Genesee river at Portage (1875) was one of the many triumphs of George S. Morison, then assistant to Octave Chanute, chief engineer of the Erie. Other bridges designed by Morison are the Illinois Central's over the Ohio at Cairo (1889), and, at Memphis, the first bridge to span the lower Mississippi (1892). James B. Eads of the Civil War rams and John Roebling are also great names in the history of American bridge-building. Roebling, in 1869, designed the Brooklyn Bridge completed by his son Washington in 1883. "In this structure," wrote Lewis Mumford, "the architecture of the past, massive and protective, meets the architecture of the future, light, aerial, open to sunlight, an architecture of voids rather than solids." Louis Sullivan and his partner Dankmar Adler acknowledged the importance of the engineer's work in learning to use new raw materials: "If they are always used where they are wanted and as they are wanted," wrote Adler, "we shall have taken the first step toward the transmutation of these utterances of scientific prose into the language of poetry and art."

First steps in doing the same with nature's own gifts of trees and shrubs, land, and water, had already been taken, fortunately for the burgeoning cities, by the great landscape architect Frederick Law Olmstead. In the meantime scholarly critics like Charles Eliot Norton were quietly inculcating new artistic values that their pupils applied in the next generation. Many Americans began to feel a craving for the beautiful, but most regarded beauty as something extrinsic to be imported. Civil War profiteers, bankers, and railroad kings invaded Europe to capture "old masters," but few had the good taste of Isabella Stewart Gardner and Martin A. Ryerson. Early bequests to the public museums of fine arts that began to spring up in the 1870's were apt to prove embarrassing in the long run.

In painting, the Hudson River School and Samuel F. B. Morse were succeeded by a group of artists who sought subjects in the life of the people. In Philadelphia worked Thomas Eakins, painter of baseball games, oarsmen, pugilists, wrestlers, and surgical operations. Winslow Homer in Boston, at Prout's Neck, Maine, and in the Bahamas, painted fishermen, Civil War scenes, gay parties in sailboats, deer hunting and canoe trips, country life and children's games, recording what he saw with exceptional simplicity of vision and in a vigorous technique. Frederic Remington accomplished for the West and the cowboy what Homer had done for the East and the sea; and two great landscapists, John La Farge and William Morris Hunt, carried on the Hudson River tradition with technique acquired at Barbizon. On a lower scale of excellence, scores of minor painters have been brought to light in Maxim Karolik's collection. The Currier and Ives establishment in New York turned out lithographs of American ships, race horses, and country scenes that are now highly prized; Fanny Palmer, one of the first American women to become a painter, was the leading artist on their staff. Cheap colored reproductions of European paintings were provided in large numbers by Lewis Prang, a German-born chromolithographer working in Boston.

It was also the age of the etching, originally a diversion of the artist's studio. A display of American and foreign etchings at the Centennial Exposition in 1876 started the craze; etching clubs were founded in the leading cities, and Seymour Haden and Philip G. Hamerton, the English Leonardo and Michaelangelo of this art form, lectured in the United States and brought out books on etching that were eagerly purchased. Winslow Homer, Joseph Baker, and J. Foxcroft Cole were the leading American etchers. "Everyone" collected etchings from 1880 to 1895, when they suddenly went out of fashion. "What has happened to all those grand treasures, so vast in size with their creamy margins punctuated with apt *remarques* or *vignettes?*" asks a biographer of Homer. "They all seem to have passed into a sort of limbo for unloved art objects." One finds them in golden-oak frames in dark corners of men's clubs, and in second-hand furniture shops. In time they will be eagerly collected, like the oils of the Hudson River School.

All the artists we have mentioned had a part of their artistic education in Europe, but returned to America to work. James McNeil Whistler, who "did not choose to have been born in Lowell, Mass." (but his famous subject, his Mother, had other views), remained an expatriate. John Singer Sargent, although flattered by the English society whose portraits he painted, never lost his attachment to America and returned to execute magnificent murals in the Boston Museum of Fine Arts and the Boston Public Library, and to paint luminous watercolors of American scenery.

At Concord, Massachusetts, when the centenary of the American Revolution came around, a twenty-five-year-old lad of the neighborhood named Daniel Chester French designed the famous statue of the Minute Man. Later he studied in Florence under Thomas Ball, and returned to design a series of sculptured groups for the Chicago World's Fair, and several statues of Lincoln. He also helped to found the American Academy at Rome. Augustus Saint-Gaudens of New York, after studying at the Beaux-Arts and in Rome, reached fame through his statue of Hiawatha at Saratoga (1871). He worked largely at Cornish, New Hampshire, where he executed his greatest works, the memorial monument to Mrs. Henry Adams in Rock Creek Park, Washington, the Shaw Memorial in Boston, and the equestrian statue of General Sherman on Fifth Avenue, New York. Comparable in sculpture to Prang's "chromos" were the "Rogers Groups," favorites in the American home, for each told a story — Checkers up at the Farm; The Favored Scholar; Coming to the Parson; Fetching the Doctor; Weighing the Baby, and the like. John Rogers designed and executed from bronze master casts these popular plaster groups, prices of which ranged from five to twenty dollars, and sold some 100,000 of them in his lifetime.

In the fields of music and drama, America was gestating. Choral societies with fiddle and flute accompaniment, such as the Handel and Haydn and the Apollo of Boston, had been in existence since the eighteenth century; but instrumental music in its highest form, the symphony orchestra, was slow to start, and slower to attain excellence. Theodore Thomas, undaunted after the ruin of his orchestra at Philadelphia in 1876, remained the country's chief musical missionary; he became conductor of the New York Philharmonic in 1880, but had to resign after a row with Leopold Damrosch, Walter's father. He then organized his own orchestra, and became musical director of the Chicago World's Fair in 1893. The Boston Symphony Orchestra, founded by Major Henry L. Higginson in 1881, quickly attained excellence. Gustav Mahler, who came from Vienna at the turn of the century, described it in a letter to Bruno Walter as of "first rank," whilst the New York Philharmonic, of which he had become the conductor, was "a regular American orchestra, talentless and phlegmatic." Cincinnati, Chicago, and Philadelphia also had symphony orchestras before the century ended. The conductors and most of the players had to be foreigners, for want of native talent; and the few native concertos and symphonies that they felt obliged to play were second-rate.

The best American music of this era, apart from folk ballads, Negro spirituals, and the like, was band music to which the war had given wide currency. Patrick Sarsfield Gilmore, author of the popular war song "When Johnny Comes Marching Home Again," organized mammoth band and vocal concerts of unprecedented size and unparalleled vulgarity. At the World Peace Jubilee in Boston in 1872 he conducted an orchestra of 1000 performers, 40 soloists, and a chorus of 10,000 men and women, their not inconsiderable din being augmented by cannon roaring, church bells pealing, and fifty firemen beating out the anvil chorus of *Il Trovatore* on real anvils. Gilmore was succeeded by more restrained bandmasters such as John Philip Sousa, composer of "The Stars and Stripes Forever." And America produced some good comic operas of the Gilbert and Sullivan type, such as Reginald De Koven's *Robin Hood* (1890) and Victor Herbert's *Babes in Toyland* and *Mlle. Modiste,* which marked the turn of the century. Grand opera was an imported art form, as it still remains after the lapse of a century, but America produced some great divas of international fame, such as Lillian Nordica and Emma Eames, both from small towns in Maine.

Foundations for the American vocal artists and composers of the twentieth century were being laid by the Peabody Conservatory of Music in Baltimore, and the New England Conservatory in Boston, both dating from the late 1860's. Of American composers during this period there was no equal to Edward MacDowell. New York born, a fellow student at the Paris *Conservatoire* with Debussy and César Franck, recipient of Liszt's blessing for his first piano concerto, for many years he taught music at Darmstadt. Coming to Boston in 1888 at the age of forty-seven, MacDowell played his own works with the Kneisel quartet and the Boston Symphony, and in 1896 received the new chair of music at Columbia University. This he resigned after eight years, disappointed both in the caliber of his pupils and the stuffiness of the trustees. But he was successful in the sale of his many compositions; and after his death in 1908 his widow developed their summer home at Peterborough, New Hampshire, into a colony where men and women may compose and write in peace. John Knowles Paine, who taught music at Harvard from 1862 to 1905, was happy in his pupils, including composers Foote, Mason, Converse, and Carpenter, whose works mostly belong to the next century. This Boston-Cambridge group produced able critics such as John Sullivan Dwight and William F. Apthorp, who labored, not in vain, to establish canons of musical criticism; and Alexander W. Thayer, whose monumental *Life of Beethoven* accomplished for the biography of the *maestro* what Parkman had done for colonial Canada; begun in 1866 it was not completed until after his death in 1897.

Americans were very partial to the theater, and the country produced some great actors and actresses such as Edwin Booth, Helena Modjeska (a leading actress of Warsaw who came to America seeking liberty in 1876), Nat Goodwin and Maxine Elliott, Julia Arthur, and Mary Madden Fiske. But a distinguished American drama lay in the future. Of the 132 plays written by Dion Boucicault, only *Rip Van Winkle* (1865) in which Joseph Jefferson starred for over thirty years, and *The Colleen Bawn*, a romantic comedy of Ireland, are remembered. As in education and music, the organizations, teachers, and promoters are more significant than the scholars and composers; actor-author-producers such as Richard Mansfield and David Belasco dominated the stage. In the absence of competition from the cinema, or the exactions of stage-hands' unions, they put on sumptuous productions of Shakespeare and adaptions of novels, often taking leading roles themselves. Richard Mansfield in *Dr. Jekyll and Mr. Hyde* made your flesh creep; his *Richard III* was so realistic that, following the royal offer to exchange his kingdom for a horse, one of the "gallery gods" shouted, "Youse can have mine fer ten bucks!" *Arms and the Man*, the first of George Bernard Shaw's plays to be staged in America, was produced by Mansfield, and he also introduced Ibsen to America. David Belasco, born in San Francisco shortly after the gold rush, wrote and presented *The Heart of Maryland*, in which Mrs. Leslie Carter swung on a big bell clapper to save her soldier lover; she found the title role in *Dubarry* more congenial. Belasco produced the stage version of *Madam Butterfly*, which Giacomo Puccini took over, as later he did *The Girl of the Golden West*, written by Belasco himself and starring Blanche Bates. American plays of that era were regarded as "corny" in the 1960's, when the favorite Broadway themes were chicanery, murder, rape, and incest; but they were feasts for the eye and ear, they catered to romance, comedy, and herosim; they gave the rising generation something to admire and emulate.

With theater seats ranging from 25 cents to $1.50, the people of this era had abundant opportunity to see the classic drama as well as modern plays. All the great English and European actors and actresses — E. H. Sothern and Julia Marlowe, Sir Henry Irving and Ellen Terry, the Salvinis, Bernhardt,

Réjane, and Duse toured the United States. Below their level were the vaude-ville houses, especially the B. F. Keith circuit which put on amusing skits (as yet devoid of smut), jugglers, ventriloquists, trained animal acts, and the earliest, very flickering, moving pictures. Then there were the dime museums and nickelodeons where one put a nickel into the slot to hear an early gramophone play from a squeaky, cylindrical record, and the "10-20-30-cent" theaters where for these modest prices one could hear old melodramas like *East Lynne* and *Uncle Tom's Cabin*, and hiss the villain.

In letters, Walt Whitman wrote some of his best work between the Civil War and his death in 1892, but it was not an age of poetry. Minor singers such as Eugene Field, Sidney Lanier, and James Whitcomb Riley kept a spark of verse alive, whilst Emily Dickinson, whose poetry has outlived theirs, wrote only for her friends and herself. Emerson, who signed off (at the age of 65) with his "Terminus": "It is time to be old, to take in sail," lived to a ripe old age, as did Lowell, Longfellow, and Holmes. But the Civil War seemed to have burned out all that was original in their genius, and they left few successors to carry on the New England tradition in poetry. Francis Parkman, whose series on New France is distinguished by scrupulous accuracy, a superb narrative style, and a feeling for the beauty of nature and the characters of Indians and French pioneers, picked up the torch of history where Prescott dropped it; and had completed the series when death took him in 1893. Henry Adams, in the meantime, had interrupted his perennial quest for education to write his remarkable *History of the United States in the Administrations of Jefferson and Madison*.

This age saw the publication of excellent American fiction and imaginative literature. Mark Twain leaped into fame with his *Jumping Frog of Calaveras County* and presently created two boys who shall neither wither nor die, *Huckleberry Finn* and *Tom Sawyer*. Henry James, at the opposite end of the literary spectrum, wrote those imperishable portraits of Americans in Europe and Europeans in America, which plumb the depths of human nature deeper than anyone except the Russian novelists dared to do. So-called "realistic" fiction (really no more realistic than *The Scarlet Letter* or *Vanity Fair*) was inaugurated by William Dean Howells's story of Silas Lapham breaking into society, James Lane Allen's *The Reign of Law* (in Kentucky), and Stephen Crane's Zola-influenced *Maggie: A Girl of the Streets*. Two other novelists whose works have survived are F. Marion Crawford, son of Thomas Crawford the sculptor, a lifelong resident of Rome who wrote a series of novels on Italian life; and Edward Bellamy, a Connecticut valley journalist who wrote the Utopian romance *Looking Backward*, well expressing the progressive optimism of the America of his day, and *The Duke of Stockbridge*, a better history of Shays's Rebellion than the formal histories.

There also flourished a school of "local colorists" who wrote stories largely in dialect (Negro, Down East, Irish, German, etc.) which flattered the "superior" reading classes, but today seem not worth the effort required to read them. A simple affirmative is never found in their pages; it is always, "yiss," "yea," "yup," "yah," "yessir," or "uh-huh." Most American fiction of this era, such as *When Knighthood Was in Flower* and *Little Lord Fauntleroy*, was super-romantic and trashy.

Lecturing as a method of popular education was still going strong, and the man who could get his name enrolled in Pond's Lecture Bureau was certain of a good income, plenty of travel and, not improbably, stomach ulcers. Declining Emerson lectured more and more feebly, rising Mark Twain lectured enthusiastically; visiting foreigners lectured — Oscar Wilde enjoyed a surprising success with an audience of miners at Leadville, Colorado, in 1881.

Organized education was fertilized by the peculiar temper and energy of this period. Free primary schools followed the frontier West and penetrated the South. Adult night schools and settlements, of which Jane Addams's Hull House at Chicago was the pioneer, helped to educate the immigrants in American ways and to protect them from the rougher sort of exploitation. The free public high school now reached the height of its prestige and (some will say) of its excellence, since "progressive" education had not yet been invented. Church-controlled boarding schools, reviving the Renaissance idea of training the whole boy, for which St. Paul's in Concord, New Hampshire, had pioneered in 1856, now multiplied; St. Mark's, Groton, and most of the now famous church schools, were established.

Seven women's colleges and girls' boarding schools were founded between 1861 and 1880, and the great Western state universities as well as most of the high schools became co-educational. These increasing opportunities of education for girls helped to bring about a social revolution, the admission of women to practically every occupation except stevedoring and the building trades, and to every profession except the police and the ministry; and they are now in those too. Prior to 1880 very few women were employed in American stores or offices. Salesladies then began to replace salesmen behind the counter, and the lady stenographer with her typewriter, which came into general use around 1895, replaced the Dickensian male clerk with his high stool, calf-bound ledger, steel pen, and tobacco quid; a great gain for the cleanliness and neatness of business offices. Public libraries at this era became instruments of popular adult education. They grew and multiplied, and were rendered more accessible by card catalogues and by librarians trained to serve the public rather than to conserve books.

American captains of industry, with some exceptions, were as generous in endowing higher learning as the princes of the Renaissance, and less inclined than they to interfere with the objects of their beneficence. University presidents of this era, such as Charles W. Eliot of Harvard, Andrew D. White of Cornell, Daniel Coit Gilman of Johns Hopkins, William R. Harper of Chicago, Francis Amasa Walker of M.I.T., towered over the men of wealth and tolerated no suggestion that unpopular professors be "fired." Under the guidance of these powerful presidents, simple colleges of liberal arts burst out with a congeries of professional schools, and new subjects were added to the curricula of undergraduates. Eliot, who had taught chemistry for a year in the Harvard Medical School and learned at first hand its deficiences, announced in his first presidential report in 1870, "The whole system of medical education in this country needs thorough reformation." And he proceeded to do just that at Harvard, with the help of Dr. Oliver Wendell Holmes. A system of lectures, clinical instruction, and practical exercises was distributed through three academic years and conducted by competent professors rather than local physicians as a part-time job, and stiff examinations were given, to weed out the incompetent. American universities, wrote James Bryce in his *American Commonwealth* (1888), were making swifter progress than any other institution, and offered "the brightest promise for the future. They are supplying exactly those things which European critics have hitherto found lacking to America." Johns Hopkins University (1876), the Columbia School of Political Science (1880), and the graduate schools of other universities, now made it possible for American scholars to study for a Ph.D. in their own country instead of Germany.

In this realm of scholarship and science, as in music and the drama, one had to wait until the next century for a harvest. Among the few Americans who gained an international reputation in science or scholarship before 1900 were J. Willard Gibbs of Yale, Basil Gildersleeve of Johns Hopkins, Charles Eliot Norton and Francis J. Child of Harvard. The American notion of a scientist still remained, as before the war, a practical inventor such as Thomas Edison; the American idea of a scholar was one who taught Latin, Greek, or mathematics in a small college. But these now forgotten teachers are not to be despised. The nation's debt to them is inestimable. Under modern circumstances, with an abundance of grants-in-aid and paid leaves of absence, they might have been productive; but they were kept so busy conveying the rudiments of a liberal education to the hordes of young barbarians who crowded their classrooms, and writing necessary textbooks, as to have no time for independent scholarship. Moreover, proper library and laboratory facilities were lacking.

4. Games, Sports, and Joining

Despite his racial heterogeneity the average American was becoming urban in environment and uniform in appearance, manners and thought. There were compensations: human dignity owes much to the Jewish organizers of the garment trades, whose cheap but stylish clothes wiped out class distinctions in dress both for men and women. Regional differences in cooking began to disappear before nation-wide distribution of canned goods and other prepared foods, which provided a more varied and (after the passage of the Pure Food and Drugs Act) more healthful diet than earlier Americans enjoyed. Advertising had not yet reached the status of a profession; but, with psychology as handmaid, it helped to build the great department stores of the Eastern cities and Chicago, St. Louis and San Francisco, with such a variety of wares and luxury in appointments that traveling Americans were no longer dazzled by the shopping splendors of London and Paris.

As the working day shortened and the number of indoor occupations increased, Americans began to show an interest in outdoor sport, which the mere business of living had afforded to their rural and frontier forebears. Games, beginning in the colleges, spread to every age and class. Baseball as an organized sport dates from the 1850's, and was seriously taken up by colleges and local clubs after the war. No distinction was then made between amateurs and professionals; the Harvard baseball team went on a "Western tour" as far as St. Louis in the summer of 1870, winning twenty-one games including one with the Chicago "White Stockings," and losing five, including one with the Cincinnati "Red Stockings." Boat racing was resumed with great enthusiasm, on Eastern lakes and rivers. College track athletics began in 1874, as a sideshow to the intercollegiate rowing regatta at Saratoga, and the Intercollegiate Association of Amateur Athletics was formed in 1876, Princeton winning the first meet. Shortly after, Evert J. Wendell first ran the 100-yard dash in 10 seconds flat. And in 1896 the American track team carried all before it in the revived Olympic games at Athens. A feature of early track meets was the two-mile race on high-wheeled bicycles. The modern "safety" bicycle, made possible by the invention of the pneumatic tire, had become a national sport by 1893 and a means for city dwellers to get out and see the country on Sundays and holidays; whilst the tandem bicycle "built for two" became a reputable vehicle for courtship. Hearst's New York *Journal* in 1895 was the first American newspaper to have a sports section; and by that time the manufacture of sporting equipment had become big business.

Hockey, played with a six-foot curved hickory stick and a baseball, entered the college scene on Jamaica Pond near Boston in 1879. The Canadian game, with a flat-faced stick, a hard rubber puck, and a "goalie" swathed in protective armor like a knight of old, was introduced in 1895. Also from Canada came the old North American Indian game of lacrosse. Basketball was invented in 1891 to provide a fast game in gymnasiums during the winter months.

Rugby football, introduced into the United States during the Civil War, became intercollegiate in 1869, when the first match was played between Princeton and Rutgers. It diverged from the English game as college strategists, notably Walter Camp of Yale, invented new formations and altered the rules to fit. Lawn tennis was introduced from Bermuda in 1874, the same year it had been patented in England; and golf was imported from Scotland in the 1880's. Both games were long considered "sissy," like smoking cigarettes. President Theodore Roosevelt never allowed a photograph of himself in tennis costume to be published, and begged his friend William H. Taft to stop injuring his presidential prospects by playing golf. In the next century both golf and tennis became so popular that towns and cities provided municipal golf courses and tennis courts.

Summer vacations, the privilege of few in 1870, had reached the clerks by 1900. Thousands of people whose parents had left homes in the country in search of more easy living, returned thither for pleasure. State, municipal, and private enterprise vied in establishing recreation parks, public bathing places, and summer resorts. The very rich built immense "cottages" at Newport, Bar Harbor, and Long Branch; the well-to-do patronized big wooden hotels in coast and mountain resorts; others boarded with farmers' families for not more than five dollars a week.

In this happy era for the capitalist, when he could get 10 per cent on his investments and paid no income tax, he indulged in various luxurious forms of expenditure, of which the most useful to the economy and the most beautiful to the eye were yachts and the breeding of race horses. Before the war there was only one American yacht club, the New York; by 1885 there were fifty in the United States and eight in Canada. Favorite type of yacht for the postwar millionaire was the big centerboard schooner, such as William Astor's 146-foot *Ambassadress*. Around 1875 the multimillionaires began building steam yachts, of which the successive queens were J. Pierpont Morgan's trio, appropriately named *Corsair*. At Bath, Maine, was built in 1879 the most gorgeous vessel that ever flew the American yacht ensign — the steel auxiliary barque *Aphrodite* (303 feet) owned by Colonel Oliver H. Payne, treasurer of the Standard Oil Company and benefactor of Cornell University.

Hundreds of yacht races were sailed every summer, but the most spectacular, viewed by thousands of spectators off Sandy Hook or Newport, were the unsuccessful attempts of British and Canadian yachtsmen to "lift" the *America's* cup. There were four of these in the 1870's. The contests of the 1880's brought into prominence Edward Burgess, a Boston naturalist who took up yacht design as a hobby. He designed the cutters *Puritan, Mayflower,* and *Volunteer,* which never lost a race to British challengers and had long subsequent careers as cruising yachts. Nathaniel G. Herreshoff of Bristol, Rhode Island, having revolutionized yacht design with long overhangs, a "spoon" bow, forefoot cut completely away, and a fin keel, designed the next challenger in 1893. His *Vigilant* easily defeated Lord Dunraven's *Valkyrie II;* his *Defender* in 1895 won three straight from *Valkyrie III,* and his *Columbia* in 1899 defeated Sir Thomas Lipton's first *Shamrock.* These handsome, gaff-headed cutters, measuring around 90 feet on the waterline and 125 feet over all, spread some 13,000 square feet of sail, exclusive of spinnakers and other "kites." They were sailed by professional skippers and crews, those of the defenders being mostly Scandinavians.

Yachting was no millionaire's privilege. In every Eastern harbor, in Puget Sound and San Francisco Bay, and on many an inland lake, there were countless small boats for racing, fishing or just fun sailing: the Cape Cod catboat immortalized by Winslow Homer, the "sandbagger," in which ballast had to be shifted quickly to avoid capsizing, the plumb-stemmed Burgess sloop, and the 21-foot knockabout.

But a sport which cost the millionaires enormous sums yet gave pleasure to everyone, was the turf. After the Civil War, Kentucky took the lead in breeding Thoroughbreds, and the Kentucky Derby was first run at Churchill Downs in 1872. Flat racing around New York City, which had got into the hands of Tammany braves and other hoodlums before the war, recovered prestige when Leonard W. Jerome (Sir Winston Churchill's American grandfather), August Belmont, and other gentleman sportsmen organized the New York Jockey Club and established a clubhouse and race track at Jerome Park. This was in Fordham, now a part of New York City but then a beautiful rolling countryside, near enough for city people to drive to in their own carriages. The stewards, by keeping race touts and other raffish elements away, made it possible for Jerome Park to become the American Longchamps or Royal Ascot. At the inaugural race meeting in 1866, Kentucky, a four-year-old by Lexington out of Magnolia, for which Jerome had paid $40,000, began a two-year winning streak. He then joined August Belmont's nursery stud at Babylon, Long Island. The Maryland Jockey Club, organized 1870, revived Baltimore racing at Pimlico; and their annual gentlemen-riders' steeplechase, the Grand National, was won five times by Preakness, another son of Lexington.

Harness trotting and pacing remained the average citizen's most popular form of horse contest. New York City had a speedway where the driving fraternity competed informally every pleasant day, skirting the Harlem river north of 155th Street. The whole country waited impatiently for a horse to make a two-minute mile in harness. In 1900, after the pneumatic-tired bicycle-wheel sulky had been invented, Lou Dillon did it. Dan Patch, a pacer foaled in 1896, first broke two minutes for that gait in 1902.

There had been informal fox hunting with horses and hounds in the South and around Philadelphia since colonial days, but not until after the Civil War was English-style hunting introduced, with trained thoroughbreds, specially bred foxhounds, huntsmen and gentlemen riders in pink and ladies in black habits on sidesaddles. This sport encountered many difficulties in America. There were never enough foxes (since the farmers *would* shoot them), so the artificial drag had to be introduced. It is said that when a fox pursued by the Myopia Hunt Club ran into Lexington, descendants of the Minute Men began taking down Revolutionary muskets from chimney breasts, assuming that the British Redcoats were back! Hunt clubs led to country clubs, horse shows, and hunt balls. By the end of the century there were thirteen organized hunts in Virginia and Maryland, which afforded the best country for this noble sport, and about fifteen more around New York, Philadelphia, and Boston. Fox hunters organized cross-country steeplechases with amateur riders, such as the Maryland Hunt Cup and the Rose Tree in Pennsylvania; horse races which have escaped the foul embrace of the underworld. From England, too, was imported the four-in-hand coach, commonly known as the "tally-ho," which furnished another luxurious sport. In these coaches jolly parties drove to country inns, announcing their presence by traditional tunes played on long brass coach horns, "tooled" their matched fours to race meets and football games, and sometimes made excursions lasting a week or more over the soft dirt roads. In New York the annual coaching parade along Fifth Avenue was an outstanding event; Mrs. Grover Cleveland graced the box seat of Perry Belmont's coach in the parade of 1890.

Except for harness racing, these were the recreations of the rich; very different was the "manly art" of pugilism, which appealed to everyone. The old-style, Queensberry rules prize-fighting with bare knuckles reached its apogee in 1889 when, as Vachel Lindsay recorded, "Nigh New Orleans, upon an emerald plain, John L. Sullivan the strong boy of Boston, fought seventy-five red rounds with Jake Kilrain." John L. held the heavyweight title until 1892, when "Gentleman Jim" Corbett, in a match fought with boxing gloves, knocked him out in the twenty-first round; five years later Corbett yielded the belt to Bob Fitzsimmons, and that fight was the subject of the first motion picture to be exhibited all over the country.

The American "joiner" now arose. Desire for distinction in a country of growing uniformity, and a human craving for fellowship among the urban middle classes, drew the descendants of stern anti-Masons into secret societies and fraternal orders. Freemasons and Odd Fellows, both of English origin, proved too exclusive to contain would-be joiners. The Elks, Royal Arcanum, Woodmen, Moose, and several others were founded in the twenty years after 1868. The Southern freedmen had their United Order of African Ladies and Gentlemen, and Brothers and Sisters of Pleasure and Prosperity. The Catholic church, embracing a movement it dared no longer defy, created the Knights of Columbus for its increasing membership. Based on race and ancestry were the patriotic societies, the Sons and Daughters of the American Revolution, Colonial Dames, Mayflower Descendants, Daughters of the Confederacy, and the like; a drawing together of the older American stock. These, nevertheless, took the lead in civic betterment, which cannot be said of those formed by the immigrants, such as the Ancient Order of Hibernians and Sons of Italy, which were then devoted to preserving old-world traditions.

These were some of the movements and tendencies that brought a new order in American life. In 1860 the average American was a land-owning yeoman farmer; since 1900 he has been an employee. In 1860, an ambitious youth fixed his sights on a farm; since 1900 and still more since 1930, he seeks a job. In 1865 only parts of New England and the Middle States had been industrialized, American technique in general was inferior to that of Great Britain, and labor combination was making a fresh start. By 1900 industry had captured the Middle West and crossed the Mississippi; agriculture, itself transformed, had conquered the Great Plains; the United States had become the greatest iron- and steel-producing country in the world, national trade unions had given labor a new dignity and greater buying power, new combinations were dominating the business and even the political world. Feverish development and ruthless competition, conducted in a framework of pioneer individualistic mores, made this age the most lawless and picturesque that America has ever known.

The Fecund Eighteen-nineties

1. *Populism and Panic*

IN 1890 AMERICAN politics lost their equilibrium and began to pitch and toss in an effort to reach stability among wild currents of protest that issued from the caverns of discontent.

Almost a generation had passed since the Civil War. The older Republicans had come to revere their "Grand Old Party" only less than the Union and the flag; to regard its leaders as the beloved generals of a victorious army. It was difficult for the leaders, representative men of the Middle West who had grown up with the country, to believe that anything was amiss. Their experience of life had been utterly different from that of any European statesman. They had seen the frontier of log cabin and stumpy clearings, sod house and unbroken prairie, replaced by frame houses and great barns, well-tilled farms, and sleek cattle. The railroad, the telegraph, the sewing machine, oil and gas lighting, and a hundred new comforts and conveniences had come within reach of all but the poorest during their lifetime. Towns with banks, libraries, high schools, mansions, and theaters had sprung up where once as barefoot boys they had hunted the squirrel and wildcat; and the market towns of their youth had grown into manufacturing cities. As young men they had taken part in the war for the Union, and returned to further progress and development. If discontented workmen and poverty-stricken farmers sometimes intruded into the picture, were not foreign agitators and the inexorable law of supply and demand the explanation? How could there be anything wrong with a government which had wrought such miraculous changes for the better, or with a Grand Old Party which had saved the nation from disaster?

Yet the quarter-century after the war had its suffering victims who, feeling something to be radically wrong, were groping for a remedy. Kansas, in 1888, began to suffer the effects of deflation after a land boom. Virgin prairie land, and peak prices of wheat and corn in 1881, had induced excessive railway construction, usually financed locally, and oversettlement of the arid western part of the state. Small towns and cities indulged in lavish expenditure, and citizens speculated wildly in building lots. The new farms were mostly bought on credit; there was one mortgage, on the average, to every other adult in the state. And in 1887 there came a summer so dry that the crops in western Kansas withered. During the next four years, one-half the people who had entered this new El Dorado trekked eastward again, with humorous mottoes on their wagon covers such as, "In God we Trusted, in Kansas we Busted." The rest made a desperate struggle to retain their farms; but with toppling prices of grain, the interest alone consumed most of the yield. Some boom towns were moved bodily out into the prairie, leaving the mortgagors to foreclose on cellar holes.

Other agricultural regions, too, were in a bad way. In one Eastern state a survey of 700 representative farms revealed an average annual yield worth $167. In the Middle West, farmers envied immigrant factory hands, who at least had their dollar a day. In the South, cotton growers struggled from year to year against a falling market and the waste of the sharecropper system. Washington Gladden, a keen observer, wrote in 1890, "The American farmer is steadily losing ground. His burdens are heavier every year and his gains are more meagre; he is beginning to fear that he may be sinking into a servile condition. Whatever he can do by social combinations or by united political action, to remove the disabilities under which he is suffering, he intends to do at once and with all his might."

A ready instrument of revolt was at hand in the Farmers' Alliances, originally fraternal and economic in purpose. The Northwestern Alliance organized a party of its own for the elections of 1890, and in Kansas this became a political crusade. Mary Lease the "Kansas Pythoness" went about advising the Kansas farmers to "raise less corn and more hell"; Jerry Simpson, the "sockless Socrates" of the prairie, defeated his silk-stockinged opponent for Congress; William A. Pfeffer, champion whisker-grower of the Northwest, was elected to the United States Senate. Two years later a convention of some 1500 delegates representing the Farmers' Alliances, the Knights of Labor, and several minor groups, founded the People's, or Populist, party. Their platform, drafted by Ignatius Donnelly (Minnesota politician, discoverer of the lost Atlantis and champion of the Baconian theory), opened with a trenchant indictment of the existing order, including such statements as "The railroad corporations will either own the people or the people must own the railroads"; and, "From the same prolific womb of governmental injustice we breed the two great classes of tramps and millionaires." The Populist planks included the free and unlimited coinage of silver at the ratio of 16 to 1; produce subtreasuries, reminiscent of the schemes of the 1780's, where farmers could deposit the yield of their farms against treasury notes; government ownership of railroads, telegraphs, and telephones; a graduated income tax; the parcel post to break the hold of the great express companies; restriction of immigration; an eight-hour day for wage earners; popular election of United States senators, the Australian ballot, and the initiative and referendum. Cries of horror greeted these "socialistic" proposals in the Eastern press; yet all but the first three were adopted within the next generation through the instrumentality of the older parties. General Weaver, a former Greenbacker of Iowa, was nominated Populist candidate for the presidency. He polled over a million votes in the presidential election of 1892 and carried four states; but

Grover Cleveland, again the Democratic candidate, carried seven Northern states together with the solid South and obtained a heavy majority in the electoral college.

2. Jim Crow in the South

The winds of agrarian revolt became really torrid when they left the prairies for the Southern savannahs and piney woods, where they were fanned to white-heat by racial fanaticism. Nowhere in the Union was the plight of the small farmer so desperate as in the one-crop region of the lower South, and nowhere else did the white farmer, the "redneck" or "cracker," hate so intensely. To quote Hodding Carter's *Angry Scar*,

He hated high-tariff Republicans and the nearby mill owners who bought his cotton so cheap and sold their bolts of cloth so dear and paid so little to the mill hands recruited from the farm homes. He hated the unbridled railroads which provided almost the only outlets to his markets. If he were a tenant he hated the landlords. He hated the local bankers and merchants for whose exclusive benefit the crop lien laws and chattel mortgages were seemingly devised, and who preyed indiscriminately on large and small landowner alike. . . . The farmer mortgaged to the merchant his future crop and stock and implements; and the merchant or banker who made the advances generally insisted that the farmer put most of his land in cotton. As the price of cotton declined, the furnish merchants became planters as well as businessmen by foreclosing upon thousands of distressed farmers. Thus did William Faulkner's tribe of Snopses so greatly replace the Sartorises and bring to its logical end whatever remained of the onetime spirit of noblesse oblige which had made more human the debilitating relationship of master and slave and landowner and tenant. But most of all the redneck hated the Negro.

When populism entered the South, it aimed at a political alliance between Negroes and poor whites to break the rule of the "Bourbons." But Tom Watson, the No. 1 demagogue of this movement, turned it against the Negro. He fought the Bourbons in Georgia all through the 1880's. Elected to Congress as a Populist in 1890 by the votes of both black and white, he was defeated for a second term. He then adopted the poor-white point of view. That class simply would not vote for a biracial party. As Watson wrote, "No matter what direction progress would like to take in the South, she is held back by the never failing cry of 'nigger.'" So, after ten years of ruminating, writing bad history, and worse biography, Tom decided to hunt with the hounds. From 1906, when he became the most popular leader in the South, he outdid every other white demagogue in Negro-baiting; he lauded lynching, described Booker T. Washington as "bestial as a gorilla," and bracketed Catholics, Socialists, and Jews with Negroes in his catalogue of hate.

We are getting ahead of the story. Throughout the lower South, professional rabblerousers and "nigger-haters" arose — Tillman, Bilbo, Vardaman, Blease, and others — to challenge the Bourbon ascendancy, exploit agrarian discontent, and seize the state governments. In one state after another, between 1890 and 1908, new constitutions which by one device or another disfranchised the Negro, were adopted by conventions but never submitted to popular ratification. Louisiana, for instance, which had the most prosperous and cultured Negroes of any Southern state, had 130,334 colored people registered as voters in 1896, but the number fell to 1342 in eight years. And every legislature elected under these new constitutions proceeded to enact a flood of jim crow laws.

Jim Crow was a blackfaced character in a popular minstrel show of the 1830's who did a song-and-dance routine of which the theme was, "Jump, Jim Crow!" After the Civil War Jim's name began to be used, like "darkey," as a slightly less insulting term than "nigger." It was now applied to the new segregation laws. Education had always been segregated in the South, and the churches too, by the Negroes' own desire; but down to 1890 there was practically no segregation in public transportation or elsewhere. The Negroes during this period 1875–90 had been quiescent, and their leader Booker T. Washington advised them to be humble and improve themselves by becoming better workers. His policy of gradualism, and never claiming social equality with white people, did the colored people no good, now that rednecks were in the saddle. And by 1900 the Negroes had lost the ballot.

Jim crow cars on passenger trains came first, then jim crow waiting rooms and lavatories, jim crow sections of streetcars and buses, jim crow entrances to circuses, factories and the like. White nurses were forbidden to attend colored patients in hospitals, and vice versa; black barbers were forbidden to cut the hair of women or children; all colored people (except as servants) were barred from lunch counters, bars, and restaurants run by whites; and when taxicabs came in, a colored driver, if he managed to obtain a license, was not allowed to carry white fares. Most of these regulations started in the lower South and worked up; but the legal zoning of cities into colored and white residential districts started in Baltimore in 1910 and worked down. Segregation as a principle received a blessing from the Supreme Court in the case of *Plessy* v. *Ferguson* (1896), which announced the "separate but equal" doctrine, that segregation was legal if those segregated enjoyed equal facilities. But the Negroes seldom obtained these. They got the old, battered schools and beat-up railroad cars, the rundown tenements and the muddy parks. Segregation reached its height in Washington under President Wilson, when all government offices, restaurants, and lavatories were segregated, and for the most part so remained until the Franklin D. Roosevelt administration.

The justification often offered for jim crow laws was sanitary or sexual; Negroes were said to be diseased, lousy, and lusting after white girls. The hypocrisy of these claims is shown by the fact that Negroes were still in great demand as nurses and domestic servants, even when they refused to "live in" and spent the night in their own homes. In these domestic relations the old friendly intimacy between the races has continued to this day; but the poor whites employed no domestic servants. The real motive of jim crow laws was to keep the Negro down and make him constantly sensible of his inferior status. That is why jim crow policy had so irresistible an appeal to the poor whites. Except for the "hill billies," who lived apart and fairly respectably, these lower-class whites of the South were a very unfortunate people — poor, illiterate, and diseased; but their feeling that the poorer of them was superior to even the most cultured Negro flattered their ego and assuaged their griefs. Custom, as well as the jim crow laws, compelled every Negro to address the lowest dirt-eating redneck, hat in hand, as "Mr.," "Sir," or "Ma'am." But the Negro no matter how respectable, had to be content with "Boy" or "Girl"; or, if elderly, "Uncle" and "Aunty" — never Mr. or Mrs. Any act of so-called insolence, such as not uncovering in the presence of whites, not stepping off a sidewalk when they approached, risked a Negro's being pulled out of his cabin and severely whipped. The Negro's daughters were free to all the lusty white lads of the neighborhood, and nothing was done about it; but if a colored man leered at a white girl of notoriously low morals, he was liable to be lynched by a mob in defense of the alleged purity of Southern woman-hood.

Altogether, the thirty years from 1890 to 1920 were the darkest for the dark people of America. And, sad to relate, a perverted form of democracy was responsible; had the "Bourbons" still been governing the South, this could not have happened.[1] But the Southern gentry who abdicated the leadership they had exerted in reconstruction days, cannot escape responsibility. Some men of courage and integrity, like Harper Lee's Atticus Finch, upheld justice to the Negro; many more deplored the situation but failed to do anything about it; others were converted to the extremist view by hate literature such as Thomas Dixon's *Clansman*, or newspapers such as Hoke Smith's *Atlanta Journal* and Josephus Daniels's *Raleigh News and Observer*. Many pandered to the red-necks in order to be elected, or to get favors from the state legislatures for railroads, cotton mills, and the like. Several Southern writers who denounced unfairness and cruelty to Negroes — notably George W. Cable and Walter Hines Page — had to move North in order to escape ostracism, or worse.

In general, the Southern Negro submitted to his own abasement and ac-cepted the degraded status that his former masters forced upon him. His fellows in the North did nothing to help him. No leaders then arose to fire his sullen heart with courage and determination to resist. For that he had to wait a century after Gettysburg.

This was an era of lynchings, which reached their apex in 1892 with 226 extra-judicial mob murders, 155 of them Negroes. From that date the number slowly dropped off, but no fewer than 50 Negroes were lynched annually until 1913, and the total count for 1889–1918 is 2522 Negroes and 702 others. Some

1. In Hawaii, where there had been an immense immigration of Oriental, European, and Puerto Rican labor to work the sugar plantations, this did not happen, precisely because the ruling class, largely descendants of New England missionaries, kept a tight political control and promptly clamped down on racial enmity.

were in Ohio, Indiana, and Illinois, a particularly bad case occuring in 1908 at Springfield, within half a mile of Abraham Lincoln's old home — property destroyed and two Negroes lynched for a crime that was never committed. Of the 702 non-Negro lynchings, including native whites, Italians, Mexicans, Indians, and Chinese, the greater part were for horse-stealing, cattle-rustling, rape, robbery, and murder in the Far West. There, lynching was resorted to in the absence or weakness of law, whilst in the South it was used in defiance of law and the courts, often after trial and conviction, to satisfy the vicious hate of the lowest elements of the population. In New Orleans, where there had been a recent influx of Sicilians, with consequent tension, an Irish chief of police who had incurred the enmity of the Mafia, was assassinated in 1891; but of 11 Italians tried by jury, not one was found guilty. Next day a mob incited by a white lawyer invaded the jail and shot down or hanged all eleven. The Italian government demanded redress; Secretary Blaine washed his hands of the affair since it was a matter of state jurisdiction, but the United States eventually paid a small indemnity. As the Italian premier remarked, "Only savages refuse to respect the inviolability of prisoners and distrust the justice of their own courts."

The common excuse for lynching is that it was resorted to only for rape, or attempted rape, of white women. The statistics prove that sexual assaults were not even alleged in more than one case in five, and that many of those lynched for it were innocent, or the alleged assault was imaginary — as in Faulkner's *Dry September*. There is a good deal of truth in what H. L. Mencken wrote, that the typical Southern lynching was one "in which, in sheer high spirits, some convenient African is taken at random and lynched, as the newspapers say, 'on general principles.' " The most abundant alleged cause was murder or suspicion of murder, as in Lillian Smith's *Strange Fruit*, but hundreds of lynchings were for theft, alleged insult, altercations between Negro tenants and white landowners, or such trivial causes as killing a white man's cow or refusing to sell cottonseed to a white man at his price. Fifty of the Negroes lynched during this period were women.

Lynchings were accompanied by incidents such as cheering crowds of men, women, and children (at Waco, Texas, in 1916) witnessing the mutilation and burning alive of a Negro already convicted and sentenced to death for murder, and carrying away collops of his flesh as souvenirs. Horrible it is to contemplate such things; but they must be recorded, if only to prove that sadistic cruelty is no monopoly of our late enemies, or of remote eras, but part of the devil that is in all of us. Not until 1918 was anyone punished in the South for taking part in a lynching. In that year, at Winston-Salem, North Carolina, the police and home guards frustrated an attempt to lynch an innocent colored man, and fifteen white men were sentenced to serve one to six years in prison for their part in the mob.

Lynching now appears to be a closed book. The leading Southern writers of the present century have exposed it, and the decent white people of the South have revolted against it. But the Negroes are no longer content with merely equal protection of the laws in cases of crime. The time has not yet arrived when the prophecy of Jeremiah xxxi.29 can be said to be fulfilled: "In those days they shall say no more, The fathers have eaten a sour grape, and the children's teeth are set on edge."

3. President Cleveland's Second Term

American society appeared to be in a state of dissolution, but the same old Grover Cleveland, a little stouter and more set in his ideas, was inaugurated President on 4 March 1893. A large proportion of his vote came from suffering farmers who looked to the Democrats for relief rather than to inexpert Populists. Cold comfort they obtained from the inaugural address! The situation, as the President saw it, demanded "prompt and conservative precaution" to protect a "sound and stable currency."

The administration was not three months old when a series of bank failures and industrial collapses inaugurated the panic of 1893. The treasury's gold reserve was depleted by an excess of imports and by liquidation of American securities in London after a panic there. Gold was subject to a steady drain by the monthly purchase of useless silver required by the Silver Purchase Act of 1890, and by the redemption of greenbacks which by law were promptly reissued and formed an "endless chain" for conveying gold to Europe. Cleveland summoned a special session of Congress to repeal that mischievous law. In so doing he flew in the face of his supporters, who demanded the directly opposite policy of inflating the currency with "free silver" at the ratio of 16 ounces of silver to one of gold, by which the silver dollars would have contained only 57 cents in bullion. Cleveland's discreet use of patronage provided enough Democratic votes at this special session to help the Republicans repeal their own Silver Purchase Act. Business and finance breathed more freely, but the farmers cried betrayal; and when Cleveland later broke the endless chain by a gold loan from J. P. Morgan and the Rothschilds, farmers and workingmen assumed that the President had sold out to Wall Street.

Cleveland's brusque manner of dealing with Congress did not help his party to redeem its pledge of tariff reduction. Vested interests had been built up under Republican protection, and Democratic senators from the East were no less averse from free trade than their Republican colleagues. The resulting Wilson tariff of 1894 took off a slice here and a shaving there, but remained essentially protective. Cleveland denounced the bill as smacking of "party perfidy and party dishonor"; but allowed it to become law without his signature. The best feature of the Act, a 2 per cent tax on incomes above $4000, was declared unconstitutional by a five to four decision of the Supreme Court, which fifteen years earlier had passed favorably and unanimously upon the wartime income tax. This decision (*Pollock* v. *Farmers' Loan & Trust Company*) made it necessary to adopt Amendment XVI (1913) before a federal income tax could be legally enacted.

The Wilson tariff went into effect during the worst industrial depression since the 1870's, and no worse came until 1929. Prices and wages struck rockbottom, and there seemed to be no market for anything. It was a period of soup kitchens, ragged armies of the unemployed, fervid soapbox oratory, desperate strikes. What was wrong with the United States, that it had to suffer these recurrent crises? The Democratic tariff, said the Republicans; gold, said the Populists; capitalism, said the socialists; the immutable laws of trade, said the economists; punishment for our sins, said the ministers. But Grover Cleveland, like Br'er Rabbit, "ain't sayin' nuffin'."

Chicago, where an army of floating labor attracted by the World's Fair could not be absorbed, became the plague spot of this depression. In the spring of 1894 employees in the Pullman car works struck against a wage cut that left them hardly any margin over their rents in the Pullman "model village." The American Railway Union supported the strike by refusing to handle Pullman cars. The General Managers Association, representing twenty-four railroads entering Chicago, refused to arbitrate and prepared for a trial of strength. At the suggestion of Cleveland's attorney general, the federal circuit court at Chicago served on the officers of the union a "blanket injunction" against obstructing the railroads and holding up the mails. Hooligans promptly ditched a mail train and took possession of strategic points in the switching yards. Cleveland then ordered a regiment of regulars to the city, declaring he would use every dollar in the treasury and every soldier in the army if necessary to deliver a single postcard in Chicago. Violence increased. Governor Altgeld of Illinois protested against this gratuitous interference of the federal government, and requested immediate withdrawal of the troops. Eugene V. Debs, president of the striking union, defied the injunction, was arrested, and sentenced for contempt of court. Gompers and the executive board of the A. F. of L. advised Debs's union that it was beaten, and by early August the strike was broken.

The dramatic events of this Pullman strike drove contending parties into positions far beyond their intentions. Cleveland saw the simple issue of law and order, and had no desire to help crush a strike; but he played into the hands of those who wanted federal troops as strikebreakers rather than state militia to preserve order. Governor Altgeld had no wish to help the strikers, but his protest against a doubtful assumption of federal authority placed him in the position of a rebel. Debs was trying to help the Pullman employees by boycotting the company, but the movement got out of his hands and became something like an insurrection. And the consequences went even further. The Supreme Court, to which Debs appealed against his sentence, upheld the government, declaring that even in the absence of statutory law it had a dormant power to brush away obstacles to interstate commerce — an implied power that would have made Hamilton and Marshall gasp. A new and potent weapon, the injunction, was legalized for use against strikers, Cleveland became the hero of American business, Debs received the Socialist nomination for the presidency, Altgeld was hounded from public life.

Cleveland believed that the manifest destiny of American expansion had been fulfilled. During Harrison's administration American settlers in the Hawaiian Islands had upset the royal house of Kamehameha and concluded a treaty of annexation to the United States. Cleveland, discovering that the American minister to Hawaii had taken an active part in these proceedings, withdrew the treaty from the Senate and let the new Hawaiian Republic shift for itself. Toward the Cuban insurrection that broke out in 1895 his attitude was neutral and circumspect. Nevertheless it fell to him to make a vigorous assertion of the Monroe Doctrine, and to risk war with Great Britain.

There was a long-standing boundary dispute between British Guiana and Venezuela. Lord Salisbury, the British foreign minister, refused to submit the question to international arbitration, owing to Venezuela's pretension to annex over half of a colony which, as he said, "belonged to the Throne of England before the Republic of Venezuela came into existence." In a message of 17 December 1895, President Cleveland informed Congress of Lord Salisbury's refusal, proposed to determine the disputed line himself, and declared that in his opinion any British attempt to assert jurisdiction beyond that line should be resisted by force. Panic ensued in Wall Street, dismay in England, and an outburst of jingoism in the United States. Secretary Olney's earlier note to England of 20 July, published with the President's message, included a definition of the Monroe Doctrine that alarmed Latin America, insulted Canada, and challenged England: "Today the United States is practically sovereign on this continent, and its fiat is law upon the subjects to which it confines its interposition. . . . Distance and three thousand miles of intervening ocean make any permanent political union between a European and an American state un-natural and inexpedient."

It has never been satisfactorily explained why the peaceful Cleveland and his gentlemanly corporation-lawyer secretary used such provocative language. Seven years later Olney explained himself on the ground "that in English eyes the United States was then so completely a negligible quantity that it was believed only words the equivalent of blows would be really effective." It must be admitted that they were; but still more effective were two other events — a panic in Wall Street over the possibility of war, and a telegram from William II, Emperor of Germany, congratulating President Kruger of the South African Republic for having repelled an unauthorized English colonists' raid on his territory. That event, a portent of the First World War, caused Lord Salisbury to adopt a conciliatory attitude. A treaty was signed between Britain and Venezuela submitting the controversy to arbitration, and the arbitral board reported subtantially in favor of the British claim. That settled it.

The party in power is always blamed for hard times. The Populists increased their vote 50 per cent at the congressional elections of 1894, and the Republicans won back their majority in the House. So certain were they of victory in 1896 as to boast that a Republican rag doll could be elected President — a boast that Mark Hanna almost made a prophecy.

Marcus Alonzo Hanna was a great figure in the "Ohio dynasty." A big business man satiated with wealth but avid of power, naturally intelligent though contemptuous of learning, personally upright but tolerant of corruption, Mark Hanna believed in the mission of the Republican party to promote "business" activity, whence prosperity would percolate to farmers and wage earners. Since 1890 he had been grooming for the President his amiable friend, Congressman William McKinley. Speaker Thomas B. Reed was far more able and experienced, but he had made enemies by his strong though necessary actions as speaker, as well as by a mordant wit; [1] and the "good and the great" of Maine were no match for the Ohio pols. So "Bill McKinley, author of the McKinley Bill, advance agent of prosperity," was nominated by the Republican convention. The convention pointed with pride to Republican achievement, viewed with horror the "calamitous consequences" of Democratic control, and came out somewhat equivocally for the gold standard.

Three weeks later, when the Democratic convention met at Chicago, it became evident that populism had permeated that party. Instead of converting the Democracy to caution, Cleveland had driven it into radicalism. While he strove for sound money the populist panacea of free silver had become an oriflamme to the discontented. Cornbelt economists concluded that gold was the cause of the hard times, and free silver the solution for all their ills. To argue that bimetallism was a world problem, that unlimited coinage of silver by the United States would avail nothing while the mints of Europe and India were closed to it, merely invited the retort that America must declare financial independence of London. Some wanted free coinage of silver in order to bring it back to par, others looked for cheap money to pay their mortgages; but all wanted free silver.

William Jennings Bryan, a thirty-six-year-old congressman from Nebraska, carried the Democratic convention off its feet by a speech which became famous for its peroration, "You shall not press down upon the brow of labor this crown of thorns, you shall not crucify mankind upon a cross of gold," and obtained the presidential nomination. The convention declared emphatically

1. To a congressman who declared his preference to be right rather than to be President, the Speaker interjected, "The gentleman need not be disturbed, he will never be either." Of two boring congressmen he said, "They never open their mouths without subtracting from the sum of human knowledge."

for free silver, and the campaign was fought on that issue. Gold Democrats bolted one way, Silver Republicans the other, and the Populists supported Bryan. Apart from the silver mining interests, it was a cleancut radical-conservative contest over the first live issue in thirty years. And the new cause had an ideal leader in the "Boy Orator of the Platte":

> The bard and the prophet of them all.
> Prairie avenger, mountain lion,
> Bryan, Bryan, Bryan, Bryan,
> Gigantic troubadour, speaking like a siege gun,
> Smashing Plymouth Rock with his boulders from the West.[1]

Radical only on the coinage issue, strictly orthodox in matters of morality and religion, Bryan was an honest, emotional crusader for humanity with the forensic fervor and political shrewdness that would have made him a good state leader in the age of Jackson. His object was merely to reform the government and curb privilege; but he was accused of "proposing to transfer the rewards of industry to the lap of indolence." In the hundreds of speeches that he delivered during a whirlwind tour of 13,000 miles, there was no appeal to class hatred. But his followers were full of it, and "Pitchfork Ben" Tillman of South Carolina called upon the people to throw off their bondage to a money power more insolent than the slave power. On the other side, Mark Hanna assessed metropolitan banks, insurance companies, and railroad corporations for colossal compaign contributions, which even the silver-mining interests could not match for Bryan. Employees were ordered to vote for McKinley on pain of dismissal, and their fears were aroused by the prospect of receiving wages in depreciated dollars. On Wall Street there was even talk of a secession of New York City from the Union if Bryan should win. The Democratic ticket carried the late Confederacy and most of the Far West; but the heavy electoral votes of the East and the Middle West gave McKinley an emphatic victory.

Now come high protection, plenty, and prosperity! Actually, the election of a Democratic administration could have served no useful purpose. They were not prepared, nor was the country ripe, for measures to bring financial giants under control. Free silver, if adopted, would have prolonged uncertainty and placed the United States in sullen financial isolation. Bryan's campaign was at once the last protest of the old agrarian order against industrialism, and the first attempt of the new order to clean house. Bryan was the bridge between Andrew Jackson and Theodore Roosevelt.

4. The Spanish-American War

William McKinley, a kindly soul in a spineless body, was inaugurated President on 4 March 1897. Mark Hanna refused a cabinet position, lest it

1. Vachel Lindsay, *Collected Poems* (1925), p. 99. By permission of The Macmillan Company, New York.

seem payment for his efforts, but 74-year-old Senator John Sherman was persuaded to take the state department so that Mark could take his seat in the Senate. Lyman J. Gage, a Chicago banker and "gold Democrat," excepted the treasury department. Other cabinet positions went to amiable contenders for the nomination, or riggers of McKinley's; only speaker Reed retired in a huff and would take nothing.

Business, breathing easily since the specter of Bryan running the government had been exorcised, was on the up and up. All omens for a peaceful administration were favorable. Since the one thing business wanted — except to be let alone — was more protection, the President promptly summoned a special session of Congress to raise the tariff. In a somewhat chastened spirit, the leaders of Congress proposed to set up more moderate schedules than those of 1890; but by the time every member had secured his pet interest, the Dingley tariff of 1897 was the highest protective tariff that had yet been enacted. So blatant were the monopoly-securing features of this tariff that the Republican party was badly in need of a new issue to divert popular attention.

Cuba provided the diversion. Cuba, which by geography is forced into an intimate relation with the United States, flared up in revolt, this time against Spain's inept (but hardly, by Cuban standards over-severe) rule. Spanish efforts to suppress the insurrection were unsuccessful and revolting. American sympathy was stirred by the plight of insurgents in concentration camps, and by atrocities which were recklessly blown up by the "yellow" journals of William Randolph Hearst and Joseph Pulitzer in their race for circulation, and by Cuban exiles in the United States. Congress had repeatedly pressed the executive to "do something" about Cuba; both Cleveland and McKinley refused to do anything. In October 1897 a new Spanish premier, Sagasta, proposed to abandon the concentration policy, recalled General Weyler who had enforced it, and promised Cuba a measure of home rule. The crisis, apparently, had passed.

Unfortunately, on 15 February 1898, U.S.S. *Maine* was blown up in Havana harbor with heavy loss of life. That started a clamor for war; and when a naval court of inquiry reported (28 March) that the cause was an external explosion by a submarine mine,[1] "Remember the *Maine!*" went from lip to lip. The next day McKinley sent to Madrid what turned out to be his ultimatum, demanding an immediate armistice, release of prisoners, and American mediation between Spain and Cuba. Spain's formal reply was unsatisfactory; but the Sagasta government, anxious to avoid war with the United States, moved toward peace with a celerity unusual at Madrid, and on 9 April the governor general of Cuba offered an armistice to the insurgents. Next day the

1. This finding was confirmed by a careful examination of the wreck in 1911 by a board of American army and navy officers. Although it is still a mystery who set and fired the mine, it is difficult to conceive what interest any Spaniard might have had in doing it, and easy to imagine that a Cuban rebel would have planned it, in order to get the United States involved with Spain.

American minister at Madrid cabled Washington that if nothing were done to humiliate Spain he could obtain a settlement of the Cuban question on the basis of autonomy, independence, or even cession to the United States. He believed that Sagasta was ready to accord Cuba the same freedom as Britain had to Canada.

Any President with a backbone would have seized this opportunity for an honorable solution. McKinley, a veteran of 1861, did not want war. Mark Hanna, Wall Street, big business, and a majority of the Republican senators backed him up. McKinley needed less firmness than John Adams had shown in the X Y Z affair, or Cleveland in the Venezuela crisis, to preserve peace. But Congress and the press, and "young Republicans" like Henry Cabot Lodge, were clamoring for war, and McKinley became obsessed with the notion that if he did not give way, the Republican party would be broken. After much prayer and hesitation, he decided to yield. A year later he confessed, "But for the inflamed state of public opinion, and the fact that Congress could no longer be held in check, a peaceful solution might have been had."

On 11 April 1898 the President sent Congress a long-winded review of the situation, making only a casual and deceptive reference to the reassuring dispatch just received from Madrid. He concluded: "I have exhausted every effort to relieve the intolerable condition of affairs which is at our doors. . . . I await your action." That action, of course, was a declaration of war.

"A splendid little war" is what John Hay called this war with Spain, which America entered upon as lightheartedly as if it were with a tribe of Indians, little reckoning the new and heavy responsibilities it would bring. Emphatically it was popular; no war was ever more emotional or less economic in motive. No important business interests were looking forward to exploiting Cuba, or had even heard of the Philippines. In declaring war, Congress also declared, "The United States hereby disclaims any disposition or intention to exercise sovereignty, jurisdiction, or control over said island except for the pacification thereof, and asserts its determination, when that is accomplished, to leave the government and control of the island to its people." It did not anticipate the series of native tyrants under whom Cuba has suffered.

Europeans took sides in this war as their parents had in the Civil War. Anatole France, in *L'Anneau d'Améthyst* depicts with matchless irony a party in a French château where the countesses beg a general of royalist views to confirm their hopes that "those American bandits" would be well thrashed. The general so predicts; America has but a tiny army, he points out, and a navy manned by stokers and mechanics, not, like the Spanish, by experienced sailors. The guests take great comfort from the rumor that the inhabitants of Boston, New York, and Philadelphia, panic-stricken over the expected appearance of a bombarding squadron, are fleeing en masse to the interior. Anatole had something there; for so apprehensive of bombardment were certain people of the Atlantic coast that the North Atlantic fleet was divided. One squadron blockaded Havana, and the other, reassuringly called the "Flying Squadron," was stationed at Hampton Roads. Senator Hale and ex-Speaker Reed of Maine so "bedevilled" the navy department, wrote assistant secretary Roosevelt, to protect Portland, that the department sent them a Civil War monitor which "quieted all that panic."

Europe came near to forming a monarchical front against the United States. Emperor William II proposed it as early as September 1897; and in Washington in April 1898, at a time when the issue of war and peace was hanging by a hair, Sir Julian Pauncefote the British ambassador sparked a joint suggestion of six European ambassadors and ministers to their respective governments that McKinley be pressured to accept the latest Spanish concessions. This move, which if carried out would have caused a fresh outburst of anglophobia in the United States, was prevented through the common sense of young Arthur James Balfour, then in charge of the British foreign office owing to the illness of Lord Salisbury. He told Sir Julian to mind his own business and stay out of any joint démarche, and the other powers did nothing, knowing that without the British navy on their side it would be impossible to influence the United States. Queen Victoria noted in her diary that the American declaration of war on Spain was "monstrous"; but almost every British political leader and journal backed the United States, realizing that England might soon need a transatlantic ally against Germany.

America rushed into this war "to free Cuba," more nearly unanimous than in any war in her history. The few who cried out against the childish jingoism, the unjust blackening of Spain's noble history, and, above all, the needlessness of the war, were dismissed as cranks or old fogies. With generous ardor young men rushed to the colors, while the bands crashed out the chords of Sousa's "Stars and Stripes Forever," and everyone sang, "There'll be a Hot Time in the Old Town Tonight! " And what a comfortable feeling of unity the country obtained at last! Democrats vied in patriotism with Republicans, Bryan was colonel of a national guard regiment, the South proved equally ardent for the fight; Joe Wheeler and Fitzhugh Lee, who ended the last war as Confederate generals, were now generals of the U. S. Army. This was a closer and more personal war to Americans than either world war; it was their own little war for liberty and democracy against all that was tyrannical, treacherous, and fetid in the Old World. Each ship of the navy, from powerful *Oregon* steaming at flank speed around the Horn to be in time for the big fight, to the absurd dynamite cruiser *Vesuvius*, was known by picture and reputation to every American boy. And what heroes the war correspondents created — Hobson who sank the *Merrimack*, Lieutenant Rowan who delivered the Message to Garcia, Commodore Dewey ("You may fire when ready, Gridley"), blaspheming Bob Evans of *Iowa*, Captain Philip of *Texas* ("Don't cheer, boys, the poor fellows are dying!"), and Teddy Roosevelt with his horseless Rough Riders.

This was no war of waiting and hope deferred. On the first day of May, one week after the declaration, Dewey steamed into Manila Bay with his Pacific

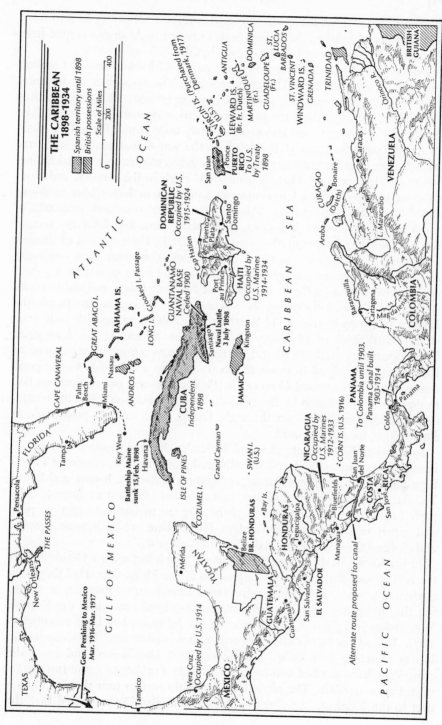

THE CARIBBEAN
1898-1934

Spanish territory until 1898

British possessions

Scale of Miles

0   200   400

TEXAS

New Orleans

THE PASSES

Pensacola

GULF OF MEXICO

Tampico

Gen. Pershing to Mexico
Mar. 1916–Mar. 1917

Vera Cruz
Occupied by U.S. 1914

Tampa

FLORIDA

CAPE CANAVERAL

Palm Beach
Miami

ANDROS I.

Nassau

BAHAMA IS.

GREAT ABACO I.

Crooked I. Passage

LONG I.

ATLANTIC

OCEAN

Key West

Battleship Maine
sunk 15, Feb. 1898

Havana

ISLE OF PINES

CUBA
Independent
1898

Grand Cayman

Santiago

Naval battle
3 July 1898

GUANTANAMO
NAVAL BASE
Ceded 1900

Cap Haitien

Port
au Prince

HAITI
Occupied by
U.S. Marines
1914–1934

Puerto
Plata

Santo
Domingo

DOMINICAN
REPUBLIC
Occupied by U.S.
1915–1924

San Juan

Ponce

PUERTO
RICO
To U.S.
by Treaty
1898

VIRGIN IS. (purchased from
Denmark, 1917)

LEEWARD IS.
(Br. Fr. Dutch)

ANTIGUA

GUADELOUPE
(Fr.)

DOMINICA

MARTINIQUE
(Fr.)

ST.
LUCIA

BARBADOS

ST. VINCENT

WINDWARD IS.

GRENADA

TRINIDAD

BRITISH
GUIANA

Orinoco R.

VENEZUELA

Caracas

CURAÇAO
(Dutch)

Bonaire

Aruba

L. Maracaibo

Barranquilla

Cartagena

COLOMBIA

Magdalena R.

PANAMA
To Colombia until 1903.
Panama Canal built
1903–1914

Panama

Colón

CARIBBEAN   SEA

Kingston

JAMAICA

SWAN I.
(U.S.)

CORN IS. (U.S. 1916)

NICARAGUA
Occupied by
U.S. Marines
1912–1933

San Juan
del Norte

Bluefields

Managua

Tegucigalpa

HONDURAS

Bay Is.

Belize
BR. HONDURAS

COZUMEL I.

YUCATÁN

Mérida

MÉXICO

GUATEMALA

Guatemala

San Salvador

EL SALVADOR

COSTA
RICA

San José

Alternate route proposed for canal

PACIFIC   OCEAN

squadron, and without losing a single man reduced the Spanish fleet to junk. After ten weeks' fighting, the United States wrested an American empire from Spain — and it was control of the ocean that did it.

Yet Spain was a formidable power on paper, with more armored cruisers and torpedo craft than the United States had. The Spanish navy, however, was inconceivably neglected, ill-armed, and untrained; whilst the United States Navy — a creation of the last fifteen years, was smart and efficient. The Army, on the contrary, was almost completely unprepared. Russell A. Alger, an elderly politician, was at the head of the war department. There were enough Krag rifles for the regulars, but the 150,000 volunteers received Spring-fields and black powder. There was no khaki cloth in the country, and thousands of troops fought a Cuba summer campaign in heavy blue uniforms issued for winter garrison duty. Volunteers neglected even such principles of camp sanitation as were laid down in Deuteronomy, and for every one of the 289 men killed or mortally wounded in battle, thirteen died of disease. Transporting 18,000 men to Cuba caused more confusion than conveying two million to France twenty years later. Yet the little expeditionary force was allowed to land on the beach unopposed (20–25 June), and the Captain-General of Cuba, with six weeks' warning, almost 200,000 troops on the Island and 13,000 in the city of Santiago, was able to concentrate only 1700 on the battlefields of El Caney and San Juan against 15,000 Americans. These Spaniards, well armed and entrenched, gave an excellent account of themselves and helped to promote Roosevelt from a colonelcy to the presidency. On 3 July Admiral Cervera's battle fleet steamed out of Santiago Bay to death and destruction by the guns of Admiral Sampson's Atlantic Squadron. Santiago surrendered on the 15th. Except for a military promenade in Puerto Rico, the war was over.

Spain asked for terms of peace and McKinley dictated them on 30 July: — immediate evacuation and definite relinquishment of Cuba, cession of Puerto Rico and an island in the Marianas, occupation of the city, harbor, and bay of Manila. Spain signed a preliminary peace to that effect on 12 August, sadly protesting, "This demand strips us of the very last memory of a glorious past, and expels us . . . from the Western Hemisphere, which became peopled and civilized through the proud deeds of our ancestors."

In the formal peace negotiations at Paris, which began on 1 October 1898, the only serious dispute was the disposition of the Philippines. Had they been contented under Spanish rule, there would have been no question of annexing this archipelago; but an insurrection was already on when the Spanish War broke. José Rizal, a noble leader of the Filipinos, had been executed in 1896. His successor, Emilio Aguinaldo, was encouraged by Commodore Dewey to return from exile after the battle of Manila Bay; and when the Americans had assaulted and captured the city (13 August), the *Insurrectos* organized a republic. The obvious thing to do was to turn the Philippines over to the Filipinos, like Cuba to the Cubans. But Dewey cabled that the

ABRAHAM LINCOLN.
Brady photograph taken during the campaign of 1860

Lieut. Gen. Ulysses S. Grant

Maj. Gen. William Tecumseh Sherman

Maj. Gen. George H. Thomas, usa

Lieut. Gen. Thomas J. Jackson, csa

CAPTAIN OLIVER WENDELL HOLMES, JR.
USA

LIEUTENANT RANDOLPH BARTON
CSA

TWO YOUNG OFFICERS IN THE WAR, AND FIFTY YEARS LATER

JUSTICE OLIVER WENDELL HOLMES (*left*), and RANDOLPH BARTON, Esq., president of the Maryland Bar Association, about 1920

Milking Time

DELINEATIONS OF COUNTRY LIFE BY WINSLOW HOMER

Shoveling Out

Rogers Group,
Coming to the Parson, 1889

POST-CIVIL WAR ARCHITECTURE AND SCULPTURE

The Syracuse, New York,
Savings Bank, 1875

Finish of the 1870 race off Staten Island. *Cambria, Dauntless, America, Idler, Magic*

America's Cup Race

Volunteer, the 1887 defender

Kentucky

TWO GREAT AMERICAN THOROUGHBREDS

Man O'War

WILLIAM McKINLEY AND THEODORE ROOSEVELT
Taken at McKinley's home, after the election of 1900

PRESIDENT WILSON AND GENERAL PERSHING
On the President's visit to the army in January 1919

A Curtiss Triad A-1 of 1912

EARLY AVIATION

NC-4 Arriving Lisbon, May 1919, after her first ocean crossing

The "Great Four" of Johns Hopkins, by John Singer Sargent

William H. Welch, William S. Halsted, William Osler, Howard A. Kelly

PRESIDENT FRANKLIN DELANO ROOSEVELT

PRESIDENT HARRY S. TRUMAN

WILLIAM LYON MACKENZIE KING

REAR ADMIRAL RICHARD E. BYRD, USN

TVA's Hiwassee Dam in North Carolina

Senator and Mrs. George W. Norris

PRESIDENT DWIGHT D. EISENHOWER

PRESIDENT JOHN F. KENNEDY

republic represented only a faction, unable to keep order within its nominal sphere. To restore the islands to Spain would be cowardly; yet few Americans wished to "take up the white man's burden," which Rudyard Kipling begged them to do. On the other hand, Germany's obvious desire to obtain "compensation" in that quarter inclined Americans to stay.

William II of Germany, a latecomer in the European competition for colonies, hoped to purchase the Philippines from Spain and put down the insurrection himself. After the Battle of Manila Bay he sent thither a more powerful squadron than Dewey's, together with a transport lifting some 1400 troops. His naval commander, Admiral von Diederichs, established close relations with the Spanish authorities ashore and even landed troops at Mariveles on the Bataan Peninsula. A touchy situation took place when Diederichs attempted to defy Dewey's blockade of Manila, and truculently paraded his ships past the American squadron with guns trained on them. A British naval squadron under Captain Sir Edward Chichester not only co-operated with Dewey, but on 13 August 1898, when the American assault on Manila began, interposed his ships between the Americans and the Germans, who showed every evidence of trying to bluff Dewey into calling off the bombardment.

Now that China seemed to be on the point of breaking up, it began to look like a good idea to many leaders of public opinion for the United States to obtain a base in the Far East. And clearly all the Philippines must be taken, or none. McKinley hesitated long and prayerfully but finally decided, as he informed a Methodist delegation, "to take them all and to educate the Filipinos, and uplift and civilize and Christianize them." Spain was persuaded to part with the archipelago for $2 million, and on 10 December 1898 cession of the archipelago was included in the Treaty of Paris. Most Americans acquiesced, but a vigorous minority of conscientious objectors, the "anti-imperialists" led by Senator Hoar, believed it a monstrous perversion of American history to conquer and rule an Oriental country, and the necessary two-thirds majority for ratification was obtained with some difficulty. Yet time has justified the words of McKinley: "No imperial designs lurk in the American mind. They are alien to American sentiment, thought and purpose. . . . If we can benefit those remote peoples, who will object? If in the years of the future they are established in government under law and liberty, who will regret our perils and sacrifices?"

This annexation of extra-continental territory populated by an alien people created a new problem in American politics and government. The islets annexed earlier had never raised, as Puerto Rico and the Philippines did, the embarrassing question whether the Constitution followed the flag. Opinions of the Supreme Court in the Insular Cases left their status very muddled; but eventually, as in the British empire, a theory was evolved from practice. Insular possessions are dependencies of, but not part of, the United States, or included in its customs barriers unless by special act of Congress. Thus the Republican party was able to eat its cake and have it: to indulge in territorial expansion, yet maintain the tariff wall against such insular products as sugar and tobacco, as foreign. Inhabitants of the dependencies are American nationals, not citizens of the United States unless expressly granted that status by the United States. Organic acts of Congress became the constitutions of the Philippines and Puerto Rico, like the British North America Act of 1867 for Canada. Only such parts of the Federal Constitution apply as were included in these organic acts, or found applicable by the federal judiciary. President and Congress, although limited in power within the United States, were almost absolute over American dependencies. The parallel with the old British empire is suggestive; and the government at Washington, like that in Westminster, refused to admit the existence of an empire. No United States colonial office was established, no secretary for the colonies appointed. Until World War II, Puerto Rico and the Philippines were administered by the war department's bureau of insular affairs, and smaller possessions like Guam were under the navy department.

Almost half a century elapsed before McKinley's confident prediction came true. The Filipinos, most of whom had been Christians for three centuries, had no desire to be "civilized" in McKinley's sense. When Aguinaldo's troops disregarded the command of an American sentry to halt (4 February 1899), the United States Army undertook the job of making them halt, and it took about two years more and several hundred lives, to put down the Philippine insurrection. Aguinaldo — still living in 1964 — finally took an oath of allegiance to the United States. General Arthur MacArthur (General Douglas MacArthur's father) acted more like an enlightened proconsul than a conqueror, announcing, "The idea of personal liberty . . . we are planting in the Orient. Wherever the American flag goes, that idea goes . . . The planting of liberty — not money — is what we seek." Military government was succeeded in 1901 by a civil Philippine Commission appointed by the President, with William H. Taft as chairman and governor general of the islands. Their population in 1900 was about seven million, of which only 4 per cent were Moslem and 5 per cent wild pagan tribes. Catholic Filipinos, the "little brown brothers" (as Governor Taft called them) who comprised the other 81 per cent, were homogeneous, intelligent, Western in ideals and civilization. Their thirst for education was keen, and Tammany Hall could teach them little about politics. Under American rule they made a remarkable advance in education, well being, and self-government. Governor Taft, on a special mission to the Vatican, paved the way for the Philippines to purchase from the religious orders 400,000 acres of agricultural land, which were sold on easy terms to some 50,000 new landowners. The Filipinos, assured of their eventual independence, co-operated with Taft and his successors to establish a new civil code, a complete scheme of education, sanitation, good roads, a native constabulary; in 1907 a representative assembly — and baseball. Seldom has there been so successful an experiment in the now despised "colonialism" or "imperialism" as American rule in the Philippines. None of the critics' predictions that the Republic had embarked on a Roman road leading to disaster, came true.

Nevertheless, acquisition of the Philippines affected America's future far more than any other settlement following the Spanish war. Cuba could be, and was, made independent, Puerto Rico was gradually advanced to commonwealth status, but responsibility for the Philippines made the United States a power in the Far East, involved her in Asiatic power politics, and made an eventual war with Japan probable. Annexing the Philippines was a major turning point in American history.

Following Japan's annexation of Formosa, and occupation of Korea, Russia, England and France began to extort from weak China permanent leases of important harbors. It became evident that unless China could be patched up, or in some way stabilized so that her vast population (six times that of Japan) would weigh in the balance of Far Eastern power, she would be sliced up by the European powers and Japan. Underlying this military menace, and the threat that each of the aggressive powers would set up barriers to American trade, there was on the part of the American people a warm feeling for China and the Chinese, fostered by medical and Christian missionaries. In the hope of arresting disintegration, Secretary of State John Hay introduced in 1899 the "open door" policy — a series of self-denying declarations by the powers that they would not interfere with vested interests and would allow a Chinese tariff commission headed by Europeans and Americans to fix and collect the customs duties. Next, in June 1900 there broke out the so-called Boxer Rebellion to cast out all "foreign devils" from China. The United States took part in a joint expeditionary force to relieve the legations at Peking; but in order to limit the objective, Hay addressed a circular note to the powers (3 July 1900), declaring it the policy of the United States "to preserve Chinese territorial and administrative entity . . . and safeguard for the world the principle of equal and impartial trade with all parts of the Chinese Empire." The powers promptly concurred, and it is claimed by Hay's admirers that this second "open door" note prevented further partition of China. His detractors, however, contend that Europe and Japan accepted the open door policy tongue-in-cheek, merely to please the American government and public, which "mistook a phrase and a promise for an event." China was so weak, and incapable of suppressing piracy and banditry, that the Empress Dowager was forced to permit the navy of each power concerned to patrol her territorial waters, even the Yangtse river.

President Cleveland, as we have seen, had defeated every earlier attempt to annex the Hawaiian Islands. Now that American expansion was on the march, annexation was consummated by joint resolution of Congress on 7 July 1898. An organic act of 1900 conferred American citizenship on all Hawaiians and the full status of a territory of the United States, eligible for eventual statehood, which was finally accorded by Congress in 1959.

Another native kingdom in the Pacific on which the United States and other powers had designs was Samoa. Here President Grant in 1878 had obtained the naval station at Pago Pago in Tutuila by treaty with native chieftains; Germany and Great Britain followed suit. In 1899 England pulled out and sovereignty over the islands was divided between Germany and the United States. In the same year, Germany obtained some consolation for her failure to acquire the Philippines by purchasing from Spain all remnants of her Pacific empire, the Marianas group (except Guam), and the Caroline Islands. American missionaries, who hitherto had conducted all the work of civilization in these islands, wanted the United States to buy them; but the state department was not interested. During the First World War, Japan easily captured them all, as well as the Marshalls, from Germany; and in the Second World War the United States had to recover them at heavy cost.

Almost everyone in Europe expected the United States to annex Cuba. Instead, Washington promptly fulfilled the promise to make Cuba really *libre*; and the insurgents under Garcia, instead of fighting us as the Filipinos did, co-operated. For over three years the island was ruled by a United States army of occupation, fewer than 6000 troops, commanded by General Leonard Wood, a highly competent and sympathetic military governor. The outstanding features of his regime were medical. In 1900 Cuba was afflicted by a severe yellow fever epidemic. General Wood appointed a commission of four army surgeons under Dr. Walter Reed to investigate the cause. Working on a theory advanced by a Cuban physician, Dr. Carlos Finlay, they proved that the pest was transmitted by the stegomyia mosquito; and two of them, Dr. James Carroll and Dr. Jesse W. Lazear, proved it with their lives. General Wood declared war on the mosquito, and by 1901 there was not a single case of yellow fever in Havana. One of the greatest scourges of the tropics had been brought under control.

The Cuban constitutional convention that met in 1900 was induced to grant to the United States the Guantanamo naval base, and to recognize the right of the United States to intervene "for the preservation of Cuban independence," or to preserve order. Two years later the United States Army was withdrawn and Cuba turned over to her own government. The treaty provisions for intervention, known as the Platt Amendment, were incorporated in the first treaty between the United States and the Republic of Cuba; and only once invoked, in 1906. On demand of the Cuban government, the United States revoked the Platt Amendment in 1934.

Puerto Rico, handicapped by a decrepit and unsatisfactory system of law and local government, overcrowded with landless *jibaros*, enervated by hookworm and discouraged by fluctuations of the sugar market, has been an economic and social rather than a political problem. Civil government, first granted by the Foraker Act of 1900, was of the old crown-colony type: an elective assembly with a governor and executive council appointed by the President. Political parties quickly developed, the American governors were unable to keep neutral, and deadlocks occurred over the budget. Another organic Act of 1917 granted American citizenship to the Puerto Ricans and a government more responsible to the people. Since that time there has been steady progress in the economy, and in self-government. In 1964 the island, under an elected governor (Luis Muñoz-Marin) is a commonwealth with a status similar to that of Canada in the British empire. Eventually Puerto Rico will become a state of the union unless she chooses independence.

As the presidential election of 1900 approached, the anti-imperialist movement waxed strong. It was led by statesmen such as Cleveland, Reed, and Bryan, financial magnates such as Andrew Carnegie, philosophers such as William James, college presidents such as Eliot and Jordan, writers such as Mark Twain and William Vaughan Moody. Although the rank and file of the Democrats were fully as proud as the Republicans of the victory over Spain and its fruits, the Democratic nominating convention adopted an anti-imperialist plank which, if implemented, would have caused the Philippines to be handed over immediately to the Filipinos. And the Democrats made much of scandalously inept administration by the war department in the Spanish war: — soldiers poisoned by putrid beef which smelled like embalmed corpses, and dying of typhoid in a discharge camp on Long Island. "Free silver" was trotted out again to catch Western and debtor votes. John Bull was given the usual kick in the teeth, this time for his Boer War, to catch the Irish vote. For the second, but not the last time, the Democrats nominated William Jennings Bryan with former Vice President Adlai E. Stevenson for second place.

Republicans held all the trump cards — victory, world prestige, booming prosperity, and Philippine insurrection well in hand by General Arthur MacArthur. McKinley, of course, received the presidential nomination, and, in a move to isolate the irrepressible Theodore Roosevelt, the bosses saw to it that he was nominated for the vice presidency. The President conducted a "front porch campaign," receiving hand-picked delegations on the verandah of his house at Canton, Ohio, hearing their carefully censored speeches of support, and delivering in reply selected passages of patriotic platitudes. "Teddy" stumped the country in a Rough Rider hat, arousing wild enthusiasm. McKinley and Roosevelt were obviously what the people wanted. Bryan carried the solid South, together with four "silver" states of the West (Colorado, Idaho, Montana, Nevada) — but he lost his own Nebraska and won only 155 electoral votes to McKinley's 292. The President's plurality was almost 900,000 votes. Prohibitionists, Socialists, and other splinter parties polled only 4 per cent of the total. Increased Republican majorities were returned to both houses of Congress, and common stocks rose to new highs.

McKinley was inaugurated for his brief second term on 4 March 1901. Before the end of April he embarked on a rail journey around the country, accompanied by Mark Hanna and several members of the cabinet. Everywhere he was received by cheering crowds, to which he delivered familiar clichés on duty, purpose, prosperity, and the glory awaiting America. The trip ended tragically on 6 September at Buffalo, where the President was opening a Pan-American Exposition. As he always prided himself on accessibility, McKinley held a public reception, guarded by only two secret service men. An anarchist who joined the line, with a loaded revolver concealed under a handkerchief, fired two shots at the President just as he had extended a welcoming hand. One shot passed through McKinley's stomach. An operation was performed, and the patient seemed to be improving; but infection set in, and as yet there were no wonder drugs to control it. His heart gave way, and on the 14th his kindly soul departed from his tired body.

Vice President Roosevelt, summoned while climbing Mount Marcy in the Adirondacks, hastened to Buffalo and was sworn in as President on 15 September. At the age of forty-three he was the youngest man ever to reach this high office. Senator Platt of New York, who had managed the vice presidential nomination to get rid of troublesome Teddy, told Mark Hanna at the inaugural ceremonies of 4 March that he had come especially "to see Theodore Roosevelt take the veil."

"Now look!" said Mark Hanna when he next met the Senator in October, "That damned cowboy is President of the United States! "

A HOT TIME IN THE OLD TOWN TONIGHT

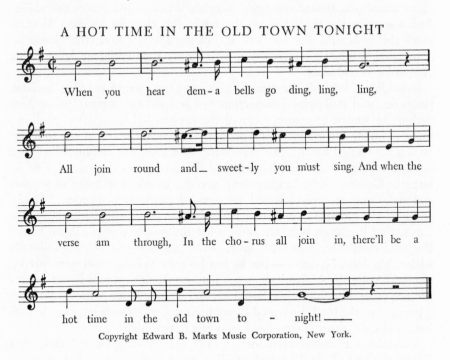

When you hear dem-a bells go ding, ling, ling,

All join round and— sweet-ly you must sing, And when the

verse am through, In the cho-rus all join in, there'll be a

hot time in the old town to - night! ——

Copyright Edward B. Marks Music Corporation, New York.

Theodore Roosevelt

1901-1909

1. *The Progressive Background and "Teddy"*

THEODORE ROOSEVELT, and after him, Presidents Taft and Wilson, were liberal conservatives. They accepted the new industrial order which had grown up since the Civil War, but wished to probe its more scabrous excrescencies, both on the political and financial levels, and bring it under government regulation. The word "constructive" was constantly on their lips; socialists and reckless agitators shared their hostility with "malefactors of great wealth" and corrupt politicians. The violent dissensions between these three men as to methods concealed the essential unity of their administrations. Theodore Roosevelt, Taft, and Wilson were successive leaders of what came to be called the Progressive Movement, which in essence was the adaptation of federal, state, and municipal governments to the changes already wrought and being wrought in American society. Roosevelt called his policies the "Square Deal," Wilson his, the "New Freedom." Their philosophy was never better stated than by Elihu Root in his presidential address before the New York State Bar Association in 1912:

The real difficulty appears to be that the new conditions incident to the extraordinary industrial development of the last half-century are continuously and progressively demanding the readjustment of the relations between great bodies of men and the establishment of new legal rights and obligations not contemplated when existing laws were passed or existing limitations upon the powers of government were prescribed in our Constitution. In place of the old individual independence of life in which every intelligent and healthy citizen was competent to take care of himself and his family, we have come to a high degree of interdependence in which the greater part of our people have to rely for all the necessities of life upon the systematized co-operation of a vast number of other men working through complicated industrial and commercial machinery. Instead of the completeness of individual effort working out its own results in obtaining food and clothing and shelter, we have specialization and division of labor which leaves each individual unable to apply his industry and intelligence except in co-operation with a great number of others whose activity conjoined to his is necessary to produce any useful result. Instead of the give-and-take of free individual contract, the tremendous power of organization has combined great aggregations of capital in enormous industrial establishments working through vast agencies of commerce and employing great masses of men in movements of production and transportation and trade, so great in the mass that each individual concerned in them is quite helpless by himself. The relations between the employer and the employed, between the owners of aggregated capital and the units of organized labor, between the small producer, the small trader, the consumer, and the great transporting and manufacturing and distributing agencies, all present new questions for the solution of which the old reliance upon the free action of individual wills appears quite inadequate. And in many directions the intervention of that organized control which we call government seems necessary to produce the same result of justice and right conduct which obtained through the attrition of individuals before the new conditions arose.

Woodrow Wilson repeated much of this in his *The New Freedom* (1913), and added, "This is nothing short of a new social age, a new era of human relationships, a new stage-setting for the drama of life."

This seems obvious half a century later, except to the more ardent Goldwater supporters; but it was then heady stuff for most lawyers, bankers, and industrialists. These, in general, approved a clean-up of politics but saw no need to regulate business, transportation, or finance. "A tree should be allowed to grow as high as it can" expressed their laissez-faire creed, even if the tree overshadowed and sucked the life out of all bushes and plants in its radius. Several university economists, such as William Graham Sumner, pointed out that former interventions of government in business, as in colonial Canada, had been disastrous. Progressives thought otherwise, and the country supported them until World War I brought reaction. The frenzied finance of the 1920's led to the great crash and the great depression. Another Roosevelt then picked up the Progressive torch, calling it the "New Deal," and this was followed by Truman's "Fair Deal," and Kennedy's "New Frontier." All were essentially the same thing: an attempt through government action to curb the arrogance of organized wealth and the wretchedness of poverty amid plenty.

As we are now concerned with the Progressive Era, to 1917, it is pertinent to inquire why it accomplished so little that a "New Deal" was necessary; much less, for instance, than the Liberals did in Great Britain under Campbell-Bannerman and Lloyd George, who were then wrestling with similar problems. One reason was the vast scale, and the federal system, through which American Progressives had to operate. But the basic reason, as Theodore Roosevelt perceived in 1911, was the Progressives' war with themselves over basic economic policy. "Half of them are really representative of a kind of rural toryism, which wishes to attempt the impossible task of returning to the economic conditions that obtained sixty years ago" — to "bust the trusts" and break up business into old-style competing units. "The other half," continued Roosevelt, wishes "to recognize the inevitableness of combinations in business, and meet it by a corresponding increase in governmental power over big business." The progressive wing represented by William Jennings Bryan and Louis Brandeis hated bigness as such and feared the tyranny of government more than the arrogance of financiers. The other, of which Herbert Croly was the leading publicist, looked forward to a "welfare state," controlled by Congress but staffed by an intelligent and dedicated bureaucracy. Although Theodore Roosevelt, in his 1911 statement, regarded this wing as the only "proper" one for a progressive, he reacted violently against it when practised by Woodrow Wilson.

Graham Wallas, like Herbert Spencer an English publicist, deeply influenced the thinking of this generation of American liberals. His *Human Nature in Politics* (1908) was followed by lecturing at Harvard, where one of his pupils was Walter Lippmann, to whom his next book *The Great Society* (1914) was dedicated. In the meantime Herbert Croly in *The Promise of American Life* (1909), and Lippmann in *A Preface to Politics* (1913) had promulgated similar ideas in the United States. Brooks Adams, a publicist who had the ear of Theodore Roosevelt, pointed out in a book entitled *A Theory of Social Revolution* (1913) that revolution had always erupted under a government so rigid that no reform could be achieved through process of law. Thus, the British Parliament claimed absolute power over its colonies, and lost them; Louis XVI dismissed Turgot and destroyed the monarchy; the cotton aristocracy of the South resisted restriction of slavery, and perished. Now, in 1913, a new capitalist class, having made untold sums through the application of steam to industry, had obtained control of the government and would meet the same fate if it acquired no sense. He expressed this with the verve worthy of a grandson of J. Q. Adams.

These heralds of the welfare state were chiefly interested in the industrial worker, whose "real" wages — i.e. wages measured not only by dollars but by rent and the prices of basic commodities — remained stationary or declined during this period of "Republican prosperity" and "the full dinner pail." Paul H. Douglas's basic work *Real Wages in the United States 1890–1926* shows that in eight of the years 1900–1914 "real" weekly earnings in all American industries were less than the average ($10.73) for the 1890's. The workers themselves, painfully aware of this, were becoming more and more skeptical of political remedies. But it would not be fair for us to denigrate the Progressives for accomplishing so little for working people, because they were the only group in the country who proposed to do anything for them, or to get away from those figments of the passing age, the "economic man" and "law of supply and demand."

One basic cause of the laborer's standstill was unrestricted immigration. In six of the ten years 1905–14 more than a million people emigrated annually to the United States. The bulk of these were no longer north Europeans, but Slavs, Jews from eastern and southern Europe, Sicilians, and Greeks. Their competition kept wages low and hampered the unions' attempts to organize; yet, low as the wages were, they were high enough to attract the poor and the ambitious from Europe. No Progressives (to my knowledge) showed any interest in this problem, and the nineteenth-century immigrant stocks — Irish, Germans, and Scandinavians — opposed restriction as likely to prevent their friends from coming over. An attempt by Congress to exclude illiterate immigrants, promoted by the unions, was vetoed by President Taft in 1913 for the sound reason that illiteracy, often due to lack of opportunity, was no test of character.

Common to all Progressives was belief in the perfectibility of man, and in an open society where mankind was neither chained to the past nor condemned to a deterministic future; one in which people were capable of changing their condition for better or worse. And they sincerely believed that they were the people chosen to make the word of Jefferson and Lincoln flesh indeed.

The Socialist party must also be counted in the Progressive group, for (unlike the later Communist party) having no obligation to hew to an international party line, it met American problems in an American manner. Starting on the local level, Socialists campaigned for municipal ownership of waterworks, gas and electric plants, and made very good progress. In 1911 Socialist candidates for mayor carried no fewer than eighteen American cities and almost won Cleveland and Los Angeles. Upton Sinclair in 1905 founded the Intercollegiate Socialist Society, which soon had chapters in the leading universities where lively young men and women discussed the new "gospel according to St. Marx." Eugene Debs, converted to socialism during his term in jail, edited the party's weekly, *Appeal to Reason,* and from 1900 through 1920, as candidate for the presidency, increased his vote almost tenfold. Norman Thomas, a Princeton graduate and Presbyterian minister in New York who succeeded Debs as perennial presidential candidate, was more typical of the party. It was an intellectual and middle-class party, rather than one of the workers. Debs himself regarded most of the country's labor leaders as a bunch of crooks — as indeed many of them proved to be.

By the time Theodore Roosevelt reached the presidency, an impressive amount of preliminary work had been done by Progressives in cities and states, and their efforts aroused the expectation of greater things on the federal level. The National Municipal League, organized in 1894, sponsored home-rule legislation for cities which enabled reform groups to free municipalities from the heavy hand of state control. Among these civic reformers were Charles R. Crane and Walter L. Fisher in Chicago, James D. Phelan and Rudolph Spreckels in San Francisco, Samuel M. "Golden Rule" Jones in Toledo, Seth Low of New York and Thomas L. Johnson of Cleveland. Lincoln Steffens's series on "The Shame of the Cities" in *McClure's Magazine,* starting in 1902, had an immense impact. Theodore Roosevelt inconsistently called Steffens and his fellow writers (such as Ida Tarbell who showed up Standard Oil, Upton Sinclair of *The Jungle* fame, and Ray Stannard Baker) "the muckrakers" — a metaphor from *Pilgrim's Progress* — but they muckraked to good purpose, exposing the evils of city and state governments, unions, business, the drug trade, and whatever was curably wrong in divers segments of American life. When this new middle-class reform strain combined with the older agrarian Populists, it accomplished something. A large proportion of these pioneer Progressives were college graduates, actuated by a genuine desire for improvement, and Theodore Roosevelt was the first President to encourage them to place their talents at the service of government, reversing the process begun under Jackson of squeezing such men out of the public service into money-making.

Robert La Follette, by defeating the Republican machine of Wisconsin in 1900, started a reaction of revolt in the Middle West, helped to make his own state a progressive commonwealth (from which it has spectacularly lapsed), and went to the United States Senate where he became a power until his death in 1925. Parallel to him were Joseph W. Folk who showed up corruption in Missouri's state government and became governor in 1904; William S. U'ren who persuaded Oregon to adopt the initiative, referendum, direct primary, and popular recall of elected officials, political reforms which the Progressives expected would return state governments to the people and end corruption — and how wrong they were! Hiram Johnson in 1910 smashed the Southern Pacific Railroad domination in California and became governor of the Golden State. This reform movement, starting in the West, gradually extended eastward. In 1905 a New York Attorney named Charles Evans Hughes exposed the rottenness of the great insurance companies and sent some of their moguls, such as James Hazen Hyde, into exile. In the Progressive period, many state governments recovered their vigor, experimenting with woman suffrage, the Australian ballot, the "I. and R.," the primary, factory and minimum wage legislation, and other expedients.

The federal government and the South were the last to feel the impact of Progressivism. But in 1901, with the accession of Theodore Roosevelt, the nation had a leader who caught its imagination. For Roosevelt was one of the most vital and virile figures of the century.

Roosevelt at forty-three still holds the record as the youngest President of the United States at his accession, although he was older when elected President than John F. Kennedy in 1960. None had been better equipped to administer the office. No President since John Quincy Adams had been as broadly cultivated as Roosevelt, and their careers are roughly parallel, although their backgrounds were not. Roosevelt liked to boast of his non-Anglo-Saxon blood; he was mostly old "Knickerbocker" Dutch and his ancestors had been city merchants, bankers, and importers for generations. Born at 10 East 28th Street (now a Roosevelt shrine), Theodore suffered as a child from asthma, defective eyesight, and other physical weaknesses, but overcame them more by force of character than medical attention. Mature, he was five feet nine inches tall, weighed about 160 pounds, and had a barrel-like chest which small boys who visited the White House were invited to pommel. His education by governesses, tutors, and trips to Europe — never did he attend a school — was such as to make him a Little Lord Fauntleroy; but basic character won. After graduating from Harvard *magna cum laude*, and an early marriage, he had enough inherited wealth to build the sprawling Sagamore Hill mansion at Oyster Bay, Long Island, raise a large family and give them everything — horses, tennis courts, yachts — that the young gentry of that era enjoyed. But he was not content with being a dilettante member of the upper class. To the British ambassador in 1901 he expressed his "feeling of contempt and anger for our socially leading people" and their "lives which vary from rotten frivolity to rotten vice." Although he loved riding to hounds with the Meadowbrook set, he would ride the fourteen miles to Hempstead and back rather than suffer their "intolerable" companionship overnight. He was devoted to his parents, but ashamed that his father had not fought in the Civil War; that may explain his burning desire to get into every war during his lifetime.

Upon graduating from Harvard, Roosevelt planned to be a naturalist; then, after the death of his first wife, he became a rancher. That experience made him an enthusiast for conserving America's natural resources. He wrote two good historical works, *The Naval History of the War of 1812*, and *The Winning of the West*. Prior to the Spanish-American War, he had been assemblyman, police commissioner in New York City, civil service commissioner in Washington, and assistant secretary of the navy. Following his spectacular military career — storming San Juan Hill with his personally recruited Rough Riders — he was elected governor of New York, and in that office struck corruption with such vigor that in self-defense Senator Platt and the machine politicians boomed him for Vice President. Roosevelt accepted the nomination to that high but innocuous office for the political oblivion that it normally meant, and was on the point of studying law in preparation for a professional career when the anarchist's fatal shot made him President.

No American President since Lincoln was more national in his interests or so universal in his friendships. Roosevelt's reading covered the range from Herodotus to Graham Wallas, and his mind was retentive; he could discuss world history with any historian, and natural history with leading naturalists like John Muir and John Burroughs. He was the idol of the younger generation, much as John F. Kennedy later became. He had identified himself with the Far West by ranching, with New England by education, with the South because his maternal uncles had been warriors in the lost cause. Roosevelt's taste was much better than the average of his class; it was on his initiative that Augustus Saint-Gaudens designed a new gold coinage and that the bureau of engraving and printing produced the classically beautiful postage stamps of 1908. He appointed a commission of artists to advise the government on plans and positions of new public buildings in Washington, which grew visibly in beauty and distinction during his administration. People everywhere loved Roosevelt as a red-blooded, democratic American whose every action showed good sportsmanship and dynamic vitality. With the heart of a boy and the instincts of a man of action, Roosevelt had the brain of a statesman. He was the only President since the Civil War who understood, even imperfectly, what had happened to the country in the last thirty years, and he had the temperament, the brains, and the energy to grapple with problems that were crying for solution.

Roosevelt's philosophy, if his largely instinctive actions can be called that, was Hamiltonian, although his objectives were not. For Jefferson he frequently expressed contempt; the more so because his critics in finance and big business began invoking Jeffersonian democracy and state rights against governmental efforts to regulate them. Roosevelt believed, as Hamilton had, in making the federal government truly national; the "general welfare clause" of the Constitution, which had earlier been considered a limitation on the taxing power, he regarded as authority to do anything for the good of the country for which the states individually were incompetent. But he intended to direct all this activity, not toward making the rich richer, but toward giving a "square deal" to the farmer, laborer, and small business man who was being squeezed by big business.

Roosevelt's ambition extended beyond the borders of his country. While reforming the domestic social order, he wished America to flex her muscles and assert her strength abroad, as a world power. He seems to have had no vision of a new world order, but he did intend to make a strong, well-armed America a guarantor of world peace. Thus his place in history is that of the first of four Presidents — himself, Wilson, the other Roosevelt, and Kennedy — who worked out a coherent domestic and foreign policy to meet the realities of the twentieth century. Theodore Roosevelt never looked back, only forward.

2. Consolidation and Reform

The "trust problem" was the popular name for the first object of Roosevelt's righteous zeal. The depression of the early 'nineties stimulated the railroads and the manufacturers to adopt various forms of combination, in order to eliminate competition and maintain prices. In 1897, just as prosperity was reviving, the Supreme Court found one of these organizations, the Trans-Missouri Traffic Association, invalid under the Sherman Anti-trust law, in a decision so sweeping that practically every pool or association became liable to criminal prosecution. Big business, in consequence, abandoned combination for consolidation. A group of bankers would organize a "trust" or super-corporation for the control of a single industry. With the help of the financiers who had large interests in the leading companies who made a certain product, the new trust would buy them out, issuing its own stock in exchange and assuming their bonds. An immense quantity of common stock would then be issued in anticipation of increased earnings and "unloaded" by the banker-promoters on the public, and up would go prices of the product. Never had there been so easy a method of making something out of nothing. Tobacco, agricultural machinery, tin cans, salt, sugar, dressed meat, and a score of basic products were consolidated in corporations with power to crush competition and mulct the public by increased prices of service and commodities, in order to pay dividends on a "watered" capitalization.

In many cases the merger of competing or complementary industries marked a technical advance. Trust methods, however suitable for industries such as meat-packing, were extended to others which were not, such as cotton-spinning, piano-making, and rope-making; and the economies of mass production were not often shared with laborer or consumer. The United States Steel Corporation, formed in 1901, combined the already swollen corporations of Frick, Carnegie, and others in a trust capitalized at $1,400 million, of which nearly one-seventh was issued to promoters for their services. Prices were maintained, although 10 to 12 per cent was being earned on the real capitalization, and the wages of steel workers were kept down by importing cheap labor from southern and eastern Europe. The great insurance companies of New York, instead of reducing premiums to their policy holders, paid salaries of $100,000 or more to chief executives who were often mere figureheads.

It did not always work. J. Pierpont Morgan endeavored to unite every steam and electric railway and steamship line of New England under one management, and succeeded in leaving the transportation system of that region a financial wreck, from which it has never recovered. E. H. Harriman purchased the bankrupt Union Pacific in 1893 with reserve funds of the Illinois Central system that he controlled, and made it one of the best railways in the country; but other lines that he absorbed were sucked dry and cast aside, after wiping out their stockholders' equities. The cordage trust collapsed, while the Plymouth firm which defied it, lived on. But often it did work. Standard Oil, consolidated through the ruthless ruining of competitors by John D. Rockefeller, paid an average annual dividend of 40 per cent in the 1890's. Neither the Cleveland nor the McKinley administrations had invoked the Sherman Anti-trust Act against these practices.

Much the same thing was going on in England and in Europe, but not to such an extent. The American theater was so vast, and American resources so boundless, that financial or industrial consolidations found greater materials to work with. American financiers and industrialists were more sanguine and audacious than their transatlantic contemporaries; and the American government was decentralized, constantly changing in personnel, lacking organic strength and administrative traditions. The future of American democracy was imperilled by no foreign enemy, but gravely menaced by corporate greed and financial imbalance, when Roosevelt took from the bewildered Bryan Democrats the torch of reform.

Not that Roosevelt applied the torch as Bryan might have tried to do. His administration began circumspectly, as his party was the favorite of big business, and he had to deal with strong Republican majorities in House and Senate. He took over McKinley's able cabinet — John Hay in state, Elihu Root and John D. Long in war and navy — and persuaded Congress to set up a new department of commerce and labor whose first duty was to gather facts for enforcing the anti-trust laws. Toward organized labor his attitude was ambiguous. In general he demanded a "square deal" for labor as for capital. He supported the unions in their demands for better wages and shorter hours, he enforced, for the first time in years, the eight-hour law for federal employees, and he persuaded Congress to pass progressive legislation for the District of Columbia. But he resented what he called the unions' "arrogant and domineering" attitude, and supported the open shop. In 1902 there came a test case — a strike in the anthracite coalfields of Pennsylvania, upon which the people of the Eastern states were then dependent for domestic fuel. Roosevelt summoned a conference of mine-owners and union leaders. The unions offered to arbitrate, the owners refused, and urged the President to break the strike with the army as Cleveland might have done. Roosevelt merely published the results of the conference, and public indignation then compelled the owners to submit to arbitration by a presidential commission. This episode not only strengthened his popularity, it taught him to use public opinion as a whip for recalcitrant congressmen no less than for captains of industry.

So lively, forthright, and "strenuous" (his favorite adjective) was Roosevelt in comparison with his predecessors that many wrongly assumed that he was radical and reckless. Impulsive indeed he was, but, unlike the stubborn Wilson, always willing to compromise with Congress on a half-measure in the hope of obtaining more later. In his first annual message (3 December 1901) he announced a policy with regard to trusts and corporations: enforce the existing laws, obtain full power for the federal government to inspect and regulate corporations engaged in interstate business. The first rested with him, the second with Congress.

Until he could obtain legislation strengthening the interstate commerce commission, this young President found plenty of work to do in cleansing his government of the unsavory garbage that had accumulated since the Civil War. Frauds in the post-office department were uncovered and punished. Upton Sinclair's *Jungle* drew popular as well as presidential attention to disgusting conditions in the Chicago stockyards. A government investigation substantiated his lurid charges, and Dr. H. W. Wiley, a chemist in the department of agriculture, proved by experiment the deleterious effect of preservatives and coloring matter in canned foods. The interests affected fought tooth and nail against "Socialist interference." ("It don't hurt the kids," said a candy manufacturer who diluted his coconut bars with shredded bone, "they like it!") But Congress strengthened the meat inspection service and passed the Pure Food and Drugs Act (1906), which gave consumers some protection.

Roosevelt's love of nature made conservation one of his leading policies. It was high time to put a brake on the greedy and wasteful destruction of natural resources that was encouraged by existing laws. The West, keen as ever for rapid "development," disliked this program. Taking advantage of an earlier law which his predecessors had largely ignored, Roosevelt set aside almost 150 million acres of unsold government timber land as national forest reserve, and on the suggestion of Senator La Follette withdrew from public entry some 85 million more in Alaska and the Northwest, pending a study of their mineral resources by the federal geological survey. The discovery of a gigantic system of fraud by which timber companies and ranchers were looting the public preserve enabled the President to obtain authority for transferring national forests to the department of agriculture, whose forest bureau under Gifford Pinchot administered them on scientific principles. Conservation was sweetened for the West by Federal projects of irrigation. A new federal reclamation service, of which F. H. Newell was the guiding spirit, added a million and a quarter acres to the arable land of the United States by 1915. Five national parks were created in Roosevelt's administration, together with two national game preserves and fifty-one wild bird refuges.

In 1902 President Roosevelt decided to challenge another form of combination, the holding company, which was outside the scope of the decision on the Trans-Missouri case. His attorney general entered suit against the Northern Securities Company, a consolidation of Hill, Morgan, and Harriman interests that controlled four of the six transcontinental railways. By a narrow margin the Supreme Court decided for the government, thereby stopping a process of consolidation that Harriman proposed to continue until every important railway in the country came under his control.

In the realm of railway regulation, much was accomplished under Roosevelt. Rebates from published freight rates were forbidden by an Act of 1903, but more scandals and disclosures were required before government could obtain control over the rates themselves. The Hepburn Act of 1906 made regulation for the first time possible, and extended its field from interstate railways to steamship, express, and sleeping-car companies. This was further enlarged in 1910 by adding telephone and telegraph companies. The Hepburn Act authorized the interstate commerce commission, upon complaint, to determine and prescribe maximum rates. Owing to respect for the ancient principle of judicial review, appeals to federal courts had to be admitted; but the burden of proof was now on the carrier, not the commission. Railways were forced to disgorge most of the steamship lines and coal mines with which they had been wont to stifle competition. Most useful of all provisions in the Hepburn Act was the requirement placed on all common carriers to file annual accounts by a standardized system, and the power given the commission to settle disputes between railroads and shippers. Yet, as Senator La Follette contended, this law did not go far enough, since it gave the commission no power to discover the value of transportation properties or the cost of service, by which alone it could determine equitable rates.

A large part of the metropolitan press attacked Roosevelt's program as socialistic and subversive of the common weal, and himself as a reckless demagogue; the editor of the *New York Sun* even forbade the name Theodore Roosevelt to be mentioned in his journal. The President, however, was steadily growing in popularity. Merely by being himself — greeting professors and pugilists with equal warmth and discussing their hobbies with the same genuine interest, playing vigorous tennis, leading perspiring major generals on a cross-country chase, praising the good, the true, and the beautiful and denouncing the base, the false, and the ugly, preaching in hundreds of short addresses all over the country, with vigorous gesture and incisive utterance, the gospel of civic virtue and intelligent democracy — Roosevelt became an institution. Even the journals most opposed to his policies were forced to advertise them willy-nilly in their news columns. When the election of 1904 came round, the "Old Guard," as the more recalcitrant Republicans began to be called, would have preferred to nominate Mark Hanna; but "Uncle Mark" died, and Roosevelt was nominated by acclamation. The Democrats, unable to compete with Roosevelt for the progressive vote, and hoping to attract disgruntled reactionaries, put up a conservative, lackluster New York judge, Alton B. Parker. He carried nothing but the solid South. Roosevelt garnered 336 electoral votes to Parker's 140, and his popular vote, 56.4 of the total, was the largest in any presidential election between Monroe's and Harding's. The minority parties — Prohibition, Socialist, etc. — polled only 6 per cent of the total. Thus, on 4 March 1905, Roosevelt began a new term with a clear mandate for what he called "my policies."

3. *Trust and Railway Regulation to 1920* [1]

Roosevelt's attitude toward the trusts, originally one of "busting," underwent a significant change. By 1906, if not earlier, he had decided that big business was here to stay, that consolidation met a legitimate need, and that regulation rather than dissolution was the proper remedy for abuses. But he was unable to obtain congressional legislation in that direction. Bills initiated by his supporters in the House died in the Senate, which was dominated by four very able and conservative men: Nelson W. Aldrich of Rhode Island, Orville H. Platt of Connecticut, John C. Spooner of Wisconsin, and William B. Allison of Iowa. These and other like-minded men were known as the "Stand-patters," from an address of Mark Hanna in 1902 advising Ohio to "stand pat and continue Republican prosperity."

"I see no promise of any immediate and complete solution of all the problems we group together when we speak of the trust question," confessed Roosevelt at the beginning of his second administration. The authority he asked for giving the federal government plenary power to regulate all corporations engaged in interstate business was not forthcoming. Big business, how-

1. Since there is no clean break in this movement prior to the Harding administration, I have carried it down to 1920, emphasizing the unity of the Progressive Era, through the Taft and Wilson administrations.

ever, was discredited by the panic of 1907 and by the discovery that the Sugar
Trust had swindled the government out of $4 million in customs duties by
false weights. Irritated by the continued attacks upon him as the destroyer of
business and author of the panic, Roosevelt issued a pungent message attributing the panic "to the speculative folly and flagrant dishonesty of a few men
of great wealth," describing the current malpractices, and concluding; "Our
laws have failed in enforcing the performance of duty by the man of property
toward the man who works for him, by the corporation toward the investor,
the wage-earner and the general public."

Without fresh legislation, the President could do little more than direct
prosecutions under the Sherman Act of 1890. Such prosecutions were infrequent, and in some instances successful; but they simply punished gross mischief after it had been committed, and did not always do that. Unscrambling
the eggs proved to be a delicate and often impossible operation. Roosevelt
was forced to conclude that the mere size and power of a combination did not
render it illegal; there were "good trusts," such as the International Harvester
Company, which traded fairly and passed economies on to consumers; and
there were bad trusts controlled by "malefactors of great wealth." This was
about what the Supreme Court decided in the Standard Oil case of 1911: that
only those acts or agreements of a monopolistic nature unduly or "unreason-
ably" affecting interstate commerce were to be construed as acts or agreements in restraint of trade, under the Anti-trust Act. This "rule of reason"
became the guiding rule of decision, notably in the case of 1920 against the
United States Steel Corporation, a consolidation from which the monopoly
feature was absent. Subsequent prosecutions have been based not on mere
size and power but on unfair and illegal use of power. President Wilson
obtained from Congress the sort of legislation that Roosevelt demanded in
vain: the Clayton Anti-trust Act proscribing certain specified trade practices,
and the federal trade commission, an administrative agency clothed with
police power to enforce the law.

As a result of the federal government's experience operating railways during
the First World War, Congress in 1920 passed a comprehensive Transportation
Act, placing the initiative and burden of rate-making on the interstate commerce commission, with a view to securing the stockholders a "fair return" on
their property, and the public just freight and passenger rates. Further, the
commission was given complete jurisdiction over the fiancing operations of
the railways in order to protect the investing public and the stockholders. In
1917 even the Supreme Court went so far as to declare, "There can be
nothing private or confidential in the activities and expenditures of a carrier
engaged in interstate commerce." A Railway Labor Board was established to
mediate disputes about wages, hours, and working conditions of railway
employees, and to settle disputes. Under plenary government regulation the
necessity for artificial competition had ended; and the railways, now chastened and impoverished by automobile and air competition, were encouraged

to combine with a view to economical operation, as Roosevelt had recommended in his annual message of 1908.

The net result of this Progressive Era for trust and railway problems was to remove them from the political arena to administrative tribunals. Law and statesmanship cannot claim full credit for this happy consummation. With the immense growth of population and wealth since 1914, some trusts have cracked of their own weight, and unexpected competition has arisen both for them and the railroads. By 1920 the "utilities," as the electrical power companies are collectively called, were getting out of hand, and the automobile industry was about to eclipse iron and steel as the nation's biggest business.

4. The Big Stick in the Caribbean

"There is a homely adage which runs: 'Speak softly, and carry a big stick; you will go far.'" This remark, which Roosevelt used in more than one speech early in his administration, provided cartoonists with another Rooseveltian emblem to add to the toothy smile, thick glasses, and Rough Rider hat. What T.R. meant by the big stick was a strong navy; but the world feared it would be used to further political and economic "imperialism," even to conquer fresh territory in the Americas. Actually it was a very appropriate symbol for the methods that he used to get the Panama Canal started, to cure troubles in certain Caribbean republics, and to settle the Canadian-Alaskan boundary. Roosevelt accomplished much to modernize and build up the army and navy, but used them as a guarantee of peace. He evacuated Cuba, as McKinley had promised to do, intervened there once — as permitted by the Platt amendment — to restore order, and evacuated again. He initiated self-government in the Philippines. He gave the Hague Tribunal its first case, the Pious Fund dispute with Mexico. He instructed the American delegation to the Second Hague Conference to work for restriction of naval armaments, returned to China America's share of the Boxer war indemnity, smoothed over a dangerous controversy with Japan, and refused to antagonize her by building a great military base in the Philippines, as the armed forces wanted. In advance of most Americans, he appreciated that the United States, having become one of the greater world powers, must gradually assume world responsibilities; and Woodrow Wilson's refusal to do so until pushed into it by events, aroused his undying wrath.

Roosevelt inherited from McKinley as secretary of state, John Hay, whose experience as ambassador in London made him eager to meet the new British policy of friendship halfway. And that friendship persisted, despite alarm over the "invasion" of England by American shoes, steel rails, and cotton goods, which was merely a dumping of surplus products during a glut in the home market. There is no truth in the oft-repeated story of a secret Anglo-American alliance, but there was in effect, during the entire Progressive Era, a good

Anglo-American understanding. Downing Street, after a brief flirtation with Huerta in Mexico, gave Washington a free hand in the New World; and in return the state department refrained from any acts or expressions inimical to British interests, and supported British diplomacy in the Far East.

A first fruit of this understanding was a treaty clearing the way for the Panama Canal. New American responsibilities in the Caribbean and the Pacific made the speedy construction of an interoceanic canal vital. The Clayton-Bulwer Treaty stood in the way, but not the British government. The Hay-Pauncefote Treaty, signed 18 November 1901 and promptly ratified, superseded that controversial pact of 1850 and gave the United States a free hand to construct, operate, and protect an isthmian canal, subject only to the Suez Canal rules which forbade discrimination in tolls against foreign ships.

This canal had been talked about for at least four centuries, and two false starts had been made in the last century — by an American company that began one over the Nicaragua route but promptly went bankrupt; and by a French company, which did a good deal of work on the Panama route but quit in 1889 after spending $260 million and sacrificing hundreds of lives to tropical diseases. That company was now eager to recoup some of its losses by selling out to the United States. In the meantime a company financed in New York had bought a concession from Nicaragua, and by 1900 had as good as convinced Congress that Panama was an impossible "pest hole," and that the northern route was both healthy and practicable. Both companies employed expensive lobbyists in Washington. After an Isthmian Canal Commission, appointed by President McKinley and headed by Rear Admiral John G. Walker, had reported strongly in favor of the Panama route on the grounds of cost, length, and freedom from volcanic disturbances, Roosevelt became a vigorous advocate of that route. As a compromise, Congress on 28 June 1902 passed the Spooner Act. This authorized the President to acquire the French concession for $40 million if Colombia would cede a strip of land across the Isthmus of Panama "within a reasonable time," and upon reasonable terms; if not, the President was to open negotiations with Nicaragua, which Roosevelt at all costs wished to avoid. The Colombian chargé at Washington then signed a treaty granting the United States a hundred-year lease of a ten-mile-wide canal zone, for the lump sum of $10 million and an annual rental of $250,000.

The Colombian government rejected this treaty on 12 August 1903, in spite of a stiff warning from Hay that something unpleasant would happen if they did. One obstacle to ratification was the cession of sovereignty; the other was the $40 million coming to the French. That company had no right to sell its concession without the permission of Colombia, which naturally demanded a cut, especially as the company's charter was about to expire, leaving it with no assets but an incomplete ditch. Roosevelt and Hay never appreciated the reluctance of patriotic Colombians to cede sovereignty. They thought it was all a holdup.

Matters had reached an impasse by the summer of 1903, when Panama business men, agents of the French company, and United States army officers, began to plan a way out — the secession of Panama from Colombia. Roosevelt and Hay officially kept clear, but the President's sympathy became notorious, and the French company's agent in Washington advised a revolutionary junta at Panama to proceed in assurance of American assistance. On 19 October three United States war vessels were ordered to the probable scene of hostilities. On 2 November their commanders were instructed to occupy the Panama railway if a revolution broke out, and to prevent Colombia from landing troops within fifty miles of the Isthmus. The secretary of state cabled the United States consul at Panama, 3 November 1903, "Uprising on Isthmus reported. Keep Department promptly and fully informed." The consul replied that afternoon, "No uprising yet. Reported will be in the night"; and, a few hours later, "Uprising occurred tonight 6; no bloodshed. Government will be organized tonight."

It was. The revolution came off according to schedule. The one Colombian gunboat on station steamed away after firing one shell which killed a sleeping Chinaman in Panama City. A landing party from U.S.S. *Nashville* confronted troops landed by the Colombian government to restore its authority; the city fire brigade formed a Panama army, a provisional government was set up, and on 4 November a declaration of Panamanian independence was read in the plaza. Two days later Secretary Hay recognized the Republic of Panama, which by cable appointed the French Company's lobbyist its plenipotentiary at Washington. With him, on the 18th, Hay concluded a treaty by which Panama leased the Canal Zone "in perpetuity" to the United States and "to the entire exclusion of the exercise by Panama of any . . . sovereign rights, power or authority," for the same sum — $10 million down and $250,000 annual rent — that he had offered to Colombia.[1] Panama retained the titular sovereignty, as Colombia would have done; this was criticized in Congress but William Howard Taft, then secretary of war, said: "I agree that to the Anglo-Saxon mind a titular sovereignty is . . . a 'barren ideality,' but to the Spanish or Latin mind — poetic and sentimental, enjoying the intellectual refinements, and dwelling much on names and forms — it is by no means unimportant." So important, in fact, that Panamanians are now willing to risk their independence for the right to fly their flag over the Canal Zone.

The Roosevelt administration defended its action by citing Polk's treaty of 1846 with Colombia, by virtue of which the United States was conceded the right to land forces on the Isthmus to restore order and keep the Panama Railway running. Under that treaty, American forces had been landed during several previous Panama revolutions. But to stretch this right into an interven-

1. By a treaty of 1955 with Panama the annual rent has been raised to $1,930,000, and Presidents Eisenhower and Kennedy agreed to fly the Panama flag beside the American within the Canal Zone; but these concessions failed to satisfy Panama, whose president on 10 January 1964 demanded a revision of the treaty of 1903.

tion to prevent Colombia from recovering her lawful authority, flew in the face of international law and morality. And this has proved to be a source of infinite vexation. By exercising patience, Colombia, then recovering from a devastating civil war, could have been persuaded within a year to sign a reasonable treaty; and although only Colombia was hit by the big stick, all Latin America trembled. Subsequently, in the Wilson administration, the United States paid Colombia $25 million as a balm; but the wound to her pride rankles to this day, and the touchy little Republic of Panama has proved to be a very difficult neighbor to the canal. The United States is paying dear today for Roosevelt's impetuosity in 1903.

Roosevelt, over-eager to "make the dirt fly," made some ill-considered appointments to the first Canal Zone commission, who nullified the work of the engineer John F. Stevens, and the dirt would have flown to little purpose had he not thrown his weight in favor of a lock canal, as Stevens wanted, and appointed Colonel George W. Goethals chief engineer and autocrat of the Canal Zone in 1907. Open to commercial traffic in August 1914 and formally completed six years later, the Panama Canal was a triumph for American engineering and organization. No less remarkable was the sanitary work of Colonel William C. Gorgas (son of the Confederacy's chief of ordnance), which the discoveries of Finlay and Reed in Cuba made possible. His efforts and those of Goethals converted this area, including the cities of Panama and Colón, earlier described by a British visitor as "a hideous dungheap of moral and physical abomination," into a community of happy, healthy workers, many of them imported Jamaican Negroes.

Elsewhere in the Caribbean Roosevelt wielded the big stick energetically. A crisis arose over the question of European intervention for the collection of the Venezuelan debt, in 1902. Great Britain, Germany, and Italy established a blockade to force General Castro, the recalcitrant dictator, to come to terms. A showdown was avoided when Germany, discreetly pressured by Roosevelt, agreed to submit her claims to arbitration. The Hague Tribunal settled the dispute satisfactorily, scaling down the demands from some $40 million to $8 million and accepting a principle advanced by the Argentine publicist Luis Drago which outlawed the use of force for the collection of such claims. Roosevelt expressed a general satisfaction with this solution in a speech in which he said that England and Germany "kept with an honorable good faith" their disclaimer of violating the Monroe Doctrine.

Even more important was the President's announcement of the so-called "Roosevelt corollary" to the Monroe Doctrine. In his annual message of 1904 he declared, "Chronic wrongdoing, or an impotence which results in a general loosening of the ties of civilized society . . . may force the United States, however reluctantly, in flagrant cases of such wrongdoing or impotence, to the exercise of an international police power." The first occasion for such "police" action arose when in 1904 the financial affairs of the Dominican Republic fell into such a desperate condition, owing to members of the government stealing the customs receipts, that she was threatened with foreclosure by European creditors. Roosevelt than announced as a "corollary" to the Monroe Doctrine that, since we could not permit European nations forcibly to collect debts in the Americas, we must ourselves assume the responsibility of seeing that "backward" states fulfilled their financial obligations. He placed an American receiver-general in charge of Dominican revenues, arranging to apply 55 per cent of customs receipts to the discharge of debts, and the rest to current expenses. This division proved to be ample for Dominican domestic needs (which the old system of stealing 90 per cent had not); but as one revolution followed another, the fiscal protectorate had to be transformed into a military occupation, and that lasted until 1924. A dangerous precedent had been established, and within a decade the United States found herself involved in domestic as well as foreign affairs of Haiti, Honduras, and Nicaragua. So burdensome did this responsibility become, so offensive to Latin America, and so utterly futile (since the evacuation by American armed forces was inevitably followed by a dictatorship or a revolution) that in 1930 the Roosevelt corollary to the Monroe Doctrine was officially repudiated by the department of state.

5. Roosevelt and World Politics

For the first time the United States had a President whom the rulers of Europe looked upon as one who understood them, and could play their game. Theodore, like his cousin Franklin, enjoyed world politics. His mediation in the Russo-Japanese War, undertaken on the suggestion of the Japanese and German emperors, is the best example. Secretary Hay being in his last illness, the President negotiated directly with premiers and crowned heads, brought the two belligerents together, and broke the deadlock from which the Treaty of Portsmouth (5 September 1905) emerged. The wisdom of that treaty is now questionable. It probably saved Japan from a beating, but her government and press persuaded the Japanese people that Roosevelt's "big stick" had done them out of vast territorial gains. And a few years later, in violation of the treaty, Japan annexed Korea. The treaty established Japan as overlord in Manchuria and enabled her to become the dominant naval power in the Pacific. Between 1941 and 1945 the United States paid heavily for the long-term results of Roosevelt's meddling, for which, ironically enough, he was awarded the Nobel peace prize.

Only thirteen months after the signing of the Treaty of Portsmouth, Japan and the United States were brought to the brink of war by segregation of the small number of Japanese children in San Francisco in a single school. These "infernal fools in California," as Roosevelt called them, aroused violent anti-American feeling in Japan; but the President, by inviting the mayor and school board to Washington and entertaining them in the White House, persuaded them to rescind their order. His part of the bargain was to conclude the "gentleman's agreement" of 1907, in which the Japanese foreign office promised to discourage further emigration to the United States. That was followed by the Root-Takahira agreement of 1908 in which both countries reaffirmed the Open Door to China and promised to maintain the status quo in the Pacific. To convince Japan that she better had, Roosevelt resorted to a typical gesture, a cruise of the United States fleet around the world in 1908–9. Sixteen post-Spanish war battleships, under the command of "Fighting Bob" Evans of Santiago fame, circled the globe, calling at four South American ports, Auckland, Sydney, and Yokohama, where the sailors had a most enthusiastic reception. This gesture convinced the world that the United States was no longer a power to be trifled with; and at the same time it showed the United States Navy, forced to fuel and provision in foreign ports, that a much better balanced fleet, with destroyer escorts and a supply train, would be required in case of war.

Roosevelt had established for his country a right that she did not yet want, to be consulted in world politics; but in the Moroccan crisis of 1905–6 he intervened to very good purpose. French extension of control over chaotic Morocco was challenged by Germany. At the suggestion of William II, the President urged France to summon a conference on the North African question, and the American representative at this Algerian Conference, Henry White, was partly responsible for a convention which kept the peace in Europe for several years. The Senate ratified this Convention reluctantly, with the qualifying amendment that it involved no departure "from the traditional American foreign policy which forbids participation by the United States in the settlement of political questions which are entirely European in their scope." President Taft, sensing the unpopularity of Roosevelt's action, refrained from participation in the second Moroccan crisis of 1911.

Roosevelt made a great mistake by announcing in 1904 that "under no circumstances" would he be a candidate for the presidency in 1908. Once having made this self-denying gesture, he lost his hold over Congress during his last two years, since the members knew that they would soon have to look elsewhere for patronage and other favors. Yet his last two years of office were fruitful in reforms to which we have already alluded, such as the Hepburn Act and the Pure Food and Drug Act. And the annual presidential message of 1907 has become a classic text on the conservation of national resources.

Roosevelt himself, as more evidence accumulated of the arrogance and occasional rottenness of big business, and as a reaction against charges of subversion, socialism, treason, and insanity hurled against him by the metropolitan press, moved further to the left and even described himself as a "radical." There had been a brief panic in the stock market in 1903; and another — the worst between 1873 and 1929 — occurred in 1907. Both were caused by overextension of credit, wild speculation in stocks, and inflexible currency, but Wall Street blamed it all on Roosevelt's "attacks on business."

Actually, his administration stopped the 1907 landslide by pumping customs receipts into the menaced New York banks, selling $150 million in bonds and notes to them on credit, and authorizing them to use these as collateral for issuing currency. This ended the drain on gold and provided money to move crops that fall. Nevertheless, the Eastern banking and business world continued to denounce Theodore in much the same terms as they later applied to his cousin Franklin. He had offended so many people that foreign observers thought he had lost his grip. But his hold on simple folk increased as time went on, and there is no doubt that he would have been triumphantly re-elected in 1908 had he not tied his hands by the 1904 promise. He was still only 50 years old, and far better equipped to be President than any possible successor.

Roosevelt controlled the Republican convention of 1908 and put over the nomination on the first ballot of his favorite candidate, William H. Taft, secretary of war. The Democrats, having failed dismally with a conservative candidate in 1904, gave William J. Bryan his third presidential nomination. The effect was to stampede all disgruntled conservatives into the Taft camp; and although Bryan polled a million more votes than Parker had in 1904, he carried only the solid South and Nebraska, Colorado, Nevada, and Oklahoma.

Never did a presidential administration afford so much fun to press and public as "Teddy's." No President prior to Kennedy showed such vitality. There was hardly a day that the White House, without benefit of a publicity staff or a press conference, did not make front-page news; for Roosevelt was constantly making pronouncements on things that were not his particular concern. Embarrassing to him was the publication of his letters to "Dear Maria" (Mrs. Bellamy) Storer, wife of the American ambassador to Italy, urging her to call on the Pope and get a red hat for Archbishop Ireland. As an example of Roosevelt's quiet benevolence and good taste, Edwin Arlington Robinson, then living in a New York hall bedroom on $12 a week, was astonished one morning in 1905 to receive a letter from the White House warmly appreciating his first book of poems, and offering him a minor post in the customs house to give him security.

Young Lieutenant Douglas MacArthur, Roosevelt's aide in 1906, asked him to what he attributed his extraordinary popularity with the masses. To which he replied, "To put into words what is in their hearts and minds but not their mouths." That was it. Lincoln had the same gift.

To William H. Taft on 4 March 1909 Theodore Roosevelt handed over a government that had grown rapidly in prestige and power during the last eight years. The entire civil service had been stimulated by Roosevelt's vitality, no less than by knowledge that efficiency and intelligence would be recognized and rewarded. The whole tone and temper of government had changed for the better, an educated and public-spirited elite had again been attracted to public life, and popular interest in public affairs had never been more keen or intelligent. Yet in one respect Roosevelt failed as a leader. He inspired loyalty to himself rather than to progressive policies; he neglected, while he still possessed the power of patronage, to build up a progressive nucleus within the Republican party. The Old Guard drew a sigh of relief when Roosevelt, wishing to avoid embarrassing President Taft, embarked on a big-game hunting expedition in Africa.

L

Taft and Wilson

1909-1917

1. Taft Takes Over

"**B**IG BILL" TAFT — he rose five feet 10½ inches and weighed 300 pounds
when in the White House — was one of the most good-humored,
lovable men ever elected President of the United States, and one of the
unhappiest in that office. Of judicial, not political temper, he had held no
elective office excepting an Ohio judgeship prior to 1909, and had set his
sights on becoming a justice of the Supreme Court, which eventually he
attained. An ambitious wife and Theodore Roosevelt, who trusted Taft to
continue "my policies," thrust him, half appreciative and half apprehensive,
into the political arena. But the results of the election were gratifying. Taft
"ran ahead of his ticket" and polled a few more votes than Roosevelt had in
1904, whilst Bryan gathered fewer than on his previous two tries, carrying
only the solid South and some of the old Populist states. Taft apparently had
a mandate to go forward with Roosevelt progressivism.

In the measure that he failed, circumstances and personality were about
equally responsible. Yet it cannot fairly be said that he did fail. His image
before the American people in 1912, when he finished a bad third in a three-
cornered contest, was that of an amiable though stupid reactionary who had
"betrayed" the Progressive cause. After fifty years have elapsed we can state
with some confidence that this image was false. It would be more nearly
correct to say that the Progressives, represented by Theodore Roosevelt,
betrayed him. But Taft did lack the energy that a President must have to be
successful; he hated the drudgery of the office, and was inept in dealing with
Congress. Nevertheless, more of the Roosevelt program was enacted in the Taft
administration than in the Roosevelt administration!

President Taft followed the right instinct in choosing his own cabinet
instead of taking over Roosevelt's; but his choices did not include a single
Progressive until 1911, when he appointed secretary of war young Henry L.
Stimson, who had just been defeated for governor of New York.

His first political action was to try to unseat, as speaker of the House,
"Uncle Joe" Cannon of Illinois, a vulgar blatherskite who had become just
such a parliamentary "czar" as the late Speaker Reed. Under existing House
rules the speaker chose the members of every committee including the rules

committee which then — as in 1964 — was the bottleneck through which every bill had to pass before reaching the floor. A group of liberal Republican congressmen led by George W. Norris of Nebraska proposed to defeat Cannon for the speakership when Congress convened, in the hope of changing the rules and giving new legislation a chance. Taft openly supported them while President-elect; then let them down when Senator Aldrich, Henry C. Payne (chairman of the ways and means committee), and Cannon himself called on the President five days after his inauguration and promised to support the tariff revision that he dearly wanted, if he would "call off his dogs" that were baiting Cannon. "Uncle Joe" was re-elected speaker, and Taft got the Payne-Aldrich tariff which fell far short of what he wanted. But in 1911 Progressive Republicans combined with Democrats to curb the speaker's power; and next year, after the Democratic victory in congressional elections, Champ Clark of Missouri replaced Cannon.

Roosevelt had cannily refused to burn his fingers on tariff revision, although he believed, as did almost all progressives, that the high protective schedules of the Dingley tariff of 1897 were the "nursing mothers of monopoly." Taft made tariff reduction his first objective, and promptly called a special session of Congress to do it. The usual thing happened. Lobbyists deprecated loss of protection against European "pauper labor," consumers were not represented, and the Aldrich Senate bill and Payne House bill, when brought together in a conference committee, provided higher rates than the 1897 act which the Republicans had promised to revise downward. At that point the President put his foot down and obtained some concessions which persuaded him to sign the bill. A notoriously high duty on gloves, inserted to please a glove manufacturer who was a friend of Cannon, was struck out; a maximum-minimum principle, to help bargaining with other countries, was inserted for the first time in any American tariff act, and free trade with the Philippines, which Taft as a former governor general ardently wanted in justice to the Filipinos, was inserted. Hides, oil, and other raw materials were put on the free list, in addition to the "curling stones, false teeth, nux vomica, bird seed, and silk-worm eggs" which "Mr. Dooley" declared to be now "within th' reach iv all." Progressives in both houses, such as Norris, Beveridge and La Follette, who had fought vigorously against the bill, expected Taft to veto it, and thought they had enough votes to sustain his veto; but to their dismay he not only signed the Payne-Aldrich compromise but declared it to be "the best tariff bill that the Republican party ever passed." In retrospect, the Payne-Aldrich tariff, while not so good as its supporters claimed, was not nearly so bad as its opponents insisted. It was a slight revision, but in the right direction, downward.

Taft next alienated the Progressives' conservationist wing in the Ballinger-Pinchot controversy of 1909. This long and complicated brawl overshadowed more important issues in the public eye. The essence of it is that Gifford Pinchot, a crusader for conservation of natural resources, Roosevelt's close friend and chief forester, accused Richard A. Ballinger, secretary of the interior, of corruptly alienating part of the national domain to a Morgan-Guggenheim syndicate. President Taft, instead of handling the business himself, tossed it to a special committee of Congress, which vindicated Ballinger. But Pinchot won in the court of public opinion, largely owing to an effective presentation of his case by Louis D. Brandeis. After half a century has elapsed, it seems that Pinchot went off half-cock and that Ballinger was innocent of the charges; but the affair was played up for far more than it was worth by the "muckraker" periodicals, and drove a wedge between President and ex-President. Taft actually did as much or more than Roosevelt for conservation. He was the first to reserve federal lands where oil had been found, including Teapot Dome which President Harding tried to give away. He asked for and obtained from Congress the authority to reserve coal lands which Roosevelt had reserved without specific authority, and set up a bureau of mines as guardian of the nation's mineral resources. Pinchot was replaced by the head of the Yale school of forestry, and his policy was continued by the purchase, in 1911, of great timbered tracts in the Appalachians.

The President's ineptitude and alienation of progressive elements should not blind us to his achievements. During his term the Mann-Elkins Act of 1910 strengthened the interstate commerce commission by empowering it to suspend rate increases until and unless the reasonableness thereof were ascertained, and created a new commerce court to hear appeals from the commission. The long overdue postal savings bank and parcel post wanted by the people but opposed by banks and express companies, were provided by Congress. The merit system was expanded by the addition of more postmasters to the civil service list. New Mexico and Arizona, last of the continental territories save Alaska, became the 47th and 48th states of the Union; Alaska was organized as a territory. Oklahoma, the 46th state, had been admitted under Roosevelt. Approximately twice as many prosecutions for violation of the Sherman Act were instituted during Taft's four years in office as during Roosevelt's seven. Significant of the rapidly expanding envelope of law were two amendments of the Federal Constitution, both of which were promoted by Taft. The income tax Amendment XVI, and Amendment XVII transferring the election of United States Senators from state legislatures to the people, were adopted by Congress in 1909 and 1912 respectively and ratified the following year.

Since Taft was temperamentally unable to take the strong lead that Roosevelt had in reform legislation, he got little credit for these achievements. The Republicans lost the congressional elections of 1910. The basic cause of this upset was a sharp rise in the cost of living owing (the economists tell us) to a world shortage of gold, without a corresponding rise in wages. "Real" wages, in fact, had been stationary or declining since the turn of the century. The retail cost of basic foods consumed by workingmen rose 30 per cent in 1900–1910, while real wages in industry rose but a fraction of one per cent. The

Democrats, attributing a world-wide phenomenon to the Payne-Aldrich tariff, made hay in these elections, won a majority in the House for the first time since 1892 and narrowed the Republican majority in the Senate. Democratic governors were elected in several Eastern states, and in New Jersey Dr. Woodrow Wilson, president of Princeton University, took his first step toward a larger presidency.

2. Canada and the Caribbean

We left the Dominion of Canada prosperous and developing a sense of nationality under Sir Wilfrid Laurier, the liberal premier. In the decade 1893–1903, three disputes between Canada and the United States were settled by arbitration. The first was over seal fisheries in the Bering Sea; the second on the perennial question of American fishermen's rights on the coast of Newfoundland. Both arbitral decisions broadly upheld the Canadian case. But the third, over the Alaska boundary, was decided against Canada, with unfortunate results.

Just where the Alaskan "panhandle" ended and British Columbia began was disputed. The boundary had been vaguely described in the Anglo-Russian treaty of 1825. Nobody bothered much about it until 1898 when a gold strike in the Yukon made Canada insistent on a port of entry to her Yukon Territory through the Lynn Canal, on which the small American settlement of Skagway was situated. The Canadians insisted on a construction of the treaty which would have left Skagway well within their borders; the Americans demanded a line some hundred miles eastward. President Roosevelt considered the Canadian case "trumped up" and in 1903 consented to its settlement by an Anglo-American tribunal, three "impartial jurists" to each side; but he truculently informed the British government, through the curious medium of Justice Holmes, that if the board did not vote his way he would secure the boundary by armed force. The Senate only consented to the arbitration after receiving word from the White House that the three "impartial jurists" on our side would be Elihu Root, a former senator from the State of Washington, and Senator Lodge, at that time a notorious anglophobe. On the other side were two leading Canadians and Lord Alverstone, Lord Chief Justice of England.

This brandishing of the "big stick" worked. Although it has never been proved, there is strong suspicion that Alverstone was ordered by the British government to vote with the Americans, as the price of continued Anglo-American friendship in the face of rising German naval power. At any rate, that is substantially what Alverstone did. The compromise line, determined by a four-to-two vote, left Skagway inside Alaska but gave Canada the heads of the Lynn, Portland, and other inlets, and considerable territory claimed by the United States. Compromise though it was, the decision aroused violent resentment in Canada: England had let her down, and truckled to the Yankees.

Like many other things in that era, reality was not so bad as appearance. Most Canadian historians now agree that their country argued a very poor case, and that the compromise did her no injury. But the controversy left a bitter taste and was partly responsible for the electorate spitting out with contempt the proffered American sugarplum of reciprocity.

President Taft in 1910 initiated a renewal of tariff reciprocity with Canada, the first since 1867, partly to ameliorate the Payne-Aldrich tariff, partly out of sheer friendliness; he owned a summer estate at Murray Bay, P.Q., and knew many leading Canadians intimately. Laurier, who had recently obtained for Canada the right to conclude her own tariff agreements, accepted the invitation, hoping thus to lower the Canadian tariff and open new markets in the United States. The Democratic majority in Congress passed a reciprocity bill which, to be valid, had to be matched by a similar bill in the Canadian parliament. For a country of 92 million population to offer practically free trade in farm, forest, and fish products to a country of 7.2 million was unprecedented, and much to the smaller country's advantage; but the "infant industries" of Canada, basking under protection, and the Canadian Pacific Railway, opposed the measure violently. Speaker Champ Clark helped whip up Canadian sentiment against it by a stupid speech in which he predicted that reciprocity would be the prelude to planting the Stars and Stripes over "every foot" of North America; and an obscure congressman proposed that Taft be instructed to open negotiations with Great Britain for the annexation of Canada. There, the "King and Country" argument was freely employed, and one of Rudyard Kipling's worst poems, "Our Lady of the Snows," was widely circulated to rebuke the impudent Yankees.

That is exactly what the Lady of the Snows did. Sir Wilfrid had to appeal to the country in a general election in September 1911. His French following, led by Henri Bourassa the eloquent Quebec nationalist, deserted the Liberal banner, and the Conservatives won 133 seats to the Liberals' 86. The *Boston Herald* thus announced the result: "Snow Lady Hits Uncle Sam in the Stomach. Grains and Foodstuffs Rise Sharply at All American Supply Centers."

Robert Laird Borden, a Nova Scotian of Scot and Loyalist ancestry and a dour, rugged personality, now succeeded suave Laurier as prime minister of the Dominion. During Sir Wilfrid's fifteen years' rule, his dream of making Canada a nation before the world had come measurably nearer fulfillment, but his hope for internal harmony had been shattered. With no statesman of his caliber to lead them, the French of Quebec became more unreasonable.

One month before "Snow Lady" handed it to Uncle Sam, President Taft submitted to the Senate two important treaties with Great Britain and France. World peace was very close to his heart, and the best method of securing it, he believed, was by judicial procedure. Hence these treaties provided for arbitration at the Hague or elsewhere of all disputes "justiciable in their nature," including those involving territory and "national honor." These treaties were received with acclamation by most of the American press as well as by Andrew Carnegie and the peace societies. But the Irish-American and German-American press, seeing their last chance of a third war with England disappearing, and encouraged by Roosevelt, led a virulent campaign against the British treaty. Both treaties were so emasculated by amendments in the Senate that the President sadly withdrew them.

The Senate was better advised in rejecting certain treaties with Caribbean countries, but the Taft administration managed to do what it wanted in that region without treaties. Philander C. Knox, secretary of state, was a corporation lawyer who cherished an odd sort of idealism to the effect that obtaining loans for the turbulent Central American republics, or pumping investment capital into them, would stabilize their governments, and cure their poverty. Knox (wrote his predecessor Root) was "antipathetic to all Spanish-American modes of thought and feeling" — a description which, unfortunately, fits many of his successors in the state department. This was illustrated by his handling of volcanic Nicaragua, where a revolution broke out against dictator Zelaya in 1909. Adolfo Díaz, who emerged triumphant (and who, miraculously, lived for 54 more years) was refused recognition until he had accepted an American bankers' loan to refund the foreign debt, and consented to American supervision of the Nicaraguan customs service. This concession occasioned, if it did not cause, an uprising against Díaz in 1912. In that civil war the intervention of about a thousand United States marines under Major Smedley D. Butler was decisive; after they had routed the rebels in a pitched battle at Coyotepe (4 October 1912), the rebellion collapsed.

Taft, in his annual message of 1912, defended this so-called "dollar diplomacy." He had gladly supported American bankers in helping "the financial rehabilitation of such countries," which needed only "a measure of stability and the means of financial regeneration to enter upon an era of peace and prosperity." Democrats and Progressives alike raised a furor against "dollar diplomacy," although it differed not from Roosevelt's with the Dominican Republic. And President Wilson continued much the same policy, even after it had been demonstrated that dollars and marines could not cure Caribbean instability.

President Taft was equally unhappy in his relations with Mexico, where *the* revolution against Porfirio Díaz, dictator for thirty-five years following the death of Juárez, broke out on 20 November 1910. Díaz had given his country order at the expense of every sort of liberty. The national domain of 135 million acres was cut up into latifundia, or used to augment the already swollen estates of fewer than a thousand great land owners, the *haciendados*. Díaz expropriated and allotted to his favorites the communal lands of the Indian villages, and the newcomers exacted free labor from landless peons by keeping them in perpetual debt for food and supplies. Education remained in the hands of the Catholic church. Generous concessions were given to foreign mining and other interests. The Mexican government was more autocratic than Czarist Russia, the ruling class more concentrated and powerful, the condition of the people worse. Taft, and Republicans generally, regarded Díaz as a great statesman, not only because he preserved order, but "for the reason" (wrote the President to Mrs. Taft) "that we have two billions American capital in Mexico that will be greatly endangered if Díaz were to die."

This revolution which, after many vicissitudes, regenerated Mexico, obtained slight sympathy in Washington, and no support. Francisco I. Madero, a gentle, dreamy liberal who succeeded Díaz, was unable to keep order or satisfy the land-hungry peons. In February 1913 a counter-revolution by half the army and most of the *haciendados* cornered Madero in Mexico City. At that juncture, a super-gangster, General Victoriano Huerta, won the support of Henry Lane Wilson the professional diplomat whom Taft had appointed ambassador to Mexico, and who with singular lack of judgment called Madero "a man of disordered intellect . . . comparable to a Nero." Wilson helped Huerta engineer a coup d'état against Madero and presented him to the diplomatic corps as the next president of Mexico. Huerta's henchmen promptly murdered both Madero and the vice president. It remained for Woodrow Wilson to try to undo what Henry Lane Wilson had done.

3. Insurgents and the Election of 1912

Theodore Roosevelt, after enjoying good hunting in Africa and a triumphal progress through Europe, returned to New York in June 1910. Greeted with hysterical enthusiasm, he settled down at Sagamore Hill to pursue his many nonpolitical interests. The weekly *Outlook,* of which he became associate editor, afforded him an organ; but the role of sage was uncongenial to "Teddy," and the public would not be denied seeing and hearing him. Before the summer was over, he was making public addresses in the West, indicating unmistakably that shooting lions and dining with crowned heads had not dulled his fighting edge for reform. His ideas, clarified and systematized as the "New Nationalism," included not merely his former policies of honesty in government, regulation of big business and conservation of natural resources, but the relatively new conception of social justice — the reconstruction of society by political action. This principle involved vigorous criticism of recent decisions of the Supreme Court as largely reconstituted by Taft (only Justices Holmes and Day remained of Roosevelt's appointees), which had nullified social legislation in the states. In his Osawatomie speech of 31 August 1910 Roosevelt announced, "I stand for the square deal . . . I mean not merely that I stand for fair play under the present rules of the game, but . . . for having those rules changed so as to work for a more substantial equality of opportunity and of reward for equally good service. . . . We must drive special interests out of politics."

Conservative Republicans shuddered and President Taft worried. "I have had a hard time," he wrote to T.R. in May 1910. "I have been conscientiously trying to carry out your policies." But the two old friends were being pulled apart. Insurgents and displaced progressives like Pinchot were continually flattering Roosevelt and entreating him to save the country in 1912, on the assumption that Taft had surrendered to the Old Guard.

After the Democratic victories of 1910 and the Republicans' loss of the House, it was clear that Taft could not succeed himself. Early in 1911 Senator La Follette, spokesman for the "insurgents," organized a National Progressive Republican League to liberalize the Republican party. Upon obtaining what he thought to be Roosevelt's promise not to run again, La Follette became a candidate for the Republican nomination. But he was unable to build up much strength outside the Mississippi valley, and when addressing a convention of nation-wide newspaper men early in 1912 he collapsed and babbled incoherently. This incident lost La Follette an influential part of his following. Insurgents who preferred Roosevelt anyway now flocked to their old leader, who on 21 February announced, "My hat is in the ring." Bored by inactivity, Roosevelt was easily persuaded that he was indispensable to carry on progressive policies. His public utterances became increasingly radical. He urged that democracy be given an economic as well as a political connotation, declared that the rich man "holds his wealth subject to the general right of the community to regulate its business use as the public welfare requires," and that the police power of the state should be broadened to embrace all necessary forms of regulation. On the political side he advocated not only the initiative and the referendum, but the recall of judicial decisions; since, as his friend Brooks Adams pointed out, the Supreme Court had arrogated the powers of a third legislative chamber to quash reform legislation. Roosevelt's radicalism alienated thousands of Republican voters and cost him the support of friends such as Lodge, Knox, Root, and Stimson.

La Follette stayed in the fight, and the three-cornered contest for the Republican nomination became unseemly and bitter. Taft denounced Roosevelt for stirring up class hatred; Roosevelt accused Taft of biting the hand that fed him; La Follette described the ex-President as a conceited playboy; and many other things were said that would better have been left unsaid. Roosevelt knew that he could not win against the regular party organization, but wherever the law permitted he entered presidential preference primaries in the hope that a display of popularity might frighten the Old Guard. Thirteen states chose delegates through popular primaries, and in these Roosevelt obtained 278 delegates, Taft 46, and La Follette 36. Roosevelt had an overwhelming support by the rank and file, but the bosses were for Taft, and the Republican "rotten boroughs" in the South returned a solid block of Taft delegates who represented little more than federal office-holders. Credentials of some 200 delegates were in dispute. The conservatives, by electing Elihu Root temporary chairman, obtained control of the convention machinery and awarded almost every contested seat to a Taft man. On the ground that he had been robbed, Roosevelt instructed his friends to walk out, and Taft was easily renominated. Old-timers thought of the split Democratic convention of 1860, and shuddered.

Roosevelt and his followers at once took steps to found a new party. On 5 August 1912 the first Progressive party convention met at Chicago amid scenes of febrile enthusiasm. "We stand at Armageddon, and we battle for the Lord!" announced Roosevelt to enraptured followers, who paraded around the convention hall singing "Onward, Christian Soldiers" and other stirring melodies. Another remark of the beloved leader, "I am feeling like a bull moose," gave the new party an appropriate symbol, beside the Republican elephant and the Democratic donkey.

Denial of the nomination to Roosevelt, and the subsequent formation of the Bull Moose party, brief though that party's life proved to be, were crucial in political history. They squeezed liberal and progressive elements out of the "Grand Old Party" and gave the Democrats their first real opportunity since the Civil War.

The Progressive party hoped to break the solid South; but Roosevelt had entertained Booker Washington at dinner at the White House, and the South had a candidate of her own. This was Woodrow Wilson, born in Staunton, Virginia, in 1856, a year earlier than Taft, two years earlier than Roosevelt. Son and grandson of Presbyterian ministers, Wilson followed a quiet academic career until 1902, when he became president of Princeton University. While Roosevelt fought political privilege in the nation, Wilson contended with social privilege at Princeton. His attempts to break up the club system and the graduate school ran afoul of wealthy alumni and foundered. Wilson then stepped off the academic vessel.

Politics in that era were considered closed to professors, even to those with a national reputation for political literature such as Wilson. But it so happened that in 1910 the Democrats of New Jersey wished to achieve respectability with a new sort of candidate. At the suggestion of George Harvey of *Harper's Weekly*, the bosses nominated Wilson and the people elected him governor. Chosen for the job of window dressing, Wilson proceeded to clean up the shop. New Jersey gasped, Harvey dropped him as an ingrate, but a silent gentleman from Texas named Edward M. House took him up, and Wilson became a leading candidate for the presidential nomination in 1912.

The Democratic party had changed singularly little since the Civil War. It was composed of a progressive Western wing represented by Bryan; Irish-Americans of the big Eastern cities and Chicago and recently naturalized immigrants who followed the Irish bosses; the solid South, including the Snopses, the rednecks, and almost every white man in the late Confederacy; and multimillionaire William Randolph Hearst with his nation-wide string of yellow journals. Only tradition and the hope of victory held these curiously incongruous elements together, but the issues of liquor and religion that split the party in 1924 had not arisen, and Southerners sympathized with rebels against Wall Street. In only one election since the Civil War (1904) had the party polled less than 43 per cent of the total vote cast for president; but it wanted leadership. Bryan had thrice failed, and the majority leaders in Congress were elderly and timid. When the Democratic national convention met in June 1912, the majority were pledged for Champ Clark of Missouri, candidate of Tammany Hall and of Hearst. Congressman Oscar W. Underwood of Alabama was candidate of the "Bourbons," as the Democratic Old Guard was called; Governor Wilson represented the progressive wing. William Jennings Bryan, still a power in his party, required all his art and eloquence to "drive the money-changers from the temple" and obtain the nomination of Woodrow Wilson on the forty-sixth ballot.

The presidential election then became a three-cornered contest between Taft, Roosevelt, and Wilson; but really between the two last as rival bidders for the popular feeling against privilege. It was a year of social unrest. A new syndicalist movement, the Industrial Workers of the World, which had organized the migratory harvest hands of the West, was now contesting the skilled-worker field with the American Federation of Labor. The I.W.W. took charge of a great strike in the polyglot textile city of Lawrence, Massachusetts, and displayed to the shocked middle class red banners with godless mottoes. Incidentally, the Lawrence strike brought out the fact that the woolen industry, which enjoyed the highest protection under the Payne-Aldrich tariff, was paying starvation wages; male operatives earned a maximum of $10 for a 54-hour week. Thus the campaign was fought with revolution looming as an alternative to reform; and in that year the Socialist party under Eugene V. Debs polled 6 per cent of the total vote, highest in their history.

Taft and the Republicans accepted the ultra-conservative role now thrust upon them, preaching checks and balances and protection of minorities as the essence of freedom. There was little to choose between the Democratic and Progressive platforms. The latter, as Roosevelt said, "represented the first effort on a large scale to translate abstract formulas of economic and social justice into concrete American nationalism." With the Roosevelt doctrine of regulation the Democrats substantially agreed; Wilson's "New Freedom" was composed of the same ingredients as Roosevelt's "New Nationalism." Their method of campaigning, however, had no more in common than their personalities. Roosevelt, with biblical imagery and a voice like a shrilling fife, stirred men to wrath, to combat, and to antique virtue; Wilson, serene and confident, lifted men out of themselves by phrases that sang in their hearts, to a vision of a better world. It was the Old Testament against the New.

The writer, who cast his first presidential ballot that year, asked a middle-aged gentleman at the polls how to vote: "Vote for Roosevelt, pray for Taft, but bet on Wilson!" was the reply. Wilson received only 42 per cent of the popular vote but won an overwhelming majority in the electoral college. Roosevelt carried California, Michigan, South Dakota, Washington, Minnesota, and Pennsylvania. Taft, with 23 per cent of the vote, carried only Utah and Vermont. Roosevelt's percentage of the vote was 27, and if that could have been added to the President's, Taft would have won.

A popular cartoon the morning after depicted a cocked-hatted Federalist, a log-cabin Whig, assorted Anti-Masons, Greenbackers, and the like, welcoming a limping elephant to "The Home for Old Parties." Ardent Progressives thought back to 1856 and ahead to 1916; Wilson would be just another bland Buchanan. But Roosevelt told a friend, "We are beaten. You can't hold a party like the Progressives together. . . . *There are no loaves and fishes.*" And how right he was! The Old Guard neither died nor surrendered. The Republicans obtained 127 members in the House as against 18 Progressives; and nothing was left but deflated enthusiasm and a defeated candidate to keep the Bull Moose alive. Many good men, such as Senator Albert J. Beveridge of Indiana, were lost to politics; but in his case at least the country benefited, because Beveridge concentrated on his classic biography of Chief Justice Marshall. President Taft became professor of constitutional law at Yale, and later attained his heart's desire, chief justiceship of the Supreme Court.

Woodrow Wilson, instead of playing the role of Buchanan, welded his party into a fit instrument of his purpose "to square every process of our national life again with the standards we so proudly set up at the beginning and have always carried at our hearts." Thus, the election of 1912 began an era in American political history that still endures, one in which the Democratic party replaced the Republican as the party of new ideas and positive leadership. After stand-patters had ousted progressives from the Republican party's organization, Wilson took them over and "stole the Bull Moose's thunder." Theodore Roosevelt's twin principles of social justice at home and vigorous leadership abroad have been forwarded by every Democratic President; whilst Republican presidents and defeated Republican presidential candidates, have tended to check reform at home and retire to isolation in foreign policy.

4. *The First Wilson Administration*

Americans like myself who were so fortunate as to be born in the late nineteenth century and brought up in the early twentieth, often look upon the years prior to 1914 as a golden age of the Republic. In part, this feeling was due to our youth; in part to the fact that the great middle class could command goods and services that are now beyond their reach. But there was also a euphoria in the air, peace among the nations, and a feeling that justice and prosperity for all was attainable through good will and progressive legislation. Even chronically pessimistic Henry Adams wrote in his *Education* that, owing to Roosevelt's successful efforts to end the Russo-Japanese War, "for the first time in 1500 years a true Roman *Pax* was in sight."

Yet few people expected more than a respectable presidency. Wilson lacked the common touch, and loved humanity in the abstract rather than people in particular. He was fully as "red-blooded" as Roosevelt; had played football at Princeton and helped coach the team when a professor. But he could not mingle with crowds to advantage or talk naturally with horse wranglers and prizefighters. Through eight years of office he was always aloof and often alone. "Wilson is clean, strong, high-minded and cold-blooded," wrote warm-hearted Franklin K. Lane who became his secretary of the interior. Wilson's warm affections embraced only family and a few friends; his puckish humor, often at his own expense, was shown only to intimates. He was very stubborn and prone to take refuge from facts in generalities. Loving the quiet places of life and preferring the slow ways of persuasion to the quick ones of force, his misfortune was to be President in an era of fierce international strife and internal discord.

Colonel House, who had earned his honorary and incongruous military title by unofficially advising a governor of Texas, now became the President's closest friend and adviser. The Colonel was no "Texas type" but a well traveled and cosmopolitan gentleman of independent means who was interested in getting things done in a progressive direction. He had published anonymously a utopian novel, *Philip Dru, Administrator*, in which one may find much of the New Freedom, and the New Deal too. House helped the President to select his cabinet. Bryan as secretary of state, which insured the support of his immense following, appeared to be a master-stroke until there was work for Bryan to do. William G. McAdoo, the President's campaign manager and future son-in-law, became secretary of the treasury. Lindley M. Garrison, a New Jersey judge whom Wilson appointed secretary of war, was dropped when war became imminent. Lane, Canadian by birth and Californian by residence, proved a good secretary of the interior to reconcile the Far West with conservation. The others were nonentities. The cabinet was not a strong group. The majority were Southerners, as by the rule of seniority were most of the chairmen of House and Senate committees. New England, for the first time since Jackson's administration was not represented, although Massachusetts, for the first time since Jefferson's, had voted with Virginia.

Wilson's inaugural address was a stirring plea for action on the tariff, conservation, banking, and regulation of "the larger economic interests of the nation," in the interest of "humanity." It concluded: "Men's hearts wait upon us; men's lives hang in the balance. . . . I summon all honest men, all patriotic, all forward-looking men, to my side. God helping me, I will not fail them, if they will counsel and sustain me."

When Congress met on 7 April 1913, President Wilson revived a practice abandoned by Jefferson, of addressing both houses in person. A slight thing in itself, this act caught popular approval. It restored the President's initiative in law-making and established good relations between "the two ends of Pennsylvania Avenue." For Wilson's power over men left him when he stepped off the rostrum; unlike Roosevelt, he could not persuade or browbeat a recalcitrant congressman in private conversation. But 114 out of 290 Democratic members of the House were there for the first time, and readily followed him.

Congress had been summoned to a special session to revise the tariff. The resulting Underwood tariff of 3 October 1913 was the lowest since the Civil War. Duties were reduced on 958 items and more than a hundred were placed on the free list. Appended to the Underwood tariff bill was a graduated federal tax on incomes above $3000, constitutional since Amendment XVI (1913) overrode the earlier Supreme Court decision that an income tax was unconstitutional. Despite the jeremiads of business, the new tariff worked admirably during the few years of peace in which it could be tested, and the income tax brought not only abundant revenue but a mass of statistical information about the distribution of the national wealth that was of immense value to lawmakers of the future. And his victory in the matter of the tariff clinched the President's control of Congress.

The greatest measure of Wilson's first year was the Federal Reserve Act of 23 December 1913, which reconstructed the national banking and currency system. The existing system, inelastic and obsolete, had contributed largely to the panic of 1907. A great central bank would have been the ideal substitute; but the tradition of Jackson's contest with the B.U.S. was still strong in the Democratic party, and federal investigation had uncovered the existence of a so-called "money trust" controlled by a handful of New York and Boston financiers. By the Federal Reserve Act, drafted by Carter Glass of Virginia, the country was divided into twelve districts, each with a federal reserve bank which was a private corporation empowered to issue banknotes against commercial paper and other liquid assets. The Federal Reserve Board, appointed by the President and connected with the treasury department, controls the rate of discount and superintends the twelve federal reserve banks, which in turn are articulated with such local banks as wish to become members of the system. That the Democratic party, with its rural constituencies, could have passed the most important piece of financial legislation since Hamilton's day was no less remarkable than the persistency with which President Wilson kept Congress to its task, even refusing a Christmas recess until this bill was ready for his signature. Wilson serenely ignored the torrent of abuse heaped on him by the big bankers; and the Federal Reserve Act is clearly the crowning achievement of his domestic legislation.

A law establishing the Federal Trade Commission and the Clayton Antitrust Act of 1914, enacted repeated recommendations by President Roosevelt — who refused to admit the connection. The Clayton Act included what Samuel Gompers called "labor's charter of freedom": a section declaring that unions could never be considered unlawful combinations *per se*; that strikes, boycotting, and picketing were not, as such, violations of federal law; and that the injunction could no longer be used by federal courts in labor disputes.

This list does not exhaust the reform and social legislation initiated by Wilson and enacted by Congress. A rural credits law, a workmen's compensation act for the federal civil service, and a law excluding from interstate commerce the products of child labor, were passed in 1916.[1] The La Follette Seamen's Act of 1915, culmination of twenty years' agitation by Andrew Furuseth of the seamen's union, did much for sailors' well-being but did not, as its advocates predicted, restore American supremacy at sea. Nor, for that matter, did the United States Shipping Board, created in 1916. All in all, the Democratic party exhibited the most harmonious co-operation between Capitol and White House since Grant's administration. It proved that statesmanship was no monopoly of the Republicans, and it took over the Progressives' weapons, lock, stock, and barrel.

5. Woodrow Wilson and Mexico

In a speech of 17 October 1913 President Wilson announced to the doubting ears of Latin America that the United States would never add a foot to her territory by conquest, nor did she; but Wilson continued in the Caribbean the "dollar diplomacy" of Taft and Knox which he had denounced. Nicaragua was persuaded to sign a treaty similar to Roosevelt's with Panama, but with no cession of sovereignty, giving the United States the exclusive right to build a Nicaragua canal, and granting a 99-year lease of two small islands and a site for a naval base, which was never used. Haiti, in a state of appalling anarchy and degradation, was occupied in 1915 by United States Marines, and nineteen years elapsed before they could complete their work of pacification and road building, and withdraw. The Dominican Republic, at the same time, was advanced from the status of a financial receivership to that of a Marine Corps occupation, which lasted until 1924. Sumner Welles of the state department then set up a democratic government which was promptly overthrown by the dictator Trujillo, who lasted until 1961. And Haiti, after being evacuated by the Marines, began slipping back into her old ways, and at the time of writing is under another cruel and ruthless dictator. In Asia, however, Wilson renounced American participation in the three-power bankers' loan to China, which Knox had arranged.

From Taft and Knox, Wilson and Bryan inherited a serious problem about Mexico. Bully Huerta, having been installed president as the result of a coup which the American minister helped to pull off, aimed to set up a regime similar to that of Porfirio Díaz, including the protection of foreign investments. England recognized him; Wilson recalled the mischievous American minister and refused recognition. At the same time there was a controversy with Britain over shipping tolls in the Panama Canal. We were obliged by treaty to treat all nations' ships equally, but Congress defiantly passed a

1. The last was declared unconstitutional by the Supreme Court, as was a second law passed in 1918, laying special taxes on factories employing children under 14. Congress in 1924 initiated a child-labor amendment to override these decisions, but it failed of ratification.

law in 1912 exempting American-flag ships from tolls. By a secret agreement between Colonel House and Sir William Tyrrell, secretary to the British foreign minister, Wilson promised to press Congress to repeal the tolls exemption — and Congress did; whilst Tyrrell agreed that the foreign office would withdraw recognition of Huerta and follow our lead in Mexico, which it did.

Apart from this sensible agreement, Wilson's Mexican policy floundered. Huerta created an "incident" by arresting the crew of Admiral Henry Mayo's barge at Tampico. Although they were promptly released, the Admiral demanded an apology and a salute to the flag; Huerta declined, and on 21 April 1914 Admiral Frank F. Fletcher, under orders from Washington, landed a force at Vera Cruz (selected for this demonstration in order to choke off Huerta's consignments of munitions from Germany), and captured the city against armed resistance, mostly sniping from buildings.

It looked as if a second Mexican War were beginning, with Wilson playing the role of Polk. Instead, Wilson adopted "watchful waiting," as he called it, and by occupying Vera Cruz and its customs house, Huerta's only source of cash was closed. This starved him out of office, he fled the country in July 1914, and American forces evacuated Vera Cruz. A victory for Wilson, apparently; but Huerta's departure made matters worse, because all Mexican political elements splintered into factions under rival leaders, each printing money, raising soldiers, killing, looting, and destroying property. The principal rivals were Emiliano Zapata, an illiterate Indian whose chief concern was to give the peons land in his state of Morelos, which he reduced to anarchy in the process; Pancho Villa, a jolly, swashbuckling bandit who controlled most of the north; and General Venustiano Carranza, a well-educated liberal with a claim to be the constitutionally elected president.

William Jennings Bryan was the strangest secretary of state in the history of the Republic. He was democratic to the extent of inviting casual visitors into his inner office to "see the wheels go round." His sincere desire to preserve peace was expressed in the promotion of compulsory arbitration treaties with all and sundry nations. He had so little sense of dignity as to go on the Chautauqua circuit, along with Tyrolean yodelers and vaudeville acts. He did not even pretend to understand Mexico; after hearing a cogent report on the situation by the President's special agent Bryan remarked, "I just can't understand why those people are fighting their brothers!" And he went so far, on one occasion, to allude to Pancho Villa, in whose presence no virtuous woman was safe, as a "Sir Galahad." So Wilson let Bryan play with arbitration treaties, and handled Mexican policy himself. He and Secretary Lansing, who succeeded Bryan in mid-1915, tried again and again, alone or with the help of the "A.B.C. Powers" — Argentine, Brazil, and Chile — to bring all Mexican revolutionists to a "get-together," make peace, and hold a fair election. Carranza thwarted all such efforts because he considered himself to be the constitutionally elected president, and saw no more reason to make tenders to Villa and Zapata than Lincoln did to Davis. Owing to this intransigence, Wilson acquired an intense dislike for Carranza, a man of his own age and similar character: honest, dogmatic, stubborn. Wilson stuck out his long chin, pursed his prim lips, and stared angrily through his pince-nez at Carranza, while Carranza, his beard bristling, glared back at Wilson through steel-rimmed glasses and refused to budge an inch.

The Mexican won. On 19 October 1915 the United States and the A.B.C. Powers, augmented by Guatemala and Uruguay, recognized Carranza as the legitimate president. But for two or three years he was unable to bring about even a truce in the civil war. Now came to the fore Pancho Villa, whom righteous Wilson and simple Bryan had favored. Since he had nothing to lose and everything to gain by embroiling his country with the United States, Villa in January 1916 murdered in cold blood seventeen American mining engineers. Two months later he raided the town of Columbus, New Mexico, set fire to it, and killed some sixteen citizens. Wilson ordered a large part of the regular army and the national guard to the border, and a column over 6000 strong under General John J. ("Black Jack") Pershing pursued Villa some 300 miles into Mexico (April 1916). The fox went to earth, and Carranza threw every obstacle in the way of the hounds, demanding their withdrawal in a bitter, insulting note. Wilson replied calmly, but required the release of twenty-three American soldiers captured by Carranza forces — or else. The Mexican yielded on that point, but won his main objective. Wilson, now that war with Germany had become probable, followed his military advisers in pulling all American troops out of Mexico by early February 1917, without taking Villa. The cost of this intervention was well worth the practice it afforded the army, but the results were nil, and Wilson had to resume "watchful waiting" as the alternative to war.

Carranza now had a respite in which he promulgated the Constitution of 1917, on which the government of Mexico rests today; but its nationalization of church and oil lands lit a fresh dispute with the United States which smoldered during the First World War, and blazed up in the 1920's. By that time Carranza, Zapata, and Villa had been assassinated, and General Álvaro Obregón was President of Mexico. Carranza, for standing stiffly on the principle of nonintervention, for letting his country work out her own destiny, has become one of the heroes of modern Mexico. That he reached that stature was due in no small measure to the patience and forbearance of the man he detested, Woodrow Wilson.

Wilson's achievements during his first term were remarkable. The Princeton professor had become leader of a party refractory to leadership and converted it from state-rights tradition to enlightened nationalism. But complaints were being voiced both from the left and the right. The Bryan wing of the party in 1913–14 demanded legislation to destroy the financial oligarchy of New York and Boston, regulate the stock exchanges, place a heavy tax on corporations, and more stringent anti-trust laws. They got none of these things, and organized labor did not obtain the restriction on unlimited immigration that it wanted. The Negroes, whose leaders had supported Wilson in 1912, got less than nothing. Racial segregation was extended to almost every federal department, and there took place a wholesale firing of Negro postmasters and other minor federal officials in the South; since (as Wilson's collector of internal revenue in Georgia announced), "A Negro's place is in the cornfield." In the congressional elections of 1914 the Democratic majorities in both houses were much reduced, mostly owing to disillusioned Progressives deserting Wilson after he had placated the bankers by putting "safe" men in charge of the federal reserve system. Judged by the test case of Mexico, Wilson had shown little capacity for leadership in world affairs; that would come under the greater test of the war in Europe. Nevertheless, according to Brooks Adams's definition of administration as "the capacity of co-ordinating . . . conflicting social energies in a single organism, so adroitly that they shall operate as a unity," Wilson had proved himself a great administrator.

The First World War: The Neutrality Period

1914-1917

1. America's Reaction to the War

BETWEEN THE FIRING on Fort Sumter and the attack on Pearl Harbor there was no shock to American public opinion comparable to that of the outbreak of the European war in August 1914. Almost every shade of American opinion had assumed that a general European war was unthinkable, because nobody cared to think about it. International arbitration was making notable progress, and the two Hague Conventions as well as the London Naval Conference of 1909 were devoted to making war unlikely to occur, or less horrible if it did. Norman Angell's *The Great Illusion* (1910) proved that modern war was unprofitable for both victors and vanquished. So who would dare to start one? There might be little wars — we were on the brink of one with Mexico — but surely no more big ones after the Russo-Japanese War? Balkan wars in 1912–13 caused some misgivings; but these, it was assumed, were just squabbles of petty princes. Surely the so-called Concert of Europe, which meant the foreign offices of the leading powers in consultation, would prevent any really big conflict from breaking out?

That Concert fell into cacophony when Austria-Hungary declared war on Serbia (28 July 1914) for presumably harboring the terrorist organization which assassinated Archduke Franz Ferdinand. Germany backed her ally Austria to the limit, Russia mobilized in the hope of protecting her small ally, and Germany declared war on Russia and on France, Russia's ally (1–3 August). German armies crashed through neutral Belgium to crush France; and Britain, honoring her pledge to defend Belgian neutrality, declared war on Germany.

The initial American reaction was horror, disgust, and determination to keep out of it. President Wilson proclaimed American neutrality on 4 August, and in a message to the Senate on the 19th declared, "The United States must be neutral in fact as well as in name. . . . We must be impartial in thought as well as in action, must put a curb upon our sentiments." Walter Hines Page, American ambassador at London, later an ardent advocate of supporting the Allies, wrote to Colonel House in August that America presented a "magnificent spectacle. . . . We escape murder, we escape brutalization." Even Theodore Roosevelt, later a strident advocate of intervention, was unmoved by the invasion of Belgium. In *The Outlook* of 22 August he wrote, "I am not now taking sides"; in September he praised the Germans as a "stern, virile and masterful people," and declared that it would be "folly to jump into the war."

America could not be "impartial in thought" in the face of such a universal catastrophe, and the public in general became divided emotionally into pro-Ally, pro-German, or pro-neutral before the war was a month old. Leaders in pro-Ally sentiment were college-educated and well-to-do people on the East and West coasts and in the South. These, mostly English in race and culture, cherished the traditional American love of France; and those who had visited Europe in the last years of peace needed no propaganda to perceive that Germany was the aggressor and that England and France had done everything honorably possible to avoid war. Canada, moreover, went to war when England did, and gave freely of her men and money. There was an immediate rush of young American college graduates to obtain commissions in the British army or the French foreign legion; to form the Lafayette Escadrille of the French air force, and to organize an American ambulance service to help the Allies. Pro-Allied bazaars and relief organizations sprang up in almost every American city; and in these circles neutral or pro-German sentiment became taboo. The educated white people of the South, who alone in America remembered the devastation of war, warmheartedly supported the Allied cause from the beginning, although somewhat shaken when England declared cotton to be contraband.

The great heart of the country, on the contrary, and working people in general, were both neutral and pacifist. Even recent immigrants embraced American isolationism with fervor; the European war represented part of what they had come over to get away from. The Mid-Westerner could think no ill of Germans because so many of them were his good neighbors. Progressives who had launched a long-range program to fulfill Herbert Croly's *Promise of American Life* loathed war not only for its waste and suffering but because it would interrupt progress toward social justice. Many simple people dismissed the war as a natural result of monarchical rivalries — Edward VII was nasty to his nephew William II, Nicholas II was jealous of the emperors of Germany and Austria. Others found the socialist, economic-determinism explanation convincing; the war was caused by rivalry for foreign markets and colonies, munitions-makers' zeal to sell their wares, and the bankers' lust to glut themselves on war profits. It followed that both sides in the European war were guilty, both were horrible; and to preserve America's integrity and perhaps regenerate an Old World exhausted from fighting, she must neither rearm nor fight. So reasoned Westerners who had won their land by fighting Indians, and Eastern progressives who accepted the Marxian argument. Henry Ford, jeered by the Eastern press but supported by warm Western hearts, even chartered a steamship, filled it with preachers, pacifists, and assorted cranks, and took it to Europe to persuade the warring governments to "get the boys out of the trenches by Christmas." And some otherwise sensible people argued that if the United States went to war, she would be torn apart by the foreign-language groups. The Hearst newspapers, the Chicago *Tribune*, Irish-Americans who cherished an implacable hostility toward Britain, and German-Americans, by and large, were determined to keep America neutral.

There was a general opinion that the war would be short. After fighting a month or two, the belligerents would be exhausted, financially and otherwise. Many American army officers believed that nothing could stop Germany, that she would crush France in a matter of weeks, then turn on Russia and invade England. The Allied victory of the Marne in September proved that France was far from "decadent"; and England's valiant efforts to build a new army out of the remnants of the "old contemptibles" compelled admiration. Allied propaganda directed at America was well handled; German propaganda was singularly truculent and ineffective. It left no doubt that Germany was autocratic and militaristic, and that her victory would impose the mailed fist on the Western world. A German patriot's "Hymn of Hate" against England was widely read and deprecated, and Kipling's reply, "The Hun is at the gate!" was appreciated; for there was no answer to his rhetorical questions, "What stands if Freedom fall? Who dies if England live?"

There now developed a controversy over neutral rights which, in other hands than Wilson's, might have drawn in the United States against the Allies.

2. Neutrality Problems

Keeping the sea lanes open was vital to England's very existence then, as in the Napoleonic Wars, and as to us in World War II and today; but it took a long time and a fresh look to convince the United States that her interest was identical with England's. Since the Allies had preponderant naval power, they used it by a blockade of Germany, which meant stopping and taking into port all neutral ships bound for Europe, and condemning those which were carrying cargoes to Germany, even if initially consigned to neutral European countries like Scandinavia. These procedures were contrary to traditional principles of freedom of the seas and neutral rights, which Americans had defended in the early days of the Republic and fought for in 1812; but (as the British made haste to point out) they were a very slight extension of the methods of blockade which the Union navy had applied to the Confederacy in 1862–65. The British government was in a dilemma — a tight blockade of Germany was essential if they were to win, but American ill will would make defeat certain. Wilson and Bryan, falling back on principles of neutral rights which had survived the age of sail, embarked on a policy of protest by diplomatic notes that recalled the equally futile note-writing by James Madison in 1807–12. Protests became fainter as the American stake in Allied victory became greater, and not only through sentiment. The Allies kept the sea lanes open and placed enormous orders for food and munitions in the United States, which relieved a serious economic recession in 1914. These purchases, moreover, were largely financed by the floating of British, French, and Russian bond issues in the United States, and by direct loans from American bankers. Not that this influenced (as the Nye Senate report of 1935 claimed it did) American desire for war. The business and financial interests who followed their pocketbooks, and Wall Street generally, remained strong for neutrality until early 1917, because that status offered them all the profits of war without the corresponding sacrifices. And the financial stake in Allied victory had no influence whatsoever on President Wilson.

Germany in 1914 as in 1939 (and like Napoleon in 1812) expected to defeat the sea powers by overrunning the continent. General Hindenburg and Ludendorff beat the Russians so badly at the Tannenberg and Masurian Lakes (26 August–15 September 1914) that Russia ceased to be an asset to the Allies. Joffre saved Paris and the Channel ports in his victory over the German army of invasion at the Marne (5–12 September). The Germans fell back to the Aisne, whence a series of bloody assaults by the Allies failed to dislodge them. By the end of 1914 the war on the western front had become a war of positions, of trenches: a ghastly, blown-up version of the Union and Confederate lines before Petersburg in 1865. In this kind of war the defense had the advantage, and every attempt of the Allies for three years to break or turn the German positions failed after grievous loss of lives.

On the oceans, England as the dominant naval power was able to contain the German high-seas fleet in port, except for hit-and-run bombardments and an occasional commerce-destroying sortie. She was able to establish and enforce an effective blockade of the Central Powers, adding greatly to the list of items to be considered contraband and so liable by international law to be taken from a neutral ship. This was reasonable, since the manufacture of modern explosives and weapons now required a vast array of new materials — copper and cotton, for instance. Germany retaliated against the blockade by commerce destroying, as the Confederacy had done in 1862. But Germany could wage war in the air and under the ocean. The U-boats, as the Germans called their submarines, confined their efforts to warships until 1915. But on 4 February 1915 the Emperor announced that all waters around the British Isles constituted a war zone in which any merchant ship attempting to trade with the Allies would be destroyed. This was what forced America into war.

The distinction between British and German violations of neutral rights was clear. No citizen of a neutral state lost his life as a result of the British blockade, and all neutral cargoes seized were paid for at war prices. But the U-boat warfare took a toll of some 200 American lives on the high seas when America was still neutral, and other neutrals suffered far more. President Wilson, foreseeing what would happen, informed the German government on 10 February 1915 that the United States would hold it "to a strict accountability" for "property endangered or lives lost." Thereby he took a stand that inevitably led to war, unless either his or the German government backed down.

Soon came tests of "strict accountablity." On 1 May 1915 the American tanker *Gulflight* was torpedoed and sunk without warning. Germany offered to make reparation for this "unfortunate accident," but refused to abandon submarine warfare. Six days later a U-boat torpedoed and sank Cunard liner *Lusitania* off the coast of Ireland, with the loss of over 1100 civilians, including 128 American citizens, some of them women. The sinking of the *Lusitania* was criminally stupid; it was no excuse to point out that the German embassy had warned passengers not to sail on the ill-fated ship, and that she carried munitions for the Allied armies. By existing laws of neutrality an enemy merchant ship captured on the high seas should have been brought into port; or if that were impractical, the passengers and crew should be taken off before scuttling. But the U-boat sank her without warning and made no effort to rescue the hapless passengers. A thrill of horror ran through America; but President Wilson, in an address on 10 May, pronounced a smug phrase that he lived to regret: "There is such a thing as a man being too proud to fight." Leaders like Theodore Roosevelt clamored for war, and the press took up the cry. That, as it turned out, might have been the best moment for the United States to have entered the war. Had she been able to bring her strength to bear in 1916, the war would probably have been over within a year; the disastrous loss of life and breakdown of civilized standards would have ended two years earlier than it did, and the Russian revolution would not have taken place, at least not then.

America was not yet emotionally prepared for war, and Wilson in 1915, like Jefferson in 1807, refused to be stampeded into it. On 13 May he demanded that the German government disavow the sinking of the *Lusitania*, make reparation, and "prevent the recurrence of anything so obviously subversive of the principles of warfare." The German reply procrastinated, and on 9 June Wilson sent a more peremptory note: "The lives of noncombatants cannot lawfully or rightfully be put in jeopardy by the capture or destruction of an unresisting merchantman." He denied altogether the legality of a "war zone," unheard of in earlier wars. Secretary Bryan, regarding this protest as dangerously close to an ultimatum, resigned rather than sign it. His own solution was to renounce responsibility for the lives of Americans who chose passage on belligerent ships. "Germany," he said, "has a right to prevent contraband from going to the Allies, and a ship carrying contraband should not rely upon passengers to protect her from an attack — it would be like putting women and children in front of an army."

3. Preparedness and the Election of 1916

Closely interwoven with the problem of defending neutral rights was the issue of military "preparedness," as it was called, for war; although usually advanced as the only way to keep America out of war. Preparedness was first advocated by those who, after the *Lusitania* sinking, believed that America must eventually intervene on the side of England and France. It was opposed by pacifists, and by all-pro-German or anti-British elements, who realized that there was no chance of America's intervening on the German side.

The preparedness people, who in general were the same as the pro-Allied interventionists, invited British veterans like Ian Hay to address meetings. But the most effective propagandists were Americans who risked or gave their lives in the Allied cause — Edouard Genet (a descendant of the "Citoyen") and others who formed the Lafayette Escadrille, Steve Galatti and his American Field Service; members of the Foreign Legion like Alan Seeger who wrote "I Have a Rendezvous with Death." The Navy League and other societies begged Congress to prepare, arguing that only strong armed forces could preserve neutrality. Long did the President remain deaf to their appeals. On the initiative of Grenville Clark, Theodore Roosevelt, Jr. and other New York business and professional men, General Leonard Wood and the war department organized in the summer of 1915 the first Plattsburg training camp, in which some 1200 civilian volunteers received instruction in modern warfare under regular army officers, paying for their own food, uniforms, and travel expenses. The idea spread, and in the following summer some 16,000 men were enrolled in a number of "Plattsburgs," thus creating a cadre of trained officers for the new army. But the Plattsburg idea received no blessing from Wilson prior to a speech of 4 November 1915 in which he set forth a program of preparedness, justifying his conversion by quoting Ezekiel xxxiii.6: "But if the watchman see the sword come, and blow not the trumpet, and the people be not warned . . . his blood will I require at the watchman's hand."

Bryan and La Follette now attempted to persuade the public that preparedness was merely a scheme of warmongers and profiteers, of whom Wilson was the dupe. Many labor and farm organizations fell in line; and their efforts were reflected in the Gore-McLemore resolutions of Congress, ordering the government to forbid American citizens to travel on armed merchant ships of belligerents. Wilson moved promptly to defeat these resolutions and succeeded, helped by press disclosures that the German-American Alliance was trying to intimidate congressmen into voting for them. In January 1916 the President toured the country to promote military preparedness and to propagate the view that the only way to "keep out of war" was to make America so strong that nobody would dare attack her. Monster preparedness parades were held in several cities, and Wilson marched in the one at Washington. On 7 March 1916 the President appointed Newton D. Baker secretary of war. As mayor of Cleveland, Baker had opposed preparedness, but he now became its vigorous and effective advocate.

During the summer of 1916 Congress, urged by Baker, Daniels, and Wilson, provided a significant strengthening of the armed forces. Most important was the "Big Navy Act" of 29 August embodying a ten-year plan of construction, which anticipated making the United States Navy equal to any two others in the world. The handicap that American trade was under, depending on foreign merchantmen to carry exports, converted the Democratic party to building up the merchant marine, and the United States Shipping Board Act of 7 September 1916 appropriated $50 million for the purchase or construction of merchant ships.

The Allies, finding the lack of defensive armament on their merchant ships to be no protection against their being sunk at sight, began arming them; the German government countered by threatening to sink all such ships without warning. Unarmed, however, was French channel steamer *Sussex*, sunk by a U-boat next month (24 March 1916) with a loss of 80 civilian lives, some of them American. Secretary Lansing on 18 April notified Germany that her methods of submarine warfare were "utterly incompatible with the principles of humanity" as well as with international law; that unless they were abandoned, diplomatic relations would be severed. This warning placed the German government in a dilemma. Was American neutrality worth the concession demanded? Was not the U-boat Germany's God-given weapon for victory? For the time being the Kaiser temporized. On 4 May he promised that U-boats would no longer sink merchantmen without sufficient warning to give their complement a chance for life — a temporary victory for Wilson.

In the wake of the *Sussex* incident came the Irish Sinn-Fein rebellion of Easter Monday, 24 April, which the British suppressed, executing several of the leaders. This produced an explosion of American anglophobia, and not only in Irish circles. Publication by the British of a blacklist of 87 American and 350 Latin-American firms which were dealing directly or indirectly with Germany, caused Wilson's attitude to harden against the Allies.

Early in that year, he had sent Colonel House on a secret mission to England, France, and Germany in the hope of persuading their governments to let him mediate and end the war. He had little encouragement in London or Paris, as the British and French army heads were confident of breaking the German lines in a spring drive; and none in Berlin, because Germany now held all the cards for victory. The Chancellor told the Colonel that he would entertain no peace offer that did not include big war indemnities and a permanent German control of Poland and Belgium.

So the slaughter continued. In February began the great Battle for Verdun. "They shall not pass!" declared General Pétain, nor did they; but the defense of Verdun cost France some 350,000 men. On 31 May–1 June occurred the Battle of Jutland, greatest sea action of the war, in which the Royal Navy drove the Imperial high seas fleet back to its mine-protected harbors, losing six capital ships in the process. On 1 July 1916 opened the Battle of the Somme, in which the tank made its debut on the field of Mars. The French paid with 200,000 lives, and the British almost double, to recover a few square miles of territory. Even heavier was the cost of a Russian offensive in Galicia, eventually stopped by the Germans and Austrians at the cost of almost a million men, and demoralization of the Russian army. By mid-November, when every contending nation had been bled white, a ghastly quiet again descended on the western front.

The presidential election had already been decided. Wilson and the Democrats planned the political campaign with unusual subtlety. They understood that the outcome would largely depend on whether the party could hold the progressives and Irish-Americans, now alienated by preparedness and fear of involvement in war on England's side. Well timed was the President's nomination of Louis D. Brandeis, foremost pro-labor and social-justice lawyer of the country, to the Supreme Court. He was confirmed by the Senate on 1 June after a bitter struggle with Republicans and big business interests. The Rural Credits Act of 17 July, creating twelve federal farm loan banks with an initial capital of $60 million, to provide cheap mortgages to farmers, came next. On 19 August, a Workmen's Compensation Act for federal employees was passed. A nation-wide railroad strike, threatened by the four railroad unions, to which management refused any concession, was prevented by the President's pushing through Congress the Adamson Act of 3 September, adopting the eight-hour day and other benefits for the railroad brotherhoods. The Jones Act of 29 August 1916 granted autonomy to the Philippines.

By this time the Democrats had appropriated almost every plank in the Bull Moose platform of 1912. And Mid-Western support of Wilson was enhanced by an incident of the Democratic nominating convention in June. Governor Martin H. Glynn of New York in a keynote speech cited one instance after another when presidential diplomacy had averted war. After each item the convention roared, "We didn't go to war!" and this, translated into the slogan "He kept us out of war!" became the oriflamme of the presidential election. But Wilson was careful to make no promise to continue neutrality under any and every condition.

Though pro-Ally in leadership, the Republican party dared not alienate Mid-Western pacifists or the "hyphenated Americans," as Theodore Roosevelt contemptuously called those whose old-world loyalties and hatreds outweighed their new-world citizenship. It nominated Charles Evans Hughes, associate justice of the Supreme Court, on a vague platform accusing Wilson of following a vacillating and timid domestic and foreign policy, truckling to the railroad brotherhoods and to Mexican bandits. For this was the summer of armed mobilization on the Mexican border and Pershing's unsuccessful pursuit of Villa. The Bull Moose party held a convention, only to expire "not with a bang but a whimper," when Theodore Roosevelt advised his followers to return as penitents to the Republican fold.

The election itself was highly exciting. Both candidates stumped the country, but Wilson had the advantage in capitalizing on neutrality and his party's legislative achievements. Hughes was a poor speaker; his full beard, suitable for a Supreme Court justice, looked comical to the younger generation of smooth-shaven voters, and his arguments in the face of Democratic legislative achievement misfired. Nevertheless, Hughes almost won; it was the closest contest since 1876. When the early returns on 7 November showed that the Republicans had made a clean sweep of the Eastern states with a heavy electoral vote, even the Democratic New York *World* conceded defeat. But California had not yet been heard from. Hughes had made several "boners" when speaking in that state, especially by not calling on Governor Hiram Johnson, the Bull Moose vice-presidential candidate in 1912, and he lost the Golden State by fewer than 4000 votes. California's electoral vote put Wilson across. The President polled 49.3 per cent of the vote, and won 277 in the electoral college; Hughes polled 46 per cent and 254 electoral votes. About half the Socialist party voted for Wilson, as did about two-thirds of the Progressives. The German-American vote divided. Hughes's surprising strength in the Eastern cities is ascribed to Irish-Americans deserting Wilson for not protesting against the execution of Irish rebels or doing anything about anti-clericalism in Mexico.

Now Wilson was free, untrammeled by political considerations, to make a final attempt to mediate in the European war; or, if that failed, to enter it on the Allied side.

4. From Wilson's Re-election to War

It is odd that Wilson, a student of history and author of an excellent book covering the Civil War, should not have seen that the European situation in 1917 was similar to that of America in 1864. Too much had been sacrificed, too much hate had been aroused, for a compromise peace. Even had European statesmen been of the caliber of Castlereagh and Talleyrand, they would not have dared disappoint the hopes of their people by "letting the enemy off easy," as the man in the street put it.

Wilson's peace effort must be set straight, because it has been distorted to mean that he thwarted a sincere attempt of Germany to end the war on fair terms. The outstanding facts are these: — On 12 December 1916, before the President was ready to start his final peace drive, Chancellor Bethmann-Hollweg anticipated him by announcing that the Imperial government was ready to negotiate with the Allies. The Kaiser, Marshal Hindenburg, General Falkenhyn, and Admiral Tirpitz allowed the chancellor to try this peace move because German victories of 1916, which included knocking Romania out of the war, put them in a strong bargaining position; yet they were frustrated (as Napoleon had been, and as Hitler would be in 1940) by "perfidious Albion's" firm control of the ocean. The only bar to a complete victory, they thought, was the Wilson-imposed shackles on the submarines. Bethmann-Hollweg, a wise and moderate man, saw clearly that if America entered the war, Germany's doom was sealed; before that happened, he must negotiate peace. But he had to promise the warlords that if this attempt did not succeed, unrestricted submarine warfare would be adopted as the last chance of breaking down England and winning the war. Suppose America did come in, argued the warlords, she could never bring her potential strength to bear before England would be brought to her knees by starvation.

Bethmann-Hollweg's announcement created a sensation and raised the question of what terms Germany would demand. Wilson now issued a note (18 December 1916) calling on all belligerents to state "the precise objects which would . . . satisfy them and their people that the war had been fought out." Lloyd George replied that Britain's terms would be "complete restitution, full reparation, and effectual guarantees" for the future. The German chancellor evaded Wilson's query because he knew that if he stated the minimum that his government had decided to accept — annexation of Luxemburg, a slice of eastern France and of Russia's Baltic provinces, protectorate over Belgium and Poland, and a vast war indemnity — neutral opinion would be alienated. His game was to use Wilson to get the Allies into a peace conference, while the Central Powers still occupied Belgium and large sections of Italy, France, and Russia. The Allied governments saw the trap and indignantly refused.

Having failed in this effort, President Wilson on 22 January 1917 delivered before the Senate his "Peace Without Victory" address. Holding forth the hope of a better world, organized in a league of peace after the war, he declared that such a peace must be a compromise, not a victorious one; a peace which would not leave the vanquished nations impoverished, bitter, and filled with feelings of revenge. He declared that he spoke "for the silent mass of mankind everywhere who have as yet had no . . . opportunity to speak their real hearts out concerning the death and ruin." Wilson's words lifted the hearts of plain people everywhere, and he became a sort of apostle. But "the silent mass of mankind" in Europe also wanted victory. They had not endured heavy sacrifices since 1914 only to be cheated out of it by noble sentiments. That, fundamentally, not machinations of "wicked" statesmen, is why the fundamental contradiction of Wilson's policy was never resolved. It was just as in 1863, when the Vice President of the Confederacy wrote that most Americans were tired of civil war and craved peace, "but as we do not want peace without independence, so they do not want peace without union."

On the last day of January 1917 the German government, through its ambassador in Washington, communicated a watered-down version of its minimum peace terms, which were bad enough; but far more deadly was the simultaneous announcement that unrestricted submarine warfare would start next day. This meant that the U-boats would be instructed to sink at sight any American or other neutral ship, armed or unarmed, that ventured into the German-declared war zone around the British Isles, or the Mediterranean. On 3 February Wilson replied by breaking diplomatic relations with Germany.

The next three weeks were a period of watchful waiting on the President's part, hoping in vain that the Germans might not dare carry out their threats. He even discouraged further military preparedness, fearing lest too much build-up would suggest to Germany that we really were preparing for war. The army bill passed by Congress on 22 February appropriated only a normal $250 million for that fiscal year. General Hugh L. Scott, the army's chief of staff, wrote (15 February), "We are not allowed to ask for any money or to get ready in a serious way, until the soft pedal is taken off." The greatest personal obstacle to adequate preparation was Josephus Daniels, secretary of the navy. He obstructed efforts of the navy to put itself on a war footing, on the ground that defensive measures might be construed by Germany as "overt acts." Even after the breach of diplomatic relations he refused to sign contracts for building new destroyers authorized by Congress, lest this "provoke" Germany. His assistant secretary, a young man named Franklin D. Roosevelt, had to persuade a New York shipping magnate to stop urging Wilson to get rid of Daniels, before the secretary would sign the contracts.

Wilson at this juncture seemed weak and vacillating, even pusillanimous, to many good citizens, but most of the country supported his every effort to evade or avoid war. We who remember those days are charitable to Woodrow Wilson, for many of us experienced the same emotional throes that he did. The years 1915–17, like 1775–76 and 1860–61, were times that tried men's souls. Should America "turn the other cheek" to Germany, to keep herself strong and free, "the hope of the world"? Or must a strong and virile nation help save her friends from being conquered by the "mailed fist"? The war on the western front had become a stalemate, a magnified Spotsylvania or Petersburg; but this affected different people different ways. It convinced the faint-hearted, as well as the ignorant, that America should virtuously stay aloof and let poor Europe destroy herself; but it strengthened stout hearts in their belief that America should play a noble part, pile in to ensure an Allied victory and, if possible, conclude the sort of peace which would prevent its happening again. Wilson himself was appalled at the prospect of war. On 1 April he told Frank Cobb, the veteran news correspondent and editor of the New York *World*, "Once lead this people into war, and they'll forget there ever was such a thing as tolerance. . . . A nation couldn't put its strength into a war and keep its head level."

So Wilson waited, hoping for something to turn up. What did turn up was a diplomatic bombshell — the "Zimmermann Note." This was a dispatch from the German minister of foreign affairs through diplomatic channels to President Carranza, proposing a German-Mexican alliance against the United States: Mexico to get New Mexico, Arizona, and Texas as her share of the loot. Carranza was further invited to detach Japan from the Allies and persuade her to attack the United States, presumably to have Hawaii as her reward. The British intercepted and decoded this dispatch and sent it to Wilson. Zimmermann's note brought to a head the entire subject of German espionage in the United States. The Austrian ambassador, two attachés of the German embassy at Washington, and others, had earlier been expelled for promoting strikes of longshoremen and explosions in munitions works. The leading German secret agent made a practice of planting time-bombs on docked ships about to carry cargoes to the Allies. American secret service unearthed documents indicating that before the end of 1915 Germany had spent $27 million in the United States for propaganda and espionage, almost half of it on General Huerta and his exiled friends to promote a counter-revolution in Mexico.

On 26 February the President addressed Congress in joint session to ask for authority to arm American merchant ships in their defense and to "employ any other instrumentalities or methods to protect them on their lawful occasions." What he had in mind was an armed neutrality or quasi-war, like the one with France in 1798; but Congress would not allow him even that. A group of die-hard pacifists, led by Senators La Follette and Norris, talked the bill to death, and the 64th Congress ended on 5 March without doing anything. "A little group of willful men," said Wilson, "have rendered the great government of the United States helpless and contemptible." The President went ahead and started arming merchant ships anyway, and summoned the 65th Congress, elected in November, to a special session on 2 April.

In the meantime, the U-boats were being hideously successful. On 18 March three unarmed American merchantmen were sunk without warning, and with heavy loss of life. This overt act, coupled with the disclosure of the Zimmermann note, started a landslide of public meetings, petitions, and manifestos for a declaration of war. News of the first Russian revolution, and the abdication of the Czar, on 15 March, not only fanned the flame but removed the last taint of autocracy from the Allied cause.

On the evening of 2 April, first day's session of the new Congress, the President reviewed his efforts to restore peace, declaring; "Neutrality is no longer feasible or desirable when the peace of the world is involved and the freedom of its peoples, and the menace to that peace and freedom lies in the existence of autocratic governments backed by organized force which is controlled wholly by their will. We have no quarrel with the German people," he added. "We have no feeling towards them but one of sympathy and friendship. . . . *The world must be made safe for democracy.*"

With a profound sense of the solemn and even tragical character of the step I am taking and of the grave responsibilities which it involves, but in unhesitating obedience to what I deem my constitutional duty, I advise that the Congress declare the recent course of the Imperial German government to be, in fact, nothing less than war against the government and people of the United States; that it formally accept the status of belligerent which has thus been thrust upon it; and that it take immediate steps not only to put the country in a more thorough state of defence, but also to exert all its power and employ all its resources to bring the government of the German Empire to terms and end the war.

He concluded with a noble peroration:

It is a fearful thing to lead this great peaceful people into war, into the most terrible and disastrous of all wars, civilization itself seeming to be in the balance.

But the right is more precious than peace, and we shall fight for the things which we have always carried nearest our hearts, — for democracy, for the right of those who submit to authority to have a voice in their own government, for the rights and liberties of small nations, for a universal dominion of right by such a concert of free peoples as shall bring peace and safety to all nations and make the world itself at last free. To such a task we can dedicate our lives and our fortunes, everything that we are and everything that we have, with the pride of those who know that the day has come when America is privileged to spend her blood and her might for the principles that gave her birth and happiness and the peace which she has treasured. God helping her, she can do no other.

Ironically, this was Holy Week. The Senate passed a declaration of war on the German Empire, 82 to 6, on 4 April; the House concurred, 373 to 50, in the small hours of Good Friday, the 6th. That afternoon the President signed the declaration, not with joy but in deep sorrow.

Not only the American declaration of war but Wilson's words heartened the people of the Allied countries, especially the young men who were fighting; for he raised their hopes anew, persuading them (alas for their disillusion!) that this new ally not only assured victory to their side but a just and lasting peace.

After the war, one frequently heard both in America and Britain that America's entry into the war was a tragic mistake; that otherwise there would have been a "peace without victory" in 1917. Now that we know more about what went on behind the scenes, we can see that this was mere wishful thinking. The only basis on which the German chancellor had been authorized by his military to conclude peace was the annexationist terms we have already mentioned; and, as the military situation continued to favor Germany through 1917, there was no reason for her to modify these terms. Had America not come in, and the Allies been so desperate as to make peace in 1917, that peace would have registered an overwhelming German victory in the west, as the Treaty of Brest-Litovsk with Russia, giving Germany the Ukraine, the Baltic provinces and Poland, actually did in the east. Germany would have kept Belgium, Luxemburg, Alsace-Lorraine, and part of France. No peace of that sort could have lasted — it would have been a mere interval between wars.

I DIDN'T RAISE MY BOY TO BE A SOLDIER

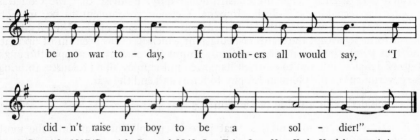

be no war to-day,   If   moth-ers all would   say,   "I

did-n't raise my boy to be a   sol - dier!" ____

© Copyright 1915/Copyright Renewal 1943, Leo Feist, Inc., New York. Used by permission.

The United States in the First World War

1917-1920

1. Naval Operations

THE UNITED STATES declared war on Germany on 6 April 1917, and the first two American republics to follow her example were Panama and Cuba. Congress at the President's recommendation declared war on the crumbling Austrian empire on 7 December 1917. It never did declare war on the other two central powers, Turkey and Bulgaria.

The old tradition of avoiding "foreign entanglements" was still so strong that the United States never formally allied with the Allies. President Wilson made it clear that we were merely "associates" in the same war. England and France, in their hours of greatest need, had concluded secret treaties with Russia, Italy, and Japan, promising them certain enemy territories after victory. Whether or not Wilson knew about these is uncertain; but, even had he not, he believed that the Allied governments contemplated a traditional peace settlement, annexing large chunks of enemy territory as Germany had done in 1871, and we in 1848. This he was determined to prevent; so he kept America's hands free of territorial commitment, bided his time, and on 8 January 1918 announced the "Fourteen Points" as a basis of peace.[1]

"President Wilson and his Fourteen Points bore me," said Clemenceau, the "tiger" of France. "Even God Almighty has only ten!"

This appearance of aloofness did not preclude full and frank interchange of views and information with the foreign offices and military and naval staffs of the Allies. But months elapsed before America contributed anything substantial in naval or military power to the war against Germany.

It happened thus, largely because "preparedness," starting late, had proceeded by halts and jerks. The fleet was far from being ready "from stem to

---

1. Wilson's Fourteen Points may thus be summarized: — (1) "Open covenants openly arrived at"; (2) Freedom of the seas; (3) No economic barriers; (4) Disarmament; (5) Adjustment of colonial claims; (6, 7, 8) Evacuation of Russia, Belgium, and France, including Alsace-Lorraine; (9) Readjustment of the Italian frontiers; (10) Autonomy of parts of the Austrian Empire; (11) Evacuation of the Balkans; (12) Emancipation of Turkey's subject peoples; (13) An independent Poland, with access to the sea; (14) A League of Nations. It should be noted that "self-determination" as a general principle was not one of the points.

stern" as Secretary Daniels claimed. Daniels's main interest in the navy was to make it a "floating university" for the bluejackets, and to improve their morals by banning alcoholic beverages from ships and shore stations. But he had a very efficient assistant secretary, Franklin D. Roosevelt; and the commander in chief of the Atlantic Fleet, Admiral Henry T. Mayo, was one of the best fleet commanders in our history. Both navy and marine corps, eager to begin fighting, were restrained by the Chief of Naval Operations, Admiral William S. Benson. A confirmed anglophobe, Benson opposed American entrance into the war (so far as his position permitted) and now proposed that the United States Navy fight a defensive war on the western side of the Atlantic. His first orders to the battle fleet were to concentrate in the Caribbean, presumably to protect the Panama Canal, and a cruiser squadron was ordered to remain in the Pacific to "watch" Japan, one of the Allies. Fortunately, the President had been prevailed upon by Ambassador Page to send to London the president of the Naval War College, Rear Admiral William S. Sims, a few days before the declaration of war. Sims was under oral orders to "keep the department posted," and Admiral Benson dispatched him with the discouraging remark, "We would as soon fight the British as the Germans."

The general situation of the Allies could hardly have been worse than in the spring of 1917. General Nivelle's offensive against the Chemin-des-Dames section of the western front was a hideous failure, provoking mutinies in several French divisions. The Canadian army was bled white taking Vimy Ridge, and the British Arras offensive, of which that was a part, also ended in mud and blood. Sims reported the Allied naval situation to be equally bad. Admiral Jellicoe, First Lord of the Admiralty, informed him that sinkings of Allied and neutral merchant and fishing vessels averaged almost 570,000 tons per month in February and March, and bade fair to reach 900,000 tons in April. They actually fell little short of that appalling figure, which the more powerful U-boats of World War II never attained. England had only three weeks' supply of food, and if something were not done promptly to stop losses and repair the lifeline, the Allies would have to throw in the sponge before the end of the year.

Before leaving Washington, Sims had been told that President Wilson was "decidedly of the opinion that ships should be convoyed." Upon arrival in England he found, to his surprise, that the Admiralty had not yet done so. Sims helped Lloyd George to put convoys across. The predicted frictions and collisions proved to be few and unimportant, and the convoy system more than any other single factor (and this is equally true of the Second World War) enabled American troops and supplies to cross the Atlantic safely.

Secretary Daniels, replying to an urgent appeal from Admiral Sims and the Royal Navy, decided in April to send destroyers to Queenstown (now Cobh), Ireland, to be used as escort-of-convoy and antisubmarine patrol under British command. The first six, under Commander J. K. Taussig, arrived on 4 May and went right to work; by 5 July there were thirty-four of them, together with six converted yachts and several ancient 400-ton torpedo boats of the Asiatic Fleet, which Lieutenant Commander Harold R. Stark had brought halfway around the world. This was the first time that American warships had operated under foreign command. The senior British naval officer at Queenstown, Vice Admiral Sir Lewis Bayly, was a crusty old sea dog; but the American destroyer officers were devoted to "Uncle Lewis"; and he, after a year had elapsed, issued an order which ended, "To command you is an honor, to work with you is a pleasure." A destroyer flotilla was sent to Brest, under Rear Admiral Henry B. Wilson, with the particular task of escorting troop-laden transports. These destroyers were equipped with underwater listening gear to detect submarines, and with depth charges which could destroy a submerged U-boat if properly placed. Both were primitive in comparison with the sonar and depth weapons of World War II, but effective against the small submarines of this war. On 17 November an American destroyer made its first kill of a U-boat. In the meantime convoys and aggressive patrolling had reduced Allied and neutral monthly shipping losses from 875,000 tons in April to 293,000 tons in November; and although they later rose to over 300,000 tons monthly, these figures were more than offset by new construction. Submarine operations now became very hazardous, and the United States could send troops and supplies abroad with confidence that they would arrive. Not one loaded transport was lost.

Admiral Mayo, with his staff officer Commander Ernest J. King, took part in a naval conference in which all the Allies including Russia and Japan were represented, at London in early September 1917. He then crossed to France and participated in a naval bombardment mission against Ostend. As a result of his experience and observations, Admiral Mayo persuaded the navy department to send more destroyers to Queenstown and Brest, to establish naval air stations in France, Ireland, and Britain to help the antisubmarine war, to take major responsibility for setting up a 250-mile mine barrage across the North Sea, and to send a battleship division to augment the British grand fleet at Scapa Flow. Rear Admiral Hugh L. Rodman commanded this contingent in U.S.S. *New York*. These battlewagons never saw action, as the German high seas fleet prudently stayed in port. A fleet of 120 subchasers of the same 110-foot model that proved serviceable twenty-five years later, was sent to European waters, beginning in June 1917. The SCs, commanded by naval ensigns or young reserve officers, carried depth-charges aft and proved their value both as patrols and escort vessels. They had one memorable battle with the Austrian navy in the Adriatic. Small-craft and destroyer service proved to be the best sort of training for future high command.

Pioneers in naval aviation, who became noted admirals by World War II, were Lieutenant Richard E. Byrd the explorer, who commanded the first

United States–Canadian naval air station at Halifax; Lieutenant "Pat" Bellinger, who made an altitude record of 10,000 feet in 1915, and Lieutenant J. H. Towers, third naval officer to win his wings, whose endurance record of 6 hours 10½ minutes airborne in 1912 stood for years. Lieutenant Artemus L. Gates, who made a remarkable rescue under shore fire of a splashed R.A.F. flyer off Dunkerque, became the first assistant secretary of the navy for air.

Naval aviation units sent to France were long dependent on foreign-built planes. One outfit was given a "flying coffin" seaplane which the French navy had rejected. Another had to go to Italy for Capronis, the flying of which to northern air bases was more hazardous than air combat, owing to the bad design and poor workmanship of their motors. Gradually these aviation units were supplied with Curtiss float planes, of which over 500 were in use by the end of the war, at 27 different European bases. These aircraft helped to protect convoys by spying lurking U-boats; some were converted to bombers and joined the army air force in its rather ineffective air raids on German military installations.

At the same time a tremendous effort was made to build up the American merchant marine, for which the shipping board, created in 1916, had done little but set up an organization. On 16 April 1917 Congress created an emergency fleet corporation with unlimited power and generous funds to requisition, purchase, construct, and operate ships without limitation. This, in co-operation with the inter-Allied shipping council, proceeded to build a "bridge to France." By seizing interned German ships, buying neutral ships, taking over all private shipping, constructing enormous new shipyards at Hog Island in the Delaware river and elsewhere, building steel ships, reviving defunct New England and West Coast yards to build wooden ships, even producing concrete ships, the emergency fleet corporation succeeded in increasing available tonnage from one to ten million tons, laying down two ships for every one sunk by the U-boats.

At the outbreak of the war, the United States Navy owned only three transports; merchantmen and freighters had to be chartered to get the initial troop contingent across the Atlantic in June. The 109 interned German ships which were commandeered were in bad shape, as their crews had done everything possible to destroy the engines; but a remarkable repair job was done by American mechanics, and these ex-German liners, starting with 54,000-ton *Vaterland* (renamed *Leviathan*) carried 558,000 troops overseas. Even so, almost half the transport tonnage used by the U.S. Army was British. About half the American troops sent to Europe were landed at British ports, mostly Liverpool, proceeding to France in a cross-channel fleet of small converted transports. The other half were landed at French outports, mostly Brest.

Naturally, the German admiralty did not take this lying down. In 1918 it sent six long-range U-boats to the American coast, in the hope of interrupting the transatlantic movement. They made a good bag of coastal schooners, fishing vessels, and small neutral freighters, cut cables and planted mines off Long Island, but never came to grips with the escorted troop convoys. All the damage inflicted on the transport fleet was done in European waters. *Tuscania* and *Moldana* were sunk, with a total loss of 222 lives; six transports homeward bound were torpedoed, and four of them sunk. Only three escort vessels of the United States Navy were lost in the course of the war. Germany, on the other hand, lost 203 U-boats; 137 of them to the British navy, three to the French, and four to the United States Navy. Thirteen of the enemy submarines were sunk by gunfire of the mystery or Q-ships, armed merchantmen with masked batteries, of which the British employed no fewer than 180 during the war. In addition, 176 U-boats surrendered to the Allies at the war's end. Submarines in World War I had a much shorter firing range than in World War II, and could not get off a torpedo without sighting the victim through a periscope; hence the most effective method of defeating them was the convoy, whose escorting destroyers and other warships drove off or kept down prowling submarines even when unable to sink them.

2. The American Expeditionary Force

Naval operations were geared to those of the army because their purpose was to control the Atlantic so that men and supplies for the Allied and associated armies could get across. The United States Army, numbering but 200,000 officers and men (133,000 regulars and 67,000 National Guard) on 1 April 1917, was probably even less prepared for war than the navy. Pershing's "punitive expedition" of 1916 had taught it something, but chasing Pancho Villa around northern Mexico was not much preparation for trench warfare on the western front.

One great obstacle to quick and abundant American reinforcement of the Allies was the need for intensive training in the sort of warfare the troops would have to wage. The 1st Infantry Division, a regular army outfit, arrived in France in time to parade down the Champs Elysées on 4 July 1917, but it was broken up into small units and distributed for training into different parts of the front. About 180,000 American troops had arrived in France by the end of the year, eight months after the declaration of war, but as yet they had done practically no fighting. The second division to arrive was the 42nd Infantry (Rainbow) of which Colonel Douglas MacArthur was chief of staff. This was an amalgamation of national guard units from twenty-six different states, to supply the necessary components for a division of 27,000 officers and men. The division sailed in October, and part of it saw action in February 1918 under French command. By that time the Allied military situation had become so desperate that a "race to France" of American forces began. Two more infantry divisions — the 2nd and the 26th (Yankee) — arrived in March. By the end of the war, the United States had created an army of 4 million men, transported more than half of them to France, and placed about 1,300,000 on the firing line. This was a tribute to the organizing genius of Newton D. Baker, secretary of war; but it took time.

General Hugh L. Scott, the army's chief of staff, persuaded President Wilson, Secretary Baker, and Congress, to adopt conscription. The Selective Service Act of 18 May 1917 required all men between the ages of 21 and 30 inclusive to register for service. Certain congressmen, recalling the draft riots of 1863, prophesied that conscription would be attended by rioting and that no draftee would ever reach the firing line; but these predictions proved mistaken. When the registration offices closed at sundown 5 June, 9.6 million men had been registered. Although this number was enlarged to 24.2 million in the registrations of 1918, which extended the age limits to 18 and 45, only 2.2 million men were actually inducted into the army by the draft. And of the twenty-nine divisions (of approximately 1000 officers and 27,000 men each) who saw action in France, only eleven were draftee divisions; the rest were seven regular and eleven national guard divisions, all volunteers.

Training these men, which took an average of eight months before action, the building of cantonments at about thirty training camps, providing them with modern weapons and equipment, and finally getting them "over there," were mighty problems not altogether solved. American field artillery largely depended on French 75s, and aviation units (as we have seen) on foreign aircraft, partly because the American equivalents were slow to get into production, partly because available shipping was crammed with beans, bullets, and soldiers. Colonel Roosevelt, as the ex-President now styled himself, created confusion by demanding that he be made commanding general of a division of "horse riflemen," as he called them, to be recruited from his friends and admirers and leap into action after six weeks' training. Clemenceau wanted it as a fillip to French morale, and President Wilson was willing to indulge Roosevelt's last grasp for glory; but General Scott and all top army generals set their faces sternly against the Colonel's scheme; he was too old for a field command, and knew nothing about modern warfare. This rejection convinced Roosevelt that Woodrow Wilson was a crafty villain, and he continued to attack him by voice and pen.

The American Expeditionary Force of 1917–18 was a jolly, singing army compared with the grim, tight-lipped American Army of 1942–45. Music and banners were not wanting; New York's tin-pan alley ground out some excellent marching songs such as Irving Berlin's "Oh, How I Hate To Get Up in the Morning!" Official propaganda aimed to make the A.E.F. feel like knights errant rescuing damsel France from the wicked Hun; "Mademoiselle from Armentières" and her sisters worked hard to make it worth their while. "We cried more over the Americans leaving for the front than over our own men," said a French peasant woman at a village near the front lines — "They were so young and looked so innocent, and were so far from home." The "doughboy" learned tactics of trench warfare surprisingly quickly; his élan, fighting spirit, and contempt for death made a deep impression on allies as well as enemies. He was far better taken care of than in earlier wars: better medicine, sanitation, field and base hospitals (but, as yet, no wonder drugs to check infection from wounds); Y.M.C.A., Red Cross, and Salvation Army; long leaves in Paris, with guided tours. And he was the better fighter because he wanted desperately to get it "over, over there" and go home.

The A.E.F. was fortunate to arrive on the western front at a time when a war of maneuver was beginning to replace the boring and deadly trench warfare. The excessive slaughter in this war was caused by an enhancement of what we have observed in the Civil War — the increased lethal power of explosives. Trenches, dugouts, barbed-wire tangles, and concrete emplacements were efforts to protect the human body, whose defenses were no better than at the dawn of history, from the effects of these explosives. But for a hundred or a thousand infantrymen, with no other armor than a steel helmet, to go "over the top" and try to take an enemy trench system by assault was suicidal, even when preceded by days of preparatory cannon fire. If Ludendorff had chosen to keep the German army sitting tight in its fixed positions across northern France, it is difficult to see how the Allies could have reached a decision, even with millions of Americans to throw in. But the war of maneuver gave American forces a chance to count. Doughboys who expected to attack the enemy in one surging, shouting line, as at Fredericksburg, watched with fascination the methodical way in which the French took out a newly established German position. Little knots of three or four men, each group with a machine-gun, would approach the enemy from different angles, and while one engaged his attention the others would make a leap forward. The Americans soon learned these tactics, and their losses were not great. Out of 1,390,000 American troops and sailors who saw active combat service, 49,000 were killed in action or died of wounds; 230,000 more were wounded. Yet, as in previous wars, deaths from disease, 57,000 in number, exceeded those from fighting. To a great extent these were caused by an influenza-pneumonia pandemic that swept through the camps in America and France in the fall of 1918.[1]

The army as well as the navy had an air arm in this war. The 1st Aero (later 1st Bombardment) Squadron was organized in 1913 with nine "pusher" biplanes, mostly Curtiss J-2s. It served with General Pershing in Mexico, making what was then a record non-stop flight of 4 hours 22 minutes. The officers and men of this unit sailed for France in 1917, where they were

---

1. L. V. Ayres, *Statistical Summary*, p. 127; but battle losses in the A.E.F. were twice those of disease. Figures for killed and died of wounds of the other combatants, as given in W. L. Langer, *Encyclopaedia of World History*, p. 960, are: Italy, 460,000; Great Britain, 947,000 (adding the Canadian and other empire losses brings it close to 1 million); Austria, 1.2 million; France, 1.4 million; Russia, 1.7 million; Germany, 1.8 million.

amalgamated with the Lafayette Escadrille and began combat duty with French Nieuports in March 1918. By the time of the Argonne offensive, this aero squadron had expanded to three, which proved very useful for observation and reconnaissance, and even tried a little bombing behind enemy lines. Lieutenant Eddie Rickenbacker, the American "ace" of this war, shot down 26 enemy planes; but the French and German aces made much higher scores. Colonel William Mitchell acquired his basic idea, that the next war could be won by air bombing alone, and Major Carl ("Tooey") Spaatz acquired the experience that led to his eminence in World War II. Major Fiorello LaGuardia, later a famous mayor of New York, commanded the A.A.F. base in northern Italy.

The army had only 55 planes and 4500 aviators when the war began. When it closed, there were 3227 U.S.A.A.F. De Haviland 4s — a British design — of which 1885 had been shipped to France, and 13,574 Liberty engines — 12-cylinder, 450 horsepower of American design — of which 5460 had been shipped abroad, over 1000 of them for the Allies. All these planes were of wood construction, and a special organization had to be set up to persuade the radical workers of the I.W.W., the "Wobblies" of the Far West, to turn out airplane fir and spruce.

At the top of the military hierarchy was President Wilson. He had only vague childhood memories of the Civil War, knew nothing of military or naval affairs, and so followed his military advisers and left them initiative and a wide discretion. Wilson's directive to Pershing simply stated that the general was "vested with all necessary authority to carry on the war vigorously," and when Foch and Haig opposed "Black Jack" and tried to appeal over him to the President, they got nowhere. But when Foch, in the crisis of 1918, was made supreme allied commander, Wilson made it clear that Pershing was subordinate to him.

The President had complete confidence in war secretary Baker, and was adamant in rejecting requests for favors from congressmen and others. But he did not have the same confidence in Secretary Daniels. After the war was over, Admiral Sims accused Daniels and Admiral Benson of delaying victory at sea by a year through their policy of feeding out mere dribs and drabs of naval power to the theater where alone it could count.

In this war, America with no plan of her own, fitted herself into the naval and western front strategy already existing. Hence Wilson was not faced as Lincoln had been, and F. D. Roosevelt would be, with the necessity of making important strategic decisions. His role was largely that of a top-level co-ordinator of military activity, and super-cheerleader of the nation.

3. The Big Push of 1918

At the time the United States entered the war, European military authorities thought that an American reinforcement of half a million men would be

ample to ensure victory. Events in the second half of 1917 upset that calculation. In October the Italian lines against Austria, which had been almost
stationary for two years, were broken at Caporetto by an Austro-German
drive. The Italian retreat became the rout so vividly described in Ernest
Hemingway's *Farewell to Arms*. The French army was unable to start a fresh

offensive after Nivelle's failure, but the British tried again. Haig's western
front offensive of 31 July to 10 November, a rain-drenched tragedy known as
the Third Battle of Ypres or Passchendaele, cost 400,000 more casualties,
made no appreciable gain, and brought the British and Canadian armies to
the verge of exhaustion.

Even worse for the Allied cause was the second Russian revolution, the most important non-military event of World War I. Russia not only left her allies cold but became the first communist state in the world, dedicated to the destruction of religion, property, and most of the values that had been built up in the Western world since ancient Greece.

Whilst this is no place to detail the causes of the Russian overturn — all being outside any possible American influence — the main events must be given in outline, since they led inexorably to the "cold war" of 1945. The inept imperial Russian government was overthrown by mutinous troops, and Emperor Nicholas II abdicated on 15 March 1917. The provisional government which succeeded, announced far-reaching reforms and pledged a vigorous prosecution of the war. That did not suit the Soviet (Workers' and Soldiers' Council) of Petrograd (now Leningrad), which demanded immediate peace negotiations. This Soviet, representing but a fraction of one per cent of the Russian people, probably would not have gone far but for a clever coup of the German government. Collecting the principal Bolshevik leaders then in exile, headed by Vladimir Lenin, it sent them to Petrograd by special train in order to undermine the Russian government. After the July offensive of the Russian army against Austria had failed, Alexander Kerensky took over the provisional government. Unable to keep order yet unwilling to make peace, he was overthrown on 6 November 1917 by the Petrograd Soviet, led by Lenin and Trotsky. These two, with Josef Stalin as one of their ministers, organized a Communist All-Russian government, cynically dissolved the constituent assembly which met on the 25th because it contained an anticommunist majority, and demanded that the Allies promptly conclude a peace on the principle of "no annexations, no indemnities."

The Allies naturally rejected this principle, when victory (with the help of America) seemed within their grasp; and when they refused, the Communists turned to the German government which, tongue in cheek, accepted and negotiated a truce on 1 December, which led to the treaty of Brest-Litovsk. Thus Russia was out of the war by December, and had been practically so since July. This meant that the Central Powers, leaving only token forces on the eastern and not much on the Italian front, could concentrate on a massive drive toward the Channel ports and Paris, to break the deadlock, as the submarine war had not done, and reach a decision before American troops arrived in strength. When her westward offensive started, Germany had 207 divisions on that front against the Allies' 173, of which only nine were American.[1]

Field Marshal Ludendorff opened this German offensive on 21 March 1918 with an assault on the British lines from Arras to La Fère. Within a week the Germans had advanced 25 to 40 miles. On 9 April came the second

1. B. H. Liddell Hart, *The Real War*, p. 366. Actually there were only 4½ U.S. divisions, but as they were almost double the strength of European divisions, his count is 9.

offensive; once again the British were hurled back on a broad front from Ypres to Armentières, and General Haig issued an appeal, "With our backs to the wall and believing in the justice of our cause, each one of us must fight on to the end." In late May the third offensive, against the French armies between Noyon and Rheims, was equally successful; the Germans were now back on the Marne, whence Joffre had expelled them in 1914, and within cannon shot of Paris; on Good Friday a shell from a "Big Bertha" 56 miles away exploded in the Paris church of St. Eustache, killing hundreds of worshippers. On 14 April the Allies placed General Ferdinand Foch in supreme command of all their forces, and on 5 June Pershing and the British commander in chief joined Foch in requesting that more American troops be sent over immediately, even if untrained. One week later this plea was supported by the premiers of Great Britain, France, and Italy, who warned Wilson, "There is great danger of the war being lost unless the numerical inferiority of the Allies can be remedied as rapidly as possible by the advent of American troops." Another 313,000 troops were shipped across in July. Wilson, Baker, and Pershing were determined that these should eventually form a separate American army, but under stress of the emergency Pershing placed all his forces at the disposal of Foch, who dispersed them among the Allied armies where they were most needed.

On 28 May the 1st Division helped to repulse the German drive on Montdidier, and captured the heights of Cantigny. A marine brigade of the 2nd Division and elements of the 3rd and 28th helped the French to stem the third German onslaught at Château-Thierry. On 6 June the marines, under Pershing's chief of staff General Harboard, with elements of two infantry divisions, took the offensive at Belleau Wood, a square mile held as a crucial strongpoint by seasoned German troops. It took them about a week to capture that bit of forest, and their losses (55 per cent) were heavy; but this action, the toughest that the Marine Corps encountered before Tarawa, astounded the Germans, and ensured the Marine Corps — then associated in the public mind with hunting Haitian bandits — a warm place in the hearts of the American people.

Ludendorff now rested his armies for three weeks, a valuable interval for the French and British to recuperate, and for the Americans to increase their strength. On 15 July opened the last phase of the German 1918 offensive, known as the Second Battle of the Marne. The Germans attacked simultaneously on both sides of Rheims. In the words of their General Walther Reinhardt, "We well-nigh reached the objectives prescribed for our shock divisions for July 15th and 16th . . . with the exception of the one division on our right wing. This encountered American units." In three days the German assault played itself out, and on 18 July Foch called upon the 1st and 2nd American Divisions, the 1st French Colonial and the Gordon Highlanders, to spearhead a counterattack at Soissons. (It was in this offensive that the poet Joyce Kilmer was killed, and buried by a tree stump — no complete tree could be found.) The counterattack, brilliantly executed, "turned the tide of war," wrote General Pershing. The German Chancellor, who on 15 July was expecting any day to receive peace overtures from the Allies, wrote, "On the 18th even the most optimistic among us knew that all was lost. The history of the world was played out in three days."

With the passing of this crisis on the Marne, Pershing on 10 August obtained Allied consent to his cherished plan for an independent American army. Colonel George C. Marshall became his operations officer. In the meantime, the British, Canadians, Australians, and Americans had delivered a successful counterattack south of the Somme which, at comparatively slight cost, made a deep penetration of the German lines. Ludendorff now told the Kaiser that he had better open peace negotiations because all chance of German victory had vanished.

While the French and British gave Ludendorff the one-two in the north, Foch assigned to Pershing the task of pinching out the Saint-Mihiel salient, south of Verdun. This place was strategically important as a rail junction and entrance to the Briey iron basin. Pershing planned the capture of Saint-Mihiel as the opening gun of an operation which would go through to Metz and eventually take over the front thence to Switzerland. But Foch, in a stormy interview with Pershing on 30 August, insisted that after taking Saint-Mihiel the new American army must come to the Allies' assistance to break the German lines to the north. Since Foch was the generalissimo, Pershing had no choice but to obey. Douglas MacArthur believed that this "was one of the great mistakes of the war," a bad example of inflexibility.

The Germans, recognizing that Saint-Mihiel was untenable in the face of a determined assault, were preparing to withdraw when, early in the morning of 12 September, blanketed by heavy fog, the American-led army, ten American and three French divisions, attacked. In two days this force wiped out the Saint-Mihiel salient, captured 15,000 prisoners and 443 guns at a cost of fewer than 8000 casualties.

General Foch's plan involved American co-operation in a gigantic Allied offensive from Ypres to Verdun. The time was propitious. The last Austrian offensive against Italy had failed, and the revived Italian army was about to resume the offensive (Battle of Vittorio-Veneto). Bulgaria cracked up in September, and Turkey would follow in October. The American First Army was assigned the sector between the Meuse and the Argonne forest, with Sedan as the ultimate objective. The Meuse-Argonne battle, launched on 26 September, was the greatest in which American troops had ever fought, and it was not until 1944 that the numbers involved — 1,031,000, of which 135,000 were French, 896,000 American — were surpassed.

The entire forward movement was a complete success. The Hindenburg line, Germany's last line of defense, was broken by the British in the northern sector. The American advance was suspended 14 October owing to logistic difficulties; but it no longer mattered, as the Central Powers were falling apart. In the hope of conciliating Wilson, Germany hastily established a parliamentary system, and Prince Max of Baden, who formed a liberal government, on 3 October addressed peace overtures to the President on the basis of his Fourteen Points. On 30 October, Austria asked Italy for an armistice. After a month of diplomatic fencing, in which the Germans were necessarily worsted, Marshal Foch was instructed by the Allied governments to negotiate an armistice. Mutiny in the German navy and revolution in Munich, the Rhine cities, and Berlin rendered the Germans impotent to offer further resistance; but in the vain hope that a complete change in the form of government might win milder terms of peace, the Kaiser was forced to abdicate. Two days later the armistice was signed in Foch's dining car on a siding in the forest of Compiègne, and at 1100 on 11 November the greatest and most costly war that the world had yet known came to an end. It happened so suddenly and spectacularly that both sides were left gasping; and a German corporal named Adolf Hitler, then hospitalized and temporarily blinded by a gas attack, sobbed bitterly and decided to become an agitator and avenge Germany.

What caused this amazingly sudden collapse of the most arrogant and powerful military nation since imperial Rome? The fortitude of the British, French, and Italians through years of uncertainty and disappointment was essential. The fresh, powerful American Expeditionary Force, which could have put over a million men into action in 1919, gave the final push. Control of the ocean by the Allies defeated the U-boats, made the transatlantic flow of men and supplies possible, and all but strangled Germany. Her people already on short rations with every prospect of their becoming shorter, were not inclined to gamble on continuing the war, even though over two million men were still under arms and full of fight.

4. The War at Home

To these exploits of American soldiers and sailors on the "field of honor," the war of opinion at home stands in painful contrast. In order to convert Americans from their traditional isolationism, the President condoned a terrific propaganda drive to make people love the war and hate the enemy.

George Creel, who headed the committee on public information established by Congress, undertook to mobilize American emotions as Bernard Baruch was mobilizing industry, and Secretary Baker the manpower. Artists, advertisers, poets, historians, photographers, educators, actors were enlisted in the campaign, the country was inundated by a flood of printed material (as yet there were very few private radio sets), while some 75,000 "four-minute men" let loose a barrage of oratory at movie houses and public gatherings. Motion pictures displayed to horrified audiences the barbarities of the "Hun"; pamphlets written by supposed experts "proved" that Germans had always been depraved, and thousands of canned editorials told the average man what to think. This whipping-up of hatred helped to defeat the President's main objective of a just and lasting peace; anyone overheard observing that there were good Germans as well as bad became suspect; speakers trying to explain that the establishment of a League of Nations after victory was the President's main object in going to war, were accused of trying to make the world soft for an unspeakable enemy.

On the excuse, or the belief, that the country was honeycombed with secret agents of the Kaiser, Congress passed the Espionage Act of 15 June 1917 and the Sedition Act of 16 May 1918, as extreme as any similar legislation in Europe. The first fixed a fine of $10,000 and 20 years' imprisonment upon anyone who interfered with the draft or encouraged disloyalty; the Sedition Act extended these penalties to anyone obstructing the sale of United States bonds, discouraging recruiting, uttering "disloyal or abusive language" about the government, the Constitution, the flag, or even the uniform. Under these laws the government arrested over 1500 persons for disloyalty, and among those convicted and sentenced to long prison terms were Eugene V. Debs the Socialist presidential candidate, for threatening that Socialists would not support the war, and Victor L. Berger, the first Socialist to be elected to Congress. Berger was re-elected to Congress in 1918 but expelled by the House — like Jack Wilkes from Parliament in the reign of George III. Even worse than the official crusade against sedition was the unofficial spy-hunting that engaged the energy of frustrated old women of both sexes. It was a wonderful opportunity to bring patriotism to the aid of neighborhood feuds and personal grudges. German-Americans, who did as much to support the war as any group, suffered the most. Stay-at-home patriots indulged in an orgy of hate, which even extended to passing state laws forbidding the teaching of German in schools or colleges, throwing German books out of public libraries, forbidding German or Austrian musicians to play in public or their music to be performed.

The bright side of the war on the home front is the control of food production and distribution under Herbert C. Hoover, a mining engineer who happened to be in England when the war broke, and who promptly organized a commission for Belgian relief. Hoover's task was to increase the production and decrease the consumption of food in America so that armies and civilians overseas might be adequately fed. He was empowered to fix the prices of staples, license food distributors, co-ordinate purchases, supervise exports, prohibit hoarding or profiteering, and stimulate production. He fixed the price of wheat at $2.20 a bushel, establishing a grain corporation to buy and sell it, organized the supply and purchase of meat, corralled the supply of sugar. But his major achievements were done by persuasion, not forced, as befitted one of Quaker background. He induced people to cut down waste and reduce consumption by voluntary wheatless Mondays, meatless Tuesdays, and the like, which became an accepted part of the war effort; to save wheat, Americans returned to the "rye 'n Injun" bread of colonial days and experimented with unattractive if nutritious substitutes such as dogfish, sugarless candy, vegetable lamb, whale meat, and horse steak. As a result of "Hooverizing," the United States was able to export in 1918 approximately thrice her normal amounts of breadstuffs, meats, and sugar.

A fuel administration, under the direction of Harry A. Garfield, introduced daylight saving and gasless days which motorists generally respected, and closed non-essential manufacturing plants in an effort to conserve coal. A war trade board licensed foreign trade and blacklisted firms suspected of trading with the enemy. A war industries board, of which Bernard M. Baruch was the leading figure, co-ordinated purchases for the government and the Allies. A labor administration regulated relations between capital and labor, arbitrated industrial disputes, fixed hours and wages in certain industries, and banned strikes as contrary to public interest. A war finance corporation was authorized to supervise the floating of security issues, and underwriting of loans to industries engaged in the production of war materials.

To keep the Allies financially viable, as well as pay for our own part in the war — which was costing about $44 million a day at the end — income and all other taxes were increased and new ones applied, and about one-third of war costs were met by taxation; the rest by loans. There was no difficulty in raising $18.5 billion in liberty and victory bonds at the low interest rates of 3.5 to 4.25 per cent. Yet the country did not go off the gold standard, and inflation was kept at a minimum, compared with World War II.

5. The Peace Conference and the League

Thus, by 11 November 1918 the war was won, so far as arms could do it. Now came the great test of what kind of peace the Allies would impose and the Central Powers accept. For a "peace without victory" had long since been ruled out, even by President Wilson.

So many mistakes were made around the beginning of peace negotiations as to support the Swedish chancellor Oxenstiern's lament *Quantula sapientia mundus regitur*, "By how little wisdom is the world governed!" First of all, the Allies, victims of their own propaganda which made the Kaiser the No. 1 villain, refused to negotiate with him; William II had to abdicate, and the moderately democratic government that followed never established itself in the hearts of the people. Germans needed someone to look up to, and in the absence of royalty they erected twin idols: Hindenburg and Hitler. Second, Wilson's unwise appeal to return only Democrats to Congress in the fall elections, which the voters disregarded, was interpreted as a repudiation of the President and all he stood for; so that when the President decided to attend the Paris Peace Conference in person, he went with diminished prestige. Republican leaders and their friends in Paris — notably Frank Simonds the war correspondent and Judson C. Welliver of the New York *Sun* — urged the French public almost daily to pay no attention to Wilson and his dreams of a League of Nations — he had been repudiated. Yet even under these discouraging circumstances Wilson's character, and the hold he had on the plain people of England, France and Italy, enabled him to obtain a peace which, if not what he had wanted, was much better than what the Allied leaders would have achieved without him.

When the fighting reached its climax in the fall of 1918, a movement for "unconditional surrender" started; super-patriots began to sport buttons with Grant's old slogan. General Pershing even protested against an armistice, wished to march right on to Berlin. But Wilson and the Allies had given Marshal Foch authority to negotiate an armistice, and that great soldier declared, "War is only a means to results. If the Germans now sign an armistice under our conditions, those results are in our possession. This being achieved, no man has the right to cause another drop of blood to be shed." This sounds very noble; but, as we can see now, signing an armistice on the basis of the Fourteen Points gave the Germans a complaint that they had been betrayed, when the ensuing treaty so little resembled said points. And simply letting the German army go home and demobilize instead of occupying the country gave Hitler the further talking point that Germany had not been beaten in 1918, only "betrayed."

The Armistice was supposed to be in force for only sixty days, which it was thought would be sufficient to conclude a treaty of peace. Actually, the Peace Conference did not even open for ten weeks, and peace-making required six months more, even though no German or Austrian delegation was allowed to debate the terms. During this time the Armistice was formally renewed monthly. And one of its severest terms, continuing the blockade until Germany signed a peace treaty, was relentlessly enforced, since the Allies wished to prevent a renewal of the war by Germany in case her government did not like the terms. This continued blockade caused more suffering in Germany than even the war, created a dangerous bitterness, and fed that desire for revenge which Hitler later exploited.

The two powerful leaders with whom Wilson had to contend at Paris were Clemenceau and Lloyd George. The "tiger of France," old and cynical — he had seen our Civil War and been through the war of 1870–71 — was willing to accept a League of Nations provided France obtained security for the future. But his one idea of security was the traditional one of leaving Germany so weak, by massive reparations and territorial cessions, that she could be no further threat to France. Lloyd George, the clever, shallow premier of Great Britain, wanted reparations for his country and continued power for himself; he had successfully waged an electoral campaign in December 1918 on the slogans "Hang the Kaiser!" and "Make Germany Pay!" Orlando, for Italy, wanted vast cessions of territory from the defunct Austrian empire; and

Mussolini later rode to power on the claim that he never got them. Wilson knew little of the seething nationalism in Europe, but he had a corps of experts (recruited by Colonel House) on every conceivable economic and territorial problem, and conscientiously tried to minimize war indemnities and obtain boundaries that would satisfy the populations. Whilst it is not true that the feature of the treaty closest to his heart, the League of Nations, prolonged the Peace Conference; it is now clear that the Allies could and should before the new year dawned, have lifted the blockade, fed the hungry, and drafted a preliminary treaty leaving the working out of a definitive treaty and league to professional diplomats at a plenary conference with those of the defeated powers.

President Wilson cherished the hope that a League of Nations, in itself, would prevent future wars; and, with no other force but international law and public opinion, enforce peace. A story circulated in Paris tells of a conversation he had with Clemenceau. It went approximately as follows:

Wilson: My one object in promoting the League of Nations is to prevent future wars.

Clemenceau: You can never prevent war by no matter what scheme or organization unless we can all agree on three fundamental principles.

Wilson: What are they?

Clemenceau: First, to declare and enforce racial equality. Japan already has a resolution to that effect before the Conference. She demands that it be incorporated in the Treaty. Do you accept?

Wilson: No, I'm afraid not. The race question is very touchy in the United States, and the Southern and West Coast senators would defeat any treaty containing such a clause.

Clemenceau: The second thing we must do is to establish freedom of immigration; no country to close her borders to foreigners wishing to come to live there. Do you agree?

Wilson: No; my country is determined to exclude Orientals absolutely, and Congress is already considering restrictions to European immigration.

Clemenceau: The third condition of an enduring peace is free trade throughout the world. How would you like that?

Wilson: I personally would like to see it, and my party has lowered the American tariff; but I could never get Congress to agree to a customs union with Europe, Asia, and Africa.

Clemenceau: Very well, then; the only way to maintain peace is to remain strong ourselves and keep our past and potential enemies weak. No conceivable League of Nations can do that.

Although Wilson had plenty of experts to tell him what was right, he made an unfortunate choice of peace commissioners. Secretary Lansing took a narrow legal point of view and disliked the League. General Tasker H. Bliss, army chief of staff, was competent for military questions only; Henry White, one of our best career diplomats, was approaching senility. The best of the commissioners, Colonel House (who for the first time had official standing), was an expert negotiator but, before the end of the Conference, he lost Wilson's confidence. A prudent President would have appointed a senator or a prominent Republican of international repute such as Taft, Elihu Root, or Hughes, who had already gone on record for a League of Nations. Mrs. Wilson apparently was jealous of House's influence on her husband and probably was the wedge that split them apart. This was unfortunate, because House's realism complemented Wilson's idealism; and when they parted, the stature of each was diminished.

Russia was the red ghost at the Peace Conference. She was represented in Paris only by committees of emigrés, ranging from socialists to monarchists; but her shadow hovered over the deliberations. The Bolsheviks (as the Russian Communists were then called) were in power, dedicated to establishing a "dictatorship of the proletariat" (meaning themselves) in Russia, and eventually throughout the world. During the Peace Conference they set up a communist regime in Hungary under Bela Kun, which was quickly snuffed out; but who could tell whether that might not happen elsewhere? Communist groups in every continental country looked to Moscow for guidance.

Wilson and Lloyd George sent a secret mission to sound out Lenin in March 1919. He was willing to negotiate, but nothing came of it, nor could any negotiation have quenched the implacable hatred the Communist party felt for the "bourgeois imperialists." The French government refused to treat in any way with the Bolsheviks because their regime, cruel and amoral beyond any in the memory of man, they believed to be certain to go. And, to make sure that it would go, the British and the French secretly supported counterrevolutionary Russian armies, which pressed into that unhappy country from three sides. President Wilson went along to the extent of sending a small American force to Archangel, ostensibly to prevent a cache of military supplies reaching Germany, and participating in a Japanese-directed invasion of Siberia, to see that Japan did not go too far. But the Russian army, reorganized by the redoubtable Trotsky, defeated all invasions and counterrevolutions; and by mid-June 1919 the Communist party was supreme in Russia.

The effect of all this on the Peace Conference, and on Wilson, was to dispose him to compromise the Fourteen Points and accept things in the treaty, such as an indefinite war indemnity, that he knew were wrong. When he felt like pulling out and telling the Allies to make peace their own way, he reflected that if he did, all Europe east of the Rhine might go Red. And, if he had quit, he would have called down on his head, his party and his country, the charge of loving "the Huns" more than the Allies. For there were other ghosts than Russia's hovering over the peace table — the spirits of millions of men killed; who, in the words of one of them, the poet John McCrae, cried

> If ye break faith with us who die
> We shall not sleep, though poppies grow
> In Flanders fields.

To blame Woodrow Wilson, in that atmosphere, for failing to do what was hard enough to do after a second world war, is palpably unfair.

Wilson successfully resisted some of the more extreme demands of the Allies. He denied Fiume to Italy — an action which caused Orlando to withdraw from the Conference in a huff, and enabled Republicans at home to mobilize Italian-Americans against the treaty. He protested against the cession of Shantung to Japan but wrung from her a promise, which Japan honored, to evacuate that Chinese province. He refused to permit the Allies to charge Germany with the whole cost of the war — a sum which Lloyd George estimated at approximately $120 billion. He resisted Clemenceau's desire to detach the entire Rhineland from Germany and set up an Alsace-Lorraine in reverse. He resisted the Polish demand for East Prussia, because it was inhabited mainly by Germans.

The Treaty of Versailles, which the Germans signed on 28 June 1919, was not so drastic as France and Italy wanted, or harsh enough to keep Germany down. It required her to admit war guilt, stripped her of all colonies and Alsace-Lorraine, imposed military and naval disarmament, saddled her with an immediate indemnity of $15 billion and a future reparations bill of indeterminate amount, and placed her economic system under temporary Allied control. Other treaties drawn up simultaneously or shortly after, set up, out of the debris of the Austro-Hungarian empire, the new republic of Czechoslovakia, restored the independence of Poland, and gave her a corridor to the Baltic. By adding the Slavic sections of the old Dual Monarchy to Serbia, that kingdom became Yugoslavia, and Romania's territory was almost doubled at the expense of Hungary. In general the revised boundaries of Europe were carefully worked out on the basis of language and race, but it was economically impractical to make every new boundary follow an ethnic line, and, in case of doubt, the Germans and Austrians naturally were the ones to suffer. Nor should it be forgotten that the fate of four debatable territories — the Saar, Schleswig, lower East Prussia, and Upper Silesia — were settled by plebiscites, three of which were won by Germany. German cries over territorial losses — enhanced to screams under Hitler — convinced many people of good will in America and Europe that grave injustice had been done; but from the viewpoint of 1964 the squawks and howls over that "horrible" Treaty of Versailles seem faintly ridiculous. Its only really bad features, which few outside Germany criticized at the time,[1] were the flexible indemnity which promoted financial instability in Germany, and the disarmament clauses

1. A notable exception was John M. Keynes's *The Economic Consequences of the Peace*, which came out in January 1920 and had an immense impact on public opinion on both sides of the Atlantic. Keynes, owing to his later heading a school of economic thought, has become a classic; but Allyn A. Young in *The New Republic*, 25 Feb. 1920, punctured several of his sophistries. It was Keynes who invented the cliché of Wilson, the simple Presbyterian elder, being "bamboozled" by those slick operators Lloyd George and Clemenceau.

which rendered the German Republic powerless to defend itself. But the treaty also set up a reparations committee which eventually let Germany off easily on the financial side, so that by 1929 such parts of the treaty as were keeping Germany poor and insolvent had been removed by mutual consent.

Wilson and most of the European statesmen agreed that through a permanent international organization for settling disputes and correcting injustices, all crooked things in the treaty could be put straight. "The settlements," said Wilson, "may be temporary, but the processes must be permanent." It was he who insisted that the League be an integral part of the treaty. On 25 January 1919 the Peace Conference sustained him and assigned to a special committee, of which he was chairman, the task of drawing up the League Covenant. The final draft was adopted by the Conference on 14 February 1919, and published immediately.

The function of the League of Nations, as set forth in the preamble, was "to promote international co-operation and to achieve international peace and security." Membership was open to all nations and self-governing dominions. An assembly, in which every member nation had a vote; a council, of which the five great powers were permanent members and four others were to be elected; a permanent secretariat at Geneva and a court of international justice at the Hague, completed the machinery for world organization. Members of the League pledged themselves to "respect and preserve as against external aggression the territorial integrity and existing political independence" of one another (Art. X); to submit to inquiry and arbitration every dispute threatening peace; to refrain from war with any nation that complied with an arbitral award by the League; and to employ military, financial, and economic sanctions against nations resorting to war in disregard of the League. In order to counter the charge of territorial aggrandizement, the League would administer the colonies of former enemies by the mandate system, a new and excellent feature of the Versailles Treaty for which Wilson and House were largely responsible. This meant that the former German colonies in Africa, China, and the Pacific, instead of being divided up as booty in the time-honored fashion, were placed under the trusteeship of England, France, Australia, New Zealand, or Japan, which were accountable to the League for promoting the welfare of the natives.

6. The Eclipse of Liberalism

In June 1919 when Wilson finally left Paris for home, House counseled him to meet the Senate in the same conciliatory spirit that he had used with Lloyd George and Clemenceau. At that suggestion the President stuck out his jaw and said he was going to fight for the treaty. That he did, to his death.

The fight had already started, and the Senate was in an ugly mood. The League was no exclusive brain-child of Wilson, nor was it "sprung" on the people unawares. In 1915 a number of leading Americans, including former

President Taft, Elihu Root, and President Lowell of Harvard, had organized a "League To Enforce Peace" society and promoted it by voice and pen. Senator Lodge delivered a commencement address on the subject in 1915 and told the League To Enforce Peace on 27 May 1916 that George Washington's warning against entangling alliances was never meant to exclude America from joining other nations in "a method . . . to diminish war and encourage peace." Even Theodore Roosevelt gave tentative support, and the Democratic platform of 1916 contained a League of Nations plank. In May 1918 there was held at Philadelphia a "win the war for Permanent Peace" convention, addressed by Taft, Lowell, Rabbi Stephen S. Wise, Charles E. Hughes, Senator John Sharp Williams, and several industrial leaders. Not only intellectuals but labor unions and financial organizations, and most of the press of the United States, had definitely endorsed the League of Nations idea well before the armistice. But during the long-drawn-out peace negotiations, hostility both to the idea of an international league, and to the actual Covenant that Wilson brought home, gathered momentum.

Many of the arguments against it were rational. Theodore Roosevelt, for instance, pointed out that the League was unlikely to preserve peace without armed forces under its exclusive control; and before condemning him, let us ask ourselves whether the United Nations could have prevented the cold war from getting hot, without NATO and American atomic power? Or whether there is now any likelihood of preserving peace without an enforceable world law? Most of the opposition, however, was irrational and emotional, compounded of personal hostility to Wilson and senatorial pique, German-American excitment over the alleged betrayal of Germany, Italian-American anger over Italy's not getting Fiume; Irish-American frenzy over Sinn Fein; conservative dislike of "leniency" toward Germany, liberal disapproval of "severity" toward Germany, and a general feeling that America, having expended her all, only to be tricked by European diplomats, should avoid future entanglements.

At one extreme in the Senate were Borah, Johnson, Knox, Moses, McCormick, La Follette and other Republicans, who were unwilling to let Wilson get away with another triumph and persuaded themselves that any departure from the traditional policy of isolation would be suicidal. At the other extreme were Democrats loyal to Wilson who felt honor bound not to let him and the Allies down, and who believed that the League was the only possible method of preventing another war. In between were members of both parties who believed in the wisdom of a few reservations, such as a declaration that Article X would not obligate the United States to go to war to preserve every new boundary set up under the Treaty of Versailles. More than three-fourths of the senators were ready to vote for the League in some form or other. If Wilson had been willing to accept a few reservations such as the one recognizing "the validity of . . . regional understandings like the Monroe Doctrine," which he himself had inserted in the Convenant, he could have obtained ratification that summer. But his basic stubbornness came to the fore, and he would yield nothing more than a few innocuous interpretations.

What a futile controversy! The Covenant proved to be far too weak to restrain a major power, and no reservations proposed in the Senate could have made it materially weaker. But it was at least worth a try.

Wilson's prideful belief that God and the people were with him — the *hubris* which in Greek tragedies always destroyed the proud — led him to make a direct appeal to the electorate. On 4 September 1919 he set out on a speaking tour through the Middle and Far West. He spoke with superb eloquence, passionate conviction, and the tongue of prophecy: "I can predict with absolute certainty that within another generation there will be another world war if the nations of the world do not concert the method by which to prevent it"; and, "What the Germans used were toys compared to what would be used in the next war." But much of the effect of his speeches was spoiled by arguments of irreconcilables who stalked him relentlessly from city to city. On 25 September he spoke at Pueblo, Colorado; that night he suffered a physical collapse. And with that vanished all hope of the United States subscribing to a new world order.

When safely back in the White House, it became clear that the President was incapacitated by arteriosclerosis and a thrombosis that paralyzed his left arm and leg. For at least two months he hovered between life and death, and his physique never fully recovered. Nobody was permitted to see him except his secretary Joseph Tumulty, his daughters, Mrs. Wilson, Dr. Grayson, his personal physician, and, occasionally, Bernard Baruch. Mrs. Wilson and Grayson acted as an informal council of regency. Colonel House's letters were not answered; some of them not opened. Even Sir Edward (now Viscount) Grey, a pioneer for the League, a liberal whom Wilson trusted and admired, sent by the British government to try to persuade him to accept reservations, was not admitted to the presence. For two months the President could do no more than scrawl a shaky signature to documents that his wife or physician thrust at him. After that, his mind became clear enough to follow what was going on, and he could dictate letters, talk for a few minutes at a time with cabinet members, and receive an occasional distinguished visitor.

This was definitely the situation envisaged by the Constitution: "In the case of" the President's "inability to discharge the powers and duties of the said office, the same shall devolve on the Vice President." But, when this was propounded by Secretary Lansing, Mrs. Wilson and Joe Tumulty opposed it so vigorously that he went no further. And who was to declare presidential disability? The Constitution and the laws said nothing about that. Moreover, Vice President Thomas R. Marshall, was a colorless character whose one utterance recorded for fame is, "What this country needs is a good five-cent cigar!" One shuddered to think of him as President, and he was terrified at the prospect himself; but the bitter irony is that if he had become President at this juncture he would have made the necessary concessions and the treaty would have been ratified. In any case, the President's disability was temporary. From about 1 November he had full control of his mental faculties.

Senator Henry Cabot Lodge, with malignant ingenuity, maneuvered the Senate to doom the treaty and the League, while pretending to favor both with reservations. On 6 November 1919 Senator Gilbert M. Hitchcock of Nebraska, who had managed the pro-League campaign, was admitted to the President's sick chamber to convey the bad news that the Democrats could not raise even a bare majority for ratification without reservations. "Is it possible?" said Wilson, groaning. "It might be wise to compromise," the Senator ventured to say. "Let Lodge compromise!" said Wilson. Even Mrs. Wilson begged him to accept the Lodge reservations. "Better a thousand times to go down fighting than to dip your colors to dishonorable compromise," he replied.

And so, fighting, the ship went down. On 19 November the Senate took a vote on ratifying the Treaty of Versailles, and the noes won. Brought up for reconsideration next session, it once more failed of two-thirds majority and on 19 March 1920 the Senate returned it to the President with formal notice of inability to ratify.

In the meantime there were sad doings on the domestic front. President Wilson's third attorney general, A. Mitchell Palmer, was a Pennsylvania politician with a presidential bee in his bonnet. Appointed alien property custodian in 1917, he sequestered some $600 million worth of German and Austrian property in the United States, and saw to it that his friends got some of the bargains when this property was sold. As attorney general, Palmer decided (like Joseph McCarthy more than thirty years later) that the way to fame and power was to crack down on the "Reds." Pro-Germans were no longer dangerous, but the success of the Bolsheviks in Russia, their provocative and threatening language, and their growing control over all socialist elements everywhere, now made them the chief target of American fears. Wilson, at the first cabinet meeting since his breakdown, in April 1920, said, "Palmer, do not let this country see red!" But Palmer had been doing just that for five months. He instigated a series of lawless raids on homes and labor headquarters, on a single night of January 1920, arresting more than 4000 alleged communists in 33 different cities. In New England, hundreds of people were arrested who had no connection with radicalism of any kind. In Detroit, 300 men were arrested on false charges, held for a week in jail and denied food for 24 hours, only to be found innocent of any involvement in revolutionary movements. The raids yielded almost nothing in the way of arms or revolutionaries, but Palmer emerged for the episode a national hero. And what made his action the more abominable is that he was a practicing Quaker, even using the traditional "thee" instead of "you." In New York, the anti-radical campaign reached its climax when the state legislature expelled five Socialist members of the assembly, although the Socialist party was legally reognized and the members were innocent of any offense. This went too far, even for conservatives; the Chicago *Tribune*, Senator Harding, and Charles Evans Hughes denounced their action. In Massachusetts the Sacco and Vanzetti case, though having nothing directly to do with the raids, was an offshoot of the same whipped-up anti-red hysteria.

Early in 1920 a movement against Palmer by the labor department, led by Secretary William B. Wilson and his assistant Louis Post, turned deportation proceedings to a saner direction. Post insisted on giving aliens proper counsel and fair hearings. He canceled action against dozens of them, and by spring released nearly half those arrested in Palmer's January raids. Palmer demanded that Post be fired for his "tender solicitude for social revolution," but when Post was haled before a congressional committee, he made such a convincing presentation that his critics were forced to back down. In the end, although 5000 arrest warrants had been sworn out, only a few more than 600 aliens were actually deported.

Palmer now let his attempts to capitalize on the "Red Menace" get out of hand. He issued a series of warnings of a revolutionary plot which would be launched on 1 May 1920, to overthrow the United States government. The National Guard was called out, and in New York City the entire police force was put on 24-hour duty. May Day passed without a single shot being fired or bomb exploded. As a result, the country concluded that Palmer had cried wolf once too often.

There was a lot more of this sort of thing going around; more hate literature, more nasty, sour, and angry groups promoting "hundred per cent Americanism" than at any earlier period of our history, or any later one prior to the 1950's. Anti-Semitism appeared openly for the first time in America, and was nourished by Henry Ford, of all people. The Dearborn newspaper that he controlled reprinted that hoary fake, "The Protocols of the Elders of Zion," supposedly proving a Jewish conspiracy to destroy civilization; and Ford either wrote or had compiled for him a book *The International Jew* (1920), which blamed the war and everything else on that race. There were also anti-Catholic pamphlets accusing the Knights of Columbus of indulging in obscene rites. The Ku Klux Klan was revived and did well, especially in the North and West; the Klan elected governors in Oklahoma and Oregon, and in 1924 practically took over Indiana. Favorite targets of the Klansmen were alcohol and adultery; but when David Stephenson, "Grand Dragon" of Indiana, who had made millions out of membership fees and selling nightshirts, was convicted of raping a young woman and causing her death, the Klan began to decline.

Another source of trouble, which the peddlers of hate whipped up, was the northward move of many Southern Negroes to work in war industries and better their condition. This, as usual, was resented by white workers, especially recent immigrants, and led to bloody riots. In one at East St. Louis, Illinois, in 1917, forty-seven people, mostly Negroes, were killed and hundreds wounded. In July of 1919, the month that President Wilson returned from Paris and submitted the Treaty to the Senate, there occurred in the capital city the most serious race riots in its history between whites and Negroes, not quelled until thousands of troops had been brought in to help the police, and six people killed. In the same month there was a three-day race riot in Chicago in which thirty-six people were killed. There were also major racial disorders that year in New York and Omaha, at least seven in the South, mostly occasioned by Negro veterans of the war having the "impudence" to demand their rights as citizens.

But for his disability, Woodrow Wilson could have been nominated for a third presidential term by the Democratic national convention. Palmer for a time thought he would get it; but he and McAdoo, the President's son-in-law, killed each other off, and Governor James A. Cox of Ohio obtained the nomination. Cox was little known nationally, like Franklin Pierce, and as unimportant. Reversing the usual procedure, his vice-presidential nominee, Franklin D. Roosevelt, was the man with a future.

Much the same happened in the Republican camp. The tycoons of the party wanted General Leonard Wood, who was exploiting a grievance of having been kept out of glory in the war, like his old friend Colonel Roosevelt. But the General and Governor Frank Lowden of Kansas could not get the necessary majority; and the bosses, after deciding on Senator Warren G. Harding of Ohio in a "smoke-filled room," put him across. They were about to impose another "pol" of the same kidney for second place, when the delegates got their backs up, and nominated Calvin Coolidge. Fame had recently thrust herself upon Governor Coolidge when, in the course of a Boston police strike, he declared that there was "no right to strike against the public safety by anybody, anywhere, anytime." This caught the imagination of a public jittery about the Red Menace.

The voters gave Harding 16,152,200 votes, with 404 in the electoral college, and Cox 9,147,353 with 127 electoral votes. The winner's plurality, 61 per cent of the total, came nearest to a political landslide in our history, prior to 1964. Harding, or whoever wrote his campaign speeches, gauged the public temper correctly when he announced, "America's present need is not heroics but healing; not nostrums but normalcy; not revolution but restoration . . . not surgery but serenity." At least half the 920,000 votes polled by Socialist candidate Debs, who was still in jail for opposing the war, registered protest by people disillusioned with Wilson but unwilling to go Republican.

So emphatic an overturn needs explanation. It was not merely dislike of the League of Nations. A group of prominent Leaguers, including Taft, Hoover, Hughes, and college presidents Nicholas Murray Butler of Columbia and Lowell of Harvard, urged people to vote for Harding as the only way to support the League — an odd piece of bad judgment that they later regretted. Walter Lippmann, who lived through those years of turmoil, in 1964 diagnosed the reaction as "the backwash of the excitement and the sacrifice, when the people were war-weary and angry at the disappointing peace which followed the war." Others have said that the poeple were tired of being "pushed around" by rationing, restrictions, drafts, and the like. Possibly so; but Herbert Hoover, as the most conspicuous pusher-arounder of the war, was elected President in 1928. Disillusion over the peace, especially by the three principal groups of "hyphenated Americans" who felt that Germany, Ireland, and Italy had been "betrayed," and the feeling that all America's sacrifices had been in vain, doubtless had much to do with the people's revulsion from the Democrats. But, in my opinion, the principal architect of Democratic defeat was George Creel and the propaganda corps. His campaign of hate during the war got the people all hopped up for fighting Germany to an unconditional surrender, marching on Berlin, hanging the Kaiser, and all that; so when the war ended abruptly before even half the armed forces had seen action, the public, suddenly let down, turned its emotions against something else. The Red Menace siphoned off a part of the hate, but most of it boomeranged on the administration which had led us into a "futile and useless war."

Whatever may have been the reason or reasons for the 1920 vote, it is certain that World War I was the most popular war in our history while it lasted, and the most hated after it was over. American books, plays, and movies on the war, such as Dos Passos's *Three Soldiers*, Hemingway's *Farewell to Arms*, and Laurence Stallings and Maxwell Anderson's *What Price Glory?* presented the war as unrelieved boredom, horror, and filth. And no general officer in the war ever received an important political office.

President Wilson, a shadow of his former self but still stern and dignified, just managed to be driven to the Capitol in an open car with President-elect Harding on 4 March 1921. He then passed into the shadows.

Woodrow Wilson, even after half a century has elapsed, is a difficult President to evaluate; especially for one who joyfully followed his leadership both in peace and war, saw him in action in Paris, suffered disillusion at the outcome, yet with the lapse of time has become tolerant of the President's mistakes. Wilson was a great leader because he sensed the aspirations of plain people and expressed them in phrases that rang like a great bronze bell. He showed flexibility, one of the attributes of statesmanship, in his shift from a pacifist to a belligerent policy, and in his negotiations at Paris; stubborness only at the end, when his efforts had worn him out. He was a prophet, foretelling that if America fell back into isolation she would surely be involved in another and more terrible war; that the only way to prevent that was to stop it from starting. His faults, which may forever deny him that veneration which the American people give to the memory of Lincoln, of Washington and even of Franklin D. Roosevelt, were a stubborn pride and a distaste for personal contacts. These were but the infirmities of a noble mind. Many turned against him for the same reason that a certain citizen of ancient Athens turned against Aristides because he was sick and tired of hearing that statesman called "the Just." Wilson's attitude about everything that he did was irritatingly virtuous.

Yet every hard thought about Wilson may vanish if we shift our attention from him to ourselves. He threw America's strength into the war, to accomplish something of transcendent benefit to his country and to mankind — an organization to ensure a peaceful solution for international conflicts. Maybe the goal was too high. Maybe he should not have made the attempt. But in that desperate gamble there is something far more admirable than what the United States Senate did, contrary to his advice and exhortation. Their action, which in some measure was forced by the people, and which the people approved in the next election, resulted in degrading America's war of 1917–18 to a mere hit-and-run operation.

OH! HOW I HATE TO GET UP IN THE MORNING

Oh! how I hate to get up in the morn - ing,

Oh! how I'd love to re - main in bed;____ For the

hard - est blow of all, is to hear the bug - ler call;____ You've

got to get up, you've got to get up, you've got to get up this morn - ing!

© Copyright 1918, Irving Berlin, 1650 Broadway, New York, N.Y.; © Copyright renewed 1945, Irving Berlin. Used by permission.

The Great Change

1902-1939

1. *The Auto and the Ad Men*

THROUGHOUT THESE crowded years of progressive legislation, violent politics, war waging and peace making, the American people were undergoing profound changes in their environment, their racial composition, their mental processes, and their moral climate. Rural America was moving to the city, horsey America was becoming motor-conscious, the American "melting pot" stopped bubbling; female America broke out of her former "only place, the home," and morally Puritan America, having put over the puritanical Amendment XVIII, became a country of wild drinking and loose morals. All these things interacted; but the invention of the internal combustion engine [1] and its multifarious applications to transport and power, was the material key to the Great Change.

The "horseless carriage," as the automobile was first called in America, was just that; a strongly built buggy with solid rubber tires and a one-cylinder gasoline engine geared to the rear axle by a bicycle chain. Just as the early steamships looked like sailing vessels, so motor vehicle designs changed slowly from those of carriages. First you had the "runabout" steered by a tiller; then you added a "tonneau" with a rear-opening door to make a "touring car." Better springs and pneumatic tires made the riding less rough; a canvas top and side-curtains protected passengers from rain; and by the end of World War I the average speed of cars had so increased that the public demanded a hardtop "limousine," "sedan," or "cabriolet," hitherto the privilege of the rich.

As these terms indicate, and also "chassis," "garage," "chauffeur," and even "automobile," France was the original home of the motor car. At the time of the Paris Exposition of 1900, cars were almost driving horses off the Champs-Elysées. But in America for eight or ten years more the automobile was an imported toy, a plaything of the rich, disliked because it was smelly, noisy, and frightened horses. Automobiling was one of those things like tennis- and golf-playing, smoking cigarettes and wearing wrist watches, which politicians did not dare to be seen doing. Theodore Roosevelt wrote in 1905 that he had

1. The gas or gasoline engine was invented by N. A. Otto in 1876, the oil or diesel engine in 1892 by Rudolf Diesel, both Germans; but, as with other basic inventions, many years elapsed before their practical application to power and transportation was consummated.

taken but two "auto rides" during his presidency and would take no more, because on the last one his chauffeur had been held up for speeding, which created undesirable publicity. Woodrow Wilson, president of Princeton in 1907, cautioned the students against indulging in the "snobbery" of motoring. "Nothing," he said, "has spread socialistic feelings in this country more" than this "picture of the arrogance of wealth."

The greatest obstacle to making the automobile popular was neither price nor prejudice but bad roads. Outside the cities these at best were macadamized, but more often just plain dirt. Maintained locally, they were full of ruts and pot-holes because farmers driving slow-moving wagons and buggies did not care to be taxed to keep them in good shape. Such roads were uncomfortable for the new vehicles at best, and impossible during snow or long wet spells. In 1902 there appeared a book by Arthur J. Eddy entitled *Two Thousand Miles on an Automobile*. Eddy drove a two-seat, one-cylinder car that could make up to 30 miles per hour but seldom went more than 20 on the roads that he encountered, and suffered a puncture and tire-change about every 100 miles. But the principal hazard was a skittish horse with timid driver. In some villages, speed limits were as low as 10 miles per hour, and the pioneer motorist was apt to be brought up short by a gate bearing the sign "No Horseless Carriages Allowed," guarded by a bearded deputy sheriff with a shotgun. The first Glidden Tour, of 34 autos in October 1903, took eight days to reach Pittsburgh from New York City.

Although there were cheap American cars before Ford's, there was no rugged, all-purpose car selling for less than $1500, until Henry Ford brought out his Model T in 1908. Six years later he invented the assembly-line method of mass production; and a few months after that, to the astonishment of the world and the indignation of other employers, Ford announced a minimum wage of $5 a day for his workers. The Model T "tin lizzie"or "flivver," as it was nicknamed, sold over half a million in 1916, two million in 1923, and by 1927 when its production ceased (Ford having unwillingly substituted the slightly more sophisticated Model A), the staggering total of 15 million cars had been sold. The price, which started at $825 for the two-seat runabout in 1908, went down to $260 in 1925. And after Ford had established an assembly plant in England, American cars began to invade the European market. A significant fact in American economic history is that in 1929 the value of automotive exports surpassed that of cotton exports, which had held first place since the Civil War.

Model T was the car that revolutionized American life. The farmer now had a vehicle that he could use for pleasure, with a pickup truck attachment to carry crops to market; or, with rear wheel jacked up and a homemade attachment, saw wood, fill the silo, do everything (it was said) but wash the dishes. The skilled worker in town or city could live miles from his job and drive his family into the country after supper or on Sundays. Even the Southern Negro's lot was bettered by the Ford car, which the most benighted

Ku-Kluxers did not deny to him, provided it was bought locally. The car not only afforded him recreation, but at a pinch his family could pile in and drive north to seek a job. The automobile, in connection with gasoline-driven agricultural machinery, emancipated the Western wheat farmer from his land. Without animals to feed, he could shut up house as soon as the crop was harvested and roll to California or Florida for the winter. Filling stations and service garages sprang up along main roads, enterprising farm wives established country restaurants to cater to "joy-riders," and small-time entrepreneurs set up dance halls for playboys and their "pick-ups." "Ye olde gifte shoppes" burgeoned to compete for the motorist's dollar, and country inns whose only patrons had been traveling salesmen, now redecorated and hung out "Old Colonial" signs. Others established tourist camps with individual cabins ("fireplace and flush toilet"), which after World War II were largely superseded by motels.

But none of these things were possible without good roads. Prior to World War I, at least nine out of ten car owners in the Northern states "put up" their cars in winter and went back to horse or steam transportation. Country doctors had to maintain a horse, buggy, and sleigh to get about when roads were impassable because of mud or snow. And at best, on dirt roads, the motorist had to wear linen duster, goggles, and veil for protection from the clouds of dust that every car raised. As late as 1920 an official of Jackson County, Missouri, named Harry Truman, when making his rounds, had to ballast the rear of his Dodge with concrete blocks to avoid being capsized in potholes. But by 1925, when more than half the families, in the North at least, either owned a car or were about to buy one on the installment plan, appropriations for hard-top roads began to pour freely out of state legislatures. The "balloon tire" made riding less rattly; and the gasoline-run bulldozer began its victorious onslaught on American scenery.

Congress in 1916 passed an act matching state appropriations for through roads, dollar for dollar. This did not satisfy the road-hungry public, and in 1954 the federal government began paying 90 per cent of the cost of roads approved by the secretary of the interior. A new and fruitful source of corruption was opened by the vast road-building programs since World War II, in the extravagant widenings, straightenings, over- and under-passes, loops and cross-country expressways, construction of which was stimulated far more by profits than by any pressing need of the traveling public. Politicians love to appropriate money for new roads; they can tip off their friends to profit by land-taking, curry favor with contractors by voting extra funds for non-contractual alterations, and with labor for overtime. The urge to get in and out of the city is ruining the city; gaping holes are torn through it to make place for urban expressways. No home is safe, no distinguished architecture of the past is spared, no amenities such as century-old trees by a quiet riverside are respected.

All earlier types of transportation suffered. The rural trolley car was the first to go; it could not compete with the faster, gasoline- or diesel-driven bus that whipped people from place to place in half the time. Livery stables, of which every small town boasted at least one, carriage and wagon factories, harness makers, grain stores and other industries that fed horse transport, went bank-rupt; hayfields where the horse's provender had been grown, reverted to brush and forest like the tobacco "old fields" of Virginia. Last horse-driven industry to be motorized was the funeral; until the 1930's it was thought indecorous for a corpse to be hustled to the grave in a motor hearse. Coastal steamboats and freighters died a lingering death, not so much owing to the change of propulsion — gasoline being too dear for freighters and the diesel engine too expensive initially — but from road-truck competition. World War I brought a last spurt in the building of wooden sailing vessels, but most of them were permanently beached in the postwar slump. Coastal steamships hung on to 1937, when the famous Fall River Line expired in its ninety-first year. The railroads, America's pride in the early part of the century, are now emitting ominous death-rattles, despite the adoption of electric-driven diesel engines and accelerated schedules.

Although Ford sold more "flivvers" than all other American cars combined, he had plenty of competition near his price range, notably the Dodge and the Maxwell. The motor-car industry in America began "all over the place" in the North and Middle West. Around 1910 thousands of mechanically minded youngsters were building their own "jalopies" in a tool-shed and dreaming of becoming another Ford; most of the tycoons of Willys-Overland, Buick, Olds-mobile, Cadillac, Packard, and Chrysler started that way. George M. Pierce of the elegant, prestigious but now defunct Pierce-Arrow, started by making bird cages, then went to bicycle manufacture, and as early as 1901 brought out his first motor car, powered by a one-cylinder French engine. Over 2000 different "makes" of autos have existed in the United States. Prior to World War I, more autos were being built in New England than in Michigan; but Ford's success attracted others to the Detroit complex, and one by one the little plants — Metz, Moon and Stanley Steamer of Boston, Winton of Cleve-land, and hundreds more — went broke or were absorbed. Cadillac survived as a name, though absorbed by General Motors, thanks to pioneering in 1912 the self-starter, which did even more than windshields and front doors to attract women drivers.

Consolidation was not confined to the motor car factories. During this era the existence of every local store became precarious. "Great Atlantic & Pa-cific" bought out over 15,000 little groceries by 1932; Woolworth, pioneer in the five-and-dime field, purchased on such an immense scale that he could undersell everybody; the success of "Piggly-Wiggly — All Over the World" sparked tens of thousands of "Stop and Shop" supermarkets to which the housewife drove in her car and served herself. Efficient, perhaps; profitable, certainly; but thousands of friendly neighborhood stores were ruined. This situation, in the 1950's, produced a series of state "fair trade" laws pegging retail prices so that small stores could survive the competition of the chains.

Ford's Model T largely sold itself, but the fierce competition among his rivals fed a relatively new business — "high-powered" salesmanship and advertising. The motor car industry did even more than drugs, cosmetics, and appliances to exalt advertising to the dignity of a profession. Prior to 1910, advertisements were relatively few and simple. In newspapers and magazines, apart from positions- and help-wanted notices, and for the department stores, advertisements were mostly of cures for physical ills — Lydia E. Pinkham's comfortable nostrum for the weaker sex, Dr. Sloan's Liniment for Man or Beast, Fletcher's Castoria ("Children Cry for It"); or bald claims for superior excellence of competing articles in daily use. But the Motor Age changed advertising to a series of prestigious urges to spend and buy: — a bigger car than your neighbor's; a luxury cruise, an all-electric kitchen, mink coat and diamonds for Mother. Emerson, over a century ago, complained that the stockjobber had supplanted the robber baron; in our time the writers of advertising copy, more highly paid than archbishops or college presidents, seem to have convinced the American public that to make money and spend it is the good life. They have become the priesthood to what William James aptly called "the bitch-goddess, Success." Bruce Barton, chairman of the board of Batten, Barton, Durstine & Osborne, in a book called *The Man Nobody Knows* (1925) presented Jesus Christ to the nation as a back-slapping good guy, a go-getter and regular rotarian.

Whilst advertising needed constant regulation to prevent defacing the countryside with billboards and claiming cure-all virtues for innocuous or harmful pills, it did contribute something positive to the economy besides employing thousands of models, photographers, and copy-writers. Advertising revenue enabled magazines and newspapers, which otherwise would have succumbed to radio competition, to survive; and some big advertisers acquired a social conscience. Texaco, for instance, has supported the broadcasting of grand opera. Advertising also promoted the revolution of rising expectations. Factory operatives by 1916 were no longer content to walk to work, wear secondhand clothes, live in cold-water "walk-ups," and have few if any recreations. Mom wanted nice new clothes for the children, and, later a radio to while away the tedium of household chores, a weekly hair-do, a vacuum cleaner, and a washing machine; Dad wanted above all things a car. Employers had to pay high enough wages for the workers to buy, and provide the leisure hours for them to enjoy, these gadgets which the advertisers had taught them it was "un-American" to be without. Nor were they denied; and by the time the big crash came, American workingmen had acquired such middle-class values that even the Great Depression did not thrust them back to the status of a helpless proletariat, as the communists hoped and predicted. Thus, advertising, more than any factor, has made the luxuries of yesterday the necessities of today; and if any profession is to be crowned or cursed for bringing about the present state of society it is that of the "ad men."

The increasing application of internal-combustion engines to power led to geographical dislocation in the economy. Certain coal-mining regions became depressed areas; oil-producing regions attracted population and wealth, and lucky land owners who happened to "strike oil" became multimillionaires of the vulgar type portrayed in Edna Ferber's *Cimarron* (1930). California, the leading oil-producing state in 1925, and Texas, which began pulling ahead of her, owe no small measure of their phenomenal increase in population to the enhanced demand for their underground riches in petroleum.

2. Aviation, 1903–1960

The successful application of the internal combustion engine to aviation took much longer than it did to road or rail transport. Substituting engine for horse to propel a wheeled vehicle, or converting a steamboat to diesel power, was simple in comparison. But man had to learn to fly before he could apply power to aircraft, and he faced far more difficult problems of engine and structural design than ever did the builders of ships and cars.

For centuries Europeans had dreamed of flying; Leonardo da Vinci designed a helicopter, Tennyson foretold "airy navies grappling in the central blue," and for decades American schoolboys had pestered their teachers with paper darts shaped like the latest delta-winged plane of 1964. Balloons had been used to some extent since the late eighteenth century. But the balloon without power was at the mercy of the wind and, with power, it led to a dead-end development — the Zeppelin and the blimp.

Active experimenting in and scientific study of aerodynamics began only in the second half of the nineteenth century. Three lines of endeavor pulled together to bring about the first powered heavier-than-air flights, in 1903. First there was the work of mathematicians and physicists such as Samuel P. Langley of the Smithsonian (whose *Experiments in Aerodynamics* of 1891 is basic), aided by experiments in kite-flying by the meteorologist A. Lawrence Rotch, and Alexander Graham Bell, inventor of the telephone. But Langley never constructed a successful "flying machine" because he relied exclusively on science, not experience. Second were the gliders, notably Otto Lilienthal of Germany who crashed fatally in 1896 after making over 2000 successful glides, and Octave Chanute whose employee Augustus M. Herring began gliding from sand dunes on Lake Michigan that year, and who lived to advise the Wrights. Third were the amateurs — writers, students, and promoters of man-made flight. These were a band of brothers, unmoved by gain, unterrified by popular skepticism and the belief that "God never meant man to fly." God made the birds, however, and all pioneers of aviation studied meticulously the flying methods of birds, especially the seagull, the stork, the albatross, and the condor; even the humble sparrow contributed by suggesting to Chanute the "tail down" landing.

Of American amateurs, the most important was James Means, a retired shoe manufacturer who founded the Boston Aëronautical Society in 1895 and the same year began the publication of the *Aëronautical Annual*. Therein professionals like Langley shared knowledge and aspirations with each other and the amateurs. Orville Wright wrote to Means early in 1908, "The old *Annuals* were largely responsible for the active interest which led us to begin experiments in aeronautics."

Orville and Wilbur Wright were the men who pulled all three lines together to produce the first powered flights. Sons of a Protestant bishop, in 1896 they were just two young men in their twenties who owned a bicycle business in Dayton, Ohio. After reading everything on the subject by Langley, Chanute, and others, they decided that the three essential problems to be solved before powered and guided flight would be possible were wing design, balance and control aloft, and the application of power. In 1900 they began gliding a plane of their own design and construction at Kitty Hawk on the outer coast of North Carolina, not far from Roanoke Island where the first Virginia colony was founded. They tried wing-warping for lateral control, and a front elevator for longitudinal control; they experimented with miniature models in a home-made wind tunnel, and in 1902 flew almost 1000 successful glides. Building their own four-cylinder, 200-pound, 12-horsepower gasoline engine — since none in the market was light enough — they fitted it to their third glider, and on the morning of 17 December 1903 made their first four powered flights — of 120 to 582 feet over the ground, lasting from twelve seconds to a minute, against a strong wind. The deed was done, and the Wrights won because they learned to fly before applying power.

But it took them five years to prove that they had won, for they were shy of the press which had sneered at their efforts, and declined financial aid. Quietly they continued experimenting, and in 1905 designed an improved airplane in which Wilbur flew over 24 miles in 38 minutes. In the meantime other aviation pioneers, mainly foreign, were receiving all the publicity, and working on the problem of stability, which the Wrights had not solved. Santos-Dumont of Brazil got into the running in 1906; and Glenn Curtiss, a former motorcycle racer, constructed a rival plane to the Wrights', which flew a mile on 4 July 1908. That fall, poker-faced Wilbur Wright took the brothers' latest airplane (35-horsepower with a pay-load of one passenger plus 100 pounds) to France, and "Vilbure Vritch," as the French pronounced his name, made a sensation, especially by his perfect control of the plane in all kinds of wind. He also established new world records for distance — 62 miles in six minutes short of two hours, and altitude — 361 feet! In the meantime, Brother Orville was demonstrating a two-seater model over Fort Myer, Virginia, which the Army had already ordered.

Few things in our history are more admirable than the skill, the pluck, the quiet self-confidence, the alertness to reject fixed ideas and to work out new ones, and the absence of pose and publicity, with which these Wright brothers made the dream of ages — man's conquest of the air — come true.

Aviation history now accelerated. Louis Blériot flew his French monoplane across the English Channel in July 1909, and next month the first international aviation meet, with Curtiss and Wright planes entered, was held at Rheims. Henry Farman won the endurance prize by a flight of 112 miles, and Curtiss took the speed prize at 43 miles an hour. "Flying circuses" of "barnstorming" aviators now became features of country fairs.

Glenn Curtiss pioneered seaplanes for water take-offs and landings; the navy ordered two in 1911 after Eugene Ely had flown one off the deck of cruiser *Birmingham*, and landed another, assisted by the first arresting hook and chain, on battleship *Pennsylvania*. In 1914 the navy established at Pensacola the first training school for aviators. Although air power was not a decisive factor in World War I, it took that war to pull aircraft construction out of the "sailcloth, sticks and string" complex into using light, tough, steel alloys, and to provide a nucleus of trained pilots.

The interest of American universities in airplane dynamics may be said to have begun in 1914 when Jerome C. Hunsaker brought back from England reports on what had been accomplished at the Teddington laboratory, and Edwin B. Wilson, first to put airplane stability into mathematical form, began to lecture on it at M.I.T. Wilson and Hunsaker's report on dynamic stability was the first to be issued by the National Advisory Committee for Aeronautics, in 1915. After the war, universities began establishing schools of flight engineering, and great progress was made in every scientific aspect of aviation. Inventors, notably Elmer A. Sperry, devised new instruments such as the automatic pilot and altimeter, to help man emulate the birds. Celestial navigation made greater strides than it had for 1000 years, owing to the air navigator's imperative need for a quick fix of his position. Lieutenant Commander Albert C. Read USN made the first transatlantic flight in 1919 in flying boat NC-4, Newfoundland to Portugal, with one stop in the Azores. A few weeks later, John Alcock and Arthur W. Brown of the R.A.F. made the first non-stop transatlantic flight, Newfoundland to Ireland, in 16 hours 12 minutes. The United States Navy established a Bureau of Aeronautics in 1921 and converted a collier to its first carrier, U.S.S. *Langley*. Two army lieutenants in a Fokker monoplane, in 1923, made the first non-stop flight across the United States, from Long Island to San Diego; it took them 26 hours 50 minutes. Three years later, Congress passed the Air Commerce Act, creating in the commerce department a bureau of aeronautics that was authorized to license planes and pilots, set up and enforce rules for air traffic, investigate accidents, and test new aircraft for safety. On 9 May 1926 Lieutenant Commander Richard E. Byrd made the first flight over the North Pole, in a plane powered by a 220-horsepower Wright Whirlwind engine. The same model engine, in the Ryan monoplane "Spirit of St. Louis" enabled twenty-five-year-old Charles A. Lindbergh to make a non-stop flight of 3735 miles from Roosevelt Field, Long Island, to Le Bourget airdrome, Paris, in 33 hours 39 minutes, on 20–21 May 1927.

Now, at last, man could emulate Walt Whitman's "Man-of-War Bird" —

> Thou born to match the gale, (thou art all wings,)
> To cope with heaven and earth and sea and hurricane . . .
> At dusk thou look'st on Senegal, at morn America.

Cross-Channel passenger air lines began both in England and France in 1919, but commercial aviation was slow to get under way in the United States; the first regularly scheduled passenger service, between Boston and New York, started in 1927. The principal aircraft designers and builders who survived those lean years were Glenn Curtiss at Garden City, Glenn Martin at Cleveland, William Boeing at Seattle, Claude Ryan at San Diego, Donald Douglas at Santa Monica, and William Stout at Detroit. Pan American Airways got its first mail contract, Key West to Cuba, in July 1927, and within three years had thrown an air loop around South America. United, American, and Trans-World Airlines were organized in 1929.

The age of the modern airliner began in 1932, when Douglas sold to T.W.A. two dozen two-engined DC-2's capable of carrying a payload of 12 passengers at 150 m.p.h., and the Boeing-247, with retractable landing gear and cowled, air-cooled engines, began to operate. These were the first two compact, all-metal planes, resembling giant birds. Douglas's DC-3 (two 900-horse-power Wright cyclone engines, payload of 21 passengers) of 1936, has been called "the Model T of aircraft." Almost 11,000 of these fast, durable planes, costing about $100,000 each, were produced in the next decade. Then came a famous trio: the Douglas DC-4 Skymaster, the Lockheed Constellation, and the Boeing-207 Stratoliner, first plane with a pressurized cabin, carrying 40 passengers at 175 miles per hour. The Skymaster, designated C-54, became the Army's workhorse in World War II.

American women were now getting into aviation. Ellen Church, the pioneer hostess, got her first job with Boeing in 1930. Amelia Earhart, pioneer aviatrix to make a non-stop transatlantic flight (1928), lost her life trying to circumnavigate the globe in 1937.

Aviation now grew at a fantastic pace. Pan American opened trans-Pacific service, San Francisco to Manila via Hawaii, Midway, Wake, and Guam, with Martin M-130 flying boats, and transatlantic service New York to Lisbon via Horta, in 1939. In the year of Pearl Harbor, American Airlines carried over 3 million passengers, and 24,000 private planes — mostly one-engine Piper Cubs and the like — were owned in the United States.

Again a great war made such demands on airplane designers, manufacturers and pilots that civilian aviation eventually profited. The air became a normal medium for transportation. Seaplanes used for transoceanic flights during the war were now replaced by faster, jet-propelled land planes. Between 1941 and 1957 the number of airports in the United States tripled, the number of certified pilots increased sixfold, the number of passengers carried rose from 3.5 to 48.5 million, the ton-miles of air cargo from 5.3 to 266.5 million.

While the airplane was helping the automobile to ruin the railroads (passenger traffic dropped from 1270 million in 1920 to 413 million in 1957), the number of automobile registrations, 30 million in 1937, rose to 67 million (one-sixth of them trucks) in 1957. Privately owned aircraft, both because of their initial cost and upkeep, and the stiff requirements for pilot licenses, had not even begun to compete with privately owned autos. There were only 84,089 of them (including 823 rotocraft and 413 gliders) in the country by 1962. Air enthusiasts look forward to the day when every American family will have a little airplane or helicopter on its roof or in its backyard. Others doubt whether there is any future for civil aviation other than the present pattern of big, fast jets, flying frequent inter-city passenger and cargo shuttles, and crossing the oceans in as many hours as a ship takes days.

3. Immigration

Two postwar policies that helped to create a revolution in American life were immigration restriction and the prohibition of alcoholic beverages.

Unlimited and unrestricted immigration, except for Orientals, paupers, imbeciles, and prostitutes, had been national policy down to World War I. The fear of labor leaders that they could never hold wage gains made during the war if it continued, was the primary pressure for reversing this policy. Labor was helped by a group of intellectuals who feared that the overwhelming number of immigrants from southern and eastern Europe, with different folkways and traditions from those of northern Europe, were a menace to American society. Kenneth Roberts the Maine novelist, in a series of articles in the *Saturday Evening Post*, argued that further unrestricted immigration would flood the country with "human parasites" and produce "a hybrid race of good-for-nothing mongrels." Such arguments appealed to "hundred per centers" after the war and determined the quota basis for the new immigration laws. The first of these, the Johnson Act of 1921, signed by President Harding after a similar law had been vetoed by President Wilson, limited the number of aliens admitted annually to 3 per cent of the number of foreign-born of that nationality already in the United States, according to the census of 1910. The total allowed was 358,000 of which 200,000 were allotted to northern European countries and 155,000 to those of southern and eastern Europe. This was cried out upon as unjust and undemocratic; but Sicilians were suspect, owing to their having imported the Mafia (now called Cosa Nostra) organization for crime, and eastern European immigration was suspect because largely Jewish and possibly "Red." So Congress in 1924 passed a new Johnson Act applying the same system more drastically. Admitted annually were 2 per cent of each foreign-born group resident in the United States in 1890, prior to the great wave of southern and eastern European immigration. After exhaustive calculations had been made of national origins of all Americans in 1890, a third act, in 1929, fixed the total annual quota at

150,000, of which 132,000 were allotted to northern Europe and only 20,000 to southern and eastern Europe and Asia. The count was made of white inhabitants only, in order to keep Africa from having any quotas. With certain exceptions, such as favoring "displaced persons" from Europe and allotting minimum quotas to Asiatic and African countries, this system is still in force in 1964.

Another restriction was the visa system adopted in the act of 1924. This meant that every prospective immigrant had to establish his right to come in under his country's quota, his eligibility respecting character, lack of communist or anarchist affiliation, and the unlikelihood of his becoming a public charge. The process required many documents, much time, and so much red tape as to discourage all but the most persistent.

This legislation did not apply to immigrants from countries in the New World, and those from Canada, Mexico and the West Indies greatly increased. "Net" immigration from Europe and Asia (that is, total number of immigrants less departures), after hovering around 200,000 to 1930, dropped during the Great Depression to a minus quantity, and only rose again to between 21,000 and 56,000 annually in the years from 1936 to World War II, when fascism produced a new crop of refugees. The total number arriving from Europe in 1933 — 23,068 — was the smallest since 1831.

The social effects of this restrictive policy were tremendous. The foreign-language press declined in numbers and influence. The so-called "ghettos" in the cities where recent immigrants congregated in search of friends and jobs, gradually faded out; but new ones have been created by the migration of Southern Negroes and Puerto Ricans to Northern cities. Absence of cheap immigrant labor permitted average "real" weekly wages in the United States, which we left at $10.73 per week in 1914, to rise to $13.14 in 1926, despite an immense increase in the cost of living; and in the same period, real wages in the largely unionized building trades rose from $18.22 to $23.94, miners' wages from $11.56 to $15.03, printers' from $19.67 to $21.63, and others in like proportion. Labor "never had it so good" as in the years between the postwar recession of 1920–21 and the crash of 1929. So good, in fact, that the unions lost a large proportion of their dues-paying members.[1]

Middle- and upper-class Americans outside the South had always been dependent on recent immigrants for domestic service; now that source was largely cut off. The number of "private household workers" — cooks, butlers, laundresses, housekeepers, and miscellaneous maids — declined between 1900 and 1950, although the total population in that period had increased 140 per cent.[2] There are probably fewer than half a million domestic workers in the

1. See above, Chapter XLIX. "Real" wages means wages in terms of purchasing power for rent and essential food. Actual money wages were far higher than these figures, because prices had risen too.
2. *Historical Statistics of U.S.*, p. 77. The figures do not include children's nurses, or their successors the baby-sitters; but do include "accommodators" and other servants who live out.

United States in 1964, although wages have risen spectacularly — from about $10 for a long week around 1900 to $65–$85 for a 5½ day week; all this without benefit of a union but with free board and lodging. The main reasons for this decline have been the reduction of immigration, and the increasing demand for women in war and other industries. This shortage of domestic "help" has been a social revolution in itself. It has increased the number of restaurants, since men and women who dislike working in a household seem to prefer the far greater drudgery in a public eatery. The rarity of domestic servants has stimulated the production of home labor-saving devices and of packaged, pre-cooked, and frozen foods to save the housewife time and trouble. Private hospitality has progressively declined; it is now evident that the "gracious living" of past generations was made possible only by a household of skilled domestic servants. Cocktail parties have become the only practicable form of home entertainment, for all but the very rich. The people upon whom the weight of this domestic revolution has fallen are the women brought up with plenty of servants who now, in middle age, must perform every household chore for which they were not trained, and which they never expected to do. The brave and successful response to this challenge by America's "thoroughbreds" is a tribute to their character, and one to which no male social scientist has yet alluded.

One prediction about the effects of immigration restriction — that the total population of the United States would level off around 1950 to about 145 million — was not realized. The total reached 179.3 million in 1960, and is estimated at 191 million for 1965. That this has happened is due primarily to the decline in the death rate, but in part to the increase of early marriages.

4. Bootlegging and Other Sports

The ratification of Amendment XIX to the Constitution in 1920, making women's suffrage national, shortly followed that of the Prohibition Amendment XVIII outlawing alcoholic beverages; and the two were closely connected. The women's rights movement, starting in the 1840's and marching to victory under Carrie Chapman Catt and Susan B. Anthony, joined forces with the Prohibition movement toward the end of the century. The Women's Christian Temperance Union founded by Frances Willard, and the Anti-Saloon League whose militant leader was Wayne B. Wheeler, determined to make the nation "dry." Evangelical churches lent vigorous support. Statewide prohibition of the manufacture, sale, and consumption of alcoholic beverages had made great strides since Neal Dow's Maine Law of 1851. Twenty-seven states were dry by 1917, and in many of the others "local option" prevailed; a county or municipality could vote itself dry even when the state at large stayed wet. The total per capita consumption of alcoholic beverages, reduced to "absolute alcohol," among the people of the United States fifteen years of age up, was 1.96 gallons in 1916–19, the lowest since the 1870's.

This orderly progress in temperance was rudely interrupted by the Volstead Act of 28 October 1919, which defined prohibited intoxicating liquors as any containing over one-half of one per cent alcohol; and by Amendment XVIII, which, after an intense and successful campaign by pressure groups, went into effect in January 1920. The reasons for so precipitate an enlargement of the federal government's power over the citizenry were many. The dry states complained that they could not enforce Prohibition when adjacent states were wet; the war induced a "spirit of sacrifice," and the German-American Alliance, by combining defense of *Bierstube* with "Hoch der Kaiser!" made drinking seem faintly treasonable. Wives of workingmen wanted their husbands to bring home their pay instead of spending half of it with "the boys" in a saloon; the liquor industry had been proved a major factor in political corruption and was tied in with prostitution, gambling, and other vices. Many business men and manufacturers favored Prohibition, hoping it would eliminate "blue Monday" absenteeism. The Anti-Saloon League printed some 100 million flyers, posters, and pamphlets, mostly to further the idea that alcohol was mainly responsible for poverty, disease, crime, insanity, and degeneracy, and that national Prohibition would empty the jails, the asylums, and the poorhouses. William Jennings Bryan, as one might expect, was always bone-dry; Theodore Roosevelt, after much hemming and hawing, went along; Taft opposed Amendment XVIII but as chief justice did his best to enforce it, as did Hughes who became chief justice in 1930. Woodrow Wilson straddled, fearing lest a stand either way defeat the League of Nations. Labor unions, in general, did not support Prohibition because it threw out of work many thousand brewers, distillers, waiters and bartenders.

No sooner had national prohibition become law than the country seemed to regret it, and a new occupation, bootlegging, sprang up to quench the public thirst. The federal government in ten years made over half a million arrests for breaking the Volstead Act, and secured over 300,000 convictions; but smuggling increased. The Canadian and Mexican borders were full of "leaks." Small craft easily ran cargoes from Cuba into Florida and the Gulf states; mountain moonshiners multiplied; obliging vineyards in California and New York provided kegs of grape juice in which, with a little time and a yeast cake, one could emulate the miracle of Cana; carloads of grapes went to Italian- and Greek-Americans to be trodden out in a traditional winepress and allowed to ferment. Off every seaport from Maine to Miami, outside the three-mile limit, rode a fleet of ocean-going ships loaded with every variety of wine and liquor. Motor launches, too fast for coast guard or enforcement agents to catch, ran these cargoes ashore, where they were transferred to trucks and cars owned by bootleggers; but the truckloads often got "hijacked" by other criminals, and in any case the strong liquor was "cut" with water before being sold. Millions of gallons of industrial alcohol, manufacture of which was permitted, were converted into bootleg whisky or gin, and bottled under counterfeit labels; poisonous wood alcohol, inexpertly "converted," caused numerous deaths. Liquor and wine imported under license for "medicinal purposes," easily found its way to the stomachs of healthy citizens. Every city became studded with "speakeasies" to replace the saloon, almost every urban family patronized a local bootlegger, and in defiant states like Rhode Island, which refused either to ratify Amendment XVIII or help enforce it, one could buy a bottle of British gin right off the shelves of a grocery store for ten dollars. Those who did not care to patronize bootleggers and so contribute to crime and political corruption, made their own "bathtub" gin at home or got along with home-brewed beer and cider. Bravado induced numerous young people to drink who otherwise would not have done so; restaurants which refused to break the law themselves provided "set-ups" of ice, soda water, and ginger ale to be energized by whatever the patrons brought.

There were many social effects of Prohibition, apart from the encouragement of lawbreaking and the building up of a criminal class that turned to gambling and drugs when Amendment XVIII was repealed in 1933. The high point in the Chicago gang war that was fed by bootlegging was the "St. Valentine's Day Massacre" of 1929. Al Capone ran one gang; George ("Bugs") Moran, the other. In four years there had been 215 unsolved murders in the Windy City. The Capone hoods, disguised as policemen, machine-gunned six of the Moran gang in a garage where they were waiting to buy a truckload of liquor from hijackers. Nobody was punished for this multiple murder; it took the federal government to get the planner, Capone, for evasion of income taxes. And the Chicago alliance between police and organized crime has never been broken.

Since beer and wine did not pay bootleggers like strong liquor, the country's drinking habits were changed from the one to the other. College students who before Prohibition would have in a keg of beer and sit around singing the "Dartmouth Stein Song," and "Under the Anheuser Busch," now got drunk quickly on bathtub gin and could manage no lyric more complicated than "How Dry I Am!" Woman, emancipated by Amendment XIX, enthusiastically connived at breaking Amendment XVIII and now helped her husband to spend on liquor the savings that formerly went to the saloon. Hip-flask drinking certainly helped the revolution in sexual standards that we shall discuss shortly. And it encouraged hypocrisy in politics.

Both major parties successfully blinked the issue for a decade. The Republicans, strongest in the rural communities and the middle classes, in general stood behind what President Hoover called "an experiment noble in motive and far-reaching in purpose." The Democrats were torn between Southern constituencies which were immovably dry because Prohibition was supposed to help "keep the Negroes in order," and Northern cities, full of Irish-, German- and Italian-Americans who were incurably wet. This division almost split the party in 1924 when the drys supported McAdoo and the wets Alfred E. Smith. The wets, having gained the upper hand by 1928, then nominated Al Smith, who proposed to abandon national prohibition and return the alcohol problem to the States. This stand was partly responsible for his spectacular success in the urban centers of the North, as well as for his defeat in the solid South and West.

President Hoover, who really tried to enforce the Volstead Act, appointed a commission to investigate the question of law enforcement. This Wickersham Commission submitted, in January 1931, a confused report to the effect that federal prohibition was unenforceable but should be enforced, that it was a failure but should be retained! By 1932 the "noble experiment" was so palpable a failure that the Republican party favored a "revision" of Amendment XVIII: the Democrats demanded outright repeal. Following Franklin D. Roosevelt's overwhelming victory, Congress in February 1933 recommended Amendment XXI repealing federal prohibition, which was promptly ratified, in December. The problem of liquor control was thus thrown back where it had been before 1917. A few states continued to be dry; but many others played around with laws forbidding drinking without a meal, or allowing fortified wine to be sold in drinking places, or keeping a state monopoly of the sale of alcoholic beverages in original packages.

Yet national prohibition did have a favorable effect on the drinking habits of the nation. The per capita consumption by those fifteen years of age and up, reduced to "absolute alcohol," was less than one gallon in 1934, the first full year after the repeal of Amendment XVIII. It rose for the first time to over two gallons ten years later, and has hovered around that figure ever since, but never approached those of 1901–15. The figure for 1962, 2.11 gallons per capita, was less than one-third that of France (which, despite the myth that the French drink only wine, is the leading consumer of alcohol among the nations), and less than that of Italy, Switzerland, the Antipodes, West Germany, and Belgium. Canada's consumption per capita is a little less than that of the United States, Britain's about 77 per cent of America's. But this is not the whole story, as only the legally sold, heavily taxed alcohol is included; there is no knowing how much "moonshine," "white mule," and other homemade and smuggled liquors have passed down the national or international gullet. Evin M. Jellinek, who has applied himself to this problem, figures that roughly 4,470,000 Americans, about 4 per cent of the population twenty years old and up, were alcoholics in 1960; no pleasant thing to contemplate.

The growth of leisure led to a vast increase in sports, especially in spectator sports like professional baseball, football, basketball, and hockey. College football, too, became professional when it spread from the older Eastern colleges to Notre Dame (whose Knute Rockne was the first of the high-pressure coaches), the Western Conference, and the South, for which Huey Long built the Sugar Bowl. Football squads lived in special quarters, practised the year round, were supported by "athletic scholarships," and graduated in physical education. "Yes, we had to go out and buy a football team," said the president of a Texas university to the writer, around 1940. "Otherwise, we could get no money for scholastic purposes out of the rich oil men."

Pugilism continued its popular appeal, especially after fights could be followed on television. Jack Johnson, in 1908, the first Negro to become heavyweight champion, kept the belt longer than any predecessor except John L. Sullivan, knocking out one "white hope" after another until Jess Willard gave him the K.O. in 1915. Jack Dempsey held the championship for seven years, 1919–26, when he was knocked out by Gene Tunney, lightest man ever to win the belt, a really scientific fighter; Gene married a New York heiress and retired from the ring. After five more championships won by white men, including the giant Italian Primo Carnera, there came an almost unbroken series of Negro winners, starting with Joe Louis and concluding with Cassius Marcellus Clay in 1964.

In professional baseball, "Ty" Cobb, the hero of the early part of the century, gave way to George Herman ("Babe") Ruth, who began belting out home runs in 1914 and so continued for 22 years, chalking up a total of 714 four-baggers — 60 in the single season of 1927 — for the New York Yankees. There never was another baseball player like "The Babe." A natural ham actor, his stream of Homeric insults to his opponents was alone worth the price of admission, and he could even dramatize striking out.

The horse, superseded for transport, was now bred entirely for hunting, hacking, and racing. Horse-racing became a favorite spectator sport and vehicle for gambling. States like Massachusetts, which had outlawed horse-racing because of its drain on the savings of those least able to afford to gamble, mindful of the revenue to be derived from pari-mutuel machines, not only legalized horse-racing in the 1930's but dog-racing too; and the once puritanical state of New Hampshire capped this by establishing an official sweepstakes in 1964. With increasing specialization, all records were broken. Citation, a bay thoroughbred, had won more than a million dollars for his owners, and many millions for the bookmakers, when he retired in 1951 at the age of six, having set up a new record of 1:33⅗ for a mile run, and won the "triple crown" — the Kentucky Derby, Preakness, and Belmont Stakes. The greatest sire in American turf history was Man o' War, by Fair Play out of Mahubah, both of the old Diomed-Lexington stock. He won $83,000 as a two-year-old in 1919, retired in 1921, and for the next 26 years at stud near Lexington, Kentucky, sired the famous steeplechaser Battleship and hundreds of other racers and hunters.

Golf and tennis, which were regarded by the American public as effete games of the idle rich around the turn of the century, now became popular. Francis Ouimet, a former caddy, by winning the open golf championship at The Country Club, Brookline, in 1913, proved that you did not have to be a Scot or a gentleman to be good at golf, and golf courses were laid out by hundreds of clubs and municipalities in every state. Golf never became wholly professionalized; contenders in tournaments still have to pay their own expenses. But tennis became semi-professionalized when the proliferating tennis clubs began paying all expenses of stars in order to attract a big "gate." The 1920's were the era of William T. ("Big Bill") Tilden, men's singles champion for seven years, and Helen Wills the women's singles champion. The international Davis Cup was won by American teams from 1922 through 1926, but for the next ten years the United States contestants had to be satisfied with second place to France or Great Britain. Skiing, hardly known in the United States before World War I, rapidly caught on after the invention of the ski-lift to save the time and effort of zig-zagging uphill. It has created new winter resorts in the West, and made the fortunes of northern New England villages which formerly hibernated. But the most popular "participation" sports, as always, were fishing and shooting. Every man of wealth on the Eastern seaboard had to have his local duckblind, join a Southern club for shooting quail and wild turkey, and a New Brunswick fishing club for taking salmon. The small-town and country lads continued to whip local streams and ponds for trout and bass, or to roam the woods with a shotgun in search of ruffed grouse and pheasant, or with a rifle for deer. New fishing developments were casting a line from beaches beyond the surf for "stripers," and catching enormous game fishes like the marlin from motor boats.

Thus the most significant developments of sport since 1902 have been the spread of gentlemanly sports to working people, the devising of new games, the growth of professionalism, and increasing public interest both as spectators and participants. At the turn of the century an ordinary citizen who wanted exercise other than shooting and fishing had a narrow choice: — "sand lot" baseball, sailing a small boat in summer, skating, snowshoeing, or gymnasium in winter. Today he has better shooting and fishing than ever, together with a choice of golf, tennis, bowling, skiing, and other sports, all with womenfolk participating; or he may stay home and gaze at a variety of games on television.

5. The Sexual Upheaval

The mores or sexual relations in European countries have fluctuated through the ages, and are a difficult subject upon which to generalize, owing to public reticence and lack of records. It is, however, fair to say that the so-called Protestant ethic — which is really the Christian ethic — in sexual morals prevailed in the United States from at least the early nineteenth century to around 1910; and that, whilst laws and principles have changed little in fifty years, practices have undergone a radical revolution.

The Protestant ethic allowed the sexual instinct to be gratified only within marriage. It disapproved of premarital intercourse as well as adultery, and regarded the Catholic countries of Europe as hopelessly immoral, although

Irish Catholics and the French bourgeoisie were, if anything, more austere in sex matters than descendants of early Puritans. Virginity before and chastity after marriage, absolute requirements for girls and women, were also enjoined on men; but for them, especially for young men whose marriages had to be postponed until they could support a wife, public opinion condoned prostitution as an outlet. Nobody can tell how far these ethics were actually respected around 1910, but they were the norm for middle-class Protestant Anglo-Saxons, Irish Catholics, and, most of the immigrants from northern Europe. Dr. Kinsey in his famous *Reports* on sexual behavior (1948–53) seems to have been surprised because sexual practices varied from class to class. Any observant boy who grew up around the turn of the century could have told him that. While middle-class intellectuals observed fairly well the principles of the Protestant ethic, the daughters of certain immigrant peoples were notoriously "easy." These were known as "chippies," in contrast to professional "tarts." And, in towns and cities, the daily visits of the iceman, who prior to mechanical refrigeration, replenished ice-chests with big blocks of pond ice, was the traditional consoler of frustrated wives and lonely widows.

The women's organizations which promoted Prohibition and female emancipation, complained of the "double standard" which required a girl to be a virgin at marriage, but not a man; they and the clergy, with some success, promoted the Christian principle that there should be a single standard of chastity for both. H. L. Mencken *In Defense of Women* (1918) snorted at this "hysterical denunciation" of the double standard. "What these virtuous beldames actually desire," he asserted, "is not that the male be reduced to chemical purity, but that the franchise of dalliance be extended to themselves." That is about what has happened. The revolution in sexual relations is one aspect of the emancipation of American women — of their escape from the Protestant purdah into business, the professions, and the arts; and from the country to the city. In that process they willingly shed the angel's wings clamped on them by sentimentalists and romantic poets.

Around 1910 there was a great to-do about prostitution and venereal disease. Houses of ill-fame to meet every taste and purse existed in the major cities (in New Orleans a guide book to them was printed annually), and there was at least one in every town. Some cities, notably San Francisco, had "red light districts," where one-dollar whores displayed their dubious charms behind windows for the benefit of sailors, lumberjacks, and cowboys whose vocations required prolonged absence from women. Many inmates were there because they preferred "woman's oldest profession" to hard work, but others were recruited by deception from the hinterland, Europe, and Mexico. Reginald Wright Kauffman's novel *The House of Bondage* (1910) created a sensation by describing the seduction of an innocent country girl into prostitution, leaving her a hopeless syphilitic. The United States Immigration Commission conducted an investigation of this "white slave" traffic, proving that girls were being imported from Europe, voluntarily or otherwise, at prices ranging from $200 to $2000; this report led Congress to pass the Mann or White Slave Traffc Act, making it a felony to bring women for immoral purposes into the United States, or across state lines. In the next four of five years, forty-five states passed laws against third persons — procurers and madams — profiting from prostitution, and some thirty cities closed their redlight districts.

These halfhearted and indifferently enforced efforts at reform were moved less by moral fervor than by the ravages of venereal disease. "Elaborate surveys," wrote one contemporary authority, "show the frequency of gonorrhea and syphilis at this period to have been one per cent among men, and almost a half of one per cent among women in the United States." Now that the religious sanction to sexual continence declined, and young people no longer feared future torment for sins observed by the All-Seeing Eye, it was hoped that fear of infection would prove a deterrent. The American Social Hygiene Association, formed in 1914, worked on sex education and the regulation of the social evil, and the League of Nations set up a committee on the white slave traffic which at least brought it into the open.

Parallel with efforts to enforce the Protestant ethic by force or fear, it was crumbling from within. The loose morals of the 1920's are generally ascribed to the First World War; but a general laxity was observable for at least seven years before America entered that war. Increased knowledge of sexual hygiene counteracted the terror of infection. The automobile offered an easy spot for courtship away from the family parlor or porch. Moving pictures were becoming more attractive and lascivious; the sight of Theda Bara very lightly clad, in close and luscious embrace with a lover, could not help but be suggestive. Dancing, formerly confined to supervised homes and ballrooms, could now be practised in all manner of night clubs and country dance halls; and instead of the sedate waltz and two-step, one now had the hesitation waltz, the Argentine tango (both banned by the Federation of Women's Clubs in 1914), the bunny-hug, the fox trot, and the turkey trot.

Women's costumes, too, were undergoing a revolution; the knee-length skirt did not arrive until after the war, but the stiff, carapace-like corset, which for generations had helped protect weak women from enterprising males, went out; girls whose parents did not allow them to follow the fashion had to discard their corsets surreptitiously in cars and dressing rooms, or risk being called "Old Ironsides" by the boys. The drinking of hard liquor by women and young girls started about the same time; dancing made them thirsty, and the more they drank the more wildly they danced. And jazz, which the Reverend Henry Van Dyke called "a sensual teasing of the strings of sensual passion" was now the principal dance music.

Thus a revolution in sexual morals was well under way before the war started, but the war quickened it. American troops who went overseas indulged in experiences denied to them by law and custom at home, and a paternal government gave them inoculations to prevent venereal disease.

Nurses, Red Cross and Y.W.C.A. workers had their eyes opened. All returned to a country where there was more of everything — money, leisure, cars, sexy movies, dance halls, jazz; not more liquor for a time, but Prohibition made drinking more exciting, and the sort of liquor one got removed inhibitions.

Coincident with the weakening of religious sanction, a pseudo-scientific version of psychology began to supplant it. Doctors Sigmund Freud of Vienna, Carl Jung of Switzerland, and Havelock Ellis of England were the prophets. Ellis's great work, *Studies in the Psychology of Sex*, a sober and scientific case book, began circulating in America around 1910. Both Freud and Jung had lectured in the United States before the war, and by 1916 there were 500 practising psychoanalysts in New York City alone. But it was not until after the war that their doctrines, through translations and popular simplifications and distortions, began to infiltrate. One of the saddest things in history is the way the doctrines of scientific innovators become distorted before they reach the mass of the people. Sir Isaac Newton was a deeply religious man, but got the reputation of postulating a purely mechanical universe; Darwin's doctrine of evolution was distorted to mean that man was descended from a monkey; Karl Marx would never have recognized the societies in which he has been substituted for God; and Dr. Freud, an austere man of impeccable morals who mainly wished to take off the wraps which prevented medical research in sex phenomena, became, in the writings of his unprofessional disciples, the prophet of promiscuity. In 1919–20 one began to hear college students comparing their dreams and prattling knowingly (as they thought) about complexes, inhibitions, infantile sexuality, introverts and extroverts, and the libido. Probably Ellis, Freud, and Jung did much good by throwing light on the dark places of the subconscious, and opening discussion. But on the young of the "lost generation" (as those of the 1920's liked to call themselves) the effect was catastrophic. By presenting inhibition or repression of natural impulses as an unmixed evil which would warp one's character and even ruin one's life, it followed that the Protestant ethic was wrong; that instead of resisting temptation and channeling the sex impulse into marriage, it should be indulged from the age of puberty. A girl who objected to being kissed and handled by her swain of the evening was apt to be silenced by a quotation alleged to be from Jung; a young man indifferent to girls would now be accused of being permanently in love with his mother; virginity became something to get rid of, chastity a medieval relic. Katherine Anthony the feminist, who had promoted the emancipation of women, was astounded in 1921 at "the wild conduct of the young, who are certainly out of bounds since the war." And the same year an ironical Irish journalist, after seeing for himself American postwar mores remarked, "Unbalanced by prolonged contemplation of the tedious virtues of New England, a generation has arisen whose great illusion is that the transvaluation of all values may be effected by promiscuity."

Chaperonage of middle- and upper-class unmarried girls was never as strict in North America as in Latin countries; but what there was now disappeared when the girls most needed protection. Emily Post's first edition of her famous book on etiquette, in 1922, devoted a chapter to "Chaperons and other Conventions." For the edition of 1937 this chapter became "The Vanished Chaperon and Other Lost Conventions." Training, said Madam Post, was replacing protection. The girls were now supposed to be sufficiently intelligent to take care of their own morals, and doubtless most of them were. Moreover, the "wages of sin" were no longer "death." Unmarried mothers were no longer driven from their homes or regarded as moral lepers. Hawthorne's Hester Prynne, or Sarah Orne Jewett's Joanna in *The Country of the Pointed Firs,* who spent her life in lonely exile to expiate one sexual slip, would have been unthinkable by 1936.

Other signs of the times were that in 1929 *The Ladies' Home Journal* first admitted advertisements of lipstick and cigarette manufacturers first dared to show pictures of women smokng. The rate of divorces to marriages doubled between 1910 and 1928, and has continued to rise.

This revolution in the sexual mores of teen-agers and the young married soon received literary expression. Francis Scott Key Fitzgerald of Minnesota, who left Princeton to serve as an infantry officer in the war, created a sensation in 1920 when he described what was going on, in his first two novels: *This Side of Paradise,* and *Flappers and Philosophers.* At the same time John Held, Jr., originally from Utah, became the artist of the flappers, as the free-and-easy girls were called. James T. Farrell in 1932 began describing the life of Chicago's no longer priest-ridden Irish-Americans in the *Studs Lonigan* trilogy, using "four-letter words" seldom before seen in print; and William Faulkner of Mississippi, after serving in the Royal Canadian Air Force, stripped the romance off the South with stark tales like *Sanctuary* (1931). These are among the best of the American novelists who informed the older generation what was going on, and the rising generation what to expect. Priests and parsons, college presidents, the Christian Endeavor Society, the Y.W.C.A., and other organizations thundered against immorality; state legislatures added new regulations to the existing sumptuary laws such as prohibiting bobbed hair or knee-length skirts. Judge Ben Lindsay of the juvenile court of Denver tried to meet the problem in 1927 by proposing to legalize birth control, and trial or "companionate" marriages; but he was howled down by believers in the older moral code. Nothing worked; the "lost generation" proceeded to go to hell or salvation in its own way.

The revolution we have been describing occurred, sooner or later, throughout the Western world. It came earlier in Sweden, Germany, and Australia than in America, about the same time in France and southern Europe; somewhat later in Britain and Latin America. European lecturers in the United States, with knowing leers, regarded developments on this side as long overdue. There was no need for sex to break out in Moslem, Hindu, or Buddhist countries, or in Japan or black Africa, where sensuousness had the sanction of religion. And nowhere in the Christian world was the revolution complete. The old mores remained, embalmed in law and preached from pulpits; and millions of people, probably a majority of the population in the United States, resisted tempting offers to rebuild their lives around a core of sex.

By the time World War II broke out, most people expected that the sexual revolution had about run its course; on the contrary, the war speeded up the movement. And during the postwar years other influences came in to relax old principles still further. The fears and tensions of the cold war tempted people to be merry, since tomorrow they might die. Stream-of-consciousness literature and movies pioneered by James Joyce's *Ulysses* increased in volume and in crudeness; the wraps were removed from frankly pornographic literature which formerly had to be smuggled; and by following "permissiveness" to its logical conclusion, crime was condoned and sexual deviation tolerated. A peculiarly nasty product of the new freedom are the teen-age monsters of both sexes who take drugs, riot, rob, and kill "just for kicks."

Another and less reprehensible development has been the prevalent very early marriage. This, in part, is owing to a desire of young men to escape the draft; in part, the supposed need of young students and working people to combine two incomes in one; in part, a praiseworthy escape into security from the social compulsion toward promiscuity.

Advocates of the new morals claim that the lifting of nineteenth-century repressions, inhibitions, etc., "freed" the rising generation, made them more natural, wholesome, and the like. Probably some oversexed persons were injured by their efforts to be faithful to the Christian ethic. But, how many of the "pure in heart" have been ruined by the present stimuli striking at them every day and from every direction, urging them to surrender to the cruder demands of the flesh? A recent glorifier of the Viennese doctor claims that Freud "demolished the ideals of the hypocritical Victorian age and turned a glaring light on the underworld by revealing the 'filth' that had been repressed into the unconscious."

Possibly that would have been the best place to have left it.

6. Letters, Arts, and Sciences

The "one hundred per cent Americans" of 1919–20 were not content to fight Reds, Parlor Pinks, Democrats, supporters of the League of Nations, and friends of England and France. Intellectuals, especially professors, attracted a good part of their hostility. The colleges and universities were accused of being hotbeds of sedition by Vice President Coolidge in a series of articles in *The Delineator* (1921); but next year Upton Sinclair in *The Goose Step* presented the same institutions as centers of reaction, literary annexes to Wall Street!

Widespread distrust of intellectuals is not surprising, for in this era the peculiarly American form of what Jacques Bendel called *la trahison des clercs*, was to attack American traditions. Charles A. Beard in his *Economic Orgins of the Constitution* (1913) paved the way for a host of writers who maintained that the Federal Constitution was the work of wealthy tricksters to keep democracy down; and in 1927 he produced his *Rise of American Civilization* to prove that there were no heroes or even leaders in American history, only economic trends. Debunking (the word was coined by William E. Woodward in his novel *Bunk*, 1923) became a literary mode; every American hero from Columbus to Coolidge was successively "debunked" — Woodward himself did it to Washington, Grant, and Lafayette. After the war, almost every American writer who had the price fled to Europe; one could find scores of them in certain Parisian cafés declaring to anyone who would listen, that America was "finished" — an "impossible" place for a "cultivated man" to live; or, in the words of T. S. Eliot (a poet whom they admired but who would have no truck with them), a "waste land." From Paris, Harold E. Stearns in 1921 edited a remarkable symposium entitled *Civilization in the United States,* one long moan by thirty solemn young men on American mediocrity, sterility, conformity, and smug prosperity. Frank M. Colby, for instance, wrote a chapter on American Humor merely to say that there was none. What, one wonders, was the matter with Peter Finley Dunne, the creator of Mr. Dooley, or Will Rogers the "Cowboy Philosopher," or Bob Benchley, or that incomparable pair of radio comedians "Amos 'n Andy."

But the greatest debunker of all — one who debunked even the other debunkers — was H. L. Mencken "the bad boy of Baltimore" whose chosen medium was *The American Mercury.* Mencken wrote in a pungent style with an original vocabulary that demanded and got attention, and he was no gentle satirist like Mr. Dooley. He lashed out at almost every group in American society — the "booboisie," the "anthropoids" of the Alleghenies; the *Gelehrten* ("as pathetic an ass as a university professor of history"), the politicians ("crooks and charlatans"), evangelists ("gaudy zanies"), orators ("the seemly bosh of the late Woodrow"), parsons and priests ("mountebanks"), and guardians of public morals ("wowsers"). Mencken was no social reformer but a saucy iconoclast who had something amusing to say about every region, class, and profession in America. He despised democracy and freely predicted that it would dissolve into despotism; he discerned very little good in American life. "Almost the only thing I believe in with a childlike and unquestioning faith," he wrote, "is free speech"; yet he refused to "sympathize with the pedagogues who . . . are heaved out of some fresh-water college for trying to exercise it," because "nothing a pedagogue says, as a pedagogue, is worth hearing." Mencken in his inimitable style emitted a good deal of sound common sense against the folderols of Dewey-inspired education in his day. His merry extravagance and cynicism might have broken down American smugness if that had been his objective; but he had no objective, so his writings had less influence than those of Beard and the ponderous debunkers.

Conrad Aiken, almost alone of Harold Stearns's contributors, found something healthy in American life, praising the "energy, vitality and confidence" of the rising generation of American poets such as Eliot, Frost, Fletcher, Sandburg, Ezra Pound, Cummings, Wheelock, Amy Lowell, Edna St. Vincent Millay, and Elinor Wylie. These and many others did their best work between the two world wars. New York, especially Greenwich Village, was a center of the English-speaking literary world disputed only by London; and Chicago, where the "New Poetry" was launched in 1910, was not far behind with the novels of Robert Herrick, Floyd Dell, and Theodore Dreiser.

Novels that successfully exploited the flatness of small-town life were Sinclair Lewis's *Main Street* (1920) and *Babbitt* (1922), which added two types to our gallery; Sherwood Anderson's *Winesburg, Ohio* (1919), *Poor White* (1920), and *Triumph of the Egg* (1922). Lewis satirized the average American but never achieved anything resembling a literary style, whilst Anderson, in singularly moving and felicitous language, described those who lived "lives of quiet desperation." The Pulitzer prizes for fiction, which began in 1918, were generally awarded, prior to World War II, to conventional novelists such as Edith Wharton (Sinclair Lewis was so angry at not getting it for *Main Street* that he refused one for *Arrowsmith*); but other Pulitzer prizes were intelligently bestowed. Most of the above-mentioned poets received one; and the prize for American biography was given to three really great books, *The Education of Henry Adams,* Beveridge's *Marshall,* and Freeman's *Lee.* The prize for the best American play was thrice awarded to the greatest dramatist of that era, Eugene O'Neill, whose *Anna Christie, Beyond the Horizon, Strange Interlude,* and *Mourning Becomes Electra,* came as close to the humor, the irony, the tragedy, and the human understanding of the ancient Greek dramatists as any playwright is likely to attain for another century.

American literature had many categories besides the above. Books like Edwin D. Slosser's *Creative Chemistry* (1919) became enormously popular, as were the works of English scientists and philosophers. There was an immense curiosity among educated Americans to learn history, philosophy, and science painlessly. H. G. Wells's *Outline of History* (1920) and Will Durant's *Story of Philosophy* (1926) were superficial and popular works which catered to this appetite.

Whilst a febrile despair, a Byronic disillusion, a belief that life had no meaning, that Western civilization was declining into chaos, characterized many of the poets and prose writers of the economically lush 1920's, the following decade of depression, which included the rise of Hitler and Stalin, persuaded most American authors that their country had something worth preserving. Sinclair Lewis in *It Can't Happen Here* (1935) painted a terrifying picture of how America could go fascist; Archibald MacLeish, who had been writing lyric poetry, came out with *The Irresponsibles* (1940), a stirring appeal to artists and men of letters to stop horsing around with strange gods and goddesses, and rally to the defense of American traditions. The same year Ernest Hemingway, after observing the death throes of the Spanish Republic, published *For Whom the Bell Tolls* as a warning to his country, and Dos Passos, after portraying in his *U.S.A.* trilogy of 1930–36 a rootless and disintegrating society, came to a halt in *The Ground We Stand On*. Edna St. Vincent Millay, having burned her "candle at both ends," turned to spiritual values in *Huntsman, What Quarry?* (1939); and Stephen Vincent Benét, who had never lost faith in America, delivered a solemn warning in "Litany for Dictatorships" (1936). John Steinbeck, after writing the Rabelaisian *Tortilla Flat* about Mexicans in California, produced *The Grapes of Wrath* in 1939. This story of a ruined family's journey from their Oklahoma dust bowl to the promised land of California was the one great novel to portray the tragedy of the Great Depression for the rural proletariat.

Painting in America remained in a healthy condition throughout this era. The Armory Show of 1913 introduced New York to the avant-garde of Europe — Gaugin, Picasso, and Duchamp's "Nude Descending a Staircase." But American artists struck out on lines of their own. Some, like Thomas Hart Benton, continued the Hudson River tradition of glorifying American scenery, but the majority depicted American life — in brisk movement, as with Waldo Peirce's "Trotting Race at a Country Fair"; with satire, as in Grant Wood's "American Gothic"; with pathos, as in George Biddle's "Sacco and Vanzetti." Biddle himself observed that in an exhibition of 1936 there were no nudes, portraits, or still-lifes among the American paintings; the majority dealt with the current scene or reflected a social criticism of American life. It was not a great age in American sculpture, largely for lack of demand; pallid busts no longer adorned the drawing-rooms of the rich, the public wanted no more statues of heroes, and architecture was becoming stark; but we had a few very distinguished works like Paul Manship's "Prometheus" at Rockefeller Center; George C. Barnard's two statues of Nature in the Metropolitan Museum, Anna Hyatt Huntington's "Joan of Arc" in New York, and Joseph Coletti's high-relief sculptures in the Baltimore Cathedral. Daniel Chester French in 1922 crowned his long career with the heroic statue in the Lincoln Memorial, which his friend Henry Bacon had designed.

In American music it was not a great age for original compositions. John Alden Carpenter of Chicago, composer in the classical tradition, came to terms with the modern age in his "Skyscrapers" ballet, produced both in New York and Munich in 1926–28. The most distinctive contributions to American music were made by Negroes. Their syncopated "rag-time" melodies developed into jazz. The Negro soldiers' bands brought jazz to Europe during the war; and before long, inspired by expert practitioners such as Duke Ellington and Bessie Smith, saxophones were wailing, trumpets shrieking, and "blues" singers moaning jazz music around the world.

The most successful American composers between-wars were New York City boys like Aaron Copland and George Gershwin, and Roy E. Harris of

Utah, who applied symphonic methods to jazz and translated this folk art into music. Gershwin's *Of Thee I Sing* (1932) was a side-splitting musical satire on American politics in the Gilbert and Sullivan manner, and his *Porgy and Bess* (1935), based on the compassionately humorous play *Porgy* by DuBose Heyward about Negro life in Charleston, has become a veritable American opera. So, too, is Rogers and Hammerstein's *Oklahoma!* Harris's Folk Song Symphonies and Walter Piston's "Third Symphony" of 1947 were in the same tradition.

Besides the works of these *maestros* there was a general dissemination of good music among the people by skilled teachers: — Archibald T. Davison and his assistant G. Wallace Woodworth, whose coaching of the Harvard Glee Club stimulated every college vocal society, and Thomas W. Surette, whose *Concord Series* of musical reprints went nationwide, and whose Concord Summer School of Music trained hundreds of teachers in the philosophy of "nothing but the best" music to be sung in schools and colleges.

Broadcasting music by radio began in 1920; forty years later there were 200 million radio and television sets in America. Discriminating listeners skipped the commercials, the "soap opera," and other trash to enjoy chamber music, symphonies, and operas. Supplementing radio were millions of phonographs playing everything from blues to Beethoven. Eighty-four new symphony orchestras were established in the depression decade, but the nation supported very few opera companies. Music conservatories flourished; great foundations like the Guggenheim patronized budding genius. And totalitarian terror brought to America some distinguished European composers and musicians such as Stravinsky, Hindemith, Bartók, and Schönberg.

American scholarship and science now came of age. The great change came after 1910 when men of wealth (notably Rockefeller, Carnegie, Guggenheim) and the foundations that they set up, endowed libraries and laboratories where scholars and scientists could labor without going to Europe, and established scholarship and research funds which enabled them to do creative work without the physical drag of teaching elements to undergraduates. Americans received no Nobel awards for physics, chemistry, or medicine prior to 1923. Thereafter, about one in three of the Nobel prizes in physics, one in five of those in chemistry, one in four of those in medicine, have gone to Americans.

The most striking advances were in the fields of astronomy, physics, and medicine. Working with the giant telescope of Mt. Wilson Observatory, which enabled them to plot thousands of new galaxies, astronomers like Harlow Shapley discovered an indefinitely expanding universe. Physicists invented the cyclotron to break down atoms, and founded the new science of nuclear physics. Einstein and Fermi were two great European physicists who found refuge in America from Hitler and Mussolini.

Of all these subjects, medical science, which closely affected the lives of the people, underwent a revolution in this period. The rural general practitioner of 1910 made endless house calls, driving long distances day and night in his buggy, as well as seeing patients in his office, which was generally at his home. Only rarely would a doctor send a patient to a hospital, of which there were few outside the great cities. Childbirth in a hospital was virtually unknown; surgeons even performed caesareans and other major operations in the patient's home, usually on the kitchen table. Specialists, mostly graduates of European universities, were available only in certain cities. The first effect of the automobile on medicine was to extend the doctor's range. Maurice H. Richardson of Boston, the country's leading specialist in appendectomy, kept two big limousines and day-and-night chauffeurs; after an urgent telephone call he would pick up a nurse, an assistant, and his instruments and be driven over abominable roads 100 miles or more into the country to perform an operation — often for nothing if the patient was poor. He once remarked to this writer, "Ten appendectomies this week; total take, $200 and a barrel of apples."

The men who did most to inaugurate an era when any patient, almost anywhere, could have the entire corpus of medical knowledge at his disposal, were a quartet of young medical geniuses who came to Johns Hopkins University during the 1890's and remained active well into the twentieth century. These were William H. Welch, pathologist; Howard A. Kelly, gynecologist; William S. Halsted, surgeon; and William Osler, beloved physician and medical scholar. All were great teachers as well as men of science; they and their pupils implemented and continued the revolution in medicine and surgery that began with Eliot's reforms at Harvard in 1870.[1]

The founding in 1903 of the Rockefeller Institute for Medical Research — one of the many institutions through which the Rockefeller family have put their ill-gotten wealth to the service of mankind — is a second landmark. For there could be little progress in medicine without research, and that required training and adequate support. The Institute was a first step leading to the vast and continuing expansion of facilities for medical research. Seven years later appeared the Flexner report on Medical Education, result of a two-year investigation initiated by the American Medical Association and financed by one of the Carnegie foundations. Dr. Abraham Flexner exposed numerous "degree mills" which even granted M.D.'s by correspondence; he found the average medical school inadequately staffed by busy general practitioners who had neither time nor inclination for research; indeed, the only first-class medical school, he said, was the Johns Hopkins. This report stimulated the good medical schools to improve, encouraged wealthy foundations and individuals to provide funds, and promoted the development of medical specialties. As an example, Boston has become the world's center for

1. Osler, a Canadian graduate of McGill, became Regius Professor of Medicine at Oxford in 1909, was created a baronet by King George V, and died in 1919. The others remained active up to their deaths: "Popsy" Welch in 1934, Halsted in 1922, and Kelly in 1943. For Eliot's reforms, see Chapter XLVII above.

children's diseases, owing to pediatricians such as Kenneth D. Blackfan and James L. Gamble, and the Children's Hospital that they served; and also for the study of tropical diseases, owing to the research and field trips of Drs. Richard P. Strong and George C. Shattuck. Another significant development was the clinic where a number of specialists gathered to minister to human ills; the Mayo Clinic at Rochester, Minnesota, is the most famous.

Diseases which had hitherto baffled the medical profession were now attacked by doctors, chemists, bacteriologists, and physicists, working in the laboratories of universities, governments, and the foundations. Results were spectacular. In the first third of the century, infant mortality in the United States declined by two-thirds, and life expectancy increased from 49 to 59 years. The death rate for tuberculosis dropped from 180 to 49 per 100,000, for typhoid from 36 to 2, for diphtheria from 43 to 2, for measles from 12 to 1, for pneumonia from 158 to 50. Sulfa drugs and penicillin made pneumonia no longer something to be dreaded. Yellow fever and smallpox were practically wiped out, and the war on malaria, pellagra, hookworm, and similar diseases was brilliantly successful. Sir Frederick Banting in Canada discovered the insulin cure for diabetes just in time to save the life of Dr. George Minot of the Harvard Medical School; Minot and his colleague William P. Murphy then proceeded to find the liver-extract treatment for pernicious anemia. Intensive research to improve anesthesia, and the perfection of avertin and cyclopropane, made possible the brain surgery of Harvey Cushing, the cardiac treatments of Paul Dudley White (which probably saved President Eisenhower's life), and the heart surgery of Alfred Blalock and Robert Gross. Rickets and tooth decay yielded to vitamin treatment, and that discovery led to general dietary reform as well as to a great deal of quackery in "wonder drugs" sold by pharmaceutical companies at staggering profits. Adrenalin proved helpful in cardiac disorders and gave relief to sufferers from asthma. Tannic acid, found to cure apparently fatal burns, saved thousands of lives of soldiers and sailors in World War II. The fight against coccus infections was sensational. English and American doctors experimented with sulfanilamide (whose therapeutic qualities were discovered by Gerhard Domagk in 1932 when working for the German dye industry) and its numerous derivatives, and found that it could be successfully used against a host of coccal infections including meningitis, gonorrhea, undulant fever, and pneumonia.

Yet it was typical of America that, side by side with the great medical schools and research laboratories there flourished throughout the country a considerable number of medical heresies, notably the chiropractors. "This preposterous quackery," wrote H. L. Mencken in 1927, which claimed to cure all human ills by "thrusts, lunges, yanks, hooks, and bounces, is now all the rage in the back reaches of the Republic, and even begins to conquer the less civilized of the big cities" — notably Los Angeles, haven of strange sects. The osteopaths, well established by 1910, though still unorthodox, have become more respectable with the lapse of years and no longer pretend to work miracles by manipulation of the spinal column.

Polar exploration was one of the most important scientific exploits of this era, and, just as all the major maritime discoveries had been made under sail, so the discovery of the two poles was made by foot and by dog.

Admiral Robert E. Peary thus attained the North Pole in 1909 as a result of exploring and studying the Arctic regions and cultivating the Eskimo for over twenty years. He decided that the best way to attain the coveted pole was to thrust as far into the Arctic ice as possible in a ship, and dash northward by dog train, establishing caches of provisions en route for the return journey. After two such attempts, which came within three degrees of the pole, he left his ship about 435 miles from the objective in March 1909, and took off with 33 men, 19 sleds, and 133 huskies. Every five days a cache was established and a section of the expedition returned. At the last of these, at lat. 87°48′ N, Peary with his Negro assistant Matthew A. Henson, four Eskimos, five sleds, and 40 dogs, made his final dash, and on 6 April reached the top of the world. Three weeks later, he was back on board his ship.

The conquest of the South Pole took more time, because there is no human life in the Antarctic, and the land is only supportable by humans with large stockpiles of food and fuel. The Norwegian Roald Amundsen did it after a decade of experience in polar regions. In 1903–5 he made the North-west Passage, Atlantic to Pacific, which the Cabots, Frobisher, and Hudson had vainly attempted, in his little sloop *Gjöa*. In 1910 he commanded a modest expedition in the ship *Fram* to the Antarctic, taking Eskimo dogs and sleds. With them he crossed the great Ross Barrier, and on 14 December 1911 raised his country's flag over the South Pole, and returned safely. The English explorer Robert F. Scott, using the same methods, arrived there a month later; but Scott with his four companions died of exposure on the return trip.

A new chapter in Antarctic exploration was opened when Richard E. Byrd, a United States naval officer, applied the internal combustion engine and the airplane. After making the first flight over the North Pole on 9 May 1926, and a transatlantic flight too, he obtained private funds for air exploration of the Antarctic. This, he rightly estimated, was of far more potential value than the Arctic, because it is a solid continent, not an ice-covered ocean. From New Zealand he jumped off in barque *Bear* to Ross Ice Shelf, where the open ocean most nearly approaches the pole and there at lat. 78°30′ S established the base that he named Little America, in October 1928. Thence, after a month of careful preparation, he departed with a crew of three in the tri-motored plane *Floyd Bennett*, flew over the South Pole on 28 November, and returned to base in less than 19 hours. Bryd, as able a writer as explorer and leader, records this exploit in his *Little America* (1930).

For Byrd, this was just a beginning. Promoted rear admiral by act of Congress, he lectured and worked for funds for several years, and in 1934 established an advanced base on lat. 80° S and spent five months there alone in the Antarctic waste to make meteorological and other observations. In addition he explored and charted a large part of Antarctica. His book *Discovery* (1935) relates his experiences. It aroused universal interest in the Antarctic for strategic and economic possibilities. President Roosevelt appointed Admiral Byrd commander of the U.S. Antarctic Service, in 1939, and for two years he made further explorations of the Southern continent by airplane and motorized sled or tractor. Then World War II interrupted his work.

The stock market crash of 1929 and the depression that followed punctuated the era that we have been describing. No quarter-century of American history had wrought so many changes in society, or so few in politics. After a crusade to "make the world safe for democracy," America turned away from Europe. After a century and a half of asking the world to "give me your tired, your poor, your huddled masses yearning to breathe free," her door was shut. After a century of increasing temperance, prohibition had been adopted, then repealed. After three centuries in which Christian morals had been maintained by law, religion, and custom, "permissiveness" had conquered St. Augustine and John Milton, becoming a dominant principle in education and sexual relations. Yet there had been gain as well as loss: the rise of real wages, the siphoning of private fortunes into research institutions, the improved quality of American literature, music, scholarship, science, and medicine. And, despite the breakdown of traditional values and virtues, America managed to weather the Great Depression and the Second World War.

OF THEE I SING

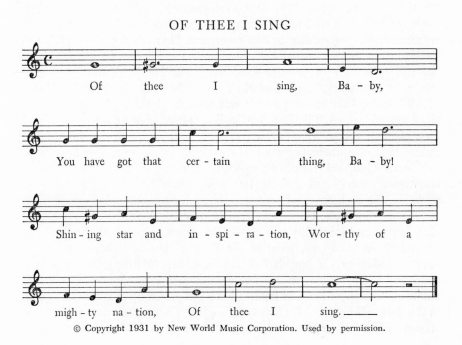

© Copyright 1931 by New World Music Corporation. Used by permission.

Republican Ascendancy

1921-1933

1. Harding and the "Ohio Gang"

EIGHT YEARS OF Democratic rule were followed by twelve of Republican ascendancy under three inept Presidents — Warren G. Harding, Calvin
Coolidge, and Herbert Hoover. Yet Hoover and Coolidge were good men and
the former had elements of greatness. Their failure to cope with difficult
problems must be shared by their party, which until 1931 controlled both
houses of Congress; the G.O.P., like the aristocrats who returned to power in
France after the fall of Napoleon, had "forgotten nothing and learned nothing." Progressive Republicans, having been piped away by Theodore Roosevelt into the Bull Moose wilderness, had to straggle back on their knees, if at
all; for the party was now in the hands of conservatives and reactionaries.
They, in general, regarded the Democratic interlude of 1913–21 as abnormal,
the war which Wilson had led them into as a failure, and his New Freedom
an unnecessary obstruction to free enterprise. Hoover's favorite cliché, "The
American system of rugged individualism," Vice President Coolidge's epigram "The business of America is business," and Harding's election slogan, a
return to "normalcy," expressed their views. McKinley's administration, to
which Harding liked to compare his, was normal; Theodore Roosevelt's and all
since were abnormal. The Harding-Coolidge plurality of 61 per cent seemed a
clear mandate for isolation in foreign policy, favoring big business in domestic
policy, and government keeping hands off individuals, no matter how rugged.

Warren Gamaliel Harding was what everyone called a "nice" man —
handsome, genial, well dressed, outwardly dignified; his big plurality was
probably due to many more women voting for him than for colorless, flat-
faced Governor Cox. He was a "typical American," son of an Ohio physician, lawyer and journalist in a small Ohio town, director of the local bank
and telephone company, pillar of the Baptist church, favorite orator, state
senator, and always a "regular" Republican. Mrs. Harding, an angular and
ambitious widow five years his senior, groomed Warren into respectability
and made his newspaper pay. Politically he had grown up as a "spieler" (orator
in the slang of that day) for Senator Joseph B. Foraker, whose intimates were
known as the "Ohio gang." Foraker, after years of feuding with Theodore

Roosevelt, had been driven from public life by the disclosure that he had been on the Standard Oil payroll while serving as senator. At that juncture Harry M. Daugherty, Foraker's hatchet man, took up Harding and managed his campaign for the Senate in 1914. Harding's senatorial career proved so satisfactory to party stalwarts and big business, that Daugherty began an astute and successful campaign to make him President of the United States. And with him the "'Ohio gang" moved into Washington.

President Harding's top cabinet appointments — Charles Evans Hughes as secretary of state, Andrew W. Mellon the Pittsburgh aluminum millionaire secretary of the treasury, Herbert Hoover secretary of commerce — were excellent. But most of the other cabinet posts and several leading administrative positions went to the gang. Harry M. Daugherty, a lobbyist by profession, became attorney general; a senatorial friend, Albert B. Fall, who looked like a ballyhoo-man at a country fair but served the oil interests well, secretary of the interior; Will N. Hays, Harding's campaign manager, postmaster general. Of the local cronies, a former county sheriff was appointed director of the mint, a Marion lawyer whose financial experience was limited to a few months' presidency of the local bank became governor of the federal reserve banking system; "Colonel" Charles R. Forbes, a chance acquaintance who, it subsequently appeared, had deserted from the army, became head of the Veterans' Bureau. A local doctor named Sawyer, who had helped Mrs. Harding (a hypochondriac and believer in soothsayers and clairvoyants) was suddenly jumped from civilian life to an army "generalcy," as the President called it, to be White House physician. A loutish fellow named Jess Smith, valet-secretary to Daugherty, was given an office in the department of justice and became the primary "fixer" of the administration. Gaston B. Means, another hanger-on, was the gang's bootlegger while holding office in the department of justice. After serving a term in the penitentiary (subsequent to Harding's death) for selling permits for "medicinal" whisky, Means disclosed that he had collected the cool sum of $7 million in bribes from bootleggers, and turned over the money to Jess Smith. But by that time Smith had committed suicide and could not deny it.

Other friends of the President were equally shady characters; there was never so raffish a "court" as that of Warren G. Harding. And what a change in the White House! In contrast to the jolly country-house atmosphere of the Theodore Roosevelt administration, the sick-room smell of the latter part of Wilson's, and the good taste and republican elegance of the future Kennedy administration, that of Harding's was of the bar-room. T.R.'s daughter Mrs. Nicholas Longworth, inadvertently straying into an upstairs room during a state reception, found a recently vacated poker table littered with cigar stubs, glasses, and partly empty whisky bottles; and if she had explored below stairs she might have found a young mistress of the President, brought in through a back door, waiting for him in a cloakroom. To escape such respectability as Mrs. Harding imposed on the White House, the President of an evening would steal away to the home of Jess Smith or some other crony, to play more poker and drink heavily.

These were indeed the "hollow men" as T. S. Eliot characterized the postwar politicians of the Western world. There was nothing in them but wind, greed, and a certain low cunning.

Congress, too, was full of hollow men, William E. Borah, perpetual senator from Idaho, was the most pretentious and the emptiest, although he looked more like a statesman than any senator since Daniel Webster. Borah would support any liberal bill with great rumbling oratory, yet in the end vote with the regular Republicans. Senator Norris said of him, "He fights until he sees the whites of their eyes." Or, for a hollow man from New England, take George Holden Tinkham, bachelor congressman from one of the Boston districts, a big-game hunter with an impressive though greasy beard. Tinkham was immovable because he did favors at Washington for most of his constituents — getting pensions for those who were not entitled to them, sending a wreath to everyone's funeral, a present for every bride, and a graduation gift to every young person in his district. No Democrat in Democratic Boston dared oppose him, and one campaign for re-election was conducted in absentia by his efficient lady secretary. Every summer Tinkham went globe-trotting, and on his return gave out pronouncements on world developments that invariably were wrong. But he could get anything he wanted from the federal government because he had taken the precaution, when Prohibition was looming, to buy a small hotel in the District and equip it with a good ten years' supply of alcoholic beverages, with which he was very generous; this being his private stock, enforcement agents did not dare touch it.

Harding was the best of the lot — a vulgar good fellow who wished to make everyone happy and saw nothing incongruous in promoting a small-town banker to the most powerful and responsible financial position in the government. That was the older American way, the Andrew Jackson way; anybody was qualified for any office, provided his politics were right. But Harding was completely out of his depth in the presidency. Typical was his outburst to a secretary after hearing his advisers discuss a financial matter: "John, I can't make a damn thing out of this tax problem. I listen to one side and they seem right, and then — God! — I talk to the other side, and they seem just as right. I know somewhere there is a book that will give me the truth, but hell, I couldn't read the book. I know somewhere there is an economist who knows the truth, but I don't know where to find him and haven't the sense to know and trust him when I find him. God! what a job!" Uncomfortable with Hughes, Mellon, and Hoover, the statesmen in his cabinet, Harding became increasingly dependent for advice on the "good fellows" — Daugherty, Hays, and Fall.

But Harding had a heart, and he wished to do something for peace. One of his first kind acts (one which Wilson had refused to do) was to pardon several victims of prosecution under the wartime Sedition Act, notably Eugene Debs who had served two years of a ten-year sentence for saying no more than the Federalist leaders had said in 1812, or the Whigs in 1846. The pardon was to have been given in 1922, but Harding upped it to the previous December "so Debs could spend Christmas with his family."

2. The Republicans and Foreign Affairs

Harding's biggest bid for peace was the Naval Disarmament Conference of 1921–22, first of several futile efforts toward disarmament. The "Big Navy" Act of 1916, if fully implemented by Congress, would have made the United States Navy "incomparably the most adequate navy in the world," as President Wilson put it. Lloyd George, instead of welcoming this development, which would partly have relieved the Royal Navy of world-wide responsibilities, chose to regard it as a challenge; and Britain, impoverished by her hard-won victory, could never match the American program. So the British premier proposed an international meeting for naval disarmament. Harding and Hughes, eager to accomplish something for peace, gladly accepted, and the conference opened at Washington on 12 November 1921, with delegates from three major (United States, Britain, Japan), two medium (France and Italy), and four minor (Belgium, Holland, Portugal, China) naval powers.

Secretary Hughes astounded the conference and electrified the world by announcing in his opening speech that the United States was prepared to scrap new naval construction on which $300 million had already been spent, if Britain and Japan would do likewise. After long bargaining, it was agreed to scrap a great deal of naval tonnage built or building, and to limit future building. The Washington treaties, signed 6 February 1922, set up a 5:5:3 ratio in battleship and aircraft carrier tonnage between Britain, America, and Japan. A ten-year "holiday" was declared on building capital ships, and the tonnage of battleships was restricted to 35,000. Although this ratio allowed Japan to become the strongest naval power in the western Pacific (since America had two, and Britain three, oceans to defend), Japanese consent had to be purchased by a supplementary agreement on military bases. The United States renounced strengthening, in a military sense, any of her bases such as Guam and Manila that lay west of Pearl Harbor; and England similarly denied the same to herself east of Singapore or north of Australia. This provision actually reversed the 5:5:3 ratio to favor Japan, as the United States and Great Britain learned to their sorrow twenty years later.

Naval limitation was undoubtedly popular. Congress never authorized naval construction up to treaty strength until the eve of World War II, and the Kellogg-Briand Peace Pact which President Coolidge added to the Republican preserve-the-peace armory was ratified by the United States Senate (15 January 1929) by a vote of 81 to 1. Initiated by the French premier Aristide Briand, supported by the British prime minister Ramsay Macdonald, this pact was negotiated for the United States by Secretary of State Frank B.

Kellogg. It provided that the contracting powers "renounce war as an instrument of national policy," and promised to solve "all disputes or conflicts of whatever nature or of whatever origin" by "pacific means." No fewer than 62 nations, including Italy, Japan, and Germany, adhered to the Kellogg-Briand Pact, which may fairly be called an attempt to keep the peace by incantation. It was taken seriously by the democratic nations, and the breach of it by the Axis powers became the basis of war criminals' trials after World War II.

These methods of preserving the peace — by naval limitation, by incantation, and (in the Roosevelt administration) by negation — would have been effective among nations that wanted peace. They were worse than useless in a world in which three nations — Germany, Italy, and Japan — wanted war; for they merely served to lull the democracies into a false feeling of security, while giving the militarists elsewhere a chance to plot, plan, and prepare for a war that would enable them to divide the world.

Uncle Sam's isolationist bark was much worse than his bite. After World War I was over, many efforts were made both by the government and private charity to relieve suffering in Europe and the Middle East. In July 1921 the Soviet government persuaded the well-known Russian writer Maxim Gorky to appeal for relief from starvation in Russia. Allegedly this was the result of drought and crop failures, but primarily it was due to the Soviet government's abolition of private property and forced collection of food from the peasants. Although Lenin had made it clear that the communists were bent on upsetting every capitalist government, and that the United States was their principal target, America responded generously to Gorky's appeals to her "bourgeois" sentiment of humanity. The American Relief Association, headed by Secretary Hoover, with funds contributed partly by private charity but mainly by the United States government, moved into Russia promptly and vigorously. By August 1922 two hundred Americans were there, directing 18,000 stations at which more than 4 million children and 6 million adults were fed. Medical assistance, too, was provided on a massive scale. A conservative estimate of the number of Russian lives saved through the efforts of the A.R.A. is 11 million. But this great effort is now written down by Soviet historians as an effort of American capitalists to overthrow the Communist regime; the most that they can admit is that A.R.A. "gave a certain help to the starving."

Near East Relief, another massive charitable effort, was financed wholly from private sources. The Rev. James L. Barton, a former missionary in Turkey, and Cleveland H. Dodge, financier and philanthropist, ran it with the help of a board of trustees that included Taft, Root, Hughes, and F. D. Roosevelt. The condition of the people around the Aegean was particularly deplorable, because, after the world war ended, hostilities continued between Greece and Turkey. These culminated in 1922 with the Greeks taking a bad beating and being forced to evacuate every person of their race and religion from Turkish territory. Almost a million and a half refugees from Asia crossed the Aegean; in revenge, all Moslems had to leave Greece. Near East Relief undertook not only to feed and clothe these "displaced persons," earliest of that unfortunate class in modern times, but to build them houses, set up schools for their children, and industries to employ them. Between 1919 and 1930 it disbursed some $91 million in money and $25 million worth of food in Greece, Turkey, Armenia, Macedonia, Persia, and Mesopotamia. About one-quarter of all this was sent to alleviate famine and disease in the Russian Caucasus, where conditions following the civil war were unspeakably bad; all this in addition to what the A.R.A. was doing in other parts of Russia.

Nor did America turn her back on Europe in the matter of war debts and German reparations. During the war, in addition to private loans, the Allies received over $7 billion from the United States government, to which $3.2 billion more were added after the armistice. These debts were to bear interest at 5 per cent. From Great Britain alone $4 billion was due; but Britain had made similar loans to other Allies amounting to $10.5 billion. Arthur Balfour proposed in 1922 that all inter-allied war debts be canceled, and to many Americans this seemed a just solution, considering how late we had entered the war and that most of the loans had been spent in the United States. But such generosity was politically explosive, and the Fordney-McCumber tariff act, an upward revision all along the line, prevented Europe from repaying her debts by the export of goods.

In 1923 Congress consented to a radical reduction of war debts, ranging from 30 per cent of both capital and interest for Britain to 80 per cent for Italy, together with extension of the time of repayment to 62 years. During the Great Depression the European governments were unable to continue these payments. President Hoover advised, and Congress consented, to a moratorium on war debts for a year. After that there was a general default, Finland and Cuba alone meeting their financial obligations in full. Americans felt that they had been very generous, but Europeans asserted that "U.S." stood for "Uncle Shylock" and mutual recriminations helped to prolong American neutrality in World War II.

German reparations, fixed at $33 billion in 1921, were inseparable from the inter-allied war debts because the Allies expected to use them to repay each other and the United States. The government of the German Republic became involved in runaway inflation, until a postage stamp cost a million marks, and suspended reparation payments in December 1922. France countered by invading the Ruhr, the German miners struck, and this attempt to collect debts by force was a dismal failure. Roland W. Boyden, a Boston lawyer of great acumen who had been unofficial "observer" for Presidents Wilson and Harding on the Reparations Commission, publicly criticized French policy and advocated that both debts and reparations be settled on the principle of "ability to pay," which finally was done. Secretary Hughes appointed a committee headed by the Chicago financier Charles G. Dawes (later Vice President under Coolidge), which arranged for an American loan to enable Germany to pay something, persuaded France to evacuate the Ruhr, and to help the German Republic establish a new and sound currency. Germany had to be bailed out again in 1929; this time it was the Wall Street financier Owen D. Young, appointed by President Hoover, who did the trick and persuaded Germany's creditors to scale down reparations to $27 billion, to be paid within 60 years. Germany met this reduced payment only by floating bonds in the United States. By 1931, when Germany finally defaulted in the depth of her depression, she had paid $4.5 billion in reparations, of which $2.5 billion had been borrowed from hopeful American investors. In the same period the Allies had paid $2.6 billion to the United States, which thus footed over half the German reparations which were actually paid, as well as allowing three-quarters of the Allied debts to go by default.

The three Republican Presidents and their secretaries of state, Hughes, Kellogg, and Henry L. Stimson, managed to maintain an uneasy peace in the Far East where the breakup of China into spheres controlled by war lords offered tempting opportunities for aggression, especially by Japan. That country, under a liberal government since the war, honored her trust commitments under the League of Nations, canceled the "Twenty-one Demands" which would have made China her satellite, withdrew her armies from Siberia, Manchuria, and the Shantung peninsula as she had promised to do, and joined in the nine-power treaty of 1922. In this treaty the powers which had Far Eastern interests promised to "safeguard the rights and interests of China," mutually agreeing to respect her sovereignty, independence, and administrative integrity, and to refrain from creating "spheres of influence" or seeking special privileges or concessions.

But the Japanese liberals, the only hope of preserving peace in the Orient, lost out to the militarists, who played up Japan's short end of the 5:5:3 ratio in the naval limitation treaties as insulting and unconstitutional, and resented the exclusion of Japanese from the United States by the Act of 1924. These things, together with too frequent instances of American intolerance toward Japanese-Americans, offended Nipponese pride and offset the gratitude for generous American help after the Tokyo earthquake of 1923. That earthquake did, however, postpone a crisis because the havoc that it created and the superstitious dread it aroused caused the military secret societies to postpone the coup d'état they had planned. The Japanese militarists, who bore a strong resemblance in methods and objectives to Hitler's Nazis, were planning to seize the government and throw the detested white man out of East Asia. World War II in the Far East really began on 18 September 1931 when General Hayashi moved his army from Korea into Manchuria. The Japanese government, ignorant of this "Manchuria Incident" until it was accomplished, was forced to acquiesce under threat of assassination, and declared Manchuria to be the independent kingdom of Manchukuo, under a puppet monarch.

All this violated treaties, the Kellogg Pact, and the League Covenant, by which Japan was bound. Without waiting for League action Secretary Stimson informed Japan that the United States would not recognize the legality of any development which impaired American treaty rights or violated the open-door policy. He would have gone further but for President Hoover's Quakerish qualms. A commission of the League of Nations condemned the Japanese aggression in September 1932; Japan countered by withdrawing from the League. The militarists consolidated their power by assassinating the Japanese premier and other important ministers of state, and entered on a vigorous program of economic and military preparation for invading China proper.

In Mexico and Central America, the Republican administrations liquidated a very sticky situation with Mexico but became deeply involved in Nicaragua.

Álvaro Obregón was elected constitutional president of Mexico in 1920 after the assassination of Wilson's old antagonist Carranza, and Plutarco Calles succeeded him in 1924. Both kept order fairly well; but both were resolved to carry out the basic principles of the Mexican Revolution — to nationalize all foreign oil, mining, and other properties, and destroy the power of the Roman Catholic church. Calles aroused resentment in the United States by conducting a heavy flirtation with the Soviets; in his era it was more profitable for Mexican politicians to make pilgrimages to Lenin's tomb in Moscow than to Our Lady of Guadalupe. American oil interests, especially those of Doheny and Sinclair which had been smirched by the Teapot Dome affair, wanted war; and Secretary Kellogg, who had negotiated the pact outlawing war, was almost converted to armed intervention. President Coolidge appeared to take the same point of view by declaring that Americans and their property abroad were part of the public domain. Thus, by the close of 1926 it looked as if another war with Mexico were about to begin. But a remarkable uprise of public sentiment, expressed by the liberal press, labor unions, Protestant church groups, and others, even converted the United States Senate, which on 25 January 1927 resolved unanimously that our differences with Mexico be settled by arbitration. "Cool Cal," sensitive to public opinion, then recalled his interventionist ambassador and appointed Dwight W. Morrow, a partner of the House of Morgan, ambassador to Mexico. Morrow succeeded in repairing most of the damage done by his predecessors there and his superiors in Washington. He really liked the Mexicans, he despised dollar diplomacy, he negotiated informally, and took Will Rogers on an inspection tour, knowing that the "cowboy philosopher's" reports would improve the average American's picture of the Mexicans. Charles Lindbergh, invited to visit Mexico City, was received with wild enthusiasm; Morrow built a house at Cuernavaca and employed Diego Rivera to decorate the town hall with murals.

The Mexican Congress now modified some of its oil and mineral legislation in line with American objections, and Morrow obtained an adjustment of land questions, claims, and the Catholic question. For several years the new understanding inaugurated by Morrow remained undisturbed, while in the United States admiration for Mexican culture and a growing appreciation of the social ideals of the Mexican revolution made a good base for the future.

Obregón, re-elected President of Mexico in 1928, was assassinated before he could take office. After three temporary presidents whom Calles promoted and sustained, Lázaro Cardenas was elected president in 1934.

Despite the reluctance of Republican administrations to get involved in Latin America, circumstances forced President Coolidge into a hot little row in Nicaragua. The previous intervention in that volcanic country, begun under President Taft, had barely been liquidated and the marines' legation guard withdrawn from Managua (August 1925) when civil war erupted. So, honoring a request from the then government of Nicaragua to help preserve order along the Corinto-Managua railroad, back came the marines — some 2000 of them by February 1927, and many more before the troubles were over. President Coolidge sent Henry L. Stimson, who had just returned from a trouble-shooting trip to the Philippines, to Managua to "straighten the matter out," which that remarkable man effected within five weeks. He brought the leaders of both sides together, obtained the "agreement of Tipitata" to stop fighting, allowed the presidential incumbent to stay in for a year and then to hold a free election supervised by the marines, who in the meantime would train a native national guard to maintain order. Stimson returned home to find that Coolidge had appointed him governor general of the Philippines.

So far, so good; but one of the twelve opposition generals, Augusto Sandino, refused to co-operate and continued the fight from his mountain redoubt in northern Nicaragua. Sandino was of different metal from the bandit chiefs with whom the marines had dealt in Hispaniola. A troublemaker from school days, he had escaped justice for murder and lived for several years in Mexico, where he made useful contacts with communists and other left-wing elements. Like the guerrillas in Viet-Nam, when hard-pressed he was always able to retire to a safe asylum over the border, recruit, and return to fight again. The Communist party played him up as a hero of liberation and not only collected arms and money for him but fooled gullible liberals in the United States and Europe into supporting Sandino as the savior of his country from the "imperialists." The New York *Nation*, edited by pacifist Oswald Garrison Villard, gave Sandino full support while he was spreading terror and torture through Nicaraguan villages. Henry Barbusse, author of *Le feu*, called Sandino "Le George Washington de l'Amérique Centrale"; and the Chinese communists named a division after him.

Sandino was a precursor of Fidel Castro; had he won, Nicaragua could have become another red satellite. "General don Augusto Cesar Sandino," as he styled himself, called his forces, "El Ejército Autonomista de Centro America," indicating that he intended to take over neighboring republics as well; and his middle name, added by himself, suggested that he proposed to play

the role of Octavian in uniting Central America against "el grotesco imperial-
ismo Yanki."

Owing largely to the marines, he did not win. Sandino never had many
troops, but his friends saw that they were well supplied with weapons and munitions. The marines had a tactical air squadron which helped turn the tide. In
November 1928, the presidential election brought about the first peaceful
change of government in Nicaraguan history. But Sandino, after spending
over a year recruiting in Mexico, struck again in 1930, financed by world-wide
contributions from left-wingers. Again repulsed, again he returned; this time
he was hurled back into Honduras by the new national guard led by Captain
Lewis B. ("Chesty") Puller USMC. Once more returning, he was arrested by
the national guard and executed by a firing squad led by Colonel Anastacio
Somoza, the guard's *jefe*. Somoza now assumed the presidency and became a
dictator. But Nicaragua was at peace; and under the "good neighbor" policy
of Franklin D. Roosevelt there were no more forcible interventions in Latin
America.

Although the Philippines were not yet "foreign," it will be convenient at
this point to follow thither Governor General Stimson. The lax and extravagant proconsulship of President Wilson's appointee, F. Burton Harrison, was
succeeded in 1921 by the severe one of General Leonard Wood, who made
the mistake of attempting to apply army discipline to an easy-going people.
Stimson quickly established friendly relations with the Filipino leaders
Osmeña, Roxas, and Quezón, and accomplished a great deal for the economy and education in the islands. What is more, he broke down racial segregation and treated the Filipinos as social equals. One good aspect of President
Coolidge's penchant for inactivity was to refrain from giving his appointees
abroad the usual stream of orders and advice. Stimson was allowed to do what
he thought best during his year as governor general, and he laid a basis for
future friendly relations between America and the Philippine Republic.

3. Postwar Canada

The Dominion of Canada, having entered the war with England and taken
part in the bloody offensive on the Western front, suffered heavier casualties
proportionally than the United States, and acquired a huge national debt
— $2.2 billion. As her population in 1921 was only 8.8 million, about the
same as that of Pennsylvania, this was more burdensome than the $24 billion
which the United States national debt reached in the same year. Canada
entered, somewhat later, the American wave of postwar prosperity, and from
1921 on the United States was her best customer.

Differences between the two countries were as significant as the resemblances. Canada's frontier of settlement had not ended in 1890, like that of
the United States. Following the war, prairie settlement placed many thou-

sand more acres under wheat cultivation in Saskatchewan, Alberta, and the Peace River district. And, when the United States began to restrict immigration, Canada encouraged it, setting up emigration offices not only in Britain, but in Paris, Warsaw, Danzig and other eastern European cities, and in many cases paying immigrants' passages. In 1926, for instance, 136,000 people emigrated to Canada, almost half as many as the United States allowed under the quota system. But more than 100,000 Canadians, on an average, emigrated to the United States annually between 1920 and 1927.

A movement similar to the earlier Populist-Progressive one in the United States, arose in Canada's prairie provinces, based upon the same agrarian discontent. A 50 per cent wartime increase of farm acreage was followed by a drop in the price of wheat from $2.19 per bushel in 1919 to 60 cents next year. This brought forth an agrarian party, called the National Progressives, which entered federal politics in 1920, captured several provincial governments, and seriously impinged on the traditional two-party system, winning 65 seats out of 235 in the Dominion House of Commons in 1921. The government proceeded to take over two great railway systems, the Canadian Northern and the Grand Trunk, which became the Canadian National. Sir Henry Thornton, a native of Indiana, who had served for twenty years in the engineering department of the Pennsylvania Railroad, became an important figure in army transportation in England during World War I. Appointed president of the Canadian National in 1922, he made it pay its running expenses. And, as another indication of close Canadian-American relations, William Howard Taft served, while professor of law at Yale, on a commission of three to appraise the value of the Grand Trunk system when it was nationalized. He dissented from the decision of the two Canadian members to give no compensation to the holders of common stock.

State socialism and welfare legislation in Canada went much further than in the United States. The street railways of Toronto were taken over by the municipality, and the Ontario Hydro-Electric Corporation, later imitated by the Tennessee Valley Authority, pioneered successfully in government ownership of electric power.

Sir Wilfrid Laurier, the Grand Old Man of Canada and leader of the Liberal party, died in 1919. William Lyon Mackenzie King, namesake and grandson of the rebellion leader of 1837, became his political heir. After graduating in law from Toronto, King took a Ph.D. in economics at Harvard, continued his studies in London, returned to Canada, and as minister of labour in the Laurier government, became responsible for an important Industrial Investigation Act. This was much admired in the United States and, after his defeat in the election of 1911, led to King's becoming a highly placed member of the Rockefeller Foundation for investigating and adjusting industrial disputes. In the United States, King was instrumental in settling major conflicts, such as a strike between coal miners and the Rockefellers' Colorado Fuel and Iron Company in which the bloody "Ludlow Massacre" occurred.

Returning again to Canada in 1919, Mackenzie King was chosen leader of the Liberals by a party convention. He was then forty-five years old, the same age as Arthur Meighen, a distinguished lawyer and member of the House of Commons who succeeded Sir Robert Borden as leader of the Unionist party in 1920. Meighen's majority in the House of Commons, eaten away by the Progressives' winning by-elections, became so tenuous that a general election was held in December 1921. The Progressives won 65 seats, the Conservatives 50, and the Liberals 117. The governor general then summoned Mackenzie King to construct a new government; but with a very slim majority he was unable to do much in the domestic area.

The Liberal party traditionally favored close and friendly relations with the United States, whilst the Unionists (generally called the Conservatives) tended toward the traditional British association. Both parties continued the earlier Canadian policy of gently but firmly pulling their country loose from imperial influence. Sir Robert Borden, prime minister at the time of the Paris Peace Conference, insisted that Canada sign and ratify the Treaty of Versailles separately from Britain, and on her receiving a seat in the League Assembly and becoming eligible to a place on the Council. The folly of the American anti-Leaguers' contention that Canada's place in the League meant a double vote for "perfidious Albion," was proved in 1922 when Lloyd George contemplated war with Turkey. The British prime minister announced that he expected Canada in the League of Nations to vote for sanctions against Turkey, but Mackenzie King refused to commit the Dominion. A year later the Canadian government, remembering how England had let her down in the Alaska boundary controversy, herself negotiated a treaty with the United States for control of the halibut fishery in the Pacific. This quasi-independence was legalized by the Imperial Conferences between Britain and her Dominions in 1923 and 1926, which agreed that any part of the British Empire might negotiate and sign treaties affecting only itself. Canada now organized her own foreign service. Early in 1927 Vincent Massey was sent to Washington as Canadian minister; and William Phillips, former undersecretary of state and ambassador to Belgium, went to Ottawa as the first United States minister to Canada. Both posts were later raised to embassies.

Mackenzie King, hampered by his slight majority, appealed to the country in 1925. The surprising results were an increase of Conservative members and disintegration of the Progressives. Canada was prosperous and wheat prices going up, the farmers having organized a system of big co-operatives and wheat pools for price support. King, with an even more slender majority than before, nevertheless decided to "muddle through" — as John Diefenbaker later did. But he was gravely embarrassed by a series of scandals paralleling those of the late President Harding.

These scandals were the indirect result of Amendment XVIII being added to the United States Constitution while Canada left the liquor question to the provinces. Several of these tried prohibition, but by the end of 1926

Ontario, Quebec, the Maritimes, and all but three prairie provinces had rejected America's "noble experiment." And the manufacture and export of alcoholic beverages had then reached stupendous proportions, owing to demands from across the border. A parliamentary committee in 1926 revealed that a rum-runner gang in Montreal had bribed excise officers and customs officials to release liquor for export without paying taxes, and in return had smuggled in American textiles, tobacco, and other articles without paying duty. Canada was rocked by the revelation of this "unholy partnership between the government and a gang of bootleggers," as the opposition described it; and although the scandals did not smirch King personally, political considerations forced him to resign. Parliament was dissolved, and a very exciting campaign ensued. There were more serious issues, but King's Harvard degree and lack of war service were brought up against him; the Liberals retorted by pointing out that Meighen had named a son after Theodore Roosevelt! (This paralleled the efforts of "Big Bill" Thompson, mayor of Chicago, and other demagogues, to drive former Rhodes scholars or anyone with British relations out of American political life.) Despite the alleged "welter of wickedness," the Liberals won; King returned to power, constructed a strong cabinet including seven French Canadians, and "cleaned house" in the customs service.

Thus Mackenzie King was premier when Canada celebrated her diamond jubilee on 1 July 1927, sixtieth anniversary of Confederation. On this occasion, in contrast to what happened in 1867, President Coolidge sent warm greetings (for him), and the United States was represented not only by Minister Phillips but by Charles Lindbergh. Immediately after the celebration at Ottawa, a new Peace Bridge between Buffalo and Fort Erie, scene of such bitter fighting in the War of 1812, was dedicated. Vice President Dawes, Secretary Kellogg, and Governor Al Smith represented the United States, and Stanley Baldwin and the Prince of Wales, Great Britain.

Although Canada was now a nation in her relations with the outside world, internally the Dominion government had lost power to the provinces; this in spite of the Canadian constitution having been expressly drafted to exorcise the specter of state rights. Owing to the profound economic and racial differences between the Canadian provinces, and the vast distances between some of them, they had acquired by 1920 prerogatives and powers far greater than the reserved rights of the American states. Certain appeals by the provinces to the supreme court of the British empire (the judicial committee of the privy council) — notably the Toronto Electric case of 1925 — resulted in several federal laws of a welfare nature being found unconstitutional. Consequently, the Dominion government had to act with circumspection and leave social experimentation largely to the provinces. Mackenzie King dominated Canadian politics for twenty years because he appreciated this situation and acted accordingly. A bachelor premier, he lacked the personal charm of Laurier or the human warmth of Macdonald, inspired slight affection, and created no personal following like that of the Roosevelts. Yet he managed to hold the volatile French Canadians in the Liberal party without alienating the Protestants; he placated the farm groups and the rising manufacturers, and accepted half-measures when it would have been unwise to demand the whole loaf. King had the blandness of Buchanan, the shrewdness of Coolidge, and a peculiar talent for easing the strains and stresses of religion, language, and sectionalism to which the Dominion was subject.

American heedlessness of the interests and aspirations of her nearest neighbor and best customer is almost incredible. One incident will suffice. Early in 1929, toward the close of the Coolidge administration, the House of Representatives began to hold hearings preliminary to jacking up tariff schedules, for which there was no excuse in that booming era. Proposed prohibitory rates on imports from Canada raised such a furor of anti-American feeling in the Canadian press, and so many threats of retaliation, that the American minister at Ottawa, William Phillips, visited Washington at the request of Mackenzie King, to see if he could do anything to moderate the greed of the tariff-mongers. Phillips called on President-elect Hoover who, as former secretary of commerce, he assumed would be interested, and pointed out that if the threatened high tariff schedules against Canadian products became law, the Conservatives would ride to power on a wave of anti-American resentment. Hoover, completely indifferent, referred the diplomat to the congressional ways and means committee, which consented to hear him. Phillips, gathering from the committee's questions that their ideas of Canadian geography were completely vague, obtained an atlas from the Library of Congress to point out where each province was located and to illustrate his exposition of their interests and powers of retaliation. He was politely dismissed with the astonishing remark that the committee was not interested in exports from the United States, only in keeping out imports.

Over a year passed and the depression struck in before the Hawley-Smoot tariff, highest in American history, was enacted, in disregard of Canadian feelings, and of many American export interests too. Objections from the American Bankers Association and a protest signed by over 1000 economists had no effect on Congress, and President Hoover signed the bill on 17 June 1930. Canada, of course, retaliated; and as one result, no fewer than 87 branch factories for American automobiles, textiles, agricultural machinery, cordage, and other manufactures were set up in Canada within a year. A catastrophic drop of United States exports to Canada, following Canadian retaliation, deepened the depression. It took Roosevelt and the New Deal to lower the barrier.

Mackenzie King initiated negotiations with the United States for building the deep-draft St. Lawrence Seaway, but did not remain in power long enough to conclude the treaty in 1932. That treaty was rejected by the United States Senate, largely because American railroads and the Eastern cities feared that the St. Lawrence, improved so that ocean freighters could steam into the

Great Lakes, would siphon away their trade.[1] Canada returned the Senate's compliment by refusing to go along with the Quoddy Project, a scheme on which President Roosevelt had set his heart, to make electric power from the tides of Passamaquoddy Bay.

In the meantime, the imperial relationship of Canada, as well as that of other British Dominions, or Commonwealths as they now began to be called, had been defined by the Statute of Westminster, passed by the Parliament of Great Britain on 11 December 1931. By virtue of this fundamental law, which embodied even more concessions than American radicals had demanded in 1775, Parliament renounced its ancient right to legislate for Canada, unless at Canada's request, as well as the royal prerogative of disallowing acts of the Canadian parliament. But the judicial committee of the Privy Council continued to act as an imperial supreme court, hearing cases appealed from the Dominion supreme court. The governor general of Canada now became a personal representative of the British crown, not the proconsul of a British government; and since the death of the much-beloved Lord Tweedsmuir (John Buchan) in 1940, most of the governors general have been Canadians. The right of Canada to conduct her own foreign relations and to decide on war or peace was implicitly if not explicitly recognized; and Canadians, while proudly clinging to their right to be British subjects, have their own Canadian citizenship.

Thus, so far as the United States and other nations were concerned, Canada had become an independent nation.

4. The Harding Scandals and the Coolidge Administration

Jess Smith's suicide was the first indication that the Ohio gang had overreached itself. Shortly after, it was brought to the President's attention that his pal "Colonel" Forbes, director of the Veterans' Bureau, had been taking a cut on the building of hospitals and profiting from the sale of excess war materials. Forbes had to resign, and in March 1923 his principal legal adviser committed suicide. All this so worried President Harding that he decided to take a trip across the country and up to Alaska. Uneasy and depressed, he fell ill of ptomaine poisoning, then of pneumonia, and died of an embolism at San Francisco on 2 August 1923.

Now the oil scandals burst forth. A Washington correspondent of the St. Louis Post-Dispatch obtained the evidence, and Senators Thomas J. Walsh and Gerald Nye made it public. Albert B. Fall, secretary of the interior, with the passive connivance of Edwin M. Denby (a complete nonentity whom Harding had made navy secretary) entered into a corrupt alliance with the Doheny and Sinclair oil interests to turn over to them valuable petroleum deposits, which President Wilson had reserved for the navy. The Elk Hill oil reserve in California was leased to Doheny and the Teapot Dome oil re-

1. The St. Lawrence Seaway was completed in 1959.

serve in Wyoming to Sinclair. In return for these favors they built some oil storage tanks for the navy in Pearl Harbor; but Fall got at least $100,000 from Doheny and $300,000 from Sinclair. The Senate investigation forced both secretaries to resign, the oil leases were canceled, and the government recovered $6 million. Criminal prosecutions sent Fall and Sinclair to prison for short terms, but the rest got off.

Other revelations besmirched the Harding administration. His appointee as custodian of alien property, who had sold valuable German chemical patents for a song, was dismissed from office and convicted of a criminal conspiracy to defraud the government. Harry Daugherty, who regarded the office of attorney general as an opportunity to reward friends and, it is said, to protect Harding from *his* friends, was dismissed for misconduct involving the illegal sale of liquor permits and pardons. A Senate committee found him guilty of these and other malpractices, but the jury that tried him could not agree. As Will Rogers remarked, it was hard to convince a jury of criminal corruption in those lush times, because most of the jurors secretly admired people who got away with it.

When these scandals and others even less savory about Harding's personal conduct were ventilated, Calvin Coolidge was President of the United States, at the age of fifty-one. The first President from New England since Franklin Pierce, born in a small farming community in the Vermont hills, he had worked his way through Amherst College, become a lawyer in Northampton, Massachusetts, and ascended from the lower to the higher brackets of state politics. Good luck, and a firm stand in the Boston police strike of 1919, made him Vice President. A mean, thin-lipped little man, a respectable mediocrity, he lived parsimoniously but admired men of wealth, and his political principles were those current in 1901. People thought Coolidge brighter than he was because he seldom said anything; but, as he admitted, he was "usually able to make enough noise" to get what he wanted. Mrs. Coolidge was a handsome and gracious lady, without whom the formal parties at the White House would have been unbearably grim. She helped this dour, abstemious, and unimaginative figure to become one of the most popular American Presidents. "Silent Cal" by his frugality, unpretentiousness, and taciturnity seems to have afforded vicarious satisfaction to a generation that was extravagant, pretentious, and voluble. Actually, Coolidge was democratic by habit rather than by conviction, and his taciturnity was calculated — "I have never been hurt by what I have not said," is one of his aphorisms. He regarded the progressive movement since Theodore Roosevelt's day with cynical distrust. Consequently, although he had a moral integrity wanting in his predecessor, there was no change in political or economic policy between the Harding and the Coolidge administrations. Policies of high tariff, tax reduction, and government support to industry were pushed to extremes, and a high plateau of prosperity was attained.

Since the President exalted inactivity to a fine art, there is not much to say about his administration except in foreign affairs, which we have already mentioned, and the prelude to the Great Depression, which is to come. He gave no lead to Congress or the country, took it easy in the White House with a long nap every afternoon, and maintained a somewhat feeble health by riding a mechanical horse. He had no intimate adviser like Wilson's House or Roosevelt's Hopkins; the nearest was his personal secretary C. Bascom Slemp, a former Republican congressman from Virginia who was an expert "fixer" and saved his boss a lot of trouble by placating petitioners for favors and jobs. Coolidge and the men whom he and Harding appointed to the great federal commissions did nothing to stop or even discourage the wild speculation that was going on. His one positive achievement was to use the presidential veto. Congress overrode him and passed a veterans' bonus, but his vetoes of the McNary-Haugen Farm relief bills in 1927–28 killed that particular measure for subsidizing the farmers, and rendered them far more vulnerable than they need have been to the Great Depression. Income and inheritance taxes were reduced during his second term, but he signed the Jones-White Act of 1928 for doubling the subsidy to builders of merchant ships, and needled Congress into building some much-needed cruisers.

In the nineteenth century, revelations such as those of Harding's administration — the worst since Grant's — would have brought a political reaction; but Coolidge's personality restored the people's confidence in the Republicans; and Coolidge, like all Vice Presidents, eager to be "President in his own right," won the Republican nomination unanimously in 1924. The Democrats hanged themselves because their nominating convention in New York was deadlocked for 102 ballots between William McAdoo the "Dry" candidate, and Al Smith the darling of the "wets"; and the sordid story, including a Tammany claque in the galleries, went to the public over the radio. Finally the convention settled on a corporation lawyer, John W. Davis, with William Jennings Bryan's innocuous brother Charles as running mate in the hope of taking off the Wall Street curse. Progressivism rose from its grave in the shape of a new party called the Conference for Political Action. This was formed by farmer groups, disgusted liberals, and radicals from both parties, allied with the Socialists; it nominated Robert La Follette for the presidency, and polled 4.8 million votes — more than Roosevelt did in 1912 — but carried only Wisconsin. "Republican prosperity" had returned, the economy was booming, and with wheat back at $2.20 the farmers were no longer after politicians' scalps. Coolidge won 54 per cent of the popular vote, and 382 in the electoral college; Davis received little more than half Coolidge's vote, and 136 in the electoral college. The Communists, who now called themselves the Workers' party, under William Z. Foster, polled only 33,000 votes.

L V

The Hoover Administration

1929-1933

1. *The Election of 1928*

WHEN THE ELECTION of 1928 approached, President Coolidge secretly aspired to a third term. But his sphinx-like announcement, "I do not choose to run," was taken as a refusal, and with ill-concealed disgust he saw his secretary of commerce, Herbert C. Hoover, run away with the Republican nomination.

Hoover, a mining engineer by profession, a graduate of Stanford University, had well earned his reputation as a humanitarian by his administration of food distribution in the war, and of Belgian and Russian relief. In the commerce department he had won the confidence of business. Although never before elected to public office, he seemed to be a new type of political leader, a socially-minded efficiency expert. People did not resent his being a millionaire, since he had been born on an Iowa farm and had worked up to success.

The Democratic nominee, Alfred E. Smith, represented a very different type of democracy. A product of "The Sidewalks of New York" (his favorite theme song) and of Tammany, he was the first man without a farm background and the first Irish Catholic to receive the presidential nomination of a major party. It was high time; the urban workers and recent immigrants had been an indispensable prop to the Democratic party since Jefferson's day. Al Smith rose superior to ward politics, and, without losing the common touch, served as governor of New York for four terms, 1919–28. Smith here showed an unexpected gift for administration; under his leadership the state government introduced an executive budget, reorganized departments and agencies, and created a cabinet system responsible to the governor. On questions of power regulation, labor, and social reform Smith was progressive; on the prohibition issue, an out-and-out "wet." In the convention his name was placed in nomination by Franklin D. Roosevelt who, paraphrasing a poem of Wordsworth, described Al as "the Happy Warrior of the political battlefield."

An exciting campaign followed. The Happy Warrior happily addressed immense, enthusiastic crowds in the cities of the North and East, but when he invaded the rural regions of the South and West he received a chill reception. Both parties raised big campaign funds, the Republicans the bigger; but it was not money that defeated Al. He carried all the great urban centers; yet Hoover, with Charles Curtis — an Osage Indian — as Vice President, received 58 per cent of the popular vote and an overwhelming electoral college majority of 357, carrying every state but eight and smashing the solid South. Explanations of this overwhelming victory are not hard to find. The average workingman was contented, the average business man prosperous, and neither had any desire for change. "You can't lick this Prosperity thing," said Will Rogers; "even the fellow that hasn't got any is all excited over the idea." Smith, as a Catholic, a Tammany brave, a New Yorker, and a wet, grated on the average rural American. His "Brooklyn accent," manners, and background did not seem proper to a President.

2. Herbert Hoover and the Boom

The stock market crash of October 1929 was a natural consequence of the greatest orgy of speculation and over-optimism since the South Sea Bubble of 1720. After a postwar recession (or minor depression) of 1920, security prices recovered, business readjusted, and a major advance began after Harding's death in 1923. Increased investment was largely responsible for the rise until 1925, when speculation raised it to a giddy height. A general euphoria drew more and more "suckers" into the speculative market; brokerage houses opened branches in small towns and near college campuses; widows, factory workers, bootblacks, and waiters risked their savings to make a "fast buck" in stocks, and even those who did not, eagerly followed *the* market, meaning the daily New York Stock Exchange quotations, which made more headlines than crime or international affairs. Probably not more than 600,000 stockbrokers' accounts, out of an estimated 1.5 million, were trading on margin — but that was enough to breed a tremendous wave of speculation.

American prosperity, Germany's remarkable recovery after 1924, and the growth of world trade justified a rise in security values, but they rose much further than was justified. And when speculation began to get out of hand, neither the federal nor the state governments did anything effective to check it. They, of course, could not check human greed and folly; but the Federal Reserve Board and Trade Commission might have applied certain brakes. The main reason they did not is that, since 1921, these bodies had been diluted by political hacks or Republican financiers who did not believe in the regulative functions which they were supposed to perform. Thus, the Federal Reserve Board was unable to make up its mind what to do, or to do anything, at critical junctures. Secretary Hoover worried about "this fever of speculation," as he called it in a press release of 1 January 1926, warned against over-extension of installment buying, and even criticized the easy credit policies of the Federal Reserve system; but when he failed to win President Coolidge or Secretary Mellon to his views, he smothered his concern and took pains to say nothing that might weaken the prevalent optimism. Coolidge, who saved money from his presidential salary, and who never gambled a nickel in a slot machine, much less a dollar in stocks, regarded the speculative orgy with detached complacency; his philosophy forbade interference with "the law of supply and demand." And no wonder people were overconfident, since even some old progressives and socialists went overboard. Walter Lippmann in 1928 praised the "unplanned activities of big business men," and early next year Lincoln Steffens, who had hailed the Russian revolution as the socialist heaven, wrote, "Big business in America is producing what the Socialists held up as their goal: food, shelter and clothing for all. . . . It is a great country this; as great as Rome."

There was a great deal wrong, besides overspeculation, with the national economy and the laws regulating it. Corporations, which as early as 1919 employed 86.5 per cent of all wage earners in industry, were proliferating under practically no control. Certain states such as Delaware and New Jersey allowed anyone paying a registration fee to incorporate a company, leaving its directors free to issue new stock, and with no obligation to make an annual report or accounting. The number of Delaware incorporations with authorized capital stock of $20 million or more, rose from 55 in 1925 to 619 in 1929. One characteristic device was to form a holding company comprising a large number of electric light and other power corporations, the "utilities" as these were called. Holding companies were often so rigged that an outsider who bought stock knew nothing of what was going on, and the insiders profited, just as railway construction groups did in the days of President Grant. Stockholders of three of the biggest — Electric Bond & Share, Standard Gas & Electric, and Cities Service (235,000 shareholders in 1925) — were not vouchsafed any information about the subsidiaries' earnings, on which theirs depended.

Stock pools burgeoned and blossomed. A group of men would get together, buy a sizeable block of stock of no matter what, then trade shares back and forth, hiking the price and pulling in outsiders who hoped to get in on the profits. When the stock reached an agreed point, members of the pool dumped it on the market, took their profits and retired, leaving the suckers to take the rap. The reverse was a "bear raid" on a stock already doing well. Rumors would be circulated that the company was being badly managed or overcapitalized, by operators who sold short, drove down the stock, and bought it back at a very attractive price. Joseph P. Kennedy, father of the late President, thwarted just such a raid on the Yellow Cab Company, then owned by John D. Hertz who became the Rent-a-Car tycoon. Hertz's friend Walter Howey, editor of the *Boston American*, enlisted Kennedy's aid to save Yellow Cab from ruin. The Bostonian installed special telephones and a ticker tape in a hotel suite, and with a borrowed $5 million placed both buy and sell orders from points all around the country, utterly confusing the raiders and stabilizing the stock at 51. This successful maneuver had the effect of attracting the favorable attention of William Randolph Hearst to Joseph P. Kennedy, with political results that we shall observe shortly.

A more typical case involving a future secretary of defense is that of a holding company called United States and Foreign Securities Corporation, chartered under the laws of Maryland by the New York investment house of Dillon, Read & Company. It had practically unlimited powers to "purchase, hold and deal with investment securities," and "engage in commercial, manufacturing and industrial enterprises." Upon its organization Dillion, Read absorbed 500,000 shares of the common stock at 20 cents a share; and of these, their partner James V. Forrestal took 37,000 shares which, after buying more later at a slightly higher price, cost him $28,539.50. Forrestal transferred about 20,000 of his shares to Beekman Company, Ltd. of Canada, a sort of ghost corporation set up by Dillon, Read and run by their employees for the particular purpose of juggling United States & Foreign Securities and other stock. Beekman Ltd. was wholly owned by the Beekman Corporation of Delaware, whose entire stock was owned by Mr. and Mrs. Forrestal. Beekman Ltd. sold 16,788 shares of Forrestal's U.S. & Foreign Securities stock to the public at 53. This stock rose to 72 before the great crash of October 1929, then went down to 1⅜ in 1932. There was also much trading and borrowing back and forth between the two Beekman corporations and Mr. Forrestal, who realized a profit of $864,000. The reason for this curious set-up, then legal, was to enable him to evade paying income tax or capital gains from the sale of this stock, which had cost him less than $29,000. Forrestal, recognizing a moral obligation, paid a large sum in back taxes after the Pecora Committee had reported the facts; but the little fellows who had bought this worthless stock, lost their shirts.

Most of the subsidiaries of the utilities' holding companies kept going more or less profitably during the depression, and the communities they served did not suffer; but there were many cases of a local industry upon which a community depended being scuttled by high finance. Organizers of a super-hardware holding company, for instance, would discover a small corporation making locks and bolts, which under conservative management made steady profits and owned a cash reserve of a million dollars. The holding company would bid up the stock, tempting local holders to sell out at a profit; then, as soon as the holding company had 51 per cent of the shares, whoosh! The cash reserve was siphoned off into its own treasury, and the locks and bolts shop closed as "uneconomical," leaving the community to support the people thus thrown out of work. This sort of thing is still going on in the 1960's, but it was much more prevalent forty years earlier.

The boom was world-wide, and the two promoters who were most successful in fleecing the American lambs were foreigners: — Samuel E. Insull, orginally from London, and Ivar Kreuger the Swedish match king; both were featured on covers of *Time* magazine as financial geniuses. Insull, who emigrated young to Chicago, became chairman of 65 company directorates which operated in the utilities field in 23 different states. He was no common crook, but a public-spirited magnate who saved the city of Chicago from bankruptcy, built it a palatial opera house, and started a natural-gas pipeline from the Texas panhandle to Lake Michigan. Regarding the depression as temporary, he continued to overextend in 1930, and his elaborate edifice crashed in April 1932 with a loss to American investors of $700 million. Insull found a pleasant asylum in Greece; extradited, he was acquitted of breaking the law. Not so nice was the career of Ivar Kreuger, who even counterfeited Italian government bonds to deceive auditors. "Uncle Ivar" looked so virtuous and claimed to be on such intimate terms with European statesmen that he was able to buy American companies like Diamond Match "on a shoestring," and to employ the old Boston firm of Lee, Higginson & Company as his American outlet. Investors as well as speculators, attracted by this respectable backing, bought about $250 million of his worthless securities; even Harvard University had a substantial slice of Kreuger & Toll in its treasury when the match king, at last found out, committed suicide in 1932.

Loans to brokers for purchasing or carrying securities had reached $8.5 billion by October 1929, and banks everywhere had made unwise loans for speculation. New issues of common stock to the unprecedented amount of $5.1 billion were floated in the United States during the twelve months before the crash.

Warnings of the coming debacle were not wanting. William Z. Ripley, Harvard economist, published two articles in *The Atlantic* in 1926 which exposed what he called the "honeyfugling, hornswoggling and skulduggery" of corporate practices; but not enough people listened. Roger W. Babson on 5 September 1929 predicted, "There is a crash coming, and it may be a terrific one," involving even "a decline of from 60 to 80 points in the Dow-Jones barometer." But *Barron's Weekly* devoted a large part of its next issue to sneering at Babson as "the Sage of Wellesley," [1] a "scaremonger," pointing out that he had advised investors to get out of the market in 1926. Alexander D. Noyes, veteran financial editor of the *New York Times*, did his utmost to prick the bubble of perpetually rising stocks and eternally increasing prosperity, only to be denounced as "trying to discredit or stop American prosperity." Herbert Hoover during the campaign of 1928 made only negligible references to speculation and predicted, "We shall soon with the help of God be in sight of the day when poverty will be banished from this nation." President Coolidge's last message, of 4 December 1928, declared that the nation might "regard the present with satisfaction and anticipate the future with optimism"; no United States Congress "has met with a more pleasing prospect

1. On 28 October 1929, after Babson's prophecy had been fulfilled by a decline of 80 points in one day, *Barron's Weekly* began taking the line that the panic was the fault of Babson and others who warned of it.

than that which appears at the present time." On 16 October 1929, Professor Irving Fisher of Yale touched the acme of prophetic folly, announcing, "Stock prices have reached what looks like a permanently high plateau."

3. The 1929 Crash and the Great Depression

The stock market had already begun to act queerly. On 23 October there was a spectacular drop during the last hour of trading, and the 24th, when almost 13 million shares changed hands, became known as "Black Thursday." Spokesmen for bankers and brokers insisted that the worst was over, but 28 and 29 October were even more terrible days, from which there was no recovery. Stocks reached new lows on 13 November, rose slightly during the early months of 1930, but in April began a downward slide that continued with only brief interruptions to rock-bottom in mid-1932.

At this point a table of the highest and lowest prices of twelve representative common stocks, and of five selected products of the soil, tell the story better than any description.

PRICES OF COMMON STOCKS [1]

	1929		1932	
	HIGHEST	LOWEST	HIGHEST	LOWEST
American Telephone & Telegraph	310¼	193¼	137⅜	69¾
Cities Service	68½	20	6⅞	1¼
Electric Bond & Share	189	50	48	5
General Electric	403	168⅛	26⅛ [2]	8½
General Motors	91¾	33½	24⅝	7⅝
Kreuger & Toll	46⅜	21⅛	(dead)	—
National Cash Register	148¾	59	18¾	6¼
Radio Corporation of America	114¾	26	13½	2½
Remington Rand	57¾	20⅜	7½	1
Sears, Roebuck	181	80	37⅜	9⅞
United States Smelting, Refining & Mining	72⅞	29⅞	22¾	10
United States Steel	261¾	150	52⅝	21¼

WHOLESALE PRICES OF SELECTED COMMODITIES
ANNUAL AVERAGES TO NEAREST HALF-CENT [3]

	1925	1929	1930	1931	1932	1933	1935	1936
Wheat, bushel	$1.435	$1.035	$0.67	$0.40	$0.38	$0.75	$0.83	$1.025
Corn, bushel	0.70	0.80	0.60	0.32	0.315	0.52	0.655	1.05
Raw cotton, pound	0.235	0.19	0.135	0.085	0.065	0.085	0.12	0.12
Wool, pound	1.40	0.985	0.765	0.62	0.46	0.665	0.725	0.88
Tobacco, pound	0.17	0.185	0.13	0.08	0.105	0.13	0.185	0.235

1. *Commercial and Financial Chronicle*, Vols. CXXX (1930) and CXXXVII (1933).
2. After issuing five new shares to each share outstanding; multiply by 5 for comparison with 1929.
3. *Historical Statistics of the U.S.*, pp. 123, 296–7, 302. The corn, wheat and tobacco prices are "season average received by farmers."

Whilst the boom of 1926–29 made the stock market crash inevitable, there was nothing inevitable about the Great Depression that followed. This reached its nadir in 1932–33. Although alleviated by the bold expedients of the New Deal, it did not really end until 1939–40 when America began to rearm. As yet there is no consensus among economists as to why a prolonged depression followed the crash. Not all agree to this writer's generalization that the national economy was honeycombed with weakness, giving "Coolidge prosperity" a fine appearance over a rotten foundation. Optimism, justified in the early 1920's, had been carried to extremes owing to lack of insight and want of courage to say "Stop!" on the part of leaders in business, finance, politics, and the universities. These, imbued with laissez-faire doctrine and overrating the importance of maintaining public confidence, refrained from making candid statements or taking steps to curb or cure the abuses, a small fraction of which we have described. At the same time, efforts were made to prevent declines of farm products and raw materials, which were the result of increasing abundance. This created world-wide overproduction of basic commodities such as wheat, rubber, coffee, cotton, sugar, copper, silver, and zinc, intensified by bumper crops in Europe in 1929.

Economic analysis, a science then in its infancy, failed to discern the serious faults in American and European economics and their increasing vulnerability to shock. Among the weak points were the tremendous volume of stock-market, mortgage, and installment-buying debts; the chaotic American banking system, precarious European currencies, and the war reparations question, supposedly but not really settled. President Hoover, in his message of 2 December 1930, rightly pointed out that soft spots in European economy infected America. But even he did not see that the American boom helped to make Europe vulnerable by checking the outflow of American capital and sucking a counter-current of European investment and call-money into New York. This depleted European gold reserves, undermined currencies, and created industrial instability.

Thus, the stock-market crash of 1929 started a downward spiral in prices, production, employment, and foreign trade, which the Hawley-Smoot tariff of 1930 and intensified protection in European countries — everyone for himself — made even worse. Collapse in commodity prices reduced buying power everywhere and increased unemployment in all industrialized countries. In 1931, when President Hoover thought he had the depression by the tail, the collapse of the *Kreditanstalt* of Vienna, and Britain's abandonment of her sacred gold standard, intensified world-wide conditions. The business world seemed to be crumbling everywhere; communists were full of glee over the imminent collapse of representative government and the capitalist system.

Efforts to arrest the avalanche were not strong enough to be effective. Many financiers appeared to be more interested in profiting from the bear market than in stopping it; Albert H. Wiggin, president of Chase National Bank, sold short 42,506 shares of his own bank, making a profit of $4 million

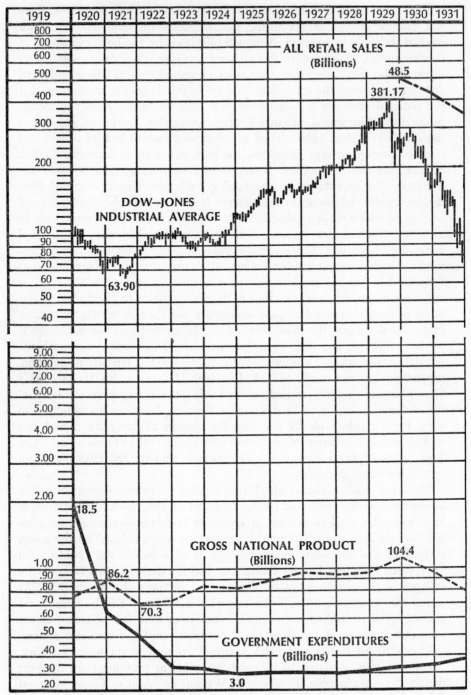

| 1919 | 1920 | 1921 | 1922 | 1923 | 1924 | 1925 | 1926 | 1927 | 1928 | 1929 | 1930 | 1931 |

ALL RETAIL SALES
(Billions)

48.5

381.17

DOW–JONES
INDUSTRIAL AVERAGE

63.90

GROSS NATIONAL PRODUCT
(Billions)

104.4

18.5

86.2

70.3

GOVERNMENT EXPENDITURES
(Billions)

3.0

From Forbes Investographs; courtesy Forbes, Inc., New York

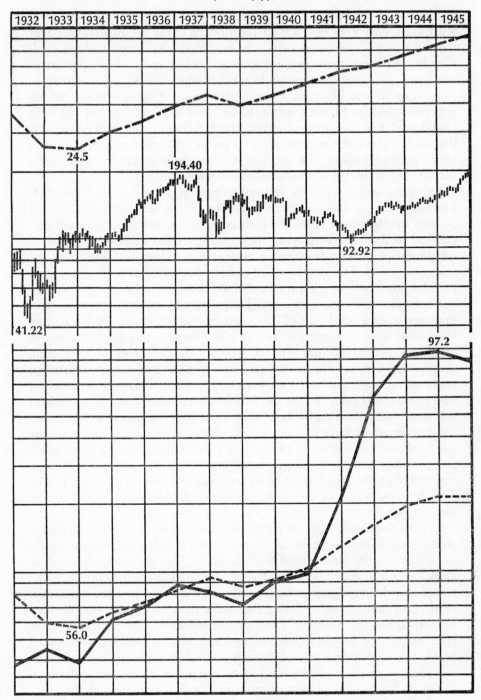

by the end of the year. By November, whatever European call money still remained in New York was recalled, contributing to the fall. Brokers called for more margin from their customers, who were unable to comply and so lost all they had ventured; banks recalled loans to brokers upon which speculation was based, and often were unable to get their money back; they also suffered from other unwise loans made during the boom. Queues formed outside perfectly sound banks, on a rumor, to withdraw deposits, and any run on a bank forced it to close its doors. Worst bank failure in American history was that of the Bank of the United States on 11 December 1930 — nine days after President Hoover in a message to Congress had stated, "The fundamental strength of the Nation's economy is unimpaired."

Before the end of 1929 the entire economy began to snowball downhill. Consumer buying declined sharply and the public, leery of banks, cached currency in safe-deposit boxes and mattresses. Every kind of business suffered, and had to discharge employees; they, unable to find other jobs, defaulted installment payments and exhausted their savings to live. To some extent the misery was relieved by the charity of employed relatives, or by returning to a parental farm; but America, unlike Britain, then had neither social security nor unemployment insurance. This tailspin of the economy went on until mid-1932 when around 12 million people, about 25 per cent of the normal labor force, were unemployed. In the cities there were soup kitchens and breadlines. Factory payrolls dropped to less than half those of early 1929. Shanty towns, where the jobless gathered to pick over a dump, grew up; bankrupt mills and garment lofts were reopened by unscrupulous promoters who paid a dollar a day to men and half that to girls. Small towns in the farm belt were almost deserted by their inhabitants. Some farmers resisted eviction and foreclosure by force of arms. On the higher level, New York apartment houses offered five-year leases for one year's rent, entire Pullman trains rolled along without a single passenger, hotels and resorts like Miami Beach were empty. For a prize understatement we nominate ex-President Coolidge's "The country is not in good condition," in his syndicated press column on 20 January 1931.

Looking backward, there is reason to believe that the Great Depression created less misery than that of 1893–96, when nothing but private charity stood between the unemployed and starvation. The researches of Joseph S. Davis bring out some alleviating factors, such as low prices stimulating the sale of household gadgetry; a higher percentage of farms acquired radio, electricity, and running water during the 1930's than in the previous decade.[1] Life expectancy continued to lengthen and the death rate to decline, especially among the Negro population, and lack of jobs induced more young people to complete high school. Popular psychology made the Great Depression seem worse than it really was because the public had so frequently been fooled by "permanent plateau of prosperity" talk that it seemed abnormal,

1. See Chapter LVI, section 3, for some of the causes of this.

unnatural, and abominable. In the 1890's, on the other hand, alternate booming and hard times were taken for granted.

No nation ever faced a business decline more optimistically than America
did this one. Nobody highly placed in government or finance admitted the
existence of a depression for six months or more after the crash. Everyone
wanted to stop the decline, but nobody knew how. Incantation was the
favorite method for the first six months. Brookmire Economic Service, heading the procession, quoted an opinion of a British industrialist after an American inspection tour of 26 October 1929: "I look on the events of the last
week as an incident . . . prices reached at the peak will look cheap . . . it is
quite impossible to be anything but optimistic about America." The National
Association of Manufacturers began covering tattered billboards with a cartoon designed by Howard Chandler Christy representing an attractive Miss
Columbia saying "Business is Good. Keep it Good. Nothing can stop US."
Old John D. Rockefeller issued a fatuous statement to the effect that "fundamental conditions of the country are sound," and that "he and his son are
accumulating shares."

President Hoover became the leading exorciser with public statements such
as, "Any lack of confidence in . . . the basic strength of business . . . is
foolish" (November 1929). "Business and industry have turned the corner"
(21 January 1930). "We have now passed the worst" (1 May 1930). On 28
June 1930, when wheat had dropped to 68 cents a bushel — and would go to
38 cents — and cotton had dropped to 13 cents a pound — and would go to
6.5 cents — James J. Davis, secretary of labor, dropped this gem: "Courage
and resource are already swinging us back on the road to recovery. And we are
fortunate in having a President who sets us a shining example of that courage and initiative."

More than talk was needed to swell the shrunken gourd and plump the
shriveled shell. President Hoover did his best according to his lights, and he had
a warm heart which responded to the suffering. But he was restrained from
taking any bold, imaginative steps by wrong estimates of the situation, and by
his laissez-faire philosophy, which taught him that nature would cure all,
whilst government intervention might ruin all. At his elbow was Andrew
Mellon, secretary of the treasury, whose one idea was to keep hands off and
let the slump liquidate itself; his formula, Hoover admitted, was "liquidate
labor, liquidate stocks, liquidate the farmer, liquidate real estate." Mellon
wanted it to go right to the bottom; thought that would be a good thing.
"People will work harder, live a more moral life. Values will be adjusted, and
enterprising people will pick up the wrecks from less competent people."
There were plenty of tycoons who had enough income from rents and bonds
to weather a prolonged depression themselves, but found consolation in the
hope that it would destroy the labor unions and bring back old times when "a
dollar a day is a white man's pay."

That was not what Hoover wanted. He aimed to end the depression promptly and to relieve present suffering. He asked for a big charity drive in the winter of 1929–30 and it yielded only a miserable $15 million. But he was unwilling to recommend, or the Congress to vote, direct relief; poor relief was traditionally the prerogative of state and local governments, churches, and private charity. Senators Costigan of Colorado, Bronson Cutting of New Mexico, and the younger La Follette of Wisconsin pled for a big federal program of public works, presenting statistics proving the breakdown of private and local charity; but every proposal was met by stubborn presidential opposition. When the House threatened to pass a bill appropriating $2 billion for public works, Hoover intervened with the warning, "This is not unemployment relief. It is the most gigantic pork-barrel ever perpetrated by the American Congress."

Not until 1932, when the Democrats controlled the House, and a coalition of Democrats and Republican progressives ran the Senate, were vital measures taken to cope with the depression. By that time an estimated one to two million men were roaming the country looking for jobs or handouts, and more than 100 cities had no relief money left. In January President Hoover signed a bill creating the Reconstruction Finance Corporation for lending money to railroads, banks, agricultural agencies, industry, and commerce. During the rest of the Hoover administration, the RFC stopped many bankruptcies by feeding in money at the top, but this did little to restore the economy. In the next three years, under Roosevelt, with vastly greater appropriations, the RFC came to the aid of 7000 banks and trust companies to the tune of $3.5 billion. Loans to mortgage-loan companies and to insurance companies and railroads took up $1 billion more. Loans to industry and to agriculture in one form or another came to over $2.6 billion.

RFC assistance to banks, mortgage and insurance companies, railroads and industries undoubtedly prevented more serious losses, and to that extent checked the downward spiral. But many loans merely put off the day of reckoning for banks that were beyond saving. And the RFC gave little relief to the people who most urgently needed it. For the theory behind it, as Will Rogers said, was "The money was all appropriated for the top in the hopes it would trickle down to the needy." Mounting figures of unemployment from 4.3 million in 1930 to 12 million in 1932,[1] figures which Hoover simply refused to believe, proved that the depression was getting worse rather than better.

President Hoover meant very well, labored hard to find solutions, and sought advice; but nothing seemed to work because, being the prisoner of fixed ideas, and surrounded by like-minded men, he refused to try anything new or bold. The year 1933, when he left office, marks the grave of the laissez-

1. These are annual averages, from *Historical Statistics of the U.S.*, p. 73; the A. F. of L. figures, as given in Lionel Robbins, *The Great Depression* (1935), p. 213, are 3 million in 1930, 10.5 million in 1932. It is significant that Germany, the only country with a larger proportion of unemployed in those years, underwent the Hitler revolution in 1933.

faire nineteenth-century state, so far as America was concerned. It had already been buried in every European country, and in Japan.

We owe admiration as well as pity to the simple folk of America who suffered so grievously under the depression. Many by mid-1932 were angry and desperate, but they still had faith in their country and its institutions; surprisingly few listened to strange voices which told them that fascism Mussolini-style, or communism Moscow-style, was the only answer. They were only waiting for a leader to show them the way out.[2]

4. The Accession of Franklin D. Roosevelt

The eruption of Franklin D. Roosevelt into the political area in 1928 was a surprise. "F.D.R.," born to a patrician Hudson river family in 1882, graduated from Groton and Harvard (where he was regarded as a playboy) and the Columbia Law School. For a few years he engaged in law and business in New York City with very moderate success; but he made a successful marriage in 1905 with Eleanor Roosevelt, niece of his remote cousin Theodore, whom he greatly admired. The Dutchess County Roosevelts to whom Franklin belonged had been Democrats since Andrew Jackson days; so, as a Democrat, "Frank," as his friends called him, was elected to the New York Senate. Support of Woodrow Wilson in the campaign of 1912 earned him the assistant secretaryship of the navy, which enabled him to counteract some of the folly of Josephus Daniels; and that, in turn, led to his vice-presidential nomination on the losing Cox ticket in 1920. Next year a sudden and severe attack of polio at his summer home in Campobello, New Brunswick, left him apparently a hopeless invalid; but during the next seven years he fought his way back to health, used his leisure for thought, study, and correspondence, and emerged from forced retirement a changed man. Still charming and jaunty in manner, he was deeply ambitious to do something for his country and lend fresh luster to the Roosevelt name.

His political comeback was signaled by nominating Al Smith in the Democratic convention of 1924 with the "happy warrior" speech; and Al later persuaded him to take the Democratic candidacy for governor of New York in 1928. To those who objected that Roosevelt was still a cripple, the Happy Warrior replied, "The Governor of New York State does not have to be an acrobat!" Although Al lost his native state in the presidential election, the magic of the Roosevelt name elected F.D.R. governor; and at Albany he did so well, with the assistance of an able staff of economists and social workers,

2. Two persistent depression myths may be mentioned here: (1) That hundreds of brokers and bankers hurled themselves out of skyscraper windows, or otherwise committed suicide after the big crash. Actually the number of suicides remained normal. (2) That the jobless were only taken care of by selling apples. What happened was that an apple growers' association in the Northwest arranged to market their surplus production by hiring unemployed men to sell apples on the streets of leading cities. This gimmick worked so well that, according to Mr. Hoover, many left good jobs to hawk apples.

that in 1930 he was re-elected by a majority of 700,000. That made him a leading contender for his party's presidential nomination.

Herbert Hoover was renominated by the Republicans as the only alternative to admitting failure. For the Democratic nomination, assumed to mean election, there was a free-for-all. Al Smith wanted it again, but the politicians recalled his poor showing in 1928 and divided their efforts between F.D.R. and "Cactus Jack" Garner of Texas, then speaker of the house. Other aspirants were William McAdoo, President Wilson's son-in-law; Newton D. Baker, Wilson's able secretary of war; Owen D. Young, who had helped put the German Republic on its financial feet; Governor Harry F. Byrd of Virginia; even Governor "Alfalfa Bill" Murray of Oklahoma. Joseph P. Kennedy, father of a future President, then a free-lance financier who had got out of the stock market in time, decided that Roosevelt was the man. Kennedy raised money for his campaign and attended the nominating convention. When it looked like a deadlock between Roosevelt and Garner, he talked on the telephone to William Randolph Hearst, who was under obligation to him for stopping the raid on Yellow Cab during the big boom. As the only California Democrat willing to spend money, Hearst controlled the California delegation. They were pledged to Garner, but Kennedy, with the help of Jim Farley, convinced the multimillionaire publisher that if he did not switch California's vote to Roosevelt, either Baker or Smith, both of whom he hated, would be nominated. Hearst switched; Garner, anxious to avoid a deadlock, released his pledged delegates, and California's 44 votes helped to nominate Roosevelt. Garner accepted the vice-presidential nomination, which was more to his liking since it gave him plenty of time for hunting and shooting in Texas.

Roosevelt, who before his nomination had seemed to many people merely "a nice man who very much wanted to be President," electrified the country by a bold, aggressive campaign. Although he now had a wide radio network at his disposal, the candidate, to prove his physical vigor and exert his personal magnetism, embarked upon an old-fashioned stumping tour which took him into almost every state of the Union. He set forth a comprehensive scheme of reform and recovery, embracing the repeal of Prohibition, unemployment relief, lower tariffs, and legislation to save agriculture, rehabilitate the railroads, protect consumers and investors, and slash government expenses; all of it contained in the party platform. The keynote was a "New Deal" to the "forgotten man." For some odd reason this last phrase aroused the fury of conservatives; even Al Smith, when he first heard Roosevelt plead for "the forgotten man at the bottom of the economic pyramid," burst out with, "This is no time for demagogues!"

President Hoover, laboring under the dead weight of the deepening depression, recited his efforts to cope with it, mumbled prophecies to the effect that a Democratic victory would mean that "The grass will grow in the streets of a hundred cities," and reaffirmed his faith in rugged individualism and the American system. "Any change of policies will bring disaster to every fireside in America."

Most of the voters, fearing that the "American system" needed desperate measures to be saved, were ready to take a chance on the New Deal. On election day Roosevelt received almost 22.8 million votes with 57.3 per cent of all cast, and won 472 electors; Hoover polled 15.8 million votes — 39.6 per cent, with only 59 votes in the electoral college. It is a tribute to the average American's faith in his country and her institutions that the Socialist and Communist parties, both insisting that capitalism had collapsed, polled fewer than a million votes. And the Democrats elected emphatic majorities to both houses of Congress. There was never a stronger popular mandate in American history for a new program or policy, or a clearer repudiation of laissez faire. As Will Rogers put it, "The little fellow felt that he never had a chance and he dident till November the Eighth. And did he grab it!"

Unfortunately the so-called "lame duck" Amendment XX to the Constitution, altering the beginning of a new presidential administration from 4 March to 20 January, and the opening of a new Congress to 3 January, was not ratified by the requisite number of states until 6 February 1933. Consequently there was an embarrassing gap between the November election and 4 March, when F.D.R. could take over. Hoover at that time made a sincere but fruitless effort to persuade the President-elect to agree to participate in an international conference to stabilize currency and exchange, and to make a public declaration against inflation, expensive government projects, and unbalancing the budget. In other words, the President-elect should (as Hoover wrote to Senator David A. Reed on 20 February) agree to "the abandoment of 90 per cent of the so-called new deal." Roosevelt refused to commit himself in advance to break his platform. It was like the situation in February 1861 when John Tyler demanded that the Republicans abandon the principles on which they were elected, as the price of union. Hoover later declared that "fear" of New Deal radicalism was what caused the governors of twenty-two states to close all banks prior to 4 March. But the banks had been falling right through the depression — almost 5000 of them since 1929; and the threatened failure of many more early in 1933 was simply the built-up result of the economic tailspin.

Before we dismiss Herbert Hoover from his unhappy four years in Washington to his happy thirty-one years of semi-retirement, we should remember that some degree of F.D.R.'s success in dealing with the depression is owed to Hoover's proving that conventional methods had failed. If Al Smith, whose economic presuppositions were the same as Hoover's, had been elected President in 1928, he probably would have repeated the same mistakes.

When Franklin D. Roosevelt took the oath of office on 4 March 1933, the stock market had already started that upswing from its all-time low which continued to 1938. But the general situation was catastrophic, and the new

President made no effort to minimize it. The first paragraph of his inaugural address sounded like a trumpet call:

First of all, let me assert my firm belief that the only thing we have to fear is fear itself — nameless, unreasoning, unjustified terror which paralyzes needed efforts to convert retreat into advance. In every dark hour of our national life a leadership of frankness and vigor has met with that understanding and support of the people themselves which is essential to victory. I am convinced that you will again give that support to leadership in these critical days.

Then came the adagio:

Values have shrunk to fantastic levels; taxes have risen; our ability to pay has fallen; government of all kinds is faced by serious curtailment of income; the means of exchange are frozen in the currents of trade; the withered leaves of industrial enterprise lie on every side; farmers find no markets for their produce; the savings of many years in thousands of families are gone. More important, a host of unemployed citizens face the grim problem of existence and an equally great number toil with little return. Only a foolish optimist can deny the dark realities of the moment.

There followed an excoriation of the "money changers" who "have fled from their high seats in the temple of our civilization"; and of the "false leadership" which had attempted to solve problems through exhortation. "They have no vision, and when there is no vision the people perish." But Roosevelt had no intention of emulating his predecessor in relying upon exhortation. "This nation," he said, "asks for action, and action now!" Setting forth a general program which he promised shortly to elaborate in detail, he warned Congress and the country that the emergency called for emergency measures; and that if "the normal balance of executive and legislative authority" prove inadequate "to meet the unprecedented task before us," he would ask Congress for "broad executive power to wage a war against the emergency as great as the power that would be given to me if we were in fact invaded by a foreign foe." He concluded:

The people of the United States . . . in their need . . . have registered a mandate that they want direct, vigorous leadership. They have asked for discipline and direction under leadership. They have made me the present instrument of their wishes. In the spirit of the gift I take it. . . . May God guide me in the days to come.

"America hasn't been as happy in three years as they are today," wrote Will Rogers in his column on 5 March. "No money, no banks, no work, no nothing, but they know they got a man in there who is wise to Congress, wise to our so-called big men. The whole country is with him." [1]

That very day I asked a New Hampshire countrywoman, in a town which always voted heavily Republican, what they thought of the new President. Here is her answer, which millions all over the land would have endorsed:

"We feel that our country has been given back to us."

1. Will Rogers, *How We Elect Our Presidents*, p. 141.

L V I

The New Deal

1. *Roosevelt Himself*

There are seasons, in human affairs, of inward and outward revolution, when new depths seem to be broken up in the soul, when new wants are unfolded in multitudes, and a new and undefined good is thirsted for. There are periods when the principles of experience need to be modified, when hope and trust and instinct claim a share with prudence in the guidance of affairs, when, in truth, *to dare* is the highest wisdom.[1]

THUS WROTE William Ellery Channing in 1829. One of those seasons had arrived, and the man who dared to dare was President of the United States. Franklin D. Roosevelt, who occupied the chief magistracy for twelve years and thirty-nine days, was one of the most remarkable characters who ever occupied that high office; and he held it during two major crises, the Great Depression and World War II. A patrician by birth and education, endowed with an independent fortune, he was a democrat not only by conviction; he really loved people as no other President has except Lincoln, and as no other American statesman had since Franklin. Appreciation he prized; opposition often angered but never soured him. Widely traveled in youth and young manhood, Roosevelt knew Europe well. A great reader, especially of American history and political science, he found time to collect postage stamps and books on the United States Navy. No American President has been a success without prior political experience; and Roosevelt had had plenty of that, in the New York assembly, the governor's chair, and as assistant secretary of the navy. In addition, he had political acumen, a sense of the "art of the possible," and knew how to work through established political machinery. Not claiming omniscience — "there is no indispensable man," he said in a campaign speech — he summoned all manner of experts to Washington to furnish ideas and formulate legislation to get the country out of its desperate plight. He combined audacity with caution; stubborn as to ultimate ends, he was an opportunist as to means, and knew when to compromise. A natural dramatist, he was able to project his personal charm both in public appearances and in those radio "fireside chats" in which he seemed to be taking the whole country into his confidence. Thus he won loyalty to his ideals as well as to his person.

Indispensable to Roosevelt's well being and success was Mrs. Roosevelt, whom the whole country before long was calling by her first name. Franklin

1. William Ellery Channing, *Complete Works* (1884), p. 459.

found traveling difficult, but Eleanor went everywhere, by car, train, and airplane, even to Pacific Ocean bases during World War II. She visited and talked to all sorts and conditions of people, giving them a feeling that the government really cared about them. She took a particular interest in the disoriented and confused young people then graduating from schools and colleges, and was instrumental in preventing thousands of them from going Red. Among the colored people she became a legendary benefactress; and, in so doing, alienated the white South. She maintained the atmosphere of a gentleman's country home in the White House, amid all the hurlyburly of the New Deal. But she never intruded upon or tried to influence the President's policy; in fact, she disapproved much of it, notably his neutrality policy toward the civil war in Spain. Eleanor Roosevelt survived her husband for eighteen years, but cheerfully continued her good works almost to the day of her death.

Roosevelt's first cabinet included two men over sixty: Cordell Hull, secretary of state who had been congressman and senator from Tennessee for thirty years, and William H. Woodin, secretary of the treasury, who came of a family of Pennsylvania ironmasters. Others were James A. Farley, who had expertly managed the campaign and thus received the postmaster-generalship, chief source of patronage; Henry A. Wallace, second-generation editor of a farm journal and the world's greatest authority on hybrid corn, secretary of agriculture; Harold L. Ickes, elderly, peppery, persnickety Bull-Mooser and conservationist from Chicago, secretary of the interior; and Frances Perkins, social worker from New York, secretary of labor. There was something odd about every one of these except Hull, a Southern statesman of the old school, and Farley, a typical Irish Democrat. Woodin played the guitar and composed songs; Wallace was a religious mystic; Ickes had a persecution complex; and although "Madam" Perkins, as she was called, had a man's brain, it was odd to have a woman in the cabinet, especially in the labor office. Several members were former Republicans. Wallace's father, Henry C. Wallace, had been secretary of agriculture in the Harding administration, and the most frustrated member of that cabinet.

Roosevelt had the same facility as Lincoln in profiting from the expertise of his advisers while overlooking their quirks; he could use the slow, ruminating mind of a Hull as well as the brittle cleverness of a Bill Bullitt. Raymond Moley of Ohio, professor of public law at Columbia, and Rexford G. Tugwell, professor of economics in the same university, became respectively assistant secretaries of state and agriculture; several others with a similar professorial background were highly placed.

Many of the unofficial cabinet, the "brain-trusters" whom Roosevelt brought to Washington, were more important than the real cabinet. Harry Hopkins, son of a Mid-Western harness maker, was the most brainy, whether in social welfare matters in which he had been trained, or in later war issues which were completely new to him. Winston Churchill once called Hopkins

"Mr. Root of the Matter," because he had an astonishing ability to get to the bottom of a problem in the shortest time. Thomas C. "Tommy the Cork" Corcoran, with his quick mind and Irish wit, and Benjamin Cohen, quiet, scholarly, and thorough, were an important part of the setup. Collectively the "New Dealers," within and without the cabinet, were well educated, at home in the world of ideas, talkers and discussers, eager to put their intelligence to the service of the government.

"I pledge you, I pledge myself, to a New Deal for the American people," said Roosevelt in his speech accepting the Democratic nomination. That theme, which he returned to frequently during the campaign, gave a collective name to his policies — the New Deal. The series of measures that he inaugurated was a natural development from his cousin's Square Deal and Wilson's New Freedom. The only really new thing about it was a conscious effort, through legislation, to enhance the welfare and eventual security of simple folk throughout the country. These, at his accession, felt completely helpless, humiliated by the business and financial barons who had deceived them, and neglected by the previous administrations.

The transfer of wealth from the rich to the poor by government action had been suggested by Theodore Roosevelt in his Bull Moose campaign; and the income and inheritance taxes now made it possible. This policy, which Roosevelt and the Democrats pursued relentlessly, led to what was named, in scorn, the Welfare State. It did not prevent rewards to the skill and organizing ability of able individuals, as the increase of great fortunes since World War II has proved; but it vastly increased the power of organized labor and gave the ordinary citizen a feeling of financial security against old age, sickness, and unemployment which he had never enjoyed, and a participation in government such as he had never felt since Lincoln's era. At the same time a large part of the middle class, especially those who had retired on pensions or annuities, felt squeezed between the upper and nether millstones.

Thus the New Deal was just what the term implied — a new deal of old cards, no longer stacked against the common man. Opponents called it near-fascism or near-communism, but it was American as a bale of hay — an opportunist, rule-of-thumb method of curing deep-seated ills. Probably it saved the capitalist system in the United States; there is no knowing what might have happened under another administration like Hoover's. The German Republic fell before Hitler largely because it kept telling the people, "The government can do nothing for you." And, as proof that the Roosevelt administration was trying to avoid excessive governmental power rather than promote socialism, in his very first measure, the Banking Act, the President refused to consider nationalization. He insisted on leaving the banks free and independent, subject only to the regulation of the Glass-Steagall Banking Act. The New Deal seemed newer than it really was, partly because progressive principles had largely been forgotten for thirteen years, but mostly because the cards were dealt with such bewildering rapidity.

2. *The Hundred Days and After*

During the first "Hundred Days" of the Roosevelt administration, the President made ten speeches, sent Congress fifteen messages, eased many laws to enactment, talked to the press twice a week, conferred personally or by telephone with foreign statesmen, and made many important decisions. Yet he remained serene, confident, and smiling. Here are the legislative and executive landmarks of those hundred days in 1933: —

9 March	Emergency Banking Act
20 March	Economy Act
31 March	Civilian Conservation Corps
19 April	Gold standard abandoned (ratified 5 June)
12 May	Federal Emergency Relief Act
"	Agricultural Adjustment Act
"	Emergency Farm Mortgage Act
18 May	Tennessee Valley Authority Act
27 May	Truth-in-Securities Act
13 June	Home Owner's Loan Act
16 June	National Industrial Recovery Act
"	Glass-Steagall Banking Act
"	Farm Credit Act

The Emergency Banking bill, which the President and Secretary Woodin had worked on with the help of directors of the Federal Reserve Board, was submitted to Congress on the very day it convened, 9 March, and passed in the record time of eight hours. It provided for reopening the banks, then closed throughout the country, under a system of licenses and conservators, and gave the treasury power to prevent hoarding gold and to issue more currency. On Sunday, 12 March, the President delivered the first of his fireside chats, in which, as Will Rogers said, he took up the complicated subject of banking "and made everybody understand it, even the bankers." The banks reopened on Monday, the stock market rose on Wednesday, and a federal bond issue was oversubscribed the first day of issue.

The Economy Act was initiated by F.D.R. and Lewis Douglas, director of the budget, to redeem a platform pledge to reduce the cost of government. All federal appointees took at least a 15 per cent salary cut, and other savings were effected. This, as it turned, out, was a false start; what the country wanted and the economy needed was more federal spending. The salary cuts were restored before the end of the year.

The Civilian Conservation Corps was a device to give unemployed young men useful work, preventing them from drifting into subversive organizations, and to help conserve natural resources. By mid-June, 1300 CCC

camps had been set up under army control and recruited by the department
of labor; by August, over 300,000 young men were at work; and before the
camps were wound up in wartime, some 2½ million men had passed
through them, 17 million acres of new forests had been planted, numerous
dams built to stop soil erosion, and an immense amount of other useful
outdoor work performed in federal and state parks. The CCC might also have
been a valuable backlog for the future army, but for pacifist pressure which
deprived the army of an opportunity to give the young men even close-order
drill. Even so, the camps vastly improved the health and well-being of the men
who would have to fight another war before long.

On 19 April the President, against the advice of most of his economic
advisers, but with the unexpected support of the House of Morgan, announced that the United States was going off the gold standard, as England
had done two years earlier. Congress backed him up on 5 June. This was the
most revolutionary act of the New Deal, since it broke the implicit contract
between government and public to the effect that all government bonds, and
bills from $20 up, were to be paid in "gold coin." But it helped foreign trade,
stopped the drain of gold to Europe, and the domestic economy reacted
buoyantly; prices and stocks rose. Winston Churchill congratulated Roosevelt
on the "noble and heroic sanity" of this step.

The off-gold order was followed by the London World Monetary and
Economic Conference on currency and exchange of June–July 1933, attended
by representatives of over fifty nations. President Hoover, who believed that
the Great Depression was essentially a world affair and that currency stabilization was the answer, had promised American participation. The professed
object of this conference was to obtain an agreement of the principal countries to peg the wildly fluctuating international exchange, and agree on gold
or some other standard for currency. Roosevelt's only positive contribution
was a proposal made to Georges Bonnet, the French finance minister, before
the conference opened: a stabilization fund to keep the dollar, the pound
sterling, and the franc in a fixed relation. But the French government turned
that down.

Every shade of opinion was represented in the large delegation that Roosevelt sent to London: senators, congressmen, bankers, economists, Democrats,
and Republicans. They argued scandalously among themselves; on one occasion, Senator Key Pittman, the Nevada free silver advocate, was seen pursuing
a "gold bug" down the hall with a drawn bowie knife! And, as if there were
not already enough confusion, over 100 members of Congress signed a petition to Roosevelt to send the radio priest Father Coughlin to London as an
"adviser"! As the President insisted on taking a summer sailing cruise along
the New England coast while this conference was going on, his influence on
it was intermittent and haphazard. Briefly, the conference became a tussle
between gold-standard countries such as France, Holland, and Belgium, and
those which had gone off gold, mainly Britain, Canada, Scandinavia, and the

United States. The former wished to protect their foreign trade by getting everyone else back on gold; the latter were determined to stay off, and to promote inflation to raise domestic prices and increase foreign trade. In the so-called Thomas amendment to the Agricultural Adjustment Act, Congress had given the President power at his discretion to devalue the dollar as much as 50 per cent, to issue fiat money, and to establish bimetallism. He was determined not to surrender those advantages by international agreement. In mid-June, after security prices had again broken in New York, F.D.R. sent Moley to London, and that economist succeeded in obtaining a rather innocuous resolution by the Conference in favor of exchange stabilization and eventual return to the gold standard. Moley urged the President to accept this; Secretary Woodin wanted it; but F.D.R., with only his yachting mates Henry Morgenthau Jr. and Louis M. Howe having the presidential ear, refused to be bound, and in a strong message from Campobello on 3 July "torpedoed" the Conference agreement. Thus lightly the President accepted a policy of managed currency and exchange, which still obtains in 1964.

Many conservative financiers at home and abroad were horrified; but Bernard Baruch and Russell Leffingwell of the House of Morgan approved, as did Winston Churchill and John M. Keynes who said, "President Roosevelt is magnificently right." After the lapse of thirty years, there can be no doubt that Roosevelt was right in protecting his administration's fiscal freedom but the manner in which he acted offended many people, and Moley had to be sacrificed to appease Cordell Hull.

The Federal Emergency Relief Act of 12 May appropriated $500 million (later increased to $5 billion) for direct relief to states, cities, towns, and counties. Harry Hopkins, who headed this, and the Civil Works Administration which grew out of it, correctly estimated that the unemployed wanted work rather than a mere dole, and organized on that basis. By January 1934 CWA had over 4 million people on its rolls, and at its peak, 400,000 separate projects were under way: roads, schoolhouses, airports (500 new ones and as many improved), parks, sewers, everything that Hopkins could think up that would be of public benefit. Work relief, as it was called, proved to be one of the best morale builders of the New Deal; it gave the recipients self-respect to feel that they were doing something useful. Governor Landon of Kansas, who contested the presidency with Roosevelt in 1936, wrote to him two years earlier, "This civil works program is one of the soundest, most constructive policies of your administration, and I cannot urge too strongly its continuance."

Next in importance came the National Industrial Recovery Act of 16 June, the (for a time) famous NRA. Title I of this law prescribed the drafting and application of "codes" to every sort of industry, with multiple objectives — recovery and reform, encouraging collective bargaining, setting up maximum hours (and sometimes prices) and minimum wages, and forbidding child labor. NRA was administered by General Hugh S. Johnson, a West Pointer who had had charge of the draft in World War I and had occupied a high place in army logistics. By hard work and persuasion, with the symbol of a blue eagle clutching a cogwheel allotted to every firm and store that adopted the system, he codified some 700 industries. Business men in general did not like NRA; they wished to be free to raise prices and cut wages as soon as they were out of the woods; and Title I was declared unconstitutional by the Supreme Court in 1935. Before that occurred, some 4 million unemployed had been reabsorbed into industry, and about 23 million workers were under codes.

The Works Projects Administration, the second part of NRA, the Supreme Court allowed to stand. Administered by Secretary Ickes, WPA spent billions on reforestation, flood control, rural electrification, water works, sewage plants, school buildings, slum clearance, and students' scholarships. A feature of the WPA which caught the public eye and became nicknamed "boondoggling," was the setting up of projects to employ artists, musicians, writers, and other "white collar" workers. Post offices and other public buildings were decorated with murals; regional and state guides were written; libraries in municipal and state buildings were catalogued by out-of-work librarians, and indigent graduate students were employed to inventory archives and copy old shipping lists, to the subsequent profit of American historians. The federal theater at its peak employed over 15,000 actors and other workers, at an average wage of $20 a week. Under the direction of John Houseman, Orson Welles, and others, new plays were written and produced, and classic dramas, too; some had long runs on Broadway and toured the "provinces." On the fine arts projects, artist George Biddle observes that they were "as humane, democratic and intelligent, as any art program the world over. . . . They had developed through trial and error. They were no brain-trust fantasy, but were suited to our needs, our tradition and our temperament."

The AAA, the Agricultural Adjustment Act of 12 May, administered by Secretary Wallace, attempted to placate the perennial grievances of our tillers of the soil. Starting with the principles of the McNary-Haugen Farm Relief bill which President Coolidge vetoed, it went even further to meet the glut of farm products and the abysmally low prices. Wheat and corn then commanded a smaller price per bushel than they had in the colonies three centuries earlier. AAA authorized the agriculture department, through a system of county agents, to reduce planting of staple commodities such as grain, cotton, tobacco, peanuts, and sugar; to plow under 10 million acres of the cotton acreage already planted (for which the owners were paid $200 million), and to reduce the breeding of pigs and neat cattle. Opponents of the New Deal made much of the slaughter of 6 million piglets that fall; but the Federal Surplus Relief Corporation froze the pork and distributed over 100 million pounds of it to families on relief. Tobacco growers who had received $43 million for their 1933 crop, got $120 million in 1934, and comparable results were attained in other farm products. The national farm income increased from $5.6 billion in 1932 to $8.7 billion in 1935. Destruction of food, and paying farmers not to produce, went against the grain; but, in the long run, no other way has been found in thirty years to meet the recurrent problem of giving the farmers an adequate return for their pains. "Agriculture cannot survive in a capitalistic society as a philanthropic enterprise," said Secretary Wallace. Sentimentalists who weep over controlled production by farmers "do not suggest that clothing factories should go on producing *ad infinitum*, regardless of effective demand for their merchandise."

On the same day, 12 May, that the AAA became law, Congress passed the Emergency Farm Mortgage Act which halted foreclosures and provided federal refunding of mortgages. One month later, Congress set up a Home Owner's Loan Corporation to refinance small mortgages on private dwellings; within a year it had approved over 300,000 loans amounting to almost $1 billion. This was the most popular enactment of the New Deal as it prevented so many citizens from losing their homes.

Legislation to reform and regulate the stock exchange and the banks began with the Truth-in-Securities Act of 27 May 1933. This bill was drafted by two law professors, Felix Frankfurter and James M. Landis, who had studied existing legislation in Great Britain. It provided that new securities be registered before a public commission, and that every offering contain full information to enable the prospective purchaser to judge the value of the issue and the condition of the corporation. Directors were made criminally liable for omitting significant information or for willful misstatement of fact.

After an interval of several months, during which the New York Stock Exchange had opportunity to curb malpractices but remained recalcitrant, two of the leading "brain-trusters," Ben Cohen and Thomas G. Corcoran, drafted a bill which speaker Sam Rayburn guided to enactment on 6 June 1934, creating the Securities and Exchange Commission. This body had power to license stock exchanges and to register all securities in which they dealt. It prohibited pools and such devices for manipulating the market, and empowered the Federal Reserve Board to determine the extension of credit for marginal and speculative loans. Subsequent legislation enlarged the authority of the Securities and Exchange Commission over the public utilities. President Roosevelt, to the consternation of many, appointed as chairman of the Securities Commission Joseph P. Kennedy, one of the leading plungers before the crash. But as one who knew all the "angles" of the market, and was convinced of the need of reform, Kennedy was the man to do it. Supported by some of the more liberal and penitent moguls of finance such as James V. Forrestal, Robert Lovett, and W. Averell Harriman, the SEC formulated rules to prevent future skulduggery, stepped up the required margin for stock trading from 10 to 45 per cent, and also worked hard to obtain new financing. For about a year the corporations were defiant, alleging that Kennedy and "That Man in the White House" had ruined business; then Swift & Company

broke the deadlock with a $43 million bond issue that was promptly sub-
scribed, and by the fall of 1935 some $800 million of new financing had been
effected. Kennedy now removed himself and his large family to the London
embassy, and saturnine James M. Landis succeeded him as head of the SEC.

When the "Fighting First" Division, United States Army, crashed through
a little Sicilian town named Nicosia in July 1943, they were not aware that it
was the birthplace of a fighting American judge, Ferdinand Pecora. In New
York City, after graduating from law school, Pecora made a name for himself
as assistant district attorney, and as a judge. Appointed counsel to the Senate
committee on banking and currency in January 1933, he conducted a sensational investigation of what had been going on in the field of investment
banking. Typically Sicilian in appearance, angry and sarcastic at times but
always in command of himself and the situation, Pecora interrogated such
titans of finance as Morgan, Dillon, Aldrich, Forrestal, Otto Kahn, and
Wiggin, uncovering the story of chicanery in high places from which we
culled a few facts for an earlier chapter. The investigation had a major influence on the Truth-in-Securities Act already mentioned, and on the Glass-
Steagall Banking Act of 16 June 1933. This law required banks to get out of
the investment business, and placed severe restrictions on the use of banking
funds for speculation. And it gave a federal guarantee for individual bank deposits. This revolutionary device, which even Roosevelt thought dangerous,
was pushed through by a group of congressmen led by Arthur A. Vandenberg
of Michigan, against the opposition of the American Bankers' Association.
Insurance of bank deposits turned to be one of the most brilliant achievements of the Hundred Days.

Many of the laws that we have briefly described were regarded by their
authors and by the President as temporary relief measures; but this banking
law, as well as the two acts regulating the securities markets, were intended as
permanent reforms and, though amended by later enactments, are in force in
1964. Of the same nature were the Social Security Act of 1935 which initiated
a comprehensive federal system of unemployment and old age insurance, and
the Public Utilities Holding Company Act of the same year, passed in spite of
a high-pressure lobby organized by Wendell Willkie. So, too, were the several
conservation measures which we shall take up shortly.

Winston Churchill, out of office and not yet acquainted with F.D.R.,
remarked on the efforts of his future partner, "The courage, the power and
the scale of his effort must enlist the ardent sympathy of every country, and
his success could not fail to lift the whole world forward with the sunlight of
an easier and more genial age. . . . Roosevelt is an explorer who has embarked on a voyage as uncertain as that of Columbus, and upon a quest which
might conceivably be as important as the discovery of the New World."

Long, exhausting, and tortuous has been that voyage in quest of peace and

security, and it may well be that none now living may sight that promised
land. But Roosevelt had at least got them through the Red Sea, with no other
miracle than the fortuitous union of courage, faith, and sagacity.

3. Conservation and the TVA

On 18 May 1933, President Roosevelt signed the Tennessee Valley Authority Act, the famous TVA, a great and permanent achievement of the New
Deal. It deserves special mention as a revolutionary attempt to do something
constructive for the poor, whom "ye have always with you." Most of the New
Deal measures were based on the theory that the only thing government
could do to relieve poverty was relief — mostly by taxing the "haves" for
benefit of the "have-nots." TVA was based on a constructive concept, to raise
the collective well-being of millions of people by controlling a mighty river in
such wise as to produce electric power, rebuild the fertility of eroded farms,
and enhance the living conditions of those inhabiting the valley.

This idea was sold to F.D.R. by Senator George Norris of Nebraska, one of
the most remarkable statesmen in our modern history. Unimpressive, simple
in his tastes — he never acquired a dinner coat during thirty years in Washington — no great orator, with arched eyebrows that gave his countenance a
look of perpetual surprise, but always a little sad over the greed and folly that
he encountered daily, Norris was a liberal progressive who linked the 1890's
with the 1930's. Always contending on the liberal side and often beaten, he
never gave up, reminding one of the warriors for Irish freedom described by
Shaemas O'Sheel:

> They went forth to battle, but they always fell;
> Something they saw above the sullen shields.

What Norris saw was "the one great central problem, the use of the earth for
the good of man." Born in Ohio in 1861, teacher, lawyer, and judge in a small
Nebraska town, Norris had served his state in Congress as representative and
senator for thirty years, always a Republican. And although he found more
support for his idea among the Democrats, he never abandoned the dream of
his youth to make the Republican party an instrument of human progress and
justice, an example of "pure and enlightened government." His first blistering
experience was that of the hard times in Nebraska in the 1890's. "Only those
who have lived in the heart of the nation's food-producing regions," he wrote,
"know fully the agony of these cycles of crop failures, heavy indebtedness
upon the land, and ruinous farm commodity prices." He followed Theodore
Roosevelt into the Progressive party, and was chosen to the Senate in 1912.
There he became interested in flood control and other aspects of conservation. For thirty years he fought the Pacific Gas & Electric Company's grab of
the Hetch Hetchy reservoir and power system in California, and lost. He
fought American entry into World War I, and lost. During the discouraging

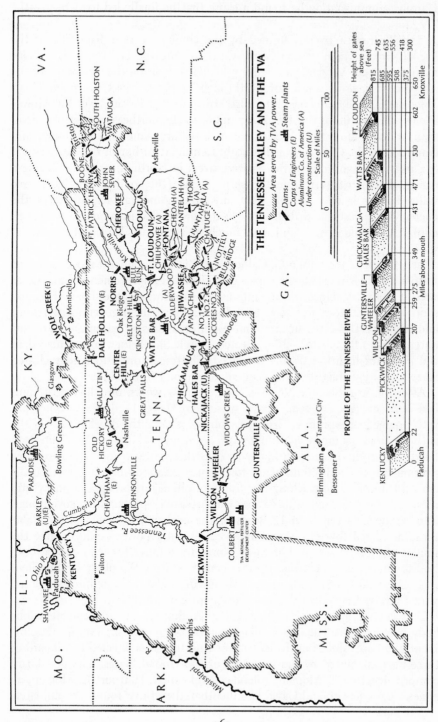

THE TENNESSEE VALLEY AND THE TVA

Harding administration he found a cause that he finally led to victory — the TVA.

The Tennessee river is formed by the confluence near Knoxville of the French Broad which rises in North Carolina, and the Holston which begins in southwestern Virginia and, fed by smaller streams on the west slope of the Appalachians, flows southwesterly through Tennessee, past Knoxville, Chattanooga, and Chickamauga, into northern Alabama. Passing over the Muscle Shoals where it drops 137 feet in 37 miles, to the northeast corner of Mississippi, it turns almost due north, passes Pittsburg Landing and Shiloh, and empties into the Ohio river at Paducah, Kentucky. Although the Tennessee is 652 miles long and one of the greatest rivers in North America, it became a raging, destructive torrent in the spring rains (the southeastern Tennessee valley having heavier rainfall than any other American region except the Pacific Northwest), and died away to a mere trickle in summer. Moreover, rainfall had eroded and gullied so much of the valley land as to render it sterile.

As far back as 1825, John C. Calhoun, still in his nationalist mood, initiated a survey of the Muscle Shoals as part of an internal improvements plan, and as a result Congress helped Alabama to build a canal around the shoals. This, too short to be effective, was soon abandoned. The federal government rebuilt and reopened this canal in 1890, but found it useless at extreme high or low water. In 1917 President Wilson selected Muscle Shoals for a government dam and plant for hydroelectrically produced nitrates, in order to render United States munitions factories independent of imports from Chile.

After the war, Senator Norris prevented these works, on which vast sums had been spent, from being leased or sold to Henry Ford or any other privately owned enterprise. He had the vision of placing the development of the entire river valley under an autonomous governmental agency. In addition to flood control, he wanted authority to construct power plants, locks to allow river navigation, and nitrate plants to produce cheap fertilizer and reclaim the eroded land. This far-reaching proposition aroused intense opposition by utilities, railroads, and all who instinctively resisted "putting the government into business." Even John L. Lewis of the coal miners' union objected because he feared that electricity produced by water power would deprive the miners of jobs! Two bills drafted by Norris for a limited scheme passed both houses but were vetoed, one by President Coolidge, the other by President Hoover. Senator Norris, who never gave up, drafted a third comprehensive bill which received President Roosevelt's signature on 18 May 1933.

This act set up the Tennessee Valley Authority, an independent public body based on the Panama Canal Commission precedent, for the development of an area three-fourths the size of England. It is directed by a board of three men appointed by the President of the United States. The first board comprised Arthur E. Morgan, a flood-control expert, Harcourt A. Morgan, an agricultural scientist, and David E. Lilienthal, then thirty-four years old, lately a member of the Wisconsin public service commission. The basic Act transferred to TVA all government-owned property at Muscle Shoals, made the Board responsible for flood control and developing navigation, and gave it authority to build and operate dams and reservoirs, to generate and sell electric power, and to manufacture and distribute fertilizer. And it made possible any number of other programs to raise the "economic and social well being of the people living in said river basin."

The Authority already owned the Wilson dam at Muscle Shoals. It started work on the first new one, appropriately named Norris, on 1 October 1933 and completed it in May 1936. This was the first of six completed before World War II. All were multi-purpose dams, including locks for navigation and a hydro-electric plant; some contributed to flood control by creating storage reservoirs on tributaries of the Tennessee.

The men who ran the Authority had the sense to see that the well being of this great valley must be promoted in a variety of ways. First, by flood control. Floods, still a hazard on the Ohio, the Connecticut, and many other American rivers, are now a thing of the past on the Tennessee. Second, by commercial navigation. By means of massive locks the haulage increased from 33 million ton-miles in 1932 — mostly short runs of gravel barges — to 2.2 billion ton-miles in 1963 — mostly diesel-power barges carrying every sort of commodity on long haul. Third, by development of cheap electric power for homes and factories. Generated at the dams on the main river and some of its tributaries, it is distributed to the ultimate consumer through 158 locally owned co-operatives, municipalities, or private companies. These deliver the current to individuals at less than one cent per kilowatt hour, compared with the average nation-wide rate of 2.4 cents charged by private utilities. By 1950 when the low-cost hydro-electric potential of the river was nearing full realization, TVA began building steam power plants operated by coal brought downstream by barge or by rail from the mines of Kentucky, Tennessee, and Illinois. Finally, by improvement of farming. A group of TVA chemists set to work to lower the cost of fertilizer by producing concentrated phosphate; and in late 1936 TVA was operating its first electric phosphorous furnace. In order to persuade farmers to use this to advantage, demonstration farms were developed with the co-operation of agricultural colleges, local bodies, and farm owners; 54,000 farms, covering more than 6.6 million acres, have participated. TVA also provided free seedlings for reforestation. With the help of state nurseries it has reforested over a million acres of valley land since 1933.

The TVA has few compulsory powers. It enjoys the right of eminent domain, and can remove obstructions to navigation, but in general operates through partnership with local authorities, and the voluntary co-operation of individuals. Although dependent on Congress for appropriations for non-revenue-producing activities, it remains independent of the Washington bureaucracy. More than 200 private companies now manufacture and market products developed by TVA. Thus it is not a super-government; both in theory and practice TVA is worlds apart from the Soviet system of forcing collectivized farming on the peasants and regulating what they sow and reap. Farmers' co-operatives were organized in all but ten of the 125 valley counties. And, since World War II, it has been the model for many similar schemes in other parts of the world.

Senator Norris could not rest after the original act received President Roosevelt's signature. He became the leader of a long and weary battle for congressional appropriations, to defend TVA from politicians who wanted to control it, and the utilities which accused it of "creeping socialism." It seemed monstrous to elderly senators such as Kenneth D. McKellar of Tennessee that this autonomous authority should operate in their bailiwick, dictate where dams and power plants should be built, and handle its personnel by the merit system. The utilities' major quarrel with TVA was probably based on its policy of providing electricity to the public at lowest possible cost, both to stimulate consumption and act as a "yardstick" for public bodies regulating the rates charged by private companies. Since the private utilities' policy was based on charging high rates for limited consumption, they considered TVA's low rate-high use policy ruinous. But in thirty years' time most of them have come to accept it.

In World War II the Oak Ridge center for atomic fission was located within the Tennessee valley to use TVA power. This, and other applications of its power to national defense, made new friends for TVA. Senator Norris noted with satisfaction that big utilities men on the National Defense Advisory Committee pressed Congress to provide funds for building Cherokee dam on the Holston river to provide power for aluminum production. This important dam, first of a number of wartime additions to TVA's power capacity, was built in the record time of sixteen months in 1940–41. Incidentally, the Authority created some fourscore public parks for boating and bathing.

This great enterprise has been one of the country's major contributions in the twentieth century. It proved that a democratic state could be progressive; that by invention, farsighted planning, and popular co-operation it could benefit the entire society within its orbit; that a great river, instead of being a destroyer, could become a boon to the dwellers on its watershed. President Kennedy, addressing an assembly at the Muscle Shoals on the thirtieth anniversary of TVA in 1963, well said: "The tremendous economic growth of this region, its private industry and its private income, make it clear to all that TVA is a fitting answer to socialism — and it certainly has not been creeping."

The Soil Conservation Act of 1936, replacing the emergency AAA, provided for the reforestation of immense areas of marginal land throughout the country. Next year Senator Norris proposed the creation of six more regional authorities like TVA, starting with the Missouri valley which needed it most. Owing in part to the failure of the states concerned to agree, in part to the utilities' lobby, none of these proposals reached law. But the Roosevelt administration is remembered for several great multi-purpose dams in the West. It completed Boulder dam on the Colorado river, begun under President Coolidge. This is a godsend to Los Angeles and Southern California as a source of electric power. The 550-foot-high Grand Coulee dam on the Columbia river in eastern Washington, completed in 1941, created a lake 150 miles long, and provided almost 2 million kilowatts' power, as well as irrigation, for a barren section of the old Oregon country known as the "Scablands." Twenty years later, the value of crops grown on this former desert was $42 million. On the lower Columbia, about 35 miles upstream from Portland, army engineers in 1938 completed Bonneville dam to tame the five-mile Cascade Rapids. These, like the Muscle Shoals, had closed a vital part of the river to shipping. And, through a series of other dams and locks, the Columbia is now navigable for boats of nine-foot draught up to Bosco, 324 miles from the bar which the ship *Columbia* was the first to cross. Several other dams and hydro-electric plants have been built on this great river by privately financed utilities. And in October 1964 a treaty with Canada, providing for joint exploitation of the upper Columbia, was ratified.

The problem of how to distribute and dispose of this newly generated electric power aroused, as we have seen in the case of TVA, a bitter controversy between the administration and the utilities. These, wedded to the "high rate–low use" concept, refused, as unprofitable, to extend light and power lines into thinly inhabited rural areas. So, in contrast to poor countries like Norway where, owing to government control of water power, almost every farmhouse had enjoyed electric light since the early years of the century, only one out of ten American farms had it in 1933; and as for electrical milking and other machines, it was clear that if the farmers were to continue dependent on privately financed utilities, they might wait forever — except in the Tennessee valley.

The Rural Electrification Administration, originally set up as a relief project, became an independent agency in 1936. REA owes as much to Morris Llewellyn Cooke as TVA does to Senator Norris; and Norris helped REA too. Cooke, a Lehigh University graduate in engineering, a main-line Philadelphian sixty-three years old, had made a power survey of Pennsylvania which convinced him that only government support would get electricity into the back-country, and sold the idea to F.D.R. and Harold Ickes. Cooke first tried to persuade the utilities to accept low-interest loans from the government for extending their lines into the country, but met with a flat refusal. He then decided to promote non-profit co-operatives among the farmers. After much opposition by the utilities' lobby, REA got the money from Congress and, by the end of 1941, had lent $434 million to rural co-operative power plants. And in five years the number of farms having electric light and power increased from about 750,000 to 2,250,000. By 1950, 90 per cent of all farms in the United States were electrified.

Conservationists got through Congress during the Hoover administration a very important law, the Shipstead-Nolan Act of 1930, "to promote better protection and highest public use of the lands of the United States." And the country now had a President and secretary of the interior who were aggressive conservationists. The Roosevelt administration promoted or completed several national parks, including the Olympic, Isle Royale, Shenandoah, and Great Smoky Mountains. Since 1927 a voluntary organization called the Quetico-Superior Council had been trying to make an international park out of the Superior National Forest in Minnesota and the Quetico Park in Ontario, to protect the lake country on both sides of the old Indian fur-trade portage between Lake Superior and Lake of the Woods. The guiding spirit of this Council was a Harvard graduate named Ernest C. Oberholtzer, who loved the wilderness and wished to preserve this last big unspoiled tract in the Middle West for posterity. Only by putting it under the National Forest Service could its natural beauty, the maze of lakes and streams, the primeval forest, the fish and game, be protected from spoliation. The Shipstead-Nolan act gave the authority, but the Quetico-Superior project, requiring concurrent action between Minnesota, the United States, Ontario, and the Dominion of Canada, was exceedingly difficult to implement. Opposition developed from Minnesota paper and pulpwood interests which wished to strip the region of its timber and ruin the lake shores by building dams so that logs could be run out at a minimum of expense. Ickes approved the Oberholtzer program, and the President instructed Secretary Hull to negotiate a treaty with Canada to carry it out; but before that could be done, World War II broke out. The state of Minnesota raised objections, but the project was completed by the Humphrey Act of June 1956, and included in the Wilderness Act of 1964.

George W. Norris, whose career is a standing reproach to those "tired liberals" who give up after defeat, died, still a senator, in 1944. His own simple conclusion to his efforts was this: "If in the peaceful years ahead new vigor comes to old and wooded hills, not only in the basin of the Tennessee but throughout America, and in other regions of the world, and laughter replaces the silence of impoverished peoples, that is well."

4. The New Deal and Foreign Affairs

We have already seen how the President "torpedoed" the London Economic Conference in the summer of 1933, in order to retain America's freedom to manipulate currency and exchange to her own advantage. The rise of Hitler, however, caused a change of heart, and Henry Morgenthau Jr., Woodin's successor in the treasury, negotiated a tripartite pact with Great Britain and France in 1936, for stabilizing the dollar-pound-franc exchange.

A constructive measure for lowering trade barriers was the Reciprocal Trade Agreements Act passed by Congress in 1934 at the earnest insistence of Secretary Hull. This allowed the President to lower customs duties against a nation as much as 50 per cent in return for similar favors. Since these agreements did not have to be ratified by the Senate, the traditional log-rolling and pressure politics were bypassed. By the end of 1938, American exports to the sixteen nations with which Hull had concluded these agreements had increased 40 per cent over the figures of 1930.

Since 1919, official American relations with Russia had been with the Kerensky government in exile. Recognition of Soviet Russia was brought about partly in the hope of trade, and also because it became clear that the communist regime was there to stay. Russia in 1933 appeared to be moving toward the "bourgeois prejudices"' which earlier she had despised; hence many Americans thought, quite erroneously, that the Russian was now going the way of the French Revolution. But Stalin and his colleagues knew exactly what they were doing. They modified the rigid communist system to make it work, but were still inseparable from the Comintern, organ of the Third International, and continued to promote world-wide revolution so far as they could, including the United States.

Recognition was accorded in November 1933 after Maxim Litvinov, the foreign minister, had visited Washington and promised not only to end communist propaganda in the United States and guarantee religious freedom in Russia, but negotiate a settlement of claims and debts. Stalin broke faith on all three counts, and the expected trade failed to materialize.

The main trend of New Deal foreign policy until 1940 was to continue to avoid European commitments, but to cultivate New World solidarity, and to attempt to persuade Japan through diplomacy to respect the integrity of China. The Latin-American aspect really worked. Secretary Hull's reciprocity agreements helped every American republic to get out of the depression, and at Montevideo in December he signed a treaty to the effect that "no state has the right to intervene in the internal or external affairs of another." This made binding Hoover's disavowal of the Roosevelt corollary to the Monroe Doctrine. In accordance with this "Good Neighbor" policy, the United States in 1934 formally renounced her right to intervene in Cuba under the Platt Amendment, withdrew the last of the marines from Haiti, and increased Panama's annuity for the Canal Zone. Roosevelt himself attended an Inter-American Conference for Peace at Buenos Aires in 1936, promising to consult with Latin-American nations "for mutual safety."

Another troublesome situation with Mexico arose in 1938, under President Cardenas, who identified himself with the interests of the peons and union labor. Partly as a result of their complaints against British and American oil companies in Mexico, Cardenas expropriated all foreign oil properties in 1938. After four years of negotiations, a commission valued the confiscated properties at $24 million — about one-tenth of what the oil companies claimed; and the companies obeyed the state department's advice to accept.

These acts implemented the Good Neighbor policy and resulted in Pan-American solidarity in World War II.

5. The Opposition and the Supreme Court

On 1 March 1934 Justice Stone of the Supreme Court wrote to Herbert Hoover, "It seems clear that the honeymoon is over, and that we may witness the beginning of real political discussion." Or, as another put it, business having emerged from its storm cellar with the help of the administration, forgot that there had ever been a storm. With the gross national product rising by 20 per cent in 1934, and the Dow-Jones index of common stock prices going from 41.2 in mid-1932 to 100 in mid-1933, the old adage came true again:

> The devil was sick, the devil a monk would be;
> The devil was well, the devil a monk was he!

Business and finance had many emotional and some legitimate grievances against the New Deal. The popular image of financiers and business men as generous promoters of the common weal had been destroyed; that of a beneficent federal government had taken its place. Industrial tycoons found it irritating to be forced to confer with "young whipper-snappers" of the "brain trust" about codes, labor relations, and the like. Railroads and trusts were used to regulation, but manufacturers, investment houses, and stock exchanges were not. Washington brain-trusters were not always tactful, and the spectacle of their drafting bills which the 74th Congress "rubber-stamped" infuriated people both in and out of Congress. Many conservatives persuaded themselves that the New Deal was destroying the historic American pattern of individual responsibility and local initiative by placing the nation's future in the hands of starry-eyed professors and power-mad bureaucrats. Soon it began to be whispered, then written, then shouted, that the Roosevelt administration was becoming totalitarian, assimilating American policy to that of Hitler or Stalin. Many a business leader began to look upon himself as Horatius at the Bridge, "facing fearful odds, for the ashes of his fathers, and the temples of his gods." The American Liberty League, founded in 1934 by a group of conservative Democrats led by Al Smith, John W. Davis, and the Du Ponts, played variations on that theme. Senator Connally of Texas expressed the popular reaction: "If the government had not got into business, there would be no business today. As soon as the business man sees a slight improvement he starts shouting, 'The government must get out of business.' "

Roosevelt made a conciliatory fireside chat on 30 September 1934 in which he declared his faith in "the driving power of individual initiative and the incentive of fair private profit," with the qualification that "obligations to the public interest" must be accepted. He had given up the hope of partnership with business, because most of the business leaders with whom he conferred simply wanted repeal of New Deal legislation, and to let laissez-faire resume its fateful course. "One of my principal tasks," wrote the President in November, was "to prevent bankers and business men from committing suicide." Wisely he elected to remain "above the battle" in the congressional elections of 1934, and forbade cabinet members — except irrepressible Jim Farley — to make campaign speeches. The election proved Roosevelt's strength. The Democrats added nine members to their majority in the House, and several new Democratic senators, including the hitherto unknown Harry Truman, were sent to the Senate.

Congress now (14 August 1935) passed one of the most far-reaching laws of the New Deal, the Social Security Act. This provided for unemployment compensation by a one per cent tax (since increased to 7¼ per cent) on payrolls, half withheld from the employee's salary, half paid by the employer; a federal bonus to state old-age assistance of half what the state paid, in addition to a straight old-age pension; grants to the states for children's health and welfare, to the blind, and to extend state public health services.

A host of cases challenging the constitutionality of these measures reached the Supreme Court. Charles Evans Hughes was still chief justice; and, of the associate justices, only Brandeis, Stone, and Cardozo could be expected to find constitutional the vast extensions of federal power assumed by President and Congress in 1933–34. In May 1935 the Supreme Court, in the Schechter poultry case, destroyed the National Industrial Recovery Act in a unanimous and sweeping decision. Congress, said the Court, cannot delegate unfettered power to the President to issue whatever edicts he thinks advisable for the good of trade or industry. The NRA constituted an improper exercise of the commerce power, for if the commerce clause were so construed, "the federal authority would embrace practically all the activities of the people and the authority of the state over its domestic concerns would exist only by sufferance." Thus ended a law which the President had described as "the most important and far-reaching ever enacted by the American Congress." Actually, NRA had run its course and done its work; the blue eagle was not greatly missed.

On 6 January 1936, the Supreme Court invalidated the AAA (Agricultural Adjustment Act) as an improper exercise of the taxing power and an invasion of the reserved rights of the states. "This is coercion by economic pressure," said Justice Roberts, who conjured up the terrifying consequences that would flow from the taxation of one part of the community for the benefit of another. But Justice Stone, dissenting, warned his colleagues against a "tortured construction of the Constitution," and observed, with some asperity, "Courts are not the only agency of government that must be assumed to have capacity to govern."

Although the Supreme Court passed favorably on TVA and other leading measures of the New Deal such as the Wagner Labor Act, it invalidated several other measures of importance to the administration. Justices of the Supreme Court are long-lived and were not then subject to a retirement age, and there had been no vacancy during President Roosevelt's first term.

F.D.R., feeling that the country could not afford to wait for the six septuagenarians on the Court to make their last decisions, in February 1937 made the startling suggestion to Congress that it authorize him to appoint one new Justice for every one over seventy years of age who had not retired. This was his first big mistake. The public may have been irritated by the obstructionism of the Supreme Court, but it did not wish that revered institution to be tampered with. From almost every quarter the proposal was denounced as an attempt to "pack" the Court, and Congress refused to pass the desired law: But, if Roosevelt lost this battle, he won the campaign. The Court itself, while the debate was under way, managed to find reasons for passing favorably on new laws differing little from those formerly under the ban: — a farm-mortgage act, the National Labor Relations Act, and Social Security. The old justices began to die or retire, and in the next four years, Roosevelt was able to appoint a virtually new court: — Senators James F. Byrnes of South Carolina and Hugo Black of Alabama, Stanley Reed of Kentucky, Professor Felix Frankfurter who had raised up a new generation of lawyers and jurists, Professor William O. Douglas, who had served on the SEC; and Governor Frank Murphy of Michigan. In 1941, when Chief Justice Hughes retired, Harlan F. Stone, a wise and tolerant associate justice, became his successor.

This new court completed the retreat from the constitutional position taken by its predecessor and renewed the tradition of Marshall and Story. It returned to that broad interpretation of the commerce, taxing, and general welfare clauses of the Constitution and of Amendment XIV which made possible the application of the Constitution to an industrial nation. The principles of those famous dissenters, Justices Holmes and Brandeis, became cornerstones for the new majority.

6. Demagogues and Deviationists

While the strongest opposition to Roosevelt came from the right, the noisiest came from the left. The depression not only spawned demagogues and cranks, each with his own panacea, but had a devastating effect on many young college graduates and other jobless intellectuals. It seemed to prove that representative government and capitalism were finished. Whither, then, to turn? Polarity being a weakness of intellectuals, many decided to save America by embracing one of the two competing ideologies in Europe — fascism and communism. Seward Collins, a graduate of Hill School and Princeton, founded *The American Review*, which became the organ of an American fascist party. Lawrence Dennis of Exeter and Harvard, a repentant Wall Street banker, turned toward Hitler as a new god; his *The Coming of American Fascism* came out in 1936. William D. Pelley of North Carolina organized the Silver Shirts, "the flower of our Protestant Christian manhood" he called these middle-class hoodlums, who imitated Hitler's storm troopers by terrorizing Jews, communists, and liberals, but with minimum success.

Pelley counted on becoming the American *Führer* when Hitler took over, and his lieutenants picked out expensive mansions from Newport to Palm Beach for future headquarters as *Gauleiter*. Other fascist groups were formed, claiming that they alone could save America from the Jews and communists toward which Franklin D. Roosevelt (Rosenveltd according to them) [1] was driving it. Those movements even enjoyed a half-hearted approval by the Hearst press in 1934–35, Hearst himself having been deeply impressed by Hitler in Berlin. Many a college student, visiting Germany during the depression, observed the *Hitler Jugend* marching, singing, and doing something, returned home to find apathy and unemployment, and became a Nazi convert. This American fascist movement never became serious, but it made some notable converts who turned traitor to the United States during the next war — the poet Ezra Pound who broadcast for Mussolini, and Fred Kaltenbach, one of Hearst's favorite European correspondents, who performed the same service for Hitler.

At the other pole was the American Communist party, which always obeyed orders from Moscow. Hitherto the Soviets followed the "hard line" — founding communist trade unions, agitating incessantly and denouncing the socialists as well as the bourgeoisie. The Communist party, following this line, organized the unions in two big textile strikes in the 1920's, at Passaic and New Bedford, and lost both. In 1934, however, Stalin, alarmed at the growing power of Hitler, adopted the "soft line" of infiltrating regular unions and cooperating with liberals and socialists to set up "Popular Front" governments in Europe. Earl Browder, head of the American Communist party, obeying his master's voice, ordered members to liquidate "every old idea that stands as an obstacle between us and the masses." The New York *Daily Worker* stopped insulting socialists but continued to attack President Roosevelt as a covert fascist, and the New Deal as "the death rattle of capitalism." Communists infiltrated the Minnesota Farmer-Labor party, and in some instances local units of the regular parties, by attending caucuses and electing themselves as delegates. Chuckleheaded union leaders — notably those of the Chicago meat packers — thought they "could use the Commies" and let them into the organization, only to find that they were the ones used. One such take-over threatened the entire structure of national defense; this was the National Maritime Union, which held up shipments to France in 1940, but became super-patriotic when Hitler attacked Russia.

Besides infiltrating labor unions, the communists joined with pacifists and other liberals in organizing "front" organizations, notably the American League Against War and Fascism, which capitalized on sentiments common to most Americans. This League held an annual congress from 1933 on, to orate and pass resolutions, on the model of the International Congress

1. One of the yarns in which many people believed during the New Deal was that F. D. R. was the descendant of a German Jew named Rosenveltd whom Peter Stuyvesant had exiled to Hyde Park because he engaged in seditious activities in New Amsterdam.

Against War at Amsterdam, organized by Barbusse and Romain Rolland. Controlled from the start by communists, this League claimed to have two million members and very likely did, as propaganda against American partici- pation in the European war fell in with the national mood. The reds also took over the National Negro Congress organized by anti-communist leaders such as Ralph Bunche; the American Student Union, which claimed 20,000 mem- bers, and the American Youth Congress, founded by vague "young" (mostly aged 40 and up) liberals, but soon captured by really young and determined communists.

Communism, presented as an ideal form of society and a gospel of all- embracing love for mankind, appealed to muddled young intellectuals, many of whom were persuaded that this, not fascism as Anne Morrow Lindbergh predicted, was "the wave of the future." They were horrified by the excesses of the Nazis but conveniently overlooked those of the Soviets — the purges and executions, the five and a half million *kulaks* (land-owning peasants) liquidated or transported to Siberia between 1928 and 1934; the five million starved in the famine of 1932–33 — because these were either concealed and denied, or were presented as a necessary prelude to an ideal society. Commu- nism also attracted young scientists whose political education had been neg- lected, because it was presented as a completely logical, scientific reorganiza- tion of government and society. Encouraged by the party, several talented young men like Whittaker Chambers and Alger Hiss sought and obtained positions — mostly unimportant ones — in the federal government. They formed a communist cell in Washington and met frequently to laugh their heads off over the futile efforts of "that cripple Roosevelt" to cure a tottering capitalist system. They attempted to ingratiate themselves with Russia by stealing government documents — mostly innocuous reports by foreign serv- ice representatives in Europe — and copying them for transmittal to Moscow. Hiss's odd typewriter became the means of his later conviction. These men confidently expected to be named top commissars of the Soviet United States, just as Hitler's supporters looked to the Fuehrer to bestow similar favors after beating America to her knees.

In the relatively temperate regions between the two political poles were bred a number of native American movements, each under a leader with a particular nostrum for ending the depression. One of the most formidable was the Reverend Charles E. Coughlin "the radio priest," Irish-Canadian rector of the parish of Royal Oak near Detroit. In 1926 he began operating the "Shrine of the Little Flower Radio Station" and preaching what he called a Christian solution of the nation's economic difficulties, namely, juggling the currency. A consummate radio orator, his Irish humor attracted attention to his theories; and as a free-silver and paper-money man he appealed to the old populist faith that gold was the root of all evil and New York bankers the devils. By 1934 ten million people were listening to Coughlin's radio broad- casts, and voluntary contributions of half a million dollars a year were rolling in to the Shrine of the Little Flower. Up to that time, Coughlin supported Roosevelt and the New Deal, which he even called "Christ's deal." But in 1934 he decided that the President had gone over to the bankers and began to attack the "Jew deal," anti-Semitism being one of Coughlin's favorite stocks in trade.

Dr. Francis E. Townsend, a sixty-six-year-old physician of Long Beach, California, was impelled into the crackpot political arena by the distressing spectacle of helpless and hopeless old folk who had lost their jobs and spent their savings and knew not where to turn. In 1933 he announced the "Townsend Plan" to cure the depression — to give everyone over sixty years of age a federal pension of $150 a month, provided he spent it. The idea went over big in California, haven of the elderly and retired; and with the aid of a real estate promoter named Robert E. Clement, Townsend Clubs spread countrywide. A Democrat named John S. McGroarty, the "poet laureate of California," introduced a bill in Congress which would give every oldster $200 a month for life. After it had been pointed out that this would channel about one-half the national income into the pockets of one-eleventh of the population, the bill was dropped.

Upton Sinclair, the most prolific author in American literary history, a Socialist for thirty years, joined the Democratic party in California to campaign for the governorship on a platform of End Poverty in California, EPIC for short. His ideas were ancient — reorganizing society in co-operative phalanstaries like Brook Farm and New Harmony, which had failed a century earlier. With the aid of a popular utopian novel that he wrote for the occasion, *I, Governor of California and How I Ended Poverty*, Sinclair captured the Democratic nomination for governor in 1934. Since he was a Democrat, the administration had to support him, as did Father Coughlin and a number of Eastern intellectuals such as Theodore Dreiser. Roosevelt rather liked Sinclair, and regarded his proposed experiments as interesting and innocuous. Not so, however, the fat cats of California. In the first of our all-out, heavily financed campaigns directed by a public relations firm of advertising men, the immense corpus of Sinclair's published literature was combed for odd or offensive statements, and documents were forged to prove him a communist and a traitor. The Republican candidate for governor stole some of his thunder by endorsing the New Deal and the Townsend Plan, and Sinclair was snowed under. That was the end of EPIC, but this state campaign was significant for proving the influence of the public relations profession. No major presidential campaign since 1948 has been waged without their fabulously expensive aid to one or both sides.

There were several other "small, sour and angry" schemes, as Emerson described their prototypes a century earlier; but the really formidable one, which had the administration trembling for a time, was "Every Man a King," led by Huey P. "Kingfish" Long of Louisiana. Huey was the most amusing and terrifying of all demagogues thrown up by the Great Depression; and, unlike the others, he had a firm state base to work from. Born into a "hill-billy" family in the piney-woods of northern Louisiana, Huey worked his way to a law degree by the age of twenty-one. When he entered state politics, the regular Democratic machine had been in power for fifty years without doing anything for the people. By appealing to the "Cajuns" (descendants of the displaced Acadians), the "sapsuckers" of the piney-woods, and the hill-billies, using a slogan he got from Bryan, "Every Man a King," Long got himself elected governor in 1928. Within a few years, having persuaded the voters to elect a "rubber stamp" legislature, and by using bribery, violence, and black-mail, he had the entire state and local government, down to the policemen and firemen, under his control. Louisiana became a government like that of Mexico under Calles or the Argentine Republic under Perón. Huey did accom-plish a lot of good. He built schools and enlarged the university, extended hard-top roads into the up-country, abolished the poll tax so that Negroes could vote; they and the poor whites adored him. But he was also a clown, a vindictive bully, and a coward who evaded the wartime draft and went about surrounded by an armed bodyguard. Aiming at national power, he got himself elected to the United States Senate in 1930 as a first step. Fellow senators, shocked by his improprieties, regarded him with his pudgy face, pug nose, pop eyes, red hair, and ungrammatical speech, as an ignorant buffoon. But they underestimated Huey, and he regarded most of them as stuffed shirts.

Long supported Roosevelt in 1932, but broke with him next year; the President, one of the first to regard him as dangerous, retaliated by denying him federal patronage. Huey retorted with what he called the Share-the-Wealth program, which outdid even Dr. Townsend, or the Social Credit people in Canada. By a capital levy on fortunes and inheritance, he would present every American family with a $5000 house, $2000 annual income, and sundry other benefits. Poor folk and crackpots all over the country poured in their praise of Share-the-Wealth, and Long announced his candidature for the presidency early in 1935. He was then only forty-two years old.

Congress adjourned at the end of August 1935, and the Kingfish returned to his kingdom. On the evening of 8 September as he was crossing the rotunda of the state capitol, he was assassinated by a man whose family he had ruined. There was a sigh of relief in Washington; but the simple folk of Louisiana sing ballads about Huey Long to this day, and his successors are still in control of the state.

The Kingfish's crown now passed to Congressman William Lemke of North Dakota. After the defeat in May 1935 of Lemke's bill to refinance farm mortgages by the issue of $8 billion worth of greenbacks, this congressman announced himself as candidate for the presidency of the Union party, or National Union for Social Justice, an inflationist organization founded (over the air) by Father Coughlin to support his views. Lemke, a Republican and a graduate of Yale Law School, aped the dress and speech of the impoverished Dakota farmers whom he championed. He characterized Roosevelt as "the bewildered Kerensky of a provisional government." Father Coughlin and Dr. Townsend supported him, and the Reverend Gerald L. K. Smith, who had been Huey Long's principal assistant in his Share-the-Wealth movement, promised to deliver the alleged six million followers of the Kingfish to the Union party. H. L. Mencken, who was present at the Union party convention in Cleveland in 1936, described Smith's speech as "a magnificent amalgam of each and every American species of rabble-rousing. . . . It ran the keyboard from the softest sobs and gurgles to the most earsplitting whoops and howls, and when it was over the 9000 delegates simply lay back in their pews and yelled." Father Coughlin was not at his best before a live audience, but when he referred to "Franklin Double-Crossing Roosevelt," the crowd went wild again. Dr. Townsend was there too, somewhat abashed because his realtor executive had skipped with $90,000 from the till. It looked as if this combination of Western agrarianism, the old folks, Huey's "Share-the-Wealth," and Coughlin's Irish brogue would make this party a mighty force. It nominated Lemke for the presidency, and for vice president Thomas C. O'Brien, a Harvard graduate who had been general counsel for the railroad brotherhoods and was counted on to get their vote.

7. The Election of 1936

As the presidential election approached, the clamor against President Roosevelt so increased both in pitch and volume that many political seers believed that the New Deal was doomed. H. L. Mencken declared in March that "this dreadful burlesque of civilized government" was at the end of its turn, that the "brain trust" had better pack up and go home, and the Republicans "begin to grasp the fact" that they can beat F.D.R. "with a Chinaman, or even a Republican!"

Governor Alfred M. Landon of Kansas, selected to do the job was thrifty, cagey, and folksy, and no fool. An old Bull Mooser, if elected he would have continued the New Deal under another name. Hoover "wowed" the Republican convention by predicting that a continuance of Democratic rule would result in "violence and outrage," "class hatred . . . preached from the White House," "despotism," "universal bankruptcy," and other horrors. Yet the platform promised to do everything that Democrats had done, without destroying "free enterprise, private competition, and equality of opportunity."

The Democratic convention met in a jubilant mood, renominated President Roosevelt by acclamation, endorsed the entire New Deal, and promised to extend and expand it.

This campaign of 1936 was very heated. The Republicans' best argument was that the New Deal had not materially increased employment — there had been 12.8 million unemployed in 1933, and were still 9 million in 1936. The Democrats answered that the numbers of jobless would have been far worse without the New Deal, and that, anyway, the upturn had come and everyone except the bankrupt bankers and speculators was feeling better. Most of the newspapers, and very many business people, supported Landon. "Save the American Way of Life" was the slogan. A poll conducted by the *Literary Digest* predicted Landon's election. Then, in one of the greatest landslides in political history, Roosevelt received 60.7 per cent of the popular vote, and won 523 presidential electors out of 531. Lemke's Union party polled 892,000 votes, about the same that Norman Thomas the Socialist candidate had received in 1932. Earl Browder the Communist leader, who had vainly tried to make a "popular front" with Thomas, obtained only 80,000 votes.

It was an old saying, "As Maine goes, so goes the nation." Jim Farley now changed this to "As Maine goes, so goes Vermont." These were the only two states that Landon carried; but his popular vote was 36 per cent of the total. The Republican minority in Congress dwindled, but still constituted strong opposition, a good thing for the country.

This unmistakable mandate for his policies encouraged Roosevelt to deal with the Supreme Court (as we have already noted) and to enlarge his methods to provide economic recovery.

The Second Roosevelt Administration

1937-1941

1. *The New Deal and Labor*

THE OVERWHELMING ENDORSEMENT of Roosevelt in 1936, followed by an almost equally strong one in 1940, did not mean that everybody loved F.D.R. Among those who did not, hatred was more bitter, vituperation more shrill, nasty rumors more prevalent, than against any President in our history — except possibly Lincoln. In most business and some professional circles it was the fashion never to mention his name — he was "That Man" or even "That Madman" in the White House. Nice old gentlemen wished he might drop dead or regretted that age and conscience prevented them from assassinating him. What reason was there for this virulence? The philosopher Alfred North Whitehead, who regarded Roosevelt as the greatest ruler since the Emperor Augustus, observed that similar things had been said in his youth about Gladstone, and for the same reason — that he was "a traitor to his class." If somebody like Bryan had been at the head of the New Deal it would have been understandable; but for a Hudson river patrician, a graduate of Groton and Harvard, to act that way, was abominable.

Big business and finance had deservedly lost status and popular respect since 1929, but blamed it on Roosevelt. And, worst of all, he had done his best to peg wages at trade-union levels. Almost every man of wealth had enough resource to tide him over any conceivable depression, but he wanted the downward spiral to hit rock bottom, smash the labor unions, and reestablish the free labor market of the previous century. Roosevelt's successful effort to prevent that was his unpardonable crime; but in the eyes of the country at large, his greatest achievement. A section of the National Industrial Recovery Act, the NRA of 1933, declared that employees had the right to collective bargaining through their own representatives, that there should be no interference, restraint, or coercion by employers in their organizing, that the "yellow dog contract" which required a worker as a condition of employment to join a company union or refrain from joining some other union, was no longer legal.

Under the impetus of the NRA, organized labor more than recovered its losses of the preceding decade, and by 1936 the A. F. of L. boasted a membership of 3.4 million. When employers who questioned the constitutionality of the NRA refused to be bound by its provisions or to accept the rulings of the Board, an epidemic of strikes and lockouts swept the country. Labor, certain of government support, presumed upon its new position and antagonized public opinion; industry, determined to recoup depression losses and unterrified by the New Deal, employed traditional weapons of strike-breakers, injunctions, and company unions. During 1934 recovery was delayed by a strike in the automobile industry, a nation-wide textile strike, and a general strike in San Francisco. All were unsuccessful, and the last two were smashed by the militia and by self-constituted vigilantes.

After the NRA had been declared unconstitutional by the Supreme Court, many of its labor provisions were re-enacted in the Wagner-Connery Act of 5 July 1935. This set up a federally appointed National Labor Relations Board, authorized to investigate complaints and issue "cease and desist" orders against "unfair practices" in labor relations. The Supreme Court sustained the constitutionality both of the Wagner-Connery Act and the NLRB. Chief Justice Hughes insisted that the connection between manufacturing and commerce was obvious and that the protection of the "right of employees to self-organization and freedom in the choice of representatives for collective bargaining" had an intimate relation with interstate commerce.

As one might have expected, the NLRB was bitterly hated and severely attacked by the great corporations and employers of labor, because it meant almost continuous government interposition between employer and employee. But the Board made an excellent record. In the five years ending January 1941, it handled some 33,000 cases involving over 7 million workers, and amicably disposed of more than 90 per cent of them. Of 3166 strikes certified to the Board, 2383 were settled peaceably. In case after case its findings were sustained by the Supreme Court. The NLRB now beat back all attempts to repeal its authority or curtail its powers, and, by the beginning of the third Roosevelt administration, the opposition was silenced if not converted.

An important development within the ranks of labor was the emergence in 1935 of the Congress of Industrial Organizations, the C.I.O., a secession from the A. F. of L. by workers impatient with Sam Gompers's cautious policy. Under the dynamic leadership of John L. Lewis of the United Mine Workers, the C.I.O. set out to unionize industries which had heretofore resisted, such as steel, automobile, textile, and public utilities. Union after union seceded from the A. F. of L. to the new organization; hundreds of thousands of unskilled and semi-skilled laborers signed up with the only union which appeared to have any interest in them; journalists and other "white collar" workers organized professional affiliates. By midsummer 1937 the C.I.O. had an estimated membership of four million. Heady with success, John L. Lewis called a series of strikes directed not toward improvement in hours and wages, but to secure the closed shop, and establish the C.I.O.'s exclusive right to represent workers in collective bargaining. He employed the new technique of the "sit-down" strike, taking possession of the premises and refusing to get out until demands had been granted. To this weapon many employers surrendered; United States Steel met the demands of the C.I.O. in March 1937. Others, notably General Motors and Republic Steel, challenged the legality of the sit-down and called upon the courts to rescue their property. The courts responded with injunctions, and when workers resisted the court orders, things erupted. The intervention of Governor Murphy of Michigan prevented widespread violence in the automobile industries of that state, but in June 1937 there was open warfare in South Chicago where police, defending the property of Republic Steel, killed ten people. Public opinion turned against the C.I.O. and the sit-down, and by midsummer 1937 it appeared that the new organization might forfeit many of its early gains.

In June 1938 Congress passed a bill drawn by Senator Black of Alabama, designed to put "a ceiling over hours and a floor under wages." This Fair Labor Standards Act had as an objective the "elimination of labor conditions detrimental to the maintenance of the minimum standards of living necessary for health, efficiency and well being of workers." It provided for an eventual maximum working week of forty hours, and minimum wage of forty cents an hour. The wage increase affected 700,000 workers, and the hours provision ultimately reached some 13 million people. President Roosevelt characterized the Fair Labor Standards Act as "the most far-reaching, far-sighted program for the benefit of workers ever adopted in this or any other country." Its constitutionality was challenged, but sustained in a unanimous opinion of the Supreme Court.

2. Canada in the Depression

Although the stock-market crash of October 1929 affected fewer people, proportionally, in Canada than in the United States, the Great Depression dug as deep or deeper in the Dominion as in the United States. As the Canadian historian A. R. M. Lower has put it, "revelry on the warm sand beaches of the 1920's was followed by the freezing rain of the 1930's, with its ghastly tale of unemployment. Only a continent as fat as North America could have stood such heating and such chilling."

Since the depression was world-wide, Canada, dependent on foreign trade, felt its effects very severely. Over one-third of her gross national product was derived from sale of products, mostly raw materials, abroad. Prices for newsprint, metals, and lumber tumbled to new lows; wheat fell from $1.60 a bushel in 1929 to 38 cents in late 1932, and the production from 567 million bushels in 1928 to 182 million in 1934. Industrial centers in Ontario, protected by the tariff, suffered from lack of consumer demand, and hundreds of thousands of workers were laid off. The Canadian National incurred deficits of over $60 million a year, and the bloated C.P.R. even passed dividends. The

Maritimes suffered least because they were poor anyway; their mixed farming and fishing at least afforded them plenty to eat even when exports fell off. British Columbia, whose fishing and lumber interests depended on foreign demand, was badly beaten down. But the prairie wheat-growing provinces suffered most, since they lost not only their markets but their crops in two years of drought. Under the weight of cumulative disaster, the promising co-operative wheat pools established in 1923–24 simply died. And the traditional Canadian resource in hard times of emigrating to the United States was no longer available because there were no jobs across the border. Over 200,000 Canadians entered the United States in 1924; only 6000 in 1933.

The Conservatives won the general election of 1930, partly as a reaction against the high United States tariff, partly because Mackenzie King refused to take radical steps to remedy unemployment or support the tumbling price of wheat. The new Conservative leader Richard B. Bennett, who spent money lavishly in the campaign, now became prime minister. Bennett, descended from a colonial Connecticut family which moved to Nova Scotia before the American Revolution, was a robust, dynamic man who, after making a personal fortune from railroads and a paper mill, had served as minister of finance under Meighen. A natural conservative like Herbert Hoover, Bennett was forced by the Great Depression to favor measures as radical as Roosevelt's.

Owing to that steady increase of provincial powers of government at the expense of the Dominion, which we have already noted, the provinces, with comparatively weak resources, now had commitments for social welfare which they could no longer bear. Bennett's first attempt to redeem Conservative campaign promises to end the depression took the form of raising customs duties, in the hope of giving Canada bargaining power to break down the high tariffs of the United States, France, Italy, and — beginning in 1931 — Great Britain. He did wrest concessions from the mother country after an imperial economic conference in 1932. The Dominion parliament also voted large sums for unemployment relief to be distributed by the provincial governments; and over a period of seven years it lent over $100 million to the prairie provinces.

Radical parties arose in the Canadian west, as in the United States, dedicated to ending the depression in one swoop. The Co-operative Commonwealth Federation (C.C.F.) led by the Reverend J. S. Woodsworth, resembled old Kansas Populism with a veneer of British Labour party philosophy. The other, the Social Credit party, was founded in Alberta by a school principal and head of a fundamentalist Bible institute named William Aberhardt. Believing that the basic trouble with Canadian society was inadequate distribution of purchasing power, this "funny money party," as opponents called it, advocated the federal government's paying every citizen a "social dividend" of $25 a month. Simple farmers who hadn't seen that much money for years were naturally impressed. Social Credit swept Alberta in 1935 but accomplished nothing because the Dominion government disallowed all provincial laws in the field of banking and currency.

Comparable to the United States Senate's Pecora investigation of banking and investment houses, was a Canadian royal commission on price spreads. Harrry H. Stevens, Bennett's minister of trade and commerce, who earlier had uncovered the customs corruption of the 1920's, presided. This commission revealed startling cases of price manipulation and stock watering, wholesale evasion of wages and hours, shops charging $2.50 each for garments made in sweatshops at $1.50 a dozen, and similar abuses. They reported "that the corporate form of business not only gives freedom from legal liability but also facilitates the evasion of moral responsibility for inequitable and uneconomic practices." Bennett tried to suppress the report, but Stevens gave it out, and made speeches emphasizing some of the more reprehensible cases of exploitation. He was forced to resign, and started a small business men's party of his own.

Now, to the astonishment of all Canada, and the dismay of Republicans across the border who had been pointing with pride to the Bennett approach as the proper one to end the depression, the Premier suddenly came out with measures out-Roosevelting Roosevelt! Apparently he had been "sold" on the New Deal by his brother-in-law William D. Herridge, whom he had appointed Canadian ambassador at Washington. Herridge was an Ottawa lawyer of great charm, and an idealist who became a sort of honorary member of the Roosevelt "brain trust." With a general election already scheduled for 1935, Bennett rocked the country with a series of radio addresses declaring that the capitalist system must be reformed by measures "more comprehensive, more far-reaching than any scheme of reform which this country has ever known." Parliament then proceeded to enact "Bennett's New Deal" — minimum wages, 48-hour week in industry and a weekly day of rest, unemployment and social insurance; and set up commissions to regulate industry, enforce business standards, and market Canadian products.

It was too late for Bennett to be the F.D.R. of Canada. Personally he was overbearing and arrogant; his sudden conversion to radicalism alienated thousands of his own party, and failed to impress the others as sincere. Mackenzie King and the Liberals swept every province except British Columbia, which the Conservatives took, and Alberta, which Social Credit won. "Funny money" and the C.C.F. obtained 24 seats in the new Parliament of 1935, and the Conservatives only 40; but the Liberals won 179, biggest majority since Confederation. Bennett retired to England where possibly the conferring of a peerage by George V consoled him for most of his New Deal measures being declared unconstitutional by the judicial committee of the Privy Council.

Mackenzie King in April 1935 again became premier of Canada and remained in office for thirteen years, through two more general elections and the Second World War. This short, thick-set man, a confirmed bachelor with a mild and diffident air, no great orator, endowed with few attributes of leadership, was nevertheless a remarkably astute statesman. He had the "feel" of Canada's ambivalent position toward the United States and Great Britain, the peculiar relation between Ottawa and the provinces, and between French Canada and English Canada. Through a French deputy premier, Ernest Lapointe, he kept the habitants of Quebec in line; by various measures he placated the embattled farmers of the west. Amd the most important of Bennett's New Deal measures, the Unemployment and Social Insurance Act, was re-enacted in 1940 after a parliamentary amendment to the British North America Act of 1867 had overridden the Privy Council decision.

Mackenzie King and Franklin D. Roosevelt, who had known each other during King's United States career, now became warm personal friends, although King (says his biographer) "was too studious, spinsterish and precious for the lusty inner White House circle." President Roosevelt, now that Canada had abandoned high protection, reciprocated, and in an agreement concluded at Washington in November 1935, United States duties on some 200 Canadian products were lowered. Secretary Hull, a glutton for reciprocal trade agreements, built on this good start with a Britain-Canada-United States conference at Washington in 1937. Out of that came a tripartite trade agreement of 17 November 1938. This was a bold stroke at the tariffs that had enhanced the depression by placing national economics in watertight compartments. And at Kingston, Ontario, in August 1938, President Roosevelt promised "that the people of the United States will not stand idly by if domination of Canadian soil is threatened by any other Empire," a promise which King reciprocated shortly after. From the outbreak of war in Europe Roosevelt passed to King by letter or telephone everything he learned that might be of interest to Canada; and that close partnership was cemented during the war.

3. New Deal for Indians and Negroes

We left the American Indian of the West in the midst of his prolonged depression which followed the passage of the well-meaning Dawes Act of 1887.[1] That situation continued to within the third decade of the twentieth century. The general assumption behind the federal government's policy was an anticipated disappearance of the Indians as a separate and distinct race. Hence it was a good thing to help the process — not, of course, by the earlier crude methods of starvation, disease, and extermination, but by promoting the breakup of reservations into individually owned allotments. Land ownership, it was believed, would make the redskins responsible citizens and assimilate them to the American Way of Life. The interior department speeded up this process through shortening by several years the time that an Indian had to occupy his allotment before receiving fee-simple title, and sell it. In one

1. See above, Chapter XLVI.

year 60 per cent of all Indians receiving titles to their allotments sold out, and most of them squandered the proceeds.

This does not, however, apply to the Five Civilized Tribes of Oklahoma. They managed to retain much of their own culture, while adapting themselves to that of the Anglo-Saxon American; and many became eminent. Will Rogers, Senator R. L. Owen, and Admiral Joseph J. ("Jocko") Clarke, a great carrier group commander in World War II, were Cherokee; Charles Curtis, Vice President under Hoover, was an Osage, and the list might be extended indefinitely by including artists, professional singers, and ballerinas.

The appointment of Albert J. Fall as secretary of the interior by President Harding boded ill for the poor Indian, now a victim marked for slaughter in that general assault on the public domain in the name of "development." Fall did not try to steal the Navajo oil lands, because by the time their leases came up for auction, he had been frightened by the Teapot Dome disclosures; but he sponsored a barefaced attempt to rob the Pueblo Indians of Arizona and New Mexico of a large proportion of their irrigated land. Since 1877 some 3000 white families had moved in on the Pueblo domain, either as squatters or by illegal purchase from individual Indians. In 1913 the Supreme Court of the United States invalidated these purchases. The white claimants then appealed for relief to Congress, which with Fall's approval drafted the so-called Bursum bill, throwing on the Indians the burden of proving ownership of their ancestral lands; failure to do so would vest title in the white squatter. This attempt at a wholesale steal caused the Pueblo Indians to act in concert for the first time since their great revolt of 1680. Forming an All Pueblo Council, they appealed to Congress and the public, and under the leadership of John Collier, a social-work director of California, not only defeated the Bursum bill but persuaded Congress to set up a fair procedure for determining ownership of the disputed property.

In an act of 1924 Congress conferred United States citizenship on all Indians born within the United States who did not already have it. This boon was received with considerable skepticism, especially as many states refused to let Indians vote — New Mexico and Arizona did not do so until 1948. What most Indians wanted was to be let alone on their diminished reservations, to live their own way. Reservation Indians, not taxed and not subject to the draft, in a sense were privileged, even if poor in goods. Most of them preferred to continue that way rather than be individual landowners with the duties that landowning imposed.

A New Deal for the Indians really began under President Coolidge when his secretary of the interior, Hubert Work, employed a private organization financed by John D. Rockefeller, Jr. to conduct a thorough investigation of the economic and social condition of reservation Indians. Their report, issued in 1928 and known by the name of the head investigator Lewis Meriam, declared, "An overwhelming majority of the Indians are poor, even extremely poor, and they are not adjusted to the . . . system of the dominant white civilization." It showed up the abuses of the allotment system, and recommended that it be abolished. It exposed the failure of the government's educational policy of placing Indian children in boarding schools where only English was spoken, and where they were suposed to learn the "three R's" and a trade. The boarding schools turned out to be regular Dotheboys Halls, where the children were overworked, undernourished (an average of 11 cents per day per capita being allowed for food), and taught very little of any use to them. Meriam urged replacement of these by day schools located within communities where their parents lived and, wherever possible, integrated with public school systems. It further declared that the Indian service should become "an efficient educational agency, devoting its main energies to the social and economic advancement of the Indians," so that they may either "be absorbed into the prevailing civilization" or "be fitted to live in the presence of that civilization" with "a minimum standard of health and decency."

The Meriam report made a deep impression. Before the Hoover administration ended, many of the boarding schools had been abolished in favor of day schools, and responsibility for health on the reservations had been transferred to the National Health Service. But Hoover's secretary of the interior was premature in predicting in 1931 that the Indian Service had "turned the corner" and would "work itself out of a job in 25 years."

For a radical change of policy, the redskins had to wait for the Roosevelt administration. Harold Ickes, the new secretary of the interior, appointed as commissioner of Indian affairs John Collier, the crusader who had helped the Pueblos. Under his aggressive leadership the administration embarked on a program of helping the Indians to stay Indian — strengthening tribal governments, fostering arts and crafts, and in general following the advice of ethnologists who believed that the Indians not only had a culture worth preserving but the right to preserve it. Congress, at the request of Ickes, passed the Indian Reorganization Act of 18 June 1934, embodying this concept and definitely repealing the allotment plan of 1887, which had reduced tribal holdings from 138 million to 48 million acres. It even provided for acquiring new land for the use of the Indian reservations which needed it. President Roosevelt accepted the thesis that the Indians were not headed for extinction; they must be helped to achieve a respected though distinctive status under the American flag. This was a return to Chief Justice Marshall's decisions in which he tried in vain to protect the Eastern Indians from the rapacity of frontiersmen and the roguery of politicians. Now the Democratic party, hostile to Indians and Negroes for a century, became the champion of both.

The American Negro probably suffered even more than whites from the Great Depression, but he benefited by the New Deal and made notable advances toward his goal of integration — the direct opposite to what most Indians wanted. Disaffection of Negroes to the party of Abraham Lincoln started in 1928 when the Republicans began to build a "lily-white" organization in the South. President Roosevelt, on the contrary, gained a large following among the colored. Segregation in federal offices in Washington, which the three Republican Presidents had allowed to stand, was abolished. Roosevelt made a beginning of integrating racially the armed forces, and insisted that in every industry, defense or otherwise, set up under the New Deal, Negroes should receive an equal chance of employment. He appointed many to office; and in almost every new commission and bureau there were one or more Negro advisers on race relations. Mrs. Roosevelt was close to Mrs. Mary Bethune, head of the National Council of Negro Women. Secretary Ickes, who had been president of the Chicago branch of the National Association for the Advancement of Colored People (NAACP), was particularly assiduous in finding posts for qualified Negroes; in 1946 there were four times the number of Negro federal employees as in 1933. Negroes benefitted equally from New Deal projects like the AAA, the TVA, and the CCC, and the housing and other welfare programs. Even a few of the labor unions which formerly had rigidly excluded Negroes from membership, now opened their doors.

Throughout this period the Communist party was playing for the Negroes, with the attractive bait of setting up an all-Negro state in the South. James W. Ford, a Negro, received second place on their presidential tickets. But the vast majority of colored citizens of the United States merely shifted their allegiance from the Republican to the Democratic Party.

Whilst the Roosevelt administration favored integration of Negroes in federal activities, it did not attempt the colossal task of forcing it on Southern states and committees, or of putting Negroes on their electoral rolls. Even in so comparatively liberal a Southern city as Richmond, Negroes were not allowed to use the public libraries until 1947. Undoubtedly the Negro made great progress toward political and economic equality between 1933 and 1945; but at the latter date he was still very far from his — or his leaders' — goal.

4. Conclusion to the New Deal

With the farm and labor legislation of 1938, the domestic program of the New Deal was rounded out. Not all the cards had been dealt, but the nature of the game was fairly well established. So, what was really accomplished?

First, the relief of distress and the rise of employment. There was a recession in 1937 and unemployment again rose above 10 million the next year; but from that time on, with the help of war orders after 1939, it dropped almost to nothing. Wages and prices remained steady.

Second, more had been done for the physical rehabilitation of the country, and to stop the waste of natural resources, than in any similar period. The

TVA, the big new dams, reforestation to halt the spread of the dust bowl, and the new national parks, reversed that earlier trend of despoiling natural resources.

Third, the thesis that the federal government is ultimately responsible for the people's welfare, employment, and security, became generally accepted. This principle, implicit in Wilson's New Freedom, received wide and general application only in the New Deal. It began with relief to the unemployed, entered the domains of agriculture and labor, and established elaborate programs of rural rehabilitation. As proof of the welfare principle's general acceptance, the Republicans adopted it from 1940 on, their quarrel being no longer with the welfare state as such but with the haphazard and wasteful way in which it was administered by the Democrats. That charge in a great measure is true; but, considering the pressing emergency and the proliferation of new boards, commissions, and administrative agencies, waste and mis-spent efforts were inevitable.

Fourth, Roosevelt reasserted the presidential leadership which had been forfeited by his three predecessors and promoted the growth of federal power which had halted since the First World War. Yet, despite all the hullaballo attributing to him dictatorship, fascism, communism, and the like, he con-sistently acted within the framework of the Constitution. When the Supreme Court declared a measure like NRA unconstitutional, the President obeyed and the blue eagle died. This was very different from President Jackson's "Marshall has made his decision, now let him execute it!" And Roosevelt's unsuccessful attempt to "pack" the Supreme Court was far less radical than Jefferson's plan to destroy it by impeachment.

Fifth, economic and social planning by the federal government became an established fact. American corporations such as General Motors and United States Steel had long planned operations for years ahead, but Americans were congenitally suspicious of governmental planning, and Roosevelt's National Resources Planning Board aroused more frenzied opposition from senators such as Taft, Tyding, and Byrd, than anything else in the New Deal. They appear to have suspected Roosevelt of attempting to put over a Russian-style "five-year plan." In the course of the 1940's, under the stress of a war that required intelligent foresight if it were to be won, planning ceased to be a dirty word and became a necessity in modern administration.

Of basic importance in the political field was a growing appreciation of the nature and function of the state. Laissez-faire, not without gallant rear-guard actions, gave way to a realization that the state was a natural medium for man's self-expression, like organized religion, fraternal orders, and social clubs. It became clear — though far from indisputably so — that there was no in-herent conflict between *imperium* and *libertas*, authority and freedom. The flexibility of the Federal Constitution was spectacularly vindicated. James Madison in *The Federalist* had predicted that only a federal government over a large area could reconcile conflicting economic interests and subordinate private to public welfare. In spite of the vastly increasing size and complexity of the United States, it now appeared that Madison was right.

Besides temporary expedients such as the employment of youth in CCC camps, the organizing of "white collar" projects and public works relief, the New Deal achieved many things of permanent benefit. Such were the conservation program, including TVA; the regulation of the stock market, the rural electrification program, and the enhanced status of union labor. This expansion of governmental functions and regulation inevitably affected the economic life of the nation. But the movement left so much scope to private enterprise that, in the end, the entire economy was strengthened. The New Deal did more to shore up and buttress a capitalist system tottering under the blows of depression, than it did to weaken or destroy it. The American system came dangerously near collapse in 1932–33, with over 12 million unemployed. Could it have stood 20 million, 30 million unemployed? Huey Long, for one, thought not; he truculently told the Senate that he might be heading a mob to storm the capitol and hang his fellow senators! Such things have happened in many countries; and there was no assurance that it could not happen here, if the people lost faith in their government.

Franklin D. Roosevelt's administration saved twentieth-century American capitalism by purging it of gross abuses and forcing an accommodation to the larger public interest. This historian, for one, believes him to have been the most effective American conservative since Alexander Hamilton, as well as the most successful democrat since Lincoln. As Roosevelt remarked in a fireside chat of 1938, democracy had disappeared in certain European nations because their governments said, "We can do nothing for you." But "We in America know that our democratic institutions can be preserved and made to work." And to this task of providing security without impairing fundamental liberties, Roosevelt devoted his major peacetime energies.

"The only sure bulwark of continuing liberty," Roosevelt further observed, "is a government strong enough to protect the interests of the people, and a people strong enough and well enough informed to maintain its sovereign control over its government." In 1940, when it became doubtful whether liberty or democracy could survive overt attempts by totalitarian states to conquer the world, it was of utmost importance to mankind that the American democracy weathered the Great Depression and emerged strong and courageous; that the American people were refreshed in their democratic faith, determined to defend it at home and to fight for it abroad. Once more the United States, in Turgot's phrase, was "the hope of the human race."

5. War in Europe and Asia

Had any pollster been looking for one idea on which the vast majority of the American people agreed, when under the New Deal experiment they agreed on nothing else, it would have been that if Europe were so wicked or stupid as to start another war, America would resolutely stay out. On this point even communists agreed with the Liberty League. Roosevelt reflected this feeling by failing even to mention foreign relations in his second inaugural address, delivered on 20 January 1937. Yet the collective security which the League of Nations supposedly had established was already giving way to uninhibited aggression by dictators or oligarchies. Hitler in 1935 denounced the German disarmament clauses in the Treaty of Versailles, one year later he occupied the Rhineland, and nobody did anything about it. Toward Italy, already at war with Ethiopia, the League of Nations applied partial economic sanctions, but by May 1936 the indestructible Emperor Haile Selassie was in exile and his country annexed to Italy. That summer, General Franco began a civil war in Spain; in the fall Hitler and Mussolini established the "Rome-Berlin Axis." And before Roosevelt's second inauguration, Japan was deeply engaged in undeclared war with China. Thus there were plenty of warnings of the next international debacle, had Roosevelt cared to allude to them. He doubtless refrained from doing so because anything he might have said would have created violent dissension among American groups and parties on whom he depended to continue his domestic program.

Of all these evil portents, the most sinister was the rise of Adolf Hitler. The hold of that uneducated paranoiac over the German people, with their long tradition of culture and decency (to which they have since returned), is a phenomenon which even the Germans themselves find hard to explain. In part, no doubt, it was due to the poverty and disorganization of Germany after her defeat in World War I; but other nations, notably Austria and Poland, had suffered even more than Germany, and made little trouble. Hitler rose on a tide of resentment over the Treaty of Versailles; but the victors had redressed most of the severities imposed by that treaty, and (with the aid of American loans) had relieved Germany from the burden of war reparations before Hitler reached power. There was much talk of *Lebensraum*, room for expansion; but the Netherlands and Scandanavia suffered similar pressures without trying to wreck the European world. Probably the conclusion that Franklin D. Roosevelt reached is the right one. Hitler, a frustrated fanatic, based his Nazi party on the residuary hatred, barbarism, and cruelty inherent in modern society. He hated the Jews, hated democracy, hated the Christian religion in which he was reared, hated all foreigners, and in general everything that was good, true, or beautiful. For brutality, sadistic cruelty, and villainy he may be compared only with Genghis Khan in ancient days, or to Stalin in ours. As Winston Churchill wrote, Hitler "called from the depths of defeat the dark and savage furies latent in the most numerous, most serviceable, ruthless, contradictory, and ill-starred race in Europe."

Never since Jefferson's time had America, and never in recorded history had England, been in so pacifist a mood as in 1933–39; Hitler was canny enough to play upon this. He pronounced President Roosevelt's speech of 16 May 1933, expressing American hopes for peace and disarmament, a "ray of comfort." Hitler and the warlords of Japan secretly worked for war but publicly advocated peace, and although this fooled the democracies, no hypocrisy was intended. For their concept of peace was as different from ours as Soviet "democracy" is from real democracy. For Hitler, peace meant getting all he wanted for Germany; in Japan, it meant a "feudal peace" of all eastern Asia under Japanese hegemony.

The Spanish civil war, exceedingly cruel and bloody, was won by General Franco early in 1939, and a fascist-type dictatorship set up. It had somewhat the same relation to World War II as "bleeding Kansas" to the American Civil War. Ernest Hemingway, who volunteered to fight for the republican cause, recalled in his novel *For Whom the Bell Tolls* the solemn words of John Donne. The bell in Spain tolled not only for that unhappy country; "*It tolls for thee.*"

We may now conclude what Winston Churchill called "the long, dismal, drawling tides of drift and surrender, of wrong measurements and feeble impulses." Unknown to anyone but the participants, Hitler at a meeting with his foreign minister and his top generals, announced his plans for conquest on 5 November 1937. His object, he said, was to acquire new territory for Germany in Europe's heartland. This could only be done by force. It was the Fuehrer's unalterable resolve to apply force by 1943 if the opportunity did not occur sooner, as he expected it would. The generals and the foreign minister who objected were dismissed.

The bell tolled for Austria in March 1938, when Hitler invaded that hapless remnant of the Hapsburg empire and annexed it to Germany; nobody stopped him. The next victim was Czechoslovakia. That secession state from the old Austro-Hungarian Empire had prospered since 1920 under the rule of able statesmen such as Masaryk and Beneš. But in its western part, the Sudeten Germans, once the ruling class under Austrian domination, regarded the Slavic Czechs and Slovaks with hatred and contempt, and hailed Hitler as the German savior who would put them in the saddle again. Czechoslovakia had a strong, well-trained army and valuable munitions works which would have been a danger to Hitler when he attacked France and Russia, as he intended to do. In May 1938 he decided to move on this country and divide or annex it. Neville Chamberlain, the British prime minister, thrice visited Hitler in September 1938, and was completely deceived by the Fuehrer's promise that he wanted only a fringe of the German-speaking part. In the final meeting at Munich on 28–29 September, Chamberlain, Mussolini, and French premier Daladier agreed to Hitler's terms; and Chamberlain returned to England, announcing cheerily "peace in our time."

In the one year 1938 Hitler had annexed and brought under his absolute rule 6.7 million Austrians and 3.5 million Sudeten Germans. And these were not annexations in the traditional sense, giving full rights to the annexed people, and at least a year's time for objectors to sell out and leave. The Czechs or Austrians who did not relish joining the German Reich had to flee, or be liquidated; the Jews were liquidated anyway.

Hitler was not yet appeased. In March 1939, again breaking solemn promises, he moved his army into Prague, divided the rest of Czechoslovakia into two German satellite states, and again cynically announced that he now had all he wanted. Mussolini followed suit by invading and seizing Albania.

These sorry episodes made Chamberlain and his inevitable umbrella figures of contempt, and "appeasement" a dirty word in the political vocabulary.

On the other side of the world the Japanese militarists, resurrecting from their dim and distant past the slogan *Hakko ichiu* — "bringing the eight corners of the world under one roof" — were riding high. Their movement had many points of resemblance to Hitler's Nazism. It entertained the same enticing ambition of wide dominion; in this instance, an empire of East Asia. Dissolving China offered a good start toward eventually bringing all Asiatic colonies or dependencies of Europe and America — India, Burma, Indonesia, Indochina, the Philippines — under Japanese hegemony. Emperor Hirohito deplored these tendencies, but was helpless before a movement that invoked his name and used his moral authority.

After the "China incident" of 7 July 1937 inaugurated undeclared war between Japan and China, the American government concentrated on diplomatic efforts to "bring Japan to her senses" and restore peace in the Far East. This was completely ineffectual, and the Japanese militarists made a concerted effort to drive American and European missionary, educational, medical, and cultural activities out of China, as the Chinese communists have since done. American churches, hospitals, schools, and colleges were bombed despite flag markings on their roofs; American missionaries and their families were killed; there were so many "accidents" of this sort that a cynic reported the most dangerous spot in an air raid to be an American mission. A small river gunboat of the navy's Yangtze river patrol, U.S.S. *Panay*, was "accidentally" bombed and sunk by Japanese planes on 12 December 1937. When the Japanese government apologized and offered to pay indemnity to the victims, a sigh of relief passed over the length and breadth of America. In a Gallup poll conducted during the second week of January 1938, 70 per cent of the American voters who were interviewed and had an opinion on the subject, favored complete withdrawal from China — Asiatic Fleet, marines, missionaries, medical missions and all.

Well, why not? the reader may ask, since that is what Mao Tse-tung's government has forced us to do in the end. Would not a China under Japanese rule have been better for the world than a Red China? Possibly; for the end is not yet in sight. But no responsible American statesman would contemplate going back on our plighted word to China, and treating her as the European powers had treated Czechoslovakia. And they knew from many historical examples, recent and remote, that militarist cliques are never satisfied, and that nothing short of the control of all Asia and the Pacific Ocean would satisfy the Japanese. We had to risk a war in the 1940's rather than take on an infinitely stronger enemy later.

In 1939 the Japanese captured Shanghai and proceeded to make life intolerable for Americans and Europeans in the international settlement. President Roosevelt now contemplated the imposition of economic sanctions on Japan to make her leaders stop, look, and listen. His first step, on 26 July 1939, was to denounce the existing treaty of commerce with Japan. This received almost unanimous approval, even from isolationists. There matters stood in the Far East when war broke out in Europe in September 1939.

That bell also tolled for the United States, but its somber notes fell dim and muffled on American ears. To threats of the war lords the average American was indifferent. He thought of Europe as decadent, given to secret diplomacy, class conflict, and evasion of debts. He was sorry for "John Chinaman" and detested the "Japs," but he felt that if 450 million Chinese could not defend themselves against 73 million Japanese there was nothing he should or could do about it. Isolationism was not so much a reasoned principle as an instinctive belief in our safety behind ocean barriers. The world was indeed out of joint, but what obligation had we to set it right?

Perversely, the American people and their Congress read awry the lessons of the First World War. First, it had been a mistake for us to enter the war, which might otherwise have ended in a draw. Second, the war was caused by competitive armaments; hence the Washington treaty of 1922 and later agreements on naval limitation. Third, the war was caused by fear, so let everyone agree, "no more war"; hence the Kellogg-Briand pact to outlaw war. Fourth, according to Senator Nye's investigation, it was caused by bankers and munitions manufacturers who made money out of war; so if we took all the profit out of war, peace could be maintained. Fifth, it was caused by the United States insisting on neutral rights; so if we renounced neutral rights we could keep out of any future war. All methods were tried — peace by isolation, peace by arms limitation, peace by incantation; and, in the Roosevelt administration, peace by negation, which was expected to dispose of the last two causes. The neutrality acts passed by Congress between 1935 and 1939, only half approved by the President but signed by him, forbade the sale or transport of arms and munitions to a belligerent, private loans to a belligerent, or the entry of American ships into war zones. Everyone ignored Woodrow Wilson's warning that the only way to prevent American involvement in another world war was to prevent it from starting.

As the poet Edna St. Vincent Millay wrote, "Longing to wed with Peace, what did we do? — Sketched her a fortress on a paper pad."

Law could have gone no further than the neutrality acts did to "keep us out of war"; but as President Roosevelt later observed, "Our arms embargo played right into the hands of the aggressor nations." Germany, Japan, and to a less degree Italy, were feverishly preparing for land, sea, and air warfare; England, France, and Russia were barely beginning to do so; and American neutrality legislation assured the Axis that when they got ready to strike, their victims would be shut off from obtaining implements of war from America.

Roosevelt was watching with growing concern the menaces to peace in Europe and Asia. Speaking in Chicago shortly after the beginning of the "China incident" in 1937, he called for a quarantine against aggressor nations. If lawlessness and violence rage unrestrained, he warned, "Let no one imagine that America will escape, that America may expect mercy, that this Western Hemisphere will not be attacked." These prophetic words awakened no popular response, and in many quarters the President was denounced as a warmonger. In January 1938 he proposed to the British government a conference of leading powers in Washington to discuss the underlying causes of turmoil in Europe. Chamberlain brushed him off; he preferred the appeasement approach to Hitler, and felt that Japan's doings in China did not concern Britain. In September the President reminded all signatory nations of their "outlawry of war" under the Kellogg-Briand pact, and appealed for arbitration of the Sudeten question. Nobody replied. On 14 April 1939 he sent a personal message to Hitler and Mussolini asking them to promise not to attack about twenty small countries in Europe during the next ten years. Hitler made an insulting reply, and then bullied some of the countries (which he was about to gobble up) into assuring Roosevelt that they had no cause to fear good neighbor Germany. Mussolini at first refused to read the message, then sneered at it before his underlings as "a result of infantile paralysis."

Hitler, far from sated with Czechoslovakia, in 1939 turned his hungry glare on Poland, with which he had recently signed a non-aggression pact. The "Polish corridor" to the Baltic was the grievance. Poland allowed German trains and cars free transit across the corridor; but to Hitler this was a degrading situation. In North American terms it was as if the United States felt insulted because trains from Buffalo to Detroit crossed the Ontario peninsula, and demanded that Canada cede her territory up to and including Toronto.

The British and French governments, now cured of their delusions about Hitler, reversed their policy and (31 March) made too late the rash move of guaranteeing against aggression Poland and Romania, which they were incapable of helping. The guarantee would have made sense if English and French diplomacy had made a partner of Russia, as Stalin was ready to do; but Chamberlain's government fiddled, Poland quibbled, and Stalin made a right-about-face. On 24 August 1939, the Western world was stupefied by the news that Stalin and Hitler, who had been violently abusing each other for five years, had shaken hands in a non-aggression pact. The world did not yet know the secret clauses, in which they also agreed to partition Poland.

After his usual preparatory propaganda of fake frontier incidents, Hitler launched his attack on Poland on 1 September 1939. Two days later, Great

Britain and France declared war on Germany. The British dominions followed suit shortly. World War II was on.

For two dreadful weeks the German mechanized army smashed through Poland in a "Blitzkrieg" without parallel in earlier warfare, while bombing planes reduced Polish towns and villages to rubble. The Russians moved in from the east, taking over what they held to be Russian Poland. Attacked from both sides by overwhelming force, with no military aid from anyone, Poland was conquered before the end of September. Germany and Russia divided the country between them. At comparatively slight cost Hitler had acquired 21 million more subjects, together with vast agricultural and industrial resources.

In the west, Germany stood securely behind the newly completed Siegfried line, while Britain and France, the one unable and the other unwilling to take the offensive, relied upon an imperfect blockade to bring her to terms. Hitler refrained from a western offensive because he hoped to buy peace with the sacrifice of Poland. There ensued a period of inaction which Senator Borah called the "phony war," and which Churchill named "the winter of illusion." It was like the "all quiet along the Potomac" period in the American Civil War. Any illusions about Russia were dispelled when Stalin picked a quarrel with his democratic neighbor Finland, and in March 1940 forced her to yield large slices of territory. Shortly after, Stalin annexed the three other Baltic states (Estonia, Latvia, Lithuania) and recovered Bessarabia and the Bukovina from Romania; thus completing, as he thought, a barrier defense against a possible change of policy by Hitler.

Early in April 1940, the phony war came to a dramatic end. Without warning Germany moved into Denmark, a nation with which Hitler had recently concluded a non-aggression pact, and then into Norway. This attack was well planned, and the co-operation of the Norse traitor Quisling almost resulted in that government's being taken over. The king escaped to England, and the British tried to help; but their efforts were "too little and too late"; within less than two months they had been driven out, and Hitler controlled Norway.

One month after the invasion of Scandinavia came the blow in the West. Here the French army, already weakened by communist and fascist propaganda, trusted to a series of modern forts, called the Maginot line after its designer. But the Maginot line ended at the frontier of Belgium, whose king was so scrupulously neutral and so eager to keep out of war that he neglected even rudimentary defense. On 10 May the German army invaded Belgium and neutral Holland, while the *Luftwaffe*, the German air force, rained death on those countries and on northeastern France. In five days the Netherlands were conquered, Rotterdam laid in ruins by air assault. Already the German Panzer (armored) divisions, slipping around the end of the Maginot line, had crashed through the Ardennes Forest, enveloped a French army, and smashed ahead toward the channel ports. On 21 May the Germans reached the English Channel, cutting off the British expeditionary force which had been rushed to the aid of Belgium and France. A week later Belgium surrendered, and the British were left to their fate. Their evacuation has well been called "the miracle of Dunkerque." Every available warship, yacht, power boat, fisherman, barge, and tug, was pressed into service; and with a suicide division holding the front and the Royal Air Force screening, 338,000 men were transported to England. But they did not take their weapons, and evacuations do not win wars.

The German army now swung south, and in two weeks cut the French army to pieces. On 10 June 1940 Mussolini, with his jackal instinct to be in at the kill, declared war on France. Five days later Paris fell, and Premier Reynaud, in desperation, appealed to Roosevelt for "clouds of planes." But Roosevelt could give only sympathy, and a hastily formed French government under the aged Marshal Pétain sued for peace. Hitler exacted a savage price. He occupied half of France, leaving the southern part to be ruled, from Vichy, by Pétain and Laval, who were forced to collaborate with the victors, even to recruit workers for German war industry and to deliver French Jews to torture and death. In one month Hitler's mechanized armies had done what the Kaiser's forces had been unable to accomplish in four years.

Now England stood alone. "We have just one more battle to win," said Hitler's propaganda minister Goebbels to cheering thousands; but Hitler was unprepared with landing craft and equipment to launch a massive amphibious operation. While these instruments were being built and assembled in northern France, the Luftwaffe under Marshal Goering tried to soften up England by bombing. In September 1940 this air assault rose to a furious crescendo. Cities like London, Coventry, and Birmingham suffered massive destruction; civilian casualties ran into the tens of thousands. England was saved by her scientists, such as Watson-Watt and Tizard, who developed radar and persuaded the government to set up a chain of radar warning posts about southern and eastern England; and by the gallantry of her Spitfire and Hurricane fighter pilots, who exacted an insupportable toll of the invaders. By October the German air force had to acknowledge that it had failed.

In this hour of mortal peril England found her soul, under the inspiration of a great leader. The reins of government, on 11 May 1940, had passed from the faltering hands of Chamberlain into the iron grip of Winston Churchill, who announced, when he took office, that he had naught to offer his countrymen but "blood, sweat, and tears." Undismayed by disaster, he confronted life with antique courage, and infused that courage into freedom-loving peoples everywhere. At the threat of invasion, he thus hurled defiance at Germany:

We shall not flag or fail, we shall go on to the end, we shall fight in France, we shall fight on the seas and oceans . . . we shall fight on the landing grounds, we shall fight in the fields and in the streets, we shall fight in the hills; we shall never surrender. And even if . . . this island . . . were subjugated and starving, then our Empire beyond the seas, armed and guarded by the British Fleet, would carry on the struggle, until, in God's good time ,the new world, with all its power and might, steps forth to the rescue and liberation of the old.

Would America respond? President Roosevelt was among the first to do so. In a speech to the graduating class of the University of Virginia, on 10 June 1940, he announced, "We will extend to the opponents of force the material resources of this nation; and, at the same time . . . speed up the use of these resources in order that we . . . in the Americas may have equipment and training equal to the task of any emergency."

6. "Short of War" to Pearl Harbor

Americans were not neutral in thought to this war, as Wilson had asked them to be in the earlier one. An overwhelming majority desired the defeat of Hitler and his satellites, but also wanted to keep out of the war. One concession, however, was wrung from a reluctant Congress — a modification of neutrality legislation which permitted belligerents to obtain war materials from this country on a "cash and carry" basis. Britain and France promptly took advantage of the new law by placing large orders with American manufacturers, but it would be months or years before tanks began to roll off assembly lines and planes out of hangers in sufficient quantity to match Germany.

The fall of France raised the distinct possibility of the fall of England too, bringing Hitler's forces within striking distance of America. Another shock was the Tripartite Pact of 27 September 1940, in which Japan formally joined the European Axis. This pact stipulated that if any one of the three got into war with the United States the other two would pitch in. For the United States Navy this posed the problem of fighting a two-ocean war with a smaller than one-ocean fleet.

President Roosevelt had a political calculating machine in his head, an intricate instrument in which Gallup polls, the strength of armed forces, and the probability of England's survival; the personalities of governors, senators, and congressmen, and of Mussolini, Hitler, Churchill, Chiang, and General Tojo the Japanese premier; the Irish, German, Italian, and Jewish votes in the approaching presidential election; the "Help the Allies" people and the "America Firsters," were combined with fine points of political maneuvering. The fall of France, fed into the F.D.R. calculating machine, caused wheels to whir and gears to click with dynamic intensity. Out came a solution: the "short of war" policy (1) to help keep England fighting in Europe (2) to gain time for American rearmament; and (3) to restrain Japan by diplomacy and naval "deterrence." Whether Roosevelt really believed that this policy would "keep us out of war" is debatable. But he had to assume that it would, until after the presidential election of 1940 in which he flouted tradition by running for a third term, and until events abroad convinced the American people that war was their only alternative to a shameful and ultimately disastrous appeasement.

In any case, an essential and most beneficial part of the "short of war" policy was to build up the navy. On 14 June 1940, the day that Hitler took Paris, President Roosevelt signed a naval expansion bill that had been under discussion for months. Three days later Admiral Stark, Chief of Naval Operations, asked Congress for $4 billion more to begin building a "two-ocean navy," and got it. The navy then had about 1.2 million tons of combatant shipping; this bill authorized a more than double increase. But, as Admiral Stark said, "Dollars cannot buy yesterday." For two years at least the Americas would be very vulnerable in the event of a German victory.

On 15 June 1940, the day after approving the first of these new navy bills, President Roosevelt appointed a group of eminent civilian scientists members of a new National Defense Research Committee. Vannevar Bush, president of the Carnegie Institution of Washington, was the chairman. From this N.D.R.C. stemmed most of the scientific research done for the armed forces during the war.

The President was ready for bolder steps, and announced them frankly. The stories built up by anti-Roosevelt fanatics like Clare Boothe Luce ("He *lied* us into war") have no foundation in fact. His radio fireside chat of 26 May 1940, his Charlottesville speech of 10 June which we have already quoted, gave fair notice that he was no longer neutral, merely non-belligerent. At the same time (June 1940), in order to make his administration bipartisan, he replaced the colorless war and navy secretaries in his cabinet with two prominent Republicans — seventy-two-year-old Henry M. Stimson, who had been secretary of war under Taft and of state under Hoover, and Frank Knox, vice-presidential candidate in 1936. By the end of 1940 there were also new and stronger Democrats in the cabinet: Frank Walker replaced Jim Farley as postmaster general; Robert H. Jackson came in as attorney general, Jesse Jones as secretary of commerce.

In pursuance of the new presidential policy came a series of bold moves. The Act of Havana, passed at a Pan American meeting in July 1940, promised protection to all America, and gave notice that any transfer of Europe's American colonies to Hitler would be resisted. In August Roosevelt conferred with Mackenzie King and concluded a United States-Canada defense pact which gave each country free use of the other's naval facilities. In mid-September Congress passed the first peacetime conscription in our history — the Burke-Wadsworth Act, providing for registration of all men between the ages of 21 and 35, and the induction into the armed services of 800,000 draftees. That month the President announced an arrangement whereby the United States transferred to Britain fifty destroyers which had been "in mothballs" for twenty years, and received in return 99-year leases on naval and air bases in the British West Indies, Argentia (Newfoundland), and Bermuda. This, said the President, was "an epochal and far-reaching act of preparation for continental defense in the face of grave danger."

It was charged, both in this country and by the Axis powers, that these measures were unneutral, which indeed they were; openly so. Attorney General Jackson advised the President that Hitler could no longer invoke the protection of international law, after successively violating the neutrality of Denmark, Norway, Belgium, and Holland. But this did not lessen our respect for the neutrality of other nations.

Although the destroyer-bases deal met with general approval, Roosevelt's foreign policy sharply divided American opinion. Critics charged that it was dragging the United States inexorably into an "imperialistic" war with which we had no legitimate concern; supporters insisted that only by helping Britain and France to defeat Hitler could we save democracy from destruction and ourselves from ultimate attack. The issue was fought out in the halls of Congress, in the press, over the radio, on public platforms, in bars, offices, and homes. Party lines were shattered, labor organizations split, business relations strained, old friendships broken. William Allen White's Committee To Defend America by Aiding the Allies organized branches in a thousand towns, sent out hundreds of speakers and millions of letters and pamphlets to arouse the nation to its danger. The opposition organization, the America First Committee, top-billing Charles Lindbergh, paraded, picketed, protested, and preached an amalgam of isolationism and pacifism, with overtones of anti-Semitism; and it came out after the war that the "America Firsters" had accepted financial support from Germany. Newspapers like the New York *Times* and *Herald-Tribune* ranged themselves behind the presidential policy, while the Chicago *Tribune* found itself in a congenial alliance with Hearst ringing an alarm-bell against "being dragged into war to save England."

In the midst of this debate came the presidential election. The Republican party, having clung to the unheroic position of isolationism, stood pat. Its three leading contenders for the presidential nomination, Senators Robert Taft of Ohio and Arthur Vandenberg of Michigan and District Attorney Thomas Dewey of New York, were isolationists in varying degree. In the meantime, a group of amateur politicians had been building up a political maverick, Wendell Willkie, a Wall Street lawyer and counsel for the big utilities. Willkie was critical of the New Deal, not of its basic principles but of its inefficiency, and a frank proponent of aid to the Allies. His sincerity and personal charm appealed to an electorate sick of political clap-trap, and inspired a devotion such as no other Republican enjoyed between "Teddy" and "Ike." When the Republican convention met at Philadelphia in June, seasoned politicians found that they could not hold the rising tide of Willkie sentiment. On the sixth ballot he was nominated.

The Democrats were in a quandary. The President had never been more popular, or his leadership more essential than in this crisis. Democratic state conventions called for his renomination. But would he accept the nomination for a third term, and would the American people acquiesce in this challenge to the sacrosanct two-term tradition? Roosevelt himself maintained an inscrutable silence. The Democratic convention, without guidance, renominated him on the first ballot. Roosevelt replied by radio that "in the face of the danger which confronts our time" he had no right to refuse. But there is no doubt that F.D.R. loved power and gladly accepted this responsibility.

Two leading Democrats were very sore about this. Jim Farley, who had even fewer qualifications for the high office than Cal Coolidge, thought he should have been nominated. Vice President Garner was persuaded to decline a third term as Vice President in the expectation he would be promoted, but the convention passed him over for both places and gave Henry Wallace the lesser one.

The campaign that followed lacked real issues, since Willkie supported the President's "short of war" measures, and most of the New Deal. It was not clear that Willkie could do better what Roosevelt was doing well, and he labored under the handicap of the support of odd-balls such as the Reverends Gerald Smith and Charles Coughlin. Although many Southern politicians disliked the New Deal because it was doing so much for the Negroes, the South in general, with its gallant tradition, applauded the President's determination to help the Allies; and, ahead of any other part of the country, prepared mentally for the war that the nation had to fight.

In the November election Roosevelt received 449 electoral votes, Willkie only 82. Apart from Maine and Vermont, the Republicans carried only the isolationist heartland of the midwest, but Willkie received 45 per cent of the popular vote. The Socialist, Communist, and other splinter parties only received one-half of one per cent. The two-term tradition had been shattered; it required Amendment XXII to the Constitution, the Republicans' posthumous revenge on F.D.R., to put it together again.

The President naturally interpreted re-election as an endorsement of his foreign as well as his domestic policies. When Congress met early in January 1941 he appealed for support of nations who were fighting in defense of what he called the Four Freedoms — freedom of speech, freedom of religion, freedom from want, freedom from fear. Four days later he submitted a program designed to circumvent existing limitations of the neutrality legislation and make American war materials immediately available to the Allies. This was the Lend-Lease Act, which authorized the President to "sell, transfer, exchange, lease, lend" any defense articles "to the government of any country whose defense the President deems vital to the defense of the United States," and made available to such nations the facilities of American shipyards. This touched off a prolonged and bitter debate which reached its nadir in Senator Burton K. Wheeler's statement that Lend-Lease "will plow under every fourth American boy." After the isolationists had had their say, administration supporters passed the bill by substantial majorities and it became law 11 March 1941. Lend-Lease made the United States the "arsenal of democracy," as F.D.R. said. Under its provisions America not only provided the enemies of the Axis with $50 billion in arms, foodstuffs, and services, but geared her own production to war needs and officially abandoned any pretense at neutrality. And Lend-Lease had the advantage of preventing another postwar controversy over debts.

Events now moved rapidly. A few weeks after the passage of Lend-Lease the United States seized all Axis shipping in American ports. In April 1941 it took Greenland under protection and announced that the navy would patrol the sea lanes in defense zones. In May came the transfer of 50 oil tankers to Britain, and, after the sinking of an American freighter by a U-boat, the proclamation of an "unlimited national emergency." In June the United States froze all Axis assets and closed the consulates. On 24 June the President announced that Lend-Lease would be extended to a new ally — Russia. For on 22 June Hitler, in one of the astounding about-faces common to dictators, broke his 1939 pact and set out to conquer that vast country. It was one of those colossal mistakes in strategy which undid all earlier faults by England and France. Now they had an ally capable of pinning down the bulk of the German army on an eastern front.

An administration bill to extend conscription for the duration of the emergency, and keep under the colors the national guard regiments then receiving training, passed the House only by a majority of one vote. Many Congressmen who voted to "send the boys home" were really for having them stay but feared the wrath of their constituents. Republicans in the House voted 133 to 21 against this selective service bill, 143 to 21 against repeal of the arms embargo, and 135 to 24 against Lend-Lease. But public opinion was hardening. And when, after a battle on 4 September between U-642 and U.S.S. *Greer*, the President ordered the navy to "shoot on sight" any German submarine encountered, most of the nation applauded. From that date, the United States was engaged in a *de facto* naval war with Germany. U.S.S. *Kearny*, torpedoed on 17 October, survived, but destroyer *Reuben James* was sunk by a U-boat 600 miles west of Iceland on the 31st. Seven American merchantmen were sunk by German warships before war was declared.

In the meantime President Roosevelt, like Wilson a generation earlier, had moved to obtain a statement of war aims from the Allies. On 14 August 1941 he and Winston Churchill met in Argentia Bay, Newfoundland, and there drew up the Atlantic Charter containing certain "common principles" on which they based "their hopes for a better future for the world." These included the already proclaimed Four Freedoms, a renunciation of territorial aggrandizement, a promise of the restoration of self-government to those deprived of it, and to all equal access to trade and raw materials.

For over a year, tension had been mounting in the Far East. The Japanese war lords, meeting unexpected resistance in China, now planned to swing south and gobble up the Philippines, Malaya, and Indonesia. In order to realize this "Greater East Asia Co-Prosperity Sphere," as they called it, Japan had to risk fighting Great Britain, France, the Netherlands, and the United States, which between them controlled the coveted territories. In the summer of 1940 Japan wrested permission to build airfields in Indochina from the helpless Vichy government of France. The United States struck back with a small loan to China and a partial embargo on exports to Japan. Congress, in July 1940, gave the President power to restrict export of war materials needed for American defense, or to license their export to friendly nations. In the same month, Congress passed the Two-Ocean Navy Act. Very cautiously, Roosevelt began imposing embargoes on various strategic materials, including scrap iron; and a Gallup poll indicated 96 per cent popular approval.

In July 1941 events began moving toward a crisis. On the 25th, Japan announced that she had assumed a protectorate of the whole of French Indochina. Next day, President Roosevelt took three momentous steps. He received the armed forces of the Philippine Commonwealth into the United States Army, appointed General Douglas MacArthur to command all army forces in the Far East, and issued an executive order freezing Japanese financial assets in the United States. Great Britain and the Netherlands followed suit, cutting off Japan's source of credit and imports of rubber, scrap iron, and fuel oil. The Japanese war lords decided to make war on these three countries within three or four months, unless the flow of oil and other strategic supplies was restored. For Japan was "eating her own tail" in the matter of oil; her armies must have fuel or evacuate the mainland, a loss of face that the military would not contemplate. This embargo on oil and credit brought Japan to the point of war.

The final negotiations were a mere sparring for time by two governments that considered war all but inevitable. The Japanese wanted time to organize their military and naval push to the south; the United States wanted time to prepare the defense of the Philippines and strengthen the navy. Through the summer and fall of 1941 Secretary Hull made it clear that Japan could have all the goods and credits she wanted, if she would begin a military evacuation of China and Indochina. Prince Konoye, the Japanese premier, on 14 October asked General Tojo, the war minister, to begin at least a token withdrawal. Tojo refused, confident that Japan could beat America, Britain, and any other country that stood in her way; and a few days later Tojo became prime minister. On 20 November he presented Japan's ultimatum. He promised to occupy no more Asiatic territory if the United States would stop reinforcing the Philippines; he would evacuate southern Indochina only if the United States would cut off aid to Chiang Kai-shek and "unfreeze" Japanese assets in the United States, leaving Japan free to complete her subjugation of China. Tojo did not expect that the United States would accept such terms, which were appropriate only for a defeated nation, and his plans for further aggression were already hardened. On 26 November 1941 the Japanese striking force of six big carriers carrying 423 planes, two battleships, two heavy cruisers, and eleven destroyers, sortied from its rendezvous in the Kurile Islands for the fatal destination of Pearl Harbor.

No inkling of even the existence of that force leaked out. A few days earlier, however, Japanese troop-laden transports and warships were reported steaming south off Formosa. Hence on 27 November, Washington sent a "war warning" message to Pearl Harbor and Manila, indicating an attack against the Philippines, Thailand, or the Malay Peninsula, but not mentioning Pearl Harbor as a possibility. Nobody in Washington thought that Japan was capable of striking a one-two blow, nor that, if she were, she would be so foolish as to drive divided America into war, united and angry. The Japanese war lords thought it necessary to destroy the Pacific Fleet, without the warning of a declaration of war, to prevent its interfering with their plans of conquest.

On 7 December at 6 a.m. the six Japanese carriers, with their escorting warships, reached their planned launching point 275 miles north of Pearl Harbor. The carriers commenced launching bombers and fighters immediately. The first attack group sighted Oahu at 7:40. "Pearl Harbor was asleep in the morning mist," wrote Commander Itaya who led the first formation. "Calm and serene inside the harbor . . . important ships of the Pacific Fleet, strung out and anchored two ships side by side."

Perfect targets. At 7:55 the bombs began to fall and aerial torpedoes aimed at the battleships to drop in the harbor. It seemed almost unbelievable to the sailors, as they rushed to man their anti-aircraft guns; confusion was almost complete, but courage was not wanting. Not until 7:58 did Rear Admiral Bellinger, the naval air commander, broadcast the message that shook the United States as nothing had since the firing on Fort Sumter:

AIR RAID, PEARL HARBOR — THIS IS NO DRILL.

LVIII

On the Defensive

1941-1942

1. World-wide Disaster

A T THE END OF THIS sad and bloody day, 7 December 1941, the "day that shall live in infamy" as President Roosevelt said of it, 2403 American sailors, soldiers, marines, and civilians had been killed, and 1178 more wounded; 149 planes had been destroyed on the ground or in the water, U.S.S. *Arizona* was destroyed beyond possible repair, *Oklahoma* shattered and capsized, four other battleships were resting on the bottom or run aground to prevent sinking, two naval auxiliaries destroyed, three destroyers and a few other vessels badly damaged. All at a cost of twenty-nine planes and pilots to the Japanese striking force, which returned undetected to its home waters.

Nor was this all. Although General MacArthur's Far Eastern command was notified of the attack on Pearl Harbor at 3:00 a.m., 8 December (corresponding to 8:00 a.m., 7 December at Oahu), a Japanese bomber attack from Formosa caught the B-17s grounded on fields near Manila at noon, and destroyed most of them. Before dawn Japanese troops landed on the Malay Peninsula, and at 8:30 a.m. Guam was bombed from nearby Saipan.

To millions of Americans, whether at breakfast in Hawaii, or reading the Sunday paper in the West, or sitting down to dinner in the East, this news of disaster after disaster seemed fantastic, incredible. As the awful details poured in, hour after hour, incredulity turned to anger and an implacable determination to avenge these unprovoked and dastardly attacks. On 8 December, Congress without one dissenting vote declared a state of war with Japan; on 11 December, Germany and Italy, faithful to the tripartite pact, declared war on the United States. President Roosevelt, in his war message following that declaration, declared, "Never before has there been a greater challenge to life, liberty and civilization."

Yet, in attacking Pearl Harbor, Japan conferred a moral benefit on the nation which was the chief object of her rage and hatred. Senator Arthur Vandenberg of Michigan, who had been one of the leading isolationists before that event, remarked five years later that Pearl Harbor "drove most of us to the irresistible conclusion that world peace is indivisible. We learned that the oceans are no longer moats around our ramparts. We learned that mass destruction is a progressive science which defies both time and space and reduces human flesh and blood to cruel impotence."

The situation in Hawaii was not so bad as first it seemed; providentially, three fleet aircraft carriers *Lexington*, *Enterprise*, and *Saratoga* were at sea. These and their air groups constituted a striking force far more valuable than the lost battleships, all but two of which were salvaged and repaired in time to fight again.

In the Far East, on the other hand, the situation was calamitous. Thailand surrendered to the Japanese, who promptly landed troops at various points on the Malay Peninsula and began a relentless march on the British base at Singapore. On 10 December the Rising Sun flag was hoisted on Guam, which had been bravely but pitifully defended by a few hundred Americans and Chamorros. The same day, England met her Pearl Harbor when the Japanese air force sank H.M.S. *Prince of Wales* and *Repulse* off the Malay Peninsula. Other Japanese task forces occupied the Gilbert Islands, captured Hong Kong, and jumped the Borneo oilfields. On Wake Island, lonely outpost in the Central Pacific, Commander W. S. Cunningham and a small marine defense force beat off a Japanese attack on 11 December, only to be overwhelmed by another on the 23rd, before the navy managed to come to their rescue. In the Philippines, on 10 December, Japanese bombers destroyed Cavite navy yard. During the seventeen days before Christmas the enemy made nine amphibious landings in the Philippines. General MacArthur evacuated Manila on 27 December, withdrew his army to the Bataan Peninsula, and set up headquarters on the island fortress of Corregidor.

The defense of Bataan and the Rock of Corregidor, although valiant and inspiring, proved to be a melancholy confirmation of Mahan's theory of sea power. The Japanese, controlling all sea and air approaches, enveloped both Peninsula and Rock in a tight blockade, landing fresh troops behind the American lines at will. After three months, over half the fighting men were disabled by wounds or by disease, and all were at the point of starvation. On 8 April the "battling bastards of Bataan," about 12,500 Americans and over 60,000 Filipinos, surrendered unconditionally. Only a couple of thousand escaped to Corregidor before the ranks of the prisoners were thinned by the infamous "death march" from Bataan to Japanese prison camps.

In the hope of restoring confidence to the Australians, President Roosevelt ordered General MacArthur to leave the Philippines and set up headquarters in the sub-continent. He left by motor torpedo boat on 11 March, promising to return, as indeed he did. On 6 May 1942, after the Japanese had captured the main defenses of Corregidor, General Jonathan M. Wainwright was forced to surrender the Rock together with its 11,000 defenders, and a Philippine army of over 50,000. There had been no such capitulations in American history since Appomattox.

In the meantime the Japanese had won their every objective in Southeast Asia. The Malay barrier (Sumatra, Java, Bali, Timor, and smaller islands), which barred the enemy from the Indian Ocean and Australia, was desperately defended by soldiers, sailors, and aviators of the United States, Great Britain, the Netherlands, and Australia under a combined command; a hopeless task. The Japanese would seize a strategic point in Borneo or Celebes, operate or build an airfield there, soften up the next objective by air bombing, occupy it with an amphibious force, and go on to the next. Admiral Hart's Asiatic Fleet, with British and Dutch allies, fought a series of valiant engagements in January and February 1942 — Balikpapan, Bali, Badung Strait, Java Sea — always greatly outnumbered, always defeated. Singapore, on which England had lavished millions of pounds, fell on 15 February. Java surrendered on 9 May; Rangoon, capital and chief seaport of Burma, had been occupied the day before. The Japanese were now in control of East Asia. India and Australia were tremblingly aware that their turn might come next.

Never in modern history has there been so quick or valuable a series of conquests; even Hitler's were inferior. The prestige of the white races fell so low that even victory over Japan could not win it back; and all countries that the Japanese conquered, though no longer Japanese, are no longer colonies.

The Atlantic sea lanes had to be kept open for supplies, and for building up a United States army in England for eventual invasion of the continent. American destroyers now helped to escort convoys all the way across, and used the sharp training facilities of the British bases in Northern Ireland. Sinkings in the North Atlantic fell off promptly; soon we knew why. Admiral Doenitz was moving wolf-packs over to the American east coast, where he rightly anticipated rich pickings from non-convoyed tankers and merchantmen. The navy, pressed to build more big ships, had neglected small vessels suitable for coastal convoy, hoping to improvise them if the need arose; but the Germans were not so accommodating as to wait.

The U-boat offensive opened on 12 January 1942 off Cape Cod, and a severe one it was. Most United States destroyers were tied to North Atlantic escort duty; only five subchasers were in commission; there were fewer than 100 planes to patrol coastal waters between Newfoundland and New Orleans; no merchantmen had yet been armed. Under these conditions, frightful destruction was wrought in shipping lanes between the Canadian border and Jacksonville. During January-April 1942, almost 200 ships were sunk in North American, Gulf, and Caribbean waters, or around Bermuda. Doenitz then shifted his wolf-packs to the Straits of Florida, the Gulf of Mexico, and the Caribbean; and in those waters 182 ships totaling over 751,000 tons were sunk in May and June 1942. Vessels were torpedoed 30 miles off New York City, within sight of Virginia Beach, off the Passes to the Mississippi, off the Panama Canal entrance. Since tourist resorts from Atlantic City to Miami Beach were not even required to turn off neon signs and waterfront lights until 18 April 1942, or to black out completely for another month, hapless freighters and tankers passing them were silhouetted for the benefit of the U-boats. Over half the victims in southern waters were tankers, the sinking of which not only fried the water-borne survivors in burning oil, but threatened the success of military operations in Europe and the Pacific. Puerto Rico suffered from inability to move crops or import necessary food; sugar and coffee had to be rationed in the United States; "good neighbors" in Latin America began to doubt big neighbor's ability to win. The north-south sea lane, along the east coast through the Caribbean to Rio de Janeiro and the River Plate, had to be maintained equally with the west-east line to Great Britain, and the Pacific sea lines. But the U-boats were knocking down the ships like tenpins. New construction of merchantmen in Allied and neutral countries amounted to less than 600,000 tons in June 1942 when the total loss almost touched 800,000 tons; and in half a year the British and American navies had sunk less than one month's production of new U-boats. Obviously, if this ratio continued, a "torpedo curtain" would soon be dropped between the United States and Europe.

Fortunately Admiral Ernest J. King, who had directed the "short of war" phase, became "Cominch," commander in chief of the United States fleet, on 20 December 1941. He took energetic measures to combat the submarine menace. The first need was for small escort vessels. The slogan "sixty vessels in sixty days" was nailed to the mast in April 1942; and 67 vessels actually came through by 4 May, when a second 60-60 program was already under way. Scientists were mobilized to find more efficient means of tracking and sinking U-boats. Inshore and offshore patrols were organized with converted yachts — the "Hooligan Navy" as it was nicknamed. As more escorts became available, an interlocking convoy system was worked out; the trunk line New York to Key West was fed freight by numerous branch lines which extended north to Canada and south to Brazil. In the second half of 1942 coastal convoys lost only 0.5 per cent of their ships; the transatlantic convoys lost only 1.4 per cent in a whole year. By April 1943 there were every day at sea in the American half of the North Atlantic, an average of 31 convoys with 145 escorts and 673 merchant ships, as well as 120 ships traveling alone and unescorted, and the heavily escorted troop convoys. There was nothing like a well-escorted convoy to bait the U-boats, or a well-equipped destroyer to kill them with depth charges or the forward-throwing hedgehog; but you had to have enough destroyers so that some of them could peel off and hunt. A big, fast, four-engined plane like the Liberator, equipped with guns, microwave radar, and depth bombs, was an effective instrument to sink a submarine, especially when it could be located by radio transmission.

It took time for these new methods and weapons to be adopted or produced in sufficient quantities to be effective. Throughout 1942 the U-boats enjoyed a succession of field days at our expense. And, in the meantime, this battle had extended into the Arctic Ocean and the South Atlantic. The first, the most dangerous and disagreeable of all convoy routes, had to be used to get lend-lease goods to Russia through Murmansk or Archangel. Although the

British navy did most of the escorting over this route — losing in that service eleven warships — about half the merchantmen concerned were American, and their losses were severe. Another extension of the Atlantic battle lay southward. Most of the Latin American nations broke relations with or declared war on the Axis and Japan, and Brazil gave the Allies substantial aid. She declared war on the Axis in August 1942, after Doenitz had sunk five Brazilian ships within sight of shore. In conjunction with the Brazilian navy, with the British naval command in West Africa, and using an airfield built by United States Army engineers on lonely Ascension Island, an effective air-sea patrol of the Atlantic Narrows was then established.

2. *The Strategy and Direction of the War*

Although America, as we have seen, learned wrong all the lessons of World War I as to how to maintain peace, the leaders of the armed forces, especially General Marshall and Admiral King, learned right how to conduct a coalition war. The first lesson was to have a plan ready if and when war came. So, before World War II engulfed America, the United States Joint Chiefs of Staff (as heads of army, navy and army air force shortly became) held a secret conference with their British opposite numbers. The resulting "ABC-1" staff agreement of 27 March 1941 set forth that, if and when America entered the war, her primary military effort would be exerted in the European theater. This concept of "Beat the Axis First" was arrived at because Germany and Italy, by knocking out France, had control of the entire western coast of Europe, and Germany's U-boats threatened to cut sea communication between the Old World and the New. Germany, too, had a greater war potential than Japan, and it was feared she might uncork some devastating secret weapon if given the time — as she did, but too late to win.

The informal alliance thus formed continued throughout the war, through the American Joint Chiefs of Staff and the British Chiefs of Staff. Meeting together as the Combined Chiefs of Staff, they, under President Roosevelt and Prime Minister Churchill, initiated strategy, drafted plans, allocated forces, and directed the war. Russia was represented by Marshal Stalin, and China by Chiang Kai-shek at two plenary C.C.S. conferences; but each of these two allies fought her own war with ample aid from England and America, but with slight regard for their strategy or wishes.

America was fortunate in having a very able war direction. Vital members of the Joint Chiefs of Staff throughout the war were General H. H. ("Hap") Arnold, head of the army air force; chief of staff General George C. Marshall, a Virginian who combined the patient wisdom of Washington with the strategic savvy of Lee; Admiral Ernest J. King, chief of naval operations and commander in chief of the fleet, a tough, experienced naval officer who took a world-wide view of strategy and seldom, if ever, made a mistake. These three in concert with President Roosevelt formed a winning team. There had been nothing like that since the Lincoln-Grant-Farragut team of 1864–65.

At the cabinet level, America was equally strong. Cordell Hull, secretary of state, was becoming slightly infirm, but he had an energetic under-secretary, Sumner Welles; Henry M. Stimson, secretary of war, was full of brains and energy. Frank Knox, secretary of the navy, also had an able under-secretary, James Forrestal, who handled all matters of procurement for the navy, as assistant secretary Robert Patterson did for the army. Forrestal succeeded Knox after the latter's death in 1944, and later became the first secretary of defense. Over these staffs and heads of departments, and also over innumerable boards and committees which dealt with various phases of the war, were Churchill and Roosevelt. The "P.M." was Britain's greatest war leader since the elder Pitt. His energy and pluck saved England in her darkest hour, which he, in his remarkable history of the war, calls "Her Finest Hour." He called leading scientists into consultation at the top levels of government. He visited every British front to give the soldiers and sailors the inspiration of his presence, always smoking a long cigar and making the "V for Victory" sign with two upraised fingers.

Roosevelt, too, was a great war President, in a class with Lincoln; and, like Lincoln's, his greatness came from a capacity to lead and inspire, rather than from skill in administration. He was an opportunist, with a flair for the attainable, rather than, as in the case of Wilson, for the ideal; but, no less than Wilson, he looked ahead to a world of peace and justice. He kept a boyish zest for life, and his courage and energy triumphed over the crippling disease of his young manhood and enabled him for twelve years to carry the greatest burden that any modern statesman has been called upon to bear. His understanding of other nations enabled him to deal successfully with Latin America, neutrals, and representatives of the overrun democracies; and his death, when victory was in sight, was almost universally mourned. He respected his military advisers, and in the few instances in which he overrode them, his judgment was sound. He sometimes worked in devious ways, through his wise but much detested confidential assistant, Harry Hopkins, and he needed the wisdom of the serpent to deal with clashing personalities and opposing interests.

Although much had been accomplished in military preparedness when Pearl Harbor broke — far more, relatively, than in 1812 or 1917 — much more remained to be done. Congress promptly repealed its prohibition against sending draftees outside the Western Hemisphere, and extended their period of service to six months after the war's end — no "three months men" in this war. All men between 18 and 45 were made liable to military service. Standards of physical fitness and intelligence were exacting, and many failed to qualify. Including voluntary enlistments, over 15 million people served in the armed forces during the war; 10 million in the army, 4 million in the navy and coast guard, 600,000 in the marine corps. About 216,000 women served as nurses, and in the auxiliary "Waves," "Wacs," "Spars," or as lady marines.

The training problem was prodigious. Morale was easier to achieve for the navy and marine corps, whose recruits were volunteers; it never seemed to occur to them that America could be defeated. But the average "G.I." (General Issue), the nickname for infantrymen in this war, was a more or less unwilling draftee, who had been brought up in a pacifist atmosphere. He could be trained *to* fight, but it was well said of General Patton that he alone could make them *want* to fight. And far more was required of the G.I. than of the "doughboy" of World War I, or the "boys in blue," or gray, of 1861. There were any number of special forces, such as the army rangers for raiding, and the navy's UDT's or "frogmen," who swam up to enemy-held beaches, made soundings, and blew obstacles. Air forces had already become highly specialized. There were fighter planes, high-level bombers, torpedo- and dive-bombers, operating both from ships and shore, and several other types, for which pilots and crewmen had to be trained. And we required an enormous amount of research to replace plane types which proved unequal to their tasks, by newer, faster, and bigger ones. To fight a global war it was necessary to build dozens of naval bases and hundreds of airfields all over the world. Specially packaged units called Lions, Cubs, Oaks, and Acorns were organized with men and matériel all ready to rush in and build a base or airfield as soon as a site was secured.

The work of the service forces was very important. In this war the average soldier required at least double the World War I equipment. An infantry division of 8000 fighting men required 6000 more to keep it fed, supplied, paid, doctored, amused, transported, and its equipment repaired. By the end of the war, so many artillery and other elements were added that a "reinforced" infantry division totaled 20,000 or more men. Remarkable progress was made by the medical corps. Infection and disease, always the bane of armies, in every war prior to 1917 had accounted for more deaths than the fighting. Thanks to abundant food, clothing, hospitals, and skillful physicians, the health of the armed forces in World War II compared favorably with that of the civilian population. The development of sulfa drugs and penicillin, the use of plasma for transfusions, control of mosquitoes and other insects, new techniques for the treatment of the terrible burns incident to bursting shells and Japanese kamikaze tactics, and prompt evacuation of wounded, reduced the death rate from wounds to less than half that of World War I, and enabled about two-thirds of all wounded to return to duty. The increasing role of artillery and the bomb in warfare is shown by the fact that, whilst 94 per cent of wounds in the Civil War were caused by rifle bullets, 72 per cent of those in the two world wars and the Korean War were inflicted by shell fragments.

The United States Navy entered the war well prepared except for anti-aircraft and antisubmarine work, which happened to be among its most pressing needs. Fortunately, in conjunction with the marines, it had undertaken training for amphibious warfare, anticipating that to deliver troops to a fighting area would be no simple matter of sea transport and landing them on a wharf, but landing under fire on enemy-held beaches. Consequently the navy began building a new line of "lettered" vessels specially designed for amphibious warfare: the 460-foot LSD (Landing Ship, Dock), which spawned loaded landing craft from a miniature lake in its bowels; the 330-foot LST (Landing Ship, Tank), a two-decker floating garage, which became the workhorse of the fleet; the 180-foot LCI (Landing Craft, Infantry) for bringing soldiers directly to a beach; and a variety of small landing craft that could be lowered by the davits of a big transport. After 1940, with money available for high wages and overtime in the shipyards, it became possible to build a destroyer in five months instead of a year, and a big carrier in fifteen months instead of thirty-five.

The Maritime Commission, created by Congress in 1936 and headed by Rear Admiral Emory S. Land, received new powers in July 1941, and drew up blueprints for an emergency freighter that could be built quickly and inexpensively. The first of these Liberty ships — appropriately named *Patrick Henry* — was launched in September, and 139 more came out that year. The bigger and faster Victory ship followed. In November 1941, when Congress repealed the Neutrality Act forbidding merchantmen to arm in self-defense, the navy began installing naval guns with bluejacket crews on freighters.

In the realm of production the United States enjoyed advantages over every other country that enabled it to become an "arsenal of democracy" while fighting the war. Lend-Lease and the big defense appropriations of 1940–41 had already added 6 million workers to the payrolls, wiping out unemployment. Yet there were ominous lags and shortages. The steel industry did not expand its capacity quickly enough, and the automobile industry was reluctant to shift from pleasure cars to war vehicles when restored prosperity released a flood of new car orders. Pearl Harbor galvanized American industry into a confusion of high-speed planning and production, which had to be straightened out by the War Production Board before anything useful could be accomplished. In 1942 the curve of production rose sharply; American industry produced not only enough matériel and weapons for the United States, but supplied the Allies. But our deficiencies were many.

Stockpiles of bauxite, aluminum, and chrome, which would have to reach America through submarine-infested waters, were lacking in 1941. Japan's quick conquests cut off the western world's principal sources of rubber, quinine, and manila fiber, and one of the chief sources of oil. As iron and horses had been essential to earlier wars, so steel, oil, and rubber were to this; armies no longer "marched on their stomachs," as Napoleon remarked, or wriggled ahead on their bellies, as in World War I, but rolled in motor vehicles on rubber tires; naval vessels were no longer fired by coal, but by black or diesel oil; high-test avgas was required for aircraft. Oil production had to be vastly increased in the United States and in Venezuela. New synthetic rubber plants, reworked tires, and wild caoutchouc imports from the Amazon lifted rubber production to over a million tons in 1944.

Mighty as America's effort was, it did not add up to total war, as the term was understood in the British Commonwealth, Germany, or Japan. There was no firm control over manpower, no conscription of women, little direction of talent to useful activities. A few edibles were rationed, but most Americans ate more heartily than before. Gasoline and tires were rationed, but hundreds of thousands of cars managed to stay on the road for purposes remotely connected with the war. Personal and corporation taxes were increased, but there was no limit on profits, or to what workers could earn, if they chose to work overtime; and as prices of most essentials were kept down, the standard of living rose. The country was never invaded, except by U-boats penetrating the three-mile limit, and a large measure of the "blood, sweat and tears" that Churchill promised his countrymen, were spared to his country's ally.

Only about 40 per cent of the cost of the war was met by taxation, the rest by borrowing; about $97 billion was subscribed in government bonds. The United States Treasury went into the red by over $40 billion annually, and borrowed freely from banks at 1 to 1.5 per cent interest — rates which would have astounded Salmon P. Chase. The national debt rose to $250 billion. Total cost of the war, exclusive of postwar pensions, interest payments, Marshall Plan, etc., came to about $350 billion, ten times that of World War I.

It was a grim, austere war for the American fighting forces, compared with World War I. No brass bands or bugles, no "Over There" or marching songs, no flaunting colors; no public farewells to boys going overseas, not even a ship's bell to mark the watches. It was typical that when the Japanese surrendered on board *Missouri* on 2 September 1945, "The Star-Spangled Banner" had to be played from a disk over the intercom system, and Admiral Halsey had only coffee to offer his guests.

3. *Turn of the Tide*

On Christmas Eve 1941 Admiral King warned, "The way to victory is long; the going will be hard." Hard indeed it was. Admiral Chester W. Nimitz, who at the same time received the command of the Pacific Fleet, was forced to bide his time until new naval construction and more trained troops gave him adequate reinforcements.

Since no British fleet remained in the Pacific, the Combined Chiefs of Staff entrusted the conduct of the Pacific war to the American Joint Chiefs of Staff, and they perforce adopted a strategy of active defense. Distances were immense, and the only hope of eventually defeating Japan was to hold fast to what we had, and prepare for future offensives. Islands still in American possession such as the Hawaiian and Samoan groups must be defended; the sea-air lanes to New Zealand and to Australia must be protected; and that meant tying up a large part of the fleet to escort transports and supply ships. Nothing much could be done for five months except to make hit-and-run raids with carrier planes. Of these the most spectacular was the air assault on Tokyo 18 April 1942. That was delivered by Colonel James H. Doolittle's B-25's from Admiral Halsey's carrier *Hornet*, a base that President Roosevelt humorously called "Shangri-La," after the idyllic land in James Hilton's *Lost Horizon*. The planes did little damage, and most of their crews had to bail out over China; but the news that Tokyo had actually been bombed lifted American morale, and encouraged the Japanese high command to retrieve face by an imprudent offensive. America learned more from adversity than Japan did from victory.

Instead of organizing their new conquests, the Japanese succumbed to what one of their admirals after the war ruefully called "victory disease." They decided to wrest more Pacific territory — Papua, Fijis, New Caledonia, Solomons, western Aleutians, Midway Island — from the Allies and set up an impregnable "ribbon defense." These islands, in connection with those that Japan already held, were near enough to one another for patrol planes to protect, and to be bases for disrupting the lifeline between the United States and the British antipodes.

Admiral Yamamoto, greatest Japanese sea lord since Togo, wished to provoke a major battle with our Pacific Fleet. A good prophet, he pointed out that the United States Navy must be annihilated, if ever, in 1942, before American productive capacity replaced the Pearl Harbor losses. He hoped that after another defeat, the "soft" American people would force their government to quit and leave Japan in possession of her most valuable conquests. Then she could proceed at her leisure to conquer the rest of China and so become the most powerful empire in the world, capable of defying even Germany, if Hitler conquered all Europe.

The Japanese navy in 1942 was, by any standards, a great navy. Japan had the two largest and most powerful battleships in the world, displacing 68,000 tons, with 18-inch guns; the American *Iowa* class, none of which were completed before 1943, were of 45,000 tons with 16-inch guns. She had a fleet of fast and powerful 8-inch gunned cruisers built in defiance of former treaty restrictions, comparable to the later American *Baltimore* class. She had the fastest and most modern destroyers, twice as many big carriers as the United States Navy, and her carrier planes were superior in the fighter and torpedo-bomber types. Japanese torpedoes were faster, more powerful, and more sure-firing than those made in the United States, and employment of them was at once more lavish and more intelligent. Japanese naval gunnery was excellent; Japanese warships were intensely trained for night fighting, as the Americans were not. They lacked only radar, which American ships began to install in 1942. Flushed with triumph after triumph in the Southwest Pacific, the Japanese army and navy were confident of victory.

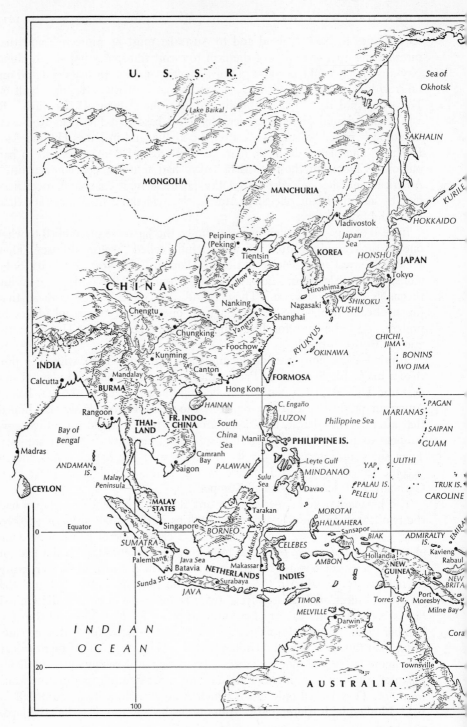

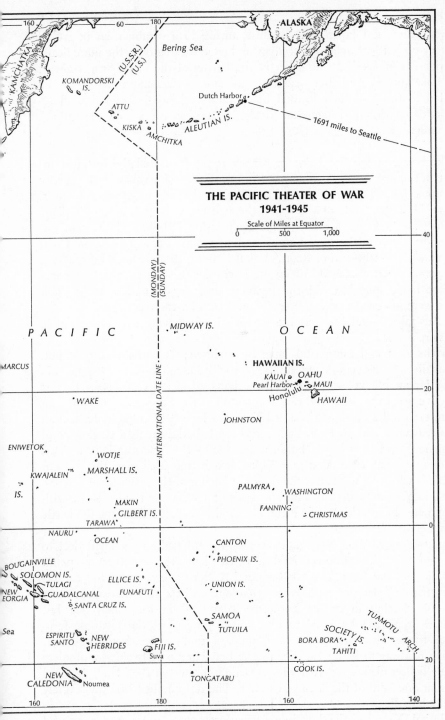

Why, then, did Japan fail? Because, owing to a combination of stupid strategy on her part and good strategy and good luck on ours, the numerically inferior Pacific Fleet defeated her in the battles of the Coral Sea, Midway, and Guadalcanal. And after 1942 it was too late, as Yamamoto predicted. The United States Navy had learned many salutary lessons, acquired unprecedented strength, and become an irresistible force in the air, on the surface, and under water.

The Battle of the Coral Sea (7–8 May 1942) frustrated the first forward lunge in the new Japanese offensive, to capture port Moresby, a strategic base in Papua, New Guinea. This was the first naval battle in which no ship of either side sighted one of the other; the fighting was done by carrier plane against carrier plane, or carrier plane against ship. Admiral Nimitz sent carriers *Lexington* and *Yorktown* and a support group of cruisers into the Coral Sea, under the command of Rear Admiral Frank Jack Fletcher. The resulting engagement was a comedy of errors. Each side in this new sort of naval warfare made mistakes, but the Japanese made more; and although their losses were inferior to ours, they dared not press on to occupy Port Moresby. For Australia, Coral Sea was the decisive battle, saving her from possible invasion.

In the next and more vital Japanese offensive, Yamamoto went all-out. Personally assuming command, he brought with him almost every capital ship of the Japanese navy except the carriers damaged in the Coral Sea. His first objective was to capture Midway, a tiny atoll at the tip end of the Hawaiian chain, 1134 miles northwest of Pearl Harbor, where the United States had an advanced naval and air base. Yamamoto wanted Midway as a staging point for air raids to render Pearl Harbor untenable by the American Pacific Fleet. Minor objectives were Attu and Kiska, two barren islands in the western Aleutians which he wanted as the northern anchor of the new ribbon defense. Yamamoto's dearest object, however, was to force Nimitz to give battle with his numerically inferior Pacific Fleet. He had his wish, but this time the battle did not go to the strong.

Nimitz guessed what Yamamoto was up to, but had only a small fleet to stop him. First, he reinforced Midway with planes to the saturation point. Next, he sent out Rear Admiral Raymond A. Spruance to command carriers *Enterprise* and *Hornet* with their attendant cruisers and destroyers; Rear Admiral Fletcher in carrier *Yorktown* (damaged in the Coral Sea but promptly repaired) hastened to join. On 4 June 1942, the Japanese four-carrier force, advancing undetected under a foul-weather front, was near enough Midway to batter the air base. A brave group of twenty-six obsolete marine fighter planes, together with anti-aircraft guns on the island, disposed of about one-third of the enemy attackers. The rest bombed Midway severely but not lethally.

Admiral Nagumo, the Japanese carrier-force commander, had a painful surprise on the morning of 4 June, when he learned from a reconnaissance plane that American flattops were approaching. Nagumo then made the fatal decision of the battle. He ordered his reserve attack group, then arming for a second strike on Midway, to be rearmed with the different sort of bombs used against ships, and turned his prows northeastward to close with the American carriers. Spruance and Fletcher already had several flights of torpedo- and dive-bombers flying toward the Japanese; and, owing to Nagumo's mistake, they had the good fortune to catch three of his four carriers in the vulnerable situation of rearming and refueling planes. But the carrier-plane battle opened ill for the Americans. Nagumo's combat air patrol of fast fighter planes shot down 35 of the 41 slow torpedo-bombers that came in first. Minutes later, the American dive-bombers hit three carriers and left them exploding and burning. The fourth Japanese carrier, *Hiryu*, unseen by the American fliers, got off two plane strikes, which found and disabled *Yorktown*. Fletcher's flagship, however, was promptly avenged, for an attack group from her deck and from *Enterprise* jumped *Hiryu* that afternoon and put her down. A lucky shot by a Japanese submarine later sank *Yorktown* as she was under tow.

Yamamoto, having lost his four best carriers, ordered a general retirement of his vast fleet. He had sustained the first defeat to the Japanese navy in modern times. The carriers and their air groups were wiped out, and the Stars and Stripes still flew over Midway. Only Kiska and Attu — consolation prizes — had been taken by a Japanese task group. The ambitious plans for capturing New Caledonia, the Fijis, and Samoa, had to be scrapped; and the Japanese high command was forced into an unaccustomed defensive position.

This glorious Battle of Midway on 4 June 1942, marked a clean-cut ending to the defensive phase in the Pacific war. For two months there was an ominous pause, each contestant licking his wounds. There then broke out a bloody and desperate six months' campaign over two focal points — Buna-Gona in New Guinea, and Guadalcanal.

4. Guadalcanal, Papua, and Africa

After the repulse of the Japanese fleet in the Battle of Midway, American and Allied armed forces were able to take the offensive in the Pacific. Admiral Nimitz's Pacific Fleet was based at Hawaii, where several infantry divisions were being trained for jungle warfare. At Nouméa in New Caledonia, and Espiritu Santo, was based the South Pacific Force, consisting largely of cruisers and destroyers, commanded (after 16 October 1942) by colorful Admiral Halsey. A few infantry divisions — one of them marine — were training there and in New Zealand. Dashing General Douglas MacArthur, Allied commander in the Southwest Pacific, was fuming at his Brisbane headquarters for lack of forces to resume the offensive. His troops were mostly Australian; and the small fleet under him was partly Australian, partly American.

Although the Japanese had been beaten back from the Coral Sea, they still held Tulagi in the Solomons, and Rabaul on New Britain. These were anchors to a formidable barrier, which for short we call the Bismarcks barrier, to an Allied advance toward Japan. The islands here are so close to one another that all approaches and surrounding waters could be controlled by land-based planes. Hence this barrier had to be breached if ever we were to approach Japan. And the campaign to do it was sparked off by the news that the Japanese had taken Buna and Gona on the north coast of Papua (the tail of the New Guinea bird), and were building an airfield on Guadalcanal, whence they would be able to bomb our advanced base at Espiritu Santo. Admiral King in Washington decided that this must not be; the South Pacific Force was hurriedly assembled, and presently nineteen transports, escorted by cruisers and destroyers, with three carriers loosely attached, were converging on the mountainous, jungle-clad Solomon Islands. On 7 August 1942, the 1st Marine Division under General Alexander A. Vandegrift landed at Tulagi and Guadalcanal, surprised the enemy, and seized the harbor of the one island and the airfield on the other.

There then began the prolonged and bloody struggle for Guadalcanal; an island hardly more valuable than the battlefield of Gettysburg, yet even more violently contested. The Japanese could not afford to let us establish a base there, and we could not afford to let it go. Ships, planes, and troops were committed by both sides. Seven major naval battles were fought until Iron-bottom Sound, as our sailors named the waters between Guadalcanal and Florida Islands, was strewn with the hulls of ships and the bodies of seamen. The first of these battles, named after Savo Island which guards the western entrance to Ironbottom Sound, was the worst defeat ever suffered by the United States Navy. Admiral Mikawa, with a force no stronger than ours, pulled off a complete surprise on the night of 9 August, sinking one Australian and three American heavy cruisers, with no loss to himself. That was Japan's great opportunity to pile in and overwhelm the marines ashore; but overconfidence led her to reinforce Guadalcanal only by dribs and drabs. One reinforcement group was defeated by Rear Admiral Norman Scott off Cape Esperance on the night of 11–12 October. And the great Naval Battle of Guadalcanal raged for two long nights between 12 and 15 November 1942, with furious daylight air-ship battles between. Rear Admirals Scott and D. J. Callaghan were killed; but Rear Admiral Willis A. Lee won the second night engagement, in U.S.S. *Washington*, by sinking a Japanese battleship. There were also two carrier actions outside the Solomons, and another surface action in Ironbottom Sound in which we lost cruiser *Northampton* to the smartest of the Japanese rear admirals, Raizo Tanaka. Every few nights a "Tokyo Express" of fast destroyer transports, crowded with troops, raced down "the Slot" — the central channel between the Solomons — dropped the troops overboard to swim ashore, and was out of American air range by morning. Every few days we did the same thing from Espiritu Santo — except that our reinforcements went ashore dryshod. On shore, the marines, reinforced by two army divisions, fought desperately and successfully. The Airsols command, comprising army, navy, and marine corps planes of the United States, Australia, and New Zealand, gradually won control of the air. And on 9 February 1943, six months after the landings, the Japanese evacuated Guadalcanal.

In this campaign, American soldiers took the measure of the supposedly invincible Japanese jungle fighters who had overrun half Eastern Asia, and found that they could be beaten. And the navy learned, the hard way, how to fight night battles and shoot down enemy planes. After Guadalcanal had been secured, the navy lost no more battles.

In the meantime, the western prong of this Japanese offensive had been stopped on the north coast of Papua, New Guinea, by American and Australian troops under Generals Eichelberger and Sir Edmund Herring. The fighting, in malaria-infested mangrove swamps against a trapped and never-surrendering enemy, was the most horrible of the entire war. With the aid of air power, the combined armies won through, and by the end of January 1943 Papua up to Huon Gulf was in Allied hands.

The counteroffensive against Japan had made a good start.

President Roosevelt and Winston Churchill, meeting in the White House in June 1942, could not agree on time or place of the first Allied offensive against the Axis, nor could their military advisers. The Americans wanted priority for a cross-channel operation against the Germans in France, a beachhead to be secured in 1942, and a strike at the heart of the Reich in 1943. They discounted the value of peripheral operations — such as the raids on Dieppe and Norway — which the British favored continuing for a couple of years before mounting any massive invasion; for the British wished at all hazards to prevent trench warfare developing. But something had to be done to help Russia, which alone of the Allies was now bearing the brunt of the war. Stalin sent Molotov to Washington to beg for a "second front, now" and all left-wing elements in England and America took up the cry. Churchill and Roosevelt could not stand the obloquy of fighting another "phony war." On 25 July 1942 they decided to occupy French North Africa — Operation "Torch." The object was to secure a strategic springboard for invading Italy. That had to do for a "second front."

Oran and Algiers on the Mediterranean, and Casablanca on the Atlantic coast of Morocco, were selected as the three harbors to be seized by amphibious forces. General Dwight D. Eisenhower was appointed commander in chief, with Admiral Sir Andrew Cunningham RN as over-all commander of naval forces. In less than four months the United States and Great Britain had to train thousands of troops for amphibious warfare, divert hundreds of ships to new duties and, as Eisenhower wrote, occupy "the rim of a continent where no major military campaign had been conducted for centuries."

On 23 October General Sir Bernard Montgomery launched the second battle of El Alamein against the German Afrika Korps under Rommel. On the same day Rear Admiral H. Kent Hewitt, commanding the Western Naval Task Force, sailed from Hampton Roads. America had invaded Africa in Jefferson's day, and Africa had been brought to America in the persons of her sons and daughters; but never before had an amphibious operation been projected across an ocean. The complex operation went like clockwork. By midnight 7–8 November all three task forces (those for Oran and Algiers under British command) had reached their destinations, unscathed and unreported. French, Spaniards, Germans, and Italians were completely surprised. Admiral Hewitt had to fight a naval battle with the French fleet off Casablanca and sink most of it, in order to get General Patton's troops ashore safely; but there was little resistance from the French army. Admiral Darlan — second to Marshal Pétain in the Vichy government — who happened to be in Algiers, was so impressed by the strength of the Anglo-American landings that Eisenhower was able to persuade him, and Marshal Pétain secretly ordered him, to issue a cease-fire order to all French forces in North Africa on 11 November.

This "Darlan deal," as it was called, aroused vicious attacks on the sincerity of Eisenhower, Roosevelt, and Churchill from left-wing elements. They were accused of compromise with fascism, yielding to the enemy, etc. But through that deal the United States and Great Britain saved thousands of their soldiers' lives and gained new bases, and support of the French in North Africa, and eventually a new ally.

Although caught flatfooted by the invasion, the Germans reacted promptly, flying 20,000 men across the Sicilian straits within a few days and establishing fighter and bomber bases on Tunisian airfields. General Eisenhower moved, too, but the difficulties he faced from mountain and desert, narrow twisting roads, the rainy reason which grounded his aircraft and, not least, from his own half-trained troops, prevented his reaching Bizerte and Tunis in 1942.

Early in January 1943 Roosevelt and Churchill and the Combined Chiefs of Staff met at Casablanca to plan future operations. For the first time Allied prospects seemed favorable; this, as Churchill said, was "the end of the beginning." The Russians had turned the tide at the decisive battle of Stalingrad, Auchinleck and Montgomery had saved Egypt, air and naval forces were fast being built up in Morocco and Algeria, Mussolini could no longer call the Mediterranean *mare nostrum*. And General de Gaulle, though furious at not being given the Allied command in Africa, consented to appear and shake hands all around.

Allied chiefs at Casablanca decided to invade Sicily as soon as Tunisia was secured, and promised "to draw as much weight as possible off the Russian armies by engaging the enemy as heavily as possible at the best selected point." And they made the momentous announcement that the war would end only with "unconditional surrender" of all enemies, European and Asiatic. That formula, borrowed from General Grant's declaration before Fort

Donelson, was the second major strategic decision of the war. Not well thought out as to the consequences, it may have been a mistake. The reasons prompting it were the failure of the armistice of 11 November 1918 to eliminate the German menace; the Darlan deal, creating suspicion that Roosevelt contemplated a similar deal with Mussolini and Hitler; and a desire to reassure Russia that we would not let her down. On Mussolini the formula had no effect, since he was almost ready to quit, but it may have helped Hitler to persuade his people to fight to the bitter end.

While Roosevelt and Churchill were discussing grand strategy, the Germans seized the initiative. Swift counterattacks and the arrival of Rommel's Afrika Korps gave them ground superiority, which Rommel exploited in brilliant fashion. On 14 February 1943 he hurled his armor through the Kasserine Pass, turned northward toward Tebessa, and threatened to cut the Allied armies in two. The untried American forces were badly beaten for a time. But General Patton, with two new armored divisions and powerful new tanks, and clearing skies that permitted the Allied air force to deliver punishing blows, turned the tide.

This was Rommel's last offensive. Montgomery had caught up with him, and the two antagonists squared off for a last round. Hammered front and rear, pounded by the most devastating aerial attack of the North African campaign, Rommel acknowledged defeat and retreated northward into Tunisia. The Allied armies, now half a million strong, closed in for the kill. Then, as Montgomery broke the German lines in the south and raced for Tunis, Omar Bradley, commanding II Corps, United States Army, smashed into Bizerte. Both cities fell on 7 May 1943. Cornered on Cape Bon, the German army still 275,000 strong, surrendered on 13 May. It was the greatest victory that British and American arms had yet won.

Now that North Africa was cleared of the enemy, the Mediterranean became open to Allied merchant ships throughout its entire length, though still subject to air attack from Italy and southern France, which the Germans occupied as soon as they heard of the Darlan deal. The now spliced lifeline of the British Empire to India through Suez made it possible to reinforce Russia via the Persian Gulf. And the way was open at last for a blow at what Churchill mistakenly called "the soft underbelly" of Europe.

5. The U-Boat Mastered, Italy Invaded

At the Casablanca conference in January 1943 the Combined Chiefs of Staff gave antisubmarine warfare number one priority. In terms of construction, this meant that American shipyards had to slow up on producing beaching and landing craft for amphibious operations, and concentrate on escort vessels, especially the new DE (destroyer-escort) and the CVE (escort or "jeep" carrier), which could carry bombing planes into submarine-infested waters.

The Battle of the Atlantic came to a head in 1943. At the turn of the year Hitler appointed to command the German navy his submarine expert Admiral Doenitz, and concentrated on producing more and better U-boats and new types which could submerge for long periods. The number operating in the Atlantic more than doubled, and their effectiveness was increased by sending big supply subs — "milch cows" — into waters around the neutral Azores, enabling U-boats to replenish without returning to France. But the number of Allied ships and planes capable of dealing with them more than quadrupled. A fresh German blitz on the North Atlantic and other routes, in March 1943, accounted for 108 merchant ships aggregating over 625,000 tons. Echelons of wolf-packs, preceded by U-boats whose sole duty was to shadow convoys, attacked by day as well as night. These sinkings, occuring at the worst season in the North Atlantic when the temperature of the water hovers around 30° F, were accompanied by heavy loss of life. The big question in mid-1943 was whether existing U-boat types could be mastered in time to enable America to get enough men and weapons across to beat Germany before the new U-boats got into production. By April 1943 the Allies were definitely ahead. At a conference with Hitler on the 11th, Doenitz admitted the loss of 40 U-boats and 6 Italian submarines since New Year's.

An increased number of convoys and escorts, many new antisubmarine devices, better training, and the work of scientists and technicians were getting results. The British put on a great drive in the Bay of Biscay against U-boats that were approaching or departing from their French bases. This, in conjunction with successes elsewhere, brought the total bag up to 41 in May. At the same time the United States began using her new escort carriers in convoys between Norfolk and the Mediterranean. These, screened by the new DE's, went out after every submarine detected within 300 miles of the convoy route and sank a considerable number, even some of the big "milch cows." The latter were already driven from their pastures when Portugal permitted the Allies to use air bases in the Azores. That closed the last stretch in the North Atlantic which long-range bomber planes had been unable to reach. And new merchant ship construction was now well ahead of losses.

Germany built 198 U-boats between 1 May 1943 and the end of the year, and lost 186. Transatlantic convoys were now so well defended that tonnage losses during these eight months were less than in the single months of June and November 1942. Admiral Doenitz, feeling that he must make a tonnage score, no matter where, now began sending his best long-legged U-boats into the Indian Ocean, where as yet there were no convoys. But he kept enough in home waters, occasionally to send wolf-packs full cry after transatlantic traffic; the Battle of the Atlantic did not end until Germany surrendered.

Operation "Torch" flickered so long that "Overlord," the invasion of Normandy, had to be postponed to 1944. Something had to be done against the Axis during the rest of 1943, or the people would howl for action; and that something obviously had to start from the newly won Allied base in North Africa.

The plan selected was to overrun Sicily, cross the Strait of Messina to Calabria, and work up the Italian peninsula. This offered a chance of complete control of the Mediterranean as well as an objective dear to Churchill's heart, knocking Italy out of the war. D-day for the attack on Sicily was set for 10 July, and General Eisenhower commanded. This was the biggest amphibious assault of the war. About 250,000 British and American troops landed simultaneously, eight divisions abreast, in deep darkness. The more numerous Italian and German defenders of Sicily were completely surprised. General Patton's American Seventh Army was put ashore by Admiral Hewitt's Eighth Fleet on the southwestern shore of Sicily; General Montgomery's British Eighth Army, which included a Canadian division, landed to the right and almost up to Syracuse. The new LST and other beaching craft, here employed in large numbers for the first time, assisted in getting troops, tanks, and field artillery ashore so promptly that within a few hours the invaders controlled 150 miles of coastline, and substantial beachheads. The smoothness with which these landings were carried off, the celerity with which enemy opposition was overwhelmed, deeply impressed the German and Italian high commands. The Germans concluded that only a delaying operation was possible; the Italians decided it was time to quit.

After a sharp battle at the Gela beachhead with a German armored division, the Seventh Army swept across Sicily, marching at a rate that matched Stonewall Jackson's "foot cavalry" in the Civil War. On 22 July General Patton made a triumphal entry into Palermo and set up headquarters in the ancient palace of the Norman kings, whence, like another Tancred or Roger, he directed the campaign along the north coast of Sicily. That big island was in the Allied bag by 17 August 1943.

Italy was heartily sick of the war into which Mussolini had forced her. On 25 July, six days after Allied air forces had delivered a 560-plane bombing raid on Rome, the little king summoned up enough courage to force *il Duce* to resign. Marshal Badoglio, who told the king that the war was absolutely and completely lost, took over the government and began to probe for peace. Owing to the Italian love of bargaining and the "unconditional surrender" slogan which made bargaining difficult, negotiations dragged along until 3 September. This gave the Germans time to rush reinforcements into Italy and to seize key points such as Genoa, Leghorn, and Rome.

General Eisenhower had already been ordered by the Combined Chiefs of Staff to invade Italy at the earliest possible date. Salerno, south of the Sorrento peninsula, was chosen for the main landing. In early September 1943 the Allied Fifth Army, commanded by General Mark W. Clark, with two British and two American infantry divisions in the assault, took off from a dozen ports between Oran and Alexandria. En route the familiar voice of

General "Ike" was heard broadcasting news of the Italian surrender, so all hands expected a walkover. They had a bitter surprise. Some very tough and unco-operative Germans were at the beachhead, and D-day at Salerno, 9 September, was very costly. The German air force was active and enterprising, and tried a new weapon, the radio-guided bomb which put several ships out of business. A series of vicious tank attacks, to divide the American from the British divisions, was thwarted by the invaders, ably assisted by naval gunfire; and on 16 September the Germans started an orderly retirement northward. Fifth Army on 1 October entered Naples, which the Germans had done their best to destroy.

Here, with the great harbor secured and the Foggia airdrome on the other side of Italy in Allied hands, the Italian campaign should have been halted. But Churchill and General Sir Alan Brooke justified continuing up the Italian "boot," on the ground that the battle of Italy pinned down and used up German divisions which might resist the Normandy landing in 1944. Actually the Italian campaign failed to draw German reserves from France, and by June 1944 the Allies were employing in Italy double the number of the Germans in that area. It developed, as General Sir Henry Wilson said, into a "slow, painful advance through difficult terrain against a determined and re-sourceful enemy, skilled in the exploitation of natural obstacles by mines and demolition." Marshal Kesselring, fighting a series of delaying operations along prepared mountain entrenchments, exploited these natural advantages to the full; and none of the Allied generals except Guillaume, who commanded a French army corps, showed much ability to cope with German tactics. From Naples to Rome is but 100 miles; yet the Allies, with numerical superiority on land and in the air, and with control of adjacent waters, took eight months to cover that ground. Fighting in the Apennines was vividly described by the war correspondent Ernie Pyle, as consisting of "almost inconceivable misery," in mud and frost. G.I.'s "lived like men of prehistoric times, and a club would have become them more than a machine gun."

Rome was the objective of the winter campaign of 1943–44, but some of the most mountainous terrain in Europe barred the way. Churchill persuaded the C.C.S. to try and break the stalemate by an amphibious landing in the rear of the Germans at Anzio, 37 miles south of Rome. Although the Anzio landing (22 January 1944) by one British and one United States division was a complete surprise, Marshal Kesselring reacted swiftly. His air force sank a number of transports and warships, and the troops had to dig into an open plain, where they were subjected to constant air and infantry counterattack. Anzio beachhead, which should have been a spearhead, became instead a beleaguered fort.

To the south, the Eighth Army launched a series of savage attacks against the ancient monastery of Monte Cassino, anchor of another German line. For three months the Allies wore themselves out in futile attempts to take the place by storm. Finally, the Eighth Army, which by this time included Ameri-

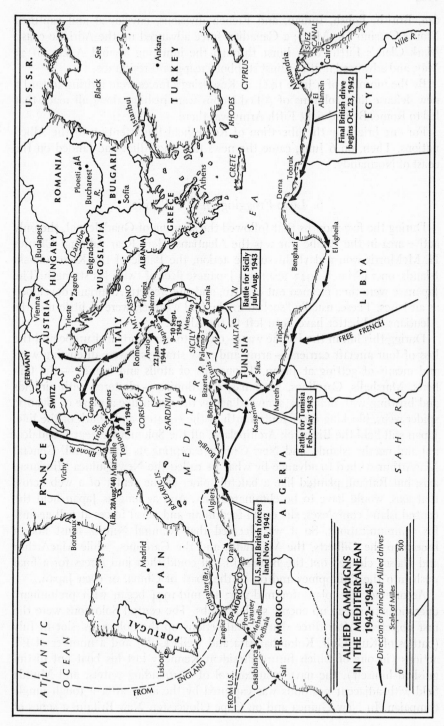

**ALLIED CAMPAIGNS
IN THE MEDITERRANEAN
1942–1945**

➤ Direction of principal Allied drives

Scale of Miles

0   500

Final British drive
begins Oct. 23, 1942

Battle for Sicily
July–Aug. 1943

Battle for Tunisia
Feb.–May 1943

U.S. and British forces
land Nov. 8, 1942

U.S.S.R.

TURKEY

Black Sea

Ankara

CYPRUS

RHODES

Istanbul

BULGARIA

Sofia

ROMANIA

Ploesti

Bucharest

Danube R.

GREECE

Athens

CRETE

ALBANIA

YUGOSLAVIA

Belgrade

Zagreb

Trieste

HUNGARY

Budapest

Vienna

AUSTRIA

GERMANY

SWITZ.

ITALY

Genoa

Po R.

MT. CASSINO

Rome

Anzio
22 Jan.
1944

Foggia

Salerno
9–10 Sept.
1943

Naples

Messina

Catania

SICILY

Palermo

MALTA

TUNISIA

Bizerte

Tunis

Sfax

Mareth

Bône

Bougie

Kasserine

Algiers

Oran

ALGERIA

SAHARA

FREE FRENCH

Tripoli

LIBYA

Benghazi

El Agheila

Derna

Tobruk

El Alamein

EGYPT

Nile R.

Cairo

Alexandria

SUEZ CANAL

MEDITERRANEAN SEA

SARDINIA

CORSICA

BALEARIC IS.

SPAIN

Madrid

PORTUGAL

Lisbon

FR. MOROCCO

SP. MOROCCO

Tangier

Gibraltar (Br.)

Casablanca

Fedhala

Mehedia

Port
Lyautey

Safi

FROM U.S.

FROM ENGLAND

FROM U.S.

FRANCE

Bordeaux

Vichy

Rhone R.

Marseille

Toulon

St.
Tropez
Aug. 1944

Cannes

(Lib. 28 Aug. '44)

ATLANTIC
OCEAN

can, British, Polish, Indian, and French divisions, enveloped and captured
Monte Cassino (19 May); a Canadian force advanced up the Adriatic coast;
Mark Clark's Fifth Army burst through the iron ring around Anzio on 25
May, and advanced north against stubborn rear-guard resistance.

By the morning of 4 June 1944, as Kesselring's forces were retiring toward a
new defense line, columns of Allied troops were rushing along all roads that
led to Rome. By midnight Fifth Army was there.

For one brief day the liberation of Rome held the attention of the Allied
nations. Then, on 6 June, came the news that the Allies had landed on the
coast of Normandy.

6. Leap-Frogging in the Pacific

During the five months that followed the securing of Guadalcanal, the only
active area in the Pacific war was the Aleutians. Here Rear Admiral Charles
H. McMorris won a daylight surface action, the Battle of the Komandorski
Islands, on 24 March 1943, against a Japanese fleet of twice his strength. The
Japanese were then cleaned out of Attu, and the western Aleutians developed
as air bases. These, usually "socked in" by foul weather, were of little use; the
Aleutians had better have been left to the Aleuts.

During this lull in the Pacific war — owing to our efforts in Europe and the
loss of four aircraft carriers — army and navy strategists were discussing ways
and means of getting at Japan. Thousands of atolls and islands — the Gilberts, Marshalls, Carolines, Marianas, and Bonins — plastered with airfields
and bristling with defenses, sprawled across the ocean like a maze of gigantic
spider webs, blocking every route north of the equator; and, south of the line,
Japan still held the Bismarck Archipelago, all the Solomons except Guadalcanal and nearby islands, and New Guinea excepting its Papuan tail. General
MacArthur wished to advance by what he called the New Guinea-Mindanao
axis; but Rabaul, planted like a baleful spider at the center of a web across
that axis, would have to be eliminated first. And as long as Japan held the
central island complexes, she could feed in air and naval forces at will against
his communications. So it was decided that Admiral Nimitz must take a
broom to the Gilberts, the Marshalls, and the Carolines, while MacArthur
and Halsey cleaned out the Bismarcks. All could then join forces for a final
push into the Philippines and on to the coast of China, or even Japan.

Accordingly the plans for mid-1943 to mid-1944 began with preliminary
operations to sweep up enemy spiders' webs. The central Solomons were the
first objective. After three sharp naval actions up the Solomons' slot in July
(battles of Kula Gulf, Kolombangara and Vella Gulf) and a number of PT
actions (in one of which future President Kennedy lost his boat but distinguished himself), the navy won control of surrounding waters, and Munda
field with adjacent positions was captured by the army after a tough jungle
campaign. In New Guinea and on Cape Gloucester, New Britain, a series of

shore-to-shore amphibious operations secured the main passage from the Coral Sea through the Bismarks barrier into the western Pacific.

Japan could now be approached in a series of bold leaps instead of a multitude of short hops. Independently, General MacArthur and Rear Admiral Theodore S. Wilkinson thought up "leap-frogging," or, as Wilkinson called it in baseball phraseology, "hitting 'em where they ain't." The essence of this strategy was to by-pass the principal Japanese strongpoints like Truk and Rabaul, sealing them off with sea and air power, leaving their garrisons to "wither on the vine," while we constructed a new air and naval base in some less strongly defended spot several hundred miles nearer Japan. After the war was over General Tojo told General MacArthur that leap-frogging, the success of United States submarines against the Japanese merchant marine, and the projection of fire power by aircraft carriers deep into enemy territory were the three main factors that defeated his country.

Now began a campaign to neutralize Rabaul. On 1 November Admiral Wilkinson's III Amphibious Force leap-frogged onto a slice of undefended coast in Bougainville and established a defensive perimeter for the Seabees to build fighter and bomber strips. A Japanese fleet based on Rabaul sortied to challenge but was decisively beaten (Battle of Empress Augusta Bay, 2 November 1943) by Rear Admiral A. S. Merrill's cruiser and destroyer force. On the 5th and 11th, planes from stately old *Saratoga* and the new carriers *Essex*, *Bunker Hill*, *Independence*, and *Princeton* pounded Rabaul, and bombers based on Bougainville continued the good work daily. Enemy air forces, even after stripping planes of carriers to defend Rabaul, were gradually worn away. On 25 November, in the Battle of Cape St. George, Captain Arleigh ("31-knot") Burke, commanding a destroyer squadron, defeated a Japanese attempt to reinforce Bougainville, and sank three of their five destroyers. Thus, by 25 March 1944, when Wilkinson's III 'Phib had taken Green Island and General MacArthur's VII 'Phib had occupied Manus in the Admiralty Islands, the Bismarcks barrier was broken, Rabaul rendered impotent, and almost 100,000 Japanese troops were neutralized.

The Gilberts and Marshalls campaigns were the first big amphibious operations in the Pacific. Some 200 sail of ships, Fifth Fleet carrying 108,0000 soldiers, sailors, marines, and aviators under the command of Rear Admirals Raymond Spruance and Kelly Turner, and Major General H. M. ("Howling Mad") Smith, converged on two coral atolls of the Gilbert group. Makin, where the enemy had no great strength, was taken early by one regiment; but Tarawa, a small, strongly defended position behind a long coral-reef apron, was a very tough nut. The lives of almost 1000 marines and sailors were required to dispose of 4000 no-surrender Japanese on an islet not three miles long. But Tarawa taught invaluable lessons for future landings, and provided another airfield.

The new Gilberts bases helped aircraft to neutralize the many Japanese airdromes in the Marshalls. Fast carrier forces under Rear Admiral Marc Mitscher roamed about the group, ships pounding and aircraft bombing. Consequently, not one Japanese plane was available in the Marshalls on D-day, 31 January 1944. Massive amphibious forces under Rear Admirals Harry Hill and Turner, with close air and gunfire support, covered landings at both ends of the great atoll of Kwajalein. On 17 February another force moved into Eniwetok, westernmost of the Marshalls. The Japanese troops, as usual, resisted to the last man; but the Marshalls not only cost many fewer casualties than tiny Tarawa, but were conquered without the loss of a single ship. The Japanese navy dared not challenge because its air arm had been sliced off to defend Rabaul; and on 20 February its capital ships and aircraft were chased out of the important naval base of Truk, with heavy loss, by a round-the-clock carrier raid.

Mobile surface forces and air power needed mobile logistics, and got them. Outstanding in the pattern for Pacific victory was the supply base — Service Squadron 10, a logistic counterpart to the fast carrier forces. While the flat-tops carried the naval air arm to within striking distance of the enemy, "Servron 10," composed of tankers, ammunition ships, refrigerator ships, re-pair ships, fleet tugs, escort carriers with replacement planes, and several other types of auxiliaries, acted as a traveling annex to Pearl Harbor to provide the fleet with food, fuel, bullets, spare parts, and spare planes. The Pacific Fleet actually recovered its independence of land bases, which had been lost when sail gave way to steam.

While Spruance and Turner were crashing through the Gilberts and Mar-shalls, "MacArthur's navy," the Seventh Fleet under Admirals Kinkaid and Barbey, was leap-frogging along the New Guinea coast. Hollandia and Aitape airfields were secured by the end of April. Biak Island, posed like a fly over the neck of the New Guinea bird, fell on 17 May 1944. Admiral Toyoda, commander in chief of the Japanese fleet (Yamamoto having been shot down over Bougainville), planned to stop the Americans right there with his two superbattleships; but before he got around to it a more dangerous American movement engaged his attention, and VII 'Phib was able to take the western end of New Guinea by 15 September 1944. MacArthur's air forces were now within bombing distance of the Philippines.

The movement that diverted Admiral Toyoda's attention was directed against the Marianas. Of this group, a bastion on Japan's inner line of de-fense, the principal islands are Saipan, Tinian, and Guam. So, when Admiral Nimitz's victorious team moved into Saipan on 15 June, Japan had to do something better than the last-ditch local resistance she had offered in the Marshalls. And by now her navy had trained new air groups.

Vice Admiral Ozawa's fleet, deploying into the Philippine Sea, comprised nine carriers, five battleships, and seven heavy cruisers. Admiral Spruance's Fifth Fleet (seven *Essex*-class and eight light carriers, seven battleships, three heavy and six light cruisers), moved out to meet him, preceded by a screen of submarines. Spruance played his usual cool game, taking risks boldly when they seemed commensurate with the damage he might inflict, yet never forgetting that his main duty was to protect the amphibious forces at Saipan. The Battle of the Philippine Sea broke at 10 a.m., 19 June 1944, when hundreds of Japanese planes were detected flying toward the American carriers, then about 100 miles northwest of Guam. Sixty miles out, Hellcat fighters intercepted the Japanese planes, and only forty broke through. The anti-aircraft fire of Spruance's ships was so accurate and deadly that these planes scored only two hits, on battleships that suffered little damage. As a result of the day's fighting, the Japanese lost over 345 planes at the cost of only 17 American aircraft. Ozawa lost three carriers (two to United States submarines), his air groups were wiped out, and he had no time to train new ones before the next great battle, in October.

Now the conquest of the Marianas could proceed without enemy interference. By 1 August 1944 the three major islands, Saipan, Tinian, and Guam, were in American possession. Airfield and harbor development went on briskly. Admiral Nimitz moved his headquarters to the hills above Agaña in Guam, and by fall, Marianas-based B-29's were bombing southern Japan.

The more sagacious Japanese now knew they were beaten; but they dared not admit it, and nerved their people to another year of bitter resistance in the vain hope that America might tire of the war when victory was within her grasp.

Victory

1944-1945

1. The Invasion of Europe

GENERAL CARL ("TOOEY") SPAATZ of the United States Army Air Force, America's foremost aviator, believed with Air Chief Marshal "Bomber" Harris of the Royal Air Force that Germany could be defeated by air bombing; no invasion would be necessary. In July and August 1943 the R.A.F. and VIII A.A.F. together inflicted the most destructive air bombing of the European war: — repeated attacks on Hamburg which wiped out over half the city, killed 42,600, and injured 37,000 people. "Those who sowed the wind are reaping the whirlwind," remarked Winston Churchill. Worse was to come; but this air offensive never became a substitute for land invasion. Bombing German cities, almost nightly by the R.A.F. and every clear day by the A.A.F., did not seriously diminish Germany's well dispersed war production, and failed to break her civilian morale. It was also frightfully expensive. In six days of October 1943, culminating in a raid on the ball-bearing plants at Schweinfurt, the VIII A.A.F. lost 148 bombers and their crews.

One reason for these heavy casualties was the lack of fighter planes long-legged enough to escort the bombers from their bases in England or Italy. But by the spring of 1944 we had the P-38 Lightning, P-47 Thunderbolt, and P-51 Mustang, which could fly to Berlin and back, fighting a good part of the way. Air power, besides obstructing the movement of enemy armies, was now applied with increasing precision and violence to the key centers of German war production.

In the week of 19–25 February 1944, 3800 heavy bombers of the VIII and XV A.A.F., escorted by fighters, attacked twelve targets vital to the German aircraft industry, as far south as Ratisbon and Augsburg. Our losses were 226 bombers, 28 fighters, and about 2600 men; but some 600 German planes were shot down. German aircraft production did recuperate, but these February bombing missions denied many hundred aircraft to the enemy when he needed them most. By 14 April, when this long-sustained bomber offensive ended, and control of the U.S. Strategic Air Forces in Europe passed to General Eisenhower, the Allied air forces had established a thirty-to-one superiority over the Luftwaffe. On Normandy D-day General Eisenhower told his

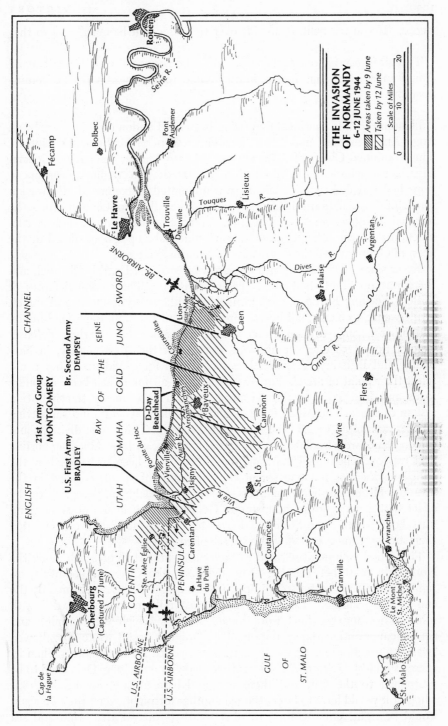

THE INVASION
OF NORMANDY
6-12 JUNE 1944

Areas taken by 9 June
Taken by 12 June

Scale of Miles
0   10   20

ENGLISH   CHANNEL

Cap de
la Hague

Cherbourg
(Captured 27 June)

COTENTIN

PENINSULA

Ste. Mère Église

U.S. AIRBORNE

U.S. AIRBORNE

La Haye
du Puits

Carentan

Coutances

GULF
OF
ST. MALO

Granville

Le Mont
St. Michel

St. Malo

Avranches

UTAH   OMAHA   GOLD   JUNO   SWORD

BAY   OF   THE   SEINE

Pointe du Hoc

Vierville

Isigny

Aure R.

D-Day
Beachhead

Armanches

Bayeux

Caumont

St. Lô

Vire R.

Vire

Flers

Caen

Orne R.

Dives

BR. AIRBORNE

Ouistreham
Courseulles
lion-sur-Mer

Falaise

Argentan

U.S. First Army
BRADLEY

Br. Second Army
DEMPSEY

21st Army Group
MONTGOMERY

Le Havre

Trouville
Deauville

Touques

Lisieux

Fécamp

Bolbec

Pont
Audemer

Seine R.

Rouen

1029

troops, "If you see fighting aircraft over you, they will be ours," and so they were.

This air war in Europe cost the lives of some 158,000 British, Canadian and American aviators, but it was indispensable to the success of the coming invasion.

Planning for the continental invasion began at London early in 1943, by an Anglo-American staff under the direction of General Sir Frederick Morgan. The Combined Chiefs of Staffs set the date for May or June 1944. General Eisenhower, who in the conduct of North African and Mediterranean operations had revealed superior talents, was appointed to command all invasion forces of both nations. In January 1944 "Ike" flew to London where he received his directive: "You will enter the continent of Europe and, in conjunction with the other United Nations, undertake operations aimed at the heart of Germany and the destruction of her armed forces."

Never since 1688 had an invading army crossed the English Channel, and there was no "Protestant wind" behind this one. The coastal defenses of Hitler's *Festung Europa* were formidable: underwater obstacles and mines, artillery emplacements, pill boxes, wire entanglements, tank traps, land mines, and other hazards to stop invaders on the beaches. Behind these defenses were stationed 58 German divisions, only 14 of them, fortunately, in Normandy and Britanny. Yet the Allies had reason for confidence. They could select their point of attack. For six weeks Allied air forces had been smashing roads and bridges in northern France, reducing the enemy transportation system to chaos. The Allied force of soldiers, sailors, aviators, and supporting services amounted to 2.8 million men in England. Thirty-nine divisions and 11,000 planes were available for the initial landings, and the Allied supporting fleet was overwhelmingly superior; the U-boats had been so handled by the Allied navies that not one got at the thousands of vessels engaged in the invasion. Hitler's army commanders, fooled by an elaborate deception to the effect that a major army group under General Patton in southeast England was about to cross the Straits of Dover to the Pas de Calais, concentrated their strongest forces on the wrong stretch of coast.

The Allied command selected as target a 40-mile strip of beach along the Normandy coast between the Orne river and the Cotentin peninsula, assigning the eastern sector to the British, the western to the Americans. By the end of May southern England was one vast military camp, crowded with soldiers awaiting the final word to go, and piled high with supplies and equipment awaiting transportation. This "mighty host," wrote Eisenhower, "was as tense as a . . . great human spring, coiled for the moment when its energy should be released." Foul weather made up on 4 June, D-day had to be postponed to the 6th, and there was a debate at supreme headquarters whether it would have to be postponed another fortnight, when the tide again would be right. On the strength of a weather forecast that wind and sea would be moderate on the 6th, General Eisenhower made the decision at 4:15 a.m., 5 June, "O.K. We'll go." During the night of 5–6 June, the assault fleet of 600 warships and 4000 supporting craft, freighted with 176,000 men from a dozen different ports, the American section commanded by Rear Admiral Alan Kirk and Lieutenant General Omar Bradley, crossed the Channel to the "far shore," a coast denied to the Allies since the fall of France. Three paratroop divisions, flown across the Channel and dropped behind the beaches, spearheaded the invasion before dawn of the ever memorable D-day, 6 June 1944. At first light the naval bombardment opened, and landing craft, lowered from transports over ten miles from shore, began their approach.

On Utah Beach, the American right, VII Corps (Major General J. Lawton Collins) landed against slight opposition and linked up with elements of the 82nd Airborne Division. But on Omaha Beach, V Corps (Major General L. T. Gerow) found the going very rough. The air force had not bombed this beach, the naval bombardment was too brief, underwater obstacles were numerous and formidable. Soldiers wading ashore fell when wounded into a maze of mined obstacles, and were drowned by the rising tide; those who reached dry land had to cross a 50-yard-wide beach exposed to cunningly contrived crossfire from concrete pill boxes that naval gunfire could not reach. Men huddled for protection under a low sea wall until company officers rallied them to root the defenders out of their prepared positions. Sheer guts and sound training saved the day at Omaha, not forgetting the naval gunfire support that rained shells on the Germans as soon as shore fire control parties were able to indicate targets.

The even bigger British assault force under Admiral Vian and General Dempsey had an easier landing on the eastern beaches, but bore the brunt of the next week's fighting. Caen, behind the British beaches, was the hinge of the Allied beachhead, where the Germans directed their main counterattacks. In both sectors the D-day assault was brilliantly successful; but the landings were only the beginning of a long and costly campaign.

In the first week the Allies landed 326,000 men, 50,000 vehicles, and over 100,000 tons of supplies, to build up an invading army faster than the Germans could reinforce theirs. They now controlled a beachhead some 7 miles in length and from five to fifteen miles in depth. Two artificial harbors called "mulberrys" built out of sunken ships with connecting pontoon units, facilitated this rapid build-up on the landing beaches, but a northwest gale which blew up on 19 June so badly damaged them that the capture of Cherbourg became highly urgent. Cherbourg surrendered on 26 June after the Germans had wrecked the harbor.

The Battle of Normandy lasted until 24 July. By that time the British had captured Caen; the Americans had taken Saint-Lô, gateway to the South. The enemy, unable to bring up reinforcements, his communications wrecked and planes grounded, was bewildered. Rommel thought the situation hopeless and was preparing to try to negotiate with Eisenhower for a separate peace when Hitler had him arrested and killed. Other high-ranking officers attempted to assassinate Hitler on 20 July, as the only way to end the war; but the Fuehrer survived, the conspirators were tortured to death, and the war went on. Hitler now trusted to secret weapons to win. His new V-1 "buzz bombs," launched from positions in Belgium and northern France, were spreading death and destruction on London, and the V-2 guided missiles were ready.

The Battle for France began on 25 July when General Patton's Third Army hit the German lines west of Saint-Lô. Within two days VII Corps had reached Coutances, hemming in remnants of the German army along the coast. By the end of July, Avranches had fallen, and the Americans stood at the threshold of Brittany. In the face of this fast and furious attack the German withdrawal turned into something like a rout. Nothing could stop Patton except running out of gas. One wing of his army turned west and within a week overran Brittany, leaving only Brest, Lorient, and Saint-Nazaire for leisurely reduction. Another wing turned east, and within two weeks reached the Loire and Le Mans. In a desperate gamble Hitler ordered the German Seventh Army to break through the American army at Avranches. Most of it was destroyed in the ensuing Battle of the Falaise Gap; only remnants of armor fought their way through and sped east to prepare for the defense of Germany.

On 15 August the Allies launched their long-awaited invasion of southern France. General Eisenhower insisted on this operation, against strong opposition from Churchill, in order to capture the major port of Marseilles for logistic supply, and deploy the American Seventh Army (Lieutenant General Alexander C. Patch) and the First French Army (General de Lattre de Tassigny) on his southern flank for the invasion of Germany. The coast of Provence was so lightly defended that the amphibious assault commanded by Admiral H. Kent Hewitt USN was a pushover. Toulon and Marseilles were soon liberated, Seventh Army rolled up the Rhone valley, captured Lyon, and by mid-September had linked with Patton's Third Army.

"Liberate Paris by Christmas and none of us can ask for more," said Churchill to Eisenhower. First Army (Lieutenant General Courtney H. Hodges) rolled to the Seine; Patton's Third boiled out into the open country north of the Loire and swept eastward through Orleans to Troyes. Paris rose against the German garrison, and with the aid of General Leclerc's 2nd Armored Division was liberated on 25 August, four months ahead of Churchill's request. General Charles de Gaulle now entered the city in triumph and assumed the presidency of a French provisional government.

Patton's spearheads reached the Marne on 28 August and overran Rheims and Verdun. To the north, Montgomery's British and Canadians pushed along the coast into Belgium, captured Brussels and entered Antwerp 4 September. By the 11th, the American First Army had liberated Luxemburg and near Aachen crossed the border into Germany. Within six weeks all France had been cleared of the enemy, and from Belgium to Switzerland Allied armies stood poised for the invasion of Germany. Hitler had lost almost half a million men, but his amazing hold over the Germans had not relaxed, and they were ready for a last counterblow that cost the Allies dear.

On other fronts, Russia had recovered most of her invaded territory, and in the spring of 1944 the Soviet armies reached the Dnieper river in the north and the Carpathians in the south. Stalin, having promised to start a new offensive when the Allies entered Normandy, on 23 June advanced along an 800-mile front from Leningrad to the Carpathians. In the space of five weeks the Russians swept across the Ukraine and Poland and up to the gates of Warsaw where they paused, despicably, instead of helping Polish patriots to liberate the capital. Romania threw in the sponge when another Red army crossed her borders, and so deprived the Germans of their last source of crude oil. In Italy the Germans were being driven back on their last line of defense, guarding the Po valley.

Although in mid-September 1944 the Allies held the initiative on the western front, they were unable to exploit it owing to a serious problem of logistics. Not only were the supply lines very, very long; the sea approach to Antwerp was still denied by a stubborn German defense of the lower Scheldt. This situation presented Eisenhower with one of his most difficult strategic problems. Field Marshal Montgomery wanted to push ahead through Holland into the heart of Germany and plunge through to Berlin. General Patton was no less confident of his ability to smash into Germany from the south. Logistical supply permitted a modest advance on a broad front, or a deep stab on a single front, but not both. Because Eisenhower deemed it essential to clear the way to Antwerp, capture Calais and Dunkerque, and overrun the V-1 and V-2 bomb emplacements which were raining guided missiles on London, priority in the scarce gasoline supply was given to Montgomery, who wasted it; and his favored operation, taking Arnhem by paratroop drop, was badly defeated, stopping the ground offensive cold. The sad prospect of another winter's campaign in Europe now loomed.

2. The Battle for Leyte Gulf

By 1 August 1944, when the Marianas and New Guinea were in American or Australian possession, the question of where to move next had virtually been decided at a conference in Honolulu between General MacArthur, Admiral Nimitz, and President Roosevelt. The President, pointing to Saipan on the map, said, "Douglas, where do we go from here?" "Leyte, Mr. President; and then Luzon!" And that is how it was done.

The Joint Chiefs of Staff first set the date for the invasion of Leyte as 20 December 1944, but at the suggestion of aggressive Admiral Halsey, with General MacArthur's glad approval, the timetable was stepped up two months. Central Pacific forces under Admirals Nimitz and Halsey, and Southwest Pacific forces under General MacArthur and Admiral Kinkaid, combined in one massive thrust into Leyte. That island was chosen as the nearest practicable base from which to begin the liberation of the Philippines, and also because land-based planes on previously captured islands could cover the invasion. Early in the morning of 20 October 1944, 73 transports and 50 LST's entered Leyte Gulf, exactly where Magellan's ships had sailed, 423 years before. The landings on Leyte by Sixth Army (Lieutenant General Walter Krueger) went off according to schedule, and that afternoon General MacArthur and President Osmeña of the Philippines splashed ashore from a landing craft. Before a microphone, MacArthur delivered an impressive liberation speech beginning, "People of the Philippines, I have returned."

He certainly had; but how long could he stay? The Japanese were not taking this lying down. At Tokyo the war lords decided to commit the entire Japanese fleet, smash American forces afloat, and so isolate MacArthur that he would be virtually back at Bataan. From that decision there resulted, on 25 October, the Battle for Leyte Gulf, greatest sea fight of this or of any other war.

Admiral Toyoda put into execution a plan based on ruse and surprise, factors dear to Japanese strategists; but his plan required a division of the Japanese fleet into three parts, which proved to be fatal. Admiral Nishimura's Southern Force of battleships and cruisers was to come through Surigao Strait, break into Leyte Gulf at daybreak 25 October, and there rendezous with Kurita's more powerful Center Force, which was to thread San Bernardino Strait and come around Samar from the north. Either separately was strong enough to make mincemeat of Admiral Kinkaid's amphibious forces in Leyte Gulf and cut off General Krueger's troops from their sea-borne lifeline. Way was to be cleared for Kurita by Admiral Ozawa's Northern Force built around four carriers, whose mission was to entice Halsey's Task Force 38, the American carrier force, up north.

That part of the plan worked only too well, but the rest of it worked not at all. Admiral Kinkaid deployed almost every battleship, cruiser, and destroyer that had supported the Leyte landings, and placed them under the command of Rear Admiral Jesse Oldendorf, to catch Nishimura as he came through Surigao Strait in the early hours of 25 October. Two destroyer torpedo attacks nicked Nishimura of one battleship and three destroyers, and what was left of his "T" was crossed by Oldendorf's battleships and cruisers. Their high-caliber fire sank the other enemy battleship, and what was left of the Southern Force fled, most of it to be harried and sunk after dawn by carrier planes. This smashing night victory — the Battle of Surigao Strait — was the battle-wagons' revenge for Pearl Harbor; five of those engaged had been sunk or grounded on 7 December 1941.

Scarcely had Surigao Strait been cleared when the most critical of the three actions began. Kurita's massive Center Force, built around his biggest

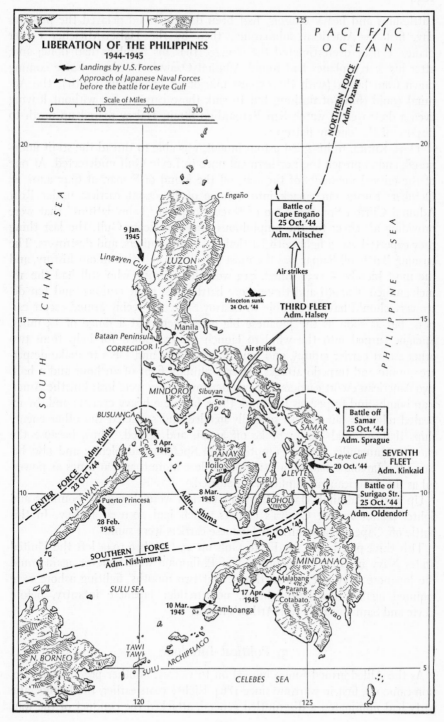

LIBERATION OF THE PHILIPPINES
1944-1945

Landings by U.S. Forces
Approach of Japanese Naval Forces
before the battle for Leyte Gulf

Scale of Miles

0   100   200   300

PACIFIC OCEAN

NORTHERN FORCE
Adm. Ozawa

SOUTH CHINA SEA

C. Engaño

9 Jan. 1945

Lingayen Gulf

LUZON

Battle of
Cape Engaño
25 Oct. '44
Adm. Mitscher

Air strikes

Princeton sunk
24 Oct. '44

THIRD FLEET
Adm. Halsey

PHILIPPINE SEA

Manila

Bataan Peninsula
CORREGIDOR I.

Air strikes

MINDORO

Sibuyan
Sea

BUSUANGA

Coron Bay

9 Apr.
1945

PANAY

Iloilo

SAMAR

Battle off
Samar
25 Oct. '44
Adm. Sprague

Leyte Gulf
20 Oct. '44

SEVENTH
FLEET
Adm. Kinkaid

CENTER FORCE — Adm. Kurita
23 Oct. '44

PALAWAN

Puerto Princesa

28 Feb.
1945

Adm. Shima

8 Mar.
1945

NEGROS

CEBU

LEYTE

BOHOL

Battle of
Surigao Str.
25 Oct. '44
Adm. Oldendorf

24 Oct. '44

SOUTHERN   FORCE
Adm. Nishimura

SULU SEA

MINDANAO

Malabang
Parang
Cotabato

17 Apr.
1945

Davao

10 Mar.
1945

Zamboanga

TAWI
TAWI

SULU ARCHIPELAGO

N. BORNEO

SULU

CELEBES   SEA

battleships and heavy cruisers, had been damaged and delayed the previous day, first by American submarines, then by the Halsey-Mitscher carrier planes. Halsey overestimated the damage that his bombers had done; and, after his search planes had found Admiral Ozawa's Northern Force coming down from Japan (with the express mission of luring him north), the Admiral could think of nothing but to sink those carriers. So, without leaving even a destroyer to watch San Bernardino Strait, Halsey roared up north to dispose of the enemy flattops.

Thus, Kurita, to his great astonishment, was able to thread the strait unopposed, and approach the northern entrance to Leyte Gulf undetected. At one of the critical moments of the war, off the island of Samar, at 6:45 a.m., 25 October, Kurita ran smack into a force of six escort carriers under Rear Admiral Clifton Sprague. One of three groups of "baby flattops" that were providing air cover for the amphibious forces in Leyte Gulf, the last thing they expected was a fight with battleships, heavy cruisers, and destroyers. The ensuing Battle off Samar was the most gallant naval action in our history, and the most bloody — 1130 killed, 913 wounded. Kurita, who still had the 18-inch-gunned *Yamato* and three more battleships, eight cruisers, and ten destroyers, should have been able to destroy Sprague's feebly armed escort carriers; but as soon as the Japanese big guns opened at a range of 14 miles, Sprague turned into the wind to launch planes, called for help from two other escort carrier groups, and sent his destroyers and DE's to make desperate gunfire and torpedo attacks. After a running fight of an hour and a half, two American escort carriers and two destroyer types were lost; but the American bombs and torpedoes had sunk three Japanese heavy cruisers and, by repeated relentless air attacks so badly mauled and scattered the other enemy ships that Admiral Kurita broke off action and retired. Thus, because the enemy commander lacked gumption, and Sprague had plenty; and also because the Japanese had no air support, a fleet more than ten times as powerful as the Americans in gunfire was defeated.

Up north, Admiral Marc Mitscher's carriers were slicing off bombers and fighter planes against Ozawa's carriers which had decoyed Halsey. In this battle off Cape Engaño, all four Japanese carriers were sunk.

This three-part battle for Leyte Gulf on 25 October 1944 left the United States Navy in complete command of Philippine waters; never again could the Japanese navy offer a real threat. But two months' fighting ashore were required against the hard-fighting, no-surrender Japanese infantry, before Leyte and Samar were in MacArthur's hands.

3. *Political Interlude*

As the Allied armed forces lunged on to victory, another presidential election came up, first in wartime since 1864. Eighty years earlier, the Democratic party had nominated a disgruntled general, attacked the conduct of the war, and called for a compromise peace. Now, in 1944, a hard core of isolationists, supported by the Chicago *Tribune* and the Hearst press, wished to reverse the "beat Germany first" decision and promote General MacArthur, supposedly a "martyr" to Roosevelt's "jealousy," for the Republican presidential nomination. But the General, although he felt slighted and hoped to become President some day, insisted first on fulfilling his promise to liberate the Philippines. A Gallup poll in the Midwest farming country in September 1943 gave General MacArthur a decided preference over Roosevelt for next President. Many voters in the old liberal-progressive farm bloc, especially German-Americans, never believed in any necessity to fight Hitler, and the Pearl Harbor attack turned all their belligerent feelings westward.

For the present, however, almost every Republican supported the war and endorsed a postwar international organization. In the 1942 congressional elections the Republicans increased their strength in the House 30 per cent, giving them high hopes of winning the presidency in 1944.

Wendell Willkie by now was a world figure, owing to several visits to Allied countries, and inspiring speeches in support of the war. But he made the tactical error of entering the presidential primary in Wisconsin, where the voters wanted no advocate of "One World," but an isolationist who would promise to "bring the boys home" from Europe. There he met a stunning defeat, and withdrew. Thomas E. Dewey, who had proved himself a competent administrator as governor of New York, was nominated by the Republican convention on the first ballot. Republican strategy was to concentrate on the argument that no party could be safely entrusted with office for more than twelve years without a hardening of political arteries, and that the country needed new and younger men for the tasks of peace and reconstruction. Respecting President Roosevelt's health the charge was only too true; but his physicians reported him still to be fit as a fiddle. The Democratic national convention renominated him on the first ballot for a fourth term, but there was a change in the second place on the ticket. Roosevelt, tired of Wallace's left-wing vagaries, gave the nod to Senator Harry Truman of Missouri — another instance of his good judgment.

The issue was never in doubt. Roosevelt carried 36 states with 432 electoral votes; Dewey, 12 states with 99 electoral votes, and Roosevelt's popular plurality was about 3.5 million. The Democrats won 242 seats in the House, as against 190 Republicans. That marked the end of isolationism as a positive political factor. But, in a sense, it "went underground," to emerge nastily as McCarthyism.

4. Victory in Europe

After the failure of the Arnhem air drop, the war lost its momentum and settled down to what General Eisenhower called "the dirtiest kind of infantry slugging." The Germans now held their strongest defensive positions since the beginning of the invasion. Rundstedt and Kesselring, their ablest generals, were now comanders in the west and in Italy. Floods, intense cold, rain and snow in the winter of 1944–45 combined to help the defense.

In the confused fighting that stretched from October to mid-December 1944 we can distinguish a series of battles, each as bitter and as costly as any since the Civil War. The first, taking them in geographical order, was the battle for the Scheldt estuary. The task of clearing the enemy out of the islands, whose possession by the Germans prevented Allied use of Antwerp, was assigned to the Canadian First Army. The reduction of Walcheren cost the Allies more casualties than the conquest of Sicily, and not until the end of November could Allied ships unload at Antwerp, and so shorten the logistics line.

The second major battle was for Aachen, near the junction of Belgium, Holland, and Germany. General Hodges's First Army launched the attack on 2 October, fighting through five miles of German fortifications. By the middle of the month the city was surrounded; then came a week of street fighting before the ancient capital of Charlemagne capitulated — first German city to fall to the Allies.

General Omar Bradley now brought Ninth Army north to co-operate with the First in a campaign to capture the Roer river dams — third of the major battles. An assault by seventeen divisions through the Hürtgen Forest to Düren failed to do it. The country was not unlike that Wilderness in which Grant and Lee had tangled eighty years earlier. Three divisions alone, the 4th, 9th, and 28th, suffered almost 13,000 casualties. The Americans reached the Roer river on 3 December, and there they were stalled until early February.

In the south, General Patton's Third Army jumped off in early November to capture Metz, northern Lorraine, and the industrial Saar basin. Only once before in modern times — in 1871 — had the fortress city of Metz fallen to an invader. Patton proved that if need be, he could be methodical, instead of dashing. First he enveloped Metz, reducing one by one the forts that encircled it. Then came a week of street fighting. The city fell on 22 November and Third Army, fighting its way through the heaviest fortifications of the Siegfried line, plunged into the Saar. This campaign cost the Americans 29,000 battle casualties, but netted them 37,000 prisoners.

In conjunction with Patton's advance, Lieutenant General Jacob L. Devers's Sixth Army Group, which incorporated Patch's and De Lattre de Tassigny's armies, entered Alsace, and Strasbourg fell on 23 November. The French then turned north along the Rhine, the Americans south. These operations, obscured by the more dramatic fighting to the north, cost the Allies 33,000 more casualties.

By mid-December the Allied armies were poised along the border from Holland to Switzerland, ready to plunge deep into Germany. Then came a dramatic change of fortune: a German counteroffensive, recalling Jubal Early's raid on Washington in 1864, but on a vast scale. Rundstedt's name was given to this desperate thrust through the Ardennes Forest, but the idea was Hitler's. His objective was to split the Allied army groups, drive through to the coast, and recapture Antwerp. Eisenhower had taken the calculated risk of spreading thin his forces in the rugged Ardennes, through which Rundstedt had crashed with his main force in May 1940. Now the Germans prepared to repeat that successful campaign. Because the bad weather prevented Allied air reconnaissance, they achieved surprise and initial success along a fifty-mile front, on 16 December. After the first shock, Allied resistance stiffened. The Germans concentrated on the center of the Allied line. They almost reached the Meuse on 26 December, but were checked at Bastogne, headquarters of General Troy Middleton's VIII Corps, focal point of a network of roads essential to the Germans. Middleton decided to hold it at all costs, without adequate forces. Late in the night of 17 December the 101st Airborne Division, then in a rest center 100 miles behind the lines, was ordered to Bastogne; the men piled into trucks and jeeps and pulled into Bastogne on the 18th, just before the German tide flooded around the town. This reinforcement beefed up the strength of the defenders to some 18,000 men.

There followed one of the fiercest land battles of the war. The Americans seized outlying villages, and set up a perimeter defense. For six days the enemy hurled armor and planes at them, persistently probing for a weak spot, and found not one. Foul weather prevented aerial reinforcement of the defenders. On 22 December the American situation appeared hopeless and the Germans presented a formal demand for surrender, to which General "Tony" McAuliffe of the 101st Airborne gave the simple answer "Nuts!" Next day the weather cleared, and planes began dropping supplies; by Christmas Eve, with bomber and fighter support, the situation looked more hopeful. In the meantime, Patton's Third Army had made a great left wheel and started pell-mell north to the rescue of the besieged garrison. On 26 December his 4th Armored Division broke through the German encirclement and Bastogne was saved. The Battle of the Bulge, as we named it, was not over, but by 15 January 1945 the original lines of mid-December had been restored. Rundstedt had held up the Allied advance by a full month, but at a cost of 120,000 men, 1600 planes, and a good part of his armor. Never thereafter were the Germans able to put up an effective defense.

At the end of January, Eisenhower regrouped his armies and resumed advance toward the Rhine. In the meantime the Russians had sprung their winter offensive, which surpassed the campaign in the west in numbers involved and territory recaptured. The Russian army jumped off on a 1000-mile front early in January, crossed the Vistula, and swept toward Germany. While one group of armies in the center took Warsaw and raced across Poland to the Oder river, others stabbed into Germany from the north and south, moved into Hungary and Czechoslovakia and threatened Vienna.

In the final Allied campaign in the west we can distinguish three stages: the advance to the Rhine, from late January to 21 March; the crossing of the

Rhine and the Battle of the Ruhr, 21 March to 14 April; and the annihilation of all enemy opposition, 14 April to the surrender on 7 May 1945. Omitting details, the 7th of March was one of the dramatic days of the war. On that day a detachment of the 9th Armored Division captured a bridge over the Rhine at Remagen, just as the Germans were about to blow it. A fleet of navy landing craft were brought up in trucks to help General Hodges's First Army get across; it then fanned out, securing the highway running south to Munich. And on 22 March Patton, beating "Monty" to the river, began crossing the Rhine at Oppenheim.

The next move after vaulting the Rhine barrier was to encircle the Ruhr. Moving at breakneck speed, First Army swung north, Lieutenant General William H. Simpson's Ninth turned south, and a giant pincer closed on the Ruhr. Encircled, pounded on all sides, hammered day and night by swarms of bombers, the German armies caught in the pocket disintegrated. By 18 April the bag of prisoners reached the total of 325,000, and organized resistance ceased. It was, said General Marshall, the largest envelopment operation in the history of American warfare; and it should be noted that this was Marshall's idea, violently opposed by Sir Alan Brooke and Montgomery, who wished to concentrate all Allied ground forces in one knifelike thrust across northern Europe. That concept, if carried out, would have created an impossible congestion and left the Ruhr in enemy hands.

Now Montgomery drove toward Bremen and Hamburg, Patton raced for Kassel, and Patch sped through Bavaria toward Czechoslovakia.

As the Allied armies penetrated Germany, Austria, and Poland, they came upon one torture camp after another — Buchenwald, Dachau, Belsen, Auschwitz, Linz, Lubin — and what they saw sickened them. These atrocious camps had been started in 1937 for Jews, gypsies, and anti-Nazi Germans and Austrians; during the war Hitler used them for prisoners of all nationalities, civilians and soldiers, men, women, and children, and for Jews rounded up in Italy, France, Holland, and Hungary. All Jews were killed in the hope of exterminating the entire race, hordes of prisoners were scientifically murdered; multitudes died of disease, starvation, and maltreatment. Much of this wholesale murder was done in the name of "science," and with the criminal collusion of German physicians, who appear to have absorbed the Nazi contempt for humanity. Nothing in their experience had prepared Americans for these revelations of human depravity; many are still incredulous. But the evidence is conclusive that the total number of civilians done to death by Hitler's orders exceeded 6 million. And the pathetic story of one of the least of these, the diary of the little Dutch girl Anne Frank, has probably done more to convince the world of the hatred inherent in the Nazi doctrine than the solemn postwar trials.

As German resistance crumbled and victory appeared certain, the Allied world was plunged into mourning by the news that a great leader had died. President Roosevelt, returning in February a sick man from the Yalta conference of the Combined Chiefs of Staff, went to his winter home in Warm Springs, Georgia, to prepare for the inauguration of the United Nations at San Francisco. On 12 April, as he was drafting a Jefferson Day address, he suffered a cerebral hemorrhage which brought instant death. The last words he wrote were an epitome of his career: "The only limit to our realization of to-morrow will be our doubts of today. Let us move forward with strong and active faith."

Now the end of Hitler's Germany approached. The Western Allies rolled unopposed to the Elbe; the Russians thrust at Berlin. Advance detachments of the two armies met at Torgau on 25 April, severing Germany. On the last day of April, Hitler died a coward's death, killing first his mistress and then himself in a bombproof bunker under Berlin. German resistance was also collapsing in northern Italy. On 4 May General Mark Clark's Fifth Army, which had fought all the way up the boot of Italy, met, at the Brenner Pass, General Patch's Seventh, coming down through Austria, and next day German resistance in Italy ceased. Italian partisans had already captured and killed Mussolini, on 28 April. Thus ended, in ruin, horror, and despair the Axis that pretended to rule the world, and the Reich which Hitler had boasted would last a thousand years.

Admiral Doenitz, Hitler's designated heir and second Fuehrer, tried desperately to arrange a surrender to the Western Allies, instead of to Russia. Loyalty to our Eastern ally — a loyalty not reciprocated — caused General Eisenhower sternly to decline these advances. On 7 May General Jodl signed an unconditional surrender at Allied headquarters in Rheims, and the war came to an end in the West.

5. Victory in the Pacific

Well before the landings on Leyte on 20 October 1944, the Joint Chiefs of Staff decided that as soon as the aircraft carrier fleet could be relieved from supporting MacArthur in the Philippines, it should help secure island bases for a final assault on Japan. Tokyo, Saipan, and Formosa make an isosceles triangle with legs 1500 miles long. The eastern leg, Saipan-Tokyo, was already being used by the B-29 Superforts to bomb the Japanese homeland, but a halfway house was wanted through which fighter support could stage, or where damaged Superforts could call. Iwo Jima fitted the bill. Kelly Turner's seasoned Fifth Fleet team, with Major General Harry Schmidt commanding the marines, landed on 19 February 1945. Mount Surabachi, scene of the famous flag-raising, was captured on 23 February; after that it was a steady, bloody advance of the marines against the holed-up enemy, with constant naval fire support. Even before organized resistance ceased on 14 March, the B-29's began using the Iwo airfields; and it is estimated that by this means thousands of American lives were saved. But Iwo Jima cost the navy and marine corps 6855 deaths and 21,000 other casualties.

In the meantime another angle of the triangle, whose apex was Tokyo, had been shifted to Okinawa in the Ryukyus, several hundred miles nearer Japan than is Formosa, and less stoutly defended. Sixty-mile-long Okinawa, where Commodore Perry had called in 1853, was an integral part of Japan. It was expected that when we attacked the Japanese would "throw the book at us," and they did. They had few warships left and American command of the sea prevented reinforcement of the island garrison; but they had plenty of planes and self-sacrificing pilots to employ the deadly kamikaze tactics. The Kamikaze ("Divine Wind") Corps was organized as a desperate expedient after the use of proximity-fuzed anti-aircraft shells by the United States Navy had made it almost impossible for a conventional bomber to hit a ship. The kamikaze pilots were trained to crash a ship, which meant certain death for a large part of its crew, and probable loss of the vessel. These tactics had already been tried in the Philippines campaign, with devastating success, and no defense against them had yet been found, except to station radar picket destroyers around the fleet, to take the rap and pass the word.

The Spruance-Turner team was in charge of the amphibious assault on Okinawa, with Lieutenant General Simon Bolivar Buckner (who lost his life there) commanding Tenth Army. American amphibious technique was now so perfected that when the four divisions went ashore on Okinawa on Easter Sunday, 1 April, the Japanese abandoned beaches and airfields and retired to prepared positions on the southern end of the island. Here they put up a desperate resistance, exacting a heavy toll of American lives, before the island was conquered late in June. In the meantime the navy, which had to cover the operation and furnish fire support, took a terrible beating from the kamikaze planes. Thirty-two ships were sunk, and sixty-one others were so badly damaged as to be out of the war; casualties were heavy even on the ships that survived. The carrier task force, besides supporting this operation, made carrier-plane raids on Tokyo and on Japanese airfields, and when the super-battleship *Yamato* sortied in early April, she was promptly sunk by air attack. Seven carriers were badly damaged by kamikazes — *Franklin*, *Wasp*, and *Bunker Hill* between them lost 2211 men killed and 798 wounded — but not one was sunk. The invasion of Okinawa cost us more than 12,500 sailors, soldiers, and aviators; but the island was indispensable as a base, not only in the closing weeks of World War II but in the cold war that followed.

Germany was now defeated and the Allies could give their undivided attention to knocking out Japan. A new British offensive, by land and sea, captured Mandalay and Rangoon in the spring of 1945 and pushed the Japanese out of Burma. While in great secrecy scientists were preparing the atomic bombs at Los Alamos, the navy and the army air force redoubled the fury of their attacks on the Japanese home islands. There were bombings by carrier planes, naval bombardments, and B-29 bombing raids. Large parts of Tokyo and other industrial cities were destroyed by incendiary bombs.

During these assaults on the outlying Japanese islands, General Eichelberger's Eighth Army and Admiral Kinkaid's Seventh Fleet — both under General MacArthur — were completing the liberation of the Philippines. They captured the ruins of Manila, where the Japanese made a house-to-house defense, on 4 March 1945. There the Philippine Commonwealth, soon to become the Philippine Republic, was already re-established by MacArthur. The General did not feel that he had redeemed his promise until the rest of the archipelago was liberated; and before Japan surrendered, Palawan, Panay, Negros, Cebu, Bohol, Mindanao, and Sulu had been taken by a series of assaults spearheaded by Rear Admiral Dan Barbey's VII 'Phib.

Nor must one forget the Pacific Fleet submarines whose destruction of merchant shipping was one of the three main factors that brought victory over Japan. Some 50 American submarines operating daily in the Pacific, in 1944 under Admiral Lockwood, were almost twice as effective as over 100 German U-boats operating daily in the Atlantic in 1942–43. Japan had 6 million tons of merchant shipping at the start of the war and added another 4 million tons by conquest and new construction; but at the end she had left only 1.8 million tons, mostly small wooden vessels in the Inland Sea, and was completely cut off from her island conquests. United States forces alone sank 2117 Japanese merchant vessels of almost 8 million tons during the war, and 60 per cent of this was done by submarines, of which 50 were lost in action. Japanese submarines sank several valuable warships but inflicted slight damage on the American merchant marine; and 128 of the Japanese submarines were lost, U.S.S. *England* sinking six in thirteen days of May 1944.

The Combined Chiefs of Staff, meeting at Quebec in September 1944, figured that it would take eighteen months after the surrender of Germany to defeat Japan. Actually, the war in the Pacific ended with a terrific bang only three months after V-E Day. President Truman and Winston Churchill, meeting with the C.C.S. at Potsdam, presented Japan with an ultimatum on 26 July 1945. The surrender must be complete, and include Allied occupation of Japan, and the return of all Japanese conquests since 1895 to their former owners. But the Japanese people were assured that the occupation would end as soon as "a peacefully inclined and responsible government" was established, and that they would neither "be enslaved as a race or destroyed as a nation." The alternative was "prompt and utter destruction." If Suzuki, the Japanese premier, had made up his mind promptly to accept the Potsdam declaration as a basis for peace, there would have been no atomic bomb explosion over Japan. But Suzuki was more afraid of the Japanese militarists than he was of American power.

The fearful consequences were the result of prolonged experiment and development in atomic fission. In 1939 Albert Einstein, Enrico Fermi, Leo Szilard, and other physicists who had sought refuge in the United States from tyranny in their native countries, warned President Roosevelt of the danger of Germany's obtaining a lead in uranium fission. The President entrusted a project of that nature to the Office of Scientific Research and Development, set up in May 1941. Before the end of that year Fermi and others achieved the first self-sustaining nuclear chain reaction, halfway mark to the atomic bomb. Army engineers under General W. S. Groves then took over and built a small city at Oak Ridge, Tennessee, for producing the atomic bomb. By 1944 research had so progressed that a special physics laboratory was erected at Los Alamos, New Mexico, for which J. R. Oppenheimer was responsible; and on 16 July 1945 the first atomic bomb was exploded there.

President Truman conveyed the news at Potsdam to Winston Churchill, who remarked, "This is the Second Coming, in wrath." That indeed it was for Japan.

We had it, but whether or not to use it was another question. President Truman's committee of high officials and top atomic scientists recommended that atomic bombs be exploded over Japan at once, and without warning. On 25 July the President issued the necessary order to the XX Army Air Force at Saipan, whither the first two bombs had been sent, to prepare to drop them at the first favorable moment after 3 August, if Japan had not by then accepted surrender. He and Secretary of State Byrnes waited in vain for word from Japan. All they got was a silly statement from Suzuki that the Potsdam Declaration was unworthy of notice. So the fateful order stood.

"Enola Gay," as the chosen B-29 was called, was commanded by Colonel Paul W. Tibbets. At 9:15 a.m., 6 August, the bomb was toggled out at an altitude of 31,600 feet over Hiroshima. This city had been given the tragic target assignment as the second most important military center in Japan. The bomb wiped out the Second Japanese Army to a man, razed four square miles of the city, and killed 60,175 people, including the soldiers. Around noon 9 August, a few hours after Russia had declared war on Japan, the second atomic bomb exploded over Nagasaki, killing 36,000 more.[1]

Although many Americans have expressed contrition over exploding the first atomic bombs, it is difficult to see how the Pacific war could otherwise have been concluded, except by a long and bitter invasion of Japan; or what difference it would have made after the war if the secret had temporarily been withheld. The explosion over Hiroshima caused fewer civilian casualties than the repeated B-29 bombings of Tokyo, and those big bombers would have had to wipe out one city after another if the war had not ended in August. Japan had enough military capability — more than 5000 planes with kamikaze-trained pilots and at least 2 million ground troops — to have made our planned invasion of the Japanese home islands in the fall of 1945 an exceedingly bloody affair for both sides. And that would have been followed by a series of bitterly protracted battles on Japanese soil, the effects of which even time could hardly have healed. Moreover, as Russia would have been a full partner in these campaigns, the end result would have been partition of Japan, as happened to Germany.

1. Official Japanese statement of 31 July 1959 for Hiroshima. Samuel Glasstone, *Effects of Nuclear Weapons* (Atomic Energy Commission, 1957), p. 455, for Nagasaki.

Even after the two atomic bombs had been dropped, and the Potsdam declaration had been clarified to assure Japan that she could keep her emperor, the surrender was a very near thing. Hirohito had to override his two chief military advisers and take the responsibility of accepting the Potsdam terms. That he did on 14 August, but even after that a military coup d'état to sequester the emperor, kill his cabinet, and continue the war was narrowly averted. Hirohito showed great moral courage; and the promise to retain him in power despite the wishes of Russia (which wanted the war prolonged and Japan given over to anarchy) was a very wise decision.

After preliminary arrangements had been made at Manila with General MacArthur's and Admiral Nimitz's staffs, an advance party was flown into Atsugi airfield near Tokyo on 28 August. Scores of ships of the United States Pacific Fleet, and of the British Far Eastern Fleet, then entered Tokyo Bay. On 2 September 1945 General MacArthur, General Umezu, the Japanese foreign minister, and representatives of Great Britain, China, Russia, Australia, Canada, New Zealand, the Netherlands, and France, signed the surrender documents on the deck of battleship *Missouri*, a few miles from the spot where Commodore Perry's treaty had been signed eighty-two years before.

At 9:25 a.m., as the formalities closed, a flight of hundreds of aircraft swept over *Missouri* and her sister ships. General MacArthur then addressed a broadcast to the people of the United States:

Today the guns are silent. A great tragedy has ended. A great victory has been won. . . .

A new era is upon us. . . . Victory itself brings with it profound concern, both for our future security, and the survival of civilization.

Men since the beginning of time have sought peace. . . . Military alliances, balances of power, leagues of nations, all in turn failed, leaving the only path to be by the way of the crucible of war. . . .

The utter destructiveness of war now blots out this alternative. We have had our last chance. If we do not devise some greater and more equitable system, Armageddon will be at our door. The problem basically is theological and involves a spiritual recrudescence. . . .

L X

The Truman Administrations

1945-1953

1. The Iron Curtain

BEFORE BEWILDERED Harry Truman takes the helm on 12 April 1945, one month before the end of the war in Europe and four months before victory in the Pacific, we must speak of relations with Russia in the latter part of the Roosevelt regime.

Almost every American admired Russia's war effort and wished to remain friendly with her government and people. But this did not suit Stalin. Churchill and Roosevelt made several basic errors in their relations with the Soviets. First, they believed that if they were "nice to Russia" and helped her to the extent of their ability, Russia would co-operate to support a free world — in the Western sense — after the war. Nothing could have been more mistaken. Stalin could, when he chose, be very pleasant and reasonable as in the conferences at Tehran and Yalta; even at Potsdam after the death of Roosevelt, who liked referring to him as "Uncle Joe." The flapdoodle written about Stalin by such people as Eric Johnson, president of the American Chamber of Commerce, and Ambassador Joseph Davies, is astounding. Davies, who lived at Moscow in an atmosphere of caviar and champagne, even declared that to question Stalin's good faith was "bad Christianity, bad sportsmanship, bad sense." Wendell Willkie glorified the Russian regime in his book *One World*. Roosevelt had the conceit to suppose that his personal charm could win over Stalin; but it bounced off that human steel like echo-ranging sonar off the hull of a U-boat. Even Truman returned from Potsdam saying, "I like Uncle Joe," and telling how they had discussed (through an interpreter) the raising of corn and pigs. Actually, Stalin never abandoned the Communist party's objective of revolutionizing the world. He naturally accepted all the help he could get from the Western powers in his war with Hitler, but he intended to control every country bordering Russia on the west, and to revolutionize the rest of Europe with the aid of communists in Italy and France; the more useful to him and dangerous to their own countries by virtue of their guerrilla experience resisting Hitler and Mussolini. Ambassador Averell Harriman and George Kennan warned Washington what would happen after the war, but nobody of importance listened, and the policy of "be nice to Russia" continued.

The second reason why the Western Allies went all out to please Stalin was the indispensability of Russia's war effort. Hitler put forth Germany's greatest strength on the eastern front, where Russia, nearly to the end of the war, engaged between 125 and 200 German divisions. It was essential for victory in the West that this vast host continue on the eastern front. Here the Western Allies paid the penalty for not having managed to beat Germany a year earlier, when they would have had far less need of Russian support.

Russia had been neutral to the war in the Pacific, but the Western Allies mistakenly assumed that Japan could not be defeated without Russian aid. Otherwise, it was feared, the Allies would have to fight a long and bloody campaign against a Japanese army in Manchuria after conquering Japan. The Combined Chiefs of Staff badly wanted Russia to declare war on Japan; even General MacArthur prior to Yalta said it was necessary. Actually, Allied military intelligence was so defective that without its knowledge the strongest elements of the Japanese army in Manchuria had been removed to defend the Marianas, Okinawa, and the home islands; by mid-1945 that army was a mere "paper tiger," to use a favorite Chinese phrase.

The final mistake was the assumption that a joint regime, communist and non-communist, would work in defeated or liberated countries, like the "popular front" governments before the war. Churchill visited Moscow in October 1944 and negotiated with Stalin a division of spheres of future influence in the Balkans. The British were to have Greece, the Russians Romania, and they would split Yugoslavia and Hungary fifty-fifty. Roosevelt and the state department did not like this, as savoring of secret treaties in World War I, but did nothing about it. The event proved that no popular front with communists could have any other result but a Communist party take-over. It was not generally known that within a month of the death of Hitler, Moscow had ordered all communists everywhere to restore the "hard line."

All these false assumptions prevailed when Churchill and Roosevelt met Stalin at Yalta in the Crimea in February 1945. The Battle of the Bulge was then barely over, the Philippines had not yet been liberated or Okinawa even invaded. Five months earlier, future lines of demarcation between the Russian and Allied armies in Germany had been agreed upon; and at the moment, when the Western Allies had not even crossed the Rhine, the Russians were fast approaching the Oder river. Moreover, the atomic bomb had not yet been tried out; the army told Roosevelt that he could not depend on it. Had it been tried and a proved success, the anxiety about Russian support either in the West or in the East would not have existed.

This is the background to the agreements at Yalta. In return for Stalin's promise to fight Japan two or three months at most after Germany surrendered, Russia was promised the southern half of Sakhalin Island, which Japan had won in her war of 1904, and the recognition of her "pre-eminent interests" in Manchuria; and the Allies promised to make Chiang recognize these interests. The touchy subject of money reparations from Germany was postponed. Poland, on which Russia had inflicted two of the dirtiest deals of the war — the Katyn massacre of captured Polish officers, and the halt of Russian armies ten miles from Warsaw to enable the Nazis to massacre Polish patriots — was "sold down the river." Stalin refused to recognize the noncommunist Polish government-in-exile which had been functioning in London for six years. His own puppet Polish government was already set up, and his only concession was to promise to add a few democratic leaders to that government. He also agreed to establish interim governments, "broadly representative of all democratic elements," in the rest of liberated Europe — Austria, Hungary, Czechoslovakia, Bulgaria, and Romania — to be followed by free elections. These agreements were merely oral, not defined in a treaty; for in the "spirit of Yalta" Roosevelt and Churchill trusted that Stalin would keep faith, which he never had any intention of doing.

The Yalta agreements, even the one about Poland, might have worked if they had been respected by Stalin; but none of them were except the promise to fight Japan, which delivered Manchuria to Russia in return for a five days' war.

Wherever Russian armies penetrated — excepting Austria and Czechoslovakia — they set up communist governments, and the local Communist Party saw to it that the elections, if held at all, would be a farce. By mid-March 1945 Winston Churchill was writing to Roosevelt that everything in Europe supposedly settled at Yalta had broken down, and F.D.R. showed signs of admitting error before his death on 12 April. In the meantime, General Eisenhower, in accordance with the Yalta agreements, had pulled Patton's army back from Prague, since Czechoslovakia was in the Soviet sphere of influence, and allowed Russian troops to take Berlin. Even if these positions had later been abandoned, they would have been good bargaining points.

Thus the cold war began as soon as the hot war was over. Earl Browder, head of the Communist party in the United States, was the first victim of the "hard line." For his continuing to preach friendly collaboration between the United States and Russia, which he had been ordered to do in 1941, he was contemptuously deposed in May 1945 by orders from Moscow. This caused all his lieutenants to weep and grovel for having "deserted the workers." Browder was replaced by William Z. Foster, willing to follow the "party line" wheresoever it might lead. The Russian government confidently expected capitalist society to collapse as a result of the war — for had not Karl Marx so prophesied? — and that the Western Allies would be unable to prevent communism from taking over one country after another. The United Nations had already been formed, but Stalin counted on neutralizing it if he could not control it.

Harry Truman, acceding to the presidency on 12 April 1945, knew little of what had been going on. He naturally tried to continue the policy of collaboration with Russia in the hope that Stalin would prove reasonable. Averell Harriman, American ambassador at Moscow, warned him that Russia was violating most of the Yalta agreements; but he thought, and Truman agreed, that Russian need for American financial aid in reconstruction would keep Stalin in line. And it was largely to obtain reassurance from Russia that Truman attended the last of the big wartime conferences, at Potsdam, on 17 July 1945. He and Clement Attlee, the new Labour premier of Great Britain (Winston Churchill having been defeated in a general election), agreed to what they supposed to be temporary arrangements, pending a general peace treaty. For occupation purposes Germany was divided down the middle, and as a result the Russians proceeded to strip East Germany of most of its machinery and set up a communist government there. West Germany was divided into three zones of occupation between Britain, the United States and France. And, as a minor reflection of this partition, both Berlin and Vienna were divided into occupation zones. The Western powers also acquiesced in Russian annexation of eastern Poland, and in the Polish Reds' occupying East Prussia and Germany up to the Neisse river.

The Potsdam agreements, concluded after the need for Russian armed help had ceased, but while Russian armies occupied most of eastern Europe, were less excusable than those of Yalta, but still defensible as one more effort to win Russia to a stable peace settlement. So it is not surprising that both agreements came to be regarded by average citizens of the United States and Great Britain — not to speak of those of Poland, Austria, and the other countries who suffered from them — as a gross betrayal of the principles for which the Western Allies had been fighting. "Yalta" became a pejorative word, a signal for booes and hisses at Republican and other rallies. These agreements and the settlements that stemmed from them were based on the fallacy that the golden rule would work on the Russian government, which regarded Christian ethics as outmoded, and agreements or treaties to be respected only so long as they aided the supposed interests of "the revolution." The enormous backlog of good will that Russia had built up in Britain and the United States, and on which she could have drawn for relief and reconstruction, was dissipated by this mad grasp for power. But it took a long time to dissipate. A strong section of the British Labour party, and hundreds of French and Italian intellectuals, continued to defend Stalin's every move and to attack the United States as a "warmongering, imperialist" power.

In America many liberal elements — notably *The Nation,* now edited by Freda Kirchwey — similarly played dupes. Charles A. Beard in his last book warned readers that Truman was trying to pick a quarrel with Russia; and in 1948 a splinter party was formed on this assumption under the aegis of former Vice President Wallace, who insisted that only continual concessions to Russia would ensure world peace. As late as 1958 Bertrand Russell, the most vocal British spokesman of this point of view, wrote that if "no alternative remains except communist domination or the extinction of the human race, the former alternative is the lesser of two evils." Translated into the slogan "Better Red than Dead," and promoted by "Ban the Bomb" parades in

England and America, this apparently inescapable dilemma made a wide appeal.

Winston Churchill, speaking before President Truman in March 1946 at Westminster College in Fulton, Missouri, said, "From Stettin in the Baltic to Trieste in the Adriatic an iron curtain has descended across the Continent." It certainly had; and presently another iron curtain would shut out most of the Asiatic continent. But years had to elapse before people recognized a basic principle: the children of a big revolution, such as Napoleon, Hitler, Mussolini, Stalin, and Mao, can never stop. To satisfy their followers they have to postulate dangers from within and without, and drive on and on until they win all, or lose all. They may make truces, but never peace. Dean Acheson, who pointed this out in 1946, and President Truman, after he had considered all possible alternatives, came to the conclusion that the only possible way to deal with Russia in such wise as to prevent another and more terrible world war, was to convince her that she could not profit by war. Congressional revival of the army draft in 1948 was one sign. Truman's decision in January 1950, to continue and intensify research and production of thermonuclear weapons, definitely marks the adoption of this policy by the United States government. From the vantage point of 1964, it appears to have succeeded.

2. Harry's First Term

Harry S Truman, almost sixty-one years old at his accession, was an inconspicuous-looking President, but one of the most conspicuously successful. He could easily have got lost in a crowd, so typically Middle-Western were his face and figure; but he had in abundance the courage and integrity which were most needed during the postwar years, and good judgment as well. By experience Truman was as well prepared for the presidency as any of his immediate predecessors — a farm and small-town childhood, service in World War I, ward politics in Kansas City, country grass-root politics, and ten years in the United States Senate. Eastern Republicans said, "Who's Truman?" just as the Whigs in 1844 said, "Who is Polk?" They soon found out.

Harry was brought up on a prosperous 440-acre farm in Jackson County, Missouri. There were all kinds of animals which the boy learned to handle, corn to shuck, wheat to thresh, and hay to pitch; and this background lasted in his speech and earthy wit. At the age of six his parents removed to Independence, the old jumping-off place of the Oregon Trail, then a typical country town. The Trumans had been Confederates in the Civil War — the President's mother said she would rather sleep on the floor of the White House than in Lincoln's bed! — and Democrats ever since. Bible readers, they indoctrinated Harry with a love of good literature, especially history; as a lad he read avidly Plutarch's Lives, Jacob Abbott's popular works, and the history of the Civil War, about which his family and neighbors were rich in stories and legends. Few statesmen have profited as much from history as Truman did; from the antics of the Republican Radicals in 1862–65 he learned how to avoid pitfalls when he became chairman of a senate committee on World War II; from Andrew Johnson's conduct he learned mistakes to be avoided when succeeding a great President; from General McClellan's case he learned how to deal with an insubordinate general; and from Jefferson's example in the Alien and Sedition hysteria of 1798 he learned to keep calm in the presence of Joe McCarthy.

As a youth Harry worked in a bank in Kansas City, joined the National Guard and, as a captain of field artillery, fought in the St. Mihiel and Meuse-Argonne campaigns of 1918. Returning to Independence, he married his early love, Bess Wallace, opened a haberdashery in Kansas City which failed in the postwar recession, and entered local politics. Under the aegis of the Pendergasts, Tammany-type bosses of Kansas City, he was elected a county official. In this office he was proud of having good modern roads constructed to help the farmers get about. Jim Pendergast, who wanted a friend in the United States Senate, helped Harry to get elected in 1934, much as Daugherty had promoted Harding; but in the Senate Truman proved to be of a different breed from the hapless good fellow of Marion. As chairman of a special committee to investigate the national defense program he attracted the attention of President and public by issuing a series of devastating though constructive reports, exposing the haphazard and wasteful manner in which war contracts had been awarded on the cost-plus basis, extortion by labor unions, and the shoving aside of small business. These led to his being on the winning ticket in 1944. Now he was President of the United States. On his first day of office Truman remarked to a newspaperman. "Did you ever have a bull or a load of hay fall on you? If you ever did, you know how I felt last night."

President Truman's native intelligence enabled him to grasp quickly the situation into which he was so suddenly thrown, and on which he had not been briefed by Roosevelt. He had to have a few boon companions from Missouri around the White House for relaxation, but he won the friendship and respect of gentlemen in politics such as Dean Acheson, soldiers such as General Marshall, and foreign statesmen such as Clement Attlee. He made good cabinet, judicial, and ambassadorial appointments; he kept a firm hand on the new department of defense and the foreign service; and with more fateful decisions than almost any President in our time, he made the fewest mistakes. Truman was always folksy, always the politician, but nobody can reasonably deny that he attained the stature of a statesman. He was magnanimous to critics and opponents — unless they did something he considered personally insulting such as criticizing his daughter Margaret's singing. Criticism of his own piano playing he did not mind.

We may now mention some domestic problems of Truman's first administration, although the situation was such that no issue could be completely isolated as domestic. Demobilization, for instance. No sooner was the war over than a popular clamor arose to "send the boys home." The army planned to discharge 5.5 million men by 1 July 1946, but this was too slow to suit the voters, and congressional pressure forced the army to speed it up. By the spring of 1950 it was down to 600,000 men and there were only ten divisions even partially ready for action — fewer than in Belgium and Holland. "It was no demobilization, it was a rout," said General Marshall. America was deprived of deterrent ground forces, and communist hopes were raised that America as a great power was slipping, by the will of the people.

To offset this impression of weakness, America confounded all the Marxist prophets by remaining prosperous. There was an enormous unsatisfied demand for consumer goods, which did not want purchasers, as almost every class in the community had money to spend. The new cars were attractive, although double the prices of 1941 models. Television, now nation-wide, dishwashing machines, and electric stoves absorbed millions of dollars. Prices went up, too, especially after Congress in 1946 removed most of the restrictions, but incomes went up even more. Even the farmers continued to benefit from high war prices for their cattle, grains, and cotton because of the demand in Europe, and the federal government's willingness to extend credit so that Europeans could buy them.

Veterans were easily absorbed into industry, and even more readily into schools. An act of Congress known as "the G.I. Bill of Rights" in 1944 offered full scholarships in colleges or universities or trade schools with subsistence, for a maximum of four years, to every able and honorably discharged member of the armed forces who applied. Some 12 million men and women availed themselves of the privilege. There was, of course, a great deal of waste in the scheme — chiropractor academies and sundry degree mills were hurriedly organized to get G.I. dollars — but on the whole it was a brilliant success, rendering several million young Americans better prepared to cope with life in an atomic age. In addition, Senator J. W. Fulbright of Arkansas fathered a bill to provide for exchange of teachers and students between American and foreign universities.

President Truman did his best to prevent a postwar reaction such as that of the 1920's. In his address of 5 September 1945 to Congress he outlined a 21-point program of progressive legislation, in accordance with a "Fair Deal," as he renamed the no longer New Deal. But Congress and the country were in no mood for more social experiments. He was also troubled by the attitude of labor. During the war the unions had been riding high, and their members made big money out of war-pressured overtime. Once the war was over and industry converted to peacetime production, management did not attempt to reduce wages but cut out overtime, and many workers were furious at having their "take-home pay" thus reduced by as much as 50 per cent. At the same time the cost of living was rising sharply because Congress refused to continue price controls as Truman requested. On the plea of the cattlemen and packers that if controls were taken off beef everyone could have beefsteak, the legal limit was removed in July 1946, and beefsteak jumped from around 50 cents to over a dollar a pound, where it has been ever since. Eight basic commodities jumped 25 per cent, and "real wages" declined 12 per cent in one year.

These were the main reasons for strikes for higher wages in coal, motor cars, steel, electric appliances, and railroads. The coal strike threatened American industry and European recovery, and John L. Lewis, the leader responsible, defied both President and courts and got away with it. The strike of the railway brotherhoods, hitherto the most conservative and responsible unions, threatened to tie up the entire transportation system; Truman ended that by promising to use the army to operate the trains. The arrogance and irresponsibility of union labor leaders, a poor return for their favors from the New Deal, produced a strong anti-union feeling in the public which was reflected in the congressional elections of 1946. A Republican majority in both houses was returned for the first time in fifteen years. And the new 80th Congress passed the Taft-Hartley Act which outlawed the closed shop, made unions liable for damages caused by breach of contract, required a 60-day "cooling-off period" before a strike, forbade unions to make political contributions or exact excessive dues, and required elected union officials to take an oath that they were not communists. It was passed over the President's veto and despite outraged cries from labor leaders that the bill meant "slavery" and "fascism" for the workers. That was nonsense, as the status of union labor in 1964 proves; but this act, which is a tribute to the political courage and integrity of Senator Robert Taft, produced a salutary purging of communists who had infiltrated the unions (not, unfortunately, of the criminal element as well) and forced the union leaders, with some notable exceptions, to be more circumspect and less greedy.

President Truman continued Harold Ickes, watchdog of the national domain, as secretary of the interior; but Ickes resigned with loud snorts in 1946 because Truman nominated as undersecretary of the navy Edwin W. Pauley, a Texas oil magnate who had his eye on the tideland oil reserves. Pauley's nomination was withdrawn and Truman defended these oil reserves, but during the Eisenhower administration Congress presented them, up to the three-mile limit, to the Gulf states and California.

Although Truman came from a former slave state, he was sympathetic with the demands of Negroes for a civil rights act to secure them their long-denied right to vote in the lower South, and at least diminish their other disabilities. Congress not only refused to pass a civil rights bill but, when the Democratic party at the presidential nominating convention of 1948 adopted a strong civil rights plank and renominated Truman, many Southern Democrats seceded from the convention, waving the Confederate battle flag, and formed a splinter party, the so-called Dixiecrats. They held a convention at Montgomery, the old Confederate capital, and nominated Governor Strom Thurmond of South Carolina for the presidency. At the other end of the political spectrum a new progressive party was formed, with former Vice President Henry Wallace as leader, on the issue that Truman was risking war with Russia. At the same time, things were going badly for the United States in China, and McCarthyism — of which more anon — was raising its ugly head. So, when the Republicans again nominated Governor Dewey, almost everyone but Harry thought that they would win.

Truman waged an aggressive campaign, denouncing the 80th Congress as only he could, and everywhere addressing enthusiastic crowds who cried, "Pour it on, Harry!" "Give it to 'em!" He won over 50 per cent of the vote and 304 electoral votes. Dewey, a poor campaigner, with an unimpressive personality, got 44 per cent of the popular vote, but only 189 in the electoral college. Thurmond carried several states of the lower South, with 39 electoral votes; Wallace, with a popular vote of over a million, carried not one state. And the Democrats recaptured control of Congress.

Harry Truman could now look forward to four years as "President in his own right" — and a troubled term indeed it was.

3. The United Nations and the Cold War

The United Nations was established shortly after Truman became President, and he entertained high hopes of its ability to quench the angry passions of postwar and prevent a new war. Secretary Hull had initiated the movement under President Roosevelt who, profiting by Woodrow Wilson's mistakes, took care to have prominent Republicans included in every committee appointed to plan this new international organization. Senator Arthur H. Vandenberg of Michigan, once a forthright isolationist, undertook the task of bringing his colleagues around to international co-operation. A meeting of representatives of Great Britain, the United States, Russia, and China at Washington in the autumn of 1944 drafted a preliminary outline, basis of the charter which issued from a plenary conference of fifty different nations at San Francisco in April 1945.

The charter of the United Nations established an international body measurably stronger than the old League of Nations. But it had the same basic defect of giving each of the "big five" on the top Security Council — the United States, Britain, Russia, China, and France — a veto on every decision. This veto was not proposed by Russia, although she exercised it *ad nauseam*; it was insisted upon by Britain and America because their respective governments knew that the people would never consent to ratification without such protection to their sovereignty. Russia also wanted a veto on discussions in the Security Council, but did not get that. Each member nation had one vote in the General Assembly, and complete freedom of discussion there. The point in which the United Nations went beyond the old League was a provision for the use of force against aggression. The Security Council could recommend the General Assembly to sever diplomatic relations, or apply economic sanctions, or go to war against an aggressor. It could even set up a permanent international military force; but owing to Russian opposition, this never came about. It had the right to appoint a commission (UNESCO) to help backward or impoverished nations, and to draw up an international Bill of Rights. Both were done, and UNESCO did a great deal of good, considering its limited budget; but the Bill of Rights has remained a dead letter to most of the members of the new league.

The Senate ratified the United Nations charter by a vote of 89 to 2 on 28 July 1945; and on 10 January 1946 the first session of the Assembly of 51 nations met in London. Next year the Sperry plant at Lake Success, Long Island, became the temporary home of the United Nations, which decided to have its permanent headquarters in the United States. After investigating various sites on the Eastern seaboard, the UN settled on New York City as its capital, and built the high building at the foot of East 43rd Street, where it has been since 1950.

Until the United Nations began functioning, the situation in Europe had to be dealt with in another manner. At Potsdam a Council of Foreign Ministers of the big powers was set up to oversee the Allied Control Council, which in turn oversaw the military administration of occupied Germany and Austria.

Efforts of the Allied Control Council to revive German industry and give the defeated people something to live for, were thwarted by Russian insistence on gutting German factories under the excuse of reparations; the real motive being to reduce that country to such a state that it would turn in despair to communism. James F. Byrnes, new secretary of state, declared in September 1946 that his country would no longer accept responsibility for "the needless aggravation of economic distress" caused by the Allied Control Council's failing to agree on anything, owing to Russia's repeated *niet*.

In the meantime, the trial of German war criminals at Nuremberg, whose records revealed an unimaginable depth of depravity, were being held, and twelve high Nazis, including Goering, Jodl, and Ribbentrop, were sentenced to death. The occupying authorities were also concerned with the "denazification" of Germany and the encouragement of the supposedly purified electorate to set up a new republican government, which was done in 1949.

An enormous relief program, abbreviated as UNRRA, was set up by the Allies before the end of the war and adopted by the United Nations. Under the successive leads of Governor Herbert H. Lehman and Mayor Fiorello H. La Guardia, UNRRA spent about a billion dollars a year — the United States contributing 68 per cent — for relief in continental Europe. UNRRA had responsibility for feeding and, if possible, resettling displaced persons, of whom there were almost ten million in Europe — Germans driven out of Poland and Czechoslovakia, Slavs who fled before advancing Russian armies, and others. It spent a large part of its effort and money transporting Jews, who saw no future for themselves in Europe, to the British-mandated territory of Palestine, thus creating a new problem for the United Nations.

The United States also initiated easing trade restrictions, stabilizing currencies, and encouraging investment. The reciprocal trade agreements which F.D.R. inaugurated in 1934 were renewed in 1945; and two years later some 40 nations, meeting at Geneva, agreed on sweeping tariff reductions. So far as the United States was concerned, the effect was to reduce duties to the 1913 level. American imports increased from a prewar average of less than $3 billion to more than $7 billion in 1948.

In 1943 the treasury department, consulting with corresponding departments in several other countries, began laying plans to stabilize currencies and provide credit for postwar international trade and investment. An international conference which met in the summer of 1944 at Bretton Woods, New Hampshire, drafted, and Congress ratified, two new agencies: the International Monetary Fund and the International Bank for Reconstruction and Development. The Fund, designed to stabilize exchange rates and discourage restrictions on international payments, was provided initially with a capital of $8.8 billion, to which the United States contributed about one-third. The International or World Bank had authority to lend and borrow money and to underwrite private loans for eligible projects.

What was to done about atomic energy and the bomb? Experiments at Bikini Atoll in the Marshall Islands in 1946 confirmed what the wartime explosions at Hiroshima and Nagasaki had indicated, that mankind had acquired a force which, if uncontrolled, could destroy civilization. At its first session the United Nations general assembly appointed an atomic energy commission on which twelve countries were represented. Bernard Baruch, the American member, presented a plan for creating an international authority to control every phase of the production of atomic energy, using it only for peaceful purposes, and forbidding the further manufacture of atomic weapons. Had this plan been adopted, America would have destroyed her stock of atomic bombs and made no more. Considering that the United States then had a monopoly of atomic weapons, this was a magnanimous proposal, and all countries on the atomic energy commission accepted it except Russia and Poland. They refused, pretending to regard as espionage the inspection necessary to enforce the plan, but really because they hoped and expected, through the work of their own scientists and the use of atomic secrets stolen from the United States, to match or surpass the American atomic arsenal. Russia made the counter-proposal that the United States destroy all her atomic weapons immediately, and every country promise to manufacture no more. As no such promise, without the sanction of inspection, was worth the paper it was written on, the Russian proposal got nowhere. But, considering the vast amount of breast-beating that there has been in the United States about the atomic bomb, we should remember that the Baruch plan offered to renounce American superiority in the race for more destructive weapons, if every country would devote atomic research to peaceful objects and permit inspection.

In Great Britain even the imposition of controls on trading by the Labour government did not prevent a financial crisis in 1947. The United States government extended a loan of $3.75 billion, but that did not recoup the loss of Britain's former export markets. At the same time, the economy of France, Italy, and other countries was teetering on the verge of collapse, with prospects of communist takeover to follow. To check this, General George C. Marshall, now secretary of state, announced at Harvard Commencement in 1947 what became known as the Marshall Plan. President Truman was behind it, and George Kennan on the policy planning staff of the state department had a good deal to do with working it out. The key idea was this: European countries which needed help should make their own reconstruction plans, not so much for immediate relief as "to permit the emergence of political and social conditions in which free institutions can exist"; the United States would provide the cash to get started. The essence, as Marshall made clear, was that the European nations must plan themselves.

Marshall's idea was taken up with enthusiasm by every European country not under communist control. Sixteen nations sent representatives to a conference in Paris, which drew up a comprehensive plan for European recovery: — new factories, new hydro-electric projects, monetary stability, lowering of trade barriers, and a thousand different things. Russia, offered the same benefits, rejected them as a cloak for American capitalist exploitation, and prevented her satellites from joining. (The real reason for Russian opposition was fear that the plan would destroy Stalin's hope for a general capitalist collapse.) Truman presented the Marshall Plan to Congress in December 1947, recommending that the United States contribute $17 billion out of the total four-year estimate of $22 billion. The leading champion of the bill in the Senate was Senator Vandenberg; the leading opponent, Senator Taft. While Congress was still arguing pro and con in February 1948, the communists pulled off a coup d'état in democratic Czechoslovakia, taking over of a country with which Americans had many strong racial and sentimental ties. America's old friend Premier Beneš was liquidated by the classic Prague method of defenestration, and the iron curtain clanged down outside that unfortunate country.

This made votes for the Foreign Assistance Act, passed by heavy majorities on 3 April 1948. Congress voted $5.3 billion immediately for the Marshall Plan, and an additional $275 million for Greece and Turkey. This was only a beginning of foreign aid by the United States, which came to $80 billion by 1 July 1961.

In retrospect, the Marshall Plan was the best thing the United States could have done for Europe; and the factor that made it work was Europe's enthusiasm and positive contribution, in brains, money, and know-how, to saving herself. Communists did their best to sabotage it by propaganda, by persuading stevedores to refuse to handle American shipments, and by other tricks of the Marxian trade; but in spite of their efforts, and of the initial skepticism of old-fashioned European industrialists, the economy of the once war-ravaged countries built up so rapidly that in a little more than a decade the balance of trade with the United States had turned in Europe's favor.

Strokes and counterstrokes in the cold war went on through 1947 and 1948. The first showdown occurred in the Mediterranean, where the West won three rounds. Russia, in an effort to expand her dependent empire of communist satellites, was putting intolerable pressure on the government of Iran (Persia), threatening Turkey, and supporting a civil war against the government of Greece; a particularly cruel war, since the communist guerrillas, invading from Albania, Yugoslavia, and Bulgaria, carried off thousands of Greek children for forced labor. Great Britain, which had been giving extensive financial and military aid to the Greek government but was now in the midst of her financial crisis, gave notice that she would have to abandon Greece and Turkey. President Truman made a quick decision to pick up both. On 12 March 1947 he sent a message to Congress embodying not only a request for appropriations for Greece and Turkey, but what came to be known as the Truman Doctrine. One of the primary objectives of the foreign policy of the United States, he said, "is the creation of conditions in which we and other nations will be able to work out a way of life free from coercion. . . . I believe that it must be the policy of the United States to support freed peoples who are resisting attempted subjugation by armed minorities or by outside pressures."

Truman felt so strongly about this that he even went in person to the House ways and means committee to lobby for aid to Greece — an unprecedented step for a President. He told me in 1960 how reporters flocked around the doors which shut them from the secret hearing; how Senator Taft, who had opposed every European commitment, got up and left the room in the middle of it, and Truman thought, "My God! he's going to give them a hostile statement and wreck the whole thing!" But Taft told them nothing and supported the appropriation for aid to Greece. All left-wing elements in the United States deplored this. They insisted that the Greek monarchy was out of date, corrupt, inept; the virile Communist party should be allowed to take over. They were disappointed. King Paul of Greece exhibited such skill and energy as to win the civil war; and Tito, the communist dictator of Yugoslavia, having broken temporarily with Stalin, refused any longer to harbor guerrillas. Turkey so strengthened her defenses as to become almost impregnable; and Stalin, deciding that this *Drang nach Osten* did not pay, stopped harassing Iran.

Another crucial spot where England abdicated was Palestine. She had held the mandate here since 1919, and in accordance with Balfour's promise of 1917, facilitated Jewish immigration to their motherland. This aroused the implacable hostility of the Arab population, which insisted on limiting the Jewish quota to a mere trickle. That was impossible to enforce after World War II, when thousands of displaced Jews from central and eastern Europe who were wanted nowhere else, were eager to go to Palestine; and many did, illegally. President Truman took an active interest in their plight, but the British government announced that it could no longer keep the peace and must give up its Palestine mandate. The United Nations now rendered a judgment of Solomon, dividing Palestine between two Arab kingdoms, Lebanon and Jordan, and a new Republic of Israel. The United States recognized Israel in January 1949. Military experts and thousands of others denounced this as a great mistake, predicting that the Arabs would soon drive the Jews into the Dead Sea. But Israel, supported by Zionists in Europe and America, has become a virile modern republic despite a constant state of war with her Arab neighbors, and the implacable enmity of Egypt.

There were strokes and counterstrokes in Europe too. After the Western Allies had helped West Germany to set up a representative government (Russia having refused to co-operate), Stalin on 24 June 1948 ordered a blockade of the non-communist zones of Berlin, hoping to squeeze out the Allies and annex their zones to East Germany. General Lucius D. Clay, the stalwart and intelligent commander of American occupation forces in Europe, warned the President that to lose Berlin would be to lose the entire Western position in Europe; and Harry saw the point. The American and British air forces promptly organized an airlift by transport planes that fed, clothed, and heated West Berlin for 321 days; 2.5 million tons of supplies were flown in, and the city's products flown out. The Berlin airlift was a striking demonstration of what air power could accomplish, and of the value of firmness and strength when confronting communists. Stalin ended the blockade on 12 May 1949, but minor hampering of trains, motor convoys, and aircraft which have to cross East Germany to reach Berlin, has continued.

This menace, in return, brought about another initiative by President Truman, resulting in the North Atlantic Treaty of 4 April 1949 between the United States, Canada, and ten nations of Western Europe. Each pledged itself to resist any armed attack against any one member. Under this treaty NATO, the North Atlantic Treaty Organization, was set up. Never before had the United States gone so far in a peacetime promise to fight under certain conditions, or to recognize a frontier extending far overseas. The Senate ratified it by a vote of 82 to 13; one of the negative votes being that of Senator Taft, who declared that NATO might seem to threaten Russia and provoke her to attack. The President's military assistance program for the NATO nations was accepted by the House, and the first shipments of arms reached Europe that month. General Eisenhower resigned the presidency of Columbia University to become supreme commander of NATO forces; Britain, France, and Italy began rearming, and in 1954 West Germany was admitted. Russia looked upon the creation of NATO as a declaration of hostility; pacifists and left-wingers everywhere deplored its existence as "shaking the mailed fist," and all that; but there can no longer be any doubt that the NATO armed forces were a major deterrent to Russia's trying any more communist putsches in Europe.

Truman's policy, "containment" as it was called, worked. Russia made no conquests in Western Europe or the Near East after her military occupations in the confused period immediately following the war. But containment was not applied early enough in the Far East.

4. China and the Occupation of Japan

The basic cause of the Pacific war of 1941–45 was the attempt of the United States to protect the integrity of China against Japan. Yet, a few years after the war was over, China became an implacable enemy of America, and within twenty years, so great a threat to world peace as to alarm even Russia. How could this have happened? The answer, in a word, is the weakness of Generalissimo Chiang Kai-shek's *kuomintang* or nationalist government, and the cleverness of the Chinese communists in exploiting that weakness.

Throughout the war, Roosevelt treated Chiang's China as a full-fledged ally, and led the way in renouncing (January 1943) the extraterritorial privileges which had been extorted from the last Manchu emperors. Churchill growled, considering Chiang a weak reed, but acquiesced. But throughout the war Mao Tse-tung maintained a communist government in North China, abstained from fighting Japan, and pinned down a large part of Chiang's army. Chiang was isolated from his allies, not only by the Reds but by Japanese blockade and conquest of Burma, Thailand, and Indochina. Just as the Western Allies made great sacrifices to send aid to Russia through the Arctic Ocean, so they flew supplies to Chiang, and to General Chennault's XIV Army Air Force, over the Himalayas "hump."

Early in the war Roosevelt sent General Joseph Stilwell to help Chiang because he was the only general officer of the army who knew the Chinese and could speak their language. Stilwell — aptly nicknamed "Vinegar Joe" — did a wonderful job training the few Chinese troops entrusted to him, but so antagonized the Generalissimo by indiscreet remarks about him and his ineffective administration that in September 1944, when F.D.R. urged Chiang to make Stilwell commander in chief of the Chinese army, Chiang demanded and obtained his recall.

When Japan surrendered in August 1945, Chiang was about at the end of his resources. He nominally controlled over half China, but runaway inflation had alienated the professional classes, and his high officials, chosen mainly from among Madame Chiang's relatives, were inept and corrupt. At this juncture General Albert C. Wedemeyer, who had relieved Stilwell as United States commander in the Chinese theater of war, proved to be the seer. In dispatches of mid-August 1945 to the Joint Chiefs of Staff he demanded priority for occupation of Manchuria and the Chinese seaports, in order to prevent the Chinese Reds from taking over. Japan, a country under orderly government, he thought could wait; but Asia was then "an enormous pot, seething and boiling, the fumes of which may readily snuff out the advancements gained by Allied sacrifices the past several years."

That is just about what happened, but neither Admiral Nimitz nor General MacArthur agreed. The latter insisted that the prompt occupation of Japan was paramount and should be given highest priority in the allotment of forces and logistics. Had Wedemeyer's advice been listened to, strong Allied forces, not really needed for the occupation of Japan, could have been landed in China to help Chiang protect himself from the Chinese Reds. Seventh Fleet did help the "G'mo" to transport troops by sea to strategic points for receiving the surrender of Japanese mainland armies, but could not reach the interior.

Trouble with Russia began immediately. A Russian army pressed through Manchuria into Jehol province, even after the Japanese cease-fire of 16 August (exactly one week after Russia declared war), and forced the Japanese forces there to surrender to them instead of to Chiang, as Stalin had agreed. For quick promise-breaking there has been nothing to equal that of a Russo-Chinese treaty of 14 August in which Stalin formed an alliance with Chiang. A few days later he decided that the Reds were going to win, and began aiding them to overthrow the Nationalist Chinese government.

Many people high in the United States government were also in favor of shifting partners. Chiang seemed hopeless, and several journalists who had been with Mao pictured his government as not really communist but bent only on distributing land to the Chinese peasants. Truman and the state department rejected the idea of dumping Chiang, but they and the Joint Chiefs of Staff were determined not to become involved in a Chinese civil war, especially since we would soon lack the military capability to intervene. Owing to popular insistence on "sending the boys home," over 3 million of them were returned from Pacific Ocean areas to the United States between September 1945 and March 1946. As General Wedemeyer put it, "America fought the war like a football game, after which the winner leaves the field and celebrates."

President Truman in December 1945 sent out General Marshall in the vain hope of mediating peace between the two Chinas and setting up a popular front government. He did obtain a cease-fire, as the Reds were now building up their strength with Russian aid. When they were ready, fighting broke out all along the line where the two forces confronted each other. Money, arms, and munitions to the tune of $2 billion were poured in by us to help Chiang, but that was not enough. He over-extended himself, many of his generals surrendered or sold out to Mao, turning their American arms against Chiang, and by the end of 1949 the Nationalist government was forced to evacuate the mainland and establish itself in Formosa (Taiwan), where it is likely long to remain. Mao promptly consolidated his position by liquidating the Chinese who would not go along, by the tens of millions; he expelled all American or European missionaries, teachers, and business men and taught, or forced, the Chinese to hate the nations who had helped them against Japan.

Such was the sad issue of World War II in China; a result profoundly shocking and distressing to the American people. All their century-long efforts to help China with medical and other missionaries, with "Open Door" and the Nine-Power treaty, and, finally, by fighting Japan, went for nought. Traditional Sino-American friendship was changed into hate, and a peaceful policy distorted into "imperialism," "war-mongering," and all the tiresome slogans that communists hurl against those who oppose their power. But the charge that traitors or fools in the American government "lost" China is fantastic. It was Chiang who lost China; not "all the king's horses and all the king's men" could protect that amiable, loyal, but inept leader against the determined drive of Mao, supported by Russia. An army of a million Americans might have done it, but that was out of the question.

Fortunately we have something pleasant to relate in the postwar Asiatic world: the military occupation of Japan. This began with the formal surrender on board U.S.S. *Missouri* (2 September 1945) and lasted until 1952. It was a brilliant success mainly for two reasons. The Western Allies had the wisdom to profit by the mistake of "hang the Kaiser" policy in 1918; and, despite outraged shrieks of communists and left-wingers, kept Emperor Hirohito, a man of peace, in power. His government, intact, faithfully carried out the occupying authority's orders, and the Japanese people, chastened by defeat but with their godlike symbol still on his throne, accepted the situation stoically, went about their business without agitation, and respected the forces of occupation.

The second wise and fortunate circumstance was the appointment of General Douglas MacArthur as SCAP (Supreme Commander Allied Powers) by President Truman, and the set-up which gave him complete authority over Japan. Russia was kept out of it by giving her a representative on an international Pacific Commission in Washington, with the proviso that if the members disagreed — as they usually did — General MacArthur could decide. Thus the dissension and frustration of the four-nation commission on occupied Germany was avoided.

His conduct of the occupation of Japan constitutes General MacArthur's greatest claim to fame; and probably he thought so, too, since he wrote, after it was over, "If the historian of the future should deem my service worthy of some slight reference, it would be my hope that he mention me not as a commander engaged in campaigns and battles, even though victorious to American arms, but rather as that one whose sacred duty it became, once the guns were silenced, to carry to the land of our vanquished foe the solace and hope and faith of Christian morals."

His task was colossal, for he had to demilitarize a military empire and give a poor and defeated people the skills and confidence to create a viable state, all within the framework of the Golden Rule. "I decided that this was to be, for the first time in history perhaps, a *Christian* occupation," said the General to me in 1950; and that it was.

Almost anyone but MacArthur would have been daunted by the problem of directing the administration of a nation of 83 million people in an area equal to California but only one-sixth arable, with a maximum of 2200 American civilians and 60,000 troops, reduced to fewer than 5000 during the Korean War. Sixty per cent of the houses in Tokyo had been destroyed. Some 4 million Japanese soldiers and sailors had to be demobilized, a cool million of them in various Pacific bases which had been bypassed in accordance with the "leap-frog" strategy. All enemy commanders in the Pacific obeyed their Emperor's orders to surrender, and their troops were returned to Japan by the United States and Australian navies, and by such Japanese transports and merchant ships as were still afloat. But about 375,000 of the Manchurian army, who had been forced to surrender to the Russians, were kept for years in Siberia doing forced labor; only in 1950 did Russia begin returning those who had been indoctrinated as communists, in the hope of disrupting the occupation policy and throwing Japan into turmoil. They did produce a number of riots and strikes but, thanks to the pervasive loyalty to the emperor, and to MacArthur's having encouraged the workers to form trade unions and giving them social security, the returning Reds fell far short of their goal.

Before there could be normal sea-traffic in Japanese waters, the thousands of mines planted both by Japan and the Allies had to be swept up and destroyed. This huge task was entrusted to no fewer than 510 minesweepers of the Pacific Fleet under Rear Admiral A. D. Struble, assisted by some 100 Japanese minesweepers, and other warships. It was concluded in March 1946 with a total catch of over 12,000 mines, and the loss of only three ships.

General MacArthur, living in the American embassy in Tokyo and using the downtown Dai-Ichi building as an office, superintended every aspect of the occupation. He got rid of the secret police, purged the civil service of unrepentant militarists, abolished the secret societies which had helped bring on the war, broke up the *zaibatsu* system of cartels which had strangled Japanese industry, and even brought about a comprehensive land reform. This confirmed tenant farmers' plots to them in full ownership and compensated the landlords, but insisted, against landlord opposition, that the deeds be registered. Over 4.5 million acres were distributed to the peasants, and a strong co-operative movement encouraged among them. All this was accomplished without undue inflation, thanks to the Diet's adopting a plan by Joseph M. Dodge of Detroit. On the political side, the General gave his blessing to a new constitution drafted by liberal Japanese elements, which set up a democratic and representative government. The Emperor, with obvious relief, renounced his divine attributes but became more popular than ever because MacArthur encouraged him to travel about the country and let the people see him. Women were given the vote, and in the first general election in 1946 they won 39 seats in the Diet. Religious discrimination was abolished, and the state religion disestablished. The occupation even tried to do something for the despised Ainu of Hokkaido, the Red Indians of Japan.

During this transition, the United States poured food, clothing, medicaments, and other supplies into Japan — $517 million in one year, 1949. The General, summoning a corps of American economists as consultants, undertook to rebuild Japanese business and find new markets for handicrafts and heavy industry. Even the arts were not neglected; a fine arts commission under SCAP saw to it that relief funds were allocated to prevent the ancient temples of Nikko, Kyoto, and other places from decaying, and the leading museums were reopened. Especially praiseworthy was the work of SCAP's public health and welfare section, headed by General C. F. Sams, a chief surgeon of the United States Army. The entire population was vaccinated twice. A control program over tuberculosis resulted in a 40 per cent reduction of deaths from the "white plague." Diphtheria, dysentery, and typhoid cases were reduced 80 to 90 per cent under the occupation; cholera ceased to be. A beginning was made to encourage cattle-raising to correct the protein deficiency in Japanese diet.

The United States Navy under Vice Admiral C. Turner Joy, an integral part of SCAP, co-operated in many ways to further the General's policy. Rear Admiral B. W. Decker, commanding the Yokosuka naval base, found jobs building furniture, boats, and yachts to occupy workers thrown out of employment by the liquidation of the Japanese navy. He even set them to growing mushrooms in the vast underground complex that the Japanese had built as a command post to resist the invasion that never came off. Ascertaining that former gangster elements had muscled into relief distribution, Decker, to the astonishment of the natives, organized the women to take over.

MacArthur became immensely popular although he kept himself rigorously aloof; crowds gathered at the exit to the Dai-Ichi building just to see him. And this, in spite of the war crimes trials for which no fewer than 720 officers and civilians were executed and 3480 given prison terms. The war crimes tribunal consisted of eleven judges, each representing an allied country or commonwealth, presided over by Sir William Webb of the Supreme Court of Queensland, Australia. Most of the convictions and executions were for torturing and beheading prisoners. General Tojo, another former premier, and five former cabinet ministers were also sentenced to death for having conspired to bring on the war. This tribunal was completely independent of SCAP. General MacArthur approved the execution of officers who had tortured prisoners, but deplored the imprisonment of civilians, particularly of foreign minister Mamoru Shigemitsu, who signed the surrender, and of the emperor's confidential adviser Koichi Kido, who had been instrumental in bringing it about. I have reason to believe that the tribunal did this to please the Russian member, in return for his voting to acquit others; and that Stalin hoped to liquidate the old governing class, as he was doing in Poland, to let in communism. Fortunately, Russian and Anglo-American leftist pressure to try the emperor as a war criminal was defeated.

On 8 September 1951 John Foster Dulles concluded for the state department a treaty with Japan that ended the state of war, and the occupation. No reparations were extorted, but the United States obtained the right to military bases and airfields at specific places in Japan and on Okinawa. Japanese good will built up under SCAP appears to have continued to the present day. The main disturbing element has been the Japanese communists who never cease their efforts to break down the democratic government and make Japan a satellite of Red China.

"Could I have but a line a century hence," wrote General MacArthur, "crediting a contribution to the advance of peace, I would yield every honor which has been accorded by war."

Here's your line, General; this historian salutes you. Your efforts for peace and good will entitle you to a place among the immortals. No proconsul, no conqueror in ancient or modern times succeeded to the degree that you did in winning the hearts of a proud and warlike people who had suffered defeat. Your victory was a dual one — military, and in the highest sense, spiritual.

5. The Korean War

A peaceful Sunday in Japan, 25 June 1950, was interrupted by very bad, surprising news. An army from North Korea had suddenly burst into South Korea and apparently was carrying everything before it.

Korea had been divided across the middle, along lat. 38° N, before the end of World War II; the northern part to be occupied by Russia and the southern by the United States. This happened before the Russians had demonstrated that by temporary occupation they meant permanent communization. They set up a Red North Korea, while the Western Allies brought back from exile the aged patriot Syngman Rhee and supported a representative government under him. Lieutenant General John R. Hodge, one of the best leaders in the Pacific war, was unable to cope with the situation, having no long-established government or well-disciplined people to deal with, as Mac-Arthur had in Japan. The Koreans, notorious individualists, organized no fewer than eighty political parties, and President Rhee, an exile since 1912, unknown to most of his compatriots, had no flair for government. He did not even have the human materials to set up a viable administration, as the Japanese had monopolized all top and middle-layer positions. At Potsdam, Stalin had promised to promote union of Korea under one government, but every effort of the United Nations to do so was foiled by the Russian veto. An assembly, boycotted by the Russians, met in 1948 and promulgated the Republic of Korea with Rhee as president, but the authority of this "R.O.K."

ended at the 38th parallel. North of it was the "People's Republic of Korea" headed by a vigorous young Moscow-trained communist named Kim Il Sung. After Russian troops evacuated North Korea, the United States pulled her garrison out of the southern half, leaving only a small military mission to help Rhee create his own army.

This evacuation of the Republic of Korea was ordered by the Joint Chiefs

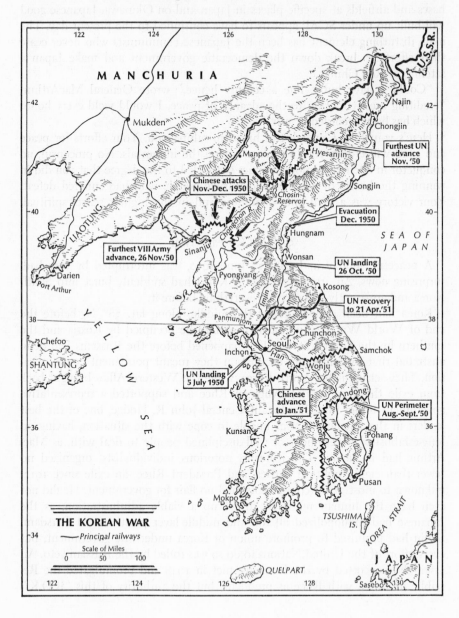

THE KOREAN WAR
—— *Principal railways*

of Staff with the approval of President Truman, General MacArthur, and the state department. The main reason for creating this sensitive power vacuum was the radical reduction in American armed forces. Moreover, the Joint Chiefs of Staff and all intelligence agencies believed that Europe was the danger point; that if war came it would be started there by Russia and be an atomic duel. Consequently, to strengthen American retaliatory power, to "get a bigger bang for a buck" as the phrase ran, the defense department built up a long-range "strategic" air force, with a stockpile of atomic bombs, but neglected both navy and ground forces. When Secretary Acheson announced in a speech of 12 January 1950 that the American defense perimeter in the Pacific included Japan, Okinawa, Formosa, and the Philippines, implying that South Korea belonged to "other areas" which would have to defend themselves initially, nobody objected.[1]

Although General MacArthur's command was braced to resist Russian aggression early in 1950, they expected it to take the form of a sudden invasion of Hokkaido; for Stalin had demanded, and Truman denied, a military occupation of this northern Japanese island. The General's military intelligence was so inadequate that 70,000 North Korean troops, complete with tanks and armor, were able to assemble behind the 38th parallel without knowledge of it reaching Tokyo. Mao of course was behind this push, which Kim would not have dared to undertake unsupported; but Stalin probably did not know what was cooking, or the Russian seat on the UN Security Council would not then have been vacant.

The communist powers counted on no interference by the United States, much less by the United Nations. But South Korea had to be defended, to protect the Korean people and because of its strategic position across the Strait of Tsushima from Japan. President Truman acted promptly and decisively. Before the end of the first day of the Red invasion — 24 June in Washington — he had sent orders to General MacArthur to do his best to help stem the tide, and brought the situation before the Security Council of the United Nations. The Council, after ordering North Korea to desist from her aggression, made this a United Nations war on the 27th by calling on all members to provide assistance to South Korea. Ten eventually did.

General MacArthur, first as SCAP and United States Commander in Chief Far East, and from 8 July Commander in Chief United Nations forces, conducted this "police action," as it was officially called. On 9 July he informed the Joint Chiefs of Staff that it was going to be a major operation, and asked that the 1st Marine Division and four army infantry divisions be sent to him at once. That took time, the Reds really got the jump, and the

1. This speech was held up against Acheson in the presidential election of 1952 as an "invitation" to the communists to overrun South Korea. He was able to prove that his perimeter was exactly the same as one previously defined by General MacArthur. Moreover, he repeatedly asked Congress to provide military aid for South Korea, even after the House on 19 January defeated the aid bill which the state department had requested.

first phase of this war went very ill for the United Nations. Before substantial forces could reach Korea, the Reds had overrun most of the peninsula, leaving the Allies only the southeastern port of Pusan and a small perimeter. This happened because of the surprise, because the South Korean ground troops were ill trained, as were the first American soldiers who arrived by airlift from Japan. Young draftees with no battle experience, they were soft from occupation duty.

A combined task force built around U.S.S. *Juneau* and H.M.S. *Jamaica* knocked out the North Korean navy and several troop-laden transports on 2 July, and from that time UN control of the sea was uncontested; but the Reds generally managed to move beyond the range of naval gunfire. The most useful contributions by the navy, other than bombardments, were helicopters and light bombers of the marine corps air wing, operating from escort carriers to give close support to ground troops, and to evacuate the wounded. The helicopter really came into its own during this war. By mid-August the United States, by drawing units from Hawaii, Puerto Rico, and the Mediterranean, had 65,000 troops, and the British Commonwealth one division, in the Pusan perimeter.

Counteroffensive began in mid-September 1950. The concept, MacArthur's own, was to bypass and cut off the Red troops south of lat. 38° by making an amphibious landing at Inchon, outport to Seoul, and then to drive up through North Korea to the Yalu. This bold gamble was suggested, said the General, by reading Parkman's account of Wolfe's assault on Quebec in 1759. His own staff didn't like it; the navy didn't like it, owing to the 30-foot range of tide at Inchon; the Joint Chiefs of Staff didn't like it; but he insisted. The navy put its best brains into the plan, and the Inchon landing, commanded by Rear Admiral Struble and effected by the 1st Marine Division on 15 September 1950, was a brilliant success. Unfortunately, it made MacArthur infallible, in his own opinion.

Inchon landing led to the capture of Seoul (25 September), cutting the Reds' communications with South Korea and forcing thousands to surrender. On 7 October the UN General Assembly approved MacArthur's crossing the 38th parallel and attempting to reunite all Korea. He had already opened his northward offensive. Eighth Army (Lieutenant General Walton H. Walker) advanced along the west coast, captured Pongyang the North Korean capital on 19 October, and pressed on to the Yalu. But MacArthur now made a grave strategic error by dividing his army and ordering X Corps to be re-embarked at Inchon and landed at Wonsan on the east coast, there to make a second northward march parallel to that of Eighth Army. The navy opposed it. Vice Admiral C. Turner Joy, the U.S. Navy's commander in the Far East, observed that X Corps could have marched the 150 miles overland to Wonsan with less effort and time than was consumed, with the limited shipping at his disposal, to lift it 800 miles around the peninsula. And the South Korean Army (the ROK) was already marching on Wonsan and took it on 10

October. But MacArthur insisted. X Corps (Major General Edward M. Almond) was landed by the navy at Wonsan on 26 October, advanced rapidly, spearheaded by the 1st Marine Division, and by 1 November was near the Chosin reservoir in northern Korea. If the two columns could meet on the Yalu, Korea would be enveloped.

This daring strategy was adopted by General MacArthur, either on the assumption that China would not intervene — at Wake Island on 14 October he assured President Truman that there was "very little chance" of it — or on the assumption that a vigorous lunge to the Yalu would convince Mao he had better not intervene. Unfortunately, Mao had decided to pile in. By mid-November some 200,000 Chinese troops had crossed the Yalu and taken up mountainous positions between Walker's Eighth Army and Almond's X Corps. The Red offensive began on 25 November, the Chinese attacking first Walker's right flank and, a week later, Almond's left.

To meet this "entirely new war" as MacArthur well called this phase of the Korean struggle, he proposed to bomb bridges over the Yalu, bomb the Chinese assembly area north of it, facilitate the invasion of China by Chiang's army on Formosa, and blockade the entire Chinese coast. It is possible, even probable, that this would have worked; for when communists are faced with resolute, determined, and superior force, they usually retreat. But would Russia have come to China's aid? That is the big question which can never be answered until communist archives yield their secrets.

The main reason MacArthur's strategy was not, indeed could not be, adopted, was UN control of the Korean War. Several members of the UN, especially Britain, insisted on keeping it a limited war and dared not risk another world conflict. Russia had exploded an atomic bomb the previous fall, and nobody knew how many she had; supposing China were invaded and Stalin decided to help his ally Mao, the first Russian counterattack would probably be a lethal rain of atomic bombs on Britain. England was indulging in a long-delayed new deal; the Labour government under Clement Attlee was apprehensive of provoking Russia; foreign secretary Ernest Bevin, and minister of labour Aneurin Bevan, who hated America, would have split the party had UN forces been allowed to invade China. Hence MacArthur's directive of 27 September 1950 ordered him under no circumstances to send planes or troops across the border into China or Russian Siberia, which touches the northeast corner of Korea.

The Labour Party in general, refusing to admit that the earlier "be nice to Russia" policy of Roosevelt and Churchill had been a dismal failure, now pressed for a "be nice to Red China" policy; they recognized the Red government at Pekin, and Attlee, at a conference with Truman in early December 1950, made the fatuous suggestion to buy off Mao by admitting Red China to the UN. Even Winston Churchill, leader of His Majesty's opposition, pointed out that to get the United States and the United Nations "entangled inextricably in a war with China" would play Stalin's game.

Nor could Korea be considered apart from other Asiatic areas in turmoil. France had half her army, some 150,000 men, trying to put down the Viet-Minh revolt in Indochina; the British were fighting communist guerrillas in Malaya; President Quirino of the independent Philippines was still fighting the "Huks," and in India fastidous, superior Nehru was doing his best to appease Mao after Red China's annexation of Tibet.

Truman, having placed this operation under UN control, had no choice but to respect our allies' wishes. Moreover, there was little military support for MacArthur's invade-China plan outside his own staff. General Eisenhower, leaving for Europe as supreme commander of NATO, opposed it; General Omar Bradley, expressing the views of the Joint Chiefs of Staff, later told Congress that MacArthur proposed "the wrong war, at the wrong place and at the wrong time, and with the wrong enemy."

The Chinese offensive that began on 25 November was not only a surprise; it took advantage of MacArthur's mistake of dividing the UN army into two columns separated by a mountainous wilderness. The Chinese who lunged into this strategic vacuum attacked each strung-out column on its exposed flank, announcing their presence in the initial engagements by eerie bugle calls, weird whistles, chirps, and howls. There then began what our troops called "the big bug-out" — a fighting retreat against attacks of vastly superior strength, through mountain passes and valleys, in bitter cold and deep snow. The story of Oliver Smith's 1st Marine Division retiring from the Chosin reservoir, beating off attacks by three Chinese armies, is one of the most glorious in the annals of that gallant corps, recalling Xenophon's retreat of the immortal ten thousand to the sea. The marines reached Hungnam on the east coast and, together with the rest of X Corps (a total of 105,000) were transferred by the navy on 11–21 December to Pusan. Eighth Army's fighting retreat, covering 300 miles in three weeks, was assisted by a combined fleet under a British admiral which evacuated several units from west coast seaports. The Reds now had ample air power, with Russian planes and pilots, to contest the UN air forces, but fortunately for us they had no naval power, and only frequent bombardments by the combined navies prevented them from exploiting their success to the point of annihilation.

December 15, when Eighth Army was back again below the 38th parallel, marks the nadir of the Korean War. The Republicans, led by Senator Taft and encouraged by gains in the fall elections, demanded the dismissal of Dean Acheson as an "appeaser" of the Reds, and cheerfully expressed their willingness to abandon the defense of Europe in order to help MacArthur in Asia.[1] Former President Hoover, proposing that American policy revert to the last century, demanded that all United States forces be withdrawn from Europe, Asia, and Africa to "Fortress America," in order to preserve this "Gibraltar of Western Civilization." His sentiment was cheered by Americans who hated

1. But several leading Republicans, such as Henry Cabot Lodge, Jr., John Foster Dulles, Thomas E. Dewey, and Harold Stassen, supported the President.

communism, hated England and Europe, hated new deals and new frontiers, and saw no need to bother with anything outside our own borders. But Truman and the Joint Chiefs of Staff stood firm. On 29 December General MacArthur received a new directive from the J. C. S. to defend all Korea, with a fresh warning that this was a limited war and there would be no blockade of China or "unleashing" Chiang from Formosa. MacArthur made a scorching reply, reiterating his plan for bombing Manchuria; Truman repeated the former directive. MacArthur replied (30 December) that this would mean the annihilation of the UN army.

A poor prophecy, indeed. The tide of battle had already turned. General Walker, killed on 23 December, was replaced as Commanding General Eighth Army by Major General Matthew B. Ridgway, who had commanded an airborne division in the 1943 invasion of Sicily. He found the morale of the now 15-nation UN army appallingly low, and bent his major efforts to improving it. By January 1951, when Ridgway had some 365,000 troops under his command, he had prepared positions ready to meet a fresh assault by Mao's half-million Chinese "volunteers" and North Koreans. Under his expert and inspiring leadership, with the Allied navies battering Chinese troop concentrations and communication lines along both coasts, the UN army advanced, recaptured Seoul on 14 March 1951, and recovered South Korea up to and a little beyond the 38th parallel. It was Ridgway who pulled victory out of defeat.

On 24 March 1951 MacArthur released to the press what he called a military appraisal containing a fresh plan to end the war. Arguing that the enemy had no industrial capability to wage modern war and that any forward move by us across the Yalu "would doom Red China to the risk of immediate military collapse," there should be no difficulty, he observed, in negotiating peace at once; and he stood ready to confer with the Chinese commander in chief to that effect. Not only was the plan foolish in itself, the release flouted an earlier presidential directive to the General to make no public statement on policy without his permission. Truman now decided that MacArthur must be relieved. The final straw was a letter from the General to Joseph Martin, Republican leader of the House, which Martin released to the press on 6 April. It said that Korea was the crucial spot where the war for global supremacy must be decided, "that here we fight Europe's war with arms while the diplomats there still fight it with words"; and ended with his favorite slogan, "There is no substitute for victory."

Truman consulted Generals Bradley and Marshall, Acheson and Harriman; all agreed that MacArthur must go. The actual orders were unnecessarily abrupt, because hurriedly drafted and dated at half past midnight 11 April in order to forestall a morning-paper scoop by the Chicago *Tribune*.

Then, what a blow-up! It reminded Winston Churchill of the dismissal of his ancestor the Duke of Marlborough by Queen Anne in 1711 — roars, groans, screams, and howls. Super-patriots half-masted American flags, Senator Nixon demanded the General's immediate reinstatement. Senator Jenner threatened to impeach the President, to "cut out this whole cancerous conspiracy out of our government." Senator McCarthy denounced Truman as "a s.o.b. who decided to remove MacArthur when drunk." A Gallup poll reported that the public favored the General against the President 69 to 29. MacArthur received wildly enthusiastic greetings on his return to the United States, culminating in an address to both houses of Congress which drew tears even from the television audience when he quoted the army ballad "Old Soldiers Never Die, They Just Fade Away."

MacArthur's egotism forced him to regard any operation that he commanded as crucial. Thus, during World War II, he objected to the war against Germany being given priority, inveighed against Admiral Nimitz being given independent authority in the Pacific, and wished the entire strength of the United States and the British Commonwealth to be directed against Japan, under his command. So, naturally, he regarded the Korean War as the center of the world-wide struggle against communism. During World War II he had largely confined his extreme views to conversations, but now he felt strong enough to appeal over the President's head to the Republican party and public opinion. He never crossed the Rubicon, to be sure, but his horse's front hoofs were in the water.

One may debate endlessly whether MacArthur's plan to crush China would or would not have brought in Russia and started a third world war. But there can be no doubt that Truman was right in relieving a general whose attitude to his civilian commander in chief had become insufferable. The only valid criticism of the President is that he did not sack the General months earlier, at the end of August 1950, when he gave a statement to the press castigating "those who invariably in the past have propagandized a policy of defeatism and appeasement in the Pacific." Everyone knew that "those" meant Truman and Acheson. The General himself told me, several years later, that a theater commander should be allowed to act independently, with no orders from President, United Nations, or anyone; and he repeated the statement so that there could be no doubt of his meaning. Any such supreme military power is incompatible with representative and responsible government.

Unable to admit a mistake, MacArthur later attributed his army's retreat in 1950 to traitors in the British embassy at Washington passing his plans to the Reds — as if the communists hadn't plenty of spies in Korea. The retreat was the result of his own bad strategy in the face of a Chinese concentration which either his intelligence service failed to report or which he and his staff disregarded.

Moreover, there is a substitute for total victory: peace, the only proper objective of war; and if Korea brought back into the international arena the concept of limited war for specific objectives, so much the better. The "unconditional surrender" kind of war was evolving into a war of mutual annihilation, as MacArthur himself told many people, including myself, before the Korean war broke. Limited war is also in the American tradition. We did not go on fighting in 1814 to conquer Canada, we did not try to take over all Mexico in 1848, we did not attempt to annex the troublesome Caribbean republics. It is regrettable that MacArthur's overweening ego prevented him, fundamentally a man of peace, from seeing this.

General Ridgway, succeeding MacArthur as SCAP, won peace in Korea. Armistice negotiations began on 10 July 1951 and continued until 5 March 1953 at Panmunjom, wearing out Admiral Joy and other negotiators. There were intermittent hostilities during that period. Cease-fire and the restoration of the 38° boundary were easy to obtain; what strung out the talks was the repatriation of prisoners, of which the UN had upward of 70,000. The Reds demanded that every one be returned to them, but the vast majority, unwilling draftees, preferred to stay out of communist territory. As a result of UN insistence that every man choose for himself, they were finally permitted to do so, and three out of four elected to stay south. On the other side, 21 American prisoners were "brainwashed" in captivity and threw in their lot with Red China. During these truce talks, the Reds pulled off a wonderful propaganda stunt, the germ warfare hoax. They accused Americans of dropping insects infected with cholera within their lines from aircraft, and supported this preposterous charge with confessions signed under torture by imprisoned aviators. This monstrous accusation was firmly believed by communists everywhere, and by thousands of fellow travelers and humanitarians. Investigation by the United Nations completely exploded it.

No formal peace treaty has so far (1964) been concluded; the situation in Korea is still an armed truce along the 38th parallel. But the Korean War was a clean-cut victory for the United States and the United Nations. It stopped a major communist lunge southward, and may well have saved Japan from being engulfed in the Red tide. It proved that the UN was no "paper tiger" — that it would and could fight if necessary. After the lapse of over a decade, it is clear that the Korean War was worth its cost in lives and money; but a major political party in the United States, and a part of the Labour party in Great Britain, took up the cry that it was a miserable failure.[1]

1. The following statistics are from David Rees, *Korea the Limited War* (1964), Appendix A: — The United States furnished seven divisions and most of her Pacific Fleet. The British furnished their Far Eastern Fleet and the Commonwealth Division, composed of units from Britain, Australia, Canada, and New Zealand. Belgium, Colombia, Ethiopia, France, Greece, Netherlands, Philippines, and Thailand each sent one infantry battalion. Turkey sent one infantry brigade — superlative fighters — and there were smaller units from Luxemburg and the Union of South Africa. The war cost the United States 33,529 killed in action, died of wounds, or in captivity. The other United Nations lost 3194 dead, 2769 missing or prisoners. Included in the UN figures are 1263 killed, 1188 missing or prisoners, in the Commonwealth Division. Of these 1263, 686 were British, 294 Canadian. I have been unable to find any reliable figures on R.O.K. forces or casualties; these were at least equal to those of the UN.

6. The Election of 1952

Eleven years after his retirement, President Truman's achievements for world peace, national security, and European reconstruction shine out from the somber postwar atmosphere, but a large section of the American public in 1950–52 could see nothing but failure. He and General Marshall had "lost" China; he and Dean Acheson then "lost" the Korean war; hero MacArthur when (by his own subsequent boast) only ten days' fighting were needed to achieve complete victory, had been brutally cashiered; the Soviets may have been "contained" in Europe, but were getting ready to leap at our throats. Public opinion, unable to understand failure following the superb victory of 1945, readily picked on Truman and the Democrats as instruments of defeat. It was helped into this frame of mind by the charges and innuendoes of the House Committee on Un-American Activities ("the most un-American thing in America in its day," wrote Truman in his *Memoirs*), and by the spectacular demagoguery of Senator Joseph McCarthy of Wisconsin.

Against this background of malaise, suspicion, and frustration, an inglorious witch hunt was sparked off by several incidents. Alger Hiss was suspected, if not proved, to have been a communist when employed by the state department; Klaus Fuchs in England was convicted of feeding atomic secrets to Russia, and Russian defector Igor Gouzenko revealed the existence of a gigantic communist spy ring in Canada. It was so sinister that Mackenzie King said he "could not believe" that Stalin "countenanced" it — an attitude which shortened but did not end King's long premiership.[1] Ten top American communists were convicted under the Smith Act of 1939 of conspiracy to overthrow the government. All this fed a neat theory to explain recent events. During "twenty years of treason," as Senator McCarthy put it, the Democrats, led by Roosevelt and Truman, had "conspired" to deliver America to the Reds. F.D.R. got into World War II mainly to help Russia, gave away everything to Stalin at Yalta; Harry presented China to the Reds and recalled General MacArthur because he was about to beat them; Alger Hisses were concealed in every government office, college, and corporation, ready to take over when Stalin pushed the button. This utterly preposterous theory almost tore the country apart then; it even played a role in later presidential campaigns. These efforts to "root out" subversives from government, colleges, and even business, ruined the careers and reputations of thousands of patriotic Americans whose only offense was to have lent their names to some "front" organizations during World War II.

1. King retired 20 April 1948 after 7619 days in office, and was succeeded as premier by his foreign secretary Louis St. Laurent. The significance of the spy disclosures is explained by the fact that Britain, Canada, and the U.S., the only three countries known to have developed atomic fission, had agreed in 1946 mutually to protect their scientists' atomic secrets. The biggest leak discovered in the United States was the Rosenbergs', for which they were convicted in 1951 and executed.

The conspiracy theory would never have been so widely received but for the histrionics and diabolical cunning of Senator Joseph R. McCarthy of Wisconsin. Estimates of him and his objectives vary, from pure white to deepest black. He was probably simply a plain rogue who wanted power to make Presidents and cabinet officials jump when he cracked the whip; but in the opinion of many he, like Huey Long, aimed at the presidency. McCarthy had none of the redeeming qualities of Huey. He was saturnine, cruel, greedy, and did nothing for the people of his native state. He was also one of the most colossal liars in our history. During a part of the war he had been air combat intelligence officer in the marines' 4th air wing; in his political campaigns, however, he claimed to have been a tail gunner on countless combat missions, responsible for killing thousands of the enemy. In competition with the younger La Follette he was elected to the Senate from Wisconsin in 1946 as a Republican. There, in search for a popular cause, he first took up that of German "martyrs" in the war criminal trials,[1] but that got him nowhere; on the advice of a prominent Catholic prelate he turned to the Red Menace. McCarthy's favorite method in speaking was to wave a document, announcing "I have in my hand" a list furnished confidentially by some patriot in the government "whose name I shall never reveal," containing the names of ten, fifty, or two hundred "card-carrying Communists" in the department of state. The document might have been a form letter or a laundry list; audiences never got a look at it.

In July 1950 a Senate committee under Millard Tydings of Maryland investigated McCarthy's charges and reported that they were "a fraud and a hoax perpetrated on the Senate of the United States and on the American people. They represent perhaps the most nefarious campaign of half-truth and untruth in the history of the Republic." McCarthy then charged the Tydings committee with being "soft" on communism, and with the aid of a big public relations firm, paid for by rightist organizations, brought so many false charges against Senator Tydings that he was defeated for re-election.

McCarthy now moved to bigger game — Dean Acheson and General Marshall, the alleged executioners of Chiang's government. He obtained valuable support from the so-called "China lobby," financed by a New York importer who anticipated a whopping trade with China if Chiang were restored. He even charged General Marshall with treason, and Dean Acheson made a perfect target for his hatred and malice. Educated as Groton, Yale, and Harvard Law School, Acheson was too handsome, well-groomed, self-assured, and ironical for the average congressman to stomach. "I look at that fellow," said Senator Hugh Butler of Nebraska, "I watch his smart-aleck manner and his British clothes and that . . . everlasting New Dealism in everything he says

1. McCarthy was three-quarters Irish blood, one-quarter German. The German-American farmers and small business men of Wisconsin, who bitterly resented being drawn into two wars against their mother country and refused to believe ill of Hitler, regarded McCarthy as their champion against the Anglo-Saxons.

and does, and I want to shout, 'Get out! Get out! You stand for everything that has been wrong with the United States for years!' "

Nobody who did not live through that period will ever believe what a sound and fury made up. McCarthy had a country-wide following. He was the idol of the Boston Irish, despite his vile attacks on men whom they had elected. Cardinal Spellman extended his blessing; rising young politicians such as John F. Kennedy hedged. Actually, not one of the hundreds of "subversives" named by McCarthy in the state department was found guilty after full investigation or trial. Many leading Republicans deplored all this, but the general run of politicians were delighted to have a new, hot issue; and the Republican platform of 1952 played up the "betrayal" of Chiang, the "loss" of the Korean War, and the "negative" nature of Truman's containment policy in Europe.

The Republicans' political strategy for 1952 was based on the inescapable fact that they had been a minority party for twenty years and were declining. Most of the rising generation regarded the G.O.P. as hopeless old fuddyduddies; many racial and occupational groups such as Negroes, Jews, and organized labor had abandoned them. Thus, to win, the Republicans must have a new issue or a glamour boy like the late Wendell Willkie, or both. McCarthy supplied the issue, but who would lead the procession? General MacArthur might have ridden the elephant. Willing enough, he was invited to give the keynote address to the Republican nominating convention at Chicago in July. It was received with slight enthusiasm, since the politicians knew that the General had no grass-roots support; he had failed as an avowed candidate in 1948 — eleven votes on the first ballot, none on the third — and veterans did not like him. Thus the most logical conservative candidate was Senator Taft — "Mr. Republican" as he was often called. None more deserved to be President, for Taft had integrity, a deep knowledge of the governmental structure, and political courage. As in the case of Henry Clay, courage lost Taft the nomination; he had made too many enemies, notably the labor union leaders, owing to the Taft-Hartley Act. Tom Dewey, twice defeated, did not care to try again, but he marshaled delegates to win the nomination for a really glamorous candidate — General Eisenhower. "Ike" had no more political experience than MacArthur, but he was well liked by the G.I.s; and his achievements in Europe, which included running two international coalitions, suggested that he had a flair for politics. He received 845 votes for the nomination, Taft had 280, Stassen 77, and MacArthur received 4. Senator Richard Nixon of California received second place on the ticket as a reward for having uncovered the former communist connections of Alger Hiss, when a member of the Un-American Activities Committee. He had no other qualifications; it was a case similar to Coolidge's winning the vice-presidential nomination for a few strong words about the Boston police strike.

Another factor that worked against the Democrats in this election was the "Truman scandals," exposed in part by congressional investigations, in part by

an article "The Scandalous Years" in *Look* magazine. These were the pardon-
ing of convicted criminals who had important Democratic friends, such as
Mayor Curley of Boston, and favors extended to and bribes received by
officeholders. A group of lobbyists known as "influence peddlers" had sprung
up in Washington. They offered, in return for a modest 5 per cent, to
connect business men who wanted contracts with the "right" person in the
administration, or to "fix" cases by persuading the department of justice to
lay off income tax evaders and other offenders. A congressional investigation
of this shady business, led by Senator Fulbright of Arkansas, discovered that
General Harry Vaughan, an old National Guard buddy whom Truman had
appointed his military aide, had befriended perfume smugglers and accepted
gifts from a grateful influence peddler, and that the wife of an examiner of
loans for the Reconstruction Finance Corporation had received a $10,000
mink coat after he had approved a loan to a Florida motel. The R.F.C. had
been a useful means of "pump priming" under the New Deal; but now,
having outlived its usefulness, it was extending loans to tottering corporations
or dubious projects such as snake farms and gambling casinos, and the arranging of such loans was a chief source of income to the 5 per centers.

Another investigation, led by Representative Cecil R. King, uncovered
many cases of "fixing" in the tax division of the department of justice, and for
which two underlings of Truman's attorney general Hannegan, and of his
administrative assistant Dawson, were eventually jailed. The picture has a
strong family resemblance to that of the "good guys" under Harding. Truman's easygoing old pals were responsible for most of the high-level corruption, but not for scandals in the tax department. Here the basic trouble,
which had been going on since 1933, was infiltration of federal tax collecting
offices in the big cities from Boston to San Francisco by dishonest members of
local Democratic machines.

President Truman was too complacent about these goings-on. Not covetous
himself, he found it hard to believe that his friends were greedy and corrupt
as the records proved. Eventually he administered mild purges to the department of justice and the bureau of internal revenue, and reorganized the
R.F.C. But the mink coat plagued him in the next campaign, like the bloody
shirt of yore.

Harry could have tried for a third term despite Amendment XXII to the
Constitution because his first term was not a full one. But, seeing how the
wind blew, he definitely declined to be a candidate in March 1952. Senator
Estes Kefauver of Tennessee, one of the leading contestants for the Democratic nomination, stumped the country in a coonskin cap to emulate Davy
Crockett, but he had two strikes against him. Advocacy of civil rights cost him
the support of the dominant white South, and by showing up the alliance
between ward politics and organized crime his name had become anathema to
Democratic bosses in the cities. Averell Harriman, governor of New York, was
thought to be too closely identified with the foreign service to win the elec-

tion. On the third ballot, Governor Adlai E. Stevenson of Illinois, grandson of the likenamed Vice President under Grover Cleveland, received the nomination.

Stevenson is an intelligent gentleman, skilled in administration, full of constructive ideas on domestic and foreign policy. He attracted the support of professors and other intellectuals (whom Eisenhower dubbed "eggheads") who thought they had found another F.D.R. Probably no Democrat could have beaten Eisenhower that year; but Stevenson's speeches were too epigrammatic and intellectual to interest the public, and the burden of the Truman scandals and malaise over the Korean War and China were too much for him to surmount or cure. General Eisenhower was no orator and his prose, even when corrected by the members of his political staff, was repetitive and obscure; but his pleasing personality and wide grin, said to have been worth several divisions during the war, attracted votes. "I Like Ike" stickers went up on cars, buildings, and trees all over the country. It was more important to know what Ike liked, but he carefully left that vague.

In the presidential election of 1952, the Eisenhower-Nixon ticket won 55.2 per cent of the popular vote, greatest plurality since 1936, and 442 electoral votes. Stevenson polled 44.5 per cent and 89 electoral votes, mostly in the South. The remaining three-tenths of one per cent was divided among six splinter parties, including a new Constitution party which nominated General MacArthur. His fanatical admirers, undismayed by his polling only 17,000 votes out of over 61 million, financed a ridiculous campaign to persuade the presidential electors to ditch General "Ike" and elect General "Doug."

After seeing General Eisenhower inaugurated, Truman retired to his native Independence. As was said in a famous Western epitaph which Harry liked to quote, "He did his damndest." Economic reconstruction of Europe, airlift to Berlin, containment of Soviet power by NATO, help to Greece and Turkey, bold acceptance of the Korean challenge, placing that war under the United Nations, maintaining the supremacy of civil over military government; all make a shining record for the little man from Missouri.

LXI

The Eisenhower Administrations

1953-1961

1. *The President and His Domestic Policy*

GENERAL OF THE ARMY Dwight D. Eisenhower became President of the United States on 20 January 1953, at the age of sixty-two. No President since George Washington entered office with a greater bank of good will on which to draw, at home and from abroad. Everyone "liked Ike" even if he did not vote for him; the British and European soldiers and statesmen who had met him during the war or as head of NATO, felt that he understood their problems; even the Soviets seemed to thaw a little when the Beria-Bulganin team succeeded Stalin. Most Americans now felt that "everything would be all right" — Korean War concluded, budget balanced, no more starry-eyed visionaries in the top ranks of government, or crypto-communists in the lower echelons, no dubious characters from city wards slinking in and out of the White House to "fix" things. And, above all, a President tested by battle, intellectual enough to be head of a great university, strong enough to bang the heads of the service chiefs together and work out a defense policy that the country could afford. Eisenhower's "historic role," wrote Walter Lippmann, was to be "restorer of peace and order after an age of violence and faction."

Eisenhower was one of the best men ever elected President of the United States, and the people endorsed his first term by re-electing him with even greater majorities in 1956. His genial character and transparent honesty inspired loyalty to himself and confidence in his administration. Yet he failed in the historic role cast for him by producer Lippmann. Peace and order were not restored abroad; violence and faction were not quenched at home. What went wrong? To put it simply, Dulles on the international scene, and the President's want of political experience on the domestic scene. Eisenhower who, like Hoover, had never occupied an elective office, disliked politics and politicians and attempted to leave sordid questions of patronage to others. And fundamentally, Eisenhower had a conception of the presidency which precluded positive leadership while leaving plenty of time for golf. Consciously or unconsciously he became a constitutional monarch, a symbolic chief of state, rather than a dynamic initiator of policy; he mediated, smoothed over difficulties, but left leadership to the Republicans in Congress. He hoped to inaugurate another Era of Good Feelings, as Monroe had done in 1820. He hoped to end the cold war and restore normal international relations. Unfortunately conditions at home and abroad were such that no dayspring of peace and tranquility could have dawned in 1953, no matter how much good will emerged from the White House, and that good will became an ill wind in the hands of his secretary of state, John Foster Dulles.

The President organized his administration somewhat like a military staff. Men below him were supposed to work out in detail what needed to be done; the President had to make the ultimate decision, but he disliked doing any preliminary thinking about it himself. Contradictory recommendations would come to him on defense and other matters from two or three different departments, each already watered down while passing up from lower echelons. The President, who studied no problem deeply himself, would return the differing recommendations and order an all-round agreement on which to base his decision; thus almost every decision was a compromise, and often a wishy-washy compromise. His health was always precarious, and in 1955 he suffered a serious heart attack which for weeks made it difficult for him to transact public business; and at all times, to maintain his strength, he spent an unusual amount of time for a president, relaxing at Camp David or his Gettysburg farm, or playing golf.

Eisenhower's cabinet appointments met with general approval, for they seemed to accord with Harding's epigram that the country needed "more business in government and less government in business." The appointment of John Foster Dulles, two years senior to Eisenhower, as secretary of state, seemed an ideal choice; on his record Dulles seemed the best equipped man in all our history to head the foreign service. Grandson of one secretary of state (John W. Foster, under the second President Harrison); nephew of another (Robert Lansing, under Wilson); Princeton graduate, member of a leading law firm of New York, Dulles had been intermittently in public life since 1907 when he played secretary to his grandfather at the Hague Convention. He had had a part in drafting the United Nations constitution, and served under Truman as consultant in the state department while still an avowed Republican. As such he negotiated the excellent treaty of peace with Japan and persuaded the Philippine Republic, which wanted a Versailles sort of treaty, to accept it. With his hunched shoulders and woeful countenance occasionally lit by a wry smile, always hard-working, always ready to fly to the ends of the earth (559,988 miles by careful count as secretary) when he thought it would do good, Dulles was a conscientious student of foreign affairs. His speech was slow and he often managed to bore rather than impress the foreign statesmen with whom he talked. His failure to attain his and Eisenhower's avowed objectives of world peace and containment of communism was due in great part to conditions beyond his control; but in good part to his pedagogical methods of handling strange and explosive situations.

For other cabinet appointments, Eisenhower sought out leaders of big business. The new department of defense, established by Congress under

Truman in the hope of co-ordinating the three armed forces, was given to Charles E. Wilson of Detroit, president since 1941 of General Motors, one of the country's biggest and most successful corporations. That sounded fine; but the President did not know that sixty-three-year-old Wilson, a mere figurehead in Detroit, had lost any capacity he might have had for business-like administration.[1] In the second Eisenhower administration Wilson was replaced by Neil H. McElroy, a Harvard graduate with a glamorous personality, president of the Procter & Gamble soap firm of Cincinnati. After this ineffective minister had served for two years he was relieved by Thomas S. Gates, Jr., a Philadelphia investment banker and former secretary of the navy, who made a really hard-working, competent defense secretary, putting in a twelve-hour day at the Pentagon. Until he came in, and to some extent even later, the method of allotting funds to the several armed services and of making up the total defense budget, was incredibly bad. A rigid fixed percentage of the total was allotted to each arm — 23 per cent to the army, 28 per cent to the navy and marines, and 46 per cent to the air force. This "vertical" budgeting resulted in each force developing its wants independent of the other two, so that the defense picture was never viewed in the aggregate. No wonder that General Maxwell D. Taylor, who relieved General Ridgway as chief of staff in 1955, found inspiration from 1 Corinthians xiv:8 for the title of his book, *The Uncertain Trumpet*.

In view of Republican promises to economize, reduce the national debt, check inflation, and promote prosperity, an appointment equal in importance to state and defense was the secretary of the treasury. George M. Humphrey of Cleveland, chairman of the board of several important steel and coal companies, was Eisenhower's choice. He was not a good team worker, consistently trying to pare down expenditures on defense during the cold war, even publicly attacking the President's budget in 1957 by announcing that the necessary taxes would produce "a depression that will curl your hair." Joseph M. Dodge, the new director of the budget, should have been given the treasury, as he had shown financial genius under Truman by stabilizing the currencies of Japan, Austria, and Germany. Both his hands and Humphrey's were tied, because the administration insisted on an independent Federal Reserve Board. This stemmed from the outmoded "free market" concept, the heart of Republican ideology. There was a severe recession in 1957–58 which might have developed into a major depression but for the controls established during the Roosevelt administrations.

1. An assistant secretary of the army has given me an account of a typical "day with Wilson." When he arrived, by appointment, with an important defense matter, Wilson instead of listening to him, insisted on discussing whether or not to fold up some petty air force facility in Georgia. In succession Admiral Radford and General Twining of the J. C. S., and Secretary Quarles of the air force, came in by appointment, each with an important subject for decision. Wilson drew them into the air force discussion, which continued during lunch, after which all four were dismissed without the important questions being brought up.

Eisenhower's first secretary of the interior, Governor Douglas MacKay of Oregon, and Postmaster General Arthur E. Summerfield were automobile distributors by profession. Adlai Stevenson remarked, "The New Dealers have all left Washington to make way for the car dealers." MacKay was a notorious foe to conservation and public power developments. Ezra Taft Benson of Utah, a graduate of Brigham Young University and one of the Twelve Apostles of the Mormon church, who strongly disapproved the welfare state, became secretary of agriculture. Despite the hostility of Western farmers who resented his efforts to reduce price supports, Benson held office through both Eisenhower terms. Sinclair Weeks, a Harvard graduate and former senator from Massachusetts, director of several New England corporations and of the National Association of Manufacturers, appropriately became secretary of commerce. He signaled the return of the *caveat emptor* concept to the federal government by firing Allen Astin, chief of the bureau of standards, who had offended several drug manufacturers and others by down-grading their products. This caused a nation-wide protest from consumers, and Astin got his job back. For cabinet lady, Eisenhower appointed to the newly established department of health, education and welfare, Mrs. Oveta Culp Hobby, wife of a wealthy Texas publisher. Nelson Rockefeller became her deputy. For attorney general, Eisenhower chose a legal aid to Governor Dewey, Herbert Brownell. To round out the picture and have one Democrat in it, the department of labor was given to Martin Durkin, president of the Journeymen Plumbers and Steamfitters' Union. As one liberal paper quipped, "Ike's cabinet consists of eight millionaires and a plumber." But Durkin was so unhappy in this company that he resigned before the year was out.

More important than the cabinet, as the turnstile through which most visitors and all business had to pass to reach the President, was Sherman Adams, Dartmouth graduate, former congressman and state governor. He had taken an active part in the Eisenhower campaign, and the President chose him as special assistant. He had cabinet rank and occupied a position similar to that of Harry Hopkins in Roosevelt's and of Harry Vaughan's in Truman's; but enjoyed far more power than either. After he had become almost indispensable to the valetudinarian President, Adams unfortunately intervened with the Federal Trade Commission and the S.E.C. on behalf of a shady manipulator and income tax evader named Bernard Goldfine, from whom he had received expensive gifts and hospitality. When this came out, the President had to accept Adams's resignation, and the "gray eminence" of the administration returned to New Hampshire to raise chickens.

Every administration, one may say, has its own pattern of corruption. "Fixing," that of Truman's, did not now altogether disappear, as the Adams-Goldfine episode reveals; but the typical thing under Eisenhower was conflict of interest. Business men who accepted cabinet appointments were supposed to "divest" themselves of pecuniary interest in companies to which government contracts might be awarded, and most of them did. But it later came out that Harold E. Talbott, president of the Dayton-Wright airplane company, who became secretary of the air force, retained half-interest in a management-engineering firm for which he solicited business while in government service; and that Robert T. Ross in the defense department awarded millions of dollars' worth to a firm of which his wife was president. Both men were forced by the defense secretary to resign, and both considered themselves "martyrs" — they had sacrificed so much money to serve the nation, why shouldn't they make a little on the side? This seems to have been a prevalent ethical attitude, well illustrated in a popular novel of the era, Sloan Wilson's *The Man in the Gray Flannel Suit*.

A somewhat different affair, which rocked the country with laughter but caused Secretary Benson great embarrassment, was the great cheese scandal. On 1 April 1954 Elder Benson dropped the price-support level for all dairy products from 90 to 75 per cent parity. Prior to that date, the big cheese distributors of Wisconsin and bordering states had contracted to sell 90 million pounds of their local "cheddar" to the government at the high support price of 37 cents per pound. Immediately after, they bought back almost the same amount from the government at $34\frac{1}{4}$ cents, making a profit of nearly $2.5 million on cheese that never left their warehouses. Neither Benson nor his subordinates profited, and they prevented its happening again.

Walter Lippmann predicted that responsibility would cure the Republicans of trying to prove that the Democrats had sold out to Moscow. So far as foreign policy was concerned, this worked; when John Foster Dulles, as Republican as Bob Taft, scrapped campaign boasts and in most essentials followed Truman's policy, the congressional Republicans fumed and growled but kept quiet. Far different was it with McCarthyism. Eisenhower extended security checks to all government agencies and purged the service of over 6900 "security risks" in seventeen months. None of these were really serious cases — mostly clerks who drank or talked too much or who had expensive girl friends. But Secretary Dulles gravely damaged the morale of his department just when America's world position required the recruitment of good men, by a pusillanimous catering to McCarthy, forcing the resignation of professional foreign service officers as punishment for giving the "wrong" advice — from the Republican point of view — about China. This display of zeal failed to appease McCarthy, who shifted his attacks to the Eisenhower administration. And no one who witnessed his appearances on TV can doubt that the Senator hoped to convict the President of being "soft on communism"; even to succeed him.

So long as McCarthy confined his smears to professors, scholars, and the foreign service, the general run of Americans, who disliked intellectuals and the "white spat boys," seemed to be with him. And the President kept silent except for attacking "book burners" in an address at Dartmouth College, which was about as effective as a speech against witch-hangers in Salem might have been.[1] But when McCarthy swung on the Protestant clergy and the

1. The allusion was to the activities of two henchmen of McCarthy in Europe, visiting

United States Army in March 1954, the administration began to take notice. Army secretary Robert Ten Broeck Stevens (one of the President's best appointments), with his attorney Joseph N. Welch, fought back vigorously; and when McCarthy demanded that he be allowed to fish in F.B.I. files for the names of new victims, Eisenhower denounced him as one who tried "to set himself above the laws of our land" and "to override orders of the President." The Senate then censured him by an emphatic vote. McCarthy himself collapsed, but the poisonous suspicion that he injected into the body politic will take many years to leach out. As Eisenhower admits in his memoirs, "McCarthyism took its toll on many individuals and on the nation. No one was safe from charges recklessly made from inside the walls of congressional immunity. Teachers, government employees, and even ministers became vulnerable. . . . The cost was often tragic." For success in dividing a country by sowing suspicion of treason in high places, there has been no one to equal Joe McCarthy since Marat in the French Revolution.

"Dynamic conservatism," a favorite phrase of the President's, was carried out in a number of ways, along the welfare line recently condemned during the election. Eisenhower canceled the few remaining price and rent controls, and wound up the discredited RFC; but with his approval Congress enlarged social security to embrace some 10 million more people — domestic servants who needed it least, farm hands who needed it most, and government employees who had it anyway. Unemployment compensation, too, was extended to an additional 4 million people. The nation-wide minimum wage was raised to a dollar an hour, laws were enacted to curb corruption and racketeering in the unions, and a moderate public housing program was passed by Congress in 1955. Next year a $40 billion highway program was launched. Eisenhower promoted a bill for federal aid to the states for building new schoolhouses, to the tune of $50 million a year; but the bill failed after being amended so that racially segregated schools were excluded.

Most amusing of unconscious tributes by Republicans to the New Deal was their adoption of Henry Wallace's "soil bank." This meant paying farmers to take marginal arable land out of cultivation and plant it with trees or put it to other uses. Soil bank, together with price supports that Elder Benson could never get rid of, shot up federal grants to farmers to $5 billion in 1959. In addition, the government lost over $1.2 billion in the years 1953–55 through purchasing and storing farm products to get rid of surpluses. The difference between Eisenhower "dynamic conservatism" and the no less dynamic liberalism of Truman, seems to have been that the Republicans passed such measures reluctantly, with sighs and groans over the political necessity, and many a backward glance to the good old days before the war.

U.S. Information Bureau libraries and designating the books of authors (such as Dos Passos, Hemingway, and Thoreau) who were on a list of "subversives" compiled by some excited old lady, to be eliminated. This sort of activity so resembled those of Hitler's brown shirts that many Europeans seriously feared that America was going fascist.

According to Lewis L. Strauss, onetime Chairman of the Atomic Energy Commission, the TVA was the "sacred cow" of the New Deal, but the Republicans regarded it as a maverick steer to be jabbed and sniped at on sight. Hence the so-called Dixon-Yates deal. The gist of this complicated affair is about as follows. In 1953 TVA proposed to build a new steam generating plant at Fulton, Tennessee, primarily to meet the growing power requirements of Memphis. President Eisenhower disapproved, Congress refused to provide funds, and as a substitute the administration backed a complex arrangement. The Atomic Energy Commission, TVA's largest single power customer, would contract with a combination of two private companies, known as "Dixon-Yates" from the names of their presidents, to provide energy which AEC would then turn over to TVA for ultimate delivery to Memphis; the basic idea being to give a private company a slice of the Authority's territory and a guaranteed profit. Although engineers demonstrated that this bizarre arrangement would cost the public $5.5 million more annually than would the proposed Fulton plant, President Eisenhower gave the deal his blessing. He also refused to reappoint Gordon Clapp, the TVA chairman who had fought for the new plant, and later replaced him by one who considered Dixon-Yates a "good deal." After AEC had signed the contract with Dixon-Yates, it came out that a consultant of the Bureau of the Budget who had helped arrange the deal was an official of the banking firm selected to finance it. The deal collapsed in 1955 when the city of Memphis declared it would build its own municipal plant rather than be dependent on Dixon-Yates. Later the department of justice found the agreement so contrary to public policy as to be "null and void." The same year, a commission headed by Herbert Hoover to recommend "streamlining" the federal government, proposed that TVA be required to sell all its steam plants to private firms. But no such law went through Congress, and the passage of an act in 1959 allowing the Authority to issue bonds to provide for expansion, guaranteed the "sacred cow" ample fodder for the future.

So many deals of the Dixon-Yates type were attempted, and enough of them succeeded, to justify the Democrats' coining the phrase "The Giveaway Program" for the Eisenhower administration's power and conservation policy. Hell's Canyon on the Snake river, for instance, was abandoned to a private utility; a bankrupt mining company was allowed to recoup its fortunes by stripping part of the Rouge River National Forest of its timber; in two years 566 leases for drilling oil wells were granted in wild life refuges. Democrats supported, Republicans defeated, a bill to set up a federal atomic power plant, and the administration farmed out Oak Ridge to Union Carbide, and the Hanford atomic energy plant to General Electric. The President, however, vetoed the biggest attempted "steal," the Natural Gas Bill which would have relieved that booming industry of price regulation. On the whole, the net picture of the Eisenhower administration on conservation is one of carelessness, not corruption, want of understanding about flood control and the preservation of mineral, oil, and forest reserves; and a disposition to let private capital exploit resources that rightfully belong to the public.

When we turn to civil rights, the picture is much brighter. President Eisenhower made some excellent appointments to the Supreme Court bench, including that of Earl Warren of California as Chief Justice, and under him the Supreme Court made several decisions safeguarding the rights of individuals in the security and loyalty cases that had been sparked off by McCarthy. All these paled in comparison with the epoch-making decision in the school segregation case.

Under Chief Justice Fuller, the Supreme Court in *Plessy* v. *Ferguson* (1896) gave legal sanction to the jim crow laws, holding that Amendment XIV to the Constitution did not forbid segregation of Negroes in schools, etc., provided that public facilities reserved for the colored were equal to those whence they were excluded. Justice Harlan of Kentucky dissented. In 1954 the principle behind his dissent became the unanimous opinion of the court, delivered by Chief Justice Warren in the case of *Brown* v. *Board of Education of Topeka*: "We conclude that in the field of public education the doctrine of 'separate but equal' has no place. Separate educational facilities are inherently unequal."

Although the Court conceded that states might move gradually toward desegregating schools, several of the former slave states resorted to every possible legal device, as well as pressure and intimidation, to block even a beginning of integration. One method, practiced in Virginia and eventually declared illegal by the Supreme Court, was to abandon the public school system and set up a series of so-called private schools for white children, the state paying the fees. In the lower South, the Supreme Court's decision was to all intents and purposes nullified and has remained so for ten years; John C. Calhoun would have been delighted! For, powerful as the federal government has become, the American system still is federal, which means that "interposition" by a state government — a word now revived from the Kentucky and Virginia Resolutions of 1798 — can thwart federal law when the great majority of the people, in this instance the Southern whites, is in violent disagreement.

Some progress was made in large cities in the upper South and the border area, such as Washington, Baltimore, Louisville, and St. Louis. There schools reopened quietly on an integrated basis. But 2300 districts, including all in the deep South and Virginia, remained segregated. In the high school of Little Rock, Arkansas, which a couple of qualified colored children tried to enter in the fall of 1957, intervention by a rabble-rousing governor and threats of mob action led President Eisenhower to send federal troops to maintain order. Protests and disorders reached their height that year and the next. The Little Rock school board appealed to the Supreme Court, which in September 1958 (case of *Cooper* v. *Aaron*) declared, "The constitutional rights [of the children] are not to be sacrificed or yielded to the violence and disorder which have followed the actions of the Governor and Legislature. . . . Law and order are not to be preserved by depriving the Negro children of their constitutional rights." President Eisenhower, after Senator Richard Russell of Georgia had insolently compared him to Hitler for sending troops to Little Rock, replied: "When a State refuses to utilize its police powers to protect persons who are peaceably exercising their rights under the Constitution as defined in such [Federal] court orders, the oath of office of the President requires that he take action to give that protection. Failure to act in such a case would be tantamount to acquiescence in anarchy and the dissolution of the Union."

It was bitterly ironical to hear all the arguments of proslavery days trotted out to prevent Negro children from mixing with whites in classrooms, or even against qualified young Negro men and women entering professional schools. God had marked the Negro as a separate race; the Negro was perfectly contented to be inferior and dependent until Northern agitators such as the NAACP and the communists stirred him up. Fortunately for the South, Negroes for the most part followed the Reverend Martin Luther King, Jr. of Georgia who, borrowing the tactics of Gandhi which won independence for India, schooled his people to non-violence and patience, starting with a bus boycott in Montgomery, Alabama.

In several cities, Negroes demonstrated successfully against segregation in streetcars and buses. In the spring of 1960 they began to "sit in" at lunch counters in drug and department stores, it being one of the peculiar tenets of jim crow philosophy that a Negro could buy goods in a white man's store, but must admit his inferiority by going humbly to a rear entrance to get a sandwich. Yet, in nearby air force bases, integrated by the President's order, white and colored worked side by side and shared the same facilities. Within a few weeks the sit-in movement had swept the South, whose authorities retaliated by wholesale arrests. The Supreme Court, in *Garner* v. *Louisana,* voided these arrests on the ground that merely to sit unserved at a lunch counter was no breach of the peace. The sit-in movement served notice that Negroes intended to claim their legal rights, and that they were prepared to use economic and political as well as legal weapons in that struggle. Presently, to the joy of the white South and discomfiture of Northern liberals, they would extend their agitation to Northern cities in search of better housing, schools, and status.

It was all very well for President Eisenhower to declare, "There must be no second-class citizens in this country" — there were, and still are. The traditional American remedy for injustice is political power. The Negro had lost his right to vote, as we have seen, in the reaction against Reconstruction; it was now felt that if he regained it, and could be elected to at least minor offices, he could improve his status and force local politicians to respect his wishes. Accordingly, in 1957 Congress after sixty-three days of debate passed a new civil rights law, first since 1870, to protect the Negro's right to vote by removing some of the obstacles imposed by state and local officials. Federal judges were empowered to enjoin state officials from refusing to register qualified persons, and to fine or even imprison them for recalcitrance. This law, of benign intent, proved far too weak to surmount the numerous tricks resorted to by dominant Southern whites, or even to overcome the average Negro's timidity. Eisenhower did complete desegregation in the armed forces, begun under F. D. Roosevelt. In other directions integration spread. TVA had desegregated all its waterside parks by 1957, and has been increasing the employment of Negroes at all levels, including the scientific staff. Between 1940 and 1957 the number of Negro professional men and women more than doubled, the number of skilled workers increased by 181 per cent, and the number of Negro clerks and salesmen more than tripled.

In other ways, Eisenhower proved himself a humanitarian and a man of peace. He played a vigorous part in obtaining, against opposition by isolationist leaders of both parties, the Refugee Relief Act of 1953, allowing him to admit during the next three years 215,000 Europeans, mostly refugees from communism, over and above the immigration quotas. These quotas had become even more restrictive under the McCarran-Walter Act of 1952, passed by Congress over President Truman's veto. Highly praiseworthy is his "Atoms for Peace" proposal to the United Nations on 8 December 1953. The idea, Eisenhower's own, was for the United States and Soviet Russia to make joint contributions from their uranium stockpiles to the United Nations. This would be administered and allocated by a UN atomic energy agency "to serve the peaceful pursuits of mankind"; especially "to provide abundant electrical energy in the power-starved areas of the world." And, in an eloquent peroration, he pledged for his country a "determination to solve the fearful atomic dilemma," to find some way to consecrate "the miraculous inventiveness of man" to his life, not his destruction. But this sincere proposal was met by the Soviet government with surly contempt. Eisenhower nevertheless promoted a unilateral development of "atoms for peace," and the world's first non-military atomic power plant was started at Shippingport, Pennsylvania, on Labor Day 1954.

Although the President's life had been despaired of for a time in 1955, he made a good recovery and decided to run for a second term in 1956. The Eisenhower and Nixon team was nominated on the first ballot at the Republican convention in San Francisco. The Democrats, meeting in Chicago, renominated Stevenson and Kefauver, despite the open opposition of Harry Truman who wanted Averell Harriman and predicted that Adlai could not win more than the nine states he carried in 1952. Actually he carried only seven states, all in the South, with 73 electoral votes; Eisenhower carried the other 41 states with 457 electoral votes. The popular vote was 35.6 to 26 million. This, the biggest plurality in twenty years, was a magnificent endorsement.

Eisenhower proved to be a better leader during his second than his first term, especially after losing his administrative assistant Adams through the Goldfine affair, and Secretary Dulles by death in May 1959. Christian Herter,

former governor of Massachusetts and assistant secretary of state who succeeded Dulles, did not enjoy robust health, and the President assumed direction of foreign policy as well as making "good will tours" as far afield as
India, Morocco, and Chile. He was received with enthusiasm everywhere.

Among the achievements of the second administration were a new Atomic
Energy Act permitting exchange of information and co-operation in atomic
research with trustworthy allies, the creation of an Aeronautics and Space
Administration to direct space research, an educational act (spurred by Russia's "sputnik" achievement) providing millions for the support of teaching
languages and science, and loans to students; and the overdue admission of
Alaska and Hawaii to statehood. The people "liked Ike" as much in December as they did in May; but they were becoming increasingly tired of the
G.O.P., as evidenced by the fact that they returned Democratic majorities to
the last three congresses of Eisenhower's two terms and increased the majority in 1958. And a number of Republican state governors and United States
senators were defeated the same year, portending a Democratic comeback.

2. Foreign Relations

During the Truman administration a new situation had been developing in
Asia and Africa, the liquidation of all colonial empires. Adding more than fifty
new independent nations to those which formed the UN in 1945, this movement constituted as great a revolution in world affairs as the spread of
communism.

Starting with the rediscovery of West Africa and India by the Portuguese,
and the discovery of America by Columbus, Spain, England, France, the
Netherlands, and Portugal had built up world-wide empires. Between 1775
and 1810 there occurred a series of revolutions by overseas colonists of the
same language and race as the mother country — the American Revolution
and the successive Latin-American revolutions. But the revolutions of 1945-65
were of entirely different character — revolts of the *indigènes*, the colored
natives, not only against the colonizing nation but against the white officials,
traders, and entrepreneurs who had come from the mother country to bring
law and order and to develop or exploit natural resources with native labor.

The Philippines, already promised independence by the United States be-
fore the war began, achieved it on 4 July 1946 and remained our good friends.
The subcontinent of India, to which Britain had brought peace and justice,
broke up into four independent states — India, Pakistan, Ceylon, and Burma.
French Indochina, of which more anon, relapsed into four turbulent little
states, Laos, Cambodia, North and South Vietnam. The Netherlands East
Indies, which the Allies had culpably neglected to occupy immediately after
World War II, threw off Dutch rule and emerged as the Republic of Indonesia under Sukarno; a child of revolution who, like others before him, stayed
in power only by demanding more and more territory, and got it. These

nationalist revolutions of the 1940's were followed by another series in Central and South Africa against England, France, and Belgium, leaving only the Portuguese colonies and the Union of South Africa, where a minority of white Africans, descendants of seventeenth-century Dutch colonists, clamped a tight lid on millions of native Negroes.

Next there came to a head three revolutions in North Africa. The old Barbary states, whose piratical activities had caused so much trouble to Presidents Washington and Jefferson, had been occupied, pacified, and colonized by France and Spain since 1830. Now they, too, threw off the foreign yoke; Morocco, Algeria, and Tunisia recovered their independence, and the native Moslems either expelled or squeezed out millions of European *colons*. General Charles de Gaulle, summoned to power to preserve *Algérie française*, was forced to acquiesce. It was as if the Tecumseh Confederacy of 1811 had succeeded in forcing all white North Americans to return to Britain. And in Egypt, to which Britain had brought peace and the rule of law in the nineteenth century, fat but friendly King Farouk was thrown out by a military junto from which emerged clever, ruthless Gamal Abdel Nasser. In the late 1950's the British West Indies began severing their imperial ties to set up little insular republics, with the consent and aid of the British government.

Beginning in the Roosevelt era and extending into the Eisenhower regime, the United States adopted a very benevolent policy toward these nationalist revolutions, partly because of popular prejudice for independence and against "colonialism," but mostly to compete with Russia for their friendship and their votes in the United Nations, and to prevent communist take-overs. Russia and Red China, however, have been strong competitors though disappointed by the results. According to the Marxian gospel, capitalism had maintained itself only through colonial expansion; but these revolutions, it turned out, saved the mother countries a great deal of trouble and expense in administration without significantly diminishing their trade. Nonetheless, the colonial breakdown lessened the world-wide power of Britain, France, and the Netherlands. The Indian army, formerly a major stabilizing power factor in Asia, has deteriorated since the British withdrew, and the British navy no longer has the force to patrol the Indian Ocean. The French can no longer draw on Africa for some of their best troops — the Zouaves, whose exploits and uniforms so impressed our Civil War ancestors; the *tirailleurs marocains*, and the *sénégalais*, who were terrors to the Germans in both world wars. Nor can Holland recruit Javanese for her navy.

Coincident with these nationalist explosions came the terrifying development of thermonuclear weapons: first the "A" atomic bomb, then the "H" hydrogen bomb, then the guided missile, land- or ship-based, with intercontinental range and warheads a hundred times more powerful than the bomb which wiped out Hiroshima.

Thus Eisenhower, like Truman, was faced almost daily by issues such as had formerly arisen only in time of war. He was buffeted from one crisis to another, in four continents. The United States could not act, or even be strong, everywhere. Which troubled theater should have priority — Central Europe, Middle East, India, Southeast Asia, Africa? And, before long, Latin America would be shouting for attention. The President was beset by differing estimates and demands by the service chiefs for concentration on this or that weapon or arm; should we go all out for very long range bombers, or rely on shorter ones, based on fields in Turkey, Morocco, Spain, and western Europe, which we held at sufferance of the several sovereign states? Should the navy be developed as an anti-submarine force (since it was known that Russia was building up a mighty submarine fleet), or a striking force for limited war, or as floating bases for launching ballistic missiles?

Russia, by boasting that she was building a great bomber fleet, goaded North America into setting up an expensive radar-warning grid across northern Canada, to detect any possible hostile flight over the North Pole. But Russia never built those bombers; instead she developed enormously powerful rockets to propel guided missiles, and in 1957 shocked the American public, as it had not been since Pearl Harbor, by launching the first satellite "Sputnik" into outer space. That exploit sparked off a feverish effort to develop bigger and better rockets and missiles here; and one of these efforts, the fleet of Polaris-equipped nuclear-powered submarines which are capable of carrying war against an enemy even if America is devastated, has probably been the major deterrent of our time. The first of this fleet, U.S.S. *Nautilus* (Commander William R. Anderson), submerged on 1 August 1958 north of Alaska, steamed for 1800 miles under the polar ice cap, emerging four days later on the European side of the Pole. The second, U.S.S.*Triton* (Captain Edward L. Beach), circumnavigated the globe under water between 16 February and 10 May 1960, broaching only twice in 84 days — to land a sick seaman at Montevideo and at Cadiz to honor the memory of Magellan, whose course she followed.

During the presidential campaign of 1952, the Republicans had made brave noises about "liberation" of captive nations. But, to do that, as General Ridgway observed, America must be able to apply air, sea, or land power, or all three, to influence any particular situation. Yet, as soon as the Korean War appeared to be about over, Wilson and Humphrey, the secretaries of defense and the treasury, insisted on cutting armed forces appropriations by some $5 billion. That basic situation, which existed through the Eisenhower regime, forced Dulles to reconsider foreign policy. As he announced it on 12 January 1954, the country would depend for its security in the future on "the deterrent of massive retaliatory power." President Eisenhower veered between the two points of view, seldom taking a strong line, but generally favoring the civilians. He undertook to play world policeman with no big stick — only the big bang of the A and H bombs which he dared not use, well knowing that they would spark off mutual destruction.

The Korean truce was signed in July 1953 after Eisenhower had been

President for six months. The Joint Chiefs of Staff anticipated that Mao, defeated here, would probe elsewhere; and before the end of the year he did so in Indochina, where the French government, unwisely refusing to follow the British example of granting immediate independence to India, fiddled around fruitlessly with attempts to set up protectorates under native princes. Here the upsetting force was the Viet Minh — a guerrilla army recruited in China and from the bordering peasants in North Vietnam. The French garrison under the war hero De Lattre de Tassigny had been driven into a stockade at Dien Bien Phu in South Vietnam and, if not shortly relieved, could not hold out. Certain military advisers of President Eisenhower, notably Admiral Arthur W. Radford, chairman of the Joint Chiefs of Staff, were in favor of our intervening militarily in Indochina as we had in Korea; and ten years later it looks as if they were right. But army chief of staff General Ridgway, who knew the terrain and predicted a struggle as tough as in Korea, and Secretary Dulles, opposed intervention as beyond the power of our reduced military establishment. While Washington debated, Dien Bien Phu fell (7 May 1954). The diplomats now took over, and the President followed their advice at the Geneva conference that summer. By agreement with Russia and Red China (20 July 1954), their followers retained control of North Vietnam but they recognized and promised to respect the independence of non-communist South Vietnam, Laos, and Cambodia. This decision created three more weak succession states to be supported by financial, economic, and military aid against attack or subversion. In the hope of preserving the status quo in this part of the world, Dulles and other members of the Geneva conference set up the Southeast Asia Treaty Organization (SEATO) between the United States, Australia, New Zealand, the United Kingdom, France, Pakistan, Thailand, and the Philippines, signing the treaty at Manila on 8 September 1954. It obliges all signatory powers to help any one of them against aggression by an outside power. When it came to a showdown in 1963, SEATO proved to be a weak reed — and the United States alone was left to defend the three non-communist states against attacks by the Viet Minh.

No sooner was the fate of Indochina handed over to the diplomats than Mao's Chinese government started to bombard two small island groups off the China coast, Quemoy and Matsu, which were still under Chiang's government in Formosa. Dulles, like Acheson before him, refused to tie his hands by signing an offensive-defensive alliance with Chiang's government in Formosa, but Congress had already given the President authority to use force if necessary to defend his territory. Should Quemoy and Matsu be considered part of Formosa? The British were very keen to put pressure on Chiang to cede the little islands to Mao in return for a Chinese pledge to settle the Formosa question peacefully. Dulles rightly prevented this, pointing out that it would smell of Munich. Mao, not caring at this point to risk war with the

United States, caused the cannonade to cease, and that neck of the woods was relatively quiet for four years.

The Matsu-Quemoy business erupted again in August 1958 when the Chinese reopened their artillery bombardment. The fainthearted argued that America should keep out of this fight and let the Reds take the islands. It was pointed out that Quemoy and Matsu were as close to China as Vancouver Island is to British Columbia, or Staten Island to New York. Should we risk an all-out war for little offshore islands which Chiang ought to evacuate anyway? All Asia was watching to see what we would do; it was a test case. The Eisenhower administration stood firm. Both navy and air force helped Chiang to reinforce and support the islands and to evacuate civilians; and the communists, lacking naval control of the Formosa strait, dared not launch an amphibious attack. The result was that they knocked off in October, and the United States gained face in the Far East.

Between the two Matsu-Quemoy crises came a much more serious one, over the Suez Canal. In 1952 King Farouk of Egypt was dethroned by an army officers' rebellion, and the Naguib-Nasser group took over. A friendly and helpful policy by the United States toward Egypt was inherited by Secretary Dulles from Secretary Acheson. But the Eisenhower-Dulles team handled the situation with incredible gaucherie and stupidity. As a starter, President Eisenhower presented General Naguib — then Nasser's partner — with a pearl-handled revolver on the day after he had denounced Britain as "the enemy." This gesture to the Arabs meant that America was on their side, to force the European nations out of Suez. After that "blooper" Eisenhower left the Suez affair completely in the hands of Dulles, who approached the subject as if he had been a Wall Street lawyer reorganizing a corporation in trouble. Dulles's hold over Eisenhower is explained by his encyclopedic knowledge of international relations, and by the fact that he appeared to have all the answers.

The Suez Canal from Port Said to the Red Sea was built by Ferdinand de Lesseps's *Compagnie Universelle* between 1859 and 1869, at a cost of about $87 million, most of which was subscribed by European governments. In 1888 an international convention between nine nations including Turkey (of which Egypt was then a part) declared the canal a neutral zone. The British government, which by 1950 had become the company's largest shareholder, maintained a small military base at Suez, by treaty with Egypt. Nobody questioned that the canal had been well and fairly managed by the company, whose board of directors included five Egyptians, or that Egyptian sovereignty had been respected. Its importance for world trade was vital; 14,555 ships passed through in 1955. The Convention of 1888 required the canal to be open to ships of all nations in war as in peace. Hitherto this stipulation had been respected; but it did not suit the Arab nations of which Nasser now became leader. In their implacable hostility to Israel they denied the canal to her ships. In 1951 the Security Council of the United Nations ordered Egypt to end this illegal prohibition, but Egypt refused to comply.

It took Dulles a long time to realize that Gamal Abdel Nasser was not a "reasonable" dictator like Tito [1] but an Arab Mussolini — the same rolling eyes, calculated rages, lust for power, and contemptuous disregard for treaty obligations or international law. Owing to pressure from Nasser, which Dulles supported, the British government agreed on 27 July 1954 to evacuate its Suez base by 1958, and did so two years earlier. It was expected, if not promised, that when this "thorn in Egypt's sovereignty" was removed, Nasser would respect the treaty of 1888.

The bait of the Western Powers to keep Nasser in line was his need for help in financing an immense dam at Aswan, to irrigate millions of acres and improve the lot of his wretched subjects; it was to cost between $1.3 and $2 billion. Negotiations between the state department, the British foreign office, and the World Bank to foot the initial bill of $70 million ($14 million from Britain, the rest from the United States), and finance the balance by loans, were complete before the end of 1955. Dulles, however, became increasingly irritated by Nasser's truculence and by his mortgaging Egypt's stocks of cotton to buy $200 million in arms from iron curtain countries. Finally, learning that he was dickering with Russia for a better financial deal for the dam, Dulles on 19 July 1956, without warning, canceled the American offer to participate in the loan. England, perforce, followed suit. This was the worst way to handle a sensitive and arrogant dictator, who could easily have been kept guessing for months. Nasser retaliated promptly. On 26 July he seized the offices and physical plant of the Suez Canal, expelled the company's employees, and began collecting the tolls for his own treasury.

Dulles, profoundly shocked by this breach of international obligations, made the mistake of imagining that Nasser could be persuaded to backtrack by diplomacy and world public opinion. He initiated two London conferences of the principal nations which used the Suez Canal. They presented to Nasser two moderate and reasonable schemes as a basis for negotiation, which he rejected with contempt. Sir Anthony Eden, the British premier, and Christian Pineau, the French foreign minister, repeatedly pointed out that force must be used to recover the canal if Nasser declined to negotiate. Dulles, who detested Eden and feared that Britain was aiming to recover her prewar position in the Middle East, refused to commit himself, but President Eisenhower, at a news conference on 31 August, did so in the worst way. He said, "We are committed to a peaceful settlement of this dispute, *nothing else*." And that came just at a moment when Robert Menzies of Australia, representing the London Conference, had persuaded Nasser to negotiate.

1. Robert Murphy of the state department, conferring with Tito, and Ambassador Clare Booth Luce conferring with the Italian government, achieved an accord on the thorny subject of Trieste in September 1954.

Nasser now felt that he had the Western Allies "over the barrel," especially since Khrushchev had assured him of Russia's support. But Britain and France were not through. Military preparations to invade the canal zone had already been started. Dulles knew about this; had been informed at least as early as 1 September. Israel, at that time suffering from raids by Nasser-supported Arab guerrillas, started hostilities by sending a military column into the Sinai peninsula of Egypt on 29 October 1956, administering a sound beating to an Egyptian army of 45,000, and in four days reaching the banks of the canal. Eden informed Eisenhower next day that England and France were about to render Israel military support. This decision was a bad diplomatic error which Eden and Pineau compounded by a confused and ineffective military action. Dulles was furious; and the President, according to Sir John Slessor (first person to talk with him after he had read Eden's note), expressed "amazed stupefaction" with the conduct of our major ally.

Nasser promptly blocked the Suez Canal by sinking ships across the channel. The communist bloc denounced the action of England, France, and Israel as "imperialist aggression," threatened to join Egypt unless there were an immediate cease-fire, and hinted at dropping atomic bombs on England and France. It was reasonable to expect that the United States would ignore these threats and give at least moral support both to Israel and the Anglo-French, who had law and right on their side. On the contrary, President Eisenhower instructed Henry Cabot Lodge, his representative at the United Nations, to support an Afro-Asian resolution meeting Russian demands and calling for an immediate cease-fire. England and France vetoed the resolution; but, faced with UN disapproval, threatened by Russia, helpless without American support, slow and bumbling in their attempts to occupy Port Said and Suez, they announced a cease-fire on 6 November and withdrew their armed forces. Israel followed early next year after the state department had threatened to stop financial aid and to invoke UN sanctions against her. Thus Israel was robbed of her well-earned military victory, and to the time of writing (September 1964) no Israeli ship has been allowed to use the Suez Canal.

As a result of the diplomacy of Eisenhower and Dulles, Russia was able to pose as Africa's great and good friend who had forced England, France, Israel — and the United States! — to yield; the NATO alliance was strained, Nasser kept and operated the canal which he had illegally seized, collected 100 per cent of the tolls, and went on to fresh trouble-making in the Middle East. The Eisenhower administration piously proclaimed that it had prevented the outbreak of a world war, but Russia's threat to start a war on this issue was a mere bluff which nobody dared call on the eve of a presidential election.

In the same October of 1956, while these events were breaking in the Middle East, Hungary revolted against her Russian masters and, for a brief period, the new government at Budapest drove out the Russian garrison. Here again was opportunity for resolute action to support freedom and justice;

again both the UN and its members muffed it. The UN merely passed resolutions of protest and Eisenhower did no more than declare, "The heart of America goes out to the people of Hungary." The heart of America was not enough. On 4 November 1956 the Russian army re-entered Hungary, stamped out the revolt, and set up a communist regime. Almost 200,000 Hungarians became refugees and many eventually reached America.

As Robert Murphy, the state department's trouble-shooter since 1939, re-marks in his memoirs, "American policy of promoting the liberation of cap-tive nations always stopped short of war, and this was well known."

Possibly a feeling of shame over Suez and Hungary is the reason why Eisenhower and Dulles applied force vigorously in 1958 when Nasser's United Arab Republic, having absorbed Syria, pulled off a coup d'état in Iraq, killing King Faisal and his family. They were preparing a similar fate for Jordan, and beginning to subvert neighboring Lebanon, whose president appealed to the UN for help. While they were debating, he turned to the United States; and Eisenhower (14 July) responded promptly by ordering Sixth Fleet (Vice Admiral J. L. Holloway) to demonstrate off the coast of Palestine, and send-ing all available marines and a group of the 187th Infantry (airborne) to land at Beirut. This was neatly accomplished within three days, during which Robert Murphy, and Robert McClintock the American ambassador to Leba-non, managed to dissuade pro-Nasser elements from firing on the marines. At the same time Britain landed 2500 paratroops in Jordan. There is no doubt that this display of strength saved Lebanon and Jordan from subversion and threw Nasser for a loss; and, strangest of all, silenced momentarily the Soviet threats. As the President well said, the Lebanon incident demonstrated "in a truly practical way that the United States was capable of supporting its friends." And the operation also proved the value of having conventional military forces trained and readied for any emergency.

Immediately after the Lebanon crisis ended by the American armed forces' withdrawal in October 1958, a new one flared, directly with Russia. Premier Khrushchev announced that if the Western powers did not get out of Berlin within six months he would turn it over to communist East Germany. This threat was removed, and a slight détente accomplished, by Khrushchev's visiting the United States in September 1959 and staying with President Eisenhower at Camp David. Arrangements were there begun for a "summit meeting" in the summer between the premiers or presidents of the United States, Britain, France, and Russia, to try to resolve the Berlin and other disputes. Unfortunately, just before the conference was to meet, the Russians shot down a U-2 high-altitude photographic plane of the United States Air Force some 1200 miles within Russia. This crisis could not have been handled worse in Washington. First, a routine statement was given out that the U-2 had simply lost its way when studying the weather, and that no photographic flights deep within Russian territory had been authorized. Then the President admitted that the Russian story was correct and that these planes had been taking photographs in order to spot Russian nuclear activities. The President's order to discontinue such flights was first announced, then denied, then confirmed. The net result was to put the United States in the wrong, to enable Khrushchev to pillory Eisenhower as an aggressor, and to break up the summit conference — as Khrushchev probably intended anyway — without accomplishing anything.

As if there were not enough old-world crises to keep the administration busy and worried, the cold war spread to the Western Hemisphere in 1954. Both postwar administrations tended to take for granted Latin American friendship, so well cultivated by F.D.R., and assumed that our sister republics were getting along all right. Canada, which had suffered more from the war than the United States, asked for nothing; why, then, should the Latin American nations need anything? Accordingly, during the seven years 1945–52, when the United States granted $44.8 billion in Marshall Plan and other foreign aid to Western Europe, all Latin America got only $6.8 billion, less than the total dispensed to Turkey and Greece ($7.3 billion), and only half again as much as the $4.4 billion largess poured into the bottomless pit of Chiang's Formosa. It was also assumed in Washington that communism was no danger to Latin America — did not the *latinos* have democratic institutions and the Roman Catholic church to keep it out? Washington was wrong again.

Latin America was suffering from a lopsided economy based on the export of minerals and products of the soil; most of the countries were too small and too hedged about with tariff restrictions to build up successful manufactures of consumer goods. And the Communist parties in Russia and China were paying court to the Americas. They did not bother with the submerged Indians, but infiltrated labor in countries like Mexico, Brazil, and Chile where the unions were strong, and also cultivated college students. These, too numerous to be absorbed in the backward economy and limited professions of their respective countries, offered fertile seedbeds for subversive movements planned in Moscow and Peking. Working in their favor was the fact that Latin American intellectuals had long regarded the "Colossus of the North" with fear, tinged by envy. Puerto Rico, having been granted commonwealth status and profiting from New Deal bounty, was an exception and a showcase of what a small, poor country could do under good government and free trade with the United States; but even Puerto Rico had a small terrorist party, which tried to assassinate President Truman, and fired pistol shots into the House of Representatives.

One strong talking point of the South American radicals was North America's alleged support of dictators. According to the non-intervention policy which began even before Roosevelt, the United States had to recognize a dictator even though his regime smelled to high heaven. President Truman burned his fingers trying to get rid of the highly unsavory dictator Perón, in powerful Argentina. During the Argentinian presidential election of 1945, the American ambassador Spruille Braden, a Yale graduate married to a Chilean lady, attempted to discredit Perón. But his efforts only served to re-elect the dictator, who lasted another ten years. Eisenhower and Dulles, however, helped pull off a successful revolt in 1954 against Jacobo Arbenz, dictator of Guatemala, who had allowed communists to control his government, and imported arms from Poland to support his power. Basing his policy on a resolution of the Organization of American States that "dominion or control of the political institutions of any American state by the international communist movement must be resisted," Dulles saw to it that Guatemalan exile groups obtained arms from the United States. They mounted an invasion, ousted Arbenz and set up a conservative, constitutional government. Among the communists who fled was an Argentine physician, Ernesto ("Che") Guevara, who later reappeared in Cuba as Fidel Castro's mentor. This indirect intervention by the United States provoked a frenzy of rage and agitation among students throughout the continent and was partly responsible for the disgraceful mobbing of Vice President and Mrs. Nixon when they visited Lima and Caracas in 1958. President Eisenhower threatened to send the marine corps into Venezuela if necessary, to get the Nixons out alive; but President Betancourt's government managed to protect its guests.

Eisenhower now adopted a policy of financial help to South America, in hope of exorcising the bitter hatred which the Nixon episode revealed. It took the form of increasing Latin America's slice of the foreign aid pie, setting up an Inter-American Development Bank with a capital of $1 billion to make loans repayable in local currencies rather than dollars, and an extended tour by Eisenhower himself, in 1960, of South America. "We are not saints," he said at Santiago de Chile, "but our heart is in the right place."

But the beloved if misunderstood "Ike" was not to leave office before having a new and apparently insoluble problem dumped on his back doorstep — Fidel Castro and communist Cuba. For years the "Pearl of the Antilles" had groaned under an unusually cruel, corrupt and ruthless dictator, Fulgencio Batista. He stopped at nothing — confiscation, blackmail, torture, murder — to stay in power; and the United States, warned by what had happened in Argentina, made no effort to oust him. In 1956 an able young revolutionary fanatic named Fidel Castro landed in Oriente Province with a tiny band of bearded guerrillas, increased his following, forced Batista to flee the country on New Year's Day 1959, entered Havana in triumph, and made himself dictator. Castro then enjoyed the support of most professional and bourgeois elements in his own country and in the United States. Herbert L. Matthews of the *New York Times*, who had visited his camp in the mountains, played him up as a democratic liberator; and when Castro visited the United States in April 1959, he received thunderous ovations at the leading universities and was offered liberal foreign aid for schools and welfare by the state department. But Fidel had other ideas. Shrewdly estimating that his share of North American financial assistance would be small, and influenced by Guevara and his communist brother Raúl, he decided that it would be more profitable for Cuba to become the first American satellite to Russia, even at the risk of breaking off her subsidized sugar trade with the United States. He expropriated all banks, sugar plantations, and major industries, threw everyone who objected into jail, closed churches, and forced at least 250,000 Cubans into exile. Khrushchev's deputy premier, Mikoyan, made Castro a state visit in 1960, extended generous credit, promised to buy the entire sugar crop, and provided enough rifles and machine guns for Castro to arm practically the entire population. This bearded revolutionary had done what Sandino had failed to do thirty years earlier — he had established a communist-supported state in the Caribbean.

Here was a crisis in foreign intervention similar to that which had provoked the declaration of the Monroe Doctrine, and probably more serious. Eisenhower protested, broke off diplomatic relations, and forbade Americans to trade with Cuba; but he was unable to obtain the unanimous support of the Organization of American States, or of Canada or the United Nations, for a policy of economic isolation. Castro became a hero to the militant Latin American students, and afforded no end of *Schadenfreude* to non-communist elements who enjoyed seeing Uncle Sam jump up and down in futile rage. And Cuba became a rallying point and breeding place for communist organizers and guerrilla specialists from the Rio Grande to Tierra del Fuego.

Secretary Dulles, who died before Castro's sun rose in Oriente, made an extraordinary defense of his and Eisenhower's foreign policy in *Life* magazine in January 1956: "The ability to get to the verge without getting into the war is the necessary art. If you cannot master it, you inevitably get into war. If you try to run away from it, if you are scared to go to the brink, you are lost. We've had to look it square in the face — on the question of enlarging the Korean War, on the question of getting into the Indochina war, on the question of Formosa. We walked to the brink and we looked it in the face. We took strong action."

The trouble with this statement is that in few instances did the Eisenhower administration act boldly. It did nothing about Castro, refused to enlarge the Korean War (as General MacArthur again urged in 1953), dropped Indochina into the Lake of Geneva, let our allies down and flinched from Russian threats over Suez, ran away from Hungary, and apologized for the U-2. The administration was demonstrably right in refusing to risk world war on these issues, especially in view of the drastic cuts in defense that the President had accepted and Congress approved; but it takes two to make a war, and it is possible that the communist powers were more scared of a nuclear war than we were. "Brinkmanship," as Dulles's critics derisively called his policy, was far short of heroic. America's relation to the world situation was comparable to that of 1905–41. At that time we had commitments to the Philippines and China; in this era, to every western European country, to the SEATO nations, and to Japan and Formosa; but in neither era were we sufficiently powerful or resolute to implement these commitments when it came to a showdown. Excepting, however, in the Quemoy-Matsu crisis.

3. The New Free Enterprise

Many and dire were the prophecies that New Deal, Fair Deal, and especially the TVA marked the beginning of the end to free enterprise, that "creeping socialism" would smother the American Way of Life. Republican orators played this theme in elections and in Congress, and they found support from three eminent economists, F. A. Hayek, John Jewkes, and Joseph Schumpeter who, like the three witches in *Macbeth*, prophesied that each deviation from economic truth would propel a nation irresistibly into socialism, and from socialism to some form of police state. Over twenty years have elapsed since the first of these three weird sisters uttered his gloomy prophecy on the barren heath of the dismal science; yet our economic Macbeth is still Thane of Glamis. Postwar developments, especially those under Eisenhower, justify the quip of Adolf Berle that instead of creeping socialism, galloping capitalism emerged from the New Deal and the war.

What the New Deal and the Great Depression really did — as the economist Arthur R. Burns pointed out back in 1936 — was to impel the United States, Canada, and Britain into a new and different form of capitalism, the development of which continued rapidly during the postwar years. Pricing, sales, and investment no longer depend on the "verdict of the market" as in laissez-faire days. Transportation services, public utilities, and fuels are now under so much public regulation in the United States, or nationalized in Canada, that pricing is often done by administrative decision, not by what business men think the market will take. Free venture capital has diminished, owing to high income taxes and social pressure to spend rather than save, so that most big corporations are financing changes and expansion by plowing in their own profits rather than by borrowing, or issuing new stock. The First National City Bank of New York estimated that in eight years, 64 per cent of the $150 billion invested in the United States to enlarge and modernize plant and equipment came out of retained earnings and reserves of the industries themselves. Most major corporations today do not seek new capital; they form it themselves out of earnings. Despite the row about "government planning" in the Roosevelt administrations, big corporate executives then and ever since have been seeking nation-wide central planning nuclei. The Interstate Oil Compact of 1935 provided for the adjustment of crude oil production to estimated demand, and was enforced by the Connally "Hot Oil Act" of 1935, which forbids the shipment of petroleum from one state to another without a certificate proving that it was produced in accordance with the controls. What a drag on free enterprise! Yet even the Texas oil industry demanded it and has worked it successfully. The American aircraft industry is in private hands, but since the United States government buys about 95 per cent of its products, government dictation as to specifications, prices, wages, and hours is complete and continuous. Electronics are in much the same situation.

In no really big American industry is competition permitted to carry through to its logical end. Whenever things get out of hand, and competition threatens to become ruinous, as when Texas oil gushers were inundating the refiners with crude oil, government is asked to step in and referee a plan to control the entire industry. Or, if the industry is international in character, an international compact is formed. That is the modern pattern. By 1956, 135 corporate Goliaths owned 45 per cent of all industrial assets of the United States and were able to finance their own growth and research. Hence, corporate Davids are becoming scarce. And the social effects are no less important than the economic. Major industries in 1910 did not want college graduates; now they send personnel experts to colleges and technical schools to recruit college graduates. The bright young man who in 1910 might invent something and start his own business, financed by a local bank, now seeks a job in a big firm and applies his brains in their laboratory; or, if not that type of young man, he takes a "personnel" job, hoping some day to be an "executive." Public admiration for executives is shown by the use of that word as an adjective in advertisements; you are offered everything from executive rugs to executive apartments.

The big concentrates, as the super-corporations are called, set and maintain prices by agreement or collusion. The recession of 1957–58 was the first slump in our history in which prices of manufactured products, and of raw materials such as copper, which the concentrates controlled, were not reduced. The concentrates simply agreed to cut production and create an artificial scarcity. Nobody in big industry really wants free competition nowadays. The thrills of the old cutthroat wars between railway and steamship companies, and Standard Oil and its competitors, are now regarded as childish. From top executive to lowliest stevedore, everyone wants a steady job, producing predictable goods at a predictable cost, to be sold at a predictable price. That is what the country now means by security, not the guarantee of liberty that it meant in the eighteenth century.

Nevertheless, competition continues in other forms, especially by advertising and salesmanship for new products. And there is competition between alternate products. For instance, anthracite coal has priced itself out of the domestic fuel market in favor of oil, and natural gas is running oil a hard race. Nylon, dacron, and other chemically produced fabrics have absorbed most of the market formerly monopolized by cotton, just as cotton in the nineteenth century replaced linen and wool. Plastics and aluminum have reduced the peacetime market for iron and steel. There is even competition from communist Russia. In April 1958 Aluminium Ltd. of Canada initiated its first price cut since 1941, and the United States aluminum industry followed. The reason, it turned out, was that Russia was undercutting the Canadian company in the British market.

The highlight of the economic picture in the Eisenhower era is the concentrate. In the manufacture of automobiles, radios, and other electrical appliances, in oil refining, meat packing, and iron and steel, a few mammoth concentrates share from one-half to three-fifths of these respective industries in the United States. The remaining half to two-fifths is shared by several competitors, so that there is no monopoly; but the pricing, production, and sales policies of the concentrates set the pace for the little fellows. Privately owned concentrates have grown by leaps and bounds since World War II; and it is they who are now invading the field of government, rather than government nationalizing them. Standard and Shell Oil, United States Steel, Reynolds Aluminum, General Motors, First National, and a score of others maintain their own foreign service officers who negotiate with similar corporations abroad, or with foreign governments, and in some cases take over governmental functions. United Fruit has been doing this for over fifty years in the Caribbean, performing services for the health and welfare of employees which the local governments were not prepared to do, and in the process becoming the target of jealousy, both communist and national.

Some of these international corporations open mines, build towns, construct roads, and improve the living standards of hitherto impoverished people by giving stimuli and scope for their ambitions. United States Steel, for instance, in order to tap a new iron ore area in Venezuela, in a few months built miles and miles of roads, a small city, and several towns, with hundreds of homes for the workers. That sort of thing is going on throughout the non-communist world. Capital investment in a country of backward economy is no longer a mere stripping of natural resources, like the old copper mining of Chile which left the Chileans nothing but the hole; it is a means of building up a local diversified economy and improving the native standard of living, as different from the Marxian theory of capitalist exploitation as white is from black.

These giant American and Canadian concentrates, either alone or in partnership with European counterparts, have been effecting an economic revolution which has become a lusty rival to the communist revolution. These are no longer mere corporations but institutions; and in spite of the governmental regulation to which they are subjected — usually by their own desire — they are free units in a free world. They still produce for profit, bargain with labor, compete with other products in the market, reward skill and initiative, and, except for the fixing of prices, satisfy every test of a free enterprise.

The success of these concentrates refutes the charge of creeping socialism; but the power that they wield is terrific, their ability to affect people's lives is frightening, and their lack of a guiding principle or philosophy is appalling. Who will regulate these giant concerns which control such immense segments of the economy? John K. Galbraith hopefully asserts that they are being automatically regulated by the "countervailing power" of labor unions and of buyers. Some of the principal purchasers of consumer goods are department and chain stores which are concentrates themselves. But what of the automobile industry, which sells directly to the public through agents? Or the building industry, before which the individual home builder is helpless? The fabulous R. Buckminster Fuller has some of the answers with his dymaxion three-wheeled car and his dymaxion steel igloo; but "Bucky" is a generation or more ahead of his time.

In the midst of the New Deal it was freely predicted by financiers and economists that the United States could not stand a national debt of more than $100 billion. The debt rose to $258.7 in 1945; Truman reduced it by a few billion before the Korean War, when it started to rise again, and throughout the Eisenhower administration it continued to rise, reaching $289 billion in 1961; but that was the lowest debt per capita since 1944. We still seem to be happily borrowing along; the debt stood at $316.3 billion in November 1964.

Prophets of doom were also worried about the growing press of people on the payroll of the federal government. The number of paid federal employees, which never exceeded a million before the Great Depression, rose to 2.9 million in 1946; and the Eisenhower administration succeeded in reducing it only by half a million. By 1963 it had risen again to 2.5 million. That is a lot of people to be "feeding at the public crib," and it does not include state or municipal employees, who would account for a couple of million more; yet the economy seems to be able to support them. "Wolf!" has been cried so often that people have come to believe that there is no wolf, but this cannot go on indefinitely. There must be a halt short of every American adult being on a government payroll, as happened in Newfoundland before it went bankrupt.

The proportion of people employed, and of goods produced, by free enterprise, is much greater than generally supposed. In 1948 about 85 per cent of the United States gross national product was contributed by private enterprise, and only 15 per cent by the federal government, including TVA. By 1963, government's share had risen to 21.5 per cent. But if defense expenditures are excluded — and those expenditures include billions in free enterprise products — the government's share was 9 per cent in 1948, 12 per cent in 1963. In Canada, the figures for 1955, including defense, were 18 per cent government, 82 per cent free enterprise. Thus there is still plenty of free enterprise in the United States and Canada, but with a great difference from the situation of 1910. Individuals are free to start new business, individuals and companies are free to buy and sell, expand or retrench, and in other ways to pursue their self-interest; but within a framework of rules established by government and labor unions, and under the high taxation of corporate income — 38 per cent in the United States, except for very small units.

4. Labor, Automation, and Antarctica

Of all the forces which check the former freedom of capitalists to pay the market wages and charge "all the traffic will bear," the great federations of union labor have probably been stronger than the government. C.I.O. and A. F. of L. merged in 1955, with a total membership of 17 million. Nevertheless, considering the enormous gains that organized labor has made since 1933, not only in higher wages and shorter hours but all manner of "fringe" benefits, union labor's feeling of responsibility for helping to maintain the economy on an even keel is still spotty. George Meany, head of the combined A. F. of L. and C.I.O., and Walter P. Reuther of the United Automobile, Aircraft and Agricultural Workers, responsible labor statesmen, have expelled the communist influences which had infiltrated their federations, and recognized the responsibility of the unions to promote a stable economy, full employment and racial integration. A few others, like "Jimmy" Hoffa of the Teamsters, are rough, tough, and corrupt, accepting bribes to call off threatened strikes, borrowing money from union funds for their own purposes, living like millionaires of the 1890's, and maintaining power over their members by strong-arm methods. So many and serious were the abuses within unions that in 1959 Congress passed a new Labor Act which set up codes of ethical practice for them and extended federal supervision to their internal affairs. On the other hand, the so-called managerial revolution, the result of studies by sociologists of human relations in industry, has brought about a better understanding of worker psychology and eased many points of friction. In the 1920's Englishmen visiting America were surprised to see workmen's automobiles parked outside factories — operatives, in their opinion, should walk to work or ride bicycles. Jan Strzelecki, a Polish communist who visited America forty years later, found dock workers in San Francisco going to work in Cadillacs, and was shocked to hear that they did not want their union newspaper mailed to their home addresses, as it might injure their middle-class status with the neighbors. Which only confirms a fact that has puzzled socialists and communists for a century: — the American workman is an expectant capitalist, not a class-conscious proletarian.

This is not to say that American labor lacks problems. The first is to complete the eradication of thugs and hoodlums from union officialdom, and the second and more serious is how to deal with technological unemployment caused by the spread of automation. That movement, so far, has fallen more heavily on the clerks and sales people, the "white collar" employees, than on the "blue-collar" workers. In 1954, when General Electric bought its first Universal Automatic Computer (UNIVAC) from Remington Rand, the *Harvard Business Review* announced, "The revolution starts this summer. Computers are taking over tasks that used to be the sole prerogative of management, and which had formerly been considered beyond the capability of machines." In UNIVAC, big business found the means to cope with the rising flood of paper work. Computers are also taking over the calculating part of the stockbroker and banking industry. "We're working toward the day when most of our employees spend their days smiling at the customers," is the way one of the big bankers put it. This means a painful dislocation of employment in the clerical branches of labor.

Automation, or mechanization as it is often called, has impoverished entire communities such as the West Virginia coal mining districts, and is seriously affecting others. Walter Reuther, in September 1963, pointed out that in the past fifteen years the automobile industry had eliminated 68,000 jobs while increasing its annual output by more than 3 million units. Estimates of the number of workers annually displaced by automation range from two to three million. This explains the anxiety of recent Presidents to speed up economic growth, the only way, it seems, to take care of the burgeoning population.

Labor, like everyone else, has benefited from the built-in safeguards to the economy, such as government control of credit and currency, unemployment and social insurance which flatten the peaks and fill in the valleys of the business cycle, and which prevented the usual postwar depression. We cannot yet appreciate what several years of continuously good employment did for the morale of the Western world, or how profoundly disappointed the Russians were at this outcome. Their diplomacy in the Stalin era was based on the expectation that American economy would go into a tailspin, followed by American withdrawal from Europe. In the United States and Canada, owing to new methods of using old materials such as oil, iron ore, and uranium; to newly invented products such as plastics, nylon, and dacron; to new gadgets for the home and for amusement; and to the extension of electric power, opportunities increased faster than population. But the problem remains of what to do with those left without jobs by automation.

Owing largely to the efforts of Admiral Richard E. Byrd, the polar explorer, a notable gain for international co-operation was made in the Antarctic during those postwar years. Byrd had long been devoted to the cause of world peace; he brooded over it during his five months' isolation in the Antarctic wastes in 1935, and seldom failed to conclude a lecture without a plea that this almost undiscovered continent, whose strategic value had been revealed by air power, might not become, like Asia and Africa, a fresh theater of discord and war between the nations.

The prospect did not seem bright in 1945, when at least six nations laid claim to the whole or part of Antarctica by right of proximity or discovery. Admiral Byrd conducted a third Antarctic expedition (Operation "High-jump") in 1946–47, significantly dropped flags of the UN over the South Pole, and then, in co-operation with scientists of several European and American nations and New Zealand, furthered the movement to establish an International Geophysical Year in 1957–58. Out of this he hoped the world might agree to make Antarctica, in his phrase, "The Great White Continent of Peace." In preparation, as commander of the American Operation "Deep-Freeze," he established seven more Antarctic bases for scientific research, invited other nations to do the same, and some eleven of them responded, establishing bases of their own or in conjunction with others. And, in this far-off corner of the world, the best of human nature triumphed over rival races, nations and ideology; American and Russian scientists and workers, for instance, became the best of friends.

Together and severally the workers in these bases have unlocked many secrets of the earth's most fertile untouched field for scientific research. Out of this co-operation came the Antarctic Treaty, signed by thirteen countries, including Russia, on 1 December 1959, and ratified unanimously the following August by the United States Senate. This significant agreement outlaws nuclear warfare in the Antarctic, adopts a workable mutual inspection system, and provides for a free exchange of scientific data and discoveries made in the southern continent.

Unfortunately the gallant Byrd died in 1957 before the International Geophysical Year began. But the Antarctic Treaty which he had worked for years to bring about, to make the Antarctic "shine forth as a continent of peace," is none the less his monument. He might well have said, like the hero in Heredia's sonnet *Plus Ultra*, "The waves of an ocean hitherto silent for all men will for me utter an imperishable murmur of glory."

President Eisenhower called the personal story of his first administration, *Mandate for Change*. The historian is entitled to ask, "What change, except in men?" There was little change in domestic affairs, apart from sniping at TVA and other New Deal institutions; all basic New Deal measures were continued and even enlarged upon. The economic developments that we have just described began before 1952, and were largely independent of government. In foreign affairs there was the same cold war challenge, which President Eisenhower and Secretary Dulles attempted to meet. No positive initiative in foreign affairs can be credited to the Eisenhower-Dulles team; Russia, China, and Egypt called the tunes to which they responded as best they could. Nevertheless, they led their country through the most critical period of the cold war and the intensified atomic race without an international disaster, which might easily have been touched off in a moment of impatience or carelessness.

So, let us not be too critical of President Eisenhower. At a relatively advanced age, devoid of political experience, he was elected largely as a symbol of what Americans admired, and he retained their confidence to the end. He took over the presidency at a time of malaise and hysteria; he left it with the country's morale restored and prosperity assured. These intangibles, apart from any positive accomplishments, make Eisenhower's eight years in the presidency memorable.

The Kennedy Administration

1961-1963

1. *The Election of 1960*

IF THE REPUBLICANS had not tied their own hands by pushing through Amendment XXII limiting presidential terms to two, Eisenhower could easily have won a third; and the improvement that he showed during his last two years, as well as the vigor that he has exhibited since his retirement, suggest that it would have been his best term. Since the Republicans could not renominate "Ike," they would have been wise to have chosen Nelson Rockefeller, governor of New York, who had been in and out of the federal government since the war. He had plenty of experience, an attractive personality, and had not yet (as one politician remarked) alienated every married woman over forty by swapping wives in midstream.

Nevertheless, political considerations decreed that Vice President Richard M. Nixon had to have it, and he got it on the first ballot. Nixon had been "groomed" for the presidency for eight years. He had sat in cabinet meetings, gone on difficult and dangerous missions for the President, and behaved with good taste and circumspection when Eisenhower's illness suggested that he was only "a heartbeat" from being called upon to take over the presidency. Yet, Eisenhower's attitude toward him was ambiguous. He called him "my boy" in 1952, but he seems to have shared to some extent the jealousy that monarchs of the House of Hanover felt toward heirs apparent. The President did little or nothing to help Nixon's campaign, and when asked by an interviewer to indicate which policies or acts of his administration had been helped by the Vice President, replied that he could not recall any! Nixon, too, was a young man for a presidential candidate, only four years older than Kennedy; but his public appearances suggested someone well over fifty and his oratory was ponderous. Nevertheless, enough of "Ike's" popularity might have rubbed off on "Dick" to ensure victory but for John Fitzgerald Kennedy.

Here was something new in national politics: a young (aged forty-three) and attractive senator with a younger and even more attractive wife, as Irish and Catholic as Al Smith of "The Sidewalks of New York," but two generations removed from the Irish ghettos of South and East Boston. His great-grandparents came over from Ireland in mid-nineteenth century. Both his grandfathers were run-of-the-mine Boston Irish politicians; more honest than

Michael J. Curley, less successful in reaching high office than Al Smith. His father, Joseph P. Kennedy, determined to break loose from the Boston Irish pattern. Joe graduated from Harvard, went into banking and investment, and was a millionaire at the age of thirty; by the time his son became a candidate, he was one of the richest men in the United States. And he took care to send his boys to leading preparatory schools instead of public or parochial schools, and to Harvard University. We have already noted the circumstances under which the elder Kennedy came to the favorable notice of President Roosevelt, who made him chairman of the Securities and Exchange Commission, and ambassador to Great Britain. During World War II his eldest son Lieutenant Commander Joseph P. Kennedy, Jr., whom he had designated as the family politician, was killed on a bombing mission for which he had volunteered, and the next younger, John F. Kennedy, was badly injured when his PT boat was knifed by a Japanese destroyer in the Solomons. But Jack showed such courage and resourcefulness in rescuing survivors of the crew that he emerged a war hero.

Financed by his father, Jack entered politics by running for Congress in 1946 from one of the Boston city districts. Old-line Boston Democrats snorted, "What has he iver done to be ilected? Has he iver got a man a job, or given a poor family a bag o' coal or a basket o' groceries?" Such was the old Tammany system; but, as one of the characters in Edwin O'Connor's *Last Hurrah* points out, the New Deal made that sort of thing obsolete; and the Boston Irish, far from being annoyed by Jack's wearing good clothes and never talking down to them, were complimented that one of theirs looked and acted like a thoroughbred. Jack was elected largely on the strength of his personality. After two terms in the House, the Massachusetts Democrats nominated him for the Senate in 1952 in opposition to the incumbent, Henry Cabot Lodge; and in the election that fall, when the Bay State went heavily for Eisenhower and elected a Republican governor, she chose Kennedy for the Senate.

Kennedy did not particularly distinguish himself in the Senate. Elder statesmen told him, "The way to get along is to go along," and for about two years he did. On McCarthy, for instance, his attitude was equivocal, possibly because his father supported Joe, probably because he feared to offend his Irish Catholic constituents who regarded McCarthy as a hero. In any case, an operation and a long convalescence in 1954 raised Kennedy's sights and gave him time to write *Profiles of Courage,* a series of thumbnail sketches of politicians from John Quincy Adams to Robert A. Taft who had exhibited that rare quality. And it is possible that Theodore Sorensen, the Unitarian from Nebraska who became Kennedy's intimate friend and private secretary, indoctrinated him with the views of the Middle-West farm belt and the idealism of George W. Norris. Kennedy's victory over Lodge made him "presidential timber," and his appearance and personality were enhanced by his marriage to Jacqueline Bouvier who belonged to the highest social circles of New York and Newport.

In the Democratic convention of 1956, Senator Kennedy was a candidate for the vice-presidential nomination but, fortunately for himself, did not get it. In 1960 he became an avowed candidate for the presidential nomination of his party, and hard he worked to get it. Adlai Stevenson, still a candidate, had kept in the public eye by traveling world-wide, making speeches, and writing articles, all very intelligent and understanding of the world situation; but the burden of two successive defeats was too much for a party that remembered Bryan. Senator Hubert Humphrey of Minnesota stood well to the left. Senator Lyndon B. Johnson of Texas, leader of the Democrats in the Senate for several years, a one-time protégé of Franklin D. Roosevelt, representing the moderate rather than the "Dixiecrat" South, and with an abundance of friends in the North as well, looked like the logical candidate. But Kennedy, liberally subsidized by his wealthy father, supported in the hustings by his pretty sisters and handsome brothers — for the Kennedys were not merely a family but a clan — entered the Democratic primaries of seven widely separated states and handily won them all. That sort of thing leads to high national office. Many politicians, remembering how Al Smith had been snowed under, were loath to risk another Catholic candidate; but Kennedy's replies to leading questions on church-state relations satisfied most of the Protestants that, if elected, he would not invite the Pope to Washington. And his youth, candor, quick wit, and grasp of political realities overcame religious prejudice. He was nominated for the presidency on the first ballot. Characteristically, he persuaded the convention to nominate for second place his chief rival Senator Johnson; and Johnson, at his earnest request, accepted.

Kennedy made an ideal candidate. His "Harvard accent" may have offended some, but his fine presence, youthful vigor, words well chosen and phrased, delivered in a strong, virile voice, appealed to voters who cared little for religion and programs but appreciated personality and character. The election, as far as issues were concerned, was not exciting, as both candidates promised about the same things — peace from strength, continuation of welfare, streamlining the federal government, etc. The most interesting feature was a TV debate between Nixon and Kennedy, in which nimble Jack ran circles around somber, jowly Dick. The popular vote, heaviest ever cast, was very close — 34.2 million for Kennedy, 34.1 million for Nixon; had New York's 45 electoral votes gone the other way, Nixon would have won. Kennedy took 303 electors to Nixon's 219. In addition, 14 "Dixiecrat" electors from the lower South voted for Senator Harry F. Byrd of Virginia, and one Oklahoma Republican who hated Nixon "crossed over" and did likewise. The religious aspect was by no means absent from the campaign; Maria Monk and all the old standbys were trotted out once more, and countercharges were directed against "Protestant bigots"; but how this actually affected the vote nobody knows. Probably about as many Protestant Democrats voted against Kennedy as the Catholic Republicans who voted for him. In any case, there was a big switch of voting habits. Other political experts believe that Kennedy and Johnson were put over by the young; for they were the first presidential team to have been born in the twentieth century. Nixon thought he had been defeated by a recession in the fall of 1960, which he and one of the economists on Eisenhower's staff predicted, but were unable to persuade the President to enlist federal credit control and public-works spending to stop.

Whatever the cause, here was something fresh and new, yet in the pattern of tradition. Millions of spectators and TV viewers felt just that on 20 January 1961 when they saw and heard venerable, white-haired Robert Frost read "The Gift Outright," and the young President — just half the age of the poet — fling out a challenging inaugural address. He opened with a promise that his administration meant "renewal" as well as change. In a very different world that confronted us from the one that confronted Washington when he took the same oath of office in 1789, "the same revolutionary beliefs for which our forebears fought are still at issue around the globe — the belief that the rights of man come not from the generosity of the state but from the hand of God."

"We dare not forget today that we are the heirs of that first revolution. Let the word go forth from this time and place, to friend and foe alike, that the torch has been passed to a new generation of Americans — born in this century, tempered by war, disciplined by a hard and bitter peace, proud of our ancient heritage — and unwilling to witness or permit the slow undoing of those human rights to which this nation has always been committed, and to which we are committed today at home and around the world."

He pledged our allies "the loyalty of faithful friends," to the poor everywhere "our best efforts to help them help themselves," to "our sister republics south of our border . . . to convert our good words into good deeds — in a new alliance for progress," to the United Nations, support and strength, to "those nations who would make themselves our adversary . . . that both sides may begin anew the quest for peace," to get away from "that uncertain balance of terror that stays the hand of mankind's final war."

"So let us begin anew — remembering on both sides that civility is not a sign of weakness, and sincerity is always subject to proof. Let us never negotiate out of fear. But let us never fear to negotiate."

Addressing again his compatriots, he said, "Now the trumpet summons us again — not as a call to bear arms, though arms we need — not as a call to battle, though embattled we are — but a call to bear the burden of a long twilight struggle year in and year out, 'rejoicing in hope, patient in tribulation' [1] — a struggle against the common enemies of man: tyranny, poverty, disease and war itself. . . . And so, my fellow Americans, ask not what your country can do for you — ask what you can do for your country."

1. Romans xii.12.

There had been no inaugural address like this since Lincoln's second. Note the recurrent theme — new, anew, renewal, recalling the motto on our Great Seal, *Novus Ordo Seculorum*, and Shelley's: "The world's great age begins anew, . . ."

But observe, also, the solemn warning not of "the long twilight struggle year in and year out." And that was the note on which his life closed; in his last speech at Fort Worth, Texas, on 21 November 1963, President Kennedy said, "This is a dangerous and uncertain world. . . . No one expects our lives to be easy — not in this decade, not in this century."

2. The Cabinet and Domestic Policy

Kennedy followed Eisenhower's principle of cabinet appointments, but with greater success in the selection. Whilst "Ike" for defense secretary chose the head of General Motors, "Jack" selected Robert S. McNamara, graduate of the University of California, president of Ford Motor Company, and a Republican; and McNamara made so acceptable a defense secretary that he was continued in office by President Johnson. C. Douglas Dillon, chairman of the board of Dillon, Reed, Eisenhower's undersecretary of state when Christian Herter was promoted, became secretary of the treasury. Dean Rusk of Georgia, a former Rhodes Scholar at Oxford, and in subordinate positions of state and war departments since 1946, became secretary of state. Arthur J. Goldberg of Chicago, a leading labor lawyer, became secretary of labor; J. Edward Day, a California insurance man, postmaster general. These major appointments were generally approved throughout the country, but there were some misgivings when the President made his fellow Harvardian, thirty-five-year-old brother Robert F., attorney general. Bob Kennedy, however, had plenty of experience, as he had practised in Washington and had been counsel to the Senate investigation of the labor rackets which exposed Jimmy Hoffa of the Teamster's Union. For special assistants, undersecretaries, and diplomats the President called to Washington any number of the despised "eggheads," drawing so heavily on members of the Harvard faculties, such as McGeorge Bundy, Arthur Schlesinger, Jr., Archibald Cox, and others, that the newspapers were inquiring. "Who is left in Cambridge to teach the students?"

There was no "gray eminence" in the Kennedy administration. He abolished the position of Assistant to the President, which Sherman Adams had held. He also abolished the staff system that President Eisenhower had installed in the White House. Instead of plans and programs being worked out by the staff and reaching the President on one sheet of paper for his approval or disapproval, Kennedy worked directly with his staff. He took an active part in the hour-by-hour work of the White House on almost every subject, and often talked on the telephone to subordinates in the departments who had never before heard a presidential voice. Although this did make the executive department seem disorderly, as in the Roosevelt administration, it enabled the

President to exert his power of decision all along the line, and made him extraordinarily well informed as to what was going on. His display in his press conferences of being well informed was a most important political asset.

There had never been such youthful euphoria in Washington since the early days of the New Deal. Kennedy's theory of the presidency was a dynamic leadership, like Roosevelt's, rather than the "Laodicean drift" (as Allan Nevins calls it) of Eisenhower. He hoped to re-create the spirit of the Hundred Days and push through Congress a series of reform measures which he called the New Frontier, similar to those of March-June 1933. To the first session of the new Congress, Kennedy sent no fewer than twenty-five messages directed toward economic recovery, stepped-up national defense and foreign aid, conservation of natural resources, federal aid for housing and schools. Comparatively few of these measures reached enactment because neither Congress nor the public felt any sense of urgency, as they had in 1933. The country was prosperous, there had been an apparent thawing of the cold war, and despite Democratic majorities in both houses, the coalition of Southern Democrats and conservative Northern Republicans which existed during the second Eisenhower administration still held firm. Only about 180 out of 260 Democrats in the House could be depended upon to vote for New Frontier measures, and a similar number to vote against them. It became blatantly evident in the Kennedy administration what had been adumbrated in the less demanding Eisenhower administration, that the two-party system had broken down, so far as Congress was concerned. The two ends of both parties, liberal and conservative, were closer together than the parties themselves; and the committee system, by putting senior members of each party on key committees like rules, and ways and means, enabled the conservatives to kill presidential proposals before they even came to a vote. As Walter Lippmann wrote in January 1964, "Congress is using a procedure of smothering and strangling, rather than of debating and voting, which violates the basic principles of representative government." Since the principal point where presidential proposals were done to death was the rules committee, presided over by Howard W. Smith of Virginia, a member since 1931 who hated the New Deal and all welfare legislation, Speaker Rayburn got through a bill increasing the membership of the rules committee from 12 to 15. That helped a little, but not much: a federal aid to education bill finally emerged from the rules committee in 1963, but the civil rights bill on which Kennedy had set his heart — "this nefarious bill" as Smith called it — remained bottled up until after Kennedy's death.

Kennedy was keenly sensitive to the "Negro revolution" that was going on, and eager to help colored citizens to secure their political rights and realize their potentialities through education. The great crisis in that revolution during his term arose over the efforts of one Negro to enroll in the hitherto lily-white University of Mississippi. The man was enrolled despite cowardly mob

THE CABINET AND DOMESTIC POLICY

efforts to intimidate him, and the President continued to protect him within the university with federal marshals. He felt intensely the injustice of excluding a qualified citizen from an American university on account of his race.

The President used patronage and personal talks to win support of the middle-of-the-road group in Congress. He exhibited the tact and patience of an old campaigner, but had to be content with somewhat less than half a loaf. A new minimum wage law raised the hourly rate from $1 to $1.25 and covered some 3.6 million more people than the old one. A housing act allotted $4.9 billion in grants or loans, for four years, to develop local transportation systems and build middle-income housing. "Medicare" for the aged failed, federal aid to education and school-building failed when it became clear that no such bill would pass unless it excluded parochial and non-integrated public schools from its benefits. Sam Rayburn, speaker for seventeen years but a friend to progressive legislation, died before Kennedy had been President a year. The new speaker, John W. McCormack, a septuagenarian who had served in Congress since 1927, came from the same background as the Kennedys and, bound to Jack by all manner of ties, used his shrewd knowledge of parliamentary law to further the presidential program. But not much grist emerged from the congressional hopper. The Southern Bourbon-Northern Republican alliance was too strong.

Kennedy entered office on the upswing from a mild slump, but the economy was sluggish; GNP (Gross National Product, that mysterious sum computed by anonymous statisticians which politicians watch as they once did the market) was not rising as fast as in several European countries. One of the President's economic advisers, Paul A. Samuelson from M.I.T., recommended more government spending, lower interest rates to stimulate building, aid to depressed areas, and a tax cut as ace-in-hole. The President did not ask for the first and the last of these, but he got most of those in between; and Khrushchev indirectly helped the American economy by resuming nuclear weapons testing, which he had promised Eisenhower not to do. This induced Congress to add another $4 billion to the defense budget. Unemployment remained fairly constant — 4.4 million or 5 per cent of the civilian working force, in March 1962. About half of it was due to automation in textiles, coal mining, motor cars, and aircraft. Kennedy tried to fill this gap by establishing new industries in chronically depressed areas and retraining the workmen replaced by machines; but very little was accomplished.

On the conservative side, Kennedy's leadership succeeded in checking the inflation which had continued, despite Republican promises, throughout the previous administration. The only time he lost his temper was in April 1962 when United States Steel and other companies announced a 3.5 per cent increase in prices after the President had persuaded striking unions to accept an infinitesimal wage increase. Steel backed down and rescinded the price raise. Big business, which had regarded Kennedy with a somewhat tolerant mistrust since his inauguration, now decided that it had an enemy to deal

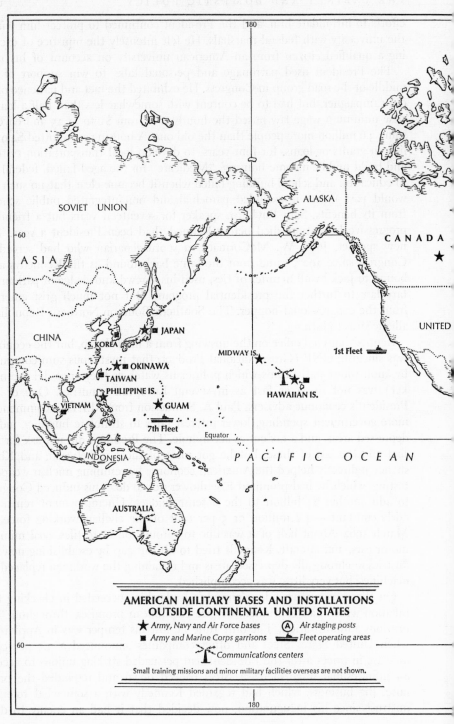

**AMERICAN MILITARY BASES AND INSTALLATIONS
OUTSIDE CONTINENTAL UNITED STATES**

★ *Army, Navy and Air Force bases*   Ⓐ *Air staging posts*

■ *Army and Marine Corps garrisons*   *Fleet operating areas*

Communications centers

Small training missions and minor military facilities overseas are not shown.

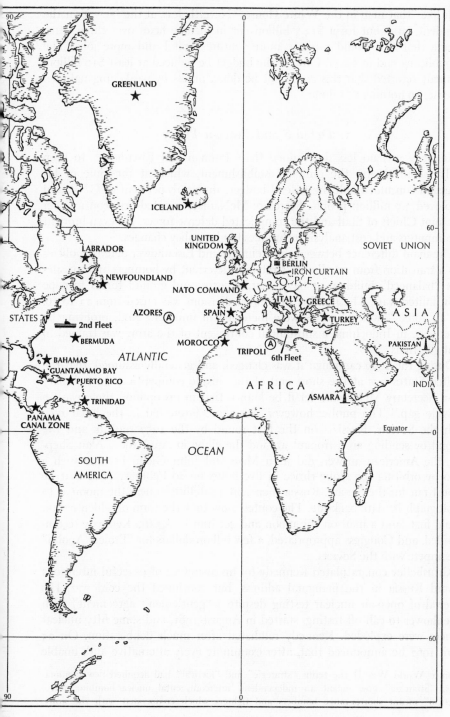

GREENLAND

ICELAND

LABRADOR

NEWFOUNDLAND

UNITED
KINGDOM

SOVIET UNION

BERLIN
IRON CURTAIN

NATO COMMAND

EUROPE

ITALY

GREECE

ASIA

STATES

AZORES Ⓐ

SPAIN

TURKEY

PAKISTAN

2nd Fleet

BERMUDA

MOROCCO

TRIPOLI Ⓐ

6th Fleet

ATLANTIC

BAHAMAS

GUANTANAMO BAY

PUERTO RICO

AFRICA

INDIA

TRINIDAD

ASMARA

PANAMA
CANAL ZONE

Equator

OCEAN

SOUTH
AMERICA

with like "that man in the White House." Nevertheless, at the New Year the President came out for a $13.5 billion cut in income taxes over three years, hoping that this would produce more venture capital and more jobs. The Republicans said in effect, O.K., if the budget be reduced at least $10 billion. Kennedy retorted that this could not be done, unless by weakening national defense. So nothing was done.

3. Defense and Foreign Policy

Kennedy was no less determined than Truman and Eisenhower to keep civilian control over the military establishment, which at the time of his accession consumed half the federal budget, almost 10 per cent of GNP, and employed 3.5 million people. Secretary McNamara asserted firm control over the Joint Chiefs of Staff and the complicated defense forces. He even brought in computers and cost-analysis techniques to plot policy changes.

The main difference between the Kennedy and Eisenhower defense policies was a transition from an all-out "strategic" deterrent by bombers and missiles to a "balanced" build-up of navy, marine corps, and ground forces to cope with limited wars. The number of combat divisions was raised from 11 to 16, the air force "tactical" wings were increased in number.[1] And, profiting by experience in Indochina, a substantial contingent of the army was trained to fight guerrillas.

During the 1960 campaign it was charged, and generally assumed, that the United States was at the short end of the missile competition. In February 1961, Secretary McNamara let it be known that in his opinion there was no "missile gap." The public, however, was more interested in the lunar race with the Soviets. Russia won the first round by the 1957 sputnik and the second by sending an astronaut around the globe in April 1961. Alan Shepard, the American answer, did it in May; and John Glenn became such a hero by orbiting the globe thrice in five hours on 20 February 1962 that he almost ran for the Senate. Russia then sent a satellite so near the moon as to photograph its dark backside. The contest now took the form of which nation would first land a man on the moon and get him back safe. Kennedy recommended, and Congress appropriated, a few billion dollars for "Project Apollo" to compete with the Soviets.

Khrushchev congratulated Kennedy for his assurance of peaceful intentions toward Russia in the inaugural address, but continued the cold war. His renewal of open-air nuclear testing despite a "gentleman's agreement" with Eisenhower to call off testing, started in August 1961, and some fifty nuclear devices were exploded. Kennedy retaliated after much deliberation. On 25 April 1962 he announced that, after examining every alternative and, unable

1. Since World War II the terms "strategic" and "tactical" had acquired new connotations. "Strategic" now meant an independent, intercontinental nuclear-bombing force; "tactical" meant shorter-range bombers and fighters which co-operated with the army.

to persuade the Soviet government to abstain, he had ordered America's armed forces to resume testing.

In April 1961 Cuba flared up again. A force of about 1500 anti-Castro Cubans, trained in Central America with logistic support from the United States, invaded Cuba at the Golfo de Cochinos, or Bay of Pigs. This force was not nearly strong enough for an invasion, much less a counter-revolution. In the showdown, Kennedy refused to commit the United States Air Force to help the invaders, who were routed by Castro's forces, supported by recently arrived T-33 jets. The whole affair was badly bungled in Washington. Kennedy should either have gone all-out to support the invasion, or prevented it from taking place by denying the rebels troop-lift. It must be remembered, however, that the invasion had been planned and assisted by President Eisenhower, and that the new President, in office only three months, was reluctant to risk another Korea, and was badly advised by the experts.

In the aftermath of this fiasco, Kennedy and Khrushchev met for the first time at Vienna in June 1961. Warily each took the other's measure. The younger man realized that he faced a ruthless, shrewd opportunist dedicated to promoting world communism by a series of "national liberation" wars to bring the leading raw-material-producing regions of the world under communist control. The elder, apparently, thought he could outwit the President. His next move seemed to confirm this. At Khrushchev's orders, on 13 August 1961 a great concrete and barbed-wire wall began knifing through Berlin between the Eastern and Western zones. Khrushchev's object, to stop the flight of Germans from communism was attained by breaking all prior agreements to preserve free access through partitioned Berlin. Once again the Russians had called the tune, and the Western powers, balancing fears of an all-out nuclear war against the risk of appeasement, did nought but protest, protest, protest.

Khrushchev took heart and tried another aggressive move. In July-August 1962, while the United States was trying to tighten her economic blockade of Cuba, some thirty Russian ships, laden with technicians, fighter planes, and ballistic missiles, landed their cargoes on Castro's shores. President Kennedy authorized high-level photographic flights to find out what was going on. On 14 October a U-2 plane brought back evidence that new missile sites were being constructed, and photographs made on succeeding days showed that this was being done faster than anything ever before accomplished in Cuba. The photos revealed short-range missiles which could have hit anywhere within an arc from Washington to Panama, and medium-range missiles with a range north to Hudson's Bay and south to Lima. On 18 October, Russian foreign minister Gromyko assured Kennedy that the installations were "purely defensive," but the photographs proved his lie. Kennedy called in his principal military and civilian advisers to discuss the situation. They recommended a tight blockade. On the 22nd the President, after briefing leaders of Congress and calling a meeting of the Organization of American States, presented over television the convincing photographic evidence of the missiles on their recently prepared sites, and announced that this "deliberately provocative and unjustified change in the status quo . . . cannot be accepted by this country." Several days of acute tension followed. Army, navy, and marine corps were mobilized in Florida and several Gulf ports. The Council of the Organization of American States on 23 October approved the blockade unanimously. The United States Navy threw an armed ring about Cuba, air force and carrier-based planes patrolled its shores; 12,000 marines stood ready, the strategic air command had nuclear-armed b-52s in the air ready to bomb, 156 ICBMs were in readiness, as well as Polaris missiles from submarines. Everything was set for an all-out invasion of Cuba and an equally massive nuclear attack on Russia if Khrushchev chose to make Castro's cause his.

Then Khrushchev crawled. On 26 October he offered to evacuate the missiles if Kennedy would promise not to invade Cuba, and Kennedy accepted. He also turned back Russian ships which were approaching Cuba. The crisis was over. By the clarity and boldness of his policy Kennedy had seized the advantage, but he was careful not to put Khrushchev in a position from which withdrawal would have been impossible. And the risk of millions of American lives was incommensurate with the advantage of ousting a dictator from Cuba. The country breathed a sigh of relief, the Russians did remove their missiles, much to Castro's rage and disappointment, and the President reached a peak of popularity at home and abroad.

Simultaneously with the Cuban crisis, Red China again made trouble, launching a series of surprise invasions over the northern Indian frontier. This was a serious blow to Jawaharlal Nehru who, ever since World War II, had followed a neutralist policy between the Western and Eastern power blocs. Nehru was a particularly irritating ruler to deal with because of his constant assumption that India's superior spiritual qualities would protect her, and that the United States was hopelessly materialistic and aggressive. And, as an alleged man of peace, Nehru was a humbug. He prevented settlement of the Kashmir border province dispute with Pakistan by a UN-supervised plebiscite; he gobbled up Portuguese Goa, whose people wished to stay Portuguese, without any right or reason. Nehru fancied that he could mediate peace in Asia and please the Chinese by letting his defense minister Menon vilify the United States on every possible occasion. When any Westerner pointed out to a leading Indian the menace of his northern neighbor, which had already grabbed Tibet, the Indian would answer with a superior smile, "*Hindi Chini bhai bhai*" — "Indians and Chinese are buddies." Now, in September 1962, Mao's army, with neither provocation nor warning, advanced across India's northern border. Nehru screamed for help from the UN and the United States, and Indian public opinion forced him to dismiss Menon. The United States promptly responded. Within a few days, air force transport planes were ferrying weapons and supplies to the Indians on the Himalayan front. China announced a truce, and Nehru went so far as to thank the "deep sympathy and practical support received from the United States," and to admit, "There is much in common between us on essentials."

Foreign aid to undeveloped countries continued through an Agency of International Development (AID), promoted by the President. Some AID projects were sheer waste; others, such as the expenditure of $43,000 in Greece under the direction of a California soil reclamation expert, were a spectacular success. Greece, a rice-importing nation, was soon providing her own needs and exporting a surplus valued at $5 million. The Alliance for Progress in Latin America encountered many snags from the Latins themselves; and in 1963 Senator Hubert Humphrey well said, "In terms of where it was a year ago, the *Alianza para el Progreso* has taken a giant leap forward. In terms of where it has yet to go, it has taken only a short, faltering step."

More successful and far less expensive is the Peace Corps organized by President Kennedy's brother-in-law Sargent Shriver. It trained and sent abroad thousands of young men and women to help undeveloped peoples to realize their potentialities. In South America, in the emerging nationalities of Africa, in the Philippines, and in Asia, these youths turned-to and helped the people build schools, roads, sanitary systems, hospitals; taught in their schools and marketed their handicraft. The Peace Corps was the best thing done in the Kennedy administration to restore the old beneficent image of the United States, after its successive blackenings by enemies abroad and extremists at home.

So many fruitless attempts to lay a basis for permanent world peace have been made by so many Presidents that one hesitates to give unqualified approval to John F. Kennedy's principal effort in that direction, the nuclear test-ban treaty with Russia. But that treaty certainly inaugurated a thaw in the cold war, and if it is succeeded by really amicable relations between the Soviet Union and the West, it may eventually be regarded as the dawn of a better day. Kennedy, at the same time, smoothed matters by approving the sale of 250 million dollars' worth of American wheat to Russia.

What seems to have happened in the diplomatic nuclear sphere is that the President and Dean Rusk shrewdly profited by the growing tension between Russia and China to renew a search for that solution which Presidents Truman and Eisenhower had sought in vain. Few thought success possible, so shortly after the hullabaloo over the U-2 being shot down. As the negotiation was drawing to a close, on 10 June 1963 the President made a notable public address in Washington. He rejected the concept of a peace imposed on the world by his own country, or by Russia. He recognized the necessity for living together in diversity: "Let us not be blind to our differences, but let us also direct attention to our common interests and the means by which these differences can be resolved. And if we cannot end our differences, at least we can help make the world safe for diversity."

After many conferences between British, American, and Russian scientists, Khrushchev was convinced by his experts that he had more to gain than lose by mutual renunciation. The troublesome inspection issue was shelved because any country could now be photographed, and nuclear testing detected, from unmanned satellites. Finally, on 5 August 1963, the nuclear test-ban treaty was signed by Russia, Great Britain, and the United States at a ceremony in the Kremlin. The signatory nations agreed to hold no more open-air or under-water tests of nuclear explosives. Next day President Kennedy announced: "Yesterday, a shaft of light cut into the darkness. . . . For the first time an agreement has been reached on bringing the forces of nuclear destruction under international control. . . . It offers to all the world a welcome sign of hope. It is not a victory for one side — it is a victory for mankind. It ended the tests which befouled the air of all men and all nations."

The United States Senate gave its advice and consent to this treaty by the emphatic vote of 80 to 19, and it went into effect on 10 October. Almost every member of the United Nations has since adhered.

4. The New Picture and the End

President Kennedy was remarkable not only for his courage and wisdom in meeting the challenges of our day; he chose to take the most important steps ever made by a President of the United States to foster literature and the arts. His admiration for accomplishment in every field led him to cultivate artists and writers. He did his best to impart to the public his respect for excellence and dislike of mediocrity. He made a good beginning of what J. Q. Adams tried and failed, the transplanting of high cultural values to the federal city. To a newly created post, special consultant on the arts, he appointed August Hecksher. Mrs. Jacqueline Kennedy, the President's fair partner in these enterprises, by her excellent taste and boundless energy, and through persuading collectors to give appropriate pieces of furniture, transformed the White House into a residence worthy of the chief magistrate of a great republic. They were the first presidential couple within the memory of White House gardeners to care about the flower gardens. Pablo Casals was invited from Puerto Rico to give a 'cello recital at the White House, his first visit to Washington since Theodore Roosevelt's time. Not only did the Kennedys by their example enhance public respect for the arts, they surrounded themselves with gay, active, intelligent people who imparted a verve and style to Washington society that it had not known in fifty years. At the same time they were an image of the typical American family, frolicking with their children and taking pleasure trips to the country or New York. American winners of Nobel prizes, never before given official recognition in Washington, together with writers, scholars, and artists of many races, were given a dinner and reception in the White House, conducted with a good taste that no European court could have surpassed; and it was typical of the President that instead of greeting his guests with a solemn address, he set a gay note by announcing, "This is the most extraordinary collection of talent . . . that has ever been gathered together at the White House — with the possible exception of when Thomas Jefferson dined alone!"

It is to Kennedy's credit that he aroused the enmity of racial, religious, and political bigots. He gave no aid and comfort to the superpatriots who wanted to get out of the United Nations, or the left-wingers who followed the Soviet party line. But, by and large, the country, and the young and perceptive people in every country, adored the presidential couple and their little children Caroline and "John-John," as the President called his son. Everything that the Kennedys did was done with grace, elegance, and style, and it all seemed natural, not forced; this was what Washington and the White House should always have been but almost never had been. Through all the crises and complexities of his short career, President Kennedy managed to seem relaxed, unhurried, confident.

In November 1963, a few months after his forty-sixth birthday, the President decided to visit first Florida and then Texas, to court votes for the election of 1964. Florida had voted against him in 1960; and Texas, though carried through the exertions of Vice President Johnson, was a stronghold of the ignorant but affluent "extreme right," which hated his policies. His visit to Florida was a continual ovation. Thence he flew to Fort Worth, where he delivered his last speech and perfected the one that he was to have given next day. In it he begged his countrymen to exercise their strength "with wisdom and restraint — that we may achieve in our time and for all time the ancient vision of 'Peace on Earth, Good Will toward men.' " For, "As was written long ago, 'Except the Lord keep the city, the watchman waketh but in vain.' " [1] American policy, he wrote, must be guided by learning and reason, "Or else those who confuse rhetoric with reality, and the plausible with the possible, will gain the popular ascendancy with their swift and simple solutions to every world problem. . . . We cannot expect that everyone . . . will 'talk sense' to the American people, but we can hope that fewer people will listen to nonsense. And the notion that this nation is headed for defeat through deficit, or that strength is but a matter of slogans, is nothing but *just plain nonsense*."

Friday, 22 November 1963, *dies irae* for America and the free world, dawned. The President and his wife made the short flight from Fort Worth to Dallas, arriving at 11:40. From the airport, accompanied by Governor Connally of Texas, they drove toward the center of the city in an open car. At 12:30 p.m. shots rang out. A wretched young man, a returned expatriate from Russia, firing a rifle from a sixth-floor window overlooking the presidential route, hit the President in the neck and the back of his head, and wounded the Governor. Jack Kennedy, his head cradled in the lap of his indomitable wife, was rushed to a hospital where he was pronounced dead one hour after noon.

Vice President Johnson, fortunately, was on hand. Not knowing whether the   assassination was an isolated act or part of a conspiracy to wipe out

1. Psalm 127:1.

the federal government, he insisted on accompanying Kennedy's body promptly to the presidential plane at Dallas airport, and taking off for Washington.

In that plane, in the presence of Mrs. Kennedy, still wearing her blood-stained suit, Lyndon B. Johnson at 2:38 p.m., 22 November 1963, took the oath of office as President of the United States.

"Let us continue!" was the theme of President Johnson's first message to Congress five days later.

With the death of John Fitzgerald Kennedy something seemed to die in each one of us. Yet the memory of that bright, vivid personality, that great gentleman whose every act and appearance appealed to our pride and gave us fresh confidence in ourselves and our country, will live in us for a long, long time.

CAMELOT

Ask ev'-ry per-son if he's heard the sto-ry; ___
___ And tell it strong and clear if he has not:
That once there was a fleet-ing wisp of glo-ry ___
___ called Cam-e-lot. Don't let it be forgot That once there was a spot For one brief shin-ing
mo-ment that was known As Cam-e-lot.

Index